THROUGHOUT EVERY CHAPTER . . . LINKS TO THE STUDY GUIDE FOR INTEGRATED LEARNING!

More than a text, this Ninth Edition gives you guidance in studying effectively for your course. Marginal notes throughout every chapter lead you to specific topic-related self-quizzes, activities, and other resources in the well-crafted *Study Guide* that is available with this book.

Fill in the blanks 15–16 →

15. Areas with rural and suburban populations are more likely to have much _____ crime rates than large _____ areas.

16. While there are most reported crimes during the _____ months, _____ and _____ occur frequently in December and January.

---

54   PART 1   THE NATURE OF CRIME, LAW, AND CRIMINAL JUSTICE

To read James Fox's reports on crime trends, you can go to his Web page:
http://www.dac.neu.edu/cj/fox/index.htm
For an up-to-date list of Web links, see http://www.wadsworth.com/product/0534573053s

United States, many under age 10; this is more than we have had for decades. Although many come from stable homes, others lack stable families and adequate supervision. Children in this age group will soon enter their prime crime years. As a result, Fox predicts a wave of youth violence.[25] Fox's predictions may be valid because the reduction in crime rate may be slowing. According to preliminary Uniform Crime Reports (released December 18, 2000) for the first six months of 2000 (the most recent data available), crime decreased by only 0.3 percent compared to the year before. Both violent crime and property crime declined by 0.3 percent when compared with the data from the same period in 1999. Some crimes (larceny and motor-vehicle theft) actually increased. Do these data portend an end to the declining crime rates?

Although Fox's arguments are persuasive, not all criminologists believe that we are in for an age-driven crime wave. Steven Levitt, for example, disputes the idea that the population's age makeup contributes as much to the crime rate as Fox and others suggest.[26] Levitt suggests that even if teens commit more crime in the future, their contribution to the crime rate may be offset by the aging of the population, which will produce a large number of senior citizens and elderly—a group with a relatively low crime rate.

Although such predictions are reassuring, there is of course no telling what changes are in store that may push crime rates either up or down. Technological developments, such as the rapid expansion of e-commerce on the Internet, have created new classes of crime. Concern about the environment in rural areas may produce a rapid upswing in environmental crimes ranging from vandalism to violence.[27] So, although crime rates have trended downward, it is still too early to predict that this trend will continue into the future.

Essay 5

CRIME PATTERNS

Criminologists look for stable crime rate patterns to gain insight into the nature of crime. If crime rates are consistently higher at certain times, in certain areas, and among certain groups, this knowledge may help explain the onset or cause of crime. For example, if criminal statistics show that crime rates are consistently higher in poor neighborhoods in large urban areas, then crime may be a function of poverty and neighborhood decline. If, in contrast, crime rates were spread evenly across the social structure, this would provide little evidence that crime has an economic basis; instead, crime might be linked to socialization, personality, intelligence, or some other trait unrelated to class position or income. In this section, we examine traits and patterns that may influence the crime rate.

Fill in the blanks 15–16

The Ecology of Crime

Most reported crimes occur during the warm summer months of July and August. During the summer, teenagers, who usually have the highest crime rates, are out of school and have greater opportunity to commit crime. People spend more time outdoors during warm weather, making themselves easier targets. Two exceptions to this trend are murders and robberies, which occur frequently in December and January (although rates are also high during the summer). Robbery rates increase in the winter partly because the Christmas shopping season means more money in the cash registers of potential targets.[28]

Crime rates may also be higher on the first day of the month than at any other time. Government welfare and Social Security checks arrive at this time, and with them come increases in such activities as breaking into mailboxes and accosting recipients on the streets. Also, people may have more disposable income at this time, and the availability of extra money may relate to behaviors associated with crime such as drinking, partying, and gambling.[29]

CHAPTER 2   THE NATURE OF CRIME AND VICTIMIZATION   55

Weather effects (such as temperature swings) may also affect violent crime rates. Crime rates increase with rising temperatures and then begin to decline at some point (85 degrees) when it may be too hot for physical exertion.[30] However, the rates of some crimes (such as domestic assault) continue to increase as temperatures rise.[31]

Large urban areas have by far the highest violence rates; rural areas have the lowest per capita crime rates.

Use of Firearms

Firearms play a dominant role in criminal activity. According to the NCVS, firearms are typically involved in about 20 percent of robberies, 10 percent of assaults, and 6 percent of rapes. In 1999, the UCR reported that almost 70 percent of all murders involved firearms; most of these weapons were handguns.

According to international criminologists Franklin Zimring and Gordon Hawkins, the proliferation of handguns and the high rate of lethal violence they cause is the single most significant factor separating the crime problem in the United States from the rest of the developed world.[32] Differences between the United States and Europe in nonlethal crimes are only modest at best.[33] Because this issue is so important, the Analyzing Criminal Justice Issues feature discusses the question of gun control.

Social Class and Crime

Crime has traditionally been thought of as a lower-class phenomenon. After all, people at the lowest rungs of the social structure have the greatest incentive to commit crimes. Those unable to obtain desired goods and services through conventional means may resort to theft and other illegal activities, such as selling narcotics,

Crimes are more common in urban areas in the West and South. Here, a police helicopter hovers over a Target store in Culver City, California, after gunmen invaded the closed discount store and ordered employees to the floor at gunpoint in a botched robbery attempt. Other police and sheriff's forces can be seen on the ground outside the store. Two people were arrested; no shots were fired, and no one was injured.

True/False 18

True/False 19
Multiple choice 17–19
Essay 6

PLUS AN ADDED BONUS . . .

FREE ONLINE ACCESS TO INFOTRAC® COLLEGE EDITION

INFOTRAC COLLEGE EDITION
FREE ONLINE ACCESS TO HUNDREDS OF PUBLICATIONS

You automatically received a four-month subscription to *InfoTrac College Edition* with every new copy of this book! Opening the door to the full text of countless articles from hundreds of publications, this online library is expertly indexed and ready to use. *InfoTrac College Edition* is updated daily with articles going back as far as four years. By entering a single key word, you can instantly search the entire *InfoTrac College Edition* database for related articles that can be read online or printed. A great resource for up-to-the-minute information on important topics such as police accountability, court cases, sentencing alternatives, and more. Available to North American college and university students only.

INTRODUCTION TO CRIMINAL JUSTICE
Ninth Edition

INTRODUCTION TO CRIMINAL JUSTICE

Ninth Edition

Joseph J. Senna, M.S.W., J. D.
Northeastern University

Larry J. Siegel, Ph.D.
University of Massachusetts—Lowell

WADSWORTH

THOMSON LEARNING   Australia • Canada • Mexico • Singapore • Spain • United Kingdom • United States

Executive Editor, Criminal Justice: Sabra Horne
Development Editor: Terri Edwards
Assistant Editor: Dawn Mesa
Editorial Assistant: Lee McCracken
Marketing Manager: Jennifer Somerville
Marketing Assistant: Karyl Davis
Project Manager, Editorial Production: Jennie Redwitz
Print/Media Buyer: Karen Hunt
Technology Project Manager: Susan DeVanna
Permissions Editor: Joohee Lee
Production Service: Cecile Joyner/The Cooper Company

Text Designer: Jeanne Calabrese
Indexer: Do Mi Stauber
Photo Researcher: Linda L Rill
Copy Editors: Betty Duncan and Peggy Tropp
Illustrators: Bob Voigts and John and Judy Waller
Cover Designer: Yvo Riezebos
Cover Image: Richard Estes, "Horn & Hardart Automat,"
    1967; © Burstein Collection/Corbis
Cover Printer: Transcontinental Printing, Inc./Metropole
Compositor: R&S Book Composition
Printer: Transcontinental Printing, Inc./Metropole

Library of Congress Cataloging-in-Publication Data
Senna, Joseph J.
    Introduction to criminal justice/Joseph J. Senna,
    Larry J. Siegel.—9th ed.
        p.   cm.
    Includes bibliographical references and index.
    ISBN 0-534-57305-3
        1. Criminal justice, Administration of—United
    States. 2. Criminal law—United States. 3. Criminal
    procedure—United States.   I. Siegel, Larry J.   II. Title.
    KF9223.S4 2001
345.73'05—dc21   2001026058

Instructor's Edition ISBN: 0-534-57306-1

For permission to use material from this text, contact us by
Web: http://www.thomsonrights.com
Fax: 1-800-730-2215
Phone: 1-800-730-2214

Wadsworth/Thomson Learning
10 Davis Drive
Belmont, CA 94002-3098
USA

For more information about our products, contact us:
Thomson Learning Academic Resource Center
1-800-423-0563
http://www.wadsworth.com

International Headquarters
Thomson Learning
International Division
290 Harbor Drive, 2nd Floor
Stamford, CT 06902-7477
USA

UK/Europe/Middle East/South Africa
Thomson Learning
Berkshire House
168-173 High Holborn
London WC1V 7AA
United Kingdom

Asia
Thomson Learning
60 Albert Street, #15-01
Albert Complex
Singapore 189969

Canada
Nelson Thomson Learning
1120 Birchmount Road
Toronto, Ontario M1K 5G4
Canada

ABOUT THE AUTHORS

Joseph J. Senna was born in Brooklyn, New York. He graduated from Brooklyn College, Fordham University Graduate School of Social Service, and Suffolk University Law School. Mr. Senna has spent over fourteen years teaching law and justice courses at Northeastern University. In addition, he has served as an Assistant District Attorney, Director of Harvard Law School Prosecutorial Program, and consultant to numerous criminal justice organizations. His academic specialties include the areas of Criminal Law, Constitutional Due Process, Criminal Justice, and Juvenile Law.

Mr. Senna lives with his wife and sons outside of Boston. He is currently working on a criminal law textbook.

Larry J. Siegel was born in the Bronx in 1947. While attending City College of New York in the 1960s he was introduced to the study of crime and justice in courses taught by sociologist Charles Winick. After graduation he attended the newly opened program in criminal justice at the State University of New York at Albany, where he earned both his M.A. and Ph.D. After completing his graduate work, Dr. Siegel began his teaching career at Northeastern University, where he worked closely with colleague Joseph Senna on a number of texts and research projects. After leaving Northeastern, he held teaching positions at the University of Nebraska–Omaha and Saint Anselm College in New Hampshire. He is currently a professor at the University of Massachusetts–Lowell.

Dr. Siegel has written extensively in the area of crime and justice, including books on juvenile law, delinquency, criminology, and criminal procedure. He is a court certified expert on police conduct and has testified in numerous legal cases. He resides in Bedford, New Hampshire, with his wife Therese J. Libby, Esq. and their children.

BRIEF CONTENTS

CONTENTS

3 COURTS AND ADJUDICATION   271

PREFACE

On Friday January 19, 2001, professional football star Rae Carruth was convicted of conspiracy to commit murder, discharging a firearm onto occupied property, and using instruments to harm an unborn child in the 1999 shooting of Cherica Adams, his former girlfriend who was carrying his child. The jury believed that Carruth had conspired with Brett Watkins, Michael Kennedy, and Stanley Drew "Boss" Abraham to kill Adams because Carruth didn't want the baby. Although the charge could keep him in prison for 25 years, the jury spared Carruth the death penalty by refusing to convict him of first-degree murder, the top charge on which he had been tried.

The Carruth case illustrates why the study of criminal justice is so fascinating to the American public. First, there are the social issues in the case. Why would a highly paid athlete enter into a conspiracy to kill a young woman with whom he had once had an intimate relationship? How can such violent acts be explained? Can anything be done to reduce or eliminate their occurrence? For example, might Cherica Adams's life have been spared if it were more difficult to obtain handguns? There are also fascinating legal and procedural elements to the case. The crime of first-degree murder requires proof of premeditation; the act must have been thought out and planned in advance. To convict Carruth as they did, the jury must have believed that he recruited Watkins, Abraham, and Kennedy to kill Adams. Nonetheless, they refused to find him guilty of first-degree murder, thus sparing his life. Did they bend the law because he was a well-known sports star? Or did they take pity on a young man who they believed deserved a second chance?

While the Carruth case is fascinating and helps focus attention on the criminal justice system, it is actually a very unusual "high profile" event. Each year the criminal justice system routinely processes millions of cases involving theft, violence, drug trafficking, and other crimes that are rarely reviewed on TV or in the newspapers. How does this vast enterprise costing billions of dollars and involving millions of people operate? What are its most recent trends and policies? How effective are its efforts to control crime? What efforts are being made to improve its efficiency? We have written this edition of *Introduction to Criminal Justice* in an attempt to help answer these questions in a forthright and objective manner.

The study of criminal justice is a dynamic, ever-changing field of scientific inquiry, and the concepts and processes of justice are constantly changing and evolving. Therefore, we have updated *Introduction to Criminal Justice* to reflect the structural and procedural changes, the most critical legal cases, research studies, and policy initiatives that have taken place during the past three years. This text provides a groundwork for the study of criminal justice by analyzing and describing the agencies of justice and the procedures used to identify and treat criminal offenders. It covers what most experts believe are the critical issues in criminal justice, and it analyzes their impact on the justice system. This edition focuses on critical policy issues in the criminal justice system, including community policing, preventive detention, alternative sentencing, jury reform, and prosecuting domestic violence.

Our primary goals in writing this Ninth Edition remain as they have been for the previous eight editions:

- To provide students with a thorough knowledge of the criminal justice system
- To be as thorough and up to date as possible
- To be objective and unbiased
- To describe current methods of social control and analyze their strengths and weaknesses

Every attempt has been made to make the presentation of material interesting, balanced, and objective. No single political or theoretical position dominates the text; instead, the many diverse views that are contained within criminal justice and characterize its interdisciplinary nature are presented. The text includes analysis of the most important scholarly works and scientific research reports, while, at the same time, it presents topical information on recent cases and events to enliven the presentation. We have tried to provide a text that is both scholarly and informative, comprehensive yet interesting, well organized and objective, and provocative and thought provoking.

Organization of the Text

This new edition has been thoroughly revised. We have made a concerted effort to make the text more concise and "leaner."

Part 1 gives a basic introduction to crime, law, and justice. The first chapter covers the problem of crime in America, agencies of justice, and the formal justice process, and introduces students to the concept of the informal justice system, which involves discretion, deal making, and plea bargains. Finally, Chapter 1 discusses the major perspectives on justice and shows how they influence the "war on drugs." Chapter 2 discusses the

nature and extent of crime and victimization: How is crime measured? Where and when does it occur? Who commits crime? Who are its victims? What social factors influence the crime rate? Chapter 3 covers both important crime patterns and types, as well as theoretical issues: Why do people commit crime? Why do some people become the victims of criminal acts? Chapter 4 provides a discussion of the criminal law and its relationship to criminal justice. It covers the legal definition of crime, the defenses to crime, changes in the insanity defense, the Federal Criminal Code, and issues in procedural law.

Part 2 provides an overview of the law-enforcement field. Its four chapters cover the history and development of criminal justice organizations, the functions of police in modern society, issues in policing, and the police and the rule of law. There is an emphasis on community policing and community crime prevention, private security, and other current issues.

Part 3 is devoted to the adjudication process, from pretrial indictment to the sentencing of criminal offenders. Chapters in this part focus on organization of the court system, an analysis of the prosecution and defense functions, pretrial procedures, the criminal trial, and sentencing. Topics included are bail reform, court reorganization, sentencing policy, three strikes laws, and capital punishment. There are also sections on the processing of felony cases, indigent defense systems, attorney competence, legal ethics, pretrial services, and bail reform.

Part 4 focuses on the correctional system, including probation and the intermediate sanctions of house arrest, intensive supervision, and electronic monitoring. The traditional correctional system of jails, prisons, community-based corrections, and parole are also discussed at length. Such issues as the prison and jail overcrowding crisis, house arrest, private corrections, correctional workers, private industry in prisons, privacy in prison, suing the parole board, parole guidelines, and parole effectiveness are discussed.

Part 5 explores the juvenile justice system. There is information on parental preventive detention of youth, waiving youths to the adult court, and the death penalty for children.

Great care has been taken to organize the text to reflect the structure and process of justice. Each chapter attempts to be comprehensive, self-contained, and orderly.

Features

To keep up with the changes in the criminal justice system, the Ninth Edition of *Introduction to Criminal Justice* has been thoroughly revised and renewed. The evolution of crime control policy has been followed by updated discussions of the criminal justice system, including recent court decisions, legislative changes, and theoretical concepts that reflect the changing orientation of the field. To help students analyze the material in greater depth, the text now contains seven different kinds of boxed inserts.

- **Analyzing Criminal Justice Issues** helps students to think critically about current justice issues. For example, in Chapter 6, *Zero Tolerance: Aggressive Policing in New York City* discusses efforts to reduce street crime using aggressive patrol techniques.
- New **Images of Justice** boxes show how the criminal justice system is portrayed in films and TV shows and also how the media influence crime and justice. *The Entertainment Media and Violence* in Chapter 3 answers the questions: Do the media influence behavior? Does broadcast violence cause aggressive behavior in viewers?
- **Law in Review** features give the facts, decisions, and significance of critical legal cases. For example, the case of *Kansas v. Hendricks* on the Sexually Violent Predator Act is covered in Chapter 4's Law in Review feature *The Constitution and the Criminal Law.*
- **International Justice** focuses on criminal justice issues around the world. *The International Use of the Death Penalty* in Chapter 13 shows that the United States is not alone in using the death penalty.
- **Race, Gender, and Ethnicity in Criminal Justice** features explore the experiences of women and minorities in the justice system. For example, *Women in Prison: Vengeful Equity* (Chapter 16) shows how women are more likely to be given prison sentences today than in the past.
- New **Criminal Justice and Technology** boxes focus on some of the latest efforts to modernize the system using contemporary technological methods. For example, in Chapter 14, *Using Technology to Monitor Offenders at Home* shows how house arrest can be made more effective by use of innovative communications gear.
- **Perspective on Justice** boxes, appearing throughout the book, show how competing views have influenced the way the system of justice operates and identify programs and policies to which they are linked. In Chapter 1, we describe competing viewpoints on what criminal justice is all about and how it should be directed. For example, some people believe that the primary mission of the justice system is to punish criminals while others focus more on their treatment and rehabilitation.
- Featured at the end of each chapter is a new element called **A Closer Look.** This feature contains short excerpts from current *InfoTrac College Edition* articles related to chapter topics. They are designed to direct readers to relevant material on the topics discussed in the chapter.

The book also contains many new figures, exhibits, and tables that make the presentation of the material easier to understand and conceptualize.

What's New in This Edition

Each chapter has been thoroughly updated.

Chapter 1: Crime and Criminal Justice
- New boxes include Analyzing Criminal Justice Issues: Is Crime a Recent Development? and Can Rehabilitation Work?
- There is a new discussion of Hollywood films that make crime seem glamorous.

Chapter 2: The Nature of Crime and Victimization
- A new chapter-opening vignette presents the interesting case of a former police officer who turns to crime, masterminding a high-tech burglary ring.
- There is updated information on recent changes in crime rates and trends.
- A new box on Analyzing Criminal Justice Issues: Debating Gun Control.
- An updated box on International Justice: International Crime Rates now includes updated information on international/transnational crime rates and Chinese crime.

Chapter 3: Understanding Crime and Victimization
- A new box on Race, Gender, and Ethnicity in Criminal Justice: Building a Bridge over the Racial Divide is presented.

Chapter 4: Criminal Law: Substance and Procedure
- A new chapter-opening vignette discusses an Internet adoption scam to sell nonexistent infants.
- A new Law in Review box discusses three recent Supreme Court cases that demonstrate court rulings declaring laws unconstitutional: *U.S. v. Morrison* (2000), *Chicago v. Morales* (1999), and *Kansas v. Hendricks* (1997).
- We include two new charts on Criminal Classification and Elements of Crime.
- A new Perspectives on Justice: The U.S. Supreme Court Role in Criminal Law and Procedure—Philosophy and Case Examples compares the Warren, Burger, and Rehnquist courts.

Chapter 5: Police in Society: History and Organization
- A new chapter-opening vignette analyzes Project Exile, an innovative Richmond, Virginia, program designed to combat gun crime.
- We present new exhibits on "The Most Notable Achievements of American Police, 1960–1999" and "Special Programs and Divisions of the FBI."

- We present new information on drug enforcement administration (including the Operation Pipeline and Operation Convoy programs) and a new section on information technology, including automatic fingerprint systems and DNA analysis.
- There is a new Criminal Justice and Technology: Crime Mapping feature.

Chapter 6: The Police: Organization, Role, and Function

- There are new boxes: Analyzing Criminal Justice Issues: Zero Tolerance: Aggressive Policing in New York City; School Resource Officers; and Civilian Review Boards.
- Sections on community policing are updated, including a successful residential police officer program initiated in Alexandria, Virginia.

Chapter 7: Issues in Policing

- A new chapter-opening vignette presents Analyzing Criminal Justice Issues: School Resource Officers.
- Images of Justice: *NYPD Blue* compares this gritty TV drama with real-life policing.
- A new exhibit features How Were Police Officers Killed in the Line of Duty?
- We present new analyses of the police corruption scandal in the Ramparts Division of the Los Angeles Police Department and disciplinary procedures of the New York City Police Department.
- There is a new box featuring Criminal Justice and Technology: Eliminating Racial Profiling.

Chapter 8: Police and the Rule of Law

- We discuss two 2000 Supreme Court cases dealing with custodial interrogation and Fourth Amendment rights: *Dickerson v. U.S.* (which reaffirms the *Miranda* rule) and *Indianapolis v. Edmond* (which struck down a state of Indiana case allowing road blocks to be used for drug search and seizure).

Chapter 9: Courts and the Judiciary

- A new chapter-opening vignette discusses controversial Massachusetts Superior Judge Maria Lopez, who rose to national attention on Sept. 6, 2000, when she sentenced a convicted kidnapper to home detention and probation rather than to jail time.
- We present the most recent data on court caseloads and the court system, updated information on judicial selection, and a new section on judicial alternatives.
- There is a new box on Criminal Justice and Technology: Technology and Court Management.

Chapter 10: The Prosecution and the Defense

- A new chapter-opening vignette offers two vivid case examples in which prosecutors make the difficult discretionary call of whether to prosecute or not to prosecute.
- There is a new personal profile of Michigan prosecutor Patricia Jessamy, new to this edition.
- A new section discusses community prosecution, a new proactive strategy that increases prosecutors' communication with the police, schools, and other community groups.
- We present updated information on public defender programs in the United States.

Chapter 11: Pretrial Procedures

- There is a new box feature Analyzing Criminal Justice Issues: The Pros and Cons of Plea Bargaining.

Chapter 12: The Criminal Trial

- A new chapter-opening vignette features the McVeigh case (Oklahoma City bombing) and the McKinney case (gay rights murder) as examples of the special difficulties of handling high-profile cases.
- There is a new chart on Defender's Constitutional Right to Trial.
- A new Table 12.2 summarizes the arguments for and against using TV cameras in courtrooms.
- We have included a new section on Trial Reform in the twenty-first century.

Chapter 13: Punishment and Sentencing

- A new chapter-opening vignette discusses child murderer/rapist Ricky McGinn's positive DNA test and ultimate execution.
- We present new sections on criticizing indeterminacy, the capital jury project, and recent data on how people are sentenced.
- There is a new box Analyzing Criminal Justice Issues: Let's Get Tough: Truth in Sentencing and Three Strikes Laws.
- There is an updated feature International Justice: The International Use of the Death Penalty.

Chapter 14: Probation and Intermediate Sanctions

- New sections appear on Why People Fail on Probation, Probationers in Prison, and Restorative Justice.
- A new box appears on International Justice: Community Sentencing Abroad.
- There is a new box Criminal Justice and Technology: Using Technology to Monitor Offenders at Home.
- There are new features Analyzing Criminal Justice Issues: Is Probation Becoming More Punitive than Prison? and Restorative Justice in the Community.

Chapter 15: Corrections: History, Institutions, and Populations

- A new chapter-opening vignette raises disturbing questions about paroling dangerous inmates and/or allowing them to conduct business on the Internet (serial killer/rapist Arthur Shawcross is highlighted).
- There are new sections on New Generation Jails and Will the Cost of Incarceration Be Reduced?
- There are new boxes on Criminal Justice and Technology: Ultra-Maximum-Security Prisons and Using Technology to Increase Prison Security.

Chapter 16: The Prison Experience: Living in and Leaving Prison

- There is a new chapter-opening vignette on The Cowboys (renegade federal corrections officers).
- There is a new box on Criminal Justice and Technology: Technocorrections: Contemporary Correctional Technology.
- We present new sections on what works in correctional rehabilitation, private health care in prisons, the Litigation Reform Act of 1996, and why people fail at parole.
- There is a new box Race, Gender, and Ethnicity in Criminal Justice: Women in Prison: Vengeful Equity.
- There is a new box Analyzing Criminal Justice Issues: Newjack.

Chapter 17: Juvenile Justice

- A new chapter-opening vignette discusses children charged with adult crimes.
- We present new information on blended sentences, waiver laws, juvenile justice reform, and the future of juvenile courts in America.
- A new figure summarizes cases involving juvenile law from the 1960s to the present.

Supplements

The most extensive package of supplemental aids for a criminal justice text accompanies this edition. The following items have been developed to enhance the course and to assist instructors and students.

Instructor's Edition A fully annotated instructor's edition will assist instructors in organizing their classroom presentations and reinforcing the themes of the course. Each chapter ties all of the supplements directly to the topics in the text.

Student Edition For the first time, Wadsworth offers a fully annotated student edition that is connected topic by topic to the book's *Study Guide.* Marginal notes throughout every chapter lead students to specific topic-related self-quizzes, activities, and other resources in the *Study Guide.* Visually inviting and innovative chapter-opening spreads are also a valuable study tool that help students easily locate important material contained within the chapter. Each chapter opener includes a list of criminal justice Web links—with page numbers—to guide students to some of the most popular Internet addresses for criminal justice–related Web sites featured throughout each chapter. Chapter openers also include an index of the chapter's boxed material so students can quickly find specific topical material within the chapter.

Instructor's Resource Manual The Instructor's Resource Manual has been revised by Charles Crawford. The manual includes resource lists, lecture outlines, and testing suggestions that will help time-pressed teachers more effectively communicate with their students and also strengthen coverage of course material. Each chapter has multiple choice, true/false, and fill-in-the-blanks test items, as well as review and discussion questions. The *Instructor's Resource Manual* is backed up by ExamView®, a computerized test bank available in Windows and Macintosh formats.

ExamView® This computerized testing software helps instructors create and customize exams in minutes. Instructors can easily edit and import their own questions and graphics, change test layout, and reorganize questions. This software also offers the ability to test and grade online. It is available for both Windows and Macintosh.

State Supplements for California, Florida, Illinois, New York, and Texas These concise booklets include state-specific topics, laws, and other criminal justice–related information as they pertain to each state. State crime enforcement, court procedures, correctional systems, and juvenile justice programs are just a few of the issues covered.

CNN® Today Video Series Exclusively from Wadsworth/Thomson Learning, the *CNN Today Video Series* offers compelling videos that feature current news footage from the Cable News Network's comprehensive archives. Volumes 1 through 4 of *Introduction to Criminal Justice* each provide a collection of three- to five-minute clips on hot topics in criminal justice, such as cybercrime, juveniles behind bars, gender and ethnicity, and much more. Available to qualified adopters, these videotapes are great lecture launchers as well as classroom discussion pieces.

The Wadsworth Criminal Justice Video Library The Wadsworth Criminal Justice Video Library offers an exciting collection of videos to enrich lectures. Qualified adopters may select from a variety of professionally prepared videos covering various aspects of policing, corrections, and other areas of the criminal justice system. The selections include videos from *Films for the Humanities & Sciences, Court TV* videos that feature provocative one-hour court cases to illustrate seminal and high-profile cases in depth, *A&E American Justice Series* videos, *National Institute of Justice: Crime File* videos, *ABC News* videos, and *MPI Home* videos.

Web Site for Introduction to Criminal Justice, Ninth Edition   Designed exclusively for this text, this text-specific Web site, located at http://cj.wadsworth.com, offers a variety of online resources for students and instructors. Students can enhance their learning experience with book-specific and chapter-based resources. Web links, periodicals, and *InfoTrac College Edition* offer valuable and reliable sources for researching specific topics. Projects and quizzing activities provide immediate feedback and can be emailed to instructors. Online homework assignments integrate Web site research with textbook activities. Student study tips provides a well-developed guide to encourage student success. Instructor downloads and Web links for professionals offer an array of resources for curriculum development.

Introduction to Criminal Justice Transparencies   To help bring key concepts of the text to the classroom, fifty full-color transparency masters for overhead projection are available in the *Criminal Justice 2001* transparency package. These transparencies help instructors fully discuss concepts and research findings with students.

Multimedia Manager for Criminal Justice: A Microsoft® PowerPoint® Link Tool   This tool is an important instrument that instructors can utilize to prepare for class lectures. The more than 450 color images included on this invaluable reference will aid instructors in visually representing to students the main concepts and ideas contained in the text.

Student Study Guide   The extensive *Student Study Guide* has been revised by Eugene Bouley, Jr. Because students learn in different ways, a variety of pedagogical aids are included in the guide to help them. Each chapter is outlined; major terms are defined; and summaries and sample tests are provided.

WebTutor Advantage™ on Web CT and Blackboard   Designed specifically for *Introduction to Criminal Justice,* Ninth Edition, WebTutor Advantage is an online resource that gives both instructors and students a virtual environment rich with study and communication tools. For instructors, WebTutor Advantage can pro-

vide virtual office hours, post syllabi, set up threaded discussions, and track student progress. WebTutor Advantage can also be customized in a variety of ways, such as uploading images and other resources and adding Web links to create customized practice materials. For students, WebTutor Advantage offers real-time access to many study aids, including flash cards, practice quizzes, online tutorials and Web links.

Careers in Criminal Justice Interactive CD-ROM   This engaging self-exploration CD-ROM provides an interactive discovery of the wide range of careers in criminal justice. The self-assessment helps steer students to suitable careers based on their personal profile. Students can gather information on various careers from the job descriptions, salaries, employment requirements, sample tests, and video profiles of criminal justice professionals presented on this valuable tool.

Crime Scenes: An Interactive Criminal Justice CD-ROM   The first CD-ROM developed specifically for the introductory criminal justice course, this highly visual and interactive program casts students as the decision makers in various roles as they explore all aspects of the criminal justice system. Exciting videos and supporting documents put students in the midst of a juvenile murder trial, a prostitution case that turns to manslaughter, and several other scenarios. This product received the gold medal in higher education and silver medal for video interface from *NewMedia Magazine's Invision Awards.*

Mind of a Killer CD-ROM   Based on Eric Hickey's book, *Serial Murderers and Their Victims,* this award-winning CD-ROM offers viewers a look at the psyches of the world's most notorious killers. Students can view confessions of and interviews with serial killers, and they can examine famous cases through original video documentaries and news footage. Included are 3-D profiling simulations, which are extensive mapping systems that seek to find out what motivates these killers.

InfoTrac® College Edition   Students receive four months of real-time access to *InfoTrac College Edition's* online database of continuously updated, full-length articles from hundreds of journals and periodicals. By doing a simple key word search, users can quickly generate a list of related articles, then select relevant articles to explore and print out for reference or further study.

Criminal Justice Internet Investigator III   This fully updated, handy brochure lists the most useful criminal justice links on the World Wide Web. It includes the most popular criminal justice sites featuring online newsletters, grants and funding information, and more.

Seeking Employment in Criminal Justice and Related Fields Written by J. Scott Harr and Kären Hess, this practical book, now in its Third Edition, helps students develop a search strategy to find employment in criminal justice and related fields. Each chapter includes "insiders' views," written by individuals in the field and addressing promotions and career planning.

Guide to Careers in Criminal Justice This concise 60-page booklet provides a brief introduction to the exciting and diverse field of criminal justice. Students can learn about opportunities in law enforcement, courts, and corrections and how they can go about getting these jobs.

Internet Guide for Criminal Justice Developed by Daniel Kurland and Christina Polsenberg, this easy reference text helps newcomers as well as experienced Web surfers use the Internet for criminal justice research.

Internet Activities for Criminal Justice This 60-page booklet shows how to best utilize the Internet for research via searches and activities.

Acknowledgments

Many people helped make this book possible. Those who reviewed this edition and made suggestions that we attempted to follow to the best of our ability include: Allen Anderson, Indiana University, Kokomo; Kelly Asmussen, Peru State College; Roger Barnes, University of the Incarnate Word; Joe Becraft, Portland Community College; Eugene Bouley, Jr., Georgia College and State University; Linda O'Daniel, Mountain View College; Edward Qualey, Hilbert College; and Robert C. Wadman, Weber State University. Those who reviewed the previous edition include: Charles Beene, Denver Business College; David Falcone, Illinois State University; Nella Lee, Portland State University; and Henry Starkel, Eastern Connecticut State University.

Our editor, Sabra Horne, who is always there for us, directed the form and content of this new edition. It has been a pleasure working with Sabra and our other colleagues at Wadsworth: Production Manager Jennie Redwitz, Production Editor Cecile Joyner, Photo Researcher Linda Rill, Marketing Manager Jennifer Somerville, Technology Project Manager Susan De-Vanna, and Assistant Editor Dawn Mesa. A lot of credit for getting this book out must go to Development Editor Terri Edwards, a wonderful person, who is always patient, kind, and sensitive.

Larry Siegel
Joseph Senna

INTRODUCTION TO CRIMINAL JUSTICE
Ninth Edition

THE NATURE OF CRIME, LAW, AND CRIMINAL JUSTICE

The case of Ernesto Miranda, shown above, versus the State of Arizona is one of the most important and influential of all Supreme Court decisions. It established the right of suspects in a criminal case to obtain legal representation to protect their Constitutional rights while in police custody. Some critics have challenged *Miranda*, arguing that it "handcuffs" the police by limiting their ability to interrogate suspects. However, in the recent case of *Dickerson vs. United States*, the Supreme Court upheld *Miranda*, stating that it has become "embedded" in the American culture. *Miranda* and other significant cases are discussed in this part, which covers the concept of criminal justice, the nature and extent of crime, and the elements of substantive and procedural criminal law.

CRIME AND CRIMINAL JUSTICE

On April 20, 1999, the nation's most deadly school shooting occurred at Columbine High School in Littleton, Colorado. Two heavily armed students—Eric Harris, age 18, and Dylan Klebold, age 17, members of a secretive student group called the "Trenchcoat Mafia"—went on a shooting spree that claimed the lives of 12 students and one teacher and wounded 24 others, many seriously. As police SWAT teams closed in, the two boys committed suicide in the school library, leaving authorities to puzzle over the cause of their deadly act. Later, their friends described Harris and Klebold as outsiders whose behavior may have been triggered by their perceived victimization at the hands of school athletes.

Such senseless acts of violence are very perplexing. While the general public has been reassured by government reports that crime rates are now in a steep decline, it continues to be buffeted by a constant drumbeat of media stories dwelling on violence and death. Incidents like the Columbine shootings convince commentators that juvenile violence is still rampant; *Newsweek* magazine heralded the "New Age of Anxiety."[1] Yet the current juvenile violent crime rate of about 30 crimes per 1,000 youths in the general population represents a significant drop from a high of 52 violent crimes per 1,000 in 1993.[2]

There is also confusion over what such violent outbursts actually signify. Do they signal the fact that many adolescents are alienated and depressed? Are disaffected youths such as Klebold and Harris liable to go on a violent rampage at the slightest provocation? Does living in our highly charged, fast-paced, technologically advanced society create overwhelming feelings of stress and anxiety?

Questions have been raised about how such crimes can be prevented. Could the Columbine shootings have been prevented if gun ownership were abolished or severely restricted? Klebold and Harris's violence was blamed in part on their interest in the entertainment media and Internet violence. Does viewing violent images on television or in the movies have a catastrophic effect on trou-

Chapter 1

© Sean Cayton/The Image Works

bled adolescents? If it does, should the depiction of violence in the media be curtailed or restricted by the government? Some politicians have demanded that the entertainment industry stop marketing violent movies, recordings, and video games to children, threatening to create legislation allowing the federal government to sanction the industry and punish transgressors if they do not police themselves.[3] To some people, such measures smack of excessive government control; to others, they are necessary measures to curb violent crimes.

Although the general public has been reassured by government reports that crime rates are now in decline, incidents of senseless violence still plague the nation. Here, two Columbine High School students, friends of slain student Rachel Scott, hug in the parking lot at Clement Park, next to Scott's red Acura Legend. The car was parked where Scott had left it before going to school the day of the shooting. It was an overpowering emotional symbol to her friend and fellow students. Following the shooting, the car was covered with flowers and other mementos.

Crime has been an ever-present fixture of American culture (see the Analyzing Criminal Justice Issues feature). To provide solutions to the crime problem and to shape the direction of crime policy, we turn to the agencies of the **criminal justice system**. This loosely organized collection of agencies is charged with, among other matters, protecting the public, maintaining order, enforcing the law, identifying transgressors, bringing the guilty to justice, and treating criminal behavior. The public depends on this vast system, employing more than 2 million people and costing taxpayers more than $130 billion a year, to protect them from evildoers and bring justice to their lives.

This text serves as an introduction to the study of criminal justice. This chapter introduces some basic issues, beginning with a discussion of the concept and the study of criminal justice. The major processes of the criminal justice system are then introduced so that you can develop an overview of how the system functions. Because there is no single view of the underlying goals that help shape criminal justice, the varying perspectives on what criminal justice really is or should be are set out in some detail.

THE CONCEPT OF A CRIMINAL JUSTICE SYSTEM

Although firmly entrenched in our culture, criminal justice agencies have existed for only 200 years or so. At first, these institutions operated independently, with little recognition that their functions could be coordinated or have common ground. Then, in 1931, President Herbert Hoover appointed the National Commission of Law Observance and Enforcement, commonly known as the Wickersham Commission, which was instructed with analyzing the American justice system in detail. The Commission uncovered the complex rules and regulations that govern the system and exposed how difficult it was for justice personnel to keep track of its legal and administrative complexity.

The modern era of criminal justice began with a series of explorations of the criminal justice process conducted under the auspices of the American Bar Foundation.[4] As a group, the Bar Foundation studies brought to light some of the hidden or low-visibility processes that were at the heart of justice system operations. They showed how informal decision making and the use of personal discretion were essential ingredients of the justice process.

Another milestone occurred in 1967, when the President's Commission on Law Enforcement and the Administration of Justice (the Crime Commission), appointed by President Lyndon Johnson, published its final report, titled *The Challenge of Crime in a Free Society*.[5] This group of practitioners, educators, and attorneys had been charged with creating a comprehensive view of the criminal justice process and offering recommendations for its reform. Its efforts resulted in passage of the Safe Streets and Crime Control Act of 1968, which provided federal funds for state and local crime control efforts. This act helped launch a massive campaign to restructure the justice system by funding the **Law Enforcement Assistance Administration (LEAA)**, an agency that provided hundreds of millions of dollars in aid to local and state justice agencies. Federal intervention through the LEAA ushered in a new era of research and development in criminal justice and established the concept that its component agencies actually make up a system.[6]

Although the LEAA is no longer in operation, its efforts helped identify the concept of a unified system of criminal justice. Rather than viewing police, court, and correctional agencies as thousands of independent institutions, it has become common to view them as components in a large, integrated, people-processing system that manages law violators from the time of their arrest through trial, punishment, and release.

criminal justice system
The various sequential stages through which offenders pass, from initial contact with the law to final disposition, and the agencies charged with enforcing the law at each of these stages.

Fill in the blanks 1–2
Multiple choice 1
Essay 1

Law Enforcement Assistance Administration (LEAA)
Agency funded by the federal Safe Streets Act that provided technical assistance and hundreds of millions of dollars in aid to local and state justice agencies between 1969 and 1982.

ANALYZING CRIMINAL JUSTICE ISSUES

Is Crime a Recent Development?

Crime and violence have been common in the United States since the nation was first formed. Guerilla activity was frequent before, during, and after the Revolutionary War. Bands supporting the British (Tories) and the American revolutionaries engaged in savage attacks on each other, using hit-and-run tactics, burning, and looting.

After the Civil War, night riders and Ku Klux Klan members were active in the South, using vigilante methods to maintain the status quo and terrorize former slaves. Some former Union and Confederate soldiers, heading west with the dream of finding gold or starting a cattle ranch, resorted to theft and robbery. Famed lawman Wyatt Earp journeyed to Tombstone, Arizona, where he was appointed deputy U.S. marshal for the Arizona Territory. Wyatt—along with his brothers, Morgan and Virgil, and their gun-slinging dentist friend, Doc Holliday—took on the "The Cowboys," a local gang of cattle thieves. The ongoing conflict culminated in the famous O.K. Corral gunfight in 1881, during which several members of the Cowboys were killed. The Cowboys were not the only gang that plied their trade in the Old West. Train robbery was popularized by the Reno Brothers of Indiana and bank robbery by the James–Younger gang of Missouri.

Population makeup and cultural values certainly played a major role in the development of this violent American culture. Until the mid-twentieth century, the U.S. population was disproportionately young and male. Most working-class immigrants were young males who typically paid for their passage from Europe by signing labor contracts. The gender ratio among Asian immigrants, mostly Chinese laborers, was an astounding 27 to 1. This extreme population imbalance meant that many men did not marry; consequently, those with aggressive natures remained unrestrained by the calming/controlling influence of family life and parental responsibility.

Nowhere were these cultural and population effects felt more acutely than on the western frontier. Here the population was predominately young bachelors, sensitive about honor, racially hostile, heavy drinkers, morally indifferent, heavily armed, and unchecked by adequate law enforcement. It is not surprising, considering this explosive mix, that 20 percent of the 89,000 miners who arrived in California during the "gold rush" of 1849 died within six months—some from disease, but many others from alcohol abuse and violence. Smoking, gambling, and heavy drinking became a cultural imperative, and those who were disinclined to indulge were considered social outcasts.

Over time, gender ratios equalized as more men brought families to the frontier and children of both sexes were born. The excess males in the population died, returned home, or drifted elsewhere. By the mid-twentieth century, America's overall male surplus was disappearing, and a balanced population helped bring the crime rate down to more reasonable levels.

Critical Thinking Skills

1. Are there cultural factors in contemporary society, similar to those that existed in the Old West, that produce crime in urban areas?
2. Does the fact that crime rates were higher in the nineteenth century refute the charge that violent entertainment is responsible for the nation's crime and violence problem?

InfoTrac College Edition Research

The Ku Klux Klan, which operated in the post–Civil War South, was later resurrected as a national organization. Read about its development in Rory McVeigh, "Structural Incentives for Conservative Mobilization: Power Devaluation and the Rise of the Ku Klux Klan, 1915–1925," *Social Forces,* June 1999, v77 i4 p1461(3)

SOURCES: David Courtwright, "Violence in America," *American Heritage* 47 (1996): 36–52, quote from p. 36; David Courtwright, *Violent Land: Single Men and Social Disorder from the Frontier to the Inner City* (Cambridge, MA: Harvard University Press, 1996); Ted Robert Gurr, "Historical Trends in Violent Crime: A Critical Review of the Evidence," in *Crime and Justice: An Annual Review of Research,* Vol. 3, ed. Michael Tonry and Norval Morris (Chicago: University of Chicago Press, 1981); Richard Maxwell Brown, "Historical Patterns of American Violence," in *Violence in America: Historical and Comparative Perspectives,* ed. Hugh Davis Graham and Ted Robert Gurr (Beverly Hills, CA: Sage, 1979).

THE CONTEMPORARY CRIMINAL JUSTICE SYSTEM

Fill in the blanks 3–5
True/False 1
Multiple choice 2
Essay 2–3

The justice system can be divided into three main components: law enforcement agencies, charged with investigating crimes and apprehending suspects; the court system, in which a determination is made whether a criminal suspect is guilty as charged; and the correctional system, charged both with treating and rehabilitating

EXHIBIT 1.1 COMPONENTS OF THE CRIMINAL JUSTICE SYSTEM

Police

Police departments are those public agencies created to maintain order, enforce the criminal law, provide emergency services, keep traffic on streets and highways moving freely, and create a sense of community safety. Police officers work actively with the community to prevent criminal behavior; they help divert members of special needs populations, such as juveniles, alcoholics, and drug addicts, from the criminal justice system; they participate in specialized units such as a drug prevention task force or anti-rape unit; they cooperate with public prosecutors to initiate investigations into organized crime and drug trafficking; they resolve neighborhood and family conflicts; and they provide emergency services, such as preserving civil order during strikes and political demonstrations.

Courts

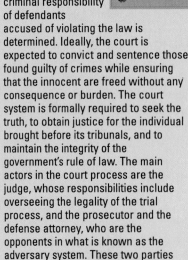

The criminal court is the scene of the trial process. Here the criminal responsibility of defendants accused of violating the law is determined. Ideally, the court is expected to convict and sentence those found guilty of crimes while ensuring that the innocent are freed without any consequence or burden. The court system is formally required to seek the truth, to obtain justice for the individual brought before its tribunals, and to maintain the integrity of the government's rule of law. The main actors in the court process are the judge, whose responsibilities include overseeing the legality of the trial process, and the prosecutor and the defense attorney, who are the opponents in what is known as the adversary system. These two parties oppose each other in a hotly disputed contest—the criminal trial—in accordance with rules of law and procedure.

Corrections

In the broadest sense, correctional agencies include community supervision or probation, various types of incarceration (including jails, houses of correction, and state prisons), and parole programs for both juvenile and adult offenders. These programs range from the lowest security, such as probation in the community with minimum supervision, to the highest security, such as 24-hour lock-down in an ultra-maximum security prison. Corrections ordinarily represent the postadjudicatory care given to offenders when a sentence is imposed by the court and the offender is placed in the hands of the correctional agency.

Despite his action-filled life, Wyatt Earp died in 1929 at the age of 80, peacefully sleeping in a rented cottage in Los Angeles. To read more about his colorful life, and to see photos of him and his associates, go to the following Web sites: http://www.techline.com/~nicks/earp.htm

http://www.thegrid.net/fern.canyon/tombston/wyatt/photos.htm

For an up-to-date list of Web links, see http://www.wadsworth.com/product/0534573053s

True/False 2–4
Essay 4

offenders and with incapacitating them so that they cannot repeat their crimes. These component agencies of the criminal justice system are set out in Exhibit 1.1.

Criminal justice agencies are political entities whose structure and function are lodged within the legislative, judicial, and executive branches of government (see Figure 1.1). The legislature defines the law by determining what conduct is prohibited and establishes criminal penalties for those who violate the law; the primary responsibility of legislatures in the justice system is to define criminal behavior and establish criminal penalties. The legislative branch of government helps shape justice policy by making appropriations for criminal justice agencies and acting as a forum for the public expression of views on criminal justice issues.

The judiciary interprets the existing law and determines whether it meets constitutional requirements. It also oversees criminal justice practices and has the power to determine whether existing laws fall within the ambit of state constitutions and, ultimately, the U.S. Constitution. The courts have the right to overturn or ban policies that conflict with constitutional rights.

Because most justice agencies fall within the executive branch of government, elected leaders have a mandate to plan programs, appoint personnel, and exercise administrative responsibility for criminal justice agencies. Executive leaders (such as the president, governors, and mayors) have the power of appointment within key justice agencies, including the right to appoint judges and heads of administrative agencies, such as police chiefs and commissioners of corrections; conversely, they can remove officials who are inefficient or ineffective.

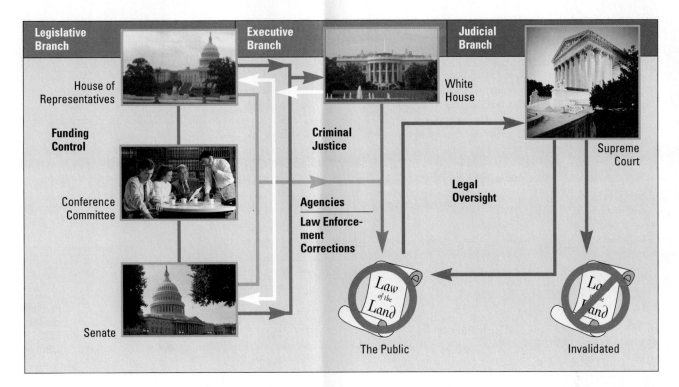

FIGURE 1.1
THE INTER-
RELATIONSHIP
AMONG THE
THREE BRANCHES
OF GOVERNMENT

SOURCE: *The United States Government Manual 1981/82 and/or 1982/83.*

The contemporary criminal justice system is monumental in size. It consists of more than 55,000 public agencies, including 17,000 police agencies, nearly 17,000 courts, more than 8,000 prosecutorial agencies, about 6,000 correctional institutions, and more than 3,500 probation and parole departments. Within the confines of these agencies, the justice system employs more than 2 million people, including about 900,000 in law enforcement.

Federal, state, and local governments spend more than $130 billion per year, or more than $400 for each U.S. resident, and the cost of operating the justice system has more than doubled since 1985 (see Exhbit 1.2 and Figure 1.2).[7] Capital costs are also growing. State jurisdictions are conducting massive correctional building campaigns, adding tens of thousands of prison cells. It costs about $70,000 to build a prison cell, and about $22,000 dollars per year to keep an inmate in prison; juvenile institutions cost about $30,000 per year per resident. Beyond the direct costs of funding police, court, and corrections, federal, state, and local governments incur many additional crime-related expenses; for example, federal drug control efforts now cost an additional $17 billion per year.[8]

The system is so big because it must process, treat, and care for millions of people each year. Although the crime rate has declined substantially during the past decade, about 15 million people are still being arrested each year, including more than 2 million for serious felony offenses.[9] In addition, about 1.5 million juveniles are handled by the juvenile courts. Today, state and federal courts convict a combined total of more than 1 million adults annually on felony charges.

Though the crime rate has declined, we are now punishing criminals more harshly and forcing them to spend more of their sentence in prison or jail cells. Consequently, the correctional system population is at an all-time high. About 6 million people are under the control of the correctional system, including almost 2 million behind bars and another 4 million in some form of community supervision. In 2000, almost 3 percent of the nation's adult population, or about 1 in every 34 adults, were incarcerated, on probation, or on parole.

 One of the best sources of information on the justice system is the Bureau of Justice Statistics: http://www.ojp.usdoj.gov/bjs/ For an up-to-date list of Web links, see http://www.wadsworth.com/product/0534573053s

EXHIBIT 1.2   THE COSTS OF CRIMINAL JUSTICE

- Federal, state, and local governments spent more than $112 billion per year for criminal and civil justice (1995).
- In 1995 the United States spent $48.6 billion for police protection and $39.8 billion for corrections, including jails, prisons, probation, and parole. The combined activities of courts, prosecution and legal services, and public defense accounted for $24.5 billion.
- The federal government alone spent more than $22 billion on criminal and civil justice in 1995, an increase of 253 percent since 1985. This included about $5.9 billion for grants to state and local governments. About $9 billion

was spent on police protection and $4.2 billion on corrections.
- Between 1985 and 1995, expenditures for operating the justice system increased from almost $65 billion to over $112 billion, an increase of about 73 percent in constant 1995 dollars.
- The justice system employed almost 2 million people, with a total 1995 October payroll of $5.8 billion.
- More than 900,000 employees worked in police protection, 401,000 were in judicial and legal services, and 656,000 worked in corrections.

SOURCE: Lea S. Gifford with assistance from Sue A. Lindgren, *Justice Expenditure and Employment in the United States, 1995* (Washington, DC: Bureau of Justice Statistics, 1999).

FIGURE 1.2 DIRECT EXPENDITURE BY CRIMINAL JUSTICE FUNCTION, 1982–1997

Direct expenditure for each of the major criminal justice functions (police, corrections, judicial) has been increasing.

NOTE: Does not include intergovernmental expenditures such as federal grants, but these dollars are included as direct expenditures by the recipient government when they are spent for salaries, supplies, and so on.

SOURCE: Sue Lindgren, *Justice Expenditure and Employment Extracts, 1997* (Washington, DC: Bureau of Justice Statistics, 2000).

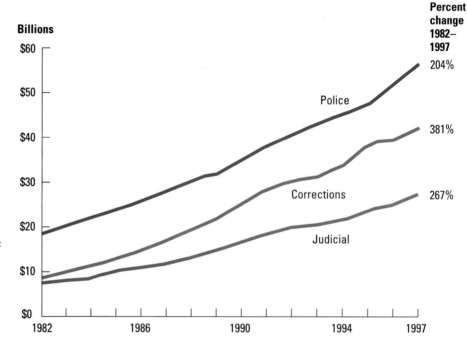

Fill in the blanks 6–11
True/False 5–16
Multiple choice 3–10
Essay 5

THE FORMAL CRIMINAL JUSTICE PROCESS

Another way of understanding criminal justice is to view it as a process that takes an offender through a series of decision points, beginning with arrest and concluding with reentry into society. During this process, key decision makers resolve whether to maintain the offender in the system or to discharge the suspect without further action. This decision making is often a matter of individual discretion, based on a variety of factors and perceptions. Legal factors—including the seriousness of the charges, available evidence, and the suspect's prior record—are usually considered legitimate influences on decision making. Troubling is the fact that such extralegal factors as the suspect's race, gender, class, and age may influence decision outcomes. Significant debate continues over the impact of extralegal factors in the decision to arrest, convict, and sentence suspects. Critics believe that a suspect's race, class, and gender often determine the direction a case will take; others argue that the system is relatively fair and unbiased.[10]

The concept of the formal justice process is important because it implies that every criminal defendant charged with a serious crime is entitled to the full range of rights under law. It is central to the American concept of liberty that every individual is entitled to his or her day in court, represented by competent counsel in a fair trial before an impartial jury, with trial procedures subject to review by a higher authority. Secret and hidden kangaroo courts and summary punishment are elements of political systems that most Americans fear and despise. The fact that most criminal suspects are actually treated informally may be less important than the fact that all criminal defendants are legally entitled to the full range of legal rights and constitutional protections.

A comprehensive view of the formal criminal process would normally include the following:

1. *Initial contact.* In most instances, the initial contact with the criminal justice system takes place as a result of a police action. For example, patrol officers observe a person acting suspiciously, conclude that the suspect is under the influence of drugs, and take him into custody. In another instance, police officers are contacted by a victim who reports a robbery; they respond by going to the scene of the crime and apprehend a suspect. In a third case, an informer tells police about some ongoing criminal activity in order to receive favorable treatment. Initial contact also may be launched by the police department's responding to the request of the mayor or other political figures to control an ongoing social problem. The police chief may then initiate an undercover investigation into corrupt practices such as gambling, prostitution, or drug trafficking.

2. *Investigation.* The purpose of the investigatory stage of justice is to gather sufficient evidence to identify a suspect and support a legal arrest. An investigation can take but a few minutes, as in the case where a police officer sees a crime in progress and apprehends the suspect within minutes. Or it can take many months

In order to make a legal arrest, police must have probable cause that the suspect committed a crime. Here, Michael McDermott of Haverhill, Massachusetts, an employee of Edgewater Technology, is led into court. McDermott was identified by police as allegedly the gunman who killed seven people in an office of Edgewater Technology on December 26, 2000.

AP/Wide World Photos

and involve hundreds of law enforcement agents, as in the FBI's pursuit of the so-called Unabomber that led to the eventual arrest of Ted Kaczynski. Investigations may be conducted at the local, state, or federal level and involve coordinated teams of law enforcement agents, prosecutors, and other justice officials.

3. *Arrest.* An arrest occurs when a person is taken into custody and consequently believes that he or she is not free to leave; the person is now a criminal suspect. An arrest is considered legal when all the following conditions exist: (1) The police officer believes there is sufficient evidence, referred to as *probable cause,* that a crime is being or has been committed and that the suspect is the person who committed it; (2) the officer deprives the individual of freedom; and (3) the suspect believes that he or she is now in the custody of the police. The police officer is not required to use the word "arrest" or any similar term to initiate an arrest, nor does the officer have to bring the suspect to the police station. To make an arrest in a misdemeanor, the officer must have witnessed the crime personally, known as the *in-presence requirement,* whereas a felony arrest can be based on the statement of a witness or victim. Arrests can also be made when a magistrate, presented with sufficient evidence by police and prosecutors, issues a warrant authorizing the arrest of a suspect.

4. *Custody.* The moment after an arrest is made, the detained suspect is considered in police custody. At this juncture, the police may wish to search the suspect for weapons or contraband, interrogate him or her in order to gain more information, find out if the person had any accomplices, or even encourage the suspect to confess to the crime. To look for further evidence, the police may wish to enter the suspect's home, car, or office. Similarly, the police may want to bring witnesses to view the suspect in a lineup or in a one-to-one confrontation. Personal information will also be taken from the suspect, including name, address, fingerprints, and photo. Because these procedures are so crucial and can have a great impact at trial, the U.S. Supreme Court has granted suspects in police custody protection from the unconstitutional abuse of police power, such as illegal searches and intimidating interrogations.

5. *Charging.* If the arresting officers and or/their superiors believe that sufficient evidence exists to charge a person with a crime, the case will be turned over to the prosecutor's office. Minor crimes (misdemeanors) are generally handled with a complaint being filed before the court that will try the case. For serious crimes (felonies), the prosecutor must decide whether to bring the case to a preliminary hearing or grand jury (depending on the procedures used in the jurisdiction). In either event, the decision to charge the suspect with a specific criminal act involves many factors, including evidence sufficiency, crime seriousness, case pressure, and political issues, as well as personal factors such as a prosecutor's specific interests and biases.

6. *Preliminary hearing/grand jury.* Because a criminal suspect faces great financial and personal costs when forced to stand trial for a felony, the U.S. Constitution mandates that, before a trial can take place, the government must first prove that there is probable cause that the accused committed the crime with which he or she is being charged. In about half the states and the federal system, this decision is rendered by a group of citizens brought together to form a grand jury, which considers the merits of the case in a closed hearing at which only the prosecutor presents evidence. If the evidence is sufficient, the grand jury will issue a bill of **indictment**, which specifies the charges on which the accused must stand trial. In the remaining states, the grand jury has been replaced with a preliminary hearing. In these jurisdictions, a charging document called an **information** is filed before a lower trial court, which then conducts an open hearing on the merits of the case. During this procedure, sometimes referred to as a *probable cause hear-*

indictment
A written accusation returned by a grand jury, charging an individual with a specified crime after determination of probable cause.

information
A formal charging document, similar to an indictment, based on probable cause as determined at a preliminary hearing.

ing, the defendant and his or her attorney may appear and dispute the prosecutor's charges. The suspect will be called to stand trial if the presiding magistrate or judge accepts the prosecutor's evidence as factual and sufficient.

7.   *Arraignment.* Before the trial begins, the defendant will be arraigned, or brought before the court that will hear the case. Formal charges are read, the defendant informed of his or her constitutional rights (for example, the right to be represented by legal counsel), an initial plea entered in the case (not guilty or guilty), a trial date set, and bail issues considered.

8.   *Bail/detention.* Bail is a money bond levied to ensure the return of a criminal defendant for trial while allowing the person pretrial freedom to prepare his or her defense. Defendants who do not show up for trial forfeit their bail. Those people who cannot afford to put up bail or who cannot borrow sufficient funds for it will remain in state custody prior to trial. In most instances, this means an extended stay in a county jail or house of correction. Most jurisdictions allow defendants awaiting trial to be released on their own recognizance (promise to the court), without bail, if they are stable members of the community and are accused of nonviolent crimes.

9.   *Plea bargaining.* Soon after an arraignment, if not before, defense counsel will meet with the prosecution to see if the case can be brought to a conclusion without a trial. In some instances, this can involve filing the case while the defendant participates in a community-based treatment program for substance abuse or receives psychiatric care. Most commonly, the defense and prosecution will discuss a possible guilty plea in exchange for reducing or dropping some of the charges or agreeing to a request for a more lenient sentence. Almost 90 percent of all cases end in a plea bargain rather than a criminal trial.

10. *Trial/adjudication.* If an agreement cannot be reached, or if the prosecution does not wish to arrange a negotiated settlement of the case, a criminal trial will be held before a judge or jury, who will decide whether the prosecution's evidence against the defendant is sufficient to prove guilt beyond a reasonable doubt. If a jury is deadlocked—that is, it cannot reach a unanimous decision—the case remains unresolved, leaving the prosecution to decide whether it should be retried at a later date.

11. *Sentencing/disposition.* If after a criminal trial the accused is found guilty as charged, he or she will be returned to court for sentencing. Possible dispositions may include a fine, probation, a period of incarceration in a penal institution, or even the death penalty.

12. *Appeal/postconviction remedies.* After conviction, the defense counsel can ask the trial judge to set aside the jury's verdict because he or she believes there has been a mistake of law. For example, in the nationally publicized Louise Woodward case, a young British nanny was convicted on a charge of second-degree murder in the death of an infant boy placed in her care. The verdict was soon set aside by the trial judge, who believed that the facts of the case did not substantiate the charge of second-degree murder; he reduced the charge to manslaughter and sentenced Woodward to time already served while she was awaiting trial.[11]

An appeal may be filed if, after conviction, the defendant believes that he or she did not receive fair treatment or that his or her constitutional rights were violated. **Appellate courts** review such issues as whether evidence was used properly, whether a judge conducted the trial in an approved fashion, whether jury selection was properly done, and whether the attorneys in the case acted appropriately. If the court rules that the appeal has merit, it can hold that the defendant be given a new trial or, in some instances, order his or her outright release.

13. *Correctional treatment.* After sentencing, offenders are placed under the jurisdiction of state or federal correctional authorities. They may serve a probationary

appellate court
Court that reconsiders a case that has already been tried to determine whether the lower court proceedings complied with accepted rules of criminal procedure and constitutional doctrines.

term, be placed in a community correctional facility, serve a term in a county jail, or be housed in a prison. During this stage of the criminal justice process, offenders may be asked to participate in rehabilitation programs designed to help them make a successful readjustment to society.

14. *Release.* Upon completion of the sentence and period of correction, the offender will be free to return to society. Most inmates do not serve the full term of their sentence but are freed via an early-release mechanism, such as parole or pardon or by earning time off for good behavior. Offenders sentenced to community supervision simply finish their term and resume their lives in the community.

15. *Postrelease.* After termination of their correctional treatment, offenders may be asked to spend some time in a community correctional center, which acts as a bridge between a secure treatment facility and absolute freedom. Offenders may find that their conviction has cost them some personal privileges, such as the right to hold certain kinds of employment. These may be returned by court order once the offenders have proven their trustworthiness and willingness to adjust to society's rules.

Criminal Justice Assembly Line

Herbert Packer has described the criminal justice process in the following terms:

> The image that comes to mind is an assembly line conveyor belt down which moves an endless stream of cases, never stopping, carrying them to workers who stand at fixed stations and who perform on each case as it comes by the same small but essential operation that brings it one step closer to being a finished product, or to exchange the metaphor for the reality, a closed file. The criminal process is seen as a screening process in which each successive stage—pre-arrest investigation, arrest, post-arrest investigation, preparation for trial, trial or entry of plea, conviction, disposition—involves a series of routinized operations whose success is gauged primarily by their tendency to pass the case along to a successful conclusion.[12]

Fill in the blanks 12–14
Multiple choice 11–12
Essay 6

According to this view, each of the stages described is actually a decision point through which cases flow (Figure 1.3). For example, at the investigatory stage, police must decide whether to pursue the case or terminate involvement because there is insufficient evidence to identify a suspect, the case is considered trivial, the victim decides not to press charges, and so on. Or at the bail stage, a decision must be made whether to set so high a bail that the defendant remains in custody, set a reasonable bail, or release the defendant on his or her own recognizance without requiring any bail at all. Each of these decisions can have a critical effect on the defendant, the justice system, and society. If an error is made, an innocent person may suffer, or a dangerous individual may be released to continue to prey upon society.

Because of this decision process, the justice system can be represented as a giant funnel (Figure 1.4). As the figure shows, most people who commit crimes escape detection, and of those who do not, many are filtered out of the system without being bound over for trial, convicted, and/or sentenced to prison.

In actual practice, many suspects are released before trial because of a procedural error, evidence problems, or other reasons that result in a dropped prosecution, or **nolle prosequi**. Other cases are dismissed by the presiding judge because of problems such as a witness's failure to appear or procedural irregularities. Thus, the justice process can be viewed as a funnel that holds a lot of cases at its mouth and relatively few at its end, narrowing down the number of offenders at each stage of the process.

Theoretically, nearly every part of the process requires that individual cases be disposed of as quickly as possible. However, the criminal justice process is slower and more tedious than desired because of congestion, inadequate facilities, limited resources, inefficiency, and the nature of governmental bureaucracy. When

nolle prosequi
Decision by a prosecutor to drop a case after a complaint has been made; reasons may include insufficient evidence, witness reluctance to testify, police error, or office policy.

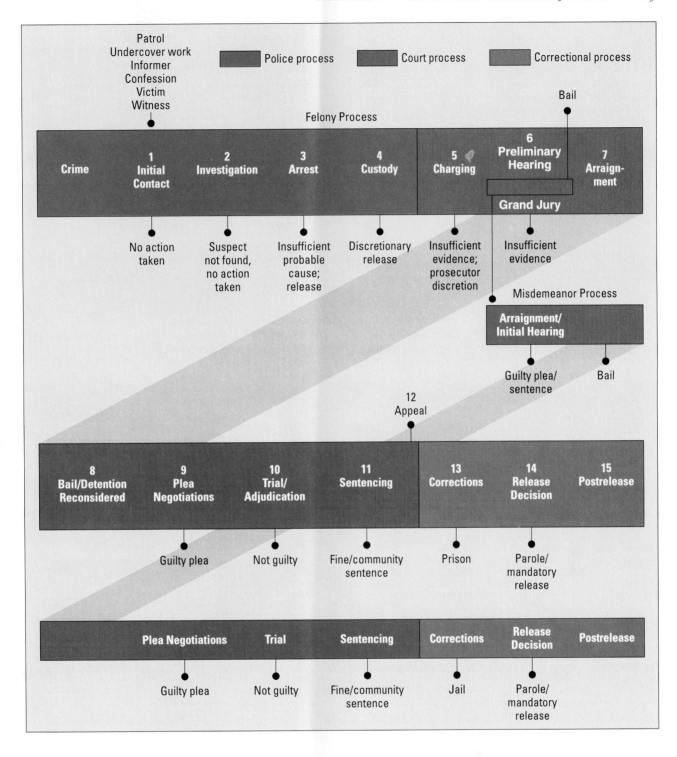

FIGURE I.3
THE CRITICAL STAGES IN THE JUSTICE PROCESS

FIGURE 1.4
THE CRIMINAL
JUSTICE FUNNEL

SOURCE: Patrick Langan and Richard Solari, *National Judicial Reporting Program,
2000* (Washington, DC: Bureau of Justice
Statistics, 2000).

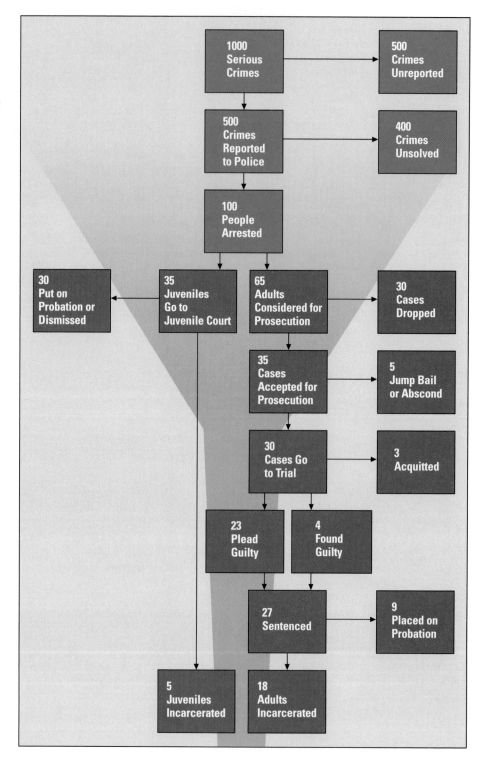

defendants are not processed smoothly, often because of the large caseloads and
inadequate facilities that exist in many urban jurisdictions, the procedure breaks
down, the process within the system fails, and the ultimate goal of a fair and efficient justice system cannot be achieved. Exhibit 1.3 shows the interrelationship
of the component agencies of the criminal justice system and the criminal justice
process.

EXHIBIT I.3 THE INTERRELATIONSHIP OF THE CRIMINAL JUSTICE SYSTEM AND THE CRIMINAL JUSTICE PROCESS

The System:
Agencies of Crime Control

1. Police

2. Prosecution and defense

3. Court

4. Corrections

The Process

1. Contact
2. Investigation
3. Arrest
4. Custody
5. Complaint/charging
6. Grand jury/preliminary hearing
7. Arraignment
8. Bail/detention
9. Plea negotiations
10. Adjudication
11. Disposition
12. Appeal/postconviction remedies
13. Correction
14. Release
15. Postrelease

THE INFORMAL CRIMINAL JUSTICE PROCESS

The public's perception of the justice system, fueled by the media, is that it is composed of daredevil, crime-fighting police officers who never ask for overtime or sick leave; crusading district attorneys who stop at nothing to send the mob boss up the river; wily defense attorneys who neither ask clients for up-front cash nor cut office visits to play golf; no-nonsense judges who are never inept political appointees; and tough wardens who rule the yard with an iron hand. Though this "ideal" model of justice still merits concern and attention, it would be overly simplistic to assume that the system works this way for every case. Although a few cases receive a full measure of rights and procedures, most are settled in an informal pattern of cooperation among the major actors in the justice process. For example, police may be willing to make a deal with a suspect in order to gain his or her cooperation, and the prosecutor bargains with the defense attorney to gain a plea of guilty as charged in return for a promise of leniency. Law enforcement agents and court officers are allowed tremendous discretion in their decisions to make an arrest, bring formal charges, handle a case informally, substitute charges, and so on. Crowded courts operate in a spirit of getting the matter settled quickly and cleanly, rather than engaging in long, drawn-out criminal proceedings with an uncertain outcome.

Although the traditional model regards the justice process as an adversary proceeding in which the prosecution and defense are combatants, the majority of criminal cases are actually cooperative ventures in which all parties get together to work out a deal; this is often referred to as the **courtroom work group**.[13] This group—made up of the prosecutor, defense attorney, judge, and other court personnel—functions to streamline the process of justice through the extensive use of plea bargaining and other alternatives. Rather than looking to provide a spirited defense or prosecution, these legal agents, who often have attended the same schools and have worked together for many years, try to work out a case to their own professional advantage. In most criminal cases, cooperation rather than conflict between prosecution and defense appears to be the norm. It is only in a few widely publicized criminal cases involving rape or murder that the adversarial

True/False 17–18

courtroom work group
All parties in the adversary process working together in a cooperative effort to settle cases with the least amount of effort and conflict.

process is called into play. Consequently, more than 80 percent of all felony cases and more than 90 percent of misdemeanors are settled without trial.

What has developed is a system in which criminal court experiences can be viewed as a training ground for young defense attorneys looking for seasoning and practice. It provides a means for newly established lawyers to receive government compensation for cases taken to get their practice going, or an arena in which established firms can place their new associates for experience before they are assigned to paying clients. Similarly, successful prosecutors can look forward to a political career or a highly paid partnership in a private firm. To further their career aspirations, prosecutors must develop and maintain a winning track record in criminal cases.

Although the courtroom work group limits the constitutional rights of defendants, it may be essential for keeping the overburdened justice system afloat. Moreover, it is not certain that informal justice is inherently unfair to both the victim and the offender. Research evidence shows that the defendants who benefit the most from informal court procedures commit the least serious crimes, while the more chronic offender gains relatively little.[14]

Samuel Walker, a justice historian and scholar, has come up with a rather dramatic way of describing this informal justice process: He compares it to a four-layer wedding cake, as depicted in Figure 1.5.[15]

Level I. The first layer of Walker's model is made up of the celebrated cases involving the wealthy and famous, such as O. J. Simpson, or the not so powerful who victimize a famous person—for example, John Hinckley, Jr., who shot President Ronald Reagan. Other cases fall into the first layer because they are widely reported in the media and become the subject of a television miniseries or movie. The media usually focus on hideous or unusual cases, such as the murder of child beauty queen JonBenet Ramsey.

Cases in the first layer of the criminal justice wedding cake usually receive the full array of criminal justice procedures, including competent defense attorneys,

FIGURE 1.5
THE CRIMINAL
JUSTICE
"WEDDING CAKE"

SOURCE: Based on Samuel Walker, *Sense and Nonsense about Crime* (Monterey, Calif.: Brooks/Cole, 1985).

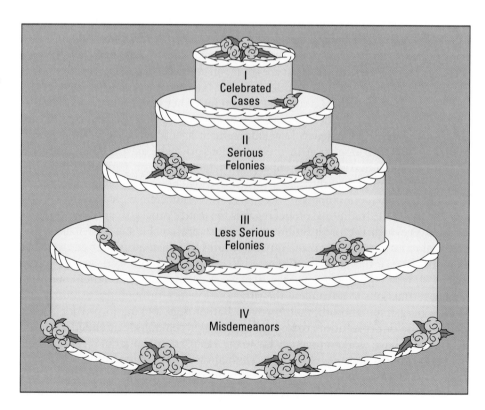

The first layer of Walker's model includes celebrated cases involving the wealthy and famous, such as O. J. Simpson. Other cases that fall into the first layer are those that are widely reported in the media, such as the murder of child beauty queen JonBenet Ramsey, whose murder remains unsolved.

© Rob Nelson/Black Star

expert witnesses, jury trials, and elaborate appeals. The media typically focus on Level I cases, giving the movie-going public the idea that most criminals are sober, intelligent people and most victims members of the upper classes—a patently false impression (see the accompanying Images of Justice feature).

Level II. In the second layer are serious felonies—rapes, robberies, and burglaries—committed by experienced offenders. Violent crimes, such as rape and assault, are vicious attacks on innocent victims and may involve a weapon and extreme violence. Robberies in this layer involve large amounts of money and suspects who brandish handguns or other weapons and are considered career criminals. Burglaries are included if the amount stolen is high and the techniques used indicate that the suspect is a professional thief. Police, prosecutors, and judges all agree that these are serious cases, worthy of the full attention of the justice system. Offenders in such Level II cases receive a full jury trial and, if convicted, can look forward to a prison sentence.

Level III. Although they can also be felonies, crimes that fall in the third layer of the wedding cake are less serious offenses, committed by young or first-time offenders and/or involving people who know each other or are otherwise related—for example, the inebriated teenager who commits a burglary and nets $50; the rape victim who had gone on a few dates with her assailant before he attacked her; the robbery that involved members of rival gangs but no weapons; the assault that was the result of a personal dispute, with some question as to who hit whom first. Agents of the criminal justice system relegate these cases to the third level because they see them as less important and less deserving of attention. Level III crimes may be dealt with by an outright dismissal, a plea bargain, a reduction in charges, and typically a probationary sentence or intermediate sanction such as victim restitution.

Hannibal

Agents of the criminal justice system routinely confront calculating, intelligent criminals who use guile and cunning to carry out their fiendish plots. Crime victims are wealthy, glamorous, highly intelligent, and well educated . . . even if they are cannibals. This is the theme of a 2001 film that focuses once again on the exploits of the media's most infamous criminal, Hannibal "The Cannibal" Lecter. As played by the distinguished British actor Anthony Hopkins, while Lecter is murderous and violent, he is also urbane, witty, and brilliant. In *Silence of the Lambs* (1991) the incarcerated Lecter locks horns with FBI Agent Clarice Starling (Jodie Foster) and helps her identify and capture a serial killer, all the while masterminding his own escape. In the 2001 hit *Hannibal,* Lecter is now free and employed as an art curator in Italy. (Why should being the most wanted man in the world stop you from getting a highly paid job that usually requires impeccable references and impressive credentials?) He is able to foil police detectives and take revenge against an old nemesis while lending a hand to his beloved Clarice (this time played by Julianne Moore).

An exciting adventure-action film, *Hannibal* is typical of the media's romanticized vision of criminals and the criminal justice system. According to Hollywood, most cases fall in the top layer of the criminal justice "wedding cake." They involve attractive victims and cunning, well-prepared criminals. The stakes are high and the law enforcement agents dedicated. Street battles and shootouts are common, lots of people die, and in the end the case is always solved. Because the victims, police, and criminals are all attractive, articulate, and well-educated (after all, they are Hollywood actors), criminals often form close bonds, friendships, or even romantic involvements with law enforcement agents.

Other films of this type include *The Jagged Edge,* in which an attorney (Glenn Close) and the client she is defending on murder charges (Jeff Bridges) become romantically involved; *Basic Instinct,* in which an accused killer (Sharon Stone) and the detective investigating the case (Michael Douglas) hook up; *The Fugitive,* in which a prison escapee (Harrison Ford), a well-known

physician, and pursuing U.S. Marshal Samuel Gerard (Tommy Lee Jones) form a bond. In *Ransom,* a billionaire's (Mel Gibson) son is kidnapped and he tracks down and kills the culprits. In *A Perfect Murder,* a multimillionaire banker (Michael Douglas) plots to kill his beautiful wife (Gwyneth Paltrow). Sometimes these formulas are so successful that they breed a score of sequels with almost identical plots. For example, *The Fugitive* was so successful that the plot was recycled in *U.S. Marshals* (1998), with Jones now pursuing an urbane secret agent named Sheridan (Wesley Snipes), and then again in *Double Jeopardy,* in which Jones plays parole officer Travis Lehman pursuing the beautiful absconder Libby Parsons (Ashley Judd) as she seeks out her supposedly dead ex-husband (Bruce Greenwood) who is really very much alive.

These films give the public a distorted view of both criminals and the criminal justice system. While it is true that some cases do involve the wealthy and glamorous, such cases are actually few and far between. The majority of victims and criminals come from the lower end of the socioeconomic scale and live in disorganized neighborhoods

Level IV. The fourth layer of the cake is made up of the millions of misdemeanors, such as disorderly conduct, shoplifting, public drunkenness, and minor assault. These are handled by the lower criminal courts in assembly-line fashion. Few defendants insist on exercising their full constitutional rights because the delay would cost them valuable time and money. Since the typical penalty is a small fine, everyone wants to get the case settled.[16]

The wedding cake model of informal justice is an intriguing alternative to the traditional criminal justice flowchart. Although criminal justice officials do handle individual cases differently, there is a high degree of consistency in the way particular types or classes of cases are dealt in most every legal jurisdiction. Police and prosecutors in Los Angeles, Boston, New York, and San Antonio will each handle the murder of a prominent citizen in a similar fashion. They will also deal with the death of an unemployed street person killed in a brawl with a peer over a pair of shoes in a likewise manner. Yet in each jurisdiction, the two cases will be

Noted British actor Anthony Hopkins plays the infamous criminal Hannibal Lecter in the 1991 film *Silence of the Lambs* and again in its 2001 sequel *Hannibal.*

Starling and match wits with the world's most notorious, and charming, killer?

Critical Thinking Skills

1. Would the public go to see movies that accurately portrayed the typical criminal as a drug-abusing teen with significant social problems?
2. Do movies such as *Hannibal* harm the justice system with their glamorized view of crime and criminals? For example, do they promote vigilante justice?

InfoTrac College Edition Research

To read more about the film *Hannibal,* use the title as a key word on InfoTrac College Edition.

rather than penthouses; few people are murdered on their yacht. Very few crimes involve millions of dollars; most criminals "earn" far less than minimum wage for their efforts. Rather than being intelligent and articulate, they are more likely to be drug abusing and desperate.

While *Hannibal* makes an exciting film, it does little to enhance the reputation of Federal law enforcement, which Lecter seems to outwit without too much effort. On the other hand, it is a great recruiting tool for the FBI. Who would not want to follow in the footsteps of Clarice

handled very differently from one another. The bigwig's killer will receive a full-blown jury trial (with details on the six o'clock news); the street person's killer will get a quick plea bargain. The model is useful because it helps us realize that, all too often, public opinion about criminal justice is formed on the basis of what happened in a celebrated case that is actually atypical.

PERSPECTIVES ON CRIMINAL JUSTICE

Even though it has been more than 25 years since the field of criminal justice began to be the subject of both serious academic study and attempts at unified policy formation, significant debate continues over the actual meaning of "criminal justice" and how the problem of crime control should be approached. Some conservative "hard-liners" seek to solve the crime problem by increasing the number of police, apprehending more criminals, and giving them long sentences in

Essay 8

maximum-security prisons. In contrast, liberals call for increased spending on social services and community organization. Others worry about giving the government too much power to regulate and control behavior and to interfere with individual liberty and freedom.

Considering the complexity of criminal justice, it is not surprising that no single view, perspective, or philosophy dominates the field. What are the dominant views of the criminal justice system today? What is the role of the justice system, and how should it approach its tasks? The different perspectives on criminal justice are discussed in the following sections.

Fill in the blanks 16
True/False 20

Crime Control Perspective

More than 20 years ago, political scientist James Q. Wilson made the persuasive argument that most criminals are not poor unfortunates who commit crime to survive but greedy people who choose theft and/or drug dealing for quick and easy profits.[17] Criminals, he argued, lack inhibition against misconduct, value the excitement and thrills of breaking the law, have a low stake in conformity, and are willing to take greater chances than the average person. If they could be convinced that their actions will bring severe punishment, only the totally irrational would be willing to engage in crime. He made this famous observation:

> Wicked people exist. Nothing avails except to set them apart from innocent people. And many people, neither wicked nor innocent, but watchful, dissembling, and calculating of their chances, ponder our reaction to wickedness as a clue to what they might profitably do.[18]

crime control perspective
A model of criminal justice that emphasizes the control of dangerous offenders and the protection of society through harsh punishment as a deterrent to crime.

Wilson's views helped define the **crime control perspective** of criminal justice. According to this view, the proper role of the justice system is to prevent crime through the judicious use of criminal sanctions. Because the public is outraged by crimes such as the shootings at Columbine High School, it demands an efficient justice system that hands out tough sanctions to those who choose to violate the law.[19] If the justice system operated in an effective manner, potential criminals would be deterred from committing law violations, and those who did commit crime would be apprehended, tried, and punished so they would never dare risk committing crime again. Crime rates trend upward, the argument goes, when criminals do not sufficiently fear apprehension and punishment. If the efficiency of the system could be increased and the criminal law could be toughened, crime rates would eventually decline. Crime control advocates attribute recent reductions in the crime rate to a "get tough" attitude toward crime, which has resulted in mandatory punishments and expanding prison populations. Although crime control may be expensive, reducing the pains of criminal activity is well worth the price.

According to the crime control perspective, the focus of justice should be on the victim of crime, not the criminal, so that innocent people can be protected from the ravages of crime. This objective can be achieved through more effective police protection, tough sentences (including liberal use of the death penalty), and the construction of prisons designed to safely incapacitate hardened criminals. If punishment was both certain and severe, few would be tempted to break the law.

Crime control advocates do not want legal technicalities to help the guilty go free and tie the hands of justice. They lobby for the abolition of legal restrictions that control a police officer's ability to search for evidence and interrogate suspects with a free hand. They are angry at judges who let obviously guilty people go free because a police officer made an unintentional procedural error. They have little patience with "bleeding heart" judges who consider an offender's troubled past when making sentencing decisions.

Unabomber victim David Gelernter holds a paintbrush in his hand damaged by Unabomber Ted Kaczynski. Crime control advocates demand that the victim's pain and suffering be considered by the justice system. They believe that the focus of justice should be on the victim of crime, not the criminal, so that innocent people can be protected from the ravages of crime.

© Brooks Kraft/CORBIS-Sygma

Advocates of the crime control perspective also question the criminal justice system's ability to rehabilitate offenders. Most treatment programs are ineffective because the justice system is simply not equipped to treat people who have a long history of antisocial behavior. Even when agents of the system attempt to prevent crime by working with young people, the results are unsatisfactory. For example, evaluations of the highly touted Drug Abuse Resistance Education (DARE) antidrug program indicate that it has little impact on students.[20] From both a moral and a practical standpoint, the role of criminal justice should be the control of antisocial people. If not to the justice system, then to whom can the average citizen turn for protection from society's criminal elements?

Rehabilitation Perspective

If crime control advocates view the justice system in terms of protecting the public and controlling criminal elements, then those who advocate the **rehabilitation perspective** may be said to see the justice system as a means of caring for and treating people who cannot manage themselves. They view crime as an expression of frustration and anger created by poverty and social inequality. The crime rate would decline if people were given the means to improve their lifestyle through conventional endeavors.

The rehabilitation concept assumes that people are at the mercy of social, economic, and interpersonal conditions and interactions. Criminals themselves are the victims of racism, poverty, strain, blocked opportunities, alienation, family

True/False 21
Multiple choice 13–14

rehabilitation perspective
A model of criminal justice that sees crime as an expression of frustration and anger created by social inequality that can be controlled by giving people the means to improve their lifestyle though conventional endeavors.

Rehabilitation advocates believe that at-risk youngsters will forgo criminal behavior if adequate alternatives to crime can be provided. Here, a police officer works with schoolchildren at a community-run summer gang-resistance program in Boston. Can such programs alone lure youths away from gangs and drugs?

© Brooks Kraft/CORBIS-Sygma

disruption, and other social problems. They live in socially disorganized neighborhoods that are incapable of providing proper education, health care, or civil services. Society must help them in order to compensate for their social problems.

Rehabilitation advocates believe that government programs can help reduce crime on both a macro (societal) and a micro (individual) level. For example, research shows that as the number of legitimate opportunities to succeed declines, people are more likely to turn to criminal behaviors, such as drug dealing, in order to survive.[21] Increasing economic opportunities through job training, family counseling, educational services, and crisis intervention are more effective crime reducers than prisons and jails. As legitimate opportunities increase, violence rates decline.[22]

Once apprehended, criminals can benefit from well-designed treatment efforts, which can reduce repeat offending. Offender rehabilitation programs that help people develop interpersonal skills, induce a prosocial change in attitudes, and improve cognitive thinking patterns have been shown to significantly reduce recidivism rates.[23]

Clearly, punishing offenders and placing them in prison does not seem to deter future criminality. Society has a choice: Pay now, by funding treatment and educational programs, or pay later, when troubled youths enter costly correctional facilities over and over again. This view is certainly not lost on the public. Although the public may want to "get tough" on crime, many are willing to make exceptions—for example, by advocating leniency for younger offenders.[24]

Multiple choice 15–17

Due Process Perspective

due process perspective
A model of criminal justice that emphasizes individual rights and constitutional safeguards against arbitrary or unfair judicial or administrative proceedings.

Falling between these extremes is the position that, regardless of its aims, the existing justice system must be made to run in an efficient and fair manner. Advocates of the **due process perspective** argue that the greatest concern of the justice system should be providing fair and equitable treatment to those accused of crime.[25] This means providing impartial hearings, competent legal counsel, equitable treatment, and reasonable sanctions. The use of discretion within the justice system should be strictly monitored to ensure that no one suffers from racial, religious, or ethnic discrimination. There are many views of what the true goals of justice should be, but there is no question that the system must operate in a fair and unbiased manner.

To learn more about the practice of racial profiling, go to the American Civil Liberties Union home page: http://www.aclu.org/profiling/

For an up-to-date list of Web links, see http://www.wadsworth.com/product/0534573053s

Those who advocate the due process perspective are quick to point out that the justice system remains an adversary process that pits the forces of an all-powerful state against those of a solitary individual accused of a crime. If concern for justice and fairness did not exist, the defendant who lacked resources could easily be overwhelmed; miscarriages of justice are common. Numerous cases have been overturned because modern technology such as DNA testing later proved that convicted criminals could not possibly have committed the crimes of which they were accused.[26] Some evidence indicates that innocent people may have been executed for crimes they did not commit: Between 1976 and 1999, 566 people were executed in the United States; during that same period of time, 82 convicts awaiting execution were exonerated—a ratio of 1 freed for every 7 put to death.[27] Since such mistakes can happen, even the most apparently guilty offender deserves all the protection the justice system can offer.

Due process advocates suggest that each citizen is entitled to a number of rights and privileges, including but not limited to the right to a fair hearing, timely notice, an impartial jury, and competent legal counsel. Although access to these rights is rarely challenged, a long-standing debate continues over the prerogatives and privileges of criminal suspects. How far should we go to protect individual rights? What happens when individual rights interfere with public safety? For example, if police officers discover incriminating evidence while searching a suspect but in so doing violate his constitutional right to privacy, should the information be excluded from his trial even if it means that a dangerous person goes free? Some might argue that it is better to free a guilty person than trample on the civil rights of citizens, even those who commit criminal acts. But what about the rights of actual or potential victims of crime? Should the needs of the victim take precedence over those of criminal offenders? And what about the quality of care? Should we provide the highest-paid private attorneys for criminal suspects, or will a novice public defender suffice?

PERSPECTIVES ON JUSTICE

Chapter 4 covers the legal rights of offenders in great detail. It also helps define the concept of due process more fully.

Nonintervention Perspective

The **nonintervention perspective** holds that justice agencies should limit their involvement with criminal defendants. Regardless of whether intervention is designed to punish or treat people, the ultimate effect of any involvement is harmful. Whatever their goals or design, programs that involve people with a social control agency—such as the police, a mental health department, the correctional system, or a criminal court—will have long-term negative effects. Once involved with such an agency, criminal defendants may be watched, people may consider them dangerous and untrustworthy, and they can develop a lasting record that has negative connotations. Eventually, they may even come to believe what their official record suggests; they may view themselves as bad, evil, outcasts, troublemakers, or crazy. Noninterventionists are concerned about the effect of **stigma** that criminal suspects bear when they are given negative labels such as "rapist" or "child abuser." These labels will stick with them forever; once labeled, people may

Multiple choice 18–20

nonintervention perspective
A model of criminal justice that favors the least intrusive treatment possible: decarceration, diversion, and decriminalization.

stigma
An enduring label that taints a person's identity and changes him or her in the eyes of others.

decriminalization
Reducing the penalty for a criminal act without actually legalizing it.

victimless crime
Public order crime that has no specific victim, such as public drunkenness or vagrancy.

deinstitutionalization
The movement to remove as many offenders as possible from secure confinement and treat them in the community.

pretrial diversion
Informal, community-based treatment programs that are used in lieu of the formal criminal process.

find it difficult to ever be accepted back into society, even after they have completed their sentence.

Fearing the harmful effects of stigma and labels, noninterventionists have tried to place limitations on the government's ability to control people's lives. They have called for the **decriminalization** (reduction of penalties) and/or legalization of nonserious **victimless crimes**, such as the possession of small amounts of marijuana for medical use, public drunkenness, and vagrancy. They demand the removal of nonviolent offenders from the nation's correctional system, a policy referred to as **deinstitutionalization**. First offenders who commit minor crimes should be instead placed in informal, community-based treatment programs, a process referred to as **pretrial diversion**.

Sometimes the passage of new criminal laws helps stigmatize offenders beyond the scope of their actual offense. For example, a person who purchases pornography on the Internet is labeled a dangerous "sex offender," or someone caught for a second time with marijuana is considered a "habitual drug abuser." Noninterventionists have fought implementation of community notification–type laws that require convicted sex offenders to register with state law enforcement officials and allow officials to make it publicly known when a registrant moves into a community. Their efforts have resulted in rulings that these laws can be damaging to the reputation and future of offenders who have not been given an opportunity to defend themselves from the charge that they are chronic "criminal sex offenders."[28] As a group, noninterventionist initiatives have been implemented to help people avoid the stigma associated with contact with the criminal justice system.

True/False 22
Multiple choice 21–22

justice perspective
A model of criminal justice that favors determinate sentencing, seeks to abolish parole, and sees prisons as places of punishment, not rehabilitation.

Justice Perspective

The core of the **justice perspective** is that all people should receive the same treatment under the law. Any effort to distinguish between criminal offenders will create a sense of unfairness that can interfere with readjustment to society. It is frustrating when two people commit the same crime but receive different sentences or punishments. The resulting anger and sense of unfairness will increase the likelihood of recidivism.

To remedy this situation, the criminal justice system must reduce discretion and unequal treatment. Law violators should be evaluated on the basis of their current behavior, not on what they have done in the past (they have already paid for their behavior) nor on what they may do in the future (future behavior cannot be accurately predicted). The treatment of criminal offenders must be based solely on present behavior: Punishment must be equitably administered and based on "just desert."

Advocates of the justice perspective have had considerable influence in molding the nation's sentencing policy. There has been an ongoing effort to reduce discretion and guarantee that every offender convicted of a particular crime receives equal punishment. Initiatives designed to achieve this result have included mandatory sentences, which require that all people convicted of a crime receive the same prison sentence. Truth-in-sentencing laws now require offenders to serve a substantial portion of their sentence in prison and limit their eligibility for early release on parole.[29]

PERSPECTIVES ON JUSTICE

Truth-in-sentencing laws will be discussed further in Chapter 13. Along with sentencing guidelines, these laws seek to create uniformity in the application of criminal punishments.

Restorative Justice Perspective

Multiple choice 23–25

According to the **restorative justice perspective**, the true purpose of the criminal justice system is to promote a peaceful and just society; the justice system should aim for peacemaking, not punishment.[30]

The restorative justice perspective draws its inspiration from religious and philosophical teachings ranging from Quakerism to Zen. Advocates of restorative justice view the efforts of the state to punish and control as crime-encouraging rather than crime-discouraging. The violent punishing acts of the state, they claim, are not dissimilar to the violent acts of individuals.[31] Therefore, mutual aid rather than coercive punishment is the key to a harmonious society. Without the capacity to restore damaged social relations, society's response to crime has been almost exclusively punitive.

According to restorative justice, resolution of the conflict between criminal and victim should take place in the community in which it originated, not in some far-off prison. The victim should be given a chance to voice his or her story, and the offender can directly communicate his or her need for social reintegration and treatment. The goal is to enable offenders to appreciate the damage they have caused, to make amends, and to be reintegrated back into society.

Restorative justice programs are now being geared to these principles. Police officers, as elements of community policing programs, are beginning to use mediation techniques to settle disputes rather than resort to formal arrest.[32] Mediation and conflict-resolution programs are common features in many communities. Financial and community-service restitution programs as an alternative to imprisonment have been in operation for more than two decades.

restorative justice perspective
A model of criminal justice that views the role of the criminal justice system as one to promote peace and justice and not to punish offenders.

PERSPECTIVES IN ACTION: CONTROLLING THE DRUG TRADE

The fact that multiple perspectives of justice exist can be most readily seen in the so-called war on drugs. Agencies of the criminal justice system have employed a number of strategies to reduce drug trafficking and the use of drugs. Some have relied on a strict crime control orientation; others feature nonintervention, justice, and rehabilitation strategies (see Figure 1.6). The following sections illustrate how each perspective influences criminal justice efforts to control or reduce the drug trade.

Crime Control Strategies

A number of strategies have been used to reduce the drug trade through strict crime control. Such strategies include source control, border control, and police crackdowns.

Source Control A major effort has been made to cut off supplies of drugs by destroying crops and arresting members of drug cartels in drug-producing countries; this approach is known as **source control**. The federal government's Drug Enforcement Administration has been in the vanguard of encouraging exporting nations to step up efforts to destroy drug crops and prosecute dealers. Translating words into deeds, however, is a formidable task. Drug lords are willing and able to fight back through intimidation, violence, and corruption. The drug cartels in Colombia and Mexico do not hesitate to use violence and assassination to protect their interests. Since 1994, enforcement efforts in Peru and Bolivia have been so successful that drug crops there have been significantly reduced. Rather than inhibiting drug shipments, however, the result has been to make Colombia the

source control
Attempting to cut off the supply of illegal drugs by destroying crops and arresting members of drug cartels in drug-producing countries.

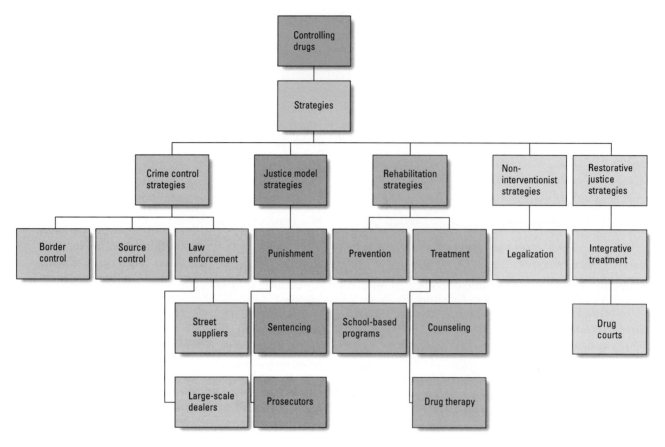

FIGURE 1.6
STRATEGIES FOR
CONTROLLING
DRUGS

To read about what the U.S. government is doing to control drug importation, and to access important data on drugs and crime, go to the Web site of the Office of National Drug Control Policy: http://www. whitehousedrugpolicy.gov/

For an up-to-date list of Web links, see http://www.wadsworth.com/product/0534573053s

premier coca-cultivating country. When the Colombian government mounted an effective eradication campaign in the traditional growing areas, the drug cartel linked up with rebel groups in remote parts of the country for their drug supply.[33] Enforcement efforts in Columbia have also promoted the emergence of Mexican drug cartels.

Border Control Another crime control approach to the drug problem has been to interdict drug supplies as they enter the country. Border patrols and military personnel using sophisticated hardware have been involved in massive interdiction efforts; many impressive multimillion-dollar seizures have been made. U.S. borders are so vast and unprotected, however, that meaningful interdiction is difficult. To aid law enforcement agencies, the U.S. military has become involved in stemming the flow of drugs across the border. The cost of staffing listening posts and patrolling borders is growing rapidly; today, interdiction and eradication strategies costs billions of dollars, yet they do little to reduce drug supplies.

Police Crackdowns Local, state, and federal law enforcement agents have also been engaged in an active fight against drugs. One approach is to direct efforts at large-scale drug rings. However, this effort has merely served to decentralize drug dealing. Law enforcement efforts have significantly reduced the strength of traditional organized syndicates. Rather than reducing the inflow of drugs, their place has been taken by Asian, Latin, and Jamaican groups, motorcycle gangs, and local street gangs. Colombian syndicates have established cocaine distribution centers on every continent, and Mexican organizations are responsible for large methamphetamine shipments to the United States. Russian, Turkish, Italian, Nigerian, Chinese, Lebanese, and Pakistani heroin-trafficking syndicates are now competing for dominance.

In terms of weight and availability, there is still no commodity more lucrative than illegal drugs. They cost relatively little to produce and provide large profit margins to dealers and traffickers. At an average street price of $100 per gram in the United States, a metric ton of pure cocaine is worth $100 million; cutting it and reducing purity can double or triple the value. It is difficult for law enforcement agencies to counteract the inducement of drug profits. When large-scale drug busts are made, supplies become scarce and market values increase, encouraging more people to enter the drug trade.

Aiming efforts at low-level dealers is also problematic. Some street-level enforcement efforts have been successful, but others are considered failures. Drug sweeps have clogged courts and correctional facilities with petty offenders while proving a costly drain on police resources. A displacement effect is also suspected: Stepped-up efforts to curb drug dealing in one area or city simply encourage dealers to seek out friendlier territory.

Justice Strategies

According to the justice perspective, if drug violations were punished with criminal sentences commensurate with their harm, then the "rational" drug trafficker would look for a new line of employment. The cornerstone of this antidrug model is the adoption of mandatory minimum sentences for drug crimes, ensuring that all offenders receive similar punishments for their acts. Justice model advocates lobby for sentencing policies that will standardize punishments. The Federal Anti–Drug Abuse Act of 1988 provides minimum mandatory prison sentences for serious drug crimes, with especially punitive sentences for anyone caught distributing drugs within 1,000 feet of a school playground, youth center, or other area where minors congregate.[34] Once convicted, drug dealers are subject to very long sentences and face seizure of their homes, automobiles, boats, and other assets used in drug trafficking.

However, these punitive efforts often have their downside. Defense attorneys consider delay tactics sound legal maneuvering in drug-related cases. Courts are so backlogged that prosecutors are anxious to plea bargain. The consequence of this legal maneuvering is that about 25 percent of people convicted on federal drug charges are granted probation or some other form of community release.[35] Even so, prisons have become jammed with inmates, many of whom were involved in drug-related cases. Many drug offenders sent to prison do not serve their entire sentences because they are released in an effort to relieve prison overcrowding.[36]

Rehabilitation Strategies

Advocates of the rehabilitation perspective have suggested strategies aimed at reducing the desire to use drugs and increasing incentives for users to eliminate substance abuse. What strategies have been tried?

AP/Wide World Photos

Law enforcement authorities at the attorney general's office in Boston display piles of cash, weapons, and drugs confiscated during an early morning drug bust that involved approximately 150 officers. State police arrested 15 people suspected of distributing drugs and seized fake placards that allowed the suspects to park in handicapped spaces. Police also seized 20 pounds of cocaine, worth between $75,000 and $100,000, several thousand Percoset pills, six luxury cars, and "a significant amount" of the drug Ecstasy. Police crackdowns like this one can bring quick results, but some critics believe they are only a short-term solution. The threat of aggressive law enforcement may simply convince criminals to relocate their operations elsewhere.

DARE
Drug Abuse Resistance Education, a school-based program designed to give students the skills to resist peer pressure to experiment with tobacco, alcohol, and illegal drugs.

Drug Prevention One approach relies on drug prevention—convincing nonusers not to start using drugs. This effort relies heavily on educational programs that teach young people to say no to drugs. The best-known program is Drug Abuse Resistance Education, or **DARE**. This elementary school course is designed to give students the skills for resisting peer pressure to experiment with tobacco, drugs, and alcohol. Evaluations of the program have been disappointing: It has increased knowledge about dangerous substances, but it has been insignificant in shaping attitudes toward drug abuse and law enforcement, increasing self-esteem, or reducing student drug use.[37]

Offender Treatment The rehabilitation model suggests that it is possible to treat known users, get them clean of drugs and alcohol, and help them reenter conventional society.

There has been an active effort to identify drug abusers in order to get them into treatment. Drug testing of arrestees is common. Public and private institutions now regularly test employees and clients to determine if they are drug abusers.

Once users have been identified, a number of drug offender treatment strategies have been implemented. One approach rests on the assumption that users have low self-esteem and holds that treatment efforts must focus on building a sense of self. In this approach, users participate in outdoor activities and wilderness training in order to create self-reliance and a sense of accomplishment.[38]

More intensive efforts use group therapy approaches, relying on group leaders who once were substance abusers. Group sessions try to give users the skills and support that can help them reject the social pressure to use drugs. These programs are based on the Alcoholics Anonymous approach: Users must find within themselves the strength to stay clean, and peer support from those who understand the users' experiences can help them achieve a drug-free life.

methadone
A synthetic narcotic used as a substitute for heroin in drug-control efforts.

Residential programs have been established for the more heavily involved users, and a large network of drug treatment centers has been developed. Some are detoxification units that use medical procedures to wean patients from the more addicting drugs to others, such as **methadone**, whose use can be more easily regulated. Methadone, a drug similar to heroin, is given to addicts at clinics under controlled conditions. Methadone programs have been undermined because some users sell their methadone on the black market, while others supplement their dosages with illegally obtained heroin.

Despite their good intentions, little evidence exists that these treatment programs are an efficient means of ending substance abuse. A stay in a treatment facility can stigmatize residents as "addicts," even though they have never used hard drugs; while in treatment, they may be introduced to hard-core users with whom they may associate upon release. Hard-core users often do not enter these programs voluntarily and have little motivation to change.[39] Even those who could be helped soon learn that there are simply more users who need treatment than there are beds in treatment facilities. Many programs are restricted to users whose health insurance will pay for short-term residential care; when the insurance coverage ends, the patients are often released before their treatment program is completed. As the Analyzing Criminal Justice Issues feature shows, if treatment strategies are to be successful, far more programs and funding are needed.

Restorative Justice Strategies

Restorative justice programs stress treatment and reintegration over punitive reactions to drug offenders. One example of this approach is the so-called drug courts first developed in Florida in the early 1990s. These serve as an alternative to traditional criminal justice prosecution for drug-related offenses and work to tailor nonpunitive, effective, and appropriate responses to offenders with drug problems. Defendants eligible for the drug court program are identified as soon as possible; if accepted into the program, they are referred immediately to a multiphased outpatient treatment program entailing multiple weekly (often daily) contacts with the treatment provider for counseling, therapy, and education and a rehabilitation program entailing vocational, educational, family, medical, and other support services.[40]

Nonintervention Strategies

Despite the massive effort to control drug usage through both crime control and rehabilitation strategies, the fight has not been successful. Getting people out of the drug trade is difficult because drug trafficking involves enormous profits and dealers and users both lack meaningful economic alternatives. Controlling drugs by convincing known users to quit is equally hard; few treatment efforts have proven successful.

Considering these problems, some commentators, relying on a noninterventionist strategy, have called for the **legalization** of drugs. If drugs were legalized, the argument goes, distribution could be controlled by the government. Price and distribution methods could be regulated, reducing addicts' cash requirements. Crime rates would be cut because drug users would no longer need the same cash flow to support their habit. Drug-related deaths would decrease because government control would reduce the sharing of needles and thus the spread of AIDS. Legalization would also destroy the drug-importing cartels and gangs. Since drugs would be bought and sold openly, the government would reap a windfall from taxes both on the sale of drugs and on the income of drug dealers, which now is untaxed as part of the hidden economy. Drug distribution would be regulated, keeping narcotics out of the hands of adolescents. Those who favor legalization point to the Netherlands as a country that has legalized drugs and remains relatively crime-free.[41]

Advocates of legalization suggest that, like it or not, drug use is here to stay because the use of mood-altering substances is customary in almost all human societies; no matter how hard we try, people will find ways of obtaining psychoactive drugs.[42] Banning drugs serves to create networks of underground manufacturers and distributors, many of whom use violence as part of their standard operating procedures. Some may charge that drug use is immoral, but is it any worse than the unrestricted use of alcohol and cigarettes, both of which are addicting and unhealthy? Far more people die each year as a result of abusing these legal substances than as a result of drug wars or abuse of illegal substances (an estimated 100,000 people per year die from alcohol-related causes and another 320,000 from tobacco).[43]

Although legalization can have the short-term effect of reducing crime, critics are wary of its social consequences. Legalization may harm the well-being of the community by creating health and social damage. Individuals do not have the right to harm society even if it means curbing their freedom and personal choices—that is, the right to use drugs. If injured by their drug use, individuals have to be cared for by the community at a very substantial cost to non–drug abusers.[44] Legalization would result in an increase in the nation's rate of drug usage, creating an even larger group of nonproductive, drug-dependent people who must be cared for by the rest of society.[45] It is likely that if drugs were legalized and freely available, drug users might significantly increase their daily intake. Countries such as Iran and Thailand, where drugs are cheap and readily available, have high rates of narcotics use.

Others argue that the problems of alcoholism should serve as a warning of what can happen when controlled substances are made readily available. The number of

legalization
The removal of all criminal penalties from a previously outlawed act.

ANALYZING CRIMINAL JUSTICE ISSUES

Can Rehabilitation Work?

One of the longest-running debates in criminal justice is whether rehabilitation can actually work or whether the justice system should be viewed as a punishment-dispensing institution aimed at deterring potential criminals. Elliot Currie, a leading rehabilitation advocate, argues forcefully in his book *Reckoning* that drug abuse and crime can be controlled by (1) emphasizing high-quality early education, such as the Head Start program; (2) expanding health and mental health services for high-risk children and adults, including prenatal and postnatal care; (3) making a greater commitment to family support programs; (4) offering adequate work opportunities; and (5) providing adequate shelter and housing for all Americans. "In the long run," he writes, "dealing with America's drug crisis means attacking the conditions which breed it—a principle we have come to accept in most other realms of life" (p. 280).

Although some critics believe that treatment and rehabilitation efforts aimed at substance abusers have had little beneficial impact, evidence shows that some programs have been highly successful. For example, the National Treatment Improvement Evaluation Study (NTIES) found that methadone detoxification and maintenance are effective in reducing heroin use. Outpatient clients receiving methadone treatment were significantly less likely to report heroin use during their posttreatment follow-up periods. The length of treatment seems to affect success rates: Clients maintained on methadone for more than 12 months and those receiving methadone treatment for 3 to 12 months had greater reductions in heroin use than did clients who remained in treatment less than 3 months.

Not only do rehabilitation efforts seem to work, but they may also be cost effective. The Drug Abuse Treatment Outcomes Study (DATOS) found that treating cocaine-dependent people in long-term residential and outpatient drug-free programs generated reductions in crime that more than offset the cost of treatment. The average cost of crime among these cocaine-addicted clients decreased 78 percent from the year before to the year after long-term residential treatment, resulting in a $21,360 average benefit per client. This is nearly twice the average treatment cost of $11,016. Outpatient drug-free clients experienced slightly lower sav-

ings: The average costs of crime decreased 28 percent from the year before to the year after treatment, resulting in a $2,217 average benefit per client—one-and-a-half times the cost of treatment.

If treatment seems to work, why is there still so much substance abuse? One reason may be that there are simply no services available for many people in need of treatment. The Substance Abuse and Mental Health Services Administration estimates that more than 5 million people in the United States are in need of treatment for severe drug abuse problems but that almost 60 percent—almost 3 million people—have not received treatment for their addiction (Figure A).

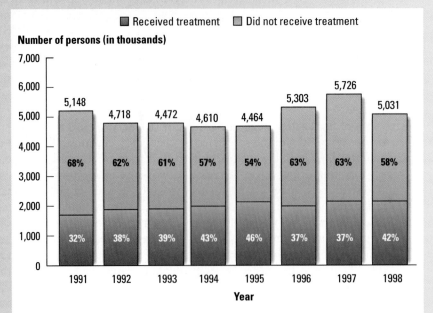

FIGURE A

ESTIMATED NUMBER OF PERSONS NEEDING TREATMENT FOR SEVERE DRUG ABUSE PROBLEMS AND THE PERCENTAGE WHO RECEIVED TREATMENT, 1991–1998

SOURCE: Office of National Drug Control Policy, "National Drug Control Strategy: 2000 Annual Report," 2000. Available online at http://www.whitehousedrugpolicy.gov/policy/ndcs.html

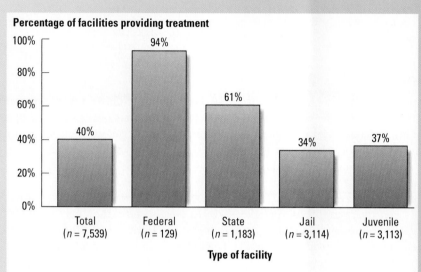

Percentage of facilities providing treatment

**FIGURE B
PERCENTAGE OF CORRECTIONAL
FACILITIES PROVIDING SUBSTANCE ABUSE
TREATMENT, 1997**

SOURCE: Substance Abuse and Mental Health Services Administration, *Substance Abuse Treatment in Adult and Juvenile Correctional Facilities: Findings from the Uniform Facility Data Set 1997 Survey of Correctional Facilities,* 2000. Available online at http://www.samhsa.gov/OAS/UFDS/CorrectionalFacilities97/CorrectionalFacilities97.pdf.

The size of this treatment gap has remained relatively unchanged over the past eight years, ranging from 54 percent to 68 percent. One reason may be that a significant number of correctional facilities, institutions that house formerly drug-dependent people, do *not* have on-site treatment facilities.

A national survey conducted in 1997 by the Substance Abuse and Mental Health Services Administration found that about 60 percent of all correctional facilities nationwide did not provide on-site substance abuse treatment to inmates or residents. Although nearly all (94%) of federal and 61 percent of state prisons provided treatment services, such as detoxification, group or individual counseling, rehabilitation, and methadone or other pharmaceutical

treatment, most jails and juvenile facilities did not. An estimated 11 percent of the adults and juveniles in these institutions received substance abuse treatment, most frequently in a general facility population program. Relatively few inmates received treatment in specialized treatment units (28%) or hospital or psychiatric inpatient units (2%).

Critical Thinking Skills

1. Even if rehabilitation efforts can work effectively, is it fair and just to spend millions of dollars of taxpayers' money on the treatment of criminal offenders who choose to use drugs and break the law while millions of nonlawbreakers still need health care, education, and other social services?

2. Cost savings related to rehabilitation efforts include the value of reduced criminal activity. What other savings can be achieved by helping substance abusers "kick the habit"?

InfoTrac College Edition Research

To learn more about the various methods of drug rehabilitation, use "substance abuse treatment" and "methadone" as search guides in InfoTrac College Edition.

SOURCES: Elliot Currie, *Reckoning: Drugs, the Cities, and the American Future* (New York: Hill and Wang, 1993); Substance Abuse and Mental Health Services Administration, "Substance Abuse Treatment in Adult and Juvenile Correctional Facilities: Findings from the Uniform Facility Data Set 1997 Survey of Correctional Facilities, 2000," available online at http://www.samhsa.gov/OAS/UFDS/CorrectionalFacilities97/CorrectionalFacilities97.pdf; Office of National Drug Control Policy, "National Drug Control Strategy: 2000 Annual Report," 2000, available online at http://www.whitehousedrugpolicy.gov/policy/ndcs.html; Center for Substance Abuse Treatment, National Evaluation Data Services, "Methadone Treatment Outcomes in the National Treatment Improvement Evaluation Study (NTIES)," June 1999, available online at http://neds.calib.com/products/pdfs/methadone.pdf; Patrick Flynn, Patricia Kristiansen, James V. Porto, and Robert L. Hubbard, "Costs and Benefits of Treatment for Cocaine Addiction in DATOS," *Drug and Alcohol Dependence* 57 (1999): 167–174; data provided by the Center for Substance Abuse Research (CESAR), 4321 Hartwick Road, Suite 501, College Park, MD 20740.

drug-dependent babies could begin to match or exceed the number who are delivered with fetal alcohol syndrome.[46] Drunk driving fatalities, which today number about 25,000 per year, could be matched by deaths caused by driving under the influence of marijuana or crack cocaine. Finally, although distribution would be regulated, adolescents likely would have the same opportunity to obtain potent drugs as they now have with beer and other forms of alcohol.

Perspectives in Perspective

The variety of tactics being used in the war on drugs aptly illustrates the impact of the various perspectives on justice on the actual operations of the criminal justice system. Advocates of each view have attempted to promote their vision of what justice is all about and how it should be. During the past decade, the crime control and justice models have dominated. Laws have been toughened, the rights of the accused have been curtailed, the prison population has grown, and the death penalty has been employed against convicted murderers. Because the crime rate has been dropping, these policies seem to be effective; they may be questioned if crime rates once again begin to rise. At the same time, efforts to rehabilitate offenders, to provide them with elements of due process, and to give them the least intrusive treatment have not been abandoned. Police, courts, and correctional agencies supply a wide range of treatment and rehabilitation programs to offenders in all stages of the criminal justice system. Whenever possible, those accused of crime are treated informally in nonrestrictive, community-based programs, and the effects of stigma are guarded against. While the legal rights of offenders are being closely scrutinized by the courts, the basic constitutional rights of the accused remain inviolate. Guardians of due process have made sure that defendants are allowed the maximum protection possible under the law. For example, criminal defendants have been awarded the right to competent legal counsel at trial; merely having a lawyer to defend them is not considered sufficient legal protection.

In sum, understanding the justice system today requires analyzing a variety of occupational roles, institutional processes, legal rules, and administrative doctrines. Each of the predominant views of criminal justice provides a vantage point for understanding and interpreting these complex issues (Figure 1.7). No single view is the right or correct one. Each individual must choose the perspective that best fits his or her own ideas and judgment—or they can all be discarded and the individual's own view substituted.

SUMMARY

The term *criminal justice* refers to the study of the agencies concerned with the prevention and control of criminal behavior. Criminal justice is both a system and a process. As a system, it ideally functions as a cooperative effort among the primary agencies—police, courts, and corrections. The process, on the other hand, consists of the actual steps the offender takes from the initial investigation through trial, sentencing, and appeal.

In many instances, the criminal justice system works informally to expedite the disposal of cases. Criminal acts that are very serious or notorious may receive the full complement of criminal justice processes, from arrest to trial. However, less serious cases are often settled when a bargain is reached between the prosecution and the defense.

The role of criminal justice can be interpreted in many ways. People who study the field or work within its agencies bring their own ideas and feelings to

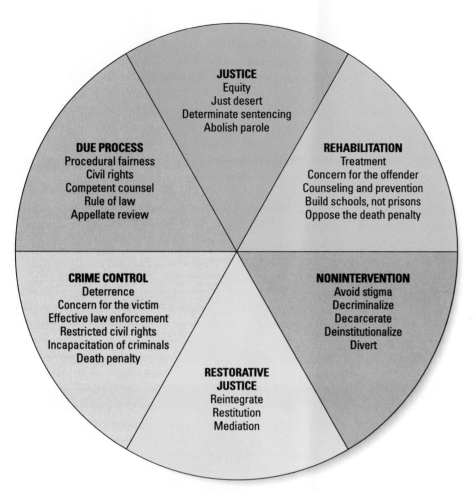

FIGURE I.7
PERSPECTIVES
ON JUSTICE: KEY
CONCERNS AND
CONCEPTS

bear when they try to decide on the right course of action to take or recommend. There are a number of different perspectives on criminal justice today. The crime control perspective is oriented toward deterring criminal behavior and incapacitating serious criminal offenders. In contrast, the rehabilitation perspective views the justice system as a treatment agency focused on helping offenders. Counseling programs are stressed over punishment and deterrence strategies. Those who hold the due process perspective see the justice system as a legal process. Their concern is that every defendant receive the full share of legal rights granted under law. The nonintervention perspective is concerned about stigma and helping defendants avoid the net of justice; advocates call for the least intrusive methods possible. Those who advocate the justice perspective are concerned with making the system equitable. The arrest, sentencing, and correction process should be structured so that every person is treated equally. Finally, the restorative justice perspective focuses on finding peaceful and humanitarian solutions to crime.

The various perspectives on justice are visible in the way the nation has sought to control substance abuse. Some programs rely on a strict crime control policy featuring the detection and arrest of drug traffickers, whereas others seek the rehabilitation of known offenders. The justice model has influenced the development of sentencing policies that emphasize mandatory punishments. Another approach is to legalize drugs, thereby reducing abusers' incentive to commit crimes, a policy that reflects a nonintervention strategy.

Key Terms

criminal justice system
Law Enforcement Assistance
Administration (LEAA)
indictment
information
appellate court
nolle prosequi
courtroom work group

crime control perspective
rehabilitation perspective
due process perspective
nonintervention perspective
stigma
decriminalization
victimless crime
deinstitutionalization

pretrial diversion
justice perspective
source control
DARE
methadone
legalization

Discussion Questions

1. Which criminal behavior patterns pose the greatest threat to the public? Should the justice system devote greater resources to combating these crimes? If so, which crime patterns should be de-emphasized?
2. Describe the differences between the formal and informal justice systems. Is it fair to treat some offenders informally?
3. What are the layers of the criminal justice "wedding cake"? Give an example of a crime for each layer.

4. What are the basic elements of each perspective on justice? Which best represents your own point of view?
5. How would each perspective on criminal justice consider the use of the death penalty as a sanction for first-degree murder?

A CLOSER LOOK

Crime control advocates believe that the state should be given a free hand to protect the rights of innocent victims; those who favor a due process orientation are concerned that, given a free hand, state authorities may tread upon the civil rights of criminal suspects. The tension between these two positions may be exacerbated as new technological breakthroughs enable state authorities to monitor potential criminal suspects. One area of concern is the accumulation of personal physical data such as an individual's DNA codes. Should the state be allowed to collect such information, or is this part of a person's medical history and therefore off limits to the government? Paul Tracy and Vincent Morgan have taken on this issue:

As law enforcement agencies the world over have been amassing huge collections of fingerprints since the closing days of the nineteenth century, so too have they recently begun to collect, organize, analyze, and store collections of DNA samples for forensic purposes. This trend, as was the case with fingerprints, has been hailed as a godsend for crime fighting, but also decried as an evil at the same time. However, as with fingerprints, it looks like DNA testing and associated databases are here to stay. Accordingly, the current proliferation of DNA databases and their likely further ex-

pansion raise three significant policy issues and attendant questions. First, how do we utilize this new technology, while protecting against misuse and abuse? The question is really much more complex than this, and it certainly covers a multitude of subissues. At the essential core of this issue is the same question which appears in virtually every facet of our daily lives today. Science and technology are progressing at exponential rates, while the ordinary citizen struggles to keep up; so, what happens when technology, and the manifold advances it spawns, transcends society's ability to regulate such technology? Further, in the absence of a serious and well-informed debate about the advisability and demonstrative value of putting into practice whatever advances new technologies may provide, will particular interest groups exert unchallenged influence, if not complete hegemony in a particular area, and successfully lobby for very large expenditures of public financing?

To read more about what they have to say, go to InfoTrac College Edition and read
Paul E. Tracy and Vincent Morgan, "Big Brother and His Science Kit: DNA Databases for 21st Century Crime Control?" *Journal of Criminal Law and Criminology,* Winter 2000, v90 i2 p635

Notes

1 "The New Age of Anxiety," *Newsweek,* 23 August 1999 p. 39.
2 Federal Interagency Forum on Child and Family Statistics, press release, Washington, DC, July 8, 1999.

3 Kevin Sack, "Gore Takes Tough Stand on Violent Entertainment," *New York Times,* 11 September 2000, p. A2.
4 For a detailed analysis of this work, see Samuel Walker, "Origins of the Contem-

porary Criminal Justice Paradigm: The American Bar Foundation Survey, 1953–1969," *Justice Quarterly* 9 (1992): 47–76.
5 President's Commission on Law Enforcement and the Administration of Justice,

The Challenge of Crime in a Free Society (Washington, DC: U.S. Government Printing Office, 1967).

6 See Public Law 90-351, Title I—Omnibus Crime Control Safe Streets Act of 1968, 90th Congress, June 19, 1968.

7 Sue Lindgren, *Justice Expenditures and Employment, 1997* (Washington, DC: Bureau of Justice Statistics, 2000).

8 Office of National Drug Control Policy, *Fact Sheet: Drug Data Summary,* February 1998; updated 1999.

9 Federal Bureau of Investigation, *Crime in the United States, 1999* (Washington, DC: U.S. Government Printing Office, 2000), p. 208.

10 For an analysis of this issue, see William Wilbanks, *The Myth of a Racist Criminal Justice System* (Monterey, CA: Brooks/Cole, 1987); Stephen Klein, Joan Petersilia, and Susan Turner, "Race and Imprisonment Decisions in California," *Science* 247 (1990): 812–816; Alfred Blumstein, "On the Racial Disproportionality of the United States Prison Population," *Journal of Criminal Law and Criminology* 73 (1982): 1259–1281; Darnell Hawkins, "Race, Crime Type and Imprisonment," *Justice Quarterly* 3 (1986): 251–269.

11 Middlesex ss Superior Court Criminal No. 97-0433 Commonwealth Memorandum and Order v. Louise Woodward, 1997.

12 Herbert L. Packer, *The Limits of the Criminal Sanction* (Stanford, CA: Stanford University Press, 1975), p. 21.

13 James Eisenstein and Herbert Jacob, *Felony Justice* (Boston: Little, Brown, 1977); Peter Nardulli, *The Courtroom Elite* (Cambridge, MA: Ballinger, 1978); Paul Wice, *Chaos in the Courthouse* (New York: Praeger, 1985); Marcia Lipetz, *Routine Justice: Processing Cases in Women's Court* (New Brunswick, NJ: Transaction Books, 1983).

14 Douglas Smith, "The Plea Bargaining Controversy," *Journal of Criminal Law and Criminology* 77 (1986): 949–967.

15 Samuel Walker, *Sense and Nonsense about Crime* (Belmont, CA: Wadsworth, 1985).

16 Malcolm Feeley, *The Process Is the Punishment* (New York: Russell Sage Foundation, 1979).

17 James Q. Wilson, *Thinking about Crime,* rev. ed. (New York: Vintage Books, 1983).

18 Ibid., p. 128.

19 John DiIulio, *No Escape: The Future of American Corrections* (New York: Basic Books, 1991).

20 Dennis Rosenbaum and Gordon Hanson, "Assessing the Effects of School-Based Drug Education: A Six-Year Multilevel Analysis of Project D.A.R.E.," *Journal of Research in Crime and Delinquency* 35 (1998): 381–412.

21 Marilyn Chandler Ford and Francis Moore, "The Impact of Policy Shifts on Correctional Populations," paper presented at annual meeting of the American Society of Criminology, Miami, November 1994.

22 Karen Parker and Patricia McCall, "Structural Conditions and Racial Homicide Patterns: A Look at the Multiple Disadvantages in Urban Areas," *Criminology* 37 (1999): 447–448.

23 Francis Cullen, John Paul Wright, and Mitchell Chamlin, "Social Support and Social Reform: A Progressive Crime Control Agenda," *Crime and Delinquency* 45 (1999): 188–207.

24 Jane Sprott, "Are Members of the Public Tough on Crime? The Dimensions of Public 'Punitiveness,'" *Journal of Criminal Justice* 27 (1999): 467–474.

25 Packer, *The Limits of the Criminal Sanction.*

26 "DNA Testing Has Exonerated 28 Prison Inmates, Study Finds," *Criminal Justice Newsletter* 17 June 1996, p. 2.

27 Caitlin Lovinger, "Death Row's Living Alumni," *New York Times,* 22 August 1999, p. 1.

28 *Doe v. Pryor, M.D.,* Ala., Civ.No. 99-T-730-N, Thompson, J. (1999).

29 This section is based on Paula M. Ditton and Doris James Wilson, *Truth in Sentencing in State Prisons* (Washington: DC: Bureau of Justice Statistics, 1999).

30 Herbert Bianchi, *Justice as Sanctuary* (Bloomington: Indiana University Press, 1994); Nils Christie, "Conflicts as Property," *British Journal of Criminology* 17 (1977): 1–15; L. Hulsman, "Critical Criminology and the Concept of Crime," *Contemporary Crises* 10 (1986): 63–80.

31 Larry Tifft, "Forward," in Dennis Sullivan, *The Mask of Love* (Port Washington, NY: Kennikat Press, 1980), p. 6.

32 Christopher Cooper, "Patrol Police Officer Conflict Resolution Processes," *Journal of Criminal Justice* 25 (1997): 87–101.

33 U.S. Department of State, *1998 International Narcotics Control Strategy Report,* February 1999.

34 Anti–Drug Abuse Act of 1988, Public Law 100-6901 21 U.S.C. 1501; Subtitle A: Death Penalty, Sec. 001, Amending the Controlled Substances Abuse Act, 21 U.S.C. 848.

35 Carol Kaplan, *Sentencing and Time Served* (Washington, DC: Bureau of Justice Statistics, 1987), p. 2.

36 Peter Rossi, Richard Berk, and Alec Campbell, "Just Punishments: Guideline Sentences and Normative Consensus," *Journal of Quantitative Criminology* 13 (1997): 267–283.

37 Dennis Rosenbaum, Robert Flewelling, Susan Bailey, Chris Ringwalt, and Deanna Wilkinson, "Cops in the Classroom: A Longitudinal Evaluation," *Journal of Research in Crime and Delinquency* 31 (1994): 3–31.

38 See, generally, Peter Greenwood and Franklin Zimring, *One More Chance* (Santa Monica, CA: Rand Corporation, 1985).

39 Eli Ginzberg, Howard Berliner, and Miriam Ostrow, *Young People at Risk: Is Prevention Possible?* (Boulder, CO: Westview Press, 1988), p. 99.

40 Drug Court Clearinghouse and Technical Assistance Project, *Looking at a Decade of Drug Courts* (Washington, DC: U.S. Government Printing Office, 1999).

41 See, generally, Ralph Weisheit, *Drugs, Crime and the Criminal Justice System* (Cincinnati: Anderson, 1990).

42 Ethan Nadelmann, "America's Drug Problem," *Bulletin of the American Academy of Arts and Sciences* 65 (1991): 24–40.

43 Ethan Nadelmann, "Should We Legalize Drugs? History Answers Yes," *American Heritage* (February–March 1993): 41–56.

44 This and other arguments are presented in Erich Goode, *Between Politics and Reason: The Drug Legalization Debate* (New York: St. Martin's Press, 1997).

45 David Courtwright, "Should We Legalize Drugs? History Answers No," *American Heritage* (February–March 1993): 43–56.

46 James Inciardi and Duane McBride, "Legalizing Drugs: A Gormless Naive Idea," *Criminologist* 15 (1990): 1–4.

AP/Wide World Photos

THE NATURE OF CRIME AND VICTIMIZATION

In 1962, a young Chicago police detective named William Hanhardt was considered a hero when he broke up a brutal burglary ring, killing two home invaders in a hail of bullets.[1] Hanhardt's skill at cracking bank robberies and burglary rings established him as a legendary crime fighter on the city's police force. He rose through the ranks from patrolman to deputy superintendent of police before he retired in 1986. Then, in October 2000, a federal indictment was handed down, stating that Hanhardt controlled some of the very criminals he was once paid to track down. He now stands accused of directing a band of seven thieves who stole about $4.8 million in gems and expensive watches. Using fake mustaches, electronic eavesdropping equipment, smoke bombs, aliases, secret codes, bulletproof vests, and a high level of computer sophistication, the ring of jewel thieves roamed the country and pulled jobs in a number of major cities. They sometimes bought cases matching those used by jewelry salespeople and were able to get into a fully locked car in a matter of seconds,

switch cases, and escape undetected. As the investigation of Hanhardt unfolded, it became evident that even during his police career he was linked to numerous organized crime figures. Despite these suspected mob connections, he rose to top command posts in the Chicago Police Department, receiving at least ten promotions after joining the police department as a patrolman in 1954.

Stories such as that of William Hanhardt convince many Americans that we live in a crime-filled society in which everyone can be a suspect, even admired police officers. If respected law enforcement officers turn to crime, then whom can we trust? Are Americans justified in their fear of crime? Should they in fact barricade themselves behind armed guards? Are crime rates rising or falling? Where do most crimes occur? To answer these and similar questions, criminologists have devised elaborate methods of crime data collection and analysis. Without accurate data on the nature and extent of crime, it would not be possible to formulate theories that explain the

Chapter Outline

Criminal Justice Links

Criminal Justice Viewpoints

Former Chicago Detective William Hanhardt has been accused of running a band of thieves who stole millions in gems and expensive watches. Why would someone with his distinguished career in law enforcement and the know-how to use electronic eavesdropping equipment and secret codes turn to a life of crime?

onset of crime or to devise social policies that facilitate its control or elimination.

In this chapter, we review how data are collected on criminal offenders and offenses and what this information tells us about crime patterns and trends. We also examine the concept of criminal careers and discover what available crime data can tell us about the onset, continuation, and termination of criminality. We begin by defining what constitutes crime and then look at how it is measured and reported.

Fill in the blanks 1–3
True/False 1
Multiple choice 1–2
Essay 1

consensus view
The view that the majority of people in a society share common ideals and work toward a common good; crimes are behaviors that conflict with the rules of the majority and the good of society.

criminal law
The body of rules that define crimes, set out their punishments, and mandate the procedures for carrying out the criminal justice process.

social control
The ability of society and its institutions to control, manage, restrain, or direct human behavior.

interactionist view
The view that crime is defined by people who hold social power and mold the law to reflect their own ideas of right and wrong.

Warren and Minnie Singleton pose amid the rubble of their home in Brooklyn, New York. The building contractor they hired to refurbish their home absconded with their money without ever intending to finish the job, an act defined by the criminal law as fraud. If the builder's actions were not defined as a crime, the Singletons would be left to their own devices to recoup their lost money. Now they can call upon law enforcement agencies to prosecute the culprits.

WHAT IS A CRIME?

There are actually three views of what constitutes a crime. According to the **consensus view**, crimes are behaviors considered harmful by a majority of citizens that, because of their potential for causing social harm, have been controlled or prohibited by the existing criminal law. The **criminal law** is a set of state-sponsored rules that are designed to control unwanted behaviors through the application of state-administered sanctions. The criminal law has a **social control** function—restraining those who would take advantage of others' weakness for their own personal gain, thereby endangering the social framework. Although differences in behavior can be tolerated within a properly functioning social system, behaviors that are considered inherently destructive and dangerous are outlawed to maintain the social fabric and ensure the peaceful functioning of society.

PERSPECTIVES ON JUSTICE

The consensus view of crime reflects the crime control perspective: The true purpose of the criminal law is to express society's revulsion toward criminals who prey upon innocent people. The punitive power of the law is what controls miscreants and protects victims.

Some scholars believe that the law, and therefore the concept of crime, is influenced by people who hold social power and use it to mold the law to reflect their way of thinking (this is referred to as the **interactionist view**). For example, various groups have tried to influence laws regulating the possession of handguns,

Ted Thai, Time, Inc.

the use of drugs and alcohol, and the availability of abortions. These **moral entrepreneurs** use their economic, social, and political influence to impose their definition of right and wrong on the rest of the population.[2] According to this view, the criminal law is a flexible instrument that may change according to the whim of powerful individuals and groups who use it to reflect their views of morality.

Another vision, called the **conflict view**, is that the criminal law is an instrument of control used by those who hold political and economic power to thwart the aspirations of the lower classes. The affluent, although small in number, use the law and the criminal justice system to maintain their wealth, advance their own causes, and control the behavior of those who oppose their ideas and values.[3]

moral entrepreneurs
Interest groups that use their economic, social, and political influence to impose their own moral values on the rest of the population.

conflict view
The view that law is an instrument of control used by those who hold economic and political power to further their own interests.

PERSPECTIVES ON JUSTICE

The conflict view of crime is the foundation of the restorative justice perspective. Law is coercive because it was originally designed to protect the rights of the privileged classes at the expense of the poor. Therefore, a new and noncoercive vision of justice is needed to protect all people, regardless of class position.

Despite these differences, there is general agreement that the criminal law defines crime, that its definition is constantly changing and evolving, that social forces mold the definition of crimes, and that the criminal law has a social control function. Therefore, as used here, the term *crime* is defined as follows:

> Crime is a violation of social rules of conduct, interpreted and expressed by a written criminal code, created by people holding social and political power. Its content may be influenced by prevailing public sentiments, historically developed moral beliefs, and the need to protect public safety. Individuals who violate these rules may be subject to sanctions administered by state authority, which include social stigma and loss of status, freedom, and, on occasion, their life.

HOW CRIME IS MEASURED

Criminal justice scholars use a variety of techniques to study crime and its consequences. Some of the major sources of crime data will be discussed in this section.

Survey Data

Survey data are typically gathered from subjects who are asked to fill out questionnaires that contain questions about their behavior, attitudes, beliefs, and abilities. Most survey data come from *probability samples,* which are made up of a limited number of subjects randomly selected from a larger population. If the sample is carefully drawn, every individual in the population has an equal chance of being selected for the study. For example, a sample of 10,000 high school seniors is selected at random and asked about the frequency of their use of alcohol and drugs. Using statistical estimation programs, their answers could be used to predict the behavior of millions of high school seniors in the United States.

Surveys provide a valuable source of information on some crime problems that otherwise would remain hidden, such as drug use, and others that are rarely reported to the police, such as school vandalism. Two important surveys of this type are the annual high school drug use survey, part of the Monitoring the Future study conducted by researchers at the University of Michigan's Institute for Social Research (ISR), and the Household Survey on Drug Abuse conducted by

Fill in the blanks 4–5
True/False 2
Multiple choice 3
Essay 2

For the latest data from the University of Michigan's Institute for Social Research (ISR) Monitoring the Future study, go to their Web site: http://monitoringthefuture.org/

For an up-to-date list of Web links, see http://www.wadsworth.com/product/0534573053s

the National Institute on Drug Abuse (NIDA), a branch of the U.S. Department of Health and Human Services.

Surveys are also an invaluable source of information on the nature and extent of criminal victimization. The National Crime Victimization Survey (NCVS) uses a large, carefully drawn sample of citizens to estimate the total number of criminal incidents that occur each year; it is one of the most important sources of crime data and is discussed at length later in this chapter.

Record Data

Fill in the blanks 6

Another significant source of criminal justice data involves analysis of official records. These records may be acquired from a variety of sources, including schools, courts, police departments, social service centers, and correctional agencies. Records can be used for a number of purposes. Prisoners' files can be analyzed in an effort to determine what types of inmates adjust to prison and what types tend to be disciplinary problems or suicidal. Parole department records are evaluated to determine the characteristics of inmates who successfully adjust to living in society and of those who fail. Educational records are important indicators of intelligence, academic achievement, school behavior, and other information that can be related to delinquent behavior patterns. However, the most important source of crime data is those records compiled by police departments and annually collected and analyzed by the Federal Bureau of Investigation (FBI) in its Uniform Crime Reports program; these are often referred to as **official crime statistics** and will be examined in the next major section of this chapter.

official crime statistics
Criminal behavior that has been recorded by the police.

Cohort Data

Fill in the blanks 7–8
True/False 3–5

cohort study
A study using a group of subjects who share a common characteristic, such as place and time of birth.

longitudinal cohort study
Research that tracks the development of a group of subjects over time.

A **cohort study** is an important research technique that measures a group (or panel) of people who share a common characteristic. For example, to conduct a **longitudinal cohort study**, researchers might select a cohort of subjects that consisted of all the boys born in Omaha, Nebraska, in 1982 and then follow their behavior patterns for an 18-year period until they reached adulthood in 2000. Cohort research may make use of the subjects' educational, police, medical, and family records. Cohort members may also be surveyed and or interviewed.

Cohort research typically involves comparing life events in order to determine what effect they had on criminal careers. For example, medical records might show an association between early childhood abuse and later criminality; educational records and interviews could indicate the effect of school failure on self-image.

Because it is extremely difficult, expensive, and time-consuming to follow a cohort over time and most of the sample do not become serious criminals, another approach is to take an intact group of known offenders and look back into their early life experiences; this format is known as a *retrospective cohort study.*

Observation Data

The systematic observation, recording, and deciphering of types of behavior within a sample or population is a common method of criminal justice data collection. Some observation studies are conducted in the field, where the researcher observes subjects in their normal environments; other observations take place in a contrived, artificial setting or a laboratory. When they conduct *participant observations,* criminologists actually join the group being studied, in order to study their behavior firsthand. This procedure allows the observer to better understand the motives that subjects may have for their behavior and attitudes and to develop a frame of reference similar to that of the subjects. Classic participant observation studies have been conducted by William F. Whyte on the lives of lower-class youths (*Street Corner Society*) and by Laud Humphreys on homosexual behavior in public places (*Tearoom Trade*).[4]

Observation is a time-consuming way to conduct research and occasionally contains some ethical risks, such as when the subjects engage in deviant behavior during the data-gathering stage of the research and the observer is faced with betraying their trust or letting a criminal act go unreported. Participant observation studies, however, do allow the researcher to gain insights into behavior that might never be available otherwise. In addition, because observation studies depend more on actual behavior than on surveyed opinions, the researcher can be fairly sure of the validity of the information because it will be more difficult for subjects to give false impressions or responses.

Interview Data

Some criminal justice researchers conduct in-depth interviews with a small sample of offenders to gain insight into their lives.

One type of interview is known as the *life history*. This method employs extensive interviewing with one or a few individuals who have had experience in crime, deviance, and other related areas. Examples of this approach are contained in two important works by Carl Klockars and Darrell Steffensmeier on the lives of two criminal *fences* (people who buy and sell stolen merchandise).[5] Life histories provide insights into the human condition that other, less personal research methods cannot hope to duplicate.

These are but a few of the various research methods used by criminal justice researchers. Each helps criminal justice experts understand the nature and extent of criminal behavior in the United States. Each source can be used independently, but taken together they provide a detailed picture of the crime problem. Although the data provided by these five sources diverge in many key areas, they have enough similarities to enable us to draw some conclusions about crime in the United States.

HOW CRIME IS REPORTED

There are three primary means of recording criminal activity. First are the official crime statistics—data from local police departments collected by the Federal Bureau of Investigation and published in its annual Uniform Crime Reports. Second are surveys of crime victims conducted by agencies of the federal government, the most prominent being the National Criminal Victimization Survey. Third are self-report surveys, typically conducted with high school students, that ask people to report on their own criminal activity and drug use. These three methods are described in the following sections.

The Uniform Crime Reports

The FBI's **Uniform Crime Reports (UCR)** are the best known and most widely cited source of aggregate criminal statistics.[6] The FBI receives and compiles records from more than 17,000 police departments serving a majority of the U.S. population.

What the UCR Reports Exhibit 2.1 defines the **index crimes** included in the UCR. The FBI tallies and annually publishes the number of reported offenses (known as Part I crimes) by city, county, standard metropolitan statistical area, and geographic divisions of the United States. In addition, the UCR shows the

Uniform Crime Reports (UCR)
The official crime data collected by the FBI from local police departments.

Fill in the blanks 9–10
True/False 6–8
Multiple choice 4–9
Essay 3

EXHIBIT 2.1   FBI INDEX CRIMES

Crime	Description
Criminal homicide	*Murder and nonnegligent manslaughter.* The willful (nonnegligent) killing of one human being by another. Deaths caused by negligence, attempts to kill, assaults to kill, suicides, accidental deaths, and justifiable homicides are excluded. Justifiable homicides are limited to: (1) the killing of a felon by a law enforcement officer in the line of duty; and (2) the killing of a felon by a private citizen.
	Manslaughter by negligence. The killing of another person through gross negligence. Traffic fatalities are excluded. While manslaughter by negligence is a Part I crime, it is not included in the crime index.
Forcible rape	The carnal knowledge of a female forcibly and against her will. Included are rapes by force and attempts or assaults to rape. Statutory offenses (no force used—victim under age of consent) are excluded.
Robbery	The taking or attempting to take anything of value from the care, custody, or control of a person or persons by force or threat of force or violence and/or by putting the victim in fear.
Aggravated assault	An unlawful attack by one person on another for the purpose of inflicting severe or aggravated bodily injury. This type of assault is usually accompanied by the use of a weapon or by means likely to produce death or great bodily harm. Simple assaults are excluded.
Burglary	Breaking or entering. The unlawful entry of a structure to commit a felony or a theft. Attempted forcible entry is included.
Larceny/theft (except motor vehicle theft)	The unlawful taking, carrying, leading, or riding away of property from the possession or constructive possession of another. Examples are thefts of bicycles or automobile accessories, shoplifting, pocket picking, or the stealing of any property or article which is not taken by force and violence or by fraud. Attempted larcenies are included. Embezzlement, "con" games, forgery, worthless checks, etc., are excluded.
Motor vehicle theft	The theft or attempted theft of a motor vehicle. A motor vehicle is self-propelled and runs on the surface and not on rails. Specifically excluded from this category are motorboats, construction equipment, airplanes, and farming equipment.
Arson	Any willful or malicious burning or attempt to burn, with or without intent to defraud, a dwelling, house, public building, motor vehicle or aircraft, personal property of another, etc.

SOURCE: Federal Bureau of Investigation, *Crime in the United States, 1999* (Washington, DC: U.S. Government Printing Office, 2000).

index crimes
The eight serious crimes—murder, rape, assault, robbery, burglary, arson, larceny, and motor vehicle theft—whose incidence is reported in the annual Uniform Crime Reports (UCR).

number and characteristics (age, race, and gender) of individuals who have been arrested for these and all other crimes except traffic violations (Part II crimes).

The UCR uses three methods to express crime data. First, the number of crimes reported to the police and arrests made are expressed as raw figures (for example, 15,533 murders occurred in 1999). Second, crime rates per 100,000 people are computed; that is, when the UCR indicates that the murder rate was 5.7 in 1999, it means that about 6 people in every 100,000 were murdered between January 1 and December 31 of 1999. This is the equation used:

$$\frac{\text{number of reported crimes}}{\text{total U.S. population}} \times 100,000 = \text{rate per } 100,000$$

Third, the FBI computes changes in the numbers and rates of crimes over time. For example, murder rates declined 9.3 percent between 1998 and 1999.

How Accurate Are the Uniform Crime Reports? The accuracy of the UCR has been suspect. Surveys indicate that fewer than half of all crime victims report incidents to police. Nonreporters may believe that the victimization was "a private matter," that "nothing could be done," or that the victimization was "not important enough."[7] Evidence also shows that local law enforcement agencies make er-

The UCR is available online at the FBI's Web site, which also contains information on current investigations, their Most Wanted list, and other types of information: http://www.fbi.gov/
For an up-to-date list of Web links, see http://www.wadsworth.com/product/0534573053s

EXHIBIT 2.2 FACTORS AFFECTING THE VALIDITY OF THE UNIFORM CRIME REPORTS

1. No federal crimes are reported.
2. Reports are voluntary and vary in accuracy and completeness.
3. Not all police departments submit reports.
4. The FBI uses estimates in its total crime projections.
5. If an offender commits multiple crimes, only the most serious is recorded. Thus, if a narcotics addict rapes, robs, and murders a victim, only the murder is recorded. Consequently, many lesser crimes go unreported.
6. Each act is listed as a single offense for some crimes, but not for others. If a man robbed six people in a bar, the offense would be listed as one robbery; but if he assaulted or murdered them, it would be listed as six assaults or six murders.
7. Incomplete acts are lumped together with completed ones.
8. Important differences exist between the FBI's definition of certain crimes and those used in a number of states.
9. Victimless crimes often go undetected.
10. Many cases of child abuse and family violence are unreported.

SOURCE: Leonard Savitz, "Official Statistics," in *Contemporary Criminology,* ed. Leonard Savitz and Norman Johnston (New York: Wiley, 1982), pp. 3–15; updated 2000.

rors in their reporting practices. Some departments may define crimes loosely—for example, reporting an assault on a woman as an attempted rape—whereas others pay strict attention to FBI guidelines.[8] Some local police departments make unintentional but systematic errors in UCR reporting; others may deliberately alter reported crimes to improve their department's public image. Police administrators interested in lowering the crime rate may falsify crime reports by, for example, classifying a burglary as a nonreportable trespass.[9] Ironically, what appears to be a rising crime rate may be simply an artifact of improved police record-keeping ability.[10] It is possible that at least one-third of all crimes reported to the police go unrecorded in their UCR reports.[11]

Methodological issues also contribute to questions regarding the UCR's validity. The complex scoring procedure used by the FBI means that many serious crimes are not counted. For example, during an armed bank robbery, the offender strikes a teller with the butt of a handgun. The robber runs from the bank and steals an automobile at the curb. The offender has technically committed robbery, aggravated assault, and motor vehicle theft—three Part I offenses; however, because robbery is the most serious, it would be the only one recorded in the UCR.[12] The most frequent issues with respect to the UCR are described in Exhibit 2.2.

PERSPECTIVES ON JUSTICE

UCR data consistently show that police are able to "solve" only one in five reported crimes. The inability of law enforcement agencies to improve arrest ratios has been one of the factors persuading police administrators to rethink the role of police as crime fighters and reorient their departments toward community service and neighborhood problem solving. The community policing models discussed in Chapter 6 reflect the restorative justice perspective on crime control.

Victim Surveys

The second source of crime data is surveys that ask crime victims about their encounters with criminals. Because many victims do not report their experiences to the police, victim surveys are considered a method of getting at the unknown

National Crime Victimization Survey (NCVS)
Annual survey conducted jointly by the U.S. Census Bureau and the Department of Justice that questions a large national sample about their experiences as victims of crime.

Fill in the blanks 11–12
True/False 9–11
Multiple choice 10–11

You can access the NCVS data at the Bureau of Justice Statistics Web site: http://www.ojp.usdoj.gov/bjs/
For an up-to-date list of Web links, see http://www.wadsworth.com/product/0534573053s

figures of crime. The **National Crime Victimization Survey (NCVS)** is the current method of assessing victimization in the United States.

The NCVS is conducted by the U.S. Bureau of the Census in cooperation with the Bureau of Justice Statistics of the U.S. Department of Justice.[13] Each year data are obtained from a nationally representative sample of roughly 45,000 households that includes more than 94,000 people. People are asked to report their victimization experiences with such crimes as rape, sexual assault, robbery, assault, theft, household burglary, and motor vehicle theft. Because of the care with which the samples are drawn and the high completion rate, NCVS data are considered a relatively unbiased, valid estimate of all victimizations for the target crimes included in the survey.

NCVS Findings The number of crimes accounted for by the NCVS (about 31 million) is considerably larger than the number of crimes reported to the FBI. For example, whereas the UCR shows that about 410,000 robberies occurred in 1999, the NCVS estimates that about 810,00 actually occurred. The reason for such discrepancies is that fewer than one-half of violent crimes, fewer than one-third of personal theft crimes (such as pocket picking), and fewer than one-half of household thefts are reported to police. Victims seem to report to the police only crimes that involve considerable loss or injury. If we are to believe NCVS findings, the official UCR statistics do not provide an accurate picture of the crime problem because so many crimes go unreported.

Is the NCVS Valid? Like the UCR, the NCVS may also suffer from some methodological problems. As a result, its findings must be interpreted with caution. Among the potential problems are the following:

- Overreporting due to victims' misinterpretation of events. For example, a lost wallet may be reported as stolen, or an open door may be viewed as a burglary attempt.
- Underreporting due to the embarrassment of reporting crime to interviewers, fear of getting in trouble, or simply forgetting an incident.
- Inability to record the personal criminal activity of those interviewed, such as drug use or gambling; murder is also not included for obvious reasons.
- Sampling errors, which produce a group of respondents who do not represent the nation as a whole.
- Inadequate question format that invalidates responses. Some groups, such as adolescents, may be particularly susceptible to error because of question format.[14]

Fill in the blanks 13
True/False 12–14
Multiple choice 12–14

self-report survey
A research approach that questions large groups of subjects, typically high school students, about their own participation in delinquent or criminal acts.

Self-Report Surveys

Self-report surveys ask people to reveal information about their own law violations. Most often, self-report surveys are administered to groups of subjects through a mass distribution of questionnaires. The basic assumption of self-report studies is that anonymity and confidentiality will be ensured, which encourages people to accurately describe their illegal activities. Self-reports are viewed as a mechanism to get at the "dark figures of crime," the figures missed by official statistics and victim surveys. Exhibit 2.3 illustrates some typical self-report items.

Most self-report studies have focused on juvenile delinquency and youth crime, for three reasons.[15] First, the school setting makes it convenient to test thousands of subjects simultaneously because they all have the means to respond to a research questionnaire (pens, desks, and time). Second, because school attendance is universal, a school-based self-report survey represents a cross-section of the commu-

EXHIBIT 2.3   SELF-REPORT SURVEY QUESTIONS

Please indicate how often in the past 12 months you did each act. (Check the best answer.)	Never did act	One time	2–5 times	6–9 times	10+ times
Stole something worth less than $50	_____	_____	_____	_____	_____
Stole something worth more than $50	_____	_____	_____	_____	_____
Used cocaine	_____	_____	_____	_____	_____
Was in a fistfight	_____	_____	_____	_____	_____
Carried a weapon such as a gun or knife	_____	_____	_____	_____	_____
Fought someone using a weapon	_____	_____	_____	_____	_____
Stole a car	_____	_____	_____	_____	_____
Used force to steal	_____	_____	_____	_____	_____
(For boys) Forced a girl to have sexual relations against her will	_____	_____	_____	_____	_____

nity. Third, juveniles have the highest reported crime rates; therefore, measuring delinquent behavior is a key to understanding the nature and extent of crime.

However, self-reports are not restricted to youth crime. They are also used to examine the offense histories of prison inmates, drug users, and other segments of the population. Also, because most self-report instruments contain items measuring subjects' attitudes, values, personal characteristics, and behaviors, the data obtained from them can be used for various purposes, including testing theories, measuring attitudes toward crime, and computing the association between crime and important social variables, such as family relations, educational attainment, and income.[16]

Self-Report Findings In general, self-reports, like victimization surveys, indicate that the number of people who break the law is far greater than the number projected by official statistics. Almost everyone questioned is found to have violated some law at some time.[17] Furthermore, self-reports dispute the notion that criminals and delinquents specialize in one type of crime or another; offenders seem to engage in a "mixed bag" of crime and deviance.[18]

Self-report studies indicate that the most common offenses are truancy, alcohol abuse, use of a false ID, shoplifting or larceny under $50, fighting, marijuana use, and damage to the property of others. What is surprising is the consistency of these findings in samples taken around the United States. Figure 2.1 contains data from a self-report study called Monitoring the Future, which researchers at the University of Michigan Institute for Social Research (ISR) conduct annually. This survey is based on the self-report responses of about 17,000 high school seniors, 15,500 tenth-graders, and 18,800 eighth-graders in hundreds of schools around the United States.

As Figure 2.1 shows, young people self-report a great deal of crime: More than 40 percent of high school seniors reported stealing in the last 12 months; 20 percent said they were involved in a gang fight; more than 10 percent injured someone so badly that the victim had to see a doctor; about 30 percent admitted shoplifting; and almost 25 percent engaged in breaking and entering. The fact that so many—at least one-third of all U.S. high school students—engaged in theft and about 20 percent committed a serious violent act during the past year shows that criminal activity is widespread and is not restricted to a few "bad apples."

FIGURE 2.1
SELF-REPORTED
DELINQUENT ACTS

SOURCE: Institute for Social Research,
Monitoring the Future, 1999 (Ann Arbor:
University of Michigan, 2000).

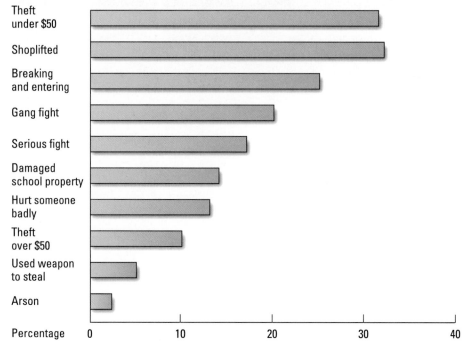

Percentage reporting doing act at least once in past 12 months

Self-Reported Drug Use Probably the most important use of self-report surveys has been to monitor adolescent drug abuse. Drug use among the general population declined from a high point around 1980 until 1990, when it began to increase once again. Usage rates for most drugs reached peak levels in the mid-1990s— inhalants in 1995; hallucinogens, including LSD and PCP, in 1996; and marijuana and amphetamines in 1996 or 1997. Since then, drug use has stabilized or receded. One particularly positive trend in drug use has been a significant drop in the use of crack cocaine among both eighth- and tenth-graders. Still, more than half of all high school seniors report drinking during the past month, more than a third use tobacco, and almost a quarter smoke marijuana.

These data indicate that, although general usage is lower than it was 20 years ago, the drug problem has not gone away and may be increasing among high school youth. Why has drug use remained a major social problem? When drug use declined in the 1980s, young people may have viewed drug taking as dangerous and risky because widespread publicity linked drug use, needle sharing, and the AIDS virus; today, the perceived risk of drug use has declined.

PERSPECTIVES ON JUSTICE

Today's baby-boomer parents may have a more relaxed attitude toward drug use than parents of an earlier generation (after all, many were drug users themselves back in the 1960s and 1970s). Not too surprisingly, their own children are unconcerned about drug abuse; such laissez-faire attitudes may be precursors for further increases in drug and alcohol use. The fact that drug use is so widespread and accepted in the general population supports a non-interventionist stance on drugs—that they should be legalized and/or de-criminalized if that's what the public wants.

Fill in the blanks 14
Multiple choice 15

Are Self-Reports Accurate? Although self-report data have profoundly affected criminological inquiry, some important methodological issues have been raised about their accuracy. Critics of self-report studies frequently suggest that it is unreasonable to expect people to candidly admit illegal acts. They have nothing to gain, and the ones taking the greatest risk are the youths with official records who may be engaging in the most criminality. On the other hand, some people may exaggerate their criminal acts, forget some of them, or be confused about what is being asked. Some surveys contain an overabundance of trivial offenses, such as shoplifting small items or using false identification, often lumped together with serious crimes to form a total crime index. Consequently, comparisons between groups can be highly misleading.

The "missing cases" phenomenon is also a concern. Even if 90 percent of a school population voluntarily participates in a self-report study, researchers can never be sure whether the few who refuse to participate or are absent that day comprise a significant portion of the school's population of persistent high-rate offenders. Research indicates that offenders with the most extensive prior criminality are also the most likely to "be poor historians of their own crime commission rates."[19] It is also unlikely that the most serious chronic offenders in the teenage population are the most willing to cooperate with university-based criminologists administering self-report tests.[20] Institutionalized youths, who are not generally represented in the self-report surveys, are not only more delinquent than the general youth population but are also considerably more misbehaving than the most delinquent youths identified in the typical self-report survey.[21] Self-reports may only be measuring nonserious, occasional delinquents while ignoring hard-core chronic offenders who may be institutionalized and unavailable for self-reports. Nonetheless, because these factors are consistent over time, self-reports are reliable measures of *changes* in drug abuse and delinquency rates. Even if they are not totally valid or accurate measures of the incidence of crime and drug abuse in the population at any given time, they can be useful in measuring patterns and trends.

© Mark Peterson/SABA

Self-report studies are essential for determining the nature and extent of drug use in the general population. School-based surveys indicate that, despite nationwide efforts to educate students about the dangers of substance abuse, adolescent recreational drug use increased in the 1990s.

Evaluating Crime Data

Each source of crime data has strengths and weaknesses. The UCR is carefully tallied and contains data on the number of murders and people arrested, information that other data sources lack. However, this survey omits the many crimes victims who choose not to report to police, and it is subject to the reporting caprices of individual police departments.

The NCVS contains unreported crime and important information on the personal characteristics of victims, but the data consist of estimates made from relatively limited samples of the total U.S. population, so that even narrow fluctuations in the rates of some crimes can have a major impact on findings. It also relies on personal recollections that may be inaccurate. The NCVS does not include data on important crime patterns, including murder and drug abuse.

Self-report surveys can provide information on the personal characteristics of offenders—such as their attitudes, values, beliefs, and psychological profiles—that is unavailable from any other source. Yet, at their core, self-reports rely on the honesty of criminal offenders and drug abusers, a population not generally known for accuracy and integrity.

Although their tallies of crimes are certainly not in synch, the crime patterns and trends they record are often quite similar.[22] For example, all three sources generally agree about the personal characteristics of serious criminals (such as age and gender) and where and when crime occurs (urban areas, nighttime, and summer months). In addition, the problems inherent in each source are consistent over time. Therefore, even if the data sources are incapable of providing a precise and valid count of crime at any given time, they do provide reliable estimates of changes and fluctuations in yearly crime rates.

What do these data sources tell us about crime trends and patterns?

CRIME TRENDS

Crime is not new to this generation.[23] Studies have indicated that a gradual increase in the crime rate, especially in violent crime, occurred from 1830 to 1860. Following the Civil War, this rate increased significantly for about 15 years. Then, from 1880 up to the time of the First World War, with the possible exception of the years immediately preceding and following the war, the number of reported crimes decreased. After a period of readjustment, the crime rate steadily declined until the Depression (about 1930), when another crime wave was recorded. Crime rates increased gradually following the 1930s until the 1960s, when the growth rate became much greater. The homicide rate, which had actually declined from the 1930s to the 1960s, also began a sharp increase that continued through the 1970s and 1980s.

In 1991, police recorded about 14.6 million crimes. Both the number and rate of crimes have been declining ever since. In 1999, about 11.6 million crimes were reported to the police, a decrease of about 7.6 percent from the preceding year. The number of reported crimes has declined more than 3 million from the 1991 peak (Figure 2.2). Even teenage criminality, a source of national concern, has been in decline during this period, declining about one-third over the past 20 years. The teen murder rate, which had remained stubbornly high, has declined during the past few years.[24] The factors that help explain the upward and downward movement in crime rates are discussed in the Analyzing Criminal Justice Issues feature on pages 50–51.

Trends in Violent Crime

The violent crimes reported in the UCR include murder, rape, assault, and robbery. In 1999, about 1.4 million violent crimes were reported to police, a rate of

FIGURE 2.2
CRIME RATE
TRENDS,
1960–1999

SOURCE: UCR, 1996; updated 1999.

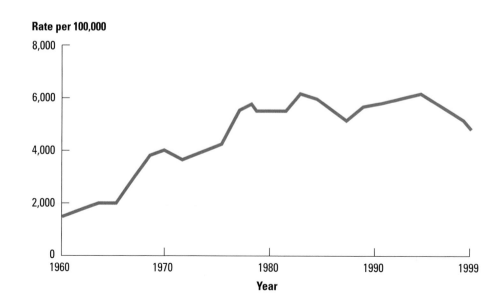

around 524 per 100,000 population. According to the UCR, violence in the United States has decreased significantly during the past decade, reversing a long trend of skyrocketing increases. The total number of violent crimes declined about 20 percent between 1994 and 1999, and the violence rate dropped more than 20 percent.

Particularly encouraging has been the decrease in the number and rate of murders. The murder statistics are generally regarded as the most accurate aspect of the UCR. Figure 2.3 illustrates homicide rate trends since 1900. Note that the rate peaked in the 1930s, then fell, rose dramatically in the 1970s, and peaked once again in 1991, when the number of murders topped 24,000 for the first time in the nation's history. Since 1990, the murder rate has declined by almost 40 percent. The decline in the violence rate has been both unexpected and welcome. Some major cities, such as New York, report a decline of more than 50 percent in their murder rates through the 1990s.

Multiple choice 16
Essay 4

Trends in Property Crime

True/False 15

The property crimes reported in the UCR include larceny, motor vehicle theft, and arson. In 1999, about 10 million property crimes were reported, a rate of about 3,742 per 100,000 population. Property crime rates have declined in recent years, though the drop has not been as dramatic as that of the violent crime rate. Between 1990 and 1999, property crime rates declined about 19 percent.

Trends in Victimization and Self-Report Surveys

True/False 16

According to the most recently available NCVS data (1999), about 30 million personal crimes occur each year. Like the UCR, the NCVS shows that crime rates underwent a major decline in the 1990s. For example, between 1993 and 1999, violent crime rates fell about 30 percent and property crime decreased about 35 percent.

Self-report results appear to be more stable. When the results of recent self-report surveys are compared with various studies conducted over a 20-year period, a uniform pattern emerges. The use of drugs and alcohol increased markedly

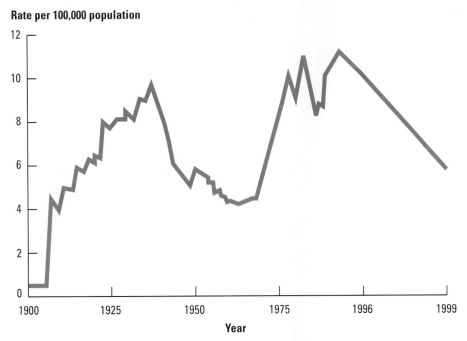

Rate per 100,000 population

FIGURE 2.3
HOMICIDE RATE
TRENDS,
1900–1999

SOURCE: UCR, 1996; updated 1999.

Why Do Crime Rates Change?

Crime experts have identified a variety of social, economic, personal, and demographic factors that influence crime rate trends. Some of the most important factors are discussed here.

Age

Crime experts view change in the population age distribution as having the greatest influence on crime trends. As a general rule, the crime rate follows the proportion of young males in the population. With the "graying" of society in the 1980s and a decline in the birth rate, it is not surprising that the overall crime rate declined between 1990 and 1999. As the teen population increases during the next decade, so too may crime rates.

Economy

Debate continues over the effects the economy has on crime rates. Some crime experts believe that a poor economy actually helps to lower crime rates because unemployed parents are at home to supervise children and guard their possessions. Because there is less to spend, a poor economy reduces the number of valuables worth stealing. Also, it seems unlikely that law-abiding, middle-aged workers will suddenly turn to a life of crime if they are laid off during an economic downturn.

Although a poor economy may lower crime rates in the short run, its long-term effects may prove the opposite. Crime rates rise during prolonged periods of economic weakness and unemployment. A long-term economic recession, such as the one that occurred in the late 1980s, may produce a climate of hopelessness in the nation's largest cities, which helps increase crime rates. Then, when the economy turned around in the 1990s, it coincided with a decade-long drop in the crime rate. Cities such as New York, which experienced an economic boom and rapid increase in real estate prices, also saw a dramatic decline in crime.

Social Problems

As the level of social problems increases—such as single-parent families, dropout rates, racial conflict, and teen pregnancies—so too do crime rates. There is a positive correlation between the homicide rate of a particular age group—for example, 17-year-olds—and the percentage of its members born to unwed mothers. The number of births by unwed single mothers has been in decline, and so too have crime rates.

Racial conflict may also increase crime rates. Areas undergoing racial change, especially those experiencing an in-migration of minorities into predominantly white neighborhoods, seem prone to significant increases in their crime rate. Whites in these areas may be using violence to protect what they view as their home turf. Racially motivated crimes actually diminish as neighborhoods become more integrated and power struggles diminish.

Abortion

In a controversial work, John Donohue and Steven Levitt found empirical evidence that the recent drop in the crime rate may be attributable to the availability of legalized abortion. In 1973, *Roe v. Wade* legalized abortion nationwide. Within a few years of this decision, more than 1 million abortions were being performed annually, or roughly one abortion for every three live births. Donohue and Levitt point out that the crime rate drop began approximately 18 years later, in 1991, when the first group of potential offenders affected by the abortion decision would have begun reaching the peak age of criminal activity. They also note that states that legalized abortion before the rest of the nation were the first to experience decreasing crime and that states with high abortion rates have seen a greater fall in crime since 1985.

The abortion-related reduction in crime is predominantly attributable to a decrease in crime per capita among the young. It is possible that the link between crime rates and abortion is the result of two mechanisms: (1) selective abortion on the part of women most at risk to have children who would engage in criminal activity, and (2) improved child-rearing or environmental circumstances resulting from better maternal, familial, or fetal circumstances because women are having fewer children. If abortion were illegal, they find, crime rates might be 10 to 20 percent higher than they currently are with abortion. If these estimates are correct, legalized abortion can explain about half of the recent fall in crime. All else being equal, they predict that crime rates will continue to fall slowly for an additional 15 to 20 years as the full effects of legalized abortion are gradually felt.

Gun Availability

The availability of firearms may influence the crime rate, especially the proliferation of weapons in the hands of teens. More guns than ever before are finding their way into the hands of young people. Surveys of high school students indicate that between 6 and 10 percent carry guns at least some of the time. Guns also cause escalation in the seriousness of crime. As the number of gun-toting students increases, so too will the seriousness of violent crime as, for example, a schoolyard fight turns into murder.

Gangs

The explosive growth in teenage gangs may have increased crime rates in the 1980s. Surveys indicate that there may be more than 700,000 gang members in the United States. Boys who are members of gangs are far more likely to possess guns than non–gang members; criminal activity increases when teens join gangs.

The recent decline in the crime rate may be tied to changing gang values. Some streetwise youths have told researchers that they now avoid gangs because of the "younger brother syndrome"—they have watched their older siblings or parents caught in gangs or drugs and want to avoid the same fate.

Drug Use

Some experts tie increases in the violent crime rate between 1980 and 1990 to the crack cocaine epidemic, which swept the nation's largest cities, and drug-trafficking gangs, which fought over drug turf. These well-armed gangs did not hesitate to use violence to control territory, intimidate rivals, and increase market share. As the crack epidemic has subsided, so too has the violence in cities such as New York and other metropolitan areas where the crack epidemic was rampant.

Justice Policy

Some law enforcement experts have suggested that a reduction in crime rates may be attributed to aggressive police practices that target "quality-of-life" crimes such as panhandling, graffiti, petty drug dealing, and loitering. By showing that even the smallest infractions will be dealt with seriously, aggressive police departments may be able to discourage potential criminals from committing more serious crimes.

It is also possible that tough laws targeting drug dealing and repeat offenders with lengthy prison terms may affect crime rates. The fear of punishment may inhibit some would-be criminals. Placing a significant number of potentially high-rate offenders behind bars may help stabilize crime rates. Some ex-criminals have told researchers that they stopped committing crime because they perceive higher levels of street enforcement and incarceration rates.

Critical Thinking Skills

1. What social policies might be most effective in bringing down the crime rate?
2. Can you identify recent social changes that may be responsible for a decline in crime rates?

InfoTrac College Edition Research

Gang activity may have a big impact on crime rates. To read about why young people join gangs, see

Benjamin B. Lahey, Rachel A. Gordon, Rolf Loeber, Magda Stouthamer-Loeber, and David P. Farrington, "Boys Who Join Gangs: A Prospective Study of Predictors of First Gang Entry," *Journal of Abnormal Child Psychology,* August 1999, v27 i4 p261

SOURCES: John J. Donohue III and Steven D. Levitt, "Legalized Abortion and Crime," unpublished paper, University of Chicago, June 24, 1999; Donald Green, Dara Strolovitch, and Janelle Wong, "Defended Neighborhoods, Integration, and Racially Motivated Crime," *American Journal of Sociology* 104 (1998): 372–403; Robert O'Brien, Jean Stockard, and Lynne Isaacson, "The Enduring Effects of Cohort Characteristics on Age-Specific Homicide Rates, 1960–1995," *American Journal of Sociology* 104 (1999): 1061–1095; Darrell Steffensmeier and Miles Harer, "Making Sense of Recent U.S. Crime Trends, 1980 to 1996/1998: Age Composition Effects and Other Explanations," *Journal of Research in Crime and Delinquency* 36 (1999): 235–274; Desmond Ellis and Lori Wright, "Estrangement, Interventions, and Male Violence Toward Female Partners," *Violence and Victims* 12 (1997): 51–68; Richard Rosenfeld, "Changing Relationships Between Men and Women: A Note on the Decline in Intimate Partner Homicide," *Homicide Studies* 1 (1997): 72–83; Bruce Johnson, Andrew Golub, and Jeffrey Fagan, "Careers in Crack, Drug Use, Drug Distribution, and Nondrug Criminality," *Crime and Delinquency* 41 (1995): 275–295; Alfred Blumstein, "Violence by Young People: Why the Deadly Nexus," *National Institute of Justice Journal* 229 (1995): 2–9; Joseph Sheley and James Wright, *In the Line of Fire: Youth, Guns, and Violence in Urban America* (New York: Aldine de Gruyter, 1995); Alan Lizotte, Gregory Howard, Marvin Krohn, and Terence Thornberry, "Patterns of Illegal Gun Carrying Among Young Urban Males," *Valparaiso University Law Review* 31 (1997): 376–394; Rosemary Gartner, "Family Structure, Welfare Spending, and Child Homicide in Developed Democracies," *Journal of Marriage and the Family* 53 (1991): 231–240.

International Crime Rates

Although the United States still has a relatively high violence rate compared to many other nations, U.S. crime rates are in decline while there is evidence of a disturbing upswing in crime abroad. For example, the murder rates in England, Germany, and Sweden have increased sharply. Racial assaults and hate crimes have risen dramatically in Germany and England. In some instances, crime rates in the United States have declined to a point where they are actually lower than in some European nations.

Gathering information on international crime rates is often difficult. One important source of international data is the United Nations Surveys of Crime Trends and Operation of Criminal Justice Systems (UNCJS). Another, more recent source is the International Crime Victims Survey (ICVS) conducted in some 60 countries across the globe and overseen by an international working group composed of the Ministry of Justice of the Netherlands, the Home Office of the United Kingdom, and the United Nations Interregional Crime and Justice Research Institute. These multinational sources tell us that crime is everywhere.

On average, crime reported to the police continued to rise in the 1990s, as it had in the 1980s. The most common crime reported was theft, followed by burglary. Around 10 to 15 percent of all reported crime involved violent acts such as homicide, assault, and robbery. The rates were higher for industrial countries than nonindustrial countries. Arab states generally reported very low rates for nearly all types of crime.

Two out of three inhabitants of big cities are victimized by crime at least once every five years. The risks of being victimized are highest in Latin America and sub-Saharan Africa. Violence against women is most prevalent in Latin America, Africa, North America, Australia, and New Zealand. Where women are more emancipated, the rates of violence against women are lower. Less than one in three female victims of violence report their victimization to the police. Reporting is particularly low in the countries of Latin America. In general, countries that have higher firearm ownership rates also have higher firearm-related death rates, including homicide rates. Firearms are frequently used in fatal domestic disputes.

Drug abuse has become an increasingly serious worldwide problem. Although only a small fraction of the world's population uses drugs, in any one year, slightly more than 1 in 1,000 persons uses heroin or other opiates, and 2 in 1,000 illicitly use cocaine. During the past two decades, drug-related crimes have increased at a faster rate than any other crime-related phenomena. The price of heroin and cocaine has fallen dramatically in recent years because, despite increased law enforcement efforts, the supply of drugs to consumers has greatly increased as a result of increased production.

The international crime rate statistics, troubling as they are, often ignore China, which, as the world's largest nation, may be the setting of untold millions of crimes. In recent years, Chinese courts have annually sentenced more than 100,000 street criminals, imposing death sentences on 1,000 and sentencing many thousands more to life in prison. The current wave of punishments is in response to a significant increase in street crimes, including robberies and drug trafficking. Although these numbers seem high, studies show that crime statistics in China may significantly underreport the actual amount of crime because of systematic errors by local police.

Violent Crime

In European nations, violence has been fueled by a dramatic growth in the number of illegal guns smuggled into these countries from the former Soviet republics. Additionally, unrestricted immigration has brought newcomers who face cultural differences, lack of job prospects, and racism. Social and economic pressures, including unemployment and cutbacks in the social welfare system, have also contributed to an increase in violence. Especially in the former communist countries of Eastern Europe, weak law enforcement institu-

in the 1970s, leveled off in the 1980s, and then began to increase in the mid-1990s until 1997, when drug use began to decline. Theft, violence, and damage-related crime rates seem more stable. Although a self-reported crime wave has not occurred, neither has there been any visible reduction in self-reported criminality.

For many years, the United States led the world in crime rates, but other nations now seem to be catching up or surpassing us. This trend is explored in the International Justice feature.

tions, rapid changes in economic laws, deteriorating economic conditions, incomplete reforms, and destabilization of social norms have contributed to rising criminality.

Increased violent activity has also been reported in Asia. For example, Japan, a nation that prides itself on low crime rates, has experienced an upsurge in juvenile crime. It is estimated that 45 percent of all crimes in Japan are committed by people under age 20, about double what it is in the United States. With so much Japanese crime committed by youths, and with the juvenile crime rate escalating, experts predict an overall increase in future crime rates.

Violence rates are also increasing in other parts of the Americas. The homicide rate in Jamaica is 32 per 100,000; in Colombia, it is about 70 per 100,000, roughly 10 times the U.S. average! As in Asia and Europe, high murder rates in the region are tied to the flourishing drug trade.

Transnational Crime

Transnational crime has emerged as a leading issue in the new millennium. It involves a garden variety of illegal activities, including illicit trafficking in arms, drugs, children, women, immigrants, body organs, cultural artifacts, flora and fauna, nuclear materials, and automobiles; terrorism; bribery, corruption, and fraud; and money laundering. Many of these acts are carried out by organized

crime groups, which now operate on a vast, global level. For example, the theft of cars, which was once confined within a particular country, is now a transnational crime because cars that are stolen in one nation are placed for sale on the international illicit market.

Typically, the direction of illicit marketing flows from the third world to affluent Western nations where demand is highest. The exception is the theft and sale of luxury cars, which, for example, are stolen in Western Europe and shipped to Eastern Europe and the Russian Federation. Very often, illicit trade is mixed in with legitimate business enterprise in order to mask criminal activities and confuse the authorities. Thus, transnational crimes are complex and difficult to record. At present, there is no systematic method of accounting for these crimes at the international level; few countries record them separately in their official statistics.

Critical Thinking Skills

1. Will countries such as Japan experience growth in their crime rates as they become more economically dominant?
2. What factors do you think contribute to the high U.S. crime rate?

InfoTrac College Edition Research

To find out about the growth of crime around the world, use

"international crime" or "international offenses" as a subject guide in InfoTrac College Edition.

SOURCES: Olivia Yu and Lening Zhang, "The Under-recording of Crime by Police in China: A Case Study," *Policing* 22 (1999): 252–264; Patrick A. Langan and David P. Farrington, *Crime and Justice in the United States and in England and Wales, 1981–96* (Washington, DC: Bureau of Justice Statistics, 1998); Michael Zielenziger, "Juvenile Crime Jumps to Record High in Japan," *Boston Globe,* 19 April 1998, p. A16; John King, "Paradise Lost? Crime in the Caribbean: A Comparison of Barbados and Jamaica," *Caribbean Journal of Criminology and Social Psychology* 2 (1997): 30–44; "With Women's Liberation Comes a Growing Involvement in Crime," *CJ International* 12 (1996): 19; "Crime Crackdown Continues as Statistics Increase," *CJ International* 12 (1996): 8; Sean Malinowski, "Battling and Emerging Crime Problem," *CJ International* 12 (1996): 3–4; "Singapore Says Delinquency Up," *Boston Globe,* 17 February 1996, p. 4; James Lynch, "A Serious Crime: Cross-National Comparison of the Length of Custodial Sentences," *Justice Quarterly* 10 (1993); Gunther Kaiser, "Juvenile Delinquency in the Federal Republic of Germany," *International Journal of Comparative and Applied Criminal Justice* 16 (1992): 185–197; Marc Mauer, *Americans Behind Bars: The International Use of Incarceration* (Washington, DC: Sentencing Project, 1994); Elizabeth Neuffer, "Violent Crime Rise Fueling Fears in a Changing Europe," *Boston Globe,* 10 April 1994, p. 1; Graeme Newman, *Global Report on Crime and Justice* (London: Oxford University Press, 1999).

What the Future Holds

True/False 17

It is always risky to speculate about the future of crime trends because current conditions can change rapidly. But some criminologists have tried to predict future patterns.

Criminologist James A. Fox predicts a significant increase in teen violence if current trends persist. There are approximately 50 million school-age children in the

To read James Fox's reports on crime trends, you can go to his Web page:
http://www.dac.neu.edu/cj/fox/index.htm
For an up-to-date list of Web links, see http://www.wadsworth.com/product/0534573053s

United States, many under age 10; this is more than we have had for decades. Although many come from stable homes, others lack stable families and adequate supervision. Children in this age group will soon enter their prime crime years. As a result, Fox predicts a wave of youth violence.[25] Fox's predictions may be valid because the reduction in crime rate may be slowing. According to preliminary Uniform Crime Reports (released December 18, 2000) for the first six months of 2000 (the most recent data available), crime decreased by only 0.3 percent compared to the year before. Both violent crime and property crime declined by 0.3 percent when compared with the data from the same period in 1999. Some crimes (larceny and motor-vehicle theft) actually increased. Do these data portend an end to the declining crime rates?

Although Fox's arguments are persuasive, not all criminologists believe that we are in for an age-driven crime wave. Steven Levitt, for example, disputes the idea that the population's age makeup contributes as much to the crime rate as Fox and others suggest.[26] Levitt suggests that even if teens commit more crime in the future, their contribution to the crime rate may be offset by the aging of the population, which will produce a large number of senior citizens and elderly—a group with a relatively low crime rate.

Although such predictions are reassuring, there is of course no telling what changes are in store that may push crime rates either up or down. Technological developments, such as the rapid expansion of e-commerce on the Internet, have created new classes of crime. Concern about the environment in rural areas may produce a rapid upswing in environmental crimes ranging from vandalism to violence.[27] So, although crime rates have trended downward, it is still too early to predict that this trend will continue into the future.

Essay 5

CRIME PATTERNS

Criminologists look for stable crime rate patterns to gain insight into the nature of crime. If crime rates are consistently higher at certain times, in certain areas, and among certain groups, this knowledge may help explain the onset or cause of crime. For example, if criminal statistics show that crime rates are consistently higher in poor neighborhoods in large urban areas, then crime may be a function of poverty and neighborhood decline. If, in contrast, crime rates were spread evenly across the social structure, this would provide little evidence that crime has an economic basis; instead, crime might be linked to socialization, personality, intelligence, or some other trait unrelated to class position or income. In this section, we examine traits and patterns that may influence the crime rate.

Fill in the blanks 15–16

The Ecology of Crime

Most reported crimes occur during the warm summer months of July and August. During the summer, teenagers, who usually have the highest crime rates, are out of school and have greater opportunity to commit crime. People spend more time outdoors during warm weather, making themselves easier targets. Two exceptions to this trend are murders and robberies, which occur frequently in December and January (although rates are also high during the summer). Robbery rates increase in the winter partly because the Christmas shopping season means more money in the cash registers of potential targets.[28]

Crime rates may also be higher on the first day of the month than at any other time. Government welfare and Social Security checks arrive at this time, and with them come increases in such activities as breaking into mailboxes and accosting recipients on the streets. Also, people may have more disposable income at this time, and the availability of extra money may relate to behaviors associated with crime such as drinking, partying, and gambling.[29]

Weather effects (such as temperature swings) may also affect violent crime rates. Crime rates increase with rising temperatures and then begin to decline at some point (85 degrees) when it may be too hot for physical exertion.[30] However, the rates of some crimes (such as domestic assault) continue to increase as temperatures rise.[31]

Large urban areas have by far the highest violence rates; rural areas have the lowest per capita crime rates.

Use of Firearms

Firearms play a dominant role in criminal activity. According to the NCVS, firearms are typically involved in about 20 percent of robberies, 10 percent of assaults, and 6 percent of rapes. In 1999, the UCR reported that almost 70 percent of all murders involved firearms; most of these weapons were handguns.

According to international criminologists Franklin Zimring and Gordon Hawkins, the proliferation of handguns and the high rate of lethal violence they cause is the single most significant factor separating the crime problem in the United States from the rest of the developed world.[32] Differences between the United States and Europe in nonlethal crimes are only modest at best.[33] Because this issue is so important, the Analyzing Criminal Justice Issues feature discusses the question of gun control.

Social Class and Crime

Crime has traditionally been thought of as a lower-class phenomenon. After all, people at the lowest rungs of the social structure have the greatest incentive to commit crimes. Those unable to obtain desired goods and services through conventional means may resort to theft and other illegal activities, such as selling narcotics,

Crimes are more common in urban areas in the West and South. Here, a police helicopter hovers over a Target store in Culver City, California, after gunmen invaded the closed discount store and ordered employees to the floor at gunpoint in a botched robbery attempt. Other police and sheriff's forces can be seen on the ground outside the store. Two people were arrested; no shots were fired, and no one was injured.

True/False 18

True/False 19
Multiple choice 17–19
Essay 6

ANALYZING CRIMINAL JUSTICE ISSUES

Debating Gun Control

More than 200 million guns are in private hands in the United States; half of all U.S. households possess a gun. An estimated 50 million of these guns are illegal.

Handguns are linked to many violent crimes, including 20 percent of all injury deaths (second only to motor vehicles) and 60 percent of all homicides and suicides. They are also responsible for the deaths of about two-thirds of all police officers who are killed in the line of duty. The association between guns and crime has spurred many Americans to advocate controlling the sale of handguns and banning the cheap mass-produced handguns known as "Saturday night specials." In contrast, gun advocates view control as a threat to personal liberty and call for severe punishment of criminals rather than control of handguns. They argue that the Second Amendment of the U.S. Constitution protects the right to bear arms.

Efforts to control handguns have many different sources. The states and many local jurisdictions have laws banning or restricting the sale or possession of guns; some regulate dealers who sell guns. The Federal Gun Control Act of 1968, which is still in effect, requires that all dealers be licensed, fill out forms detailing each trade, and avoid selling to people prohibited from owning guns, such as minors, ex-felons, and drug users. On November 30, 1993, the Brady Handgun Violence Prevention Act (named after former presidential press secretary James Brady, who was severely wounded in the 1981 attempted assassination of President Ronald Reagan) was enacted. The Brady law imposes a waiting period of five days before a licensed importer, manufacturer, or dealer may sell, deliver, or transfer a handgun to an unlicensed individual. The Brady law provides for an instant check on whether a prospective buyer is prohibited from purchasing a weapon. Federal law bans gun purchases by people convicted of or under indictment for felony charges, fugitives, the mentally ill, those with dishonorable military discharges, those who have renounced U.S. citizenship, illegal aliens, illegal drug users, and those convicted of domestic violence misdemeanors or who are under domestic violence restraining orders; individual state laws may create other restrictions.

Some state jurisdictions have tried to reduce gun violence by adding extra punishment, such as a mandatory prison sentence for any crime involving a handgun. California's "10-20-life" law mandates an additional 10 years in prison for carrying a gun while committing a violent felony, 20 years if the gun is fired; if someone is injured, the penalty is 25 years to life in prison.

Even if guns are outlawed or severely restricted, the government's ability to control them is problematic. Although gun control advocates see federal and state legislation as a good first step, some question whether any gun control measures will ultimately curb gun violence. For example, when Jens Ludwig and Philip Cook compared two sets of states—32 that implemented the Brady law in 1994 and 18 states plus the District of Columbia that already had similar laws prior to 1994—they found no evidence that the Brady law had contributed to a reduction in homicide.

What problems face gun control efforts? Private citizens can still sell, barter, or trade handguns. Unregulated gun fairs and auctions are common throughout the United States; many gun deals are made at gun shows with few questions asked. Regulating dealers is

---

instrumental crime
A criminal act intended to improve the financial or social position of the criminal.

expressive crime
A criminal act that serves to vent rage, anger, or frustration.

to obtain them. These activities are referred to as **instrumental crimes**. Those living in poverty are also believed to engage in disproportionate amounts of **expressive crimes**, such as rape and assault, as a means of expressing their rage, frustration, and anger against society. Alcohol and drug abuse, common in impoverished areas, helps fuel violent episodes.[34]

Official police statistics (arrest records) have consistently shown that crime rates in inner-city, high-poverty areas are higher than those in suburban or wealthier areas.[35] Another official indicator of a class–crime relationship comes from surveys of prison inmates, which consistently find that prisoners were members of the lower class and unemployed or underemployed in the years before their incarceration.

An alternative explanation for these findings is that the relationship between official crime and social class is a function of law enforcement practices, not actual criminal behavior patterns. Police may devote more resources to poor areas,

difficult, and tighter controls on them would only encourage private sales and bartering. Corrupt dealers can circumvent the law by ignoring state registration requirements or making unrecorded or misrecorded sales to individuals and unlicensed dealers. Even a few corrupt dealers can supply tens of thousands of illegal handguns.

Not all experts are convinced that strict gun control is a good thing. Criminologist Gary Kleck argues that guns may actually inhibit violence because they allow criminals to scare their victims, who are unlikely to fight back and be injured when facing the threat of a gun. Victims can back down without losing face because it is socially acceptable to retreat from an armed assailant. Conversely, arming people may help reduce crime because criminals are afraid of gun-toting victims. When John Lott analyzed the effects on crime in 23 states that made it easier for citizens to arm themselves by carrying concealed weapons, he found a significant yearly drop in crimes such as murder and rape.

Although these arguments are persuasive, the recent spate of gun violence in public schools makes a powerful statement against gun ownership. Studies show that many people who seek to

buy guns legally and/or purchase licenses to carry concealed weapons have prior criminal records and engage in patterns of heavy drinking. Strict control of gun purchases by this high-risk group might help reduce the rate of violent crimes.

Critical Thinking Skills

1. Should the sale and possession of handguns be banned?
2. Which of the gun control methods discussed do you feel would be most effective in deterring crime?

 InfoTrac College Edition Research

Conservatives are adamant about keeping their guns, charging that liberals spread false stories about gun violence. To check out this perspective, read Dave Kopel, "An Army of Gun Lies: How the Other Side Plays," *National Review,* 17 April 2000, v52 i7 For an opposing, more liberal view, see Michael Warfel, "Why Gun Control? An Individual's Right to Own and Bear Arms Must

Be Balanced by the Greater Social Needs of a Society," *America,* 15 April 2000, v182 i13 p18

SOURCES: Jens Ludwig and Philip Cook, "Homicide and Suicide Rates Associated with the Implementation of the Brady Violence Prevention Act," *Journal of the American Medical Association* 284 (2000): 585–591; John R. Lott, Jr., *More Guns, Less Crime: Understanding Crime and Gun-Control Laws* (Chicago: University of Chicago Press, 1998); Julius Wachtel, "Sources of Crime Guns in Los Angeles, California," *Policing* 21 (1998): 220–239; Gary Kleck and Michael Hogan, "National Case-Control Study of Homicide Offending and Gun Ownership," *Social Problems* 46 (1999): 275–293; Garen Wintemute, Mora Wright, Carrie Parham, Christina Drake, and James Beaumont, "Denial of Handgun Purchase: A Description of the Affected Population and a Controlled Study of Their Handgun Preferences," *Journal of Criminal Justice* 27 (1999): 21–31; Shawn Schwaner, L. Allen Furr, Cynthia Negrey, and Rachelle Seger, "Who Wants a Gun License?" *Journal of Criminal Justice* 27 (1999): 1–10; "Gun Crime Mandatory Sentences Take Effect in California," *Criminal Justice Newsletter,* 15 December 1997; Gary Kleck and Marc Gertz, "Armed Resistance to Crime: The Prevalence and Nature of Self-Defense with a Gun," *Journal of Criminal Law and Criminology* 86 (1995): 150–187; Gary Kleck, "The Incidence of Gun Violence Among Young People," *Public Perspective* 4 (1993): 3–6.

and consequently apprehension rates may be higher there. Similarly, police may be more likely to formally arrest and prosecute lower-class citizens than those in the middle and upper classes, which may account for the lower class's overrepresentation in official statistics and the prison population.

Class and Self-Reports Self-report data have been used extensively to test the class–crime relationship. If people in all social classes self-report similar crime patterns, but only those in the lower class are formally arrested, that would explain higher crime rates in lower-class neighborhoods. However, if lower-class people report greater criminal activity than their middle- and upper-class peers, it would indicate that official statistics accurately represent the crime problem.

Surprisingly, self-report studies generally do not find a direct relationship between social class and youth crime.[36] Socioeconomic class is related to official processing by police, courts, and correctional agencies, but not to the actual commission of crimes. Although lower- and middle-class youths self-reported equal amounts of crime, the lower-class youths had a greater chance of getting arrested, convicted, and incarcerated and thus becoming official delinquents.[37] More than 20 years ago, Charles Tittle, Wayne Villemez, and Douglas Smith found little if any support for the contention that crime is primarily a lower-class phenomenon. They concluded that official statistics probably reflect class bias in processing lower-class offenders.[38]

Weighing the Evidence for a Class–Crime Relationship Tittle's research has sparked significant debate. Many self-report instruments include trivial offenses such as using a false ID or drinking alcohol. Their inclusion may obscure the true class–crime relationship because affluent youths frequently engage in trivial offenses such as petty larceny, drug use, and simple assault. Those who support a class–crime relationship suggest that if only serious felony offenses are considered, a significant association can be observed.[39] Studies showing middle- and lower-class youths to be equally delinquent rely on measures weighted toward minor crimes (for example, using a false ID or skipping school); when serious crimes, such as burglary and assault, are compared, lower-class youths are significantly more delinquent.[40] There is also debate over the most appropriate measure of class. Should it be income? Occupation? Educational attainment? Findings may be skewed if the measure of class used is inappropriate or invalid. Research also shows that class affects minority subgroups in the population more than it affects whites.[41]

The debate over the true relationship between class and crime will most likely continue. The weight of evidence seems to suggest that serious, official crime is more prevalent among the lower classes, whereas less serious and self-reported crime is spread more evenly throughout the social structure.[42] Income inequality, poverty, and resource deprivation are all associated with the most serious violent crimes, including homicide and assault.[43] Communities that lack economic and social opportunities also produce high levels of frustration; residents, seeing themselves as deprived relative to those in more affluent areas, may turn to criminal behavior to relieve their frustration.[44] Family life is disrupted and law-violating youth groups thrive in a climate that undermines adult supervision.[45] Conversely, when the poor are provided with economic opportunities via welfare and public assistance, crime rates drop.[46]

PERSPECTIVES ON JUSTICE

Income inequality, poverty, and resource deprivation are all associated with the most serious violent crimes, including homicide and assault. The finding that crime rates may be lowered by efforts to rehabilitate neighborhoods and provide legitimate job opportunities supports the rehabilitation perspective on justice.

Although crime rates may be higher in lower-class areas, poverty alone cannot explain why a particular individual becomes a chronic violent criminal. If it could, the crime problem would be much worse than it is.[47]

Age and Crime

There is general agreement that age is inversely related to criminality.[48] Regardless of economic status, marital status, race, or sex, younger people commit crime more often than older people; research indicates that this relationship has been stable across time periods ranging from 1935 to the present.[49] Official statistics tell us that young people are arrested at a rate disproportionate to their numbers in the population; victim surveys generate similar findings for crimes in which assailant age can be determined. Whereas youths aged 13 to 17 collectively make up about 6 percent of the total U.S. population, they account for about 25 percent of index crime arrests and 17 percent of arrests for all crimes. As a general rule, the peak age for property crime is believed to be 16, and for violence, 18 (see Figure 2.4). In contrast, adults 45 and over, who make up more than 30 percent of the population, account for less than 10 percent of index crime arrests. The elderly are particularly resistant to the temptations of crime; they make up more than 12 percent of the population and less than 1 percent of arrests. Elderly men, age 65 and over, are predominantly arrested for alcohol-related matters (public drunkenness and drunk driving) and elderly women for larceny (shoplifting). The elderly crime rate has remained stable for the past 20 years.[50] The fact that people commit less crime as they mature is referred to as **aging out** or **desistance**.

Why does aging out occur? One view is that there is a direct relationship between aging and crime. Psychologists note that young people, especially the indigent and antisocial, tend to discount the future.[51] They are impatient, and because their future is uncertain, they are unwilling or unable to delay gratification. As they mature, troubled youths are able to develop a long-term life view and resist the need for immediate gratification.[52] Young people may view crime as fun—a risky but exciting social activity. As they grow older, life patterns such as job and marriage become inconsistent with criminality; people literally grow out of crime.[53]

James Q. Wilson and Richard Herrnstein argue that aging out is a function of the natural history of the human life cycle.[54] Deviance in adolescence is fueled by the need for conventionally unobtainable money and sex and reinforced by close relationships with peers who defy conventional morality. At the same time, teenagers are becoming independent from parents and other adults who enforce conventional standards. They have a new sense of energy and strength and are involved with peers who are similarly vigorous and frustrated. Adults, on the other

aging out
The reduction in criminal behavior as people get older.

desistance
The reduction in criminal behavior as people get older; aging out.

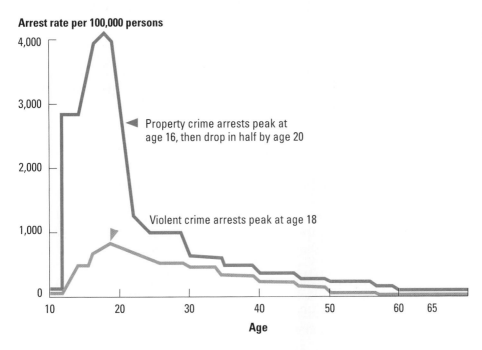

Arrest rate per 100,000 persons

Property crime arrests peak at age 16, then drop in half by age 20

Violent crime arrests peak at age 18

Age

FIGURE 2.4
THE RELATIONSHIP BETWEEN AGE AND SERIOUS CRIME ARRESTS

SOURCE: UCR, 1999.

hand, develop the ability to delay gratification and forgo the immediate gains that law violations bring. They also start wanting to take responsibility for their behavior and to adhere to conventional mores, such as establishing long-term relationships and starting a family.[55] Research shows that teenagers may turn to crime as a way to solve the problems of adolescence—loneliness, frustration, fear of peer rejection. As they mature, conventional means of problem solving become available, and their life experience helps them seek out nondestructive solutions to their personal travails.[56]

Although most people age out of crime, some do pursue a criminal career. Yet even people who actively remain in a criminal career will eventually slow down as they age. Crime is too dangerous, physically taxing, and unrewarding (and punishments too harsh and long-lasting) to become a long-term way of life for most people.[57] By middle age, even the most chronic offenders terminate their criminal behavior.

Gender and Crime

Fill in the blanks 18–19
Multiple choice 21
Essay 7

masculinity hypothesis
The view that women who commit crimes have biological and psychological traits similar to those of men.

The three main sources of crime data agree that male crime rates are much higher than female rates. In more than 80 percent of all violent personal crimes, victims report that their assailant was male. UCR arrest statistics indicate that the overall male–female arrest ratio is about 3.5 male offenders to 1 female offender; for serious violent crimes, the ratio is closer to 5 males to 1 female; for murder arrests, it is 8 to 1. Self-report data collected by the ISR also show that males commit more serious crimes, such as robbery, assault, and burglary, than females. However, although the patterns in self-reports parallel official data, the ratios seem smaller. In other words, males self-report more criminal behavior than females, but not to the degree suggested by official data.

Why are there gender differences in the crime rate? Early criminologists pointed to emotional, physical, and psychological differences between males and females to explain the differences in crime rates. They maintained that because females were weaker and more passive, they were less likely to commit crimes. Cesare Lombroso argued that the small group of female criminals lacked "typical" female traits of "piety, maternity, undeveloped intelligence, and weakness."[58] Lombroso's theory became known as the **masculinity hypothesis;** in essence, a few "masculine" females were responsible for the handful of crimes that women committed.[59]

Although these early writings are no longer taken seriously, some criminologists still consider trait differences a key determinant of crime rate differences. For example, some criminologists link antisocial behavior to hormonal influences, arguing that male sex hormones (androgens) account for more aggressive male behavior and that gender-related hormonal differences can thus explain the gender gap in the crime rate.[60]

By the mid-twentieth century, criminologists commonly portrayed gender differences in the crime rate as a function of socialization. Female criminals were described as troubled individuals, alienated at home, who pursued crime as a means of compensating for their disrupted personal lives.[61] The streets became a "second home" to girls whose physical and emotional adjustment was hampered by a strained home life marked by such conditions as absent fathers or overly competitive mothers. The relatively few females who commit violent crimes report having home and family relationships that are more troubled than those experienced by males.[62]

In the 1970s, liberal feminists focused their attention on the social and economic role of women in society and its relationship to female crime rates.[63] They suggested that the traditionally lower crime rate for women could be explained by their "second-class" economic and social position. They further contended that as women's social roles changed and their lifestyles became more like those of males, their crime rates would converge.[64]

Although male arrest rates are still considerably higher than female rates, female arrest rates seem to be increasing at a faster pace. Between 1990 and 1999, male arrests actually decreased 5 percent, while female arrests increased by about 18 percent. More important, arrests of teenage girls increased 32 percent between 1990 and 1999, while arrests of teenage boys increased by about 5 percent, suggesting that young girls are increasing their offense rates at a pace even greater than their older sisters.

PERSPECTIVES ON JUSTICE

At one time it was believed that male police officers were reluctant to arrest female offenders in order to protect them from the rigors of the criminal justice system; this was referred to as the "chivalry hypothesis." Higher female arrest rates may actually reflect a new trend in police work with less resistance to formally arresting female offenders. This change in social policy would conform both to the due process perspective, which asks that all offenders be treated equally before the law, and the justice perspective, which calls for standardized treatment.

Race and Crime

Official crime data indicate that minority-group members are involved in a disproportionate share of criminal activity. According to UCR reports, African Americans make up about 12 percent of the general population, yet they account for about 41 percent of index violent crime arrests and 34 percent of property crime arrests. They also are responsible for a disproportionate number (29 percent) of Part II arrests (except for alcohol-related arrests, which involve primarily white offenders).

Self-Reports and Race Another approach to examining this issue is to compare the racial differences in self-report data with those found in official delinquency records. Charges of racial discrimination in the arrest process would be supported if racial differences in self-report data were insignificant.

Nationwide youth surveys have found few racial differences in crime rates, although black youths are much more likely to be arrested and taken into custody.[65] These self-report studies seem to indicate that the criminal behavior rates of black and white teenagers are generally similar and that differences in arrest statistics may indicate a differential selection policy by police.[66]

Causes of Racial Disparity Racial differences in crime rates remain an extremely sensitive issue. Although official arrest records indicate that African Americans are arrested at a higher rate than members of other racial groups, some question whether this is a function of crime rate differences, racism by police, or faulty data collection.[67] Research shows that suspects who are poor, minority, and male are more likely to be formally arrested than suspects who are affluent, white, and female.[68] Some critics charge that police officers routinely use "racial profiling" to stop African Americans and search their cars without probable cause or reasonable suspicion. Some cynics have gone so far as to suggest that police officers have created a new form of traffic offense called DWB—*driving while black*.[69]

Fill in the blanks 20
Multiple choice 22–23
Essay 8

Although the UCR may reflect discriminatory police practices, African Americans are arrested for a disproportionate amount of violent crime, such as robbery and murder, and it is improbable that police discretion alone could account for these proportions. It is doubtful that police routinely ignore white killers, robbers, and rapists while arresting violent black offenders.

Today, many crime experts concede that recorded differences in the black and white violent crime arrest rates cannot be explained away solely by racism or differential treatment within the criminal justice system.[70] To do so would be to ignore the social problems that exist in the nation's inner cities.

Racism and Crime How, then, can racial patterns be explained? Most explanations focus on the effects of economic deprivation, social disorganization, subcultural adaptations, and the impact of racism and discrimination on personality and behavior.[71] The fact that U.S. culture influences African American crime rates is underscored by the fact that black violence rates are much lower in other nations—both those that are predominantly white, such as Canada, and those that are predominantly black, such as Nigeria.[72]

African Americans have suffered through a long history of racism in the United States that has left long-lasting emotional scars.[73] Racism is still an element of daily life in the African American community, undermining faith in social and political institutions and weakening confidence in the justice system. Such fears are supported by empirical evidence that, in at least some jurisdictions, young African American males are treated more harshly by the criminal justice system than members of any other group.[74] In some legal jurisdictions, African Americans, especially those who are indigent or unemployed, receive longer prison sentences than European Americans. It is possible that some judges view poor blacks as "social dynamite," considering them more dangerous and likely to recidivate than white offenders.[75] Yet when African Americans are victims of crime, their predicament receives less public concern and media attention than that afforded white victims.[76]

PERSPECTIVES ON JUSTICE

The conflict view of crime suggests that minority crime rates are fueled both by police discrimination and by the income inequality produced by the capitalist economy. If racism and capitalism were ended, crime rates would converge.

Is Convergence Possible? Considering these overwhelming social problems, is it possible that racial crime rates will soon converge? One argument is that if economic conditions improve in the minority community, then differences in crime rates will eventually disappear.[77] A trend toward residential integration, underway since 1980, may also help reduce race-based crime rate differentials.[78] Despite economic disparity, there are actually few racial differences in attitudes toward crime and justice today. Convergence in crime rates will occur if economic and social obstacles can be removed.

In sum, the weight of the evidence shows that although there is little difference in the self-reported crime rates of racial groups, African Americans are more likely to be arrested for serious violent crimes. The causes of minority crime have been linked to poverty, racism, hopelessness, lack of opportunity, and urban problems experienced by all too many African Americans.

Victims and Crime

Not only do the data sources tell us about the characteristics of criminals, but they also let us know something about the victims of crime. According to the NCVS, criminal acts are not random events but exhibit stable long-term patterns, indicating that they are shaped by personal and ecological factors. What are these patterns?

Social Ecology The NCVS shows that violent crimes are slightly more likely to take place in (1) an open, public area, such as a street, a park, or a field, (2) in a school building, or (3) at a commercial establishment such as a tavern during the daytime or early evening hours. The more serious forms of these crimes, such as rape and aggravated assaults, typically take place after 6 P.M. Less serious forms of violence, such as unarmed robberies and personal larcenies like purse snatching, are more likely to occur during the daytime. Approximately two-thirds of rapes and sexual assaults occur at night, from 6 P.M. to 6 A.M.

Neighborhood characteristics influence the chances of victimization. Those living in the central city had significantly higher rates of theft and violence than suburbanites; people living in nonmetropolitan, rural areas had a victimization rate almost half that of city dwellers. The NCVS tells us that larger, higher income, African American, western, and urban areas are the most vulnerable to crime. In contrast, poor, rural white homes in the northeast are the least likely to contain crime victims or be the target of theft offenses, such as burglary or larceny. People who own their homes are less vulnerable than renters.

Victim Characteristics Social and demographic characteristics also distinguish victims and nonvictims. Except for the crimes of rape and sexual assault, males are much more likely than females to suffer violent crime. Men were twice as likely as women to experience aggravated assault and robbery. Women, however, were six times more likely than men to be victims of rape or sexual assault.

Victim data reveal that young people face a much greater victimization risk than do older persons; victim risk diminishes rapidly after age 25. The elderly, who are thought of as the helpless targets of predatory criminals, are actually much safer than their grandchildren. People over 65, who make up about 15 percent of the population, account for only 1 percent of violent victimizations; teens 12–19, who also make up 15 percent of the population, typically account for more than 30 percent of victimizations.

CRIMINAL CAREERS

Multiple choice 24–25
Essay 9

Crime data show that most offenders commit a single criminal act and, upon arrest, discontinue their antisocial activity. Others commit a few less serious crimes. A small group of criminal offenders, however, accounts for a majority of all criminal offenses. These persistent offenders are referred to as **career criminals**.

The concept of the career criminal is most closely associated with the research efforts of Marvin Wolfgang, Robert Figlio, and Thorsten Sellin.[79] In their landmark 1972 study, *Delinquency in a Birth Cohort,* they used official records to follow the criminal careers of a cohort of 9,945 boys born in Philadelphia in 1945 from the time of their birth until they reached 18 years of age in 1963. Official police records were used to identify delinquents. About one-third of the boys (3,475) had some police contact; the remaining two-thirds (6,470) had none.

The best-known discovery of Wolfgang and his associates was what they called **chronic offenders**. These 627 boys, each of whom had been arrested five times or more, were involved in the most dramatic amounts of delinquent behavior: They

career criminal
A persistent repeat offender who organizes his or her lifestyle around criminality.

chronic offender
As defined by Wolfgang, a delinquent arrested five or more times before the age of 18 who commits a disproportionate amount of all criminal offenses.

were responsible for 5,305 offenses, or 51.9 percent of all the offenses committed by the cohort. Even more striking was the involvement of chronic offenders in serious criminal acts. Of the entire sample, they committed 71 percent of the homicides, 73 percent of the rapes, 82 percent of the robberies, and 69 percent of the aggravated assaults. Wolfgang and his associates found that arrests and court experience did little to deter the chronic offender. In fact, punishment was inversely related to chronic offending: The more stringent the sanction chronic offenders received, the more likely they were to engage in repeated criminal behavior. Wolfgang's pioneering effort to identify the chronic career offender has been replicated by a number of other researchers in a variety of locations in the United States and abroad.[80]

The findings of the cohort studies and the discovery of the chronic offender raise some challenging issues. If relatively few offenders become chronic, persistent criminals, then perhaps they possess some individual trait that is responsible for their behavior. Most people exposed to troublesome social conditions, such as poverty, do not become chronic offenders, so it is unlikely that social conditions alone can cause chronic offending. Traditional theories of criminal behavior have failed to distinguish between chronic and occasional offenders. They concentrated more on explaining why people begin to commit crime and paid scant attention to why people stop offending. The discovery of the chronic offender forced crime experts to consider such issues as persistence and desistance in their explanations of crime; more recent theories account not only for the onset of criminality but also for its termination.

SUMMARY

There are three primary sources of crime statistics: The Uniform Crime Reports (UCR) are based on police data accumulated by the FBI. The National Crime Victimization Survey (NCVS) samples more than 50,000 people annually to estimate the total number of criminal incidents, including those not reported to police. Self-report surveys ask people to anonymously reveal their participation in criminal activity. Each data source has its strengths and weaknesses, and although quite different from one another, they generally agree on the nature of criminal behavior. They tell us that there is quite a bit of crime in the United States, although the amount has been decreasing for about a decade.

The data sources show stable patterns in the crime rate. Ecological patterns show that some areas of the country are more crime-prone than others, that there are seasons and times for crime, and that these patterns are quite stable. There are also gender and age gaps in the crime rate: Men commit more crime than women, and young people commit more crime than the elderly. Crime data show that people commit less crime as they age, but the significance and cause of this pattern are still not completely understood.

Racial and class patterns also appear in the crime rate. However, it is still unclear whether these are true differences or a function of discriminatory law enforcement. Some experts suggest that institutional racism, such as police profiling, accounts for the racial differences in the crime rate. Others believe that high African American crime rates are a function of living in a racially segregated society.

One of the most important findings is the existence of chronic offenders—repeat criminals responsible for a significant amount of all law violations. Chronic offenders begin their careers early in life and, rather than aging out of crime, persist into adulthood. The discovery of the chronic offender has led to the study of developmental criminology—why people persist, desist, terminate, or escalate their deviant behavior.

Key Terms

consensus view

criminal law

social control

interactionist view

moral entrepreneurs

conflict view

official crime statistics

cohort study

longitudinal cohort study

Uniform Crime Reports (UCR)

index crimes

National Crime Victimization Survey
    (NCVS)

self-report survey

instrumental crime

expressive crime

aging out

desistance

career criminal

chronic offender

Discussion Questions

1. Would you answer honestly if a national crime survey asked you about your criminal behavior, including drinking and drug use? If not, why?
2. How would you explain gender differences in the crime rate? That is, why do you think males are more violent than females?
3. Assuming that males are more violent than females, does that mean that crime has a biological rather than a social basis (because males and females share a similar environment)?
4. The UCR tells us that crime rates are higher in large cities than in small towns. Yet teens everywhere watch the same movies and television shows and listen to the same music CDs. What does this tell us about the effect of TV, movies, and music on teenage behavior?

A CLOSER LOOK

Some experts have expressed the view that drugs should be legalized. Doing so would reduce the amount of crime committed by abusers and allow the government to control the supply and distribution of illegal drugs. Governor Gary Johnson of New Mexico embraces the legalization idea as a means of drug control. Here's what he has to say:

> I am a "cost–benefit" analysis person. What's the cost and what's the benefit? A couple of things scream out as failing cost–benefit criteria. One is education. The other is the war on drugs. We are presently spending $50 billion a year to combat drugs. I'm talking about police, courts, and jails. For the amount of money that we're putting into it, I want to suggest, the war on drugs is an absolute failure. My "outrageous" hypothesis is that under a legalized sce-

nario, we could actually hold drug use level or see it decline.

Sometimes people say to me, "Governor, I am absolutely opposed to your stand on drugs." I respond by asking them, "You're for drugs, you want to see kids use drugs?" Let me make something clear. I'm not pro-drug. I'm against drugs. Don't do drugs. Drugs are a real handicap. Don't do alcohol or tobacco, either. They are real handicaps.

To read more, go to InfoTrac College Edition and read Gary E. Johnson, "The Case for Drug Legalization: We Need to Make Drugs a Controlled Substance Just Like Alcohol," *World and I,* February 2000, v15 i2 p34

Notes

1 Associated Press, "Ex-detective Linked to Jewel Thefts," *New York Times,* 22 October 2000, p. 2.
2 Howard Becker, *Outsiders,* 2d ed. (New York: Macmillan, 1972).
3 For a general discussion of Marxist thought, see Michael Lynch and W. Byron Groves, *A Primer in Radical Criminology,* 2d ed. (New York: Harrow and Heston, 1990), pp. 6–26.
4 William F. Whyte, *Street Corner Society: The Social Structure of an Italian Slum* (Chicago: University of Chicago Press, 1955); Laud Humphreys, *Tearoom Trade: Impersonal Sex in Public Places,* rev. ed. (Chicago: Aldine, 1975).
5 Carl Klockars, *The Professional Fence* (New York: Free Press, 1976); Darrell

Steffensmeier, *The Fence: In the Shadow of Two Worlds* (Totowa, NJ: Rowman and Littlefield, 1986).
6 Federal Bureau of Investigation, *Crime in the United States, 1998* (Washington, DC: U.S. Government Printing Office, 1999).
7 Craig Perkins and Patsy Klaus, *Criminal Victimization, 1994* (Washington, DC: Bureau of Justice Statistics, 1996).
8 Duncan Chappell, Gilbert Geis, Stephen Schafer, and Larry Siegel, "Forcible Rape: A Comparative Study of Offenses Known to the Police in Boston and Los Angeles," in *Studies in the Sociology of Sex,* ed. James Henslin (New York: Appleton Century Crofts, 1971), pp. 169–193.
9 David Seidman and Michael Couzens, "Getting the Crime Rate Down: Political

Pressure and Crime Reporting," *Law and Society Review* 8 (1974): 457.
10 Robert O'Brien, "Police Productivity and Crime Rates: 1973–1992," *Criminology* 34 (1996): 183–207.
11 Barbara Warner and Glenn Pierce, "Re-examining Social Disorganization Theory Using Calls to the Police as a Measure of Crime," *Criminology* 31 (1993): 493–517.
12 FBI, *UCR Handbook* (Washington, DC: U.S. Government Printing Office, 1998), p. 33.
13 Callie Marie Rennison, *Criminal Victimization 1998: Changes 1997–98 with Trends 1993–98* (Washington, DC: Bureau of Justice Statistics, 1999).
14 L. Edward Wells and Joseph Rankin, "Juvenile Victimization: Convergent

Validation of Alternative Measurements," *Journal of Research in Crime and Delinquency* 32 (1995): 287–307.

15 A pioneering effort in self-report research is A. L. Porterfield, *Youth in Trouble* (Fort Worth, TX: Leo Potishman Foundation, 1946); for a review, see Robert Hardt and George Bodine, *Development of Self-Report Instruments in Delinquency Research: A Conference Report* (Syracuse, NY: Syracuse University Youth Development Center, 1965). See also Fred Murphy, Mary Shirley, and Helen Witner, "The Incidence of Hidden Delinquency," *American Journal of Orthopsychology* 16 (1946): 686–696.

16 For an example of this utility, see G. David Curry, "Self-Reported Gang Involvement and Officially Recorded Delinquency," *Criminology* 38 (2000): 1253–1275.

17 For example, the following studies have noted the great discrepancy between official statistics and self-report studies: Martin Gold, "Undetected Delinquent Behavior," *Journal of Research in Crime and Delinquency* 3 (1966): 27–46; James Short and F. Ivan Nye, "Extent of Undetected Delinquency: Tentative Conclusions," *Journal of Criminal Law, Criminology and Police Science* 49 (1958): 296–302; Michael Hindelang, "Causes of Delinquency: A Partial Replication and Extension," *Social Problems* 20 (1973): 471–487.

18 D. Wayne Osgood, Lloyd Johnston, Patrick O'Malley, and Jerald Bachman, "The Generality of Deviance in Late Adolescence and Early Adulthood," *American Sociological Review* 53 (1988): 81–93.

19 Leonore Simon, "Validity and Reliability of Violent Juveniles: A Comparison of Juvenile Self-Reports with Adult Self-Reports Incarcerated in Adult Prisons," paper presented at the annual meeting of the American Society of Criminology, Boston, November 1995, p. 26.

20 Stephen Cernkovich, Peggy Giordano, and Meredith Pugh, "Chronic Offenders: The Missing Cases in Self-Report Delinquency Research," *Journal of Criminal Law and Criminology* 76 (1985): 705–732.

21 Terence Thornberry, Beth Bjerregaard, and William Miles, "The Consequences of Respondent Attrition in Panel Studies: A Simulation Based on the Rochester Youth Development Study," *Journal of Quantitative Criminology* 9 (1993): 127–158.

22 Alfred Blumstein, Jacqueline Cohen, and Richard Rosenfeld, "Trend and Deviation in Crime Rates: A Comparison of UCR and NCVS Data for Burglary and Robbery," *Criminology* 29 (1991): 237–248. See also Michael Hindelang, Travis Hirschi, and Joseph Weis, *Measuring Delinquency* (Beverly Hills, CA: Sage, 1981).

23 Clarence Schrag, *Crime and Justice, American Style* (Washington, DC: U.S. Government Printing Office, 1971), p. 17.

24 Thomas Bernard, "Juvenile Crime and the Transformation of Juvenile Justice: Is There a Juvenile Crime Wave? *Justice Quarterly* 16 (1999): 336–356.

25 James A. Fox, *Trends in Juvenile Violence: A Report to the United States Attorney General on Current and Future Rates of Juvenile Offending* (Boston: Northeastern University, 1996).

26 Steven Levitt, "The Limited Role of Changing Age Structure in Explaining Aggregate Crime Rates," *Criminology* 37 (1999): 581–599.

27 Ralph Weisheit and L. Edward Wells, "The Future of Crime in Rural America," *Journal of Crime and Justice* 22 (1999): 1–22.

28 Peter Van Koppen and Robert Jansen, "The Time to Rob: Variations in Time of Number of Commercial Robberies," *Journal of Research in Crime and Delinquency* 36 (1999): 7–29.

29 Ellen Cohn, "The Effect of Weather and Temporal Variations on Calls for Police Service," *American Journal of Police* 15 (1996): 23–43.

30 R. A. Baron, "Aggression as a Function of Ambient Temperature and Prior Anger Arousal," *Journal of Personality and Social Psychology* 21 (1972): 183–189.

31 Ellen Cohn, "The Prediction of Police Calls for Service: The Influence of Weather and Temporal Variables on Rape and Domestic Violence," *Journal of Environmental Psychology* 13 (1993): 71–83.

32 See, generally, Franklin Zimring and Gordon Hawkins, *Crime Is Not the Problem: Lethal Violence in America* (New York: Oxford University Press, 1997).

33 Ibid., p. 36.

34 Robert Nash Parker, "Bringing 'Booze' Back In: The Relationship Between Alcohol and Homicide," *Journal of Research in Crime and Delinquency* 32 (1995): 3–38.

35 Victoria Brewer and M. Dwayne Smith, "Gender Inequality and Rates of Female Homicide Victimization Across U.S. Cities," *Journal of Research in Crime and Delinquency* 32 (1995): 175–190.

36 R. Gregory Dunaway, Francis Cullen, Velmer Burton, and T. David Evans, "The Myth of Social Class and Crime Revisited: An Examination of Class and Adult Criminality," *Criminology* 38 (2000): 589–632.

37 Ivan Nye, James Short, and Virgil Olsen, "Socio-economic Status and Delinquent Behavior," *American Journal of Sociology* 63 (1958): 381–389; Robert Dentler and Lawrence Monroe, "Social Correlates of Early Adolescent Theft," *American Sociological Review* 63 (1961): 733–743. See also Terence Thornberry and Margaret Farnworth, "Social Correlates of Criminal Involvement: Further Evidence of the Relationship Between Social Status and Criminal Behavior," *American Sociological Review* 47 (1982): 505–518.

38 Charles Tittle, Wayne Villemez, and Douglas Smith, "The Myth of Social Class and Criminality: An Empirical Assessment of the Empirical Evidence," *American Sociological Review* 43 (1978): 643–656. See also Charles Tittle and Robert Meier, "Specifying the SES/Delin-quency Relationship," *Criminology* 28 (1990): 271–301.

39 Delbert Elliott and Suzanne Ageton, "Reconciling Race and Class Differences in Self-Reported and Official Estimates of Delinquency," *American Sociological Review* 45 (1980): 95–110.

40 See also Delbert Elliott and David Huizinga, "Social Class and Delinquent Behavior in a National Youth Panel: 1976–1980," *Criminology* 21 (1983): 149–177. For a similar view, see John Braithwaite, "The Myth of Social Class and Criminality Reconsidered," *American Sociological Review* 46 (1981): 35–58; Hindelang, Hirschi, and Weis, *Measuring Delinquency*, p. 196.

41 R. Gregory Dunaway, Francis Cullen, Velmer Burton, and T. David Evans, "The Myth of Social Class and Crime Revisited: An Examination of Class and Adult Criminality," *Criminology* 38 (2000): 589–632.

42 Judith Blau and Peter Blau, "The Cost of Inequality: Metropolitan Structure and Violent Crime," *American Sociological Review* 147 (1982): 114–129; Richard Block, "Community Environment and Violent Crime," *Criminology* 17 (1979): 46–57; Robert Sampson, "Structural Sources of Variation in Race-Age-Specific Rates of Offending Across Major U.S. Cities," *Criminology* 23 (1985): 647–673.

43 Chin-Chi Hsieh and M. D. Pugh, "Poverty, Income Inequality, and Violent Crime: A Meta-Analysis of Recent Aggregate Data Studies," *Criminal Justice Review* 18 (1993): 182–199.

44 Robert Agnew, "A General Strain Theory of Community Differences in Crime Rates," *Journal of Research in Crime and Delinquency* 36 (1999): 123–155.

45 Bonita Veysey and Steven Messner, "Further Testing of Social Disorganization Theory: An Elaboration of Sampson and Groves's Community Structure and Crime," *Journal of Research in Crime and Delinquency* 36 (1999): 156–174.

46 Lance Hannon and James Defronzo, "Welfare and Property Crime," *Justice Quarterly* 15 (1998): 273–288.

47 Alan Lizotte, Terence Thornberry, Marvin Krohn, Deborah Chard-Wierschem, and David McDowall, "Neighborhood Context and Delinquency: A Longitudinal Analysis," in *Cross National Longitudinal Research on Human Development and Criminal Behavior*, ed. E. M. Weitekamp and H. J. Kerner (Stavernstr, Netherlands: Kluwer, 1994), pp. 217–227.

48 Travis Hirschi and Michael Gottfredson, "Age and the Explanation of Crime," *American Journal of Sociology* 89 (1983): 552–584, at p. 581.

49 Darrell Steffensmeier and Cathy Streifel, "Age, Gender, and Crime Across Three Historical Periods: 1935, 1960 and 1985," *Social Forces* 69 (1991): 869–894.

50 For a comprehensive review of crime and the elderly, see Kyle Kercher, "Causes and Correlates of Crime Committed by the Elderly," in *Critical Issues in Aging Policy*, ed. E. Borgatta and R. Montgomery (Bev-

erly Hills, CA: Sage, 1987), pp. 254–306; Darrell Steffensmeier, "The Invention of the 'New' Senior Citizen Criminal," *Research on Aging* 9 (1987): 281–311.

51 Margo Wilson and Martin Daly, "Life Expectancy, Economic Inequality, Homicide, and Reproductive Timing in Chicago Neighbourhoods," *British Journal of Medicine* 314 (1997): 1271–1274.

52 Edward Mulvey and John LaRosa, "Delinquency Cessation and Adolescent Development: Preliminary Data," *American Journal of Orthopsychiatry* 56 (1986): 212–224.

53 Gordon Trasler, "Cautions for a Biological Approach to Crime," in *The Causes of Crime: New Biological Approaches,* ed. Sarnoff Mednick, Terrie Moffitt, and Susan Stack (Cambridge: Cambridge University Press, 1987), pp. 7–25.

54 James Q. Wilson and Richard Herrnstein, *Crime and Human Nature* (New York: Simon and Schuster, 1985), pp. 126–147.

55 Ibid., p. 219.

56 Timothy Brezina, ""Delinquent Problem-Solving: An Interpretive Framework for Criminological Theory and Research," *Journal of Research in Crime and Delinquency* 37 (2000): 3–30.

57 Walter Gove, "The Effect of Age and Gender on Deviant Behavior: A Biopsychosocial Perspective," in *Gender and the Life Course,* ed. A. Ross (Chicago: Aldine, 1985), p. 131.

58 Cesare Lombroso, *The Female Offender* (New York: Appleton, 1920), p. 122.

59 Lombroso, *The Female Offender.*

60 Alan Booth and D. Wayne Osgood, "The Influence of Testosterone on Deviance in Adulthood: Assessing and Explaining the Relationship," *Criminology* 31 (1993): 93–118.

61 Gisela Konopka, *The Adolescent Girl in Conflict* (Englewood Cliffs, NJ: Prentice-Hall, 1966); Clyde Vedder and Dora Somerville, *The Delinquent Girl* (Springfield, IL: Charles C. Thomas, 1970).

62 Robert Hoge, D. A. Andrews, and Alan Leschied, "Tests of Three Hypotheses Regarding the Predictors of Delinquency," *Journal of Abnormal Child Psychology* 22 (1994): 547–559.

63 Rita James Simon, *The Contemporary Woman and Crime* (Washington, DC: U.S. Government Printing Office, 1975).

64 David Rowe, Alexander Vazsonyi, and Daniel Flannery, "Sex Differences in Crime: Do Mean and Within-Sex Variation Have Similar Causes?" *Journal of Research in Crime and Delinquency* 32 (1995): 84–100; Michael Hindelang,

"Age, Sex, and the Versatility of Delinquency Involvements," *Social Forces* 14 (1971): 525–534; Martin Gold, *Delinquent Behavior in an American City* (Belmont, CA: Brooks/Cole, 1970); Gary Jensen and Raymond Eve, "Sex Differences in Delinquency: An Examination of Popular Sociological Explanations," *Criminology* 13 (1976): 427–448.

65 David Huizinga and Delbert Elliott, "Juvenile Offenders: Prevalence, Offender Incidence, and Arrest Rates by Race," *Crime and Delinquency* 33 (1987): 206–223. See also Dale Dannefer and Russell Schutt, "Race and Juvenile Justice Processing in Court and Police Agencies," *American Journal of Sociology* 87 (1982): 1113–1132.

66 Paul Tracy, "Race and Class Differences in Official and Self-Reported Delinquency," in *From Boy to Man, from Delinquency to Crime,* ed. Marvin Wolfgang, Terence Thornberry, and Robert Figlio (Chicago: University of Chicago Press, 1987), p. 120.

67 Phillipe Rushton, "Race and Crime: An International Dilemma," *Society* 32 (1995): 37–42; for a rebuttal, see Jerome Neapolitan, "Cross-National Variation in Homicides: Is Race a Factor?" *Criminology* 36 (1998): 139–156.

68 Miriam Sealock and Sally Simpson, "Unraveling Bias in Arrest Decisions: The Role of Juvenile Offender Type-scripts," *Justice Quarterly* 15 (1998): 427–457.

69 "Law Enforcement Seeks Answers to 'Racial Profiling' Complaints," *Criminal Justice Newsletter* 29 (1998): 5.

70 Daniel Georges-Abeyie, "Definitional Issues: Race, Ethnicity and Official Crime/Victimization Rates," in *The Criminal Justice System and Blacks,* ed. D. Georges-Abeyie (New York: Clark Boardman, 1984), p. 12; Robert Sampson, "Race and Criminal Violence: A Demographically Disaggregated Analysis of Urban Homicide," *Crime and Delinquency* 31 (1985): 47–82.

71 Barry Sample and Michael Philip, "Perspectives on Race and Crime in Research and Planning," in *The Criminal Justice System and Blacks,* ed. D. Georges-Abeyie (New York: Clark Boardman, 1984), pp. 21–36.

72 Candace Kruttschnitt, "Violence by and Against Women: A Comparative and Cross-National Analysis," *Violence and Victims* 8 (1994): 1–28, at p. 4.

73 Fox Butterfield, *All God's Children: The Bosket Family and the American Tradition of Violence* (New York: Avon, 1996).

74 Michael Leiber and Jayne Stairs, "Race, Contexts and the Use of Intake Diversion," *Journal of Research in Crime and Delinquency* 36 (1999): 56–86; Darrell Steffensmeier, Jeffery Ulmer, and John Kramer, "The Interaction of Race, Gender, and Age in Criminal Sentencing: The Punishment Cost of Being Young, Black, and Male," *Criminology* 36 (1998): 763–798.

75 Tracy Nobiling, Cassia Spohn, and Miriam DeLone, "A Tale of Two Counties: Unemployment and Sentence Severity," *Justice Quarterly* 15 (1998): 459–486.

76 Alexander Weiss and Steven Chermak, "The News Value of African-American Victims: An Examination of the Media's Presentation of Homicide," *Journal of Crime and Justice* 21 (1998): 71–84.

77 Roy Austin, "Progress Toward Racial Equality and Reduction of Black Criminal Violence," *Journal of Criminal Justice* 15 (1987): 437–459.

78 Reynolds Farley and William Frey, "Changes in the Segregation of Whites from Blacks During the 1980s: Small Steps Toward a More Integrated Society," *American Sociological Review* 59 (1994): 23–45.

79 Marvin Wolfgang, Robert Figlio, and Thorsten Sellin, *Delinquency in a Birth Cohort* (Chicago: University of Chicago Press, 1972).

80 Paul Tracy and Robert Figlio, "Chronic Recidivism in the 1958 Birth Cohort," paper presented at the annual meeting of the American Society of Criminology, Toronto, October 1982; Marvin Wolfgang, "Delinquency in Two Birth Cohorts," in *Perspective Studies of Crime and Delinquency,* ed. Katherine Teilmann Van Dusen, and Sarnoff Mednick (Boston: Kluwer-Nijhoff, 1983), pp. 7–17. See also Lyle Shannon, *Criminal Career Opportunity* (New York: Human Sciences Press, 1988); D. J. West and David P. Farrington, *The Delinquent Way of Life* (London: Hienemann, 1977); Marvin Wolfgang, Terence Thornberry, and Robert Figlio, eds., *From Boy to Man, from Delinquency to Crime* (Chicago: University of Chicago Press, 1987); Paul Tracy and Kimberly Kempf-Leonard, *Continuity and Discontinuity in Criminal Careers* (New York: Plenum Press, 1996); Susan Martin, "Policing Career Criminals: An Examination of an Innovative Crime Control Program," *Journal of Criminal Law and Criminology* 77 (1986): 1159–1182; D. J. West and David P. Farrington, *The Delinquent Way of Life* (London: Hienemann, 1977).

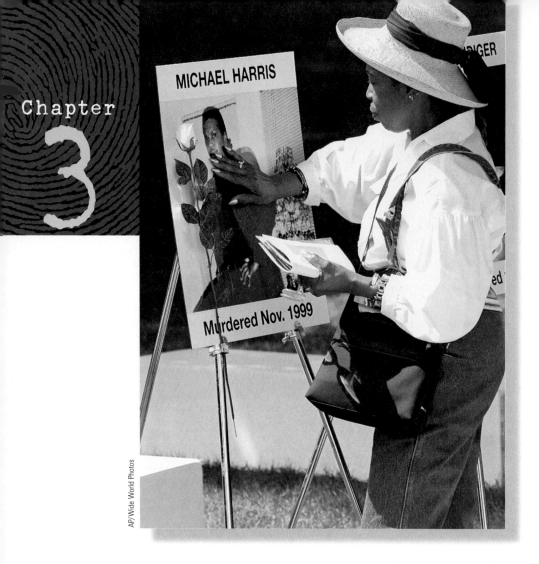

MICHAEL HARRIS

Murdered Nov. 1999

AP/Wide World Photos

UNDERSTANDING CRIME
AND VICTIMIZATION

When Robert Spangler learned he was dying of cancer in August 2000, police detectives did not wait long to come to his home, hoping he would confess to crimes for which he had long been a suspect. The investigators were not disappointed.[1] In October 2000, Spangler admitted killing his first wife and their two children in 1978 and also confessed to pushing his third wife to her death at the Grand Canyon 15 years later. The 67-year-old Spangler was placed under arrest on murder charges.

To his friends and neighbors, Spangler appeared to be just a normal, hardworking guy. He refereed youth soccer and acted in dinner-theater productions. Over the years, Spangler worked for Honeywell Corporation's camera and instruments division, was public relations director for a

nonprofit organization, and was a part-time disc jockey at a radio station.

In the mid-1950s, Spangler married his high school sweetheart, and they moved to the Denver area, where they raised two children. In 1978, Spangler's wife and children were found dead in their home. A gun and type-written suicide note were found near their mother's body, and police believed their deaths were the result of a murder-suicide. Prosecutors later claimed that Spangler killed his first wife and children because he was dissatisfied with family life; why he killed his third wife remains a mystery. As one neighbor who knew Spangler put it, "Obviously there was a side to him that none of us know. Everybody was duped."

Chapter

3

Chapter Outline

Criminal Justice Links

Criminal Justice Viewpoints

AP/Wide World Photos

A handcuffed and shackled Robert Spangler is escorted from the U.S. Federal Building in Grand Junction, Colorado, after a detention and identification hearing. After Spangler learned that he was dying of cancer, he admitted killing his family in 1978 and pushing his third wife to her death at the Grand Canyon 15 years later.

The Spangler case highlights the diversity of crime, its complexity, and how baffling it sometimes is to understand its cause. Police were suspicious of Spangler but perplexed: How could an educated person with a stable job commit such terrible acts? The Spangler case shows that crime touches all segments of society. Both the poor and the affluent engage in criminal activity. Crime cuts across racial, class, and gender lines. It involves some acts that shock the conscience and others that may seem to be relatively harmless human foibles.

Criminal acts may be the work of strangers, so-called predatory criminals who care little for the lives of their victims. News accounts have focused on "thrill killings," impulsive acts of violence in which a stranger is killed as an act of "daring" or recklessness—for example, adolescents who throw a boulder from a highway overpass onto an oncoming car.[2] Stories of devil-worshiping groups ordered by their leaders to kill nonbelievers have also appeared in the news—though some experts suggest that these lurid stories of murderous cults may be more a product of fear than reality.[3] In contrast, many crimes—including date rape and spouse, child, elderly, and sexual abuse—involve family members, friends, or trusted associates. Such acts are referred to as intimate violence.

CRIME IN THE UNITED STATES

Crime is an all too familiar and disturbing aspect of life in the United States. Surveys indicate that people fear crime and are suspicious of the criminal justice system's ability to reduce its incidence. What are the major forms of crime that concern most Americans?

Essay 1

Violent Crime

Americans are bombarded with television news stories and newspaper articles featuring grisly accounts of violent gangs, terrorism, serial murder, child abuse, and rape. Although rates of violent crime have declined significantly, violence rates in the United States still exceed those of most other industrialized nations. What are the forms of violence that most people fear?

Fill in the blanks 1
True/False 1

Gang Violence   After remaining dormant for many years, organized youth gangs today terrorize neighborhoods in urban communities around the United States. From Boston to Los Angeles, gangs have become actively involved in drug distribution, extortion, and violence.

Whereas youth gangs once relied on group loyalty and emotional involvement with neighborhood turf to encourage membership, modern gangs seem more motivated by the quest for drug profits and street power. It is common for drug cliques to form within gangs or for established drug dealers to make use of "gang bangers" for protection and distribution services. Today's more sophisticated gang members have replaced the traditional weapons of gangs—chains, knives, and homemade guns—with readily available handguns and automatic weapons. As a consequence, gang-related killings have become so commonplace that the term *gang homicide* is now recognized as a separate and unique category of criminal behavior.[4]

At one time, gang activity was restricted to the nation's largest cities, especially Philadelphia, New York, Detroit, Los Angeles, and Chicago. These cities still have large gang populations, but today smaller cities—such as Cleveland and Columbus, Ohio, and Milwaukee, Wisconsin—also have been the locus of gang activity. One reason that gang populations are swelling is that established urban gang members now migrate to other locales to set up local branches. A number of national surveys of gang membership conducted over the past two decades in-

How can gang activity be prevented? To find out, go to the Office of Juvenile Justice Web site at http://www.ncjrs.org/html/ojjdp/2000_9_2/page3.html
For an up-to-date list of Web links, see http://www.wadsworth.com/product/0534573053s

dicate that national gang membership is rising rapidly and that more than 700,000 youths are now gang members.[5]

Serial and Mass Murder   On March 13, 1995, ex–Boy Scout leader Thomas Hamilton took four high-powered rifles into the primary school of the peaceful Scottish town of Dunblane and slaughtered 16 children and their teacher. This horrific crime shocked the British Isles into implementing strict controls on all guns.[6]

Fill in the blanks 2
True/False 2

Mass murderers, such as Hamilton, and serial killers, such as Jeffrey Dahmer of Milwaukee, have become all too familiar to the American public.[7] The threat of the unknown, random, and deranged assailant has become a part of modern reality. Some roam the country killing a particular type of victim; others, such as Richard Ramirez, the Satan-worshiping Los Angeles "Night Stalker," terrorize a city. A third type of serial murderer—such as hospital orderly Donald Harvey, who murdered 54 patients—kills so cunningly that many victims are dispatched before the authorities even realize that the deaths can be attributed to a single perpetrator.

There is no single explanation for serial or mass murder. Such widely disparate factors as mental illness, sexual frustration, neurological damage, child abuse and neglect, smothering maternal relationships, and childhood anxiety have been suggested as possible causes. However, most experts view serial killers as sociopaths who from early childhood demonstrated bizarre behavior (such as torturing animals), enjoy killing, are immune to their victims' suffering, and bask in the media limelight when caught.[8]

Terrorism   The tragic bombing in Oklahoma City on April 19, 1995, made the country aware of the threat that domestic political terrorism presents to the public. Political terrorism is directed at people or groups opposed to the terrorists' political ideology or seen as "outsiders" who must be destroyed. The U.S. government has been a target because its agents enforce laws (for example, collecting taxes and controlling firearms) that are unpopular with some groups. Political terrorists tend to be heavily armed groups organized around such themes as white supremacy, Nazism, militant tax resistance, and religious revisionism.

Intimate Violence   With the arrest of O. J. Simpson in 1994, the nation was made aware of the growing threat of intimate violence.[9] Although violent attacks by strangers produce the most fear and create the graphic headlines, Americans actually face greater physical danger from people with whom they are in close and intimate contact: spouses, other relatives, and dating partners. In one survey, as many as 16 percent of families had experienced such assaults; in some jurisdictions, more than half of all evening calls for police service involve domestic violence.[10]

True/False 3
Multiple choice 1

One area of intimate violence that has received a great deal of media attention is child abuse, a term that describes any physical or emotional trauma to a child for which no reasonable explanation, such as an accident or ordinary disciplinary practices, can be found. Child abuse can result from physical beatings administered by hands, feet, weapons, belts, or sticks, or from burning.

The American Humane Society estimates that 3 million cases of child abuse are reported to authorities each year, and after investigation, about half of reported cases are considered valid.[11] Estimating the incidence of child sexual abuse is more difficult, but surveys have found that more than one-third of all women had experienced intra- or extrafamilial sexual abuse by the time they reached age 18.[12]

Substance Abuse

The United States is currently waging a "war on drugs." The most commonly abused substance, alcohol, is easily obtained and suspected of being involved in

Fill in the blanks 3

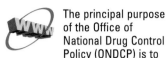

The principal purpose of the Office of National Drug Control Policy (ONDCP) is to establish policies, priorities, and objectives for the nation's drug control program, the goals of which are to reduce illicit drug use, manufacturing, and trafficking; drug-related crime and violence; and drug-related health consequences. To read more about their efforts, go to their Web site: http://www.whitehousedrugpolicy.gov

For an up-to-date list of Web links, see http://www.wadsworth.com/product/0534573053s

half of all U.S. murders, suicides, and accidental deaths. Alcohol-related deaths number 100,000 a year, far more than deaths by all other illegal drugs combined. There are strong links between alcohol abuse and violent crime and other antisocial behaviors; for example, drinking among college students is closely associated with episodes of assaultive behavior and vandalism.[13] There also are strong links between alcohol consumption and certain types of homicide, especially those that occur during robberies and other criminal offenses.[14]

Although drug use has stabilized in the general population, it is still quite prevalent in the offender population—evidence of the association between drug use and crime. The federally sponsored Arrestee Drug Abuse Monitoring (ADAM) program, which drug-tests people who have been arrested, is active in 34 cities.[15] The most recent ADAM data (2000) show overall drug-use rates of 50 to 77 percent or greater among arrestees. In 27 of the 34 sites measured, more than 60 percent of the arrestees tested positive for drugs, and more than 60 percent of all women tested positive.

Multiple choice 2

Economic Crimes

Millions of property- and theft-related crimes occur each year; most are the work of amateur or occasional criminals whose decision to steal is spontaneous and whose acts are unskilled, unplanned, and haphazard. Many thefts, ranging in seriousness from shoplifting to burglary, are committed by school-age youths who are unlikely to enter into a criminal career.

Added to the pool of amateur thieves are the millions of adults whose behavior may occasionally violate the criminal law—shoplifters, pilferers, tax cheats—but whose main source of income comes from conventional means and whose self-identity is noncriminal. Most of these property crimes occur when there is an immediate opportunity, or *situational inducement,* to commit crime.[16]

Professional thieves, in contrast, derive a significant portion of their income from crime. Professionals do not delude themselves that their acts are impulsive, one-time efforts; nor do they employ elaborate rationalizations to excuse the harmfulness of their action ("Shoplifting doesn't really hurt anyone"). Professionals pursue their craft with vigor, attempting to learn from older, experienced criminals the techniques that will earn them the most money with the least risk. Their numbers are relatively few, but professionals engage in crimes that produce greater losses to society and perhaps cause more significant social harm. Typical forms include pickpocketing, burglary, shoplifting, forgery and counterfeiting, extortion, and swindling.[17]

True/False 4

White-Collar Crime As events in the past decade have shown, some of the most costly and damaging economic crimes are not the violent acts of inner-city gang youths or deranged serial killers but the white-collar crimes of upper-class bankers, brokers, corporate officers, and government officials. Unfortunately, the public still clings to the notion that these crimes are less harmful and dangerous than street crimes.[18]

One of the most devastating examples of white-collar criminality involved the looting of the savings and loan industry. For more than 10 years, the owners and managers of some of the nation's largest savings and loan banks defrauded investors, depositors, and the general public out of billions of dollars. It has been conservatively estimated that over the next 40 years the cost of rectifying savings and loan fraud cases could total $500 billion, a number almost too staggering to imagine. More than 1,000 banks eventually collapsed, and ongoing criminal activity was a central factor in 70 to 80 percent of these cases.[19]

The motives for white-collar crimes sometimes seem mystifying. Why would otherwise respected and often wealthy business executives and government officials risk all to secure illegal payments and profits?[20] Some experts view their actions as a function of an organizational climate in which senior managers wink at behaviors that violate business regulations but make a profit and believe that the end always justifies the means.[21] Another view is that white-collar criminals are simply greedy people who impulsively break the law to make a lot of money.[22]

Organized Crime Organized crime involves the criminal activity of people and organizations whose acknowledged purpose is economic gain through illegal enterprise.[23] These criminal cartels provide those outlawed goods and services demanded by the general public: prostitution, narcotics, gambling, loan sharking, pornography, and untaxed liquor and cigarettes. In addition, organized criminals infiltrate legitimate organizations, such as unions, to drain off their funds and profits for illegal purposes.

Some organized gangs are enterprise groups that provide illegal goods and services such as prostitution, gambling, and pornography. Others are organized as power groups, providing no tangible goods or services but preying on the public and on other criminals through fear, violence, and extortion. Power groups sell protection, demand a percentage of the profits of legitimate businesses, muscle in on unions and other organizations, and carry out large-scale burglaries and robberies.[24]

Federal and state agencies have been dedicated to wiping out organized crime, and some well-publicized arrests have resulted in the imprisonment of important leaders. It is estimated that the membership of the traditional Italian and Irish crime families has dropped 50 percent over a 20-year period. It seems unlikely, however, that the organized crime problem will ever be eradicated. As long as profits can be made from narcotics, prostitution, pornography, gambling, and other illegal

Fill in the blanks 4
True/False 5

Former Gambino crime family member Sammy "the Bull" Gravano's testimony about mob activity helped convict John Gotti, known as the "Dapper Don."

AP/Wide World Photos

enterprises, people will be willing to risk becoming involved in them. Although many leaders of "traditional" ethnic crime organizations have been given long prison sentences, new groups—including Russian and Eastern European, Hispanic, and African American gangs—have filled the vacuum created by federal prosecutors.

THE CAUSE OF CRIME

criminology
The scientific study of the nature, extent, cause, and control of criminal behavior.

Despite years of study and research, criminologists are still uncertain about why people commit crime or why some people become crime victims. One of the enduring goals of **criminology** is to develop an understanding of the nature and cause of crime and victimization. Without knowing why crime occurs, it would be difficult to create effective crime reduction programs. We would never be sure if efforts were being aimed at the proper audience or, if they were, whether the prevention efforts were the ones most likely to cause positive change. For example, a crime prevention program based on providing jobs for unemployed teenagers would only be effective if in fact crime is linked to unemployment. Similarly, a plan to reduce prison riots by eliminating the sugar intake of inmates is feasible only if research shows a link between diet and violence.

In the following sections, each of the most important theoretical perspectives in criminology is briefly described.

Fill in the blanks 5
True/False 6
Essay 2

BECAUSE THEY WANT TO: CHOICE THEORY

One prominent view of criminality is that people choose to commit crime after weighing the potential benefits and consequences of their criminal act: They will commit a crime if they believe it will provide immediate benefits without the threat of long-term risks. For example, before concluding a drug sale, experienced traffickers will mentally balance the chances of making a large profit against the probability of being apprehended and punished for drug dealing. They know that most drug deals are not detected and that the potential for enormous, untaxed profits is great. They evaluate their lifestyle and determine how much cash they need to maintain their standard of living, which is usually extravagant. They may have borrowed to finance the drug deal, and their creditors are not usually reasonable if loans cannot be repaid promptly. They also realize that they could be the target of a "sting" operation by undercover agents and, if caught, will get a long mandatory sentence in a forbidding federal penitentiary. If the greedy culprits conclude that the potential for profits is great enough, their need for cash urgent, and the chances of apprehension minimal, they will carry out the deal. If, however, they believe that the transaction will bring them only a small profit and a large risk of apprehension and punishment, they may forgo the deal, believing it too risky. Crime, then, is a matter of rational decision making in which a motivated offender weighs the potential costs and benefits of crime before deciding to take action.

deterrent
Preventing crime before it occurs by means of the threat of criminal sanctions.

According to choice theory, to deter crime, punishment must be sufficiently strict, sure, and swift to outweigh any benefits of law violation. For example, a 30-year prison sentence should deter potential bank robbers, regardless of the amount of money in the bank's vault. However, no matter how severely the law punishes a criminal act, it will have little **deterrent** effect if potential law violators believe they have little chance of being caught or that the wheels of justice are slow and inefficient.

The Rational Criminal

The decision to commit a specific crime, then, is a matter of personal decision making based on the evaluation of available information. For example, offenders are likely to desist from crime if they believe that (1) their future criminal earnings will be relatively low and (2) attractive and legal opportunities to generate income are available.[25] In contrast, criminals may be motivated when they know people who have made "big scores" and are successful at crime. Although the prevailing wisdom is that "crime does not pay," a small but significant subset of criminals earn close to $50,000 a year from crime, and their success may help motivate other would-be offenders.[26] In this sense, rational choice is a function of a person's perception of conventional alternatives and opportunities.

The rational criminal may also decide to forgo or desist from illegal behaviors. Such criminals may fear apprehension and punishment: A target appears too well protected; the police in the area are very active; local judges have vowed to crack down on crime; they simply cannot find a safe site to break the law.[27]

AP/Wide World Photos

Autumn Jackson (left) was convicted in 1997 for trying to extort $40 million from comedian Bill Cosby after claiming to be his "love child." Though he admitted to having an affair with her mother, Cosby maintained that he was not Jackson's father. Was Jackson, who served a prison term for her efforts, a rational, calculating criminal?

Rational Crimes That crime is rational can be observed in a wide variety of criminal events. White-collar and organized crime figures engage in elaborate and well-planned conspiracies, ranging from international drug deals to the looting of savings and loan institutions. But even predatory street criminals exhibit stealth and planning in their criminal acts. Burglars may try to determine which homes are easy targets by reading newspaper stories about weddings or social events that mean the attendees' homes will be unguarded. They choose houses that are easily accessible and screened from public view and offer good escape routes—for example, at the end of a cul-de-sac abutting a wooded area. They target high-value homes that do not have burglar alarms or other security devices.[28] Burglars seem to prefer "working" between 9 A.M. and 11 A.M. and in midafternoon, when parents are either working or dropping off or picking up children at school. Burglars appear to monitor car and pedestrian traffic and avoid selecting targets on heavily traveled streets.[29]

Even violent criminals exhibit elements of rationality. For example, armed robbers choose targets close to their homes or in areas that they routinely travel. Familiarity with the area gives them knowledge of escape routes; this is referred to as their "awareness space."[30] Robbers also report being wary of people who are watching the community for signs of trouble; robbery levels are relatively low in neighborhoods where residents keep a watchful eye on their neighbors' property.[31] Robbers avoid freestanding buildings because they can more easily be surrounded by police; others select targets that are known to do a primarily cash business, such as bars, supermarkets, and restaurants.[32]

Robbers and other violent criminals refrain from attacking people they believe to be carrying handguns.[33] Even the most disturbed criminals, such as mass murderers, choose victims who pose little threat of resistance, such as children, vagrants, or prostitutes; serial killers rarely target karate experts or weight lifters.[34]

If crime is a rational choice, how can it be prevented or controlled?

Make 'Em Afraid I: The Concept of General Deterrence

Fill in the blanks 6
True/False 7
Multiple choice 3
Essay 3

general deterrence
A crime control policy that depends on the fear of criminal penalties.

If crime is a matter of choice, it follows that it can be controlled by convincing criminals that breaking the law is indeed a bad or dangerous choice to make. If people believe that they are certain to be apprehended by the police, quickly tried, and severely penalized, they will most likely forgo any thought of breaking the law.[35] In other words, people will not choose crime if they fear legal punishment. This principle is referred to as **general deterrence**.

If the justice system could be made more effective, those who care little for the rights of others would be deterred by fear of the law's sanctioning power.[36] Only by reducing the benefits of crime through sure, swift, and certain punishment can society be sure that a group of new criminals will not emerge to replace the ones who have already been dealt with.[37]

Research shows that some people who report that they fear punishment will be deterred from committing certain crimes.[38] However, there is still little hard evidence that fear of the law alone can be a general deterrent to crime.[39] Even the harshest punishment, the death penalty, appears to have little effect on the murder rate.[40]

What factors inhibit the sanctioning power of the criminal law? One is the lack of efficiency of the justice system. About 20 percent of serious reported crimes result in an arrest. Relatively few criminals are eventually tried, convicted, and sentenced to prison.[41] Chronic offenders and career criminals may believe that the actual risk of apprehension and imprisonment is limited and conclude that the certainty of punishment, a key element in deterrence, is minimal. Even if they do fear punishment, their anxiety may be neutralized by the belief that a crime gives them a significant chance for large profit. When criminologists Alex Piquero and George Rengert interviewed active burglars, they were told that fear of capture and punishment was usually neutralized by the hope of making a " big score"— greed overcomes fear.[42]

The concept of general deterrence assumes a rational criminal—an offender who carefully weighs and balances the pains and benefits of the criminal act. However, a majority of arrested criminals are under the influence of drugs or alcohol at the time of their arrest. Many offenders, therefore, may be incapable of having the rational thought patterns upon which the concept of general deterrence rests. Relatively high rates of substance abuse, including alcohol and illegal drugs, may render even the harshest criminal penalties for violent crimes ineffective deterrents.[43]

In sum, the theory of rational choice predicts that criminals are calculating individuals who can be deterred by the threat of punishment. Research has so far failed to turn up clear and convincing evidence that the threat of punishment or its actual implementation can deter would-be criminals.

Make 'Em Afraid II: Specific Deterrence

Fill in the blanks 7
Multiple choice 4

specific deterrence
Punishment severe enough to convince convicted offenders never to repeat their criminal activity.

Even if the threat of punishment cannot deter would-be criminals, actual punishment at the hands of the justice system should be sufficient to convince arrested offenders never to repeat their criminal acts. If punishment were severe enough, a convicted criminal would never dare repeat his or her offense. What rational person would? This view is referred to as **specific deterrence**. Prior to the twentieth century, specific deterrence was a motive for the extreme tortures and physical punishments commonly used on convicted criminals. By breaking the convicts physically, legal authorities hoped to control their spirit and behavior.[44]

Although our more enlightened society no longer uses such cruel and unusual punishments, we do impose long prison sentences in dangerous and forbidding prisons. Yet such measures do not seem to deliver the promise of crime control inherent in the specific deterrence concept. A majority of inmates repeat their criminal acts soon after returning to society, and most inmates have served time previously.[45]

Why have these punishments failed as a specific deterrent? Specific deterrence also assumes a rational criminal, someone who learns from experience. It is possible that many offenders have impulsive personalities that interfere with their ability to learn from experience. And if they do learn, it may be from more experienced offenders who encourage them to commit crime once they are released. A majority of criminal offenders have lifestyles marked by heavy substance abuse, lack of formal education, and disturbed home lives, which inhibit conventional behavior. The pains of imprisonment and the stigma of a prison record do little to help an already troubled person readjust to society. Rather than deter crime, a prison sentence may encourage future law violations.

Make It Difficult: Situational Crime Prevention

Some advocates of rational choice theory argue that crime prevention can be achieved by reducing the opportunities people have to commit particular crimes, a technique known as *situational crime prevention.*

Situational crime prevention was first popularized in the United States in the early 1970s by Oscar Newman, who coined the term *defensible space.* The idea is that crime can be prevented or displaced through the use of residential architectural designs that reduce criminal opportunity, such as well-lit housing projects that maximize surveillance.[46] Contemporary choice theorists maintain that situational crime prevention can be achieved by creating a strategy or overall plan to reduce specific crimes and then developing specific tactics to achieve those goals. Ronald Clarke sets out the four main types of crime prevention tactics in use today:

- Increase the effort needed to commit the crime.
- Increase the risks of committing the crime.
- Reduce the rewards for committing the crime.
- Induce guilt or shame.[47]

Increasing the effort needed to commit crimes involves using target-hardening techniques and access control: placing steering locks on cars; putting unbreakable glass on storefronts; locking gates and fencing yards; having owners' photos on credit cards; controlling the sale of spray paint (to reduce grafitti); providing caller IDs (to reduce the number of obscene or crank calls).

It is also possible to increase the risks of crime by improving surveillance lighting, creating neighborhood watch programs, controlling building entrances and exits, putting in burglar alarms and security systems, and increasing the number and effectiveness of private security officers and police patrols. For example, research shows that crime rates are reduced when police officers use aggressive crime reduction techniques and promote community safety by increasing lighting and cleaning up vacant lots.[48] A Dallas Police Department initiative to aggressively pursue truancy and enforce curfew laws has resulted in lower rates of gang violence.[49]

Target reduction strategies include making car radios removable so they can be taken into the home at night, marking property so that it is more difficult to sell when stolen, and having gender-neutral phone lists to discourage obscene phone calls.

Inducing guilt or shame might include such techniques as embarrassing offenders (for example, publishing "John lists" in the newspaper to punish those arrested for soliciting prostitutes), or facilitating compliance by providing trash bins whose easy access might "shame" chronic litterers into using them. When caller

Fill in the blanks 8
Multiple choice 5
Essay 4

ID, a device that displays the telephone number of the party placing the call, was installed in New Jersey, the number of obscene phone calls reported to police declined significantly because of the threat of exposure.[50]

At their core, situational crime prevention efforts seek clearly defined solutions to specific crime problems. Rather than changing criminals, they seek to change the environment so that criminality becomes more difficult and consequently less profitable.

PERSPECTIVES ON JUSTICE

Choice theory is the philosophical cornerstone of the crime control perspective of justice. It has been used to justify the "get tough" law-and-order approach that is predominant today. If criminals choose crime, then it follows that increasing the level of criminal punishment should deter and lower crime. Law enforcement agencies now establish task forces to locate and apprehend chronic offenders, prosecutors target career criminals, and state legislatures enact laws providing lengthy prison sentences for recidivists. Long prison sentences are believed to be the best way to keep repeaters "out of circulation," to convince prospective offenders that crime does not pay, and to teach those who decide to commit crimes a lesson not soon forgotten.

True/False 8–10
Multiple choice 6
Essay 5

BECAUSE THEY'RE DIFFERENT: BIOLOGICAL THEORIES

As the nineteenth century came to a close, some criminologists began to suggest that crime was caused not so much by human choice but by inherited and uncontrollable biological and psychological traits: intelligence, body build, personality, diet. The newly developed scientific method was applied to the study of social relations, including criminal behavior.

The origin of scientific criminology is usually traced to the research of Cesare Lombroso (1836–1909). Lombroso, an Italian army physician fascinated by human anatomy, became interested in finding out what motivated criminals to commit crimes. He physically examined hundreds of prison inmates and other criminals to discover any similarities among them. On the basis of his research, Lombroso proposed that criminals manifest *atavistic anomalies:* primitive, animal-like physical qualities such as an asymmetric face or excessive jaw, eye defects, large eyes, a receding forehead, prominent cheekbones, long arms, a twisted nose, and swollen lips.[51]

Lombroso's views were discredited in the twentieth century, and biological explanations of crime were abandoned. Today, the biology of crime has gained a resurgence of interest, and a number of criminologists are looking once again at the biological underpinnings of crime. At their core, biological theories assume that variation in human physical traits can explain behavior.[52] Rather than being born equal and influenced by social and environmental conditions, each person possesses a unique biochemical, neurological, and genetic makeup. People may develop physical or mental traits at birth, or soon after, that affect their social functioning over the life course and influence their behavior choices. For example, low-birth-weight babies have been found to suffer poor educatonal achievement later in life; academic deficiency has been linked to delinquency and drug abuse.[53]

Today, biocriminologists are attempting to link physical traits with tendencies toward violence, aggression, and other antisocial behavior. Their work, which is still in the early stages of development, can be divided into three broad areas of focus: biochemical factors, neurological problems, and genetic influence.

 James Cook University in Australia has an interesting Web site devoted to health issues that covers the work of Lombroso and cross-references it with views of his contemporaries: http://www.cimm.jcu.edu.au/hist/stats/lomb/
For an up-to-date list of Web links, see http://www.wadsworth.com/product/0534573053s

It's in the Blood: Biochemical Factors

Some biocriminologists focus on the influence of biochemical factors on criminal behavior. Some research efforts have linked vitamin and mineral deficiencies, improper diet, environmental contaminants, and allergies to antisocial behavior.[54] Research focusing on the behavior of jailed inmates has shown that subjects who maintain high levels of sugar and caffeine in their diet are more likely to engage in antisocial behavior than control-group subjects whose diets are low in those substances.[55]

Another area of biological research focuses on hypoglycemia, a condition that occurs when blood glucose (sugar) falls below levels necessary for normal and efficient brain functioning. Symptoms of hypoglycemia include irritability, anxiety, depression, crying spells, headaches, and confusion. Research shows that persistent abnormality in the way the brain metabolizes glucose is linked to substance abuse.[56]

Hormonal imbalance has been linked to aggressive behavior. Research shows that children who have low levels of the stress hormone cortisol tend to be more violent and antisocial than those with normal levels.[57] A growing body of evidence suggests that hormonal changes are also related to mood and behavior and that adolescents experience more intense mood swings, anxiety, and restlessness than their elders, explaining in part the high violence rates found among teenage males.[58]

In sum, biochemical studies suggest that criminal offenders have abnormal levels of organic or inorganic substances that influence their behavior and in some way make them prone to antisocial behavior.

The Abnormal Brain: Neurological Problems

True/False 11
Multiple choice 7

Another area of interest to biocriminologists is the relationship of brain activity to behavior. Electroencephalograms (EEGs) have been used to record the electrical impulses given off by the brain. Preliminary studies indicate that 5 to 15 percent of the general teenage population have abnormal EEG ratings, but 50 to 60 percent of those with behavioral disorders display abnormal recordings.[59] Studies of problem children have found that almost half have abnormal EEG

© Christopher Morris/Black Star

Some children become involved in violent crimes at a very early age. Does this suggest that violence is the result of a biological trait, present at birth, that determines future behavior patterns throughout the life span?

ratings; studies using adult subjects have found that abnormal EEG patterns are associated with hostile, nonconforming, and impulsive behavior.[60] Tests of convicted murderers show that a disproportionate number manifest abnormal EEG ratings.[61]

Psychologist Dorothy Otnow Lewis and her associates found that murderous youths suffer signs of major neurological impairment (such as abnormal EEGs, multiple psychomotor impairment, and severe seizures).[62] In her 1998 book *Guilty by Reason of Insanity,* Lewis reports that death row inmates have a history of mental impairment and intellectual dysfunction.[63] Other research efforts show that spouse abusers exhibit a variety of neuropsychological disorders and cognitive deficits; many suffered brain injuries in youth.[64]

People with an abnormal cerebral structure referred to as minimal brain dysfunction (MBD) may experience periods of explosive rage.[65] Brain dysfunction is sometimes manifested as an attention-deficit hyperactivity disorder (ADHD), another suspected cause of antisocial behavior. Several studies have shown that children with attention problems experience increased levels of antisocial behavior and aggression during childhood, adolescence, and adulthood.[66] The condition may cause poor school performance, bullying, stubbornness, and a lack of response to discipline. Although the origin of ADHD is still unknown, suspected causes include neurological damage, prenatal stress, and even food additives and chemical allergies. Research shows that youths with ADHD who grow up in a dysfunctional family are the most vulnerable to chronic delinquency that continues into their adulthood.[67]

The National Attention Deficit Disorder Association disseminates information and policy updates at their Web site: http://www.add.org/

For an up-to-date list of Web links, see http://www.wadsworth.com/product/0534573053s

True/False 12

The Bad Seed: Genetic Factors

Although the earliest biological studies of crime tried and failed to discover a genetic basis for criminality, modern biocriminologists are still concerned with the role of heredity in producing crime-prone people.

If inherited traits are related to criminality, twins should be more similar in their antisocial activities than other sibling pairs. Because most twins are brought up together, however, determining whether behavioral similarities are a function of environmental influences or genetics is difficult. To overcome this problem, biocriminologists usually compare identical, or monozygotic (MZ), twins with fraternal, or dizygotic (DZ), twins of the same sex. MZ twins are genetically identical, so their behavior would be expected to be more similar than that of DZ twins; preliminary studies have shown that this is indeed true.[68] There is some evidence that genetic makeup is a better predictor of criminality than either social or environmental variables.[69]

Another approach has been to evaluate the behavior of adopted children. If an adopted child's behavior patterns run parallel to those of his or her biological parents, it would be strong evidence to support a genetic basis for crime. Preliminary studies conducted in Europe have indicated that the criminality of the biological father is a strong predictor of a child's antisocial behavior.[70] The probability that a youth will engage in crime is significantly enhanced when both biological and adoptive parents exhibit criminal tendencies.

IT'S IN THEIR HEADS: PSYCHOLOGICAL THEORIES

The view that criminals may be suffering from psychological abnormality or stress has also had a long history. Today, psychological views of crime can be divided into four major areas.

The Disturbed Mind: Psychoanalytic Theory

Fill in the blanks 9
Essay 6

Psychoanalysis, the creation of Viennese physician Sigmund Freud (1856–1939), still holds a prominent position in psychological thought.[71] According to the psychoanalytic view, some people encounter problems during their early development that cause an imbalance in their personality. *Neurotics* are people who are extremely anxious and fear that repressed, unacceptable impulses may break through and control their behavior (today, the term *mood disorder* is used). *Psychotics* are people whose primitive impulses have broken through and actually control their personality; they may hear voices telling them what to do or see visions. One type of psychosis is *schizophrenia,* a condition marked by incoherent thought processes, a lack of insight, hallucinations, and feelings of persecution.

Psychoanalysts believe that law violators may have suffered damage to their egos or superegos early in their development that renders them powerless to control their impulses and urges. They may suffer delusions and feel persecuted, worthless, and alienated.[72] Psychosis is often associated with violent episodes, but even nonviolent criminals may be motivated by a lack of insight and control caused by personality disorders.[73] As a result, they seek immediate gratification of their needs without considering right and wrong or the needs of others.

Although a link between mental instability and criminality seems logical (and a popular topic in horror movies), little empirical evidence actually exists that mentally ill people are any more criminal than the mentally sound. Studies focusing on the criminal activity of the mentally ill have failed to establish a clear link between crime and psychiatrically diagnosed problems.[74] Mentally disordered inmates may actually pose less risk to society upon their release than the typical inmate.[75] Nonetheless, it is still possible that some link exists. Existing data suggest that certain symptoms of mental illness are connected to violence—for example, the feeling that others wish the person harm, that the person's mind is dominated by forces beyond his or her control, or that thoughts are being put into the person's head by others.[76] There are even bizarre cases in which people who commit murder hope to be executed for their crimes, a form of "suicide-murder."[77]

Currently, major assessments and research studies are ongoing; results should soon determine the true link between mental illness and crime.[78]

Learning to Commit Crime: Behavioral Theory

Fill in the blanks 10
Multiple choice 8

A second branch of psychological theory views behavior as learned through interactions with others. Behavior that is rewarded becomes habitual; behavior that is punished becomes extinguished. One branch of behavioral theory of particular relevance to criminology is **social learning theory**. According to social learning theorists, people act aggressively because, as children, they modeled their behavior after the violent acts of adults.[79] Later in life, antisocial behavioral patterns are reinforced by peers and other acquaintances.[80]

social learning theory
The view that human behavior is learned through observation of human social interactions, either directly from those in close proximity or indirectly from the media.

Social learning theorists conclude that the antisocial behavior of potentially violent people can be triggered by a number of different influences: verbal taunts and threats; the experience of direct pain; and perceptions of relative social disability, such as poverty and racial discrimination. Those who have learned violence and have seen it rewarded are more likely to react violently under these stimuli than those who have not.

One area of particular interest to social learning theorists is whether the entertainment media can influence violence. This topic is discussed in the Images of Justice feature.

The Entertainment Media and Violence

Young viewers of television and movies are constantly barraged with media depictions of demented and crazed killers who use grotesque violence to dispatch their victims. Depicted in gory detail are the violent acts of crazed baby-sitters (*Hand That Rocks the Cradle*), deranged roommates (*Single White Female*), unhinged police officers (*Kiss the Girls*), doctors (*Silence of the Lambs*), and cab drivers (*The Bone Collector*); abnormal girlfriends (*Fatal Attraction*) and boyfriends (*Fear*), unstable husbands (*Sleeping with the Enemy*) and wives (*Black Widow*), loony fathers (*The Stepfather*), mothers (*Friday the 13th, Part 1*) and grandmothers (*Hush*); unbalanced crime victims (*I Know What You Did Last Summer*); and unsound high school friends (*Scream*) who grow into murderous college classmates (*Scream II*). Has viewing this collection of gore on television, in video rentals, or in movie theaters created a generation of violence-prone adolescents? Do the entertainment media influence behavior? Politicians seem to think so, and media violence became a significant issue in the 2000 presidential campaign.

If there is in fact a television–violence link, the problem is indeed alarming. Systematic viewing of television begins at 2½ years of age and continues at a high level throughout the preschool and early school years. It has been estimated that children ages 2 to 5 watch television an average of 27.8 hours per week; children ages 6 to 11, 24.3 hours per week; and teens, 23 hours per week. Marketing research indicates that adolescents aged 11 to 14 rent violent horror movies at a higher rate than any other age group. Children this age use older peers and siblings and apathetic parents to gain access to R-rated movies. More than 40 percent of U.S. households now have cable television, which features violent movies and shows. Even children's programming is saturated with violence.

The fact that children watch so much violent television is not surprising, considering the findings of a well-publicized 1995 study conducted by UCLA researchers. They found that of the 161 made-for-television movies that year, 23 raised concerns about their use of violence, violent theme, violent title, or inappropriate portrayals of a scene; of the 118 theatrical movies shown that season, 50 raised concerns about their use of violence. Even some children's television shows have worrisome signs, featuring "sinister combat" as the theme of the show. The characters are usually happy to fight and frequently do so with little provocation. A University of Pennsylvania study found that children's programming contained an average of 32 violent acts per hour, 56 percent had violent characters, and 74 percent had characters who became the victims of violence (though "only 3.3 percent had characters who were actually killed"). In all, the average child views 8,000 television murders before finishing elementary school.

Numerous cases of violence have been linked, at least anecdotally, to television and movies. In 1977, Ronald Zamora killed an elderly woman and then pleaded not guilty by reason of insanity. His attorney claimed that Zamora was addicted to television violence and could no longer differentiate between reality and fantasy. The jury did not buy the defense, and Zamora was found guilty as charged. John Hinckley shot President Ronald Reagan because of his obsession with actress Jodie Foster, which developed after he watched her play a prostitute in the movie *Taxi Driver*. Hinckley had seen the movie at least 15 times.

Although the general public believes that violence on television can cause violence "in real life," psychologists do not believe that media violence, in itself, *causes* violent behavior; if it did, there would be millions of incidents daily in which viewers imitated the aggression they watched on television or in movies. However, most psychologists agree that media violence *contributes* to aggression. There are several explanations for the effects of television and movie violence on behavior:

- Media violence can provide aggressive "scripts" that children store in memory. Repeated exposure to these scripts can increase their retention and lead to changes in attitudes.
- Children learn from what they observe. In the same way that they learn cognitive and social skills from their parents and friends, children learn to be violent from television.
- Television violence increases the arousal levels of viewers and makes them more prone to act aggressively. Studies measuring the galvanic skin response of subjects—a physical indication of arousal based on the amount of electricity conducted across the palm of the hand—have found that viewing violent television shows leads to increased arousal levels in young children.

- Watching television violence promotes such negative attitudes as suspiciousness and the expectation that the viewer will become involved in violence. Those who watch television frequently come to view aggression and violence as common and socially acceptable behavior.

- Television violence allows aggressive youths to justify their behavior. It is possible that, instead of causing violence, television helps violent youths rationalize their behavior as a socially acceptable and common activity.

- Television violence may disinhibit aggressive behavior, which is normally controlled by other learning processes. Disinhibition takes place when adults are viewed as being rewarded for violence and when violence is seen as socially acceptable. This contradicts previous learning experiences in which violent behavior was viewed as wrong.

Such distinguished bodies as the American Psychological Association, the National Institute of Mental Health, and the National Research Council support the television–violence link. They base their conclusion on research results: Watching violence on television leads to increased levels of violence in laboratory settings as well as in natural settings. Watching violence on television has at least a short-term impact on behavior; subjects who view violent television shows are likely to exhibit aggressive behavior almost immediately.

A number of critics argue that the evidence simply does not support the claim that watching violence on television or in movies, or listening to heavy metal music, is related to antisocial behavior. There is little evidence that areas with the highest levels of violent television viewing also have higher rates of violent crime. Millions of children who watch violence every night do not become violent criminals. If violent television shows did cause interpersonal violence, then there should be few ecological and regional patterns in the crime rate. How can regional differences in the violence rate be explained when people all across the nation watch the same television shows and movies?

Although these arguments are persuasive, the weight of the experimental results indicates that violent entertainment does have an immediate impact on people with a preexisting tendency toward crime and violence.

Even though the evidence linking television violence to aggression is still unclear, concern has caused the television industry to join with the movie industry to place advisory warnings on shows that have objectionable content. Such labels may help guide some parents, but they do little to restrict television watching when children are home alone (though it may soon be possible to equip television sets with computer chips that prevent the reception of shows designated as having violent themes). Critics charge that any attempt to control or regulate television content may run afoul of the First Amendment guarantee of free speech; who is to say when a television show is too violent?

Critical Thinking Skills

1. Should the government control the content of television shows and limit the amount of weekly violence? How could the national news be shown if violence were omitted? What about boxing matches or hockey games?

2. How can we explain the fact that millions of children watch violent television shows and remain nonviolent? If there is a television–violence link, how can we explain the fact that violence rates may have been higher in the "Old West" than they are today? Do you think that members of violent youth gangs stay home and watch television shows?

InfoTrac College Edition Research

What lessons did the media learned from the Columbine massacre? To find out, go to the following article on InfoTrac College Edition: Dan Trigoboff, "Lessons of Columbine," *Broadcasting & Cable*, 3 April 2000, v130 p26

SOURCES: Dave Grossman and Gloria Degaetano, *Stop Teaching Our Kids to Kill: A Call to Action Against TV, Movie, and Video Game Violence* (New York: Random House, 1999); Richard Rhodes, "Hollow Claims About Fantasy Violence," *New York Times,* 17 September 2000, p. A31; Lawrie Mifflin, "Many Researchers Say Link Is Already Clear on Media and Youth Violence," *New York Times,* 9 May 1999, p. B1; UCLA Center for Communication Policy, *Television Violence Monitoring Project* (Los Angeles, 1995); Garland White, Janet Katz, and Kathryn Scarborough, "The Impact of Professional Football Games upon Violent Assaults on Women," *Violence and Victims* 7 (1992): 157–171; Wendy Wood, Frank Wong, and J. Gregory Chachere, "Effects of Media Violence on Viewers' Aggression in Unconstrained Social Interaction," *Psychological Bulletin* 109 (1991): 371–383.

True/False 13

Developing Criminal Ideas: Cognitive Theory

Cognitive psychologists are concerned with the way people perceive and mentally represent the world in which they live. Some focus on how people process and store information, viewing the operation of human intellect as similar to the way computers analyze available information; the emphasis is on *information processing*. Aggressive people may actually base their behavior on faulty information. They perceive other people to be more aggressive than they actually are; consequently, they are more likely to be vigilant, on edge, or suspicious. When they attack victims, they may believe they are defending themselves, when they are simply misreading the situation.[81] The college student who rapes his date may have a cognitive problem, rendering him incapable of distinguishing behavioral cues; he misidentifies rejection as a come-on or "playing hard to get."

Another area of cognitive psychology is *moral development theory*. According to this theory, people go through a series of stages beginning early in childhood and continuing through their adult years.[82] Each stage is marked by a different view of right and wrong. For example, a child may do what is right simply to avoid punishment and censure. Later in life, the same person will develop a sensitivity to others' needs and do what is right to avoid hurting others. On reaching a higher level of maturity, the same person may behave in accordance with his or her perception of universal principles of justice, equality, and fairness.

According to developmental psychologists, criminals may lack the ability to make moral judgments. Criminals report that their outlooks are characterized by self-interest and impaired moral development; they are unlikely to consider the rights of others, nor are they concerned with maintaining the rules of society.[83]

Fill in the blanks 11
True/False 14
Multiple choice 9

Personality and Crime: The Psychopath

Some psychologists view criminal behavior as a function of a disturbed personality structure. Personality can be defined as the reasonably stable patterns of behavior, including thoughts and emotions, that distinguish one person from another.[84] An individual's personality reflects characteristic ways of adapting to life's demands and problems. The way we behave is a function of how our personality enables us to interpret life events and make appropriate behavioral choices.

Psychologists have explored the link between personality and crime. Evidence suggests that aggressive youths have unstable personality structures, often marked by hyperactivity, impulsiveness, and instability. Suspected traits include impulsivity, hostility, and aggressiveness.[85]

One area of particular interest to criminology is the identification of the *psychopathic* (also called *antisocial* or *sociopathic*) personality. **Psychopaths** are believed to be dangerous, aggressive, antisocial individuals who act in a callous manner. They neither learn from their mistakes nor are deterred by punishments.[86] Although they may appear charming and have at least average intelligence, psychopaths lack emotional depth, are incapable of caring for others, and maintain an abnormally low level of anxiety. They are likely to be persistent alcohol and drug abusers.[87] Violent offenders often display psychopathic tendencies such as impulsivity, aggression, dishonesty, pathological lying, and lack of remorse.[88] Psychopathy has also been linked to chronic recidivism and serial murder.[89] A high proportion of serial rapists and repeat sexual offenders exhibit psychopathic personality structures.[90]

A number of factors are believed to contribute to the development of a psychopathic personality.[91] They include having a psychopathic parent, parental rejection and lack of love during childhood, and inconsistent discipline. Some psy-

psychopath
A person whose personality is characterized by a lack of warmth and feeling, inappropriate behavioral responses, and an inability to learn from experience; also called *sociopath* or *antisocial personality*.

Serial killer suspect Orville Lynn Majors, in handcuffs, smiles as he is led by police. Majors is suspected of killing more than 100 patients while working as a nurse. Is it possible that serial killers like Majors are mentally healthy? Could someone kill 100 people and not be suffering some psychological impairment?

chologists suspect that psychopaths suffer from a low level of arousal as measured by the activity of their autonomic nervous system. It is possible, therefore, that psychopaths are thrill seekers who engage in high-risk antisocial activities to raise their general neurological arousal level. Another view is that the psychopathic personality is imprinted at birth and is relatively unaffected by socialization.[92]

PERSPECTIVES ON JUSTICE

Biological and psychological explanations of crimes seem to mesh with the crime control perspective: If criminals are "damaged goods"—genetically damaged or psychologically bent—then it stands to reason that they should be incarcerated for long periods of time if the public is to be protected. However, a supporter of rehabilitation might argue that trait theory suggests that criminals are not responsible for their actions and can be helped by psychological counseling or other efforts to change their behavior.

SOCIETY IS THE REAL CULPRIT: SOCIOLOGICAL THEORIES

Official, self-report, and victim data all indicate social patterns in the crime rate.[93] Some regions are more crime-prone than others; there are distinct differences in crime rates across states, cities, and neighborhoods. If crime rates are higher in California than Vermont, it is probably not because Californians are more likely to suffer personality defects or eat more sugar than Vermonters. Crime rates are higher in large urban areas that house concentrations of the poor than they are in sparsely populated rural areas in which residents are relatively affluent. Prisons are filled with the poor and the hopeless, not the rich and the famous. Because crime patterns have a decidedly social orientation, sociological explanations of crime have predominated in criminology.

Sociological criminology is usually traced to the pioneering work of sociologist Émile Durkheim (1858–1917), who viewed crime as a social phenomenon.[94] In formulating his theory of **anomie**, Durkheim held that crime is an essential part of society and a function of its internal conflict. As he used the term, *anomie* means the absence or weakness of rules and social norms in any person or group; without these rules or norms, an individual may lose the ability to distinguish between right and wrong.

As the field of sociological criminology emerged in the twentieth century, greater emphasis was placed on environmental conditions, while the relationship between crime and physical and/or mental traits was neglected. Equating the cause of criminal behavior with social factors, such as poverty and unemployment, was instrumental in the development of treatment-oriented crime prevention techniques. If criminals are in fact made and not born—if they are forged in the crucible of societal action—then it logically follows that crime can be eradicated by the elimination of the social elements responsible for crime. The focus of crime prevention shifted from punishing criminals to treatment and rehabilitation.

We now turn to some of the most important criminological theories that have a sociological base.

Because They're Poor: Social Structure Theory

According to **social structure** theory, the United States is a stratified society. Social strata are created by the unequal distribution of wealth, power, and prestige. Social classes are segments of the population whose members have relatively similar attitudes, values, and norms, and an identifiable lifestyle. In U.S. society, people can be identified as belonging to the upper, middle, or lower class, with a broad range of economic variation in each group.

The contrast between the lifestyles of the wealthiest members of the upper class and the poorest segment of the lower class is striking. According to the U.S. Census Bureau, from 1998 to 1999, median household income adjusted for inflation increased 2.7 percent to $40,800—meaning that half of all households had incomes above $40,800, and half below. Despite this improvement, more than 32 million people still live below the poverty line, defined by the government as an income of $17,029 for a family of four, or $13,290 for a family of three. There are also racial differences in the poverty rate: About 23 percent of Hispanics and African Americans live in poverty, as compared with about 8 percent of European Americans.[95] About 20 million high school dropouts face dead-end jobs, unemployment, and social failure. Because of their meager economic resources, lower-class citizens are often forced to live in slum areas marked by substandard housing, inadequate health care, poor educational opportunities, underemployment, and despair. They live in areas with deteriorated housing and abandoned buildings, which research shows are "magnets" for crime, drug dealing, and prostitution.[96]

True/False 15
Multiple choice 10–12

anomie
The absence or weakness of rules, norms, or guidelines as to what is socially or morally acceptable.

Fill in the blanks 12
True/False 16

social structure
The stratifications, classes, institutions, and groups that characterize a society.

The problems of lower-class culture are particularly acute for racial and ethnic minorities. Research indicates that their disproportionate representation in the poverty class may be a result of negative racial stereotyping among potential employers, which results both in lower employment opportunities and greater income inequality.[97]

The crushing burden of urban poverty leads to the development of a **culture of poverty**.[98] This subculture is marked by apathy, cynicism, helplessness, and distrust. The culture is passed from one generation to the next, creating a permanent underclass, referred to as the "truly disadvantaged."[99]

Considering the social disability suffered by the lower-class, it is not surprising that some people turn to crime as a means of support and survival. According to the social structure approach, a significant majority of people who commit violent crimes and serious theft offenses live in the lower-class culture, and a majority of all serious crimes occur in inner-city areas. The social forces operating in lower-class, inner-city areas produce high-crime rates. What are these forces, and how do they produce crime?

The Disorganized Neighborhood Crime is a product of neighborhoods that are characterized both by physical deterioration and by conflicting values and social systems. Disorganized neighborhoods are undergoing the disintegration of their existing culture and services, the diffusion of cultural standards, and successive changes from purely residential to a mixture of commercial, industrial, transient, and residential populations. In these areas, the major sources of informal social control—family, school, neighborhood, civil service—are broken and ineffective.

Urban areas are believed to be crime-prone because their most important social institutions cannot function properly. These neighborhoods are unable to realize the common values of their residents or to solve commonly experienced problems.[100] Disorganized neighborhoods have high population density, large numbers of single-parent households, unrelated people living together, and a lack of employment opportunities.[101] Their residents perceive significant levels of fear, alienation, and social dissatisfaction. These high-crime areas typically have rapid population turnover and lack the ability to socially integrate their residents.[102] Constant population turnover makes it difficult for these communities to understand or assimilate their newest members; hence, they acquire the reputation of being a "changing neighborhood."

The social, economic, and physical conditions that develop in disorganized neighborhoods have been associated with escalating crime rates. Areas that experience a high rate of housing abandonment, neighborhood decline, increased population density, and urban growth have also been found to have increasing crime rates.[103] Even in rural areas, which normally have low crime rates, signs of social disorganization such as residential instability (a large number of people moving in an out), family disruption, and changing ethnic composition are linked to high crime rates.[104] The crime-producing influence of these economic disadvantages are felt by all residents, both male and female.[105] However, minority-group members living in these areas suffer the added disadvantages of race-based income inequality and institutional racism.[106] The fact that significant numbers of African Americans are forced to live under these conditions can help explain the distinct racial patterns in the official crime statistics. The powerful effect of living in racially segregated poverty areas is discussed in the Race, Gender, and Ethnicity in Criminal Justice feature.

Unfortunately, the problems found in disorganized areas are stubborn and difficult to overcome. Even when an attempt is made to revitalize a neighborhood—for example, by creating institutional support programs such as community centers and better schools—the effort may be countered by the enduring lack of economic and social resources.[107]

culture of poverty
The view that people in the lower class of society form a separate culture with its own values and norms that are in conflict with those of conventional society.

Fill in the blanks 13
True/False 17–18
Multiple choice 13

RACE, GENDER, AND ETHNICITY IN CRIMINAL JUSTICE

Building a Bridge over the Racial Divide

In his famous 1987 book, *The Truly Disadvantaged,* William Julius Wilson provided a description of the plight of the lowest levels of the underclass. Wilson portrayed members of this group as socially isolated people who dwell in urban inner cities, occupy the bottom rung of the social ladder, and are the victims of discrimination. They live in areas in which the basic institutions of society—family, school, housing—have long since declined. Their decline triggers similar breakdowns in the strengths of inner-city areas, including a loss of community cohesion and the ability of people living in the area to control the flow of drugs and criminal activity. For example, in a more affluent area, neighbors might complain to parents that their children were acting out. In distressed areas, this element of informal social control may be lacking because parents are under stress or, all too often, absent. These effects magnify the isolation of the underclass from mainstream society and promote a ghetto culture and behavior.

Since the truly disadvantaged rarely come into contact with the actual source of their oppression, they direct their anger and aggression at those with whom they are in close and intimate contact, such as neighbors, businesspeo-ple, and landlords. Members of this group, plagued by under- or unemployment, begin to lose self-confidence, a feeling supported by the plight of kin and friendship groups who also experience extreme economic marginality. Self-doubt is a neighborhood norm, overwhelming those forced to live in areas of concentrated poverty.

In his 1996 publication, *When Work Disappears,* Wilson assessed the effect of joblessness and underemployment on residents of poor neighborhoods on Chicago's South Side. He noted that, for the first time in the twentieth century, most adults in inner-city ghetto neighborhoods were not working during a typical week. He found that inner-city life was only marginally affected by the surge in the nation's economy, brought about by new industrial growth connected with technological development. Poverty in these inner-city areas is eternal and unchanging and, if anything, worsening as residents are further shut out of the economic mainstream.

He suggests that as difficult as life was for African Americans in the 1940s and 1950s, they at least had a reasonable hope of steady work. Now, because of the globalization of the economy, those opportunities have evaporated. Although in the past racial segregation had limited opportunity, growth in the manufactur-ing sector fueled upward mobility and provided the foundation of today's African American middle-class. Those opportunities no longer exist because manufacturing plants have moved to nonaccessible rural and overseas locations where the cost of doing business is lower. With manufacturing opportunities all but obsolete in the United States, service and retail establishments that depended on blue-collar spending have similarly disappeared, leaving behind an economy based on welfare and government support. In less than 20 years, formerly active African American communities have become crime-infested slums.

When work becomes scarce, the discipline and structure it provides are absent. Community-wide underemployment destroys social cohesion, increasing the presence of neighborhood social problems ranging from drug use to educational failure. Schools in these areas cannot teach basic skills, and because desirable employment is lacking, there are few adults to serve as role models. In contrast to more affluent suburban households, where daily life is organized around job and career demands, children in inner-city areas are not socialized in the workings of the mainstream economy.

In his newest book, *The Bridge over the Racial Divide: Rising Inequality and*

Fill in the blanks 14
True/False 19
Essay 8

Deviant Values and Cultures Living in deteriorated inner-city neighborhoods, forced to endure substandard housing and schools, and cut off from conventional society, lower-class slum dwellers are faced with a constant assault on their self-image and sense of worth. While the media bombard them with images glorifying a materialistic lifestyle, they cannot purchase fine clothes, a luxury automobile, or their own home. Residents may become resentful and angry when they realize that they are falling further and further behind the social mainstream.[108] How is it possible for them to adjust and satisfy their needs?

One method of adjusting is to create an independent value system. Whereas middle-class values favor education, hard work, sexual abstinence, honesty, and sobriety, lower-class values in slum areas applaud goals that are realistically ob-

Coalition Politics (1999), Wilson argues that despite economic gains, inequality is growing in American society, and ordinary families of all races and ethnic origins are suffering. Whites, Latinos, African Americans, Asians, and Native Americans must therefore begin to put aside their differences and concentrate more on what they have in common—their aspirations, problems, and hopes. There needs to be mutual cooperation across racial lines.

One reason for this set of mutual problems is that the government tends to aggravate rather than ease the financial stress being placed on ordinary families. Monetary policy, trade policy, and tax policy are harmful to working-class families. A multiracial citizens' coalition could pressure national public officials to focus on the interests of ordinary people. As long as middle- and working-class groups are fragmented along racial lines, such pressure is impossible.

Wilson finds that racism is becoming more subtle and harder to detect. Whites believe that African Americans are responsible for their inferior economic status because of their cultural traits. Because even affluent whites fear corporate downsizing, they are unwilling to vote for government assistance to the poor. Whites live mainly in the sub-

urbs, further isolating poor minorities in central cities and making their problems seem distant and unimportant. The changing marketplace, with its reliance on sophisticated computer technologies, is continually decreasing demand for low-skilled workers, which affects African Americans more negatively than other, better-educated groups.

Wilson argues for a cross-race, class-based alliance of working- and middle-class Americans to pursue policies that will benefit them rather than the affluent. These include full employment, programs to help families and workers in their private lives, and a reconstructed "affirmative opportunity" program that benefits African Americans without antagonizing whites.

With these three volumes, Wilson provides probably the best description of the plight of the poor within an affluent American society and what must be done to bring them within the mainstream.

Critical Thinking Skills

1. Is it unrealistic to assume that a government sponsored public works program can provide needed jobs in this era of budget cutbacks?

2. What are some of the hidden costs of unemployment in a community setting?

3. How would a biocriminologist explain Wilson's findings?

InfoTrac College Edition Research

For more on Wilson's view of poverty, unemployment, and crime, check out Gunnar Almgren, Avery Guest, George Immerwahr, and Michael Spittel, "Joblessness, Family Disruption, and Violent Death in Chicago, 1970–90," *Social Forces,* June 1998, v76 i4 p1465 William Julius Wilson, "Inner-City Dislocations," *Society,* January–February 1998, v35 i2 p270

SOURCES: William Julius Wilson, *The Truly Disadvantaged* (Chicago: University of Chicago Press, 1987); *When Work Disappears: The World of the Urban Poor* (New York: Knopf, 1996); *The Bridge over the Racial Divide: Rising Inequality and Coalition Politics* (Berkeley: University of California Press, 1999).

---

tainable in a disorganized society: being cool, promiscuous, intemperant, and fearless. Thus, lower-class **focal concerns** include scorning authority, living for today, seeking excitement, and scoffing at formal education (see Exhibit 3.1).[109]

Some people living in disorganized areas band together to form an independent lower-class subculture—small reference groups that provide members with a unique set of values, beliefs, and traditions distinct from those of conventional society. Within this subculture, lower-class youths can achieve success unobtainable within the larger culture, while gaining a sense of identity and achievement. Members of the criminal subculture adopt a set of norms and principles in direct opposition to middle-class society. They engage in short-run hedonism, living for today by taking drugs, drinking, and engaging in unsafe sex. They resist

focal concerns
Central values and goals that, according to Miller, differ by social class.

EXHIBIT 3.1 MILLER'S LOWER-CLASS FOCAL CONCERNS

Trouble In lower-class communities, people are evaluated by their actual or potential involvement in making trouble. Getting into trouble includes such behavior as fighting, drinking, and sexual misconduct. Dealing with trouble can confer prestige—for example, when a man establishes a reputation for being able to handle himself well in a fight. Not being able to handle trouble, and having to pay the consequences, can make a person look foolish and incompetent.

Toughness Lower-class males want local recognition of their physical and spiritual toughness. They refuse to be sentimental or soft and instead value physical strength, fighting ability, and athletic skill. Those who cannot meet these standards risk getting a reputation for being weak, inept, and effeminate.

Smartness Members of the lower-class culture want to maintain an image of being streetwise and savvy, using their street smarts, and having the ability to outfox and outcon the opponent. Although formal education is not admired, knowing essential survival techniques, such as gambling, conning, and outsmarting the law, is a requirement.

Excitement Members of the lower class search for fun and excitement to enliven an otherwise drab existence. The search for excitement may lead to gambling, fighting, getting drunk, and sexual adventures. In between, the lower-class citizen may simply "hang out" and "be cool."

Fate Lower-class citizens believe that their lives are in the hands of strong spiritual forces that guide their destinies. Getting lucky, finding good fortune, and hitting the jackpot are all slum dwellers' daily dreams.

Autonomy Being independent of authority figures, such as the police, teachers, and parents, is required; losing control is an unacceptable weakness, incompatible with toughness.

SOURCE: Walter Miller, "Lower-Class Culture as a Generating Milieu of Gang Delinquency," *Journal of Social Issues* 14 (1958): 5–19.

efforts by family members and other authority figures to control their behavior and instead join autonomous peer groups and gangs.[110] Members may be prone to violence, for example, because the routine activities of their subculture require them to frequent locations, such as bars and dance clubs, where aggressive behavior is the norm and where they are exposed to other violence-prone people.[111]

Multiple choice 14
Essay 9

strain
The emotional turmoil and conflict caused when people believe they cannot achieve their desires and goals through legitimate means.

Strain In lower-class neighborhoods, **strain**, or status frustration, occurs because legitimate avenues for success are all but closed. Frustrated and angry, with no acceptable means of achieving success, people may use deviant methods, such as theft or violence, to achieve their goals.

The concept of strain can be traced to the pioneering work of famed sociologist Robert Merton, who recognized that members of the lower-class experience anomie, or normlessness, when the means they have for achieving culturally defined goals, mainly wealth and financial success, are insufficient.[112] As a result, people will begin to seek alternative solutions to meet their need for success: they will steal, sell drugs, or extort money. Merton referred to this method of adaptation as *innovation*—the use of innovative but illegal means to achieve success in the absence of legitimate means. Other youths, faced with the same dilemma, might reject conventional goals and choose to live as drug users, alcoholics, and wanderers; Merton referred to this as *retreatism*. Still others might join revolutionary political groups and work to change the system to one of their liking; Merton refers to this as *rebellion*. Criminologist Robert Agnew has expanded anomie theory by recognizing other sources of strain in addition to failure to meet goals. These include both negative experiences, such as child abuse, and the loss of positive supports, such as the end of a stable romantic relationship (see Figure 3.1).[113]

Research has linked these sources of strain to criminal and delinquent behaviors.[114] People who report feelings of stress- and strain-related anger are more likely to interact with deviant peers and engage in criminal behaviors.[115] There is also evidence that people who fail to meet success goals are more likely to engage in criminal activities.[116]

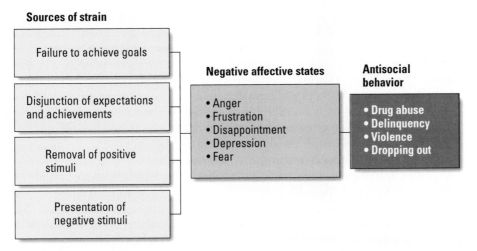

FIGURE 3.1 AGNEW'S SOURCES OF STRAIN AND THEIR CONSEQUENCES

PERSPECTIVES ON JUSTICE

Social structure theory is linked to the rehabilitation perspective on justice. If poverty and strain cause crime, then efforts to improve economic opportunity can help reduce crime rates. Job and social welfare programs are part of the government's effort to give members of the lower class opportunities to succeed legitimately. Of course, efforts to reduce crime rates by revitalizing a community's social and economic health are extremely difficult to achieve because the problems of decayed, transitional neighborhoods are overwhelming. Rehabilitation efforts are dwarfed by the social problems ingrained in these areas.

Socialized to Crime: Social Process Theories

True/False 20–21
Multiple choice 15–16

Not all criminologists agree that the root cause of crime can be found solely within the culture of poverty.[117] After all, self-report studies indicate that many middle- and upper-class youths take drugs and commit serious criminal acts. As adults, they commit white-collar and corporate crimes. Conversely, the majority of people living in the poorest areas hold conventional values and forgo criminal activity. These patterns indicate that forces must be operating in all strata of society that influence individual involvement in criminal activity.

If crime is spread throughout the social structure, then it follows that the factors that cause crime should be found within all social and economic groups. People commit crimes as a result of the experiences they have while they are being socialized by the various organizations, institutions, and processes of society. People are most strongly influenced toward criminal behavior by poor family relationships, destructive peer-group relations, educational failure, and labeling by agents of the justice system. Although lower-class citizens have the added burdens of poverty, strain, and blocked opportunities, middle- or upper-class citizens also may turn to crime if their socialization is poor or destructive.

Social process theorists point to research efforts linking family problems to crime as evidence that socialization, not social structure, is the key to understanding the onset of criminality. The quality of family life is considered a significant determining factor in adolescent development.[118] Among the most important research efforts are those showing that inconsistent discipline, poor supervision and discipline, and a lack of warm parent–child relationships are closely related to a child's deviant behavior.[119] Children who grow up in homes where parents use severe discipline and also lack warmth and involvement are prone to engage in antisocial behavior.[120] In contrast, positive parental relationships can insulate children from criminogenic influences in the environment.[121] It has also been suggested that child abuse is related both to delinquency and to the perpetuation of abusive behavior; abused children grow up to become child abusers themselves.[122]

Educational experience has also been found to have a significant impact on behavioral choices. Schools contribute to fostering criminality when they set problem youths apart by creating a track system that labels some as college bound and others as academic underachievers. Studies show that chronic delinquents do poorly in school, lack educational motivation, and are frequently held back.[123] Research indicates that high school dropouts are more likely to become involved in crime than those who complete their education.[124]

Associating with deviant peers also exerts tremendous influence on behavior, attitudes, and beliefs.[125] Deviant peers provide friendship networks and support behaviors such as riding around, staying out late, and partying; they provide the opportunity to commit deviant acts.[126] Because delinquent friends tend to be, as criminologist Mark Warr puts it, "sticky" (once acquired, they are not easily lost), peer influence may continue through the life span.[127] The more antisocial the peer group, the more likely its members will be to engage in delinquency; nondelinquent friends help moderate delinquency.[128] People who maintain close relations with antisocial peers will sustain their own criminal behavior into adulthood. If peer influence dimishes, so too does criminal activity.[129]

In sum, significant evidence exists that the direction and quality of interpersonal interactions and relationships influence behavior throughout the life span. However, there is disagreement over the direction this influence takes. Some crime experts maintain that all people are "born innocent," but some are exposed to and learn criminal techniques and attitudes from peers and family members. Another view is that all people have the potential to engage in antisocial behavior, but most are controlled by the bonds they form with society. Still another view is that crime is a by-product of social stigma and the formation of a deviant identity. Each of these three branches of social process theory will be described.

differential association theory
The view that criminal acts are related to a person's exposure to antisocial attitudes and values.

Students of Crime: Learning Theories Those who advocate learning theories hold that people enter into a life of crime when, as adolescents, they are taught the attitudes, values, and behaviors that support a criminal career. They may learn the techniques of crime from a variety of intimates, including parents and family members.[130]

The best-known example of the learning perspective is Edwin Sutherland's **differential association theory**.[131] Sutherland, considered by many to be the preeminent American criminologist, believed that the attitudes and behaviors that cause crime are learned in close and intimate relationships with significant others. People learn to commit crime in the same way they learn any other behavior. For example, children learn to ride a bike by observing more experienced riders, practicing riding techniques, and hearing how much fun it is to ride. In the same fashion, adolescents learn from more experienced drug users how to buy drugs, how to use them properly, and how to behave when they are high. Adolescents who are exposed to an excess of attitudes ("definitions") in support of deviant behavior will eventually view those behaviors as attractive, appropriate, and suitable and engage in a life of crime.

Testing the principles of differential association theory is difficult, but several notable research efforts have supported its core assumptions. Differential associ-

Courtesy of DARE America

According to those who advocate learning theories, behavior can be modified by exposure to prosocial or antisocial experiences and interactions. Adults can provide role models for conventional behaviors and help young people say no to drugs and violence.

ation measures have been correlated with the onset of substance abuse and a career in the drug trade. Adolescent drug users are likely to have intimate relationships with a peer friendship network that supports their substance abuse and teaches them how to deal with the drug world.[132] Differential association has also been found to be a significant predictor of criminal behavior in adult felons.[133]

They're Out of Control: Control Theories When we were in high school, most of us knew a few people who seemed detached and alienated from almost everything and everyone. They did not care about school, they had poor relationships at home, and, although they may have belonged to a tough crowd, their relationships with their peers were superficial and often violent. Very often these same people got into trouble at school, had run-ins with the police, and were involved in drugs and antisocial behaviors.

These observations form the nucleus of **social control theory**. This approach to understanding crime holds that all people may have the inclination to violate the law but most are held in check by their relationships to conventional institutions and individuals, such as family, school, and peer group. For some people, when these relationships are strained or broken, they become free to engage in deviant acts that otherwise would be avoided. Crime occurs when the influence of official and informal sources of social control is weakened or absent.

The most influential advocate of control theory is sociologist Travis Hirschi, who suggests that people's social bonds are formed from a number of different elements (see Figure 3.2). According to Hirschi, people whose bond to society is secure are unlikely to engage in criminal misconduct because they have a strong stake in society. Those who find their social bond weakened are much more likely to succumb to the temptations of criminal activity. After all, crime does have rewards, such as excitement, action, material goods, and pleasures. Hirschi does not give a definitive reason for what causes a person's social bond to weaken, but the process has two likely main sources: disrupted home life and poor school ability (leading to subsequent school failure and dislike of school).

Ongoing research efforts have attempted to test Hirschi's theory about social control and crime. Although results vary, a number of studies have supplied data

Fill in the blanks 16
Multiple choice 18–19
Essay 11

social control theory
The view that most people do not violate the law because of their social bonds to family, peer group, school, and other institutions; if these bonds are weakened or absent, they become free to commit crime.

FIGURE 3.2
ELEMENTS OF THE
SOCIAL BOND

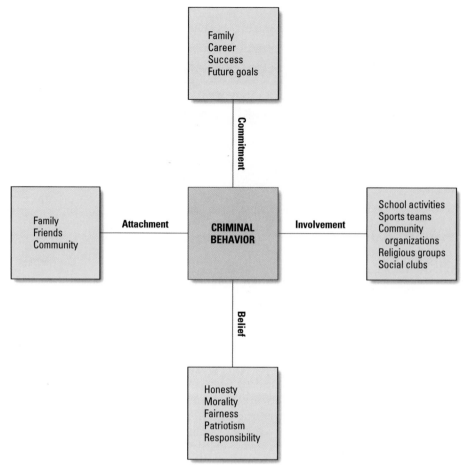

that support Hirschi's view.[134] For example, youths who maintain positive attachments with others also report low rates of delinquency.[135] Those adolescents who are committed to school are less likely to engage in delinquent acts than youths who fail at school and are detached from the educational experience.[136]

PERSPECTIVES ON JUSTICE

Control theory has been linked to the rehabilitation perspective. Programs have been designed to present alternative values and lifestyles to youths who have bought into a delinquent way of life. These programs often use group process and counseling to attack the criminal behavior orientations of their clients and help them learn conventional values and beliefs. Rehabilitation advocates suggest that community-based programs designed to strengthen young people's bonds to society will insulate them from crime. Family development, counseling programs, and school-based prevention programs are often utilized. In addition, various state youth and adult correctional authorities maintain inmate treatment programs that stress career development, work and educational furloughs, and self-help groups, all designed to help reestablish social bonds.

True/False 22–23
Multiple choice 20
Essay 12

The Outsider: Labeling Theory According to **labeling theory**, officially designating people as "troublemakers," stigmatizing them with a permanent deviant label, leads many to become criminals. People who commit undetected antisocial acts are called "secret deviants" or "primary deviants." Their illegal act has little influence or impact on their lifestyle or behavior. However, if another person commits the same act and his or her behavior is discovered by social control agents, the labeling process may be initiated. That person may be given a deviant label, such as "mentally ill" or "criminal." The deviant label transforms him or her into an outsider, shunned by the rest of society. In time, the stigmatized person may believe that the deviant label is valid and assume it as a personal identity. For example, the student placed in special education classes begins to view himself as "stupid" or "backward," the mental patient accepts society's view of her as "crazy," and the convicted criminal considers himself "dangerous" or "wicked."

Accompanying the deviant label are a variety of degrading social and physical restraints—handcuffs, trials, incarceration, bars, cells, and a criminal record—which leave an everlasting impression on the accused. These sanctions are designed to humiliate and are applied in what labeling experts call *degradation ceremonies,* in which the target is made to feel unworthy and despised.

Labels and sanctions work to define the whole person, meaning that a label evokes stereotypes that are used to forecast other aspects of the labeled person's character. A person labeled "mentally ill" is assumed to be dangerous, evil, cruel, or untrustworthy, even though he or she has exhibited none of these characteristics.

Faced with such condemnation, negatively labeled people may begin to adopt their new, degraded identity. They may find no alternative but to seek others who are similarly stigmatized and form a deviant subculture. Supported by a deviant peer group that sports similar labels, they enter into a deviant or criminal career. Rather than deterring crime, labeling begins a deviance amplification process. If apprehended and subjected to even more severe negative labels, the offender may be transformed into a "real" deviant—one whose view of self is in direct opposition to conventional society. The deviant label may become a more comfortable and personally acceptable social status than any other. The individual whose original crime may have been relatively harmless is transformed by social action into a career deviant, a process referred to as *secondary deviance.* The entire labeling process is illustrated in Figure 3.3.

Labeling theorists also believe that there is racial, gender, and economic discrimination in the labeling

labeling theory
The view that society produces criminals by stigmatizing certain individuals as deviants, a label that they come to accept as a personal identity.

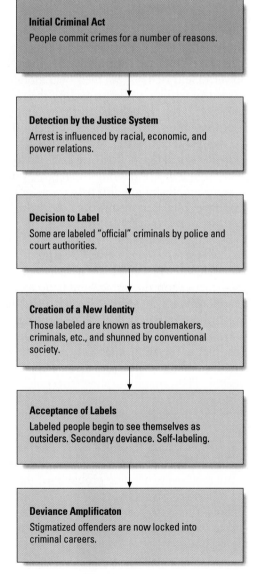

Initial Criminal Act
People commit crimes for a number of reasons.

Detection by the Justice System
Arrest is influenced by racial, economic, and power relations.

Decision to Label
Some are labeled "official" criminals by police and court authorities.

Creation of a New Identity
Those labeled are known as troublemakers, criminals, etc., and shunned by conventional society.

Acceptance of Labels
Labeled people begin to see themselves as outsiders. Secondary deviance. Self-labeling.

Deviance Amplificaton
Stigmatized offenders are now locked into criminal careers.

FIGURE 3.3
THE LABELING
PROCESS

process. For example, judges may sympathize with white defendants and help them avoid criminal labels, especially if they seem to come from "good families," whereas minority youths are not afforded that luxury.[137] This may help explain racial and economic differences in the crime rate.

PERSPECTIVES ON JUSTICE

Labeling theory principles support the noninterventionist view that an offender's interface with the criminal justice system should be limited. Among the most prominent policy initiatives based on labeling theory are efforts to divert first offenders away from the normal justice process and into treatment programs, to order offenders to pay victim restitution rather than enter into the justice process, and to deinstitutionalize nonviolent offenders (that is, remove them from the prison system).

IT'S POLITICAL: CONFLICT THEORY

conflict theory
The view that crime results from the imposition by the rich and powerful of their own moral standards and economic interests on the rest of society.

Multiple choice 21–24
Essay 13

Conflict theory views the economic and political forces operating in society as the fundamental cause of criminality. The criminal law and criminal justice system are seen as vehicles for controlling the poor. The criminal justice system helps the powerful and rich impose their own morality and standards of good behavior on the entire society, while protecting their property and physical safety from the have-nots, even though the cost may be the legal rights of the lower class. Those in power control the content and direction of the law and the legal system. Crimes are defined in a way that meets the needs of the ruling classes; thus, the theft of property worth five dollars by a poor person can be punished much more severely than the misappropriation of millions by a large corporation. Those in the middle class are drawn into this pattern of control because they are led to believe they, too, have a stake in maintaining the status quo and should support the views of the upper-class owners of production.[138]

Conflict theory has a number of subdivisions. One approach—known as *conflict criminology*—views crime as a product of the class conflict that can exist in any society.[139] A second subbranch—called *critical, radical,* or *Marxist criminology*—focuses on the crime-producing forces contained within the capitalist system. Both branches agree that the law and justice systems are mechanisms through which those in power control the have-not members of society.

Conflict theorists devote their research efforts to exposing discrimination and class bias in the application of laws and justice. They trace the history of criminal sanctions to show how those sanctions have corresponded to the needs of the wealthy. They attempt to show how police, courts, and correctional agencies have served as tools of the powerful members of society.

left realism
A branch of conflict theory that accepts the reality of crime as a social problem and stresses its impact on the poor.

radical feminism
A branch of conflict theory that focuses on the role of capitalist male dominance in female criminality and victimization.

peacemaking criminology
A branch of conflict theory that stresses humanism, mediation, and conflict resolution as means to end crime.

Critical criminology is now undergoing significant evolution, and a number of new subbranches have gained popularity. **Left realism** attempts to reconcile critical views with the social realities of crime and its impact on the lower class. Left realists recognize that predatory crimes are not "revolutionary" acts and that crime is an overwhelming problem for the poor. Regardless of its origins, according to left realists, crime must be dealt with by the police and courts.[140] **Radical feminism** has tried to explain how capitalism places particular stress on women and to explicate the role of male dominance in female criminality.[141] **Peacemaking criminology** views crime as just one form of violence among others, such as war and genocide. Peacemakers call for universal social justice as a means of eliminating antisocial acts.[142]

PERSPECTIVES ON JUSTICE

Conflict theory resonates with the restorative justice perspective. Rather than being adversarial and punitive, the justice system should strive to restore damaged social relations. Harsh punishments have become the norm. An alternative would be mediation, arbitration, restitution, and forgiveness. This call for social justice has helped focus attention on the plight of the poor, women, and minority groups when they confront the agencies of the justice system. Programs that have been developed as a result include free legal services for indigent offenders, civilian review boards to oversee police, laws protecting battered women, and shelters for victims of domestic abuse.

IT'S A MATTER OF DEVELOPMENT: INTEGRATED THEORIES

To derive more powerful and robust explanations of crime, some criminologists are now integrating individual factors into complex theories that seek to blend seemingly independent concepts into coherent explanations of criminality. One of the many reasons for the recent popularity of integrated theory is that the questions criminologists ask about crime are changing. They are concerned not only with why people begin committing crimes (criminal onset) but why most criminals age out or desist from crime. Although a single factor—whether poverty, intelligence, greed, strain, or learning—can be useful for explaining the onset of crime, it is more difficult for a single factor to explain its termination. For example, if criminality is a function of intelligence, as some criminologists claim, why do most delinquents fail to become adult criminals? It seems unlikely that intelligence level increases as young offenders mature; therefore, some other factor must explain adult desistance from crime. Two popular versions of integrated theory are *latent trait theory* and *developmental theory*.

Latent Trait Theory

According to latent trait theory, a certain percentage of the population possesses a personal characteristic that controls their propensity to offend.[143] Suspected latent traits include defective intelligence, impulsive personality, and genetic makeup—characteristics that may be present at birth or established early in life and remain stable over time.[144] Because latent traits are stable, people who are antisocial during adolescence are the ones most likely to remain criminals throughout their life span. Factors that produce crime early in life are therefore also responsible for antisocial behavior that persists into adulthood.

The best-known latent trait theory is Michael Gottfredson and Travis Hirschi's general theory of crime (see Figure 3.4).[145] In the general theory, Gottfredson and Hirschi argue that individual differences in the tendency to commit criminal acts can be found in a person's level of self-control. People with limited self-control tend to be impulsive, insensitive, physical (rather than mental), risk-taking, short-sighted, and nonverbal. They have a "here and now" orientation and refuse to work for distant goals; they lack diligence, tenacity, and persistence in a course of

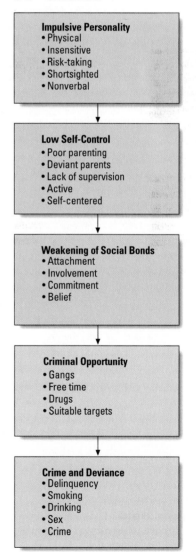

FIGURE 3.4
GENERAL THEORY
OF CRIME

Fill in the blanks 17
Multiple choice 25
Essay 14–15

action. People lacking self-control tend to be adventuresome, active, physical, and self-centered. As they mature, they have unstable marriages, jobs, and friendships.

Criminal acts are attractive to such individuals because they provide easy and immediate gratification—or, as Gottfredson and Hirschi put it, "money without work, sex without courtship, revenge without court delays." Given the opportunity to commit crime, they will readily violate the law; under the same set of circumstances, nonimpulsive people will refrain from antisocial behavior.

Criminal activity diminishes when the opportunity to commit crime is limited. People age out of crime because the opportunity to commit crimes diminishes with age: Teenagers simply have more opportunity to commit crimes than the elderly, regardless of their intelligence. Here the general theory integrates the concepts of latent traits and criminal opportunity: Possessing a particular trait + having the opportunity to commit crime = the choice to commit crime.

Developmental Theory

True/False 24
Multiple choice 26

Developmental criminologists chart the natural history of a criminal career. Why do some offenders escalate their criminal activities, whereas others decrease or limit law violations? Why do some offenders "specialize" in a particular crime, whereas others become "generalists"? Why do some criminals reduce criminal activity and then resume it once again? By integrating a variety of ecological, socialization, psychological, biological, and economic factors into a coherent structure, criminologists are now attempting to answer these complex questions.

According to the developmental (sometimes called the life course) view, a criminal career is an evolutionary process, and the role of "criminal" is always changing. Some criminals may desist from crime, only to resume their activities at a later date. Some commit offenses at a steady pace, whereas others escalate the rate of their criminal involvement. Offenders can begin to specialize in one type of crime or become "generalists" who commit a variety of illegal acts. The reasons people commit crimes and the frequency of their criminal activity change over the course of their lives. Criminals may be influenced by family matters, financial needs, and changing lifestyle and interests. Latent traits may be important, but they do not alone determine the direction of criminal careers.

Developmental theory recognizes that as people mature, the factors that influence their behavior also undergo change. At first, family relations may be most influential; in later adolescence, school and peer relations predominate; in adulthood, marital relations may be the most critical influence. Some antisocial youths who are in trouble throughout their adolescence may be able to find stable work and maintain intact marriages as adults; these life events help them desist from crime. In contrast, those who develop arrest records, get involved with the wrong crowd, and can only find menial jobs are at risk for criminal careers. Social forces that are critical at one stage of life may have little meaning or influence at another.

Two of the leading life course theorists, criminologists Robert Sampson and John Laub, have sought to identify the "turning points" in a criminal career; two of the most important are marriage and career.[146] As they mature, people who have had significant problems with the law are able to desist from crime if they can become attached to a spouse who supports and sustains them. They may encounter employers who are willing to give them a chance despite their record. People who cannot sustain secure marital relations or are failures in the labor market are less likely to desist from crime. Getting arrested can help sustain a criminal career because it reduces the chances of marriage, employment, and job stability, factors that are directly related to crime.

According to Sampson and Laub, these life events help people build **social capital**—positive relations with individuals and institutions that are life sustaining. For example, a successful marriage creates social capital when it improves a per-

social capital
Positive relations with individuals and institutions that foster self-worth and inhibit crime.

son's stature, creates feelings of self-worth, and encourages people to take a chance on him or her. Getting a good job inhibits crime by creating a stake in conformity—why commit crimes when you are doing well at your job? The relationship is reciprocal: Persons chosen as employees return the "favor" by doing the best job possible; those chosen as spouses blossom into devoted partners. Building social capital and strong social bonds reduces the likelihood of long-term deviance.

Sampson and Laub's research indicates that people can undergo change and that events that occur in later adolescence and adulthood do in fact influence people's propensity to commit crime. Life events help terminate or sustain deviant careers.

IT'S HOW YOU LIVE: THEORIES OF VICTIMIZATION

For many years, criminological theory focused on the actions of the criminal offender; the role of the victim was virtually ignored. Then a number of scholars found that the victim is not a passive target in crime but someone whose behavior can influence his or her own fate. Hans Von Hentig portrayed the crime victim as someone who "shapes and molds the criminal."[147] The criminal may be a predator, but the victim may help the criminal by becoming a willing prey. Stephen Schafer continued this approach by focusing on the victim's responsibility in the "genesis of crime."[148] Schafer accused some victims of provoking or encouraging criminal behavior, a concept now referred to as **victim precipitation**. These early works helped focus attention on the role of the victim in the crime problem and led to further research efforts that have sharpened the image of the crime victim.

victim precipitation
The role of the victim in provoking or encouraging criminal behavior.

Victim Precipitation

Multiple choice 27–28
Essay 16

Victims may actually precipitate the confrontations that lead to their injury or death. A victim may provoke or threaten an attacker, use "fighting words," or even attack first. The concept of victim precipitation was popularized by Marvin Wolfgang's 1958 study of criminal homicide. Wolfgang found that crime victims were often intimately involved in their demise, and as many as 25 percent of all homicides could be classified as victim precipitated.[149]

There are two types of victim precipitation. *Active precipitation* occurs when victims act provocatively, use threats or fighting words, or even attack first.[150] For example, some experts have suggested that female rape victims contribute to their attacks by dressing provocatively or pursuing a relationship with the rapist.[151] Although this finding has been disputed, courts have continued to return not guilty verdicts in rape cases if a victim's actions can in any way be construed as consenting to sexual intimacy.[152]

Passive precipitation occurs when the victim exhibits some personal characteristic that unintentionally either threatens or encourages the attacker. The crime may occur because of personal conflict; for example, a woman may become the target of intimate violence when she increases her job status and her success results in a backlash from a jealous spouse or partner.[153] Passive precipitation may also occur when the victim belongs to a group whose mere presence threatens the attacker's reputation, status, or economic well-being. For example, hate crime violence may be precipitated by immigrants' arriving in the community to compete for jobs and housing.[154]

Lifestyle Theory

Essay 17

Some criminologists believe that people may become crime victims because their lifestyle increases their exposure to criminal offenders. Victimization risk is increased

Six friends carry the coffin of 17-year-old Kenya LaShawn McClendon, killed by a drug dealer's stray bullet in West Palm Beach, Florida. Victimization rates are higher in open public areas, especially during the evening hours. People may be at risk for violent victimization when their lifestyles place them in dangerous areas.

© Greg Lovett/*Palm Beach Post*

by such behaviors as associating with violent young men, going out in public places late at night, and living in an urban area. Those who have histories of engaging in serious delinquency, getting involved in gangs, carrying guns, and selling drugs have an increased chance of being shot and killed themselves.[155] Lifestyle risks continue into young adulthood. College students who spend several nights each week partying and who take recreational drugs are much more likely to suffer violent crime than those who avoid such risky lifestyles.[156]

Lifestyle theory suggests that a person can reduce the chances of victimization by reducing risk-taking behavior: staying home at night, moving to a rural area, staying out of public places, earning more money, and getting married. The basis of this theory is that crime is not a random occurrence but rather a function of the victim's lifestyle.

Routine Activities Theory

Routine activities theory, a variation on the lifestyle model, holds that the incidence of criminal activity and victimization is related to the nature of normal, everyday patterns of human behavior. According to this view, predatory crime rates can be explained by three factors (see Figure 3.5): the supply of *motivated offenders* (such as large numbers of unemployed teenagers); *suitable targets* (goods that have value and can be easily transported, such as VCRs); and the absence of *effective guardians* (protections such as police and security forces or home security devices).[157]

The routine activities view of victimization suggests that people's daily activities may put them at risk. If people leave unguarded valuables in their home, they increase the likelihood of becoming burglary victims; if they walk at night in public places, they increase the risk of becoming targets of violence.[158]

According to this approach, the likelihood of victimization is a function of both criminal motivation and the behavior of potential victims. For example, if average family income increases because of an increase in the number of working mothers, and consequently the average family is able to afford more luxury goods such as portable computers and digital cameras, we might expect a comparable increase in the crime rate because the number of suitable targets has expanded while the number of capable guardians left to protect the home has been reduced.[159] In contrast, crime rates may go down during times of high unemployment, because there is less to steal and more people are at home to guard their

Fill in the blanks 18
Essay 18

routine activities theory
The view that crime is a product of three everyday factors: motivated offenders, suitable targets, and a lack of capable guardians.

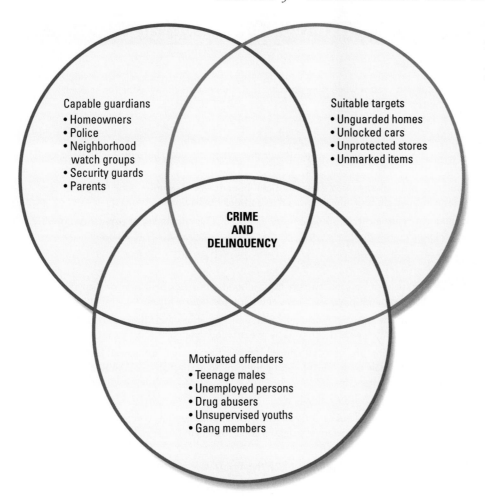

FIGURE 3.5
ROUTINE
ACTIVITIES
THEORY

possessions. The routine activities approach seems a promising way of understanding crime and victimization patterns and predicting victim risk.

SUMMARY

This chapter has reviewed some of the most important theoretical models in criminology (see Exhibit 3.2). Clearly, there is more than one approach to understanding the cause of crime and its consequences. Debate continues over whether crime is a social, economic, psychological, biological, or personal problem; whether it is a matter of free choice or the product of uncontrollable social and personal forces; and whether it can be controlled by the fear of punishment or the application of rehabilitative treatment. Consequently, a number of different and diverse schools of criminological theory exist—some focusing on the individual, and others viewing social factors as the most important element in producing crime.

Choice theories assume that criminals carefully choose whether to commit criminal acts. People are influenced by their fear of the criminal penalties associated with being caught and convicted for law violations. The more severe, certain, and swift the punishment, the more likely it is to control crime. Deterrence theory holds that if criminals are indeed rational, an inverse relationship should exist between punishment and crime. Specific deterrence theory holds that the crime rate can be reduced if known offenders are punished so severely that they never commit crimes again.

EXHIBIT 3.2 CONCEPTS AND THEORIES OF CRIMINOLOGY: A REVIEW

Theory	Major Premise
Choice Theory	People commit crimes when they perceive that the benefits of law violation outweigh the threat and pain of punishment.
Biosocial Theories	
Biochemical	Crime, especially violence, is a function of diet, vitamin intake, hormonal imbalance, or food allergies.
Neurological	Criminals and delinquents often suffer brain impairment. Attention deficit disorder and minimum brain dysfunction are related to antisocial behavior.
Genetic	Delinquent traits and predispositions are inherited. The criminality of parents can predict the delinquency of children.
Psychological Theories	
Psychoanalytic	The development of personality early in childhood influences behavior for the rest of a person's life. Criminals have weak egos and damaged personalities.
Social learning	People commit crimes when they model their behavior after others they see being rewarded for the same acts. Behavior is enforced by rewards and extinguished by punishment.
Cognitive	Individual reasoning processes influence behavior. Reasoning is influenced by the way people perceive their environment and by their moral and intellectual development.
Social Structure Theories	
Social disorganization	The conflicts and problems of urban social life and communities control the crime rate. Crime is a product of transitional neighborhoods that manifest social disorganization and value conflict.
Strain	People who adopt society's goals but lack the means to attain them seek alternatives, such as crime.
Social Process Theories	
Learning	People learn to commit crimes from exposure to antisocial behaviors. Criminal behavior depends on the person's experiences with rewards for conventional behaviors and punishments for deviant ones. Being rewarded for deviance leads to crime.

Trait theories hold that biological conditions such as biochemical makeup, neurological deficits, and/or genetic abnormalities control crime. In contrast to these views, sociologists believe that crime is a product of environmental influences. Some argue that people living in disorganized inner-city neighborhoods are at risk to commit crime because their environment gives them little hope of achieving success through conventional means; they may become angry and frustrated. Another view is that people become socialized to crime because of their upbringing and social learning. Still another view is that the conflict inherent in a capitalist society is a direct cause of antisocial behavior. Some theorists believe that there is an underlying trait that causes crime. Still another view is that crime is a developmental process and that the conditions that cause criminal behavior at one point in the life cycle change radically as people mature.

There are also a number of theories of victimization. One view, called victim precipitation, is that victims actually provoke criminals and are at least partially responsible for their victimization. More common are lifestyle theories that suggest that victims put themselves in danger by engaging in high-risk activities, such as going out late at night, living in a high-crime area, and associating with high-risk peers. The routine activities theory maintains that a pool of motivated offenders exists and that these offenders will take advantage of suitable, unguarded targets.

Theory	Major Premise
Social Process Theories (continued)	
Social control	A person's bond to society prevents him or her from violating social rules. If the bond weakens, the person is free to commit crimes.
Conflict Theories	
Conflict	People commit crimes when the law, controlled by the rich and powerful, defines their behavior as illegal. The immoral actions of the powerful go unpunished.
Left realism	Crime is a function of relative deprivation; criminals prey on the poor.
Radical feminism	The capital system creates patriarchy, which oppresses women. Male dominance explains gender bias, violence against women, and repression.
Peacemaking	Peace and humanism can reduce crime; conflict resolution strategies can work.
Integrated Theories	
Latent trait: general theory of crime	Crime and criminality are separate concepts. People choose to commit crime when they lack self-control. People lacking in self-control will seize criminal opportunities.
Developmental	Criminals go through lifestyle changes during their offending career. As people mature, the factors that influence their propensity to commit crime change. In childhood, family factors are critical; in adulthood, marital and job factors are key.
Victimization Theories	
Victim precipitation	Victims trigger criminal acts by their provocative behavior. Active precipitation involves fighting words or gestures. Passive precipitation occurs when victims unknowingly threaten their attackers.
Lifestyle	Victimization risk is increased when people have a high-risk lifestyle. Placing oneself at risk by going out to dangerous places results in increased victimization.
Routine activities	Crime rates can be explained by the availability of suitable targets, the absence of capable guardians, and the presence of motivated offenders.

Key Terms

criminology	**social structure**	**conflict theory**
deterrent	**culture of poverty**	**left realism**
general deterrence	**focal concerns**	**radical feminism**
specific deterrence	**strain**	**peacemaking criminology**
social learning theory	**differential association theory**	**social capital**
psychopath	**social control theory**	**victim precipitation**
anomie	**labeling theory**	**routine activities theory**

Discussion Questions

1. What factors are present in a disorganized urban area that produce high crime rates?
2. If research could show that the tendency to commit crime is inherited, what should be done with the young children of violence-prone criminals?
3. It seems logical that biological and psychological factors might explain why some people commit crime. Why would these factors fail to explain crime patterns and trends?
4. Are criminals impulsive? How could impulsivity be used to explain white-collar and organized crime?
5. If crime is a routine activity, what steps should you take to avoid becoming a crime victim?

A CLOSER LOOK

Elliot Currie, a noted liberal criminologist, believes that the term *radical criminology* is inaccurate and misleading. Criminologists who define themselves as radical undercut their own work and reduce the chances of achieving more humane criminal justice. As a result, they have enhanced the influence of right-wing criminologists who advocate crime control policies.

Today, the way the field of criminology is structured in the United States is something like this: there is a large, rather technocratic, "middle" contingent, the "mainstream," which often produces quite useful work, but is only rarely engaged in the public arena and shies away from sticking its neck out; there is the small but extremely effective right wing that has an extraordinary amount of presence and influence, less within the profession than in the media and among politicians, despite a quarter-century of the failure of its most basic ideas; and there is a self-defined "radical" contingent, complete with its own separate organizations and sections of organizations, that has a lot less influence than the power of its ideas should warrant—in part because it has too often gone along with the definition of itself as a fringe, or as a kind of subspecialization within the larger field.

To read more of Currie's ideas, go to InfoTrac College Edition and look for

Elliott Currie, "Radical Criminology or Just Criminology—Then, and Now," *Social Justice,* Summer 1999, v26 i2 p16

Notes

1 Catherine Tsai, "Man Dying of Cancer Charged in 4 Slayings: Police Say He Admits Killing Two Wives and Two Children," *Boston Globe,* 23 October 2000, p. A2.

2 For an analysis of "stranger" crimes, see Kenneth Polk, "Observations on Stranger Homicide," *Journal of Criminal Justice,* 21 (1993): 573–582.

3 Charles Patrick Ewing, *When Children Kill* (Lexington, MA: Lexington Books, 1990), p. 22.

4 Gary Bailey and N. Prabha Unnithan, "Gang Homicides in California: A Discriminant Analysis," *Journal of Criminal Justice* 22 (1994): 267–275.

5 G. David Curry, Richard Ball, and Scott Decker, "Estimating the National Scope of Gang Crime from Law Enforcement Data," in *Gangs in America,* 2d ed., ed. C. Ronald Huff (Newbury Park, CA: Sage, 1996); Malcolm Klein, *The American Street Gang: Its Nature, Prevalence, and Control* (New York: Oxford University Press, 1995), p. 30.

6 Stryker McGuire, "The Dunblane Effect," *Newsweek,* 28 October 1996, p. 46.

7 James A. Fox and Jack Levin, *Mass Murder,* 2d ed. (New York: Plenum, 1991).

8 Ibid.

9 For an unusual perspective on this issue, see Helen Birch, ed., *Moving Targets: Women, Murder and Representation* (Berkeley: University of California Press, 1994).

10 Richard Gelles and Murray Straus, *Intimate Violence* (New York: Simon and Schuster, 1988), p. 27.

11 *Current Trends in Child Abuse Reporting and Fatalities: The Results of the 1998 Annual Fifty-State Survey* (Chicago: National Committee to Prevent Child Abuse, 1999).

12 Diana Russell, "The Incidence and Prevalence of Intra-familial and Extra-familial Sexual Abuse of Female Children," *Child Abuse and Neglect* 7 (1983): 133–146.

13 Ruth Engs and David Hanson, "Boozing and Brawling on Campus: A National Study of Violent Problems Associated with Drinking over the Past Decade," *Journal of Criminal Justice* 22 (1994): 171–180.

14 Robert Nash Parker, "Bringing 'Booze' Back In: The Relationship between Alcohol and Homicide," *Journal of Research in Crime and Delinquency* 32 (1993): 3–38.

15 ADAM (Arrestee Drug Abuse Monitoring Program), *1999 Annual Report on Drug Use Among Adult and Juvenile Arrestees* (Washington, DC: National Institute of Justice, 2000).

16 John Hepburn, "Occasional Criminals," in *Major Forms of Crime,* ed. Robert Meier (Beverly Hills, CA: Sage, 1984), pp. 73–94.

17 James Inciardi, "Professional Crime," in *Major Forms of Crime,* ed. Robert Meier (Beverly Hills, CA: Sage, 1984), p. 223.

18 Tony Poveda, *Rethinking White-Collar Crime* (Westport, CT: Praeger, 1994), pp. 1–8.

19 Kitty Calavita and Henry Pontell, "Heads I Win, Tails You Lose: Deregulation, Crime, and Crisis in the Savings and Loan Industry," *Crime and Delinquency* 36 (1990): 309–341; Rich Thomas, "Sit Down Taxpayers," *Newsweek,* 4 June 1990, p. 60; L. Gordon Crovitz, "Milken's Tragedy: Oh How the Mighty Fall Before RICO," *Wall Street Journal,* 2 May 1990, p. A17.

20 For an excellent review of this issue, see Katherine Jamieson, *The Organization of Corporate Crime: The Dynamics of Antitrust Violation* (Thousand Oaks, CA: Sage, 1994).

21 John Braithwaite, "Toward a Theory of Organizational Crime," paper presented at the annual meeting of the American Society of Criminology, Montreal, November 1987.

22 Travis Hirschi and Michael Gottfredson, "Causes of White Collar Crime," *Criminology* 25 (1987): 969–974.

23 See, generally, Jay Albanese, *Organized Crime in America,* 2d ed. (Cincinnati: Anderson, 1989), p. 68.

24 Alan Block, *East Side/West Side* (New Brunswick, NJ: Transaction Books, 1983), vol. 7, pp. 10–11.

25 Liliana Pezzin, "Earnings Prospects, Matching Effects, and the Decision to Terminate a Criminal Career," *Journal of Quantitative Criminology* 11 (1995): 29–50.

26 Pierre Tremblay and Carlo Morselli, "Patterns in Criminal Achievement: Wilson and Abrahamse Revisited," *Criminology* 38 (2000): 633–660.

27 Gordon Knowles, "Deception, Detection, and Evasion: A Trade Craft Analysis of Honolulu, Hawaii's Street Crack Cocaine Traffickers," *Journal of Criminal Justice* 27 (1999): 443–455.

28 Andrew Buck, Simon Hakim, and George Rengert, "Burglar Alarms and the Choice Behavior of Burglars: A Suburban Phenomenon," *Journal of Criminal Justice* 21 (1993): 497–507; Julia MacDonald and Robert Gifford, "Territorial Cues and Defensible Space Theory: The Burglar's Point of View," *Journal of Environmental Psychology* 9 (1989): 193–205; Paul Cromwell, James Olson, and D'Aunn Wester Avary, *Breaking and Entering: An Ethnographic Analysis of Burglary* (Newbury Park, CA: Sage, 1991), pp. 48–51.

29 Matthew Robinson, "Lifestyles, Routine Activities, and Residential Burglary Victimization," *Journal of Criminal Justice* 22 (1999): 27–52.

30 William Smith, Sharon Glave Frazee, and Elizabeth Davison, "Furthering the Integration of Routine Activity and Social Disorganization Theories: Small Units of Analysis and the Study of Street Robbery as a Diffusion Process," *Criminology* 38 (2000): 489–521.

31 Paul Bellair, "Informal Surveillance and Street Crime: A Complex Relationship," *Criminology* 38 (2000): 137–167.

32 John Gibbs and Peggy Shelly, "Life in the Fast Lane: A Retrospective View by Commercial Thieves," *Journal of Research in Crime and Delinquency* 19 (1982): 229–230.

33 James Wright and Peter Rossi, *Armed and Considered Dangerous: A Survey of Felons and Their Firearms* (New York: Aldine, 1986).

34 Jennifer Browdy, "Interview with Ann Rule," *Law Enforcement News,* 21 May 1984, p. 12.

35 James Q. Wilson, *Thinking about Crime* (New York: Basic Books, 1975); Ernest Van den Haag, *Punishing Criminals* (New York: Basic Books, 1975).

36 Herbert Packer, *The Limits of the Criminal Sanction* (Stanford, CA: Stanford University Press, 1968).

37 Ernest Van den Haag, "Could Successful Rehabilitation Reduce the Crime Rate?" *Journal of Criminal Law and Criminology* 73 (1985): 1022–1035.

38 Steven Klepper and Daniel Nagin, "Tax Compliance and Perceptions of the Risks of Detection and Criminal Prosecution," *Law and Society Review* 23 (1989): 209–240.

39 Raymond Paternoster, "Decisions to Participate in and Desist from Four Types of Common Delinquency: Deterrence and the Rational Choice Perspective," *Law and Society Review* 23 (1989): 7–29; "Examining Three-Wave Deterrence Models: A Question of Temporal Order and Specification," *Journal of Criminal Law and Criminology* 79 (1988): 135–163.

40 Jon Sorenson, Robert Wrinkle, Victoria Brewer, and James Marquart, "Capital Punishment and Deterrence: Examining the Effect of Executions on Murder in Texas," *Crime and Delinquency* 45 (1999): 481–493.

41 Ibid.

42 Alex Piquero and George Rengert, "Studying Deterrence with Active Residential Burglars," *Justice Quarterly* 16 (1999): 451–462.

43 Robert Nash Parker, "Bringing 'Booze' Back In."

44 Michel Foucault, *Discipline and Punishment* (New York: Random House, 1978).

45 David J. Levin, Patrick A. Langan, and Jodi M. Brown, *State Court Sentencing of Convicted Felons, 1996* (Washington, DC: Bureau of Justice Statistics, 2000); Allen Beck and Bernard Shipley, *Recidivism of Young Parolees* (Washington, DC: Bureau of Justice Statistics, 1987).

46 Oscar Newman, *Defensible Space: Crime Prevention through Urban Design* (New York: Macmillan, 1972).

47 Ronald Clarke, *Situational Crime Prevention* (Albany, NY: Harrow and Heston, 1992).

48 Anthony Braga, David Weisburd, Elin Waring, Lorraine Green Mazerolle, William Spelman, and Francis Gajewski, "Problem-Oriented Policing in Violent Crime Places: A Randomized Controlled Experiment," *Criminology* 37 (1999): 541–580.

49 Eric Fritsch, Tory Caeti, and Robert Taylor, "Gang Suppression Through Saturation Patrol, Aggressive Curfew, and Truancy Enforcement: A Quasi-Experimental Test of the Dallas Anti-Gang Initiative," *Crime and Delinquency* 45 (1999): 122–139.

50 Ronald Clarke, "Deterring Obscene Phone Callers: The New Jersey Experience," *Situational Crime Prevention,* ed. Ronald Clarke (Albany, NY: Harrow and Heston, 1992), pp. 124–132.

51 See, generally, Cesare Lombroso, *Crime: Its Causes and Remedies* (Montclair, NJ: Patterson Smith, 1968).

52 Daniel Nagin and David Farrington, "The Stability of Criminal Potential from Childhood to Adulthood," paper presented at the annual meeting of the American Society of Criminology, San Francisco, November 1991.

53 Dalton Conley and Neil Bennett, "Is Biology Destiny? Birth Weight and Life Chances," *American Sociological Review* 654 (2000): 458–467.

54 Leonard Hippchen, "Some Possible Biochemical Aspects of Criminal Behavior," *Journal of Behavioral Ecology* 2 (1981): 1–6.

55 B. D'Asaro, C. Grossback, and C. Nigro, "Polyamine Levels in Jail Inmates," *Journal of Orthomolecular Psychiatry* 4 (1975): 149–152.

56 Diana Fishbein, "Neuropsychological Function, Drug Abuse, and Violence: A Conceptual Framework," *Criminal Justice and Behavior* 27 (2000): 139–159.

57 Keith McBurnett et al., "Aggressive Symptoms and Salivary Cortisol in Clinic-Referred Boys with Conduct Disorder," *Annals of the New York Academy of Sciences* 794 (1996): 169–177.

58 Christy Miller Buchanan, Jacquelynne Eccles, and Jill Becker, "Are Adolescents the Victims of Raging Hormones? Evidence for Activational Effects of Hormones on Moods and Behavior at Adolescence," *Psychological Bulletin* 111 (1992): 62–107.

59 D. Williams, "Neural Factors Related to Habitual Aggression: Consideration of Differences between Habitual Aggressives and Others Who Have Committed Crimes of Violence," *Brain* 92 (1969): 503–520.

60 R. S. Aind and T. Yamamoto, "Behavior Disorders of Childhood," *Electroencephalography and Clinical Neurophysiology* 21 (1966): 148–156.

61 Z. A. Zayed, S. A. Lewis, and R. P. Britain, "An Encephalographic and Psychiatric Study of 32 Insane Murderers," *British Journal of Psychiatry* 115 (1969): 1115–1124.

62 Dorothy Otnow Lewis, Ernest Moy, Lori Jackson, Robert Aaronson, Nicholas Restifo, Susan Serra, and Alexander Simos, "Biopsychosocial Characteristics of Children Who Later Murder," *American Journal of Psychiatry* 142 (1985): 1161–1167.

63 Dorothy Otnow Lewis, *Guilty by Reason of Insanity* (New York: Fawcett Columbine, 1998).

64 Ronald Cohen, Alan Rosenbaum, Robert Kane, William Warneken, and Sheldon Benjamin, "Neuropsychological Correlates of Domestic Violence," *Violence and Victims* 15 (2000): 397–410.

65 R. R. Monroe, *Brain Dysfunction in Aggressive Criminals* (Lexington, MA: D. C. Heath, 1978); L. T. Yeudall, *Childhood Experiences as Causes of Criminal Behavior* (Senate of Canada, issue no. 1, Thirteenth Parliament, Ottawa, Canada, 1977).

66 Rolf Loeber and Dale Hay, "Key Issues in the Development of Aggression and Violence from Childhood to Early Adulthood," *Annual Review of Psychology* 48 (1997): 371–410.

67 Terrie Moffitt and Phil Silva, "Self-Reported Delinquency, Neuropsychological Deficit, and History of Attention Deficit Disorder," *Journal of Abnormal Child Psychology* 16 (1988): 553–569.

68 See S. A. Mednick and Karl O. Christiansen, eds., *Biosocial Bases of Criminal Behavior* (New York: Gardner Press, 1977).

69 David Rowe and D. Wayne Osgood, "Heredity and Sociological Theories of Delinquency: A Reconsideration," *American Sociological Review* 49 (1984): 526–540.

70 B. Hutchings and S. A. Mednick, "Criminality in Adoptees and Their Adoptive and Biological Parents: A Pilot Study," in *Biosocial Bases of Criminal Behavior,* ed. S. A. Mednick and Karl O. Christiansen (New York: Gardner Press, 1977).

71 For an analysis of Freud, see Spencer Rathus, *Psychology* (New York: Holt, Rinehart & Winston, 1990), pp. 412–420.

72 August Aichorn, *Wayward Youth* (New York: Viking, 1965).

73 Seymour Halleck, *Psychiatry and the Dilemmas of Crime* (New York: Harper & Row, 1967), pp. 99–115.

74 John Monahan and Henry Steadman, *Crime and Mental Disorder* (National Institute of Justice Research Brief, Washington, DC, September 1984); David Tennenbaum, "Research Studies of Personality and Criminality," *Journal of Criminal Justice* 5 (1977): 1–19.

75 Carmen Cirincione et al., "Mental Illness as a Factor in Criminality: A Study of Prisoners and Mental Patients," paper presented at the annual meeting of the American Society of Criminology, San Francisco, November 1991.

76 John Monahan, *Mental Illness and Violent Crime* (Washington, DC: National Institute of Justice, 1996).

77 Katherine Van Wormer and Chuk Odiah, "The Psychology of Suicide-Murder and the Death Penalty," *Journal of Criminal Justice* 27 (1999): 361–370.

78 See Monahan, *Mental Illness and Violent Crime.*

79 This discussion is based on three works by Albert Bandura: *Aggression: A Social Learning Analysis* (Englewood Cliffs, NJ: Prentice-Hall, 1973); *Social Learning Theory* (Englewood Cliffs, NJ: Prentice-Hall, 1977); "The Social Learning Perspective:

Mechanisms of Aggression," in *The Psychology of Crime and Criminal Justice,* ed. H. Toch (New York: Holt, Rinehart & Winston, 1979), pp. 198–326.

80 Mark Warr and Mark Stafford, "The Influence of Delinquent Peers: What They Think or What They Do?" *Criminology* 29 (1991): 851–866.

81 J. E. Lockman, "Self and Peer Perception and Attributional Biases of Aggressive and Nonaggressive Boys in Dyadic Interactions," *Journal of Consulting and Clinical Psychology* 55 (1987): 404–410.

82 See, generally, Jean Piaget, *The Moral Judgement of the Child* (London: Kegan Paul, 1932).

83 Lawrence Kohlberg et al., *The Just Community Approach in Corrections: A Manual* (Niantic: Connecticut Department of Corrections, 1973).

84 Walter Mischel, *Introduction to Personality,* 4th ed. (New York: Holt, Rinehart & Winston, 1986), p. 1.

85 Edelyn Verona and Joyce Carbonell, "Female Violence and Personality," *Criminal Justice and Behavior* 27 (2000): 176–195.

86 See, generally, Albert Rabin, "The Antisocial Personality: Psychopathy and Sociopathy," in *The Psychology of Crime and Criminal Justice,* ed. H. Toch (New York: Holt, Rinehart & Winston, 1979), pp. 236–251.

87 Steven Smith and Joseph Newman, "Alcohol and Drug Abuse: Dependence Disorders in Psychopathic and Nonpsychopathic Criminal Offenders," *Journal of Abnormal Psychology* 99 (1990): 430–439.

88 Richard Rogers, Randall Salekin, Kenneth Sewell, and Keith Cruise, "Prototypical Analysis of Antisocial Personality Disorder," *Criminal Justice and Behavior* 27 (2000): 234–255.

89 Jack Levin and James Alan Fox, *Mass Murder* (New York: Plenum, 1985).

90 Stephen Porter, David Fairweather, Jeff Drugge, Huues Herve, Angela Birt, and Douglas Boer, "Profiles of Psychopathy in Incarcerated Sexual Offenders," *Criminal Justice and Behavior* 27 (2000): 216–233.

91 David Lykken, "Psychopathy, Sociopathy, and Crime," *Society* 34 (1996): 30–38.

92 Samuel Yochelson and Stanton Samenow, *The Criminal Personality* (New York: Jason Aronson, 1977).

93 See, generally, Terance Miethe and Robert Meier, *Crime and Its Social Context: Toward an Integrated Theory of Offenders, Victims, and Situations* (Albany: State University of New York Press, 1994).

94 Émile Durkheim, *The Division of Labor in Society* (New York: Free Press, 1964); *Rules of the Sociological Method,* trans. S. A. Solvay and J. H. Mueller, ed. G. Catlin (New York: Free Press, 1966).

95 "Poverty Rate Lowest in 20 Years, Household Income at Record High, Census Bureau Reports," U.S. Department of the Census news release, September 26, 2000.

96 William Spelman, "Abandoned Buildings: Magnets for Crime," *Journal of Criminal Justice* 21 (1993): 481–495.

97 William Julius Wilson, "Poverty, Joblessness, and Family Structure in the Inner City: A Comparative Perspective," paper presented at the annual meeting of the American Society of Criminology, San Francisco, November 1991.

98 Oscar Lewis, "The Culture of Poverty," *Scientific American* 215 (1966): 19–25.

99 William Julius Wilson, *The Truly Disadvantaged* (Chicago: University of Chicago Press, 1987).

100 Robert Bursik, "Social Disorganization and Theories of Crime and Delinquency: Problems and Prospects," *Criminology* 26 (1988): 519–551, at p. 521.

101 Robert Sampson, "Structural Sources of Variation in Race-Age-Specific Rates of Offending across Major U.S. Cities," *Criminology* 23 (1985): 647–673; Janet Heitgerd and Robert Bursik, Jr., "Extracommunity Dynamics and the Ecology of Delinquency," *American Journal of Sociology* 92 (1987): 775–787; Ora Simcha-Fagan and Joseph Schwartz, "Neighborhood and Delinquency: An Assessment of Contextual Effects," *Criminology* 24 (1986): 667–703.

102 E. Britt Patterson, "Poverty, Income Inequality, and Community Crime Rates," *Criminology* 29 (1991): 755–776.

103 Leon Pettiway, "Urban Spatial Structure and Incidence of Arson: Differences between Ghetto and Nonghetto Environments," *Justice Quarterly* 5 (1988): 113–129.

104 D. Wayne Osgood and Jeff Chambers, "Social Disorganization Outside the Metropolis: An Analysis of Rural Youth Violence," *Criminology* 38 (2000): 81–117.

105 Darrell Steffensmeier and Dana Haynie, "Gender, Structural Disadvantage, and Urban Crime: Do Macrosocial Variables Also Explain Female Offending Rates?" *Criminology* 38 (2000): 403–438.

106 Karen Parker and Matthew Pruitt, "Poverty, Poverty Concentration, and Homicide," *Social Science Quarterly* 81 (2000): 555–582.

107 Ruth Peterson, Lauren Krivo, and Mark Harris, "Disadvantage and Neighborhood Violent Crime: Do Local Institutions Matter?" *Journal of Research in Crime and Delinquency* 37 (2000): 31–63.

108 Beverly Stiles, Xiaoru Liu, and Howard Kaplan, "Relative Deprivation and Deviant Adaptations: The Mediating Effects of Negative Self-Feelings," *Journal of Research in Crime and Delinquency* 37 (2000): 64–90.

109 Walter Miller, "Lower Class Culture as a Generating Milieu of Gang Delinquency," *Journal of Social Issues* 14 (1958): 5–19; see also Thorsten Sellin, *Culture Conflict and Crime,* bulletin no. 41 (New York: Social Science Research Council, 1938).

110 Richard Cloward and Lloyd Ohlin, *Delinquency and Opportunity* (Glencoe, IL: Free Press, 1960).

111 Leslie Kennedy and Stephen Baron, "Routine Activities and a Subculture of Violence: A Study of Violence on the Street," *Journal of Research in Crime and Delinquency* 30 (1993): 88–112.

112 Robert Merton, "Social Structure and Anomie," in *Social Theory and Social Structure,* ed. Robert Merton (Glencoe, IL: Free Press, 1975).

113 Robert Agnew, "Foundation for a General Strain Theory of Crime and Delinquency," *Criminology* 30 (1992): 47–87; "Stability and Change in Crime over the Life Course: A Strain Theory Explanation," in *Advances in Criminological Theory: Vol. 7. Developmental Theories of Crime and Delinquency,* ed. Terence Thornberry (New Brunswick, NJ: Transaction Books, 1994).

114 Raymond Paternoster and Paul Mazerolle, "General Strain Theory and Delinquency: A Replication and Extension," *Journal of Research in Crime and Delinquency* 31 (1994): 235–263.

115 Paul Mazerolle, Velmer Burton, Francis Cullen, T. David Evans, and Gary Payne, "Strain, Anger, and Delinquent Adaptations: Specifying General Strain Theory," *Journal of Criminal Justice* 28 (2000): 89–101.

116 Stephen Cernkovich, Peggy Giordano, and Jennifer Rudolph, "Race, Crime and the American Dream," *Journal of Research in Crime and Delinquency* 37 (2000): 131–170.

117 Charles Tittle, Wayne Villemez, and Douglas Smith, "The Myth of Social Class and Criminality: An Empirical Assessment of the Evidence," *American Sociological Review* 43 (1978): 643–656.

118 Rolf Loeber and Magda Stouthamer-Loeber, "Family Factors as Correlates and Predictors of Juvenile Conduct Problems and Delinquency," in *Crime and Justice,* vol. 7, ed. Michael Tonry and Norval Morris (Chicago: University of Chicago Press, 1986), pp. 29–151.

119 John Laub and Robert Sampson, "Unraveling Families and Delinquency: A Reanalysis of the Gluecks' Data," *Criminology* 26 (1988): 355–380.

120 Ronald Simons, Chyi-In Wu, Kuei-Hsiu Lin, Leslie Gordon, and Rand Conger, "A Cross-Cultural Examination of the Link Between Corporal Punishment and Adolescent Antisocial Behavior," *Criminology* 38 (2000): 47–79.

121 Joan McCord, "Family Relationships, Juvenile Delinquency, and Adult Criminality," *Criminology* 29 (1991): 397–419.

122 Lawrence Rosen, "Family and Delinquency: Structure or Function?" *Criminology* 23 (1985): 553–573.

123 Lyle Shannon, *Assessing the Relationship of Adult Criminal Careers to Juvenile Careers: A Summary* (Washington, DC: U.S. Government Printing Office, 1982); Donald J. West and David P. Farrington, *The Delinquent Way of Life* (London: Heineman, 1977); Marvin Wolfgang, Robert Figlio, and Thorsten Sellin, *Delinquency in a Birth Cohort* (Chicago: University of Chicago Press, 1972).

124 Terence Thornberry, Melanie Moore, and R. L. Christenson, "The Effect of Drop-

ping Out of High School on Subsequent Criminal Behavior," *Criminology* 23 (1985): 3–18.

125 Scott Menard, "Demographic and Theoretical Variables in the Age-Period Cohort Analysis of Illegal Behavior," *Journal of Research in Crime and Delinquency* 29 (1992): 178–199.

126 D. Wayne Osgood, Janet Wilson, Patrick O'Malley, Jerald Bachman, and Lloyd Johnston, "Routine Activities and Individual Deviant Behavior," *American Sociological Review* 61 (1996): 635–655.

127 Mark Warr, "Age, Peers, and Delinquency," *Criminology* 31 (1993): 17–40.

128 Sara Battin, Karl Hill, Robert Abbott, Richard Catalano, and J. David Hawkins, "The Contribution of Gang Membership to Delinquency Beyond Delinquent Friends," *Criminology* 36 (1998): 93–116.

129 David Fergusson, L. John Horwood, and Daniel Nagin, "Offending Trajectories in a New Zealand Birth Cohort," *Criminology* 38 (2000): 525–551.

130 Denise Kandel and Mark Davies, "Friendship Networks, Intimacy, and Illicit Drug Use in Young Adulthood: A Comparison of Two Competing Theories," *Criminology* 29 (1991): 441–467.

131 Edwin Sutherland and Donald Cressey, *Criminology* (Philadelphia: J. B. Lippincott, 1970), pp. 71–91.

132 Denise Kandel and Mark Davies, "Friendship Networks, Intimacy, and Illicit Drug Use in Young Adulthood: A Comparison of Two Competing Theories," *Criminology* 29 (1991): 441–467.

133 Leanne Fiftal Alarid, Velmer Burton, and Francis Cullen, "Gender and Crime among Felony Offenders: Assessing the Generality of Social Control and Differential Association Theory," *Journal of Research in Crime and Delinquency* 37 (2000) 171–199.

134 See, for example, Randy La Grange and Helen Raskin White, "Age Differences in Delinquency: A Test of Theory," *Criminology* 23 (1985): 19–45; Marvin Krohn and James Massey, "Social Control and Delinquent Behavior: An Examination of the Elements of the Social Bond," *Sociological Quarterly* 21 (1980): 529–544.

135 Bobbi Jo Anderson, Malcolm Holmes, and Erik Ostresh, "Male and Female Delinquents' Attachments and Effects of Attachments on Severity of Self-Reported Delinquency," *Criminal Justice and Behavior* 26 (1999): 435–452.

136 Patricia Jenkins, "School Delinquency and the School Social Bond," *Journal of Research in Crime and Delinquency* 34 (1997): 337–367.

137 Christina DeJong and Kenneth Jackson, "Putting Race into Context: Race, Juvenile Justice Processing, and Urbanization," *Justice Quarterly* 15 (1998): 487–504.

138 W. Byron Groves and Robert Sampson, "Critical Theory and Criminology," *Social Problems* 33 (1986): 58–80.

139 Gresham Sykes, "The Rise of Critical Criminology," *Journal of Criminal Law and Criminology* 65 (June 1974): 206; see also Ian Taylor et al., *The New Criminology: For a Social Theory of Deviance* (New York: Harper & Row, 1973).

140 See, generally, Jock Young, *Realist Criminology* (London: Sage, 1989).

141 Kathleen Daly and Meda Chesney-Lind, "Feminism and Criminology," *Justice Quarterly* 5 (1988): 438–497.

142 Harold Pepinsky, "Violence as Unresponsiveness: Toward a New Conception of Crime," *Justice Quarterly* 5 (1988): 539–587.

143 David Rowe, D. Wayne Osgood, and W. Alan Nicewander, "A Latent Trait Approach to Unifying Criminal Careers," *Criminology* 28 (1990): 237–270.

144 David Rowe and Daniel Flannery, "An Examination of Environmental and Trait Influences on Adolescent Delinquency," *Journal of Research in Crime and Delinquency* 31 (1994): 374–389.

145 Michael Gottfredson and Travis Hirschi, *A General Theory of Crime* (Stanford, CA: Stanford University Press, 1990).

146 Robert Sampson and John Laub, *Crime in the Making: Pathways and Turning Points through Life* (Cambridge, MA: Harvard University Press, 1993).

147 Hans Von Hentig, *The Criminal and His Victim: Studies in the Sociobiology of Crime* (New Haven, CT: Yale University Press, 1948), p. 384.

148 Stephen Schafer, *The Victim and His Criminal* (New York: Random House, 1968), p. 152.

149 Marvin Wolfgang, *Patterns of Criminal Homicide* (Philadelphia: University of Pennsylvania Press, 1958).

150 Ibid.

151 Menachem Amir, *Patterns in Forcible Rape* (Chicago: University of Chicago Press, 1971).

152 Susan Estrich, *Real Rape* (Cambridge, MA: Harvard University Press, 1987).

153 Edem Avakame, "Females' Labor Force Participation and Intimate Femicide: An Empirical Assessment of the Backlash Hypothesis," *Violence and Victims* 14 (1999): 277–283.

154 Rosemary Gartner and Bill McCarthy, "The Social Distribution of Femicide in Urban Canada, 1921–1988," *Law and Society Review* 25 (1991): 287–311.

155 Rolf Loeber, Mary DeLamatre, George Tita, Jacqueline Cohen, Magda Stouthamer-Loeber, and David Farrington, "Gun Injury and Mortality: The Delinquent Backgrounds of Juvenile Offenders," *Violence and Victims* 14 (1999): 339–351.

156 Bonnie Fisher, John Sloan, Francis Cullen, and Chunmeng Lu, "Crime in the Ivory Tower: The Level and Sources of Student Victimization," *Criminology* 36 (1998): 671–710.

157 Lawrence Cohen and Marcus Felson, "Social Change and Crime Rate Trends: A Routine Activities Approach," *American Sociological Review* 44 (1979): 588–608; Lawrence Cohen, Marcus Felson, and Kenneth Land, "Property Crime Rates in the United States: A Macrodynamic Analysis, 1947–1977, with Ex-Ante Forecasts for the Mid-1980's," *American Journal of Sociology* 86 (1980): 90–118; for a review, see James LeBeau and Thomas Castellano, "The Routine Activities Approach: An Inventory and Critique," unpublished paper, Center for the Studies of Crime, Delinquency and Corrections, Southern Illinois University, Carbondale, 1987.

158 Steven Messner and Kenneth Tardiff, "The Social Ecology of Urban Homicide: An Application of the 'Routine Activities' Approach," *Criminology* 23 (1985): 241–267; Philip Cook, "The Demand and Supply of Criminal Opportunities," in *Crime and Justice,* vol. 7, ed. Michael Tonry and Norval Morris (Chicago: University of Chicago Press, 1986), pp. 1–28; Ronald Clarke and Derek Cornish, "Modeling Offenders' Decisions: A Framework for Research and Policy," in *Crime and Justice,* vol. 6, ed. Michael Tonry and Norval Morris (Chicago: University of Chicago Press, 1985), 147–187.

159 Cohen, Felson, and Land, "Property Crime Rates in the United States."

CRIMINAL LAW:
SUBSTANCE AND PROCEDURE

John and Terri Nakai had been waiting a year with a local adoption agency when, in June 2000, a fellow subscriber to America Online emailed them. A self-styled Philadelphia-based adoption facilitator named Sonya Furlow had a baby they could adopt quickly, the email said. They emailed Furlow and within a few weeks sent her $4,500, the first installment of her $8,500 adoption fee. Then Furlow dropped out of sight. There never was any child.

A few months later, Furlow conned $9,500 from another family. She told them to fly from Nebraska to Philadelphia to pick up a baby. She met them at a hospital pretending to have just come from a birth. After letting the couple wait in the hotel for days, she told them the mother had changed her mind.

Furlow's cruel hoax of using the Internet to sell fictitious babies continued into September 2000, when Jill and Steven Hopster of Redmond, Washington, saw Internet postings offering the very same baby they were about to adopt to others.

The Internet has made the complex business of adoptions easier, but it has also spawned heartbreaking cases of adoption fraud. Furlow pled guilty and received a 2-year prison sentence. Her Web site was still up when she went to prison.

Chapter Outline

Criminal Justice Links

Criminal Justice Viewpoints

Cases such as Furlow's underscore why the criminal law remains of vital importance to the criminal justice system.[1] The criminal law defines crimes, dictates punishments, and controls the procedures used to process criminal offenders through the justice system. It is the ultimate weapon to deter unacceptable behavior—including such modern variants as Internet crime.

This chapter focuses on the basic principles of the substantive criminal law, which regulates conduct in our society. In addition, constitutional criminal procedure, the law that governs the judicial process, will be discussed to show how the rules of procedure, laid out in the U.S. Constitution and interpreted over time by the Supreme Court, control the operations of the justice system.

The **substantive criminal law** defines crime in U.S. society. Each state government, and the federal government as well, has its own criminal code, developed over many generations and incorporating moral beliefs, social values, political and economic matters, and other societal concerns. The criminal law is a living document, constantly evolving to keep pace with society and its needs.

Fill in the blanks 1
Multiple choice 1
Essay 1

substantive criminal law
A body of specific rules that declare what conduct is criminal and prescribe the punishment to be imposed for such conduct.

procedural law
The rules that define the operation of criminal proceedings, from obtaining a warrant or making an arrest through trial, sentencing, and appeal.

The rules designed to implement the substantive law are known as **procedural law**. It is concerned with the *criminal process*—the legal steps through which an offender passes—commencing with the initial criminal investigation and concluding with the release of the offender. Elements of the law of criminal procedure include the rules of evidence, the law of arrest, the law of search and seizure, questions of appeal, and the right to counsel. Many of the rights extended to offenders over the past three decades lie within procedural law.

In our modern society, the rule of law governs almost all phases of human enterprise, including commerce, family life, property transfer, and the regulation of interpersonal conflict. It contains elements that control personal relationships between individuals and public relationships between individuals and the government. The former is known as *civil law*; the latter is *criminal law*.

HISTORICAL DEVELOPMENT OF THE CRIMINAL LAW

The roots of the criminal codes used in the United States can be traced to such early legal charters as the Babylonian Code of Hammurabi (2000 B.C.), the Mosaic Code of the Israelites (1200 B.C.), and the Twelve Roman Tables. During the sixth century, under the leadership of Byzantine emperor Justinian, the first great codification of law in the Western world was prepared. Justinian's Corpus Juris Civilis, or body of civil law, summarized the system of Roman law that had gradually developed over a thousand years. Rules and regulations to ensure the safety of the state and the individual were organized into a code and served as a basis for future civil and criminal legal classifications. Centuries later, French emperor Napoleon I created the French civil code using Justinian's code as a model. France and other countries that modeled their legal systems on French and Roman law have civil law systems. Thus, the concepts of law and crime have evolved over thousands of years.[2]

Before the Norman Conquest in 1066, the legal system among the early Anglo-Saxons was decentralized. The law often varied from county to county, and there was very little written law, except for those covering crimes. Prior to the year 1000, crimes were viewed as personal wrongs, and compensation was often paid to the victim. Major violations of customs and law included violent acts, thefts, and disloyalty to the lord. For certain actions, such as treason, the penalty was often death. For other crimes, such as theft, compensation could be paid to the victim. Thus, to some degree, the early criminal law sought to produce an equitable solution to both private and public disputes.[3]

Fill in the blanks 2
True/False 1

The Common Law

A more immediate source for much U.S. law is the English system of jurisprudence that developed after the Norman Conquest. Before the ratification of the U.S. Constitution in 1788 and the development of the first state legal codes, formal law in the original colonies was adapted from existing English law, known today as **common law**.

Common law first came into being during the reign of King Henry II (1154–1189) when royal judges were appointed to travel to specific jurisdictions to hold court and represent the crown. Known as circuit judges, they followed a specific route (circuit) and heard cases that previously had been under the jurisdiction of local courts.[4] The royal judges began to replace local custom with a national law that was followed in courts throughout the country; thus, the law became "common" to the entire nation. The common law developed when English judges ac-

common law
Early English law, developed by judges, that incorporated Anglo-Saxon tribal customs, feudal rules and practices, and the everyday rules of behavior of local villages; basis of U.S. criminal law.

tually created many crimes by ruling that certain actions were subject to state control and sanction. The most serious offenses, such as murder, rape, treason, arson, and burglary, which had been viewed largely as personal wrongs (torts for which the victim received monetary compensation from the offender), were redefined by the judges as offenses against the state, or crimes.

The English common law continually evolved to fit specific incidents that the judges encountered. Legal scholars have identified specific cases in which judges created new crimes, some of which exist today. For example, in the *Carriers* case (1473), an English court ruled that a merchant who had been hired to transport merchandise was guilty of larceny (theft) if he kept the goods for his own purposes.[5] Before the *Carriers* case, the common law had not recognized a crime when people kept something that was voluntarily placed in their possession, even if the rightful owner had only given them temporary custody of the merchandise. Breaking the legal tradition, the court recognized that the commercial system could not be maintained unless the law of theft was changed. Thus, larcenies defined by separate and unique criminal laws, such as embezzlement, extortion, and false pretenses, came into existence.

Over time, common law decisions made by judges in England produced a body of rules and legal principles about crime and punishment that formed the basis of the early American legal system.[6] Today, criminal behavior is defined primarily by statute.

The Principle of Stare Decisis

One of the principal components of the common law was its recognition of the law of precedent. Once a decision had been made by a court, that judicial decision was generally binding on other courts in subsequent cases. Thus, judicial decisions became the basis for judge-made, or case, law. For example, if a homeowner who killed an unarmed intruder was found not guilty of murder on the grounds that he had a right to defend his property, that rule would be applied in subsequent cases involving the same set of facts. In other words, a decision on the issue of self-defense in that case would be followed in that jurisdiction by the same court or a lesser court in future cases presenting the same legal problem.

Because the common law represented decisions handed down by judges, as distinguished from law that is determined by statutes, it was essential that the rule of precedent be followed. This legal principle, known as **stare decisis,** originated in England and is still used as the basis for deciding legal cases in the United States. The courts are generally bound by the principle of stare decisis to follow criminal law as it has been judicially determined in prior cases in the justice system. This principle is also used in interpreting evidence given in trials and in determining trial outcomes. The advantage of this legal doctrine is that it promotes predictability and uniformity in the process of making legal decisions.

Criminal Law and Civil Law

In modern U.S. society, all laws can be divided into two broad categories: criminal law and civil law. All law other than criminal law is known as **civil law**; it includes **tort law** (personal wrongs and damages), property law (the law governing the transfer and ownership of property), and contract law (the law of personal agreements).

The differences between criminal law and civil law are significant, because criminal proceedings are completely separate from civil actions. The major objective of the criminal law is to protect the public against harm by preventing criminal offenses. The primary concern of the civil law—in the area of private wrongs

Fill in the blanks 3–4
True/False 2–3

stare decisis
To stand by decided cases; the legal principle by which the decision or holding in an earlier case becomes the standard by which subsequent similar cases are judged.

Multiple choice 2–5
Essay 2

civil law
All law that is not criminal, including tort, contract, personal property, maritime, and commercial law.

tort law
The law of personal wrongs and damage; includes negligence, libel, slander, assault, and trespass.

Civil law can involve both inter-personal agreements and conflicts. Here, Regina Lewis, daughter of former Boston Celtics star Reggie Lewis, rests in her mother's arms during closing arguments in the Reggie Lewis medical malpractice trial. Donna Harris-Lewis sued her late husband's primary cardi-ologist, Dr. Gilbert Mudge, for damages following Lewis's tragic death. The jury found for Dr. Mudge even though the basketball star had died while in his care.

AP/Wide World Photos

or torts, for example—is that the injured party be compensated for any harm done. The injured person usually initiates proceedings to recover monetary dam-ages. In contrast, when a crime is committed, the state initiates the legal process and imposes a punishment in the form of a criminal sanction. Furthermore, in criminal law, the emphasis is on the intent of the individual committing the crime; a civil proceeding gives primary attention to affixing the blame each party de-serves for producing the damage or conflict.

Despite these major differences, criminal and civil law share certain features. Both seek to control people's behavior by preventing them from acting in an un-desirable manner, and both impose sanctions on those who commit violations of the law. The payment of damages to the victim in a tort case, for example, serves some of the same purposes as the payment of a fine in a criminal case. The criminal law sentences offenders to prison, whereas the civil law also im-poses confinement on such individuals as the mentally ill, alcoholics, and the mentally defective. In addition, many actions, such as assault and battery, vari-ous forms of larceny, and negligence, are the basis for criminal as well as civil actions. Table 4.1 summarizes the similarities and differences between the crim-inal law and tort law.

TABLE 4.1 A COMPARISON OF CRIMINAL AND TORT LAW

Similarities

- Goal of controlling behavior
- Imposition of sanctions
- Some common areas of legal action—for example, personal assault, control of white-collar offenses such as environmental pollution

Differences

Criminal Law	*Tort Law*
Crime is a public offense.	Tort is a civil or private wrong.
The sanction associated with criminal law is incarceration or death.	The sanction associated with tort law is monetary damages.
The right of enforcement belongs to the state.	The individual brings the action.
The government ordinarily does not appeal.	Both parties can appeal.
Fines go to the state.	The individual receives damages as compensation for harm done.

SOURCES OF THE CRIMINAL LAW

The three major sources of the criminal law are (1) common law, statutes, and case decisions, (2) administrative rules and regulations, and (3) constitutional laws.[7]

Essay 3

Common Law, Statutes, and Case Decisions

True/False 4–5

The common law crimes adopted into state codes form one major source of the substantive criminal law today. Under common law, crimes had a general meaning, and everyone basically understood the definitions of such actions as murder, larceny, and rape. Today, statutes enacted by state and federal legislative bodies have built on these common law meanings and often contain more detailed and specific definitions of the crime. Statutes are thus a way in which the criminal law is created, modified, or expunged.

 Crime data are reported in the annual Uniform Crime Reports (UCR). Find out which crimes are considered the most serious at the FBI Web site: http://www.fbi.gov/ucr.htm

For an up-to-date list of Web links, see http://www.wadsworth.com/product/0534573053s

Case law and judicial decision making also change and influence laws. For example, a statute may define murder as the "unlawful killing of one human being by another with malice." Court decisions might help to explain the meaning of the term *malice* or clarify whether a *human being* includes a fetus. A judge may rule that a statute is vague, deals with an act no longer of interest to the public, or is an unfair exercise of state control over an individual.

Administrative Rule Making

True/False 6

Administrative agencies with rule-making authority also develop measures to control conduct in our society. Some agencies regulate taxation, health, environment, and other public functions; others control drugs, illegal gambling, or pornographic material. The listing of prohibited drugs by various state health boards, for example, is an important administrative control function. Parole boards are administrative agencies that implement the thousands of parole regulations that govern the conduct of criminal offenders after their release from prison.

Constitutional Law and Its Limits

Fill in the blanks 5–6
Multiple choice 6–7

Regardless of its source, all criminal law in the United States must conform to the rules and dictates of the U.S. Constitution. Any criminal law that conflicts with the various provisions and articles of the Constitution will eventually be challenged in the appellate courts and stricken from the legal code by judicial order (or modified to adhere to constitutional principles). As Chief Justice John Marshall's opinion in *Marbury v. Madison* indicated, "If the courts are to regard the constitution and the constitution is superior to any ordinary act of the legislature, the constitution and not such ordinary act must govern the case to which they apply."[8]

ex post facto law
A law that makes an act criminal after it was committed or retroactively increases the penalty for a crime.

Among the general limitations set by the Constitution are those that forbid the government to pass **ex post facto laws**. Such laws create crimes (or penalties) that can be enforced retroactively (although civil penalties, such as those set in tax laws, can be retroactive). The Constitution also forbids *bills of attainder,* legislative acts that inflict punishment without a judicial trial.[9] In addition, criminal laws have been interpreted as violating constitutional principles if they are too vague, or broad, to give clear meaning of their intent.

In general, the Constitution has been interpreted to forbid any criminal law that violates a person's right to be treated fairly and equally; this principle is referred to as *substantive due process.* Usually, this means that before a new law can be created, the state must show that there is a compelling need to protect public safety or morals. The Law in Review feature discusses three cases that deal with the constitutionality of the criminal law.

CRIMES: CLASSIFICATIONS AND LEGAL DEFINITIONS

To find out more about the legal definition of various crimes, review state criminal codes at http://www.findlaw.com
For an up-to-date list of Web links, see http://www.wadsworth.com/product/0534573053s

Essay 4

Fill in the blanks 7
True/False 7
Multiple choice 8–9

The decision of how a crime should be classified rests with the individual jurisdiction. Each state has developed its own body of criminal law and consequently determines its own penalties for the different crimes. Thus, the criminal law of a given state defines and grades offenses, sets levels of punishment, and classifies crimes into different categories. Over the years, crimes have generally been grouped into two types of classifications: (1) felonies, misdemeanors, and violations; and (2) other statutory classifications, such as juvenile delinquency, sex-offender categories, and multiple- or first-offender classifications.

Felonies and Misdemeanors

felony
A more serious crime that carries a penalty of incarceration in a state or federal prison, usually for one year or more.

The most common classification in the United States is the division between felonies and misdemeanors. This distinction is based primarily on the seriousness of the crime. Simply put, a **felony** is a serious offense, and a **misdemeanor** is a less serious one.

misdemeanor
A less serious crime usually punishable by a fine or incarceration in a local jail for less than one year.

Each jurisdiction in the United States determines by statute what types of conduct constitute felonies or misdemeanors. The most common definition of a felony is that it is a crime punishable by death or imprisonment in a state or federal prison. Another statutory definition is that a felony is any crime punishable by imprisonment for more than one year. In the former definition, the place of imprisonment is critical; in the latter, the length of the prison sentence distinguishes a felony from a misdemeanor.

Kansas v. Hendricks (1997)

Facts

Leroy Hendricks, an admitted pedophile, has a 40-year history of sexually molesting children. In 1984, Hendricks was convicted in Kansas of sexually abusing two 13-year-old boys.

Shortly before his scheduled release in 1994, Kansas enacted the Sexually Violent Predator Act. The act defines a sexually violent predator as someone who (1) has been convicted or charged with committing a sexually violent act (rape, sexual assault, or sexual exploitation of a child) and (2) has a mental abnormality. The act defines mental abnormality as the inability to control one's sexual conduct to a degree that the person constitutes a menace to the health and safety of others.

The act provides for the involuntary and indeterminate commitment of any person classified as a sexually violent predator. If committed under the statute, the person is placed in a mental health institution, not a prison. It also provides for a number of procedural safeguards to protect the due process rights of any offender committed under the statute: (1) The state must prove beyond a reasonable doubt that the individual is a sexually deviant predator; (2) the individual is entitled to the right to counsel and a jury trial; and (3) the individual is entitled to an annual judicial review where the state must prove again beyond a reasonable doubt that he or she continues to meet the definition of a sexually dangerous individual.

After serving his 10-year prison sentence, Hendricks was involuntarily committed to a mental hospital as a sexually deviant predator after a jury trial under the Kansas statute. Hendricks appealed his civil conviction, and the Kansas Supreme Court struck down the act as a violation of the due process clause. The Kansas court said that a person must be dangerous and mentally ill before being committed involuntarily.

Decision

The U.S. Supreme Court reversed the Kansas court in a 5-to-4 decision written by Justice Clarence Thomas. Thomas ruled that (1) the act did not violate substantive due process and was not punitive in nature, and (2) the act did not violate the double jeopardy clause of the U.S. Constitution, rejecting the defendant's claim that the civil commitment constituted a second punishment. The Court said that Hendrick's diagnosis as a pedophile qualifies as a mental abnormality under the Kansas statute and plainly satisfies due process of law. Defendants like Hendricks can be held indefinitely if considered mentally abnormal. Therefore, the Court ruled that violent sexual predators who are believed to be dangerous can be locked up indefinitely in mental hospitals against their will after completing their sentence, even if not mentally ill. The Kansas Sexually Violent Predator Act did not violate the due process and double jeopardy clauses and was determined to be constitutional.

Significance of the Case

This case will serve as a powerful impetus for states to adopt sexual predator statutes. According to law enforcement officials, the case represents a major victory for crime control in dealing with the problem of recidivist sexual offenders.

Critical Thinking Skills

Each of these cases deals with the ability of the government to regulate the behavior of citizens. These instances are not unique, and there are many other examples of recent governmental efforts to control behaviors that sometimes fall on the borderline of criminality. For example, parental responsibility laws are designed to punish parents for the misbehavior of their children. Do such measures go too far and pose a threat to personal freedoms? Should the ability of the government to control behavior be restricted to only those acts that are actually law violations and not those that merely show a potential for committing future illegal acts? If you answered "yes," then must you disagree with the *Hendricks* decision?

InfoTrac College Edition Research

In the case of *United States v. Morrison,* the U.S. Supreme Court held to the principle that federal statutes that impinge on state responsibility are unconstitutional. Will these kinds of decisions curtail the movement to use the federal criminal law to prevent crime? For answers to this question, see Douglas Husak, "Philosophical Analysis and Limits of Substantive Criminal Law," *Criminal Justice Ethics,* 1999, v18 p58

SOURCES: *United States v. Morrison,* 120 S.Ct. 1740 (2000); *Chicago v. Morales,* 119 S.Ct. 246 (1999); *Kansas v. Hendricks,* 117 S.Ct. 2072 (1997).

FIGURE 4.2
THREE BASIC
ELEMENTS OF
ANY CRIME

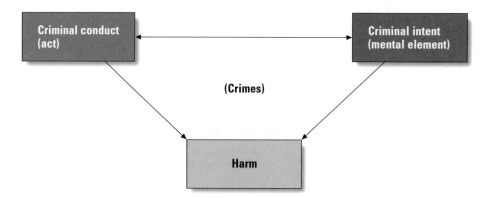

corpus delicti
The body of the crime; all the elements that together constitute a crime, including the criminal act, criminal intent, and the relationship between the two.

that the act was intentional. These elements form what is known as the **corpus delicti**, or "body of the crime." The term is often misunderstood; some people, for instance, wrongly believe that it refers to the body of the deceased in a homicide. Corpus delicti describes all the elements that together constitute a crime; it includes the criminal act, the criminal intent, and the relationship between the two. Together, these elements form the basis for criminal liability (see Figure 4.2).

actus reus
An illegal act, or failure to act when legally required.

Actus Reus The term **actus reus**, which translates as "guilty act," refers to the forbidden act itself. The criminal law uses it to describe the physical crime and/or the commission of the criminal act (or the omission of the lawful act). In *Criminal Law,* Wayne LaFave and Austin Scott state:

> Bad thought alone cannot constitute a crime, there must be an act, or an omission to act where there is a legal duty to act. Thus, the criminal law crimes are defined in terms of act or omission to act and statutory crimes are unconstitutional unless so defined. A bodily movement, to qualify as an act forming the basis of criminal liability, must be voluntary.[11]

The physical act in violation of the criminal statute is usually clearly defined within each offense. For example, in the crime of manslaughter, the unlawful killing of a human being is the physical act prohibited by a statute; in burglary, it is the actual breaking and entering into a dwelling house or other structure for the purpose of committing a felony.

Many jurisdictions hold a person accountable if a legal duty to act exists and the offender avoids it. In most instances, the duty to act is based on a defined relationship such as parent–child or on a contractual duty such as lifeguard–swimmer. The law, for example, recognizes that a parent has a legal duty to protect a child. If a parent refuses to obtain medical attention for the child and the child dies, the parent's actions constitute an omission to act, and that omission is a crime.

Finally, the actus reus must be a measurable act; thought alone is not a crime. However, planning, conspiring, and soliciting for criminal purposes is considered an actus reus, even if the actual crime is never carried out or completed.

mens rea
A guilty mind; the intent to commit a criminal act.

Mens Rea The second element basic to the commission of any crime is the **mens rea**, translated as "guilty mind." Mens rea is the element of the crime that deals with the defendant's intent to commit a criminal act and also includes such states of mind as concealing criminal knowledge, recklessness, negligence, and criminal purpose.[12] A person ordinarily cannot be convicted of a crime unless it is proven that he or she intentionally, knowingly, or willingly committed the criminal act.

The following case illustrates the absence of mens rea. A student at a university took home some books, believing them to be her own, and subsequently found that the books belonged to her classmate. When she realized that the books did not belong to her, she returned them to their proper owner. The student could not be prosecuted for theft because she did not intend to steal the books in the first place; she did not knowingly take someone else's books and therefore lacked sufficient knowledge that her act was unlawful.

Other variations on the concept of criminal intent exist. Different degrees of intent are used to determine the mental state necessary for an individual to commit a particular crime. Where a criminal homicide occurs, it may be necessary to prove that a mental state of premeditation and malice existed in the accused before a judgment of first-degree murder can be reached; for a judgment of second-degree murder, it may be necessary to prove malice; and for a judgment of third-degree murder, it may be necessary to prove guilty knowledge or criminal negligence.

Mens rea conditions also differ among the types of crime when considering whether a general or specific intent to commit the crime exists. For most crimes, a **general intent** on the part of the accused to act purposefully or to accomplish a criminal result must be proved. A **specific intent** requires that the actor intended to accomplish a specific purpose as an element of the crime. Burglary, for example, involves more than the general intent of breaking and entering into a dwelling house; it usually also involves the specific intent of committing a felony, such as stealing money or jewels. Many other crimes such as robbery, larceny, assault with intent to kill, false pretense, and even kidnapping may require a specific intent.

> **general intent**
> Action that on its face indicates a criminal purpose.
>
> **specific intent**
> The intent to accomplish a specific criminal purpose.

In sum, for there to be a criminal violation, criminal intent must ordinarily exist along with criminal conduct. Criminal intent is when a defendant willfully and knowingly acts based on conscious wrongdoing. It consists of two key elements: (1) intent to do an act and (2) knowledge of circumstances that make the act a criminal offense.

Relationship of Mens Rea to Actus Reus The third element needed to prove the corpus delicti of a crime is the relationship of the act to the criminal intent or result. The law requires that the offender's conduct must be the proximate cause of any injury resulting from the criminal act. If, for example, a man chases a victim into the street intending to assault him and the victim is struck and killed by a car,

© Ted Fitzgerald/*The Boston Herald*

To be found guilty of a crime, a person must commit the guilty act (actus reus) and at the same time have sufficient intent (mens rea) as required by law. Here, British au pair Louise Woodward, on trial for the death of Matthew Eappen, the baby left in her care, reacts to the jury's verdict of guilty of second-degree murder. The guilty verdict was later overturned by the trial judge, who ruled that the prosecution had not adequately proved all the elements of the crime.

EXHIBIT 4.1   THE JURY'S CHOICES

The jury in the Massachusetts murder trial of British au pair Louise Woodward, who was accused of killing the baby she was caring for, had four choices:

1. *First-degree murder:* intent to kill or cause harm or injury, or atrocity and extreme cruelty
2. *Second-degree murder:* defendant acted with malice
3. *Not guilty:* the prosecution failed to prove guilt beyond a reasonable doubt
4. *Hung jury:* unable to agree on a verdict

After the jury found her guilty of second-degree murder, Judge Hiller Zobel reduced the verdict to manslaughter because neither the intent to do bodily harm nor malice was present. Involuntary manslaughter is a killing with no intention to cause serious bodily harm, such as acting without proper caution.

The *Commonwealth v. Woodward* case raises a number of criminal law and procedure questions, including:

1. Does a judge have the power to change criminal jury verdicts?
2. Why did the government exercise discretion in its charge against the defendant?
3. Was the interest of justice served in this case?

Suppose you are a criminal attorney and have been assigned the task of coming up with information on criminal homicide. See if you can figure out the distinctions between first- and second-degree murder, as well as voluntary and involuntary manslaughter.

---

the accused could be convicted of murder if the court feels his actions make him responsible for the victim's death. If, however, a victim dies from a completely unrelated illness after being assaulted, the court must determine whether the death was a probable consequence of the defendant's illegal conduct or whether it would have resulted even if the assault had not occurred.

In addition, to prove a crime, the state must show that the external physical act and the internal mental state were in some way connected to each other. For example, if a man breaks into another person's house to escape a violent storm and while in the home notices some jewels and steals them, he cannot be found guilty of the crime of burglary, because he did not intend to commit a crime at the time he broke into the house. Nevertheless, he could be convicted of larceny and criminal trespass, because he had the necessary intent at the time he committed these crimes.

strict liability crime
A criminal violation—usually one that endangers the public welfare—that is defined by the act itself, irrespective of intent.

Strict Liability Existence of a criminal intent and a wrongful act must both be proved before an individual can be found guilty of committing a crime. However, certain statutory offenses exist in which mens rea is not required. These offenses fall within a category known as public welfare crimes, or **strict liability crimes**. A person can be held responsible for such a violation independent of any intent to commit the offense. Strict liability criminal statutes generally include narcotics control laws, traffic laws, health and safety regulations, sanitation laws, and other regulatory statutes. For example, a driver could not defend himself against a speeding ticket by claiming that he was unaware of how fast he was going or did not intend to speed, nor could a bartender claim that a juvenile to whom she sold liquor looked quite a bit older. No state of mind is generally required where a strict liability statute is violated.[13]

Table 4.2 presents some categories of major substantive crimes common to all jurisdictions. The basic elements of each crime are contained within its definition.

CRIMINAL RESPONSIBILITY

The idea of criminal responsibility is essential to any discussion of criminal law. The law recognizes that certain conditions of a person's mental state might excuse him or her from acts that otherwise would be considered criminal. These factors have been used in legal defenses to negate the intent required for the commission of the crime. For example, a person who kills another while insane may argue in

TABLE 4.2 COMMON LAW CRIMES

	Crime	Definition	Example
Crimes against the person	First-degree murder	Unlawful killing of another human being with malice aforethought and with premeditation and deliberation.	A woman buys some poison and pours it into a cup of coffee her husband is drinking, intending to kill him. The motive—to get the insurance benefits of the victim.
	Voluntary manslaughter	Intentional killing committed under extenuating circumstances that mitigate the killing, such as killing in the heat of passion after being provoked.	A husband coming home early from work finds his wife in bed with another man. The husband goes into a rage and shoots and kills both lovers with a gun he keeps by his bedside.
	Battery	Unlawful touching of another with intent to cause injury.	A man seeing a stranger sitting in his favorite seat in the cafeteria goes up to that person and pushes him out of the seat.
	Assault	Intentional placing of another in fear of receiving an immediate battery.	A student aims an unloaded gun at her professor who believes the gun is loaded. The student says she is going to shoot.
	Rape	Unlawful sexual intercourse with a female without her consent.	After a party, a man offers to drive a young female acquaintance home. He takes her to a wooded area and, despite her protests, forces her to have sexual relations with him.
	Robbery	Wrongful taking and carrying away of personal property from a person by violence or intimidation.	A man armed with a loaded gun approaches another man on a deserted street and demands his wallet.
Inchoate (incomplete) offenses	Attempt	An intentional act for the purpose of committing a crime that is more than mere preparation or planning of the crime. The crime is not completed, however.	A person intending to kill another places a bomb in the second person's car, so that it will detonate when the ignition key is used. The bomb is discovered before the car is started. Attempted murder has been committed.
	Conspiracy	Voluntary agreement between two or more persons to achieve an unlawful object or to achieve a lawful object using means forbidden by law.	A drug company sells larger-than-normal quantities of drugs to a doctor, knowing that the doctor is distributing the drugs illegally. The drug company is guilty of conspiracy.
Crimes against property	Burglary	Breaking and entering of a dwelling house of another in the nighttime with the intent to commit a felony.	Intending to steal some jewelry and silver, a young man breaks a window and enters another's house at 10 P.M.
	Arson	Intentional burning of a dwelling house of another.	A secretary, angry that her boss did not give her a raise, goes to her boss's house and sets fire to it.
	Larceny	Taking and carrying away the personal property of another with the intent to steal the property.	While a woman is shopping, she sees a diamond ring displayed at the jewelry counter. When no one is looking, the woman takes the ring and walks out of the store.

court that he or she was not responsible for the criminal conduct. Similarly, a child who violates the law may not be treated as an adult offender. Three major types of criminal defense are detailed in this section: insanity, intoxication, and age.

Insanity

Criminal **insanity** is a legal defense involving the use of rules and standards to determine if a person's state of mental balance negates criminal responsibility. Insanity is a legal concept, not a mental health term. Consequently, there are no

Fill in the blanks 12–14
True/False 10
Multiple choice 12–13
Essay 7

insanity
A legal defense that maintains that the defendant was incapable of forming criminal intent owing to a defect of reason or mental illness.

M'Naghten rule
A legal test that defines insanity as not knowing what one is doing or being unable to distinguish between right and wrong.

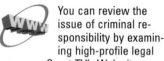 You can review the issue of criminal responsibility by examining high-profile legal cases on Court TV's Web site: http://courttv.com/index.html
For an up-to-date list of Web links, see http://www.wadsworth.com/ product/0534573053s

standard symptoms of insanity or any specific behaviors that determine its existence. Instead, each legal jurisdiction defines insanity as it sees fit and then, at trial, attempts to determine whether the defendant meets the standards set forth in the state's criminal code. Usually, people who claim they are insane are examined by psychologists and psychiatrists who will testify at the trial on the defendant's mental condition.

Legal Definition of Insanity Over the years, the legal system has struggled to define the rules relating to the use of insanity as a defense in a criminal trial. The different tests for criminal responsibility involving insanity followed by U.S. courts are the M'Naghten rule, the irresistible impulse test, the Durham rule, and the substantial capacity test.

The **M'Naghten rule**, or the right–wrong test, is based on the decision in the *M'Naghten* case.[14] In 1843, Daniel M'Naghten shot and killed Edward Drummond, believing Drummond to be Sir Robert Peel, the British prime minister. M'Naghten was prosecuted for murder. At his trial, he claimed that he was not criminally responsible for his actions because he suffered from delusions at the time of the killing. M'Naghten was found not guilty by reason of insanity. Because of the importance of the case and the unpopularity of the decision, the House of Lords reviewed the decision and asked the court to define the law with respect to crimes committed by persons suffering from insane delusions. The court's answer became known as the M'Naghten rule and subsequently became the primary test for criminal responsibility in the United States.

The M'Naghten rule can be stated as follows:

A defendant may be excused from criminal responsibility if at the time the act is committed the accused party suffered under a defect of reason, from a disease of the mind, so as not to know the nature and quality of the act he was doing, or if he did know it, that he did not know that he was doing what was wrong.

Thus, according to the M'Naghten rule, a person is legally insane if, as a result of some mental disability, he or she is unable to distinguish between right and wrong.

Over the years, the courts have become critical of the M'Naghten rule. Many insane individuals are able to distinguish between right and wrong. Also, the courts have never clearly determined the meaning of such phrases as "disease of the mind" and "the nature and quality of the act." As a result, many jurisdictions that follow the M'Naghten rule have supplemented it with the *irresistible impulse test.* This rule excuses from criminal responsibility a person whose mental disease makes it impossible to control personal conduct. The criminal may be able to distinguish between right and wrong but unable to exercise self-control because of a disabling mental condition. Approximately 20 states use a combined M'Naghten rule–irresistible impulse test.

Another test for determining criminal insanity is known as the *Durham rule.* Originally created in New Hampshire in 1871, this standard was reviewed and subsequently adopted by the Court of Appeals for the District of Columbia in 1954 in the case of *Durham v. United States.*[15] In that opinion, Judge David Bazelon rejected the M'Naghten formula and stated that an accused is not criminally responsible if the unlawful act was the product of mental disease or defect. This rule, also known as the *products test,* is based on the contention that insanity is the product of many personality factors.

The Durham rule has been viewed with considerable skepticism, primarily because the problem of defining mental disease, or defect, and product does not give the jury a reliable standard by which to make its judgment. Consequently, it has been dropped in the jurisdictions that experimented with it.

TABLE 4.3 VARIOUS INSANITY DEFENSE STANDARDS

Test	Legal Standard of Mental Illness	Final Burden of Proof	Who Bears Burden of Proof
M'Naghten	"didn't know what he was doing or didn't know it was wrong"	Balance of probabilities	Defense
Irresistible impulse	"could not control his conduct"	Beyond reasonable doubt	Prosecutor
Durham	"The criminal act was caused by his mental illness."	Beyond reasonable doubt	Prosecutor
Substantial capacity	"lacks substantial capacity to appreciate the wrongfulness of his conduct or to control it"	Beyond reasonable doubt	Prosecutor
Present federal law	"lacks capacity to appreciate the wrongfulness of his conduct"	Clear and convincing evidence	Defense

SOURCE: National Institute of Justice, *Crime Study Guide: Insanity Defense,* by Norval Morris (Washington, DC: U.S. Department of Justice, 1986), p. 3.

Another test for criminal insanity is the *substantial capacity test.* As presented in Section 4.01 of the American Law Institute's Model Penal Code, this test states:

> A person is not responsible for criminal conduct if at the time of such conduct as a result of mental disease or defect he lacks substantial capacity to appreciate the criminality (wrongfulness) of his conduct or to conform his conduct to the requirements of law.[16]

This rule is basically a broader restatement of the M'Naghten rule–irresistible impulse test. The most significant feature of this test is that it requires only a lack of "substantial capacity," rather than complete impairment of the defendant's ability to know and understand the difference between right and wrong. Many states use the substantial capacity test as defined by the American Law Institute.

For a summary of various rules for determining criminal insanity, see Table 4.3.

Debate over the Insanity Defense   The insanity defense has been controversial for many years. It has been criticized on the grounds that it (1) spurs crime, (2) releases criminal offenders, (3) requires extensive use of expert testimony, and (4) commits more criminals to mental institutions than to prisons.[17] In addition, according to Norval Morris, defendants end up with a double stigma—that they are "bad and mad"—when they are found not guilty by reason of insanity.[18]

Multiple choice 14–15

In the early 1980s, the case of John Hinckley, Jr., heightened the debate over the insanity plea. Charged with the attempted murder of President Ronald Reagan in 1981, Hinckley pleaded insanity.

Today, many prosecutors, judges, and even mental health experts believe that the Hinckley case points up the need for a verdict of "guilty but insane." Under this provision, if a person uses the insanity defense but a judge or jury finds the evidence insufficient for legal insanity, they can return a verdict of guilty but mentally ill. This indicates that the defendant is suffering from an emotional disorder severe enough to influence behavior but insufficient to render him or her insane. After such a finding, the court can impose any sentence it could have used on the crime charge. The convicted defendant is sent to prison, where the correctional authorities are required to provide therapeutic treatment. If the mental illness is cured, the offender is returned to the regular prison population to serve out the remainder of the sentence.

John Salvi is shown at his trial for murder, stemming from attacks on women's clinics in the Boston area. Salvi, who appeared to be mentally disturbed, was found guilty as charged; he committed suicide while in custody. Should troubled people such as Salvi be found "guilty but mentally ill" and sent to hospitals rather than prisons?

AP/Wide World Photos

Some states provide for a verdict of guilty but mentally ill.[19] John Du Pont, a Pennsylvania multimillionaire, for instance, was found guilty of third-degree murder but mentally ill in the shooting of Olympic wrestler David Schultz in 1996. Du Pont escaped a life sentence because the jury found that his mental illness, identified as paranoid schizophrenia, played a role in the murder. Du Pont was sent to a mental hospital indefinitely. If cured, he will be jailed for 20 to 40 years.

Finally, the federal government has adopted a test of criminal responsibility known as the *appreciation test.* It resembles the M'Naghten test by relying on cognitive incapacity and differs from the substantial capacity test in that the defendant is not required to show lack of control regarding behavior. It also shifts the burden of proof to the defense, who must prove the defense of insanity by clear and convincing evidence.

Despite efforts to ban its use, the insanity plea is probably here to stay. Most crimes require mens rea, and unless we are willing to forgo that standard of law, we will be forced to find not guilty those people whose mental state makes it impossible for them to rationally control their behavior.

Fill in the blanks 15
True/False 11

Intoxication

As a general rule, intoxication, which may include drunkenness or being under the influence of drugs, is not considered a defense. However, a defendant who becomes involuntarily intoxicated under duress or by mistake may be excused for the crimes committed. Voluntary intoxication may also lessen the degree of the crime—for example, a judgment may be decreased from a first- to a second-degree murder because the defendant may use intoxication to prove the lack of the critical element of mens rea, or mental intent. Thus, the effect of intoxication upon criminal liability depends on whether the defendant uses alcohol or drugs voluntarily. For example, a defendant who enters a bar for a few drinks, becomes intoxicated, and strikes someone can be convicted of assault and battery. On the other hand, if the defendant ordered a nonalcoholic drink that was spiked by someone else, the defendant may have a legitimate legal defense.

Given the frequency of drug- and alcohol-related criminal offenses, the impact of intoxication on criminal liability is a common issue in the criminal justice system. The connection between drug use or alcoholism and violent street crime has been well documented. Although those in law enforcement and the judiciary tend to emphasize the use of the penal process in dealing with problems of chronic alcoholism and drug use, others in corrections and crime prevention favor approaches that depend more on behavioral theories and the social sciences. For example, in *Robinson v. California* (1962), the U.S. Supreme Court struck down a California statute making addiction to narcotics a crime on the grounds that it violated the defendant's rights under the Eighth and Fourteenth Amendments to the U.S. Constitution.[20] On the other hand, the landmark decision in *Powell v. Texas* (1968) placed severe limitations on the behavioral science approach when it rejected the defense of chronic alcoholism of a defendant charged with the crime of public drunkenness.[21] The *Powell* case made clear, however, that punishment for a status is unconstitutional.

Age

True/False 12
Multiple choice 16

The law holds that a child is not criminally responsible for actions committed at an age that precludes a full realization of the gravity of certain types of behavior. Under common law, there is generally a conclusive presumption of incapacity for a child under age 7; a reliable presumption for a child between the ages of 7 and 14; and no presumption for a child over the age of 14. This means that, in general, a child under 7 years old who commits a crime will not be held criminally

A student reacts with horror to the carnage at Heath High School in Paducah, Kentucky, where 14-year-old Michael Carneal killed three of his classmates. Should the age of violent juvenile offenders be considered in determining their criminal responsibility? Should a 14-year-old who intentionally kills three people be subject to the death penalty?

AP/Wide World Photos

responsible and a child between 7 and 14 may be held responsible. These common law rules have been changed by statute in most jurisdictions. Today, the maximum age of criminal responsibility for children ranges from 14 to 17, while the minimum age may be set at 7 or under 14.[22]

Every U.S. jurisdiction has established a juvenile court system to deal with juvenile offenders and children in need of court and societal supervision. The mandate of the juvenile justice system is to provide for the care and protection of children under a given age established by state statute. In certain situations, a juvenile court may transfer a more serious chronic youthful offender to the adult criminal court. With the growth of the juvenile law system in the twentieth century, the common law rules on infancy have been modified by juvenile statutes. (The juvenile court system is discussed in Chapter 17.)

CRIMINAL DEFENSE: JUSTIFICATION AND EXCUSE

Criminal defenses may also be based on the concept of *justification* or *excuse*; that is, the commission of a crime may be legally justified or excused on the grounds of fairness and public policy. In these instances, defendants normally acknowledge that they committed the act but claim that they cannot be prosecuted because they were justified in doing so. Four major types of criminal defenses involving justification or excuse are described here—consent; self-defense; entrapment; and mistake, compulsion, and necessity—along with some newer, more exotic defenses (see Table 4.4).

True/False 13

Consent

As a general rule, the victim's consent to a crime does not justify or excuse the defendant who commits the action. The type of crime involved generally determines the validity of consent as an appropriate legal defense. Such crimes as common law rape and larceny require lack of consent on the part of the victim. A rape does not occur if the victim consents to sexual relations; similarly, a larceny cannot occur if the owner voluntarily consents to the taking of the property. In such crimes, lack of consent is an essential element of the crime, and consent is a valid defense where it can be shown that it existed at the time the crime was committed. In statutory rape, however, consent is not a valid defense, because the state presumes that young people are not capable of giving consent.

Multiple choice 17

Self-Defense

In certain circumstances, a defendant who admits to the act that constitutes a crime may claim to be not guilty because of **self-defense**. To establish the neces-

TABLE 4.4 MAJOR DEFENSES

Personal Responsibility	Justification or Excuse	Exotic Defenses
Age	Consent	Euthanasia
Insanity	Self-defense	Civil disobedience
	Entrapment	Mental distress
	Double jeopardy	Premenstrual syndrome
	Mistake	XYY chromosome
	Necessity	Black rage

sary elements to constitute self-defense, the defendant must have acted under a reasonable belief that he or she was in danger of death or great harm and had no means of escape from the assailant.

As a general legal rule, a person defending himself or herself may use only such force as is reasonably necessary to prevent personal harm. A person who is assaulted by another with no weapon is ordinarily not justified in hitting the assailant with a baseball bat. A person verbally threatened by another is not justified in striking the other party. If a woman hits a larger man, generally speaking, the man would not be justified in striking the woman and causing her physical harm. To exercise the self-defense privilege, the danger to the defendant must be immediate. In addition, the defendant is obligated to look for alternative means of avoiding the danger, such as escape or retreat or seeking assistance from others.

The case of Bernhard Goetz, the celebrated "subway shooter," is a well-known example of legal self-defense versus unlawful vigilantism in an urban setting.[23] Goetz, a 37-year-old businessman, shot four black teenagers on a New York City subway train after being asked for $5. Three of the teens were carrying sharpened screwdrivers and had prior arrest records; they had allegedly threatened Goetz. New York state law allows a victim to shoot in self-defense only if there is reasonable belief that the assailant will use deadly force and if the victim cannot escape.

After a much publicized refusal by a first grand jury to indict Goetz for attempted murder, Goetz was subsequently indicted, tried, and acquitted in 1987 of attempted murder and assault but was convicted of illegal possession of an unlicensed concealed handgun. Goetz claimed that he shot the four youths in self-defense because he feared he was about to be robbed. According to the prosecution, Goetz had taken the law into his own hands; Goetz maintained that society needs to be protected from criminals. This bitter and controversial case finally came to an end in January 1989, when Goetz was given a one-year jail sentence for the illegal handgun charge.

Today, there is a good deal of debate over the application of self-defense to a woman who is physically abused by her husband and then kills him. This is known as *battered-wife syndrome* (or in cases involving child abuse, *battered-child syndrome*). Self-defense in such cases often requires the presence of imminent danger and the inability to escape from the assailant.

Entrapment

Entrapment refers to a defense that excuses a defendant from criminal liability when law enforcement agents use traps, decoys, and deception to induce criminal action. It is generally legitimate for law enforcement officers to set traps for criminals by getting information about crimes from informers, undercover agents, and codefendants. Police officers are allowed to use ordinary opportunities for defendants to commit crime and to create these opportunities without excessive inducement and solicitation to commit and involve a defendant in a crime. However, when the police instigate the crime, implant criminal ideas, and coerce individuals into bringing about a crime, defendants can use the defense of entrapment. Entrapment is not a constitutional defense but one created by court decision and statute in most jurisdictions.

The degree of government involvement in a criminal act leading to the entrapment defense has been defined in a number of U.S. Supreme Court decisions, beginning with the 1932 case of *Sorrells v. United States*.[24] During Prohibition, a federal officer passing himself off as a tourist gained the defendant's confidence. The federal agent eventually enticed the defendant to buy illegal liquor for him. The defendant was then arrested and prosecuted for violating the National Prohibition Act. The Supreme Court held that the officer used improper inducements

self-defense
A legal defense that claims a criminal act was justified by an imminent and unavoidable threat to oneself or another person.

True/False 14–15

entrapment
A legal defense that maintains the police originated the criminal idea or initiated the criminal action.

that amounted to entrapment. In deciding this case, the Court settled on the "subjective" view of entrapment, which means that the predisposition of the defendant to commit the offense is the determining factor in entrapment. Following the *Sorrels* case, the Supreme Court stated in *Sherman v. United States* (1958) that the function of law enforcement is to prevent crime and to apprehend criminals, not to implant a criminal design that originates with the officials of the government in the mind of an innocent person.[25]

In 1973, the U.S. Supreme Court again ruled on the issue of entrapment in *United States v. Russell.*[26] In this case, an agent of the Federal Bureau of Narcotics offered to supply defendants with the ingredients necessary to manufacture the drug "speed." The defendants showed the agent the laboratory where speed was produced. The agent eventually obtained a search warrant and arrested the defendants for unlawful manufacture, sale, and delivery of drugs. Defendant Russell raised the defense of entrapment in his criminal trial. The Court ruled that the participation of the narcotics agent was not entrapment in this case and rejected the "objective" test of entrapment, which looks solely to the police conduct to determine if a law-abiding citizen has been persuaded to commit a crime.

In a 1976 case, *Hampton v. United States,* the Court ruled that the defendant's predisposition rendered the entrapment defense unavailable to him even though a federal informant had provided the heroin that the defendant was charged with selling.[27] "The police conduct in Hampton no more deprived the defendant of any right secured to him by the U.S. Constitution than did the police conduct in *Russell* deprive Russell of any rights."

In the most recent entrapment case, *Jacobson v. United States* (1992), a defendant who ordered magazines depicting nude boys was pursued by the government for more than two-and-a-half years for violating a new law relating to minors. In this case, the Court held that the defendant was entrapped because a predisposition to break the law was the result of government coaxing.[28]

Thus, the major legal rule today considers entrapment primarily in light of the defendant's predisposition to commit a crime. A defendant with a criminal record would have a tougher time using this defense successfully than one who had never been in trouble before.

Mistake, Compulsion, and Necessity

Fill in the blanks 16
True/False 16–17

Mistake or ignorance of the law is generally no defense to a crime. According to the great legal scholar William Blackstone, "Ignorance of the law, which everyone is bound to know, excuses no man."[29] Consequently, a defendant cannot present a legitimate defense by saying he or she was unaware of a criminal law, had misinterpreted the law, or believed the law to be unconstitutional.

On the other hand, mistakes of fact, such as taking someone else's coat that is similar to your own, may be a valid defense. If the jury or judge determines that criminal intent was absent, such an honest mistake may remove the defendant's criminal responsibility.

Compulsion or coercion may also be a criminal defense under certain conditions. In these cases, the defendant is forced into committing a crime. For this defense to be upheld, a defendant must show that the actions were the only means of preventing death or serious harm to self or others. For example, a bank employee might be excused from criminal liability in taking bank funds if she can prove that her family was being threatened and that consequently she was acting under duress. However, duress as a defense has limitations; there is widespread agreement, for example, that duress is no defense for an intentional killing.

Closely connected to the defense of compulsion is that of necessity. Necessity may be an acceptable defense, provided the harm to be avoided is greater than the offense charged; it is justified when the crime was committed because other

Acting out of a medical necessity is a defense for crime. Here, Renee Emry-Wolfe arrives by wheelchair at Superior Court in Washington, D.C., for her trial on charges of smoking marijuana in the office of Rep. Bill McCollum (R-Fla.). Emry-Wolfe, 38, of Ann Arbor, Michigan, who suffers from multiple sclerosis, smoked the marijuana to protest an anti–medicinal marijuana resolution introduced by Rep. McCollum. Should her criminal action be excused because of her medical need?

AP/Wide World Photos

circumstances could not be avoided. For example, a husband steals a car to bring his pregnant wife to the hospital for an emergency delivery, or a hunter shoots an animal of an endangered species that was about to attack her. The defense has been found inapplicable, however, where defendants sought to shut down nuclear power plants or abortion clinics or to destroy missile components under the belief that their actions were necessary to save lives or prevent a nuclear war. Even those who use a controlled substance such as marijuana for medicinal purposes often cannot claim vindication based on medical necessity. The classic topic for discussion on necessity is the English case of the *Queen v. Dudley and Stephens,* in which the defendants killed a cabin boy and ate his remains as a necessity for survival while they awaited rescue in a lifeboat on the high seas. Should the defendants have been convicted of murder?[30] (They were convicted but were later pardoned.)

Exotic Defenses

True/False 18

The courts have also grappled with such controversial defenses as euthanasia (mercy killing), civil disobedience, and the cultural defense (taking into account the beliefs, customs, and traits of a specific racial or ethnic group).[31]

Today, mental distress seems to be a favorite maneuver in high-profile criminal cases. Lorena Bobbitt was acquitted by convincing a jury that physical and

Public Policy through Lawmaking

Of all the industrialized nations, the United States has one of the highest rates of violent crime. U.S. lawmakers are increasingly disposed to prevent and control antisocial behavior by passing new and often tougher criminal statutes. A number of these anticrime measures are summarized here.

Domestic or family violence legislation. Abuse of family members has become a major public issue; in all states today, it is a criminal offense. Courts have expanded sentencing powers in domestic abuse cases, and the new legislation often defines more broadly the victims and the crimes against them. Experts believe that omnibus family statutes are an essential way to strengthen and support individuals and families at risk from domestic violence and abuse.

Tough recidivist statutes. Many jurisdictions have enacted "three strikes" laws to increase the period of imprisonment for persons previously convicted of two felony offenses. There are even "two strikes" measures that impose life without parole for a second violent offense. Such criminal laws, enacted through both legislation and voter initiative, express the intent to abrogate judges' authority in the interest of justice and public safety. Such statutes are often attacked as being in violation of the cruel and unusual punishment clause of the state and federal constitutions.

Gun laws. Although legislators often shy away from laws limiting or banning guns, particularly because of the gun lobby led by the National Rifle Association, the federal government has made progress in restricting and regulating gun use in the past few years, as have many states. There is now a five-day waiting period on handgun purchases as a result of the Brady Handgun Violence Prevention Act, and a 10-year federal ban on the manufacture, trade, and possession of 19 semiautomic assault weapons. The Supreme Court has ruled on numerous occasions that gun restrictions do not violate individual rights.

Community notification laws. Innovative criminal statutes are being passed requiring that residents be made aware of ex-felony offenders, such as convicted sex offenders, who move into their neighborhood. One such statute, known as Megan's Law, was passed in New Jersey after the killing of a child by a convicted sex offender who, unknown to the community, had moved in across the street from the victim.

Drug laws. Congress and state legislatures keep passing laws dealing with possession, use, and sale of illegal drugs. More individuals are incarcerated today for drug offenses than for all violent crimes, and today's prisons are filled wall-to-wall with drug dealers and addicts. Legalizing drugs does not appear to be in the future, so it is likely that conservative legislators will use the criminal laws to incarcerate even more drug violators while providing only marginal treatment and aftercare. In addition, the majority of states have instituted unusual statutes against HIV-positive people who don't take precautions or don't tell sex partners about the risks of infection.

Stalking statutes. Recent laws have designated stalking as a criminal offense. States typically define stalking as the willful, malicious, and repeated following and harassing of another person. Although many of these new laws were passed to protect women terrorized by former boyfriends or husbands, the laws also often apply to women or men stalked by casual acquaintances or even strangers.

sexual abuse removed her responsibility for the mutilation of her husband. The Menendez brothers' trial, in which they used a defense of childhood abuse, resulted in a hung jury. A good deal of debate rages over the application of self-defense to a woman who is battered by her husband and then kills him.

Alan Dershowitz, the well-known Harvard Law School professor, dubs such defenses the "abuse excuses" or soft defenses.[32] They include premenstrual syndrome, posttraumatic stress, black rage, cocaine-induced psychosis, XYY chromosome, and many others. All of these defenses boil down to one thing—an effort by a defense attorney to limit individual criminal responsibility. Prosecutors believe that defendants are raising almost any kind of excuse for their behavior—that if everyone is a victim, there can be no criminals. Thus, the principles of criminal responsibility are often the central element of criminal jurisprudence. Most of these bizarre and unusual defenses, however, are unacceptable in the criminal trial.

Software piracy. Computers and technology play a significant role in our society, and technology is viewed as an increasingly important development in the fight against crime (fingerprint analysis, DNA profiling, and so on). At the same time, however, defendants are being charged with violating laws against illegal computer software use for commercial gain. Federal and state governments are passing statutes against illegally distributing software and infringing on software copyrights. In recent years, indictments for illegally copying software have been prosecuted under wire fraud statutes, but this often means that home computer users who make a single copy of a software program for their own use would be subject to criminal prosecution. This underscores the need to develop criminal statutes allowing for the prosecutuion of software theft by computer, as well as Internet violations, on a global basis.

Critical Thinking Skills

1. In recent years, policymakers have concentrated heavily on laws crafted to deal with violent crime and domestic abuse, with punishment as the theme. Might not some people be unfairly punished under such statutes? What really distinguishes the "three strikes" acts from other laws involving chronic offenders? Should domestic violence laws require treatment responses and assistance to families in addition to incarceration?

2. Ensuring the right to due process is an issue in virtually all new criminal law regulation. What constitutional issues are raised by antistalking legislation, recidivism statutes, gun control laws, and domestic violence codes?

InfoTrac College Edition Research

New criminal statutes often provoke more debate than any other criminal justice issue. To learn more about the statutory perspective on crime control, read
John Schafer, "The Deterrent Effect of Three Strikes Laws," *FBI Law Enforcement Bulletin,* 1999, v68 p5

Another policy issue involving the criminal law is whether states can develop effective stalking statutes. A major survey reveals that the stalking problem is more prevalent than previously believed. More than 1,000,000 women (over 8%) and 370,000 men (2%) are stalked at some time in their lives. Many state laws are inadequate to deal with the problem. For more information, see
National Violence Against Women Survey, "Stalking in America," *Journal of State Government,* 1998, v71 p20

SOURCES: Donna Hunzeker, "Significant State Anti-Crime Legislation," *National Conference of State Legislatures* 19 (1994): 1–90; Joseph Califano, "It's Drugs, Stupid," *New York Times Magazine,* 29 January 1995, p. 41; National Conference of State Legislatures, *1997 State Legislative Summary* (Denver: National Conference, 1997); Michael Higgins, "Is Capital Punishment for Killers Only?" *American Bar Association Journal* 83 (1997): 30; U.S. Department of Justice, *Stalking and Domestic Violence* (Washington, DC: Office of Justice Programs, 1998); "America under the Gun: Special Report," *Newsweek,* 23 August 1999.

SUBSTANTIVE CRIMINAL LAW REFORM

In recent years, many states and the federal government have been examining and revising their substantive and procedural criminal codes. An ongoing effort has been made to update legal codes so that they provide an accurate reflection of public opinion, social change, technological innovation, and other important social issues.

What kind of criminal statutes do we need today? Should it be a crime to aid and abet a suicide? What about stalking statutes that make it a crime to harass or follow someone? In the Violent Crime Control and Law Enforcement Act of 1994, the federal government increased its jurisdiction over many crimes traditionally within state police powers, such as crimes committed with guns, gang crimes, and offenses involving frauds and the adult prosecution of juvenile offenders.[33] The proliferation of such new laws is discussed in the Analyzing Criminal Justice Issues feature.

Some actions considered a crime years ago—such as performing an abortion—are no longer a crime today. In this instance, clouds of protest continue to surround the issue as pro- and antiabortion groups argue the merits of government intervention in such decisions.

One aspect of criminal law reform involves weeding out laws that seem archaic in light of what is now known about human behavior; for example, alcoholism is now considered a disease that should be treated, not an offense that should be punished. Many experts believe that offenses such as drunkenness, disorderly conduct, vagrancy, gambling, and minor sexual and drug violations are essentially social problems and should not be dealt with by the criminal justice system.

True/False 19

The RICO Statute

Racketeer Influenced and Corrupt Organization Act (RICO)
Federal legislation that enables prosecutors to bring additional criminal or civil charges against people whose multiple criminal acts constitute a conspiracy.

In an effort to control organized crime, Congress passed the **Racketeer Influenced and Corrupt Organization Act (RICO)**. This law prevents people from acquiring or maintaining an interest in an ongoing enterprise, such as a union or legitimate business, with funds derived from illegal enterprises and racketeering activities.[34]

RICO did not create new categories of crime, but it did create new categories of offenses in racketeering activity, which it defined as involvement in two or more acts prohibited by 24 existing federal statutes and 8 state statutes. The offenses listed in RICO include such state-defined crimes as murder, kidnapping, gambling, arson, robbery, bribery, extortion, and narcotic violations and such federally defined crimes as bribery, counterfeiting, transmission of gambling information, prostitution, and mail fraud.

An individual convicted under RICO is often subject to a long prison term and a huge fine. Additionally, the accused must forfeit to the U.S. government any interest in a business in violation of RICO. These penalties are much more potent than simple conviction and imprisonment. In addition, a separate civil provision of the law permits private parties to sue for racketeering and obtain treble damages.[35]

Using RICO, U.S. attorneys have attacked the leadership of major organized crime families and obtained convictions of high-ranking mafiosi for insider trading, stock fraud, and software piracy. The major target of the RICO statute, however, continues to be the infiltration of legitimate business by organized crime.

Fill in the blanks 17

Federal Crime Legislation: 1984–2000

One of the most significant criminal law revisions in the last two decades was the 1984 Comprehensive Crime Control Act.[36] This federal legislation reformed a code that had been criticized for its complexity and inconsistency. Among the most important changes is the treatment of the insanity defense. In the past, federal prosecutors had the burden of proving that a defendant was sane; now, the burden of proof for insanity has shifted to the defendant. In addition, the new federal code eliminates parole and requires that criminal punishments be imposed more fairly and evenhandedly. Another important provision allows judges to retain offenders in jail before trial if they are considered a danger to the community or themselves; preventive detention is a significant change in the nation's bail system.

Amid much national concern about drugs, Congress passed the Omnibus Drug Law of 1988.[37] Earmarking billions of dollars for antidrug activities, the law called for increased drug education and treatment programs and broader federal drug interdiction efforts. This legislation is in large measure the basis for U.S. drug enforcement policy today.

In 1990, Congress passed the Omnibus Crime Control Act. Some significant provisions of this act are (1) improvements in public defender services; (2) the implementation of "shock incarceration" programs in federal and state correctional systems; (3) reforms in the investigation of child abuse cases; (4) efforts to aid crime victims through the Victims Rights and Restitution Act of 1990; (5) authorization for a study of mandatory sentencing by the U.S. Sentencing Commission; (6) provisions dealing with drugs; and (7) the development of new offenses and penalties relating to the savings and loan scandals.[38]

The desire to be tough on crime has been a top priority among politicians. Federal crime legislation under the Clinton administration included the Brady Handgun Violence Prevention Act of 1993 and the Violent Crime Control and Law Enforcement Act of 1994.[39] The largest crime bill in U.S. history, the 1994 law expanded the scope of the death penalty and authorized billions of dollars for more police officers, prisons, and crime prevention programs. The Brady law, which requires a waiting period before an individual can buy a handgun, has stopped some stalkers, felons, and drug users from acquiring handguns. The law's overall effect on crime is still being debated.

The Brady law came under constitutional review in the 1997 case of *Printz v. United States*.[40] The law mandated local law enforcement officials to conduct background checks on prospective gun purchasers until a federal computerized checking system could be completed. Local sheriffs argued that this provision illegally forced them to administer a federal regulatory program. The Supreme Court agreed and declared the part of the Brady law requiring background checks unconstitutional because it violated state sovereignty under the Tenth Amendment.

Two recent pieces of crime legislation are the Antiterrorism and Effective Death Penalty Act and the Violence Against Women Act, both passed in 1996. The antiterrorism law was a direct response to the 1995 bombing of the federal building in Oklahoma City. Many of its provisions relate to terrorist activity, but it also revises federal habeas corpus proceedings. Known as the *great writ*, habeas corpus is a procedure for obtaining judicial determination of the legality of an individual's custody. The new legislation seeks to reduce the delay often attributable to habeas corpus proceedings in capital cases.[41] The Violence Against Women Act provides for federal criminal prosecution of gender-based violent crimes and civil suits for sexual assault.[42]

CONSTITUTIONAL CRIMINAL PROCEDURE

Whereas substantive criminal law primarily defines crimes, the law of criminal procedure consists of the rules and procedures that govern the pretrial processing of criminal suspects and the conduct of criminal trials. The principles that govern criminal procedure flow from the relationship between the individual and the state. They include (1) a belief in the presumption of innocence, (2) the right to a defense against criminal charges, and (3) the requirement that the government act in a lawful manner. Based on the U.S. Constitution, these policies are generally mandated by the provisions of state constitutions.

A sound understanding of criminal procedure requires an awareness of constitutional law. The basic principles of constitutional criminal procedure follow; the key cases involving criminal procedure and the police are discussed in Chapter 8.

True/False 20–21

The U.S. Constitution

The U.S. Constitution has played and continues to play a critical role in the development of the criminal law used in the criminal justice system.

The forerunner of the Constitution was the Articles of Confederation, adopted by the Continental Congress in 1781. The articles were found to be generally inadequate as the foundation for effective government because they did not create a proper balance of power between the states and the central government. As a result, in 1787 the Congress of the Confederation adopted a resolution calling for a convention of delegates from the original states. Meeting in Philadelphia, the delegates' express purpose was to revise the Articles of Confederation. The work of that convention culminated in the drafting of the Constitution; it was ratified by the states in 1788 and put into effect in 1789.

In its original form, the Constitution consisted of a preamble and seven articles. The Constitution divided the powers of government into three independent but equal parts: the executive, the legislative, and the judicial branches. The purpose of the separation of powers was to ensure that no single branch of the government could usurp power for itself and institute a dictatorship. The measures and procedures initiated by the framers of the Constitution have developed over time into our present form of government.

How does the Constitution, with its formal set of rights and privileges, affect the operations of the criminal justice system? One way is to guarantee that no one branch of government can in and of itself determine the fate of those accused of crimes. The workings of the criminal justice process illustrate this principle. A police officer, who represents the executive branch of the government, makes an arrest on the basis of laws passed by the legislative branch, and the accused is subsequently tried by the judiciary. In this way, citizens are protected from the arbitrary abuse of power by any single element of the law.

Fill in the blanks 18
True/False 22–23
Multiple choice 18–21

The Bill of Rights

In addition to providing protection by ensuring a separation of powers within the government, the Constitution also controls the operations of the criminal justice system. It does this by guaranteeing individual freedoms in the 10 amendments added to it on December 15, 1791, known collectively as the Bill of Rights.[43]

The Bill of Rights was added to the Constitution to prevent any future government from usurping the personal freedom of citizens. In its original form, the Constitution contained few specific guarantees of individual rights. The Founders, aware of the past abuses perpetrated by the British government, wanted to ensure that the rights of U.S. citizens would be safe in the future. The Bill of Rights only protected individual liberties from abuse by the national government, however; it did not apply to the actions of state or local officials. This oversight resulted in abuses that have been rectified only with great difficulty and even today remain the subject of court action.

Over the past four decades, the U.S. Supreme Court's interpretation of the Constitution has served as the basis for the creation of legal rights of the accused. The principles that govern criminal procedures are required by the U.S. Constitution and the Bill of Rights. Of primary concern are the Fourth, Fifth, Sixth, and Eighth Amendments, which limit and control the manner in which the federal government operates the justice system. In addition, the due process clause of the Fourteenth Amendment has helped define the nature and limits of government action against those accused on the state level. Because these key amend-

If citizens were not protected by constitutional guarantees, they would be at the mercy of overzealous law enforcement agencies. Here, Richard Jewell, accompanied by his mother, speaks to the press after having been cleared by the FBI of any involvement in the bombing in Atlanta during the 1996 Olympics. Jewell's case illustrates what can happen to innocent people when police are under intense pressure to identify suspects and make arrests.

© John Kuntzer/Sipa Press

ments furnish the basis for our system of criminal procedure, they will each be examined in turn.

The Fourth Amendment The Fourth Amendment to the U.S. Constitution provides some of the major limits on police behavior. It states:

> The right of the people to be secure in their persons, houses, papers, and effects, against unreasonable searches and seizures, shall not be violated, and no warrants shall issue, but upon probable cause, supported by oath or affirmation, and particularly describing the place to be searched, and the persons or things to be seized.

The Fourth Amendment is especially important for the criminal justice system because it means that police officers cannot indiscriminately use their authority to investigate a possible crime or arrest a suspect unless either or both actions are justified by the law and the facts of the case. Stopping, questioning, or searching an individual without legal justification represents a serious violation of the Fourth Amendment right to personal privacy.

The Fifth Amendment Limiting the admissibility of confessions that have been obtained unfairly is another method of controlling police behavior. The right against **self-incrimination** is frequently asserted by a defendant in an effort to exclude confessions or admissions that might be vital to the government's case. In such instances, the meaning of the Fifth Amendment to the U.S. Constitution is critical. The amendment states:

self-incrimination
A person's spoken or written statement that can be used against him or her as evidence in a criminal matter; such statements may not be coerced.

> No person shall be held to answer for a capital, or otherwise infamous crime, unless on a presentment or indictment of a grand jury, except in cases arising in the land or naval forces, or in the militia, when in actual service in time of war or public danger; nor shall any person be subject for the same offense to be twice put in jeopardy of life or limb; nor shall be compelled in any criminal case to be a witness against himself, nor be deprived of life, liberty, or property, without due process of law; nor shall private property be taken for public use, without just compensation.

The Fifth Amendment has had a tremendous impact on the U.S. criminal justice system. In 1966, for instance, in the landmark case of *Miranda v. Arizona,* the

U.S. Supreme Court held that a person accused of a crime has the right to refuse to answer questions when placed in police custody.[44]

The Sixth Amendment   The Sixth Amendment states:

> In all criminal prosecutions, the accused shall enjoy the right to a speedy and public trial, by an impartial jury of the state and district wherein the crime shall have been committed, which district shall have been previously ascertained by law, and to be informed of the nature and cause of the accusation; to be confronted with the witnesses against him; to have compulsory process for obtaining witnesses in his favor; and to have the assistance of counsel for his defense.

One of the goals of the framers of the Constitution was to ensure that criminal defendants received a fair trial. Their concerns stemmed from abuses to human rights that had occurred in England and other European nations. For example, in the seventeenth century, an English court known as the Star Chamber tried persons charged with political crimes in secret and judged them with little regard to fairness or due process of law. To protect U.S. citizens from such practices, the Sixth Amendment sets out rights guaranteed to all people facing criminal charges.

Many Supreme Court decisions regarding the Sixth Amendment have concerned the individual's right to counsel. The right of a defendant to be represented by an attorney has been extended to numerous stages of the criminal justice process, including pretrial custody, identification and lineup procedures, preliminary hearing, submission of a guilty plea, trial, sentencing, and postconviction appeal.

The Eighth Amendment   According to the Eighth Amendment,

> Excessive bail shall not be required, nor excessive fines imposed, nor cruel and unusual punishments inflicted.

bail
A monetary amount set by a judge as a condition of pretrial release to ensure the defendant's appearance at subsequent proceedings; if the defendant fails to appear, bail is forfeited.

Bail is a money bond put up by the accused to attain freedom between the time of arrest and the trial. Bail is meant to ensure a trial appearance, so the bail money is forfeited if the defendant misses the trial date.

The Eighth Amendment does not guarantee a constitutional right to bail but rather prohibits the exactment of excessive bail. Nevertheless, because many state statutes place no precise limit on the amount of bail a judge may impose, many poorer defendants cannot make bail and are placed in detention while awaiting trial.

cruel and unusual punishment
Treatment that degrades human dignity, is disproportionately severe, or shocks the general conscience; prohibited by the Eighth Amendment to the U.S. Constitution.

The Eighth Amendment also forbids the use of torture and excessive physical punishment. In the early history of Europe, convicted criminals were often subjected to bizarre and cruel methods of execution, including burning, being slowly crushed with heavy objects, and even being pulled apart by horses. Consequently, the prohibition against **cruel and unusual punishment** was added to the Eighth Amendment. This prohibition has affected the imposition of the death penalty and other criminal dispositions and has become a guarantee that serves to protect accused and convicted offenders from actions regarded as unacceptable by a civilized society.

True/False 24–25
Multiple choice 22
Essay 8

THE STATE CRIMINAL JUSTICE SYSTEM UNDER THE U.S. CONSTITUTION

The Fourteenth Amendment has been the vehicle most often used to apply the protection of the Bill of Rights to the states. The Fourteenth Amendment states:

> All persons born or naturalized in the United States, and subject to the jurisdiction thereof, are citizens of the United States and of the state wherein they reside. No state

shall make or enforce any law which shall abridge the privileges or immunities of citizens of the United States; nor shall any state deprive any person of life, liberty, or property, without due process of law; nor deny to any person within its jurisdiction the equal protection of the laws.

The most important aspect of this amendment is the clause that says no state shall "deprive any person of life, liberty, or property, without due process of law." This means that the same general constitutional restrictions previously applicable only to the federal government are also applicable to the states.

It is essential to keep the following constitutional principles in mind while examining the Fourteenth Amendment:

1. The Bill of Rights originally applied only to the federal government. These amendments to the U.S. Constitution were designed to protect citizens against injustices inflicted by federal authorities. The Bill of Rights restricts the actions of the federal government; it does not apply to the states.
2. The Fourteenth Amendment's due process clause applies to state governments. It has been used to provide individuals in all states with the basic liberties guaranteed by the Bill of Rights.
3. The U.S. Supreme Court has expanded the rights of defendants in the criminal justice system by interpreting the due process clause to mean that the states must be held to standards similar to those made applicable to the federal government by the Bill of Rights.

Through a long series of decisions, the Supreme Court has held that the guarantees of the First, Fourth, Fifth, Sixth, and Eighth Amendments apply to the states as well as to the federal government. The movement to make the Bill of Rights applicable to the states gained impetus during the second half of the twentieth century. It is based on a number of legal theories that describe the relationship of the Bill of Rights to the Fourteenth Amendment.

The first theory, known as the **incorporation theory**, states that all the provisions of the Bill of Rights are incorporated into the Fourteenth Amendment's due process clause. Thus, the fundamental rights such as freedom from unreasonable search and seizure, the right to a jury trial, and the right to counsel are all considered binding on the states through the Fourteenth Amendment. The idea of total incorporation has never received majority support in any Supreme Court decision, however; nor has it been accepted in any substantial way by legal scholars and historians. Those supporting total incorporation argue that an individual is a citizen of both the federal government and a state government and should receive similar protections from each. Those arguing against this position believe that states should be allowed to develop their own criminal procedures.

The most widely recognized theory of constitutional responsibility is the theory of **selective incorporation**, which states that the Bill of Rights does apply to the states through the due process clause of the Fourteenth Amendment but only on a case-by-case basis. Advocates of this theory believe that some of the provisions of the Bill of Rights may be binding on the states—such as the right to a jury trial or the right to be free from self-incrimination—but that these should apply only after a careful consideration of the facts, or merits, of each case.

Under this formula, the incorporation of the provisions of the Bill of Rights into the Fourteenth Amendment has moved forward slowly on a case-by-case basis, accelerating in 1953 when Earl Warren became chief justice of the Supreme Court. Under his leadership, the due process movement reached its peak. The Court decided numerous landmark cases focusing on the rights of the accused and brought about a revolution in the area of constitutional criminal procedure.

Today, the Fourteenth Amendment's due process clause has been interpreted by the U.S. Supreme Court to mean that an accused in a state criminal case is

incorporation theory
The view that all provisions of the Bill of Rights are incorporated into the Fourteenth Amendment's due process clause and are therefore binding on the states.

selective incorporation
The view that the rights and privileges in the Bill of Rights can be applied to the states through the due process clause of the Fourteenth Amendment, but only on a case-by-case basis.

FIGURE 4.3
RELATIONSHIP
OF THE BILL OF
RIGHTS AND THE
FOURTEENTH
AMENDMENT
TO THE
CONSTITUTIONAL
RIGHTS OF THE
ACCUSED

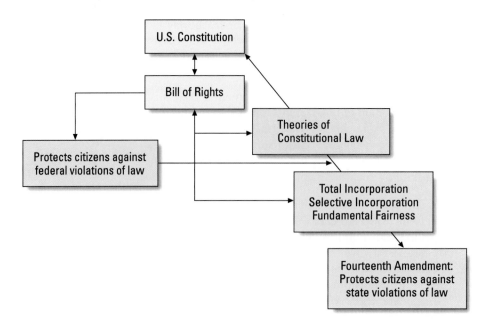

entitled to the same protections available under the federal Bill of Rights. A diagram of the relationship between the Bill of Rights and the Fourteenth Amendment is presented in Figure 4.3.

PROCEDURAL DUE PROCESS OF LAW

due process
Constitutional safeguards against arbitrary and unfair state procedures in judicial or administrative proceedings.

Multiple choice 23
Essay 9

The concept of **due process** has been used as a basis for incorporating the Bill of Rights into the Fourteenth Amendment. Due process has also been used to evaluate the constitutionality of legal statutes and to set standards and guidelines for fair procedures in the criminal justice system. In seeking to define the meaning of the term, most legal experts believe that it refers to the essential elements of fairness under law.

This definition is based on the legal system's need for rules and regulations that protect individual rights. The actual objectives of due process help define the term even more explicitly. Due process seeks to ensure that no person will be deprived of life, liberty, or property without notice of charges, assistance from legal counsel, a hearing, and an opportunity to confront those making the accusations. Basically, due process is intended to guarantee that fundamental fairness exists in each individual case. However, abstract definitions are only one aspect of due process. Much more significant are the procedures that give meaning to due process in the everyday practices of the criminal justice system. These procedural due process safeguards are listed in Exhibit 4.2.

Exactly what constitutes due process in a specific case depends on the facts of the case, the federal and state constitutional and statutory provisions, previous court decisions, and the ideas and principles that society considers important at a given time and in a given place. The degree of loss suffered by the individual (victim or offender) balanced against the state's interests also determines which and how many due process requirements are ordinarily applied. The essence of

EXHIBIT 4.2 PROCEDURAL DUE PROCESS RIGHTS

- Notice of charges
- A formal hearing
- The right to counsel or some other representation
- The opportunity to respond to charges
- The opportunity to confront and cross-examine witnesses and accusers
- The right to be free from self-incrimination
- The opportunity to present one's own witnesses
- A decision made on the basis of substantial evidence and facts produced at the hearing
- A written statement of the reasons for the decision
- An appellate review procedure

due process, however, is adequate notice and a fair hearing in both the civil and the criminal law.

FUTURE DIRECTIONS IN CRIMINAL LAW AND PROCEDURE

Multiple choice 24–25

Despite current problems with the criminal justice system, much progress has been made in the field of criminal law and constitutional procedure over the past 30 years. The future direction of the criminal law in the United States remains unclear. There seems to be less tolerance for government corruption, more public interest in fixed sentences and capital punishment, and more conservative decision making by judicial bodies. More attention will probably be paid to the substantive nature of criminal law, particularly where it seems important to the preservation of U.S. society. For example, special prosecutors, using criminal statutes involving conspiracy, perjury, and fraud, were able to uncover the illegal operations in the Nixon administration of the 1970s and to examine the Reagan administration's activities in the 1980s. In the Bush and Clinton administrations of the 1990s, efforts were made to prosecute such diverse crimes as those involved in the savings and loan scandals and the alleged infiltration of legitimate businesses by organized crime. The criminal law system has demonstrated amazing resilience in its ability to prosecute public officials and private citizens whose behavior has damaged the government.

An expansion of the criminal law itself can also be anticipated. Areas of expansion will probably include a greater emphasis on controlling career criminals. Laws making it easier for states to punish serious juvenile offenders and incarcerate them in secure adult institutions will probably be passed. More attention will be given to white-collar crimes, as well as to drug-related crimes and terrorism. Corporations are almost certainly going to be held accountable for their illegal acts, especially those that result in physical as well as economical harm. Stock market and computer activities will receive close scrutiny by law enforcement agencies, as will child abuse and domestic violence.

Software piracy in particular is receiving greater emphasis as computers and technology play an ever-increasing role in our society. This will lead to the development of criminal statutes allowing for the prosecution of software theft by computer, as well as Internet violations, on a global basis.

Finally, the legal system will continue to be faced with difficult challenges involving AIDS. Some criminal laws specifically attempt to control the activities of prisoners, prostitutes, drug users, and criminal defendants who are HIV positive, to protect others from contracting the disease.

Regardless of what changes occur in the future, the criminal law system will continute to deal with four fundamental problems: (1) defining and classifying antisocial behavior; (2) establishing appropriate criminal sanctions or punishments; (3) applying the proper degree of criminal responsibility; and (4) determining what departures from due process safeguards may require the reversal of a conviction.

More than any other factor, the role of the Supreme Court will dominate the future direction of criminal law and procedure in the United States. In the second half of the twentieth century, the Court was the setting for a number of important developments in the administration of criminal justice. During the Earl Warren era of the 1960s, the Court took a decidedly liberal turn in granting individual rights for the accused. In the 1970s and 1980s, Nixon's conservatives—Justices Warren Burger and William Rehnquist—curbed the growth of criminal procedure rights. With the replacement of liberal Justice William Brennan by moderate David Souter of New Hampshire in 1990 and the controversial appointment of conservative Clarence Thomas to replace Thurgood Marshall in

More biographical information about U.S. Supreme Court justices, their philosophies, and voting can be found at http://oyez.nwu.edu/justices/justices.cgi

For an up-to-date list of Web links, see http://www.wadsworth.com/product/0534573053s

1. **The Warren Court**
Chief Justice Earl Warren
1953–1969
Philosophy: The Warren Court was instrumental in granting new constitutional rights to those accused of crimes and extended due process protections to defendants throughout various stages of the justice system.
Case Examples: *Mapp v. Ohio* (1961)—evidence obtained by illegal means cannot be used in a criminal trial; *Miranda v. Arizona* (1966)—an accused person must be informed of his or her constitutional rights before being questioned.

2. **The Burger Court**
Chief Justice Warren Burger
1969–1986
Philosophy: The Burger Court helped moderate the liberal direction that the Court had taken under Chief Justice Warren. It removed long-standing restrictions on the police and prosecuting attorneys and upheld the use of capital punishment, while supporting the right to counsel for all defendants.

Case Examples: *Greg v. Georgia* (1976)—the death penalty is constitutional when state statutes provide fair procedures for its use; *Argersinger v. Hamlin* (1972)—no person can be imprisoned for any offense, whether classified as a misdemeanor or a felony, without benefit of counsel.

3. **The Rehnquist Court**
Chief Justice William Rehnquist
1986–Present
Philosophy: The Rehnquist Court has centered around a conservative philosophy on such issues as police surveillance, right to counsel, and trial procedures. However, the appointment of Justices Ginsberg (1993) and Breyer (1994) has produced a more moderate direction in judicial decisions.
Case Examples: *Dickerson v. U.S.* (2000)—*Miranda* warnings remain a necessary constitutional step to confession admissability; *Illinois v. Wardlow* (2000)—a defendant's flight from a police officer in a high-crime area raises reasonable suspicion sufficient for the officer to search the individual for weapons.

1991, the Court continues to hand down legally conservative opinions favoring state law enforcement over criminal defendants.[45] (See Exhibit 4.3.)

More recently, the philosophical direction of the Court seems to be veering toward a middle course. President Clinton's appointment of Ruth Bader Ginsburg in 1993 to succeed Justice Byron White tempered the Court's conservatism. In 1994, Clinton appointed Stephen Breyer, a Boston federal appellate court judge, to replace Justice Harry Blackmun. Because Breyer does not have a distinct ideology, his addition adds to the moderate bent of the Court.

Today, the nine-member Court is made up of competing blocs of four liberal-to-moderate judges (John Paul Stevens, Ruth Bader Ginsberg, Stephen Breyer, and David Souter) and three conservative justices (Antonin Scalia, Clarence Thomas, and Chief Justice William Rehnquist). In the middle are Sandra Day O'Connor and Anthony Kennedy, who often are the deciding votes on criminal law and procedure cases.[46] Figure 4.4 identifies how the individual justices on the Court might view actual cases on criminal justice issues for years to come.

Finally, President George W. Bush may have the opportunity to nominate two or even three justices to the Supreme Court, possibly affecting the orientation of the nine-member Court well into the twenty-first century.

SUMMARY

The purpose of criminal law is to regulate behavior and maintain order in society. What constitutes a crime is defined primarily by the state and federal legislatures and reviewed by the courts. A crime is a public wrong against the state, and the criminal law imposes sanctions in the form of fines, probation, or imprisonment. Crimes are generally classified as felonies or misdemeanors, depending on their seriousness.

Under the criminal law, all adults are presumed to be aware of the consequences of their actions, but the law does not hold an individual blameworthy unless that person is capable of intending to commit the crime of which he or she is

1 Ruth Bader Ginsburg
Age: 67   1993*
Moderate on criminal
justice issues

2 David H. Souter
Age: 60   1990
In moderate camp on
criminal procedure

3 Clarence Thomas
Age: 52   1991
Conservative
Republican

4 Stephen Breyer
Age: 61   1994
Mixed on criminal
procedure

5 Antonin Scalia
Age: 64   1986
A constitutional scholar

6 John Paul Stevens
Age: 80   1975
Middle of the road on
rights of the underdog

7 William H. Rehnquist
Age: 75   1972
Leader of conservative
crime and justice
revolution

8 Sandra Day O'Connor
Age: 70   1981
Generally votes to limit
criminals' rights

9 Anthony M. Kennedy
Age: 63   1988
Often upholds states'
position on criminal
procedure

*Year appointed to Supreme Court

FIGURE 4.4
THE LAW AND
ORDER COURT OF
THE TWENTY-
FIRST CENTURY?

accused. Such facotrs as insanity, a mental defect, or age mitigate a person's criminal responsibility.

Procedural laws deal with the rules for processing an offender from arrest through trial, sentencing, and release. An accused person must be provided with the guarantees of due process under the Fifth and Fourteenth Amendments to the U.S. Constitution. Federal and state governments periodically revise and update the substantive criminal law and procedural laws in their penal codes.

Key Terms

substantive criminal law	corpus delecti	entrapment
procedural law	actus reus	Racketeer Influenced and Corrupt
common law	mens rea	Organization Act (RICO)
stare decisis	general intent	self-incrimination
civil law	specific intent	bail
tort law	strict liability	cruel and unusual punishment
ex post facto law	insanity	incorporation theory
felony	M'Naghten rule	selective incorporation
misdemeanor	self-defense	due process

Discussion Questions

1. What are the specific aims and purposes of the criminal law? To what extent does the criminal law control behavior?
2. What kinds of activities should be labeled criminal in contemporary society? Why?
3. What is a criminal act? What is a criminal state of mind? When are individuals liable for their actions?
4. Discuss the various kinds of crime classifications. To what extent or degree are they distinguishable?
5. In recent years, numerous states have revised their penal codes. What are some of the major categories of substantive crimes you think should be revised?

6. What legal principles can be used to justify self-defense? Considering that the law seeks to prevent crime, not promote it, are such principles sound?
7. What are the minimum standards of procedure required in the criminal justice system?
8. Discuss the relationship between the U.S. Constitution and the Bill of Rights. What particular provisions does the incorporation theory involve?
9. What is the current philosophical orientation of the U.S. Supreme Court regarding criminal justice issues?

A CLOSER LOOK

The criminal law applies in an action taken by the local, state, or federal government against an individual who has been accused of committing a crime. The civil law comes into play when an individual or group seeks monetary compensation for harmful actions committed by another individual or group. The single characteristic that distinguishes the criminal law from the civil law is punishment.

Sanford Kadish, an expert in criminal law, notes with disapproval the recent trend away from rehabilitation and toward severe retributive punishment for those convicted of crimes. The displacement of reform and corrections by severe retribu-

tion, according to Kadish, has resulted in skyrocketing prison populations in the United States. Will the number of people in prison spiral even higher?

To learn more about the role of the criminal law in crime deterrence and punishment, go to InfoTrac College Edition and read

Sanford Kadish, "Criminal Law and Society: A Symposium," *California Law Review,* 1999, v87 p943

Markus Dubber, "Reforming American Penal Law," *Journal of Criminal Law and Criminology,* 1999, v90 p49

Notes

1 Kim Clark, "The Web's Dark Side," *U.S. News and World Report,* 28 August 2000, p. 39.
2 Some of the historical criminal law concepts are a synthesis of those contained in Fred Inbua, James Thompson, and James Zagel, *Criminal Law and Its Administration* (Mineola, NY: Foundation Press, 1974); Jerome Hall, *General Principles of Criminal Law* (Charlottesville, VA: Michie, 1961); Richard Singer and Martin Gardner, *Crimes and Punishments: Cases, Materials and Readings in Criminal Law* (New York: Matthew Bender, 1989).

3 See, generally, Sanford Kadish and Monrad Paulsen, *Criminal Law and Its Processes* (Boston: Little, Brown, 1975); also J. Dressler, *Understanding Criminal Law* (New York: Matthew Bender, 1987).
4 See T. F. Pluckett, *A Concise History of the Common Law* (Boston: Little, Brown, 1956); also E. Allan Farworth, *An Introduction to the Legal System of the United States* (New York: Oceana, 1963).
5 *Carriers Case Yearbook,* 13 Edward IV 9.pL.5 (1473).
6 Lord Irvine of Lairg, "Common Origins, Common Future: Shared Principles of

English and American Law," *American Bar Association Journal* 86 (2000): 54–56.
7 See, generally, Wayne R. LaFave and Austin W. Scott, *Criminal Law* (St. Paul, MN: West, 1986).
8 *Marbury v. Madison,* 5 U.S. (1 Cranch) 137, 2 L.Ed. 60 (1803).
9 Thomas Gardner and Terry Anderson, *Principles and Cases of Criminal Law,* 5th ed. (St. Paul, MN: West, 1992), pp. 15–18.
10 See *Massachusetts General Laws,* chap. 274, sec. 1.

11 LaFave and Scott, *Criminal Law,* 2d ed., p. 177; see, generally, Frank Miller et al., *Cases and Materials on Criminal Justice Administration,* 3d ed. (New York: Foundation Press, 1988).

12 See American Law Institute, Model Penal Code, Sec. 2.02; see also *United States v. Bailey,* 444 U.S. 394, 100 S.Ct. 624, 62 L.Ed.2d 575 (1980).

13 See *United States v. Balint,* 258 U.S. 250, 42 S.Ct. 301, 66 L.Ed. 604 (1922); see also *Morissette v. United States,* 342 U.S. 246, 72 S.Ct. 240, 96 L.Ed. 288 (1952).

14 8 *English Reporter* 718 (1843).

15 214 F.2d 862 (1954).

16 American Law Institute, Model Penal Code, Sec. 4.01.

17 "The Insanity Defense: Should It Be Abolished?" *Newsweek,* 24 May 1982, pp. 56–70.

18 See, generally, Norval Morris, *Madness and the Criminal Law* (Chicago: University of Chicago Press, 1982), chap. 2; see also Rita Simon and David Aaronson, *The Insanity Defense: A Critical Assessment of Law and Policy in the Post-Hinckley Era* (New York: Praeger, 1988), p. 45.

19 See John Klofas and Janette Yandrasits, "Guilty but Mentally Ill and the Jury Trial: A Case Study," *Criminal Law Bulletin* 24 (1989): 424.

20 370 U.S. 660, 82 S.Ct. 1417, 8 L.Ed.2d 758 (1962).

21 392 U.S. 514, 88 S.Ct. 2145, 20 L.Ed.2d 1254 (1968).

22 Samuel M. Davis, *Rights of Juveniles: The Juvenile Justice System* (New York: Boardman, 1994), chap. 2; Larry Siegel and Joseph Senna, *Juvenile Delinquency: The-ory, Practice and Law,* 7th ed. (Belmont, CA: Wadsworth, 2000).

23 *People v. Goetz,* 68 N.Y.2d 96, 497 N.Ed.2d 41, 506 N.Y.S.2d 18 (1986); see also "New York Upholds Goetz Gun Conviction," *Boston Globe,* 23 November 1988, p. 5.

24 287 U.S. 435, 53 S.Ct. 210, 77 L.Ed. 413 (1932).

25 356 U.S. 369, 78 S.Ct. 819, 2 L.Ed.2d 848 (1958).

26 411 U.S. 423, 93 S.Ct. 1637, 36 L.Ed.2d 366 (1973).

27 425 U.S. 484, 96 S.Ct. 1646, 48 L.Ed.2d 113 (1976).

28 503 U.S. 540, 112 S.Ct. 1535, 118 L.Ed.2d 174 (1992).

29 William Blackstone, *Commentaries on the Law of England,* vol. 1, ed. Thomas Cooley (Chicago: Callaghan, 1899), pp. 4, 26. Blackstone was an English barrister who lectured on the English common law at Oxford University in 1753.

30 14 QBD 273 (1884).

31 See "Note," *Harvard Law Review* 99 (1986): 1293, which gives several examples of whether a defendant's cultural background has a bearing on criminal responsibility.

32 Stephanie Goldberg, "Fault Lines," *American Bar Association Journal* 80 (1994): 40–46.

33 "Violent Crime Control and Law Enforcement Act of 1994," *The Criminal Law Reporter* 55 (1994): 2305–2430.

34 18 U.S.C. XXX 1961–1968 (1970). Enterprise includes both legitimate and illegitimate associations.

35 See John Brooks, *The Takeover Game* (New York: E. P. Dutton, 1987), p. 319. See also James Stewart, *Den of Thieves* (New York: Simon & Schuster, 1991); this book is a complete analysis of the insider trading scandal.

36 Comprehensive Crime Control Act of 1984, Title 18, U.S.C.; also Albert P. Melone, "The Politics of Criminal Code Revision," *Capital U.S. Review* 15 (1986): 191.

37 Omnibus Drug Law, H5210, *Congressional Quarterly,* 29 October 1988, p. 3145.

38 Tom Smith, "Legislative and Legal Developments in Criminal Justice," *Journal of Criminal Justice* 5 (1991): 36–37; see also Omnibus Crime Control Act of 1990, Public Law No. 101–647.

39 John DiIulio, Jr., "A Crime Bill That Would Work," *Wall Street Journal,* 15 February 1995.

40 117 S.Ct. 2365 (1997).

41 Antiterrorism and Effective Death Penalty Act of 1996, Public Law No. 104-132 (1996).

42 Violence Against Women Act, 42 U.S.C. sec. 13981 (1966).

43 Marvin Zalman and Larry Siegel, *Criminal Procedure: Constitution and Society* (Belmont, CA: West/Wadsworth, 1997).

44 384 U.S. 436, 86 S.Ct. 1602, 16 L.Ed.2d 694 (1966).

45 David Garrow, "Justice Souter Emerges," *New York Times Magazine,* 25 September 1994, p. 36.

46 "The High Court Rules—The Law of the Land Changes," *New York Times,* 2 July 2000, p. 5.

THE POLICE
AND LAW ENFORCEMENT

CNN.

The charge that police use racial profiling
when they detain suspects has captured headlines around the nation. While police administrators reject the charge that a person's
race influences the decision to stop automobiles and question drivers, some civil libertarians maintain that the practice is so
widespread that it has created a new crime
category: "DWB"—Driving While Black. Complaints of racial bias seem to decline when
police behavior comes under official
scrutiny and data are collected on police behavior. The subject of charges of racial bias
is just one of the topics covered in this part,
which focuses on the history of police agencies, police operations and activities, and
the critical issues police must confront in
the new millennium.

Chapter

5

© Nancy Richmond/The Image Works

POLICE IN SOCIETY:
HISTORY AND ORGANIZATION

A few years ago, the Richmond, Virginia, homicide rate was the second highest in the nation; gun toting had become a way of life.[1] Then the local police, in cooperation with the U.S. Bureau of Alcohol, Tobacco and Firearms, created Project Exile. This innovative program was designed to combat gun crime in a simple and direct fashion. Anytime Richmond police found a gun on a drug dealer, user, convicted felon, or suspect in a violent crime, the case would be tried under federal statutes that carry mandatory sentences of at least five years without parole—and longer for repeat or aggravated offenses. To publicize the program, its slogan, "An Illegal Gun Gets You 5 Years in Federal Prison," was splashed across billboards in high-crime neighborhoods and on city buses. A

TV campaign spread the word over the airwaves. Since the program began, 647 people have been indicted, 762 guns have been removed from the street, and more than 400 offenders have been sent to prison. Much to the program creators' delight, murders in Richmond dropped sharply, from 140 in 1997 to 94 in 1998 and 72 in 1999. Armed robberies showed a similar decline. Because of its success, Project Exile–type programs are being adopted in Atlanta; Birmingham, Alabama; Fort Worth, Texas; New Orleans; Norfolk, Virginia; Philadelphia; Rochester, New York; and San Francisco. In Fort Worth, the program's motto is "Gun Crime Means Hard Time"; in Rochester, billboards on the side of city buses read "You + Illegal Gun = Federal Prison."

Chapter 5

Chapter Outline

Criminal Justice Links

Criminal Justice Viewpoints

AP/Wide World Photos

The Exile programs are an example of aggressive, proactive police work. Here, Texas Attorney General John Cornyn holds up a gun confiscated from a convicted drug dealer under the Texas Exile program, during a rally in Houston in October 2000 marking the first anniversary of the program. Texas Exile is a crime-control initiative that uses existing state and federal gun laws to get at the root cause of gun violence—criminals who illegally carry and use weapons. Those convicted of a gun crime can add at least five years to their sentence.

Fill in the blanks 1–2
True/False 1
Multiple choice 1
Essay 1

pledge system
In early England, the system in which neighbors aided each other and protected the settlement.

tithings
During the Middle Ages, groups of about ten families responsible for maintaining order among themselves and dealing with disturbances, fire, wild animals, or other threats.

hue and cry
In medieval England, a call for mutual aid against trouble or danger.

hundred
In medieval England, a group of 100 families responsible for maintaining order and trying minor offenses.

Fill in the blanks 3–5
True/False 2–5
Multiple choice 2–4
Essay 2

constable
In early English towns, an appointed peacekeeper who organized citizens for protection and supervised the night watch.

shire reeve
In early England, the senior law enforcement figure in a county, forerunner of today's sheriff.

watch system
In medieval England, men organized in church parishes to guard at night against disturbances and breaches of the peace under the direction of the local constable.

Programs such as Project Exile typify the effort of modern police agencies to take an aggressive stance against crime. Rather than simply react after a crime occurs, local police are now cooperating with other government agencies and working in partnership with the general public to reduce area crime rates. Cracking down on gun crimes, patrolling crime-ridden schools, and acting as community change agents are but a few of the roles of the modern police.

The changing police role is of critical importance for the criminal justice system. The police are the gatekeepers of the criminal justice process. They initiate contact with law violators and decide whether to formally arrest them and start their journey through the criminal justice system, to settle the issue in an informal way (such as by issuing a warning), or to simply take no action at all. The strategic position of law enforcement officers, their visibility and contact with the public, and their use of weapons and arrest power have kept them in the forefront of public thought for most of the twentieth century.

Although the public may applaud police efforts that have brought the crime rate down, they are also concerned by media reports of police officers who abuse their power by using unneccessary force and brutality or who routinely violate the civil rights of suspects. Such concern may be warranted. For example, some critics charge that police officers routinely induce or force confessions from criminal suspects. Later, at trial, these false confessions may influence jurors, even if they seem inconsistent with the facts of the case.[2] Another concern is that police are racially and ethnically biased and use "racial profiling" to routinely stop African Americans and search their cars. Some cynics suggest that police have created a new crime: DWB (driving while black).[3] Despite these concerns, the majority of citizens, both whites and minority-group members, give their police force high marks.[4] Citizens are especially likely to look favorably on police if they credit local law enforcement agencies with keeping their neighborhood safe.[5]

In this and the following three chapters, we will evaluate the history, role, organizational issues, and procedures of police agents and agencies and discuss the legal rules that control police behavior.

THE HISTORY OF POLICE

The origin of U.S. police agencies, like that of the criminal law, can be traced to early English society.[6] Before the Norman conquest, there was no regular English police force. Every person living in the villages scattered throughout the countryside was responsible for aiding neighbors and protecting the settlement from thieves and marauders. This was known as the **pledge system**. People were grouped in collectives of ten families, called **tithings**, and were entrusted with policing their own minor problems. When trouble occurred, the citizen was expected to raise a **hue and cry**. Ten tithings were grouped into a **hundred**, whose affairs were supervised by a **constable** appointed by the local nobleman. The constable, who might be considered the first real police officer, dealt with more serious breaches of the law.[7]

Shires, which resembled the counties of today, were controlled by a **shire reeve** appointed by the Crown or local landowner to supervise the territory and ensure that order would be kept. The shire reeve, a forerunner of today's sheriff, soon began to pursue and apprehend law violators as part of his duties.

In the thirteenth century, the **watch system** was created to help protect property in England's larger cities and towns. Watchmen patrolled at night and helped protect against robberies, fires, and disturbances. They reported to the area constable, who became the primary metropolitan law enforcement agent. In larger cities, such as London, the watchmen were organized within church parishes and were usually members of the parish they protected.

In 1326, the office of **justice of the peace** was created to assist the shire reeve in controlling the county. Eventually, these justices took on judicial functions in addition to their primary role as peacekeeper. The local constable became the operational assistant to the justice of the peace, supervising the night watchmen, investigating offenses, serving summonses, executing warrants, and securing prisoners. This system helped delineate the relationship between police and the judiciary that has continued for 500 years.

Eighteenth-Century Developments

As the eighteenth century began, rising crime rates encouraged a new form of private "monied police," who were able to profit both legally and criminally from the lack of formal police departments. These private police agents, referred to as **thief takers**, are discussed in the International Justice feature.

In 1829, Sir Robert Peel, England's home secretary, guided through Parliament an "Act for Improving the Police in and near the Metropolis." The Metropolitan Police Act established the first organized police force in London. Composed of more than 1,000 men, the London police force was structured along military lines; its members would be known from then on as **bobbies**, after their creator. They wore a distinctive uniform and were led by two magistrates, who were later given the title of commissioner. However, the ultimate responsibility for the police belonged to the home secretary and, consequently, to Parliament.

The early bobbies suffered many of the same problems that had befallen their predecessors. Many were corrupt, they were unsuccessful at stopping crime, and they were influenced by the wealthy. Owners of houses of ill repute, who in the past had guaranteed their undisturbed operations by bribing watchmen, now turned their attention to the bobbies. Metropolitan police administrators fought constantly to terminate cowardly, corrupt, and alcoholic officers, dismissing in the beginning about one-third of the bobbies each year.

Despite its recognized shortcomings, the London experiment proved a vast improvement over what had come before. It was considered so successful that the metropolitan police soon began providing law enforcement assistance to outlying areas that requested it. Another act of Parliament allowed justices of the peace to establish local police forces, and by 1856, every borough and county in England was required to form its own police force.

Law Enforcement in Colonial America

Law enforcement in colonial America paralleled the British model. In the colonies, the county sheriff became the most important law enforcement agent. Besides keeping the peace and fighting crime, sheriffs collected taxes, supervised elections, and handled a great deal of other legal business.

The colonial sheriff did not patrol or seek out crime. Instead, he reacted to citizens' complaints and investigated crimes that had occurred. His salary was related to his effectiveness and was paid on a fee system. Sheriffs received a fixed amount for every arrest made. Unfortunately, their tax-collecting chores were more lucrative than fighting crime, so law enforcement was not one of their primary concerns.

In the cities, law enforcement was the province of the town marshal, who was aided, often unwillingly, by a variety of constables, night watchmen, police justices, and city council members. However, local governments had little power of administration, and enforcement of the criminal law was largely an individual or community responsibility.

After the American Revolution, larger cities relied on elected or appointed marshals or constables to serve warrants and recover stolen property, sometimes

justice of the peace
Official appointed to act as the judicial officer in a county.

Fill in the blanks 6–7
True/False 6–8
Multiple choice 5–6
Essay 3

thief takers
In eighteenth-century London, organized groups of private police who earned a living by catching wanted felons.

bobbies
Members of the London police force, named after its founder, Sir Robert Peel.

 To learn more about the history of the London Metropolitan Police, go to their Web site: http://www.met.police. uk/police/mps/mps/history/ mishist0.htm

For an up-to-date list of Web links, see http://www.wadsworth.com/ product/0534573053s

Fill in the blanks 8–10
True/False 9–10
Multiple choice 7–8

INTERNATIONAL JUSTICE

The Thief Takers of London

By the eighteenth century, the Industrial Revolution had lured thousands of people from the English countryside to work in the factory towns. The swelling population of urban poor, whose minuscule wages could hardly sustain them, resulted in increased crime rates. In London and its surrounds, law enforcement was provided by *thief takers*—organized groups of private police who earned a living by catching wanted felons and collecting rewards for their capture. According to research by John McMullan, by the mid-eighteenth century, between 30 and 40 thief takers were active in London. Among them was the infamous rascal Jack Wild, who used his position to enrich himself in all manner of criminal enterprise.

Most thief takers started as prison turnkeys, constables, court bailiffs, or other minor court officers. These monied police were universally corrupt, taking profits not only from catching and informing on criminals, but also from receiving stolen property, theft, intimidation, perjury, and blackmail. They often relieved their prisoners of money and stolen goods, and made more income by accepting hush money, giving perjured evidence, swearing false oaths, and operating extortion rackets. Petty debtors were especially easy targets for those who combined thief taking with the keeping of alehouses and taverns. While incarcerated, the health and safety of prisoners were entirely at the whim of the keepers/thief catchers, who were virtually free to charge what they wanted for board and other necessities. Court bailiffs who also acted as thief

takers were the most passionately detested legal profiteers. They seized debtors and held them in small lockups, where they forced their victims to pay exorbitant prices for food and lodging.

The thief takers' use of violence was notorious. They went armed and were prepared to maim or kill in order to gain their objectives. Before he was hanged in 1725, Jack Wild "had two fractures in his skull and his bald head was covered with silver plates. He had seventeen wounds in various parts of his body from swords, daggers and gunshots, [and] . . . his throat had been cut in the course of his duties."

Henry Fielding, author of *Tom Jones,* along with Saunders Welch and Sir John Fielding, sought to clean up the thief-taking system. Appointed a city magistrate in 1748, Fielding operated his own group of monied police out of Bow Street in London, directing and deploying them throughout the city and its environs, deciding which cases to investigate and what streets to protect. His agents were carefully instructed on their legitimate powers and duties. Fielding's Bow Street Runners were a marked improvement over the earlier monied police because they were subject to an administrative structure with better record-keeping and investigative procedures. Despite these improvements, Fielding's forces were not adequate, and by the nineteenth century state police officers were needed.

Critical Thinking Skills

1. Does the thought of private police agents who profit from catching criminals seem repugnant? If so,

think about their modern-day counterparts involved in the commercial aspects of justice: private security firms, private prison operators, bail bondsmen, and bounty hunters. Is it wrong to profit from justice? After all, we think nothing of going to a private hospital, which is also involved in the privatization of what is essentially a public service.

2. Do you find it ironic that some politicians call on the government to privatize services—for example, by replacing police officers with private security firms, or publicly run prisons with private institutions? Would such measures herald the return of thief takers, with all the problems they presented 300 years ago? Have we not moved ahead as a civilization to the point where the government can provide help to those in need without contracting for private services?

InfoTrac College Edition Research

Use "private police" and "private security" as search guides to learn more about the contemporary versions of thief takers.

SOURCE: John L. McMullan, "The New Improved Monied Police: Reform, Crime Control, and the Commodification of Policing in London," *British Journal of Criminology* 36 (1996): 85–108.

in cooperation with the thieves themselves. Night watchmen, referred to as "leatherheads" because of the leather helmets they wore, still patrolled the streets, calling out the hour; they were equipped with a rattle to summon help and a nightstick to ward off lawbreakers. Watchmen were not widely respected: Rowdy young men enjoyed tipping over the watch houses with the leatherheads inside, and a favorite saying in New York was "While the city sleeps, the watchmen do too."[8]

In rural areas of the South, "slave patrols" charged with recapturing escaped slaves were an early if loathsome form of law enforcement.[9] In the western territories, individual initiative was encouraged by the practice of offering rewards for the capture of felons. If trouble arose, the town "vigilance committee" might form a posse to chase offenders. These **vigilantes** were called on to eradicate social problems, such as theft of livestock, through force or intimidation. The San Francisco Vigilance Committee actively pursued criminals in the mid-nineteenth century.

As cities grew, it became increasingly difficult for local leaders to organize ad hoc citizen vigilante groups. Moreover, the early nineteenth century was an era of widespread urban unrest and mob violence. Local leaders began to realize that a more structured police function was needed to control demonstrators and keep the peace.

vigilantes
In the Old West, members of a vigilance committee or posse called upon to capture cattle thieves or other felons.

Early Police Agencies

By the mid-nineteenth century, wealthy industrialists perceived a growing threat to the existing social order from the so-called dangerous classes—Irish and German immigrants, free blacks, unionists, and the urban poor in general. These groups were perceived as menacing because of their growing numbers and deteriorating social and economic position. Mob violence became commonplace, and existing law enforcement mechanisms were unable to suppress the frequent riots, demonstrations, and strikes.

The modern police department was born out of urban mob violence that wracked the nation's cities in the nineteenth century. Boston created the first formal U.S. police department in 1838. New York formed its police department in 1844; Philadelphia, in 1854. The new police departments replaced the night watch system and relegated constables and sheriffs to serving court orders and running jails.

 From 1936 to 1938, more than 2,300 former slaves from across the American South were interviewed by writers and journalists. These former slaves, most born in the last years of the slave regime or during the Civil War, provided firsthand accounts of their experiences on plantations, in cities, and on small farms. To learn more, go to http://xroads.virginia.edu/~hyper/wpa/wpahome.html For an up-to-date list of Web links, see http://www.wadsworth.com/product/0534573053s

PERSPECTIVES ON JUSTICE

The fact that police agencies grew out of the desire of the upper classes to suppress the social behavior and economic aspirations of the lower classes supports the restorative justice perspective that American justice is traditionally coercive and must be changed in order to become humanistic.

At first, the urban police departments inherited the functions of the institutions they replaced. For example, Boston police were charged with maintaining public health until 1853; in New York, the police were responsible for street sweeping until 1881. Politics dominated the departments and determined the recruitment of new officers and promotion of supervisors. An individual with the right connections could be hired despite a lack of qualifications. Early police agencies were corrupt, brutal, and inefficient.[10]

In the late nineteenth century, police work was highly desirable because it paid more than most other blue-collar jobs. By 1880, the average factory worker earned $450 a year, while police in large cities made $900 annually. For immigrant groups, having enough political clout to be appointed to the police department was an important step up the social ladder.[11] However, job security was uncertain, because it depended on the local political machine's staying in power.

Police work itself was primitive. There were few of even the simplest technological innovations common today, such as call boxes or centralized record keeping. Most officers patrolled on foot, without backup or the ability to call for help. Officers were commonly taunted by local toughs and responded with force

Fill in the blanks 11–13
True/False 11–12
Multiple choice 9–11
Essay 4

Thomas Nast, Jr. "The Position of Police Inspector—Nothing to 'Do' But—Everybody," 1907. #47.242.4 © Museum of the City of New York

Although some experts mourn the "good old days" when police officers walked a beat and knew everyone in the neighborhood, others point out that the "good old days" were filled with corruption and incompetence. Here, a newspaper cartoon from 1907 blasts police corruption.

and brutality. The long-standing conflict between police and the public was born out of the difficulty that untrained, unprofessional officers had in patrolling the streets of nineteenth-century American cities and in breaking up and controlling labor disputes. Police were not crime fighters as we know them today. Their major role was maintaining order, and their power was almost unchecked. The average officer had little training, no education in the law, and a minimum of supervision, yet the police became virtual judges of law and fact with the ability to exercise unlimited discretion.[12]

At mid-nineteenth century, the detective bureau was set up as part of the Boston police. Until then, thief taking had been the province of amateur bounty hunters, who hired themselves out to victims for a price. When professional police departments replaced bounty hunters, the close working relationships that developed between police detectives and their underworld informants produced many scandals and, consequently, high personnel turnover.

Police during the nineteenth century were regarded as incompetent and corrupt and were disliked by the people they served. The police role was only minimally directed at law enforcement. Its primary functions were serving as the enforcement arm of the reigning political power, protecting private property, and keeping control of the ever-rising numbers of immigrants.

Police agencies evolved slowly through the second half of the nineteenth century. Uniforms were introduced in 1853 in New York. The first technological breakthroughs in police operations came in the area of communications. The linking of precincts to central headquarters by telegraph began in the 1850s. In 1867, the first telegraph police boxes were installed; an officer could turn a key in a box, and his location and number would automatically register at headquarters. Other technological advances were made in transportation. The Detroit Police Department outfitted some of its patrol officers with bicycles in 1897. By 1913, the motorcycle was being used by departments in the eastern part of the nation. The first police car was used in Akron, Ohio, in 1910, and the police wagon became popular in Cincinnati in 1912.[13] Nonpolice functions, such as care of the streets, began to be abandoned after the Civil War.

At first, big-city police were not respected by the public, unsuccessful in their role as crime stoppers, and uninvolved in progressive activities. The control of police departments by local politicians impeded effective law enforcement and fostered an atmosphere of graft and corruption. The concern about police behavior expressed by advocates of the due process perspective has its roots during this period.

Fill in the blanks 14–15
True/False 13–14
Multiple choice 12–13
Essay 5

Twentieth-Century Reform

At the turn of the twentieth century, American police agencies—in response both to the perceived threat of social revolution and a crisis of legitimacy in police agencies considered both corrupt and incompetent—entered a period of reform. Professionalization entailed a radical reorganization of police agencies, including the creation of standards for recruiting and training, greater discipline for police officers, increased centralization, bureaucratization, a greater division of labor, new technology, and extraordinary increases in the numbers of officers. By 1905, most urban police departments were 6 to 10 times their size in 1865.

In an effort to reduce police corruption, civic leaders in a number of jurisdictions created police administrative boards to reduce local officials' control over the police. These tribunals were responsible for appointing police administrators and controlling police affairs. In many instances, these measures failed because the private citizens appointed to the review boards lacked expertise in the intricacies of police work.

Another reform movement was the takeover of some big-city police agencies by state legislators. Although police budgets were financed through local taxes, control of police was usurped by rural politicians in the state capitals. New York City temporarily lost authority over its police force in 1857. Despite such efforts, even when the administration of police forces improved, the effects were mostly temporary. Political interference would simply not go away as long as the "bosses" profited from selective police vice enforcement. Reformers who tried to alleviate the situation by passing laws against gambling, prostitution, and Sunday drinking in saloons only served to create new opportunities for graft as tavern owners and gamblers offered payoffs in order to operate and the local beat cop demanded payments from saloon or brothel keepers. It was not until the first decades of the twentieth century that cities regained control of their police forces.

The Boston police strike of 1919 heightened interest in police reform. The strike came about because police officers were dissatisfied with their status in society. Other professions were unionizing and increasing their standards of living, but police salaries lagged behind. The Boston police officers' organization, the Boston Social Club, voted to become a union affiliated with the American Federation of Labor. The officers struck on September 9, 1919. Rioting and looting broke out, resulting in Governor Calvin Coolidge's mobilization of the state militia to take over the city. Public support turned against the police, and the strike was broken. Eventually, all the striking officers were fired and replaced by new recruits. The Boston police strike ended police unionism for decades and solidified power in the hands of reactionary, autocratic police administrators. In the aftermath of the strike, various local, state, and federal crime commissions began to investigate the extent of crime and the ability of the justice system to deal with it effectively and made recommendations to improve police effectiveness.[14] However, with the onset of the Depression, justice reform became a less important issue than economic revival, and for many years, little changed in the nature of policing.

The Emergence of Professionalism

Fill in the blanks 16–17
True/False 15–16
Multiple choice 14–15

Around the turn of the twentieth century, a number of nationally recognized leaders called for measures to help improve and professionalize the police. In 1893, a professional society, the **International Association of Chiefs of Police (IACP)**, was formed. Under the direction of its first president, District of Columbia Chief of Police Richard Sylvester, the IACP became the leading voice for police reform during the first two decades of the twentieth century. The IACP called for creating a civil service police force and for removing political influence and control. It also advocated centralized organizational structure and record keeping to curb the power of politically aligned precinct captains. Still another professional reform the IACP fostered was the creation of specialized units, such as delinquency control squads.

The most famous police reformer of the time was August Vollmer. While serving as police chief of Berkeley, California, Vollmer instituted university training

International Association of Chiefs of Police (IACP)
The professional organization of local police agencies.

for young officers. He also helped develop the School of Criminology at the University of California at Berkeley, which became the model for justice-related programs around the United States. Vollmer's disciples included O. W. Wilson, who pioneered the use of advanced training for officers when he took over and reformed the Wichita (Kansas) Police Department in 1928. Wilson was also instrumental in applying modern management and administrative techniques to policing. His text, *Police Administration,* became the single most influential work on the subject.

During this period, police professionalism was equated with an incorruptible, tough, highly trained, rule-oriented department organized along militaristic lines. The most respected department was that in Los Angeles, which emphasized police as incorruptible crime fighters who would not question the authority of the central command.

Fill in the blanks 18–19
True/False 17–18
Multiple choice 16–19
Essay 6

THE MODERN ERA OF POLICING: 1960–2000

The modern era of policing emerged during the decade of the 1960s. The following sections trace some of the major events that have occurred from that time to the present.

Policing in the 1960s

Turmoil and crisis were the hallmarks of policing during the 1960s. Throughout the decade, the Supreme Court handed down a number of decisions designed to control police operations and procedures. Police officers were now required to obey strict legal guidelines when questioning suspects, conducting searches, wiretapping, and so on. As the civil rights of suspects were significantly expanded, police complained they were being "handcuffed by the courts."

Also during the 1960s, civil unrest produced a growing tension between police and the public. African Americans, who were battling for increased rights and freedoms in the civil rights movement, found themselves confronting police lines. When riots broke out in New York, Detroit, Los Angeles, and other cities be-

Police in the 1960s were continually involved in trying to suppress political and social protests, a job for which they were unsuited and poorly trained. The results, such as this clash outside the 1968 Democratic Party convention in Chicago, were often chaotic, and an entire generation of young people grew up mistrusting the police.

© Dennis Brack/Black Star

tween 1964 and 1968, the spark that ignited conflict often involved the police. And when students across the nation began marching in anti–Vietnam War demonstrations, local police departments were called on to keep order. Police forces were ill equipped and poorly trained to deal with these social problems; it is not surprising that the 1960s were marked by a number of bloody confrontations between the police and the public.

Confounding these problems was a rapidly rising crime rate. The number of violent and property crimes increased dramatically during the 1960s. Drug addiction and abuse grew to be national concerns, common in all social classes. Urban police departments could not control the crime rate, and police officers resented the demands placed on them by dissatisfied citizens.

Policing in the 1970s

The 1970s witnessed many structural changes in police agencies themselves. The end of the Vietnam War significantly reduced tensions between students and police. However, the relationship between police and minorities was still rocky. Local fears and distrust, combined with conservative federal policies, encouraged police departments to control what was perceived as an emerging minority "threat."[15]

Increased federal government support for criminal justice greatly influenced police operations. During the 1970s, the Law Enforcement Assistance Administration (LEAA) devoted a significant portion of its funds to police agencies. Although a number of police departments used this money to purchase little-used hardware, such as antiriot gear, most of it went to supporting innovative research on police work and advanced training for police officers. Perhaps most significant, LEAA's Law Enforcement Education Program helped thousands of officers further their college education. Hundreds of criminal justice programs were developed on college campuses around the country, providing a pool of highly educated police recruits. LEAA funds were also used to import or transfer technology originally developed in other fields into law enforcement. Technological innovations involving computers transformed the way police kept records, investigated crimes, and communicated with one another. State training academies improved the way police learn to deal with such issues as job stress, community conflict, and interpersonal relations.

The 1970s also saw more women and minorities recruited to police work. Affirmative action programs helped alter, albeit slowly, the ethnic, racial, and gender composition of U.S. policing.

Policing in the 1980s

As the 1980s began, the police role seemed to be changing significantly. A number of experts acknowledged that the police were not simply crime fighters and called for police to develop a greater awareness of community issues. This resulted in the emergence of the community policing concept.[16]

Police unions, which began to grow in the late 1960s, continued to have a great impact on departmental administration in the 1980s. Unions fought for and won increased salaries and benefits for their members. In many instances, unions eroded the power of the police chief to make unquestioned policy and personnel decisions. During the 1980s, chiefs of police commonly consulted with union leaders before making major decisions concerning departmental operations.

Although police operations improved markedly in the 1980s, police departments were also beset by problems that impeded their effectiveness. State and local budgets were cut back during the Reagan administration, while federal support for innovative police programs was severely curtailed with the demise of the LEAA.

EXHIBIT 5.1   THE MOST NOTABLE ACHIEVEMENTS OF CONTEMPORARY AMERICAN POLICE

- The intellectual caliber of the police has risen dramatically. American police today at all ranks are smarter, better informed, and more sophisticated than police in the 1960s.
- Senior police managers are more ambitious for their organizations than they used to be. Chiefs and their deputies want to leave their own distinctive stamp on their organizations. Many recognize that management is a specialized skill that must be developed.
- An explicit scientific mind-set has taken hold in American policing that involves an appreciation of the importance of evaluation and the timely availability of information.
- The standards of police conduct have risen. Despite recent well-publicized incidents of brutality and corruption, American police today treat the public more fairly, more equitably, and less venally than police did 30 years ago.

- Police are remarkably more diverse in terms of race and gender than a generation ago. This amounts to a revolution in American policing, changing both its appearance and, more slowly, its behavior.
- The work of the police has become intellectually more demanding, requiring an array of new specialized knowledge about technology, forensic analysis, and crime. This has had profound effects on recruitment—notably, civilianization—organizational structure, career patterns, and operational coordination.
- Civilian review of police discipline has gradually become accepted by police. Although the struggle is not yet over, expansion is inevitable as more and more senior police executives see that civilian review reassures the public and validates their own favorable opinion of the overall quality of police performance.

SOURCE: David H. Bayley, "Policing in America," *Society* 36 (December 1998): 16–20.

In the 1980s, police–community relations continued to be a major problem. Riots and incidents of urban conflict occurred in some of the nation's largest cities.[17] They triggered continual concern about what the police role should be, especially in inner-city neighborhoods.

Policing in the 1990s

As the 1990s began, several police experts declared that the nation's police forces should be evaluated not on their crime-fighting ability but on their courteousness, deportment, and helpfulness. Interest renewed in reviving an earlier style of police work featuring foot patrols and increased citizen contact. Police departments began to embrace new forms of policing that stressed cooperation with the community and problem solving. Ironically, urban police departments began to shift their focus to becoming community organizers at a time when technological improvements increased their ability to identify suspects.

Police corruption continued to be an issue, and the rogue cops of the 1990s were even more brazen and violent than the corrupt cops of 20 years earlier. New York, Philadelphia, Los Angeles, and other large cities continued to experience incidents of police corruption and abuse of power. Even in smaller cities, police procedures were questioned regarding overenforcement in minority communities.[18] Minority citizens seemed to be the target of incidents of extreme violence and misconduct.[19]

Despite these troubling incidents, police experts such as David Bayley believe that the police have made many notable strides over the past three decades. Some of the most important achievements are listed in Exhibit 5.1.

CONTEMPORARY LAW ENFORCEMENT

Law enforcement today is divided into four broad categories—federal, state, county, and local—with many subcategories. There is no real hierarchy; each branch has its own sphere of operations, though overlap may exist.

Federal Law Enforcement Agencies

The federal government has a number of law enforcement agencies designed to protect the rights and privileges of U.S. citizens. No single agency has unlimited jurisdiction, and each has been created to enforce specific laws and cope with particular situations. Federal law enforcement agencies have no particular rank order or hierarchy of command or responsibility, and each reports to a specific department or bureau (se Figure 5.1).

Department of Justice The **Department of Justice (DOJ)** is the legal arm of the U.S. government. Headed by the attorney general, it is empowered to (1) enforce all federal laws, (2) represent the United States when it is party to court action, and (3) conduct independent investigations through its law enforcement services.

The Department of Justice maintains several separate divisions that are responsible for enforcing federal laws and protecting U.S. citizens. The Civil Rights Division proceeds legally against violations of federal civil rights laws that protect citizens from discrimination on the basis of their race, creed, ethnic background, age, or sex. Areas of greatest concern include discrimination in education, housing, and employment, including affirmative action cases. The Tax Division brings legal actions against tax violators. The Criminal Division prosecutes violations of the Federal Criminal Code.

The Justice Department first became involved in law enforcement when the attorney general hired investigators to enforce the Mann Act (forbidding the transportation of women between states for immoral purposes). These investigators were formalized in 1908 into a distinct branch of the government, the Bureau of Investigation; the agency was later reorganized into the **Federal Bureau of Investigation (FBI)**, under the direction of J. Edgar Hoover (1924–1972).

Federal Bureau of Investigation Today's FBI is not a police agency but an investigative agency with jurisdiction over all matters in which the United States is, or may be, an interested party. It limits its jurisdiction, however, to federal laws, including all federal statutes not specifically assigned to other agencies. Areas covered by these laws include espionage, sabotage, treason, civil rights violations, murder and assault of federal officers, mail fraud, robbery and burglary of federally insured banks, kidnapping, and interstate transportation of stolen vehicles and property.

The FBI has been the most glamorous and widely publicized law enforcement agency. In the 1920s and 1930s, its agents pursued such gangsters as John Dillinger, "Mad Dog" Coll, Bonnie and Clyde, "Machine Gun" Kelly, and "Pretty Boy" Floyd. During World War II, they hunted Nazi agents and prevented any major sabotage on U.S. military bases. After the war, they conducted a crusade against Soviet intelligence agents and investigated organized crime figures. They have been instrumental in cracking tough criminal cases, which has brought the FBI enormous public respect.

Today, the FBI offers a number of important services to local law enforcement agencies. A few of its many services and subsections are described in Exhibit 5.2.

Fill in the blanks 20
True/False 19
Multiple choice 20–24
Essay 7–8

Department of Justice (DOJ)
The legal arm of the U.S. government, headed by the attorney general, empowered to enforce federal laws, represent the federal government in court, and conduct independent investigations.

Although police agencies are learning from the mistakes of the past, racial and ethnic conflict and charges of police brutality are still quite common. Here, police speak to protesters rallying against racial profiling and police brutality in front of the Ramparts police station in downtown Los Angeles. Some of the protesters, who urged police to arrest them, were later arrested peacefully.

AP/Wide World Photos

FIGURE 5.1
FEDERAL LAW
ENFORCEMENT
PERSONNEL

SOURCE: Brian Reaves and Timothy Hart, *Federal Law Enforcement Officers, 1998* (Washington, DC: Bureau of Justice Statistics, 2000).

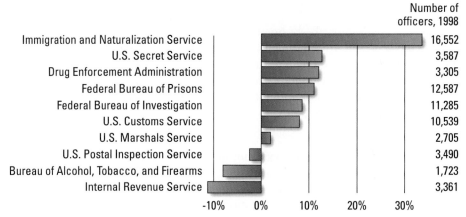

Number of officers, 1998

Immigration and Naturalization Service	16,552
U.S. Secret Service	3,587
Drug Enforcement Administration	3,305
Federal Bureau of Prisons	12,587
Federal Bureau of Investigation	11,285
U.S. Customs Service	10,539
U.S. Marshals Service	2,705
U.S. Postal Inspection Service	3,490
Bureau of Alcohol, Tobacco, and Firearms	1,723
Internal Revenue Service	3,361

Percent change in the number of federal officers with arrest and firearm authority, 1996–1998

Federal Bureau of Investigation (FBI)
The arm of the Justice Department that investigated violation of federal law, gathers crime statistics, runs a comprehensive crime laboratory, and helps train local law enforcement officers.

Drug Enforcement Administration (DEA)
The federal agency that enforces federal drug control laws.

Drug Enforcement Administration Government interest in drug trafficking can be traced back to 1914, when the Harrison Act established federal jurisdiction over the supply and use of narcotics. A number of drug enforcement units, including the Bureau of Narcotics and Dangerous Drugs, were charged with enforcing drug laws. In 1973, these agencies were combined to form the **Drug Enforcement Administration (DEA)**.

DEA agents assist local and state authorities in investigating illegal drug use and carrying out independent surveillance and enforcement activities to control the importation of narcotics. For example, DEA agents work with foreign governments in cooperative efforts aimed at destroying opium and marijuana crops at their source—hard-to-find fields tucked away in the interiors of Latin America, Asia, Europe, and Africa. The DEA also conducts a variety of operations in the United States. For example, Operation Pipeline is a nationwide highway interdiction program that focuses on private motor vehicles. Similarly, Operation Convoy targets drug transportation organizations that use truck and commercial vehicles to transport drugs and employs long-term surveillance undercover operations aimed at illicit transportation organizations. The Mobile Enforcement Team (MET) helps local law enforcement attack the violent drug organizations in their neighborhoods by identifying major drug traffickers and organizations that commit homicide and other violent crimes; collecting, analyzing, and sharing intelligence with state and local counterparts; conducting investigations against violent drug offenders and gangs; arresting drug traffickers and assisting in the arrests of violent offenders and gangs; seizing the assets of violent drug offenders and gangs; and providing support to state, local, and federal prosecutors.

Other Justice Department Agencies Other federal law enforcement agencies under the direction of the DOJ include the U.S. Marshals, the Immigration and Naturalization Service, and the Organized Crime and Racketeering Unit. The U.S. Marshals are court officers who help implement federal court rulings, transport prisoners, and enforce court orders. The Immigration and Naturalization Service is responsible for the administration of immigration laws governing the exclusion and deportation of illegal aliens and the naturalization of aliens lawfully present in the United States. This service also maintains border patrols to prevent illegal aliens from entering the United States. The Organized Crime and Racketeering Unit, under the direction of the U.S. attorney general, coordinates

EXHIBIT 5.2   SPECIAL PROGRAMS AND DIVISIONS OF THE FEDERAL BUREAU OF INVESTIGATION

- **Criminal Justice Information Services (CJIS).** Located in Clarksburg, West Virginia, the CJIS centralizes criminal justice information. It serves as the national repository for fingerprint information and criminal record data and also manages Law Enforcement On-Line (LEO), a law enforcement intranet that provides secure communications, distance learning, and information services to the law enforcement community. It operates the National Instant Check System (NICS), mandated by the Brady law to check on the backgrounds of people desiring to purchase firearms. It is currently developing the Integrated Automated Fingerprint Identification System (IAFIS).

- **Crime Laboratory.** The FBI Crime Laboratory—one of the largest and most comprehensive forensic laboratories in the world—examines evidence free of charge for federal, state, and local law enforcement agencies. Among its activities are
  - Scientific analysis of physical evidence submitted for examination, followed by expert testimony in court
  - Operational and technical support to investigations
  - Research and development of forensic techniques and procedures
  - Development and deployment of new forensic technologies

  - Training programs and symposia for U.S. and international crime laboratory practitioners and law enforcement personnel

- **Child Abduction and Serial Killer Unit (CASKU).** Created in 1994, CASKU responds upon request from local law enforcement agencies to kidnappings and to serial killer cases.

- **Combined DNA Index System (CODIS).** CODIS is a national database of DNA profiles from convicted offenders, unsolved crime scenes, and missing persons. CODIS enables state and local law enforcement crime labs to exchange and compare DNA profiles electronically.

- **Critical Incident Response Group (CIRG).** CIRG is ready to assist law enforcement agencies in hostage-taking and barricade situations, terrorist activities, and other critical incidents.

- **Uniform Crime Reports (UCR).** Another service of the FBI, the UCR is an annual compilation of crimes reported to local police agencies, arrests, police killed or wounded in action, and other information.

- **National Crime Information Center (NCIC).** A computerized network linked to local police departments, the NCIC provides ready information on stolen vehicles, wanted persons, stolen guns, and other crime-related materials.

SOURCE: Federal Bureau of Investigation, *FBI Facts and Figures* (Washington, DC: FBI, 2000).

federal efforts to curtail organized crime, primarily through the use of federal racketeering laws.

Treasury Department   The U.S. Treasury Department maintains the following enforcement branches:

- *Bureau of Alcohol, Tobacco and Firearms (BATF).* The BATF helps control sales of untaxed liquor and cigarettes and, through the Gun Control Act of 1968 and the Organized Crime Control Act of 1970, has jurisdiction over the illegal sale, importation, and criminal misuse of firearms and explosives.

- *Internal Revenue Service (IRS).* The IRS, established in 1862, enforces violations of income, excise, stamp, and other tax laws. Its Intelligence Division actively pursues gamblers, narcotics dealers, and other violators who do not report their illegal financial gains as taxable income. For example, the career of 1920s gangster Al Capone was brought to an end through the efforts of IRS agents.

- *Customs Service.* The Customs Service guards points of entry into the United States and prevents smuggling of contraband into (or out of) the country. It ensures that taxes and tariffs are paid on imported goods and helps control the flow of narcotics into the country.

- *Secret Service.* The Secret Service was originally charged with enforcing laws against counterfeiting. Today, it is also responsible for protecting the president and vice-president and their families, presidential candidates, and former presidents. The Secret Service maintains the White House Police Force, which is responsible for protecting the executive mansion, and the Treasury Guard, which protects the mint.

Fill in the blanks 21
True/False 20–22

state police
Agencies that enforce state law outside of metropolitan areas and have jurisdiction over highway patrol.

State Police Agencies

Unlike municipal police departments, **state police** were legislatively created to deal with the growing incidence of crime in nonurban areas—a consequence of increased population mobility and personalized mass transportation in the form of the automobile. County sheriffs—elected officials with occasionally corrupt or questionable motives—had proven to be ineffective in dealing with the wide-ranging criminal activities that developed during the latter half of the nineteenth century. In addition, most local police agencies were unable to effectively protect against highly mobile lawbreakers who randomly struck at cities and towns throughout a state. In response to citizens' demands for effective and efficient law enforcement, state governors began to develop plans for police agencies that would be responsible to the state, instead of being tied to local politics and possible corruption.

The Texas Rangers, created in 1835, was one of the first state police agencies formed. Essentially a military outfit that patrolled the Mexican border, it was followed by the Massachusetts State Constables in 1865 and the Arizona Rangers in 1901. Pennsylvania formed the first truly modern state police in 1905.[20]

Today, about 23 state police agencies have the same general police powers as municipal police and are territorially limited in their exercise of law enforcement regulations only by the state's boundaries. In some jurisdictions, state police are also given special police powers; for example, some states use state police to serve civil process, while others provide emergency medical services. The remaining state police agencies are primarily responsible for highway patrol and traffic law enforcement. Some state police, such as those in California, direct most of their attention to the enforcement of traffic laws; others, such as those in South Dakota, have no responsibility for traffic control.

State police typically handle both law enforcement and traffic-related duties. Here, an Indiana state trooper photographs a rifle lying on the road in Terre Haute. The Terre Haute city police car behind him was rammed by Ben Nevins, 17, who died of gunshot wounds from a police officer.

AP/Wide World Photos

Most state police organizations are restricted by legislation from becoming involved in the enforcement of certain areas of the law. For example, in some jurisdictions, state police are prohibited from becoming involved in strikes or other labor disputes, unless violence erupts.

The nation's 80,000 state police employees (55,000 officers and 25,000 civilians) not only are involved in law enforcement and highway safety but also carry out a variety of other functions, including maintaining a training academy and providing emergency medical services. State police crime laboratories aid local departments in investigating crime scenes and analyzing evidence. State police also provide special services and technical expertise in such areas as bomb-site analysis and homicide investigation. Other state police departments, such as California's, are involved in highly sophisticated traffic and highway safety programs, including the use of helicopters for patrol and rescue, the testing of safety devices for cars, and the conducting of postmortem examinations to determine the causes of fatal accidents.

County Police Agencies

Most of the nation's county police departments, with their 265,000 employees (including 153,000 sworn officers), are independent agencies whose senior officer, the **sheriff**, is (in all states except Rhode Island and Hawaii) an elected political official.[21] The county sheriff's role has evolved from that of the early English shire reeve, whose primary duty was to assist the royal judges in trying prisoners and enforcing sentences. From the time of the westward expansion in the United States until municipal departments were developed, the sheriff was often the sole legal authority over vast territories.

The duties of a county sheriff's department vary according to the size and degree of development of the county. The standard tasks of a typical sheriff's department are serving civil process (summons and court orders), providing court security, operating the county jail, and investigating crimes. Less commonly, sheriff's departments may serve as coroners, tax collectors, overseers of highways and bridges, custodians of the county treasury, and providers of fire, animal control, and emergency medical services; in years past, sheriff's offices also conducted executions. Typically, a sheriff's department's law enforcement functions are restricted to unincorporated areas within a county, unless a city or town police department requests its help.

Some sheriff's departments are exclusively law enforcement oriented; some carry out court-related duties only; some are involved solely in correctional and judicial matters. However, a majority are full-service programs that carry out judicial, correctional, and law enforcement activities. As a rule, agencies serving large population areas (over 1 million) are devoted to maintaining county correctional facilities, while those in smaller population areas are focused on law enforcement.

In the past, sheriffs' salaries were almost always based on the fees they received for the performance of official acts. They received fees for every summons, warrant, subpoena, writ, or other process they served; they were also compensated for summoning juries or locking prisoners in cells. Today, sheriffs are salaried to avoid conflict of interest.

In some jurisdictions, the county sheriff's department has primary law enforcement duties. Here, Trumbull County (Ohio) sheriff's deputies, along with police from Brookfield, Howland, and Johnston, search a 140-car train that passed by the Corrections Corporation of America prison in Youngstown shortly after six inmates escaped.

Fill in the blanks 22–23

sheriff
The chief law enforcement officer in a county.

Multiple choice 25–26

Local Police Agencies

Local police comprise the majority of the nation's authorized law enforcement personnel. Metropolitan police departments range in size from the New York City Police Department, with more than 30,000 sworn officers and 10,000 civilian employees, to rural police departments with a single officer. In all, local police departments have an estimated 530,000 full-time employees, including at least 410,000 sworn personnel and more than 100,000 civilian employees (see Table 5.1). Local police employment rose an average of about 3 percent per year from 1993 to 1997, compared to about 1 percent per year from 1987 to 1993. Racial and ethnic minorities comprised 21.5 percent of full-time sworn officers in local police departments in 1997, compared to 19.1 percent in 1993, 17.0 percent in 1990, and 14.6 percent in 1987.[22]

Although most TV police shows feature the trials of big-city police officers, the overwhelming number of departments actually have fewer than 50 officers and serve a population of under 25,000. A total of 70 agencies employ 1,000 or more full-time sworn officers, including 15 state, 12 county, 41 local, and 2 special police agencies. In contrast, 2,245 agencies have just 1 full-time officer, and another 1,164 rely solely on part-time officers.[23]

The cost of maintaining these police forces is high. The average police officer costs taxpayers about $62,000 a year, including salary, benefits, and other costs; this amounts to an annual cost of more than $130 for every resident in the jurisdiction. Residents in larger jurisdictions who want and receive greater police protection pay about 40 percent more each year for police services than those living in small towns.

Regardless of size, most metropolitan police departments perform a standard set of functions and tasks and provide similar services to the community. These include traffic enforcement, accident investigation, patrol and peacekeeping, property and violent crime investigation, death investigation, narcotics and vice control, radio communications, crime prevention, fingerprint processing, and search and rescue. The police role is expanding, and procedures are being developed to aid special-needs populations, including HIV-infected suspects, the homeless, and victims of domestic and child abuse.[24]

These are only a few examples of the multiplicity of roles and duties assumed today in some of the larger urban police agencies around the nation. Smaller agencies may have trouble carrying out these tasks effectively, and the hundreds of

TABLE 5.1 PERSONNEL IN STATE, COUNTY, AND LOCAL LAW ENFORCEMENT

Type of Agency	Number of Agencies	Number of Full-time Sworn Officers
Total		738,028
All state and local	18,769	663,535
Local police	13,578	410,956
Sheriff	3,088	152,922
Primary state police	49	54,587
Special police	1,316	43,082
Texas constable		1,988
Federal*		74,493

*Nonmilitary federal officers authorized to carry firearms and make arrests.
NOTE: Special police category includes both state-level and local-level agencies. Five consolidated police-sheriffs are included under local police category.
SOURCE: Brian Reaves and Timothy Hart, *Law Enforcement Management and Administrative Statistics, 1999* (Washington, DC: Bureau of Justice Statistics, 2000), p. 1.

small police agencies in each state often provide duplicative services. Whether unifying smaller police agencies into "superagencies" would improve services is often debated among police experts. Smaller municipal agencies can provide important specialized services that might have to be relinquished if they were combined and incorporated into larger departments. Another approach has been to maintain smaller departments but to link them via computerized information sharing and resource management networks.[25]

LAW ENFORCEMENT IN THE TWENTY-FIRST CENTURY

Future trends in law enforcement include broader community involvement and the use of increasingly sophisticated technology.

Departmental Changes

One view is that police departments will reshape their role, de-emphasizing crime fighting and stressing community organization and revitalization.[26] Around the country, citizens are demanding that police departments reconsider their image as disinterested outsiders. Community leaders are asking that, instead of riding around anonymously in patrol cars, police officers become actively involved in neighborhood affairs. Programs that do this include neighborhood-based ministations and foot patrols.

Fill in the blanks 24
True/False 23–24
Essay 9

PERSPECTIVES ON JUSTICE

Police departments are evolving because leaders recognize that traditional crime control models have not been effective: The streets are still not safe; the fear of crime has not declined; respect for the justice system has not increased. In the future, the police role may shift more toward a restorative justice perspective, moving away from a legalistic style that isolates officers from the public to a service orientation that holds officers accountable to the community and encourages them to learn from the people they serve. This means that the police must actively create a sense of community where none has existed and recruit neighborhood cooperation for crime prevention activities.

Police agencies will continue to emphasize the decentralization of command through the creation of specialized units, substations, and direct response teams. Decentralization does not automatically ensure greater citizen cooperation, but it is believed to increase sensitivity to citizen needs, create special knowledge of and commitment to the area served, and foster heightened community trust in the police.

Departments are also increasing their use of civilian employees, thereby freeing sworn officers for law enforcement tasks. As police salaries and benefits increase, civilian employees will become an economic necessity. In addition, employing citizens from the community can help police departments become sensitive to the cultural environment they serve.[27]

Police departments will become increasingly proactive and focus their attention on solving community problems such as domestic violence, drug dealing, and drunk driving. Police administrators believe that arrests for these crimes may help reduce recidivism, and vocal community groups demand action against violators.

CRIMINAL JUSTICE AND TECHNOLOGY

Crime Mapping

Crime maps offer police administrators graphic representations of where crimes are occurring in their jurisdiction. Like the archaic pin maps they replace, computerized crime maps help police detect patterns of crimes and pathologies of related problems. Enabling police to work with multiple layers of information and scenarios, crime maps are far more successful in identifying emerging hot spots of criminal activity and helping police target their resources accordingly.

The simplest maps display crime locations or concentrations and help direct police to where they are most needed. (Figure A, for example, shows the distribution of serious crimes in Tempe, Arizona, during the month of August 1999.) More complex maps can be used to chart trends in criminal activity and have even proven valuable in solving individual criminal cases. For example, a serial rapist may be caught by observing and understanding his crime pattern so that detectives can predict where he will strike next and stake out the area with police decoys.

According to a survey conducted by the National Institute of Justice, 36 per-cent of agencies with 100 or more sworn officers are now using some form of computerized crime mapping, including a number of the nation's largest departments. The New York City Police Department's CompStat process relies on computerized crime mapping to identify crime hot spots and hold individual officers accountable for crime reduction, along with the department's chain of command. The department credits CompStat for dramatic and continuing reductions in crime in New York City. The Chicago Police Department has developed ICAM (Information Collection for Automated Mapping) to help officers analyze and solve neighborhood crime problems. Operational in all of the department's 25 police districts, ICAM lets beat officers and other police personnel quickly and easily generate maps of timely, accurate crime data for individual beats or larger units. ICAM makes it easier for police to share crime information with the community, thus supporting the department's community policing philosophy.

Some mapping efforts cross jurisdictional boundaries. Examples of this approach include the Regional Crime Analysis System in the greater Baltimore–Washington area and the multijurisdictional efforts of the Greater Atlanta PACT Data Center. The Charlotte–Mecklenburg (North Carolina) Police Department uses data collected by other city and county agencies in its crime-mapping efforts. By coordinating the tax assessor's, public works, planning, and sanitation departments, Charlotte–Mecklenburg departmental analysts have made links between disorder and crime that have been instrumental in supporting the department's community policing philosophy.

Critical Thinking Skills

1. Crime mapping represents one of the latest technological advances in the allocation of police resources to fight crime effectively. Is it possible that recent downturns in the crime rate reflect this emphasis on technology?

2. Does a growing police technology capability present a danger to personal privacy? How far should the police go to keep tabs on potentially dangerous people? For example, should DNA samples be taken at birth from all people and kept on

---

Police agencies will also have to deal with new categories of high-tech crimes, ranging from theft of information and data to electronic counterfeiting. Agencies that now train police officers to prevent burglaries may someday have to create high-tech forensic labs that can identify suspects involved in the theft of genetically engineered cultures from biomedical laboratories.[28]

The demographic structure of policing will also evolve. The numbers of minority and female police officers should continue to grow. In the past, white males followed their fathers into a police career. A new generation of minorities and females will now be able to follow their parents into police work.

Information Technology

True/False 25

Criminal investigation will be enhanced by the application of sophisticated electronic gadgetry: computers, cellular phones, and digital communication devices.[29]

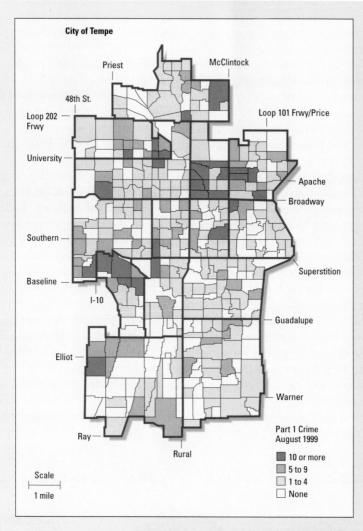

City of Tempe

Priest

McClintock

48th St.

Loop 202 Frwy

Loop 101 Frwy/Price

University

Apache

Broadway

Southern

Superstition

Baseline

I-10

Guadalupe

Elliot

Warner

Part 1 Crime August 1999

Ray

■ 10 or more

Rural

▨ 5 to 9

Scale

▢ 1 to 4

□ None

1 mile

file to match with genetic materials collected at crime scenes?

InfoTrac College Edition Research

To read more about developments in police technology, see Christina Couret, "Police and Technology: The Silent Partnership," *American City and County,* August 1999, v114 i9 p31

SOURCES: William W. Bratton and Peter Knobler, *Turnaround: How America's Top Cop Reversed the Crime Epidemic* (New York: Random House, 1998), p. 289; Jeremy Travis, *Computerized Crime Mapping* (Washington, DC: National Institute of Justice, 1999).

FIGURE A
CRIME MAP OF
TEMPE, ARIZONA,
AUGUST 1999

SOURCE: Courtesy of Tempe (Arizona) Police Department.

Budget realities demand that police agencies make the most effective use of their forces, and technology seems to be an important method of increasing productivity at a relatively low cost. The introduction of technology has already been explosive. In 1964, for example, only one city, St. Louis, had a police computer system; by 1968, 10 states and 50 cities had criminal justice information systems; today, almost every city of more than 50,000 has some sort of computer support services.[30]

One way that technology is being used to improve the effectiveness of police resources is crime mapping.[31] It is now recognized that a majority of predatory crimes are concentrated in certain geographic "hot spots." Computer mapping programs that translate addresses into map coordinates help law enforcement agencies identify problem areas for particular crimes, such as drug dealing. Computer maps enable police to identify the location, time of day, and linkage among criminal events and concentrate their forces accordingly.[32] Crime mapping is discussed in the Criminal Justice and Technology feature.

True/False 26

True/False 27–30
Multiple choice 27

For news about police technology and other related issues, go to the Police Officer Internet Directory at http://www.officer.com

For an up-to-date list of Web links, see http://www.wadsworth.com/product/0534573053s

FIGURE 5.2 COMPUTER-GENERATED COMPOSITES FOR IDENTIFYING SUSPECTS

Computer-generated composites can be used to help a witness create a precise sketch of criminal suspects. The Compusketch© program developed by the Visatex Corporation of Campbell, California, contains thousands of facial features and details.

Criminal Identification

One of the most important computer-aided tasks is the identification of criminal suspects. Some police departments are using computerized imaging systems to replace mug-shot books. Photos or sketches stored in computer memory can be easily retrieved for viewing.

Several software companies have developed identification programs that help witnesses create a composite picture of a suspect (see Figure 5.2). A vast library of photographed or drawn facial features can be stored in computer files and easily retrieved for viewing on a monitor. Witnesses can scan through thousands of noses, eyes, and lips until they find those that match the suspect's. Eyeglasses, mustaches, and beards can be added; skin tones can be altered. Once the composite has been created, it can be printed out for distribution.[33]

Computer systems now used in the booking process can also help in the suspect identification process. During booking, a visual image of the suspect is stored in a computer's memory, along with other relevant information. Police can then easily create a "photo lineup" by calling up on the computer monitor color photos of all suspects having a particular characteristic described by a witness.

Computer software now being developed allows two-dimensional mug shots to be re-created in three dimensions. This technology divides the human face into 64 features. For each of these features, such as nose, mouth, or chin, the program offers 256 different variations to choose from. The result is that virtually any face can be re-created according to a witness's or victim's description. Once re-created, the image can be compared with more than 1 million mug shots in less than a second to search for a match. A two-dimensional mug shot can be enhanced to generate a three-dimensional image, and effects such as lighting and angles can also be changed to simulate the environment in which a crime has taken place.[34]

New techniques are constantly being developed. Soon, through the use of genetic algorithms (mathematical models), it will be possible to construct a com-

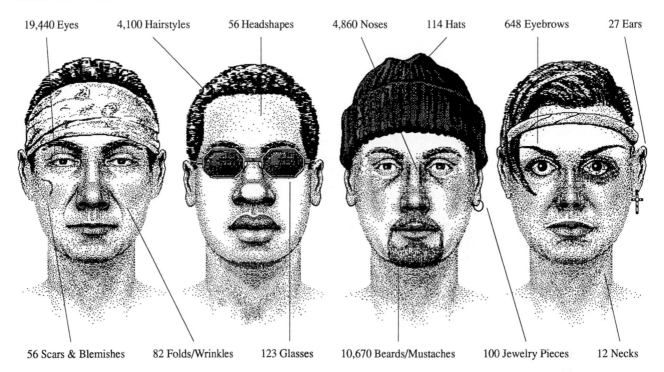

19,440 Eyes   4,100 Hairstyles   56 Headshapes   4,860 Noses   114 Hats   648 Eyebrows   27 Ears

56 Scars & Blemishes   82 Folds/Wrinkles   123 Glasses   10,670 Beards/Mustaches   100 Jewelry Pieces   12 Necks

puterized composite image of a suspect's face from relatively little information.[35] Digitization of photographs will enable the reconstruction of blurred images. Videotapes of bank robbers or blurred photos of license plates, or even bite marks, can be digitized using highly advanced mathematical models.

Computers are also being used to expedite the analysis of evidence. Los Angeles police can instantly cross-reference computer databases—for example, comparing files on suspects who own brown Chevrolets with those who have facial scars.[36]

PERSPECTIVES ON JUSTICE

In the future, police departments will be relying more heavily on the new technologies for investigation efficiency. The use of improved computer-based record keeping and long-range electronic surveillance devices creates the fear that police will have carte blanche to intrude into the private lives of citizens. How much information will go on police databases? Some now question the wisdom of emphasizing the technological aspects of police productivity at the expense of public service. As technology improves, the threat to privacy and security will increase, pitting crime control advocates against due process–oriented civil libertarians.

Automatic Fingerprint Systems The use of computerized fingerprint systems is growing around the United States. Using mathematical models, an automated fingerprint identification system (AFIS) can classify fingerprints and identify up to 250 characteristics (minutiae) of the print.[37] This automated system uses high-speed silicon chips to plot each point of minutiae and count the number of ridge lines between that point and its four nearest neighbors, which substantially improves its speed and accuracy over earlier systems. Some police departments, such as the District of Columbia's, report that computerized fingerprint systems are allowing them to make more than 100 identifications a month from fingerprints taken at a crime scene. AFIS files have been regionalized. For example, the Western Identification Network serves Alaska, California, Idaho, Nevada, Oregon, Utah, Washington, and Wyoming.[38]

If these computerized fingerprint files become standardized and a national database is formed, it will be possible to check records in all 50 states to determine whether the suspect's fingerprints match those taken at the crime scene of previously unsolved cases. A national fingerprint identification system is likely to become an even more effective tool because laser technology should vastly improve fingerprint analysis. Investigators will soon be able to recover prints that in the past were too damaged to be used as evidence. New breeds of fingerprint analysis will soon be available. As noted in Exhibit 5.2, the FBI is in the midst of creating an Integrated Automated Fingerprint Identification System that will enable local departments to scan fingerprints, send them electronically to a national depository, and receive back identification and criminal history of suspects.

DNA Testing Advanced technology is also spurring new forensic methods of identification and analysis.[39] The most prominent technique is **DNA profiling**, a procedure that gained national attention because of the O. J. Simpson case. This technique allows suspects to be identified on the basis of the genetic material

DNA profiling
The identification (or elimination) of criminal suspects by comparing DNA samples (genetic material) taken from them with specimens found at crime scenes.

found in hair, blood, and other bodily tissues and fluids. When DNA is used as evidence in a rape trial, DNA segments are taken from the victim and the suspect and from blood and semen found on the victim. A DNA match indicates a 4-billion-to-1 chance that the suspect is the offender.

Two methods of DNA matching are used. The most popular technique, known as RFLP (restriction fragment length polymorphism), uses radioactive material to produce a DNA image on an X-ray film. The second method, PCR (polymerase chain reaction), amplifies DNA samples through molecular photocopying.[40]

DNA fingerprinting is now used as evidence in criminal trials in more than 20 states.[41] The use of DNA evidence to gain convictions has also been upheld on appeal.[42] The use of DNA in criminal trials received a boost in 1997 when the FBI announced that DNA evidence has become so precise that experts no longer have to supply a statistical estimate of accuracy ("The odds are 1 in a billion that this is the culprit") when testifying at trial; they can now state in court that there exists "a reasonable degree of scientific certainty" that evidence came from a specific suspect.[43]

As you may recall from Exhibit 5.2, the FBI is now operating the Combined DNA Index System (CODIS), which allows DNA taken at a crime scene to be searched electronically to find matches against (1) samples taken from convicted offenders and (2) samples taken from other crime scenes. In 1999, the FBI announced that the system had made its first "cold hit" by linking evidence taken from crime scenes in Jacksonville, Florida, and Washington, D.C., thereby tying nine crimes to a single offender.[44]

Although DNA is a very useful tool, ethical and practical questions arise concerning its use. Critics such as Paul Tracy and Vincent Morgan report that the cost of maintaining a national DNA database is significant, rising into the hundreds of millions of dollars, while the number of criminals identified using DNA is relatively small.[45] They argue that DNA databases cannot be used to solve the vast majority of serious crimes, and solve few if any nonserious ones. Even if crime scenes contain DNA evidence, local law enforcement agencies do not have the necessary resources to collect evidence and identify criminals. Tracy and Morgan also warn that having DNA evidence on file poses a serious threat to civil liberties. Should a person who is arrested for placing a bet on a football game have his DNA kept on file with convicted rapists and child molesters?

Communications

Computers now link neighboring agencies so that they can share information on cases, suspects, and warrants. One such system is the Police Information Network, which electronically links the 93 independent law enforcement agencies in the San Francisco area, enabling them to share information. In addition, local departments now use computerized databases to record not only crime-related information but also motor vehicle and business data, workers' compensation files, and other public records that can be used to locate and track wanted felons.[46] On a broader jurisdictional level, the FBI in 1967 implemented the National Crime Information Center. This system, which provides rapid collection and retrieval of data about persons wanted for crimes anywhere in the 50 states, is currently undergoing a major overhaul and upgrading.

Computer technology is enhancing communications and information dissemination. For example, the St. Petersburg, Florida, police department has equipped all of its officers with portable computers, which has significantly cut down on the time needed to write and duplicate reports.[47] Police can now use terminals to draw accident diagrams, communicate with city traffic engineers, and merge their incident reports into other databases. Pen computing, in which officers write directly

Police departments around the nation are turning to technology to improve service delivery. Here, Scarborough (Maine) Police Department Officer Joe Giacomantonio demonstrates a computer program called Reverse 911. In emergency situations, police can use the program to quickly alert whole neighborhoods about potential problems.

on a computer screen, eliminates paperwork and increases the accuracy of reports.[48] To make this material more accessible to the officer on patrol, head-up display (HUD) units now project information onto screens located on patrol car windshields so that police officers can access computer readouts without taking their eyes off the road.[49]

Officers are using cellular phones in their cars to facilitate communication with victims and witnesses.[50] Departments that cover wide geographical areas and maintain independent precincts and substations are experimenting with teleconferencing systems that provide both audio and video linkages. Police agencies can also use advanced communications gear to track stolen vehicles. Car owners can buy transmitters that emit a signal that can then be monitored and tracked.[51] Finally, some departments are linking advanced communications systems with computers, making use of electronic bulletin boards that link officers in an active online system, enabling them to communicate faster and more easily.[52]

PRIVATE SECURITY

Because police alone can have only a limited influence on controlling crime and protecting victims, their efforts are often supplemented by those of private security forces. In the next decade, such private security forces are likely to have an even greater effect on law enforcement.

In the United States today, more than $50 billion is being spent annually on more than 10,000 private security firms, employing some 1.5 million guards. These firms range from the one-person operation to the offices of Pinkerton, the country's oldest and second-largest security firm, which employs more than 45,000 people internationally.

Much of what is known about the national trends in private policing comes from the Hallcrest Report. This government-financed survey of the industry found that the use of private security falls into two major areas.[53] Proprietary security, undertaken by an organization's own employees, includes both plainclothes and uniformed agents directed by the organization's head of security. The second type of private

Fill in the blanks 25
Multiple choice 28–29
Essay 10–11

AP/Wide World Photos

security is contractual services, such as guards, investigators, and armored cars, provided by private companies such as Wackenhut and Pinkerton's. Also included within the category of contractual security is the wide variety of security products, such as safes, electronic access-control devices, and closed-circuit television.

Private security forces take on responsibilities that are also within the domain of local police agencies. These include responding to burglar alarms, investigating misdemeanors, enforcing parking restrictions, and providing court security. Despite this overlap, little contact or cooperation used to occur between private and public policing agents. In the 1980s, the International Association of Chiefs of Police, the National Sheriffs' Association, and the American Society for Industrial Security began joint meetings to improve relations between the public and private sectors. In 1986, the Joint Council on Law Enforcement and Private Security Associations was formed.

One reason that public–private cooperation is essential is the rise of a movement to privatize services that have been within the jurisdiction of public police agencies. Candidates for privatization include public building security, parking enforcement, park patrol, animal control, special event security (such as rock concerts), funeral escorts, prisoner escorts, and public housing security. About 18 states have already privatized some police functions. In some small towns, private police may even replace the town police force. Reminderville, Ohio, experimented with an all-private police force and found that it produced great savings without any decrease in service. In 1971, some 5,000 federal police provided security at government buildings around the country; today, most of that work is handled privately.

One area that may be ideal for privatization is responding to private security systems. With rapid growth in the number of private security systems has come a corresponding increase in the number of false alarms. Today, about 20 percent of all homes have security systems, and in some jurisdictions, 30 percent of all calls for police service are false alarms. One approach has been to fine or charge homeowners for repeat false alarm calls. Another is to have private firms contracted to handle alarm calls and screen out false alarms before notifying police. The technology that supports this field will grow rapidly, with more sophisticated alarm systems, access control, and closed-circuit television.

The expanded role of private security is not without its perils. Many law enforcement executives are critical of the quality of private security and believe it has little value as a crime control mechanism. One complaint heard by the Hallcrest researchers was the lack of training and standards in the profession. Still another source of contention between private security and local police agencies is the increasing number of police calls that are a function of private security measures.

The Hallcrest Report recommended a number of strategies to improve the quality of private security: upgrading employee quality; creating statewide regulatory bodies and statutes for controlling security firms; requiring mandatory training; increasing police knowledge of private security; expanding the interaction between police and private security providers, such as information sharing; and transferring some police functions, such as burglar alarm checking, to the private sector. The report recommended that the industry establish its own standards similar to those adopted by the British Security Industry Association to professionalize the trade.

SUMMARY

Present-day police departments evolved out of early European and colonial American crime control forces.

Many types of organizations are involved in law enforcement activities on the local, state, and federal levels of government. The most visible law enforcement agencies are local police departments, which carry out patrol, investigative, and traffic functions, as well as many support activities.

In the coming years, police departments will rely increasingly on advanced computer-based technologies to identify suspects and collate evidence. Automated fingerprint systems and computerized identification systems will become more widespread. At the same time, some people fear that technology may make police overly intrusive and interfere with civil liberties.

In addition to public law enforcement agencies, a large variety of private policing enterprises have developed. These include a multibillion-dollar private security industry and the private employment of public police.

Key Terms

pledge system	justice of the peace	Federal Bureau of Investigation (FBI)
tithings	thief takers	Drug Enforcement Administration
hue and cry	bobbies	(DEA)
hundred	vigilantes	state police
constable	International Association of Chiefs of	sheriff
shire reeve	Police (IACP)	DNA profiling
watch system	Department of Justice (DOJ)	

Discussion Questions

1. List the problems faced by police departments today that were also present during the early days of policing.
2. Distinguish between the duties of state police, sheriffs' departments, and local police departments.
3. What are some of the technological advances that should help the police solve more crimes? What are the dangers of these advances?
4. Discuss the trends that will influence policing during the coming decade. What other social factors may affect policing?
5. Why has the private security industry blossomed? What factors will influence the role of private policing during the coming decade?

A CLOSER LOOK

Wilbur Miller, a professor of history at the State University of New York, Stony Brook, and the author of *Revenuers and Moonshiners: Enforcing Federal Liquor Law in the Mountain South, 1865-1900,* has written extensively on police history. He describes the origin and development of big-city police and the social forces that shaped their directions. Here is what he has to say about their earliest development:

> Before the rise of large cities and mass immigration in the nineteenth century, policing relied heavily on community consensus and the willingness of citizens to assist in capturing criminals. Able-bodied men were liable for service in the ancient institution of the sheriff's posse, and for election (or conscription in some places) as constables. County sheriffs were usually more occupied with collecting taxes or supervising elections than leading posses or serving warrants. Night-time, always regarded as an especially

> dangerous time, was enlivened by nightwatchmen calling the hour and sometimes giving weather reports while they were looking out for suspicious characters. The heart of colonial policing was not policemen but punishments. Public punishments—the ducking stool for gossips, stocks for petty criminals, branding of thieves, hanging for murderers and other serious offenders—were meant to induce shame in the people and provide moral lessons for the spectators. Jails were only pens for holding offenders between arrest and trial, or trial and sentencing, not places of punishment or rehabilitation.

To read more of what Miller has to say, go to InfoTrac College Edition and look up
Wilbur Miller, "The Good, the Bad, and the Ugly: Policing America," *History Today,* August 2000, v50 i8 p29

Notes

1 "Have Gun? Will Travel: Criminals Are Afraid to Arm Themselves in a Virginia City That Simply Enforced the Law," *Time,* 16 August 1999, p. 30.

2 Richard A. Leo and Richard J. Ofshe, "The Consequences of False Confessions: Deprivations of Liberty and Miscarriages of Justice in the Age of Psychological Interrogation," *Journal of Criminal Law and Criminology* 88 (1998): 429–496.

3 "Law Enforcement Seeks Answers to 'Racial Profiling' Complaints," *Criminal Justice Newsletter* 29 (1998): 5.

4 Liqun Cao, James Frank, and Francis Cullen, "Race, Community Context and Confidence in the Police," *American Journal of Police* 15 (1996): 3–15.

5 Thomas Priest and Deborah Brown Carter, "Evaluations of Police Performance in an African American Sample," *Journal of Criminal Justice* 27 (1999): 457–465.

6 This section relies heavily on the following sources: Malcolm Sparrow, Mark Moore, and David Kennedy, *Beyond 911: A New Era for Policing* (New York: Basic Books, 1990); Daniel Devlin, *Police Procedure, Administration, and Organization* (London: Butterworth, 1966); Robert Fogelson, *Big City Police* (Cambridge, MA: Harvard University Press, 1977); Roger Lane, *Policing the City: Boston 1822–1885* (Cambridge, MA: Harvard University Press, 1967); Roger Lane, "Urban Police and Crime in Nineteenth-Century America," in *Crime and Justice,* vol. 2, ed. Norval Morris and Michael Tonry (Chicago: University of Chicago Press, 1980), pp. 1–45; J. J. Tobias, *Crime and Industrial Society in the Nineteenth Century* (New York: Schocken Books, 1967); Samuel Walker, *A Critical History of Police Reform: The Emergence of Professionalism* (Lexington, MA: Lexington Books, 1977); Samuel Walker, *Popular Justice* (New York: Oxford University Press, 1980); President's Commission on Law Enforcement and the Administration of Justice, *Task Force Report: The Police* (Washington, DC: U.S. Government Printing Office, 1967), pp. 1–9.

7 Devlin, *Police Procedure, Administration, and Organization,* p. 3.

8 Wilbur Miller, "The Good, the Bad, and the Ugly: Policing America," *History Today* 50 (2000): 29–32.

9 Phillip Reichel, "Southern Slave Patrols as a Transitional Type," *American Journal of Police* 7 (1988): 51–78.

10 Walker, *Popular Justice,* p. 61.

11 Ibid., p. 8.

12 Dennis Rousey, "Cops and Guns: Police Use of Deadly Force in Nineteenth-Century New Orleans," *American Journal of Legal History* 28 (1984): 41–66.

13 Law Enforcement Assistance Administration, *Two Hundred Years of American Criminal Justice* (Washington, DC: U.S. Government Printing Office, 1976).

14 National Commission on Law Observance and Enforcement, *Report on the Police* (Washington, DC: U.S. Government Printing Office, 1931), pp. 5–7.

15 Pamela Irving Jackson, *Minority Group Threat, Crime, and Policing* (New York: Praeger, 1989).

16 James Q. Wilson and George Kelling, "Broken Windows," *Atlantic Monthly,* March 1982, pp. 29–38.

17 Frank Tippett, "It Looks Just Like a War Zone," *Time,* 27 May 1985, pp. 16–22; "San Francisco, New York Police Troubled by Series of Scandals," *Criminal Justice Newsletter* 16 (1985): 2–4; Karen Polk, "New York Police: Caught in the Middle and Losing Faith," *Boston Globe,* 28 December 1988, p. 3.

18 John Klofas, "Drugs and Justice: The Impact of Drugs on Criminal Justice in a Metropolitan Community," *Crime and Delinquency* 39 (1993): 204–224.

19 Steven Tuch and Ronald Weitzer, "The Polls: Trends: Racial Differences in Attitudes Toward the Police," *Public Opinion Quarterly* 61 (1997): 642–663.

20 Bruce Smith, *Police Systems in the United States* (New York: Harper & Row, 1960), p. 72.

21 *Sheriffs' Departments, 1997* (Washington, DC: Bureau of Justice Statistics, 1999).

22 *Local Police Departments, 1997* (Washington, DC: Bureau of Justice Statistics, 1999).

23 Brian A. Reaves and Andrew L. Goldberg, *Census of State and Local Law Enforcement Agencies, 1996* (Washington, DC: Bureau of Justice Statistics, 1998).

24 See, for example, Susan Martin and Edwin Hamilton, "Police Handling of Child Abuse Cases: Policies, Procedures and Issues," *American Journal of Police* 9 (1990): 1–16.

25 See, for example, Robert Keppel and Joseph Weis, *Improving the Investigation of Violent Crime: The Homicide Investigation and Tracking System* (Washington, DC: National Institute of Justice, 1993).

26 This section leans heavily on Jerome Skolnick and David Bayley, *The New Blue Line* (New York: Free Press, 1986), pp. 210–230.

27 See Stephen Mastrofski, "The Prospects of Change in Police Patrol: A Decade in Review," *American Journal of Police* 9 (1990): 1–69.

28 Larry Coutorie, "The Future of High-Technology Crime: A Parallel Delphi Study," *Journal of Criminal Justice* 23 (1995): 13–27.

29 Bill Clede, "Cellular Digital Packet Data: CDPD," *Law and Order* 43 (1995): 36–37.

30 Mark Birchler, "Computers in a Small Police Agency," *FBI Law Enforcement Bulletin,* January 1989, pp. 7–9.

31 Lois Pliant, "Information Management," *Police Chief* 61 (1994): 31–35.

32 J. Thomas McEwen and Faye Taxman, *Applications of Computerized Mapping to Police Operations* (Alexandria, VA: Institute for Law and Justice, 1994).

33 See Judith Blair Schmitt, "Computerized ID Systems," *Police Chief* 59 (1992): 33–45.

34 "Spotlight on Computer Imaging," *Police Chief* 66 (1999): 6–8.

35 Richard Rau, "Forensic Science and Criminal Justice Technology: High-Tech Tools for the 90s," *NIJ Reports,* June 1991, pp. 6–10.

36 Kristen Olson, "LAPD's Newest Investigative Tool," *Police Chief* 55 (1988): 30.

37 William Stover, "Automated Fingerprint Identification: Regional Application of Technology," *FBI Law Enforcement Bulletin* 53 (1984): 1–4.

38 Schmitt, "Computerized ID Systems," p. 35.

39 See generally, Ryan McDonald, "Juries and Crime Labs: Correcting the Weak Links in the DNA Chain," *American Journal of Law and Medicine* 24 (1998): 345–363; "DNA Profiling Advancement," *FBI Law Enforcement Bulletin* 67 (1998): 24.

40 Rau, "Forensic Science and Criminal Justice Technology."

41 "California Attorney General Endorses DNA Fingerprinting," *Criminal Justice Newsletter,* 1 March 1989, p. 1.

42 *State v. Ford,* 301 S.C. 485, 392 S.E.2d 781 (1990).

43 "Under New Policy, FBI Examiners Testify to Absolute DNA Matches," *Criminal Justice Newsletter,* 15 October 1997, pp. 1–2.

44 "FBI's DNA Profile Clearinghouse Announce First 'Cold Hit,' " *Criminal Justice Newsletter,* 16 March 1999, p. 5.

45 Paul Tracy and Vincent Morgan, "Big Brother and His Science Kit: DNA Databases for 21st Century Crime Control?" *Journal of Criminal Law and Criminology* 90 (2000): 635–690.

46 John Schmitz, "Criminals Versus Computers," *Law and Order* 42 (1994): 80–84.

47 Brewer Stone, "The High-Tech Beat in St. Pete," *Police Chief* 55 (1988): 23–28.

48 "Pen Computing: The Natural 'Next Step' for Field Personnel," *Law and Order* 43 (1995): 37.

49 Miller McMillan, "High Tech Enters the Field of View," *Police Chief* 62 (1994): 29.

50 Ibid., p. 24.

51 Mark Thompson, "Police Seeking Radio Channel for Stolen Auto Tracking System," *Criminal Justice Newsletter,* 15 March 1989, p. 1.

52 John Davis, "Information at Your Fingertips," *Law and Order* 43 (1995): 54–56.

53 William Cunningham and Todd Taylor, *The Growing Role of Private Security* (Washington, DC: U.S. Government Printing Office, 1984).

AP/Wide World Photos

THE POLICE: ORGANIZATION, ROLE, AND FUNCTION

On October 5, 2000, a federal jury awarded more than $3 million to Irma Morales, a 51-year-old Bronx woman who had been beaten by an undercover New York City police officer when she was mistakenly arrested in a drug case in 1998.[1] Although Morales was released a short time after her arrest, when another police officer pointed out the mistake, evidence showed that she suffered bruises on her arms and legs. During the trial, Morales testified that she had been walking to a bus near east 183rd Street and Prospect Avenue, to go to the dentist that morning, when a man grabbed her and dragged her into an unmarked car. The man, she later learned, was a New York police detective who did not identify himself at the time; she resisted arrest, not realizing that he was a police officer. She testified that she had started to struggle with him because she wanted him to let her go. "He grabbed me harder, and I started to scream because I was very scared, scared of being kidnapped or hurt. I thought my world was coming to an end. I didn't know what

he wanted with me." The detective, Anthony Leone, a veteran of more than 15 years on the force, told the jury that he had acted appropriately, identifying himself to Morales and treating her as he would any suspect. He was part of a team of officers arresting suspects whose descriptions were being radioed from another officer who was making undercover drug purchases. Morales was stopped because she matched a description of a woman involved in a drug deal. He denied using force sufficient to cause injuries. The jury awarded Morales $2.75 million for excessive force, $250,000 for false arrest, and $7,500 in punitive damages.

This incident illustrates the difficulty some police officers have in carrying out their role. They are told to be enforcers of the law in some of the toughest areas in urban America, yet are criticized or even jailed when their tactics become too aggressive. Is it unrealistic to expect police officers to fulfill society's demand for order while maintaining a tight grip on their behavior and emotions?

174

PERSPECTIVES ON JUSTICE

A crime control advocate would consider the Morales case typical of efforts by the courts to handcuff police officers, make their job more difficult, and stifle their initiative. According to this perspective, if police are constantly wary of lawsuits, they will not be able to do their job in an effective manner.

This chapter describes the organization of police departments and their various operating branches: patrol, investigation, service, and administration. It discusses the realities and ambiguities of the police role and how the concept of the police mission has been changing radically. The chapter concludes with a brief overview of some of the most important administrative issues confronting U.S. law enforcement agencies.

THE POLICE ORGANIZATION

Fill in the blanks 1–2
True/False 1–3
Multiple choice 1–2

Most municipal police departments in the United States are independent agencies within the executive branch of government, operating without specific administrative control from any higher governmental authority. On occasion, police agencies will cooperate and participate in mutually beneficial enterprises, such as sharing information on known criminals, or they may help federal agencies investigate interstate criminal cases. Aside from such cooperative efforts, police departments tend to be functionally independent organizations with unique sets of rules, policies, procedures, norms, budgets, and so on. The unique structure of police agencies greatly influences their function and effectiveness.

Although many police agencies are in the process of rethinking their organization and goals, the majority are still organized in a militaristic, hierarchical manner, as illustrated in Figure 6.1. Within this organizational model, each element of the department normally has its own chain of command. For example, in a large municipal department, the detective bureau might have a captain as the director of a particular division (such as homicide), a lieutenant overseeing individual cases and acting as liaison with other police agencies, and sergeants and inspectors carrying out the actual fieldwork. Smaller departments may have a captain as head of all detectives, with lieutenants supervising individual subsystems (such as rob-

FIGURE 6.1
ORGANIZATION OF A TRADITIONAL METROPOLITAN POLICE DEPARTMENT

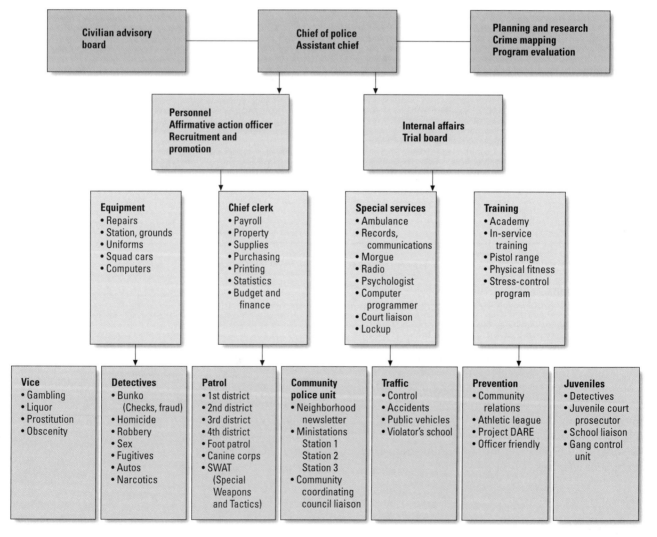

bery or homicide). At the head of the organization is the **chief of police**, who sets policy and has general administrative control over all of the department's various operating branches.

The typical police department's organizational structure has a number of problems. First, it is often difficult for citizens to determine who is actually responsible for the department's policies and operations. Second, the large number of operating divisions and the lack of any clear relationship among them almost guarantee that the decision-making practices of one branch will be unknown to another; two divisions may unknowingly compete with each other over jurisdiction on a particular case.

Most departments also follow a military-like system in promoting personnel within the ranks; at an appropriate time, a promotion test may be given, and based on his or her scores and recommendations, an officer may be advanced in rank. This organizational style frustrates some police officers from furthering their education, since a college or advanced degree may have little direct impact on their promotion potential or responsibilities. Furthermore, some otherwise competent officers are unable to increase their rank because of their inability to take tests well.

Most police departments employ a **time-in-rank system** for determining promotion eligibility. This means that before moving up the administrative ladder, an officer must spend a certain amount of time in a given rank; a sergeant cannot become a captain without serving an appropriate amount of time as a lieutenant. Although this system is designed to promote fairness and limit favoritism, it also restricts administrative flexibility. Unlike the private sector, where talented people can be pushed ahead in the best interests of the company, the time-in-rank system prohibits rapid advancement. A police agency would probably not be able to hire a computer systems expert with a PhD and give her a command position in charge of its data analysis section. The department would be forced to hire the expert as a civilian employee under the command of a ranking senior officer who may not be as technically proficient.

Under this rank system, a title can rarely be taken away or changed once it is earned. Police administrators become frustrated when qualified junior officers cannot be promoted or reassigned to appropriate positions because they lack time in rank or because less qualified officers have more seniority. Inability to advance through the ranks convinces numerous educated and ambitious officers to seek private employment. The rank system also means that talented officers cannot transfer to other departments or sell their services to the highest bidder. Time in rank ensures the stability—for better or worse—of police agencies.

THE POLICE ROLE

In countless books, movies, and television shows, the public has been presented with a view of policing that romanticizes police officers as fearless crime fighters who think little of their own safety as they engage in daily shoot-outs with Uzi-toting drug runners, psychopathic serial killers, and organized crime assassins. Occasionally, but not often, fictional patrol officers and detectives seem aware of departmental rules, legal decisions, citizen groups, civil suits, or physical danger. They are rarely faced with the economic necessity of moonlighting as security guards, caring about an annual pay raise, or griping when someone less deserving gets promoted ahead of them for political reasons.

How close is this portrayal of a selfless crime fighter to "real life"? Not very, according to most research efforts. Police officers are asked to deal with hundreds of incidents each year. For example, the Los Angeles Police Department receives more than 3.5 million calls for service each year, an average of 593 per officer;

chief of police
The head of a police agency who sets policy and has control over operations.

time-in-rank system
The promotion system in which a police officer can advance in rank only after spending a prescribed amount of time in the preceding rank.

Fill in the blanks 3
True/False 4
Multiple choice 3–5

Copsonline is a police Internet resource. It provides information on how to become a police officer, as well as information on the latest books, training, and jobs. http://www.copsonline.com
For an up-to-date list of Web links, see http://www.wadsworth.com/product/0534573053s

police in Dallas receive more that 1.6 million calls, or 665 per officer. In some places, the load is even more staggering; the Lawrence (Massachusetts) Police Department, for example, receives more than 1,500 calls for service per officer each year![2]

Most research shows that a police officer's crime-fighting efforts are only a small part of his or her overall activities. Studies of police work indicate that a significant portion of an officer's time is spent handling minor disturbances, service calls, and administrative duties. Studies conducted over the past two decades have found that social service and administrative tasks consume more than half of a police officer's time and account for more than half of his or her calls. Police work, then, involves much more than "catching criminals."[3]

These results are not surprising when UCR (Uniform Crime Reports) arrest data are considered. Currently, about 600,000 local, county, and state police officers make about 14 million arrests annually, an average of about 20 each. Of these, about 2 million are for serious index crimes (Part I), or less than 4 yearly per officer. Assuming an even distribution of arrests, then, the average police officer makes 2 arrests per month, and perhaps 1 arrest for a serious crime every three months.

These figures should be interpreted with caution because not all police officers are engaged in activities that allow them to make arrests, such as patrol or detective work. About one-third of all sworn officers in the nation's largest police departments are in such units as communications, antiterrorism, administration, and personnel and are therefore unlikely to make arrests. Even if the number of arrests per officer were adjusted by one-third, it would still amount to less than 10 serious crime arrests per officer per year. So although police handle thousands of calls each year, relatively few result in an arrest for a serious crime, such as a robbery and burglary; in suburban and rural areas, years may go by before a police officer arrests someone for a serious crime.

The evidence, then, shows that the police role involves a preponderance of non-crime-related activities and is similar in both large and small departments. Although officers in large urban departments may be called on to handle more felony cases than those in small towns, they too will probably find that the bulk of their daily activities are not crime related. In the future, officers will probably spend even more of their time learning to deal with the social problems exploding across the United States, ranging from women who have been battered in domestic disputes to runaway children. More attention will be paid to special-needs populations: substance abusers, the homeless, the mentally ill, and the disabled.[4] Unlike their fictional counterparts who arrest 10 people per hour, most officers rarely spend their days directly fighting crime.

The activities of most police departments are listed in Figure 6.1. As this figure shows, large metropolitan police departments carry out a wide variety of tasks and maintain a number of highly specialized roles. The most important of these, the patrol and investigation (detective) functions, are described in the next sections.

THE PATROL FUNCTION

Regardless of style of policing, uniformed patrol officers are the backbone of the police department, usually accounting for about two-thirds of a department's personnel.[5] Patrol officers are the most highly visible components of the entire criminal justice system. They are charged with supervising specific areas of their jurisdiction, called **beats**, whether on foot, in a patrol car, or by motorcycle, horse, helicopter, or even boat (see Table 6.1). Each beat, or patrol area, is covered 24 hours a day by different shifts. The major purposes of patrol are to

Fill in the blanks 4–7
True/False 5–9
Multiple choice 6–9
Essay 1

beat
A designated police patrol area.

TABLE 6.1 TYPES OF PATROL USED BY LOCAL POLICE DEPARTMENTS, BY SIZE OF POPULATION SERVED*

Population Served	Any Type	Auto-mobile	Foot	Bicycle	Motor-cycle	Marine	Horse
	Agencies Using Each Type of Patrol on a Routine Basis (%)						
All sizes	99	99	50	28	9	3	1
1,000,000 or more	100	100	94	87	88	62	69
500,000–999,999	100	100	58	88	88	50	42
250,000–499,999	100	100	61	74	85	17	54
100,000–249,999	100	100	50	70	79	13	21
50,000–99,999	100	100	43	68	52	6	6
25,000–49,999	100	100	54	64	38	6	2
10,000–24,999	100	100	49	52	14	6	—
2,500–9,999	99	99	54	29	4	3	1
Under 2,500	99	98	49	13	1	1	—

*— = less than 0.5%.
SOURCE: *Local Police Departments, 1997* (Washington, DC: Bureau of Justice Statistics, 2000).

- Deter crime by maintaining a visible police presence
- Maintain public order (peacekeeping) within the patrol area
- Enable the police department to respond quickly to law violations or other emergencies
- Identify and apprehend law violators
- Aid individuals and care for those who cannot help themselves
- Facilitate the movement of traffic and people
- Create a feeling of security in the community[6]

Patrol officers' responsibilities are immense; they may suddenly be faced with an angry mob, an armed felon, or a suicidal teenager and be forced to make split-second decisions on what action to take. At the same time, they must be sensitive to the needs of citizens who are often of diverse racial and ethnic backgrounds.

Patrol Activities

Most experts agree that the great bulk of police patrol efforts is devoted to **order maintenance**, or **peacekeeping**: maintaining order and civility within their assigned jurisdiction, or "handling the situation."[7] Police encounter many troubling incidents that need some sort of "fixing up."[8] Enforcing the law might be one tool a patrol officer uses; threat, coercion, sympathy, understanding, and apathy might be others. Most important is keeping the situation under control so that no one complains that the officer is doing nothing or doing too much. The "real" police role, then, may be as a community problem solver.

Police officers actually practice a policy of selective enforcement, concentrating on some crimes but handling the majority in an informal manner. An officer is supposed to know when to take action and when not to, whom to arrest and whom to deal with by issuing a warning or some other informal action. If a mistake is made, the officer can be severely criticized by peers and superiors, as well as the general public. Consequently, the patrol officer's job is extremely demanding and often unrewarding and unappreciated. It is not surprising that the attitudes of police officers toward the public are sometimes characterized as ambivalent and cynical.[9]

order maintenance (peacekeeping) Maintaining order and authority without the need for formal arrest; "handling the situation"; keeping things under control by means of threats, persuasion, and understanding.

Police officers make an arrest outside a Los Angeles laundromat. Some experts believe that strong action on "lifestyle crimes," such as loitering and panhandling, can help reduce the overall crime rate. Although these tactics may work, how do they affect the social climate? How aggressive should police officers be in cracking down on crime?

© David Butow/SABA

Does Patrol Deter Crime?

It is assumed that a large, visible police patrol is a deterrent to criminal behavior and that the rapid deployment of police officers to the scene of a crime is a particularly effective law enforcement technique. Is patrol a successful crime deterrent?

The most widely heralded attempt at measuring patrol effectiveness was undertaken during the early 1970s in Kansas City, Missouri, under the sponsorship of the Police Foundation, a private institute that studies police behavior.[10] To evaluate the effectiveness of patrol, the researchers divided 15 separate police districts into three groups: One group retained normal police patrol; in the second (proactive) group, districts were supplied with two to three times the normal amount of patrol forces; in the third (reactive) group, preventive patrol were eliminated, and police officers responded only when summoned by citizens to the scene of a particular crime.

Data from the Kansas City study indicated that these variations in patrol techniques had little effect on the crime patterns in the 15 districts. The presence or absence of patrol did not seem to affect residential or business burglaries, motor vehicle thefts, larcenies involving auto accessories, robberies, vandalism, or other criminal behavior.[11] Variations in police patrol techniques also appeared to have little influence on citizens' attitudes toward the police, their satisfaction with police, or their fear of future criminal behavior.[12]

Proactive Patrol The Kansas City study suggested that the mere presence of police may not be sufficient to deter crime. As a consequence, police departments scrambled to find more effective methods of using their patrol forces to reduce crime rates. Some began using a proactive, aggressive law enforcement style, encouraging officers to stop motor vehicles to issue citations and to aggressively arrest and detain suspicious persons; these tactics have been related to crime rate reductions.[13] Departments that more actively enforce minor regulations, such as disorderly conduct and traffic laws, are also more likely to experience lower felony rates.[14] Another approach is to target areas with extremely high crime rates ("hot spots") with saturation patrols.[15]

Pinpointing why proactive policing works effectively is difficult. It may have a deterrent effect: Aggressive policing increases community perception that police arrest many criminals and that most violators get caught; criminals are afraid to commit crimes in a town that has such an active police force. Proactive policing may also help control crime because it results in conviction of more criminals. Because aggressive police arrest more suspects, there are fewer left on the street to commit crime; fewer criminals produce lower crime rates.

PERSPECTIVES ON JUSTICE

These results are encouraging to crime control enthusiasts, but the downside of aggressive tactics must be considered before a general policy of vigorous police work can be adopted. Proactive police strategies may cause resentment in minority areas where citizens believe they are being unfairly targeted by police. Aggressive police tactics such as stopping and frisking and rousting teenagers who congregate on street corners may be the seeds from which racial conflict grows. Overly aggressive officers may also be the ones who are continually involved in incidents of unnecessary brutality, which concerns due process advocates. Despite such reservations, many large police jurisdictions have adopted a crime control philosophy by having patrol officers become more aggressive and concentrate on investigating and deterring crimes.

Not all aggressive patrol efforts have proven to be successful, but they have been a critical success with local city officials aiming for a "get tough" policy on crime.[16] The downturn in the New York City violent crime rate during the 1990s has been attributed to aggressive police work aimed at "lifestyle" crimes—vandalism, panhandling, and graffiti—and helped elevate the reputation of both Mayor Rudolph Giuliani and William Bratton, the police commissioner who instigated the program.[17] However, as the Analyzing Criminal Justice Issues feature shows, aggressive police work may have its downside.

Targeting Crimes Evidence also shows that targeting specific crimes can be successful. One aggressive patrol program, known as the Kansas City Gun Experiment, was directed at restricting the carrying of guns in high-risk places at high-risk times. Working with academics from the University of Maryland, the Kansas City (Missouri) Police Department focused extra patrol attention on a "hot spot" high-crime area identified by computer analysis of all gun crimes. Over a 29-week period, the gun patrol officers made thousands of car and pedestrian checks and traffic stops and made more than 600 arrests. Using frisks and searches, they found 29 guns; an additional 47 weapons were seized by other officers in the experimental area.

The target beat experienced 169 gun crimes in the 29 weeks prior to the gun patrol, but only 86 while the experiment was underway—a decrease of 49 percent. Drive-by shootings dropped significantly, as did homicides, without any displacement to other areas of the city. It is possible that the weapons seized were taken from high-rate offenders who were among the most likely perpetrators of gun-related crimes; their "lost opportunity" to commit violent crimes may have resulted in an overall rate decrease. It is also possible that the gun sweeps caused some of the most violent criminals to be taken off the streets. And as word of the patrol got out, there may have been a general deterrent effect: People contemplating violent crime may have been convinced that apprehension risks were unacceptably high.[18]

ANALYZING CRIMINAL JUSTICE ISSUES

Zero Tolerance: Aggressive Policing in New York City

During the 1990s, New York City experienced a significant reduction in street crime. Much of the crime reduction has been attributed to a concerted effort by the New York Police Department (NYPD) to rid the city of seemingly minor lifestyle offenses such as prostitution, low-level drug dealing, and panhandling. City and law enforcement officials believe that dangerous criminals will be deterred if they get tough on these crimes and maintain a policy of zero tolerance toward any offense. Criminologist Judith Greene has explored whether the NYPD's zero tolerance approach is truly responsible for the rather impressive reduction in urban crime.

When Mayor Rudolph Giuliani took office in 1993, he promised to make New York City a safer place. One of Giuliani's first acts was to hire then Boston Police Chief William Bratton to run the NYPD. At the time of Bratton's appointment, many people thought that a significant crime reduction was impossible, believing that the NYPD was too big to manage effectively.

Bratton, however, brought a fresh approach to policing. He helped update the technology of the NYPD by creating the crime-mapping CompStat program, which put crime data into the hands of precinct commanders. Bratton held commanders accountable if crime problems were not taken care of in a timely fashion and replaced officers whose performances he deemed inadequate. Finally, Bratton increased the freedom of police officers to stop, search, and question those who had violated the law, even if infractions were not especially serious. Law enforcement officials believed that stopping and questioning a suspect on an unimportant law violation might turn up a weapon or lead to information about a more serious crime that was about to take place.

The numbers seemed to support the new police practices, as the city saw dramatic reductions in the numbers of murders, nonnegligent homicides, robberies, and burglaries from 1993 to 1997. New York also saw its place on the FBI Index fall from 87th in 1993 to 150th in 1997.

Although the numbers appear to support a zero tolerance approach, Greene reports that the city paid a heavy price for adopting an aggressive crime control strategy. Filings of civil rights complaints against the NYPD climbed 75 percent in four years after the zero tolerance strategy was introduced. By 1996, citizen complaints filed with New York's Civilian Complaint Review Board had risen by 60 percent. Complaints against the police in cases in which no arrests were made doubled within a year of implementation of the zero tolerance approach; most incidents occurred in minority neighborhoods. Amnesty International claimed that New York had problems with police brutality and the use of unjustifiable force.

The zero tolerance approach seemed to reduce crime in New York, but Greene points out that during the early 1990s, other urban areas achieved similar results using less aggressive police tactics. For example, the San Diego Police Department (SDPD) took a more community-oriented approach to crime prevention by adopting a Neighborhood Policing Philosophy. This model has law enforcement personnel work in conjunction with community organizations such as Neighborhood Watch programs to prevent and control crime. The SDPD works closely with citizens and businesses to try to bring about change in areas with chronic crime problems. Information sharing is the norm, and teams work with residents to find solutions to long-term problems.

The crime reduction results achieved by San Diego's Neighborhood Policing Philosophy are similar to those attained with New York City's heralded zero tolerance program. However, the results were achieved at less cost and with fewer negative consequences. New York's 37.4 percent drop in crime from 1990 to 1995 was bolstered by a 39.5 percent increase in personnel; San Diego's 36.8 percent crime rate drop during the same time period was accomplished with a 6.2 percent increase in staff. Perhaps even more important to the community, San Diego's crime rate decrease was accompanied by a decrease in the number of citizen complaints filed against the police.

Critical Thinking Skills

1. Would you want to live in a city with extremely aggressive police officers who routinely stop and frisk suspicious looking people and use their arrest power for every violation of the law, no matter how minor or petty?
2. If police become overly aggressive, are charges of minority harassment and racial profiling inevitable?

 InfoTrac College Edition Research

To find out more about the dangers of zero tolerance policing, read Dorothy E. Roberts, "Foreword: Race, Vagueness, and the Social Meaning of Order-Maintenance Policing," *Journal of Criminal Law and Criminology,* Spring 1999, v89 p775

SOURCE: Judith Greene, "Zero Tolerance: A Case Study of Police Policies and Practices in New York City," *Crime and Delinquency* 45 (1999): 171–188.

More Patrol Officers, Less Crime? One reason patrol activity may be less effective than desired is the lack of adequate resources. Does adding more police help bring the crime rate down? Comparisons of police expenditures in U.S. cities indicate that cities with the highest crime rates also spend the most on police services.[19] The actual number of law enforcement officers in a jurisdiction seems to have little effect on area crime.[20] However, there is some evidence that cities that have more officers per capita than the norm also experience lower levels of violent crime.[21]

Adding police resources may improve the overall effectiveness of the justice system. Communities with relatively high crime rates and inadequate law enforcement resources find that many cases are dropped before they ever get to trial.[22] It is possible that prosecutors in these jurisdictions are forced to drop cases because police lack the resources to gather sufficient evidence to ensure convictions.

Do Arrests Deter Crime?

If the mere presence of police is not sufficient to deter crime, is it possible that more formal police action, such as an arrest, can help reduce the frequency of illegal acts?

A number of experts have expressed doubt that formal police action can have any general deterrent effect or, if it does, that it would be anything but short-lived and temporary.[23] However, a few research studies do show that contact with the police may cause some offenders to forgo repeat criminal behavior; under some circumstances, formal police action such as arrest may in fact deter future criminality.[24]

Some of the most significant tests of the deterrent effect of police arrest power have focused on the ability to reduce repeated domestic violence. These cases are particularly vexing for police administrators because they typically involve repeat incidents and situations in which it is difficult for the officer on the scene to respond effectively.

To test the most appropriate response, police officers who participated in a study conducted in Minneapolis randomly assigned treatments to the domestic assault cases they encountered on their beat.[25] One approach was to give some sort of advice and mediation; another was to send the assailant from the home for eight hours; the third was to arrest the assailant.

The Minneapolis data indicate that when police took formal action (arrest), the chance of repeat offending, or **recidivism**, was substantially less than when they took less punitive measures, such as warning offenders or ordering them out of the house for a cooling-off period. A six-month follow-up found that only 10 percent of those who were arrested repeated their violent behavior, compared with 19 percent of those advised and 24 percent of those sent away.

recidivism
Repetition of criminal behavior; habitual criminality.

To supplement the official police data, 205 of the victims were personally interviewed. The victims also reported that an arrest had the greatest benefit in controlling domestic assaults. Nineteen percent of the women whose men had been arrested reported their mates had assaulted them again, compared with 37 percent of those whose mates had been advised and 33 percent of those whose mates had been sent away. In sum, the Minnesota experiment indicates that a formal arrest was the most effective means of controlling domestic violence, regardless of what happened to the offender in court.

Although the results of the Minneapolis experiment received quick acceptance, government-funded research replicating the experimental design in other locales, including Omaha, Nebraska, and Charlotte, North Carolina, failed to duplicate the results: Formal arrest was no greater a deterrent to domestic abuse than warning or advising the assailant.[26] And even when research has found that arrest can be a deterrent under some circumstances, the effect soon dissipates and violence eventually recurs.[27]

THE INVESTIGATION FUNCTION

Fill in the blanks 8–9
True/False 10–11
Multiple choice 10–12
Essay 2–3

Since the first independent detective bureau was established by the London Metropolitan Police in 1841,[28] criminal investigators have been romantic figures vividly portrayed in novels, movies such as *Lethal Weapon* (Mel Gibson and Danny Glover) and television shows such as *Columbo, NYPD Blue,* and *Law & Order.* The fictional police detective is usually depicted as a loner, willing to break departmental rules, perhaps even violate the law, to capture the suspect. The average fictional detective views departmental policies and U.S. Supreme Court decisions as unfortunate roadblocks to police efficiency. Civil rights are either ignored or actively scorned.[29]

Although every police department probably has a few "hell-bent for leather" detectives who take matters into their own hands at the expense of citizens' rights, the modern criminal investigator is most likely an experienced civil servant, trained in investigatory techniques, knowledgeable about legal rules of evidence and procedure, and at least somewhat cautious about the legal and administrative consequences of his or her actions.[30] Although detectives are often handicapped by limited time, money, and resources, they are certainly aware of how their actions will one day be interpreted in a court of law. In fact, police investigators are sometimes accused of being more concerned with the most recent court cases regarding search and seizure and custody interrogation than with engaging in shoot-outs with suspected felons.

Detectives investigate the causes of crime and attempt to identify the individuals or groups responsible for committing particular offenses. They may enter a case after patrol officers have made the initial contact, such as when a patrol car interrupts a crime in progress and the offenders flee before they can be apprehended. They may investigate a case entirely on their own, sometimes by following up on leads provided by informants.

Conducting Investigations

vice squad
Police officers assigned to enforce morality-based laws, such as those on prostitution, gambling, and pornography.

Detective divisions are typically organized into sections or bureaus, such as homicide, robbery, or rape. Some jurisdictions maintain morals sections, or **vice squads**, which are usually staffed by plainclothes officers or detectives specializing in victimless crimes, such as prostitution or gambling. Vice squad officers may set themselves up as customers for illicit activities to make arrests. For example, male undercover detectives may frequent public men's rooms and make advances toward entering men; those who respond are arrested for homosexual soliciting. In other instances, female police officers may pose as prostitutes. These covert police activities have often been criticized as violating the personal rights of citizens, and their appropriateness and fairness have been questioned.

Detective work can be viewed as dealing with four types of situations:

1. A suspect has been apprehended or a subject placed under control, and there is adequate information about the person's behavior.
2. There is reliable information that a crime has been committed, but the suspect has not been identified or, if identified, has not been apprehended. This is the classic problem of detection: to discover reliable information that will permit the identification and arrest of a perpetrator.
3. A suspect or subject is known or even under continuous observation or control, but there is no reliable or adequate information about this person's past behavior, present connections, or future intentions. The investigators are not sure that a crime has been committed but are hoping to discover a crime that can implicate a targeted individual or his or her confederates.
4. The detectives have neither an identified subject nor adequate information. However, they have reason to believe, ranging from a hunch and the tips of

untested informants to the implications of other investigative reports, that something may be up or something bears watching.[31]

Sting Operations Another approach to detective work, commonly referred to as a **sting**, involves organized groups of detectives who deceive criminals into openly committing illegal acts or conspiring to engage in criminal activity. Numerous sting operations have been aimed at capturing professional thieves and seizing stolen merchandise. Undercover detectives pose as fences, set up ongoing fencing operations, and encourage thieves interested in selling stolen merchandise. Transactions are videotaped to provide prosecutors with strong cases. Sting operations have netted millions of dollars in recovered property and resulted in many arrests.

Although these results seem impressive, sting operations do have drawbacks.[32] By its very nature, a sting involves deceit by police agents that often comes close to entrapment. Sting operations may encourage criminals to commit new crimes because they have a new source for fencing stolen goods. Innocent people may hurt their reputations by buying merchandise from a sting operation when they had no idea the items had been stolen. By putting the government in the fencing business, such operations blur the line between law enforcement and criminal activity.

sting
An undercover police operation in which police pose as criminals to trap law violators.

Undercover Work Sometimes detectives go undercover to investigate crime.[33] Undercover work can take a number of forms. A lone agent can infiltrate a criminal group or organization to gather information on future criminal activity. For example, a DEA (Drug Enforcement Administration) agent may go undercover to gather intelligence on drug smugglers. Undercover officers can also pose as victims to capture predatory criminals who have been conducting street robberies and muggings.

Undercover work is considered a necessary element of police work, although it can prove quite dangerous for the agent. Police officers may be forced to engage in illegal or immoral behavior to maintain their cover. They also face significant physical danger in playing the role of a criminal and dealing with mobsters, terrorists, and drug dealers. In far too many cases, undercover officers are mistaken for real criminals and are injured by other law enforcement officers or private citizens trying to stop a crime. Arrest situations involving undercover officers may also provoke violence when suspects do not realize they are in the presence of police and therefore violently resist arrest.

Undercover officers may also experience psychological problems. Being away from home, keeping late hours, and always worrying that their identity will be uncovered all create enormous stress. Officers have experienced postundercover stress resulting in trouble at work and, in many instances, ruined marriages and botched prosecutions. Associating with criminals for a long period of time, becoming their friends, and earning their trust can also have a damaging psychological impact.

Evaluating Investigations

Serious criticism has been leveled at the nation's detective forces for being bogged down in paperwork and relatively inefficient in clearing cases. One famous study of 153 detective bureaus found that a great deal of a detective's time was spent in nonproductive work and that investigative expertise did little to solve cases; half of all detectives could be replaced without negatively influencing crime clearance rates.[34]

Although some question remains about the effectiveness of investigations, police detectives do make a valuable contribution to police work because their skilled interrogation and case-processing techniques are essential to eventual criminal conviction.[35] Nonetheless, a majority of cases that are solved are done so when the perpetrator is identified at the scene of the crime by patrol officers. Research shows that if a crime is reported while in progress, the police have about a 33 percent chance of making an arrest; the arrest probability declines to about 10 percent if the crime is reported 1 minute later, and to 5 percent if more than 15 minutes have elapsed. As the time between the crime and the arrest grows, the chances of a conviction are also reduced, probably because the ability to recover evidence is lost. Put another way, once a crime has been completed and the investigation is put in the hands of detectives, the chances of identifying and arresting the perpetrator diminish rapidly.[36]

Improving Investigations

A number of efforts have been made to revamp and improve investigation procedures. One practice has been to give patrol officers greater responsibility for conducting preliminary investigations at the scene of the crime. In addition, the old-fashioned precinct detective has been replaced by specialized units, such as homicide or burglary squads, that operate over larger areas and can bring specific expertise to bear. Technological advances in DNA and fingerprint identification have also aided investigation effectiveness.

One reason for the ineffectiveness of investigation is that detectives often lack sufficient resources to carry out a lengthy ongoing probe of any but the most serious cases. Research shows the following:

- *Unsolved cases.* Almost 50 percent of burglary cases are screened out by supervisors and never assigned to a detective for a follow-up investigation. Of those assigned, 75 percent are dropped after the first day of the follow-up investigation. Robbery cases are more likely to be assigned to detectives, but 75 percent of them are also dropped after one day of investigation.
- *Length of investigation.* The vast majority of cases are investigated for no more than four hours stretching over three days. An average of 11 days elapses between the initial report of a crime and suspension of the investigation.
- *Sources of information.* Early in an investigation, the focus is on the victim; as the investigation is pursued, emphasis shifts to the suspect. The most critical information for determining case outcome is the name and description of the suspect and related crime information. Victims are most often the source of information; witnesses, informants, and members of the police department are consulted far less often. However, when these sources are tapped, they are likely to produce useful information.
- *Effectiveness.* Preliminary investigations by patrol officers are critical. In situations where the suspect's identity is not known immediately after the crime is committed, detectives are able to make an arrest in less than 10 percent of all cases.[37]

These findings suggest that detective work may be improved if greater emphasis is placed on collecting physical evidence at the scene of the crime, identifying witnesses, checking departmental records, and using informants. The probability of successfully settling a case is improved if patrol officers carefully gather evidence at the scene of a crime and effectively communicate it to detectives working on the case. Police managers should pay more attention to screening cases, monitoring case flow and activity, and creating productivity measures to make sure that individual detectives and detective units are meeting their goals. Also recommended is the use of targeted investigations that direct attention at a few individuals, such as career criminals, who are known to have engaged in the behavior under investigation.

CHANGING CONCEPTS OF THE POLICE ROLE

Many police officers feel unappreciated by the public they serve, which may be due to the underlying conflicts inherent in the police role. Police may want to be proactive crime fighters who initiate actions against law violators; yet most remain reactive, responding when a citizen calls for service. The desire for direct action is often blunted because police are expected to perform many civic duties that in earlier times were the responsibility of every citizen: keeping the peace, performing emergency medical care, dealing with family problems, and helping during civil emergencies.[38] The public wants the police to perform those duties that the average citizen finds distasteful or dangerous, such as breaking up domestic quarrels. At the same time, the public resents the power the police have to use force, to arrest people, and to deny people their vices. Put another way, the average citizen wants the police to crack down on undesirable members of society, while excluding his or her own behavior from legal scrutiny. Not surprisingly, faced with this role conflict, some police officers feel ambivalent and uncertain about the public they are sworn to protect.

Because of this ambivalence and role conflict, more communities are adopting new models of policing that reflect the changing role of the police. Some administrators now recognize that police officers are better equipped to be civic problem solvers than effective crime fighters. Rather than ignore, deny, or fight this reality, police departments are being reorganized to maximize their strengths and minimize their weaknesses. What has emerged is the community policing movement, a new concept of policing designed to bridge the gulf between police agencies and the communities they serve.

Bonnie Campbell, former Iowa attorney general, heading a federal program, Violence Against Women Act, meets with Seattle police officers. In the future, police officers must become more aware of lingering social problems, such as domestic violence, if they are to gain the cooperation of the general public.

"Broken Windows": The Development of Community Policing

For more than 30 years, police agencies have been trying to gain the cooperation and respect of the communities they serve. At first, these efforts involved programs with the general title of **police–community relations (PCR)**. These initial PCR programs, developed at the station house and departmental levels, were designed to make citizens more aware of police activities, alert them to methods of self-protection, and improve general attitudes toward policing.

Although PCR efforts showed a willingness on the part of police agencies to cooperate with the public, some experts believed that law enforcement agencies needed to undergo a significant transformation in order to create meaningful partnerships with the public. These views were articulated in a critical 1982 paper by two justice policy experts, George Kelling and James Q. Wilson. Kelling and Wilson formulated a new approach to improving police–community relations that has come to be known as the **broken windows model**,[39] based on the following three points:

1. *Neighborhood disorder creates fear.* Urban areas filled with street people, youth gangs, prostitutes, and the mentally disturbed are the ones most likely to maintain a high level of crime.

Fill in the blanks 10–11
True/False 12
Multiple choice 13
Essay 4

police–community relations (PCR)
Programs designed to bring police and the public closer together and create a more cooperative working environment between them.

broken windows model
Role of the police as maintainers of community order and safety.

2. *Neighborhoods give out crime-promoting signals.* A neighborhood filled with deteriorated housing, unrepaired broken windows, and untended disorderly behavior gives out crime-promoting signals. Honest citizens live in fear in these areas, and predatory criminals are attracted to them.

3. *Police need citizens' cooperation.* If police are to reduce fear and successfully combat crime in these urban areas, they must have the cooperation, support, and assistance of the citizens.

community-oriented policing (COP)

A police strategy that emphasized fear reduction, community organization, and order maintenance rather than crime fighting.

The resulting policies have come to be known as **community-oriented policing (COP)**. According to this approach, community relations and crime control effectiveness cannot be the province of a few specialized units housed within a traditional police department. Instead, the core police role must be altered if community involvement is to be won and maintained. To accomplish this goal, urban police departments should return to the earlier style of policing in which officers on the beat had intimate contact with the people they served. Modern police departments generally rely on motorized patrol to cover wide areas, to maintain a visible police presence, and to ensure rapid response time. Though effective and economical, the patrol car removes officers from the mainstream of the community, alienating people who might otherwise be potential sources of information and assistance to the police.

PERSPECTIVES ON JUSTICE

According to the broken windows model, police administrators should deploy their forces where they can encourage public confidence, strengthen feelings of safety, and elicit cooperation from citizens. Community preservation, public safety, and order maintenance—not crime fighting—should become the primary focus of patrol. Just as physicians and dentists practice preventive medicine and dentistry, police should help maintain an intact community structure, rather than simply fight crime. This model has shifted policing from a purely crime control perspective to one that embraces elements of rehabilitation and restorative justice.

Fill in the blanks 12
True/False 13–15
Multiple choice 14

foot patrol

Police patrol that takes officers out of cars and puts them on a walking beat to strengthen ties with the community.

The School of Criminal Justice at Michigan State University maintains a comprehensive Web site devoted to community policing. It contains an extensive collection of full-text papers on all aspects of community policing. You can access it at http://www.ssc.msu.edu/~cj/cp/cptoc.html

For an up-to-date list of Web links, see http://www.wadsworth.com/product/0534573053s

Community-Oriented Policing in Practice

The COP concept was originally implemented through a number of innovative demonstration projects.[40] Among the most publicized were experiments in **foot patrol**, which took officers out of cars to walk beats in the neighborhood. Foot patrol efforts were aimed at forming a bond with community residents by acquainting them with the individual officers who patrolled their neighborhood, letting them know that police were caring and available. The first foot patrol experiments were conducted in cities in Michigan and New Jersey. An evaluation of foot patrol indicated that, although it did not bring the crime rate down, residents perceived greater safety and were less afraid of crime.[41]

Since the advent of these programs, hundreds of communities have adopted innovative forms of decentralized, neighborhood-based community policing. Recent surveys indicate that COP activities have increased significantly in recent years and that certain core programs, such as crime prevention activities, have become embedded in the police role.[42]

COP programs have been implemented in large cities, suburban areas, and rural communities.[43] The most successful programs give officers the time to meet with local residents to talk about crime in the neighborhood and to use personal initiative to solve problems (see Exhibit 6.1).

EXHIBIT 6.1 RESIDENTIAL POLICE OFFICER PROGRAM, ALEXANDRIA, VIRGINIA

One successful community policing initiative has been implemented in Alexandria, Virginia: the Residential Police Officer (RPO) program, in which veteran police officers live in and patrol areas that have problems such as elevated levels of crime, nuisance activities, dilapidated buildings, graffiti, and absentee landlords.

RPOs work closely with residents to create and implement effective crime- and problem-reduction strategies. By working with citizens, rather than for them, the police hope not only to reduce the number of crimes but also to reduce residents' fear of crime and increase their quality of life.

To determine its effectiveness, the RPO program was evaluated in one of the city's oldest communities—Arlandria, home to more than 4,500 people who were concerned about

drugs, juvenile gangs, and other crime and nuisance activities. The results of surveys given to Arlandria residents in 1992 and 1998 were compared in order to gauge the impact of the RPO program. In addition, reported crimes, nuisance incidents, and calls for service were charted from 1992 when the RPOs first arrived. In the 1992 survey, residents complained about drug dealing in the streets, lack of police presence, and fear of crime. By 1998, citizens were less concerned about crime and gangs and more concerned about quality-of-life issues such as trash and loitering. All three measures of criminal activity indicated a decrease in crime. Between 1992 and 1998, reported crime dropped by 17 percent, the number of reported nuisance incidents declined by almost 19 percent, and the number of calls for service dropped 12 percent.

SOURCES: "Expanding Alexandria's Residential Police Officer Program," *Police Chief,* October 1999; Police Department Correspondence, 2001.

Not all programs work (police–community newsletters and cleanup campaigns do not seem to do much good), but the overall impression has been that patrol officers can actually reduce the level of fear in the community. Some COP programs assign officers to neighborhoods, organize training programs for community leaders, and feature a bottom-up approach to dealing with community problems: Decision making involves the officer on the scene, not a directive from central headquarters. Others have created programs for juveniles who might ordinarily have little to do but get involved in gangs but are now directed into such activities as neighborhood cleanup efforts.[44] In Spokane, Washington, for example, the community policing effort created a program called COPY Kids, a summer outreach program for disadvantaged youths that promotes a positive work ethic, emphasizes the value of community involvement, and helps create a positive image of the police department.[45]

In Washington, D.C., Howard University's Violence Prevention Project aims to create a safety net that protects youths against social risk factors. The project relies on a team approach that involves parents, teachers, mental health professionals, business owners, and local police. The police component of the project, called the Youth Trauma Team, requires that police officers, along with psychologists, respond to violent incidents that occur at night. They talk to children who have been a part of or have witnessed violence and afterward link them with services as needed. Police officers involved in the project receive training in conflict resolution, cultural sensitivity, and crisis de-escalation. They also have networked or partnered extensively with existing social service providers in the community in a multidisciplinary team effort to provide comprehensive care.[46]

Neighborhood Policing Community policing means more than implementing direct action programs. It also refers to a philosophy of policing that requires departments to reconsider their recruitment, organization, and operating procedures. What are some of the most important community policing concepts? First, COP emphasizes results, not bureaucratic process. Rather than react to problems in the community, police departments take the initiative in identifying issues and actively treating their cause. Problem-solving and analysis techniques replace

The foundation of community policing is to develop cooperation between law enforcement agencies and the general public. Here, a Poughkeepsie (New York) police officer talks with a city business owner as part of a program to keep police informed of what's happening in the community.

© Kathy McLaughlin/The Image Works

innovative neighborhood-oriented policing (INOP)
A model in which police solve problems at the neighborhood level.

To find the latest information, training, advice, and discussion related to community policing, go to http://www.policing.com

For an up-to-date list of Web links, see http://www.wadsworth.com/product/0534573053s

emphasis on bureaucratic detail. There is less concern with "playing it by the book" and more with getting the job done.

To achieve the goals of COP, some agencies have tried to decentralize, an approach sometimes referred to as **innovative neighborhood-oriented policing (INOP)**.[47] Problem solving is best done at the neighborhood level where issues originate, not at a far-off central headquarters. Because each neighborhood has its own particular needs, police decision making must be flexible and adaptive. For example, neighborhoods undergoing change in racial composition experience high levels of racially motivated violence.[48] Police must be able to distinguish these neighborhood characteristics and allocate resources to meet their needs.

Changing the Police Role Community policing also stresses sharing power with local groups and individuals. A key element of the COP philosophy is that citizens must actively participate with police to fight crime.[49] This participation might involve providing information in areawide crime investigations or helping police reach out to troubled youths.

Community policing also means the eventual redesign of police departments. Management's role must be reordered to focus on the problems of the community, not the needs of the police department. The traditional vertical police organizational chart must be altered so that top-down management gives way to bottom-up decision making. The patrol officer becomes the manager of his or her beat and a key decision maker. Figure 6.2 shows how one police department is organized for community policing.

Community policing requires that police departments alter their recruitment and training requirements. Future officers must develop community-organizing and problem-solving skills, along with traditional police skills. Their training must prepare them to succeed less on their ability to make arrests or issue citations and more on their ability to solve problems, prevent crime effectively, and deal with neighborhood diversity and cultural values.[50]

Not only is the COP concept catching on in the United States (see Exhibit 6.2), it has also captured the interest of police departments around the world.[51] Community policing is being used in numerous countries, including Denmark, Finland, and Great Britain.

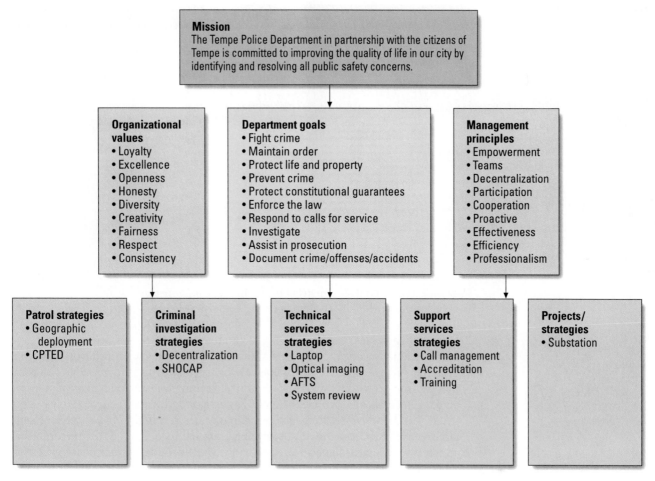

Mission
The Tempe Police Department in partnership with the citizens of Tempe is committed to improving the quality of life in our city by identifying and resolving all public safety concerns.

Organizational values
- Loyalty
- Excellence
- Openness
- Honesty
- Diversity
- Creativity
- Fairness
- Respect
- Consistency

Department goals
- Fight crime
- Maintain order
- Protect life and property
- Prevent crime
- Protect constitutional guarantees
- Enforce the law
- Respond to calls for service
- Investigate
- Assist in prosecution
- Document crime/offenses/accidents

Management principles
- Empowerment
- Teams
- Decentralization
- Participation
- Cooperation
- Proactive
- Effectiveness
- Efficiency
- Professionalism

Patrol strategies
- Geographic deployment
- CPTED

Criminal investigation strategies
- Decentralization
- SHOCAP

Technical services strategies
- Laptop
- Optical imaging
- AFTS
- System review

Support services strategies
- Call management
- Accreditation
- Training

Projects/ strategies
- Substation

FIGURE 6.2 TEMPE (ARIZONA) POLICE DEPARTMENT PLANNING MODEL

SOURCE: Tempe Police Department, 2000.

Problem-Oriented Policing

Closely associated with, yet independent of, the COP concept is **problem-oriented policing**. Traditional police models focus on responding to calls for help in the fastest possible time, dealing with the situation, and then getting on the street again as soon as possible.[52] In contrast, the core of problem-oriented policing is a proactive orientation.

Problem-oriented police strategies require police agencies to identify long-term community problems—street-level drug dealers, prostitution rings, gang hangouts—and develop strategies to eliminate them.[53] As with COP, problem-oriented policing requires that police departments rely on local residents and private resources. This means that police managers must learn how to develop community resources, design cost-efficient and effective solutions to problems, and become advocates as well as agents of reform.[54]

Problem-oriented policing models are supported by the fact that a great deal of urban crime is concentrated in a few "hot spots."[55] A significant portion of all police calls in metropolitan areas typically radiate from a relatively few locations: bars, malls, the bus depot, hotels, certain apartment buildings.[56] By implication, concentrating police resources on these hot spots could appreciably reduce crime.[57]

The new community policing models are essentially problem oriented, and both efforts can be combined. For example, in Vancouver, Canada, community police officers assigned to reduce and control street prostitution actually included prostitutes in their planning activities and were able to reduce neighborhood

Fill in the blanks 13
Multiple choice 15–16
Essay 5

problem-oriented policing
A style of police management that stresses proactive problem solving rather than reactive crime fighting.

EXHIBIT 6.2   EXTENT OF COMMUNITY POLICING

A majority of local police departments serving a population of 50,000 or more had a full-time COP unit, and a majority of the departments serving a population of 10,000 or more had personnel assigned to COP activities. A majority of sheriffs' departments serving 250,000 or more residents had personnel so assigned.

By 1997, among municipal police departments employing 100 or more officers,

- 61 percent had a formally written COP plan.
- 71 percent had a COP unit with sworn personnel assigned full-time.

- 74 percent operated one or more community substations.
- 79 percent had full-time school resource officers.
- 91 percent trained at least some of their in-service officers in COP.
- 80 percent trained all their new officer recruits in COP.
- 69 percent offered COP training to citizens.
- 68 percent formed problem-solving partnerships with local groups or agencies.

SOURCE: *Local Police Departments, 1997* (Washington, DC: Bureau of Justice Statistics, 2000).

conflict by mediating between residents and prostitutes. They included both groups to help control collateral problems such as drug dealing and pornography.[58]

Problem-oriented strategies can also be developed within traditional police organizations.[59] The Jersey City (New Jersey) Police Department has applied a variety of aggressive crime-reducing techniques in some of the city's highest-crime areas. Evaluations of the program show that crime rates were reduced when police officers used aggressive problem solving (such as drug enforcement) and community improvement (increased lighting, cleaning vacant lots) in a high-crime area.[60] The Dallas Police Department has assigned officers to aggressively pursue truancy and curfew enforcement, a tactic that has resulted in lower rates of gang violence.[61] The accompanying Analyzing Criminal Justice Issues feature describes another program, designed to reduce a problem of growing national concern—school violence.

Programs such as these seem to be successful, but the effectiveness of any street-level problem-solving efforts must be interpreted with caution.[62] It is possible that criminals will be displaced to other, "safer" areas of the city and will return shortly after the program is called a success and the additional police forces have been pulled from the area.[63] Nonetheless, the evidence shows that merely saturating an area with police may not deter crime, but focusing efforts at a particular problem may have a crime-reducing effect.

Multiple choice 17
Essay 6

The Challenge of Community Policing

The core concepts of police work are changing as administrators recognize the limitations and realities of police work in modern society. A majority of larger police agencies now employ community policing officers and engage in community police activities (see Figure 6.3). If they are to be successful, however, community policing strategies must be able to react effectively to some significant administrative problems:

1. *Defining community.* Police administrators must be able to define the concept of community in terms of an ecological area defined by common norms, shared values, and interpersonal bonds.[64] After all, the main focus of COP is to activate the community norms that make neighborhoods more crime resistant. To do so requires identification of distinct ecological areas. If, in contrast, COP projects cross the boundaries of many different neighborhoods, any hope of learning and accessing community norms, strengths, and standards will be lost.[65] Even if natural community structures can be identified, it will be necessary for police agencies to continually monitor the changing norms, values, and attitudes of the com-

ANALYZING CRIMINAL JUSTICE ISSUES

School Resource Officers

Horrific outbursts of school violence, such as the shootings at Columbine High School in 1999, have prompted school administrators to improve security at schools around the nation. To assist in keeping students safe, some school systems have called upon local police to serve as School Resource Officers (SROs).

The goal of placing SROs in city schools is to create an atmosphere in which students and teachers can focus on learning without fear. SROs are expected to reduce the number of weapons in schools, prohibit drug abuse, counsel students with problems, and because of their visible presence, secure school buildings from nonstudents. SROs are expected to deter offenses on school grounds before they happen.

Ida Johnson analyzed the effectiveness of the SRO program in a southern school district. She compared weekly school disciplinary records for the 1994–1995 school year, the year before officers were assigned to schools on a permanent basis, with incident reports and disciplinary records for the 1995–1996 school year. In addition, interviews were conducted with administrators, teachers, students, and officers to assess the work of the SROs.

Johnson evaluated the impact of the SROs on three types, or levels, of student misbehavior. Level 1 offenses included harassment and intimidation of other students, chronic tardiness, use of

profanity, and minor disturbances on a school bus. Level 2 offenses included such acts as fighting, larceny, use of tobacco, trespassing, propositioning of sexual acts, and leaving school without permission. Level 3 offenses, deemed the most serious, included arson, aggravated battery, possession of firearms or other weapons, grand theft, and burglary.

The study found that 3,760 offenses occurred in the district during the 1995–1996 school year, a drop of nearly 300 from the year before the SRO program was initiated. Declines were recorded in all three offense levels, and the number of misdemeanor and felony arrests occurring on school grounds decreased.

Interviews with administrators and students indicated support for the presence of SROs in schools. Administrators perceived that the use of weapons had declined and that levels of marijuana, gambling, fighting, and illicit sexual behavior were down since SROs were placed in schools. Students reported feeling more secure and that having an SRO in school deterred classmates from committing disciplinary infractions.

SROs also reported having a positive relationship with students. Officers counseled students on career choices and encouraged them to excel academically. SROs made daily contact with the parents of at-risk students. Nearly all the SROs believed that parents and teachers responded positively to them.

The SRO concept has great promise as a means of reducing school crime. Efforts should be made to expand officer training, increase the number of officers hired, increase communication between SROs and other community members, and have regular counseling sessions between SROs and the students, teachers, and parents they serve.

Critical Thinking Skills

1. What do you think of having police officers patrol school buildings on a regular basis? Will it ensure order and security, or might it create a hostile environment that reduces school spirit and the enjoyment of education?
2. Should SROs arrest young people for getting into a school yard fight that would otherwise go unrecorded?

InfoTrac College Edition Research

To read more about SROs, see Connie Mulqueen, "School Resource Officers More Than Security Guards," *American School & University,* July 1999, v71 i11 pSS17

SOURCE: Ida Johnson, "School Violence: The Effectiveness of a School Resource Officer," *Journal of Criminal Justice* 27 (1999): 173–193.

munity they serve, a process that has the positive side effect of creating positive interactions between the community and the police.[66]

2. *Defining roles.* Police administrators must establish the exact role of COP officers. How should they integrate their activities with those of regular patrol forces? For example, should foot patrols have primary responsibility for policing in an area, or should they coordinate their activities with officers assigned to patrol cars? Should COP officers be solely problem identifiers and neighborhood organizers, or should they also be law enforcement agents who get to the crime

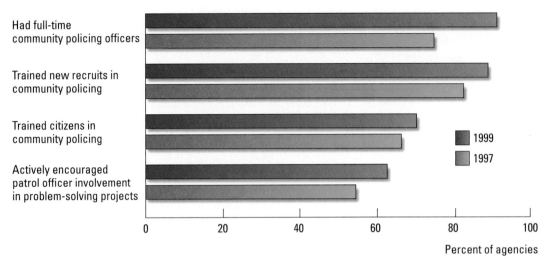

FIGURE 6.3
COMMUNITY
POLICING
ACTIVITIES OF
LOCAL LAW
ENFORCEMENT
AGENCIES, 1997
AND 1999

Law enforcement agencies with
100 or more full-time sworn personnel

SOURCE: Brian Reaves and Timothy Hart,
*Law Enforcement Management and Ad-
ministrative Statistics, 1999* (Washington,
DC: Bureau of Justice Statistics, 2000),
p. v.

scene rapidly and later do investigative work? Can COP teams and regular patrols work together, or must a department abandon traditional police roles and
become purely community policing oriented?

3. *Changing the command structure.* Some supervisors are wary of COP because it
supports a decentralized command structure. This would mean fewer supervisors
and, consequently, less chance for promotion and a potential loss of authority.[67]

4. *Reorienting police values.* Research shows that police officers who have a traditional crime control orientation are less satisfied with community policing efforts than those who are public service oriented.[68] Although this finding comes
as no surprise, it is indicative of the difficulty police managers will face in convincing experienced officers, many of whom hold traditional law-and-order values, to embrace COP models.

5. *Revising training.* Because the COP model calls for a revision of the police
role, from law enforcer to community organizer, police training must be revised
to reflect this new mandate. If COP is to be adopted on a wide scale, a whole new
type of police officer must be recruited and trained in a whole new way.

6. *Reorienting recruitment.* The success of community policing depends on recruiting and training midlevel managers who are receptive to and can implement
community-change strategies.[69] The selection of new recruits must be guided by a
desire to find individuals with both skills and attitudes that support COP. They
must be open to the idea that COP can help them understand the community, gain
skill and experience, and engage in proactive problem solving.[70] Selecting people
who find these values attractive and then providing training that accentuates the
community vision of policing are essential to the success of the COP model.

Although results are encouraging, there are still obstacles to overcome before
community policing becomes a norm. It is still unclear whether COP is the crime
control panacea that its backers claim.[71] Crime rate reductions in cities that have
used COP may be the result of an overall downturn in the nation's crime rate or
some other factor such as an improved economy. Some of its most cherished programs, such as police officers' meeting with community groups and going door-
to-door to reduce neighborhood crime rates, have not proven effective.[72] Also
troubling are the results of a recent evaluation of community policing efforts in
Indianapolis, Indiana, and St. Petersburg, Florida, which found that COP officers
actually spend more time on administrative work than regular patrol officers—
meaning that some COP officers spend less time with citizens than do patrol officers.[73] Another survey of COP programs in Florida found that although numerous departments considered themselves "community oriented," each had its

Community policing efforts use a variety of innovative techniques to reach out to the public. Here, two Syracuse (New York) police officers ride 21-speed bicycles, providing high visibility to store owners and citizens.

own distinct view of what community policing was all about; no single, definitive model of community policing could be found.[74]

Although these issues remain unresolved, numerous police experts believe that community- and problem-oriented policing can work and fit well with traditional forms of policing.[75] COP efforts have been credited with helping reduce crime rates in large cities such as New York and Boston while providing a motivating force for police officers involved in the programs.[76]

POLICE SUPPORT FUNCTIONS

As the model of a typical police department in Figure 6.1 indicates, not all members of a department engage in what the general public regards as "real" police work—patrol, detection, and traffic control. Even in departments that are embracing community- and problem-oriented policing, a great many police resources are actually devoted to support and administrative functions. Of these many and varied tasks, only the most important are described here.

Many police departments maintain their own personnel service, which carries out such functions as recruiting new officers, creating exams to determine the most qualified applicants, and handling promotions and transfers. New and innovative selection techniques are constantly being developed and tested. For example, the Behavioral-Personnel Assessment Device (B-PAD) requires police applicants to view videotaped scenarios and respond as if they were officers handling the situation; reviews indicate that this procedure may be a reliable and unbiased method of choosing new recruits.[77]

Larger police departments often maintain an **internal affairs** branch, charged with policing the police. Internal affairs officers process citizen complaints of police corruption, investigate what may be the unnecessary use of force by police officers, and even probe police participation in criminal activity, such as burglaries or narcotics violations. In addition, internal affairs divisions may assist police managers when disciplinary action is brought against individual officers. Internal affairs is a controversial function: Investigators are feared and distrusted by fellow officers, and citizens may question whether internal investigations are rigorous and

Fill in the blanks 14
True/False 16–17
Multiple choice 18–22
Essay 7–8

internal affairs
Unit that investigates allegations of police misconduct.

ANALYZING CRIMINAL JUSTICE ISSUES

Civilian Review Boards

Two Rochester, New York, police officers arrested two young males, allegedly for dealing drugs. During the melee, one of them was pushed through a plate glass window. One youth's mother claims that these innocent young men were the victims of police brutality: The young men were innocently walking along the street when the officers approached. At a hearing, the city's citizen review board finds that the arrestees had drugs in their possession, that the officers remained polite and professional throughout the encounter, and that it was actually one of the boys who pushed the officer into the store window. The officers are exonerated by the review board.

Citizen oversight of police conduct can be a critical method of improving community relations, but it has also caused conflict with police officers. Nonetheless, there has been a considerable increase in citizen oversight of police in the United States.

Oversight systems typically follow one of four models:

1. Citizen review board investigates allegations of police misconduct and recommends findings to the head of the agency.
2. Officers investigate allegations and develop findings; citizen board reviews findings and recommends that the head of the agency approve or reject them.
3. Complainants may appeal agency findings to citizen board, which reviews them and makes recommendations to the head of the agency.
4. An auditor investigates the process the agency uses to accept and investigate complaints and reports to the agency and the community the thoroughness and fairness of the process.

These basic models have many variations. For example, the Minneapolis civilian review process operates in two stages. First, paid professional investigators and a director examine citizen complaints to determine if there is reasonable evidence that police misconduct has occurred. Then, in probable cause cases, volunteer board members conduct closed-door hearings to decide whether they should support the allegations that came from the initial screening process. In Orange County, Florida, a nine-member volunteer citizen review board holds hearings, open to the public and the media, on all cases involving the alleged use of excessive force and abuse of power after the sheriff's department has conducted an investigation.

Police agencies in some communities have embraced citizen review; others find it troublesome. Departmental opposition is most likely when oversight procedures represent outside interference, oversight staff lack experience with and understanding of police work, and oversight processes are unfair. Most police administrators believe that their agencies should have the final say in matters of discipline, policies and procedures, and training, and some bridle at any hint of outside interference by nonprofessionals. In some communities, local governments have established oversight bodies that act only in an ad-

fair or simply amount to a cover-up. Because of these concerns, it has become commonplace for police departments to institute citizen oversight of police practices, creating civilian review boards with the power to listen to complaints and conduct investigations. Civilian oversight is the subject of the accompanying Analyzing Criminal Justice Issues feature.

Most police departments are responsible for the administration and control of their own budgets. These financial tasks include administering payroll, purchasing equipment and services, planning budgets for future expenditures, and auditing departmental financial records.

Police departments maintain separate units that are charged with maintaining and disseminating information on wanted offenders, stolen merchandise, traffic violators, and so on. Modern data management systems enable police to use their records in a highly sophisticated fashion. For example, officers in a patrol car who spot a suspicious-looking vehicle can instantly receive a computerized rundown on whether it has been stolen. If property is recovered during an arrest, police can determine who reported the loss of the merchandise and arrange for its return.

Another important function of police communication is the effective and efficient dispatching of patrol cars. Again, modern computer technologies have been used to make the most of available resources.[78]

visory capacity and make nonbinding recommendations to law enforcement agencies.

Another familiar complaint is that civilians cannot understand the complexities of police work. To compensate, candidates for the review board in Rochester, New York, attend a condensed version of a police academy run by the police department. The 48-hour course includes three hours every evening for two weeks plus two all-day Saturday sessions. The members use a shoot/don't shoot simulator, practice handcuffing, and learn about departmental policies and procedures, including the use-of-force continuum.

In addition to these issues, many officers believe that review members hold them accountable for minor infractions, such as placing the wrong offense code on a citation or failing to record the end mileage on a vehicle transport. Many officers also believe that the review process is too lengthy; delays both harm the credibility of the oversight process and cause officers considerable stress as they wait for their cases to be decided.

To forestall such problems, some police administrators have taken the initiative by helping set up a citizen oversight system before being required to do so, thus becoming involved in the planning process.

Despite serious reservations about citizen oversight, many law enforcement administrators have identified positive outcomes from having a review board in place. These include improving community relations, enhancing an agency's ability to police itself, and most important, improving an agency's policies and procedures. Citizen oversight bodies can recommend changes in the way the department conducts its internal investigation into alleged misconduct, as well as improvements in departmental policies governing officer behavior.

Critical Thinking Skills

1. Research shows that a civilian review board is not a panacea that will eliminate or significantly reduce citizen complaints. One reason is police resistance to civilian oversight. If you were the chief of police, would you want civilians to oversee how you ran your department and/or handled citizen complaints?

2. If you were the head of a civilian review board, how would you get the local police to accept your authority?

InfoTrac College Edition Research

What can happen if police behavior gets out of control? Read Sidney L. Harring, "The Diallo Verdict: Another 'Tragic Accident' in New York's War on Street Crime?" *Social Justice,* 2000, v27 I1 p9

SOURCES: Liqun Cao and Bu Huang, "Determinants of Citizen Complaints Against Police Abuse of Power," *Journal of Criminal Justice* 28 (2000): 203–213; Peter Finn, "Getting Along with Citizen Oversight," *FBI Law Enforcement Bulletin* 69 (2000): 22–27.

In many police departments, training is continuous throughout an officer's career. Training usually begins at a police academy, which may be run exclusively for a large police department or be part of a regional training center servicing smaller jurisdictions. More than 90 percent of all police agencies require preservice training, including almost all departments in larger cities (population over 100,000). The average officer receives more than 500 hours of preservice training, including 400 hours in the classroom and the rest in field training. Police in large cities receive more than 1,000 hours of instruction, divided almost evenly between classroom and field instruction.[79] Among the topics usually covered are law and civil rights, firearms handling, emergency medical care, and restraint techniques.[80]

After assuming their police duties, new recruits are assigned to field-training officers, who break them in on the job. However, training does not stop here. On-the-job training is a continuous process in the modern police department and covers such areas as weapons skills, first aid, crowd control, and community relations. Some departments use roll-call training, in which superior officers or outside experts address junior officers at the beginning of the workday. Other departments allow police officers time off to attend annual training sessions to sharpen their skills and learn new policing techniques.

To be effective, police departments must provide officers with continuous in-service training. Here, the Traverse City (Michigan) Police Department holds a police K-9 seminar. Twenty law enforcement departments from five states participated in the training, enabling current police dog handlers to solve minor problems in need of correction or just challenge their dogs in a new environment.

AP/Wide World Photos

Police departments provide emergency aid to the ill, counsel youngsters, speak to school and community agencies on safety and drug abuse, and provide countless other services designed to improve citizen–police interactions.

Larger police departments maintain specialized units that help citizens protect themselves from criminal activity. For example, they advise citizens on effective home security techniques or conduct Project ID campaigns—engraving valuables with an identifying number so that they can be returned if recovered after a burglary. Police also work in schools teaching young people how to avoid drugs.[81]

Police agencies maintain (or have access to) forensic laboratories that enable them to identify substances to be used as evidence and classify fingerprints.

Planning and research functions include designing programs to increase police efficiency and strategies to test program effectiveness. Police planners monitor recent technological developments and institute programs to adapt them to police services.

Fill in the blanks 15
True/False 18–20
Multiple choice 23–25

IMPROVING POLICE PRODUCTIVITY

Police administrators have sought to increase the productivity of their line, support, and administrative staff. As used today, the term *police productivity* refers to the amount of order maintenance, crime control, and other law enforcement activities provided by individual officers and by police departments as a whole. By improving productivity, a department can keep the peace, deter crime, apprehend criminals, and provide useful public services without necessarily increasing costs. This goal is accomplished by having each officer operate with greater efficiency, thus using fewer resources to achieve greater effectiveness.

Despite the emphasis on increasing police effectiveness, serious questions have been raised about how the police accomplish their assigned tasks.[82] One basic complaint has been that the average patrol officer spends relatively little time on "real" police work. More often than not, highly skilled officers can be found writing reports, waiting in court corridors, getting involved in domestic disputes, and handling "miscellaneous noncriminal matters."

Police departments are now experimenting with cost-saving reforms that maximize effectiveness while saving taxpayer dollars. For example, J. David Hirschel and Charles Dean describe a program to summon offenders to court via a "field citation" that is considerably cheaper than a formal arrest. Factoring in the cost of rearresting offenders who fail to appear in court, a citation program would save about $72 per case. Considering the millions of arrests made each year, such a program could produce considerable savings, not to mention the cost-saving effect on the overcrowded jail system.[83] Other cost-saving productivity measures include consolidation, informal arrangements, sharing, pooling, contracting, police service districts, use of civilian employees, multiple tasking, special assignment programs, budget supplementation, and differential police responses.[84]

Consolidation One way to increase police efficiency is to consolidate police services. This means combining small departments (usually with fewer than 10 employees) in adjoining areas into a superagency that services the previously fragmented jurisdictions. Consolidation has the benefit of creating departments large enough to use expanded services, such as crime labs, training centers, communications centers, and emergency units, that are not cost-effective in smaller departments. This procedure is controversial, because it demands that existing lines of political and administrative authority be drastically changed. Nonetheless, consolidation of departments or special services (such as a regional computer center) has been attempted in California (the Los Angeles County Sheriff's Department), Massachusetts, New York, and Illinois.[85]

Informal Arrangements Unwritten cooperative agreements may be made between localities to perform a task collectively that would be mutually beneficial (such as monitoring neighboring radio frequencies so that needed backup can be provided). An example is the Metro Task Force program implemented in New Jersey that commits state troopers to help local police officers in urban areas for limited times and assignments.[86]

Sharing Sharing is the provision or reception of services that aid in the execution of a law enforcement function (such as the sharing of a communications system by several local agencies). Some agencies form mutual aid pacts so that they can share infrequently used emergency services such as SWAT and Emergency Response Teams.[87] Some states have gone as far as setting up centralized data services that connect most local police agencies into a statewide information net.[88]

Pooling Some police agencies pool the resources of two or more agencies to perform a specified function under a predetermined, often formalized arrangement with direct involvement by all parties. An example is the use of a city–county law enforcement building or training academy or the establishment of a crime task force.

Contracting Another productivity measure, contracting, is a limited and voluntary approach in which one government enters into a formal binding agreement to provide all or certain specified law enforcement services (such as communications or patrol service) to another government for an established fee. Many communities that contract for full law enforcement service do so at the time they incorporate to avoid the costs of establishing their own police capability. For example, in Florida, the five small towns of Pembroke Park, Lauderdale Lakes,

Tamarac, Dania, and Deerfield Beach contract with the Broward County Sheriff's Department to provide law enforcement for their communities; contracting saves each town millions of dollars.[89]

Service Districts Some jurisdictions have set aside areas, usually within an individual county, where a special level of service is provided and financed through a special tax or assessment. In California, residents of an unincorporated portion of a county may petition to form such a district to provide more intensive patrol coverage than is available through existing systems. Such service may be provided by a sheriff, another police department, or a private person or agency. This system is used in Contra Costa and San Mateo counties in California and Suffolk and Nassau counties in New York.

Civilian Employees One common cost-saving method is to use civilians in administrative support or even in some line activities. Civilians' duties have included operating communications gear; performing clerical work, planning, and research; and staffing traffic control (meter monitors). Using civilian employees can be a considerable savings to taxpayers, because their salaries are considerably lower than those of regular police officers. In addition, it allows trained, experienced officers to spend more time on direct crime control and enforcement activities.

Another form of civilian help comes in the form of COP programs that use civilian volunteers to supplement police services. For example, the Code Blue program in Fort Worth, Texas, organizes neighborhood watch groups that supplement police patrol while providing on-site services unavailable before the program was instituted.[90]

Multiple Tasking Some police officers are trained to carry out other functions of municipal government. For example, in a number of smaller departments, the roles of firefighter and police officer have been merged into a job called *public safety officer*. The idea is to increase the number of people trained in both areas to have the potential for putting more police at the scene of a crime or more firefighters at a blaze than was possible when the two tasks were separated. The system provides greater coverage at far less cost.[91]

Special Assignments Some departments train officers for special assignments that are required only occasionally. For example, the Special Enforcement Team in Lakewood, Colorado, is trained in a variety of police tasks, such as radar operation, surveillance, traffic investigation, and criminal investigations, but specializes in tactical operations, such as crowd control and security.[92]

Budget Supplementation Municipal agencies often seek out innovative sources of income to supplement the department's limited budget. For example, Chicago police instituted a private fund drive that raised more than $1.5 million to purchase protective clothing. Other departments have created private foundations to raise funds to support police-related activities. Additional budget-supplementing activities include conducting fund-raising events, using traffic fines for police services, enacting special taxes that go directly for police services, and auctioning goods forfeited by crime-involved individuals.

Differential Police Response These strategies maximize resources by differentiating among requests for service and providing different types of response. Some calls will result in the dispatch of a sworn officer, others in the dispatching of a less highly trained civilian; calls considered low priority are handled by asking citizens to walk in or to mail in their requests.[93]

SUMMARY

Today's police departments operate in a military-like fashion, with policy generally emanating from the top of the hierarchy. Most police officers, therefore, use a great deal of discretion when making on-the-job decisions.

The most common law enforcement agencies are local police departments, which carry out patrol and investigation functions, as well as many support activities.

Many questions have been raised about the effectiveness of police work, and some research seems to indicate that police are not effective crime fighters. However, aggressive police work, the threat of formal action, and cooperation between departments can have a measurable impact on crime. To improve effectiveness, police departments have developed new methods of policing that stress community involvement and problem solving. They have also been concerned with developing more effective and productive methods for using their resources.

Key Terms

chief of police	vice squad	foot patrol
time-in-rank system	sting	innovative neighborhood-oriented
beat	police–community relations (PCR)	policing (INOP)
order maintenance (peacekeeping)	broken windows model	problem-oriented policing
recidivism	community-oriented policing (COP)	internal affairs

Discussion Questions

1. Should the primary police role be law enforcement or community service?
2. Should a police chief be permitted to promote an officer with special skills to a supervisory position, or should all officers be forced to spend time in rank?
3. Do the advantages of proactive policing outweigh the disadvantages?
4. Can the police and the community ever form a partnership to fight crime? Does the COP model remind you of early forms of policing?

A CLOSER LOOK

Are COP officers like the physicians of an earlier era, who did not hesitate to make house calls and get to know their patients and did not worry about insurance companies or malpractice suits? Police expert Joseph Harpold makes the following observations:

> In the past, doctors had closer relationships with their patients than they do now. They knew them all by name, and they even made house calls. Today, the practice of medicine has given way to health maintenance organizations, where doctors may see hundreds of patients and may never get to know them on a first-name basis. American policing has evolved in much the same manner. The desire to create an ethical and efficient police force moved officers from foot beats to patrol cars. The pendulum has swung back as police departments adopt community policing principles.

Although the small-town doctor may have become a relic, police departments would do well to take their cues from the medical profession. Physicians know a great deal about disease and the nature of injuries; they treat patients based on the collective knowledge and experience in the treatment of illness. They observe the symptoms present in the patient, diagnose the disease, prescribe the treatment, then monitor the patient's progress. At the same time, they practice preventive medicine and educate the public. To treat the causes of illness in the community, the police must do the same.

To learn more about what he has to say, go to InfoTrac College Edition and read

Joseph Harpold, "Medical Model for Community Policing," *FBI Law Enforcement Bulletin,* June 2000, v69 i6 p23

Notes

1 Benjamin Weiser, "$3 Million Award in Police Brutality Case," *New York Times,* 6 October 2000, p. B1.

2 Brian Reaves and Andrew Goldberg, *Law Enforcement Management and Administrative Statistics, 1997: Data for Individual State and Local Law Enforcement Agencies with 100 or More Officers* (Washington, DC: Bureau of Justice Statistics, 1999).

3 Velmer Burton, James Frank, Robert Langworthy, and Troy Barker, "The Prescribed Roles of Police in a Free Society: Analyzing State Legal Codes," *Justice Quarterly* 10 (1993): 683–695.

4 David Carter and Allen Sapp, "Police Experiences and Responses Related to the Homeless," *Journal of Criminal Justice* 16 (1993): 87–96; Peter Finn and Monique Sullivan, *Police Response to Special Populations* (Washington, DC: National Institute of Justice, 1988).

5 Brian Reaves and Pheny Smith, *Law Enforcement Management and Administrative Statistics, 1993: Data for Individual State and Local Agencies with 100 or More Officers* (Washington, DC: Bureau of Justice Statistics, 1995).

6 American Bar Association, *Standards Relating to Urban Police Function* (New York: Institute of Judicial Administration, 1974), standard 2.2.

7 Albert J. Reiss, *The Police and the Public* (New Haven, CT: Yale University Press, 1971), p. 19.

8 James Q. Wilson, *Varieties of Police Behavior: The Management of Law and Order in Eight Communities* (Cambridge, MA: Harvard University Press, 1968).

9 See Harlan Hahn, "A Profile of Urban Police," in *The Ambivalent Force,* ed. A. Niederhoffer and A. Blumberg (Hinsdale, IL: Dryden Press, 1976), p. 59.

10 George Kelling, Tony Pate, Duane Dieckman, and Charles Brown, *The Kansas City Preventive Patrol Experiment: A Summary Report* (Washington, DC: Police Foundation, 1974).

11 Ibid., pp. 3–4.

12 Ibid.

13 James Q. Wilson and Barbara Boland, "The Effect of Police on Crime," *Law and Society Review* 12 (1978): 367–384.

14 Robert Sampson, "Deterrent Effects of the Police on Crime: A Replication and Theoretical Extension," *Law and Society Review* 22 (1988): 163–191.

15 Lawrence Sherman and David Weisburd, "General Deterrent Effects of Police Patrol in Crime 'Hot Spots': A Randomized, Controlled Trial," *Justice Quarterly* 12 (1995): 625–648.

16 Kenneth Novak, Jennifer Hartman, Alexander Holsinger, and Michael Turner, "The Effects of Aggressive Policing of Disorder on Serious Crime," *Policing* 22 (1999): 171–190.

17 For a thorough review of this issue, see Andrew Karmen, "Why Is New York City's Murder Rate Dropping So Sharply?" John Jay College, New York, 1996.

18 Lawrence Sherman, James Shaw, and Dennis Rogan, *The Kansas City Gun Experiment* (Washington, DC: National Institute of Justice, 1994).

19 Craig Uchida and Robert Goldberg, *Police Employment and Expenditure Trends* (Washington, DC: Bureau of Justice Statistics, 1986).

20 Colin Loftin and David McDowall, "The Police, Crime, and Economic Theory: An Assessment," *American Sociological Review* 47 (1982): 393–401.

21 David Jacobs and Katherine Woods, "Interracial Conflict and Interracial Homicide: Do Political and Economic Rivalries Explain White Killings of Blacks or Black Killings of Whites?" *American Journal of Sociology* 105 (1999): 157–190.

22 Joan Petersilia, Allan Abrahamse, and James Q. Wilson, "A Summary of RAND's Research on Police Performance, Community Characteristics and Case Attrition," *Journal of Police Science and Administration* 17 (1990): 219–229.

23 H. Lawrence Ross, *Deterring the Drunk Driver: Legal Policy and Social Control* (Lexington, MA: D. C. Heath, 1982); Samuel Walker, *Sense and Nonsense About Crime* (Belmont, CA: Wadsworth, 1985), pp. 82–85.

24 Mitchell Chamlin, "Crime and Arrests: An Autoregressive Integrated Moving Average (ARIMA) Approach," *Journal of Quantitative Criminology* 4 (1988): 247–255.

25 See Richard Berk, Gordon Smyth, and Lawrence Sherman, "When Random Assignment Fails: Some Lessons from the Minneapolis Spouse Abuse Experiment," *Journal of Quantitative Criminology* 4 (1989): 209–223.

26 J. David Hirschel, Ira Hutchison, and Charles Dean, "The Failure of Arrest to Deter Spouse Abuse," *Journal of Research in Crime and Delinquency* 29 (1992): 7–33; Franklyn Dunford, David Huizinga, and Delbert Elliott, "The Role of Arrest in Domestic Assault: The Omaha Experiment," *Criminology* 28 (1990): 183–206; David Hirschel, Ira Hutchinson, Charles Dean, Joseph Kelley, and Carolyn Pesackis, *Charlotte Spouse Abuse Replication Project: Final Report* (Washington, DC: National Institute of Justice, 1990).

27 Lawrence Sherman, Janell Schmidt, Dennis Rogan, Patrick Gartin, Ellen Cohn, Dean Collins, and Anthony Bacich, "From Initial Deterrence to Long-Term Escalation: Short-Custody Arrest for Poverty Ghetto Domestic Violence," *Criminology* 29 (1991): 821–850.

28 See Belton Cobb, *The First Detectives* (London: Faber & Faber, 1957).

29 See, for example, James Q. Wilson, "Movie Cops—Romantic vs. Real," *New York Magazine,* 19 August 1968, pp. 38–41.

30 For a view of the modern detective, see William Sanders, *Detective Work: A Study of Criminal Investigations* (New York: Free Press, 1977).

31 James Q. Wilson, *The Investigators: Managing FBI and Narcotics Agents* (New York: Basic Books, 1978), pp. 21–23.

32 Robert Langworthy, "Do Stings Control Crime? An Evaluation of a Police Fencing Operation," *Justice Quarterly* 6 (1989): 27–45.

33 Mark Pogrebin and Eric Poole, "Vice Isn't Nice: A Look at the Effects of Working Undercover," *Journal of Criminal Justice* 21 (1993): 385–396; Gary Marx, *Undercover: Police Surveillance in America* (Berkeley: University of California Press, 1988).

34 Peter Greenwood and Joan Petersilia, *Summary and Policy Implications,* vol. 1 of *The Criminal Investigation Process* (Santa Monica, CA: Rand Corporation, 1975).

35 Mark Willman and John Snortum, "Detective Work: The Criminal Investigation Process in a Medium-Size Police Department," *Criminal Justice Review* 9 (1984): 33–39.

36 Police Executive Research Forum, *Calling the Police: Citizen Reporting of Serious Crime* (Washington, DC: Author, 1981).

37 John Eck, *Solving Crimes: The Investigation of Burglary and Robbery* (Washington, DC: Police Executive Research Forum, 1984).

38 Egon Bittner, *The Functions of Police in Modern Society* (Cambridge, MA: Oelgeschlager, Gunn & Hain, 1980), p. 8; see also James Q. Wilson, "The Police in the Ghetto," in *The Police and the Community,* ed. Robert F. Steadman (Baltimore: Johns Hopkins University Press, 1974), p. 68.

39 George Kelling and James Q. Wilson, "Broken Windows: The Police and Neighborhood Safety," *Atlantic Monthly* 249 (1982): 29–38.

40 For a general review, see Robert Trojanowicz and Bonnie Bucqueroux, *Community Policing: A Contemporary Perspective* (Cincinnati: Anderson, 1990).

41 Police Foundation, *The Newark Foot Patrol Experiment* (Washington, DC: Author, 1981).

42 Jihong Zhao, Nicholas Lovrich, and Quint Thurman, "The Status of Community Policing in American Cities," *Policing* 22 (1999): 74–92.

43 Albert Cardarelli, Jack McDevitt, and Katrina Baum, "The Rhetoric and Reality of Community Policing in Small and Medium-Sized Cities and Towns," *Policing* 21 (1998): 397–415.

44 Quint Thurman, Andrew Giacomazzi, and Phil Bogen, "Research Note: Cops, Kids, and Community Policing—An Assessment of a Community Policing Demonstration Project," *Crime and Delinquency* 39 (1993): 554–564.

45 Quint Thurman and Phil Bogen, "Research Note: Spokane Community Policing Officers Revisited," *American Journal of Police* 15 (1996): 97–114.

46 Diana Fishbein, "The Comprehensive Care Model," *FBI Law Enforcement Bulletin* 67 (1998): 1–5.

47 Susan Sadd and Randolph Grinc, *Implementation Challenges in Community Policing* (Washington, DC: National Institute of Justice, 1996).

48 Donald Green, Dara Strolovitch, and Janelle Wong, "Defended Neighborhoods, Integration and Racially Motivated Crime," *American Journal of Sociology* 104 (1998): 372–403.

49 Walter Baranyk, "Making a Difference in a Public Housing Project," *Police Chief* 61 (1994): 31–35.

50 Michael Palmiotto, Michael Birzer, and Prabha Unnithan, "Training in Community Policing: A Suggested Curriculum," *Policing* 23 (2000): 8–21.

51 Jerome Skolnick and David Bayley, *Community Policing: Issues and Practices Around the World* (Washington, DC: National Institute of Justice, 1988).

52 Ibid., p. 17.

53 Herman Goldstein, "Improving Policing: A Problem-Oriented Approach," *Crime and Delinquency* 25 (1979): 236–258.

54 Skolnick and Bayley, *Community Policing*, p. 12.

55 Lawrence Sherman, Patrick Gartin, and Michael Buerger, "Hot Spots of Predatory Crime: Routine Activities and the Criminology of Place," *Criminology* 27 (1989): 27–55.

56 Ibid., p. 45.

57 Dennis Roncek and Pamela Maier, "Bars, Blocks, and Crimes Revisited: Linking the Theory of Routine Activities to the Empiricism of 'Hot Spots,'" *Criminology* 29 (1991): 725–753.

58 E. Nick Larsen, "Community Policing and the Control of Street Prostitution," paper presented at the annual meeting of the American Society of Criminology, Chicago, November 1996.

59 Herman Goldstein, "Toward Community-Oriented Policing: Potential, Basic Requirements, and Threshold Questions," *Crime and Delinquency* 33 (1987): 6–30.

60 Anthony Braga, David Weisburd, Elin Waring, Lorraine Green Mazerolle, William Spelman, and Francis Gajewski, "Problem-Oriented Policing in Violent Crime Places: A Randomized Controlled Experiment," *Criminology* 37 (1999): 541–580.

61 Eric Fritsch, Tory Caeti, and Robert Taylor, "Gang Suppression Through Saturation Patrol, Aggressive Curfew, and Truancy Enforcement: A Quasi-Experimental Test of the Dallas Anti-Gang Initiative," *Crime and Delinquency* 45 (1999): 122–139.

62 Bureau of Justice Assistance, *Problem-Oriented Drug Enforcement: A Community-Based Approach for Effective Policing* (Washington, DC: National Institute of Justice, 1993).

63 Ibid., pp. 64–65.

64 Jack R. Greene, "The Effects of Community Policing on American Law Enforcement: A Look at the Evidence," paper presented at the International Congress on Criminology, Hamburg, Germany, September 1988, p. 19.

65 Roger Dunham and Geoffrey Alpert, "Neighborhood Differences in Attitudes Toward Policing: Evidence for a Mixed-Strategy Model of Policing in a Multi-Ethnic Setting," *Journal of Criminal Law and Criminology* 79 (1988): 504–522.

66 Mark E. Correia, "The Conceptual Ambiguity of Community in Community Policing: Filtering the Muddy Waters," *Policing* 23 (2000): 218–233.

67 Scott Lewis, Helen Rosenberg, and Robert Sigler, "Acceptance of Community Policing Among Police Officers and Police Administrators," *Policing* 22 (1999): 567–588.

68 Amy Halsted, Max Bromley, and John Cochran, "The Effects of Work Orientations on Job Satisfaction Among Sheriffs' Deputies Practicing Community-Oriented Policing," *Policing* 23 (2000): 82–104.

69 Lisa Riechers and Roy Roberg, "Community Policing: A Critical Review of Underlying Assumptions," *Journal of Police Science and Administration* 17 (1990): 105–113 at pp. 112–113.

70 John Riley, "Community-Policing: Utilizing the Knowledge of Organizational Personnel," *Policing* 22 (1999): 618–633.

71 Jihong Zhao, Ni He, and Nicholas Lovrich, "Value Change Among Police Officers at a Time of Organizational Reform: A Follow-up Study of Rokeach Values," *Policing* 22 (1999): 152–170.

72 See for example, Lawrence Sherman, "Policing for Crime Prevention," in *Preventing Crime: What Works, What Doesn't, What's Promising* (Washington, DC: Bureau of Justice Programs, 1997).

73 Roger Parks, Stephen Mastrofski, Christina DeJong, and M. Kevin Gray, "How Officers Spend Their Time With the Community," *Justice Quarterly* 16 (1999): 483–519.

74 Gerasimos Gianakis and G. John Davis, "Reinventing or Repackaging Public Services? The Case of Community-Oriented Policing," *Public Administration Review* 58 (1998): 485–505.

75 David Kessler, "Integrating Calls for Service with Community- and Problem-Oriented Policing: A Case Study," *Crime and Delinquency* 39 (1993): 485–508.

76 L. Thomas Winfree, Gregory Bartku, and George Seibel, "Support for Community Policing Versus Traditional Policing Among Nonmetropolitan Police Officers: A Survey of Four New Mexico Police Departments," *American Journal of Police* 15 (1996): 23–47.

77 William Doerner and Terry Nowell, "The Reliability of the Behavioral-Personnel Assessment Device (BPAD) in Selecting Police Recruits," *Policing* 22 (1999): 343–352.

78 See, for example, Richard Larson, *Urban Police Patrol Analysis* (Cambridge, MA: MIT Press, 1972).

79 Brian Reaves, *State and Local Police Departments, 1990* (Washington, DC: Bureau of Justice Statistics, 1992), p. 6.

80 Philip Ash, Karen Slora, and Cynthia Britton, "Police Agency Officer Selection Practices," *Journal of Police Science and Administration* 17 (1990): 258–269.

81 Dennis Rosenbaum, Robert Flewelling, Susan Bailey, Chris Ringwalt, and Deanna Wilkinson, "Cops in the Classroom: A Longitudinal Evaluation of Drug Abuse Resistance Education (DARE)," *Journal of Research in Crime and Delinquency* 31 (1994): 3–31.

82 Greenwood and Petersilia, *Summary and Policy Implications*; Peter Greenwood et al., *Observations and Analysis*, vol. 3 of *The Criminal Investigation Process* (Santa Monica, CA: Rand Corporation, 1975).

83 J. David Hirschel and Charles Dean, "The Relative Cost-Effectiveness of Citation and Arrest," *Journal of Criminal Justice* 23 (1995): 1–12.

84 Adapted from Terry Koepsell and Charles Gerard, *Small Police Agency Consolidation: Suggested Approaches* (Washington, DC: U.S. Government Printing Office, 1979).

85 Thomas McAninch and Jeff Sanders, "Police Attitudes Toward Consolidation in Bloomington/Normal, Illinois: A Case Study," *Journal of Police Science and Administration* 16 (1988): 95–105.

86 James Garofalo and Dave Hanson, *The Metro Task Force: A Program of Intergovernmental Cooperation in Law Enforcement* (Washington, DC: National Institute of Justice, 1984).

87 Mike D'Alessandro and Charles Hoffman, "Mutual Aid Pacts," *Law and Order* 43 (1995): 90–93.

88 Leonard Sipes, Jr., "Maryland's High-Tech Approach to Crime Fighting," *Police Chief* 61 (1994): 18–20.

89 Nick Navarro, "Six Broward County Cities Turn to the Green and Gold," *Police Chief* 59 (1992): 60.

90 Greg Givens, "A Concept to Involve Citizens in the Provision of Police Services," *American Journal of Police* 12 (1993): 1–9; for a review, see Stephen Mastrofski, "Varieties of Community Policing," *American Journal of Police* 12 (1993): 65–75.

91 For a detailed review of this issue, see John Crank, "Patterns of Consolidation Among Public Safety Departments, 1978–1988," *Journal of Police Science and Administration* 17 (1990): 277–288.

92 Kenneth Perry, "Tactical Units Reduce Overtime Costs," *Police Chief* 52 (1985): 57–58.

93 Robert Worden, "Toward Equity and Efficiency in Law Enforcement: Differential Police Response," *American Journal of Police* 12 (1993): 1–24.

AP/Wide World Photos

ISSUES IN POLICING

Society's trashy behavior winds up in cops' hands.

—*William Bennett*[1]

On October 4, 2000, federal investigators looking into the activities of the New York Police Department's Street Crime Unit issued a report claiming that its officers had been singling out African American and Hispanic citizens as they conducted an aggressive campaign of street searches, a practice known as *racial profiling*.[2] The elite undercover unit had come under official scrutiny in the aftermath of the highly publicized 1999 shooting death of Amadou Diallo, an unarmed black man. Not taking the accusations lightly, New York Mayor Rudolph Giuliani charged that if police were forced to stop and search people based on their representation in the city's population, then about 17 percent of those detained must be senior citizens! He argued that although the federal report said that about 85 percent of the people searched by police were

African American or Hispanic, in truth about 89 percent of the criminal suspects in New York City were identified by victims as being African American or Hispanic.[3] Were members of the Street Crime Unit behaving in a racist fashion, or did their behavior merely reflect the sad realities of urban life in which the poor and minority-group members are disproportionately involved in criminal behavior?

The issue of racial profiling has become one of many critical issues facing big-city police departments. These incidents highlight the critical and controversial role police play in the justice system and the need for developing a professional, competent police force. The police are the gatekeepers of the criminal justice process. They initiate contact with law violators and decide whether to formally arrest them and start their journey through the criminal justice system, to settle the issue in an informal way (such as by issuing a warning), or to simply take no action at all. The strategic position of law enforcement

Chapter 7

The Diallo shooting raised serious questions about the police use of racial profiling to identify suspects.

officers, their visibility and contact with the public, and their use of weapons and arrest power kept them in the forefront of public thought for most of the twentieth century. This chapter reviews these important issues and presents a picture of the problems and concerns of police in society and some of the efforts being made by administrators to solve them and improve police services.

The general public is not the only group concerned about police attitudes and behavior. Police administrators and other law enforcement experts have focused their attention on issues that may influence the effectiveness and efficiency of police performance in the field. Some of their concerns are outgrowths of the development of policing as a profession: Does an independent police culture exist, and what are its characteristics? Do police officers develop a unique "working personality," and if so, does it influence their job performance? Are there police officer "styles" that make some police officers too aggressive and others inert and passive? Is policing too stressful an occupation?

The Police Foundation is a nonprofit organization dedicated to conducting research on law enforcement. To check out their activities and publications, go to their Web site at http://www.policefoundation.org/ For an up-to-date list of Web links, see http://www.wadsworth.com/ product/0534573053s

Fill in the blanks 1–2
True/False 1–2
Essay 1

blue curtain
The secretive, insulated police culture that isolates officers from the rest of society.

Another area of concern is the social composition of police departments: Who should be recruited as police officers? Are minorities and women being attracted to police work, and what have their experiences been on the force? Should police officers have a college education?

Important questions are also being raised about the problems police departments face when interacting with the society they are entrusted with supervising: Are police officers too forceful and brutal, and do they discriminate in their use of deadly force? Are police officers corrupt, and how can police deviance be controlled?

THE POLICE PROFESSION

All professions have unique characteristics that distinguish them from other occupations and institutions. Policing is no exception. Police experts have long sought to understand the unique nature of the police experience and to determine how the challenges of police work shape the field and its employees. In this section, some of the factors that make policing unique are discussed in detail. The Images of Justice feature discusses how the media portray police work and the police profession.

Police Culture

Police experts have found that the experience of becoming a police officer and the nature of the job itself cause most officers to band together in a police subculture, characterized by cynicism, clannishness, secrecy, and insulation from others in society—the so-called **blue curtain**. Police officers tend to socialize together and believe that their occupation cuts them off from relationships with civilians. Joining the police subculture means always having to stick up for fellow officers against outsiders, maintaining a tough, macho exterior personality, and distrusting the motives and behavior of outsiders.[4] Six core beliefs are viewed as being the heart of the police culture today:

1. Police are the only real crime fighters. The public wants the police officer to fight crime; other agencies, both public and private, only play at crime fighting.
2. No one else understands the real nature of police work. Lawyers, academics, politicians, and the public in general have little concept of what it means to be a police officer.
3. Loyalty to colleagues counts above everything else. Police officers have to stick together because everyone is out to get the police and make the job more difficult.
4. It is impossible to win the war against crime without bending the rules. Courts have awarded criminal defendants too many civil rights.
5. Members of the public are basically unsupportive and unreasonably demanding. People are quick to criticize police unless they need police help themselves.
6. Patrol work is the pits. Detective work is glamorous and exciting.[5]

These cultural beliefs make it difficult for police to accept new ideas and embrace innovative concepts, such as community policing. The forces that support a police culture generally are believed to develop from on-the-job experiences. Most officers, both male and female, originally join police forces because they want to help people, fight crime, and have an interesting, exciting, prestigious career with a high degree of job security.[6] Recruits often find that the social reality of police work does not mesh with their original career goals. They are unprepared for the emotional turmoil and conflict that accompany police work today.

IMAGES OF JUSTICE

NYPD Blue

Hard-charging police officers have long been the focus of films and TV shows. Representative of the genre is the gritty police drama *NYPD Blue,* which presents the ongoing saga of a group of streetwise New York City detectives assigned to the One-Five precinct. The show's core figure is Detective Andy Sipowicz (Dennis Franz), a recovering alcoholic who lost both his family and his self-respect after battling the bottle for decades. Now sober, Sipowicz is easily enraged by the deadbeats he meets on the job. He exhibits multiple personality traits—at times, a coarse racist, and at other times, a kind, good-hearted man with high morals.

Over the lifetime of the show, a number of detectives have been paired with Sipowicz—most recently, Danny Sorenson (Rick Schroder), who although young has a lot of "street smarts" and heart. Among other detectives in the precinct is Diane Russell (Kim Delany), also a recovering alcoholic, the widow of Sipowicz's former partner. She was joined in 2001 by another female detective, Connie McDowell (Charlotte Ross). The squad's able leader, Lt. Arthur Fancy (James McDaniel), was promoted

The central figure of the 15 precinct is Lt. Andy Sipowitz, played by Dennis Franz.

and replaced by Lt. Rodriquez (Esai Morales). Rounding out the cast are Detective Baldwin Jones (Henry Simmons), a young, idealistic African American officer, and Detective Greg Medavoy (Gordon Clapp) who, despite being a walking bundle of neuroses and insecurity, is a good investigator who has managed to earn the respect of his coworkers.

NYPD Blue aims for authenticity by using New York City street scenes and characters. Unlike so many other police shows and movies, few criminals are affluent, highly educated society folk. The detectives rarely use their weapons, engage in high-speed chases, or pursue criminals by jumping from one rooftop to another. They rarely sustain injury or get beaten to a pulp by criminals only to be on the job an hour later. In other words, *NYPD Blue* avoids the ludicrous vision of police officer as action hero that is the stock in trade of Bruce Willis (*Die Hard* series) and Mel Gibson (*Lethal Weapon* series). In fact, the thought of Sipowicz jumping from one rooftop to another or pursuing a criminal down the street is ludicrous: It is doubtful whether he can bend over to lace up his own shoes.

Like their real-life counterparts, the detectives have myriad social and personal problems, including obesity and alcoholism, conditions that rarely afflict superheroes (Medavoy and Sipowicz are always dieting; Sipowicz and Russell are members of Alcoholics Anonymous). Sipowicz has to confront his racist attitudes, which constantly entangle him with African Americans both on the job and off. During the last few seasons, he has lost two former partners—John Kelly (David Caruso) to an internal af-

fairs investigation and Bobby Simone (Jimmy Smits) to a fatal heart infection. Sipowicz's oldest son, Andy Jr., was killed by a pair of armed robbers, and his wife, Sylvia, died after being hit by a stray bullet in a courthouse shoot-out. There is little question that Sipowicz has faced the personal and job-related stress that plagues all too many police officers. The show's constant turnover of personnel in fact reflects the stress and job burnout suffered by the 15th squad's real-life counterparts.

Although *NYPD Blue* aims for realism, the plots often stray into a media version of police work. The squad almost always solves its cases, gets the bad guys to talk, and can concentrate on a single case for days on end until it is solved. If every arrestee were willing to write a confession, as they are when captured by detectives of the 15th squad, then we would have no need for the prosecutors who appear regularly on the competing show *Law & Order.*

Critical Thinking Skills

1. Knowing what you do about police, how different is the daily routine of officers in the 15th squad from that of a "normal" police detective?
2. Is it necessary for police detectives to begin their career as patrol officers, or should they be considered a separate branch of law enforcement and given totally separate training and skills?

InfoTrac College Edition Research

To read a critique of the "Sipowicz style" of policing, see William J. Bratton, "The Legacy of Detective Sipowicz," *Time,* 6 2000 March, v155 i9 p34

Membership in the police culture helps recruits adjust to the rigors of police work and provides the emotional support needed for survival.[7] The culture encourages decisiveness in the face of uncertainty and the ability to make split-second judgments that may later be subject to extreme criticism. The police culture has developed in response to the insulated, dangerous lifestyle of police officers. Policing is a dangerous occupation, and the availability of unquestioned support and loyalty of their peers is not something officers could readily do without.[8]

Police Personality

Police officers develop a unique set of personality traits that distinguish them from the average citizen. The typical police personality has been described as dogmatic, authoritarian, suspicious, racist, hostile, insecure, conservative, and cynical.[9] **Cynicism** has been found on all levels of policing, including chiefs of police, and throughout all stages of a police career.[10] Maintenance of these negative values and attitudes is believed to cause police officers to be secretive and isolated from the rest of society, producing the blue curtain.[11]

The police officer's "working personality" is shaped by constant exposure to danger and the need to use force and authority to reduce and control threatening situations.[12] Police feel suspicious of the public they serve and defensive about the actions of their fellow officers.

There are two opposing viewpoints on the cause of this phenomenon. One position holds that police departments attract recruits who are by nature cynical, authoritarian, secretive, and so on.[13] Other experts maintain that socialization and experience on the police force itself cause these character traits to develop in police officers.

Since the first research measuring police personality was published, numerous efforts have been made to determine whether the typical police recruit does indeed possess a unique personality that sets him or her apart from the average citizen. The results have been mixed.[14] Some research concludes that police values are different from those of the general adult population; other studies have found that police officers are actually more psychologically healthy than the general population, less depressed and anxious, and more social and assertive.[15] In general, research on police personality finds that police recruits value such personality traits as warmth, flexibility, and emotion; these traits are far removed from rigidity and cynicism.[16]

If recruits share values with the general population, then how can the cynicism of experienced officers be explained? In what is probably the classic study of police personality, *Behind the Shield* (1967), Arthur Niederhoffer examined the assumption that most police officers develop into cynics as a function of their daily duties.[17] Among his most important findings were that (1) police cynicism increases with length of service, (2) college-educated patrol officers become cynical if they are denied promotion, and (3) military-like police academy training causes new recruits to quickly become cynical about themselves. For example, Niederhoffer found that nearly 80 percent of first-day recruits believed that the police department was an "efficient, smoothly operating organization"; two months later, less than 33 percent professed that belief. Similarly, 50 percent of new recruits believed that a police superior was "very interested in the welfare of his subordinates"; two months later, that number had declined to 13 percent.[18]

The development of negative attitudes by police officers may have an extremely damaging effect on their job performance. A police officer's feelings of cynicism seem to intensify the need to maintain respect and exert authority over others.[19] As police escalate their use of authority, citizens learn to distrust and fear them. These feelings of hostility and anger in turn create feelings of potential danger among police officers, resulting in "police paranoia."[20] Cynical attitudes make

Fill in the blanks 3–4
True/False 3

cynicism
The belief that most people's actions are motivated solely by personal needs and selfishness.

police very conservative and resistant to change, factors that interfere with the efficiency of police work.[21]

Police Style

Fill in the blanks 5–7
True/False 4–6
Multiple choice 1–4
Essay 2

Policing encompasses a multitude of diverse tasks, including peacekeeping, criminal investigation, traffic control, and providing emergency medical service. Part of the socialization as a police officer is developing a working attitude, or **style**, through which he or she approaches policing. For example, some police officers may view their job as a well-paid civil service position that stresses careful compliance with written departmental rules and procedures. Other officers may see themselves as part of the "thin blue line" that protects the public from wrongdoers. They will use any means to get the culprit, even if it involves such cheating as planting evidence on an obviously guilty person who so far has escaped arrest. This is referred to as the "Dirty Harry problem," after the Clint Eastwood movie character who routinely violates all known legal standards of police work.[22]

Several studies have attempted to define and classify police styles into behavioral clusters.[23] An examination of the literature suggests that four styles of police work seem to fit the current behavior patterns of most police agents: the **Crime Fighter**, the **Social Agent**, the **Law Enforcer**, and the **Watchman**. These four styles are described in Exhibit 7.1.

Do police styles actually exist? As you may recall, the police role involves a great deal of time spent in noncrime service-related activities, ranging from providing

style
Working attitude through which a police officer approaches policing. Four styles that have been identified are the Crime Fighter, the Social Agent, the Law Enforcer, and the Watchman.

Crime Fighter
A style of policing that stresses dealing with serious crimes and arresting dangerous criminals.

EXHIBIT 7.1   THE FOUR BASIC STYLES OF POLICING

- **The Crime Fighter**   To Crime Fighters, the most important aspect of police work is investigating serious crimes and apprehending criminals. Their focus is on the victim, and they see effective police work as the only force that can keep society's "dangerous classes" in check. They are the "thin blue line" protecting society from murderers and rapists. They consider property crimes to be less significant and believe that such matters as misdemeanors, traffic control, and social service functions would be better handled by other government agencies. The ability to investigate criminal behavior that poses a serious threat to life and safety, combined with the power to arrest criminals, separates a police department from other municipal agencies. They see diluting these functions with minor social-service and nonenforcement duties as harmful to police efforts to create a secure society.

- **The Social Agent**   Social Agents believe that police should be involved in a wide range of activities without regard for their connection to law enforcement. Rather than viewing themselves as criminal catchers, they consider themselves problem solvers. They are troubleshooters who patch the holes that appear where the social fabric wears thin. They are happy to work with special-needs populations, such as the homeless, schoolchildren, and those in need of emergency services. The Social Agent fits well within a community policing unit.

- **The Law Enforcer**   According to this view, duty is clearly set out in law, and Law Enforcers stress playing it "by the book." Since the police are specifically charged with apprehending all types of lawbreakers, they see themselves as generalized law enforcement agents. Although they may prefer working on serious crimes, which are more intriguing and rewarding in terms of achievement, prestige, and status, they see the police role as one of enforcing all statutes and ordinances. They perceive themselves neither as community social workers nor as vengeance-seeking vigilantes; quite simply, they are law enforcement officers who perform the functions of detecting violations, identifying culprits, and taking the lawbreakers before a court. Law Enforcers are devoted to the profession of police work and are the officers most likely to aspire to command rank.

- **The Watchman**   The Watchman style is characterized by an emphasis on the maintenance of public order as the police goal, rather than on law enforcement or general service. Watchmen choose to ignore many infractions and requests for service unless they believe that the social or political order is jeopardized. Juveniles are "expected" to misbehave and are best ignored or treated informally. Motorists will often be left alone if their driving does not endanger or annoy others. Vice and gambling are problems only when the currently accepted standards of public order are violated. The Watchman is the most passive officer, more concerned with retirement benefits than with crime rates.

SOURCES: William Muir, *Police: Streetcorner Politicians* (Chicago: University of Chicago Press, 1977); James Q. Wilson, *Varieties of Police Behavior* (Cambridge, MA: Harvard University Press, 1968).

Social Agent
A style of policing that sees police work as a helping profession involved in a wide range of activities, not just law enforcement.

Law Enforcer
A style of policing that stresses the detection and apprehension aspects of police work, enforcement of all statutes and ordinances, and going "by the book."

Watchman
A style of policing that reacts to calls for service rather than aggressively pursuing crime.

emergency medical care to directing traffic. Although officers who admire one style of policing may emphasize one area of law enforcement over another, their daily activities will likely require them to engage in police duties they consider trivial or unimportant. Although some pure types exist, an officer probably cannot specialize in one area of policing while ignoring the others.[24] It is possible that today's police officer is more of a generalist than ever before and that future police recruits understand that they will be required to engage in a great variety of police tasks. Style and role orientation may influence how police officers carry out their duties and the way they use their discretion.[25]

PERSPECTIVES ON JUSTICE

Police officer style is a good example of how people holding different views of justice may be forced to work together within the same agency and perform similar tasks. On an individual level, some officers adhere to a strict crime control perspective and seek admission to the SWAT team, whereas others desire a placement in the community policing initiative. On the departmental level, some law enforcement agencies favor aggressive tactics to control would-be criminals, whereas others take a more humanistic approach and view policing as a helping profession. Thus, there are differences within and between police departments on what direction law enforcement policy should take.

Police Discretion

Police have the ability to deprive people of their liberty, to arrest them and take them away in handcuffs, and even to use deadly force to subdue them. A critical aspect of this professional responsibility is the personal **discretion** each officer has in carrying out his or her daily activities. Discretion can involve the selective enforcement of the law, as when a vice squad plainclothes officer decides not to take action against a tavern that is serving drinks after hours. Patrol officers use discretion when they decide to arrest one suspect for disorderly conduct but escort another home.

The majority of police officers use a high degree of personal discretion in carrying out daily tasks, sometimes referred to as "low-visibility decision making" in criminal justice.[26] This terminology suggests that, unlike members of almost every other criminal justice agency, police are neither regulated in their daily procedures by administrative scrutiny nor subject to judicial review (except when their behavior clearly violates an offender's constitutional rights). As a result, the exercise of discretion by police may sometimes deteriorate into discrimination, violence, and other abusive practices. The following sections describe the factors that influence police discretion and review suggestions for its control.

discretion
The use of personal decision making and choice in carrying out operations in the criminal justice system.

Fill in the blanks 8
True/False 7–10
Multiple choice 5–8
Essay 3

PERSPECTIVES ON JUSTICE

Police discretion is a good example of the decision making that concerns due process advocates. Are people who commit the same violations or crimes being treated differently by police officers, and if so, on what basis? Do race, gender, and class enter into the equation?

Legal Factors   Police discretion is inversely related to the severity of the offense. There is far less personal discretion available when police confront a suspect in a case involving murder or rape than there is with a simple assault or trespass. The likelihood of a police officer's taking legal action, then, may depend on how the individual views offense severity. Other legal factors that might influence police are the use of a weapon, seriousness of injury, and the presence of alcohol or drugs.

Victim–Offender Relationship   The relationship between the parties involved influences decision making. An altercation between two friends or relatives may be handled differently than an assault on a stranger. A case in point is policing domestic violence cases. Research indicates that police are reluctant to even respond to these kinds of cases because they are a constant source of frustration and futility. Victims, they believe, often fail to get help or change their abusive situation.[27] Even when they do respond, police are likely to treat domestic violence cases more casually than other assault cases.[28] Evidence shows that police intentionally delay responding to domestic disputes, hoping that by the time they get there the problem will be settled.[29] Yet, when domestic abuse involves extreme violence, especially if a weapon is brandished or used, then police are more likely to respond with a formal arrest.[30]

Environmental Factors   The degree of discretion an officer will exercise is at least partially defined by his or her living and working environment.[31] Police officers may work or dwell within a community culture that either tolerates eccentricities and personal freedoms or expects extremely conservative, professional, nononsense behavior on the part of its civil servants. For example, research now shows that people are becoming less tolerant of spouse abuse.[32] It would not be surprising to find that police officers assigned to an area whose residents are particularly disapproving of domestic violence will become more proactive in their enforcement of spouse abuse laws.

An officer who lives in the community he or she serves is probably strongly influenced by and shares a large part of the community's beliefs and values and is likely to be sensitive to and respect the wishes of neighbors, friends, and relatives. Conflict may arise, however, when the police officer commutes to an assigned area of jurisdiction, as is often the case in inner-city precincts. The officer who holds personal values in opposition to those of the community can exercise discretion in ways that conflict with the community's values and result in ineffective law enforcement.[33]

Treatment Alternatives   In an environment that has a proliferation of social agencies—detoxification units, drug control centers, and child-care services, for example—a police officer will obviously have more alternatives from which to choose when deciding whether to make the arrest. Referring cases to these alternative agencies, in fact, saves the officer both time and effort—records do not have to be filled out, and court appearances can be avoided. Thus, social agencies provide greater latitude in police decision making. A case in point is domestic violence cases. Police in communities that provide training in domestic violence prevention and maintain local shelters for battered women are more likely to take action in cases involving spouse abuse.[34]

Departmental Influences   The policies, practices, and customs of the local police department are another influence on discretion. These conditions vary from department to department and strongly depend on the judgment of the chief and others in the organizational hierarchy. For example, departments can issue directives aimed at influencing police conduct. Patrol officers may be asked to issue more tickets and make more arrests or to refrain from arresting under certain circumstances. Occasionally, a directive will instruct officers to be particularly alert for certain types of violations or to make some sort of interagency referral when specific events occur. For example, the department may order patrol officers to crack down on street panhandlers or to take formal action in domestic violence cases.[35] These factors affect the decisions of the police officer, who has to produce appropriate performance statistics by the end of the month or be prepared to offer justification for following a course of action other than that officially prescribed.

The ratio of supervisory personnel to subordinates may also influence discretion: Departments with a high ratio of sergeants to patrol officers may experience fewer officer-initiated actions than one in which fewer eyes are observing the action in the streets. The size of the department may also determine the level of officer discretion. In larger departments, looser control by supervisors seems to encourage a level of discretion unknown in smaller, more tightly run police agencies.

Peer Pressure Police discretion is also subject to peer pressure.[36] Police officers suffer a degree of social isolation because the job involves long and often irregular hours, including being on 24-hour call, and their authority and responsibility to enforce the law cause embarrassment during social encounters. At the same time, officers must handle irregular and emotionally demanding encounters involving the most personal and private aspects of people's lives. As a result, officers turn to their peers for both on-the-job advice and off-the-job companionship, essentially forming a subculture to provide a source of status, prestige, and reward.

The peer group affects how police officers exercise discretion on two distinct levels. First, in an obvious, direct manner, other officers dictate acceptable responses to street-level problems by displaying or withholding approval in office discussions. Second, the officer who takes the job seriously and desires the respect and friendship of others will take their advice, abide by their norms, and seek out the most experienced and most influential patrol officers on the force and follow their behavioral models.

Situational Factors How a crime is detected, the nature of the crime, and the circumstances that the police encounter at the crime scene can all influence police discretion. If, for example, a police officer stumbles on an altercation or break-in, the discretionary response may be quite different from a situation in which the officer is summoned by police radio. If an act has received official police recognition, such as the dispatch of a patrol car, police action must be taken or an explanation given as to why it was not. If a matter is brought to an officer's attention by a citizen observer, the officer can either ignore the request and risk a complaint or take discretionary action. When an officer chooses to become involved in a situation without benefit of a summons or complaint, maximum discretion can be used. Even in this circumstance, however, the presence of a crowd or of witnesses may influence the officer's decision making.

The nature and target of the crime may alter police action. Suspects in domestic violence cases are more likely to face arrest if they are present at the time the police arrive at the scene than if they have already left the premises. Police officers may be unwilling to spend the time to track down absconders; they also may be aware that victims are much less likely to participate in prosecution if the attacker has left before the police arrive.[37] Research also shows that police are more likely to make arrests in serious domestic violence cases if there are multiple offenders and/or victims and if the victim is a spouse rather than a girlfriend or boyfriend.[38]

demeanor
The way in which a person outwardly manifests his or her personality.

Attitude and Demeanor It is a long-standing belief among police experts that a suspect's **demeanor** and attitude will weigh heavily on the use of discretionary powers: If a suspect is rude, talks back, has an attitude problem, or otherwise challenges an officer's authority, formal action is more likely to be taken.[39] This belief has been challenged, however, by research by David Klinger, who finds that police officers are used to people who have bad attitudes and that more than angry words are needed to affect police decision making.[40] Klinger suggests that the person who struggles or touches police during a confrontation is a likely candidate for arrest; merely having a "bad attitude" is not enough to generate police retaliation. Although Klinger's data are persuasive, there are still those suspects whose negative demeanor will result in formal police action.[41]

Race and Ethnicity   One often-debated issue is whether police take personal characteristics into account when making arrest decisions. The prevailing wisdom is that police are more likely to arrest the young, males, minorities, and the poor while favoring the old, whites, females, and the affluent.[42] Because this issue is so important, it is the topic of the Race, Gender and Ethnicity in Criminal Justice feature.

Police discretion is one of the most often debated issues in criminal justice (see Figure 7.1). On its face, the unequal enforcement of the law smacks of unfairness and violates the Constitution's doctrines of due process and equal protection. Yet if some discretion were not exercised, police would be forced to function as robots merely following the book. Administrators have sought to control discretion so that its exercise may be both beneficial to citizens and nondiscriminatory.[43]

 How do police use their discretion, and what can be done to control behaviors that violate community standards? Answers to these questions can be found in a publication of the National Institute of Justice, "'Broken Windows' and Police Discretion" by criminologist George Kelling: http://www.ncjrs.org/pdffiles1/nij/178259.pdf

For an up-to-date list of Web links, see http://www.wadsworth.com/product/0534573053s

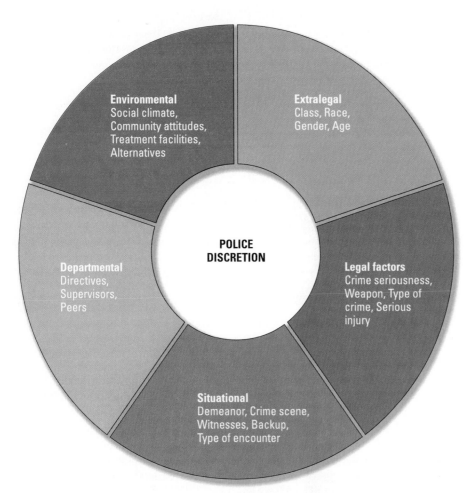

FIGURE 7.1
INFLUENCES
ON POLICE
DISCRETION

SOURCE: Brian Reeves & Andrew Goldberg, *Local Police Departments 1997* (Washington, DC: Bureau of Justice Statistics, 2000)

RACE, GENDER, AND ETHNICITY IN CRIMINAL JUSTICE

Does Race Influence the Police Use of Discretion?

In the late summer of 1997, New Yorkers were shocked as an astounding case of police brutality began to unfold in the daily newspapers. Abner Louima, age 33, a Haitian immigrant, had been arrested outside Club Rendez-vous, a Brooklyn nightclub, on August 9, 1997, after a fight had broken out. Louima later claimed that the arresting officers had become furious when he protested his arrest, twice stopping the patrol car to beat him with their fists. When they arrived at the station house, two officers, apparently angry because some of the club goers had fought with the police, led Louima to the men's room, removed his trousers, and attacked him with the handle of a toilet plunger, first shoving it into his rectum and then into his mouth, breaking teeth—while Louima screamed, "Why are you doing this to me? Why? Why?" The officers also shouted racial slurs at Louima, who was later rushed to a hospital for emergency surgery to repair a puncture in his small intestine and injuries to his bladder. Louima, who witnesses said had no bruises or injuries when officers took him into custody, arrived at the hospital three hours later, bleeding profusely.

In the aftermath of the case, New York Police Department investigators granted departmental immunity to nearly 100 officers in order to gain information. After this cracking of the "blue curtain" of silence, a number of police officers were given long prison sentences on charges of sexual abuse and first-degree assault.

The Louima case and other incidents involving police and the minority community have reignited the long debate over whether police take extralegal factors such as race into account when making arrest decisions. The question is whether police discretion works against the young, males, the poor, and minority-group members and favors the wealthy, the politically connected, and majority-group members.

There are two opposing views on this point. Some experts question whether racial discrimination actually exists. Police expert Ronald Weitzer finds that although some law enforcement officers may discriminate against racial minorities, the frequency and scope of police discrimination may be less than anticipated. Sociologists Matt De Lisi and Bob Regoli provide data showing that whites are nine times more likely to suffer DWI (driving while intoxicated) arrests than blacks. For a crime where it would be very easy for police to discriminate, whites—not blacks—are disproportionately arrested. Although discrimination may have existed in the past, according to legal experts Dan Kahan and Tracey Meares, we no longer need to worry about racial discrimination because minorities now possess sufficient political status to protect them within the justice system. Finally, as Harvard University law professor Randall Kennedy forcefully argues, even if a law enforcement policy exists that disproportionately affects African American suspects, it might be justified as a "public good" because law-abiding African Americans are statistically more often victims of crimes committed by other African Americans.

In contrast, after thoroughly reviewing the literature on police bias, Samuel Walker, Cassia Spohn, and Miriam DeLone conclude that police discriminate against racial minorities and that significant problems persist between the police and racial and ethnic communities in the United States. Similarly, constitutional scholar David Cole conclusively argues in his recent book, *No Equal Justice: Race and Class in the American Criminal Justice System,* that despite efforts to create racial neutrality, a race-based double standard operates in virtually every aspect of criminal justice, including the use of police discretion. These disparities allow the privileged to enjoy constitutional protections from police power, without extending these protections across the board to minorities and the poor.

These two polar positions on race discrimination by police are reflected in the literature, which yields research supporting both sides of the issue. A number of studies have found that race does in fact play an important role in police discretion. For example, a significant body of literature shows that police are more likely to "hassle" or arrest poor, African American males. Darlene Conley's research found evidence that police frequently stop and question youths of color

WHO ARE THE POLICE?

The composition of the nation's police forces is changing. Traditionally, police agencies were composed of white males with a high school education who viewed policing as a secure position that brought them the respect of their family and friends and a step up the social ladder. It was not uncommon to see police families in which one member of each new generation would enter the force. This picture has been changing and will continue to change. As criminal justice programs turn out thousands of graduates every year, an increasing number of police officers have at least some college education. In addition, affirmative action programs

walking down the streets of their neighborhoods or standing on corners. Neighborhood youths told her how suspicion produces crime: If you're going to be harassed and "messed with," you might as well not care and commit crime.

In contrast to these findings, a number of studies have produced data indicating that racial bias does not influence the decision to arrest and process a suspect. According to this view, it is prior record, crime seriousness, and other legal factors that control police decision making, not a suspect's race, ethnicity, or gender. Suspects who are intoxicated and belligerent are more likely to evoke the ire of police officers, regardless of their race or ethnicity. This claim of racially unbiased police behavior is supported by a survey conducted by Ronald Weitzer in three Washington, D.C., neighborhoods. Weitzer found that residents in African American neighborhoods do not distinguish in their qualitative evaluations of black and white police officers and, if anything, value racially integrated police services. Similarly, Thomas Priest and Deborah Brown Carter have found that the African American community is supportive of the local police, especially when they respond quickly to calls for service. It is unlikely that African Americans would appreciate rapid service or the presence of white officers if police routinely practiced racial discrimination.

One reason for these contrasting views is that racial influences on police

decision making are often subtle and hard to detect. For example, it may be that the victim's race, not the criminal's, is the key to racial bias: Police officers are more likely to take formal action when the crime victim is white than when the victim is a minority-group member. These data suggest that any study of police discretion must take into account both victim and offender characteristics if it is to be truly valid.

Regardless of which position is correct, all police officers do not operate in an unfair and unjust manner, nor can all police departments be accused of operating with a racial bias. Evidence shows that the influence of race on police discretion varies from jurisdiction to jurisdiction and may be a function of the professionalism of the individual department.

Critical Thinking Skills

1. What, if anything, can be done to reduce racial bias on the part of police? Would adding minority officers help? Would it be a form of racism to assign minority officers to minority neighborhoods?

2. Would research showing that police are more likely to make arrests in interracial incidents than in intraracial incidents constitute evidence of racism?

 InfoTrac College Edition Research

Use "racial profiling" as a keyword to review articles on race

as a determining factor in the police use of discretion.

SOURCES: Ronald Weitzer "White, Black, or Blue Cops? Race and Citizen Assessments of Police Officers," *Journal of Criminal Justice* 28 (2000): 313–324; Thomas Priest and Deborah Brown Carter, "Evaluations of Police Performance in an African American Sample," *Journal of Criminal Justice* 27 (1999): 457–465; Matt De Lisi and Bob Regoli, "Race, Conventional Crime, and Criminal Justice: The Declining Importance of Skin Color," *Journal of Criminal Justice* 27 (1999): 549–557; David Cole, *No Equal Justice: Race and Class in the American Criminal Justice System* (New York: New Press, 2000); Randall Kennedy, *Race, Crime and the Law* (New York: Vintage Books, 1998); Dan M. Kahan and Tracey L. Meares, "The Coming Crisis of Criminal Procedure," *Georgetown Law Journal* 86 (1998): 1153–1184; David Kocieniewski, "Man Says Officers Tortured Him After Arrest," *New York Times,* 13 August 1997, p. A1; John Kavanagh, "The Occurrence of Resisting Arrest in Arrest Encounters: A Study of Police–Citizen Violence," *Criminal Justice Review* 22 (1997): 16–29; Ronald Weitzer, "Racial Discrimination in the Criminal Justice System: Findings and Problems in the Literature," *Journal of Criminal Justice* 24 (1996): 309–322; Samuel Walker, Cassia Spohn, and Miriam DeLone, *The Color of Justice: Race, Ethnicity, and Crime in America* (Belmont, CA: Wadsworth, 1996), p. 115; Sandra Lee Browning, Francis Cullen, Liqun Cao, Renee Kopache, and Thomas Stevenson, "Race and Getting Hassled by the Police: A Research Note," *Police Studies* 17 (1994): 1–10; Darlene Conley, "Adding Color to a Black and White Picture: Using Qualitative Data to Explain Racial Disproportionality in the Juvenile Justice System," *Journal of Research in Crime and Delinquency* 31 (1994): 135–148.

have helped slowly change the racial and gender composition of police departments to reflect community makeup. The following sections explore these changes in detail.

College-Educated Police Officers

In recent years, many police experts have argued that police recruits should have a college education. This development is not unexpected, considering that higher education for police officers has been recommended by national commissions since 1931.[44]

True/False 11–12
Essay 4

Although education is valued, most law enforcement agencies do not require recruits to have an advanced degree. Today, 16 percent of state police agencies require a two-year college degree, and 4 percent require a four-year degree. Among large municipal police agencies, 9 percent had a degree requirement, with 2 percent requiring a four-year degree. Among sheriffs' departments, 6 percent required a degree, including 1 percent with a four-year degree requirement.[45]

What are the benefits of higher education for police officers? Better communication with the public, especially minority and ethnic groups, is believed to be one benefit. College-educated officers write better and more clearly and are more likely to be promoted. Police administrators believe that higher education enables officers to perform more effectively, generate fewer citizen complaints, show more initiative in performing police tasks, and generally act more professionally.[46] In addition, college-educated officers are less likely to have disciplinary problems and are viewed as better decision makers.[47] Studies have shown that college-educated police officers generate fewer citizen complaints and have better behavioral and performance characteristics than their less-educated peers.[48] Research by John Krimmel indicates that educated officers are more likely to rate themselves higher on most performance indicators—signifying that, if nothing else, higher education is associated with greater self-confidence and assurance.[49]

There is little evidence, however, that college-educated officers are more effective crime fighters; education appears to have relatively little influence on police officer behavior.[50] The diversity of the police role, the need for split-second decision making, and the often boring and mundane tasks police are required to do are all considered reasons why higher education may be a waste of time.[51] However, superiors find educated officers to be more reliable employees and better report writers, and citizens find them to be exceptional in the use of good judgment and problem solving.[52]

Although they may not require officers to have a college education, most police departments seem to value academic experience.[53] However, a tight labor market has forced some departments, such as New York City, to loosen or waive educational requirements in an effort to encourage job applications. Normally, the city requires recruits to have at least 60 college credits, but will now (as of 2001) waive that prerequisite for those recruits with two or more years of honorable military service and those who have served as traffic enforcement and school safety agents.[54] It would be ironic if a healthy economy hampers efforts to upgrade the education level of the nation's police departments.

 To learn more about police education, read what Jeremy Travis of the National Institute of Justice has to say: http://www.ojp.usdoj.gov/nij/ speeches/police.htm

For an up-to-date list of Web links, see http://www.wadsworth.com/ product/0534573053s

 Fill in the blanks 9–14
True/False 13–15
Multiple choice 9–10
Essay 5

Minority Police Officers

For the past two decades, U.S. police departments have made a concerted effort to attract minority police officers, and there have been some impressive gains. As might be expected, cities with large minority populations are the ones that have a higher proportion of minority officers in their municipal police departments.[55]

The reasons for this effort are varied. Viewed in its most positive light, police departments recruit minority citizens to field a more balanced force that truly represents the communities they serve. Most citizens seem to approve of their local law enforcement agents, yet approval is often skewed along racial lines.[56] African Americans generally have less confidence in the police than European Americans and are skeptical of their ability to protect them from harm. [57]African Americans also seem to be more adversely affected than European Americans when well-publicized incidents of police misconduct occur.[58] It comes as no surprise, then, that public opinion polls and research surveys show that African American citizens report having less confidence in the police than either Hispanics or European Americans.[59] African American juveniles seem particularly suspicious of police, even when they deny having had a negative encounter with a police officer.[60]

Middle-class African Americans seem even more critical of police than their working class peers, perhaps because they believe that their class position should shield them from police misconduct and are disappointed when it does not.[61]

A heterogeneous police force can be instrumental in gaining the minority community's confidence by helping dispel the view that police departments are generally bigoted or biased organizations. Furthermore, minority police officers possess special qualities that can serve to improve police performance. For example, Spanish-speaking officers can help with investigations in Hispanic neighborhoods, and Asian officers are essential for undercover or surveillance work with Asian gangs and drug importers. Figure 7.2 shows the racial and gender breakdown of the nation's largest police departments.

Work History of Minority Police Officers   The earliest known hiring of an African American police officer was 1861 in Washington, D.C.; Chicago hired its first black officer in 1872.[62] By 1890, an estimated 2,000 minority police officers were employed in the United States. At first, black officers suffered a great deal of discrimination. Their work assignments were restricted, as were their chances for promotion. Minority officers were often assigned solely to black neighborhoods, and in some cities they were required to call a white officer to make an arrest. White officers held highly prejudicial attitudes, and as late as the 1950s some refused to ride in patrol cars with black officers.[63]

The experience of African American police officers has not been an easy one. In his classic 1969 book, *Black in Blue,* Nicholas Alex pointed out that black police officers of the time suffered from what he called **double marginality**.[64] On the one hand, black officers had to deal with the expectation that they would give members of their own race a break. On the other hand, they often experienced overt

double marginality
According to Nicholas Alex, the social burden African American police officers carry by being both minority-group members and law enforcement officers.

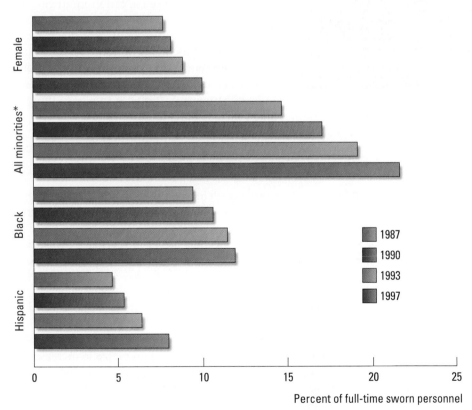

FIGURE 7.2
FEMALE AND
MINORITY LOCAL
POLICE OFFICERS,
1987, 1990,
1993, AND 1997

*Includes Blacks, Hispanics, Asians, Pacific Islanders,
American Indians, and Alaska Natives

Atlanta police chief Beverly Harvard was the first woman to head a big-city police department.

racism from their police colleagues. Alex found that black officers' adaptation to these pressures ranged from denying that black suspects should be treated differently from whites to treating black offenders more harshly than white offenders to prove their lack of bias. Alex offered several reasons for some black officers' being tougher on black offenders: They desired acceptance from their white colleagues, they were particularly sensitive to any disrespect given them by black teenagers, and they viewed themselves as protectors of the black community. Supportive evidence can be found in a study conducted by criminologist Kim Michelle Lersch, who discovered that minority citizens are actually more likely to accuse a minority officer than a white officer of misconduct.[65]

These conflicts have become more muted as minority representation has increased. As Figure 7.2 shows, by 1997 racial and ethnic minorities made up about 22 percent of full-time sworn officers in local police departments, up from 15 percent in 1987.[66] The number of African American officers in some of the nation's largest cities is now proportionate to minority representation in the population. For example, Los Angeles, Washington, Boston, and Pittsburgh, among other cities, now have police forces that represent their population.[67]

As their level of representation improves, minority officers now seem more self-assured and less willing to accept any discriminatory practices by the police department; as a consequence, race-based job differences may be eroding.[68] For example, the reporting rates of minority officers feeling job-related stress and strain are similar to those of white officers.[69] Black and white police officers seem to share similar attitudes toward important issues such as community policing.[70] This convergence may be trickling down to the general public: Some research finds that the general public perceives few differences in the performance of white and black officers.[71]

Affirmative Action Despite these positive changes, minority police officers have been victims of intentional and sometimes unintentional departmental discrimination. For example, some departments, in an effort to provide representative coverage to minority areas of the city, assign all their black, Hispanic, or Asian officers to a single patrol area or beat, a practice ruled discriminatory by federal courts.[72] Minority police officers have resorted to lawsuits to seek relief from what they consider to be discriminatory or demeaning activity.[73]

A series of legal actions brought by minority representatives has resulted in local, state, and federal courts' ordering police departments to create affirmative action programs to increase minority representation in police departments. One method has been to reformulate entrance exams and requirements to increase minority hiring. Court-ordered hiring was deemed necessary because, as late as 1940, less than 1 percent of all police officers were minorities and by 1950 the numbers had increased to only 2 percent.[74]

Numerous hiring plans have been implemented under court supervision. Sometimes the drive to recruit and promote minority officers forces police and city officials to reevaluate the results of normal testing procedures.[75] In 1987, in the case of *United States v. Paradise,* the Supreme Court upheld racial quotas as a means of reversing the effects of past discrimination. Ordering the Alabama Department of Public Safety to promote an equal number of black and white highway patrol officers, the Court said, "Discrimination at the entry level necessarily precluded blacks from competing and resulted in a departmental hierarchy dominated exclusively by nonminorities." The Alabama State Patrol had no minority majors, captains, lieutenants, or sergeants, and only 4 of 66 corporals were black. The Court justified its ruling on the grounds that only qualified people would be promoted, the restriction was temporary, and it did not require layoffs of white officers.[76]

Court-ordered hiring has sometimes generated resentment among white officers who view affirmative action hiring and promotion programs as a threat to their job security. Despite the presence of such attitudes, many departments have voluntarily complied with minority hiring plans.[77] Minorities will continue to increase their presence on police forces, especially if the recruitment mechanisms ordered by courts are used. At the same time, police administrators will be challenged to encourage minority youths to consider careers in law enforcement, considering the fact that many hold negative attitudes about police.[78]

Female Police Officers

Fill in the blanks 15–16
True/False 16–17
Multiple choice 11–12

In 1910 Alice Stebbins Wells became the first woman to hold the title of police officer (in Los Angeles) and to have arrest powers.[79] For more than half a century, female officers endured separate criteria for selection, were given menial tasks, and were denied the opportunity for advancement.[80] Some relief was gained with the passage of the Civil Rights Act of 1964 and its subsequent amendments. Courts have consistently supported the addition of women to police forces by striking down entrance requirements that eliminated almost all female candidates but could not be proven to predict job performance (such as height and upper-body strength).[81] Women do not do as well as men on strength tests and are much more likely to fail the entrance physical than male recruits; critics contend that many of these tests do not reflect the actual tasks that police do on the job.[82] Nonetheless, the role of women in police work is still restricted by social and administrative barriers that have been difficult to remove. Today, about 6 percent of all sworn officers are women.

Women continue to be underrepresented in the senior administrative ranks, and many believe they are assigned duties that underutilize their skills and training.[83] If they aspire to rise in police organizations, policewomen become frustrated when they begin to recognize that few women get promoted to command positions. Female recruits often lack successful female role models on which to shape their career aspirations.[84] It may not be surprising, then, that female officers report significantly higher levels of job-related stress than male officers.[85]

Work Performance Gender bias is certainly not supported by existing research, which indicates that women are highly successful police officers.[86] In an important study of recruits in the Metropolitan Police Department of Washington, D.C., policewomen were found to display extremely satisfactory work performances.[87] Compared with male officers, women were found to respond to similar types of calls, and the arrests they made were as likely to result in conviction. Women were more likely than their male colleagues to receive support from the community and were less likely to be charged with improper conduct. Policewomen seem to be more understanding and sympathetic to crime victims than male officers and are more likely to offer them treatment.[88]

Research has also debunked another enduring myth about female officers: Because they are less capable of subduing a suspect physically, they will be more likely to use their firearms. Actually, the opposite is true: Policewomen are less likely to use firearms in violent confrontations than their male partners, are more emotionally stable, are less likely to seriously injure a citizen, and are no more likely to suffer injuries than their male partners.[89] These generally positive results are similar to findings developed in other studies conducted in major U.S. cities.[90]

Gender Conflicts Despite the overwhelming evidence supporting their performance, policewomen have not always been fully accepted by their male peers or the general public. Male officers complain that female officers lack the emotional and physical strength to perform well in situations involving violence.[91] Some officers' wives resent their husbands' having a female partner because they consider the policewoman not only a sexual threat but inadequate support in a violent encounter.[92]

Studies of policewomen indicate that they are still struggling for acceptance, believe that they do not receive equal credit for their job performance, and report that it is common for them to be sexually harassed by their co-workers.[93] Female officers may also be targeted for more disciplinary actions by administrators and, if cited, are more likely to receive harsher punishments than male officers; that is, a greater percentage receive punishments greater than a reprimand.[94]

Surveys of male officers show that only one-third actually accept a woman on patrol and that more than one-half do not think that women can handle the physical requirements of the job as well as men.[95] This form of bias is not unique to the United States. Research shows that policewomen in England report being excluded from full membership on their force because of gender inequality; their aspirations are frequently frustrated in favor of male officers.[96] Similarly, female officers in New Zealand, compared with their male counterparts, believe that their superiors are not fair in making decisions or treating people fairly.[97]

Defining the Female Police Role Those female officers who fail to catch on to the unwritten police subculture are often written off as "bad police material."[98] Women who prove themselves tough enough to gain respect as police officers are then labeled as "lesbians" or "bitches" to neutralize their threat to male dominance, a process referred to as **defeminization**.[99] Male officers also generally assume that female officers who adopt an aggressive style of policing will be quicker to use deadly force than their male counterparts. Women working in this male-dominated culture may experience stress and anxiety.[100] It is not surprising, then, that significantly more female than male officers report being the victim of discrimination on the job. Male officers who claim to have experienced gender-based discrimination suggest that it comes at the hands of female officers who use their "sexuality" for job-related benefits.[101]

These perceptions of female officers are often based on gender stereotypes and are consequently incorrect.[102] Nonetheless, policewomen are frequently caught in the classic "catch-22" dilemma: If they are physically weak, male partners view them as a risk in street confrontations; if they are actually more powerful and aggressive than their male partners, they are regarded as an affront to the policeman's manhood.

Minority Female Officers African American policewomen, who account for only about 2 percent of all police officers, occupy a unique status. A study of black women serving in five large municipal departments, conducted by Susan Martin, found that many minority women do in fact perceive significantly more racial discrimination than both other female officers and African American male officers.[103] Martin found that black policewomen often incur the hostility of both white women and black men who feel threatened that they will take their place. On patrol, black female officers are treated differently from white female officers by male officers: Although neither group of women is viewed as equals, white policewomen are protected and coddled, whereas black policewomen are viewed as pas-

defeminization
The process by which policewomen become enculturated into the police profession at the expense of their feminine identity.

sive, lazy, and unequal. In the station house, male officers show little respect for black female officers, who face "widespread racial stereotypes as well as outright racial harassment."[104] Black female officers also report having difficult relationships with black male officers, their relationships strained by tensions and dilemmas "associated with sexuality and competition for desirable assignments and promotions."[105] Surprisingly, there was little unity among the female officers.

THE DOWNSIDE OF POLICING: STRESS, VIOLENCE, AND CORRUPTION

Law enforcement is not an easy job. The role ambiguity, social isolation, and threat of danger present in "working the street" are the police officer's constant companions. What effects do these strains have on police? This section discusses three of the most significant problems: stress, violence, and corruption.

Police Stress

Fill in the blanks 17
Multiple choice 13–16
Essay 6

The complexity of their role, the need to exercise prudent discretion, the threat of using violence and having violence used against them, and isolation from the rest of society all take a toll on law enforcement officers. It is not surprising that

AP/Wide World Photos

While most police work involves routine tasks, the threats of danger and violence are always present. Here, officers are called on to control angry protesters. Even if properly handled, such confrontations are bound to increase stress levels.

police officers experience tremendous stress, a factor that leads to alcoholism, divorce, depression, and even suicide.

The Cause of Stress A number of factors have been associated with police stress.[106] The pressure of being on duty 24 hours a day leads to stress and emotional detachment from both work and public needs. Police stress has been related to internal conflict with administrative policies that deny officers support and a meaningful role in decision making. For example, stress may occur when an officer is forced to adapt to a department's new methods of policing, such as COP (community-oriented policing), and they are opposed or skeptical about the change in policy.[107] In addition, officers suffer stress in their personal lives when they bring the job home or when their work hours are shifted, causing family disruptions.[108] Other stressors include poor training, substandard equipment, inadequate pay, lack of opportunity, job dissatisfaction, role conflict, exposure to brutality, and fears about competence, success, and safety.[109] Some officers may feel stress because they believe that the court system favors the rights of the criminal and "handcuffs" the police; others may be sensitive to a perceived lack of support from government officials and the general public.[110] Some officers believe that their superiors care little about their welfare.[111]

Police psychologists have divided these stressors into four distinct categories:

- *External stressors,* such as verbal abuse from the public, justice system inefficiency, and liberal court decisions that favor the criminal. What are perceived to be antipolice judicial decisions may alienate officers and reduce their perceptions of their own competence.[112]
- *Organizational stressors,* such as low pay, excessive paperwork, arbitrary rules, and limited opportunity for advancement.
- *Duty stressors,* such as rotating shifts, work overload, boredom, fear, and danger.
- *Individual stressors,* such as discrimination, marital difficulties, and personality problems.[113]

The effects of stress can be shocking. Police work has been related to both physical and psychological ailments. Police officers have a significantly high rate of premature death caused by such conditions as coronary heart disease and diabetes. They also experience a disproportionate number of divorces and other marital problems. Research indicates that officers in some departments, but not all, have higher suicide rates than the general public.[114] Nor are stress disorders limited to American policing. For example, studies of Australian police departments indicate that such stress-related factors as years of service, job satisfaction, and perceived control within the job are significant predictors of an officer's alcohol consumption.[115]

How Can Stress Be Combated? Police departments are now attempting to neutralize job-related stress by training officers to cope with its effects. Today, stress training includes diet information, biofeedback, relaxation and meditation, and exercise. Many departments include stress management as part of an overall "wellness" program designed to promote physical and mental health, fitness, and good nutrition.[116] Some programs have included family members because they may be better able to help the officer cope if they have more knowledge about the difficulties of police work. Still other efforts promote "total wellness programming," which enhances the physical and emotional well-being of officers by emphasizing preventive physical and psychological measures.[117] Research also shows that since police perceive many benefits of their job and enjoy the quality of life it provides, stress-reduction programs may help officers focus on the positive aspects of police work.[118]

Stress is a critically important aspect of police work. Further research is needed to create valid methods of identifying police officers under considerable stress and to devise effective stress-reduction programs.[119]

Police Violence

Fill in the blanks 18–20
True/False 18–20
Multiple choice 17–22
Essay 7

Since their creation, U.S. police departments have wrestled with the charge that they are brutal, physically violent organizations. Early police officers resorted to violence and intimidation to gain the respect that was not freely given by citizens. In the 1920s, the Wickersham Commission detailed numerous instances of police brutality, including the use of the third degree to extract confessions.

Police violence first became a major topic for discussion in the 1940s, when rioting provoked serious police backlash. Former Supreme Court Justice Thurgood Marshall, when he was chief counsel of the National Association for the Advancement of Colored People's Legal Defense Fund, referred to the Detroit police as a "gestapo" after a 1943 race riot left 34 people dead.[120] Twenty-five years later, excessive police force was again an issue when television cameras captured police violence against protestors at the Democratic National Convention in Chicago.

Today, police brutality continues to be a concern, especially when police use excessive violence against members of the minority community. The nation looked on in disgust when a videotape was aired on network newscasts showing members of the Los Angeles Police Department beating, kicking, and using electric stun guns on Rodney King. Earlier, Los Angeles police stopped using a restraining choke hold that cuts off circulation of blood to the brain after minority citizens complained that it caused permanent damage and may have killed as many as 17 people. It is not surprising that three-quarters of all complaints filed against the police for misconduct tend to be nonwhite males under the age of 30.[121]

The question of police use of force has two main aspects: (1) Are typical police officers generally brutal, violent, and disrespectful to the citizens with whom they come in daily contact? (2) Are the police overzealous and discriminatory in their use of deadly force when apprehending suspected felons? Let's examine each of these issues separately.

Police Brutality   The term **police brutality** refers to such actions as using abusive language, making threats, using force or coercion unnecessarily, prodding with nightsticks, and stopping and searching people to harass them. Charges of generalized police brutality were common between the 1940s and 1960s. Surveys undertaken by the President's Commission on Law Enforcement and the Administration of Justice and other national commissions found that many citizens believed that police discriminated against minorities when they used excessive force in handling suspects, displayed disrespect to innocent bystanders, and so on.[122] However, by 1967 the President's Commission concluded that the police use of physical brutality had somewhat abated.[123]

police brutality
Actions such as using abusive language, making threats, using force or coercion unnecessarily, prodding with nightsticks, and stopping and searching people to harass them.

Charges of police brutality continue to be made in many jurisdictions, but the evidence suggests that actual instances of physical abuse of citizens by police officers are less frequent than commonly imagined.[124] Numerous studies have found that violent interactions are actually atypical.[125] Studies of individual police departments have found that, when force is used, it usually involves grabbing and restraining; weapons are rarely used.[126] For example, a study of the Phoenix (Arizona) Police Department found that physical force was used in only 22 percent of arrests and that when force was used it was typically at a minimal level; weapons of any kind, such as flashlights, were used in only 2 percent of arrests.[127]

National surveys on police use of force have also found that use of force is rare.[128] For example, the International Association of Chiefs of Police (IACP), a national organization devoted to professional policing, is conducting an ongoing survey of the police use of violence in 150 police departments. Preliminary findings from the project include the following:

- The police use-of-force rate is 4.19 per 10,000 responded-to calls for service, or 0.0419 percent.
- About 87 percent of use-of-force incidents involve officers using physical force. Officers use chemical force in 7 percent of the incidents, firearms in about 5 percent.
- About 10 percent of officers using force sustained injuries, less than 1 percent serious. About 38 percent of subjects in force incidents were injured, with 1.5 percent sustaining major injuries.[129]

Research by the federal government estimates that 144 million contacts occur between the police and the public each year, and of these only 500,000 involve some force (Figure 7.3). Other research indicates that the use of force appears to be unrelated to an officer's personal characteristics, such as age, gender, and ethnicity. It is more likely to be situational—for example, when police are trying to make an arrest and the suspect is resisting. Force is also more likely to be used with special populations, such as people under the influence of alcohol or drugs or mentally ill individuals.

Brutality Incidents Although these national data indicate an overall decline in brutality incidents, brutality incidents continue to stain metropolitan police agencies. One sore point is the unrestrained use of choke holds. Some suspects have died during the application of this method of restraint, and the procedure is known to carry the risk of asphyxia. In June 1999, Gregory Riley died after allegedly being placed in a choke hold during a struggle with Chicago police officers trying to arrest him for a drug offense. The Cook County medical examiner found the cause of death to be "asphyxia due to compression of the neck and

FIGURE 7.3 POLICE–COMMUNITY CONTACT AND THE USE OF FORCE

*Figures may not add to 100% because of rounding and the exclusion of those persons classified as "other" from the presentation. **Most of the 500,000 also said they were handcuffed.

SOURCE: Lawrence Greenfield, Patrick Langan, and Steven Smith, *Police Use of Force* (Washington, DC: Bureau of Justice Statistics, 1997), 3.

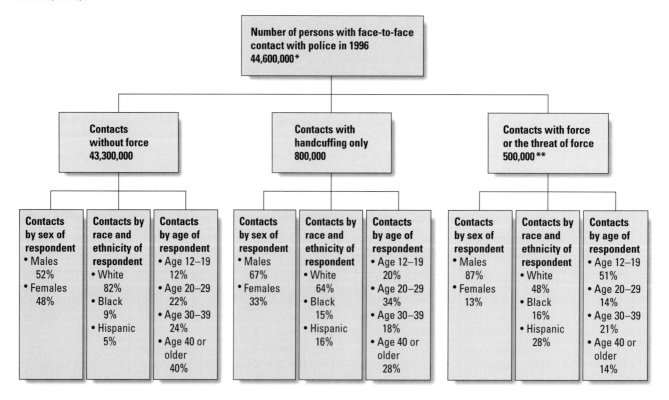

chest" and ruled it a homicide. There have been at least 14 other restraint-related deaths of suspects in the Chicago area in the past decade.[130]

Who Are the Problem Cops?   Evidence shows that a small proportion of officers are disproportionately involved in use-of-force incidents.[131] What kind of police officer gets involved in problem behavior? Are some officers "chronic offenders"? Research conducted in a southeastern city by Kim Michelle Lersch and Tom Mieczkowski found that a few officers (7%) were in fact chronic offenders who accounted for a significant portion of all citizen complaints (33%). Those officers receiving the bulk of the complaints tended to be younger and less experienced and had been accused of harassment or violence after a proactive encounter that they had initiated. Although repeat offenders were more likely to be accused of misconduct by minority citizens, there was little evidence that attacks were racially motivated.[132] In another study, Lersch and Mieczkowski found that rather than condemning officers who were the target of multiple complaints, police administrators actually praised them as more productive, aggressive officers performing their duties to the best of their abilities; citizen complaints may be viewed as an indicator of productivity and not malfeasance.[133]

Curbing Brutality   Because incidents of brutality undermine efforts to build a bridge between police and the public, police departments around the United States have instituted specialized training programs to reduce them. Urban police departments are now implementing or considering implementing neighborhood and community policing models to improve relations with the public. In addition, detailed rules of engagement that limit the use of force are now common in major cities. However, the creation of departmental rules limiting behavior is often haphazard and is usually a reaction to a crisis situation (for example, a citizen is seriously injured) rather than part of a systematic effort to improve police–citizen interactions.[134]

Some cities are taking an aggressive, proactive stance to curb violent officers. Since 1997, the New York City Police Department has been operating a Force-Related Integrity Testing program in which undercover officers pose as angry citizens in elaborate sting operations intended to weed out officers with a propensity for violence. In a typical encounter, police officers responding to a radio call on a domestic dispute confront an aggressive husband who spews hatred at everyone around, including the police. The "husband" is actually an undercover officer from the Internal Affairs Bureau, who is testing whether the officers, one of whom has had a history of civilian complaints, will respond to verbal abuse with threats or violence. The NYPD conducts about 600 sting operations each year to test the integrity of its officers, including several dozen devoted to evaluating the conduct of officers with a history of abuse complaints.[135]

PERSPECTIVES ON JUSTICE

The vicious attack on Abner Louima by New York City police officers in 1997, which involved beatings and sodomy, made headlines around the nation. One police officer was sentenced to life in prison. The fact that the NYPD quickly investigated the case, identified the culprits, and took swift legal action indicates that police administrators are now sensitive to the due process perspective on justice.

Some police departments have developed sophisticated systems for identifying and monitoring officers involved in persistent misconduct cases. For example, as a result of civil lawsuits, detailed tracking systems have been established in the Pittsburgh (Pennsylvania) and Steubenville (Ohio) Police Departments. These include keeping records of officers' disciplinary, training, and complaints history, as well as data on arrests, traffic stops, race, and use-of-force incidents. Both the Los Angeles Sheriff's Department and the Los Angeles Police Department have established detailed computerized monitoring programs to keep tabs on high-risk officers.[136]

Perhaps the greatest single factor that can control the use of police brutality is the threat of lawsuits and civil judgments against individual officers who use excessive force, police chiefs who ignore or condone violent behavior, and the cities and towns that employ them. This issue is discussed further in the Analyzing Criminal Justice Issues feature on "Suing the Police."

deadly force
Police killing of a suspect who resists arrest or presents a danger to an officer or the community.

Deadly Force As commonly used, the term **deadly force** refers to the actions of a police officer who shoots and kills a suspect who is fleeing from arrest, assaulting a victim, or attacking the officer.[137] The justification for the use of deadly force can be traced to English common law, in which almost every criminal offense was a felony and bore the death penalty. The use of deadly force in the course of arresting a felon was considered expedient, saving the state the burden of trial (the "fleeing felon" rule).[138]

Although the media depict hero cops in a constant stream of deadly shootouts in which scores of "bad guys" are killed, the actual number of people killed by the police each year is most likely between 250 and 300. However, some researchers believe that the actual number of police shootings is far greater and may be hidden or masked by a number of factors. For example, coroners may be intentionally or accidentally underreporting police homicides by almost one-half.[139]

Factors Related to Police Shootings Is police use of deadly force a random occurrence, or are there social, legal, and environmental factors associated with its use? The following patterns have been related to police shootings.

1. *Exposure to violence.* Most police shootings involve suspects who are armed and who either attack the officer or are engaged in violent crimes. A number of studies have found that fatal police shootings were closely related to reported violent crime rates and criminal homicide rates; police officers kill civilians at a higher rate in years when the general level of violence in the nation is higher.[140] The perception of danger may contribute to the use of violent means for self-protection.[141]
2. *"Death by cop."* Police officers may become exposed to violence when they are forced to confront the emotionally disturbed. Some distraught people attack police as a form of suicide, an event that has become so common that the term "death by cop" has been coined to denote victim-precipitated killings by police.[142] In a majority of these incidents, police officers or bystanders are threatened with lethal force, and officers feel compelled to shoot. Ironically, police are more likely to feel threatened and use deadly force against people who confront them with nonloaded weapons or props.[143] In some jurisdictions, more than 10 percent of police shooting incidents are considered "death by cop" situations.[144]
3. *Workload.* A relationship exists between police violence and the number of police on the street, the number of calls for service, the number and nature of police dispatches, the number of arrests made in a given jurisdiction, and police exposure to stressful situations.
4. *Firearm availability.* Cities that experience a large number of crimes committed with firearms are also likely to have high police violence rates. A strong association has been found between police use of force and "gun density" (the proportion of suicides and murders committed with a gun).[145]

5. *Social variables.* Research suggests that many individuals shot by police are transients or nonresidents caught at or near the scenes of robberies or burglaries of commercial establishments.[146] The greatest number of police shootings occur in areas that have great disparities in economic opportunity and a resulting high level of income inequality.[147]

6. *Administrative policies.* The philosophy, policies, and practices of individual police chiefs and departments significantly influence the police use of deadly force.[148] Departments that stress restrictive policies on the use of force generally have lower shooting rates than those that favor tough law enforcement and encourage officers to shoot when necessary. Poorly written or ambivalent policies encourage shootings because they allow the officer at the scene to decide when deadly force is warranted, often under conditions of high stress and tension.

7. *Race and police shootings.* No other issue is as important to the study of the police use of deadly force as that of racial discrimination. A number of critics have claimed that police are more likely to shoot and kill minority offenders than they are whites. In a famous statement, Paul Takagi charged that police have "one trigger finger for whites and another for blacks."[149] Takagi's complaint was supported by a number of research studies that showed that a disproportionate number of police killings involved minority citizens—almost 80 percent in some of the cities surveyed.[150]

Do these findings alone indicate that police discriminate in the use of deadly force? Some pioneering research by James Fyfe helps provide an answer to this question. In his study of New York City shootings over a five-year period, Fyfe found that police officers were most likely to shoot suspects who were armed and with whom they became involved in violent confrontations. Once such factors as being armed with a weapon, being involved in a violent crime, and attacking an officer were considered, the racial differences in the police use of force ceased to be significant. In fact, Fyfe found that black officers were almost twice as likely as white officers to have shot citizens. Fyfe attributes this finding to the fact that (1) black officers work and live in high-crime, high-violence areas where shootings are more common and (2) black officers hold proportionately more line positions and fewer administrative posts than white officers, which would place them more often on the street and less often behind a desk.[151]

Limiting Deadly Force Police use of deadly force is a serious problem, and ongoing efforts have been made to control it.

One of the most difficult problems in controlling the use of deadly force was the continued use of the fleeing felon rule in a number of states. In 1985, however, in the case of *Tennessee v. Garner,* the Supreme Court ruled that the use of deadly force against apparently unarmed and nondangerous fleeing felons is an illegal seizure of their person under the Fourth Amendment. Deadly force may not be used unless it is necessary to prevent the escape and the officer has probable cause to

Demonstrators rally after New York City police were accused of beating Abner Louima in a highly publicized 1997 brutality case. Although incidents of brutality are relatively rare, racially tinged incidents such as the Louima case can give the public the impression that police are insensitive and violent.

ANALYZING CRIMINAL JUSTICE ISSUES

Suing the Police

There is perhaps no sizable police department in the country that has not been sued in state or federal court for damages or injunctive relief.
—Rolando del Carmen (1993)

Anthony Baez was playing touch football in the street with his brothers in December 1994 when an errantly thrown ball struck New York City police officer Francis Livoti's patrol car. The officer tried to stop the game, and Baez, age 29, of Orlando, Florida, died in the ensuing struggle. A police department investigation found that Livoti had used an illegal choke hold to subdue Baez. Though Livoti was acquitted in 1996 of negligent homicide, he was fired from the force and in June 1998 was convicted in federal court of violating Baez's civil rights. On October 1, 1998, the city agreed to pay nearly $3 million to settle lawsuits filed by the Baez family.

It has become routine for civilians to file civil actions against police departments when they believe that an officer has violated their civil rights. Police may be sued when victims believe that excessive force was used during their arrest or custody. They may collect damages if they can show that the force used was unreasonable, considering all the circumstances known to the officer at the time he or she acted. Excessive-force suits commonly occur when police use a weapon, such as a gun or baton, to subdue an unarmed person who is protesting his or her treatment.

In contrast, a suit can also be brought if the police fail to act in a matter, as when despite a (court) restraining order, they fail to arrest a husband who is battering his wife or if they fail to give aid to the victim of a crime.

It is also possible to sue the police for abandonment. This occurs when individuals who should be taken into custody by the police are left to fend for themselves and consequently suffer injuries. For example, police have been held liable when a parent is taken into custody and minor children, left at the scene of the crime without care, suffer injury. The police have also been found liable when they have taken a drunk driver into custody while leaving an obviously intoxicated passenger in possession of the car and the passenger then becomes a drunk driver. Liability has also been attached when law enforcement officers abandon an individual who is in the process of being assaulted, especially when the victim pleads for the officers' help. Courts seem willing to assess damages if an officer's actions (or inaction) enhanced or created the danger or if departmental policies contributed to the injuries.

Suits are now being brought when police officers take sexual advantage of people falling under their control—for example, when people are unnecessarily "strip-searched" after arrest. Police departments are liable for the sexual misconduct of their employees when the activity is committed under the guise of agency authority or to further its activities and objectives. Other areas of police civil liability include suicide of a suspect who should have been closely monitored while in police detention, failure to arrest drunk drivers who are later injured or killed, infliction of emotional distress, and wrongful sudden deaths in police custody. It has also been common to file actions when, while in "hot pursuit" of a vehicle, an officer uses excessive speed and that negligent behavior results in the death or injury of suspects or innocent bystanders. Police may also be sued if they arrest a person when a reasonable officer should have known there were no legal grounds for an arrest (false arrest).

Legal Rights

Civil suits became common after the Supreme Court ruled in 1978 (*Monell v.* *Department of Social Services*) that local agencies could be held liable under the federal Civil Rights Act (42 USC 1983) for actions of their employees if those actions were part of an official custom or practice. Before *Monell,* attorneys were reluctant to file civil actions against police officers because even if the case could be won, there was often no way to collect damages from individuals who in most instances were without attachable financial resources. After *Monell,* police agencies, with their "deep pockets," could be held liable if in some way the officer's behavior could be attributed to an official policy or behavior. Liability increases if the policy or behavior is sanctioned by a high-ranking official, such as the chief.

A victim can seek redress against the department and the municipality it serves if he or she can show that the incident stemmed from a practice that, although not necessarily an official policy, was so widespread that it had become a "custom" that fairly represented official policy. To make the department liable under this standard, the victim might show that the actions that led to the injury were practices accepted by supervisors, that many police officers frequently engaged in these practices, that the police department failed to investigate or discipline officers involved in similar incidents, and that the department knew about such practices and did little to prohibit them. For example, a municipality could be held liable under the Civil Rights Act if police officers made it a custom to use excessive force in making arrests, police officials ignored the problem despite many complaints and incidents, brutality complaints were rarely investigated, and neither rules to limit force nor special training programs to aid police in making arrests were created.

Training

One area of particular concern has been the failure of police departments to properly train officers. Municipalities have been held liable if an officer uses excessive force and that officer has not been trained in the use of force or the training was forgotten, obsolete, and inadequate. The Supreme Court in *Canton v. Harris* ruled that to be liable for their failure to train, police departments must be "deliberately indifferent" to the needs of people injured by the untrained officers. Some commentators believe that *Harris* made suing police more difficult because of the need to prove deliberate indifference, not mere negligence or misconduct.

Although it is difficult to define "deliberate indifference," it is usually thought to contain a number of distinct elements. First, the training must be considered "inadequate," and this ongoing inadequacy must represent standard municipal policy. Second, the deficiency in training must be related to the injury; that is, the failure to train must be the cause of harm. Third, the training must address regular and ongoing tasks officers routinely face. In other words, the need for training must be so obvious that its absence seems a clear-cut violation of constitutional rights; for example, a police officer is not given any firearms training after leaving the police academy, even though the department has switched its standard weapon from the .38-caliber revolver to the 9mm automatic. Deliberate indifference might also involve failure to train officers in dealing with a particular crime problem, such as domestic abuse, even though police officials should recognize it as a significant area of concern.

The Threat of Civil Litigation

The threat to police departments posed by civil litigation is significant. Not only are they liable for large dollar awards to victims, but they must also pay hefty legal fees. It is not uncommon for a plaintiff in a civil rights case to be awarded a nominal amount of damages, with ten times that amount going to his or her attorney in legal fees. Research by Victor Kappeler and his associates found that about half the cases brought are successful and awards can be in the millions; findings of liability based on claims of excessive force averaged $187,503!

Today, relatively few citizen complaints against the police are sustained by internal police investigations. A study conducted by the Police Foundation, an organization that does research on policing, found that fewer than 13 percent of citizen complaints about excessive force were sustained by the departments themselves. In about one-fourth of the city departments, officers were not required to provide information to investigators. The threat of large civil penalties generated from civilian judges and juries may prove the most effective deterrent yet to the police use of excessive force. It will certainly cause police departments to carefully consider whom they hire, how they train, when they investigate, and what action they take against officers who are brutal or negligent.

Critical Thinking Skills

1. Policing is a dangerous, stressful job. Is it fair to hold officers and towns liable for the occasional use of excessive force?
2. Many offenders are disrespectful to officers and provoke violent responses. Even Rodney King, who was brutally beaten by police, resisted being handcuffed and flailed his arms around, rather than meekly consenting to arrest. Would the threat of civil suits prevent officers from taking the necessary steps to subdue dangerous criminals?
3. People want police to make neighborhoods safe, even if it means putting their lives at risk. Research has found that many officers have a real fear of lawsuits and maintain an "us versus them" mentality. Will these concerns undermine police–community relations at a time when they are seen as critical to effective policing? Should officers be immune from punishment if they use too much force in this dangerous undertaking?

InfoTrac College Edition Research

To see how the threat of lawsuits influences police policy, read Lisa Gelhaus, "Civil Suits Against Police Change Domestic Violence Response," *Trial,* September 1999, v35 i9 p103

SOURCES: Darrell L. Ross, "Emerging Trends in Police Failure to Train Liability," *Policing* 23 (2000): 192–211; Associated Press, "NY Pays $3M To Police Victim Kin," *New York Times,* 2 October 1998; Kevin Flynn, "Record Payouts in Settlements of Lawsuits"; Michael Vaughn, "Police Sexual Violence: Civil Liability Under State Tort Law," *Crime and Delinquency* 45 (1999): 334–357; "Suits Against the New York City Police Are Set for Year," *New York Times,* 1 October 1999, p. 12; David Griswold, "Complaints Against the Police: Predicting Dispositions," *Journal of Criminal Justice* 22 (1994): 215–221; Michael Vaughn, "Police Civil Liability for Abandonment in High-Crime Areas and Other High-Risk Situations," *Journal of Criminal Justice* 22 (1994): 407–424; Victor Kappeler, Stephen Kappeler, and Rolando Del Carmen, "A Content Analysis of Police Civil Liability Cases: Decisions of the Federal District Courts, 1978–1990," *Journal of Criminal Justice* 21 (1993): 325–337; Police Foundation, *Police Use of Force: Official Reports, Citizen Complaints, and Legal Consequences* (Washington, DC: Police Foundation, 1993).

believe that the suspect poses a significant threat of death or serious injury to the officer or others. The majority opinion stated that where the suspect poses no immediate threat to the officer and no threat to others, the harm resulting from failing to apprehend the suspect does not justify the use of deadly force to do so: "A police officer may not seize an unarmed, nondangerous suspect by shooting him dead."[152]

With *Garner,* the Supreme Court effectively put an end to any local police policy that allowed officers to shoot unarmed or otherwise nondangerous offenders if they resisted arrest or attempted to flee from police custody. However, the Court did not ban the use of deadly force or otherwise control police shooting policy. In *Graham v. Connor,* the Court created a reasonableness standard for the use of force: Force is excessive when, considering all the circumstances known to the officer at the time he or she acted, the force used was unreasonable.[153] For example, a police officer is approached in a threatening manner by someone wielding a knife. The assailant fails to stop when warned and is killed by the officer. The officer would not be held liable if it turns out that the shooting victim was deaf and could not hear the officer's command but the officer at the time of the incident had no way of knowing the person's disability.

Individual state jurisdictions still control police shooting policy. Some states have adopted statutory policies that restrict the police use of violence. Others have upgraded training in the use of force. The Federal Law Enforcement Training Center has developed the FLETC use-of-force model, illustrated in Figure 7.4, to teach officers the proper method to escalate force in response to the threat they face. As the figure shows, resistance ranges from compliant (cooperative) to assaultive with the threat of serious bodily harm or death. Officers are taught via lecture, demonstration, computer-based instruction, and training scenarios to assess the suspect's behavior and apply an appropriate and corresponding amount of force.[154]

Another method of controlling police shootings is through internal review and policymaking by police administrative review boards. For example, New York's Firearm Discharge Review Board was established to investigate and adjudicate all

FIGURE 7.4
THE FEDERAL LAW
ENFORCEMENT
TRAINING
CENTER'S USE-OF-
FORCE MODEL

SOURCE: Franklin Graves and Gregory Connor, The Federal Law Enforcement Training Center, Glynco, Georgia.

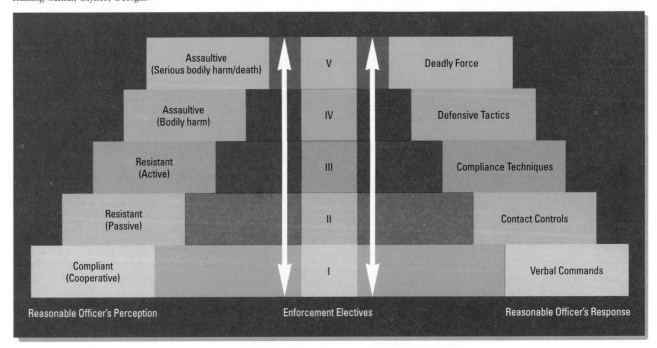

police firearm discharges. Among the dispositions available to the board are the following:

1. The discharge was in accordance with law and department policy.
2. The discharge was justifiable, but the officer should be given additional training in the use of firearms or in the law and department policy.
3. The shooting was justifiable under law but violated department policy and warrants department disciplinary action.
4. The shooting was in apparent violation of law and should be referred to the appropriate prosecutor if criminal charges have not already been filed.
5. The officer involved should be transferred (or offered the opportunity to transfer) to a less sensitive assignment.
6. The officer involved should receive drug testing or alcoholism counseling.[155]

The review board approach is controversial because it can mean that the department recommends that one of its own officers be turned over for criminal prosecution, an outcome with which some legal scholars disagree.[156]

Police departments are also developing nonlethal methods to control suspects in an effort to provide officers with an alternative to deadly force. One common approach is to arm officers with "pepper spray," which seems to be a highly effective, nondeadly means of incapacitating resisting offenders.[157] However, police administrators are cautioned that even nonlethal weapons such as pepper spray present the danger of overuse if officers become convinced that that these new weapons are "safe" and make liberal use of them even in situations that do not require the use of any weapon.[158]

Police Victimization

Although police officers are often taken to task for being too violent, the public sometimes forgets that police are all too often injured and killed by armed assailants. More than 65,000 officers are attacked and 23,000 seriously injured each year.[159] In 1999 (the most recent year for which data are available), 42 law enforcement officers lost their lives as a result of criminal action, the lowest recorded figure in more than 35 years; 61 were killed in 1998, and 71 in 1997.[160] Data suggest that officers are at significant risk for injury when they use force, particularly when they strike a suspect with their fists (48% chance) or use their hands and arms to control a suspect (43% chance).[161]

A long-held belief has been that police officers who answer domestic violence calls are at risk of violence against them; when confronted, one of the two battling parties turns on the outsider who dares to interfere in a "private matter." Research conducted in Charlotte, North Carolina, however, indicates that domestic violence calls may be no more dangerous than many other routine police interactions.[162] So although police officers should be on their guard when investigating a call for assistance from an abused spouse, the risk of violence against them may be no greater than when they answer a call for a burglary or car theft (see Exhibit 7.2). The issue of when police are injured or killed in the line of duty is further explored in the Analyzing Criminal Justice Issues feature "In the Line of Fire."

EXHIBIT 7.2 HOW WERE POLICE OFFICERS KILLED IN THE LINE OF DUTY?

- 12 officers lost their lives during arrest situations
- 7 investigating suspicious persons or circumstances
- 7 answering disturbance calls
- 6 serving arrest warrants
- 6 encountering ambush situations
- 3 attempting to prevent robberies or apprehend robbery suspects
- 2 investigating drug-related situations
- 2 handling prisoners
- 1 attempting to apprehend a burglary suspect
- 1 enforcing traffic laws

SOURCE: "Lowest Number of U.S. Police Deaths in 35 Years," *FBI Law Enforcement Bulletin* 69 (2000): 13.

ANALYZING CRIMINAL JUSTICE ISSUES

In the Line of Fire: Shootings of Police

Although police officers are often taken to task for being too violent, the public sometimes forgets that police are all too often injured and killed by armed assailants. Professional criminals and drug dealers armed with automatic weapons, such as Uzi machine guns, pose a significant hazard to law enforcement officers. Most officers are slain during arrest situations, such as attempting to prevent robberies or apprehend robbery suspects. In addition, police officers are slain while answering disturbance calls, encountering ambush situations, enforcing traffic laws, investigating suspicious persons or circumstances, and handling prisoners. Another seventy to eighty officers are killed each year in job-related incidents, such as traffic accidents.

What are the factors that predict the shooting of police officers? The majority of incidents are initiated by the officers themselves, as opposed to an unexpected attack by a hidden assailant; black officers have a greater risk of getting killed than white officers, and by black assailants. Police officers face the greatest danger when they are attempting to arrest an armed assailant. Ecological patterns may also be present when a police officer becomes the victim of violent crime. Southern cities, with high violence and gun-ownership rates, experience the highest numbers of police officer fatalities.

Research also shows that off-duty police and plainclothes officers are very likely to be shot. One reason is that off-duty officers, who are usually armed, are expected to take appropriate action yet suffer tactical disadvantages, such as a lack of communication and backup. Plainclothes officers are often mistaken for perpetrators or unwanted interveners.

An FBI report shows that police officers may get killed because they fail to follow proper procedures, perhaps because they are too trusting and let their "guard down": They fail to call for backup, act alone, fail to search the suspect completely, and in an effort to make the suspect more comfortable, fail to secure handcuffs properly. When interviewed by the FBI, slain officers' peers described them as friendly to everyone and quick to look for good in people. Their slayers, in contrast, suffered personality disorders that rendered them incapable of obeying social norms or having a conscience, feelings, or remorse.

The FBI report has been criticized by William King and Beth Sanders as methodologically flawed. It is possible, they suggest, that the difference between fatal and nonfatal shooting incidents is actually "luck, a bullet-proof vest, or closer medical facilities." Clearly, more research is needed to understand the circumstances of why police get killed in the line of duty.

Critical Thinking Skills

1. Would police be less or more likely to be shot in the line of duty if, like British police officers, they were unarmed?

2. Do you consider police work to be a dangerous profession? After all, there are more than 500,000 police and relatively few are killed in the line of duty each year. On the other hand, how many teachers, accountants, or dentists are killed in the "line of duty"?

 InfoTrac College Edition Research

To find out more about the police use of force, use "police shooting" as a subject guide.

SOURCES: Anthony Pinizzotto, Edward F. Davis, and Charles E. Miller III, "In the Line of Fire: Learning from Assaults on Law Enforcement Officers," *FBI Law Enforcement Bulletin* 67 (1998):15–24; FBI, *Killed in the Line of Duty: A Study of Selected Felonious Killings of Law Enforcement Officers* (Washington, DC: U.S. Government Printing Office, 1992); William King and Beth Sanders, "Nice Guys Finish Last: A Critical Review of *Killed in the Line of Duty*," *Policing* 20 (1997): 392–408.

Police Corruption

Fill in the blanks 21
Multiple choice 23–25
Essay 8

In July 1996, members of an elite antigang unit from the Rampart Division of the Los Angeles Police Department (LAPD) raided gang-infested apartments at Shatto Place; their target was the notorious 18th Street Gang, one of Los Angeles's most violent gangs. During the raid, police officers killed one gang member and wounded another. A departmental investigation found nothing wrong and exonerated the police involved. Then, in 1999, Rafael Perez, an officer who took part in the raid, was caught stealing eight pounds of cocaine from police evidence lockers. After pleading guilty in September 1999, he bargained for a lighter sentence by telling LAPD investigators about police brutality, perjury, planted evidence, drug corruption, and attempted murder within the Rampart Division and its antigang unit, known as CRASH (Community Resources Against Street Hoodlums). Perez told authorities that during the Shatto raid, officers thought that the gang members may have been unarmed, so the raiding officers resorted to a "throwdown"— slang for a weapon planted by police to make a shooting legally justifiable. Perez's testimony resulted in at least 12 Rampart officers' being fired or relieved from duty. Perez also said he and his partner, Niño Durden, shot an unarmed 18th Street Gang member named Javier Ovando, then planted a semiautomatic rifle on the unconscious suspect and claimed that Ovando had tried to shoot them during a stakeout. Their testimony helped get Ovando, confined to a wheelchair for life because of the shooting, a 23-year sentence for assault. Ovando has now been freed from prison

Nestor Zeteno talks to reporters in April 2000. He sued the Los Angeles Police Department on the grounds that he was taken into custody by officers from the Ramparts Division and falsely charged with firearms possession. Standing beside Zeteno is his attorney, Samuel Pez.

and is suing the city for more than $20 million. The Rampart's scandal has rocked the LAPD to its core.[163] A number of police officers face criminal charges in the case, and more than 100 convicted offenders have been released from prison.[164]

From their creation, U.S. police departments have wrestled with the problem of controlling illegal and unprofessional behavior by their officers. Corruption pervaded the American police when the early departments were first formed. In the nineteenth century, police officers systematically ignored violations of laws related to drinking, gambling, and prostitution in return for regular payoffs. Some actually entered into relationships with professional criminals, especially pickpockets. Illegal behavior was tolerated in return for goods or information. Police officers helped politicians gain office by allowing electoral fraud to flourish; some senior officers sold promotions to higher rank within the department.[165]

Since the early nineteenth century, scandals involving police abuse of power have occurred in many cities, and elaborate methods have been devised to control or eliminate the problem. Although most police officers are not corrupt, the few who are dishonest bring discredit to the entire profession. Unfortunately, the number of officers being convicted on corruption charges has increased significantly in recent years: In 1994, about 107 police officers were in federal prisons; by 1999, that number had grown to more than 650.[166]

Varieties of Police Corruption Police deviance can include a number of activities. In a general sense, it involves misuse of authority by police officers in a manner designed to produce personal gain for themselves or others.[167] However, debate continues over whether a desire for personal gain is an essential part of corruption. Some experts argue that police misconduct also involves such issues as the unnecessary use of force, unreasonable searches, or an immoral personal life and that these should be considered as serious as corruption motivated by economic gain.

Knapp Commission
A public body that conducted an investigation into police corruption in New York City in the early 1970s and uncovered a widespread network of payoffs and bribes.

meat eater
A term used to describe a police officer who actively solicits bribes and vigorously engages in corrupt practices.

grass eater
A term used for a police officer who accepts payoffs when everyday duties place him or her in a position to be solicited by the public.

Mollen Commission
An investigative unit set up to inquire into police corruption in New York City in the 1990s.

Scholars have attempted to create typologies categorizing the forms that the abuse of police powers can take. For example, when investigating corruption among police officers in New York, the **Knapp Commission** classified abusers into two categories: "meat eaters" and "grass eaters."[168] **Meat eaters** aggressively misuse police power for personal gain by demanding bribes, threatening legal action, or cooperating with criminals. Across the country, police officers have been accused, indicted, and convicted of shaking down club owners and other businesspeople.[169] In contrast, **grass eaters** accept payoffs when their everyday duties place them in a position to be solicited by the public. For example, police officers have been investigated for taking bribes to look the other way while neighborhood bookmakers ply their trade.[170] The Knapp Commission concluded that the vast majority of police officers on the take are grass eaters, although the few meat eaters who are caught capture all the headlines. In 1993, another police scandal prompted formation of the **Mollen Commission**, which found that some New York City police officers were actively involved in violence and drug dealing.

Other police experts have attempted to create models to better understand police corruption. It may be possible to divide police corruption into four major categories:[171]

1. *Internal corruption.* This is corruption that takes place among police officers themselves, involving both the bending of departmental rules and the outright performance of illegal acts. For example, some Chicago police officers conspired to sell relatively new police cars to other officers at cut-rate prices, forcing the department to purchase new cars unnecessarily. A major scandal hit the Boston Police Department when a police captain was indicted in a promotional-exam tampering and selling scheme. Numerous officers bought promotion exams from the captain, and others had him lower the scores of rivals who were competing for the same job.[172]

2. *Selective enforcement/abuse of power.* This form occurs when police abuse or exploit their discretion. If an officer frees a drug dealer in return for valuable information, that would be considered a legitimate use of discretion; if the police officer does so for personal or political reasons, that would be an abuse of police power. Corruption may involve abuse of power where police routinely use excessive force against suspects or use racial profiling to make traffic stops. Though these practices are feared to be commonplace, police departments around the nation are taking steps to eliminate them, as the Criminal Justice and Technology feature illustrates.

PERSPECTIVES ON JUSTICE

Some police officers may engage in abuse of power because they are so intent on controlling crime that they lose sight of citizens' rights. Their corruption is based not on greed but on zeal. This is an example of the dark side of the crime control perspective.

How do police themselves feel about the abuse of power? To find out, read the findings of a national survey on police attitudes toward abuse of authority: http://www.ncjrs.org/pdffiles1/nij/181312.pdf

For an up-to-date list of Web links, see http://www.wadsworth.com/product/0534573053s

3. *Active criminality.* This is participation by police in serious criminal behavior. Police may use their positions of trust and power to commit the very crimes they are entrusted with controlling. For example, between 1994 and 1997, U.S. Justice Department attorneys won 52 convictions against Chicago police officers who were robbing drug dealers and/or selling narcotics.[173]

4. *Bribery and extortion.* This includes practices in which law enforcement roles are exploited specifically to raise money. Bribery is initiated by the citizen; extortion is initiated by the officer. Bribery or extortion can be a one-shot transaction, as when a traffic violator offers a police officer $20 to forget about issuing a summons. Or the relationship can be an ongoing one, in which the officer solicits (or

CRIMINAL JUSTICE AND TECHNOLOGY

Eliminating Racial Profiling

A number of police departments and law enforcement agencies have been rocked by accusations that they engage in a type of abuse of power known as *racial profiling*: stopping vehicles simply because the driver and passengers are members of racial or ethnic minorities whom they believe are more likely to commit certain types of crimes. Due process advocates condemn such practices as violating the civil rights of people who have committed no crime but are suspects simply because of their skin color. The practice has become so widespread that the phrase "driving while black" (DWB) is commonly used.

One reason for the spread of racial profiling has been the issuance of official guidelines that use race as a criterion for identifying potential drug couriers. For example, the Florida Highway Patrol in 1985 issued guidelines that included the use of rental cars, drivers "who do not fit the vehicle," drivers who wear "lots of gold," and "ethnic groups associated with the drug trade." The Drug Enforcement Administration's Operation Pipeline, a program taught to more than 25,000 officers, has been criticized for explicitly or implicitly targeting minorities.

To help eliminate racial profiling, a number of jurisdictions are now insisting that police officers record the race, gender, and ethnicity of all drivers they

stop on the road. Software companies such as Information Technologies, Inc., are now developing database programs that allow departments to analyze these data in spreadsheet form. The statistics can then be measured against community demographic characteristics to determine whether the agency's traffic enforcement policies are consistent with the population demographics. These programs allow police administrators to review each officer individually to determine whether stops are being made consistently throughout the department. In some cases, a single officer may be violating departmental policy and skewing the efforts to eliminate profiling.

Using database software can also help police administrators investigate such issues as whether there is gender bias in the issuance of citations. If a male officer exhibits a very low enforcement rate against female violators when compared with his peers, supervisors may want to determine if he is just being "easy" on women or if he is on the prowl for coerced sexual favors.

Database software may become a low-cost method of ending racial profiling while yielding other management benefits.

Critical Thinking Skills

1. Might police departments be reluctant to adopt this technology because

they do not want this information to become public knowledge, especially if it shows that officers are stopping a disproportionate number of minority citizens?

2. Is it possible that officers would misreport the racial makeup of the people they stop in an effort to foil monitoring by their supervisors?

InfoTrac College Edition Research

To read more about racial profiling, check out "Race, Crime, and Justice," *Christian Century,* 5 April 2000, v117 i11 p379

"Police and Racial Profiling," *New York Times Upfront,* 6 September 1999, v132 i1 p36

Tammerlin Drummond, "It's Not Just in New Jersey: Cops across the U.S. often search people just because of their race, a study says," *Time,* 14 June 1999, v153 i23 p61

SOURCE: Neil Kurlander, "Software to Track Traffic Stop Data," *Law Enforcement Technology* (July 2000): 148–153.

---

is offered) regular payoffs to ignore criminal activities, such as gambling or narcotics dealing. This is known as "being on the pad."

Sometimes police officers accept routine bribes and engage in petty extortion without considering themselves corrupt; they consider these payments as some of the unwritten "benefits" of police work. For example, "mooching" involves receiving free gifts of coffee, cigarettes, meals, and so on in exchange for possible future acts of favoritism. "Chiseling" occurs when officers demand admission to entertainment events or price discounts; "shopping" involves taking small items, such as cigarettes, from a store whose door was accidentally left unlocked after business hours.[174]

Corrupt Departments It has also been suggested that entire police departments can be categorized on the basis of the level and type of corruption existing within them.[175] Three types of departments may exist:

1. *Rotten apples and rotten pockets.* This type of police department has a few corrupt officers ("rotten apples") who use their position for personal gain. When these corrupt officers band together, they form a "rotten pocket." Robert Daley described the activities of such a group in his book *Prince of the City.*[176] Agents of New York City's Special Investigations Unit kept money they confiscated during narcotics raids and used illegal drugs to pay off informers. *Prince of the City* tells the story of New York Detective Frank Leuci, whose testimony against his partners before investigating committees made him an outcast in the police department. Rotten pockets help institutionalize corruption because their members expect newcomers to conform to their illegal practices and to a code of secrecy.

2. *Pervasive unorganized corruption.* This type of department contains a majority of personnel who are corrupt but have little relationship to one another. Though many officers are involved in taking bribes and extortion, they are not cooperating with one another for personal gain.

3. *Pervasive organized corruption.* This describes a department in which almost all members are involved in systematic and organized corruption. The Knapp Commission found this type of relationship in New York City's vice divisions, where payoffs and bribes were an organized and accepted way of police life.

The Causes and Control of Corruption No single explanation satisfactorily accounts for the various forms that abuse of power takes. One view puts the blame on the type of person who becomes a police officer. This position holds that policing tends to attract lower-class individuals who do not have the financial means to maintain a coveted middle-class lifestyle. As they develop the cynical, authoritarian police personality, accepting graft seems an all-too-easy method of achieving financial security.

A second view is that the wide discretion that the police enjoy, coupled with the low visibility they maintain with the public and their own supervisors, makes them likely candidates for corruption. In addition, the "code of secrecy" maintained by the police subculture helps insulate corrupt officers from the law. Similarly, police managers, most of whom have risen through the ranks, are reluctant to investigate corruption or punish wrongdoers. Thus, corruption may also be viewed as a function of police institutions and practices.[177]

A third position holds that corruption is a function of society's ambivalence toward many forms of vice-related criminal behavior that police officers are sworn to control. Unenforceable laws governing moral standards promote corruption because they create large groups with an interest in undermining law enforcement. These include consumers—people who gamble, wish to drink after the legal closing hour, or patronize prostitutes—who do not want to be deprived of their chosen form of recreation. Even though the consumers may not actively corrupt police officers, their existence creates a climate that tolerates active corruption by others.[178] Since vice cannot be controlled and the public apparently wants it to continue, the police officer may have little resistance to inducements for monetary gain offered by law violators.

How can police misconduct be controlled? One approach is to strengthen the internal administrative review process within police departments. A strong and well-supported internal affairs division has been linked to lowered corruption rates.[179] However, asking police to police themselves is not a simple task. Police officers are often reluctant to discipline their peers. For example, a 1999 review of disciplinary files found that hundreds of New York City police officers escaped punishment when their cases were summarily dismissed by the police department without ever interviewing victims or witnesses or making any other efforts to examine the strength of the evidence.[180]

Another approach, instituted by then New York Commissioner Patrick Murphy in the wake of the Knapp Commission, is the **accountability system**. This holds that supervisors at each level are directly accountable for the illegal behav-

accountability system
A method of dealing with police corruption by making superiors responsible for the behavior of their subordinates.

iors of the officers under them. Consequently, a commander can be demoted or forced to resign if one of his or her command is found guilty of corruption.[181] Close scrutiny by a department, however, can lower officer morale and create the suspicion that the officers' own supervisors distrust them.

Some departments have set up guidelines to help reduce corruption. In 1996, the city of Philadelphia agreed to implement a set of reforms to combat corruption in order to settle a lawsuit brought by civil rights organizations. Among the measures taken to reduce corruption were the following:

- A policy mandating that all citizens' complaints be forwarded for investigation by the internal affairs division
- Development of computer files containing all types of complaints and suits against individual officers that could be easily accessed during investigations
- A policy requiring that internal affairs give a high priority to any police officer's claim that another officer was corrupt or used excessive force
- Mandatory reporting and recording of all incidents in which an officer used more than incidental force
- Training of officers to treat citizens without racial bias, with a deputy commissioner to be assigned to monitor charges of race discrimination
- Review of all policies and practices to ensure they do not involve or have the potential for race bias[182]

Another approach is to create outside review boards or special prosecutors, such as the Mollen Commission in New York and the Christopher Commission in Los Angeles, to investigate reported incidents of corruption. However, outside investigators and special prosecutors are often limited by their lack of intimate knowledge of day-to-day police operations. As a result, they depend on the testimony of a few officers who are willing to cooperate, either to save themselves from prosecution or because they have a compelling moral commitment. Outside evaluators also face the problem of the blue curtain, which is quickly closed when police officers feel their department is under scrutiny.

A more realistic solution to police corruption, albeit a difficult one, might be to change the social context of policing. Police operations must be made more visible, and the public must be given freer access to controlling police operations. All too often, the public finds out about police problems only when a scandal hits the newspaper. Some of the vice-related crimes the police now deal with might be decriminalized or referred to other agencies. Although decriminalization of vice cannot in itself end the problem, it could lower the pressure on individual officers and help eliminate their moral dilemmas.

SUMMARY

Police departments today are faced with many critical problems in their development and relationship with the public. Police are believed to be insulated from the rest of society. Some experts hold that police officers have distinct personality characteristics marked by authoritarianism and cynicism. It is also alleged that police maintain a separate culture with distinct rules and loyalties. A police personality also influences their working style. Four distinct police styles have been identified, and each influences police decision making. The complexity and danger of the police role produce an enormous amount of stress that harms police effectiveness.

Social concerns also affect police operations. Today, many police officers are seeking higher education. The jury is still out on whether college-educated police officers are actually more effective. Women and minorities are now being recruited into the police in increasing numbers. Research indicates that, with few exceptions, they perform as well as or even better than white male officers. The percentage of minorities on police forces reflects their representation in the general population, but the number of female officers still lags behind. Of greater importance is increasing the number of women and minorities in supervisory positions.

Police departments have also been concerned about limiting police stress and improving police–community relations. One critical concern is the police use of deadly force. Research indicates that antishooting policies can limit deaths resulting from police action. Another effort has been to identify and eliminate police corruption, which still mars the reputation of police forces.

Key Terms

blue curtain	Watchman	deadly force
cynicism	discretion	Knapp Commission
style	demeanor	meat eater
Crime Fighter	double marginality	grass eater
Social Agent	defeminization	Mollen Commission
Law Enforcer	police brutality	accountability system

Discussion Questions

1. Should male and female officers have exactly the same duties in a police department?
2. Do you think that an officer's working the street will eventually produce a cynical personality and distrust for civilians?
3. How can higher education help police officers?
4. Should a police officer who accepts a free meal from a restaurant owner be dismissed from the force?
5. A police officer orders an unarmed person running away from a burglary to stop; the suspect keeps running and is shot and killed by the officer. Has the officer committed murder?
6. Would you like to live in a society that abolished police discretion and used a full enforcement policy?

A CLOSER LOOK

Police use of racial profiles to stop motorists and pedestrians has become a national issue. Sociologist Jackson Toby presents his view of racial profiling which, because it fails to condemn the practice as unreasonable, may prove highly controversial:

It is not clear why minorities were caught disproportionally in this net. It could have been that, even in the absence of an official policy to target minorities for extra scrutiny, individual troopers believed that blacks and Hispanics were more likely to be traffickers and acted on their belief without reasonable cause to make a stop.

Unfair, yes, but not entirely unreasonable. Here is a more sympathetic interpretation of the disproportionate arrests of minorities on the New Jersey Turnpike: Much higher proportions of black children than white are born to single mothers and grow up economically and educationally disadvantaged. No surprise that some

male blacks are more tempted to break society's rules than luckier white males. Although blacks are only 12% of the American population, they were in a recent year 56% of the nationwide arrests for murder, 42% of the arrests for rape, 61% of the arrests for robbery, 39% of the arrests for aggravated assault, 31% of the arrests for burglary, 33% of the arrests for larceny, and 40% of the arrests for motor vehicle theft. Why shouldn't they be overrepresented in drug trafficking too, as the Drug Enforcement Administration has alleged? If so, the police don't need to be prejudiced to arrest a higher proportion of black and Hispanic than of white motorists stopped because of minor traffic violations; police simply have to know the telltale indications of a possible courier.

To read more, go to InfoTrac College Edition and read Jackson Toby, "Are Police the Enemy?" *Society,* May 2000, v37 4 p38

Notes

1 John Hoffman, "Society's Trashy Behavior Winds Up in Cop's Hands: An Interview with Former Drug Czar William J. Bennett," *Law and Order* 42 (1994): 28–33.
2 Benjamin Weiser, "Federal Inquiry Finds Racial Profiling in Street Searches," *New York Times,* 5 October 2000, p. 1.

3 Thomas J. Lueck, "Mayor Disputes Finding of Profiling by Police," *New York Times,* 6 October 2000, p. B2.
4 See, for example, Richard Harris, *The Police Academy: An Inside View* (New York: Wiley, 1973); John Van Maanen, "Observations on the Making of a Policeman," in

Order Under Law, ed. R. Culbertson and M. Tezak (Prospect Heights, IL: Waveland Press, 1981), pp. 111–126; Jonathan Rubenstein, *City Police* (New York: Ballantine Books, 1973); John Broderick, *Police in a Time of Change* (Morristown, NJ: General Learning Press, 1977).

5 Malcolm Sparrow, Mark Moore, and David Kennedy, *Beyond 911: A New Era for Policing* (New York: Basic Books, 1990), p. 51.

6 M. Steven Meagher and Nancy Yentes, "Choosing a Career in Policing: A Comparison of Male and Female Perceptions," *Journal of Police Science and Administration* 16 (1986): 320–327.

7 Michael K. Brown, *Working the Street* (New York: Russell Sage Foundation, 1981), p. 82.

8 Egon Bittner, *The Functions of Police in Modern Society* (Cambridge, MA: Oelgeschlager, Gunn & Hain, 1980), p. 63.

9 Richard Lundman, *Police and Policing* (New York: Holt, Rinehart & Winston, 1980); see also Jerome Skolnick, *Justice Without Trial* (New York: Wiley, 1966).

10 Robert Regoli, Robert Culbertson, John Crank, and James Powell, "Career Stage and Cynicism Among Police Chiefs," *Justice Quarterly* 7 (1990): 592–614.

11 William Westly, *Violence and the Police: A Sociological Study of Law, Custom, and Morality* (Cambridge, MA: MIT Press, 1970).

12 Skolnick, *Justice Without Trial*, pp. 42–68.

13 Milton Rokeach, Martin Miller, and John Snyder, "The Value Gap Between Police and Policed," *Journal of Social Issues* 27 (1971): 155–171.

14 Bruce Carpenter and Susan Raza, "Personality Characteristics of Police Applicants: Comparisons Across Subgroups and with Other Populations," *Journal of Police Science and Administration* 15 (1987): 10–17.

15 Larry Tifft, "The 'Cop Personality' Reconsidered," *Journal of Police Science and Administration* 2 (1974): 268; David Bayley and Harold Mendelsohn, *Minorities and the Police* (New York: Free Press, 1969); Robert Balch, "The Police Personality: Fact or Fiction?" *Journal of Criminal Law, Criminology, and Police Science* 63 (1972): 117.

16 Lowell Storms, Nolan Penn, and James Tenzell, "Policemen's Perception of Real and Ideal Policemen," *Journal of Police Science and Administration* 17 (1990): 40–43.

17 Arthur Niederhoffer, *Behind the Shield: The Police in Urban Society* (Garden City, NY: Doubleday, 1967).

18 Ibid., pp. 216–220.

19 Robert Regoli and Eric Poole, "Measurement of Police Cynicism: A Factor Scaling Approach," *Journal of Criminal Justice* 7 (1979): 37–52.

20 Ibid., p. 43.

21 Ibid., p. 44.

22 Carl Klockars, "The Dirty Harry Problem," *Annals* 452 (1980): 33–47.

23 Jack Kuykendall and Roy Roberg, "Police Manager's Perceptions of Employee Types: A Conceptual Model," *Journal of Criminal Justice* 16 (1988): 131–135.

24 Ellen Hochstedler, "Testing Types: A Review and Test of Police Types," *Journal of Criminal Justice* 9 (1981): 451–466.

25 For a thorough review, see Eric Rikssheim and Steven Chermak, "Causes of Police Behavior Revisited," *Journal of Criminal Justice* 21 (1993): 353–383.

26 Skolnick, *Justice Without Trial*.

27 Peter Sinden and B. Joyce Stephens, "Police Perceptions of Domestic Violence: The Nexus of Victim, Perpetrator, Event, Self and Law," *Policing* 22 (1999): 313–326.

28 Helen Eigenberg, Kathryn Scarborough, and Victor Kappeler, "Contributory Factors Affecting Arrest in Domestic and Nondomestic Assaults," *American Journal of Police* 15 (1996): 27–51.

29 Leonore Simon, "A Therapeutic Jurisprudence Approach to the Legal Processing of Domestic Violence Cases," *Psychology, Public Policy and Law* 1 (1995): 43–79.

30 Robert Kane, "Patterns of Arrest in Domestic Violence Encounters: Identifying a Police Decision-Making Model," *Journal of Criminal Justice* 27 (1999): 65–79.

31 Gregory Howard Williams, *The Law and Politics of Police Discretion* (Westport, CT: Greenwood Press, 1984).

32 Ida Johnson and Robert Sigler, "Public Perceptions: The Stability of the Public's Endorsements of the Definition and Criminalization of the Abuse of Women," *Journal of Criminal Justice* 28 (2000): 165–179.

33 Douglas Smith and Jody Klein, "Police Control of Interpersonal Disputes," *Social Problems* 31 (1984): 468–481.

34 Dana Jones and Joanne Belknap, "Police Responses to Battering in a Progressive Pro-Arrest Jurisdiction," *Justice Quarterly* 16 (1999): 249–273.

35 Ibid.

36 Westly, *Violence and the Police*.

37 Amanda Robinson and Meghan Chandek, "The Domestic Violence Arrest Decision: Examining Demographic, Attitudinal and Situational Variables," *Crime and Delinquency* 46 (2000): 18–37.

38 Catherine Connolly, Snehalata Huzurbazar, and Tillie Routh-McGee, "Multiple Parties in Domestic Violence Situations and Arrest," *Journal of Criminal Justice* 28 (2000): 181–188.

39 Nathan Goldman, *The Differential Selection of Juvenile Offenders for Court Appearance* (New York: National Council on Crime and Delinquency, 1963).

40 David Klinger, "Demeanor or Crime? Why 'Hostile' Citizens Are More Likely to Be Arrested," *Criminology* 32 (1994): 475–493.

41 Richard Lundman, "Demeanor or Crime? The Midwest City Police–Citizen Encounters Study," *Criminology* 32 (1994): 631–653; Robert Worden and Robin Shepard, "On the Meaning, Measurement, and Estimated Effects of Suspects' Demeanor Toward the Police," paper presented at the annual meeting of the American Society of Criminology, Miami, November 1994.

42 Matt De Lisi and Bob Regoli, "Race, Conventional Crime, and Criminal Justice: The Declining Importance of Skin Color," *Journal of Criminal Justice* 27 (1999): 549–557; R. Steven Daniels, Lorin Baumhover, William Formby, and Carolyn Clark-Daniels, "Police Discretion and Elder Mistreatment: A Nested Model of Observation, Reporting and Satisfaction," *Journal of Criminal Justice* 27 (1999): 209–225.

43 Brown, *Working the Street*, p. 290.

44 See Larry Hoover, *Police Educational Characteristics and Curricula* (Washington, DC: U.S. Government Printing Office, 1975).

45 Brian Reaves and Andrew Goldberg, *Law Enforcement Management and Administrative Statistics, 1997: Data for Individual State and Local Law Enforcement Agencies with 100 or More Officers* (Washington, DC: Bureau of Justice Statistics, 1999).

46 Bruce Berg, "Who Should Teach Police? A Typology and Assessment of Police Academy Instructors," *American Journal of Police* 9 (1990): 79–100.

47 David Carter and Allen Sapp, *The State of Police Education: Critical Findings* (Washington, DC: Police Executive Research Forum, 1988), p. 6.

48 See, for example, B. E. Sanderson, "Police Officers: The Relationship of a College Education to Job Performance," *Police Chief* 44 (1977): 62.

49 John Krimmel, "The Performance of College-Educated Police: A Study of Self-Rated Police Performance Measures," *American Journal of Police* 15 (1996): 85–95.

50 Robert Worden, "A Badge and a Baccalaureate: Policies, Hypotheses, and Further Evidence," *Justice Quarterly* 7 (1990): 565–592.

51 See Lawrence Sherman and Warren Bennis, "Higher Education for Police Officers: The Central Issues," *Police Chief* 44 (1977): 32.

52 Worden, "A Badge and a Baccalaureate," pp. 587–589.

53 Carter and Sapp, *The State of Police Education*.

54 C. J. Chivers, "Police Relax Requirements for Recruits," *New York Times*, 28 September 2000, p. B1.

55 Jihong Zhao and Nicholas Lovrich, "Determinants of Minority Employment in American Municipal Police Agencies: The Representation of African American Officers," *Journal of Criminal Justice* 26 (1998): 267–278.

56 John Klofas, "Drugs and Justice: The Impact of Drugs on Criminal Justice in a Metropolitan Community," *Crime and Delinquency* 39 (1993): 204–224.

57 David Murphy and John Worrall, "Residency Requirements and Public Perceptions of the Police in Large Municipalities," *Policing* 22 (1999): 327–342.

58 Steven Tuch and Ronald Weitzer, "The Polls—Trends: Racial Differences in Attitudes Toward the Police," *Public Opinion Quarterly* 61 (1997): 642–663.

59 Sutham Cheurprakobkit, "Police–Citizen Contact and Police Performance: Attitudinal Differences Between Hispanics and Non-Hispanics," *Journal of Criminal Justice* 28 (2000) 325–336; Kathleen Maguire and Ann L. Pastore, eds., *Sourcebook of Criminal Justice Statistics* (1999) [Online], http://www.albany.edu/sourcebook.

60 Yolander G. Hurst, James Frank, and Sandra Lee Browning, "The Attitudes of Juveniles Toward the Police: A Comparison of Black and White Youth," *Policing* 23 (2000): 37–53.

61 Ronald Weitzer and Steven Tuch, "Race, Class and Perceptions of Discrimination by the Police," *Crime and Delinquency* 45 (1999): 494–507.

62 Jack Kuykendall and David Burns, "The Black Police Officer: An Historical

Perspective," *Journal of Contemporary Criminal Justice* 1 (1980): 4–13.

63 Ibid.

64 Nicholas Alex, *Black in Blue: A Study of the Negro Policeman* (New York: Appleton-Century-Crofts, 1969).

65 Kim Michelle Lersch, "Predicting Citizens' Race in Allegations of Misconduct Against the Police," *Journal of Criminal Justice* 26 (1998): 87–99.

66 *Local Police Departments, 1997: Executive Summary* (Washington, DC: Bureau of Justice Statistics, 1999).

67 Samuel Walker and K. B. Turner, "A Decade of Modest Progress: Employment of Black and Hispanic Police Officers, 1983–1992," unpublished manuscript, Department of Criminal Justice, University of Nebraska, Omaha, 1993.

68 Stephen Leinen, *Black Police, White Society* (New York: New York University Press, 1984); Nicholas Alex, *New York Cops Talk Back* (New York: Wiley, 1976).

69 Robin Haarr and Merry Morash, "Gender, Race, and Strategies of Coping with Occupational Stress in Policing," *Justice Quarterly* 16 (1999): 303–336.

70 Donald Yates and Vijayan Pillai, "Race and Police Commitment to Community Policing," *Journal of Intergroup Relations* 19 (1993): 14–23.

71 Meghan Stroshine Chandek, "Race, Expectations and Evaluations of Police Performance: An Empirical Assessment," *Policing* 22 (1999): 675–695.

72 *Baker v. City of St. Petersburg*, 400 F.2d 294 (5th Cir. 1968).

73 See, for example, *Allen v. City of Mobile*, 331 F.Supp. 1134 (1971), affirmed 466 F.2d 122 (5th Cir. 1972).

74 Kuykendall and Burns, "The Black Police Officer."

75 "The Police Exam That Flunked," *New York Times*, 24 November 1985, p. 20.

76 *United States v. Paradise*, 480 U.S. 149, 107 S.Ct. 1053, 94 L.Ed.2d 203 (1987).

77 Michael Charles, "Resolving Discrimination in the Promotion of Fort Wayne Police Officers," *American Journal of Police* 10 (1991): 67–87.

78 Robert Kaminski, "Police Minority Recruitment: Predicting Who Will Say Yes to an Offer for a Job as a Cop," *Journal of Criminal Justice* 21 (1993): 395–409.

79 For a review of the history of women in policing, see Dorothy Moses Schulz, "From Policewoman to Police Officer: An Unfinished Revolution," *Police Studies* 16 (1993): 90–99; Cathryn House, "The Changing Role of Women in Law Enforcement," *Police Chief* 60 (1993): 139–144.

80 Susan Martin, "Female Officers on the Move? A Status Report on Women in Policing," in *Critical Issues in Policing*, ed. Roger Dunham and Geoffery Alpert (Grove Park, IL: Waveland Press, 1988), pp. 312–331.

81 *Le Boeuf v. Ramsey*, 26 FEP Cases 884 (9/16/80).

82 Michael Birzer and Delores Craig, "Gender Differences in Police Physical Ability Test Performance," *American Journal of Police* 15 (1996): 93–106.

83 Carole Garrison, Nancy Grant, and Kenneth McCormick, "Utilization of Police Women," *Police Chief* 55 (1988): 32–33.

84 Eric Poole and Mark Pogrebin, "Factors Affecting the Decision to Remain in Policing: A Study of Women Officers," *Journal of Police Science and Administration* 16 (1988): 49–55.

85 Haarr and Morash, "Gender, Race, and Strategies of Coping with Occupational Stress in Policing."

86 Merry Morash and Jack Greene, "Evaluating Women on Patrol: A Critique of Contemporary Wisdom," *Evaluation Review* 10 (1986): 230–255.

87 Peter Bloch and Deborah Anderson, *Policewomen on Patrol: Final Report* (Washington, DC: Police Foundation, 1974).

88 Robert Homant and Daniel Kennedy, "Police Perceptions of Spouse Abuse: A Comparison of Male and Female Officers," *Journal of Criminal Justice* 13 (1985): 49–64.

89 Sean Grennan, "Findings on the Role of Officer Gender in Violent Encounters with Citizens," *Journal of Police Science and Administration* 15 (1988): 78–85.

90 See, for example, Jack Molden, "Female Police Officers: Training Implications," *Law and Order* 33 (1985): 62–63.

91 Joseph Balkin, "Why Policemen Don't Like Policewomen," *Journal of Police Science and Administration* 16 (1988): 29–38.

92 Anthony Bouza, "Women in Policing," *FBI Law Enforcement Bulletin* 44 (1975): 2–7.

93 James Daum and Cindy Johns, "Police Work from a Woman's Perspective," *Police Chief* 61 (1994): 46–49.

94 Matthew Hickman, Alex Piquero, and Jack Greene, "Discretion and Gender Disproportionality in Police Disciplinary Systems," *Policing* 23 (2000): 105–116.

95 Mary Brown, "The Plight of Female Police: A Survey of NW Patrolmen," *Police Chief* 61 (1994): 50–53.

96 Simon Holdaway and Sharon K. Parker, "Policing Women Police: Uniform Patrol, Promotion and Representation in the CID," *British Journal of Criminology* 38 (1998): 40–48.

97 L. Thomas Winfree, Jr., and Greg Newbold, "Community Policing and the New Zealand Police: Correlates of Attitudes Toward the Work World an a Community-Oriented National Police Organization," *Policing* 22 (1999): 589–618.

98 Adriane Kinnane, *Policing* (Chicago: Nelson-Hall, 1979), p. 58.

99 Bruce Berg and Kimberly Budnick, "De-feminization of Women in Law Enforcement: A New Twist in the Traditional Police Personality," *Journal of Police Science and Administration* 14 (1986): 314–319.

100 Curt Bartol, George Bergen, Julie Seager Volckens, and Kathleen Knoras, "Women in Small-Town Policing: Job Performance and Stress," *Criminal Justice and Behavior* 19 (1992): 245–259.

101 Susan Martin, " 'Outsider Within' the Station House: The Impact of Race and Gender on Black Women Police," *Social Problems* 41 (1994): 383–400.

102 Michael Charles, "Women in Policing: The Physical Aspects," *Journal of Police Science and Administration* 10 (1982): 194–205.

103 Martin, " 'Outsider Within' the Station House," p. 387.

104 Ibid., p. 392.

105 Ibid., p. 394.

106 For an impressive review, see Richard Farmer, "Clinical and Managerial Implications of Stress Research on the Police," *Journal of Police Science and Administration* 17 (1990): 205–217.

107 Lawrence Travis III and Craig Winston, "Dissension in the Ranks: Officer Resistance to Community Policing and Support for the Organization," *Journal of Crime and Justice* 21 (1998): 139–155.

108 Francis Cullen, Terrence Lemming, Bruce Link, and John Wozniak, "The Impact of Social Supports on Police Stress," *Criminology* 23 (1985): 503–522.

109 Farmer, "Clinical and Managerial Implications of Stress Research on the Police"; Nancy Norvell, Dale Belles, and Holly Hills, "Perceived Stress Levels and Physical Symptoms in Supervisory Law Enforcement Personnel," *Journal of Police Science and Administration* 16 (1988): 75–79.

110 Donald Yates and Vijayan Pillai, "Attitudes Toward Community Policing: A Causal Analysis," *Social Science Journal* 33 (1996): 193–209.

111 Harvey McMurray, "Attitudes of Assaulted Police Officers and Their Policy Implications," *Journal of Police Science and Administration* 17 (1990): 44–48.

112 Robert Ankony and Thomas Kelley, "The Impact of Perceived Alienation of Police Officers' Sense of Mastery and Subsequent Motivation for Proactive Enforcement," *Policing* 22 (1999): 120–132.

113 John Blackmore, "Police Stress," in *Policing Society*, ed. Clinton Terry (New York: Wiley, 1985), p. 395.

114 Rose Lee Josephson and Martin Reiser, "Officer Suicide in the Los Angeles Police Department: A Twelve-Year Follow-Up," *Journal of Police Science and Administration* 17 (1990): 227–230.

115 Jeremy Davey, Patricia Obst, and Mary Sheehan, "Work Demographics and Officers' Perceptions of the Work Environment Which Add to the Prediction of At Risk Alcohol Consumption Within an Australian Police Sample," *Policing* 23 (2000): 69–81.

116 Rosanna Church and Naomi Robertson, "How State Police Agencies Are Addressing the Issue of Wellness," *Policing* 22 (1999): 304–312.

117 Farmer, "Clinical and Managerial Implications of Stress Research on the Police," p. 215.

118 Peter Hart, Alexander Wearing, and Bruce Headey, "Assessing Police Work Experiences: Development of the Police Daily Hassles and Uplifts Scales," *Journal of Criminal Justice* 21 (1993): 553–573.

119 Vivian Lord, Denis Gray, and Samuel Pond, "The Police Stress Inventory: Does It Measure Stress?" *Journal of Criminal Justice* 19 (1991): 139–149.

120 Samuel Walker, *Popular Justice* (New York: Oxford University Press, 1980), p. 197.

121 Richard R. Johnson, "Citizen Complaints: What the Police Should Know," *FBI Law Enforcement Bulletin* 67 (1998): 1–6.

122 See, for example, President's Commission on Law Enforcement and the Administration of Justice, *Task Force Report: The Police* (Washington, DC: U.S. Government Printing Office, 1967), pp. 181–182; National Advisory Commission on Civil Disorders, *Police and the Community* (Washington, DC: U.S. Government Printing Office, 1968), pp. 158–159.

123 President's Commission on Law Enforcement and the Administration of Justice, *Task Force Report: The Police,* pp. 181–182.

124 Lawrence Sherman, "Causes of Police Behavior: The Current State of Quantitative Research," *Journal of Research in Crime and Delinquency* 17 (1980): 80–81.

125 David Bayley and James Garofalo, "The Management of Violence by Police Patrol Officers," *Criminology* 27 (1989): 1–27.

126 Joel Garner, John Buchanan, Tom Schade, and John Hepburn, *Understanding the Use of Force by and Against the Police* (Washington, DC: National Institute of Justice, 1996).

127 Ibid.

128 Antony Pate and Lorie Fridell, *Police Use of Force: Official Reports, Citizen Complaints, and Legal Consequences* (Washington, DC: Police Foundation, 1993).

129 Kenneth Adams, Geoffrey P. Alpert, Roger G. Dunham, Joel H. Garner, Lawrence A. Greenfeld, Mark A. Henriquez, Patrick A. Langan, Christopher D. Maxwell, and Steven K. Smith, *Use of Force by Police: Overview of National and Local Data* (Washington, DC: National Institute of Justice and Bureau of Justice Statistics, 1999).

130 *Summary of Amnesty International's Concerns on Police Abuse in Chicago* (Washington, DC: Amnesty International, November 1999).

131 Adams et al., *Use of Force by Police.*

132 Kim Michelle Lersch and Tom Mieczkowski, "Who Are the Problem-Prone Officers? An Analysis of Citizen Complaints," *American Journal of Police* 15 (1996): 23–42.

133 Kim Michelle Lersch and Tom Mieczkowski, "An Examination of the Convergence and Divergence of Internal and External Allegations of Misconduct Filed Against Police Officers," *Policing* 23 (2000): 54–68.

134 Samuel Walker, "The Rule Revolution: Reflections on the Transformation of American Criminal Justice, 1950–1988," Working Papers, Series 3, Institute for Legal Studies, University of Wisconsin Law School, Madison, December 1988.

135 Kevin Flynn, "New York Police Sting Tries to Weed Out Brutal Officers," *New York Times,* 24 September 1999, p. 2.

136 *Summary of Amnesty International's Concerns on Police Abuse in Chicago.*

137 Lawrence Sherman and Robert Langworthy, "Measuring Homicide by Police Officers," *Journal of Criminal Law and Criminology* 4 (1979): 546–560.

138 Ibid.

139 Ibid.

140 Richard Kania and Wade Mackey, "Police Violence as a Function of Community Characteristics," *Criminology* 15 (1977): 27–48.

141 John MacDonald, Geoffrey Alpert, and Abraham Tennenbaum, "Justifiable Homicide by Police and Criminal Homicide: A Research Note," *Journal of Crime and Justice* 22 (1999): 153–164.

142 Richard Parent and Simon Verdun-Jones, "Victim-Precipitated Homicide: Police Use of Deadly Force in British Columbia," *Policing* 21 1998: 432–449.

143 Robert Homant, Daniel Kennedy, and R. Thomas Hupp, "Real and Perceived Danger in Police Officer Assisted Suicide," *Journal of Criminal Justice* 28 (2000): 43–52.

144 "10% of Police Shootings Found to Be 'Suicide by Cop,'" *Criminal Justice Newsletter* 29 (1998): 1.

145 Sherman and Langworthy, "Measuring Homicide by Police Officers."

146 Ibid.

147 David Lester, "Predicting the Rate of Justifiable Homicide by Police Officers," *Police Studies* 16 (1993): 43; Jonathan Sorenson, James Marquart, and Deon Brock, "Factors Related to Killings of Felons by Police Officers: A Test of the Community Violence and Conflict Hypotheses," *Justice Quarterly* 10 (1993): 417–440; David Jacobs and David Britt, "Inequality and Police Use of Deadly Force: An Empirical Assessment of a Conflict Hypothesis," *Social Problems* 26 (1979): 403–412.

148 James Fyfe, "Police Use of Deadly Force: Research and Reform," *Justice Quarterly* 5 (1988): 165–205 at p. 181.

149 Paul Takagi, "A Garrison State in a 'Democratic' Society," *Crime and Social Justice* 5 (1974): 34–43.

150 Mark Blumberg, "Race and Police Shootings: An Analysis in Two Cities," *Contemporary Issues in Law Enforcement,* ed. James Fyfe (Beverly Hills, CA: Sage 1981), pp. 152–166.

151 James Fyfe, "Shots Fired," Ph.D. dissertation, State University of New York, Albany, 1978.

152 *Tennessee v. Garner,* 471 U.S. 1, 105 S.Ct. 1694, 85 L.Ed.2d 889 (1985).

153 *Graham v. Connor,* 490 U.S. 386, 109 S.Ct. 1865, 104 L.Ed.2d 443 (1989).

154 Franklin Graves and Gregory Connor, "The FLETC Use-of-Force Model," *Police Chief* 59 (1992): 56–58.

155 See James Fyfe, "Administrative Interventions on Police Shooting Discretion: An Empirical Examination," *Journal of Criminal Justice* 7 (1979): 313–325.

156 Frank Zarb, "Police Liability for Creating the Need to Use Deadly Force in Self-Defense," *Michigan Law Review* 86 (1988): 1982–2009.

157 R. Kaminski, S. Edwards, and J. Johnson, "The Deterrent Effects of Oleoresin Capsicum on Assaults Against Police: Testing the Velcro-Effect Hypothesis," *Police Quarterly* 1 (1998): 1–20; "Assessing the Incapacitative Effects of Pepper Spray During Resistive Encounters with the Police," *Policing* 22 (1999): 7–29.

158 Michael R. Smith and Geoffrey P. Alpert, "Pepper Spray: A Safe and Reasonable Response to Suspect Verbal Resistance," *Policing* 23 (2000): 233–245.

159 National Law Enforcement Officers Memorial Fund, press release, Washington, DC, 7 February 1996.

160 "Lowest Number of U.S. Police Deaths in 35 Years," *FBI Law Enforcement Bulletin* 69 (2000): 13.

161 Adams et al., *Use of Force by Police.*

162 J. David Hirschel, Charles Dean, and Richard Lumb, "The Relative Contribution of Domestic Violence to Assault and Injury of Police Officers," *Justice Quarterly* 11 (1994): 99–118.

163 John Cloud, "L.A. Confidential, for Real: Street Cops Accused of Frame-Ups in Widening Scandal," *Time,* 27 September 1999, p. 44; "L.A.'s Dirty War on Gangs: A Trail of Corruption Leads to Some of the City's Toughest Cops," *Newsweek,* 11 October 1999, p. 72.

164 Ann W. O'Neill, "Fingerprint Evidence Bogus, Witness Says: Inmate Says Rampart Police Pressed Fellow Gang Member's Fingertips Against a Gun to Frame Him," *Los Angeles Times,* 25 October 2000, p. 1.

165 Walker, *Popular Justice,* p. 64.

166 Richard Willing and Kevin Johnson, "More Law Enforcers Becoming Law Breakers," *USA Today,* 29 July 1999, p. A4.

167 Herman Goldstein, *Police Corruption* (Washington, DC: Police Foundation, 1975), p. 3.

168 Knapp Commission, *Report on Police Corruption* (New York: George Braziller, 1973), pp. 1–34.

169 Elizabeth Neuffer, "Seven Additional Detectives Linked to Extortion Scheme," *Boston Globe,* 25 October 1988, p. 60.

170 Kevin Cullen, "U.S. Probe Eyes Bookie Protection," *Boston Globe,* 25 October 1988.

171 Michael Johnston, *Political Corruption and Public Policy in America* (Monterey, CA: Brooks/Cole, 1982), p. 75.

172 William Doherty, "Ex-Sergeant Says He Aided Bid to Sell Exam," *Boston Globe,* 26 February 1987, p. 61.

173 Willing and Johnson, "More Law Enforcers Becoming Law Breakers."

174 Ellwyn Stoddard, "Blue Coat Crime," in *Thinking About Police,* ed. Carl Klockars (New York: McGraw-Hill, 1983), pp. 338–349.

175 Lawrence Sherman, *Police Corruption: A Sociological Perspective* (Garden City, NY: Doubleday, 1974).

176 Robert Daley, *Prince of the City* (New York: Houghton Mifflin, 1978).

177 Sherman, *Police Corruption,* pp. 40–41.

178 Samuel Walker, *Police in Society* (New York: McGraw-Hill, 1983), p. 181.

179 Sherman, *Police Corruption,* p. 194.

180 Kevin Flynn, "Police Dept. Routinely Drops Cases of Officer Misconduct, Report Says," *New York Times,* 15 September 1999, p. 1.

181 Barbara Gelb, *Tarnished Brass: The Decade After Serpico* (New York: Putnam, 1983); Candace McCoy, "Lawsuits Against Police: What Impact Do They Have?" *Criminal Law Bulletin* 20 (1984): 49–56.

182 "Philadelphia Police Corruption Brings Major Reform Initiative," *Criminal Justice Newsletter* 27 (1996, October 1): 4–5.

POLICE AND THE RULE OF LAW

Defendant and two other individuals were in an automobile stopped for speeding and a faulty brake light in the early morning hours of July 23, 1995.[1] The driver had a syringe in his shirt pocket. When asked about it, the driver, with refreshing candor, replied that he used it to take drugs. The officer then checked inside the car, saw defendant's purse on the seat, searched it, and found a vial of liquid methamphetamine. She was arrested, tried, and convicted of drug possession.

It took four years for defendant's case to reach the U.S. Supreme Court for review. The state appeals court overturned the conviction, but the Supreme Court upheld it, ruling that the police officer had probable cause (reason to believe a crime was committed) to search the purse of a presumably innocent passenger. According to the Court, effective law enforcement would be impaired without the ability to search a passenger's personal belongings when there is reason to believe contraband is hidden.

In a different type of case, a federal border patrol agent boarded a bus near the Texas–Mexico border to check the immigration status of the passengers.[2] As he was leaving the bus, he squeezed the soft luggage that passengers had placed in the overhead storage space. When he squeezed a canvas bag belonging to the defendant, he noticed that it contained a "brick-like" object. Defendant consented to a search of the bag, the agent discovered a "brick" of methamphetamine, and defendant was charged with and convicted of possession. The Court of Appeals ruled that the agent's manipulation of the bag was not a "search" under the Fourth Amendment.

On appeal, however, the Supreme Court held that the agent's manipulation of the bag violated the Fourth Amendment's rule against unreasonable searches. Personal luggage, according to the Court, is protected under the Fourth Amendment. The defendant had a privacy interest in his bag, and his right to privacy was violated by the police search.

Chapter Outline

Criminal Justice Links

Criminal Justice Viewpoints

Thousands of incidents like these two cases occur each year. Traditional police power to strictly enforce traffic laws is often used as a way to search for drugs on the roadway. The U.S. Supreme Court has given police officers greater leeway to stop cars, to detain drivers and their passengers, and to search vehicles and luggage—often with the intent of finding illegal drugs.

The two cases illustrate the complex Fourth Amendment issues that the police and courts face in modern society. Should privacy rights be secondary to public safety? Should the Fourth Amendment be a check on police power? The question presented to the Supreme Court in the first case was whether the so-called automobile exception to the Fourth Amendment allows the police to conduct a warrantless search of a passenger's belongings when there is no apparent evidence that the passenger is involved in a crime. The question in the second case was whether squeezing a bus passenger's luggage was a "search" and a violation of the right to privacy. These are two examples of the many different types of cases involving the law of search and seizure, which is discussed in this chapter.

The police are charged with preventing crime before it occurs and identifying and arresting criminals who have already broken the law. To carry out these tasks, police officers want a free hand to search for evidence, to seize contraband such as guns and drugs, to interrogate suspects, and to have witnesses and victims identify suspects. They know their investigation must be thorough. For any trial, they will need to provide the prosecutor with sufficient evidence to prove guilt "beyond a reasonable doubt." Therefore, soon after the crime is committed, they must make every effort to gather physical evidence, obtain confessions, and take witness statements that will be adequate to prove the case in court. Police officers also realize that evidence the prosecutor is counting on to prove the case, such as the testimony of a witness or co-conspirator, may evaporate before the trial begins. Then the case outcome may depend on some piece of physical evidence or a suspect's statement taken early in the investigation.

The need for police officers to gather conclusive evidence can conflict with the constitutional rights of citizens. For example, although police want a free hand to search homes and cars for evidence, the Fourth Amendment restricts police activities by requiring that they obtain a warrant before conducting a search. When police want to vigorously interrogate a suspect, they must honor the Fifth Amendment's prohibition against forcing people to incriminate themselves.

POLICE AND THE COURTS

Once a crime has been committed and the purpose of the investigation has been determined, the police may use various means to collect the evidence needed for criminal prosecution. With each crime, police must decide how best to investigate it. Should surveillance techniques be employed to secure information? Is there reasonable suspicion to justify stopping and frisking a suspect? Has the investigation shifted from a general inquiry and begun to focus on a particular suspect so that police can start a legally appropriate interrogation? Depending on the circumstances, one investigative technique may be more appropriate than another.

Fill in the blanks 1–2

Criminal detection, apprehension, and arrest are the primary investigative functions performed by law enforcement officers.[3] Proper police investigations involve collecting facts and information that will lead to the identification, arrest, and conviction of the criminal. Many police operations are informational—such as referring an alcoholic to a hospital or resolving a family dispute—and based on agency policy or police discretion. In contrast, the primary techniques of investigation—such as stopping and questioning people or interrogating a suspect—are controlled by statute and constitutional case law and are subject to review by the courts.

The U.S. Supreme Court has taken an active role in considering the legality of police operations. The Court has reviewed numerous appeals charging that police violated a suspect's rights during the investigation, arrest, and custody stages of the justice process. Of primary concern has been police conduct in obtaining and serving search and arrest warrants and in conducting postarrest interrogations and lineups. In some instances, the Court has expanded police power—for example, by increasing the occasions when police can search without a warrant. In other cases, the Court has restricted police operations—for example, by ruling that every criminal suspect has a right to an attorney when being interrogated by police. Changes in the law often reflect such factors as the justices' legal philosophy, their emphasis on the ability of police to control crime, their views on public safety, and their commitment to the civil liberties of criminal defendants. The issues and cases discussed in the following sections reflect the endless ebb and flow of judicial decision making and its impact on the law enforcement process.

The Supreme Court often gets several cases each term requiring it to elaborate on standards for searches and seizures, as well as confessions. In recent years, it has frequently struck the balance in favor of police officers, with some exceptions.

SEARCH AND SEIZURE

Evidence collected by the police is governed by the **search and seizure** requirements of the Fourth Amendment to the U.S. Constitution.[4] The Fourth Amendment protects the defendant against unreasonable searches and seizures resulting from unlawful activities. Although there are exceptions, the general rule regarding the application of the Fourth Amendment is that any search or seizure undertaken without a validly obtained search warrant is unlawful. Furthermore, the amendment provides that no warrant shall be issued unless there is probable cause to believe that an offense has been or is being committed. A police officer concerned with investigating a crime can undertake a proper search and seizure if a valid search warrant has been obtained from the court, or if the officer is functioning under one of the many exceptions to the search warrant requirement.

Fill in the blanks 3–6
True/False 1–2
Multiple choice 1–5

search and seizure
The legal term, contained in the Fourth Amendment to the U.S. Constitution, that refers to the searching for and carrying away of evidence by police during a criminal investigation.

Bridgeport, Connecticut, police search an apartment for drugs after arresting suspected dealers. Under normal circumstances, police must have a legal warrant to search a dwelling for contraband.

© Bob Strong/The Image Works

A great site for U.S. Supreme Court decisions on criminal procedure is http://www.law.cornell.edu
For an up-to-date list of Web links, see http://www.wadsworth.com/product/0534573053s

search warrant
An order, issued by a judge, directing officers to conduct a search of specified premises for specified objects or persons and to bring them before the court.

A **search warrant** is an order from a court authorizing and directing the police to search a designated place for property stated in the order and to bring that property to court. The order must be based on a sworn testimony of the police officer that the facts on which the request for the search warrant is made are trustworthy.

PERSPECTIVES ON JUSTICE

It has been said that one of the most essential principles of our freedom is the freedom to be secure in one's home. "A man's home is his castle, while he is quiet he is as well guarded as a prince in his castle." Is this what the framers had in mind when they adopted the Fourth Amendment? Two important clauses are contained in the Fourth Amendment: the prohibition against unreasonable searches and seizures, and the warrant clause. The due process perspective has extended the individual protections of the Fourth Amendment beyond one's home.

Search Warrant Requirements

Three critical concepts in the Fourth Amendment are directly related to the search warrant: reasonableness, probable cause, and particularity.

reasonableness
Requirement, under the Fourth Amendment, for a search and seizure; there must be probable cause to believe that the item being searched for was involved in criminal activity and is located at the place to be searched.

probable cause
The evidentiary criterion necessary to sustain an arrest or the issuance of an arrest or search warrant; a set of facts, information, circumstances, or conditions that would lead a reasonable person to believe that an offense was committed and that the accused committed that offense.

particularity
The requirement that a search warrant state precisely where the search is to take place and what items are to be seized.

Reasonableness in searches and seizures generally refers to whether an officer has exceeded the scope of police authority. Most unreasonable actions are those in which the police officer did not have sufficient information to justify the search. Reasonableness requires the existence of **probable cause** to believe that the item being searched for was involved in criminal activity and will be located at the site to be searched. The Fourth Amendment provides clearly that no warrants shall be issued unless probable cause is supported by oath or affirmation; in other words, a search warrant can be obtained only if the request for it is supported by facts that convince the court that a crime has been or is being committed.

Particularity generally refers to the specificity of the search. The Fourth Amendment requires that a search warrant specify the place to be searched and the reasons for searching it. When the police request a search warrant, it must identify the premises and the personal property to be seized, and it must be signed under oath by the officer requesting it. The essential facts and information justifying the need for the search warrant are set out in an affidavit requesting the warrant.

In practice, law enforcement officers often do not rely on a search warrant to enter a home or search a person, but in certain kinds of cases—such as investigations of organized crime, gambling, drugs, and pornography—search warrants are particularly useful. Police also request warrants during investigations of other offenses when they are reasonably sure that the evidence sought cannot be removed from the premises, destroyed, or damaged by the suspect. The police are generally reluctant to seek a warrant, however, because of the stringent evidentiary standards courts require for obtaining one and the availability of search-and-seizure alternatives, such as warrantless searches, that have been approved by the U.S. Supreme Court (discussed later).

Use of Informers

The U.S. Supreme Court has played an active role in interpreting the legal requirements of a search warrant. One of the major issues considered by the Court has been the reliability of the evidence contained in the affidavit. In many instances, the evidence used by the police in requesting a search warrant originates with a police informer, rather than with the police officer. Such information is normally referred to as **hearsay evidence**.

    The Supreme Court has determined that hearsay evidence must be corroborated to serve as a basis for probable cause and thereby justify the issuance of a warrant. In the case of *Spinelli v. United States* (1969), the Supreme Court held that when an informer has previously supplied truthful information, statements that he or she now has personal knowledge of the facts about a crime are sufficient corroboration.[5] In an earlier case, *Aguilar v. Texas* (1964), the Court articulated a two-part test for issuing a warrant on the word of an informant: The police had to show (1) why they believed the informant and (2) how the informant acquired personal knowledge of the crime.[6] Later, in *Illinois v. Gates* (1983), the Court eased the process of obtaining search warrants by developing a new test. The "two-pronged test" of *Spinelli* and *Aguilar* was replaced with a *totality of the circumstances* test to determine probable cause for issuing a search warrant. To obtain a warrant, the police must prove to a judge that, considering the "totality of the circumstances," an informant has relevant and factual knowledge that a fair probability exists that evidence of a crime will be found in a certain place.[7]

    In sum, to obtain a search warrant, the following procedural requirements must be met:

1. The police officer must request the warrant from the court.
2. The officer must submit an affidavit establishing the proper grounds for the warrant.
3. The affidavit must state the place to be searched and the property to be seized.

Whether the affidavit contains sufficient information to justify issuing the warrant is what determines the validity of the warrant once it is issued.

hearsay evidence
Testimony that is not firsthand but relates information told by a second party.

For frequently asked questions about search and seizure, go to http://www.lawinfo.com/legalfaqs/search_seizure.html

For an up-to-date list of Web links, see http://www.wadsworth.com/product/0534573053s

---

PERSPECTIVES ON JUSTICE

In executing a search warrant authorizing the search of a person's home, there is the common law rule that the officer must knock on the door and announce his or her presence before using force to obtain entry. The *Wilson v. Arkansas* case, 514 U.S. 927 (1995), held that circumstances might exist that could justify a no-knock exception to the knock-and-announce rule. Following this case, the state of Wisconsin held that there is a blanket felony-drug exception to the knock-and-announce rule, so that officers executing warrants for felony-level drug cases are never required to knock and announce their presence. But the Supreme Court in *Richards v. Wisconsin*, 65 U.S.L.W. 4283 (1997), ruled that law enforcement officials must justify no-knock searches on a case-by-case basis. In the no-knock Wisconsin case, the Court moved to a due process perspective requiring the police, even in drug cases, to justify their intrusion.

WARRANTLESS SEARCHES

There are some significant exceptions to the search warrant requirement of the Fourth Amendment. Two critical exceptions are (1) searches incident to a lawful arrest and (2) field interrogations. Other specialized warrantless searches include automobile searches, consent searches, and drug courier profiles. These exceptions, as well as the doctrine of plain view and the law of electronic surveillance, will be discussed.

Fill in the blanks 7
True/False 3–4
Multiple choice 6
Essay 1

Searches Incident to a Lawful Arrest

Traditionally, a search without a warrant is permissible if it is made incident to a lawful arrest. For example, if shortly after the armed robbery of a grocery store, officers arrest a suspect with a briefcase hiding in the basement, a search of the suspect's person and of the briefcase would be a proper **search incident to a lawful arrest** without a warrant. The legality of this type of search depends almost entirely on the lawfulness of the arrest. The arrest will be upheld if the police officer observed the crime being committed or had probable cause to believe that the suspect committed the offense. If the arrest is found to have been invalid, then any warrantless search made incident to the arrest would be considered illegal, and the evidence obtained from the search would be excluded from trial.

The police officer who searches a suspect incident to a lawful arrest must generally observe two rules. First, it is important that the officer search the suspect at the time of or immediately following the arrest. Second, the police may search only the suspect and the area within the suspect's immediate control; the search may not legally go beyond the area where the person can reach for a weapon or destroy any evidence. The U.S. Supreme Court dealt with the permissible scope of a search incident to a lawful arrest in *Chimel v. California.*[8] According to the *Chimel* doctrine, the police can search a suspect without a warrant after a lawful arrest to protect themselves from danger and to secure evidence.

On the afternoon of September 13, 1965, three police officers arrived at the Santa Ana, California, home of Ted Chimel with a warrant authorizing his arrest for the burglary of a coin shop. The officers knocked on the door, identified themselves to Chimel's wife, and asked if they could come inside. She admitted the officers into the house, where they waited 10 or 15 minutes until Chimel returned home from work. When he entered the house, one of the officers handed him the arrest warrant and asked for permission to look around. Chimel objected but was advised that the officers could conduct a search on the basis of the lawful arrest. No search warrant had been issued.

Accompanied by Chimel's wife, the officers then looked through the entire three-bedroom house. The officers told Chimel's wife to open drawers in the master bedroom and sewing room and "to physically move contents of the drawers from side to side so that [they] might view any items that would have come from [the] burglary." After completing the search, the officers seized numerous items, including some coins. The entire search took between 45 minutes and an hour.

At the defendant's subsequent state trial on two charges of burglary, the coins taken from his house were admitted into evidence against him over his objection that they had been unconstitutionally seized. He was convicted, and the judgment was affirmed by the California Supreme Court.

The U.S. Supreme Court decided that the search of Chimel's house went far beyond any area where he might conceivably have obtained a weapon or destroyed any evidence and that no constitutional basis existed for extending the search to all areas of the house. The Court concluded that the scope of the search was unreasonable under the Fourth Amendment as applied through the Fourteenth Amendment, and Chimel's conviction was overturned.

Field Interrogation: Stop and Frisk

Another important exception to the rule requiring a search warrant is the **threshold inquiry**, or the **stop-and-frisk** procedure. Police examination of a suspect on the street does not always occur during or after arrest; officers frequently stop persons who appear to be behaving in a suspicious manner or are the source of complaints. Ordinarily, police are not required to have sufficient evidence for an arrest to stop a person for brief questioning. If the only way in which the police could stop a person was by making an arrest, they would be prevented from investigating many potentially criminal situations. For this reason, the courts have given the police the authority to stop a person, ask questions, and search the person in a limited way, such as frisking for a concealed weapon. The courts have concluded that it is unreasonable to expect a police officer to decide immediately whether to arrest a suspect. With a limited power to stop and frisk, the police officer is able to investigate suspicious persons and situations without having to meet the probable cause standard for arrest. Without this authority, many innocent individuals would probably be arrested.

The threshold inquiry, or the stop-and-frisk procedure, applies to an important point of contact between the police officer and the citizen—the street encounter. Stopping a suspect allows for brief questioning of the person, while frisking affords the officer an opportunity to avoid the possibility of attack. For instance, a police officer patrolling a high-crime area observes two young men loitering outside a liquor store after dark. The two men confer several times and stop to talk to a third person who pulls up alongside the curb in an automobile. From this observation, the officer may conclude that the men are casing the store for a possible burglary. He can then stop the suspects and ask them for some identification and an explanation of their conduct. If, after questioning the suspects, the officer has further reason to believe that they are planning to engage in criminal activity and that they are a threat to his safety, the officer can conduct a proper frisk, or a carefully limited search of the suspects' outer clothing.

In the case of *Terry v. Ohio* (1968), the Supreme Court upheld the right of the police to conduct brief threshold inquiries of suspicious persons when they have reason to believe that such persons may be armed and dangerous to the police or others.[9] The Court's intention was to allow the officer, who interacts with members of the community many times each day, to conduct proper investigations where necessary, while at the same time keeping invasions of personal rights to a minimum and protecting the officer from harm.

The field interrogation process is based primarily on the ability of the police officer to determine whether suspicious conduct exists that gives the officer reason to believe that a crime is about to be committed. Some jurisdictions have enacted legislation authorizing the stop-and-frisk procedure, thereby codifying the standard established in *Terry v. Ohio*. Courts have ruled that frisking must be limited to instances in which the police officer determines that his or her safety or that of others is at stake. The stop-and-frisk exception cannot be used to harass citizens or conduct exploratory searches.

The Supreme Court has continued to treat the *Terry v. Ohio* ruling as an exception to the general rule requiring probable cause for arrest, and even extended it in the 1993 case of *Minnesota v. Dickerson.*

The case began when two Minneapolis police officers noticed Timothy Dickerson acting suspiciously after leaving an apartment building they believed to be a "crack house." The officers briefly stopped Dickerson to question him and conducted a pat-down search for weapons. The search revealed no weapons, but one officer felt a small lump in the pocket of Dickerson's nylon jacket. The lump turned out to be one-fifth of a gram of crack cocaine, and Dickerson was arrested and charged with drug possession.

At issue before the Court was whether the Fourth Amendment permits the seizure of contraband detected through a police officer's sense of touch during such a protective pat-down search. Extending the Supreme Court's ruling in *Terry v. Ohio,* the Court added to its "plain view" doctrine (under which officers may make a warrantless seizure of contraband found in plain view during a lawful search for other items) a "plain touch" or "plain feel" corollary. The pat-down,

threshold inquiry
A term used to describe a stop and frisk.

stop and frisk
The situation in which police officers who are suspicious of an individual run their hands lightly over the suspect's outer garments to determine if the person is carrying a concealed weapon; also called a threshold inquiry or pat-down.

however, must be limited to a search for weapons, and the officer may not extend the "feel" beyond that necessary to determine if it is a weapon.[10]

PERSPECTIVES ON JUSTICE

Does the U.S. Supreme Court shed more light on the meaning of the Fourth Amendment and due process of law when it decides cases like the following?

Defendant Wardlow was walking on the street in an area known for narcotics trafficking. When he made eye contact with a police officer riding in a marked police car, he ran away. The officer caught up with defendant on the street, stopped him, and conducted a protective pat-down search for weapons. He said he did this because, in his experience, there were usually weapons in the vicinity of narcotics transactions. A handgun was discovered in the frisk, and defendant was convicted of unlawful use of a weapon by a felon. The Supreme Court of Illinois ruled that the frisk violated *Terry v. Ohio* because flight may simply be an exercise of the right to "go on one's way" and does not constitute reasonable suspicion.

The U.S. Supreme Court, in *Illinois v. Wardlow,* 120 S.Ct. 673 (2000), reversed the state court ruling that a person's presence in a "high crime area," standing alone, is not enough to support a reasonable, particularized suspicion of criminal activity. It held that a location's characteristics are sufficiently suspicious to warrant further investigation, and in this case, the additional factor of defendant's unprovoked flight added up to reasonable suspicion. The officers found that defendant possessed a handgun and, as a result of the pat-down and search, had probable cause to arrest him for violation of a state law. The frisk and arrest were thus proper under *Terry v. Ohio.*

The case represents the inherent conflict between the crime control and due process perspectives.

Multiple choice 9–11

Automobile Searches

The U.S. Supreme Court has also established that certain situations justify the warrantless search of an automobile on a public street or highway. For example, evidence can be seized from an automobile when a suspect is taken into custody in a lawful arrest. In *Carroll v. United States,* which was decided in 1925, the Supreme Court ruled that distinctions should be made between searches of automobiles, persons, and homes. The Court also concluded that a warrantless search of an automobile is valid if the police have probable cause to believe that the car contains evidence they are seeking.[11]

The legality of searching automobiles without a warrant has always been a trouble spot for police and the courts. Should the search be limited to the interior of the car, or can the police search the trunk? What about a suitcase in the trunk? What about the glove compartment? Does a traffic citation give the police the right to search an automobile? These questions have produced significant litigation over the years. To clear up the matter, the Supreme Court decided the landmark case of *United States v. Ross* in 1982.[12]

In *Ross,* the Court held that, if probable cause exists to believe that an automobile contains criminal evidence, a warrantless search by the police is permissible, including a search of closed containers in the vehicle.

In sum, the most important requirement for a warrantless search of an automobile is that it must be based on the legal standard of probable cause that a crime

Police search a vehicle incident to an arrest. In *Ross v. United States,* the U.S. Supreme Court ruled such searches could be conducted without a warrant if there was probable cause that the vehicle had been involved in a crime and contained criminal evidence.

related to the vehicle has been or is being committed. Under such conditions, the car may be stopped and searched, the contraband seized, and the occupant arrested.

Roadblock Searches

Police departments often wish to set up roadblocks to check drivers' licenses or the condition of drivers. Is such a stop an illegal search and seizure? In *Delaware v. Prouse* (1979), the Supreme Court forbade the practice of random stops in the absence of any reasonable suspicion that some traffic or motor vehicle law has been violated.[13] Unless there is at least reasonable belief that a motorist is unlicensed, that an automobile is not registered, or that the occupant is subject to seizure for violation of the law, stopping and detaining a driver to check his or her license violates the Fourth Amendment.

One important purpose of the *Prouse* decision was to eliminate the individual police officer's use of discretion to stop cars. However, what has developed from this case is tacit approval for police roadblocks that are set up to stop cars in some systematic fashion. As long as the police can demonstrate that the checkpoints are conducted in a uniform manner and that the operating procedures have been determined by someone other than the officer at the scene, roadblocks can be used to uncover violators of even minor traffic regulations.

Roadblocks have recently become popular for combating drunk driving. Courts have ruled that police can stop a predetermined number of cars at a checkpoint and can request each motorist to produce his or her license, registration, and insurance card. While doing so, they can check for outward signs of intoxication. Nevertheless, some state jurisdictions find that such procedures intrude on citizens' privacy. Stopping an automobile without suspicion is ordinarily unreasonable under the Fourth Amendment; there must be reason to believe the motorist is unlicensed, the vehicle is not registered, or the vehicle or the occupant is in violation of some law.

Can police officers randomly stop vehicles and then use drug-sniffing dogs to spot narcotics traffickers? In *City of Indianapolis v. Edmund,* the Court ruled that

Fill in the blanks 9
True/False 6
Multiple choice 12

ANALYZING CRIMINAL JUSTICE ISSUES

Traffic Stops: Undercutting the Fourth Amendment

Of special concern to the police and the public are the constitutional rules regarding traffic stops. In 1977, the Supreme Court ruled in *Pennsylvania v. Mimms* that officers could order drivers out of their cars during routine traffic stops; officers' safety outweighed the intrusion on individual rights.[14] It came as no surprise in 1997 when the Court held in *Maryland v. Wilson* (1997) that the police had the same authority with respect to passengers. In the *Wilson* case, a state patrol officer lawfully stopped a vehicle for speeding. While the driver was producing his license, the front-seat passenger, Wilson, was ordered out of the vehicle. As he exited, crack cocaine dropped to the ground. Wilson was arrested and convicted of drug possession. His attorney moved to suppress the evidence, and the Maryland Appeals Court agreed. But the U.S. Supreme Court disagreed and extended the *Mimms* rule to passengers. The Court noted that lawful traffic stops had become progressively more dangerous to police officers; from 1994 to 1996, 5,700 officers had been assaulted and 11 killed during such stops. The decision means that passengers must comply when ordered out of a lawfully stopped vehicle.

In two other decisions, the Court further bolstered police powers in traffic stops. The legality of pretext stops (those in which police use traffic violations as an excuse to stop a vehicle) was challenged in *Whren v. United States* (1966). Two black defendants claimed that plainclothes police officers used traffic violations as an excuse to stop

their vehicle because the officers lacked objective evidence that they were drug couriers. The Court ruled, however, that if probable cause exists to stop a person for a traffic violation, the motivation of the officers is irrelevant.

In *Ohio v. Robinette* (1996), the key issue was whether police officers must inform detained drivers that they are "free to go" before asking consent to search the vehicle. The Court concluded that no such warning is needed to make consent to a search reasonable. Robinette was stopped for speeding. After checking his license, the officer asked if Robinette was carrying any illegal contraband in the car. When the defendant answered in the negative, the officer asked for and received permission to search the car. The search turned up illegal drugs. The Supreme Court said that the Ohio rule that an officer may not obtain consent to search in a valid traffic stop situation without first notifying the defendant that he or she is free to go is illegal. According to the Court, the touchstone of the Fourth Amendment is reasonableness, which is assessed by examining the totality of the circumstances, not by applying rigid rules.

Critical Thinking Skills

1. The Supreme Court has decided that police are allowed to make pretext stops without knowing that a search will produce drugs. They can order drivers and passengers out of cars during routine traffic stops. Further, they are not required to tell drivers that they are free to go before asking for consent to search a vehicle. What

is the impact of these Court decisions?

2. Legal experts believe that the public interest in protecting an officer's safety outweighs the intrusion on a driver's rights. Do you agree?

3. Think about how many thousands of innocent passengers are involved in traffic stops every day. Is the risk to the police outweighed by the intrusion on the privacy rights of so many citizens?

4. One of the major issues in this line of cases is whether it will be easier for police to target minority motorists for traffic stops. Do you think it will be?

InfoTrac College Edition Research

Use InfoTrac College Edition to read more about automobile searches. Look under "probable cause," "search warrant," and "electronic surveillance" to broaden your understanding of Fourth Amendment law. In particular, see Aaron Mendelsohn, "The Fourth Amendment and Traffic Stops," *Journal of Criminal Law and Criminology*, 1998, v88 p930

SOURCES: *Maryland v. Wilson*, 65 U.S.L.W. 4124 (February 19, 1997); *Ohio v. Robinette*, 117 S.Ct. 417 (1996); *Whren v. United States*, 116 S.Ct. 1769 (1996); Mark Hansen, "Rousting Miss Daisy?" *American Bar Association Journal* 83 (1997): 22; *Wyoming v. Houghton*, 199 S.Ct. (1999).

Fill in the blanks 10
True/False 7–9
Multiple choice 13

the police may not routinely stop all motorists in the hope of finding a few drug criminals.[15] The general rule is that any seizure must be accompanied by individualized suspicion; the random stopping of cars to search for drugs is illegal.

One of the most important issues associated with roadblock searches is the legality of pretext traffic stops, discussed in the Analyzing Criminal Justice Issues feature.

Consent Searches

True/False 10
Multiple choice 14
Essay 3

Police officers may also undertake warrantless searches when the person in control of the area or object voluntarily consents to the search. Those who consent to a search essentially waive their constitutional rights under the Fourth Amendment. Ordinarily, courts are reluctant to accept such waivers and require the state to prove that the consent was voluntarily given. In addition, the consent must be given intelligently, and in some jurisdictions, consent searches are valid only after the suspect is informed of the option to refuse consent.

The major legal issue in most consent searches is whether the police can prove that consent was given voluntarily. For example, in the case of *Bumper v. North Carolina* (1968), police officers searched the home of an elderly woman after informing her that they possessed a search warrant.[16] At the trial, the prosecutor informed the court that the search was valid because the woman had given her consent. When the government was unable to produce the warrant, the court decided that the search was invalid because the woman's consent was not given voluntarily. On appeal, the U.S. Supreme Court upheld the lower court's finding that the consent had been illegally obtained by the false claim that the police had a search warrant.

In most consent searches, however, voluntariness is a question of fact to be determined from all the circumstances of the case. In *Schneckloth v. Bustamonte* (1973), for example, where the defendant actually helped the police by opening the trunk and glove compartment of the car, the Court said this demonstrated that the consent was voluntarily given.[17] Furthermore, the police are usually under no obligation to inform a suspect of the right to refuse consent. Failure to tell a suspect of this right does not make the search illegal, but it may be a factor used by the courts to decide if the suspect gave consent voluntarily.

The Bus Sweep

Multiple choice 15

Today, consent searches have additional significance because of their use in drug control programs. On June 20, 1991, the U.S. Supreme Court, in *Florida v. Bostick,* upheld the drug interdiction technique known as the **bus sweep**, in which police board buses and, without suspicion of illegal activity, question passengers, ask for identification, and request permission to search luggage.[18] Police in the *Bostick* case boarded a bus bound from Miami to Atlanta during a stopover in Fort Lauderdale. Without suspicion, the officers picked out the defendant and asked to inspect his ticket and identification. After identifying themselves as narcotics officers looking for illegal drugs, they asked to inspect the defendant's luggage. Although there was some uncertainty about whether the defendant consented to the search in which contraband was found and whether he was informed of his right to refuse consent, the defendant was convicted.

The Supreme Court was faced with deciding whether consent was freely given or whether the nature of the bus sweep negated the defendant's consent. The Court concluded that drug enforcement officers, after obtaining consent, may search luggage on a crowded bus without meeting the Fourth Amendment requirements for a search warrant or probable cause.

This case raises fundamental questions about the legality of new techniques used to discourage drug trafficking. Law enforcement officials are concerned about intercepting large amounts of drugs and sums of money. Bus sweeps are one answer to the drug menace. But is the Supreme Court also compromising individual Fourth Amendment rights when it considers these encounters between police and citizens to be consensual in nature?

Look for a moment at the specific facts in *Bostick.* First, when the officers entered the bus, the driver exited and closed the door, leaving the defendant and

bus sweep
Police investigation technique in which officers board a bus or train without suspicion of illegal activity and question passengers, asking for identification and seeking permission to search their baggage.

passengers alone with two officers. Second, Bostick was seated in the rear of the bus, and officers literally blocked him from exiting the bus. Third, one of the officers was clearly holding his handgun in full view. In light of these circumstances, was this a consensual or coercive search?

Bostick also raises the issue of expanding police officers' searches in public housing projects. Supporters of "gun sweeps" argue that the danger of gun violence in the urban projects constitutes an emergency circumstance in which the Supreme Court may uphold such a warrantless search.

Multiple choice 16–18

The Doctrine of Plain View and Curtilage

One final instance in which police can search for and seize evidence without benefit of a warrant is if it is in plain view. For example, if a police officer is conducting an investigation and notices while questioning some individuals that one has drugs in her pocket, the officer can seize the evidence and arrest the suspect. Or if the police are conducting a search under a warrant authorizing them to look for narcotics in a person's home and they come upon a gun, the police can seize the gun, even though it is not mentioned in the warrant. The 1986 case of *New York v. Class* illustrates the **plain view doctrine**.[19] A police officer stopped a car for a traffic violation. Wishing to check the vehicle identification number (VIN) on the dashboard, he reached into the car to clear away material that was obstructing his view. While clearing the dash, he noticed a gun under the seat—"in plain view." The U.S. Supreme Court upheld the seizure of the gun as evidence because the police officer had the right to check the VIN; therefore, the sighting of the gun was legal.

The doctrine of plain view was applied and further developed in *Arizona v. Hicks* in 1987.[20] Here, the Court held that moving a stereo component in plain view a few inches to record the serial number constituted a search under the Fourth Amendment. When a check with police headquarters revealed that the item had been stolen, the equipment was seized and offered for evidence at Hicks's trial. The Court held that a plain-view search and seizure could only be justified by prob-

plain view doctrine
Evidence that is in plain view of police officers may be seized without a search warrant.

According to the plain-view doctrine, police can seize illegal contraband without a warrant if, while investigating crime, they view it in "plain sight." If, for example, police officers spot drugs on the front seat of a car they stopped for a traffic violation, they may seize the illegal substances even though they do not have a warrant to search the vehicle.

© Bob Strong/Sipa Press

able cause, not reasonable suspicion, and suppressed the evidence against the defendant. In this case, the Court decided to take a firm stance on protecting Fourth Amendment rights. The *Hicks* decision is uncharacteristic in an era when most decisions have tended to expand the exceptions to the search warrant requirement.

An issue long associated with plain view is whether police can search open fields that are fenced in but otherwise open to view. In *Oliver v. United States* (1984), the U.S. Supreme Court distinguished between the privacy granted persons in their own home or its adjacent grounds (**curtilage**) and a field. The Court ruled that police can use airplane surveillance to spot marijuana fields and then send in squads to seize the crops, or they can peer into fields from cars for the same purpose.[21]

In *California v. Ciraola* (1986), the Court expanded the police ability to spy on criminal offenders. In this case, the police received a tip that marijuana was growing in the defendant's backyard.[22] The yard was surrounded by fences, one of which was ten feet high. The officers flew over the yard in a private plane at an altitude of 1,000 feet to ascertain whether it contained marijuana plants. On the basis of this information, a search warrant was obtained and executed, and using the evidence, Ciraola was convicted on drug charges. On appeal, the Supreme Court found that the defendant's privacy had not been violated.

This holding was expanded in 1989 in *Florida v. Riley,* when the Court ruled that police do not need a search warrant to conduct even low-altitude helicopter searches of private property.[23] The Court allowed Florida prosecutors to use evidence obtained by a police helicopter that flew 400 feet over a greenhouse in which defendants were growing marijuana plants. The Court said the search was constitutionally permissible because the flight was within airspace legally available to helicopters under federal regulations.

These cases illustrate how the concepts of curtilage and open fields have added significance in defining the scope of the Fourth Amendment in terms of the doctrine of plain view.

curtilage
Grounds or fields attached to a house.

ELECTRONIC SURVEILLANCE

The use of wiretapping to intercept conversations between parties has significantly affected police investigative procedures. Electronic devices allow people to listen to and record the private conversations of other people over telephones, through walls and windows, and even over long-distance phone lines. Using these devices, police are able to intercept communications secretly and obtain information related to criminal activity.

The earliest and most widely used form of electronic surveillance is wiretapping. With approval from the court and a search warrant, law enforcement officers place listening devices on telephones to overhear oral communications of suspects. Such devices are also often placed in homes and automobiles. The evidence collected is admissible and used in the defendant's trial.

More sophisticated devices have come into use in recent years. A pen register, for instance, is a mechanical device that records the numbers dialed on a telephone. "Trap and tracer" devices ascertain the number from which calls are placed to a particular telephone. Law enforcement agencies also obtain criminal evidence through electronic communication devices, such as electronic mail, video surveillance, and computer data transmissions, and even through thermal imaging devices that can do infrared searches of dwellings. A case currently before the U.S. Supreme Court (*Kyllo v. United States*) will discuss whether the police need a warrant before using a thermal imaging device to detect heat patterns in a home. Whatever the "star wars" capacity of this technology, the Court needs to decide if it is an illegal intrusion.

Fill in the blanks 11–12
True/False 11–13
Multiple choice 19–20
Essay 4

Electronic eavesdropping, however, represents an invasion of an individual's right to privacy unless a court gives prior permission for law enforcement personnel to intercept conversations in this manner. Police can obtain criminal evidence by eavesdropping only if such activities are controlled under rigid guidelines established under the Fourth Amendment, and they must normally request a court order based on probable cause before using electronic eavesdropping equipment.

Many citizens believe that electronic eavesdropping through hidden microphones, radio transmitters, telephone taps, and bugs represents a grave threat to personal privacy.[24] Although the use of such devices is controversial, the police are generally convinced of their value in investigating criminal activity. Opponents, however, believe that these techniques are often used beyond their lawful intent to monitor political figures, harass suspects, or investigate cases involving questionable issues of national security.

In response to concerns about invasions of privacy, the U.S. Supreme Court has increasingly limited the use of electronic eavesdropping in the criminal justice system. *Katz v. United States* (1967) is the classic example of a case in which the government failed to meet the requirements necessary to justify electronic surveillance.[25] The *Katz* doctrine is usually interpreted to mean that the government must obtain a court order if it wishes to listen in on conversations in which the parties have a reasonable expectation of privacy, such as in their own homes or on the telephone; public utterances or actions are fair game. *Katz* concluded that electronic eavesdropping is a search, even though there is no actual trespass. Therefore, it is unreasonable and a warrant is needed.

Congress has passed legislation to control the interception of oral communications. The Omnibus Crime Control Act (Title III) of 1968 initially prohibited interceptions except by warrant or with consent.[26] It established procedures for judicial approval to be obtained based on probable cause and upon application

A robbery suspect is caught on video surveillance while leaving a Citizens First bank branch in Oshkosh, Wisconsin. Police said a man who told a bank teller he had a gun robbed the bank for an undisclosed amount five minutes before the bank closed, then was videotaped leaving the bank on foot. Such photographic evidence could be used in a trial because the defendant has no expectation of privacy and therefore no warrant is required.

AP/Wide World Photos

by the attorney general or a designate. Statutory provisions also provide for the suppression of evidence when recordings are obtained in violation of the law.

The federal electronic surveillance law was modified by the Electronic Communications Privacy Act of 1986.[27] In light of technological changes, Title III of the new act was expanded to include not only all forms of wire and oral communications but virtually all types of nonaural electronic communication. The law added new offenses to the previous list of crimes for which electronic surveillance could be used and liberalized court procedures for permitting such surveillance and issuing court orders.

The United States has more than 80 million people on the Internet. The advent of e-commerce, for instance, endangers privacy and gives criminals the opportunity to steal Social Security and credit card numbers and passwords, wage cyberwar, and commit software piracy. Since almost 50 percent of Americans send or receive email every day, new legislation will be needed in the future to deal with crimes unheard of today.

The basic principle of the law of electronic surveillance is that wiretapping and other devices that violate privacy are contrary to the Fourth Amendment. As a result of technological advances, such devices probably pose a greater threat to personal privacy than do physical searches. The U.S. Supreme Court has permitted only narrow exceptions, such as court-ordered warrants and consensual monitoring.[28]

ARREST

The **arrest** power of the police involves taking a person into custody in accordance with lawful authority and holding that person to answer for a violation of the criminal law. For all practical purposes, the authority of the police to arrest a suspect is the basis for crime control; without such authority, the police would be powerless to implement the criminal law.

The power to arrest is used primarily by law enforcement officers. Generally, all enforcement personnel are employed by public police agencies, derive their authority from statutory laws, and take an oath to uphold the laws of their jurisdiction. Most police officers have complete law enforcement responsibility and unrestricted powers of arrest in their jurisdictions; they carry firearms, and they give evidence in criminal trials. In the United States, private citizens also have the right to make an arrest, generally when a crime is committed in their presence. Private citizens rarely exercise their power of arrest, except when they apprehend offenders who have committed crimes against them.

An arrest, the first formal police procedure in the criminal justice process, occurs when a police officer takes a person into custody or deprives a person of freedom for having allegedly committed a criminal offense. The police stop unlimited numbers of people each day for a variety of reasons, so the time when an arrest actually occurs may be hard to pinpoint. Some persons are stopped for short periods of questioning; others are informally detained and released; and still others are formally placed under arrest. An actual arrest occurs when the following conditions exist:

1. The police officer believes that sufficient legal evidence exists that a crime is being or has been committed and intends to restrain the suspect.
2. The police officer deprives the individual of freedom.
3. The suspect believes that he or she is in the custody of the police officer and cannot voluntarily leave.

Arrests can be initiated with or without an arrest warrant and must be based on probable cause. The **arrest warrant**, an order issued by the court, determines

arrest
Taking a person into legal custody for the purpose of restraining the accused until he or she can be held accountable for the offense at court proceedings.

Fill in the blanks 13–14
True/False 14–17
Essay 5–6

arrest warrant
Written court order authorizing and directing that an individual be taken into custody to answer criminal charges.

that an arrest should be made and directs the police to bring the named person before the court. An arrest must be based on probable cause that the person to be arrested has committed or is attempting to commit a crime. The police will ordinarily go before a judge and obtain a warrant where no danger exists that the suspect will leave the area, where a long-term investigation of organized crime is under way, or where a probable cause exists to arrest the suspect.

Most arrests are made without a warrant. The decision to arrest is often made by the police officer during contact with the suspect. However, an arrest may be made without a warrant only in the following circumstances:

1. The arresting officer is able to establish probable cause that a crime has been committed and that the defendant is the person who committed it.
2. The law of a given jurisdiction allows for arrest without a warrant.

In the case of a felony, most jurisdictions provide that a police officer may arrest a suspect without a warrant where probable cause exists, even though the officer was not present when the offense was committed. In the case of a misdemeanor, probable cause and the officer's presence at the time of the offense are required. When there is some question as to the legality of an arrest, it usually involves whether the police officer has probable cause or a reasonable belief based on reliable evidence that the suspect has committed a crime. The issue is reviewed by the judge when the suspect is brought before the court for a hearing.

As a general rule, if the police make an arrest without a warrant, the person arrested must be brought before a magistrate promptly for a probable cause hearing. The U.S. Supreme Court dealt with the meaning of "promptly" in the 1991 case of *Riverside County v. McLaughlin*.[29] The Court said that the police may detain an individual arrested without a warrant for up to 48 hours without a court hearing on whether the arrest was justified. This decision takes into account the state's interest in taking suspects into custody and the individual's concern about prolonged custody affecting employment and family relations.

PERSPECTIVES ON JUSTICE

In Texas, police may arrest drivers for failing to wear a seat belt. An officer stopped Gail Atwater for this offense as she drove her two children home from soccer practice in Lago Vista, near Austin. The officer had recently mistakenly stopped Atwater for not wearing a seat belt, but he got her this time.

Under Texas law, she had committed a misdemeanor. She alleged that the officer yelled at her and frightened her children, ages 4 and 6. A friend took the children home, but the officer handcuffed Atwater and took her to the station. She was there for an hour while her mug shot was taken. Atwater was also found to be driving without a license and lacked proof of insurance.

The standards for determining whether the police action was reasonable under the circumstances in this case is difficult. Some might argue that Atwater's traffic violation was not a breach of the peace, while others might suggest that Atwater's arrest was legal because she had violated the state statute. Whatever your opinion is, in April 2001 the Supreme Court upheld the right to arrest a suspect for a traffic violation. This decision appears to be a victory for those holding the crime-control perspective. (See no. 99-1408, U.S. Supreme Ct. 2000–2001.)

CUSTODIAL INTERROGATION

A suspect taken into police custody—on the street, in a police car, or at the police station—must be warned at the time of arrest of the right under the Fifth Amendment to be free from self-incrimination before police conduct any questioning.

The *Miranda* Warning

In the landmark case of *Miranda v. Arizona* (1966), the Supreme Court held that the police must give the *Miranda* warning to a person in custody before questioning begins.[30] Suspects in custody must be told that they have the following rights:

Fill in the blanks 14
True/False 18
Multiple choice 21
Essay 7

1. They have the right to remain silent.
2. If they decide to make a statement, the statement can and will be used against them in a court of law.
3. They have the right to have an attorney present at the time of the interrogation, or they will have an opportunity to consult with an attorney.
4. If they cannot afford an attorney, one will be appointed for them by the state.

Some suspects choose to remain silent, and because oral as well as written statements are admissible in court, police officers often do not elicit any statements without making certain a defense attorney is present. If an accused decides to answer any questions, he or she may also stop at any time and refuse to answer further questions. A suspect's constitutional rights under *Miranda* can be given up (waived), however. Consequently, a suspect should give careful consideration before abrogating any custodial rights under the *Miranda* warning.

Read the full text of the *Miranda v. Arizona* opinion at http://laws.findlaw.com/us/384/436.html
For an up-to-date list of Web links, see http://www.wadsworth.com/product/0534573053s

More than 30 years have passed since this warning was established by the Warren Court. During this time, U.S. appellate courts have heard literally thousands of cases involving alleged violations of the *Miranda* rights, including custodial interrogation, right to counsel, and statements made to persons other than the police. Some experts believe felons have been freed because *Miranda* protects the right to be free from self-incrimination. What follows is an analysis of this often litigated and hotly contested legal issue.

Historical Perspective on *Miranda*

Prior to the *Miranda* safeguards, a confession could be obtained from a suspect who had not consulted with an attorney. An early ruling in *Brown v. Mississippi* (1936) held that statements obtained by physical coercion were inadmissible evidence, but it also limited the use of counsel to aid the accused at this early stage of the criminal process.[31] Not until 1964, in *Escobedo v. Illinois,* was the groundwork laid for the landmark *Miranda* decision.[32] In *Escobedo,* the Supreme Court finally recognized the critical relationship between the Fifth Amendment privilege against self-incrimination and the Sixth Amendment right to counsel. Danny Escobedo was a convicted murderer who maintained that the police interrogation forced him to make incriminating statements that were regarded as a voluntary confession. The Court recognized that he had been denied the assistance of counsel, which was critical during police interrogation. With this decision, the Court made clear its concern that the accused be guaranteed certain due process rights during interrogation.

Fill in the blanks 15
True/False 19–21
Multiple choice 22

Two years later came the *Miranda* decision, which had a historic impact on police interrogation practices at the arrest stage of the criminal justice process. Prior to *Miranda,* the police often obtained confessions through questioning methods that violated the constitutional right against self-incrimination. The

Supreme Court declared in *Miranda* that the police have a duty to inform defendants of their rights. Certain specific procedures (that is, the *Miranda* warning) must be followed, or any statements by a defendant will be excluded from evidence. The purpose of the warning is to implement the basic Fifth Amendment right to be free from self-incrimination.

As a result, the interrogation process is protected by the Fifth Amendment; if the accused is not given the *Miranda* warning, any evidence obtained during interrogation is not admissible to prove the state's case. It is important to note, however, that the *Miranda* decision does not deny the police the opportunity to ask a suspect general questions as a witness at the scene of an unsolved crime, as long as the person is not in custody and the questioning is of an investigative and nonaccusatory nature. In addition, a suspect can still offer a voluntary confession after the *Miranda* warning has been issued.

After the *Miranda* decision, many people became concerned that the Supreme Court under Chief Justice Earl Warren had gone too far in providing procedural protections to the defendant. Some nationally prominent persons expressed opinions that made it seem as if the Supreme Court were emptying the prisons of criminals. Law enforcement officers throughout the nation generally have been disturbed by the *Miranda* decision, believing that it seriously hampers their efforts to obtain confessions and other self-incriminating statements from defendants. On the other hand, some research indicates that the decision has had little effect on the number of confessions obtained by the police, and that it has not affected the rate of convictions.[33] Since *Miranda,* little empirical evidence has been produced showing that the decision has had a detrimental impact on law enforcement efforts. Instead, it seems apparent that the police formerly relied too heavily on confessions to prove a defendant's guilt. Other forms of evidence, such as witness statements, physical evidence, and expert testimony, have proved adequate to win the prosecution's case. Blaming *Miranda* for increased crime rates is debatable.[34] The real reasons crime may be out of control lie in the drug problem and an overwhelmed justice system, not the enforcement of constitutional rights.

The *Miranda* decision is summarized in the Law in Review feature, along with the case of *Dickerson v. United States* (2000),[35] which reaffirmed the *Miranda* rule. Table 8.1 summarizes a number of the most significant Fourth and Fifth Amendment Supreme Court decisions that have had an impact on law enforcement practices and individual rights.

Multiple choice 23–24
Essay 8

booking
The administrative record of an arrest listing the offender's name, address, physical description, date of birth, employer, time of arrest, offense, and name of arresting officer; also includes photographing and fingerprinting of the offender.

lineup
Placing a suspect in a group for the purpose of being viewed and identified by a witness.

THE PRETRIAL IDENTIFICATION PROCESS

After the accused is arrested, he or she is ordinarily brought to the police station, where the police list the possible criminal charges. At the same time, they obtain other information, such as a description of the offender and the circumstances of the offense, for booking purposes. The **booking** process is a police administrative procedure in which generally the date and time of the arrest are recorded; arrangements are made for bail, detention, or removal to court; and any other information needed for identification is obtained. The defendant may be fingerprinted, photographed, and required to participate in a lineup.

In a **lineup**, a suspect is placed in a group for the purpose of being viewed and identified by a witness. Lineups are one of the primary means the police have of identifying suspects. Others are show-ups, which occur at the crime scene, and photo displays or mug shots of possible suspects. In accordance with the U.S. Supreme Court decisions in *United States v. Wade* (1967) and *Kirby v. Illinois* (1972), the accused has the right to have counsel present at this postindictment lineup or identification procedure.[36]

TABLE 8.1 NOTABLE CASE DOCTRINES AND EXCEPTIONS TO THE FOURTH AMENDMENT (SEARCH AND SEIZURE) AND FIFTH AMENDMENT (SELF-INCRIMINATION) CLAUSES

	Case Decision	Holding
Fourth Amendment Doctrine		
Expectation of privacy	*Katz v. United States* (1968)	Electronic eavesdropping is a search.
Plain view	*Arizona v. Hicks* (1967)	Fourth Amendment may not apply when the object is in plain view.
Open fields	*Oliver v. United States* (1984)	To what extent can police search a field and curtilage?
Warrant Requirements		
Probable cause	*Illinois v. Gates* (1983)	Probable cause to issue a warrant is based on a "totality of circumstances."
Exceptions to the Warrant Requirement		
Federal requirement of exclusionary rule	*Weeks v. United States* (1914)	U.S. Supreme Court applied the exclusionary rule to federal prosecutions.
State application	*Mapp v. Ohio* (1961)	U.S. Supreme Court applied the exclusionary rule to state prosecutions.
Automobile search	*United States v. Ross* (1982)	Warrantless search of an auto is permissible when it is based on probable cause.
Search incident to arrest	*Chimel v. California* (1969)	Permissible scope for a search is the area "within the arrestee's immediate control."
Fourth Amendment Doctrine		
Stop and frisk	*Terry v. Ohio* (1967)	Police are authorized to stop and frisk suspicious persons.
Consent	*Schneckloth v. Bustamonte* (1973)	Consent to search must be voluntarily given.
Bus sweep	*Florida v. Bostick* (1991)	Police, after obtaining consent, may conduct a search of luggage without a search warrant or probable cause.
Exceptions to the Exclusionary Rule		
Good faith	*United States v. Leon* (1984)	When police rely on "good faith" in a warrant, the evidence seized is admissible even if the warrant is subsequently deemed defective.
Good faith	*Arizona v. Evans* (1995)	Even though police arrested a man based on an erroneous warrant that resulted from a court employee's computer error, the evidence they found in a subsequent search is admissible.
Fifth Amendment Doctrine		
Self-incrimination	*Miranda v. Arizona* (1966)	Defendant must be given the *Miranda* warning before questioning begins.
Miranda warning	*Dickerson v. United States* (2000)	Congress cannot overrule the requirements that *Miranda* rights be read to criminal suspects.

Miranda v. Arizona (1966) and *Dickerson v. U.S.* (2000)

Miranda v. Arizona is a landmark decision that climaxed a long line of self-incrimination cases in which the police used unlawful methods to obtain confessions from suspects accused of committing a crime.

Facts

Ernesto Miranda, a 25-year-old mentally retarded man, was arrested in Phoenix, Arizona, and charged with kidnapping and rape. Miranda was taken from his home to a police station, where he was identified by a complaining witness. He was then interrogated and, after about two hours, signed a written confession. Miranda was subsequently convicted and sentenced to 20 to 30 years in prison. His conviction was affirmed by the Arizona Supreme Court, and he appealed to the U.S. Supreme Court, claiming that he had not been warned that any statement he made would be used against him and that he had not been advised of any right to have counsel present at his interrogation.

The *Miranda* case was one of four cases heard simultaneously by the U.S. Supreme Court that dealt with the legality of confessions obtained by the police from a suspect in custody. In *Vignera v. New York,* the defendant was arrested in connection with a robbery and taken to two different detective headquarters, where he was interrogated and subsequently confessed after eight hours in custody. In *Westover v. United States,* the suspect was arrested by the Kansas City police, placed in a lineup, and booked on a felony charge. He was interrogated

by the police during the evening and in the morning and by the FBI in the afternoon, when he signed two confessions. In *California v. Stewart,* the defendant was arrested at his home for being involved in a robbery. He was taken to a police station and placed in a cell, where over a period of five days he was interrogated nine times. The U.S. Supreme Court in *Miranda* described the common characteristics of these four cases:

> In each, the defendant was questioned by the police in a room in which he was cut off from the outside world. In none of these cases was the defendant given a full and effective warning of his rights at the outset of the interrogation process. In all the cases, the questioning elicited oral admissions, and in three of them, signed statements as well which were admitted at their trials. They all thus share salient features—incommunicado interrogation of individuals in a police-dominated atmosphere, resulting in self-incriminating statements without full warnings of constitutional rights.

Decision

The major constitutional issue in *Miranda,* as in the other three cases, was the admissibility of statements obtained from a defendant questioned while in custody or while otherwise deprived of his freedom. The Fifth Amendment provides that no person shall be compelled to be a witness against himself. This means that a defendant cannot be required to testify at his trial and that a suspect who is questioned before trial cannot be subjected to any physical or psychological pressure to confess.

In the opinion of Chief Justice Earl Warrant in the *Miranda* case, the "third degree method was still 'sufficiently widespread to be the object of concern.'" Of greater concern, he believed, was the increased use of sophisticated psychological pressures on suspects during interrogation. Thus, in a 5-to-4 decision, Miranda's conviction was overturned, and the Court established specific procedural guidelines for police to follow before eliciting statements from persons in police custody.

The Court's own summary of its decision was as follows:

> Our holding will be spelled out with some specificity in the pages which follow but briefly it is this: the prosecution may not use statements, whether exculpatory or inculpatory, stemming from custodial interrogation of the defendant unless it demonstrates the use of procedural safeguards effective to secure the privilege against self-incrimination. By custodial interrogation, we mean questioning initiated by law enforcement officers after a person has been taken into custody or otherwise deprived of his freedom of action in any significant way. As for the procedural safeguards to be employed, unless fully effective means are devised to inform accused persons of their right of silence and to assure a continuous opportunity to exercise it, the following measures are required. Prior to any questioning the person must be warned that he has a right to remain silent, that any statement he does make may be used as evidence against him, and that he has a right to the presence of an attorney, either retained or appointed. The defendant may waive effectuation of

these rights, provided the waiver is made voluntarily, knowingly and intelligently. If, however, he indicates in any manner and at any stage of the process that he wishes to consult with an attorney before speaking there can be no questioning. Likewise, if the individual is alone and indicates in any manner that he does not wish to be interrogated, the police may not question him. The mere fact that he may have answered some questions or volunteered some statements on his own does not deprive him of the right to refrain from answering any further inquiries until he has consulted with an attorney and thereafter consents to be questioned.

Significance of the Case

The *Miranda* decision established that the Fifth Amendment right against self-incrimination requires that a criminal suspect in custody or in any other manner deprived of freedom must be informed of his or her rights. If the suspect is not warned, then any evidence given is not admissible by the government to prove its case.

Dickerson v. United States (2000)
Facts

Charles Dickerson, a Maryland resident, voluntarily confessed to a series of bank robberies before he was read his *Miranda* warning. The federal district court ruled the confession inadmissible, but the Court of Appeals ruled that a confession that is determined to be voluntary may be admitted as evidence despite a technical violation of the *Miranda* warning.

Decision

On appeal, the Supreme Court ruled that *Miranda* governs the admissibility of statements made during custodial interrogation in both state and federal courts. Even though Congress had passed 18 USC §3501 in 1968, ostensibly overruling *Miranda* and making voluntariness the sole standard for the admissibility of confessions, that standard was largely ignored by prosecutors and the federal courts over the years.

The Court stated that *Miranda* is a constitutional decision that cannot be overruled by an Act of Congress. It noted that remedies are available for curbing abusive police conduct and did not agree that Section 3501 was sufficient to replace *Miranda* warnings for protecting the right against self-incrimination.

Significance of the Case

In declining to overrule *Miranda,* the Court made three major points:
1. Prior decisions by the Court applying the case narrowly did not justify a conclusion that *Miranda* was not a constitutional mandate.
2. The *Miranda* warnings are now imbedded in police practices and procedures, and there would be little value in changing them today.
3. The rule of *stare decisis,* which discourages the overruling of long-standing constitutional precedent, militated against overruling *Miranda* after it had been the law of the land for more than 34 years.

The Court's decision was a complete reaffirmation of the *Miranda v. Arizona* decision.

In short, those who had long awaited an opportunity for eliminating the warning/waiver requirements of *Miranda* received no solace from the Court in the *Dickerson* decision. The Court reemphasized that due process voluntariness is the touchstone for confession admissibility but retained the *Miranda* warning and waiver as necessary to the admission of a confession.[37]

InfoTrac College Edition Research

Many experts consider the *Miranda* case the hallmark decision of the Warren Court. To learn more about this landmark case, go to InfoTrac College Edition and read

Richard Leo, "*Miranda* Revisited," *Journal of Criminal Law and Criminology,* 1996, v86 p621

Donald Dripps, "Is *Miranda* Case Law Inconsistent? A Fifth Amendment Synthesis," *Constitutional Community,* 2000, v17 p19

During the booking process, police identify suspects, take their fingerprints, bring in witnesses for purposes of identification, and interrogate suspects about their suspected criminal activities.

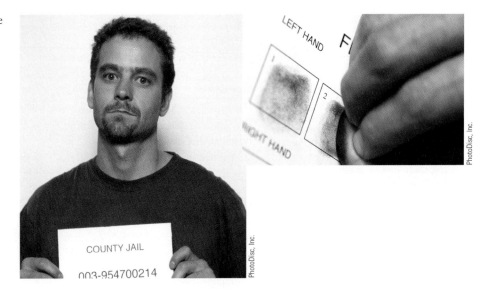

In the *Wade* case, the Supreme Court held that a defendant has a right to counsel if the lineup takes place after the suspect has been formally charged with a crime. This decision was based on the Court's belief that the postindictment lineup procedure is a critical stage of the criminal justice process. In contrast, the suspect does not have a comparable right to counsel at a pretrial lineup where a complaint or indictment has not been issued. Right to counsel does not apply until judicial proceedings have begun and the defendant is formally charged with a crime. When the right to counsel is violated, the evidence of any pretrial identification must be excluded from the trial.

One of the most difficult legal issues in this area is determining if the identification procedure is "suggestive" and consequently in violation of the due process clause of the Fifth and Fourteenth Amendments. According to Zalman and Siegel, "the ability to identify the criminal defendant as the person who committed the crime charged is a necessary element in the prosecution of offenders."[38] In *Simmons v. United States* (1968), the Supreme Court said, "The primary evil to be avoided is a very substantial likelihood of irreparable misidentification."[39] In its decision in *Neil v. Biggers* (1972), the Court established the following general criteria to judge the suggestiveness of a pretrial identification procedure:

1. The opportunity of the witness to view the criminal at the time of the crime
2. The degree of attention by the witness and the accuracy of the prior description by the witness
3. The level of certainty demonstrated by the witness
4. The length of time between the crime and the confrontation[40]

Weighing all these factors, the Court determines the substantial likelihood of misidentification.

True/False 22–24
Multiple choice 25–27

exclusionary rule
The principle that prohibits using illegally obtained evidence in a trial.

THE EXCLUSIONARY RULE

No review of the legal aspects of policing would be complete without a discussion of the **exclusionary rule**, the principal means used to restrain police conduct. The Fourth Amendment guarantees individuals the right to be secure in their persons, homes, papers, and effects against unreasonable searches and seizures. The exclusionary rule provides that all evidence obtained by illegal searches and seizures is inadmissible in criminal trials. Similarly, it excludes the use of illegal confessions under Fifth Amendment prohibitions.

For many years, evidence obtained by unreasonable searches and seizures that consequently should have been considered illegal was admitted by state and federal governments in criminal trials. The only criteria for admissibility were whether the evidence was incriminating and whether it would assist the judge or jury in ascertaining the innocence or guilt of the defendant. How the evidence was obtained was unimportant; its admissibility was determined by its relevance to the criminal case.

In 1914, however, the rules on the admissibility of evidence underwent a change of direction when the Supreme Court decided the case of *Weeks v. United States*.[41] The defendant, Freemont Weeks, was accused by federal law enforcement authorities of using the mail for illegal purposes. After his arrest, the home in which Weeks was staying was searched without a valid search warrant. Evidence in the form of letters and other materials was found in his room and admitted at the trial. Weeks was then convicted of the federal offense based on the incriminating evidence. On appeal, the Supreme Court held that evidence obtained by unreasonable search and seizure must be excluded in a federal criminal trial.

Thus, for the first time, the Court held that the Fourth Amendment barred the use of evidence obtained through illegal search and seizure in a federal prosecution. With this ruling, the Court established the exclusionary rule. The rule was based not on legislation but on judicial decision making. Can the criminal go free because the constable blunders? That became the question.

In 1961, the Supreme Court made the exclusionary rule applicable to the state courts in the landmark decision of *Mapp v. Ohio*. Because of the importance of the *Mapp* case, it is highlighted in the Law in Review feature.[42]

Read the full text of the *Mapp v. Ohio* decision at http://laws.findlaw.com/us/367/643.html

For an up-to-date list of Web links, see http://www.wadsworth.com/product/0534573053s

Current Status

In the 1980s, a more conservative U.S. Supreme Court gradually began to limit the scope of the exclusionary rule. In *Illinois v. Gates* (1983), the Court made it easier for police to search a suspect's home, by allowing an anonymous letter to be used as evidence in support of a warrant.[43] In another critical case, *United States v. Leon* (1984), the Court ruled that evidence seized by police relying on a warrant issued by a detached and neutral magistrate can be used in a court proceeding, even if the judge who issued the warrant may have relied on less than sufficient evidence.[44] In this case, the Court articulated a **good faith exception** to the exclusionary rule: Evidence obtained with a less-than-adequate search warrant may be admissible in court if the police officers acted in good faith on obtaining court approval for their search. However, deliberately misleading a judge or using a warrant that the police know is unreasonably deficient would be grounds to invoke the exclusionary rule. Although prosecutors initially applauded the *Leon* decision and defense lawyers feared that police would be inclined to secure warrants from sympathetic judges, both groups agree that *Leon* has had little practical effect on the processing of criminal cases. Further, most experts believe that no important data exist to prove that the exclusionary rule has had a direct impact on police behavior.

In 1995, in one of the most important exclusionary rule cases since *Leon* (1984), *Arizona v. Evans* presented a compelling argument for further applying the good faith exception.[45]

The facts in *Evans* are relatively simple. Phoenix police officers stopped the defendant for a vehicular violation and ran a computer check, which showed an outstanding arrest warrant. As Evans was being arrested, he dropped a marijuana cigarette; more of the drug was seized after being found in the car.

There was one problem with the seizure. Seventeen days earlier, the Phoenix Justice Court had quashed the arrest warrant; it was unclear why the arrest

good faith exception
The principle that evidence may be used in a criminal trial even though the search warrant used to obtain it was technically faulty, so long as the police acted in good faith when they sought the warrant from a judge.

LAW IN REVIEW

Mapp v. Ohio (1961)

In this historic case, the U.S. Supreme Court held that all law enforcement agents, federal and state, are affected by the exclusionary rule, which bars the admission of illegally obtained evidence in a criminal trial.

Facts

On May 23, 1957, three police officers arrive at Dolree Mapp's residence after receiving information that "a person [was] hiding out in the home, who was wanted for questioning in connection with a recent bombing, and that there was a large amount of police paraphernalia being hidden in the home." Mapp and her daughter by a former marriage lived on the top floor of the two-family dwelling. The officers knocked on the door and demanded entrance, but Mapp, after telephoning her attorney, refused to admit them without a search warrant.

The officers again sought entrance three hours later when four or more additional officers arrived on the scene. When Mapp did not immediately come to the door, the police forcible opened one of the doors to the house and gained admittance. Meanwhile, Mapp's attorney arrived, but the officers would not permit him to see Mapp or to enter the house. Mapp was halfway down the stairs when the officers broke into the hall. She demanded to see the search warrant. One of the officers waved a piece of paper and claimed it was the search warrant. She grabbed the "warrant" and placed it in her bosom. A struggle ensued in which the officers recovered the piece of paper and handcuffed Mapp.

Mapp was then forcibly taken upstairs to her bedroom, where the officers searched a dresser, a chest of drawers, a closet, and some suitcases. They also looked into a photo album and through personal papers belonging to her. The search spread to the rest of the second floor, including the child's bedroom, the living room, the kitchen, and the dinette. In the course of the search, the police officers found pornographic literature. Mapp was arrested and subsequently convicted in an Ohio court of possessing obscene materials.

Decision

The question in the *Mapp* case was whether the evidence was seized in violation of the search-and-seizure provisions of the Fourth Amendment and therefore inadmissible in the state trial, which had resulted in an obscenity conviction. The Supreme Court of Ohio found the conviction valid. However, the U.S. Supreme Court overturned it, stating that the Fourth Amendment's prohibition against unreasonable searches and seizures, enforceable against the states through the due process clause, had been violated. Justice Tom Clark, delivering the majority opinion of the Court, made clear the importance of this constitutional right in the administration of criminal justice:

> There are those who say, as did Justice (then Judge) Cardozo, that under our constitutional exclusionary doctrine "(t)he criminal is to go free because the constable has blundered." In some cases this will undoubtedly be the result. But . . . there is another consideration—the imperative of judicial integrity. . . . The criminal goes free, if he must, but it is the law that sets him free. Nothing can destroy a government more quickly than its failure to observe its own laws, or worse its disregard of the charter of its own existence.

Significance of the Case

In previous decisions, the U.S. Supreme Court had refused to exclude evidence in state court proceedings based on Fourth Amendment violations of search and seizure. The *Mapp* case overruled such decisions, including *Wolf v. Colorado,* and held that evidence gathered in violation of the Fourth Amendment would be inadmissible in a state prosecution. For the first time, the Court imposed federal constitutional standards on state law enforcement personnel. In addition, the Court reemphasized the point that a relationship exists between the Fourth and Fifth Amendments, which forms the constitutional basis for the exclusionary rule.

InfoTrac College Edition Research

The exclusionary rule operates to exclude from admission in a trial evidence determined to be the product of an unconstitutional search or seizure; in the *Mapp* case, the Supreme Court applied the exclusionary rule to the states. For more on this controversial rule, go to InfoTrac College Edition and check under such terms as "search and seizure," "Fourth Amendment," and "exclusionary rule." In particular, see

Timothy Lynch, "In Defense of the Exclusionary Rule," *USA Today Magazine,* 1999, v129, p22

John Wasowicz, "Future of the Exclusionary Rule," *Trial Magazine,* 1998, v34 p79

warrant had not been removed from the police computer. The trial judge refused to admit the evidence gathered during the traffic stop on grounds that the computer error was caused by negligence of the law enforcement authorities. The Arizona Supreme Court affirmed the trial court, stating that it is repugnant to the principles of a free society that a person should ever be taken into custody because of a careless computer error.

In a close vote, the U.S. Supreme Court ruled that the evidence did not have to be suppressed under the exclusionary rule. The exclusionary rule was designed as a means of deterring police misconduct, not mistakes by employees, and it does not apply where police have acted in objectively reasonable reliance on an apparently valid warrant.

In these and other cases, the Court has made it easier for the police to conduct searches of criminal suspects and their possessions and then use the seized evidence in court proceedings. The Court has indicated that, as a general rule, the protection afforded the individual by the Fourth Amendment may take a back seat to concerns about public safety if criminal actions pose a clear threat to society.

The Future of the Exclusionary Rule   Essay 9

The exclusionary rule has long been a controversial subject in the administration of criminal justice. It was originally conceived to control illegitimate police practices, and that remains its primary purpose today. It is justified on the basis that it deters illegal searches and seizures. Yet most experts believe that no impartial data exist to prove that the rule has a direct impact on police behavior. This is by far the most significant criticism of the rule. By excluding evidence, the rule has a more direct effect on the criminal trial than on the police officer on the street. Furthermore, the rule is powerless when the police have no interest in prosecuting the accused or in obtaining a conviction. In addition, it does not control the wholesale harassment of individuals by law enforcement officials bent on disregarding constitutional rights.

The most popular criticism of the exclusionary rule, however, is that it allows guilty defendants to go free. Because courts frequently decide in many types of cases (particularly those involving victimless offenses, such as gambling and drug use) that certain evidence should be excluded, the rule is believed to result in excessive court delays and to negatively affect plea-bargaining negotiations. However, the rule appears to result in relatively few case dismissals.

Suggested approaches to dealing with violations of the exclusionary rule include the following:

1. Criminal prosecution of police officers who violate constitutional rights
2. Internal police control
3. Civil lawsuits against state or municipal police officers
4. Federal lawsuits against the government under the Federal Tort Claims Act

An individual using any of these alternatives, however, would be faced with such obstacles as the cost of bringing a lawsuit, proving damages, and dealing with a bureaucratic law enforcement system.

In the end, of all the civilized countries in the world, only the United States applies an exclusionary rule to illegal searches and seizures of material evidence. Whether the Supreme Court or legislative bodies adopt any more significant changes to the rule will depend largely on efforts by police to discipline themselves. It will also depend on a tough civil tort remedy that allows lawsuits and claims for damages against offending police officers.

The fate of the exclusionary rule remains difficult to predict. Although it is a simple rule of evidence, it involves complex issues of fairness, justice, and crime control.[46] Modifications to the exclusionary rule are a perennial issue before legislators and the courts.

PERSPECTIVES ON JUSTICE

Throughout the past decade, the U.S. Congress has tried to legislate the admissibility of evidence from illegal searches and seizures. Do you think such evidence should be admissible even if the police deliberately violate the Constitution? Which branch of government, legislative or judicial, do you believe is more powerful in the area of criminal justice? Curtailing the use of the exclusionary rule would widen the scope of the justice and crime control perspective but reduce due process protections for the defendant.

SUMMARY

Law enforcement officers use many different investigatory techniques to detect and apprehend criminal offenders, including searches, electronic eavesdropping, interrogation, informants, surveillance, and witness identification procedures. Over the past three decades, in particular through U.S. Supreme Court decisions, serious constitutional limitations have been place on the pretrial process. Under interpretations of the Fourth Amendment, for example, police are required to use warrants to conduct searches except in some clearly defined situations. The exceptions to the search warrant rule include searches of automobiles used in a crime, stop and frisk, searches incident to an arrest, and searches of material in plain view.

Police interrogation procedures have also been reviewed extensively. Through the *Miranda* rule, the Supreme Court established a procedure required for all custodial interrogations. Many issues concerning *Miranda* continue to be litigated. Lineups and other suspect identification practices have also been subject to court review. The degree to which a defendant's rights should be protected at the pretrial stage while maintaining the government's interest in crime control remains a source of constant debate in the criminal justice system.

The exclusionary rule continues to be one of the most controversial issues in the criminal justice system. Even though the courts have curtailed its application in recent years, it still generally prohibits the admission of evidence obtained in violation of the defendant's constitutional rights. The exclusionary rule is an example of a federal rule that has been made binding on the states—a judicial remedy dating back more than three-quarters of a century.

The National Criminal Justice Reference Service links to additional resources related to U.S. Government, Supreme Court, and specific decisions: http://www.ncjrs.org

For an up-to-date list of Web links, see http://www.wadsworth.com/product/0534573053s

Key Terms

search and seizure	search incident to a lawful arrest	arrest
search warrant	threshold inquiry	arrest warrant
reasonableness	stop and frisk	booking
probable cause	bus sweep	lineup
particularity	plain view doctrine	exclusionary rule
hearsay evidence	curtilage	good faith exception

Discussion Questions

1. Should obviously guilty persons go free because police originally arrested them with less than probable cause?
2. Should illegally seized evidence be excluded from trial, even though it is conclusive proof of a person's criminal acts?
3. Should police be personally liable if they violate a person's constitutional rights? How might this influence their investigations?
4. Should a person be put in a lineup without the benefit of counsel?
5. Have criminals been given too many rights? Should courts be more concerned with the rights of the victims or the rights of offenders?
6. Does the exclusionary rule effectively deter police misconduct?
7. Can a search and seizure be "reasonable" if it is not authorized by a warrant?
8. What is the purpose of the *Miranda* warnings?
9. What is a pretrial traffic stop?

A CLOSER LOOK

For much of the past three decades, law enforcement has ruled at the Supreme Court. The Court has given police more power to stop motorists, search homes, and put defendants in jail. Except for landmark cases such as *Miranda v. Arizona* and *Mapp v. Ohio,* the justices have allowed the police to crack down on crime and expand their power.

But there has been a modest reversal in recent years. New criminal disputes have produced surprisingly lopsided decisions favoring defendants. None was more symbolic than the 2000 ruling backing the *Miranda* requirement.

Several other recent rulings suggest that the Court has become increasingly suspicious about aggressive techniques police are using to counter drugs and gun violence. In one case, the Court ruled that police may not stop and frisk someone simply because an anonymous tipster said he was carrying a gun. The decision rejected the argument that the danger posed by illegal guns should give the police more latitude (see *Florida v. J.L.,* 120 S.Ct. 1375, 2000). In another dispute, the

Court ruled that police cannot look for drugs by randomly squeezing the luggage of bus passengers (*Bond v. United States,* 120 S.Ct. 1462, 2000).

Cases reaching the Supreme Court continue to determine how far police officers can go to crack down on crime. Read the following articles from InfoTrac College Edition:

George Thomas, "The End of the Road for *Miranda v. Arizona*?" *American Criminal Law Review,* 2000, v37 p1

Jerry Riggs, "Excluding Automobile Passengers from the Fourth Amendment," *Journal of Criminal Law and Criminology,* 1998, v88 p957

Both articles raise important questions regarding the history and future of rules for police interrogation and search and seizure law.

What standards does the Court use to balance the interests of police officers versus defendants when determining the reasonableness of an inquiry?

Notes

1. *Wyoming v. Houghton,* 119 S.Ct. 1297 (1999); also David Savage, "Privacy Rights Pulled Over," *American Bar Association Journal* 86 (1999): 42.
2. *Bond v. United States,* 120 S.Ct. 1462 (2000).
3. William Greenhalgh, *The Fourth Amendment Handbook: A Chronological Survey of Supreme Court Decisions* (Chicago: American Bar Association Section on Criminal Justice, 1995); see Robert Greenberger, "Next President to Tip Balance of Supreme Court," *Wall Street Journal,* 2 October 2000, p. A36.
4. See Wayne LaFave, *Arrest: The Decision to Take a Suspect into Custody* (Boston: Little, Brown, 1965); Lawrence P. Tiffany, Donald McIntyre, and Daniel Rotenberg, *Detection of Crime: Stopping and Question, Search and Seizure* (Boston: Little, Brown,

1967); Wayne LaFave, *Search and Seizure: A Treatise on the Fourth Amendment* (St. Paul, MN: West Publishing, 1978); also William A. Grimes, *Criminal Law Outline—1996* (Reno: University of Nevada, National Judicial College, 1996).
5. 393 U.S. 410, 89 S.Ct. 584, 21 L.Ed.2d 637 (1969).
6. 378 U.S. 108, 84 S.Ct. 1509, 12 L.Ed.2d 723 (1964).
7. 462 U.S. 213, 103 S.Ct. 2317, 76 L.Ed.2d 527 (1983).
8. 395 U.S. 752, 89 S.Ct. 2034, 23 L.Ed.2d 685 (1969).
9. 392 U.S. 1, 88 S.Ct. 1868, 20 L.Ed.2d 899 (1968).
10. 508 U.S. 366, 113 S.Ct. 2130, 124 L.Ed.2d 334 (1993).
11. 267 U.S. 132, 45 S.Ct. 280, 69 L.Ed.2d 543 (1925); also James Rodgers, "Poi-

soned Fruit: Quest for Consistent Rule on Traffic Stop Searches," *American Bar Association Journal* 81 (1995): 50–51.
12. 456 U.S. 798, 102 S.Ct. 2157, 72 L.Ed.2d 572 (1982); see also Barry Latzer, "Searching Cars and Their Contents: *U.S. v. Ross,*" *Criminal Law Bulletin* 6 (1982): 220; Joseph Grano, "Rethinking the Fourth Amendment Warrant Requirements," *Criminal Law Review* 19 (1982): 603.
13. 440 U.S. 648, 99 S.Ct. 1391, 59 L.Ed.2d 660 (1979); see also Lance Rogers, "The Drunk-Driving Roadblock: Random Seizure or Minimal Intrusion?" *Criminal Law Bulletin* 21 (1985): 197–217.
14. 434 U.S. 106, 98 S.Ct. 330, 54 L.Ed.2d 331 (1977).
15. No. 99-1030, U.S. Supreme Court, 2000–2001.

16 391 U.S. 543, 88 S.Ct. 1788, 20 L.Ed.2d 797 (1968).

17 412 U.S. 218, 93 S.Ct. 2041, 36 L.Ed.2d 854 (1973).

18 *Florida v. Bostick,* 501 U.S. 429, 111 S.Ct. 2382, 115 L.Ed.2d 389 (1991).

19 475 U.S. 106, 106 S.Ct. 960, 89 L.Ed.2d 81 (1986).

20 480 U.S. 321, 107 S.Ct, 1149, 94 L.Ed.2d 347 (1987).

21 466 U.S. 170, 104 S.Ct. 1735, 80 L.Ed.2d 214 (1984).

22 476 U.S. 207, 106 S.Ct. 1809, 90 L.Ed.2d 210 (1986).

23 488 U.S. 445, 109 S.Ct. 693, 102 L.Ed.2d 835 (1989).

24 Gary T. Marx, *Undercover: Police Surveillance in America* (Berkeley: University of California Press, 1988).

25 389 U.S. 347, 88 S.Ct. 507, 19 L.Ed.2d 576 (1967).

26 Omnibus Crime Control Act, Title III, 90th Congress 1968; 18 U.S.C. (2511–2520.

27 Electronic Communications and Privacy Act of 1986, Public Law No. 99-508, title 18 U.S.C. (2510.

28 See Michael Goldsmith, "The Supreme Court and Title III: Rewriting the Law of Electronic Surveillance," *Journal of Criminal Law and Criminology* 74 (1983): 76–85.

29 500 U.S. 44, 111 S.Ct. 1661, 114 L.Ed.2d 49 (1991).

30 384 U.S. 436, 86 S.Ct. 1602, 16 L.Ed.2d 694 (1966).

31 297 U.S. 278, 56 S.Ct. 461, 80 L.Ed.2d 682 (1936).

32 378 U.S. 478, 84 S.Ct. 1758, 12 L.Ed.2d 977 (1964).

33 Michael Wald et al., "Interrogations in New Haven: The Impact of *Miranda,*" *Yale Law Journal* 76 (1967): 1519; see also Walter Lippman, "*Miranda v. Arizona*—Twenty Years Later," *Criminal Justice Journal* 9 (1987): 241; Stephen J. Schulhofer, "Reconsidering *Miranda,*" *University of Chicago Law Review* 54 (1987): 435–461; also Paul Cassell, "How Many Criminals Has *Miranda* Set Free?" *Wall Street Journal,* 1 March 1995, p. A12.

34 "Don't Blame *Miranda,*" *Washington Post,* 2 December 1988, p. A26; also Scott Lewis "*Miranda* Today: Death of a Talisman," *Prosecutor* 28 (1994): 18–25; Richard Leo, "The Impact of *Miranda* Revisited," *Journal of Criminal Law and Criminology* 86 (1996): 621–648.

35 No. 99-5525 (2000).

36 388 U.S. 218, 87 S.Ct. 1926, 18 L.Ed.2d 1149 (1967); 406 U.S. 682, 92 S.Ct. 1877, 32 L.Ed.2d 40 (1972).

37 *Dickerson v. United States,* 120 S.Ct. 158 (2000).

38 Marvin Zalman and Larry Siegel, *Key Cases and Comments on Criminal Procedure* (St. Paul. MN: West Publishing, 1994).

39 390 U.S. 377, 88 S.Ct. 967, 19 L.Ed.2d 1247 (1968).

40 409 U.S. 188, 93 S.Ct. 375, 34 L.Ed.2d 401 (1972).

41 232 U.S. 383, 34 S.Ct. 341, 58 L.Ed. 652 (1914).

42 367 U.S. 643, 81 S.Ct. 1684, 6 L.Ed.2d 1081 (1961).

43 462 U.S. 213, 103 S.Ct. 2317, 76 L.Ed.2d 527 (1983).

44 468 U.S. 897, 104 S.Ct. 3405, 82 L.Ed.2d 677 (1984).

45 *Arizona v. Evans,* 514 U.S. 260, 115 S.Ct. 1185, 131 L.Ed.2d 34 (1995).

46 See "The Exclusionary Rule," *American Bar Association Journal* 19 (1983): 3; "Rule Prohibiting Illegal Evidence Faces Limitation," *Wall Street Journal,* 30 November 1982, p. 42; Bradford Wilson, *Exclusionary Rule* (Washington, DC: U.S. Government Printing Office, 1986); Jana Nestlerode, "Distinguishing the Exclusionary Rule Exceptions," *Journal of National Associations of District Attorneys* 24 (1991): 29–35; Lawrence Crocker, "Can the Exclusionary Rule Be Saved?" *Journal of Criminal Law and Criminology* 84 (1993): 310; Harold Rothwax, *The Collapse of Criminal Justice* (New York: Random House, 1996); Tom Smith, "Legislative and Legal Developments," *American Bar Association Journal of Criminal Justice* 11 (1996): 46–47.

COURTS AND ADJUDICATION

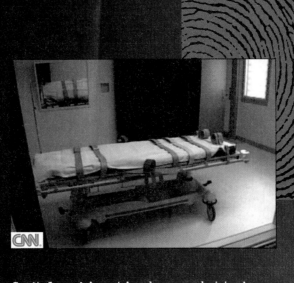

Capital punishment has become a hot topic because a growing number of death-row inmates have been found to be not guilty of the crime of which they were convicted. Abolitionists charge that the system is flawed and innocent people may be executed. Some lawyers who handle capital cases are incompetent, and consequently their clients cannot receive fair trials. The death penalty is just one of the many critical topics contained in this part, which covers the criminal court process.

Chapter

9

Alinari/Regione Umbria/Art Resource, NY

COURTS AND THE JUDICIARY

When Judge Maria Lopez, a Cuban emigré, was nominated in 1993 to the Superior Court bench in Massachusetts by Republican Gov. William Weld, she became the first Hispanic woman on the state Superior Court.[1] A local celebrity, Lopez was routinely featured in the society columns. Lopez became a lightning rod of controversy when, on September 6, 2000, she sentenced Charles Horton, 22, a transgendered male, to one year of home detention and four more years of probation. Horton had been convicted for kidnapping a 12-year-old Dorchester boy, holding a screwdriver to his neck, and attempting to rape him. The decision drew outrage from local residents who believed that Horton deserved jail time for his heinous behavior, especially since it involved a minor.

The Boston Bar Association issued a call for the legislature to have more control over criminal sentencing. Its president said:

> Confronted with a highly publicized sentencing decision, within [Lopez's] discretion but shocking to a significant segment of the public, those of us who stand before the bar are

berated for our professional association and besieged to explain the judge's conduct.

Massachusetts Governor Paul Cellucci claimed that the decision had so eroded public confidence in the state judiciary that prosecutors should be granted legal authority to protest or overturn outrageously lenient judicial sentences.[2]

When legal groups called for the ouster of Judge Lopez, the Massachusetts Association of Criminal Defense Lawyers (MACDL) defended her and issued a statement calling inappropriate attempts by politicians to censure or remove Judge Lopez for meting out a lenient yet legal sentence. The MACDL called the attacks on Lopez "an outrageous and alarming attack on the independence of the judiciary."[3] To the dismay of her detractors and relief of her supporters, efforts to oust Judge Lopez eventually proved futile.

Was Horton's sentencing too lenient? About 5 percent of convicted murderers and 20 percent of convicted rapists avoid prison sentences.[4] Judge Lopez may have been lenient, but she is certainly not unique.

Chapter 9

Chapter Outline

Criminal Justice Links

Criminal Justice Viewpoints

Copyright 1994 Globe Newspaper Company, Inc. Republished with permission of Globe Newspaper Company, Inc.

Judge Maria Lopez, a superior court judge, was the center of controversy in Massachusetts because of her lenient sentencing practices. Is it appropriate for politicians to criticize judicial decision making, or does such second-guessing undermine the objectivity of the justice process?

Fill in the blanks 1–2
True/False 1–4
Multiple choice 1

adjudication
The determination of guilt or innocence; a judgment concerning criminal charges.

Judge Lopez's story played out within the confines of the criminal court process. This is the setting in which many of the most important decisions in the criminal justice system are made; bail, trial, plea negotiations, **adjudication**, and sentencing all involve court-rendered decisions. Within the confines of the court, those accused of crime (defendants) call on the tools of the legal system to provide them with a fair and just hearing, with the burden of proof resting on the state; crime victims ask the government to provide them with justice for the wrongs done them and the injuries they have suffered; and agents of the criminal justice system attempt to find solutions that meet the needs of the victim, the defendant, and society in general.

PERSPECTIVES ON JUSTICE

The court process is designed to provide an open and impartial forum for deciding the truth of the matter and reaching a solution that, though punitive, is fairly arrived at and satisfies the rule of law. This is the heart of the due process perspective on justice.

appeal
A review of lower court proceedings by a higher court.

Regardless of the parties or issues involved, the presence of these parties in a courtroom should guarantee them that a hearing will be conducted under fair, equitable, and regulated rules of procedure; that the outcome of the hearing will be clear; and that the hearing will take place in an atmosphere of legal competence and objectivity. If either party, prosecution or defense, feels that these ground rules have been violated, they can take the case to a higher court, where the procedures of the original trial will be examined. If, upon **appeal**, a determination is made that criminal procedure has been violated, the appellate court may deem the findings of the original trial improper and either order a new hearing or provide some other remedy—for example, the court may dismiss the charge outright.

PERSPECTIVES ON JUSTICE

In today's crowded court system, such abstract goals are often impossible to achieve. In reality, the U.S. court system is often the scene of accommodation rather than an arena for a vigorous criminal defense. **Plea negotiations** and other nonjudicial alternatives, such as diversion, are far more common than the formal trial process. In a sense, caseload pressure interferes with due process and in many cases makes the court system an instrument of nonintervention.

plea negotiation/plea bargaining
Discussions between defense counsel and prosecution in which the accused agrees to plead guilty in exchange for certain considerations, such as reduced charges or a lenient sentence.

In this and the following four chapters, the structure and function of the court system will be closely examined. Here, we set out the structure of the U.S. court system and discuss its guiding hand, the judge. The following chapters cover the prosecutor and the defense attorney, the pretrial process, the trial, and finally, sentencing and punishment.

CRIMINAL COURT PROCESS

The court is a complex social agency with many independent but interrelated subsystems, each of which has a role in the court's operation: police, prosecutor, defense attorney, judge, and probation department.[5] It is also the scene of many important elements of criminal justice decision making: bail, detention, charging, jury selection, trial, and sentencing.

There are two ways to view the criminal court process. In the traditional model, the court is seen as a setting for an **adversarial procedure** that pits the defendant against the state, the defense counsel against the prosecutor. Procedures are fair and formalized, controlled by the laws of criminal procedure and the rules of evidence. In the second model, the court is viewed as a system that encourages settling matters in the simplest, quickest, and most efficient manner possible. Rather than being adversaries, prosecutors and defense attorneys form a "work group" with the judge and other court personnel that tries to handle the situation with as little fuss as possible. This usually involves dropping the case if the defendant agrees to make restitution or enter a treatment or diversion program, plea bargaining, or some other "quick fix."

In Malcolm Feeley's classic study of a lower court in Connecticut, not one defendant in 1,640 cases analyzed insisted on having a jury trial, and only half made use of legal counsel. Because cases dragged on endlessly, people were encouraged to plea bargain. And the haphazard nature of justice produced a situation in which the defendant's prior criminal record and the seriousness of the current charge had little influence on case outcome. Felons with prior records fared as well as first-time misdemeanants.[6]

THE STRUCTURE OF THE STATE COURT SYSTEM

The U.S. court system has evolved over the years into an intricately balanced legal process that has recently come under siege because of the sheer numbers of cases it must consider and the ways in which it is forced to handle such overcrowding. Overloaded court dockets have given rise to charges of assembly-line justice, in which a majority of defendants are induced to plead guilty, jury trials are rare, and the speedy trial is highly desired but unattainable.

Overcrowding causes the poor to languish in detention, whereas the wealthier go free on bail. This increases the possibility that an innocent person may be frightened into pleading guilty and, conversely, that a guilty person may be released because a trial has been delayed too long.[7] Whether providing more judges or new or enlarged courts will solve the problem of overcrowding remains to be seen. Meanwhile, diversion programs, decriminalization of certain offenses, and bail reform provide other avenues of possible relief. More efficient court management and administration is also seen as a step that might ease the congestion of the courts. These issues are extremely important if defendants are going to view their experience as a fair one in which they were able to present their side of the case and influence its outcome.

True/False 5–6
Multiple choice 2
Essay 1

adversarial procedure
Method of determining truth in the adjudication of guilt or innocence in which the prosecution advocates for the state, the defense advocates for the accused, and the judge is a neutral arbiter of the legal rules.

The National Center for State Courts is an independent nonprofit organization dedicated to the improvement of justice. NCSC activities include developing policies to enhance state courts, advancing state courts' interests within the federal government, fostering state court adaptation to future changes, securing sufficient resources for state courts, strengthening state court leadership, facilitating state court collaboration, and providing a model for organizational administration. To access their Web site, go to http://www.ncsc.dni.us

For an up-to-date list of Web links, see http://www.wadsworth.com/product/0534573053s

PERSPECTIVES ON JUSTICE

Ironically, there is evidence that an informal justice system, which is often deplored by experts, may provide criminal suspects a greater degree of satisfaction than the more formal criminal trial. This belief is the core of the restorative justice perspective, whose advocates want the community to play a greater role in the justice process.

To house this rather complex process, each state maintains its own state court organization and structure (Figure 9.1). Usually three (or more) separate court systems exist within each state jurisdiction. Descriptions of each follow.

Fill in the blanks 3–4
True/False 7

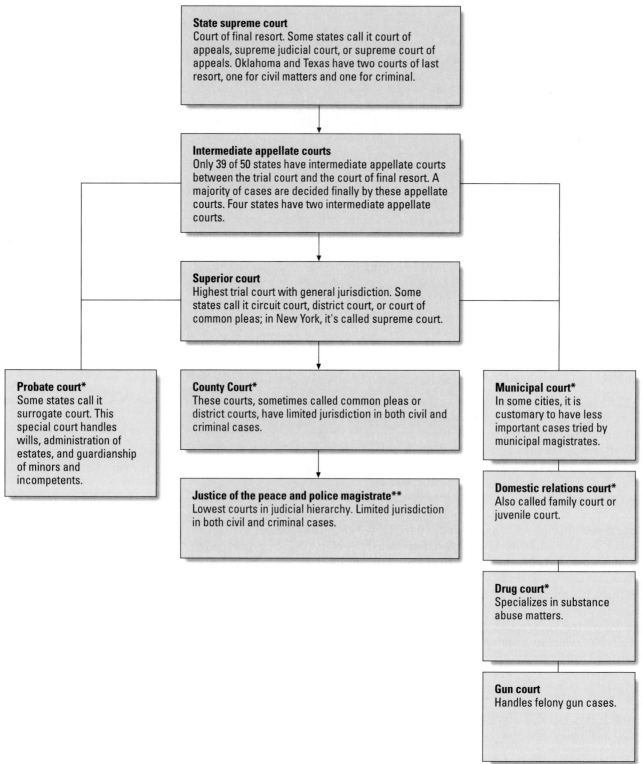

FIGURE 9.1
A MODEL OF A STATE JUDICIAL SYSTEM

*Courts of special jurisdiction, such as probate, family, or juvenile courts, and the so-called inferior courts, such as common pleas or municipal courts, may be separate courts or part of the trial court of general jurisdiction.

**Justices of the peace do not exist in all states. Where they do exist, their jurisdictions vary greatly from state to state.

SOURCES: American Bar Association, *Law and the Courts* (Chicago: ABA, 1974), 20; Bureau of Justice Statistics, *State Court Organization—1998* (Washington, DC: Department of Justice, 2000).

Lower Trial Courts: Courts of Limited Jurisdiction

There are approximately 13,000 **courts of limited jurisdiction** in the United States. Most (87%) are organized along town, municipal, and county lines of government; about 700 are controlled by state governments.

Courts of limited jurisdiction (sometimes called misdemeanor courts, municipal courts, or lower courts) are restricted in the types of cases they can hear. Usually, they handle misdemeanor criminal infractions, including assault, shoplifting, violations of municipal ordinances, traffic violations, and civil suits where the damages involve less than a certain amount of money (usually $10,000). These courts also conduct preliminary hearings for felony criminal cases—that is, probable cause hearings to determine whether a trial should be held.

The **lower criminal courts** are restricted in the criminal penalties they can impose. Most can levy a fine of $1,000 or less and incarcerate a person for 12 months or less in the local jail.

Included within the category of courts of limited jurisdictions are special courts, such as juvenile, family, and probate courts (divorce, estate issues, and custody). Some states separate limited courts into those that handle civil cases only and those that settle criminal cases.

The nation's lower courts are the ones most often accused of providing assembly-line justice. Because the matters they decide involve minor personal confrontations and conflicts—family disputes, divorces, landlord–tenant conflicts, barroom brawls—the goal is handling the situation and resolving the dispute. Social commentator Charles Silberman describes his experience in such a criminal court:

> My first visit to a criminal court, in fact, reminded me of nothing quite so much as a long evening spent in the emergency room of a large city hospital, trying to get medical care for an elderly relative who had been knocked down by an automobile. In the courtroom, defendants, witnesses, and complainants, along with their families, sat in hard-backed chairs, waiting with the same air of resignation that patients and their families had displayed in the hospital emergency room; waiting sometimes seems to be a principal occupation of the poor.[8]

Malcolm Feeley describes the lower courts as a "world apart . . . their facilities are terrible. Courtrooms are crowded, chambers are dingy, and libraries are virtually nonexistent. Even the newer courtrooms age quickly, worn down by hard use and constant abuse."[9] Lower courts are basically informal institutions in which all parties work together to settle the situation in an equitable fashion. In this respect, the criminal process is similar to the civil justice system. According to Feeley, the "process is the punishment in lower courts." By this, he means that nothing much happens by way of formal punishment in the lower courts. Just having to go to hearings, retain counsel, miss work, and so on is the real punishment for offenders. So many cases are settled by plea bargains because defendants are trying to avoid the pains of the court process, not the pains of imprisonment. Defendants are aided in this by the court personnel, who practice accommodative rather than adversarial justice. Sometimes, because of the way justice is handed down in these overcrowded courts, dangerous offenders slip through the cracks of justice.

Felony Courts: Courts of General Jurisdiction

Approximately 3,200 **courts of general jurisdiction**, or felony courts, exist in the United States; they process more than 5 million criminal cases each year. About 90 percent of the general courts are state administered, and the remainder are controlled by counties or municipalities. The overwhelming majority (95%) of general courts hear both serious civil and criminal matters (felonies).

True/False 8–10
Multiple choice 3–6
Essay 2

court of limited jurisdiction
A court that handles misdemeanors and minor civil complaints.

lower criminal court
A court that has jurisdiction over misdemeanors and conducts preliminary investigations of felony charges.

True/False 11–12
Multiple choice 7

court of general jurisdiction
A court that tries felony cases and more serious civil matters.

About three-fourths of the courts of general jurisdiction are also responsible for reviewing cases on appeal from courts of limited jurisdiction. After reviewing the transcript of the trial, the higher court has the power to grant a new trial, known as a trial *de novo.*

Specialty Courts

True/False 13
Multiple choice 8
Essay 3

A growing phenomenon in the United States is the creation of specialty courts that focus on one type of criminal act—for example, drug courts and gun courts. All cases within the jurisdiction that involve this particular type of crime are funneled to the specialty court, where presumably they will get prompt resolution.

One well-known example is the Gun Court in Providence, Rhode Island. All felony cases in Bristol and Providence counties are automatically routed to Gun Court where, once a preliminary hearing has begun, the cases must be heard within 60 days. The purpose is to make sure that violent felons are not lost in the shuffle of crowded urban courts, where witnesses disappear and offenders are free to abscond.[10]

drug court
A specialty court with jurisdiction over cases involving illegal substances, often providing treatment alternatives for defendants.

Another specialty court is the **drug court**, which has jurisdiction over the burgeoning number of cases involving substance abuse and trafficking. The aim is to place nonviolent first offenders into intensive treatment programs rather than send them to jail or prison. One such court, the Drug Night Court program in Cook County, Illinois, was set up in 1975 as an emergency measure to deal with the rapidly expanding number of narcotics cases being filed. Today, there are 327 drug courts across 43 states, the District of Columbia, and Puerto Rico.[11] Some early evaluations have praised the drug court program, indicating that it is an efficient method for processing cases, dramatically reducing the processing time of drug cases.[12] However, recent research finds that drug courts may not be as effective as originally believed and that recidivism for drug court participants is significantly higher than for similar offenders who are processed in traditional courts. It is possible that drug courts stigmatize defendants as substance abusers and, consequently, impede their rehabilitation.[13]

By 1998, all but 17 states had family courts that served some number of counties or districts, or were statewide. These courts typically had jurisdiction over domestic and marital matters such as divorce, child custody and support, and domestic violence. In addition, there are currently more than 450 tribal justice forums among the 556 federally recognized tribes in the United States. Sixteen states have assumed mandatory or optional jurisdiction over tribal lands, pursuant to Public Law 280.[14] There are also juvenile courts, which specialize in cases of underage minors who violate the criminal law (*juvenile delinquents*), who are uncontrollable or unmanageable (*status offenders,* including truants and runaways), or who are not provided with adequate care by their parents (*neglected children*). Some states have created comprehensive family courts, which handle all problems involving youths and their families, including custody issues. The juvenile court will be discussed more fully in Chapter 17.

Appellate Courts

True/False 14–15
Multiple choice 9–10

If defendants believe that the procedures used in their case violated their constitutional rights, they can appeal the outcome. For example, defendants can file an appeal if they believe that the law they were tried under violates constitutional standards (for example, it was too vague) or if the procedures used in the case contravened principles of due process and equal protection or were in direct opposition to a constitutional guarantee (for example, the defendants were denied the right to have competent legal representation).

CHAPTER 9 COURTS AND THE JUDICIARY 279

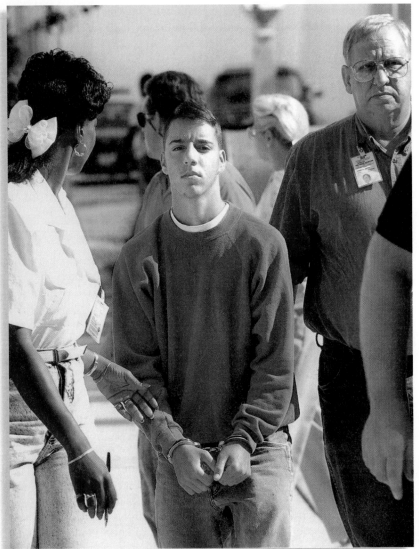

Victor Brancaccio, age 16, who killed a woman who criticized his rap music, is led into St. Lucie County courthouse in Ft. Pierce, Florida. Should violent children be tried in juvenile courts, or do their actions warrant their being punished as adults?

© Paul Milette/*Palm Beach Post*

Appellate courts do not try cases; they review the procedures of the case to determine whether an error was made by judicial authorities. Judicial error can include admitting into evidence illegally seized material, improperly charging a jury, allowing a prosecutor to ask witnesses improper questions, and so on. The appellate court can either order a new trial, allow the defendant to go free, or uphold the original verdict.

State criminal appeals are heard in one of the 94 appellate courts in the 50 states and the District of Columbia. Each state has at least one court of last resort, usually called a state supreme court, which reviews issues of law and fact appealed from the trial courts; two states, Texas and Oklahoma, have two high courts, one for civil appeals and the other for criminal cases. In addition, 36 states have established intermediate appellate courts to review decisions by trial courts and administrative agencies before they reach the supreme court stage. Five states, including New York, Pennsylvania, and Indiana, have established more than one type of intermediate appellate court. In Hawaii, Idaho, Iowa, Oklahoma, and South Carolina, intermediate courts do not have original jurisdiction over appeals but are assigned cases when the supreme court's caseload overflows.

In all, there are 132 courts of appeal, including the U.S. Supreme Court and U.S. Courts of Appeal; more than 1,400 judges now sit on the appellate bench.[15]

PERSPECTIVES ON JUSTICE

Crime control advocates believe that criminal appeals clog the nation's court system because so many convicted criminals try to "beat the rap" on a technicality. Actually, criminal appeals represent a small percentage of the total number of cases processed by the nation's appellate courts. For example, less than 20 percent of the appeals in federal courts are criminal matters. The right to appeal an unjust conviction lies at the heart of the due process perspective.

Although criminal cases make up only a small percentage of appellate cases, they are still of concern to the judiciary. Steps have been taken to make appealing more difficult. For example, the Supreme Court has tried to limit the number of appeals being filed by prison inmates.

Variations in State Court Structure

Multiple choice 11

Each state has a tiered court organization (lower, upper, and appellate courts), but states vary in the way they have delegated responsibility to a particular court system.

For example, take a look at the court structures of Texas (Figure 9.2) and New York (Figure 9.3). Note the complexity of their organization in comparison with the "model" court structure. Texas separates its highest appellate division into civil and criminal courts: The Texas Supreme Court hears civil, administrative, and juvenile cases, whereas an independent Court of Criminal Appeals has the final say on criminal matters. New York's unique structure features two separate intermediate appellate courts with different geographic jurisdictions and an independent Family Court, which handles both domestic relations (such as guardianship and custody, neglect, and abuse) and juvenile delinquency. New York's Surrogates' Court handles adoptions and settles disagreements over estate transfers. The Court of Claims handles civil matters in which the state is a party. In contrast to New York, which has ten independent courts, six states (Idaho, Illinois, Iowa, Massachusetts, Minnesota, and South Dakota) have unified their trial courts into a single system.

THE STRUCTURE OF THE FEDERAL COURTS

The legal basis for the federal court system is contained in Article 3, section 1, of the U.S. Constitution, which provides that "the judicial power of the United States shall be vested in one Supreme Court, and in such inferior courts as the Congress may from time to time ordain and establish." Article 3, section 2, specifies that the federal courts have jurisdiction over the laws of the United States and treaties and cases involving admiralty and maritime jurisdiction, as well as over controversies between two or more states and citizens of different states.[16] This complex language generally means that state courts have jurisdiction over all legal matters unless they involve a violation of a federal criminal statute or a civil suit between citizens of different states or between a citizen and an agency of the federal government.

Fill in the blanks 5–6
Multiple choice 12
Essay 4

Within this authority, the federal government has established a three-tiered hierarchy of court jurisdiction that, in order of ascendancy, consists of (1) U.S.

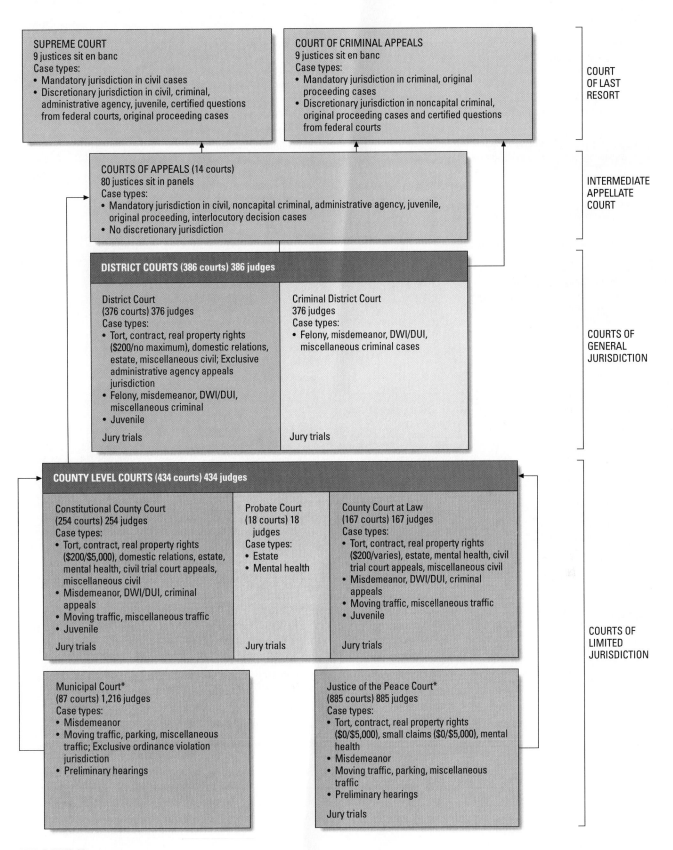

FIGURE 9.2
TEXAS COURT STRUCTURE

NOTE: *Some municipal and justice of the peace courts may appeal to the district court.

SOURCE: David Rottman et al., *State Court Organization, 1998* (Washington, DC: Bureau of Justice Statistics, 2000), 392.

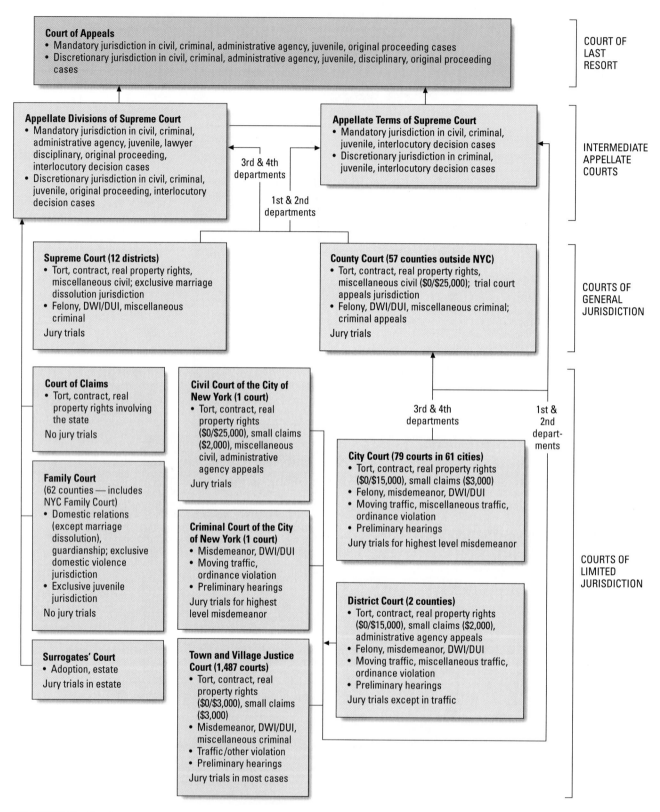

FIGURE 9.3
NEW YORK COURT STRUCTURE

SOURCE: David Rottman et al., *State Court Organization, 1998* (Washington, DC: Bureau of Justice Statistics, 2000), 380.

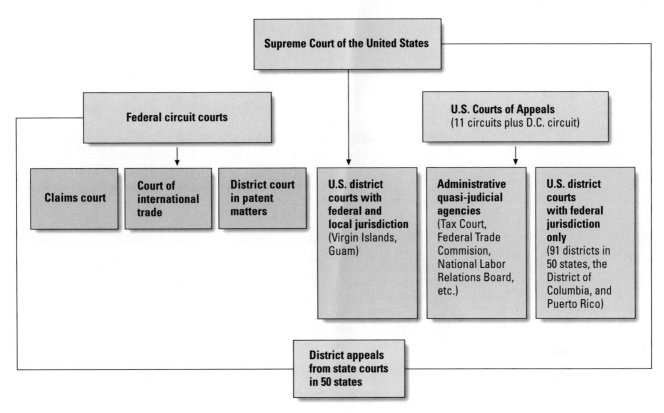

FIGURE 9.4
THE FEDERAL
JUDICIAL SYSTEM

SOURCE: American Bar Association, *Law and the Courts* (Chicago: ABA, 1974), 21. Updated information provided by the Federal Courts Improvement Act of 1982 and West Publishing Company, St. Paul, Minnesota.

district courts, (2) U.S. courts of appeals (circuit courts), and (3) the U.S. Supreme Court (see Figure 9.4).

Federal District Courts

The 94 **federal district courts** are the trial courts of the federal system. They have jurisdiction over cases involving violations of federal laws, including civil rights abuses, interstate transportation of stolen vehicles, and kidnappings. They can also hear cases on questions involving citizenship and the rights of aliens. The jurisdiction of federal district courts occasionally overlaps that of state courts. For example, citizens who reside in separate states and are involved in litigation of an amount in excess of $10,000 can choose to have their cases heard in either of the states or in federal court. Finally, federal district courts hear cases in which one state sues a resident (or firm) of another state, one state sues another, or the federal government is a party in a suit.

Federal district courts were organized by Congress in the Judicial Act of 1789. Originally, each state was allowed one court; as the population grew, however, so did the need for courts. Now each state has from one to four district courts, and the District of Columbia has one, for a total of 94 independent courts.

In most cases, a single judge presides over trials; a defendant may request that a jury also be present. In complex civil matters, a three-judge panel may be convened.

federal district court
A trial court of the federal system.

Multiple choice 13–14

Federal Appellate Courts

Approximately 35,000 appeals from the district courts are heard each year in the 12 federal courts of appeals, sometimes referred to as **U.S. circuit courts**. Circuit court offices are usually located in major cities, such as San Francisco and New York, and attorneys must bring cases to these locations to be heard.

Fill in the blanks 7–8
Multiple choice 15

U.S. circuit court
A court that handles the first level of appeal in the federal system.

The circuit court is empowered to review federal and state appellate court cases on substantive and procedural issues involving rights guaranteed by the Constitution. Circuit courts do not actually retry cases, nor do they determine whether the facts brought out during trial support conviction or dismissal. Instead, they analyze judicial interpretations of the law, such as the charge (or instructions) to the jury, and reflect on the constitutional issues involved in each case they hear.

Federal appellate courts also enforce orders of federal administrative agencies, such as the Food and Drug Administration and the Securities and Exchange Commission. Federal decisions in these matters are final, except when reviewed by the U.S. Supreme Court. Any dissatisfied litigant in a federal district court has the right to appeal the case to a circuit court.

The U.S. Supreme Court

The U.S. Supreme Court is the nation's highest appellate body and the **court of last resort** for all cases tried in the various federal and state courts. The Supreme Court is composed of nine justices appointed for lifetime terms by the president with the approval of the Senate.

The Supreme Court is unique in several respects. First, it is the only court established by constitutional mandate, rather than federal legislation. Second, it decides basic social and political issues of grave consequence and importance to the nation. Third, the Court's nine justices shape the future meaning of the U.S. Constitution. Their decisions specify the rights and liberties of citizens throughout the United States.

In its early years, the Supreme Court did not review state court decisions involving issues of federal law. Even though Congress had given the Supreme Court jurisdiction to review state decisions, much resistance and controversy surrounded the relationship between the states and the federal government. However, in a famous decision, *Martin v. Hunter's Lessee* (1816), the Supreme Court reaffirmed the legitimacy of its jurisdiction over state court decisions when such courts handled issues of federal or constitutional law.[17] This decision allowed the Supreme Court to actively review actions by states and their courts and reinforced the Court's power to make the supreme law of the land. Since that time, a defendant who indicates that government action—whether state or federal—violates a constitutional law is in a position to have the Supreme Court review the action.

To carry out its responsibilities, the Court had to develop a method of dealing with a large volume of cases coming from the state and federal courts for final review. In the early years of its history, the Court sought to review every case filed. Since the middle of the twentieth century, however, the court has used the **writ of certiorari** to decide what cases it should hear. *Certiorari* is a Latin term that means "to bring the record of a case from a lower court up to a higher court for immediate review." Four of the nine justices must vote to hear a case brought by a writ of certiorari; generally, these votes are cast in a secret meeting attended only by the justices. However, the Supreme Court must accept jurisdiction in a few instances, such as decisions of a three-judge federal district court on reapportionment or cases involving the Voting Rights Act.

More than 90 percent of the cases heard by the Supreme Court are brought by petition for a writ of certiorari, and the Court may choose to hear only those it deems important, appropriate, and worthy of its attention. Over the years, the Court has reduced the number of cases it reviews: In 1976, it heard arguments in 176 cases and gave a full opinion in 154; today, it hears arguments and issues full opinions in fewer than 100 cases each year.[18]

Fill in the blanks 9–11
True/False 16
Multiple choice 16–17
Essay 5

court of last resort
A court that handles the final appeal on a matter; in the federal system, the U.S. Supreme Court.

The Supreme Court maintains a Web site with a wealth of information on its history, judges, procedures, case filings, rules, handling guides, opinions, and other court-related material. To access the site, go to http://www.supremecourtus.gov For an up-to-date list of Web links, see http://www.wadsworth.com/product/0534573053s

Fill in the blanks 12
True/False 17–18
Multiple choice 18–19
Essay 6

writ of certiorari
An order of a superior court requesting that a record of an inferior court (or administrative body) be brought forward for review or inspection.

Karla Faye Tucker in prison in Gatesville, Texas, waits during the last days of her life to see if the Supreme Court will hear her case. Tucker was executed in 1998 when the Supreme Court failed to uphold her appeals.

© Mark Graham/CORBIS-Sygma

When the Court grants a writ of certiori, it requests a transcript of the case proceedings for review. Attorneys are then normally asked to present written arguments, or *legal briefs,* and oral arguments to the Court in Washington, D.C. After reviewing the written materials and hearing the oral arguments, the justices usually meet in a *case conference,* where they discuss the case and vote to reach a decision.

In reaching a decision, the Supreme Court justices reevaluate and reinterpret state statutes, the U.S. Constitution, and previous case decisions. Based on a review of the case, the Court either affirms or reverses the decision of the lower court. When the justices reach a decision, the chief justice assigns one of the majority group to write the opinion. Another justice normally writes a *dissent,* or minority opinion. In the final analysis, the justices join with either the majority opinion or the dissenting opinion.

Fill in the blanks 13

When the U.S. Supreme Court rules on a case, its majority decision becomes a precedent that must be honored by all lower courts. For example, if the Court grants a particular litigant the right to counsel at a police lineup, then all similarly situated clients must be given the same right. This type of ruling is often referred to as a **landmark decision**. The use of precedents in the legal system gives the Supreme Court power to influence and mold the everyday operating procedures of the police, trial courts, and corrections agencies. In the past, this influence was not nearly as pronounced as it was during the tenure of Chief Justices Earl Warren and Warren Burger, who greatly amplified and extended the power of the Court to influence criminal justice policies. Under Chief Justice William Rehnquist, the Court has continued to influence criminal justice matters, ranging from the investigation of crimes to the execution of convicted criminals.

landmark decision
A decision of the Supreme Court that establishes a significant precedent for similar legal issues.

The Court's action is the final step in settling constitutional criminal disputes throughout the nation. By discretionary review through a petition for a writ of certiorari, the U.S. Supreme Court requires state courts to accept its interpretation of the federal Constitution. In doing so, the Court has changed the day-to-day operations of the criminal justice system.

The steps involved in appealing a case to the Supreme Court are summarized in Figure 9.5.

FIGURE 9.5
TRACING THE
COURSE OF A
CASE TO THE U.S.
SUPREME COURT

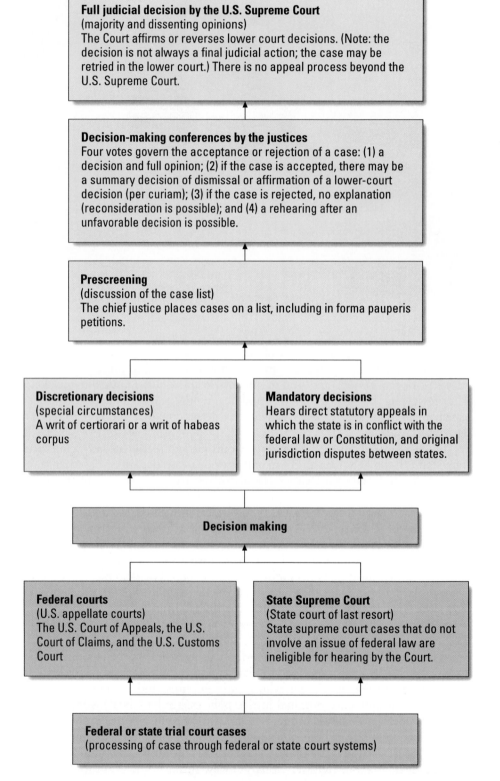

Full judicial decision by the U.S. Supreme Court
(majority and dissenting opinions)
The Court affirms or reverses lower court decisions. (Note: the decision is not always a final judicial action; the case may be retried in the lower court.) There is no appeal process beyond the U.S. Supreme Court.

Decision-making conferences by the justices
Four votes govern the acceptance or rejection of a case: (1) a decision and full opinion; (2) if the case is accepted, there may be a summary decision of dismissal or affirmation of a lower-court decision (per curiam); (3) if the case is rejected, no explanation (reconsideration is possible); and (4) a rehearing after an unfavorable decision is possible.

Prescreening
(discussion of the case list)
The chief justice places cases on a list, including in forma pauperis petitions.

Discretionary decisions
(special circumstances)
A writ of certiorari or a writ of habeas corpus

Mandatory decisions
Hears direct statutory appeals in which the state is in conflict with the federal law or Constitution, and original jurisdiction disputes between states.

Decision making

Federal courts
(U.S. appellate courts)
The U.S. Court of Appeals, the U.S. Court of Claims, and the U.S. Customs Court

State Supreme Court
(State court of last resort)
State supreme court cases that do not involve an issue of federal law are ineligible for hearing by the Court.

Federal or state trial court cases
(processing of case through federal or state court systems)

COURT CASELOADS

The state courts handle about 90 million civil, criminal, and traffic cases each year, resulting in backlogs, delays, and what is sometimes called "assembly-line justice."[19] Of these cases, approximately 14 million were criminal matters; the remainder were juvenile, civil, traffic, and so on. These figures have been inflated by the sharp increase in both civil and criminal litigation in the past few years. Figure 9.6 shows the increase in caseloads for the period 1994 to 1998. With the exception of traffic violations, all types of case filings increased at a significant pace, far outstripping the nation's population growth during this period. These increases explain in part why court dockets are so overloaded. In the nation's largest counties, it can take up to a year to adjudicate a murder case and six months for a robbery.[20]

The federal court system has also witnessed explosive growth. In 1900, a total of 13,605 cases were filed in federal district courts, and 1,093 in courts of appeals. In 1999, more than 320,194 cases were filed in federal district courts, more than 54,600 in courts of appeals, and more than 1.3 million in federal bankruptcy courts.[21]

The significant increases in both criminal and civil litigation have forced federal, state, and local governments to allocate ever greater resources to the courts. Court services, including the judiciary, prosecution, legal services such as public defenders, and other court-related services (juries, stenographers, clerks, bailiffs, maintenance) now cost about $20 billion annually. Heavy workloads have also taken their toll in job-related tension and stress.

What causes court caseloads to overflow? One problem is the excessive number of continuances demanded by attorneys and the increasing number of pretrial motions on evidentiary and procedural issues. As the law becomes more complex and involves more complex issues, such as computer crimes, the need for a more involved court process has escalated. Ironically, efforts being made to reform the criminal law may also be helping to overload the courts. For example, the increase

Essay 7

Multiple choice 20

FIGURE 9.6 CASES FILED IN STATE COURTS, 1994–1998

Source: Brian Ostrom and Neal Kavder, *Examining the Work of State Courts, 1998* (Williamsburg, VA: National Center for State Courts, 2000).

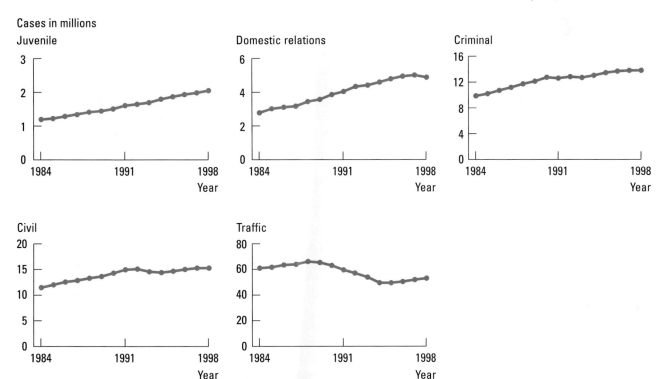

in mandatory prison sentences for some crimes may reduce the use of plea bargaining and increase the number of jury trials because defendants fear that a conviction will lead to an incarceration sentence and must therefore be avoided at all costs. An explosion in civil litigation has added to the backlog because most courts handle both criminal and civil matters.

If relief is to be found, it will probably be in the form of better administrative and management techniques that improve the use of existing resources. For example, it may be possible for legal jurisdictions to create policies mandating speedy trials to reduce trial delay. An analysis of the federal Speedy Trial Act of 1974 and Rule 50(b) of the Federal Rules of Criminal Procedure, policy initiatives designed to facilitate federal case processing, shows that these initiatives actually produced a significant reduction in the processing time of federal criminal cases.[22]

Another possible way of creating a more efficient court system is to unify existing state courts into a single administrative structure employing modern management principles. Massachusetts, Illinois, Iowa, Minnesota, South Dakota, and Idaho have implemented unified court systems. In contrast, 14 states have complex court systems in which several courts have overlapping jurisdiction with other courts.

THE JUDICIARY

The judge is the senior officer in a court of criminal law. His or her duties are quite varied and are actually far more extensive than might be expected. During trials, the judge rules on the appropriateness of conduct, settles questions of evidence and procedure, and guides the questioning of witnesses. In a jury trial, the judge must instruct jurors on which evidence is proper to examine and which should be ignored. The judge also formally charges the jury, instructing its members on what points of law and evidence they must consider to reach a decision of either guilty or not guilty. When a jury trial is waived, the judge must decide whether to hold for the complainant or the defendant. Finally, if a defendant is found guilty, the judge must decide on the sentence (unless it is legislatively determined)—the type of sentence, its length, and in the case of probation, the conditions under which it may be revoked.

Beyond these stated duties, the trial judge has extensive control and influence over other agencies of the court: probation, the court clerk, the police, and the district attorney's office. Probation and the court clerk may be under the judge's explicit control. In some courts, the operations, philosophy, and procedures of these agencies are within the magistrate's administrative domain. In others—for example, where a state agency controls the probation department—the attitudes of the county or district court judge greatly influence the way a probation department is run and how its decisions are made. Judges often consult with probation staff on treatment decisions, and many judges are interested in providing the most innovative and up-to-date care possible.[23]

Police and prosecutors are also directly influenced by the judge, whose sentencing discretion affects the arrest and charging processes. For example, if a judge usually hands down minimal sentences (such as a fine) for a particular offense, the police may be reluctant to arrest offenders for that crime, knowing that doing so will basically be a waste of their time. Similarly, if a judge is known to have an open mind toward police discretion, then the police may be more inclined to push the limit, engaging in practices that border on entrapment or pursuing cases through easily obtained wiretaps. However, a magistrate oriented toward strict use of due process guarantees would stifle such activities by dismissing all cases involving apparent police abuses of personal freedoms. The district attorney's office may also be sensitive to judicial attitudes, forgoing indictments in

True/False 19–21
Multiple choice 21
Essay 8

The purposes of the American Judges Association are to improve the effective and impartial administration of justice, to enhance the independence and status of the judiciary, to provide for continuing education of its members, and to promote the interchange of ideas of a judicial nature among judges, court organizations, and the public. Visit their Web site at http://aja.ncsc.dni.us

For an up-to-date list of Web links, see http://www.wadsworth.com/product/0534573053s

cases that the presiding magistrate expressly considers trivial or quasi-criminal and in which the judge has been known to take only token action, such as the prosecution of pornographers.

Finally, the judge considers requests by police and prosecutors for leniency (or severity) in sentencing. The judge's reaction to these requests is important if the police and the district attorney are to honor the bargains they may have made with defendants to secure information, cooperation, or guilty pleas. For example, when police tell informers that they will try to convince the judge to go easy on them to secure required information, they will often discuss the terms of the promised leniency with representatives of the court. If a judge ignores police requests, then the department's bargaining power is severely diminished and communication within the criminal justice system is impaired.

There is always concern that judges will discriminate against defendants on the basis of their gender, race, or class. Although this issue is of great social concern, most research efforts have failed to find consistent bias in judicial decision making; judges tend to dismiss cases that they consider weak and less serious.[24] The role of the judge in guiding the outcome of a high-profile criminal case is nowhere better illustrated than in the trial of Louise Woodward, the British au pair accused in 1997 of killing her eight-month-old charge, Matthew Eappen. This case is discussed in the Images of Justice feature.

Judicial Qualifications

Fill in the blanks 14
Multiple choice 22

The qualifications for appointment to one of the existing 28,000 judgeships vary from state to state and court to court. Typically, the potential judge must be a resident of the state, licensed to practice law, a member of the state bar association, and at least 25 and less than 70 years of age.[25] However, the basic qualifications may vary, depending on the level of court jurisdiction. Almost every state requires judges to have a law degree if they are to serve on appellate courts or courts of general jurisdiction, but it is not uncommon for municipal or town court judges to lack a legal background, even though they maintain the power to incarcerate criminal defendants. Surprising as it may seem, thousands of these municipal or town judges are not trained attorneys; yet they routinely handle criminal matters. In contrast, 14 states, including California, Florida, Nebraska, and New Jersey, make possession of a law degree or being "learned in the law" a requirement for all judicial appointments.

Many states require judges to participate in some form of legal education beyond the Continuing Legal Education expected of all members of the state bar. Eighteen states, the District of Columbia, Puerto Rico, and the Navajo Nation make formal provisions for an ongoing evaluation of judicial performance. Evaluations are conducted in states that select judges through nonpartisan elections (Michigan, Minnesota, and Tennessee) and also in those where judges are appointed (Connecticut, Delaware, Massachusetts, New Hampshire, Rhode Island, South Carolina, and Vermont).[26]

Judicial Selection

Multiple choice 23–25
Essay 9

State Judicial Selection Many different methods are used to select state judges, depending on the level of court jurisdiction. In some jurisdictions, the governor simply appoints judges. In others, the governor's recommendations must be confirmed by either (1) the state senate, (2) the governor's council, (3) a special confirmation committee, (4) an executive council elected by the state assembly, or (5) an elected review board. More than 30 states now use some form of judicial nominating commission that submits names to the governor for approval.

Commonwealth v. Woodward

On February 4, 1997, British au pair Louise Woodward called the police and said that Matthew Eappen, the eight-month-old baby she had been hired to care for, was having difficulty breathing. The 18-year-old Woodward had been hired by two Newton, Massachusetts, doctors, Sunil and Deborah Eappen, in November 1996 to care for their two young sons. When paramedics arrived at the Eappen household, they found that the baby had a two-and-a-half-inch skull fracture. Matthew's eyes were also bulging, a possible sign of "shaken baby syndrome." The baby spent four days on life support before dying on February 9.

Newton police officers on the scene later claimed that Woodward admitted to handling the baby roughly and "dropping" him on the floor, causing the skull fracture. The belief that this rough treatment had caused the death

AP/Wide World Photos

of a child convinced prosecutors to charge Woodward with first-degree murder on the grounds that her behavior was heinous and cruel.

At the trial, Woodward's high-powered defense team claimed that her alleged mishandling of the baby did not cause Matthew Eappen's death but that a preexisting medical condition might have killed the baby. Defense experts testified that the skull fracture detected during the autopsy was actually three weeks old and could have opened spontaneously. On the stand, Louise claimed that she might have shaken Matthew, but only to revive a baby already in distress. Moreover, the police officers on the scene did not hear her correctly. Rather than saying she "dropped" the baby on the floor, she actually had said she had "popped" the baby down, an English expression misunderstood by American police officers.

Despite the scientific evidence and Louise Woodward's dramatic testimony, the jury found her guilty of second-degree murder, a charge that carries a minimum of 15 years in prison. Then, in a dramatic turn of events, Judge Hiller Zobel reversed the jury's decision and found Louise guilty of involuntary manslaughter. Even more surprising to the prosecution, he sentenced her to "time served," allowing for her immediate release. Judge Zobel explained his reasoning as follows:

> Judges must follow their oaths and do their duty, heedless of editorials,

Judge Hiller Zobel—standing—instructs the jury as Louise Woodward sits beneath him in the witness box, October 23, 1997.

letters, telegrams, picketers, threats, petitions, panelists, and talk shows. In this country, we do not administer justice by plebiscite. A judge, in short, is a public servant who must follow his conscience, whether or not he counters the manifest wishes of those he serves; whether or not his decision seems a surrender to the prevalent demands.

The test here is no longer narrowly legal. The judge, formerly only an umpire enforcing the rules, now must determine whether, under the special circumstances of this case, justice requires lowering the level of guilt from murder to manslaughter (or even to battery). The facts, as well as the law, are open to consideration.

In deciding this issue, the judge must, above all, use the power sparingly, and with restraint, taking care not to act arbitrarily or unreasonably. The judge does not sit as a second jury, or even as a thirteenth juror; he should not second-guess the jury. Nonetheless, he is entitled to consider testimony that the jury may have disbelieved, including such of Defendant's own testimony as he finds credible.

After considering the law and the evidence of the whole case "broadly," to determine whether "there was any miscarriage of justice," the judge's duty requires: weighing "the fundamental fairness of the result," deciding whether a reduced verdict would be more consonant with justice, and determining whether justice "will be more nearly achieved" by a reduction, rather than by allowing the jury's verdict to stand. In short, the court may reduce the level of the conviction, for any reason that justice may require. This in turn means that the judge must decide whether failing to reduce the verdict raises a substantial risk that justice has miscarried. The scope of review may be even broader than requiring Defendant to show "grave prejudice" or "substantial likelihood" that a miscarriage of justice has occurred.

The Court may not, however, take into account the feelings of those the death has affected; the judge must focus entirely on the events of the trial. Thus although as a father and grandfather I particularly recognize and acknowledge the indescribable pain Matthew Eappen's death has caused his parents and grandparents, as a judge I am duty-bound to ignore it. I must look only at the evidence and the defendant.

Viewing the evidence broadly, as I am permitted to do, I believe that the circumstances in which Defendant acted were characterized by confusion, inexperience, frustration, immaturity and some anger, but not malice (in the legal sense) supporting a conviction for second-degree murder. Frustrated by her inability to quiet the crying child, she was "a little rough with him," under circumstances where another, perhaps wiser, person would have sought to restrain the physical impulse. The roughness was sufficient to start (or restart) a bleeding that escalated fatally.

Having considered the matter carefully, I am firmly convinced that the interests of justice mandate my reducing the verdict to manslaughter.

I do this in accordance with my discretion and my duty. After intensive, cool, calm reflection, I am morally certain that allowing this defendant on this evidence to remain convicted of second-degree murder would be a miscarriage of justice.

The Woodward case is fascinating for many reasons. It was televised around the globe, making it an international spectacle. The extensive use of expert witnesses who supplied forensic evidence was a key element in the case. Is it possible that only defendants who can afford to hire experts (some of whom charged $900 per hour) may be in a position to acquire evidence sufficient to counteract the prosecution's case (Woodward raised $100,000 in donations to pay for her defense)? But the most important element of the case was the discretion used by the presiding judge. The defense had the option to include manslaughter in the charge to the jury but chose not to, mistakenly believing that no jury could find their client guilty of the malicious killing of a child; but they were wrong. If they had allowed the prosecution to include manslaughter, the jury might have convicted on that lesser charge. It was left, then, to the judge to use his discretion both to reduce the jury's verdict and to hand down an extremely lenient sentence. This aspect of judicial power is not invoked very often; Judge Zobel had only overturned two verdicts in 18 years.

Critical Thinking Skills

The Eappen case illustrates the power that judges have to shape the criminal process. As Judge Zobel states in his decision, the power to change jury verdicts is part of the judicial duty to render fair and impartial justice. He believes that a judge's duty requires "weighing 'the fundamental fairness of the result'" of jury decisions, "deciding whether a reduced verdict would be more consonant with justice, and determining whether justice 'will be more nearly achieved' by a reduction." Do you agree with this approach, or do you feel it undermines the jury process? After all, why spend so much time and effort serving on a jury if a judge can later decide to ignore your decision?

InfoTrac College Edition Research

To learn more about the Eappen case, read

Suzanne Fields, "Why Is Matthew Eappen Sharing Victim Status?" *Insight on the News,* 8 December 1997, v13 i45 p48

Wray Herbert, "Why Did Matthew Die?" *U.S. News & World Report,* 24 November 1997, v123 i20 p41

SOURCES: Sarah Lyall, "An American Jury Shocks Britain," *New York Times,* 5 November 1997; Matt Richtel, "Judge in Au Pair Trial Plans to Use Net to Unveil Decision," *New York Times,* 2 November 1997, p. 1; Middlesex ss Superior Court Criminal No. 97-0433, *Commonwealth Memorandum and Order v. Louise Woodward.*

Judicial selection should be structured so that only the most competent people, who can sift through complex evidence, are able to sit on the bench. Spokane County Superior Court Judge Linda Tompkins, seen in January 2001 in Spokane, Washington, rejected motions to seal records and close pretrial hearings in a case involving the abductions of five Japanese college students and rape of two of them in two separate incidents late last year. Tompkins said she could find no evidence that reporting had jeopardized the three defendants' rights to a fair trial.

Another form of judicial selection is popular election. In some jurisdictions, judges run as members of the Republican, Democratic, or other parties; in others, they run without party affiliation. Thirteen states have partisan elections for selecting judges in courts of general jurisdiction, 17 states have nonpartisan elections, and in the remainder, upper trial court judges are appointed by the governor or the legislature.

Fourteen states have adopted some form of the **Missouri Plan** (or Merit Plan) to select appellate court judges, and six states also use it to select trial court judges. This plan consists of three parts: (1) nomination of candidates by a judicial nominating commission, (2) appointment of judges by an elected official (usually in the executive branch) from the list submitted by the commission, and (3) subsequent nonpartisan and noncompetitive elections in which incumbent judges run on their records and voters can choose to either retain or dismiss them (typically after 12 years).[27]

Some states use a variety of methods for selecting judges. For example, in New York, judges of the highest appellate court are appointed by the governor from a group of candidates selected by a judicial nominating commission and serve for 14 years; judges in the two intermediate appellate courts are selected by a screening committee, appointed by the governor, and serve for 5 years; partisan elections are held to select general jurisdiction, limited jurisdiction, and family court judges, with terms ranging from 6 to 14 years; the mayor appoints criminal court and family court judges in New York City; and mayors appoint local town judges.

General jurisdiction trial judges are selected through nonpartisan elections in 18 states, through partisan elections in 10 states, by gubernatorial appointment in 15 states, and by state legislatures in 3 states; the remaining states vary in their method of selection.[28] Appellate judges are selected by gubernatorial appointment in 21 states, by legislative appointment in 3 states, by nonpartisan elections in 14 states, by partisan elections in 8 states, and by retention elections in 4 states.

Federal Judicial Selection By constitutional mandate, federal judges, including Supreme Court justices, court of appeals judges, and district court judges, are nominated by the President and confirmed by the United States Senate. Potential nominees are often recommended by members of the Senate, or sometimes the House, who are of the President's political party. The Senate Judiciary Committee typically conducts confirmation hearings for each nominee.

On occasion, new federal judgeships are created by legislation that must be enacted by Congress. New judgeships were last created in December 1990, under Public Law 101-650, which established 11 new court of appeals and 74 new district court judgeships.

Problems of Judicial Selection The quality of the judiciary is a concern. Although merit plans, screening committees, and popular elections are designed to ensure a competent judiciary, it has often been charged that many judicial appointments are made to pay off political debts or to reward cronies and loyal friends. Also not uncommon are charges that those desiring to be nominated for judgeships are required to make significant political contributions. Another problem is the limited

Missouri Plan

A method of judicial selection that combines a judicial nominating commission, executive appointment, and nonpartisan confirmation elections.

requirements for judicial appointments, with some jurisdictions not requiring municipal or town judges to be attorneys, to be members of the bar, or to have any legal experience at all.

A great deal of concern has been raised about the qualifications of judges. In most states, people appointed to the bench have had little or no training in how to be a judge. Others may have held administrative posts and may not have appeared before a court in years. Although judicial salaries may seem impressive, they certainly cannot compare with the high salaries paid to partners in large urban law firms. It may be difficult to attract the most competent attorneys to a relatively low-paying judgeship.

A number of agencies have been created to improve the quality of the judiciary. The National Conference of State Court Judges and the National College of Juvenile Justice both operate judicial training seminars and publish manuals and guides on state-of-the-art judicial technologies. Their ongoing efforts are designed to improve the quality of the nation's judges.

Judicial Alternatives

Increased judicial caseloads have prompted the use of alternatives to the traditional judge. For example, to expedite matters in civil cases, it has become common for both parties to agree to hire a retired judge and abide by his or her decision. Jurisdictions have set up dispute resolution systems for settling minor complaints informally upon the agreement of both parties. An estimated 700 dispute resolution programs are now handling domestic conflicts, landlord–tenant cases, misdemeanors, consumer–merchant disputes, and so on.[29]

To read about judicial issues, including attacks on the judiciary, defending judicial independence, controversial judicial opinions, federal judicial selection, state judicial elections, judicial appointments in the states, impeachment and disciplining of judges, and judicial reform, go to the home page of the Brennan Judicial Center at New York University: http://brennancenter.org/

For an up-to-date list of Web links, see http://www.wadsworth.com/product/0534573053s

Fill in the blanks 15
True/False 22
Essay 10

PERSPECTIVES ON JUSTICE

The use of mediation is one of the key components of the restorative justice perspective. By removing cases from the court setting, mediation is designed to both be a money-saving device and a forum in which conflicts can be solved in a nonadversarial manner.

Other jurisdictions have created new quasi-judicial officers, such as referees or magistrates, to relieve the traditional judge of time-consuming responsibilities. The Magistrate Act of 1968 created a new type of judicial officer in the federal district court system who handles pretrial duties.[30] Federal magistrates also handle civil trials if both parties agree to the arrangement.[31]

Other jurisdictions use part-time judges. Many of these are attorneys who carry out their duties pro bono—for no or limited compensation. These "judicial adjuncts" assist the courts on a temporary basis while maintaining an active law practice.[32] The use of alternative court mechanisms should continue to grow as court congestion increases.

COURT ADMINISTRATION

Former Chief Justice Warren Burger wrote:

> The days are . . . past when a chief judge, with the help of a secretary and the clerk of the court, can manage the increasingly complex tasks required of them to keep courts functioning effectively. We must be constantly alert to new ideas, new methods, new ways of looking at the judiciary.[33]

Fill in the blanks 16
Essay 11

CRIMINAL JUSTICE AND TECHNOLOGY

Technology and Court Management

Computers are becoming an important aid in the administration and management of courts. Rapid retrieval and organization of data can be used for such functions as

- maintaining case histories and statistical reporting
- monitoring and scheduling cases
- preparing documents
- indexing cases
- issuing summonses
- notifying witnesses, attorneys, and others of required appearances
- selecting and notifying jurors
- preparing and administering budgets and payrolls

The federal government has encouraged the states to experiment with computerized information systems. Federal funds were used to begin a 50-state consortium for the purpose of establishing a standardized crime-reporting system called SEARCH (Systems for the Electronic Analysis and Retrieval of Criminal Histories).

Computer technology is also being applied in the courts in such areas as videotaped testimonies, new court-reporting devices, information systems, and data-processing systems to handle such functions as court docketing and jury management. In 1968, only 10 states had state-level automated information systems; today, all states employ such systems for a mix of tasks and duties. A survey of Georgia courts found that 84 percent used computers for three or more court administration applications.

Another modern technology being used for court administration is the facsimile (fax) machine. In Minnesota, fax machines allow the courts to relay criminal arrest or search warrants, juvenile warrants, and temporary restraining orders instantly to police officers. The Minnesota Supreme Court even allows fax documents to be filed as permanent court documents.

Court jurisdictions are also cooperating with police departments in the installation of communication systems that allow defendants to be arraigned via closed-circuit television while they are in police custody. Closed-circuit television has also been used for judicial conferences and scheduling meetings. Courts are using voice-activated cameras to record all testimony during trials; these are the sole means of keeping trial records. Four videos are made: one each for the prosecution and the defense and two for the court records.

Case management will soon be upgraded. In the 1970s, municipal courts installed tracking systems that used databases to manage court data. These older systems were limited and could not process the complex interrelationships of information pertaining to persons, cases, time, and financial matters that occur in court cases. Contemporary relational databases now provide the flexibility to handle such complex case management. To help programmers define the multiplicity of relationships that occur in a court setting, the National Center for State Courts in Williamsburg, Virginia, has developed a methodology for structuring a case management system that tracks a person to the case or cases in which he or she is a defendant, the scheduling of the cases to avoid any conflicts, and of increasing importance, the fines that have been levied and the accounts to which the money goes.

Other technologies being used include:

- *Videoconferencing.* About 400 courts across the country have videoconferencing capabilities. This technology is now being employed for juvenile detention hearings, expert witness

The need for efficient management techniques in an ever-expanding criminal court system has led to the recognition of improved court administration as a way to relieve court congestion. Management goals include improving organization and scheduling of cases, devising methods to allocate court resources efficiently, administering fines and monies due the court, preparing budgets, and overseeing personnel.

The federal courts have led the way in creating and organizing court administration. In 1939, Congress passed the Administrative Office Act, which established the Administrative Office of the United States Courts. Its director was charged with gathering statistics on the work of the federal courts and preparing the judicial budget for approval by the Conference of Senior Circuit Judges. One clause of the act created a judicial council with general supervisory responsibilities for the district and circuit courts.

Unlike the federal government, the states have experienced a slow and uneven growth in the development and application of court management principles.

testimony at trial, oral arguments on appeal, and parole hearings.

- *Evidence presentation.* More than 50 high-tech courtrooms are now equipped for real-time transcription and translation, video preservation of the court record, remote witness participation, computer graphics displays, television monitors for jurors, and computers for counsel and judge.
- *CD-ROM briefs.* Attorneys in the case of *Yukiyo v. Watanabe,* 114 F.3d 1207 (9th Cir. 1997) filed an appellate brief on a CD-ROM containing hot links to the entire trial transcript, the deposition record, the full opinions of all cases cited by the attorneys, and replications of all exhibits used by expert witnesses during trial. Though the CD-ROM brief was dismissed after opposing counsel objected to its use, it provides a glimpse of how technology can change the court process.
- *Internet.* The Internet has begun finding its way into the court system. For example, in the federal judiciary, an intranet site, J-Net, makes it easier for judges and court personnel to access important information in a timely fashion. The federal courts' Administrative Office has begun

sending official correspondence by electronic mail (email), providing instantaneous communication of important information. In 1999, an automated library management system was developed that enables judges to access a Web-based virtual law library. A Web-based electronic public access network, providing the public with access to court records and other information via the Internet, was also implemented.

The computer cannot replace the judge, but it can be used as an ally to help speed the trial process by identifying backlogs and bottlenecks that can be eradicated by applying intelligent managerial techniques. Just as a manager must know the type and quantity of goods on hand in a warehouse, so an administrative judge must have available information concerning those entering the judge's domain, what happened to them once they were in it, and how they have fared since judgment was rendered.

Critical Thinking Skills

1. What technological breakthroughs might speed the court process? In the future, could expert witnesses testify via satellite from far-off

reaches of the planet without having to travel to court? Could juries evaluate evidence online?
2. If you could, would you replace the jury system with a group of highly trained, technologically sophisticated decision makers who might use their skills to make better decisions?

InfoTrac College Edition Research

What are the issues in court administration and technology? To find out, use "court administration" and "court management" as subject guides in InfoTrac College Edition.

SOURCE: Donald C. Dilworth, "New Court Technology Will Affect How Attorneys Present Trials," *Trial* 33 (1997): 100–114.

The first state to establish an administrative office was North Dakota in 1927. Today, all states employ some form of central administration.

Almost every state is now implementing technology to aid in the administration of their court services. In most jurisdictions, centralized court administrative services perform numerous functions with the help of sophisticated computers that free the judiciary to fulfill their roles as arbiters of justice. This issue is discussed in the Criminal Justice and Technology feature.

SUMMARY

The U.S. court system is a complex social institution. There is no set pattern of court organization, and court structure varies considerably among the various state jurisdictions.

Courts are organized on the federal, state, county, and local levels of government. States commonly handle felony and misdemeanor cases separately, as well as operate independent trial and appellate courts. This structure is repeated on the federal level of jurisdiction. However, federal appellate courts also rule on state cases, and the U.S. Supreme Court is the court of last resort for all cases decided in the United States.

Directly supervising the nation's courts is the judiciary. Judges have a variety of backgrounds, skills, and qualifications. Their functions vary according to the courts on which they sit; some rule at the trial level, others handle appellate cases. Judges also serve as decision makers in administering probation departments and in working with district attorneys and police. Some judges are appointed by the state's chief executive, the governor, whereas others are elected to office by popular vote.

A recent trend has been the creation of administrative bodies to oversee court operations. Within this operational sphere are court administrators, who are using sophisticated computer operations and communications technology to ease the flow of cases and improve court efficiency.

Key Terms

adjudication	lower criminal court	court of last resort
appeal	court of general jurisdiction	writ of certiorari
plea negotiation/plea bargaining	drug court	landmark decision
adversarial procedure	federal district court	Missouri Plan
court of limited jurisdiction	U.S. circuit court	

Discussion Questions

1. What qualities should a judge have? Should the judgeship be a lifetime appointment, or should judges be reviewed periodically?
2. Do the pomp and formality of a courtroom impede justice by setting it apart from the common person?
3. What is meant when we say that the Supreme Court is "the court of last resort"?
4. Should all judges be lawyers? When can people with no legal training be of benefit to the court system?
5. What are the benefits and drawbacks of holding judicial elections?

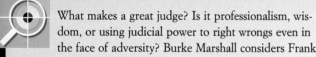

A CLOSER LOOK

What makes a great judge? Is it professionalism, wisdom, or using judicial power to right wrongs even in the face of adversity? Burke Marshall considers Frank M. Johnson, Jr., and John Minor Wisdom, senior judges on the United States Courts of Appeals for the Eleventh and Fifth Circuits, "great judges" because of their efforts to further the cause of racial equality first articulated in the landmark case of *Brown v. Board of Education:*

> This adjective can be used without qualification not just because of the superb intellectual energy and high professional standards that each brought to the bench. These two extraordinarily gifted men also met the very special—indeed, burdensome without parallel—tasks the Supreme Court thrust upon them and their colleagues, especially those sitting in the old Fifth Circuit (now the Eleventh and Fifth), as well as others in the Fourth, Sixth, and Eighth Circuits and throughout the federal court system. The Supreme Court's mandate to the inferior courts was contained—

obscurely, indirectly, and without any specific guidelines or instructions—in the final paragraph of the second *Brown* opinion, ordering a remand. I say this without hesitation because even though that paragraph could be taken, and might possibly have been intended to be taken, as referring only to the four cases before the Court, I have always interpreted it to reflect the Court's vision of the future. That final paragraph articulates the duty of the inferior courts to exercise their judicial discretion and to bring their experience to bear not just on segregated school systems, but also on other state-controlled institutions that perpetuated the monstrous subjugation of black people.

To read more of Marshall's views, go to InfoTrac College Edition and read
Burke Marshall, "In Remembrance of Judges Frank M. Johnson, Jr., and John Minor Wisdom," *Yale Law Journal,* April 2000, v109 i6 p1207

Notes

1 David Weber, "Lopez Flap Renews Hub Bar's Call for Sentence Guidelines," *Boston Herald,* 26 September 2000, p. 3.

2 Brian MacQuarrie, "Cellucci Seeks Tougher Courts: His Appeals Bill Seen as Too Broad," *Boston Globe,* 28 September 2000, p. 6.

3 Marcella Bombardieri, "Lawyers Alarmed by Calls to Oust Lopez," 18 September 2000, p. 5.

4 David J. Levin, Patrick A. Langan, and Jodi M. Brown, *State Court Sentencing of Convicted Felons, 1996* (Washington, DC: Bureau of Justice Statistics, 2000).

5 Data on court process in this chapter come from David B. Rottman, Carol R. Flango, Melissa T. Cantrell, Randall Hansen, and Neil LaFountain, *State Court Organization, 1998* (Washington, DC: Bureau of Justice Statistics, 2000). Hereinafter cited as *State Court Organization, 1998.*

6 Malcolm Feeley, *The Process Is the Punishment* (New York: Russell Sage Foundation, 1979), pp. 9–11.

7 Thomas Henderson, *The Significance of Judicial Structure: The Effect of Unification on Trial Court Operations* (Washington, DC: National Institute of Justice, 1984).

8 Charles Silberman, *Criminal Violence/ Criminal Justice* (New York: Vintage Books, 1980), p. 347.

9 Feeley, *The Process Is the Punishment,* p. 3.

10 John Larrabee, " 'You're Going to Jail Fast' in Nation's First Gun Court," *USA Today,* 19 December 1994, p. 3.

11 *State Court Organization, 1998.*

12 Bureau of Justice Assistance, *Drug Night Courts: The Cook County Experience* (Washington, DC: National Institute of Justice, 1994).

13 Terance Miethe, Hong Lu, and Eric Reese, "Reintegrative Shaming and Recidivism Risks in Drug Court: Explanations for Some Unexpected Findings," *Crime and Delinquency* 46 (2000): 522–541.

14 *State Court Organization, 1998.*

15 Ibid.

16 U.S. Constitution, Article 3, sec. 1 and 2.

17 1 Wheaton 304, 4 L.Ed. 97 (1816).

18 Administrative Office of the United States Courts, *Annual Report of the Director, 1996* (Washington, DC: U.S. Government Printing Office, 1996), p. 82.

19 Brian Ostrom and Neal Kavder, *Examining the Work of State Courts, 1998* (Williamsburg, VA: National Center for State Courts, 2000).

20 Brian A. Reaves and Pheny Z. Smith, *Felony Defendants in Large Urban Counties, 1992* (Washington, DC: Bureau of Justice Statistics, 1995).

21 "The 1999 Year End Report on the Federal Judiciary," *The Third Branch: Newsletter of the Federal Courts* 32, no. 1 (January 2000), p. 1.

22 Joel Garner, "Delay Reduction in the Federal Courts: Rule 50(B) and the Federal Speedy Trial Act of 1974," *Journal of Quantitative Criminology* 3 (1987): 229–250.

23 Robert Sigler, Joan Crowley, and Ida Johnson, "Judicial and Prosecutorial Endorsement of Innovative Techniques in the Trial of Domestic Abuse Cases," *Journal of Criminal Justice* 18 (1990): 443–453.

24 Huey-Tsyh Chen, "Dropping In and Dropping Out: Judicial Decisionmaking in the Disposition of Felony Arrests," *Journal of Criminal Justice* 19 (1991): 1–17.

25 *State Court Organization, 1998.*

26 Ibid.

27 Sari Escovitz with Fred Kurland and Nan Gold, *Judicial Selection and Tenure* (Chicago: American Judicature Society, 1974), pp. 3–16.

28 *State Court Organization, 1998.*

29 "State Adoption of Alternative Dispute Resolution," *State Court Journal* 12 (1988): 11–15.

30 Public Law 90-578, Title I, sec. 101, 82 Stat. 1113 (1968), amended; Public Law 94-577, sec. 1, Stat. 2729 (1976); Public Law 96-82, sec. 2, 93 Stat. 643 (1979).

31 See, generally, Carroll Seron, "The Professional Project of Parajudges: The Case of U.S. Magistrates," *Law and Society Review* 22 (1988): 557–575.

32 Alex Aikman, "Volunteer Lawyer-Judges Bolster Court Resources," *NIJ Reports,* January 1986, pp. 2–6.

33 Warren Burger, "Rx for Justice: Modernize the Courts," *Nation's Business,* September 1974, p. 62.

THE PROSECUTION
AND THE DEFENSE

Alex Hunter was the District Attorney of Boulder County, Colorado, where 6-year-old JonBenet Ramsey was found murdered in her home in 1997.[1] The case drew instant national attention because of the age of the victim, the fact that she was a child beauty contest winner, and the many confusing aspects of the crime.

A great deal of pressure was placed on Hunter to prosecute JonBenet's parents for the murder, despite a lack of convincing evidence. The prosecutors would have liked to hand down indictments; it probably would have made their job a lot easier. But in our system of justice, an individual is innocent until proven guilty, and the government must be able to prove beyond a reasonable doubt that the defendant committed the crime. The results of DNA and lie dectector tests raised serious doubts regarding the sufficiency of the evidence against the parents. Hunter refused to indict them, and the prosecution remains faced with the still-unsolved murder.

In a different type of case, Allan Elias, owner of a chemical processing plant in Idaho, ordered employees to clean sludge from the bottom of a 25,000-gallon tank. The tank contained sodium cyanide, and the workers were given no safety equipment. Scott Dominquez, a robust young man of 20, was overcome by cyanide gas. By the time he was rescued from the tank, he was changed forever. Now suffering an illness that resembles Parkinson's disease, he speaks with great difficulty and struggles to complete even the simplest physical tasks.

Elias was tried and found guilty of environmental crimes and could remain in prison for a decade or more.[2] Just a few years ago, environmental lawbreakers were not even indicted, and they rarely ended up behind bars. Compared with a decade ago, prosecutors are charging many more individuals with environmental crimes.

These cases illustrate the dilemmas facing the American prosecutor and his or her counterpart, the defense at-

Chapter Outline

Criminal Justice Links

Criminal Justice Viewpoints

AP/Wide World Photos

torney. Can the Ramseys, described as rich and influental, ever be indicted for their child's murder? Would a defense attorney easily get the charges dismissed for insufficint evidence? Are environmental polluters dangerous criminals? Is it because the American public fear environmental crimes that prosecutors are taking them more seriously today?

The JonBenet Ramsey case remains one of the most controversial in United States history. Here Boulder District Attorney Alex Hunter announces that the Grand Jury investigating the death of JonBenet Ramsey has been dismissed and no charges will be filed against anybody they investigated. Looking on at right is special prosecutor Michael Cane who presented the case of JonBenet's death to the Grand Jury.

prosecutor
The public official who presents the government's case against a person accused of a crime.

This chapter examines the role of the prosecutor and the defense attorney in the criminal process. The **prosecutor**, to a great extent, is the person who single-handedly controls the "charging" decision. To charge or not, and for what offense, is the prosecutor's greatest discretionary authority. The defense acts in a different capacity. Although defendants have a right to defend themselves, most are represented by a lawyer who is knowledgeable about the criminal law. The criminal lawyer has a legal obligation to make every effort to provide a competent and adequate defense.

THE PROSECUTOR

Fill in the blanks 1–2
True/False 1–3
Multiple choice 1–3

Depending on the level of government and the jurisdiction in which he or she functions, the prosecutor may be known as a district attorney, a county attorney, a state's attorney, or a U.S. attorney. Whatever the title, the prosecutor is ordinarily a member of the practicing bar who has been appointed or elected to be a public prosecutor.

The prosecutor is a participant, with the judge and defense attorney, in the adversary process. The prosecutor is responsible for bringing the state's case against the accused. He or she focuses the power of the state on those who disobey the law by charging them with a crime, releasing them from prosecution, or eventually bringing them to trial.

Although the prosecutor's primary duty is to enforce the criminal law, his or her fundamental obligation as an attorney is to seek justice as well as convict those who are guilty. For example, if the prosecutor discovers facts suggesting that the accused is innocent, he or she must bring this information to the attention of the court. The American Bar Association's *Model Code of Professional Responsibility,* Canon 7-103, addresses the ethical duties of the attorney as a public prosecutor:

> Dr 7-103 Performing the Duty of Public Prosecutor or Other Government Lawyer
>   A. A public prosecutor or other government lawyer shall not institute or cause to be instituted criminal charges when he knows or it is obvious that the charges are not supported by probable cause.
>   B. A public prosecutor or other government lawyer in criminal litigation shall make timely disclosure to counsel for the defendant, or to the defendant, if he has no counsel, of the existence of evidence, known to the prosecutor or other government lawyer, that tends to negate the guilt of the accused, mitigate the degree of the offense, or reduce the punishment.[3]

The senior prosecutor must make policy decisions on the exercise of prosecutorial enforcement powers in a wide range of cases in criminal law, consumer protection, housing, and other areas. In so doing, the prosecutor determines and ultimately shapes the manner in which justice is exercised in society.[4]

Individual prosecutors are often caught between being compelled by their supervisors to do everything possible to obtain a guilty verdict and acting as a concerned public official to ensure that justice is done. Sometimes this conflict can lead to prosecutorial misconduct. According to some legal authorities, unethical prosecutorial behavior is often motivated by the desire to obtain a conviction and by the fact that prosecutorial misbehavior is rarely punished by the courts.[5] Some prosecutors may conceal evidence or misrepresent it or influence juries by impugning the character of opposing witnesses. Even where a court may instruct a jury to ignore certain evidence, a prosecutor may attempt to sway the jury or the judge by simply mentioning the tainted evidence. Appellate courts generally uphold convictions where such misconduct is not considered serious (the *harmless error doctrine*), so prosecutors are not penalized for their behavior, nor are they held personally liable for their conduct. Overzealous, excessive, and even cruel prosecutors, motivated by political gain or notoriety, produce wrongful convictions, thereby abusing their office and the public trust.[6] According to legal expert Stanley Fisher, prosecutorial excesses appear when the government

1. Always seeks the highest charges
2. Interprets the criminal law expansively
3. Wins as many convictions as possible
4. Obtains the most severe penalties[7]

Local Prosecution: A Statistical Profile

True/False 4–6
Multiple choice 4–5

The Bureau of Justice Statistics (BJS) reports that local and state prosecutor's offices employ approximately 67,000 total staff, with a median budget of almost $226,000. The median professional staff includes three prosecuting attorneys. More than three-quarters of the nation's prosecutor's offices have a full-time chief prosecutor.

As might be expected, local prosecutor's offices are generally very small but active in terms of workload. Offices of prosecutors who try felony cases in state courts close about 200 felony cases and nearly 500 misdemeanor cases annually, with an overall conviction rate of about 85 percent.

The BJS survey also found that more than one-quarter of the prosecutor's offices experience a work-related threat or assault, usually directed at the chief prosecutor.

Other major findings of the BJS report include the following:

One of the best sources of current information on prosecution is the Bureau of Justice Statistics: http://www.ojp.usdoj.gov/bjs/pros.htm
For an up-to-date list of Web links, see http://www.wadsworth.com/product/0534573053s

1. At least three-quarters of the prosecutor's offices use videotapes or polygraph tests, and one-fourth use DNA evidence.
2. A majority of prosecutors handle new categories of offenses, including statutes dealing with child abuse, rape, environmental crimes, and domestic violence (discussed in more detail later).
3. Three-quarters experience dismissal of some felony cases because of constitutional violations, witness unavailability, or speedy trial time restrictions.[8]

The picture that emerges is of a local prosecutor who is often the single most powerful individual in local government. Because the prosecutor's office is the heart of the law enforcement and adjudication function, it interacts with the entire criminal justice system. The emphasis on a locally functioning prosecutor continues to mirror the traditional role of the office. Because the criminal law is largely the creation of state government, there is often considerable appeal to a statewide system of prosecution. However, a prosecutor who is a local official can be responsive to local conditions.

Politics and Prosecutors

Fill in the blanks 3–4
True/False 7

In the United States, federal prosecutors are appointed, but state prosecutors are often elected, and the overwhelming majority of jurisdictions elect prosecutors on a local level. Thus, the prosecutor is a political figure in the criminal justice system. He or she normally has a party affiliation, a constituency of voters and supporters, and a need to respond to community pressures and interest groups. In this regard, the American Bar Association's *Standards for Criminal Justice: Prosecution Function and Defense Function* states:

> The political process has played a significant part in the shaping of the role of the American prosecutor. Experience as a prosecutor is a familiar stepping-stone to higher political office. The "DA" has long been glamorized in fiction, films, radio, television, and other media. Many of our political leaders had their first exposure to public notice and political life in this office. A substantial number of executive and legislature officials as well as judges have served as prosecuting attorneys at some point in their careers.[9]

PERSONAL PROFILE: PATRICIA JESSAMY

Patricia Jessamy became a prosecutor by accident, literally. The incident that changed her career and life occurred one morning in 1978 on an icy patch of highway during a typically harsh Michigan winter. She was on her way to work at a law firm in Pontiac, and it was a long drive. Suddenly her car started to slide on the slippery highway, then spun around four times before landing in a ditch. Jessamy emerged unhurt, but decided to find a job closer to her home. She joined the Genesee County prosecuting attorney's office in Flint, and as she later remarked, "I took to it like a duck to water."

Seven years later, Jessamy moved to Baltimore to become assistant state's attorney, and from that point her rise was rapid. In 1986 she was named chief of the economic crimes unit, and a year later she was appointed deputy state's attorney for administration, with direct responsibility for all special investigative units and fiscal matters. In 1995, when her boss retired, Jessamy was the unanimous choice to succeed him.

Today, as chief prosecutor of the nation's 16th largest city (estimated population 675,000), she oversees close to 200 attorneys and 158 support personnel. Baltimore has what she describes as "intentionally" one of the most racially and ethnically diverse prosecutor's offices in the nation, reflecting the city's diverse population.

Although many large cities are reporting declining murder rates, Baltimore is not. Jessamy attributes this largely to the city's unusually large number of drug addicts—an estimated 60,000, close to 9 percent of the population.

To combat the problem, Jessamy says, her office is doing "a lot of innovative and creative things." These include an adaption of Boston's highly successful Operation Cease Fire. Baltimore's version, called Operation Safe Neighborhoods, involves attacking the drug and murder problems at the neighborhood level with a combination of preventive measures and treatment. She has also established a Firearms Investigation/Violence Enforcement Unit, whose top priority is to investigate and prosecute repeat offenders who illegally possess and use handguns in the commission of violent crimes.

A firm believer in a prosecutor's role as a community leader, Jessamy has used a federal block grant program to establish a network of community coordinators who work with neighborhood representatives to identify and prosecute so-called quality of life nuisance crimes.

Asked about what she considers her most significant achievement since becoming state's attorney, Jessamy has a one-word answer: automation. Her office has an up-to-date computer system with a terminal on every desk, an office network as well as an Internet connection, plus a computerized case management database. She also now has a computer lab for training staff members and a Web site.

Jessamy says that prosecutors in general face two common challenges—one material, the other perceptive. "We all need more resources." At the same time, she says, "A lot of adverse things that are happening in the criminal justice system as a whole, and especially to law enforcement agencies, spill over into the public's perception that prosecutors are responsible for handling all of the community's problems. People can accomplish a lot when they take a stand for themselves."

Patricia Jessamy's road to the state attorney's office in Baltimore began in Hollandale, Mississippi, where her father managed the family's dry-cleaning business. Jessamy went to Jackson State University to earn her bachelor's degree, then earned her J.D. from the University of Mississippi School of Law. She worked in a small law firm in Mississippi and then in various law positions as she followed her husband Howard's career as a health care administrator to Michigan and Kansas City and finally to Baltimore.

Jessamy says she has found that prosecution attracts lawyers with the highest ideals and principles. "Most of the people who leave our office do so only to make more money," she says. "They tell me, 'I don't want to leave because I have a high degree of job satisfaction. And I would stay here forever if I could make more money. I'm leaving only because I have to do more for my family and I have children who are going to go to college.'"

As for herself, Jessamy declares, "This is the best job I've ever had. Every day you go home and have the feeling that you've done something to help society. It's a very good feeling."

SOURCE: "The Prosecutor," *National District Attorney Association Journal* 34 (2000): 14.

The political nature of the prosecutor's office can heavily influence decision making. When deciding if, when, and how to handle a case, the prosecutor cannot forget that he or she may be up for election soon and have to answer to an electorate who will scrutinize those decisions. For example, in a murder trial involving a highly charged issue such as child killing, the prosecutor's decision to ask for the death penalty may hinge on his or her perception of the public's will. The Images of Justice feature highlights the partisan political process in a famous murder trial.

Essay 1–2

The Duties of the Prosecutor

The prosecutor is the chief law enforcement officer of a particular jurisdiction. His or her participation spans the entire gamut of the justice system, from the time search and arrest warrants are issued or a grand jury is impaneled to the final sen-

IMAGES OF JUSTICE

The Sacco and Vanzetti Case: Anarchism, Ethnicity, and Inadequate Evidence

The Sacco and Vanzetti case was a controversial murder trial held in Massachusetts in 1921. Two Italian immigrants—Nicola Sacco, a shoemaker, and Bartolomeo Vanzetti, a fish peddler—were both tried, convicted, and executed for the armed robbery and murder of two payroll guards outside a shoe factory in Braintree, Massachusetts. The robber grabbed the payroll, jumped into a Buick, and sped away, shooting wildly and shouting at the crowd.

Three weeks after the crime, witnesses identified both Sacco and

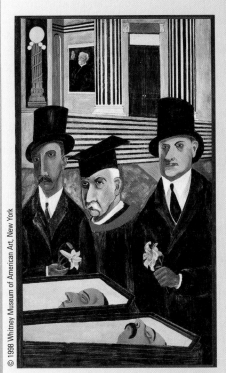

Ben Shahn's painting *Passion of Sacco and Vanzetti*.

Vanzetti as the murderers. They were carrying pistols when arrested, and Sacco's gun was of the same caliber as the one used to kill one of the murder victims. Both defendants also supported a political philosophy known as *anarchism,* which called for the overthrow of all systems of government. They explained that they were often attacked for their political beliefs, and that the pistols they were carrying at the time of their arrest were used to protect themselves.

Prior to the trial, the police chief declared that the murders could only have been committed by anarchists. Judge Webster Thayer shared the views of many people who assumed that Sacco and Vanzetti were guilty. He made it clear that the nation needed to be protected from such men. When the jury convicted both defendants, Thayer sentenced them to the electric chair. Appeals and legal reviews lasted six years, and they were finally put to death in 1927.

Many people believed there was not enough evidence to prove that Sacco and Vanzetti were guilty. The evidence was confusing. Eyewitness identification was uncertain. The trial was filled with political testimony, with much emphasis placed on the defendants' ethnicity. Many people argued that Sacco and

Vanzetti were convicted mainly because they were Italian anarchists.

Critical Thinking Skills

What is the truth about this case? Were Sacco and Vanzetti innocent men framed and tried in a kangaroo court by a prejudicial trial judge? The case was a "cause célèbre" for decades. In 1997, the governor of Massachusetts signed a proclamation that recognized the faults of the trial and cleared the names of both defendants. In recent years, new evidence has surfaced—ballistics tests on Sacco's gun, opened FBI files, and private papers from Sacco's family—suggesting that Sacco may have been guilty and that Vanzetti was probably innocent. The true story of this crime may never be known. Today, we realize that the primary responsibility of the prosecutor is to see that justice is accomplished, and a prosecution similar to that in the Sacco case would be a violation of state and federal law.

InfoTrac College Edition Research

For an interesting case history and analysis of the racial effects in sentencing, as opposed to political discrimination, see Jill Neimark, "Crime and Punishment," *Psychology Today,* July–August 1995, v28 p54

tencing decision and appeal. General duties of a prosecutor include (1) enforcing the law, (2) representing the government, (3) maintaining proper standards of conduct as an attorney and court officer, (4) developing programs and legislation for law and criminal justice reform, and (5) being a public spokesperson for the field of law. Of these, representing the government while presenting the state's case to the court is the prosecutor's central activity. Some of the main prosecutorial tasks in this regard are listed in Exhibit 10.1.

EXHIBIT 10.1 PROSECUTORIAL TASKS

1. Investigates possible violations of the law
2. Cooperates with police in investigating a crime
3. Determines what the charge will be
4. Interviews witnesses in criminal cases
5. Reviews applications for arrest and search warrants
6. Subpoenas witnesses
7. Represents the government in pretrial hearings and in motion procedures
8. Enters into plea bargaining negotiations
9. Tries criminal cases
10. Recommends sentences to courts upon convictions
11. Represents the government in appeals

Fill in the blanks 5–6
True/False 8–9
Multiple choice 6–7

The American Bar Association has published a set of *Standards for Criminal Justice*—a compilation of more than 20 volumes dealing with every aspect of justice. Go to the ABA home page and review the standards for prosecution and defense: http://www.abanet.org/abapubs/crimlaw.html

For an up-to-date list of Web links, see http://www.wadsworth.com/product/0534573053s

The American Prosecutors Research Institute (APRI) of the National District Attorneys Association (NDAA) conducts research and provides consultation to state and local prosecutors. To learn more about current research on prosecutorial issues, visit NDAA and APRI at http://www.ndaa-apri.org

For an up-to-date list of Web links, see http://www.wadsworth.com/product/0534573053s

Priority Prosecution in the Twenty-First Century

Many jurisdictions have established special programs aimed at seeking indictments and convictions of those committing major felonies, violent offenses, rapes, and white-collar crimes. In a recent national survey of prosecutorial practices, Michael Benson and his colleagues found an apparent increase in local prosecution of corporate offenders.[10] According to Benson, the federal government historically played a dominant role in controlling white-collar crime, but there appears to be an increased willingness to prosecute corporate misconduct on a local level if an offense causes substantial harm.

According to the Department of Justice, environmental crime prosecution—a field that mixes elements of law, public health, and science—has emerged as a new area of specialization. Not only federal prosecutions (see Table 10.1) but also local environmental crime prosecutions have increased dramatically.[11] Approximately half of all U.S. jurisdictions now operate special environmental units.

The most common environmental offenses being prosecuted today involve waste disposal. Such cases, often involving the illegal disposal of hazardous wastes, are referred to the prosecutor by local law enforcement and environmental regulatory agencies. The two most important factors in deciding to prosecute these crimes are the degree of harm posed by the offense and the criminal intent of the offender. If the prosecutor decides not to prosecute, it is usually because of a lack of evidence, or problems with evidentiary standards and the use of expert witnesses.

The National District Attorneys Association has responded to the concerns of prosecutors faced with the need to enforce complex environmental laws by creating the National Environmental Crime Prosecution Center. This center, modeled after the National Center for Prosecution of Child Abuse, lends assistance to district attorneys who are prosecuting environmental crimes.[12]

Another area of priority prosecutions in many jurisdictions is often called the *career criminal prosecution program.* Such programs involve identifying those dangerous offenders who commit a high proportion of crime so that prosecutors can target them for swift prosecution.[13]

Local prosecutors' handling of rape crimes continues to undergo changes. In the 1980s, most states imposed a heavy burden on rape victims, such as prompt reporting of the crime to police, corroboration by witnesses, and the need to prove physical resistance by the victim. In recent years, many states have removed these restrictions and have also made the victims' sexual history inadmissible as evidence at trial. In addition, the definition of rape has been expanded to include other

TABLE 10.1 CRACKDOWN ON ENVIRONMENTAL CRIME

Referrals to the Justice Department by the Environmental Protection Agency have increased since 1990, as have the number of prosecutions and the length of prison sentences for environmental crimes.

	1990	1991	1992	1993	1994	1995	1996	1997	1998	1999
Referrals	65	81	107	140	220	256	262	278	266	241
Defendants charged	100	104	150	161	250	245	221	322	350	324
Months sentenced	745	963	1,135	892	1,188	888	1,116	2,351	2,074	2,486

SOURCE: *Department of Justice Environmental Crime Report, 1999* (Washington, DC: 2000).

forms of penetration of the person, and laws now exist making the rape of a woman by her husband a crime. Other areas in which the justice system is expanding its rape prosecution capabilities include (1) more vigorous prosecution of acquaintance rape, (2) testing of defendants for the AIDS virus and for DNA profiling, and (3) improved coordination among police, prosecutors, rape crisis centers, and hospitals.[14]

Donald Rebovich points out that local prosecutors have also assumed the role of protector of the public health.[15] Today, they are responsible for such areas as prosecution of physician-assisted suicide, cases in which AIDS transmission is used as a weapon, violence against the elderly, cases in which pregnant women are known drug abusers, and health care fraud cases. Other new, nontraditional prosecutorial roles are listed in Table 10.2. Figure 10.1 reports data from a recent study on the extent of computer crime in the United States, and computer crime is also the focus of the Analyzing Criminal Justice Issues feature.

TABLE 10.2 FIVE MAJOR NONTRADITIONAL PROSECUTION EFFORTS

Area	Types of Statute
Domestic violence	Stalking, hate crimes, child abuse
Juvenile crime	Transfer to adult courts, capital punishment, gang prosecution
Elderly protection	Health care fraud, nursing home violence
Drunk driving	Lower blood alcohol levels, drunk boating laws, mandatory jail sentences
Computer fraud	Internet statutes, theft of trade secrets, computer seizures and viruses

Types of Prosecutors

In the federal system, prosecutors are known as U.S. attorneys and are appointed by the President. They are responsible for representing the government in federal district court. The chief prosecutor is usually an administrator, whereas assistants normally handle the actual preparation and trial work. Federal prosecutors are professional civil service employees with reasonable salaries and job security.

On the state and county levels, the **attorney general** and the **district attorney**, respectively, are the chief prosecutorial officers. Again, the bulk of the criminal prosecution and staff work is performed by scores of full- and part-time attorneys, police investigators, and clerical personnel. Most attorneys who work for prosecutors on the state and county levels are political appointees who earn low salaries, handle many cases, and in some jurisdictions maintain private law practices. Many young lawyers take these staff positions to gain the trial experience that will qualify them for better opportunities. In most state, county, and municipal jurisdictions, however, the office of the prosecutor can be described as having the proper standards of professional skill, personal integrity, and adequate working conditions.

In urban jurisdictions, the structure of the district attorney's office is often specialized, with separate divisions for felonies, misdemeanors, and trial and appeal assignments. In rural offices, chief prosecutors handle many of the criminal cases themselves. Where assistant prosecutors are employed in such areas, they often work part time, have limited

Fill in the blanks 7
True/False 10–11
Multiple choice 8

attorney general
The chief legal officer and prosecutor of each state and of the United States.

district attorney
The county prosecutor who is charged with bringing offenders to justice and enforcing the criminal laws of the state.

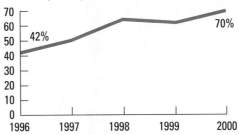

Percentage who reported an unauthorized use of their computer systems within the past 12 months

42%

70%

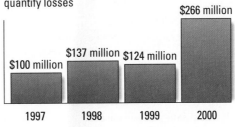

Total amount reported by respondents willing to quantify losses

$266 million

$100 million $137 million $124 million

1997   1998   1999   2000

FIGURE 10.1 SURVEY OF COMPUTER CRIME

SOURCE: Computer Security Institute, *FBI Computer Crime and Security Survey* (Washington, DC: 2000).

ANALYZING CRIMINAL JUSTICE ISSUES

Cybercrime

What do you do when the crime scene is a computer? Ordinarily, the goal of the crime scene unit is to secure the crime area, collect and preserve physical evidence, and complete reports, sketches, and photographs. With the computer crime, where do you look for the weapon?

Computer crime basically falls into two categories: theft of computer hardware, and misappropriation of information stored on computer systems. The stealing of a computer system is easily prosecuted under existing larceny statutes. But the theft of computer software or information might be more difficult.

Today, computer criminals are able to use the Internet to steal credit card numbers, manipulate the stock market, or even make sexual advances to minors. Computer crime is now among the top three white-collar crimes. Businesses lose millions of dollars each year to high-tech criminals who steal trade secrets or plant computer viruses.

Years ago, criminal statutes were often inadequate to deal with the theft of stored computer information or the use of viruses to invade computer software. Even though the criminal law applies to any medium, including the Internet, some computer crimes have avoided prosecution. For instance, making sexual overtures to minors or supplying indecent material online are the types of offenses that do not easily fit into existing criminal laws. Statutes for such crimes

are also often challenged by the courts. First Amendment proponents argue that you cannot regulate the Internet because that would violate free speech.

To deal with these problems, many states are forming High Technology Crime Units staffed by prosecutors and computer specialists to protect private industry. The federal government passed one of the first computer criminal law statutes in 1984, known as the Computer Fraud and Abuse Act. This act protects access to government computers and makes illegal interstate entry into a computer a federal crime. The Electronic Communications Privacy Act of 1986 also prohibits unauthorized interception of computer communications. The Violent Crime Control and Law Enforcement Act of 1994 added further computer crime categories for prosecution.

Critical Thinking Skills

1. A *virus* is a program that disrupts or destroys existing programs or networks. Often this high-tech vandalism is the work of *hackers,* who consider their efforts pranks. In one such case, a 25-year-old computer whiz unleashed a program that destroyed a nationwide mail network. His efforts netted him probation, a fine, and community service. Prosecutors felt the punishment was too lenient. How do you deter future virus predators?

2. It is likely that computer-related crime will increase as business and

society become more dependent on computers. One of the major new roles of the prosecutor will be to use the high-tech crime statutes to uncover and prosecute computer violations. Cybercrooks are often intelligent individuals. Do you believe local prosecutors have the skills for job?

InfoTrac College Edition Research

In the new millennium a whole new breed of cyber criminals are applying their skills for criminal gain. Information theft, attack by destructive code, denial of service, and access violations threaten companies worldwide. To find out what is being done to thwart cyber criminals, go to InfoTrac College Edition and read Luis Ramiro Hernandez, "Integrated Risk Management in the Internet Age." *Risk Management,* June 2000 v47 i6 p29

SOURCES: Computer Fraud and Abuse Act of 1984, Public Law 98-473 Title II (1984); Jon Jefferson, "Deleting Cybercrooks," *American Bar Association Journal* 83 (1997): 69; Scott Harshbarger, "Fighting High Tech Crime," *Massachusetts Bar Association Journal,* October 1997, p. 5; Christine Dugas, "Agents Armed with Computers Nab Robbers," *USA Today,* 3 March 1998, pp. B1–2; David Hamilton and David Cloud, "The Internet Under Siege," *Wall Street Journal,* 10 February 2000, p. B1.

professional opportunities, and depend on the political patronage of chief prosecutors for their positions. See Figure 10.2 for an organizational chart of a county district attorney's office.

The personnel practices, organizational structure, and political atmosphere of many prosecutor's offices often restrict the effectiveness of individual prosecutors in investigating and prosecuting criminal offenses. For many years, prosecutors have been criticized for bargaining justice away, for using their positions as a stepping-stone to higher political office, and often for failing to investigate or simply dismissing criminal cases. Lately, however, the prosecutor's public image has

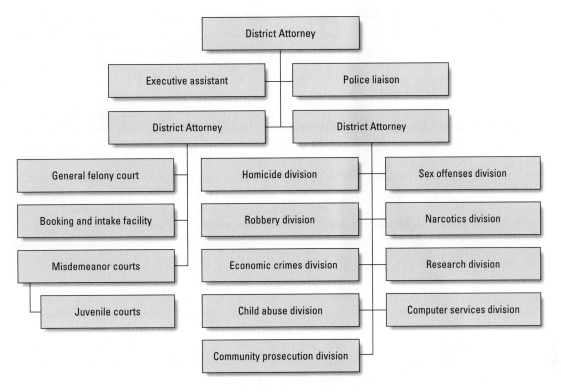

FIGURE 10.2
COUNTY DISTRICT
ATTORNEY'S
OFFICE

improved. Violations of federal law, such as white-collar crime, drug peddling, and corruption, are being more aggressively investigated by the 94 U.S. attorneys and nearly 2,000 assistant U.S. attorneys. The National Drug Prosecution Center of the National District Attorneys Association, for instance, is assisting state and federal prosecutors in enforcing complex drug laws.

Aggressive federal prosecutors in New York have made extraordinary progress in the war against insider trading and securities fraud on Wall Street, using information, wiretaps, and the federal racketeering law. Through RICO (Racketeer Influenced and Corrupt Organization Act, detailed in Chapter 4), the government has also successfully obtained convictions of important Mafia gangsters.[16]

The Law Enforcement Role of Prosecutors

True/False 12–13
Multiple choice 9–10

One of the most important of the prosecutor's many functions involves the relationship between the prosecutor and the police officer. The prosecutor has broad discretion in decisions to charge a suspect with a crime and is generally the chief law enforcement official of the jurisdiction. When it comes to processing everyday offenses and minor crimes, the prosecutor often relies on law enforcement officers to provide and initiate the formal complaint. With more serious offenses, such as some felonies, the prosecutor is involved in the criminal investigation. Some district attorney's offices carry out special investigations of organized crime, corruption of public officials, and corporate and white-collar crime, as well as vice and drug offenses. Much of the investigative work is handled by police personnel.

Police and prosecutorial relationships vary from one jurisdiction to another and often depend on whether the police agency is supplying the charge or the district attorney is investigating the matter. In either case, the prosecutor is required to maintain regular contact with the police department to develop the criminal prosecution properly. Some of the areas in which the police officer and the prosecutor work together include the following:

1. *The police investigation report.* This report is one of the most important documents in the prosecutor's file. It is basically a statement by the police of the details of the crime, including all the evidence needed to support each element of the offense. It is a critical first step in developing the government's case against a suspect.

2. *Providing legal advice.* Often the prosecutor advises the police officer about the legal issues in a given case. The prosecutor may also assist the officer by limiting unnecessary court appearances, informing the officer of the disposition of the case, and preparing the officer for pretrial appearances. As an officer of the court, the prosecutor enjoys civil immunity when assisting the police in criminal cases. This means that he or she is not liable to a criminal defendant in a civil suit.

3. *Training police personnel.* In many jurisdictions, prosecutors help train police officers in securing warrants, making legal arrests, interrogating persons in custody, and conducting legal lineups. Some police departments have police legal advisers who work with the prosecutor in training new and experienced police personnel in legal matters.[17]

Although the police and the prosecutor work together in many ways, in others they function with minimal cooperation and even distrust because of their different roles. The police and the prosecutor often compete with each other in seeking credit for the successful arrest, prosecution, and conviction of a particular defendant. In some cases, the prosecutor is insensitive to the problem of unnecessary court appearances by police officers. And in some jurisdictions, the police and the prosecutor may be outright antagonistic toward each other if there is little or no exchange of information about a particular case. The police may be unwilling to understand the prosecutor's decision not to charge a suspect with a crime after they have put much work into an investigation. The police may not agree with alternative procedures developed by the prosecutor and may prefer to press for full enforcement in the charging decision. In some cases, the prosecutor may not handle the witnesses or informants properly, which may place the police officer in an embarrassing position. On the other hand, the prosecutor may believe that the police have legally bungled an investigation and mishandled evidence. Such problems between prosecutors and police officers vary in degree from one jurisdiction to another.

At the same time, the prosecutor, as the chief law enforcement official of a jurisdiction, ordinarily depends on police and other investigative agencies for information on criminal violations. A large part of the prosecutor's work comes from complaints made by citizens or arrests made directly by police agencies. Consequently, the prosecutor needs the cooperation of the police in processing the case. Even when the prosecutor initiates investigations of suspected criminal acts, the investigations are generally conducted by police personnel. Most prosecutors willingly cooperate with law enforcement personnel so that they have the most impact possible on the investigation and a higher probability of successfully prosecuting their cases.

Fill in the blanks 8–9
True/False 14
Multiple choice 11
Essay 3

The Community Prosecution Role

The concept of **community prosecution** recognizes that crime reduction is built on community partnerships.[18] It is not just a program, but a new strategy for prosecutors to do their job. Just as police officers no longer simply make arrests (see Chapter 6), prosecutors need to do more than try cases. They become problem solvers looking to improve the overall safety and well-being of the communities over which they have jurisdiction.

The traditional prosecutorial model is case-oriented and reactive to crime, not problem-oriented and proactive. Prosecutors are centrally located and assigned to teams focusing on specific types of crime (homicide, narcotics, sex offenses, misdemeanors, and so on), with the most senior prosecutors handling the most serious felonies. Most prosecutions are arrest-generated. There is not much direct interaction among prosecutors, police, and members of the community outside of specific cases.

The lack of direct involvement by prosecutors in the community, when combined with an arrest-generated, case-oriented approach, often leads to an inefficient allocation of criminal justice resources. Often, there is no effort to allocate resources on a geographical basis or to assign prosecutors where they are needed. To align resources with community needs, some prosecutors need to be in the community daily. In this way, the prosecutor can gauge the seriousness of the crime problem and play a positive role in its solution, along with other law enforcement and community groups. Community prosecution requires that "field" prosecutors work directly with the police to improve public safety in a particular district.

The main components of such a program include (1) placing prosecutors in selected communitites to work at police stations; (2) increasing communication with police and with community groups, schools, and other organizations so prosecutors can be made aware of which cases and problems need the most attention; and (3) using prosecutorial resources to solve community problems, not just to prosecute individual cases.

What is the role of community prosecutors? They meet with the police daily to discuss law enforcement problems, strategize about the methods used to approach criminal behaviors, attend community meetings to learn about criminal incidents ranging from nuisances to felonies, and screen citizen complaints by diverting those cases that should not be in the criminal justice system.

In short, field prosecutors build partnerships with the police, citizen groups, schools, and businesses to ensure public safety for the community.

Community prosecution programs have been started in many jurisictions, with notable accomplishments. For example, prosecutors working with police and business leaders reduced the incidence of robberies near a local theater by implementing measures to make the area less attractive to criminals (better lighting, removal of pay phones, stricter enforcement of trespass laws, and increased police surveillance). In another example, community prosecutors, police, and housing inspectors closed and condemned a drug house where illegal drug activities were consistently taking place.[19]

Establishing partnerships with the community and law enforcement, as well as strong working relationships with other public and private agencies, is the key to a successful community prosecution approach. Community prosecution is not a new program, but rather an important new philosophy. It is the result of consistent efforts similar to community policing to provide better criminal justice service to the community.

Finally, one of the greatest challenges facing community prosecution is the task of evaluating its effectiveness. What is the best measure of success for a prosecutor? Is it the number of prosecutions? What about the percentage of cases won in court? Is it how many offenders are given prison time? Or is it whether crime is actually reduced in the community? Each of these factors provide a useful measure for determining the success or failure of community prosecution efforts.

community prosecution
A prosecutorial philosophy that emphasizes community support and cooperation with other agencies in preventing crime, and a less centralized and more proactive role for local prosecutors.

Community prosecution is considered community policing's legal partner. The Chicago Police Department recently launched a Web site granting users public access to a wide range of crime information. Can the same concept be applied to community prosecution? To find out, access Chicago's Web site at http://www.ci.chi.il.us/communitypolicing

For an up-to-date list of Web links, see http://www.wadsworth.com/product/0534573053s

PROSECUTORIAL DISCRETION

One might expect that after the police arrest and bring a suspect to court, the entire criminal court process would be mobilized. This is often not the case, however. For a variety of reasons, a substantial percentage of defendants are never brought to trial. The prosecutor decides whether to bring a case to trial or to

True/False 15
Multiple choice 12
Essay 4

Prosecutors have the discretion to determine whether a suspect will be brought to trial and then decide on the specific charges. Here, prosecutor Sheila Ross Finley, left, shows witness Wesley Silliman, right, knife packaging on May 23, 2000, during the murder trial of Ray Lewis, Reginald Oakley, and Joseph Sweeting at Fulton Superior Court in Atlanta, Georgia. Silliman was managing a Sports Authority store in Gwinnett County the day Lewis was there to sign autographs during Super Bowl Week in January.

AP/Wide World Photos

grand jury
A group of citizens chosen to hear charges against persons accused of crime and to determine whether there is sufficient evidence to bring the persons to trial.

dismiss it outright. Even if the prosecutor decides to pursue a case, the charges may later be dropped, in a process called *nolle prosequi,* if conditions are not favorable for a conviction.

Even in felony cases, the prosecutor ordinarily exercises considerable discretion in deciding whether to charge the accused with a crime.[20] After a police investigation, the prosecutor may be asked to review the sufficiency of the evidence to determine if a criminal complaint should be filed. In some jurisdictions, this may involve presenting the evidence at a preliminary hearing. In other cases, the prosecutor may decide to seek a criminal complaint through a **grand jury** or other information procedure. These procedures, representing the formal methods of charging the accused with a felony offense, are discussed in Chapter 11.

There is little question that prosecutors exercise a great deal of discretion in even the most serious cases. Barbara Boland collected the data for a study of the differences in how prosecutors handle felony arrests.[21] Although procedures were different in three districts, prosecutors used their discretion to dismiss a high percentage of the cases before trial. However, when cases were forwarded for trial, very few defendants were acquitted, indicating that prosecutorial discretion was exercised to screen out the weakest cases. Of those cases accepted for prosecution, a high percentage ended with the defendant pleading guilty. All the evidence here points to the conclusion that prosecutorial discretion is used to reduce potential trial cases to a minimum.

The reasons some cases are rejected or dismissed are summarized in Exhibit 10.2. Evidence problems are the most common reason for rejecting cases; many other cases are dropped because defendants plead guilty to lesser crimes. U.S. prosecutors have great discretionary power to decide not to prosecute—and are often immune from review by other officials and the courts. The key question is: When prosecutors exercise their discretion, are they more concerned with fairness, the likelihood of conviction, or political considerations?

The prosecutor may also play a limited role in exercising discretion in minor offenses, consulting with the police after their investigation results in the filing of a complaint against the accused. In such instances, the decision to charge a person with a crime may be left primarily to the discretion of the law enforcement agency. The prosecutor may decide to enter this type of case after an arrest has

EXHIBIT 10.2 WHAT ARE THE MOST COMMON REASONS FOR REJECTION OR DISMISSAL OF A CRIMINAL CASE?

Many criminal cases are rejected or dismissed because of

1. **Insufficient evidence**—a failure to find sufficient physcial evidence linking the defendant to the offense.
2. **Witness problems**—for example, when a witness fails to appear, gives unclear or inconsistent statements, is reluctant to testify, or is unsure of the identity of the offender, or when a prior relationship exists between the victim/witness and the offender.
3. **The interests of justice**—deciding not to prosecute certain types of offenses, particularly those that violate the letter but not the spirit of the law (for example, offenses involving insignificant amounts of property damage).
4. **Due process problems**—violations of the constitutional requirements for seizing evidence and for questioning the accused.
5. **A plea on another case**—for example, when the accused is charged in several cases and the prosecutor agrees to drop one or more of the cases in exchange for a plea of guilty on another case.
6. **Pretrial diversion**—agreeing to drop charges when the accused successfully meets the conditions for diversion, such as completion of a treatment program.
7. **Referral for other prosecution**—when there are other offenses, perhaps of a more serious nature, in a different jurisdiction, or deferring to a federal prosecution.

been made and a complaint has been filed with the court and subsequently determine whether to adjust the matter or proceed to trial. In some minor crimes, the prosecutor may not even appear until the trial stage of the process (if at all); the police officer sometimes handles the entire case, including its prosecution.

The Exercise of Discretion

Fill in the blanks 10

The power to institute or discontinue formal charges against the defendant is the key to the prosecutorial function, representing the control and power the prosecutor has over an individual's liberty. The prosecutor has broad discretion in the exercise of his or her duties; this discretion is subject to few limitations and often puts the prosecutor in the position of making difficult decisions without appropriate policies and guidelines. Nearly 70 years ago, Newman Baker commented on the problems of prosecutorial decision making:

> "To prosecute or not to prosecute?" is a question which comes to mind of this official scores of times each day. A law has been contravened and the statute says he is bound to commence proceedings. His legal duty is clear. But what will be the result? Will it be a waste of time? Will it be expensive to the state? Will it be unfair to the defendant (the prosecutor applying his own ideas of justice)? Will it serve any good purpose to society in general? Will it have good publicity value? Will it cause a political squabble? Will it prevent the prosecutor from carrying the offender's home precinct when he, the prosecutor, runs for Congress after his term as prosecutor? Was the law violated a foolish piece of legislation? If the offender is a friend, is it the square thing to do to reward friendship by initiating criminal proceedings? These and many similar considerations are bound to come to the mind of the man responsible for setting the wheels of criminal justice in motion.[22]

Once involved in a case, the prosecutor must also determine the formal charge. Deciding whether or not to charge a person with a crime is often not easy—nor is determining the appropriate charge. Should a 17-year-old boy be charged with burglary or handled as a juvenile offender in the juvenile court? Would it be more appropriate to reduce a drug charge from the sale of marijuana to mere possession? Should an offense be considered mayhem, battery, or simply assault?

What, then, are the factors that influence prosecutorial decision making?

System Factors In determining what course of action to take, the prosecutor has a significant effect on the criminal justice system. Initiating formal charges against all defendants arrested by the police would clog the courts with numerous petty crimes and cases with little chance of conviction. The prosecutor would waste time on minor cases that could have been better spent on the investigation and prosecution of more serious crimes. Effective screening by prosecutors can eliminate from the judicial system many cases in which convictions cannot reasonably be obtained or that may be inappropriate for criminal action, such as petty thefts, minor crimes by first offenders, and criminal acts involving offenders in need of special services (for example, emotionally disturbed or mentally retarded offenders). The prosecutor can then concentrate on bringing to trial offenders who commit serious personal and property crimes, such as homicide, burglary, rape, and robbery.

Essay 5

Case Factors Because they are ultimately responsible for deciding whether to prosecute, prosecutors must be aware of the wide variety of circumstances that affect their decisions. Frank Miller, in his classic work *Prosecution: The Decision to Charge a Suspect with a Crime,* identified the factors that affect discretion and the charging decision. Among these factors are

1. The attitude of the victim
2. The cost of prosecution to the criminal justice system
3. The avoidance of undue harm to the suspect
4. The availability of alternative procedures
5. The use of civil sanctions
6. The willingness of the suspect to cooperate with law enforcement authorities[23]

Evidence also indicates that the relationship between the victim and the criminal may greatly influence whether a prosecutor wishes to pursue a case. Barbara Boland found that conviction rates were much lower in cases involving friends (30%) or relatives (19%) than they were in cases involving strangers (48%).[24] Prosecutors who are aware of the lower conviction probability in friend/relative cases may be reluctant to pursue them unless they involve serious offenses.

Fill in the blanks 11
True/False 16–17
Multiple choice 13

Disposition Alternatives In determining which cases should be eliminated from the criminal process or brought to trial, the prosecutor has the opportunity to select alternative actions if they are more appropriate. For example, offenders may be alcoholics or narcotic addicts; they may be mentally ill; or they may have been led into crime by their family situation or their inability to get a job. If they are not helped, they may well return to crime. In many cases, only minimal intrusions on defendants' liberty seem necessary. Often it will be enough simply to refer offenders to the appropriate agency in the community and hope that they will take advantage of the help offered. The prosecutor might, for example, be willing to drop charges if a man goes to an employment agency and makes a bona fide effort to get a job, seeks help from a social service agency, or resumes his education. The prosecutor retains legal power to file a charge until the period of limitations has expired, but as a practical matter, unless the offense is repeated, reviewing the initial charge would be unusual.

Today, particularly in those jurisdictions where alternative programs exist, prosecutors are identifying and diverting offenders to community agencies in cases where the full criminal process does not appear necessary. This may occur in certain juvenile cases, with alcoholic and drug offenders, and in nonsupport paternity, prostitution, and gambling offenses. The American Bar Association recommends the use of social service programs as an appropriate alternative to prosecution.[25]

Dealing with the accused in a noncriminal fashion has come to be known as pretrial **diversion**. In this process, the prosecutor postpones or eliminates criminal prosecution in exchange for the alleged offender's participation in a rehabili-

diversion
The use of a noncriminal alternative to trial, such as referral to treatment or employment programs.

tation program.[26] In recent years, the reduced cost and general utility of such programs have made them an important factor in prosecutorial discretion and a major part of the criminal justice system. A more detailed discussion of pretrial diversion is found in Chapter 11.

The Role of Prosecutorial Discretion

Fill in the blanks 12
True/False 18
Multiple choice 14

The proper exercise of prosecutorial discretion can improve the criminal justice process, preventing unnecessarily rigid implementation of the criminal law. Discretion allows the prosecutor to consider alternative decisions and humanize the operation of the criminal justice system. If prosecutors had little or no discretion, they would be forced to prosecute all cases brought to their attention. According to Judge Charles Breitel, "If every policeman, every prosecutor, every court, and every postsentence agency performed his or its responsibility in strict accordance with the rules of law, precisely and narrowly laid down, the criminal law would be ordered but intolerable."[27]

On the other hand, too much discretion can lead to abuses that result in the abandonment of law. One of the nation's most eminent legal scholars, Roscoe Pound, defined discretion as

> an authority conferred by law to act in certain conditions or situations in accordance with an official's or an official agency's considered judgment and conscience. It is an idea of morals, belonging to the twilight between law and morals.[28]

In terms of prosecutorial practices, this definition of discretion implies the need to select and choose among alternative decisions—to move cases from the criminal process, to modify criminal charges, or to prosecute to the fullest intent of legal authority. Because there is no easy way to make these decisions, the prosecutor needs to establish standards for evaluating whether criminal proceedings should be brought against an accused. The most important decision in any criminal case—especially in a capital case—is the discretionary decision made by the prosecution to charge someone with a felony. In the famous 1997 Louise Woodward trial (the au pair case), the district attorney obtained an indictment for second-degree murder. It is doubtful whether the prosecutors believed they could sustain a conviction. Yet their decision was probably based on legal tactical advantages (no bail, a jury compromise on manslaughter) as well as the political environment. Whatever happened in this case, overcharging set the stage for judicial discretion and a political outcry. Proactive prosecution strategies may cause public resentment and inappropriate interference by the trial judge.

PERSPECTIVES ON JUSTICE

The charging decision is a major prosecutorial function. Broad discretion is given to the prosecutor in deciding to bring charges against a defendant. Can the exercise of this discretion be reduced to some clearly defined formula?

An alternative to prosecution is diversion. Diversion programs often allow prosecutors to use the rehabilitative persective on justice, because there is an official suspension of the criminal process. But the use of a noncriminal disposition incorporates procedures that permit the prosecutor to proceed with the case at a future time. The authority to institute diversion proceedings is an important part of the prosecutor's discretion. Note how a public official can move from one theoretical perspective to another.

THE DEFENSE ATTORNEY

The **defense attorney** is the counterpart of the prosecuting attorney in the criminal process. The accused has a constitutional right to counsel; if the defendant cannot afford an attorney, the state must provide one.

For many years, much of the legal community looked down on the criminal defense attorney and the practice of criminal law. This attitude stemmed from the kinds of legal work a defense attorney was forced to do—working with shady characters, negotiating for the release of known thugs and hoodlums, and often overzealously defending alleged criminals in the criminal trial. Lawyers were reluctant to specialize in criminal law because they received comparatively low pay and often provided services without compensation. In addition, law schools in the past seldom offered more than one or two courses in criminal law and trial practice.

In recent years, however, with the implementation of constitutional requirements regarding the right to counsel, interest has grown in criminal law. Almost all law schools today have clinical programs that employ students as voluntary defense attorneys. They also offer courses in trial tactics, brief writing, and appellate procedures. In addition, legal organizations such as the American Bar Association, the National Legal Aid and Defenders Association, and the National Association of Criminal Defense Lawyers have assisted in recruiting able lawyers to do criminal defense work. As the American Bar Association has noted, "An almost indispensable condition to fundamental improvement of American criminal justice is the active and knowledgeable support of the bar as a whole."[29]

The Role of the Criminal Defense Attorney

The defense counsel is an attorney as well as an officer of the court. As an attorney, the defense counsel is obligated to uphold the integrity of the legal profession and to observe the requirements of the *Model Rules of Professional Conduct* in the defense of a client. According to the *Rules,* the duties of the lawyer to the adversary system of justice are as follows:

> Our legal system provides for the adjudication of disputes governed by the rules of substantive, evidentiary, and procedural law. An adversary presentation counters the natural human tendency to judge too swiftly in terms of the familiar that which is not yet fully known; the advocate, by his zealous preparation of facts and law, enables the tribunal to come to the hearing with an open and neutral mind to render impartial judgments. The duty of the lawyer to his client and his duty to the legal system are the same: To represent his client zealously within the boundaries of the law.[30]

The defense counsel performs many functions while representing the accused in the criminal process. Exhibit 10.3 lists some of the major duties of a defense attorney, whether privately employed by the accused, appointed by the court, or serving as a public defender.

Because of the way the U.S. system of justice operates today, criminal defense attorneys face many role conflicts. They are viewed as the prime movers in what is essentially an adversary process: The prosecution and the defense engage in conflict over the facts of the case, with the prosecutor arguing the case for the state and the defense counsel using all the means at his or her disposal to aid the client. This system can be compared to a sporting event in which the government and the accused are the players and

defense attorney
Legal counsel for the defendant in a criminal case, representing the accused person from arrest to final appeal.

Fill in the blanks 13
True/False 19

 Combining nearly a century of tradition with innovation, the National Legal Aid and Defenders Association offers leadership skills to support public defender services. To learn more about this organization, go to the NLADA home page: http://www.nlada.org/html
For an up-to-date list of Web links, see http://www.wadsworth.com/product/0534573053s

True/False 20
Multiple choice 15
Essay 6

EXHIBIT 10.3 FUNCTIONS OF THE DEFENSE ATTORNEY

- Investigating the incident
- Interviewing the client, police, and other witnesses
- Discussing the matter with the prosecutor
- Representing the defendant at the various pretrial procedures, such as arrest, interrogation, lineup, and arraignment
- Entering into plea negotiations
- Preparing the case for trial, including developing tactics and strategy
- Filing and arguing legal motions with the court
- Representing the defendant at trial
- Providing assistance at sentencing
- Determining the appropriate basis for appeal

the judge and the jury are the referees. As members of the legal profession, defense counsel must also be aware of their role as officers of the court. As attorneys, defense counsel are obligated to uphold the integrity of the legal profession and to rely on constitutional ideals of fair play and professional ethics to provide adequate representation for a client.

Ethical Issues

Essay 7

As an officer of the court, along with the judge, prosecutors, and other trial participants, the defense attorney seeks to uncover the basic facts and elements of the criminal act. In this dual capacity as both a defense advocate and an officer of the court, the attorney is often confronted with conflicting obligations to his or her client and profession. Monroe Freedman identifies three of the most difficult problems involving the professional responsibility of the criminal defense lawyer:

1. Is it proper to cross-examine for the purpose of discrediting the reliability or credibility of an adverse witness whom you know to be telling the truth?
2. Is it proper to put a witness on the stand when you know he will commit perjury?
3. Is it proper to give your client legal advice when you have reason to believe that the knowledge you give him will tempt him to commit perjury?[31]

There are other, equally important, issues with respect to a lawyer's ethical responsibilities. Suppose a client confides that he is planning to commit a crime. What are the defense attorney's ethical responsibilities in this case? Obviously, the lawyer would have to counsel the client to obey the law; if the lawyer assisted the client in engaging in illegal behavior, the lawyer would be subject to charges of

An unruly defendant, Christopher Charles Lightsey, has his mouth taped after he screamed obscenities during trial. A defense attorney is legally obligated to uphold the integrity of the legal profession and give the best defense possible even if the client's behavior is shocking or loathsome. Lightsey was sentenced to death for murder.

© Henry A. Barrios/*The Bakersfield Californian*

unprofessional conduct and even criminal liability. Suppose the defense attorney is aware that the police made a procedural error and that the guilty client could be acquitted on a technicality. What are the attorney's ethical responsibilities in this case? The criminal lawyer needs to be aware of these troublesome situations to properly balance the duties of being an attorney with those of being an officer of the court.

Because the defense attorney and the prosecutor have different roles, their ethical dilemmas may also differ. The defense attorney must maintain confidentiality and advise his or her client of the constitutional requirements of counsel, the privilege against self-incrimination, and the right to trial. The prosecutor represents the public and is not required to abide by such restrictions in the same way. In some cases, the defense counsel may even be justified in withholding evidence by keeping the defendant from testifying at the trial. In addition, whereas prosecutors are prohibited from expressing a personal opinion on the defendant's guilt during summation of the case, defense attorneys are not barred from expressing their belief about a client's innocence.

As a practical matter, therefore, ethical rules may differ because the state is bringing the action against the defendant and must prove the case beyond a reasonable doubt. This is also why a defendant who is found guilty can appeal, whereas a prosecutor must live with an acquittal, and why defense lawyers generally have more latitude in performing their duties on behalf of their clients. However, neither side should encourage unethical practices.[32]

PERSPECTIVES ON JUSTICE

The role of counsel for the accused is complex, involving multiple obligations. Toward the client, the defense lawyer is a counselor and advocate; toward the prosecutor, the lawyer is a professional adversary; and toward the court, the lawyer is both advocate for the client and officer of the court. The defense attorney advocates the use of a due process perspective because it provides fair and equitable treatment to those accused of a crime. Public defenders use hearings, notices, motions, and other legal devices in gaining outcomes for their clients (acquittals, charge reductions, and shorter prison sentences).

THE RIGHT TO COUNSEL

Multiple choice 16–19

Over the past decade, the rules and procedures of criminal justice administration have become extremely complex. Bringing a case to court involves a detailed investigation of the crime, knowledge of court procedures, the use of rules of evidence, and skills in criminal advocacy. Both the state and the defense must have this specialized expertise, particularly when an individual's freedom or even life is at stake. Consequently, the right to the assistance of counsel in the criminal justice system is essential if the defendant is to have a fair chance of presenting a case in the adversary process.

indigent
A poor defendant who lacks the funds to hire a private attorney and is therefore entitled to free counsel.

One of the most critical issues in the justice system has been whether an **indigent** defendant has the right to counsel. Can an accused person who is poor and cannot afford an attorney have a fair trial without the assistance of counsel? Is counsel required at preliminary hearings? Should the convicted indigent offender be given counsel at state expense in appeals of the case? Questions such as these have arisen constantly in recent years. The federal court system has long provided counsel to indigent defendants on the basis of the Sixth Amendment to the U.S. Constitution, unless he or she waives this right. This constitutional mandate clearly applies to the federal courts, but its application to state criminal proceedings has been less certain.

In the landmark case of *Gideon v. Wainwright* in 1963, the U.S. Supreme Court took the first major step on the issue of right to counsel by holding that state courts must provide counsel to indigent defendants in felony prosecutions.[33] Nine years later, in *Argersinger v. Hamlin* (1972), the Court extended the obligation to provide counsel to all criminal cases in which the penalty includes imprisonment— regardless of whether the offense is a felony or a misdemeanor.[34] These two major decisions apply to the Sixth Amendment right to counsel when presenting a defense at the trial stage of the criminal justice system.

In numerous Supreme Court decisions since *Gideon,* the states have been required to provide counsel for indigent defendants at virtually all other stages of the criminal process, beginning with the arrest and concluding with the defendant's release from the system.

Today, the Sixth Amendment right to counsel and the Fourth Amendment guarantee of due process of law have been judicially interpreted together to require state-provided counsel in all types of criminal proceedings. The right to counsel begins at the earliest stages of the justice system, usually when a criminal suspect is interrogated while in police custody; *Miranda v. Arizona* (see Chapter 8) held that any statements made by the accused when in custody are inadmissible at trial unless the accused has been informed of the right to counsel and, if indigent, the right to have an attorney appointed by the state.[35]

The Supreme Court also has extended the right to counsel to postconviction and other collateral proceedings, such as probation and parole revocation and appeal. When, for example, the court intends to revoke a defendant's probation and impose a sentence, the probationer has a right to counsel at the deferred sentence hearing.[36] Where the state provides for an appellate review of the criminal conviction, the defendant is entitled to the assistance of counsel for this initial appeal.[37] However, the defendant does not have the right to counsel for an appellate review beyond the original appeal or for a discretionary review to the U.S. Supreme Court. The Supreme Court has also required states to provide counsel in other proceedings that involve the loss of personal liberty, such as juvenile delinquency hearings[38] and mental health commitments.[39]

Areas still remain in the criminal justice system where the courts have not required assistance of counsel for the accused. These include (1) preindictment lineups; (2) booking procedures, including the taking of fingerprints and other forms of identification; (3) grand jury investigations; (4) appeals beyond the first review; (5) disciplinary proceedings in correctional institutions; and (6) postrelease revocation hearings. Nevertheless, the general rule of thumb is that no person can be deprived of freedom without representation by counsel.

Today, the scope of representation for the indigent defendant is believed to cover virtually all areas of criminal process and most certainly those critical points at which a person's liberty is at stake. Justice Hugo Black, one of the greatest Supreme Court justices of the twentieth century, acknowledged the need for public defenders when he wrote, in his dissent in *Betts v. Brady,* "A fair trial is impossible if an indigent is not provided with a free attorney."[40]

Table 10.3 summarizes the major U.S. Supreme Court decisions granting defendants the right to counsel throughout the criminal justice system. The Law in Review feature on page 319 discusses the landmark *Gideon v. Wainwright* case, which guaranteed the right to counsel in felony trials.

TABLE 10.3 MAJOR U.S. SUPREME COURT CASES GRANTING THE RIGHT TO COUNSEL

Case	Stage and Ruling
Escobedo v. Illinois, 378 U.S. 478 (1964)	The defendant has the right to counsel during the course of any police interrogation.
Miranda v. Arizona, 384 U.S. 436 (1966)	Procedural safeguards, including the right to counsel, must be followed at custodial interrogation to secure the privilege against self-incrimination.
Massiah v. United States, 377 U.S. 201 (1964)	The defendant has the right to counsel during postindictment interrogation.
Hamilton v. Alabama, 368 U.S. 52 (1961)	The arraignment is a critical stage in the criminal process, so that denial of the right to counsel is a violation of due process of law.
Coleman v. Alabama, 399 U.S. 1 (1970)	The preliminary hearing is a critical stage in a criminal prosecution requiring the state to provide the indigent defendant with counsel.
United States v. Wade, 388 U.S. 218 (1967)	A defendant in a pretrial, postindictment lineup for identification purposes has the right to assistance of counsel.
Moore v. Michigan, 355 U.S. 155 (1957)	The defendant has the right to counsel when submitting a guilty plea to the court.
Brady v. United States, 397 U.S. 742 (1970)	Counsel is required during the plea bargaining process.
Powell v. Alabama, 287 U.S. 45 (1932)	Defendants have the right to counsel at their trial in a state capital case.
Gideon v. Wainwright, 372 U.S. 335 (1963)	An indigent defendant charged in a state court with a noncapital felony has the right to the assistance of free counsel at trial under the due process clause of the Fourteenth Amendment.
Argersinger v. Hamlin, 407 U.S. 25 (1972)	A defendant has the right to counsel at trial whenever he or she may be imprisoned, even for one day, for any offense, whether classified as a misdemeanor or a felony.
Faretta v. California, 422 U.S. 806 (1975)	The defendant has a constitutional right to defend herself or himself if her or his waiver of the right to counsel is knowing and intelligent.
In re Gault, 387 U.S. 1 (1967)	Procedural due process, including the right to counsel, applies to juvenile delinquency adjudication that may lead to a child's commitment to a state institution.
Townsend v. Burke, 334 U.S. 736 (1948)	A convicted offender has a right to counsel at the time of sentencing.
Douglas v. California, 372 U.S. 353 (1963)	An indigent defendant granted a first appeal from a criminal conviction has the right to be represented by counsel on appeal.
Mempa v. Rhay, 389 U.S. 128 (1967)	A convicted offender has the right to assistance of counsel at probation revocation hearings where the sentence has been deferred.
Gagnon v. Scarpelli, 411 U.S. 778 (1973) *Morrissey v. Brewer,* 408 U.S. 471 (1972)	The defendant has a right to counsel in the court's discretion at probation revocation and parole board revocation hearings.

True/False 21
Multiple choice 20

The Private Bar

Today, the lawyer whose practice involves a substantial proportion of criminal cases is often considered a specialist in the field. Most lawyers are not prepared in law school for criminal work, so their skill often results from their experience in the trial courts. Lawyers such as Alan Dershowitz, Gerry Spencer, and Roy Black are the elite of the private criminal bar; they are nationally known criminal defense attorneys who often represent defendants for large fees in celebrated and widely publicized cases. Attorneys like these are relatively few in number and do

Gideon v. Wainwright (1963)

Facts

Clarence Gideon was charged in a Florida state court with having broken into and entered a poolroom with intent to commit a misdemeanor. This offense is a felony under Florida law. Appearing in court without funds and without a lawyer, the petitioner asked the court to appoint counsel for him. The court replied that it could not appoint counsel because under Florida law the court could appoint counsel for a defendant only when that person was charged with a capital offense.

In his jury trial, Gideon conducted his defense about as well as could be expected from a layperson. He made an opening statement to the jury, cross-examined the state's witnesses, presented witnesses in his own defense, decline to testify himself, and made a short argument emphasizing his innocence of the charge. The jury returned a verdict of guilty, and Gideon was sentenced to serve five years in the Florida state prison.

Gideon filed a habeas corpus petition in the Florida Supreme Court attacking his conviction and sentence on the grounds that the trial court's refusal to appoint counsel for him denied him rights guaranteed by the Constitution and the Bill of Rights. Relief was denied.

Gideon then filed an *in forma pauperis* appeal to the U.S. Supreme Court, which granted certiorari and appointed counsel to represent him. The Supreme Court took on this case to review its earlier decision in *Betts v. Brady* (1942), which held that the refusal to appoint counsel is not so "offensive to the common and fundamental ideas of fairness" as to amount to a denial of due process.

The issues faced by the Supreme Court were simple but of gigantic importance: (1) Is an indigent defendant charged in a state court with a noncapital felony entitled to the assistance of a lawyer under the due process clause of the Fourteenth Amendment? (2) Should *Betts v. Brady* be overruled?

Decision

Justice Hugo Black delivered the opinion of the Court:

> We accept *Betts v. Brady*'s assumption, based as it was on our prior cases, that a provision of the Bill of Rights which is fundamental and essential to a fair trial is made obligatory upon the States by the Fourth Amendment. We think the Court in *Betts v. Brady* was wrong, however, in concluding that the Sixth Amendment's guarantee is not one of the fundamental rights. In our adversary system of criminal justice, any person brought into court, who is too poor to hire a lawyer, cannot be assured a fair trial unless counsel is provided for him. That government hires lawyers to prosecute and defendants who have the money to hire lawyers to defend, are the strongest indications of the widespread belief that lawyers in criminal court are necessi-
> ties, not luxuries. The right of one charged with crime to counsel may not be deemed essential to fair trial in some countries, but it is in ours.

Significance of the Case

The U.S. Supreme Court unanimously overruled its earlier decision in *Betts v. Brady* and explicitly held that the right to counsel in criminal cases is fundamental and essential to a fair trial and as such applicable to the states by way of the Fourteenth Amendment. The *Gideon* decision thus guarantees the right to counsel in criminal cases in both federal and state proceedings. The refusal to appoint counsel for indigent defendants consequently violates the due process clause of the Fourteenth Amendment and the right to counsel of the Sixth Amendment.

InfoTrac College Edition Research

For further information on the right to counsel, see Martin Gardner, "Sixth Amendment Right to Counsel and Its Underlying Values," *Journal of Criminal Law and Criminology,* 2000, v90 p397

not regularly defend the ordinary criminal defendant. Johnnie Cochran and Robert Shapiro are two high-profile California attorneys with considerable trial experience and public exposure who handled the O. J. Simpson double murder case. Barry Scheck participated in the Simpson trial and was lead counsel in the 1997 Louise Woodward (nanny) murder case.

In addition to this limited group of well-known criminal lawyers, some lawyers and law firms serve as house counsel for such professional criminals as narcotics dealers, gamblers, prostitutes, and even big-time burglars. These lawyers, however, constitute a very small percentage of the private criminal bar.

A large number of criminal defendants are represented by lawyers who often accept many cases for small fees. These lawyers may belong to small law firms or work alone, but a sizable portion of their practice involves representing those accused of crime. Other private practitioners occasionally take on criminal matters as part of their general practice. Criminal lawyers often work on the fringe of the legal business, and they receive little respect from colleagues or the community as a whole.

All but the most eminent criminal lawyers are bound to spend much of their working lives in overcrowded, physically unpleasant courts, dealing with people who have committed questionable acts, and attempting to put the best possible construction on those acts. It is not the sort of working environment that most people choose. Finally, the professional status of the criminal lawyer tends to be low. Generally, the criminal lawyer is identified unjustifiably in the public eye with the client he or she represents.

Another problem associated with the private practice of criminal law is that the fee system can create a conflict of interest. Private attorneys are usually paid in advance and do not expect additional funds whether their client is convicted or acquitted. Many are aware of the guilt of their client before the trial begins, and they earn the greatest profit if they get the case settled as quickly as possible. This usually means bargaining with the prosecutor rather than going to trial. Even if attorneys win the case at trial, they may lose personally because the time expended will not be compensated by more than the gratitude of their client. And, of course, many criminal defendants cannot afford even a modest legal fee and therefore cannot avail themselves of the services of a private attorney. For these reasons, an elaborate, publicly funded legal system has developed.

Legal Services for the Indigent

To satisfy the constitutional requirement that indigent defendants be provided with the assistance of counsel at various stages of the criminal process, the federal government and the states have had to evaluate and expand criminal defense services. Prior to the Supreme Court's mandate in *Gideon v. Wainwright,* public defense services were provided mainly by local private attorneys appointed and paid for by the court, called **assigned counsel**, or by limited **public defender** programs. In 1961, for example, public defender services existed in only 3 percent of the counties in the United States, serving only about one-quarter of the country's population.[41] The general lack of defense services for indigents traditionally stemmed from these causes, among others:

1. Until fairly recently, laws of most jurisdictions did not require the assistance of counsel for felony offenders and others.
2. Only a few attorneys were interested in criminal law practice.
3. The organized legal bar was generally indifferent to the need for criminal defense assistance.
4. The caseloads of lawyers working in public defender agencies were staggering.
5. Financial resources for courts and defense programs were limited.

However, since the *Gideon* case in 1963 and the *Argersinger* decision in 1972, the criminal justice system has been forced to increase public defender services. Today, about 3,000 state and local agencies are providing indigent legal services in the United States.

Providing legal services for indigent offenders is a huge undertaking; more than 4.5 million offenders are given free legal services annually. And although most states have a formal set of rules for determining who is indigent, and many require repayment to the state for at least part of their legal services (known as **recoupment**), indigent legal services still cost more than $1.5 billion annually.

Multiple choice 21–22
Essay 8

assigned counsel
A private attorney appointed by the court to represent a criminal defendant who cannot afford to pay for a lawyer.

public defender
An attorney employed by the government to represent criminal defendants who cannot afford to pay for a lawyer.

recoupment
Process by which the state later recovers some or all of the cost of providing free legal counsel to an indigent defendant.

Programs providing assistance of counsel to indigent defendants can be divided into three major categories: public defender systems, assigned counsel systems, and contract systems. Other approaches to the delivery of legal services include mixed systems, such as representation by both public defenders and the private bar; law school clinical programs; and prepaid legal services. Of the three major approaches, assigned counsel systems are the most common; a majority of U.S. courts use this method. However, public defender programs seem to be on the increase, and many jurisdictions use a combination of programs statewide.

Fill in the blanks 14–15
True/False 22
Multiple choice 23–24

Public Defenders   The first public defender program in the United States opened in 1913 in Los Angeles. Over the years, primarily as a result of efforts by judicial leaders and bar groups, the public defender program became the model for the delivery of legal services to indigent defendants in criminal cases throughout the country.

Most public defender offices can be thought of as law firms whose only clients are criminal offenders. However, they are generally administered at one of two government levels: statewide or county. About one-third of the states have a statewide public defender's office headed by a chief public defender who administers the system. In some of these states, the chief defender establishes offices in all counties around the state; in others, the chief defender relies on part-time private attorneys to provide indigent legal services in rural counties. Statewide public defenders may be organized as part of the judicial branch, part of the executive branch, an independent state agency, or even a private, nonprofit organization.

Assigned Counsel System   In contrast to the public defender system, the assigned counsel system involves the use of private attorneys appointed by the court to represent indigent defendants. The private attorney is selected from a list of attorneys maintained by the court and is reimbursed by the state for any legal services rendered to the client. Assigned counsels are usually used in rural areas, which do not have sufficient caseloads to justify a full-time public defender staff.

There are two main types of assigned counsel systems. In the first, the presiding judge appoints attorneys on a case-by-case basis; this is referred to as an *ad hoc* assigned counsel system. In a *coordinated* assigned counsel system, an administrator oversees the appointment of counsel and sets up guidelines for the administration of indigent legal services. The fees awarded assigned counsels can vary widely, ranging from a low of $10 per hour for handling a misdemeanor out of court to a high of $100 per hour for a serious felony. Some jurisdictions may establish a maximum allowance per case of $750 for a misdemeanor and $1500 for a felony. Average rates seem to be between $40 and $80 per hour, depending on the nature of the case. Proposals for higher rates are pending. Restructuring the attorney fee system is undoubtedly needed to maintain fair standards for the payment of such legal services.

The assigned counsel system, unless organized properly, suffers from such problems as unequal assignments, inadequate legal fees, and the lack of supportive or supervisory services. Other disadvantages

Public defenders are appointed to help clients who are indigent and cannot afford a proper legal defense. Here, Julie Ann S. Barnes confers with one of her lawyers, Louis R. Aloise, during her arraignment in Worcester Superior Court February 2000, in connection with the December 3, 1999, Worcester Cold Storage Warehouse Fire. Barnes pleaded innocent to six counts each of manslaughter for starting a deadly warehouse fire that killed six firefighters. Her attorneys were able to convince the judge that the fire was an accident, and Barnes was released. In Massachusetts there is no legal obligation to report a fire.

AP/Wide World Photos

are the frequent use of inexperienced attorneys and the tendency to use the guilty plea too quickly. Some judicial experts believe that the assigned counsel system is still no more than an ad hoc approach that raises serious questions about the quality of representation. However, the assigned counsel system is simple to operate. It also offers the private bar an important role in providing indigent legal services, because most public defender systems cannot represent all needy criminal defendants. Thus, the appointed counsel system gives attorneys the opportunity to do criminal defense work.

contract system
Provision of legal services to indigent defendants by private attorneys under contract to the state or county.

Contract System The **contract system** is a relative newcomer in providing legal services to the indigent; it is being used in a small percentage of the counties around the United States. In this system, a block grant is given to a lawyer or law firm to handle indigent defense cases. In some instances, the attorney is given a set amount of money and is required to handle all cases assigned. In other jurisdictions, contract lawyers agree to provide legal representation for a set number of cases at a fixed fee. A third system involves representation at an estimated cost per case until the dollar amount of the contract is reached. At that point, the contract may be renegotiated, but the lawyers are not obligated to take new cases.

The contract system is used quite often in counties that also have public defenders. Such counties may need independent counsel when a conflict of interest arises or when there is a constant overflow of cases. It is also used in sparsely populated states that cannot justify the structure and costs of full-time public defender programs. Experts have found that contract attorneys are at least as effective as assigned counsel and are most cost-effective.[42]

The per-case cost in any jurisdiction for indigent defense services is determined largely by the type of program offered. In most public defender programs, funds are obtained through annual appropriations. Assigned counsel costs relate to legal charges for the appointed counsel, and contract programs negotiate a fee for the entire service. No research currently available indicates which is the most effective way to represent the indigent on a cost-per-case basis. However, Lawrence Spears reports that some jurisdictions have adopted the contract model with much success. Advantages include the provision of comprehensive legal services, controlled costs, and improved coordination in counsel programs.[43]

Mixed Systems A mixed system uses both public defenders and private attorneys in an attempt to draw on the strengths of both. In this approach, the public defender system operates simultaneously with the assigned counsel system or contract system to offer total coverage to the indigent defendant. This need occurs when the caseload increases beyond the capacity of the public defender's office. In addition, many counties supply independent counsel to all co-defendants in a single case to prevent a conflict of interest. In most others, separate counsel will be provided if a co-defendant requests it or if the judge or the public defender perceives a conflict of interest.

Other methods of providing counsel to the indigent include the use of law school students and prepaid legal service programs (similar to comprehensive medical insurance). Most jurisdictions have a student practice rule of procedure; third-year law school students in clinical programs provide supervised counsel to defendants in nonserious offenses. In *Argersinger v. Hamlin,* Supreme Court Justice William Brennan suggested that law students are an important resource in fulfilling constitutional defense requirements.[44]

Costs of Defending the Poor Over the past decade, the justice system has faced Essay 9 extreme pressure to provide counsel for all indigent criminal defendants. However, inadequate funding has made implementation of this Sixth Amendment right an impossible task. The chief reasons for underfunded defender programs are

1. Caseload problems
2. Lack of available attorneys
3. Legislative restraints. Increasing numbers of drug cases, mandatory sentencing, and even overcharging have put tremendous stress on defender services.

The system is also overloaded with appeals by indigent defendants convicted at the trial level whose representation involves filing complex briefs and making oral arguments. Such postconviction actions often consume a great deal of time and result in additional backlog problems. Death penalty litigation is another area in which legal resources for the poor are strained.

The indigent defense crisis is a chronic problem. In some jurisdictions, attorneys are just not available to provide defense work. Burnout from heavy caseloads, low salaries, and poor working conditions are generally the major causes for the limited supply of attorneys interested in representing the indigent defendant. Some attorneys even refuse to accept appointments in criminal cases because the fees are too low.

Lack of government funding is the most significant problem today. Although the entire justice system is often underfunded, the indigent defense system is usually in the worst shape. Ordinarily, providing funding for indigent criminal defendants is not the most politically popular thing to do. Yet indigent defense services are a critical component of the justice system. If there is growing disparity in the resources allocated to police, courts, and correctional agencies, then very few cases will go to trial, and most will have to be settled by informal processing, such as plea bargaining or diversion.[45]

According to Robert Spangenberg and Tessa Schwartz, noted experts on public defense programs, total justice spending in the 1990s was about $75 to $100 billion per year; of this amount, only 3 percent was spent on the indigent defense system. All too often, the limited criminal justice resources available are used to place more police officers on the streets and build more prisons, while ignoring prosecution, courts, and public defense.[46] As we enter the twenty-first century, the resources spent on public defense are not much higher.

Current funding for defender programs is ordinarily the responsibility of state and local governments. As a result of an amendment to the Crime Control Act of 1990, however, federal funds are also available through the Drug Control Act of 1988.[47] No effort was made to increase available funds in the 1994–95 federal crime legislation, but the Anti-Terrorism Act of 1996 authorizes $300 million to improve the federal judiciary's public defender program (Public Law 104-132, 1996). According to most experts on public defender spending, jurisdictions whose legislatures have been relatively generous in funding such programs in the past have continued to do so, whereas underfunded programs have become more seriously hampered.

In 1997, the National Institute of Justice reported that a new Public Defenders in the Neighborhood program has improved the overall quality of justice for indigent clients while reducing the cost of such services. Indigent defendants are often dissatisfied with court-appointed attorneys because of the pressure for quick plea bargains. Known as the Neighborhood Defender Service (NDS), this program has several benefits: (1) lawyers and clients are more accessible to each other; (2) there is more contact with the client's family during criminal investigation; (3) team representation (lawyers, investigators, and support staff) enables the use of a broad range of social and legal resources; and (4) savings are realized because defendants spend less time in jail or prison. The impact of NDS programs builds on the right of indigent defendants to free counsel.[48] NDS takes cases only from its surrounding vicinity because it believes that staff can acquire a deeper knowledge of clients and their problems this way, as opposed to traditional public defender agency operations.

THE DEFENSE LAWYER AS A PROFESSIONAL ADVOCATE

Essay 10

The problems of the criminal bar are numerous. Private attorneys are often accused of sacrificing their clients' interests for pursuit of profit. Many have a bad reputation in the legal community because of their unsavory clientele and reputation as "shysters" who hang out in court hoping for referrals. Attorneys who specialize in criminal work base their reputation on their power and influence. A good reputation is based on their ability to get obviously guilty offenders acquitted on legal technicalities, to arrange the best deal for clients who cannot hope to evade punishment, and to protect criminals whose illegal activities are shocking to many citizens. Consequently, the private criminal attorney is not often held in high esteem by his or her colleagues.

Public defenders are often young attorneys who are seeking trial practice before going on to high-paying jobs in established law firms. They are in the unenviable position of being paid by the government, yet acting in the role of the government's adversary. Generally, they find themselves at the bottom of the legal profession's hierarchy because they represent clients without social prestige for limited wages. Forced to work under bureaucratic conditions, public defenders can only do routine processing of their cases. Large caseloads prevent them from establishing more than a perfunctory relationship with their clients. To keep their caseload under control, they may push for the quickest and easiest solution to a case—a plea bargain.

Assigned counsel and contract attorneys may also be young lawyers just starting out and hoping to build their practice by taking on indigent cases. Because

Some defense attorneys achieve national prominence due to their courtroom exploits. Roy Black, representing Eller Media Co., shows the jury an enlargement of the bus bench where a 12-year-old was electrocuted while waiting for a bus, in a courtroom in Miami, March 2, 2001. Black claimed lightning—not faulty wiring—killed the boy. Eller Media Co., the company that built the bus shelter, and unlicensed electrician Victor Garcia, 39, were charged with causing the death of Jorge Luis Cabrera, who prosecutors said was electrocuted when he stepped on a conduit pipe at the bus stop. Black is one of the nation's most famous criminal defense attorneys.

AP/Wide World Photos

their livelihood depends on getting referrals from the court, public defender's office, or other government body, they risk the problem of conflict of interest. If they pursue too rigorous a defense or handle cases in a way not approved by the presiding judge or other authorities, they risk being removed from the assigned counsel lists.

Very often, large firms contribute the services of their newest members for legal aid to indigents, referred to as **pro bono** work. Although such efforts may be made in good spirit, they mean that inexperienced lawyers are handling legal cases in which a person's life may be at stake.

pro bono
The practice by private attorneys of taking the cases of indigent offenders without fee as a service to the profession and the community.

The Informal Justice System

What has emerged is a system in which plea bargaining predominates because little time and insufficient resources are available to give criminal defendants a full-scale defense. Moreover, because prosecutors are under pressure to win their cases, they are often more willing to work out a deal than pursue a case trial. After all, half a loaf is better than none. Defense attorneys, too, often find it easier to encourage their clients to plead guilty and secure a reduced sentence or probation rather than seek an acquittal and risk a long prison term.

These conflicts have helped erode the formal justice process. As you may recall, the formal justice system is based on the adversary system, in which prosecutors and defense attorneys meet in the arena of the courtroom to do battle over the merits of the case. Through the give-and-take of the trial process, the truth of the matter becomes known. Guilty defendants are punished, and the innocent go free. Yet the U.S. legal system seldom works that way. Because of the pressures faced by defense attorneys and prosecutors, the prosecution and the defense more often work together in a spirit of cooperation to get the case over with, rather than "fight it out," wasting each other's time and risking an outright loss. In the process of this working relationship, the personnel in the courtroom—judge, prosecutor, defense attorney—form working groups that leave the defendant on the outside. Criminal defendants may find that everyone they encounter in the courtroom seems to be saying "plead guilty," "take the deal," "let's get it over with."

The informal justice system revolves around the common interest of its members to move the case along and settle matters. In today's criminal justice system, defense attorneys share a common history, goals, values, and beliefs with their colleagues in the prosecution. They are alienated by class and social background from the clients they defend. Considering the reality of who commits crime, who are its victims, and who defends, prosecutes, and tries the case, it should not be surprising that the adversary system has suffered. The key question is whether the adversary system impedes public safety while safeguarding the rights of the accused.

The Competence of Defense Lawyers

The presence of competent and effective counsel has long been a basic principle of the adversary system. With the Sixth Amendment's guarantee of counsel for virtually all defendants, the performance of today's attorneys has come into question.

Inadequacy of counsel may occur in a variety of instances. The attorney may refuse to meet regularly with his or her client, fail to cross-examine key government witnesses, or fail to investigate the case properly. A defendant's plea of guilty may be based on poor advice, where the attorney may misjudge the admissibility of evidence. When co-defendants have separate counsel, conflicts of interest between defense attorneys may arise. On an appellate level, the lawyer may decline to file a brief, instead relying on a brief submitted for one of the co-appellants. Such problems as these are being raised with increasing frequency.

Even a legally competent attorney sometimes makes mistakes that can prejudice a case against his or her client. For example, in *Taylor v. Illinois* (1988), a defense lawyer sprung a surprise witness against the prosecution.[49] The judge ruled the witness out of order (invoking the *surprise witness rule*), thereby depriving the defendant of valuable testimony and evidence. The Supreme Court affirmed the conviction despite the defense attorney's error in judgment because the judge had correctly ruled that surprising the prosecution was not legally defensible. The key issue is the level of competence that should be required of defense counsel in criminal cases.

reasonable competence standard
Minimally required level of functioning by a defense attorney such that defendants are not deprived of their rights to counsel and to a fair trial.

Essay 11

In recent years, the courts have adopted a **reasonable competence standard**, but differences exist in the formulation and application of this standard. For example, is it necessary for defense counsel to answer on appeal every nonfrivolous issue requested by his or her convicted client? What if counsel does not provide the court with all the information at the sentencing stage and the defendant feels counsel's performance is inadequate? Whether counsel should be considered incompetent in such circumstances is a question that requires court review.

Finally, the concept of attorney competence was defined by the Supreme Court in the case of *Strickland v. Washington* in 1984.[50] Strickland had been arrested for committing a string of extremely serious crimes, including murder, torture, and kidnapping. Against his lawyer's advice, Strickland pleaded guilty and threw himself on the mercy of the trial judge at a capital sentencing hearing. He also ignored his attorney's recommendation that he exercise his right to have an advisory jury at his sentencing hearing.

In preparing for the hearing, the lawyer spoke with Strickland's wife and mother but did not otherwise seek character witnesses. Nor was a psychiatric examination requested because, in the attorney's opinion, Strickland did not have psychological problems. The attorney also did not ask for a presentence investigation because he believed that such a report would contain information damaging to his client.

Although the presiding judge had a reputation for leniency in cases where the defendant confessed, he sentenced Strickland to death. Strickland appealed on the grounds that his attorney had rendered ineffective counsel, citing his failure to seek psychiatric testimony and present character witnesses.

The case eventually went to the Supreme Court, which upheld Strickland's sentence. The justices found that a defendant's claim of attorney incompetence must have two components. First, the defendant must show that the counsel's performance was deficient and that such serious errors were made as to eliminate the presence of counsel guaranteed by the Sixth Amendment. Second, the defendant must also show that the deficient performance prejudiced the case to such an extent that the defendant was deprived of a fair trial (that is, a trial with reliable results). In *Strickland,* the Court found insufficient evidence that the attorney had acted beyond the boundaries of professional competence. Although the strategy he had adopted might not have been the best one possible, it certainly was not unreasonable, considering minimum standards of professional competence.

The Court recognized the defense attorney's traditional role as an advocate of the defendant's cause, which includes such duties as consulting on important decisions, keeping the client informed of important developments, bringing knowledge and skill to the trial proceeding, and making the trial a reliable adversary proceeding. But the Court found that a mechanical set of rules to define competency would be unworkable.

Relations between Prosecutor and Defense Attorney

In the final analysis, the competence of the prosecutor and the defense attorney depends on their willingness to work together in the interest of the client, the criminal justice system, and the rest of society. However, serious adversarial conflicts have arisen between them in recent years.

The prosecutor, for instance, should exercise discretion in seeking to **subpoena** other lawyers to testify about any relationship with their clients. Although not all communication between a lawyer and his or her client is privileged, confidential information entrusted to a lawyer is ordinarily not available for prosecutorial investigation. Often, however, overzealous prosecutors try to use their subpoena power against lawyers whose clients are involved in drug or organized crime cases to obtain as much evidence as possible. Prosecutors interested in confidential information about defendants have subpoenaed lawyers to testify against them. Court approval should be needed before a lawyer is forced to give information about a client. Otherwise, the defendant is really not receiving effective legal counsel under the Sixth Amendment. In addition, prosecutors should refrain from using their grand jury subpoena power to obtain information from private investigators employed by the defense attorney. Judicial remedies for violations of these rules often include suppression of subpoenaed evidence and even dismissal of a criminal indictment.

By the same token, some criminal defense lawyers ignore situations in which a client informs them of his or her intention to commit perjury. The purpose of the defense attorney's investigation is to learn the truth from the client. The defense attorney also has a professional responsibility to persuade the defendant not to commit perjury, which is a crime.

It is the duty of the prosecutor to seek justice and not merely to obtain a conviction; this goal also applies to the criminal defense attorney. As legal scholar David G. Bress so aptly put it, "A defense attorney does not promote the attainment of justice when he secures his client's freedom through illegal and improper means."[51]

A current critical issue in the relationship between prosecutors and defense attorneys is the presentation of scientific evidence in the courtroom and the standards regarding the admissibility of such evidence. This issue is discussed in the Criminal Justice and Technology feature.

Often, the public image of prosecutors and defense attorneys is shaped by television programs, movies, and newspaper stories. You may hear of a prosecutor who takes a campaign donation and ignores a politician's crime. A defense attorney may use improper influence in representing a client. Unfortunately, corruption is still a fact of life in the justice system. Doing everything possible to deter such behavior is an important feature of a fair justice system.

subpoena
A court order requiring a witness to appear in court at a specified time and place.

SUMMARY

The judge, the prosecutor, and the defense attorney are the major officers of justice in the judicial system. The judge approves plea bargains, tries cases, and determines the sentence given the offender. The prosecutor, who is the people's attorney, has discretion to decide the criminal charge and disposition. The prosecutor's daily decisions have a significant impact on police and court operations.

CRIMINAL JUSTICE AND TECHNOLOGY

Admissibility of Scientific Evidence

The long-standing test for the admissibility of scientific evidence was articulated in 1923 in the case of *Frye v. United States.* The **Frye test**, adopted by the federal and state courts, is whether the technique has general acceptance in the field to which it belongs. However, in 1993, the *Daubert v. Merrill Dow Pharmaceuticals, Inc.* case replaced the *Frye* standard in the federal courts, and in many state courts as well. In *Daubert,* the Court decided to allow expert testimony concerning scientific or technical knowledge that assists the trier of fact to understand the evidence. This more flexible **Daubert test** can be significant in the prosecution and defense of many types of cases, including paternity cases, child abuse crimes, rapes, and murder, where information and testimony about the scientific evidence may not be needed.

No area is questioned more than DNA profiling, where DNA (deoxyribonucleic acid) evidence is used to link defendants to a crime. An individual's distinct genetic pattern is carried in his

or her DNA. Under the Frye test, the prosecutor often had a difficult time with the admissibility of DNA because the process would fail the test of general acceptance in the scientific community. Under the less stringent Daubert test, the court can use its discretion to admit DNA evidence more easily.

The admissibility of DNA testing has become one of the most controversial issues in the prosecutor–defense relationship. In the O. J. Simpson case, for instance, the results of DNA testing of blood drops found at the crime scene were critical evidence linking the defendant to the crime. Under the *Daubert* decision, DNA evidence is subject to cross-examination, the presentation of opposing evidence, and careful jury instructions, making it more likely to be admitted than under the *Frye* standard. The prosecution argued in the Simpson case, for example, that the DNA tests on blood at the murder scene and in Simpson's Ford Bronco positively identified Simpson as the killer; the defense attacked the DNA tests as unreliable. The defense subsequently acknowl-

edged that Simpson's blood was at the crime scene but questioned the police's handling of the evidence. The outcome of DNA decisions significantly increases the likelihood of a conviction or acquittal. Despite early controversies and challenges by defense attorneys, the admission of DNA test results in the courtroom has become routine today.

Some states still apply the *Frye* test, which says that the evidence is admissible if the methodology is generally accepted in the scientific community. But the *Frye* test is no longer used in the federal courts, where the *Daubert* decision takes precedence, and in most state courts. Consequently, questions about the validity and reliability of forensic DNA continue to be addressed by prosecutors and defense attorneys. More than 200 published court opinions support its use.

Today, all 50 states have laws authorizing them to collect DNA from convicts and match it via a computer database to unsolved crimes. All states draw DNA from sex offenders, and most take it from murderers. But some states col-

---

Fill in the blanks 16
Multiple choice 25–27

Frye test
A rule that allows scientific evidence to be admitted in court only if the technique used has general acceptance in its field.

Daubert test
A rule that gives courts wider discretion in admittting scientific evidence if it helps the judge or jury to understand the evidence.

The role of the defense attorney in the criminal justice system has grown dramatically during the past few decades. Today, providing defense services to the indigent criminal defendant is an everyday practice. Under landmark decisions of the U.S. Supreme Court, particularly *Gideon v. Wainwright* and *Argersinger v. Hamlin,* all defendants who could face imprisonment for any offense must be afforded counsel at trial. Methods of providing counsel include assigned counsel systems, where an attorney is selected by the court to represent the accused, and public defender programs, where public employees provide legal services. Lawyers doing criminal defense work have discovered an increasing need for their services, not only at trial, but also at the pre- and postjudicial stages of the criminal justice system. Consequently, the issue of defense lawyer competence has become an important one for judicial authorities.

The prosecutor and the defense attorney are the principal adversaries in the courtroom because they represent the public and the accused. How they fulfill

lect DNA from a varity of lesser criminals—robbers, burglars, even white-collar criminals. DNA left at crime scenes is then compared with database samples to check for a match. The goal is twofold: (1) to help free wrongly convicted prisoners and (2) to introduce DNA evidence in court to convict offenders accused of crimes. The problem is that although all states have authorized collection of DNA evidence, fewer than half of the states are part of the DNA database.

DNA evidence still has many critics. One of the most important issues concerns the right of privacy, particularly when taking samples from those who are not suspects. In addition, not all DNA evidence is admitted in court. Despite these problems, DNA profiling is being used routinely during trials to obtain convictions and has been upheld by the appellate courts.

Another controversial issue in dealing with scientific evidence is the use of polygraph evidence in a criminal trial. The polygraph or "lie detector" is an electromechanical device that measures and records physiological changes in the body, such as heart rate and breathing, that may be involuntarily caused by a person's efforts to deceive the questioner. Because of their unreliability, virtually all courts today reject the results of a polygraph when offered in evidence to establish guilt or innocence. The 1997 case of *United States v. Scheffer,* however, provided the first full-scale examination of the reliability and use of lie detector evidence in criminal trials.[55] In that case, the United States Supreme Court rejected the request of a military defendant to introduce favorable lie detector results in a court martial on drug charges, because scientific studies cast doubt on the reliability of polygraphs. But the Court did not rule out the use of polygraph evidence in states that are considering its use.

Critical Thinking Skills

One of the most controversial issues regarding DNA profiling concerns the privacy rights of those tested. To what extent do the constitutional rights of criminals balance with the responsibility to control crime? At what point does DNA testing constitute an illegal search and seizure?

InfoTrac College Edition Research

InfoTrac College Edition provides access to extensive literature on DNA testing. Use DNA Testing as a keyword. For a very informative article, read John Smialek, Charlotte Word, and Arthur Westveer. "The Microscopic Slide." *The FBI Law Enforcement Bulletin,* Nov 2000 v69 i11 p18

SOURCES: *Frye v. United States,* 293 F. 1013 (1923); *Daubert v. Merrill Dow Pharmaceuticals, Inc.,* 509 U.S. 579, 13 S.Ct. 2786, 125 L.Ed.2d 469 (1993); Jerry Bishop, "How DNA Scientists Help Track Criminals and Clear the Innocent," *Wall Street Journal,* 6 January 1995, p. A1; Victor Weedn and John Hicks, "The Unrealized Potential of DNA Testing," *National Institute of Justice Journal* 234 (1997): 16; *United States v. Scheffer,* No. 96-1113, 117 S.Ct. 56, 65 U.S.L.W. 3761 (1997).

their respective roles and responsibilities affects society's fundamental ability to control crime and the public's perception of the justice system. The need to deal with complex issues involving the admissibility of scientific evidence has only heightened the adversarial nature of their relationship.

Key Terms

prosecutor	defense attorney	pro bono
attorney general	indigent	reasonable competence standard
district attorney	assigned counsel	subpoena
community prosecution	public defender	Frye test
grand jury	recoupment	Daubert test
diversion	contract system	

Discussion Questions

1. Should attorneys disclose information given them by their clients concerning participation in earlier unsolved crimes?
2. Should defense attorneys cooperate with prosecutors if it means that their clients will go to jail?
3. Should prosecutors have absolute discretion over which cases to proceed on and which to drop? Do you believe prosecutors should have a great deal of discretion? Why?
4. Should clients be made aware of an attorney's track record in court?

5. Does the assigned counsel system present an inherent conflict of interest because attorneys are hired and paid by the institution they are to oppose?
6. Which kinds of cases do you think are most likely to be handled informally?
7. Explain the following: "It is the duty of the prosecutor to seek justice, not merely a conviction."
8. What are the differences between community prosecution and the traditional approach to prosecution?

A CLOSER LOOK

In the 1980s, a quiet revolution was shaping American policing; it was the development of community policing. Organized at the station house level, the initial community policing programs were designed to make citizens aware of police activities, alert them to methods of self-protection, and improve general attitudes toward policing.

In the 1990s, many prosecutors are implementing the notion of community prosecution. Both approaches want to make neighborhoods safe.

Go to InfoTrac College Edition and read the following two articles:

Catherine M. Coles and George L. Kelling, "Prevention through Community Prosecution: New Approaches to Fighting Crime," *The Public Interest,* 1999, v36 p69

Susan P. Weinstein, "Community Prosecution: Community Policing's Legal Partner," *FBI Law Enforcement Bulletin,* 1998, v67 p19

Review these articles carefully. Learn about the similarities and differences between community policing and community prosecution.

Notes

1 National District Attorneys Association, "The Prosecutor," *Names in the News* 34 (2000): 20.

2 Tom Kenworthy, "It's a New World: Polluters Go to Prison," *USA Today,* 21 April 2000, p. A3.

3 American Bar Association, *Model Code of Professional Responsibility* (Chicago: ABA, 1986), p. 87; John Jay Douglas, *Ethical Issues in Prosecution* (Houston: University of Houston Law Center, National College of District Attorneys, 1988); National District Attorneys Association, *National Prosecution Standards,* 2d ed. (Alexandria, VA: NDAA, 1991).

4 *Berger v. United States,* 295 U.S. 78, 88, 55 S.Ct. 629, 633, 79 L.Ed. 1341 (1935).

5 See Bennett Gershman, "Why Prosecutors Misbehave," *Criminal Law Bulletin* 22 (1986): 131–143; also Joan Jacoby, "The American Prosecutor—from Appointive to Elective Status," *Prosecutor* 31 (1997): 25.

6 American Bar Association, *Model Rules of Professional Conduct* (Chicago: ABA, 1983), Rule 3.8; see also Stanley Fisher, "In Search of the Virtuous Prosecutor: A Conceptual Framework," *American Journal of Criminal Law* 15 (1988): 197.

7 Stanley Fisher, "Zealousness and Overzealousness: Making Sense of the

Prosecutor's Duty to Seek Justice," *Prosecutor* 22 (1989): 9; see also Bruce Green, "The Ethical Prosecutor and the Adversary System," *Criminal Law Bulletin* 24 (1988): 126–145.

8 John Dawson, Steven Smith, and Carol DeFrances, *Prosecution in State Courts* (Washington, DC: Bureau of Justice Statistics, 1992), 1–15; also Bureau of Justice Statistics, *1996 Prosecution Statistics* (Washington, DC: U.S. Department of Justice, 1998).

9 American Bar Association, *Standards for Criminal Justice: Prosecution Function and Defense Function* (Washington, DC: ABA, 1993), pp. 18–19. Reprinted with permission of the American Bar Association, which authored these standards and holds the copyright.

10 Michael Benson, Francis Cullen, and William Maakestad, "Local Prosecutors and Corporate Crime," *Crime and Delinquency* 36 (July 1990): 356–372.

11 "Environmental Crime Prosecution: Results of a National Survey," *National Institute of Justice Research in Brief* (1994): 1–12.

12 "NDAA Establishes Environmental Center," *National District Attorneys Association Bulletin* 10 (October 1991): 1.

13 Marcia Chaiken and Jan Chaiken, *Priority Prosecutors of High-Rate Dangerous Offenders* (Washington, DC: National Institute of Justice, 1991).

14 Bureau of Justice Statistics, *The Criminal Justice and Community Response to Rape* (Rockville, MD: National Criminal Justice Reference Service, 1994).

15 Donald Rebovich, "Expanding the Role of Local Prosecution," *National Institute of Justice Journal Research in Action* 28 (1994): 21–24.

16 "Litigator's Legacy," *Wall Street Journal,* 11 January 1989, p. 1; Selwyn Raab, "A Battered and Ailing Mafia Is Losing Its Grip on America," *New York Times,* 22 October 1990, p. 1; also Gerard O'Neill and Dick Lehr, *The Underboss: The Rise and Fall of a Mafia Family* (New York: St. Martin's Press, 1989).

17 *Standards for Criminal Justice: Prosecution Function and Defense Function;* also *Standards for Criminal Justice: Providing Defense Sources,* 3d ed. (Washington, DC: American Bar Association, 1993).

18 Eric Holden, "Community Prosecution," *The Prosecutor* 34 (2000): 31.

19 Douglas Gansler, "Implementing Community Prosecution in Montgomery County, Maryland," *The Prosecutor* 34 (2000): 30.

20 Kenneth C. Davis, *Discretionary Justice* (Baton Rouge: Louisiana State University Press, 1969), p. 180; see also James B. Stewart, *The Prosecutor* (New York: Simon and Schuster, 1987).

21 Barbara Boland, *The Prosecution of Felony Arrests* (Washington, DC: U.S. Government Printing Office, 1983).

22 Newman Baker, "The Prosecutor—Initiation of Prosecution," *Journal of Criminal Law, Criminology, and Police Science* 23 (1933): 770–771.

23 Frank W. Miller, *Prosecution: The Decision to Charge a Suspect with a Crime* (Boston: Little Brown, 1970); see also Harvey Wallace, "A Prosecutor's Guide to Stalking," *Prosecutor* 29 (1995): 26–30.

24 Boland, *The Prosecution of Felony Arrests.*

25 American Bar Association, *Standards for Criminal Justice: Prosecution Function and Defense Function,* standard 3.8, p. 33.

26 See, generally, "Pretrial Diversion from the Criminal Process," *Yale Law Journal* 83 (1974): 827.

27 Charles D. Breitel, "Control in Criminal Law Enforcement," *University of Chicago Law Review* 27 (1960): 427.

28 Roscoe Pound, "Discretion, Dispensation, and Mitigation: The Problem of the Individual Special Case," *New York University Law Review* 35 (1960): 925; "Unleashing the Prosecutor's Discretion: *United States v. Goodwin,*" *American Criminal Law Review* 20 (1983): 507.

29 American Bar Association, *Report of Standing Committee on Legal Aid and Indigent Defendants* (Chicago: ABA, 1991).

30 See American Bar Association, *Model Rules of Professional Conduct* (Chicago: ABA, 1994), Rule 12.

31 Monroe H. Freedman, "Professional Responsibility of the Criminal Defense Lawyer: The Three Hardest Questions," *Michigan Law Review* 64 (1966): 1468.

32 Bennett Brummer, *Ethics Resource Guide for Public Defenders* (Chicago: ABA, February 1992).

33 372 U.S. 335, 83 S.Ct. 792, 9 L.Ed.2d 799 (1963).

34 407 U.S. 25, 92 S.Ct. 2006, 32 L.Ed.2d 530 (1972).

35 384 U.S. 436, 86 S.Ct. 1602, 16 L.Ed.2d 694 (1966).

36 *Mempa v. Rhay,* 389 U.S. 128, 88 S.Ct. 254, 19 L.Ed.2d 336 (1967).

37 *Douglas v. California,* 372 U.S. 353, 83 S.Ct. 814, 9 L.Ed.2d 811 (1963).

38 *In re Gault,* 387 U.S. 1, 875 S.Ct. 1428, 18 L.Ed.2d 527 (1967).

39 *Specht v. Patterson,* 386 U.S. 605, 87 S.Ct. 1209, 18 L.Ed.2d 326 (1967).

40 See *Betts v. Brady,* 316 U.S. 455, 62 S.Ct. 1252, 86 L.Ed. 1595 (1942). Justice Black subsequently wrote the majority opinion in *Gideon v. Wainwright,* guaranteeing defendants' right to counsel and overruling the *Betts* case.

41 See F. Brownell, *Legal Aid in the United States* (Chicago: National Legal Aid Defender Association, 1961); for an interesting study of Cook County, Illinois, Office of Public Defenders, see Lisa McIntyre, *Public Defenders: Practice of Law in Shadows of Dispute* (Chicago: University of Chicago Press, 1987).

42 Pauline Houlden and Steven Balkin, "Quality and Cost Comparisons of Private Bar Indigent Defense Systems: Contract vs. Ordered Assigned Counsel," *Journal of Criminal Law and Criminology* 76 (1985): 176–200; see John Arrango,

"Defense Services for the Poor," *American Bar Association Journal on Criminal Justice* 12 (1998): 35.

43 Lawrence Spears, "Contract Counsel: A Different Way to Defend the Poor—How It's Working in North Dakota," *American Bar Association Journal on Criminal Justice* 6 (1991): 24–31.

44 407 U.S. 25, 92 S.Ct. 2006, 32 L.Ed.2d 530 (1972).

45 Timothy Murphy, "Indigent Defense and the War on Drugs: The Public Defender's Losing Battle," *American Bar Association Journal on Criminal Justice* 6 (1991): 14–20.

46 Robert Spangenberg and Tessa J. Schwartz, "The Indigent Defense Crisis Is Chronic," *Criminal Justice Journal* 9 (1994): 13–16; *Sourcebook of Criminal Justice Statistics: 1998* (Washington, DC: U.S. Department of Justice, 1999).

47 See Drug Control Act of 1988, 42 U.S.C. §375 (G)(10).

48 David Anderson, *Public Defenders in the Neighborhood* (Washington, DC: Office of Justice Programs, March 1997); also Roger Hanson et al., *Indigent Defenders: Get the Job Done and Done Well* (Williamsburg, VA: National Center for State Courts, 1992).

49 *Taylor v. Illinois,* 484 U.S. 400, 108 S.Ct. 646, 98 L.Ed.2d 798 (1988).

50 *Strickland v. Washington,* 466 U.S. 688, 104 S.Ct. 2052, 80 L.Ed.2d 674 (1984).

51 David G. Bress, "Professional Ethics in Criminal Trials," *Michigan Law Review* 64 (1966): 1493; John Mitchell, "The Ethics of the Criminal Defense Attorney," *Stanford Law Review* 32 (1980): 325.

© Mark Richards/Contact Press Images

PRETRIAL PROCEDURES

What exactly did Michael Milken do wrong? Milken was a wealthy broker for Drexel Burnham Lambert, a highly respected securities firm. In the late 1980s, his earnings amounted to millions of dollars a year. Under Milken's influence, Drexel became the leading underwriter of *junk bonds,* which were sold to institutional investors. Junk bonds were high-yield bonds of less than investment quality, and the corporate takeover game of the 1980s was based on the junk-bond market. Junk bonds often made it possible for corporate raiders to buy huge corporations without putting up their own cash or borrowing money from banks. Once acquired, the corporations' assets were stripped and sold to service (pay for) the bond debt. This practice diverted assets that could have been used for research and job creation.

In 1986, a Drexel employee, Dennis Levine, was accused of *insider trading* (stock trading based on nonpublic information that has been misappropriated) by the Securities and Exchange Commission. Levine implicated Ivan Boesky, a market speculator, who in turn helped the SEC secure evidence against Milken. Milken was indicted for insider trading, racketeering, market manipulation, price fixing, and other criminal stock market activities, as was his firm. He was identified as the leader of a conspiracy to defraud clients, shareholders, and the public through insider trading, fee gouging, and illegal profit taking.

In 1990, Milken entered into plea bargaining and agreed to a guilty plea. He was sentenced to prison and ordered to pay millions of dollars in fines. The federal court imposed a prison sentence of 10 years to prevent and deter

Chapter 11

Michael Milken and his wife and attorneys walking into court past a roped off crowd of photographers and onlookers, November 1990.

others from similar criminal activity. Milken denied that he had done anything wrong, but the government contended that his product, the junk bond, was a fraud because it was not secured and bore high interest rates. The high interest rates, the government argued, inflicted what was for many corporations insurmountable debt. Michael Milken ended up a high-profile white-collar criminal.

Many legal experts consider the Ted Kaczynski case one of the most bizarre criminal cases of the twentieth century. Other crimes have been more horrible or deadlier, but few crimes have taken so many years to solve. The case began when a bomb went off at Northwestern University in 1978. More bombs were sent to universities and airlines in the early 1980s. The FBI subsequently came up with the nickname Unabomber, partly because it appeared that all the attacks were the work of one individual and partly because only university and airline personnel were targeted. By the time he was captured in 1996, Ted Kaczynski had committed 16 Unabomber attacks, killing three people and injuring 22 others. The FBI reviewed more than 200 suspects and received many thousands of phone calls, eventually leading to his arrest.

Who was Ted Kaczynski? Born in Chicago in 1942, Kaczynski was a brilliant student who became a mathematics professor at the University of California after graduating from Harvard and receiving his M.A. and Ph.D. degrees at the University of Michigan. After resigning from teaching, Kaczynski dropped out of society, built a small cabin in rural Lincoln, Montana, and lived off the land. He then began his crusade to disrupt industrial society.

Kaczynski's downfall occurred when he sent a 35,000-word manifesto against modern civilization to the *New York Times* and the *Washington Post.* When it was published, David Kaczynski, Ted's brother, recognized its similarity to some of his brother's letters and alerted the FBI

that his brother could be the Unabomber. When the FBI searched Kaczynski's house, they found bomb parts, chemicals, wires, and hand drawn diagrams for bombs.

Kaczynski was charged with being the Unabomber. Lengthy negotiations followed between the prosecution and the defense over whether Kaczynski was competent to stand trial. In addition, Kaczynski feuded with his lawyers over their plans to use the insanity defense and to tell the jury he was a paranoid schizophrenic. When Kaczynski attempted suicide and then sought to handle his own defense, the court conducted a competency examination. Even though Kaczynski was a paranoid schizophrenic and lived like a hermit, the court psychiatrist said he was competent to stand trial. The only legal standard for competency is whether a defendant is able to understand the charges and help in his defense. The psychiatric report became the turning point in whether Kaczynski would be brought to trial. Prosecutors knew they would have a difficult time persuading a jury to execute a mentally ill person.

In exchange for the government's dropping its demand for a trial and death sentence, Kaczynski agreed to enter a guilty plea and receive a life sentence without parole. Thus, the longest and most expensive manhunt for a serial killer in U.S. histroy ended in a plea bargain. The plea bargain avoided the trial process, eliminated the cost of the trial, and shortened the time required for resolving the case.

Fill in the blanks 1–2
True/False 1–2

The plea bargain, described in the Milken and Kaczynski cases, is just one of a series of events that are critical links in the chain of justice. These include arraignments, grand jury investigations, bail hearings, plea bargaining negotiations, and predisposition treatment efforts (see Exhibit 11.1). These pretrial procedures are important components of the justice process because the great majority of all criminal cases are resolved informally at this stage and never come before the courts. Although television and the news media like to focus on the elaborate jury trial, with its dramatic elements and impressive setting, formal criminal trials are relatively infrequent. The adversary system is not a myth, but the social reality of justice in the United States is that it is more often handled than fought over. Consequently, understanding the events that take place during the pretrial period is essential to grasping the reality of criminal justice policy.

Cases are settled during the pretrial stage in a number of ways. Prosecutors can use their discretion to drop cases before formal charges are filed because of insufficient evidence, office policy, witness

EXHIBIT 11.1 STEPS IN THE PRETRIAL PROCESS

1. **Arrest:** suspect taken into custody
2. **Booking:** administrative record of arrest
3. **Initial appearance:** notice of charge, advice of rights, setting of bail
4. **Preliminary hearing:** test of evidence against defendant
5. **Grand jury/information:** review of evidence by grand jury; charge filed by prosecution
6. **Arraignment:** appearance for plea; defendant elects trial by jury or judge
7. **Guilty plea/trial**: plea accepted or trial scheduled

conflicts, or similar problems. Even if charges are filed, the prosecutor can decide not to proceed against the defendant (nolle prosequi) because of a change in the circumstances of the case.

The prosecutor and the defense almost always meet to try to arrange a nonjudicial settlement of the case. Plea bargaining, in which the defendant exchanges a guilty plea for some consideration such as a reduced sentence, is commonly used to terminate the formal processing of the case. The prosecution and/or the defense may believe, for example, that a trial is not in the best interests of the victim, the defendant, or society because the defendant is physically or emotionally incapable of understanding the charges or controlling his or her behavior. In this instance, the defendant may have a competency hearing before a judge and be placed in a secure treatment facility until ready to stand trial. Or the prosecutor may waive further action so that the defendant can be placed in a special treatment program.

PROCEDURES FOLLOWING ARREST

After arrest, the accused is ordinarily taken to the police station, where the police list the possible criminal charges against him or her and obtain other information for booking purposes. This may include a description of the suspect and the circumstance of the offense. The suspect may then be fingerprinted, photographed, and required to participate in a lineup.

Fill in the blanks 3–4
True/False 3–5
Multiple choice 1–4

complaint
A sworn written statement addressed to a court or judge by the police, prosecutor, or individual alleging that an individual has committed an offense and requesting indictment and prosecution.

Individuals arrested on a misdemeanor charge are ordinarily released from the police station on their own recognizance to answer the criminal charge before the court at a later date. They are usually detained by police until it is decided whether a criminal complaint will be filed. The **complaint** is the formal written document identifying the criminal charge, the date and place where the crime occurred, and the circumstances of the arrest. The complaint is sworn to and signed under oath by the complainant, usually a police officer. The complaint requests that the defendant be present at an **initial hearing** to be held soon after the arrest is made. (In some jurisdictions, this may be referred to by other names, such as arraignment.) At the initial hearing, the defendant is informed of the formal charge. If unable to afford an attorney, the defendant is provided one and then asked to plead guilty or not guilty. If the plea is guilty, the case may be disposed of immediately. If the plea is not guilty, a date in the near future is set for the trial, and the defendant is generally released on bail or on his or her own recognizance to await trial.

initial hearing
Appearance before a magistrate that occurs within 24 hours after a defendant's arrest, at which the defendant is informed of the charge, counsel is appointed, a plea is taken, and bail is considered.

Felony Procedures

When a more serious crime or felony is involved, the U.S. Constitution requires an intermediate step before a person can be tried. It must be proved to an objective body that there is probable cause to believe that a crime has taken place and that the accused should be tried on the matter. This step of the formal charging process requires an *indictment* from a grand jury or an *information* issued by a lower court. An indictment is a written accusation that is drawn up by a prosecutor and submitted to a grand jury charging a person with a crime. The grand jury, after considering the evidence presented by the prosecutor, votes to endorse or deny the indictment. An information is a charging document drawn up by the prosecutor in jurisdictions that do not employ the grand jury system. The information is brought before a lower court judge in a **preliminary hearing** (sometimes called a **probable cause hearing**). The prosecutor is required to present the case at this hearing so that the judge can determine whether the defendant should be held to answer for the charge in a felony court.

preliminary hearing (probable cause hearing)
Hearing before a magistrate to determine if the government has sufficient evidence to show probable cause that the defendant committed the crime.

arraignment
Initial trial court appearance at which accused is read the charges, advised of his or her rights, and asked to enter a plea.

After an indictment or information is filed, the accused is brought before the trial court for **arraignment**, during which the judge informs the defendant of the charge, ensures that the accused is properly represented by counsel, and determines whether he or she should be released on bail or some other form of release pending a hearing or trial.

The defendant who is arraigned on an indictment or information can ordinarily plead guilty, not guilty, or **nolo contendere** (no contest), which is equivalent to a guilty plea but cannot be used as evidence against the defendant in a civil case on the same matter. For example, a plea of nolo contendere in a rape case could not be used as an admission of guilt if the offender is later sued for damages by the victim.

If a guilty plea is entered, the defendant admits to all the elements of the crime, and the court begins a review of the person's background for sentencing purposes. A plea of not guilty sets the stage for a trial on the merits or for negotiations between the prosecutor and the defense attorney, known as plea bargaining.

Before discussing these issues, it is important to address the question of pretrial release and bail, which may arise at the police station, at the initial court appearance in a misdemeanor, or at the arraignment in most felony cases.

Pretrial Services

As we have described, many jurisdictions today are faced with significant increases in criminal cases, particularly those involving drugs. The police have responded with an unprecedented number of arrests, which has clogged an already burdened jail system. Of these arrestees, the justice system must determine which can safely be released pending trial. *Pretrial services* help courts deal with this problem. At the pretrial stage, the system is required to balance the often conflicting goals of ensuring community safety and respecting the rights of the arrestee.

Pretrial services are those practices and programs that screen arrestees to provide the bail-setting magistrate concise summaries of the arrestees' personal background as it relates to bail.[1] These programs are distinguished from *diversion,* in which criminal prosecution is bypassed in favor of alternative measures, such as treatment or counseling; diversion is discussed at the end of this chapter.

Pretrial service programs seek to

1. Improve the release/detention decision process in criminal courts by providing complete, accurate, nonadversarial information to judicial officers
2. Identify those for whom alternative forms of supervision may be more appropriate than incarceration
3. Monitor released pretrial arrestees to ensure they comply with the conditions of release imposed by the judicial officer for the benefit of public safety[2]

Virtually all jurisdictions in the United States have pretrial release in one form or another. Court-administered programs compose the greatest percentage of pretrial programs (38%); probation-administered programs constitute the next largest segment (24%). The general criteria used to assess eligibility for release center around the defendant's community ties and prior criminal justice involvement. According to a recent report prepared by the National Association of Pretrial Services, more than three-quarters of the programs in the United States have a wide variety of release options.[3] Many jurisdictions have conditional and supervised release and third-party custody release, in addition to release on a person's own recognizance.

In recent years, many states have begun to rely on programs to detect illicit drug use by defendants. The aim is to provide a judge with an objective measure of a defendant's drug use for pretrial release determination and to serve as a tool for controlling possible misconduct during the pretrial release period. Judges and magistrates generally believe that pretrial drug testing is a valuable tool in implementing the statutory requirements of any pretrial release program.

Effective pretrial release programs benefit the justice system in many ways. Judicial officers are able to make more effective decisions about who may be re-

nolo contendere
A plea of "no contest"; the defendant submits to sentencing without any formal admission of guilt that could be used against him or her in a subsequent civil suit.

Fill in the blanks 5–6
True/False 6–8
Multiple choice 5–6
Essay 1

pretrial services
Programs that screen arrestees and provide judges with information relevant to the granting of bail or other pretrial release.

To learn more about pretrial release and detention statistics, go to http://www.ojp.usdoj.gov/bjs/pretrial.htm
For an up-to-date list of Web links, see http://www.wadsworth.com/product/0534573053s

For a summary of new pretrial programs, go to the Pretrial Services Resource Center: http://www.pretrial.org/html
For an up-to-date list of Web links, see http://www.wadsworth.com/product/0534573053s

TABLE 11.1   PRETRIAL RELEASE MECHANISMS

Stage	Mechanism	Description
Police	Field citation release	An arresting officer releases the arrestee on a written promise to appear in court, at or near the actual time and location of the arrest. This procedure is commonly used for misdemeanor charges and is similar to issuing a traffic ticket.
Police	Station house citation release	The determination of an arrestee's eligibility and suitability for release and the actual release of the arrestee are deferred until after he or she has been removed from the scene of an arrest and brought to the station house or police headquarters.
Police/pretrial	Jail citation release	The determination of an arrestee's eligibility and suitability for citation release and the actual release of the arrestee are deferred until after he or she has been delivered by the arresting department to a jail or other pretrial detention facility for screening, booking, and/or admission.
Pretrial/court	Direct release authority by pretrial program	To streamline release processes and reduce the length of stay in detention, courts may authorize pretrial programs to release defendants without direct judicial involvement. Where court rules delegate such authority, the practice is generally limited to misdemenaor charges, but felony release authority has been granted in some jurisdictions.
Police/court	Bail schedule	An arrestee can post bail at the station house or jail according to amounts specified in a bail schedule. The schedule is a list of all bailable charges and a corresponding dollar amount for each. Schedules may vary widely from jurisdiction to jurisdiction.
Court	Judicial release	Arrestees who have not been released either by the police or the jailer and who have not posted bail appear at the hearing before a judge, magistrate, or bail commisioner within a set period of time. In jurisdictions with pretrail release programs, program staff often interview arrestees detained at the jail prior to the first hearing, verify the background information, and present recommendations to the court at arraignment.

SOURCE: Andy Hall, *Pretrial Release Program Options* (Washington, DC: National Institute of Justice, 1984).

leased safely. The compliance of pretrial arrestees with their conditions of release can be monitored. In addition, pretrial programs can operate at different stages of the judicial process, thereby increasing the number of release options available to the courts. Table 11.1 describes a number of pretrial release mechanisms.

BAIL

Bail is money or some other security provided to the court to ensure the appearance of the defendant at every subsequent stage of the criminal justice process. Its purpose is to obtain the release from custody of a person charged with a crime. Once the amount of bail is set by the court, the defendant is required to deposit all or a percentage of the entire amount in cash or security (or to pay a professional bonding agent to submit a bond). If the defendant is released on bail but fails to appear in court at the stipulated time, the bail deposit is forfeited. A defendant who fails to make bail is confined in jail until the court appearance.

Fill in the blanks 7
True/False 9–10
Multiple choice 7–8

The Legal Right to Bail

The Eighth Amendment to the Constitution does not guarantee a constitutional right to bail but rather prohibits "excessive bail." Many state statutes place no precise limit on the amount of bail a judge may impose, and many defendants who cannot make bail are placed in detention while awaiting trial. It has become apparent over the years that the bail system is discriminatory because defendants who are financially well-off are able to make bail, whereas indigent defendants languish in *pretrial detention* in the county jail. In addition, keeping a person in jail imposes serious financial burdens on local and state governments—and, in turn, taxpayers—who must pay for the cost of confinement. These factors have given rise to bail reform programs that depend on the defendant's promise to appear in court for trial (recognizance), rather than on financial ability to meet bail. These reforms have enabled many deserving but indigent offenders to go free. Another trend has been to deny people bail on the grounds that they are a danger to themselves or others in the community.

PERSPECTIVES ON JUSTICE

Bail is controversial because it penalizes the indigent offender who does not have the means to pay the bond. Detention centers are dreary, dangerous places, and those who are held in them can become victims of the justice system even though they are innocent of all charges. Experts on bail agree that pretrial detention is the most pervasive denial of equal protection and equal rights in U.S. law.

    Denying a defendant bail represents a crime control perspective. Release on recognizance, on the other hand, represents the due process perspective. In most cases, accused persons have the right to be released on reasonable bail to prepare their defense and continue their life in the community.

The Eighth Amendment restriction on excessive bail may also be interpreted to mean that the sole purpose of bail is to ensure that the defendant returns for

Sometimes hearings are held in order to determine whether a suspect should receive bail. Here Baltimore Ravens owner Art Modell is sworn in to testify as a character witness during a bond hearing for Ravens linebacker Ray Lewis in Fulton County Superior Court in Atlanta, February 14, 2000. Lewis, 24, and two companions were charged with murder in the stabbing deaths of two Atlanta men in the early morning hours after Super Bowl XXXIV.

AP/Wide World Photos

trial; bail may not be used as a form of punishment, nor may it be used to coerce or threaten a defendant. In most cases, a defendant has the right to be released on reasonable bail. Many jurisdictions also require a bail review hearing by a higher court in cases in which the initial judge set what might be considered excessive bail.

The U.S. Supreme Court's interpretation of the Eighth Amendment's provisions on bail was set out in the case of *Stack v. Boyle* (1951).[4] In that case, the Supreme Court found bail to be a traditional right to freedom before trial that permits unhampered preparation of a defense and prevents the criminal defendant from being punished prior to conviction. The Court held that bail is excessive when it exceeds an amount reasonably calculated to ensure that the defendant will return for trial. The Court indicated that bail should be in the amount that is generally set for similar offenses. Higher bail can be imposed when evidence supporting the increase is presented at a hearing, where the defendant's constitutional rights can be protected. Although *Stack* did not mandate an absolute right to bail, it did set guidelines for state courts to follow: If a crime is bailable, the amount set should not be frivolous, unusual, or beyond a person's ability to pay under similar circumstances. In this regard, there is an old saying, "The rich get bail, and the poor get jail."

Receiving Bail

Whether a defendant can be expected to appear at the next stage of the criminal proceeding is a key issue in determining bail. Bail cannot be used to punish an accused, nor can it be denied or revoked at the indulgence of the court. Many experts believe that money bail is one of the most unacceptable aspects of the criminal justice system: It is discriminatory because it works against the poor; it is costly because the government must pay to detain those offenders who are unable to make bail but would otherwise be in the community; it is unfair because a higher proportion of detainees receive longer sentences than people released on bail; and it is dehumanizing because innocent people who cannot make bail suffer in the nation's deteriorated jail system.

Does discrimination occur in setting the amount of bail? Are minorities asked to pay larger amounts of bail, increasing the probability that they will be detained in jail and receive longer prison sentences upon conviction? A survey of bail practices in federal courts conducted by William Rhodes sheds some light on this issue.[5] The study found, contrary to the fears of some critics, little actual relationship between the amount of bail and a person's race, age, economic status, and/or other social variables. Instead, Rhodes found that the amount of bail requested by judges was more closely associated with the seriousness of the offense and the defendant's prior record, two factors that by most legal standards should legitimately influence the bail decision.

How successful are bail and pretrial release? The answer depends on your perspective. Mary Toborg evaluated bail procedures in eight state urban jurisdictions and found that about 85 percent of all defendants received bail. Of these, about 15 percent did not return for trial because they absconded. An additional 15 percent were rearrested for another crime prior to their trial date. Thus, about 30 percent of those released on bail could be considered failures for one reason or another.[6]

Other studies found that about 10 percent of the defendants released by federal trial courts failed to honor their bail; the reasons included rearrest, failure to appear, or violation of the conditions of bail.[7] Those rearrested tended to (1) be on bail longer (nine months or more); (2) have a serious prior record; (3) abuse drugs; (4) have a poor work record; and (5) be disproportionately young, male, and minority-group members.

Fill in the blanks 8
True/False 11–12
Multiple choice 9

TABLE 11.2 FELONY DEFENDANTS HELD UNTIL CASE DISPOSITION (BY MOST SERIOUS ARREST CHARGE, 1996)

Most Serious Arrest Charge	Number of Defendants	Percent of Defendants		
		Total	Released before Case Disposition	Detained until Case Disposition
All offenses	50,241	100%	62%	38%
Violent offenses	12,897	100	55	45
Murder	500	100	21	79
Rape	525	100	53	47
Robbery	3,842	100	43	57
Assault	5,858	100	66	34
Other violent	2,172	100	56	44
Property Offenses	15,574	100%	64%	36%
Burglary	4,417	100	47	53
Theft	5,720	100	68	32
Other property	5,436	100	74	26
Drug offenses	17,491	100%	66%	34%
Trafficking	7,468	100	61	39
Other drug	10,023	100	70	30
Public-order offenses	4,279	100%	64%	36%
Weapons	1,967	100	64	36
Driving-related	1,210	100	70	30
Other public-order	1,101	100	56	44

SOURCE: Brian A. Reaves, *Felony Defendants in Large Urban Counties, 1996* (Washington, DC: Bureau of Justice Statistics, 1999).

The differences between the state and federal studies may be attributed to the type of offenders who pass through their jurisdictions. The federal courts probably see more white-collar offenders and fewer violent offenders. Thus, although state statistics are less encouraging, the 10 percent failure rate recorded by the federal government indicates that pretrial release has been quite successful in some jurisdictions.

A study by the National Pretrial Reporting Program found that about 24 percent of released defendants failed to appear in court and about 15 percent were rearrested for a felony while on pretrial release. These findings were based on a 1994 sample of state felony cases drawn from the 75 most populous counties in the United States. About 53,000 defendants were involved, of which more than two-thirds, or almost 35,000, were released prior to trial.[8] Some of the conclusions resulting from this important study are that (1) significant numbers of defendants are given pretrial release; (2) the failure-to-appear rate varies according to the type of arrest charge and the type of release; and (3) defendants in different age groups and those with different criminal backgrounds are rearrested at different rates. The overall rates of rearrest and of failure to appear are similar to results of previous research in this area. The study presents further evidence that pretrial release continues to be a effective component of the criminal justice system, providing pivotal services at key stages of the criminal process.

To improve success rates, further research is probably needed on pretrial personnel and how judges handle bail decisions. One approach to limiting disparity and improving decision making is the use of bail guidelines. Table 11.2 shows the percentage of felony defendants facing various charges who were released by the court prior to the disposition of their cases. The percentage of defendants given pretrial release in five major felonies is highlighted in Figure 11.1.

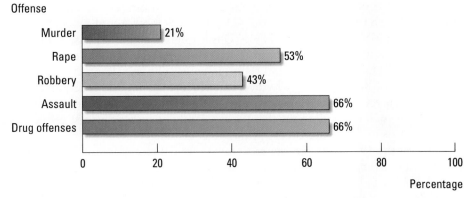

Offense

FIGURE 11.1
PERCENTAGE OF
STATE
DEFENDANTS
GIVEN PRETRIAL
RELEASE FOR
MAJOR FELONY
OFFENSES

SOURCE: Brian A. Reaves, *Felony Defendants in Large Urban Counties, 1994* (Washington, DC: Bureau of Justice Statistics, 1998), p. 17.

Bail Bonding

Essay 2

A parallel development associated with the bail system is the use of a **bail bond** to secure a defendant's release. For a fee, **bail bonding** agents lend money to people who cannot make bail on their own. Powerful ties exist between bonding agents and the court, with the result that defendants are steered toward particular bonding agents. Charges of kickbacks and cooperation accompany such arrangements, and allegations of corruption associated with the bail bonding system have been made. Consequently, many states have abolished bonding agents, replacing them with bail systems in which the state acts as a bonding agency. Defendants put up 10 percent of the total bail but are responsible for paying the entire amount if they abscond. This is referred to as the "10 percent cash match," or **deposit bail**, system. Nevertheless, an estimated 5,000 professional bail bonding agents operate in the United States today. The potential for abuse inherent in the system has led many critics to suggest that, in many instances, the traditional bail system is an unsatisfactory pretrial release procedure.

bail bond
An instrument executed by another party promising to forfeit money to the court if the defendant fails to appear for future criminal proceedings.

bail bonding
The business of providing bail to needy offenders, usually at very high rates of interest.

deposit bail
System in which the state acts as a bonding agency; defendants put up 10 percent of the total bail but are responsible for paying the entire amount if they abscond.

Bail Reform

Multiple choice 10–12
Essay 3–4

Efforts have been made to reform and even eliminate many bails and reduce the importance of bonding agents. Until the early 1960s, the justice system relied on money bonds as the principal form of pretrial release. In effect, defendants with financial means were able to post bail to secure pretrial release, whereas indigent defendants had to remain in custody. Today, however, many states allow defendants to be released on their own recognizance without any money bail.

Release on recognizance (ROR) was pioneered by the Vera Institute of Justice in an experiment called the Manhattan Bail Project, which began in 1961 with the cooperation of New York City criminal courts and local law students.[9] This project found that if the court had sufficient background information about the defendant, it could make a reasonably good judgment about whether the accused would return to court. When release decisions were based on such information as the nature of the offense, family ties, and employment record, most defendants returned to court when released on their own recognizance. The results of the Vera Institute's initial operation showed a default rate of less than seven-tenths of 1 percent. The bail project's experience suggested that releasing a person on the basis of verified information more effectively guaranteed appearance in court than did money bail. Highly successful ROR projects were set up in major cities around the country, including Philadelphia and San Francisco. By 1980, more than 120 formal programs were in operation, and today they exist in almost every major jurisdiction.[10]

release on recognizance (ROR)
A pretrial release in which a defendant with ties to the community is not required to post bail but promises to appear at all subsequent proceedings.

The Vera Institute, a nonprofit organization in New York, introduced the concept of ROR and sponsors pretrial release programs. Visit their Web site at http://broadway.vera.org/html

For an up-to-date list of Web links, see http://www.wadsworth.com/product/0534573053s

The success of the early ROR programs resulted in further bail reforms that culminated with the enactment of the federal Bail Reform Act of 1966, the first change in federal bail laws since 1786.[11] This legislation sought to ensure that release would be granted in all noncapital cases where there was sufficient reason to believe that the defendant would return to court. The law clearly established a presumption of ROR that must be overcome before money bail is required, authorized 10 percent deposit bail, introduced the concept of conditional release, and implemented the philosophy that release should be under the least restrictive method necessary to ensure court appearance.

During the 1970s, the pretrial movement was hampered by public pressure over crimes committed by those on pretrial release. As a result, the Bail Reform Act of 1984 mandated that no defendants should be kept in pretrial detention simply because they could not afford money bail, established the presumption of ROR in all cases in which a person is bailable, and formalized restrictive preventive detention provisions (discussed later in this chapter).[12] The 1984 act required that community safety, as well as the risk of flight, be considered in the release detention decision.

A number of innovative alternative bail programs are described in Exhibit 11.2. The most often used are (1) personal reocognizance, (2) unsecured or personal bond, (3) surety or cash bond, and (4) percentage or deposit bail.

Bail reform is considered one of the most successful programs in the recent history of the criminal justice system. However, critics suggest that emphasis should be placed on controlling the behavior of serious criminals, rather than on

For an online listing of pretrial service agencies, go to http://www.napsa.org/html

For an up-to-date list of Web links, see http://www.wadsworth.com/product/0534573053s

EXHIBIT 11.2   INNOVATIVE BAIL SYSTEMS

Nonfinancial Release

- **Release on recognizance**. The defendant is released on a promise to appear, without any requirement of money bond. This form of release is unconditional—that is, without the imposition of any special conditions, supervision, or specially provided services. The defendant must simply appear in court for all scheduled hearings.
- **Conditional release**. The defendant is released on a promise to fulfill some state requirements that go beyond those associated with release on recognizance. Four types of conditions are placed on defendants, all of which share the common aims of increasing the defendant's likelihood of returning to court and/or maintaining community safety: (1) status quo conditions, such as requiring that the defendant maintain residence or employment status; (2) restrictive conditions, such as requiring that the defendant remain in the jurisdiction, stay away from the complainant, or maintain a curfew; (3) contact conditions, such as requiring that the defendant report by telephone or in person to the release program or a third party at various intervals; (4) problem-oriented conditions, such as requiring that the defendant participate in drug or alcohol treatment programs.

Financial Release

- **Unsecured bail**. The defendant is released with no immediate requirement of payment. However, if the defendant fails to appear, he or she is liable for the full amount.
- **Privately secured bail.** A private organization or individual posts the bail amount, which is returned when the defendant appears in court. In effect, the organization provides services akin to those of a professional bonding agent, but without cost to the defendant.
- **Property bail**. The defendant may post evidence of real property in lieu of money.
- **Deposit bail**. The defendant deposits a percentage of the bail amount, typically 10 percent, with the court. When the defendant appears in court, the deposit is returned, sometimes minus an administrative fee. If the defendant fails to appear, he or she is liable for the full amount of the bail.
- **Surety bail**. The defendant pays a percentage of the bond, usually 10 percent, to a bonding agent, who posts the full bail. The fee paid to the bonding agent is not returned to the defendant if he or she appears in court. The bonding agent is liable for the full amount of the bond should the defendant fail to appear. Bonding agents often require posting of collateral to cover the full bail amount.
- **Cash bail**. The defendant pays the entire amount of bail set by the judge to secure release. The bail is returned to the defendant when he or she appears in court.

SOURCE: Adapted from Andy Hall, *Pretrial Release Program Options* (Washington, DC: National Institute of Justice, 1984), pp. 32–33.

making sure that nondangerous defendants are released prior to their trials. In addition, research conducted by John Goldkamp has uncovered evidence that race and other social variables may play an important role in the decision to grant ROR.[13] This is particularly troubling, given that the suspicion of social bias in granting bail was among the most important reasons for bail reform in the first place. Because of these considerations, recent efforts have concentrated on improving the standards for bail, rather than on easing its application.

The Preventive Detention Controversy

Those who promote bail reform point to the Eighth Amendment of the Constitution as evidence that bail should be made available to almost all people accused of committing a crime. The presumption of the right to bail is challenged by those who believe that releasing dangerous criminals before trial poses a threat to public safety. They point to the evidence showing that many people released on bail commit new crimes while at large and often fail to appear for trial. One response to the alleged failure of the bail system to protect citizens has been **preventive detention** statutes. These statutes require that certain dangerous defendants be confined prior to trial for their own protection and that of the community.

Does the federal Bail Reform Act of 1984 allow preventive detention?[14] Although the act does contain provisions for ROR, it also allows judges to order preventive detention if they determine "that no condition or combination of conditions will reasonably assure the appearance of the person as required and the safety of any other person and the community." The decision to detain is evaluated at a hearing where the accused has the right to counsel, to testify, and to confront and cross-examine witnesses, and the government must present clear and convincing evidence of the dangers the defendant presents. If it is determined that the defendant is dangerous, the magistrate can preventively detain him or her for the safety of the community and deny bail.[15]

In addition to the federal act, a number of state jurisdictions have incorporated elements of preventive detention into their bail systems. These provisions include (1) exclusion of certain crimes from bail eligibility; (2) definition of bail to include appearance in court and community safety; and (3) limitations on the right to bail for those previously convicted. Although most of them do not constitute outright preventive detention, they serve to narrow the scope of bail eligibility.

Preventive detention has been a source of concern for civil libertarians, who believe that holding a person in custody before proof of guilt violates the due process clause of the U.S. Constitution. The U.S. Supreme Court has disagreed with this analysis. In *United States v. Salerno* (1987), the Court upheld the Bail Reform Act's provision on preventive detention.[16] According to Chief Justice William Rehnquist, the statute conforms to the principle that "in our society, liberty is the norm, and detention prior to trial or without trial is the carefully limited exception."[17] Because of the importance of this case, it is analyzed in the Law in Review feature.

PRETRIAL DETENTION

Whereas preventive detention keeps defendants in jail prior to trial to protect the community, defendants who are ineligible for bail or ROR because they might not return for trial are subject to **pretrial detention**.

Pretrial custody accounts for more people in incarceration in the United States than does imprisonment after sentencing.[18] In the late 1990s, on any given day in the United States, more than 300,000 people were held in more than 35,000 local

Fill in the blanks 9–10
Multiple choice 13
Essay 5

preventive detention
Holding without bail a defendant believed to be dangerous or likely to commit a crime if released before trial.

True/False 13–14
Multiple choice 14–16

pretrial detention
Holding a defendant in jail without bail to ensure his or her appearance at trial.

United States v. Salerno (1987)

In this case, the U.S. Supreme Court held that the use of preventive detention is constitutionally permissible.

Facts

On March 21, 1986, Anthony Salerno and co-defendant Vincent Cafaro were charged in a 29-count indictment alleging various racketeering violations, including gambling, wire fraud, extortion, and conspiracy to commit murder. At their arraignment, the government moved to have them detained on the grounds that no condition of release could ensure community safety. At a detention hearing, the prosecution presented evidence that Salerno was the "boss" of the Genovese crime family and that Cafaro was a "captain." Wiretap evidence indicated that the two men had participated in criminal conspiracies, including murder. The court heard testimony from two witnesses who had personally participated in the murder conspiracies. In rebuttal, Salerno provided character statements, presented evidence that he had a heart condition, and challenged the veracity of the government's witnesses. Cafaro claimed the wiretaps had merely recorded "tough talk." The trial court allowed the detention on the grounds that the defendants wanted to use their pretrail freedom to continue their "family" business and "when business as usual involves threats, beatings, and murder, the present danger such people pose to the community is self-evident."

On appeal, the U.S. Court of Appeals for the Second Circuit agreed with the defendants' claim that the government could not detain suspects simply because they were thought to represent a danger to the community. The circuit court found that the criminal law system holds people accountable for their past deeds, not their anticipated future actions. The government appealed this decision to the Supreme Court.

Decision

The Supreme Court held that the preventive detention act had a legitimate and compelling regulatory purpose and did not violate the due process clause. Preventive detention was not designed to punish dangerous individuals but to find a solution for the social problem of people committing crimes while on bail; preventing danger to the community is a legitimate societal goal.

The Court also stated that society's need for protection can outweigh an individual's liberty interest and that, under some circumstances, individuals can be held without bail. The act provides that only the most serious criminals can be held and mandates careful procedures to ensure that the judgment of future dangerousness is made after careful deliberation. Finally, the Court found that the Eighth Amendment does not limit the setting (or denial) of bail simply to prohibit defendants' flight to avoid trial and held that considerations of dangerousness are a valid reason to deny pretrial release.

Significance of the Case

Salerno legitimizes the use of preventive detention as a crime control method. It permits the limitations on bail already in place in many state jurisdictions to continue. *Salerno* further illustrates a growing concern for community protection. It is a good example of the recent efforts by the Court to give the justice system greater control over criminal defendants. At this time, it is still unclear how often judges will rely on preventive detention statutes that require a hearing on the facts, or whether they will simply continue to set extremely high bail for defendants they wish to remain in pretrial custody.

Critical Thinking Skills

1. Preventive detention remains one of the most controversial issues in criminal justice. Under preventive detention a person may be incarcerated not because of what they did in the past but because of what they may do in the future. As a result, some people are detained who, had they been released, might have posed little danger to society. Is it possible to truly assess future behavior? What methods would you employ? Are clinical tests by psychologists reliable? Would you simply rely on past behavior as an indicator of future behaviors?

2. Suppose a person is a known drug dealer with no history of violent or aggressive behavior. He has been picked up for the tenth time on drug trafficking charges. Would you recommend preventive detention even though he has no history of violence and probably poses little direct threat to society? What about a person who has ten prior sex offenses (exposing himself to women)? What about a person who has cheated on his income tax ten times? Do you see differences among these examples?

InfoTrac College Edition Research

The Supreme Court also upheld a statute allowing the placement of children in preventive detention before their adjudication. The Court concluded that it was not unreasonable to detain juveniles for their own protection (see *Schall v. Martin* 467 U.S. 253 (1984)). Read the following article comparing the adult and juvenile process: Jeffrey Fagan and Martin Guggenheim, "Preventive Detention and Judicial Determination," *Journal of Criminal Law and Criminology*, 1996, v2 p415

jails. Over the course of a year, many times that number passed through these jails. More than 50 percent of those held in local jails have been accused of crimes but not convicted; they are pretrial detainees. In the United States, people are detained at a rate twice that of neighboring Canada and three times that of Great Britain.

The jail has long been a trouble spot for the criminal justice system. Conditions tend to be poor and rehabilitation nonexistent. Hundreds of jails are overcrowded, and some are under court orders to reduce their populations and improve conditions. This national jail-crowding crisis has worsened over the years.[19] Local jails now hold approximately 500,000 adults, either awaiting trial or serving a sentence. Further data on the jail population are found in Chapter 15.

Jails are often considered the weakest link in the criminal justice process. They are frequently dangerous, harmful, decrepit, and filled by the poor and friendless. Costs of holding a person in jail range up to more than $100 a day and $40,000 a year. In addition, detainees are often confined with those convicted of crimes. Many felons are transferred to jails from state prisons to ease crowding. In the same cell, it is possible to find in close quarters a convicted rapist, a father jailed for nonpayment of child support, and a person awaiting trial for a crime that he did not actually commit. Thus, jails contain a mix of inmates that can lead to violence, brutality, and suicide.

Why does the jail crisis persist? Societal problems such as drug use, the prevalence of mentally ill people in open society, and cutbacks in federal and state social service funding are probably all contributing factors.

People who are detained before trial tend to receive longer prison sentences if convicted than those who are released on bail. The relationship between bail and conviction is less clear. John Goldkamp's well-known study of bail in Philadelphia found a small correlation between defendants' custody status before trial and the probability of conviction at trial. However, Goldkamp found that convicted offenders who were denied bail were much more likely to receive prison terms than those who were released before trial.[20]

Information from the Department of Justice supports these findings regarding adjudication and higher conviction rates of detained versus released defendants.

Fill in the blanks 11–13
True/False 15–16

© Alon Reininger/Contact Press Images

Inmates in the Los Angeles county jail. People who cannot make bail are not only subject to incarceration before they are tried, but they also suffer higher rates of conviction and incarceration than defendants who had been released on bail. Bail reform has attempted to remedy this problem by reducing the number of detained defendants.

Overall, a higher percentage of detained defendants (79%) than released defendants (61%) were convicted in this 1992 study. Among defendants who were detained until their case was disposed, 67 percent were sentenced to incarceration, compared with 29 percent of those who were released.[21] In other words, detained defendants have a much higher probability of being imprisoned than those released into the community.

How can these relationships be explained? It is possible that people who do not make bail are the more violent chronic offenders who, upon conviction, are punished more severely by sentencing judges. However, this explanation would not apply to individuals involved in white-collar crimes, such as fraud and forgery; it is unlikely that detainees for those crimes are more dangerous than those receiving bail. It is likely that judges are reluctant to give probation or even a relatively short prison sentence to people who have already been detained in jail. The justice system would look foolish if a person who has already spent a considerable period behind bars did not receive a prison sentence that at least matched the jail time.

It is also likely that judges' decision making is influenced by the pretrial behavior of bailees. People who make bail have a chance to demonstrate that they can adjust to society and make use of community social services; detainees are not afforded this opportunity to prove themselves. Whereas bailees can demonstrate that they have refrained from any further criminal activity, detainees are not given a chance to show their trustworthiness. Consequently, detainees may receive a greater period of secure confinement than bailees, who may be considered better risks.

In sum, the evidence suggests that, if convicted, people who were detained before trial are much more likely to be sent to prison and to do more time than those who avoided pretrial detention. More information on the issue of local jails is contained in Chapter 15.

THE INDICTMENT PROCESS

Fill in the blanks 14–16
True/False 17–20
Multiple choice 17–18
Essay 6

It is the government's responsibility to prove that there is probable cause to believe that the accused committed the crime with which he or she is charged. The grand jury review and the preliminary hearing are two alternative procedures for evaluating the evidence against the accused.

The Grand Jury

The grand jury was an early development of the English common law. Under the Magna Carta (1215), no "freeman" could be seized and imprisoned unless he had been judged by his peers. To determine fairly who was eligible to be tried, a group of freeman from the district where the crime was committed would be brought together to examine the facts of the case and determine whether the charges had merit. Thus, the grand jury was created as a check against arbitrary prosecution by a judge who might be a puppet of the government.

The concept of the grand jury was brought to the American colonies by early settlers and later incorporated into the Fifth Amendment of the U.S. Constitution, which states that "no person shall be held to answer for a capital, or otherwise infamous crime, unless on a presentment or indictment of a grand jury."

Today, the use of the grand jury is diminishing. Only a small number of states require a grand jury indictment to begin all felony proceedings. Some states allow a grand jury to be called at the option of the prosecutor. The federal government employs both the grand jury and the preliminary hearing systems.

The grand jury today has two roles. First, the grand jury has the power to act as an independent investigating body. In this capacity, it examines the possibility of criminal activity within its jurisdiction. These investigative efforts are directed toward general rather than individual criminal conduct. After completing its investigation, the grand jury issues a report called a **presentment**, which contains its findings and also usually a recommendation of indictment.

The grand jury's second and better-known role is accusatory in nature. In this capacity, the grand jury acts as the community's conscience in determining whether an accusation by the state (the prosecution) justifies a trial. The grand jury relies on the testimony of witnesses called by the prosecution through its subpoena power. After examining the evidence and the testimony of witnesses, the grand jury decides whether probable cause exists for prosecution. If it does, an indictment, or **true bill**, is affirmed. If the grand jury fails to find probable cause, a **no bill** (meaning that the indictment is ignored) is passed. In some states, a prosecutor can present evidence to a different grand jury if a no bill is returned; in other states, this action is prohibited by statute.

A grand jury is ordinarily made up of 16 to 23 individuals, depending on the requirements of the jurisdiction. This group theoretically represents a county. Selection of members varies from state to state, but for the most part, they are chosen at random (for example, from voting lists). To qualify to serve on a grand jury, an individual must be at least 18 years of age, a U.S. citizen, and a resident of the jurisdiction for one year or more and possess sufficient English-speaking skills for communication.

The grand jury usually meets at the request of the prosecution. Hearings are closed and secret. The prosecuting attorney presents the charges and calls witnesses who testify under oath to support the indictment. Usually, the accused individuals are not allowed to attend the hearing unless they are asked to testify by the prosecutor or the grand jury.

The effectiveness and efficiency of the grand jury procedure have been questioned for a number of reasons. One common complaint is that the grand jury is costly in terms of space, personnel, and money. The members must be selected, notified, sworn, housed, fed, and granted other considerations. More important, the grand jury has been criticized as being a "rubber stamp" for the prosecution. The presentation of evidence is under prosecutorial control, and the grand jury merely assents to the actions of the prosecutor. Studies of grand jury effectiveness have noted that the grand jury indicts almost all cases presented to it and has a negligible effect—other than delay—on the criminal process. The general view is that the grand jury should be avoided except in cases where a community voice is needed in a troublesome or notorious case. It is generally agreed, however, that the investigative role of the grand jury is a valuable and necessary function that should be not only maintained but expanded.

Because the grand jury is often controlled solely by the state prosecutor, some legal experts believe that the system should provide the defendant with more due process protection. The American Bar Association's *Grand Jury Policy and Model Act* suggests the following changes in state grand jury statutes: (1) Witnesses should have their own attorneys when they give testimony; (2) prosecutors should be required to present evidence that might show that a suspect is innocent; (3) witnesses should be granted constitutional privileges against self-incrimination; and (4) grand jurors should be informed of all the elements of the crimes being presented against the suspect.[22]

The Preliminary Hearing

The preliminary hearing is used in about half the states as an alternative to the grand jury. Although the purpose of preliminary and grand jury hearings is the same—to establish whether probable cause is sufficient to merit a trial—the procedures differ significantly.

presentment
The report of a grand jury investigation, which usually includes a recommendation of indictment.

true bill
The action by a grand jury when it votes to indict an accused suspect.

no bill
The action by a grand jury when it votes not to indict an accused suspect.

True/False 21–23
Essay 7

The preliminary hearing is conducted before a magistrate or inferior court judge and, unlike the grand jury hearing, is open to the public unless the defendant requests otherwise. Also present at the preliminary hearing are the prosecuting attorney, the defendant, and the defendant's counsel, if already retained. The prosecution presents its evidence and witnesses to the judge. The defendant or the defense counsel then has the right to cross-examine witnesses and to challenge the prosecutor's evidence.

After hearing the evidence, the judge decides whether there is probable cause to believe that the defendant committed the alleged crime. If there is, the defendant is bound over for trial, and the prosecuting attorney's information (same as the indictment) is filed with the superior court, usually within 15 days. If probable cause is not established, the charges are dismissed, and the defendant is released from custody.

A unique aspect of the preliminary hearing is the defendant's right to waive the proceeding. In most states, the prosecutor and the judge must agree to this **waiver**. A waiver has advantages and disadvantages for both the prosecutor and the defendant. In most situations, a prosecutor will agree to a waiver because it avoids revealing evidence to the defense before trial. However, if the state believes it needs to obtain a record of witness testimony because of the possibility that a witness or witnesses may be unavailable for the trial or unable to remember the facts clearly, the prosecutor may override the waiver. In this situation, the record of the preliminary hearing can be used at the trial.

The defendant will most likely waive the preliminary hearing if he or she (1) has already decided to plead guilty; (2) wants to speed up the criminal process; or (3) hopes to avoid the negative publicity that might result from the hearing. On the other hand, the preliminary hearing is of obvious advantage to the defendant who believes that it will result in a dismissal of the charges. In addition, the preliminary hearing gives the defense the opportunity to learn what evidence is available to the prosecution. Figure 11.2 outlines the significant differences between the grand jury and the preliminary hearing processes.

waiver
The voluntary and deliberate relinquishing of a known right, such as those guaranteed under the Fifth and Sixth Amendments.

Essay 8

Arraignment

An arraignment takes place after an indictment or information is filed following a grand jury or preliminary hearing. At the arraignment, the judge informs the defendant of the charges against him or her and appoints counsel if it has not yet been retained. According to the Sixth Amendment of the U.S. Constitution, the accused has the right to be informed of the nature and cause of the accusation; thus, the judge at the arraignment must make sure that the defendant clearly understands the charges.

After the charges are read and explained, the defendant is asked to enter a plea. If a plea of not guilty or not guilty by reason of insanity is entered, a trial date is set. When a defendant pleads guilty or nolo contendere, a date for sentencing is arranged. The magistrate then either sets bail or releases the defendant on personal recognizance.

Essay 9

The Plea

Ordinarily, a defendant in a criminal trial will enter one of the following pleas: guilty, not guilty, or nolo contendere.

Guilty More than 90 percent of defendants appearing before the courts plead guilty prior to the trial stage. A guilty plea has several consequences. It serves not only as an admission of guilt but also as a surrender of the entire array of consti-

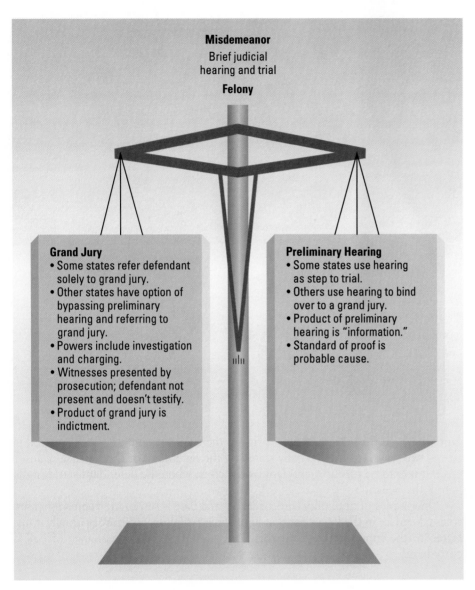

Misdemeanor
Brief judicial
hearing and trial
Felony

Grand Jury
- Some states refer defendant solely to grand jury.
- Other states have option of bypassing preliminary hearing and referring to grand jury.
- Powers include investigation and charging.
- Witnesses presented by prosecution; defendant not present and doesn't testify.
- Product of grand jury is indictment.

Preliminary Hearing
- Some states use hearing as step to trial.
- Others use hearing to bind over to a grand jury.
- Product of preliminary hearing is "information."
- Standard of proof is probable cause.

FIGURE 11.2
CHARGING THE
DEFENDANT WITH
A CRIME

Note the differences between the grand jury and preliminary hearing.

tutional rights designed to protect a criminal defendant against unjustified conviction, including the right to remain silent, the right to confront witnesses against him, the right to a trial by jury, and the right to be proven guilty by proof beyond a reasonable doubt.

As a result, a judge must observe certain procedures when accepting a plea of guilty. First, the judge must clearly state to the defendant the constitutional guarantees automatically waived by this plea. Second, the judge must believe that the facts of the case establish a basis for the plea and that the plea is made voluntarily. Third, the judge must inform the defendant of the right to counsel during the pleading process. In many felony cases, the judge will insist on the presence of defense counsel. Finally, the judge must inform the defendant of the possible sentencing outcomes, including the maximum sentence that can be imposed.

After a guilty plea has been entered, a sentencing date is arranged. In a majority of states, a guilty plea may be withdrawn and replaced with a not guilty plea at any time prior to sentencing if good cause is shown.

Sometimes arraignments don't go as planned. Here, handcuffed murder suspect Alfred Gaynor, 31, left, lies slumped over a Springfield District Courtroom railing April 30, 1998, in Springfield, Massachusetts, after being struck with a chair by a man at the start of Gaynor's pretrial hearing in connection with the murder of two Springfield women. Gaynor's assailant was Eric Downs, son of one of the victims.

AP/Wide World Photos

Not Guilty At the arraignment or prior to the trial, a not guilty plea is entered in one of two ways: (1) It is verbally stated by the defendant or the defense counsel, or (2) it is entered for the defendant by the court when the defendant stands mute before the bench.

Once a plea of not guilty is recorded, a trial date is set. In misdemeanor cases, trials take place in the lower court system, whereas felony cases are normally transferred to the superior court. At this time, a continuance or issuance of bail is considered.

Nolo Contendere The nolo contendere plea, which means "no contest," is essentially a plea of guilty. This plea has the same consequences as a guilty plea, with one exception: It may not be held against the defendant as proof in a subsequent civil matter because technically there has been no admission of guilt.

PLEA BARGAINING

One of the most common practices in the criminal justice system today, and a cornerstone of the "informal justice" system, is *plea bargaining.* More than 90 percent of criminal convictions are estimated to result from negotiated pleas of guilty. Even in serious felony cases, some jurisdictions will make about four bargains for every trial.

Plea bargaining has been defined concisely as the exchange of prosecutorial and judicial concessions for pleas of guilty.[23] Normally, a bargain can be made between the prosecutor and the defense attorney in four ways: (1) The initial charge may be reduced to that of a lesser offense, thus automatically reducing the sentence imposed. (2) In cases where many counts are charged, the prosecutor may reduce the number of counts. (3) The prosecutor may promise to recommend a lenient sentence, such as probation. (4) When the charge carries a strong nega-

Multiple choice 19
Essay 10–11

tive label (for example, child molester), the prosecutor may alter the charge to a more "socially acceptable" one (assault) in exchange for a plea of guilty. In a jurisdiction where sentencing disparities exist between judges, the prosecutor may even agree to arrange for the defendant to appear before a lenient judge in exchange for a plea; this practice is known as *judge-shopping*.

Because of excessive criminal court caseloads and the personal and professional needs of the prosecution and the defense (to get the case over with in the shortest amount of time), plea bargaining has become an essential if controversial part of the administration of justice. Proponents contend that plea bargaining actually benefits both the state and the defendant in the following ways: (1) The overall financial costs of the criminal prosecution are reduced; (2) the administrative efficiency of the courts is greatly improved; (3) the prosecution is able to devote more time to serious cases; and (4) the defendant avoids possible detention and an extended trial and may receive a reduced sentence. Those who favor plea bargaining believe it is appropriate to enter into plea discussions where the interests of the state in the effective administration of justice will be served.

Opponents of the plea bargaining process believe that the negotiated plea should be eliminated. Some argue that plea bargaining is objectionable because it encourages defendants to waive their constitutional right to trial. In addition, some experts suggest that sentences tend to be less severe when a defendant enters a guilty plea rather than goes to trial, and that plea bargains result in even greater sentencing disparity. Particularly in the eyes of the general public, this allows the defendant to "beat the system" and further tarnishes the criminal process. Plea bargaining also raises the danger that an innocent person will be convicted of a crime if he or she is convinced that the lighter treatment from a guilty plea is preferable to the risk of conviction with a harsher sentence following a formal trial.

It is unlikely that plea negotiations will be eliminated or severely curtailed in the near future. Why? The pressure of caseloads in contemporary courts outweighs the legal principle of evenhanded justice for all. Supporters of the total

Defendants plead guilty in order to obtain favorable sentences. Here, former U.S. Olympic figure skater Tonya Harding is led by police Capt. Paul Pearce to a police car outside Camas-Washougal Municipal Court in Camas, Wash., May 18, 2000. She pled guilty to disorderly conduct and malicious mischief for attacking her boyfriend, Darren Silver, on Feb. 22, 2000, and was sentenced to 3 days in jail, 10 days of community service on a work crew, and $822 in fines and court costs.

AP/Wide World Photos

ANALYZING CRIMINAL JUSTICE ISSUES

Pros and Cons of Plea Bargaining

Plea bargaining is so widespread that it is recognized as one of the major elements of the criminal justice system. Despite its prevalence, its merits are hotly debated. Those opposed to the widespread use of plea bargaining assert that it is coercive in its inducement of guilty pleas, that it encourages the unequal exercise of prosecutorial discretion, and that it complicates sentencing as well as the job of correctional authorities. Others argue that it is unconstitutional and that it results in cynicism and disrespect for the entire system.

Proponents of plea bargaining contend that the practice ensures the flow of guilty pleas essential to administration efficiency. It allows the system the flexibility to individualize justice and inspires respect for the system because it is associated with certain and prompt punishment.

In recent years, efforts have been made to convert plea bargaining into a more visible, understandable, and fair dispositional process. Many jurisdictions have developed safeguards and guidelines to prevent violations of due process and to ensure that innocent defendants do not plead guilty under coercion. Such safeguards include the following:
1. Uniform plea practice
2. Time limits on plea negotiations
3. Presence of defense counsel to advise defendant
4. Open discussions about plea between prosecutor and defense attorney
5. Full information regarding offender and offense
6. Judicial questioning of defendant before accepting plea
7. Judicial supervision of plea

Critical Thinking Skills

Research shows that plea bargaining is the key to managing criminal caseloads. If plea bargaining were eliminated, wouldn't legislatures have to provide the courts with more resources and possibly build additional prisons?

InfoTrac College Edition Research

To learn more about the pros and cons of plea bargaining, see George Fisher, "Plea Bargaining Triumphs," *Yale Law Review,* 2000, v109 p855

SOURCE: Stephen Schulhofer, "Is Plea Bargaining Inevitable?" *Harvard Law Review* 97 (1984): 125.

---

abolition of plea bargaining are in the minority. As a result of abuses, however, efforts are being made to improve the process. Proposed reforms include (1) the development of uniform plea practices, (2) representation by counsel during plea negotiations, and (3) the establishment of time limits on plea negotiations. The Analyzing Criminal Justice Issues feature discusses the pros and cons of plea bargaining in more detail.

Multiple choice 20–27

Legal Issues in Plea Bargaining

The U.S. Supreme Court has reviewed the propriety of plea bargaining in several decisions, particularly with regard to the voluntariness of guilty pleas. Defendants are entitled to the effective assistance of counsel to protect them from pressure and influence. The Court ruled in *Hill v. Lockhart* (1985) that to prove ineffectiveness of counsel the defendant must show a "reasonable probability that, but for counsel's errors, he would not have pleaded guilty and would have insisted on going to trial."[24]

In *Boykin v. Alabama* (1969), the Court held that an affirmative action (such as a verbal statement) that the plea was made voluntarily must exist in the record before a trial judge can accept a guilty plea.[25] This is essential because a guilty plea basically constitutes a waiver of the defendant's Fifth Amendment privilege against self-incrimination and Sixth Amendment right to a jury trial. The voluntariness of the defendant's plea is one of the key ingredients in the plea bargaining process. Subsequent to *Boykin,* the Court ruled in *Brady v. United States* (1970) that a guilty plea is not invalid merely because it is entered to avoid the possibility of the death penalty.[26]

When the question arose about whether a guilty plea could be accepted by a defendant who was maintaining his or her innocence, the Supreme Court, in *North Carolina v. Alford* (1970), said that such an action was appropriate where a defendant was seeking a lesser sentence. In other words, a defendant could plead guilty without admitting guilt.[27] This is known in many jurisdictions as the *Alford plea.* Prosecutors often believe that such a plea presents problems of perception for victims and their families, who consider the defendant's acknowledgment of guilt to be an essential part of punishment. Yet *Alford* pleas remain constitutionally sound.

In *Santobello v. New York* (1971), the Court held that the prosecutor's promise must be kept and that the breaking of a plea bargaining agreement by the prosecutor required a reversal for the defendant.[28] In *Ricketts v. Adamson* (1987), the Court ruled that defendants must also keep their side of a bargain to receive the promised offer of leniency. In this case, the defendant was charged with first-degree murder but was allowed to plead guilty to second-degree murder in exchange for testifying against his accomplices. The testimony was given, but the co-defendants' conviction was later reversed on appeal. Ricketts refused to testify a second time, and the prosecutor withdrew the offer of leniency. On appeal, the Supreme Court allowed the recharging and held that Ricketts had to suffer the consequences of his voluntary choice not to retestify.[29]

How far can prosecutors go to convince a defendant to plead guilty? The Supreme Court ruled in the 1978 case of *Bordenkircher v. Hayes* that a defendant's due process rights are not violated when a prosecutor threatens to reindict the accused on more serious charges if he or she does not plead guilty to the original offense.[30]

In 1995, the U.S. Supreme Court decided the case of *United States v. Mezzanatto.*[31] In *Mezzanatto,* the Court declared that statements made by the defendant during plea bargaining can be used at trial for impeachment purposes. This means that a prosecutor can refuse to plea bargain with a defendant unless the defendant agrees that any statements made during the negotiations can be used to impeach him at trial. The Court narrowly interpreted Rule 410 of the Federal Rules of Evidence, which says that statements made during plea bargaining are inadmissible at trial. Although the ruling applies only to federal trials, it has been adopted by some state court systems that watch Supreme Court decisions and follow suit.

From repeated actions by the Supreme Court, we realize that plea bargaining is a constitutionally accepted practice in the United States. Table 11.3 summarizes the major Supreme Court decisions regulating plea bargaining practices.

Plea Bargain Decision Making
Essay 12

Because the plea bargaining process is largely informal, lacking in guidelines, and discretionary in nature, some effort has been made to determine how much information, of what kinds, is used by the prosecutor to make plea bargaining decisions. Research has found that certain information weighs heavily in the prosecutorial decision to accept a plea negotiation.[32] Such factors as the offense, the defendant's prior record and age, and the type, strength, and admissibility of evidence are considered important in the plea bargaining decision. The attitude of the complainant is also an important factor in the decision-making process: In victimless cases, such as heroin possession, the police attitude is most often considered, whereas in victim-related crimes, such as rape, the attitude of the victim is of primary concern. The research also revealed that prosecutors in low-population

TABLE 11.3 NOTABLE U.S. SUPREME COURT CASES ON THE REGULATION OF PLEA BARGAINING

Case	Decision
Boykin v. Alabama (1969)	The defendant must make an affirmative statement that the plea is voluntary before the judge can accept it.
Brady v. United States (1970)	Avoiding the possibility of the death penalty is not grounds to invalidate a guilty plea.
North Carolina v. Alford (1970)	Accepting a guilty plea from a defendant who maintain his or her innocence is valid.
Santobello v. New York (1971)	The promise of a prosecutor that rests on a guilty plea must be kept in a plea bargaining agreement.
Bordenkircher v. Hayes (1978)	A defendant's constitutional rights are not violated when a prosecutor threatens to reindict the accused on more serious charges if he or she is not willing to plead guilty to the original offense.
Hill v. Lockhart (1985)	To prove ineffectiveness of defense counsel, the defendant needs to show a reasonable probability that, except for counsel's errors, the defendant would not have pleaded guilty.
Ricketts v. Admason (1987)	The defendant is required to keep his or her side of the bargain to receive the promised offer of leniency, because plea bargaining rests on an agreement between the parties.
United States v. Mezzanatto (1995)	A defendant who wants to plea bargain in federal court can be required to agree that, if he testifes at trial, his statements during the plea bargain negotiations can be used against him.

or rural jurisdictions not only use more information in making their decisions but also seem more likely than their urban counterparts to accept bargains. It was suggested that "this finding tends to dispute the notion that plea bargaining is a response to overcrowding in large urban courts." Where caseload pressures are less, it appears that the acceptance of a plea bargain is actually more probable.

A study by William McDonald of plea bargaining in six court jurisdictions reached similar conclusions. McDonald found that plea negotiations were not conducted in a haphazard manner, nor were they used by prosecutors to engage in frauds or other deceptive practices. For example, prosecutors did not overcharge suspects with the idea of forcing them to plead to a more reasonable charge.[33]

Figure 11.3 shows how decisions made by police, prosecutors, and defense attorneys play a critical role in disposing of criminal felony cases prior to trial. Taken from a study of 100 typical cases, it shows that most cases are not brought to trial but are handled by guilty pleas, diversion, or dismissal.

The Nature of Plea Bargaining

A federal study of plea negotiations sheds some light on the plea bargaining process. The study by Boland and Forst looked at 14 jurisdictions around the country and found a wide discrepancy in the use of pleas.[34] Although the overall average was one trial for every 11 plea bargains, the range was from one for every 37 in Geneva, Illinois, to one for every 4 in Portland, Oregon. Interestingly, the high plea bargain jurisdictions were not exclusively high-crime areas where case pressure was a factor; some of the jurisdictions that hold a large number of trials, such as Washington, D.C., St. Louis, and New Orleans, are big cities with high caseloads. Thus, case pressure does not seem to play as important a role in plea negotiations as might have been thought. The study also found that jurisdictions that hold a great many trials tend to be more selective in the cases they process and are more likely to screen out weak cases before trial.

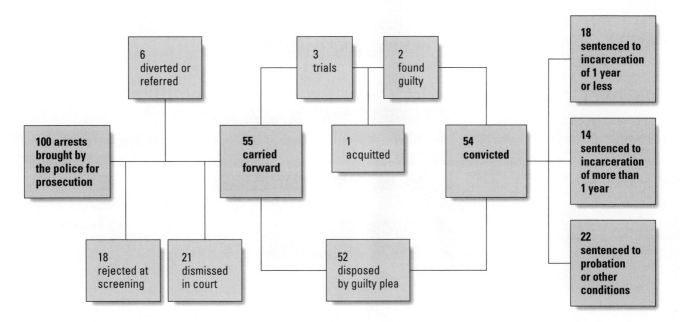

The data collected for this report indicate that for every 100 adult arrests for a felony, 54 will result in a conviction for either a felony or a misdemeanor. Of those 54:
- 52 will be guilty pleas, and
- 2 will be convictions at trial.

Of the 54 arrests resulting in conviction, 32 will lead to a sentence of incarceration:
- 18 will result in a sentence of 1 year or less, and
- 14 will result in a sentence of more than 1 year.

Of the 46 arrests that do not result in convictions:
- 6 will result in the defendants' being referred to diversion programs or to other courts for prosecution;
- 18 will be rejected for prosecution at screening, before court charges are filed;
- 21 will be dismissed in court; and
- 1 will result in an acquittal at trial.

FIGURE 11.3
WHAT HAPPENS
TO FELONY
ARRESTS

SOURCE: Barbara Boland, Paul Mahanna, and Ronald Sones, *The Prosecution of Felony Arrests, 1989* (Washington, DC: Bureau of Justice Statistics, 1992), p. 2.

One of the most important issues regarding the nature of plea bargaining is its effect on sentencing. Many people believe that "copping a plea" lets a criminal "get away with murder." This charge is supported by research conducted by Mark Cuniff in 28 large jurisdictions. Cuniff found that people convicted after a plea bargain were much less likely to be sent to prison than those convicted after a jury trial. Interestingly, those convicted after a bench trial (before a judge alone) had the same probability of being sent to prison as defendants who plea bargained.[35] Also, those who plea bargained received lower average prison terms than those who went to trial, which supports the argument that plea bargaining helps the defendant avoid punishment.

Other research, however, indicates that plea bargains may not be helpful to criminal defendants. Douglas Smith's study of almost 3,500 felony cases in six separate jurisdictions found that the probability of receiving an incarceration sentence was roughly equal for those who pleaded guilty and those who actually went to trial.[36] The defendants who seemed to benefit the most from plea bargaining were those who had committed the least serious offenses and had the best prior records.

Another project conducted by the federal government found that about 60 percent of the defendants pleaded guilty to the top charge filed against them; this did not necessarily mean the absence of negotiation or concession.[37] The study found that bargaining often included judicial agreement to give a more lenient sentence than might be expected if the defendant went to trial. In other cases, the negotiation involved the dropping of other charges or pending cases. Sometimes the lesser charges involved acts that required add-ons to a sentence, such as possession

FIGURE 11.4
TYPES AND
LENGTHS OF
SENTENCES BASED
ON GUILTY PLEAS

Types of sentences imposed by
state courts, by nature of
conviction. A prison sentence was
the result in 64 percent of trial
convictions versus in 43 percent of
guilty plea convictions.

SOURCE: Patrick A. Langan and Richard
Solari, *National Judicial Reporting Program, 1990* (Washington, DC: Bureau of
Justice Statistics, 1993).

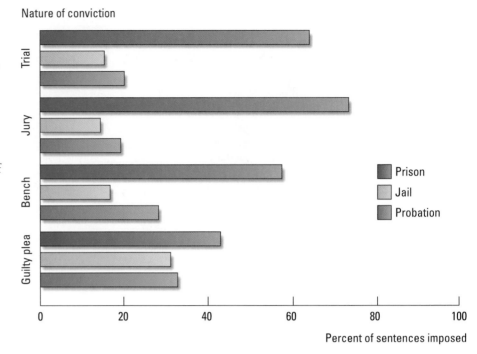

Nature of conviction

Percent of sentences imposed

of a handgun; dropping the lesser offense automatically shortened the defendant's
prison term. People who pleaded guilty were also less likely to do their time in a
state prison and more likely to be sent to a less restrictive correctional facility, such
as a county jail. This conclusion is supported by McDonald's study of plea bargaining in six jurisdictions. He found that in five of six jurisdictions people who
did not plead guilty increased their chances of receiving a prison sentence and also
received significant prison terms.[38]

In sum, although punishment is a certainty when defendants decide to plead
guilty, it is likely to be somewhat less severe than if they are found guilty after a
trial (see Figure 11.4). The plea bargaining process reflects the "wedding cake"
model of justice: Pleas are a quick and efficient way of disposing of cases that fall
into the bottom layers. Plea bargains also reduce the time the defendant is involved with the justice system: Cases that go to trial take significantly longer than
those that are bargained. So defendants, especially those placed in pretrial detention, have the extra burden of remaining within the justice system if they refuse
to plea bargain, a burden that few wish to bear. Plea bargaining, driven primarily
by the high volume of criminal cases, is thus an inevitable part of the justice system in the United States.

Essay 13

The Role of the Prosecutor in Plea Bargaining

The major players in the plea negotiations are (1) the prosecutor, (2) the defense
attorney, (3) the judge, (4) the defendant, and (5) the victim.

The prosecutor in the U.S. system of criminal justice has broad discretion in
the exercise of his or her responsibilities. Such discretion includes deciding
whether to initiate a criminal prosecution, determining the nature and number of
the criminal charges, and choosing whether to plea bargain a case and under what
conditions. Plea bargaining is one of the major tools the prosecutor uses to control and influence the criminal justice system (the other two are the decision to

initiate a charge and the ability to take the case to trial). Few states have placed limits on the discretion prosecutors have in plea bargaining situations. The prosecutor generally is free to weigh competing alternatives and factors, such as the seriousness of the crime, the attitude of the victim, the police report of the incident, and applicable sentencing provisions. Plea bargaining frequently occurs in cases where the government believes the evidence is weak—for example, when a key witness seems unreliable or unwilling to testify. Bargaining permits a compromise settlement in a weak case where the criminal trial outcome is in doubt.

On a case-by-case basis, the prosecutor determines the concessions to be offered in the plea bargain and seeks to dispose of each case quickly and efficiently. However, the prosecutor's role in plea bargaining is also important on a statewide or systemwide basis, because it involves exercising leadership in setting policy. The assistant prosecutor evaluates and moves individual cases, but the chief prosecutor must establish plea bargaining guidelines for the entire office or district. In the Manhattan district attorney's office, for example, guidelines cover such matters as avoiding overindictment, controlling nonprovable indictments, reducing felonies to misdemeanors, and bargaining with defendants.

Plea bargaining guidelines vary among jurisdictions. For instance, a given office may be required to define the types of cases and offenders that may be suitable for plea bargaining. In other jurisdictions, approval by a senior attorney may be required before plea bargaining. Other controls might include procedures for the chief prosecutor to review decisions and the use of written memorandums to document the necessity and acceptability of a plea bargain in a given case. In some jurisdictions, pleas are offered on a "take it or leave it" basis: In each case, a special prosecutor, whose job it is to screen cases, sets the bargaining terms. If the defense counsel cannot accept the agreement, there is no negotiation, and the case must go to trial. Only if complications arise in the case, such as witnesses' changing their testimony, can negotiations be reopened.

The most extreme example of a chief prosecutor's influencing the plea negotiation process has occurred where the prosecutor has attempted to eliminate plea bargaining. Such efforts can meet with resistance from assistant prosecutors and others in the system—namely, judges and defense attorneys. The more moderate approach by prosecutors involves establishing guidelines for assistant prosecutors to follow in evaluating cases for plea bargaining. Thus, the prosecutor plays a role in setting plea bargaining policy, as well as in using the technique on a case-by-case basis.

The Role of the Defense Counsel in Plea Bargaining

Both the U.S. Supreme Court and such organizations as the American Bar Association in its *Standards Relating to Pleas of Guilty* have established guidelines for the court receiving a guilty plea and for the defense counsel representing the accused in plea negotiations.[39] No court should accept a guilty plea unless the defendant has been properly advised by counsel and the court has determined that the plea is voluntary and has a factual basis; the court has the discretion to reject a plea if it is inappropriately offered.

The defense counsel—a public defender or a private attorney—is required to play an advisory role in plea negotiations. The defendant's counsel is expected to be aware of the facts of the case and of the law and to advise the defendant of the alternatives available. The defense attorney is responsible for making certain that the accused understands the nature of the plea bargaining process and the guilty plea. This means that the defense counsel should explain to the defendant that by pleading guilty, he or she is waiving certain rights that would be available on going to trial. In addition, the defense attorney has the duty to keep the defendant informed of developments and discussions with the prosecutor regarding plea bargaining. Furthermore, the attorney for the accused cannot misrepresent evidence or mislead the client into making a detrimental agreement.

In reality, most plea negotiations occur in the judge's chambers, in the prosecutor's office, or in the courthouse hallway. Under these conditions, it is often difficult to assess the actual roles played by the prosecutor and the defense attorney. Even so, it is fundamental that a defendant should not be required to plead guilty until advised by counsel and that a guilty plea should not be made unless it is done with the consent of the accused. Where the lawyers disagree, it often appears that judges play an active role in settling the plea negotiation process, even though that is a controversial approach.

The Judge's Role in Plea Bargaining

One of the most confusing problems in the plea bargaining process has been the proper role of the judge. Should the judge act only in a supervisory capacity or actually enter into the negotiation process? Leading national legal organizations, such as the American Bar Association, are opposed to judicial participation in plea negotiations.[40] In addition, the Federal Rules of Criminal Procedure prohibit federal judges from participating in plea negotiations.[41] A few states disallow any form of judicial involvement in plea bargaining, but others permit the judge to participate.

The American Bar Association objects in general to the judge's participating in plea negotiations because of his or her position as chief judicial officer. A judge should not be a party to arrangements for the determination of a sentence, whether as a result of a guilty plea or a finding of guilt based on proof. Furthermore, judicial participation in plea negotiations (1) creates the impression in the mind of the defendant that he or she could not receive a fair trial; (2) lessens the ability of the judge to make an objective determination of the voluntariness of the plea; (3) is inconsistent with the theory behind the use of presentence investigation reports; and (4) may induce an innocent defendant to plead guilty because he or she is afraid to reject the disposition desired by the judge.[42]

Those who suggest that the judge should participate directly in plea bargaining argue that such an approach would make sentencing more uniform and ensure that the plea bargaining process would be fairer and more efficient.

It appears that judges play an active role in the negotiation process in most jurisdictions in the United States. Where judges simply supervise plea bargaining, they oversee the taking of the guilty plea, determine a factual basis for the plea, inform the defendant of the sentencing consequences, and control the withdrawal of the plea. This type of judicial involvement can have a beneficial effect, but judges usually play an extremely neutral role and do not look into how a plea was arrived at or examine the strength of the state's case.

The Victim and Plea Bargaining

Related to the issue of prosecutorial discretion, discussed in Chapter 10, is the proper role of the victim in influencing plea bargaining. Often defense attorneys criticize prosecutors for treating victims' interests as paramount and oppose the practice of seeking approval for the proposed plea from a victim or family member. Some suggest that the system today is too "victim driven." Others maintain that the victim plays an almost secondary role in the process.

In reality, the victim is not "empowered" at the pretrial stage of the criminal process. Statutes do not require that the prosecutor defer to the victim's wishes, and there are no legal consequences for ignoring the victim in plea bargaining decisions. Even the American Bar Association's *Model Uniform Victims of Crime Act* only suggests that the prosecutor "confer" with the victim.[43]

Victims are certainly not in a position to veto a plea bargain. Most of the work of the victims' rights movement in the justice system is devoted to securing financial compensation from the state and some restitution when possible from the defendant. Currently, it is at the trial stage that the victim has the greatest influence. Here, the victim often has the right to offer a victim-impact statement after a guilty determination and before the court imposes a sentence.

There is no question that the prosecutor should consider the impact that a plea bargain may have on the victim or the victim's family. Some victims' groups even suggest that the victim's family should have statutory authority to approve or disapprove any plea bargain between the prosecutor and the defense attorney in criminal homicide cases. Given the volume of plea bargains (more than 90 percent of all criminal cases), it appears that the victim should have greater control and participation.[44] Plea bargaining is inevitable and essential to the continued functioning of the criminal process; therefore, it must be conducted fairly. As George Fletcher, a noted legal scholar at Columbia Law School, indicates, it should be done "with due consideration of the victim whose complaint initiates the action."[45]

PERSPECTIVES ON JUSTICE

Former Red Sox outfielder Wilfredo Cordero pleaded guilty on November 10, 1997, in Middlesex County (Massachusetts) District Court to assaulting his wife during a domestic dispute. Upon investigation, it was found that Cordero had also battered his first wife.

Cordero received a suspended sentence of 90 days and was required to complete a 40-week course given by the state to convicted batters. Cordero pleaded guilty to four charges, including assault and battery with a dangerous weapon (felony). Cordero's wife was unwilling to testify for the state. Her testimony was important to corroborate the facts of the crime. Cordero was released by the Red Sox at the end of the baseball season. The dominant views of the justice system in the case are crime control, rehabilitation, and restorative justice. What role do you think the victim, Mrs. Cordero, played in the settlement of the case? In this type of case, the state estimates the sentence that seems likely after a conviction, discounts the sentence by the possibility of an acquittal, and balances that sentence against the one achieved through a plea bargain.

PRETRIAL DIVERSION

Another important feature of the early court process is the placing of offenders into noncriminal *diversion* programs prior to their normal trial or conviction. Pretrial diversion programs were first established in the late 1960s and early 1970s, when it became apparent that a viable alternative to the highly stigmatized criminal sentence was needed. In diversion programs, formal criminal proceedings against an accused are suspended while that person participates in a community treatment program under court supervision. Diversion helps the offender avoid the stigma of a criminal conviction and enables the justice system to reduce costs and alleviate prison overcrowding.

Essay 14

Drug courts have become a popular form of diversion. Access these types of programs at the Drug Courts Program Office:
http://www.ojp.usdoj.gov/dcpo.htm
For an up-to-date list of Web links, see http://www.wadsworth.com/product/0534573053s

Many diversion programs have been established throughout the United States. These programs vary in size and emphasis but generally pursue the same goal: to constructively bypass criminal prosecution by providing a reasonable alternative in the form of treatment, counseling, or employment programs.

The prosecutor often plays a central role in the diversion process. Decisions about nondispositional alternatives are based on

1. The nature of the crime
2. Special characteristics of the offender
3. Whether the defendant is a first-time offender
4. Whether the defendant will cooperate with a diversion program
5. The impact of diversion on the community
6. Consideration for the opinion of the victim[46]

Diversion programs can take many forms. Some are separate, independent agencies that were originally set up with federal funds but are now being continued with county or state assistance. Others are organized as a part of a police, prosecutor, or probation department's internal structure. Still others are a joint venture between the county government and a private, nonprofit organization that actually carries out the treatment process.

Diversion is considered after the arrest and arraignment of the individual but before the trial. The defendant chosen for a diversion program is released on a *continuance*—that is, the trial is postponed—if the relevant court personnel (judge, probation officer, assistant district attorney, arresting officer) and the program representative agree on the potential of the accused to succeed in the program. During this initial period, the program's staff assesses the potential client's suitability for the program. Acceptance may begin with a long continuance (the time limit varies from program to program) without entry of a plea and on the written waiver by the defendant of the right to a speedy trial.

First viewed as a panacea that could reduce court congestion and help treat minor offenders, diversion programs have come under fire for their alleged fail-

A counselor confers with a problem youth during a counseling session in a program designed to steer youth away from criminal lifestyles. Diversion programs can have both treatment and economic benefits since they are typically far less costly to operate than the traditional prison system.

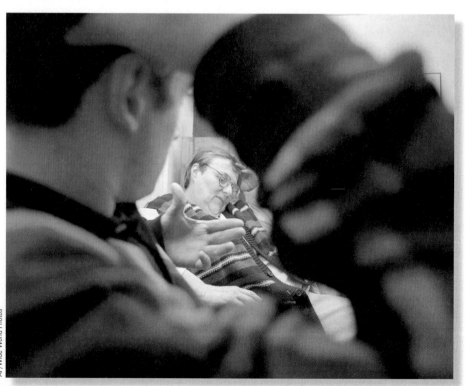

AP/Wide World Photos

ures. Some national evaluations have concluded that diversion programs are no more successful at avoiding stigma and reducing recidivism than traditional justice processing.[47] The most prominent criticism is that they help **widen the net** of the justice system. By this, critics mean that the people put in diversion programs are the ones most likely to have been dismissed after a brief hearing with a warning or small fine. Those who ordinarily would have received a more serious sentence are not eligible for diversion anyway. Thus, rather than limiting interface with the system, the diversion programs actually increase it. Of course, not all justice experts agree with this charge, and some, such as Arnold Binder and Gilbert Geis, have championed diversion as a worthwhile exercise of the criminal justice system's rehabilitation responsibility.[48] As supporters such as Binder and Geis point out, although diversion may not be a cure-all for criminal behavior, it is an important effort that continues to be made in most jurisdictions across the United States.

widen the net
To enmesh more offenders for longer periods in the criminal justice system—a criticism of pretrial diversion programs.

SUMMARY

Many important decisions about what happens to a defendant are made prior to trial. Hearings, such as before the grand jury and the preliminary hearing, are held to determine if probable cause exists to charge the accused with a crime. If so, the defendant is arraigned; enters a plea; is informed of his or her constitutional rights, particularly the right to assistance of counsel; and is considered for pretrial diversion. The use of money bail or other alternatives, such as release on recognizance, enables most defendants to remain free pending their trial. Bail provisions are beginning to be toughened, resulting in the preventive detention of people awaiting trial. Preventive detention has been implemented because many believe that significant numbers of criminals violate their bail and commit further crimes while on pretrial release.

The issue of discretion plays a major role at this stage of the criminal process. Research indicates that most cases never go to trial but are bargained out of the system; many defendants agree to plea bargains or are placed in diversion programs. Not enough judges, prosecutors, defense attorneys, and courts exist to try every defendant accused of a crime. As a result, subsystems such as plea bargaining and diversion are essential elements in the administration of the criminal justice system. Similarly situated defendants should be afforded substantially equal plea agreement opportunities. Although plea bargaining has been criticized, efforts to control it have not met with success. Similarly, diversion programs have not been overly successful, yet they continue to be used throughout the United States.

Key Terms

complaint	pretrial services	pretrial detention
initial hearing	bail bond	presentment
preliminary hearing (probable cause hearing)	bail bonding	true bill
arraignment	deposit bail	no bill
nolo contendere	release on recognizance (ROR)	waiver
	preventive detention	widen the net

Discussion Questions

1. Should criminal defendants be allowed to bargain for reduced sentences in exchange for a guilty plea?
2. Should those accused of violent acts be subjected to preventive detention instead of bail, even though they have not been convicted of a crime?
3. What purpose does a grand jury or preliminary hearing serve in felony offenses?
4. Should a judge participate in plea bargaining? Is this a conflict of interest?

5. Do rehabilitation-oriented programs, such as pretrial diversion, create a whole new set of problems for people, such as net widening, or are they essentially beneficial?

6. What are some of the legal issues in plea bargaining?

7. What is the purpose of bail? of preventive detention?

8. Is plea bargaining constitutional?

9. Do most criminals "cop a plea" to escape long sentences?

A CLOSER LOOK

Isn't preventive detention punishing an individual who has not been found guilty of the allegations made by the state? At the same time, aren't justice officials required to protect the community? A preventive detention statute is an example of the crime control perspective and the judicious use of a serious criminal sanction—jail. Denying defendants the right to bail because they are dangerous is the basis of the preventive detention law. Merely accusing a person of a crime and keeping the person incarcerated has caused critics to question the legality of such a practice. Yet the Supreme Court upheld the constitutionality of the preventive detention statute in *Salerno.*

You can learn more about the arguments regarding preventive detention by using InfoTrac College Edition to research the topics of bail, release on recognizance, and preventive detention. Read also "Investigative Detentions," *FBI Law Enforcement Bulletin,* 1998, v67 p26

Notes

1 D. Alan Henry, "Pretrial Services: Today and Yesterday," *Federal Probation* (June 1991): 54.

2 Bureau of Justice Assistance, *Pretrial Services Program* (Washington, DC: U.S. Government Printing Office, 1990), p. 3.

3 Kristen Segebarth, *Pretrial Services and Practices in the 1990s* (Washington, DC: Pretrial Resource Center, March 1991), p. 3.

4 342 U.S. 1, 72 S.Ct. 1, 96 L.Ed. 3 (1951).

5 William Rhodes, *Pretrial Release and Misconduct* (Washington, DC: Bureau of Justice Statistics, 1985).

6 Mary Toborg, *Pretrial Release: A National Evaluation of Practices and Outcomes* (Washington, DC: National Institute of Justice, 1982).

7 Rhodes, *Pretrial Release and Misconduct.*

8 Brian A. Reaves, *Felony Defendants in Large Urban Counties, 1994* (Washington, DC: Bureau of Justice Statistics, 1998), p. 15; see also *Felony Defendants in Large Urban Counties, 1996* (Washington, DC: Bureau of Justice Statistics, 1999).

9 Vera Institute of Justice, *1961–1971: Programs in Criminal Justice* (New York: Vera Institute of Justice, 1972).

10 Chris Eskridge, *Pretrial Release Programming* (New York: Clark Boardman, 1983), p. 27.

11 Public Law 89-465, 18 U.S.C. §3146 (1966).

12 18 U.S.C. §3142 (1984).

13 John Goldkamp, "Judicial Reform of Bail Practices: The Philadelphia Experiment," *Court Management Journal* 17 (1983): 16–20.

14 18 U.S.C. §3142 (1984).

15 See, generally, Fred Cohen, "The New Federal Crimes Control Act," *Criminal Law Bulletin* 21 (1985): 330–337; also Thomas Scott, "Pretrial Detention under Bail Reform Act of 1984," *American Criminal Law Review* 21 (1989): 19.

16 481 U.S. 739, 107 S.Ct. 2495, 95 L.Ed.2d 697 (1987).

17 Ibid., at 742, 107 S.Ct., at 2098.

18 Susan Kline, *Jail Inmates, 1987* (Washington, DC: Bureau of Justice Statistics, 1988); also Allen Beck, Thomas Bonczar, and Darrell Gilliard, *Jail Inmates, 1992* (Washington, DC: Bureau of Justice Statistics, 1993).

19 "Jail Crowding," *Pretrial Reporter* (Washington, DC: Pretrial Services Resource Center, October–November 1991), pp. 8–9; Kathleen Maguire and Ann L. Pastore, *Sourcebook of Criminal Justice, 1998* (Washington, DC: U.S. Government Printing Office, 1999); Bureau of Justice Statistics, *Key Facts at a Glance: Number of Jail Inmates by Age and Gender* (Washington, DC: Bureau of Justice Statistics, 1999).

20 John Goldkamp, *Two Classes of Accused* (Cambridge, MA: Ballinger, 1979); also Ellen Steury and Nancy Frank, "Gender Bias and Pretrial Release," *Journal of Criminal Justice* 18 (1990): 417–432.

21 Brian A. Reaves, *Felony Defendants in Large Urban Counties, 1994* (Washington, DC: U.S. Department of Justice, 1994), pp. 16–17; Andrea Gerlin, "Criminal Defendants Released without Bail Spark Heated Debate," *Wall Street Journal,* 9 July 1996, p. A1.

22 American Bar Association, *Grand Jury Policy and Model Act* (Chicago: American Bar Association, 1982); also Deborah Day Emerson, *Grand Jury Reform: A Review of Key Issues* (Washington, DC: National Institute of Justice, 1983).

23 Alan Alschuler, "The Prosecutor's Role in Plea Bargaining," *University of Chicago Law Review* 36 (1968): 50–112; see also William Gibbons, "Instituting a No Plea Bargaining Policy," *The Prosecution* 40 (1999): 36–40.

24 474 U.S. 52, 106 S.Ct. 366, 88 L.Ed.2d 203 (1985).

25 395 U.S. 238, 89 S.Ct. 1709, 23 L.Ed.2d 274 (1969).

26 397 U.S. 742, 90 S.Ct. 1463, 25 L.Ed.2d 747 (1970).

27 400 U.S. 25, 91 S.Ct. 160, 27 L.Ed.2d 162 (1970).

28 404 U.S. 257, 92 S.Ct. 495, 30 L.Ed.2d 427 (1971).

29 483 U.S. 1, 107 S.Ct. 2680, 97 L.Ed.2d 1 (1987).

30 434 U.S. 357, 98 S.Ct. 663, 54 L.Ed.2d 604 (1978).

31 *United States v. Mezzanatto,* 513 U.S. 196, 116 S. Ct. 1480, 134 L.Ed.2d 687 (1995).

32 Stephen Lagoy, Joseph J. Senna, and Larry J. Siegel, "An Empirical Study on Information Usage for Prosecutorial Decision Making in Plea Negotiations," *American Criminal Law Review* 13 (1976): 435–471.

33 William McDonald, *Plea Bargaining: Critical Issues and Common Practices* (Washington, DC: U.S. Government Printing Office, 1985).

34 Barbara Boland and Brian Forst, *The Prevalence of Guilty Pleas* (Washington, DC: Bureau of Justice Statistics, 1984).

35 Mark Cuniff, *Sentencing Outcomes in 28 Felony Courts, 1984* (Washington, DC: Bureau of Justice Statistics, 1987), p. 25.

36 Douglas Smith, "The Plea Bargaining Controversy," *Journal of Criminal Law and Criminology* 77 (1986): 949–967.

37 Boland and Forst, *The Prevalence of Guilty Pleas.*

38 McDonald, *Plea Bargaining: Critical Issues and Common Practices,* p. 97.

39 See American Bar Association, *Standards Relating to Pleas of Guilty,* 2d ed. (Chicago: American Bar Association, 1988); see also *North Carolina v. Alford,* 400 U.S. 25, 91 S.Ct. 160, 27 L.Ed.2d 162 (1970).

40 American Bar Association, *Standards Relating to Pleas of Guilty,* std 3.3.

41 Federal Rules of Criminal Procedure, Rule 11, Titles 18 and 28, U.S. Code.

42 American Bar Association, *Standards Relating to Pleas of Guilty,* p. 73; see also Alan Alschuler, "The Trial Judge's Role in Plea Bargaining," *Columbia Law Review* 76 (1976): 1059.

43 American Bar Association, *Model Uniform Victims of Crime Act* (Chicago: American Bar Association, 1992).

44 Candace McCoy, *Politics and Plea Bargaining: Victims' Rights in California* (Philadelphia: University of Pennsylvania Press, 1993).

45 George P. Fletcher, *With Justice for Some: Protecting Victims' Rights in Criminal Trials* (New York: Addison-Wesley, 1995), pp. 190–193.

46 National District Attorneys Association, *National Prosecution Standards,* 2d ed. (Alexandria, VA: National District Attorneys Association, 1991), p. 130.

47 Franklyn Dunford, D. Wayne Osgood, and Hart Weichselbaum, *National Evaluation of Diversion Programs* (Washington, DC: U.S. Government Printing Office, 1982).

48 Arnold Binder and Gilbert Geis, "Ad Populum Argumentation in Criminology: Juvenile Diversion as Rhetoric," *Criminology* 30 (1984): 309–388.

AP/Wide World Photos

THE CRIMINAL TRIAL

On April 19, 1995, at 9:02 A.M, a truck bomb destroyed the Alfred Murrah Building in Oklahoma City. About 90 minutes later, Timothy McVeigh was stopped for driving with no license plate near Billings, Oklahoma, and was jailed for carrying a concealed weapon. Just before being released, McVeigh was recognized as a bombing suspect and turned over to the FBI. After further investigation, McVeigh was charged and indicted in the bombing. In a trial that lasted less than six weeks, he was convicted of the worst act of domestic terror in U.S. history. In the photograph above, one of his lawyers looks at the front page of a newspaper reporting that McVeigh received the death penalty.

How did McVeigh's trial, for all its complexity, proceed so rapidly? Who was responsible for the efficiency of the trial, which resulted in McVeigh's conviction on all 11 counts of murder and conspiracy in the bombing that killed 168 people?

From the beginning, the U.S. Justice Department was determined to streamline the trial and avoid the choas of other high-profile criminal cases. Some of the procedures used to accomplish this were (1) moving the trial to Denver, 700 miles from Oklahoma City; (2) applying the rule of the federal courts not to televise criminal trials; (3) using a federal prosecutor known for being efficient and avoiding publicity; and (4) selecting a no-nonsense trial judge who rejected defense requests for delays, refused to allow additional peremptory challenges, held hearings on weekends, and protected jury privacy.

Trial experts agree that the McVeigh trial was a model of judicial efficiency. Testimony was direct, the trial was not interrupted by evidentiary or discovery arguments, and the lawyers and jurors acted appropriately. The government presented 137 witnesses in eight days, and the defense presented 25 witnesses in four days. Much of the evidence was overwhelmingly in favor of conviction.

Chapter

12

McVeigh's fingerprints were on a receipt for the purchase of explosive ammonium nitrate; sworn testimony was given that he had threatened to destroy the Murrah Building; and traces of explosives were found on his clothing. In addition, when the prosecution trimmed its case by not using all its evidence, the defense was limited in its cross-examination of government witnesses and was never really able to "poke holes" in the case.

The circus-free trial of Timothy McVeigh has restored some faith in the U.S. criminal justice system.[1]

In another highly publicized crime, in October 1998, Matthew Shepard, age 21, an openly gay student at the

University of Wyoming, was savagely beaten and left to die. Tied for 18 hours to a rural fence, he died five days later in a local hospital. Prosecutors said that Aaron McKinney and a friend, who subsequently pled guilty, lured Shepard from a bar and drove him to a remote spot; there McKinney pistol-whipped him into a coma. The government claimed that robbery was the primary motive but that the victim was singled out because he was gay.

In a case that drew nationwide attention, McKinney was indicted for robbery, kidnapping, and first-degree murder. During the criminal trail before a jury of seven men and five women, the prosecutors portrayed McKinney as a bloodthristy person intent on killing a gay man in a blind rage, triggered by his own drug addiction. Testimony from the co-defendant substantiated the fact that McKinney had fatally beaten the victim.

The defense attorney argued that Shepard went with the defendant willingly and even sexually groped him, which caused McKinney to explode violently against Shepard and kill him. According to the defense, the criminal homicide was not premeditated murder because Shepard provoked McKinney. The defense attempted to use a "gay panic" strategy, based on the theory that a person with latent homosexual tendencies will have an uncontrollable violent reaction when propositioned by a homosexual. This argument was barred by the court.

After many hours of deliberation, the jury convicted McKinney of felony murder—that is, a killing while committing other crimes, in this case kidnapping and aggravated robbery. The jury acquitted McKinney on the charge of first-degree murder but convicted him of second-degree murder, which means they didn't believe the killing was premeditated. McKinney was sentenced to life imprisonment but spared the death penalty.[2]

Cases such as McVeigh's and McKinney's point out why the criminal trial process remains a matter of vital importance to the criminal justice system. It must render fair, impartial justice in deciding the outcome of a conflict between the state and the accused, even in the most heinous crimes. The opportunity to go to trial provides the foremost safeguard against abuse of informal processing and serves as the basis of public faith in the system. Is the judicial system capable of handling high-profile cases like the McVeigh case? Why did the O. J. Simpson trial leave such a poor impression of the justice system? Did both defendants receive a fair trial?

Fill in the blanks 1–2
True/False 1
Multiple choice 1

To review U.S. Supreme Court, other federal, and state decisions, briefed for the special interest of criminal justice practitioners and students, visit the Web site of the National District Attorneys Association http://www.ndaa-apri.org
For an up-to-date list of Web links, see http://www.wadsworth.com/product/0534573053s

continuance
Adjournment of a court case to a future time.

The *adjudication* stage of the criminal justice process begins with a hearing that seeks to determine the truth of the facts of the case. This process is usually referred to as the *criminal trial,* as described in the McVeigh and McKinney cases. The classic jury trial of a criminal case is an uncommon occurrence. The overwhelming majority of individuals charged with crimes, nearly 90 percent, plead guilty. Another 5 percent are dealt with by other methods. Many have their cases dismissed by judges for a variety of reasons: The government may decide not to prosecute; the accused may be found emotionally disturbed and unable to stand trial; or the court may be unwilling to attach the stigma of a criminal record to a particular defendant.

Still other defendants waive their constitutional right to a jury trial. In this situation, which occurs daily in the lower criminal courts, the judge may initiate a number of formal or informal dispositions, including dismissing the case, finding the defendant not guilty, finding the defendant guilty and imposing a sentence, or even continuing the case indefinitely. The judge's decision may depend on the seriousness of the offense, the background and previous record of the defendant, and the judgment of the court as to whether the case can be properly dealt with through the criminal process.

In minor cases in some jurisdictions, for example, the **continuance** is a frequently used disposition. In this instance, the court holds a case in abeyance, without a finding of guilt, to induce the accused to improve his or her behavior in the community; if the defendant's behavior does improve, the case is ordinarily closed within a certain amount of time.

Thus, the number of actual trials is small in comparison to all the cases processed through the criminal justice system; fewer than 5 percent ever reach the trial stage. Those cases that are actually tried before a jury often involve serious crimes. Such crimes require a formal inquiry into the facts to determine the guilt or innocence of the accused.

Even though proportionately few cases are actually tried by juries, the trial process remains a focal point in the criminal justice system. It symbolizes the U.S. system of jurisprudence, in which an accused person can choose to present a defense against the government's charges. The fact that the defendant has the option of going to trial significantly affects the operation of the criminal justice system. A federal government commission put it this way:

> Although most criminal prosecutions do not involve the adversary determination of guilt or innocence that occurs at a formal trial of a criminal case, the trial process remains a matter of vital importance to the criminal justice system. Whether or not a defendant chooses to invoke his right at trial, he has an interest in the trial process because in many cases it represents to him a legal option guaranteed by the Constitution of the United States. The opportunity to go to trial provides a valuable safeguard against abuse of informal processing and a basis for encouraging a faith in the system.[3]

LEGAL RIGHTS DURING TRIAL

Underlying every trial are constitutional principles, complex legal procedures, rules of court, and interpretation of statutes, all designed to ensure that the accused will receive a fair trial. This section discusses the most important constitutional rights of the accused at the trial stage of the criminal justice system and reviews the legal nature of the trial process. The major legal decisions and statutes involving the rights to jury trial, counsel, self-representation, and a speedy and public trial are all examined.

The Right to Confront Witnesses

The Sixth Amendment states, "In all criminal prosecutions, the accused shall enjoy the right . . . to be confronted with the witnesses against him."[4] The **confrontation clause** is essential to a fair criminal trial because it restricts and controls the admissibility of hearsay evidence. Secondhand evidence, which depends on a witness not available in court, is ordinarily limited; the personal knowledge of a witness or victim of a crime is preferred. The framers of the Constitution sought face-to-face accusations in which the defendant has a right to see and cross-examine all witnesses against him or her. The idea that it is always more difficult to tell lies about people to their face than behind their back underlies the point of the confrontation clause. A witness in a criminal trial may have more difficulty repeating his or her testimony when facing the accused in a trial than in providing information to the police during an investigation. The accused has the right to confront any witnesses and challenge their assertions and perceptions: Did they really see what they believe? Are they biased? Can they be trusted? What about the veracity of their testimony? Generally speaking, the courts have been nearly unanimous in their belief that the right to confrontation and cross-examination is an essential requirement for a fair trial.[5]

This face-to-face presence was reviewed by the Supreme Court in a case involving a child as a witness in criminal proceedings. In *Coy v. Iowa* (1988), the Supreme Court limited the protection available to child sex victims at the trial stage.[6] In *Coy,* two girls were allowed to be cross-examined behind a screen that separated them from the defendant. The Court ruled that the screen violated the defendant's right to confront witnesses and overturned his conviction. However, in her supporting opinion, Justice Sandra Day O'Connor made it clear that ruling out the protective screen did not bar the states from using videotapes or closed-circuit television. Although Justice O'Connor recognized that the Sixth

Fill in the blanks 3
True/False 2
Multiple choice 2–4

confrontation clause
The constitutional right of a criminal defendant to see and cross-examine all the witnesses against him or her.

The right to confront witnesses is critical, because all too often mistakes can be made when identifying criminal suspects. Here, Jennifer Thompson talks with Ronald Cotton in Greensboro, N.C., on September 14, 2000. In 1984 Thompson identified Cotton as the man who raped her. After serving 11 years of a life sentence, Cotton was released from prison when DNA testing revealed his innocence.

AP/Wide World Photos

Amendment right to confront witnesses was violated, she indicated that an exception to a literal interpretation of the confrontation clause might be appropriate.

In *Maryland v. Craig* (1990), the second case in this area, the Supreme Court carved out an exception to the Sixth Amendment confrontation clause by deciding that alleged child abuse victims could testify by closed-circuit television if face-to-face confrontation would cause them trauma.[7] In allowing the states to take testimony via closed-circuit television, the Supreme Court found that circumstances exist in child sex abuse cases that override the defendant's right of confrontation.

As a result of these decisions, it appears that the confrontation clause does not guarantee criminal defendants the absolute right to a face-to-face meeting with witnesses at their trial. Instead, according to *Maryland v. Craig,* it reflects a preference for such a guarantee. *Craig* signals that the Court is willing to compromise a defendant's right to confront his or her accuser to achieve a social objective, the prosecution of a child abuser.

Fill in the blanks 4
True/False 3
Multiple choice 5–8

The Right to a Jury Trial

The defendant has the right to choose whether the trial will be before a judge or a jury. Although the Sixth Amendment to the U.S. Constitution guarantees the defendant the right to a jury trial, the defendant can and often does waive this right. A substantial proportion of defendants, particularly those charged with misdemeanors, are tried before the court without a jury.

The major legal issue surrounding jury trial has been whether all defendants, those accused of misdemeanors as well as felonies, have an absolute right to a jury trial. Although the U.S. Constitution is silent on this point, the U.S. Supreme Court has ruled that all defendants in felony cases have this right. In *Duncan v. Louisiana* (1968), the Court held that the Sixth Amendment right to a jury trial is applicable to all states, as well as to the federal government, and that it can be interpreted to apply to all defendants accused of serious crimes.[8] The Court in *Duncan* based its holding on the premise

> that in the American states, as in the federal judicial system, a general grant of jury trial for serious offenses is a fundamental right, essential for preventing miscarriages of justice and for assuring that fair trials are provided for all defendants.[9]

The *Duncan* decision did not settle whether all defendants charged with crimes in state courts are constitutionally entitled to jury trials. It seemed to draw the line at only those charged with serious offenses, leaving the decision to grant jury trials to defendants in minor cases to the discretion of the individual states.

In 1970, in *Baldwin v. New York,* the Supreme Court departed from the distinction of serious versus minor offenses and decided that a defendant has a constitutional right to a jury trial when facing a possible prison sentence of six months or more, regardless of whether the crime committed was a felony or a misdemeanor.[10] Where the possible sentence is six months or less, the accused is not entitled to a jury trial unless it is authorized by state statute. In most jurisdictions, the more serious the charge, the greater likelihood of trial—and of a trial by jury.

The latest U.S. Supreme Court decision on jury trials is *Lewis v. United States* (1996).[11] As noted, the Supreme Court has used six months' potential imprisonment as the dividing line between petty offenses for which the Sixth Amendment gives no right to jury trial and "serious" offenses that enjoy such a legal right. In the *Lewis* case, the Court faced the unusual problem of multiple petty offenses which, when added together, could lead to imprisonment in excess of six months. The defendant argued that he was constitutionally entitled to a jury trial. But the Supreme Court said there was no Sixth Amendment right to a jury trial for a string of petty offenses tried together, even when the potential total sentence could exceed six months. The Court's reasoning was that (1) the legislature was responsible for the design of an offense with a maximum possible penalty, and (2) the prosecutor has the right to exercise discretion to join different offenses in one trial without defeating the legislative intent to distinguish between petty and serious offenses.

In sum, the Sixth Amendment guarantees the right to a jury trial. The accused can waive this right and be tried by a judge, who then becomes the fact-finder as well as the determiner of the law.

Other important issues related to the defendant's rights in a criminal jury trial include the right to a jury of 12 people and the right to a unanimous verdict.

Jury Size The actual size of the jury has been a matter of great concern. Can a defendant be tried and convicted of a crime by a jury of fewer than 12 persons? Traditionally, 12 jurors have deliberated as the triers of fact in criminal cases involving misdemeanors or felonies. However, the U.S. Constitution does not specifically require a jury of 12 persons. As a result, in *Williams v. Florida* (1970), the U.S. Supreme Court held that a six-person jury in a criminal trial does not deprive a defendant of the constitutional right to a jury trial.[12] The Court made clear that the 12-person panel is not a necessary ingredient of the trial by jury and upheld a Florida statute permitting the use of a six-person jury in a robbery trial. The majority opinion in the *Williams* case traced the Court's rationale for its decision:

> We conclude, in short, as we began: the fact that a jury at common law was composed of precisely twelve is a historical accident, unnecessary to effect the purposes of the jury system and wholly without significance "except to mystics."[13]

Justice Byron White, writing further for the majority, said,

> In short, while sometime in the 14th century the size of the jury came to be fixed generally at 12, that particular feature of the jury system appears to have been a historical accident, unrelated to the great purpose which gave rise to the jury in the first place.[14]

On the basis of this decision, many states are using six-person juries in misdemeanor cases, and some states, such as Florida, Louisiana, and Utah, even use them in felony cases (except in capital offenses). In the *Williams* decision, Justice White emphasized, "We have an occasion to determine what minimum number can still constitute a jury, but do not doubt that six is above the minimum."[15]

The six-person jury can play an important role in the criminal justice system because it promotes court efficiency and also helps implement the defendant's rights to a speedy trial. However, the Supreme Court has ruled that a jury comprising fewer than six people is unconstitutional[16] and that if a six-person jury is used in serious crimes, its verdict must be unanimous.[17] *Williams v. Florida,* decided more than 30 years ago, offered a welcome measure of relief to an overburdened crime control system. Today, jury size can be reduced for all but the most serious criminal cases.

Unanimity In addition to the convention of 12-person juries in criminal trials, tradition had also been that the jurors' decision must be unanimous. However, in *Apodaca v. Oregon* (1972), the Supreme Court held that the Sixth and Fourteenth Amendments do not prohibit criminal convictions by less than unanimous jury verdicts in noncapital cases.[18] In the *Apodaca* case, the Court upheld an Oregon statute requiring only 10 of 12 jurors to convict the defendant of assault with a deadly weapon, burglary, and grand larceny.

Nonunanimous verdicts are not unusual in civil matters, but much controversy remains regarding their place in the criminal process. Those in favor of less-than-unanimous verdicts argue, as the Court stated in *Apodaca,* that unanimity does not materially contribute to the exercise of commonsense judgment. Some also believe that it would be easier for the prosecutor to obtain a guilty plea verdict if the law required only a substantial majority to convict the defendant. Today, the unanimous verdict remains the rule in the federal system and all but two state jurisdictions. Unanimity is required in six-person jury trials.

True/False 4
Multiple choice 9–11

The Right to Counsel at Trial

Through a series of leading U.S. Supreme Court decisions (*Powell v. Alabama* in 1932,[19] *Gideon v. Wainwright* in 1963,[20] and *Argersinger v. Hamlin* in 1972[21]), the right of a criminal defendant to have counsel in state trials has become fundamental in the U.S. criminal justice system. Today, state courts must provide counsel at trial to indigent defendants who face the possibility of incarceration.

It is interesting to note the historical development of the law regarding right to counsel, because it shows the gradual process of decision making in the Supreme Court. It also reiterates the relationship between the Bill of Rights, which protects citizens against federal encroachment, and the Fourteenth Amendment, which provides that no state shall deprive any person of life, liberty, or property without due process of law. A difficult constitutional question has been whether the Fourteenth Amendment incorporates the Bill of Rights and makes its provisions binding on individual states.

In *Powell v. Alabama* (also known as the Scottsboro Boys case), nine young black men were charged in an Alabama court with raping two young white women. They were tried and convicted without the benefit of counsel. The U.S. Supreme Court concluded that the presence of a defense attorney is so vital to a fair trial that the failure of the Alabama trial court to appoint counsel was a denial of due process of law under the Fourteenth Amendment. In this instance, due process meant the right to counsel for defendants accused of a capital offense.

More than 30 years later, in *Gideon v. Wainwright,* the Supreme Court in a unanimous and historic decision stated that, although the Sixth Amendment does not explicitly lay down a rule binding on the states, the right to counsel is so fundamental to a fair trial that states are obligated to abide by it under the Fourteenth Amendment's due process clause. Thus, the Sixth Amendment requirement regarding the right to counsel in the federal court system is also binding on the states. The Law in Review feature in Chapter 10 examined the *Gideon* case in detail.

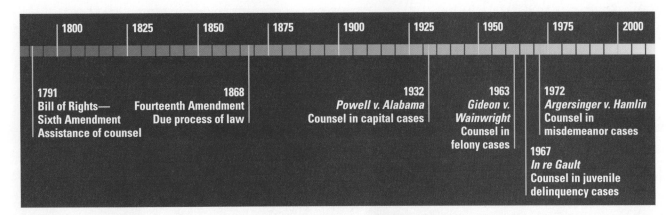

FIGURE 12.1
HISTORICAL TIME
LINE OF RIGHT
TO COUNSEL

Almost two centuries were needed
to establish that adults and juveniles have a right to counsel at
trial.

The *Gideon* decision made it clear that a person charged with a felony in a
state court has an absolute constitutional right to counsel. But whereas some states
applied the *Gideon* ruling to all criminal trials, others did not provide a defendant
with an attorney in misdemeanor cases. Then, in 1972, in the momentous decision of *Argersinger v. Hamlin,* the Supreme Court held that no person can be imprisoned for any offense—whether classified as a petty offense, a misdemeanor,
or a felony—unless he or she is offered representation by counsel at trial. The decision extended this right to virtually all defendants in state criminal prosecutions.

The time line in Figure 12.1 tracks the almost 200 years it has taken to establish what the U.S. Constitution stated in 1791: "In all criminal prosecutions,
the accused shall enjoy the right . . . to have the assistance of counsel for his
defense."[22]

PERSPECTIVES ON JUSTICE

Tremendous indigent defense caseload increases have far outpaced increases in funding. Underfunding is the major problem for virtually all of the
public defender offices in America. Yet, the emergence and growth of professional criminal defense attorneys for indigent defendants are among the
most important contemporary developments in the criminal justice system.
Today, criminal defendants are granted the right to an attorney at almost all
stages of the legal process. The success of indigent defenders is attributable
to the use of the due process model.

The Right to Self-Representation

Fill in the blanks 5
Multiple choice 12–13

Are criminal defendants guaranteed the right to represent themselves—that is, to
act as their own lawyers? Prior to the U.S. Supreme Court decision in *Faretta v.
California* in 1975,[23] defendants in most state courts and in the federal system
claimed the right to proceed **pro se**, or for themselves, by reason of federal and
state statutes and on state constitutional grounds. This permitted defendants to
choose between hiring counsel or conducting their own defense. Whether a constitutional right to represent oneself in a criminal prosecution existed remained
an open question until the *Faretta* decision.

The defendant, Anthony Faretta, was charged with grand theft in Los Angeles County. Before his trial, he requested that he be permitted to represent himself. The judge told Faretta that he believed this would be a mistake but accepted

pro se
To present one's own defense in a
criminal trial; self-representation.

Judges will allow a defendant to proceed pro se when they are reasonably certain the defendant has the ability and knowledge to conduct an adequate defense. Here, Frank Grano, 65, leans on a parking meter in San Francisco. Grano, facing a life sentence in a "three strikes" theft case, defended himself and persuaded a jury to acquit him of all charges. Grano credits the victory to long hours in the jail law library. His two-day trial started Dec. 27, 1999. Jurors deliberated overnight before coming back with an acquittal.

his waiver of counsel. The judge then held a hearing to inquire into Faretta's ability to conduct his own defense and subsequently ruled that Faretta had not made an intelligent and knowing waiver of his right to assistance of counsel. As a result, the judge appointed a public defender to represent Faretta, who was brought to trial, found guilty, and sentenced to prison. He appealed, claiming that he had a constitutional right to self-representation.

Upon review, the U.S. Supreme Court recognized Faretta's pro se right on a constitutional basis, while making it conditional on a showing that the defendant could competently, knowingly, and intelligently waive his right to counsel. The Court's decision was based on the belief that the right of self-representation is supported by the Sixth Amendment, as well as by English and colonial jurisprudence from which the amendment emerged. Thus, in forcing Faretta to accept counsel against his will, the California trial court deprived him of his constitutional right to conduct his own defense.

It is important to recognize that the *Faretta* case dealt only with the constitutional right to self-representation. It did not provide guidelines for administering the right during the criminal process. For instance, how was it that Colin Ferguson, the convicted murderer of six people in the Long Island, New York, train shooting rampage, was allowed to defend himself at his trial in 1995? Viewers watched on Court TV as Ferguson questioned witnesses in the third person. Legal and psychiatric experts contended Ferguson was paranoid and delusional. But the trial judge ruled that he met the minimum standards for competency to stand trial: (1) He understood the charges, and (2) he intelligently and voluntarily waived counsel. Therefore, the trial court was obligated to allow Ferguson to defend himself because of existing Supreme Court opinions.

Today, a defendant in a criminal trial is able to waive the right to the assistance of counsel. Generally, however, the courts have encouraged defendants to accept counsel so that criminal trials may proceed in an orderly and fair manner. When defendants ask to be permitted to represent themselves and are found competent to do so, the court normally approves their requests. The defendants in these cases are almost always cautioned by the courts against self-representation. When pro se defendants' actions are disorderly and disruptive, the court can terminate their right to represent themselves.

There has been no ruling, similar to *Faretta,* that a defendant has a federal constitutional right to prosecute his own criminal appeal. In *Martinez v. Court of Appeals of California* (2000),[24] the U.S. Supreme Court indicated that historical and practical differences between trials and appeals convinced them that due process does not require a recognition of the right to self-representation in criminal appeals.

The Right to a Speedy Trial

Fill in the blanks 6
Multiple choice 14
Essay 1–2

The requirement of the right to counsel at trial in virtually all criminal cases often causes delays in the formal processing of defendants through the court system. Counsel usually seeks to safeguard the interests of the accused and in doing so may employ a variety of legal devices—pretrial motions, plea negotiations, trial procedures, and appeals—that require time and extend the decision-making period in a particular case. The involvement of counsel, along with inefficiencies in the court process—such as the frequent granting of continuances, poor scheduling procedures, and the abuse of time by court personnel—has made the problem of delay in criminal cases a serious constitutional issue. According to the American Bar Association's *Standards Relating to Speedy Trial,* "Congestion in the trial courts of this country, particularly in urban centers, is currently one of the major problems of judicial administration."[25]

The Sixth Amendment guarantees a criminal defendant the right to a speedy trial in federal prosecutions. This right was made applicable to the states by the decision in *Klopfer v. North Carolina* (1967).[26] In this case, the defendant Klopfer was charged with criminal trespass. His original trial ended in a mistrial, and he sought to determine if and when the government intended to retry him. The prosecutor asked the court for a *nolle prosequi with leave,* a legal device discharging the defendant but allowing the government to prosecute him in the future. The U.S. Supreme Court held that the government's attempt to postpone Klopfer's trial indefinitely without reason denied him the right to a speedy trial guaranteed by the Sixth and Fourteenth Amendments.

In *Klopfer,* the Supreme Court emphasized the importance of the speedy trial in the criminal process, stating that this right was "as fundamental as any of the rights secured by the Sixth Amendment."[27] Its primary purposes are

1. To improve the credibility of the trial by seeking to have witnesses available for testimony as early as possible
2. To reduce the anxiety for the defendant in awaiting trial, as well as to avoid pretrial detention
3. To avoid extensive pretrial publicity and questionable conduct of public officials that would influence the defendant's right to a fair trial
4. To avoid any delay that can affect the defendant's ability to defend himself or herself

Since the *Klopfer* case in 1967, the Supreme Court has dealt with the speedy trial guarantee on numerous occasions. One example is the 1992 case of *Doggett v. United States,* in which the Court found that a delay of eight-and-a-half years between indictment and arrest was a prejudicial to the defendant and required a dismissal of the charges.[28]

Because of court backlogs, the government has been forced to deal with the problem of how to meet the constitutional requirement of a speedy trial. The President's Commission on Law Enforcement and the Administration of Justice in 1967 suggested that nine months would be a reasonable period of time in which to litigate the typical criminal felony case through appeal. The process from arrest through trial would take four months, and the decision of an appeals court an additional five months.[29] In 1973, the National Advisory Commission on Criminal

Justice Standards and Goals recommended that the period from the arrest of the defendant in a felony prosecution to the beginning of the trial should generally not be longer than 60 days and that the period from arrest to trial in a misdemeanor prosecution should be no more than 30 days.[30]

Today, most states and the federal government have statutes fixing the period of time during which an accused must be brought to trial. These requirements ensure that a person's trial cannot be unduly delayed and that the suspect cannot be held in custody indefinitely. The federal Speedy Trial Act of 1974 established the following time limits:

1. An information or indictment charging a person with a crime must be filed within 30 days of the time of arrest.
2. The arraignment must be held within 10 days of the time of the information or indictment.
3. The trial must be held within 60 days of the arraignment.[31]

This means that the accused must be brought to trial in the federal system within 100 days of arrest. Other special provisions of the Speedy Trial Act include the gradual phasing in of time standards, the use of fines against defense counsels for causing delays, and the allocation of funds with which to plan speedy trial programs in the federal judicial districts. The Speedy Trial Act was amended in 1979 to more precisely define what constitutes the guarantee of a speedy trial and to encourage state jurisdictions to adopt similar procedures. Many state speedy trial statutes provide even shorter time limits when a defendant is detained in jail.

Long delays have been a central feature of the U.S. justice system. In the 1992 case of *Doggett v. United States,*[32] the Supreme Court declared that a delay of eight-and-a-half years between indictment and arrest was prejudicial to the defendant and required dismissal under the Sixth Amendment. Many states have found that dramatic results can be achieved in reducing such extreme delays by establishing special drug and even homicide courts. These courts aim to get cases to trial within 60 days of a defendant's initial appearance. The results often include (1) shortened disposition time, (2) reduced case backlogs, (3) increased convictions, and (4) lowered pretrial jail costs. The success of speedy trial courts also enhances the quality of justice for defendants and the public by getting victims and witnesses to attend court proceedings and to give reliable and accurate testimony.

FAIR TRIAL VERSUS FREE PRESS

Every person charged with a crime has a fundamental right to a fair trial. What does it mean to have a fair trial in the criminal justice system? A fair trial is one before an impartial judge and jury in an environment of judicial restraint, orderliness, and fair decision making. Although it is not expressly stated in the U.S. Constitution, the right of the accused to a fair trial is guaranteed by the due process clause of the Fifth Amendment.

This fair trial right can be violated in a number of ways. A hostile courtroom crowd, improper pressure on witnesses, or any behavior that produces prejudice toward the accused can preclude a fair trial. When a defendant was required to go to trial in prison clothing, for example, the U.S. Supreme Court found a violation of the due process clause of the Fourteenth Amendment.[33] Adverse pretrial publicity can also deny a defendant a fair trial. The release of premature evidence by the prosecutor, extensive and critical reporting by the news media, and vivid and uncalled-for details in indictments can all prejudice a defendant's case.

Recently, one of the most controversial issues involving the conduct of a trial has been the apparent conflict between the constitutional guarantees of fair trial and freedom of the press. When there is widespread pretrial publicity, as in the

AP/Wide World Photos

Is it possible for well-known celebrity defendants to receive a fair trial after they are the subject of a media blitz? Can jurors truly remain unbiased? Here, witness Van Brett Watkins, left, points out Cherica Adams' apartment in a photograph held by prosecutor David Graham Dec. 20, 2000, in Charlotte, N.C., at the capital murder trial of former Carolina Panthers player Rae Carruth. Watkins testified that he rode in a car driven by codefendant Michael Eugene Kennedy past the apartment with Kennedy's son, Stanley Abraham, Rae Carruth, and Panthers player Hannibal Navies. Carruth was convicted of murder in the death of Adams, his former girlfriend and mother of his child.

Menendez brothers murder case and the Rodney King police brutality case, can an accused defendant get a fair trial as guaranteed by the Fifth, Sixth, and Fourteenth Amendments? Think about the intense media coverage in the O. J. Simpson double murder trial, the Timothy McVeigh Oklahoma City bombing case, and the Louise Woodward child murder case. The murder conviction of Dr. Sam Sheppard more than 30 years ago was reversed by the U.S. Supreme Court because negative publicity generated by the government denied Sheppard a fair trial.[34] In one of the most highly publicized trials in U.S. history, Claus von Bulow was acquitted of the attempted murder of his wife after two trials.[35] Both the prosecution and the defense used the media to reflect their side. Press conferences, leaked news stories, and daily television and radio coverage all contributed to a media sideshow. Even jury sequestration was not successful because many of the jurors had prior knowledge of the case. In the end, the media played a critical role in both the initial conviction and the subsequent acquittal on retrial of the defendant.

Judges involved in newsworthy criminal trials have attempted to place restraints on media coverage to preserve the defendant's right to a fair trial; at the same time, it is generally believed that the media have a constitutional right to provide news coverage. Judge Lance Ito faced these issues in limiting the media's access in the O. J. Simpson trial. He threatened a television blackout, temporarily banned the *Los Angeles Times* for their early release of the juror questionnaire, and even tinkered with television cameras after a broadcast showed jurors from another trial. This represents the classic conflict between the Constitution's First Amendment guarantee of press freedom and the Sixth Amendment guarantee of a fair trial.

Some critics of the media have suggested that the media should be prohibited from reporting about ongoing criminal trials. Such an approach, however, would inhibit the role of the press under the First Amendment. Public information about criminal trials, the judicial system, and other areas of government is an indispensable characteristic of a free society. At the same time, trial by the media violates a defendant's right to a fair trial. Still, publicity is essential to preserving confidence in the trial system, even though this principle may occasionally clash with the defendant's right to a fair trial.

True/False 5
Multiple choice 15–17

The Law of Fair Trial

The U.S. Supreme Court dealt with the fair trial–free press issue in *Nebraska Press Association v. Stuart* (1976).[36] The Court ruled unconstitutional a trial judge's order that prohibited the press from reporting confessions implicating the defendant in the crime. The Court's decision was based primarily on the principle that "prior restraints on speech and publication are the most serious and least tolerable infringement on First Amendment rights."[37]

In *Gannett Co. v. DePasquale* (1979), the Court was asked to decide if the public had an independent constitutional right of access to a pretrial hearing, even though all the parties agreed to closure to guarantee a fair trial.[38] Justice Potter Stewart, writing for the Court, said that the trial court was correct in finding that the press had a right of access of constitutional dimensions but that this right was outweighed by the defendant's right to a fair trial.[39] The Court balanced competing social interests and found that denial of access to the public did not violate the First (free press), Sixth (fair trial), or Fourteenth (due process) Amendment rights of the defendant. The interests of justice requires that the defendant's case should not be jeopardized, and the desire for a fair trial far outweighed the public's right of access to a pretrial suppression hearing. The *Gannett* decision is not ordinarily cited as a precedent to determine whether a right of access to trials is constitutionally guaranteed, because the Court believes that pretrial hearings are not trials.

The question of the First Amendment right of access to preliminary hearings was raised again in *Press-Enterprise Co. v. Superior Court* (1986).[40] The defendant, charged with murder, agreed to have the preliminary hearing closed to the press and the public. But the Supreme Court said that closure is permissible under the First Amendment only if there is a substantial probability that the defendant's right to a fair trial would be prejudiced by publicity that closed proceedings would prevent. According to the Court, preliminary hearings have traditionally been open to the public and should remain so. The *Press-Enterprise* case clearly established the First Amendment right of access to criminal trials.

In an important 1993 case involving pretrial hearings, a reporter for the largest newspaper in Puerto Rico was denied access to a probable cause hearing because of a rule in the Commonwealth of Puerto Rico requiring that the hearings be held privately. The Supreme Court held that this rule violated the First Amendment to the Constitution and, based on the *Press-Enterprise* case, indicated that a pretrial hearing cannot be closed to the press unless prejudice will result to the accused.[41]

True/False 6
Multiple choice 18–19

The Right to a Public Trial

The U.S. Supreme Court has also interpreted the First Amendment to mean that members of the press (and the public) have a right to attend trials. The most important case on this issue is *Richmond Newspapers, Inc. v. Commonwealth of Virginia* (1980).[42] Here, the Supreme Court clearly established that criminal trials must remain public.

Although the Court has ruled that criminal trials are open to the press, the right to a public trial is basically for the benefit of the accused.[43] The familiar language of the Sixth Amendment clearly states that "the accused shall enjoy the right to a speedy and public trial." This provision is rooted in the principle that justice cannot survive behind walls of silence.[44] It was enacted because the framers of the Constitution distrusted secret trials and arbitrary proceedings. Settlers brought this concept to colonial America from England, where the wisdom of holding criminal trials in public predates the Norman conquest.

In the 1948 case of *In re Oliver,* the Supreme Court held that the secrecy of a criminal contempt trial violated the right of the defendant to a public trial under the Fourteenth Amendment.[45] Thus, the Court recognized the constitutional guarantee of a public trial for defendants in state as well as federal courts. Three decades later, the *Richmond Newspapers* decision clearly affirmed the right of the public and the press to attend criminal trials.[46] Thus, criminal trials may not be closed unless findings are sufficient to overcome the presumption of openness.

Table 12.1 summarizes the decisions guaranteeing the defendant's constitutional rights at trial.

Televising Criminal Trials

Other fair trial–free press issues remain, however. Whether jury trials should be televised, for instance, is one of the most controversial questions in the criminal justice system today. The legal community was divided over the use of television cameras in the courtroom for the highly publicized 10-day rape trial of William Kennedy Smith.[47] Smith's acquittal also raised the question of whether the media should protect the privacy rights of the rape victim (name and picture).

In another case that received a great deal of media coverage, Mike Tyson, the former heavyweight boxing champion, was convicted in 1992 of raping a Miss Black America contestant who said he lured her to his hotel room and overpowered her. Because of the interest in the trial, closed-circuit television was used to accommodate the more than 100 news organizations that covered the trial.

Judges involved in such high-profile trials are faced with placing restrictions not only on press coverage but also on television coverage. In the Tyson trial, the State of Indiana, which normally does not allow television cameras in its courts, acquiesced in the use of closed-circuit television. Colorado, on the other hand, refused to allow television coverage of the Timothy McVeigh trial. In the so-called trial of the century, *People v. O. J. Simpson,* unedited television coverage allowed Americans to see the entire trial. Television coverage was also permitted in the *Commonwealth of Massachusetts v. Louise Woodward* murder case. This courtroom drama was seen on two continents and received worldwide attention. Like the Simpson and Kennedy trials, the Woodward case was a television event. Cases of this magnitude have intense emotional appeal, provoke arguments, and generate enormous public interest.

Today, many state courts permit such coverage, often at the judge's discretion, but the use of television cameras, video recorders, and still photography is banned in the federal court system.[48] In addition, Chief Justice William Rehnquist opposes televising Supreme Court proceedings. After a two-year study, the U.S. Judicial Conference decided in 1995 to continue to ban cameras in the federal courts. Camera advocates may try to get federal legislation passed to permit cameras in the federal system.[49]

Televising criminal proceedings could have significant advantages: Judges would be better prepared; the public would be informed about important legal issues; and the proceedings would serve an educational function, offsetting the simplistic views offered by such television programs as *The People's Court, Perry Mason, Law & Order,* and *Ally McBeal.* The extent to which judges, witnesses, and the accused would be influenced by the use of modern technology in the courtroom remains unknown, however, and is the major argument against adopting total media coverage. In extreme cases, the judge might ban the media if televising the case risked igniting violence or if the rights of the accused and the state might be at risk. Also, under the statutes of different jurisdictions, spectators and

TABLE 12.1 DECISIONS AFFIRMING THE DEFENDANT'S CONSTITUTIONAL RIGHTS AT TRIAL

Constitutional Right	Decision
Confrontation of witnesses	*Coy v. Iowa*
Jury trial	*Duncan v. Louisiana*
Right to counsel	*Gideon v. Wainwright*
Self-representation	*Faretta v. California*
Speedy trial	*Klopfer v. North Carolina*
Fair trial/free press	*Nebraska Press Association v. Stuart*
Public trial	*Richmond Newspapers, Inc. v. Commonwealth of Virginia*

Fill in the blanks 7
True/False 7
Multiple choice 20
Essay 3

the press might be excluded from the trial of juvenile cases, certain sordid sex crimes, or national security offenses.

Regardless of the kind of crime committed, a defendant is always permitted to have family, close associates, and legal counsel at his or her trial. Still, the Supreme Court has held, in *Chandler v. Florida* (1981), that subject to certain safeguards, a state may allow electronic media coverage by television stations and still photography of public criminal proceedings over the objection of the defendant in a criminal trial.[50] The Supreme Court did not maintain in *Chandler* that the media had a constitutional right to televise trials; it left it up to state courts to decide whether they wanted trials televised in their jurisdictions.

The controversy surrounding the televising of trials has prompted bar and media groups to develop standards in an attempt to find an acceptable middle ground between the First and Sixth Amendment rights concerning public trials. The defendant has a constitutional right to a public trial, and it is equally imperative that the media exercise their First Amendment rights. Above all, the court must seek to protect the rights of the accused to a fair trial by an unbiased jury. Televising these courtroom dramas has also resulted in a boom in lawyer-centered talk shows, including *Burden of Proof* on CNN, *Cochran and Co.* on Court TV, and *Rivera Live* on CNBC. The public debates legal, political, and social issues through these trials.

Exhibit 12.1 summarizes current laws and policies regarding television cameras in the courtroom, along with the arguments for and against televising criminal trials.

THE TRIAL PROCESS

Fill in the blanks 8–9
Essay 4

The trial of a criminal case is a formal process conducted in a specific and orderly fashion in accordance with rules of criminal law, procedure, and evidence. Unlike what transpires in popular television programs involving lawyers—where witnesses are often asked leading and prejudicial questions and where judges go far beyond their supervisory role—the modern criminal trial is a complicated and often time-consuming technical affair. It is a structured adversary proceeding in which both the prosecution and defense follow specific procedures and argue the merits of their cases before the judge and jury.

Each side seeks to present its own case in the most favorable light. When possible, the prosecutor and the defense attorney object to evidence they consider

EXHIBIT 12.1   TELEVISING CRIMINAL TRIALS

Current Laws and Policies Regarding Television Cameras in the Courtroom

- Most state courts allow television cameras, with various restrictions.
- Cameras are not allowed in federal courts.
- A commercial court TV network offers the most sensationalized criminal trials.
- A noncommercial court TV network has been proposed to focus on educational trials and to expose the judicial process to proper public scrutiny.
- Camera advocates have tried to get state and federal legislation to permit cameras in all state and federal courtrooms, to no avail.
- The U.S. Supreme Court has decided that no rule prohibits television cameras in state courts.

Arguments in Favor

- Public trials encourage participants to do a better job.
- The public should have access to all trials in a democratic society.
- Television coverage contributes to educating the public.

Arguments Against

- Jurors and potential jurors are exposed to media coverage that may cause prejudgment.
- In-court media coverage, especially television cameras, can increase community and political pressure on participants and even cause grandstanding.
- Media coverage can erode the dignity and decorum of the courtroom.

damaging to their positions. The prosecutor uses direct testimony, physical evidence, and a confession, if available, to convince the jury that the accused is guilty beyond a reasonable doubt. The defense attorney rebuts the government's case with his or her own evidence, makes certain that the rights of the criminal defendant under the federal and state constitutions are considered during all phases of the trial, and determines whether an appeal is appropriate if the client is found guilty. The defense attorney uses his or her skill at cross-examination to discredit government witnesses: Perhaps they have changed their statements from the time they gave them to the police, perhaps their memory is faulty, perhaps their background is unsavory, and so on. From the beginning of the process to its completion, the judge promotes an orderly and fair administration of the criminal trial.

Although each jurisdiction in the United States has its own trial procedures, all jurisdictions conduct criminal trials in a generally similar fashion. The basic steps of the criminal trial, which proceed in an established order, are described in this section and outlined in Figure 12.2.

Jury Selection

Jurors are selected randomly in both civil and criminal cases from tax assessment, driver's license, or voter registration lists within each court's jurisdiction. Advocates of more diverse jury pools contend that such lists often do not accurately reflect a state's ethnic composition. As a result, some jurisdictions are requiring that its poll of prospective jurors include people drawn from welfare and unemployment rolls.

Few states impose qualifications on those called for jury service; many states do mandate a residency requirement.[51] Most jurisdictions also prohibit convicted felons from serving on juries, as well as others exempted by statute, such as public officials, medical doctors, and attorneys. The initial list of persons chosen— called **venire** or *jury array*—provides the state with a group of capable citizens able to serve on a jury. Many states, by rule of law, review the venire to eliminate unqualified persons and to exempt those who by reason of their profession are not allowed to be jurors. The actual jury selection process begins with those remaining on the list.

The court clerk, who handles the administrative affairs and documents related to the trial, randomly selects enough names (sometimes from a box) to fill the required number of places on the jury. In most cases, the jury in a criminal trial consists of 12 persons, with two alternate jurors standing by to serve should one of the regular jurors be unable to complete the trial. There is little uniformity in the amount of time served by jurors, with the term ranging from one day to months, depending on the nature of the trial.

Once the prospective jurors are chosen, they undergo a process known as **voir dire** (French for "to tell the truth"), in which they are questioned by both the prosecution and the defense to determine their appropriateness to sit on the jury. They are examined under oath by the government, the defense, and sometimes the judge about their background, occupation, residence, and possible knowledge of or interest in the case. Detailed questionnaires are also used for this purpose. A juror who acknowledges any bias for or prejudice against the defendant (if the defendant is a friend or relative, for example, or if the juror has already formed an opinion about the case) is removed "for cause" and replaced with another. Thus, any prospective juror who declares that he or she cannot be impartial and render a verdict solely on the evidence to be presented at the trial may be removed by either the prosecution or the defense. Because normally no limit is placed on the number of **challenges for cause**, it often takes considerable time to select a jury for controversial and highly publicized criminal cases.

Jury selection in the 1990 Iran–Contra trial of Oliver North lasted for more than three months, and hundreds of prospective jurors were examined. The voir

Fill in the blanks 10–12
True/False 8–12
Multiple choice 21–29

venire
The group called for jury duty from which jury panels are selected.

voir dire
The process in which a potential jury panel is questioned by the prosecution and the defense to select jurors who are unbiased and objective.

challenge for cause
Dismissal of a prospective juror by either the prosecution or the defense because he or she is biased, has prior knowledge about a case, or for other reasons that demonstrate the individual's inability to render a fair and impartial judgment.

FIGURE 12.2
THE STEPS IN A
JURY TRIAL

SOURCE: Marvin Zalman and Larry
Siegel, *Criminal Procedure: Constitution
and Society* (St. Paul, MN: West Publishing, 1991), p. 655.

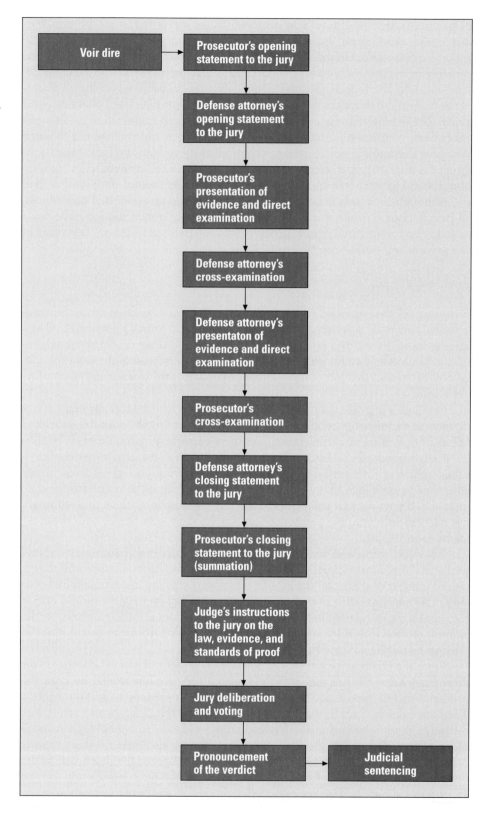

dire process was made especially difficult because the trial judge insisted on dis-
qualifying all jurors who had heard or read anything about the defendant's public testimony before congressional committees. According to some experts, this is
an example of an extreme application of the impartiality requirement (no knowl-

edge of the case), as opposed to simply determining that a jury lacks any prejudice toward the accused. In other front-page cases, hundreds of potential jurors were screened in the Menendez murder trial, and extensive questionnaires (more than 75 pages) were used in the Simpson case. Jury selection lasted about two weeks in the McVeigh trial—a more appropriate time frame for a high-profile criminal case.

In certain instances, the court may also want to ask prospective jurors "content" questions about how they became familiar with a particular case. In *Mu'Min v. Virginia* (1991), a highly publicized murder case, the trial judge did not allow questions from the defendant concerning the content of the prospective jurors' acquired information.[52] Although the jurors were asked whether they had read or heard about the case and formed an opinion based on outside information, content questions that would give legal depth to a finding of impartiality were not asked. Should the judge have asked about the type and extent of pretrial information that would disqualify a juror? The Supreme Court said such content questions are not constitutionally compelled in a voir dire hearing, unless the failure to ask them would result in an unfair trial. Thus, the failure to ask such questions in those cases involving pretrial publicity is not ordinarily a violation of the defendant's Sixth Amendment right to an impartial jury.

Peremptory Challenges In addition to challenges for cause, both the prosecution and the defense are allowed **peremptory challenges**, which enable the attorneys to excuse jurors for no particular reason or for undisclosed reasons. For example, a prosecutor might not want a bartender as a juror in a drunk-driving case, believing that a person with that occupation would be sympathetic to the accused. Or the defense might excuse a prospective male juror because the attorney prefers to have a predominantly female jury. The number of peremptory challenges permitted is limited by state statute and often varies by case and jurisdiction.

The peremptory challenge has been criticized by legal experts who question the fairness and propriety with which it has been used.[53] The most significant criticism is that it has been used to exclude blacks from hearing cases in which the defendant is also black. In *Swain v. Alabama* (1965), the U.S. Supreme Court upheld the use of peremptory challenges in isolated cases to exclude jurors by reason of racial or other group affiliation.[54] This policy was extremely troublesome because it allowed what seemed to be legally condoned discrimination against minority-group members. In 1986, the Court struck down the *Swain* doctrine in *Batson v. Kentucky,*[55] holding that the use of peremptory challenges by prosecutors in criminal cases, if based on race, violated the Constitution. Because of the importance of this landmark case, it is discussed in the Law in Review feature.

In an analysis of the peremptory challenge after the *Batson* decision, James Archer suggested that this legal procedure can still be used fairly, with improved systematic jury selection, appropriate judicial discretion, and the identification of prima facie (evident "on its face") constitutional violations in the jury process.[56] Other authors believe that the success of the *Batson* standard depends primarily on the discretion of the trial judge.[57] Marvin Steinberg makes a case for eliminating peremptory challenges altogether to end racial discrimination in the jury system.[58]

Since the *Batson* decision, the issue of racial discrimination in the use of peremptory challenges has been raised by defendants in numerous cases. In *Powers v. Ohio* (1991) for instance, the Supreme Court was faced with deciding the legality of peremptory challenges involving jurors not of the same race as the defendant. The Court held that a defendant may object to the race-based removal of a juror even when the defendant is a member of a different racial group. The equal protection clause prohibits a prosecutor from using the peremptory challenge

peremptory challenge
Dismissal of a prospective juror by either the prosecution or the defense for unexplained, discretionary reasons.

LAW IN REVIEW

Batson v. Kentucky (1986)

Facts

During the criminal trial of a black defendant in Kentucky, the prosecutor used his peremptory challenges to remove four blacks from the venire. Consequently, an all-white jury was selected. Although defense counsel protested that this deprived Batson, his client, of a fair jury representing a cross section of the community, the trial judge denied the motion. Batson was ultimately convicted. The Kentucky Supreme Court relied on the *Swain* doctrine in upholding the case, arguing that the defense did not demonstrate systematic exclusion of black jurors in other cases.

Decision

The U.S. Supreme Court held that defendants have no right to a jury composed of members in whole or in part of their own race. However, the Fourteenth Amendment's equal protection clause guarantees that the state will not exclude jury members on account of race or under the false assumption that members of the defendant's own race cannot render a fair verdict. This would also discriminate against the jury members and undermine public confidence in the jury system. Thus, the state is for-

bidden to preempt jurors solely on the basis of their race.

In addition, if defendants want to prove racism in the use of the peremptory challenge, they no longer must show a pattern of discrimination as the *Swain* doctrine indicated. Defendants may show purposeful racial discrimination in selection of the venire by relying solely on the facts of their own case. They must show that they are members of a particular race and that the prosecutor has exercised his or her peremptory challenges to remove members of that racial group from the jury. They may rely on the fact that such practices permit "those to discriminate who have a mind to discriminate." The burden is then on the prosecutor to come forward with a neutral explanation for challenging the jurors.

Finally, the Court argued that the peremptory challenge can still play an important role in the adversarial process. It can be used in most criminal cases as long as it is not employed in a racially biased manner.

Significance of the Case

Batson strikes down a legal procedure that was out of sync with modern ideas of justice and fairness. It prevents an el-

ement of racial discrimination from entering into the trial stage of justice, which is one of the cornerstones of American freedom. Yet it preserves, under controlled circumstances, the use of the peremptory challenge, which is an integral part of the jury selection process.

Critical Thinking Skills

The Supreme Court has limited the ways the prosecution and defense can exercise peremptory challenges based on race or gender. In what other areas can we expand the *Batson* rule?

InfoTrac College Edition Research

Jury selection is often the most important part of a case. Preparation, evidence, and eyewitnesses don't mean anything unless you have a good jury. For a discusson of this issue, go to InfoTrac College Edition and read Kathryn Barnett, "Letting Focus Groups Work for You," *Trial,* 1999, v35 p74

to exclude qualified and unbiased persons from a jury solely by reason of race. In so ruling, the Court rejected the government's contention that the rule only applied to jurors of the same race as the defendant. Similarly, in the 1992 case of *Georgia v. McCollum,* the Supreme Court found that criminal defendants may not seek to exclude potential jurors strictly on the basis of race. Race-based peremptory challenges to potential jurors in civil lawsuits have also been declared unconstitutional.[59]

In 1994, the Supreme Court, in *J. E. B. v. Alabama,* ruled that prosecutors and defense attorneys may not use peremptory challenges to strike men or women from juries solely on the basis of gender. Such discrimination also violates the equal protection clause of the Fourteenth Amendment, the Court said.[60] Supreme Court decisions regarding peremptory challenges are summarized in Table 12.2.

TABLE 12.2 U.S. SUPREME COURT DECISIONS REGARDING THE PEREMPTORY CHALLENGE

Batson v. Kentucky (1986)	Under the Fourteenth Amendment, the Supreme Court ruled that prosecutors were barred from using peremptory challenges to remove black jurors because of their race.
Powers v. Ohio (1991)	The Supreme Court concluded that a defendant has the standing to object to race-based exclusion of jurors by the use of peremptory challenges on the grounds of equal protection, even if the defendant is not of the same race as the challenged jurors.
Edmonson v. Leesville Concrete Co. (1991)	The Court held that the *Batson* ruling applies to attorneys in civil lawsuits. A private party in a civil action may not raise peremptory challenges to exclude jurors on the basis of race.
Georgia v. McCollum (1992)	On the basis of *Batson,* the Court prohibited the exercise of race-based peremptory challenges by defense attorneys in criminal cases.
J. E. B. v. Alabama (1994)	The Supreme Court held that the equal protection clause of the Fourteenth Amendment bars discrimination in jury selection on the basis of sex. Discrimination in jury selection, whether based on race or gender, causes harm to the litigants, the community, and the individual jurors who are wrongfully excluded from participation in the judicial process.

Some state courts have ruled that peremptory challenges cannot be based on religion. Some day, states may rule that they can't be based on age or disability.[61]

Impartial Juries   The Sixth Amendment provides for the right to a speedy trial by an *impartial* jury, but the concept of an impartial jury has always been controversial. Research indicates that jury members often have little in common with their criminal "peers." Moreover, remaining impartial may be a struggle; studies of jury deliberations indicate that the dynamics of decision making often involve pressure to get the case over with and convince recalcitrant jurors to join the majority. Nevertheless, jurors also appear to take cases seriously and to reach decisions not too different from those made by legal professionals.[62] Judges, for instance, often agree with jury decisions. However, jurors often have problems understanding judicial instructions and legal rule-making in criminal trials, and this may cause confusion in determining the appropriate verdict.

The Supreme Court has sought to ensure compliance with the constitutional mandate of impartiality by eliminating racial discrimination in jury selection. For instance, in *Ham v. South Carolina* (1973), the Court held that the defense counsel of a black civil rights leader was entitled to question each juror on the issue of racial prejudice.[63] In *Taylor v. Louisiana* (1975), the Court overturned the conviction of a man by an all-male jury because a Louisiana statute allowed women but not men to exempt themselves from jury duty.[64]

The issue of racial composition of the jury is particularly acute in cases involving the death penalty. In *Turner v. Murray* (1986), the Court ruled that a defendant accused of an interracial crime in which the death penalty is an option can insist that prospective jurors be informed of the victim's race and be questioned on the issue of their bias. A trial judge who refuses this line of questioning during voir dire risks having the death penalty vacated, but not having the conviction reversed.[65] These and other, similar decisions have had the effect of providing safeguards against jury bias.

Jury selection can be even more difficult in capital punishment cases, where jurors are asked about their views on the death penalty. In *Lockhart v. McCree* (1986), the Supreme Court decided that jurors who strongly oppose capital punishment may be disqualified from determining a defendant's guilt or innocence in capital cases.[66] The *Lockhart* decision raises certain questions, however. Juries are not supposed to represent only one position or another. An impartial jury of one's peers is rooted in the idea that the defendant should be judged by a cross section of members of the local community. Their views should not be disproportionate

RACE, GENDER, AND ETHNICITY IN CRIMINAL JUSTICE

Jury Selection and Peremptory Challenges

Jury selection often accounts for a large share of criminal trial time, particularly in high-profile cases involving serious crimes. Jury selection procedures include (1) the voir dire examination, in which prospective jurors are questioned for the purpose of ascertaining their fitness to serve on the jury; (2) the challenge for cause, in which jurors are eliminated because of prejudice; and (3) the peremptory challenge, an objection to a juror for no apparent reason.

Of all these procedures, the peremptory challenge poses the greatest actual and potential risk of jury discrimination. The U.S. Supreme Court, in *Batson v. Kentucky,* recognized the widespread abuses of peremptory challenges by deciding that purposeful discrimination in their use is a violation of the defendant's right to an impartial jury. The Court later extended the *Batson* rule beyond racial discrimination to the category of gender.

Despite the expansion of the *Batson* rule, peremptory challenges may still involve discrimination along other dimensions. Race-neutral explanations may be used to justify what may be discriminatory peremptory challenges of minorities. For instance, it may be possible to strike Spanish-speaking minorities if a prosecutor claims that they would have difficulty understanding the testimony. It is also possible that the social class of jurors is as important as race and gender in explaining disproportionate jury representation.

Based on the cases addressing peremptory challenges decided by the U.S. Supreme Court, it is clear that excluding potential jurors from criminal trials because of race or gender violates the defendant's rights under the Fourteenth Amendment. Justice Thurgood Marshall recognized the seriousness of this issue when he suggested in the *Batson* case that peremptory challenges should be eliminated entirely from the criminal justice system.

Professor Charles Ogletree points out that the seemingly neutral explanations of prosecutors for peremptory challenges undermine the protection against jury discrimination established by the *Batson* case. Ogletree suggests that the following procedural protections be implemented: (1) If a prosecutor violates *Batson,* the criminal case should be dismissed. (2) Prosecution peremptory challenges should be eliminated. However, it seems unlikely that such rules would be established by a state court or legislature.

Critical Thinking Skills

1. Would criminal trials be fairer without peremptory challenges?
2. There are differences in the number of peremptory challenges available in each state and in the federal court system. The American Bar Association has recommended allowing ten peremptory challenges per side in capital cases, five per side if a sentence of imprisonment of more than six months may be imposed, and three per side if the maximum sentence is incarceration of six months or less. Are these standards reasonable?
3. Should social class indicators (income, occupation, and authority position of prospective jurors) be considered in determining jury participation?

**InfoTrac College
Edition Research**

The peremptory challenge has been weakened in recent decades by U.S. Supreme Court decisions holding that challenges based on either race or gender violate the equal protection clause of the Fourteeenth Amendment. But the Court has not yet considered the constitutionality of religion-based challenges. See Jean Hellwege, "Religion-Based Peremptory Challenges Are Unconstitutional," *Trial Magazine,* 1999, v35 p15

SOURCES: Charles Ogletree, "Just Say No! A Proposal to Eliminate Racially Discriminatory Uses of Peremptory Challenges," *American Criminal Law Review* 31 (1994): 1099–1511; Marvin Zalman and Larry Siegel, *Criminal Procedure: Constitution and Society,* 2d ed. (Belmont, CA: West/Wadsworth, 1997); Hiroshi Fukurai, "Race, Social Class, and Jury Participation: New Dimensions for Evaluating Discrimination in Jury Service," *Journal of Criminal Justice* 24 (1996): 71–88.

on any one issue. Consequently, a ruling such as *Lockhart* could theoretically result in higher conviction rates in murder cases.

The Supreme Court has not yet fully answered all of the important questions regarding impartiality in the role and qualifications of jurors in criminal cases. The Race, Gender, and Ethnicity in Criminal Justice feature provides additional information on discrimination in jury selection.

Another safeguard against bias, used in highly publicized and celebrated cases, is to **sequester** jury members, once selected, for the duration of the trial, isolating them from contact with the outside world. Sequestration is discretionary with the trial judge, and most courts believe "locking a jury up" is needed only in sensational cases, such as the O. J. Simpson trial.

sequester
To insulate jurors from the outside world so that their decision making cannot be influenced or affected by events outside the courtroom.

True/False 13–14

Opening Statements

Once the jury has been selected and has heard the criminal complaint read by the court clerk, the prosecutor and the defense attorney may each make an opening statement to the jury. The purpose of the prosecutor's statement is to introduce the judge and jury to the particular criminal charges, to outline the facts, and to describe how the government will prove the defendant guilty beyond a reasonable doubt. The defense attorney reviews the case and indicates how the defense intends to show that the accused is innocent of the charge. The defense attorney's opening statement ordinarily follows that of the prosecution.

The opening statement gives the jury a concise overview of the evidence that is to follow. In the opening statement, neither attorney is allowed to make prejudicial remarks or inflammatory statements or to mention irrelevant facts. Both are free, however, to identify what they will eventually prove by way of evidence—witnesses, physical evidence, and expert testimony. The actual content of the statement is left to the discretion of the trial judge. As a general rule, the opening statements used in jury trials are important because they provide the finders of fact (the jury) with an initial summary of the case. They are less effective and are infrequently used in **bench trials**, however, where juries are not employed. Most lower-court judges have handled hundreds of similar cases and do not need the benefit of an opening statement.

bench trial
The trial of a criminal matter by a judge without a jury.

Presentation of the Prosecutor's Evidence

Fill in the blanks 13
True/False 15

Following the opening statements, the government begins its case by presenting evidence to the court through its witnesses. Those called as witnesses, such as police officers, victims, or experts, provide testimony via **direct examination**. During direct examination, the prosecutor questions the witness to reveal the facts believed pertinent to the government's case. Testimony involves what the witness actually saw, heard, or touched and does not include opinions. However, a witness's opinion can be given in certain situations, such as when describing the motion of a vehicle or indicating whether a defendant appeared to act intoxicated or insane. Witnesses may also qualify to give opinions because they are experts on a particular subject relevant to the case; for example, a psychiatrist may testify about a defendant's mental capacity at the time of the crime.

direct examination
The initial questioning of one's own (prosecution or defense) witness during a trial.

After the prosecutor finishes questioning a witness, the defense may **cross-examine** the same witness by asking questions that seek to clarify the defendant's role in the crime. The right to cross-examine witnesses is an essential part of a trial, and except in extremely unusual circumstances (such as a person's being hospitalized), witness statements will not be considered unless they are made in court and open for question. For example, in *Lee v. Illinois* (1986), the U.S. Supreme Court ruled that a confession made to police by a co-defendant in a criminal trial cannot be used in court unless the person making the confession is available for cross-examination.[67] If desired, the prosecutor may seek a second direct examination after the defense attorney has completed cross-examination; this allows the prosecutor to ask additional questions about information brought out during cross-examination. Finally, the defense attorney may question or cross-examine the witness once again. All witnesses for the trial are sworn in and questioned in the same basic manner.

cross-examination
The questioning of a prosecution witness by the defense, or of a defense witness by the prosecution.

During his or her presentation of the evidence, the prosecutor may call expert witnesses to help the jury understand complex scientific data. Here, Dr. Joseph Cohen, the medical examiner who did the autopsy on Amadou Diallo, shows the jury the bullet hole in the right shoe that Diallo was wearing when he was shot. Cohen testified in the trial of four New York City police officers, Feb. 8, 2000, in Albany, N.Y. The officers were found not guilty of intentionally killing Diallo.

© Philip Kamrass/Albany Times Union/The Image Works

Fill in the blanks 14–15
True/False 16–17

real evidence
Any object, such as a weapon or a photograph, produced for inspection at a trial; physical evidence.

circumstantial evidence
Indirect evidence from which a fact may be inferred.

Types of Evidence at a Criminal Trial

In addition to testimonial evidence given by police officers, citizens, and experts, the court also acts on **real** (nonverbal) **evidence**.[68] Real or physical evidence may include exhibits such as a revolver that may have been in the defendant's control at the time of a murder, tools found in the possession of a suspect charged with a burglary, a bottle allegedly holding narcotics, or blood samples from a murder victim. The criminal court judge will also review documentary evidence, such as writings, government reports, public records, and business or hospital records.

In general, the primary test for the admissibility of evidence in either a criminal or civil proceeding is its relevance. The court must ask itself whether the gun, shirt, or photograph, for instance, has relevant evidentiary value in determining the issues of the case. Ordinarily, evidence that establishes an element of the crime is acceptable to the court. For example, in a prosecution for possession of drugs, evidence that shows the defendant to be a known drug user might be relevant.

Circumstantial (indirect) **evidence** is also often used in trial proceedings. Such evidence is often inferred or used indirectly to prove a fact in question. On the issue of malice in a criminal murder trial, for instance, it would be appropriate to use circumstantial evidence to prove the defendant's state of mind. Such evidence has often been the controversial issue in many celebrated criminal cases. More than a century ago, the disappearance of Dr. George Parkman attracted national attention when Parkman's colleague at Harvard University, Dr. Webster, was convicted of murder after Parkman disappeared.[69] Because there was no *corpus delicti* (in this case, a body), Webster's conviction was based on circumstantial evidence.

In the famous Sacco and Vanzetti trial of the 1920s, two men were tried and convicted of murder and finally executed seven years later based on circumstantial evidence (and possibly because they were Italian anarchists).[70] Circumstantial evidence bearing on or establishing the facts in a crime is ordinarily admissible, but evidence that is prejudicial, remote, or unrelated to the crime should be excluded by the court. In general, the admissibility of such evidence remains governed by constitutional law, such as the right to be free from unreasonable search and seizure, the privilege against self-incrimination, and the right to counsel.

In recent years, a considerable amount of real evidence has come from video recordings. Courtroom use of videotape originated with undercover surveillance operations. Today, citizens are being filmed regularly. Security cameras are mounted everywhere. The plethora of cameras makes evidentiary videotape widely available and an important part of the technology of criminal evidence collection.[71]

Motion for a Directed Verdict

Once the prosecution has provided all the government's evidence against a defendant, it will inform the court that it rests the people's case. The defense attorney at this point may enter a motion for a **directed verdict**. This is a procedural device by which the defense attorney asks the judge to order the jury to return a verdict of not guilty. In essence, the defense attorney argues that the prosecutor's case against the defendant is insufficient to prove the defendant guilty beyond a reasonable doubt. The judge must rule on the motion and will either sustain it or overrule it, depending on whether he or she believes that the prosecution has proved all the elements of the alleged crime. If the motion is sustained, the trial is terminated. If it is rejected, the case continues with the defense portion of the trial.

The defense usually makes a motion for a directed verdict so that a finding of guilt can later be appealed to a higher court. If the judge refuses to grant the motion, this decision can be the focus of an appeal charging that the judge did not use proper procedural care in making his or her decision. In some cases, the judge may reserve decision on the motion, submit the case to the jury, and consider a decision on the motion before the jury verdict.

Presentation of Evidence by the Defense Counsel

The defense attorney has the option of presenting many, some, or no witnesses on behalf of the defendant. In addition, the defense attorney must decide if the client should take the stand and testify in his or her own behalf. In a criminal trial, the defendant is protected by the Fifth Amendment right against self-incrimination, which means that a person cannot be forced by the state to testify against himself or herself in a criminal trial. However, defendants who choose voluntarily to tell their side of the story can be subject to cross-examination by the prosecutor.

After the defense concludes its case, the government may then present *rebuttal evidence.* This normally involves bringing evidence forward that was not used when the prosecution initially presented its case. The defense may examine the rebuttal witnesses and introduce new witnesses in a process called a *surrebuttal.* After all the evidence has been presented to the court, the defense attorney may again submit a motion for a directed verdict. If the motion is denied, both the prosecution and the defense prepare to make closing arguments, and the case on the evidence is ready for consideration by the jury.

Closing Arguments

The attorneys use closing arguments to review the facts and evidence of the case in a manner favorable to each of their positions. At this stage of the trial, both the prosecution and the defense are permitted to draw reasonable inferences and to show how the facts prove or refute the defendant's guilt. Both attorneys have a

Fill in the blanks 16
Essay 5

directed verdict
A judge's order directing a jury to acquit a defendant because the state has not proven the elements of the crime or otherwise has not established guilt according to law.

Fill in the blanks 17
True/False 18–19

relatively free hand in arguing about the facts, issues, and evidence, including the applicable law. They cannot comment on matters not in evidence, however, nor on the defendant's failure to testify in a criminal case. Normally, the defense attorney makes a closing statement first, followed by the prosecutor. Either party can elect to forgo the right to make a final summation to the jury. Because the prosecution gives the opening statement first and makes the closing argument last, some experts believe that the government has a decided advantage over the defense.

Instructions to the Jury

Fill in the blanks 18
True/False 20

charge
Instructions to a jury on the principles of law that ought to guide their decision; also, the specific crime a defendant is accused of committing.

In a criminal trial, the judge will instruct, or **charge**, the jury members on the principles of law that ought to guide and control their decision on the defendant's innocence or guilt. Included in the charge is information about the elements of the alleged offense, the type of evidence needed to prove each element, and the burden of proof required for a guilty verdict. Although the judge commonly provides the instruction, he or she may ask the prosecutor and the defense attorney to submit instructions for consideration; the judge then uses discretion in determining whether to use any of their instructions. The instructions that cover the law applicable to the case are particularly important because they may serve as the basis for a subsequent appeal.

A good example of an improper jury instruction that voided a conviction occurred in *Sullivan v. Louisiana* (1993).[72] In this murder case, the defendant's lawyer argued that there was reasonable doubt concerning the identity of the killer. The trial judge in his instructions said that reasonable doubt must have a "substantial" basis that would give rise to a grave uncertainty that Sullivan was the killer. The Supreme Court declared that this instruction violated the Fifth Amendment due process clause because it downplayed the duty of the state to prove all the elements of a crime beyond a reasonable doubt. Thus, even the use of one word can create further confusion in interpreting the reasonable doubt standard.

The Verdict

True/False 21–22

verdict
The finding of a trial jury or judge on the question of fact: guilty or not guilty.

Once the charge is given to the jury members, they retire to deliberate on a **verdict**. The verdict in a criminal case is usually required to be unanimous. A review of the case by the jury may take hours or even days. The jurors are always sequestered during their deliberations, and in certain lengthy and highly publicized cases, they are kept overnight in a hotel until the verdict is reached. In less sensational cases, the jurors may be allowed to go home, but they are cautioned not to discuss the case with anyone.

The rules of procedure for most jurisdictions permit only two possible verdicts in a criminal trial: *guilty* and *not guilty*. In a criminal trial, it is the government's responsibility to convince the judge or jury that the defendant is guilty. If the government fails, the defendant is then found not guilty. Contrary to what is often observed on television or in the movies, where a person accused of a crime is found "innocent," criminal courts do not make such a determination. If a verdict cannot be reached, the trial may result in a **hung jury**; if the prosecution still wants a conviction, it must bring the defendant to trial again.

hung jury
A jury whose members are unable to agree on a verdict.

If found not guilty, the defendant is released from the criminal process. If the defendant is found guilty, the judge normally orders a presentence investigation by the probation department before imposing a sentence. Prior to sentencing, the defense attorney will probably submit a motion for a new trial, alleging that legal errors occurred in the trial proceedings. The judge may deny the motion and impose a sentence immediately, a practice quite common in misdemeanor offenses. In felony cases, however, the judge sets a date for sentencing and the defendant is either released on bail or held in custody until that time.

At the completion of a trial the jury verdict is publicly announced. Here, a packed courtroom in Las Vegas listens as guilty verdicts on all charges for the murder of casino heir Ted Binion are read May 19, 2000. From left, defense attorney John Momot, defendants Sandy Murphy and Rick Tabish, Tabish's attorney Louis Palazzo, attorney Rob Murdock, and Linda Norvell show little emotion. Prosecutors say Binion was forced to ingest a lethal dose of heroin and the prescription antidepressant Xanax, then was suffocated by Murphy, who was Binion's live-in girlfriend, and Tabish, who became her lover.

AP/Wide World Photos

The Sentence

True/False 23

Imposing the criminal **sentence** is normally the responsibility of the trial judge. In some jurisdictions, the jury may determine the sentence or make recommendations for leniency for certain offenses. Often, the sentencing decision is based on information and recommendations given to the court by the probation department after a presentence investigation of the defendant. The sentence itself is determined by the statutory requirements for the particular crime, as established by the legislature; in addition, the judge ordinarily has a great deal of discretion in sentencing. The different criminal sanctions available include fines, probation, imprisonment, and even commitment to a state hospital, as well as combinations of these. Sentencing is discussed in detail in the following chapter.

sentence
The criminal sanction or punishment imposed by the court on a convicted defendant, usually in the form of a fine, incarceration, or probation.

The Appeal

Defendants have three possible avenues of appeal: the direct appeal, federal court review, and postconviction remedy.[73] Both the direct appeal and federal court review provide the convicted person with the opportunity to appeal to a higher state or federal court on the basis of an error that affected the conviction in the trial court. Extraordinary trial court errors, such as the denial of the right to counsel or the inability to provide a fair trial, are subject to the "plain error" rule of the federal courts.[74] "Harmless errors," such as the use of innocuous identification procedures or the denial of counsel at a noncritical stage of the proceeding, would not necessarily result in overturning a criminal conviction.

A postconviction remedy, on the other hand—often referred to as a "collateral attack"—is the primary means by which state prisoners can have their conviction or sentence reviewed in federal court. It takes the form of a legal petition,

Fill in the blanks 19
True/False 24
Essay 6

 A great deal of research is being conducted regarding criminal sanctions. One of the best sources of information is the Sentencing Project: http://www.sentencingproject.org
For an up-to-date list of Web links, see http://www.wadsworth.com/product/0534573053s

writ of habeas corpus
A judicial order requiring a review of the legal reasons for a person's detention and confinement.

 Take a look at the appeal petition in the famous Woodward child abuse case:
http://www.courttv.com/trials/woodward/appeal.html
For an up-to-date list of Web links, see http://www.wadsworth.com/product/0534573053s

in forma pauperis
An appeal "in the form of a pauper"; if granted, a criminal defendant is entitled to assistance of counsel at state expense.

such as for a **writ of habeas corpus**. A writ of habeas corpus (meaning "you should have the body") seeks to determine the validity of detention by asking the court to release the person or give legal reasons for the incarceration.

In most jurisdictions, direct criminal appeal to an appellate court is a matter of right. This means that the defendant has an automatic right to appeal a conviction based on errors that may have occurred during the trial proceedings. A substantial number of criminal appeals are the result of disputes over points of law, such as the introduction at the trial of illegal evidence detrimental to the defendant or statements made during the trial that were prejudicial to the defendant. Through objections made at the pretrial and trial stages of the criminal process, the defense counsel preserves specific legal issues on the record as the basis for appeal. A copy of the transcript of these proceedings serves as the basis on which the appellate court will review any errors that may have occurred during the lower court proceedings. Although the defendant has an automatic right to an appeal in the first instance, all further appeals are discretionary, including an appeal "all the way to the U.S. Supreme Court."

Because an appeal is an expensive, time-consuming, and technical process, involving a review of the lower court record, the research and drafting of briefs, and the presentation of oral arguments to the appellate court, the defendant has been granted the right to counsel at this stage of the criminal process. In *Douglas v. California* (1963), the Supreme Court held that an indigent defendant has a constitutional right to the assistance of counsel on a direct first appeal.[75] If the defendant appeals to a higher court, the defendant must have private counsel or apply for permission to proceed **in forma pauperis**, meaning that the defendant may be granted counsel at public expense if the court believes the appeal has merit.

The right of appeal normally does not extend to the prosecution in a criminal case. At one extreme are states that grant no right of appeal to the prosecution in criminal cases. At the other, some jurisdictions permit the prosecution to appeal in those instances that involve the unconstitutionality of a statute or a motion granting a new trial to the defendant. However, the prosecutor cannot bring the defendant to trial again on the same charge after an acquittal or a conviction; this would violate the defendant's right to be free from double jeopardy under the Fifth Amendment. As discussed in Chapter 4, the purpose of the double jeopardy guarantee is to protect the defendant from a second prosecution for the same offense.

After an appeal has been fully heard, the appeals court renders an opinion on the procedures used in the case. If an error of law is found, such as an improper introduction of evidence or an improper statement by the prosecutor that was prejudicial to the defendant, the appeals court may reverse the decision of the trial court and order a new trial. If the lower court's decision is upheld, the case is finished, unless the defendant seeks a discretionary appeal to a higher state or federal court.

Over the past decade, criminal appeals have increased significantly in almost every state and the federal courts. Criminal case appeals make up a majority of the state appellate and federal caseload, which includes prisoner petitions and ordinary criminal appeals. Today, a substantial number of these appeals involve drug-related cases.

EVIDENTIARY STANDARDS

Essay 8–9

beyond a reasonable doubt
Standard of proof required for conviction of a criminal defendant; conclusive proof of guilt, with no realistic possibility of innocence.

The standard required to convict a defendant at the trial stage of the criminal process is proof **beyond a reasonable doubt**. This requirement dates back to early American history, and over the years has become the accepted measure of persuasion needed by the prosecutor to convince the judge or jury of the defendant's guilt. Many twentieth-century U.S. Supreme Court decisions have reinforced this standard by making "beyond a reasonable doubt" a constitutional due process requirement.[76]

The reasonable doubt standard is an essential ingredient of the criminal justice process. It is the prime instrument for reducing the risk of convictions based on factual errors. The underlying premise of this standard is that it is better to release a guilty person than to convict someone who is innocent. In applying the reasonable doubt standard to juvenile trials, in *In re Winship* (1970), the Supreme Court noted:

> If the standard proof for a criminal trial were preponderance of evidence rather than proof beyond a reasonable doubt, there would be a smaller risk of factual errors that result in freeing guilty persons, but a far greater risk of factual errors that result in convicting the innocent.[77]

Because the defendant is presumed innocent until proven guilty, this standard forces the prosecution to overcome the presumption of innocence with the highest standard of proof. Unlike the civil law, where a mere **preponderance of the evidence** is the standard, the criminal process requires proof beyond a reasonable doubt for each element of the offense. These and other evidentiary standards of proof are defined and compared in Table 12.3.

Over the years, the courts have struggled to define many of the standards of evidence, particularly reasonable doubt. The Federal Judicial Center's model standard states its best:

> Proof beyond a reasonable doubt is proof that leaves you firmly convinced of the defendant's guilt. There are very few things in this world that we know with absolute certainty, and in criminal cases the law does not require proof that overcomes every possible doubt. If, based on your consideration of the evidence, you are firmly convinced that the defendant is guilty of the crime charged, you must find him guilty. If, on the other hand,

preponderance of the evidence
Standard of proof in civil cases; greater weight of evidence on one side than the other.

TABLE 12.3   EVIDENTIARY STANDARDS OF PROOF: DEGREES OF CERTAINTY

Standard	Definition	Where Used
Absolute certainty	No possibility of error; 100 percent certainty	Not used in civil or criminal law
Beyond a reasonable doubt; moral certainty	Conclusive and complete proof, without leaving any reasonable doubt as to the guilt of the defendant; allowing the defendant the benefit of any possibility of innocence	Criminal trial
Clear and convincing evidence	Prevailing and persuasive to the trier of fact	Civil commitments, insanity defense
Preponderance of evidence	Greater weight of evidence in terms of credibility; more convincing than an opposite point of view	Civil trial
Probable cause	U.S. constitutional standard for arrest and search warrants, requiring existence of facts sufficient to warrant that a crime has been committed	Arrest, preliminary hearing, motions
Sufficient evidence	Adequate evidence to reverse a trial court	Appellate review
Reasonable suspicion	Rational, reasonable belief that facts warrant investigation of a crime on less than probable cause	Police investigations
Less than probable cause	Mere suspicion; less than reasonable to conclude that criminal activity exists	Prudent police investigation where safety of an officer or others is endangered

you think there is a real possibility that he is not guilty, you must give him the benefit of the doubt and find him not guilty.[78]

PERSPECTIVES ON JUSTICE

During closing arguments, both the prosecution and the defense outline and summarize their case for the jury. The prosecutor explains why he or she has proven the case beyond a reasonable doubt; the defense focuses on any holes in the evidence and reminds the jury that if there is any doubt in their minds, they must find for the defendant and render a "not guilty" verdict. If a verdict cannot be reached, the trial may result in a hung jury.

The trial of Eric and Lyle Menendez, charged with the shotgun slaying of their parents, resulted in a hung jury and a new trial. A second trial found both guilty of criminal homicide. The verdict and retrial contain elements of both crime control and due process perspectives.

The trial of Ted Kaczynski, the Unabomber, also contained similar elements. The prosecution sought the death penalty, whereas the defense claimed that Kaczynski was mentally ill. He eventually pleaded guilty.

TRIAL REFORM IN THE TWENTY-FIRST CENTURY

Essay 7

Criminal trial practices will likely undergo considerable change during coming decades. What innovations can we expect in the twenty-first century? What are the trends in the trial process, and in the role of the jury? Where is the criminal trial heading?

Trials will likely continue to be adversarial in nature. Prosecutors, defense attorneys, and judges will reshape their roles, stressing community organization, sentencing reform, and mediation of criminal cases. The number of minority and female members of the judiciary should continue to grow.

Another change that will continue to have an impact on the trial is the use of DNA evidence. DNA profiling involves scientifically matching the genetic material from hair, blood and other bodily tissues and fluids found at a crime scene with samples taken from known suspects. (See Chapter 4.)

The use of DNA profiling in criminal trials received a boost in 1997 when the FBI announced that DNA testing has become so precise that experts no longer have to supply statistical estimates of accuracy while testifying at trial. They can now state in court that there exists "a reasonable degree of scientific certainty" that evidence came from a single suspect.

The FBI has implemented a combined DNA index system (CODIS). This computerized database allows DNA taken at a crime scene to be searched electronically to find matches against samples taken from convicted offenders and from other crime scenes. One database allows suspects to be identified; the second allows investigators to establish links between crimes. So far there have been more than 100 instances in which offenders have been linked to unsolved cases. In addition, 67 convicts (some on death row) have been exonerated by DNA evidence.[79] The use of DNA evidence should become commonplace in the twenty-first century.

Trial courts also are tapping into new communication technologies to improve the effectiveness of the criminal trial. Cellular phones, fax machines, computers, and teleconferencing systems that provide both audio and video linkages are routinely used by judges, prosecutors, and defense attorneys. Legal experts are still uncertain about the viability of televising all criminal trials. Some support the idea, because it exposes the judicial process to public scrutiny. Others believe the tabloid approach of a commercial enterprise like Court TV will continue to scare off the federal courts from ever allowing cameras into the courtroom.

According to some legal experts, the present U.S. criminal trial process is inadequate because it is too complicated and requires an inordinate amount of time. The accuracy of jury verdicts is often questioned by the public, and serious questions remain regarding the use of unanimous verdicts and peremptory challenges. The past decade has seen serious criticism of the jury system by the legal profession, the press, and the public.[80] Two areas of the jury system that require attention are (1) jury selection procedures and (2) jury service during conduct of the trial.[81]

The peremptory challenge has led to scientific jury selection and has even given birth to a new profession, jury consulting. Selecting a jury has become a very complicated process, as attorneys seek to stack the jury with people who fit their ideal demographic profile. Even the unlimited "for cause" challenges delay the trial process and often lead the courts to search for the least informed citizens to serve as jurors. The present system has put an increased time burden on the judicial system and decreased public confidence in the accuracy of jury verdicts.

The treatment of jurors during the trial is also a problem. Most jurors consider jury service a hassle; it means taking time off from work or finding someone to care for children at home. It may even mean a loss of money. Jurors need to be treated with respect and consideration in keeping with their critical role in the legal system. Consequently, shortening the in-court voir dire examination of prospective jurors would make practical sense. Allowing the jury to ask questions during the trial and to discuss evidence among themselves would also be very helpful, particularly in complex cases with scientific testimony.

Another question is whether judges need to summarize the law and the facts for the jury. Presently, judges read to the jury a statement of the law along with a definition of reasonable doubt. Research has found that jurors often have a poor understanding of the judge's instructions. Jurors often need assistance in applying the law to the facts in a given case. These reforms would give the jury more information when it seeks the truth and also create a more efficient jury system.[82]

Yet another issue is whether jury verdicts should always be unanimous. As we have seen, the U.S. Supreme Court has ruled that the Sixth Amendment's guarantee of a jury trial does not require a unanimous verdict. Proponents of less than unanimous jury verdicts argue that such an approach would largely eliminate hung juries and even reduce the possibility of one juror's corrupting the jury process. Opponents counter that nonunanimous verdicts tend to reduce juror deliberation and devalue dissenting opinions.

The International Justice feature considers the similarities and differences on many of these points between the American and English criminal trial systems.

For information on violations of civil liberties in criminal trial practice, as well as on racial profiling in the justice system, visit the Web site of the American Civil Liberties Union (ACLU) http://www.aclu.org

For an up-to-date list of Web links, see http://www.wadsworth.com/product/0534573053s

SUMMARY

The number of cases disposed of by trials is relatively small in comparison to the total number that enter the criminal justice system. Nevertheless, the criminal trial provides the defendant with a very important option. Unlike other steps in the system, the criminal trial allows the accused to assert the right to a day in court. The defendant may choose between a trial by jury or before a judge only. In either case, the purpose of the trial is to adjudicate the facts, ascertain the truth, and determine the guilt or innocence of the accused.

Criminal trials represent the adversary system at work. The state uses its authority to seek a conviction, and the defendant is protected by constitutional

INTERNATIONAL JUSTICE

A Comparison of the American and English Trial Processes

How do criminal trial procedures in the United States compare with those in England? According to some legal experts, the present U.S. legal system is inadequate. Jury selection is a very complicated process. Criminal cases require an inordinate amount of time. The accuracy of jury verdicts is being questioned by the public. Serious questions exist regarding peremptory challenges and unanimous verdicts.

Although the immediate source of the U.S. trial system is the English system of jurisprudence, the disparity between the two systems has become more pronounced over time. For instance, the English criminal code was revised in 1967 to permit 19-to-2 jury verdicts and to eliminate peremptory challenges. These experiments seem to have proven successful.

The accompanying table summarizes the basic similarities and differences in trial procedures between the American and English systems.

Critical Thinking Skills

1. Assume that the United States has a far greater crime rate than England. What trial innovations can be developed to bring the rate down? What reforms will strengthen the American jury system?
2. Extensive media publicity often accompanies high-profile criminal cases in the United States. How is it possible to limit media coverage in the English system but not in the American system?
3. Do current U.S. court rules do justice to the jury system in modern times?

InfoTrac College Edition Research

For more suggestions on how to improve the American jury system, see Thomas Hogan, Gregory Mize, and Kathleen Clark, *World and I,* 1998, v13 p64

SOURCES: Eugene Sullivan and Akhil Amar, "Jury Reform: A Return to the Old Country," *American Criminal Law Review* 33 (1996): 141; Benjamin Austin, "Right to Jury Trial," *Georgetown University Law Review* 85 (1997): 1240; Alan Dershowitz, "Divided by Common Judiciary," *Boston Globe,* 9 November 1997, p. D1.

A COMPARISON OF THE AMERICAN AND ENGLISH CRIMINAL TRIAL SYSTEMS

Similarities

- Adversarial
- Trial by jury
- Presumption of innocence
- Proof beyond a reasonable doubt
- Independent judiciary
- Constitutional due process

Major Differences

American System	*English System*
Appointed or elected judges with political background	Appointed legal barristers
Prosecutors with political aspirations	Prosecutors are career civil servants
Freedom of the press	Limited media coverage
States permit television coverage	Prohibition on television coverage
Jury publicity in selection procedures	Limited attention given to jury process
Use of jury consultants in high-profile cases	No jury consultants
Government use of overcharging and plea bargaining	Limited use of overcharging
Little judicial influence over jury verdict	Judicial influence over jury
Jury unanimity required	Less than unanimous verdicts allowed
Extensive voir dire procedures	Voir dire handled outside the courtroom
Discussion of evidence during trial not permitted	Review of evidence allowed during trial
No questions permitted	Written questions permitted
Judicial instructions on law only	Judicial summary of facts and law
Extensive use of peremptory challenges	No peremptory challenges

rights, particularly those under the Fifth and Sixth Amendments. When they involve serious crimes, criminal trials are complex legal affairs. Each jurisdiction relies on rules and procedures that have developed over many years. As the U.S. Supreme Court has extended the rights of the accused, these procedures have undoubtedly contributed to the complexities and delays within the system. Some suggested solutions include using smaller juries; eliminating peremptory challenges; and reducing time delays between arrest, indictment, and trial.

An established order of steps is followed throughout a criminal trial, beginning with the reading of the complaint, proceeding through the introduction of evidence, and concluding with closing arguments and a verdict. The criminal trial serves both a symbolic and a pragmatic function for defendants who require a forum of last resort to adjudicate their differences with the state.

Under the U.S. system of justice, the defendant is presumed innocent until proven guilty. The standard of proof in a criminal case is proof beyond a reasonable doubt.

Key Terms

continuance	bench trial	hung jury
confrontation clause	direct examination	sentence
pro se	cross-examination	writ of habeas corpus
venire	real evidence	in forma pauperis
voir dire	circumstantial evidence	beyond a reasonable doubt
challenge for cause	directed verdict	preponderance of the evidence
peremptory challenge	charge	
sequester	verdict	

Discussion Questions

1. Identify the steps involved in the criminal trial. Consider the pros and cons of a jury trial versus a bench trial.
2. What are the legal rights of the defendant in the trial process? Trace the historical development of the right of counsel at the trial stage of the criminal justice system.
3. Discuss the significance of the Supreme Court decisions in *Gideon v. Wainwright* and *Argersinger v. Hamlin.*
4. In the adversary system of criminal justice, the burden of proof in a criminal trial is on the government to show that the defendant is guilty beyond a reasonable doubt. Explain the meaning of this statement in terms of other legal standards of proof.
5. If a 17-year-old youth is tried by a jury, should the jurors also be under 21 years of age to maintain fairness?
6. Devise a charge to the jury for a first-degree murder case.
7. What factors support televising criminal trials? Why don't we televise federal court trials?
8. What do you believe is the area of greatest concern in jury selection?
9. What are the characteristics of the criminal trial in the twenty-first century?

A CLOSER LOOK

The United States is not alone in using juries in criminal trials. Many other nations, including Great Britain, also make use of juries.

In an article on the role of juries in the American and British justice systems, Zakaria Erinchoglu questions the assumption that trial by jury is superior to trial by a judge. According to her analysis, the jury trial may not always promote the emergence of truth and justice. She points to numerous cases of miscarriage of justice caused by a jury's returning an irrational verdict. Among the questions she raises are the following:

1. Do we wish to abolish the right of a defendant to a trial by jury for all minor crimes?
2. Would actions to restrict the use of trial by jury arouse the fury of civil liberties groups and ethnic minorities?
3. Does the jury trial live up to its exalted reputation?
4. Do we need to reevaluate the jury system?

For her discussion of these questions, go to InfoTrac College Edition and read

Zakaria Erinchoglu, "The Role of Juries in the Justice System," *Contemporary Review,* 1999, v274 p297

Notes

1 A year after the Oklahoma City bombing, Congress passed the Anti-Terrorism and Effective Death Penalty Act of 1996, P.L. No. 104-132 (1996); see also David Kopel and Joseph Olson, "Preventing a Reign of Terror: Civil Liberties Implications of Terrorism Legislation," *Oklahoma City University Law Review* 21 (1996): 247.

2 Patrick O'Driscoll, "Man Guilty of Murdering Gay Student," *USA Today*, 4 November 1999, p. 3A.

3 National Advisory Commission on Criminal Justice Standards and Goals, *Courts* (Washington, DC: U.S. Government Printing Office, 1973), p. 66; see also Donald Newman, *Conviction: The Determination of Guilt or Innocence without Trial* (Boston: Little, Brown, 1966).

4 U.S. Constitution, Amend. VI.

5 *Pointer v. State of Texas,* 380 U.S. 400, 85 S.Ct. 1065, 13 L.Ed.2d 923 (1965).

6 487 U.S. 1012, 108 S.Ct. 2798, 101 L.Ed.2d 867 (1988).

7 497 U.S. 836, 110 S.Ct. 3157, 111 L.Ed.2d 666 (1990).

8 391 U.S. 145, 88 S.Ct. 1444, 20 L.Ed.2d 491 (1968).

9 Ibid., at 157–58, 88 S.Ct., at 1451–52.

10 399 U.S. 66, 90 S.Ct. 1886, 26 L.Ed.2d 437 (1970).

11 See *Blanton v. City of Las Vegas,* 489 U.S. 538, 109 S.Ct. 1289, 103 L.Ed.2d 550 (1989); also *Lewis v. United States,* 116 S.Ct. 2163 (1996).

12 399 U.S. 78, 90 S.Ct. 1893, 26 L.Ed.2d 446 (1970).

13 Ibid., at 102–3, 90 S.Ct., at 1907.

14 Ibid., at 101, 90 S.Ct., at 1906.

15 Ibid., at 102, 90 S.Ct., at 1907.

16 *Ballew v. Georgia,* 435 U.S. 223, 98 S.Ct. 1029, 55 L.Ed.2d 234 (1978).

17 *Burch v. Louisiana,* 441 U.S. 130, 99 S.Ct. 1623, 60 L.Ed.2d 96 (1979).

18 406 U.S. 404, 92 S.Ct. 1628, 32 L.Ed.2d 184 (1972).

19 287 U.S. 45, 53 S.Ct. 55, 77 L.Ed. 158 (1932).

20 372 U.S. 335, 83 S.Ct. 792, 9 L.Ed.2d 799 (1963); see also Yale Kamisar, "*Gideon v. Wainwright,* a Quarter Century Later," *Pace Law Review* 10 (1990): 343.

21 407 U.S. 25, 92 S.Ct. 2006, 32 L.Ed.2d 530 (1972).

22 U.S. Constitution, Amend. VI.

23 422 U.S. 806, 95 S.Ct. 2525, 45 L.Ed.2d 562 (1975).

24 120 S.Ct. 684, 2000.

25 See American Bar Association, *Standards Relating to Speedy Trial* (New York: Institute of Judicial Administration, 1986), p. 1.

26 386 U.S. 213, 87 S.Ct. 988, 18 L.Ed.2d 1 (1967).

27 Ibid., at 223, 87 S.Ct., at 993.

28 *Doggett v. United States,* 505 U.S. 647, 112 S.Ct. 2686, 120 L.Ed.2d 520 (1992).

29 President's Commission on Law Enforcement and the Administration of Justice,

30 National Advisory Commission on Criminal Justice Standards and Goals, *Courts,* pp. xx–xxi; see also Gregory S. Kennedy, "Speedy Trial," *Georgetown Law Journal* 75 (1987): 953–964.

31 18 U.S.C.A. § 3161 (Supp. 1975). For a good review of this legislation, see Marc I. Steinberg, "Right to Speedy Trial: The Constitutional Right and Its Applicability to the Speedy Trial Act of 1974," *Journal of Criminal Law and Criminology* 66 (1975): 229; see also Thomas Schneider and Robert Davis, "Speedy Trial and Homicide Courts," *American Bar Association Journal of Criminal Justice* 9 (1995): 24.

32 See *Doggett v. United States,* 505 U.S. 647, 112 S.Ct. 2686, 120 L.Ed.2d 520 (1992).

33 *Estelle v. Williams,* 425 U.S. 501, 96 S.Ct. 1691, 48 L.Ed.2d 126 (1976).

34 *Sheppard v. Maxwell,* 384 U.S. 333, 86 S.Ct.1507, 16 L.Ed.2d 600 (1966).

35 See *State v. von Bulow,* 475 A.2d 995 (R.I. 1984); see also Alan Dershowitz, *Reversal of Fortune: The von Bulow Affair* (New York: Random House, 1986).

36 427 U.S. 539, 96 S.Ct. 2791, 49 L.Ed.2d 683 (1976).

37 Ibid., at 547, 96 S.Ct., at 2797.

38 443 U.S. 368, 99 S.Ct. 2898, 61 L.Ed.2d 608 (1979).

39 Ibid., at 370, 99 S.Ct., at 2900.

40 478 U.S. 1, 106 S.Ct. 2735, 92 L.Ed.2d 1 (1986).

41 *Carribbean International News Corp. v. Puerto Rico,* 508 U.S. 147, 113 S.Ct. 2004, 124 L.Ed.2d 60 (1993).

42 448 U.S. 555, 100 S.Ct. 2814, 65 L.Ed.2d 1 (1980).

43 Nicholas A. Pellegrini, "Extension of Criminal Defendant's Right to Public Trial," *St. John's University Law Review* 611 (1987): 277–289.

44 U.S. Constitution, Amend. VI.

45 *In re Oliver,* 333 U.S. 257, 68 S.Ct. 499, 92 L.Ed. 682 (1948).

46 448 U.S. 555, 100 S.Ct. 2814, 65 L.Ed.2d 1 (1980)

47 See *Chandler v. Florida,* 449 U.S. 560, 101 S.Ct. 802, 66 L.Ed.2d 740 (1981).

48 T. Dyk and B. Donald, "Cameras in the Supreme Court," *American Bar Association Journal* 75 (1989): 34.

49 "Rally for Court Cameras Falls Short," *American Bar Association Journal* 81 (1995): 30.

50 449 U.S. 560, 101 S.Ct. 802, 66 L.Ed.2d 740 (1981).

51 Conference of State Court Administrators, *State Court Organization, 1987* (Williamsburg, VA: National Center for State Courts, 1988).

52 500 U.S. 415, 111 S.Ct. 1899, 114 L.Ed.2d 493 (1991); also Walter Olson, "The Jury Selection Ordeal," *Wall Street Journal,* 7 December 1994, p. A14.

53 George Hayden, Joseph Senna, and Larry Siegel, "Prosecutorial Discretion in Peremptory Challenges: An Empirical Investigation of Information Use in the Massachusetts Jury Selection Process," *New England Law Review* 13 (1978): 768.

54 380 U.S. 202, 85 S.Ct. 824, 13 L.Ed.2d 759 (1965).

55 476 U.S. 79, 106 S.Ct. 1712, 90 L.Ed.2d 69 (1986).

56 James Archer, "Exercising Peremptory Challenges after *Batson,*" *Criminal Law Bulletin* 24 (1988): 187–211.

57 Brian Sern and Mark Maney, "Racism, Peremptory Challenges, and Democratic Jury: The Jurisprudence of Delicate Balance," *Journal of Criminal Law and Criminology* 79 (1988): 65.

58 Marvin Steinberg, "The Case for Eliminating Peremptory Challenges," *Criminal Law Bulletin* 27 (1991): 216–229.

59 *Powers v. Ohio,* 499 U.S. 400, 111 S.Ct. 1364, 113 L.Ed.2d 411 (1991); *Georgia v. McCollum* 505 U.S. 42, 112 S.Ct. 2348, 120 L.Ed.2d 33 (1992).

60 *J. E. B. v. Alabama,* ex rel. T. B., 511 U.S. 142, 114 S.Ct. 1419, 128 L.Ed.2d 89 (1994).

61 "Peremptory Challenges Can't Be Based on Religion," *Lawyers Weekly USA,* 13 February 1995, p. 1.

62 For a review of jury decision making, see John Baldwin and Michael McConville, "Criminal Juries," in *Crime and Justice,* vol. 2, ed. Norval Morris and Michael Tonry (Chicago: University of Chicago Press, 1980), pp. 269–320: see also Reid Hastie, ed., *Inside the Juror* (New York: Cambridge University Press, 1993).

63 409 U.S. 524, 93 S.Ct. 848, 35 L.Ed.2d 46 (1973).

64 419 U.S. 522, 95 S.Ct. 692, 42 L.Ed.2d 690 (1975).

65 476 U.S. 28, 106 S.Ct. 1683, 90 L.Ed.2d 27 (1986). See James Gobert, "In Search of an Impartial Jury," *Journal of Criminal Law and Criminology* 79 (1988): 269.

66 476 U.S. 162, 106 S.Ct. 1758, 90 L.Ed.2d 137 (1986).

67 476 U.S. 530, 106 S.Ct. 2056, 90 L.Ed.2d 514 (1986).

68 See Charles McCormick, *Handbook on Evidence* (St. Paul, MN: West Publishing, 1987), chap. 1.

69 See the fascinating case study of the *"State's Case v. Dr. Webster,"* in Helen Thomson, *Murder at Harvard* (Boston: Houghton-Mifflin, 1971).

70 See Francis Russell, *Sacco and Vanzetti: The Case Resolved* (New York: Harper & Row, 1986).

71 Deborah Mahan, "Forensic Image Processing," *American Bar Association Journal of Criminal Justice* 10 (1995): 2.

72 *Sullivan v. Louisiana,* 508 U.S. 275, 113 S.Ct. 2078, 124 L.Ed.2d 182 (1993).

73 Bureau of Justice Statistics, *Report to the Nation on Crime and Justice,* 2d ed. (Washington, DC: U.S. Government Printing Office, 1988), p. 88.

74 *Chapman v. California,* 386 U.S. 18, 87 S.Ct. 824, 17 L.Ed.2d 705 (1967).

75 372 U.S. 353, 83 S.Ct. 814, 9 L.Ed.2d 811 (1963).

76 See *Brinegar v. United States,* 338 U.S. 160, 69 S.Ct. 1302, 93 L.Ed. 1879 (1949); *Speiser v. Randall,* 357 U.S. 513, 78 S.Ct. 1332, 2 L.Ed.2d 1460 (1958); *In re Winship,* 397 U.S. 358, 90 S.Ct. 1068, 25 L.Ed.2d 368 (1970).

77 See *In re Winship,* 397 U.S. 358, 90 S.Ct. 1068, 25 L.Ed.2d 368 (1970).

78 *Model Jury Standards for Criminal Trial* (Washington, DC: Federal Judicial Center, 1987); also Michael Higgins, "Not So Plain English," *American Bar Association Journal* 84 (1998): 40.

79 Barry Scheck, Peter Newfeld, and Jim Dugen, *Actual Innocence* (New York: Doubleday, 2000).

80 Benjamin Austin, "Right to Jury Trial," *Georgetown University Law Review* 85 (1997): 1240.

81 Sandra Day O'Connor, "Juries: They May Be Broken—but We Can Fix Them," *Federal Lawyer* 44 (1997): 20.

82 Eugene Sullivan and Akhil Amar, "Jury Reform: A Return to the Old Country," *American Criminal Law Review* 33 (1996): 1141.

AP/Wide World Photos

PUNISHMENT AND SENTENCING

In the midst of a hotly contested 2000 presidential campaign, Gov. George W. Bush of Texas came under pressure from death penalty opponents, who charged that Texas led the nation in the use of capital punishment.[1] Lawyers for Ricky McGinn, scheduled to die for the 1993 rape and murder of his 12-year-old stepdaughter, begged the governor for a stay of execution so he could have a DNA test that would prove his innocence. Bush, a proponent of capital punishment, granted the reprieve, probably because he was concerned about anti–capital punishment backlash in the midst of a presidential campaign. This was the first stay Bush had granted during his entire time in office; during this five-year period, 131 people were executed in Texas.[2] Ironically, though Bush's act of mercy and McGinn's protestation of innocence received a great

deal of national attention, the DNA test proved that McGinn was actually the killer! He was executed on September 27, 2000.

The McGinn case illustrates the difficulty of finding proper and fair sentences for criminal offenders. When popular opinion, fueled by the media, demands revenge, politicians establish "get tough" measures such as mandatory sentences for drug offenders and the death penalty for murder. Yet even hardcore proponents of capital punishment may rethink their positions under intense political pressure.

Historically, the punishments inflicted on criminal defendants included disfigurement, torture, branding, whipping, and for most felony offenses, death. During the Middle Ages, the philosophy of punishment was to

Chapter 13

AP/Wide World Photos

Ricky McGinn stares from a visiting room cell shortly before his execution. Does the introduction of DNA evidence make executions less risky because it provides hard scientific evidence that can substantiate the defendant's guilt?

EXHIBIT 13.1 FORMS OF PUNISHMENT

- **Fine**—monetary payment made to the court reflecting the cost to society of the criminal act
- **Community sentence**—period of supervision in the community during which the criminal is required to obey predetermined rules of behavior and may be asked to perform tasks such as making restitution to the victim
- **Incarceration**—a period of confinement in a state or federal prison, jail, or community-based treatment facility
- **Capital punishment**—death in the electric chair or gas chamber or by lethal injection

Fill in the blanks 1
True/False 1

"torment the body for the sins of the soul."[3] People who violated the law were considered morally corrupt and in need of strong discipline. Harsh punishment would convince offenders never to repeat their mistakes. Punishment was also viewed as a spectacle that taught a moral lesson. The more gruesome and public the sentence, the greater the impact it would have on the local populace.[4] Harsh physical punishment would control any thoughts of rebellion or dissent against those who held political and economic control.

Such barbaric use of state power is, of course, no longer tolerated in the United States. The most important forms of criminal punishment used in the United States today are listed in Exhibit 13.1.

Punishing criminal offenders continues to be one of the most complex and controversial issues in the criminal justice system. Its complexity stems from the wide variety of sentences available and the discretion judges have in applying them. Some believe that this task is too difficult for an individual judge and have suggested that sentencing decisions be based on "scientific" prediction methods, classifying defendants based on their past behavior. If potentially dangerous offenders could be identified, the argument goes, they could be singled out for long prison sentences, a procedure called *selective incapacitation.*[5] But critics claim that these predictions are unreliable: Dangerous criminals are often classified as low risk, and low-rate offenders are mislabeled as dangerous.[6] Although prediction schemes seem unreliable, it has become the norm to punish people harshly if their past behavior labels them as potentially dangerous.

The controversy over punishment involves both its nature and extent: Are too many people being sent to prison? Do people receive widely different sentences for similar crimes? Does sentencing reflect discrimination based on race, gender, or social class?[7] These are but a few of the most significant issues in the sentencing process.

This chapter first examines the history of punishment and then focuses on incarceration and capital punishment, the two most punitive forms of criminal sanction used today. Chapter 14 reviews alternative sentences that have been developed to reduce the strain on the overburdened correctional system. These sentences, including probation and other forms of community correction, provide intermediate sanctions designed to control people whose behavior and personality make incarceration unnecessary.

HISTORY OF PUNISHMENT

The punishment and correction of criminals has changed considerably through the ages, reflecting custom, economic conditions, and religious and political ideals.[8]

True/False 2–3

Fill in the blanks 2–3
Multiple choice 1–3

From Exile to Fines, Torture to Forfeiture

In early Greece and Rome, the most common state-administered punishment was banishment or exile. Only slaves were commonly subjected to harsh physical punishment for their misdeeds. Interpersonal violence, even when an attack resulted in death, was viewed as a private matter. These ancient peoples typically used economic punishments, such as fines, for crimes such as assault on a slave, arson, or housebreaking.

During the Middle Ages (fifth to eleventh centuries), there was little law or government control. Offenses were settled by blood feuds carried out by the families of the injured parties. When possible, the Roman custom of settling disputes by fine or an exchange of property was adopted as a means of resolving interpersonal conflicts with a minimum of bloodshed. After the eleventh century, during the feudal period, forfeiture of land and property was a common punishment for persons who violated law and custom or who failed to fulfill feudal obligations to their lord. The word *felony* actually comes from the twelfth century, when the term *felonia* referred to a breach of faith with one's feudal lord.

During this period, the main emphasis of criminal law and punishment was on maintaining public order. If in the heat of passion or while intoxicated a person severely injured or killed a neighbor, freemen in the area would gather to pronounce judgment and make the culprit do penance or pay compensation, called *wergild.* The purpose of the fine was to pacify the injured party and ensure that the conflict would not develop into a blood feud and anarchy. The inability of the peasantry to pay fines led to the use of corporal punishment, such as whipping or branding, as a substitute penalty.

The development of the common law in eleventh-century England brought some standardization to penal practices. However, corrections remained an amalgam of fines and brutal physical punishments. Capital and corporal punishment were used to control the criminal poor. While the wealthy could buy their way out of punishment and into exile, the poor were executed and mutilated at ever-increasing rates. Execution, banishment, mutilation, branding, and flogging were used on a whole range of offenders, from murderers and robbers to vagrants and gypsies. Punishments became unmatched in their cruelty, featuring a gruesome variety of physical tortures, often part of a public spectacle, presumably so that the sadistic sanctions would act as deterrents. But the variety and imagination of the tortures inflicted on even minor criminals before their death suggest that retribution, sadism, and spectacle were more important than deterrence.

Forced Labor

By the end of the sixteenth century, the rise of the city and overseas colonization provided vast markets for manufactured goods and spurred the need for labor. Punishment of criminals changed to meet the demands created by these social conditions. Instead of being tortured or executed, many offenders were made to do hard labor for their crimes. Poor laws, developed at the end of the sixteenth century, required that the poor, vagrants, and vagabonds be put to work in public or private enterprise. Houses of correction were developed to make it convenient to assign petty law violators to work details. In London, a workhouse was developed at Brideswell in 1557; its use became so popular that by 1576, Parliament ordered a Brideswell-type workhouse be built in every county in England. Many convicted offenders were pressed into sea duty as galley slaves. Galley slavery was considered a fate so loathsome that many convicts mutilated themselves rather than submit to servitude on the high seas.

The constant shortage of labor in the European colonies also prompted authorities to transport convicts overseas. In England, an Order in Council of 1617 granted a reprieve and stay of execution to people convicted of robbery and other felonies who were strong enough to be employed overseas. Although **transportation** in lieu of a death sentence may seem an attractive alternative, transported prisoners endured enormous hardships. Those who were sent to Australia suffered incredible physical abuse, including severe whippings and mutilation.

Transporting convicts to the colonies became increasingly popular. It supplied labor, cost little, and was actually profitable for the government, since manufacturers and plantation owners paid for convicts' services. The Old Bailey Court in

Fill in the blanks 4
True/False 4

transportation
Exile of convicted criminals to overseas colonies in lieu of execution.

London supplied at least 10,000 convicts between 1717 and 1775. Similar measures were used in France and Italy to recruit galley slaves and workers.

The American Revolution ended the transportation of felons to North America, but transportation to Australia and New Zealand continued. Between 1787 and 1875, when the practice was finally abandoned, more than 135,000 felons were transported to Australia.

Multiple choice 4–7

The Rise of the Prison

Between the American Revolution in 1776 and the first decades of the nineteenth century, the population of Europe and the United States increased rapidly. Transportation of convicts to North America was no longer an option. The increased use of machinery made industry capital- rather than labor-intensive. As a result, there was less need for unskilled laborers in England, and many workers could not find suitable employment.

The gulf between poor workers and wealthy landowners and merchants widened. The crime rate rose significantly, prompting a return to physical punishment and increased use of the death penalty. During the later part of the eighteenth century, 350 types of crime in England were punishable by death. Although many people sentenced to death for trivial offenses were spared the gallows, the use of capital punishment was extremely common in England during the mid-eighteenth century.

Prompted by the excessive use of physical and capital punishment, legal philosophers argued that physical punishment should be replaced by periods of confinement. Jails and workhouses were commonly used to hold petty offenders, vagabonds, the homeless, and debtors. However, these institutions were not meant for hard-core criminals. One solution to imprisoning a growing criminal population was to keep prisoners in abandoned ships anchored in rivers and harbors throughout England. The degradation under which prisoners lived in these ships inspired John Howard, the sheriff of Bedfordshire, to write *The State of the Prisons* in 1777. As a result, Parliament passed legislation mandating the construction of secure and sanitary structures to house prisoners.

incarceration
Confinement in a correctional institution, such as a jail or prison.

By 1820, long periods of **incarceration** in walled institutions called *reformatories* or *penitentiaries* began to replace physical punishment in England and the United States. These institutions were considered liberal reforms during a time when harsh physical punishment and incarceration in filthy holding facilities were the norm. The history of correctional institutions will be discussed further in Chapter 15.

Incarceration has remained the primary mode of punishment for serious offenses in the United States since it was introduced early in the nineteenth century. Ironically in our high-tech society, some of the institutions constructed soon after the Revolutionary War are still in use today. In recent times, prison as a method of punishment has been supplemented by sentences of community supervision for less serious offenders, while the death penalty is reserved for those crimes considered to be the most serious and dangerous.

THE GOALS OF CRIMINAL PUNISHMENT

When we hear about a notorious criminal, such as serial killer Jeffery Dahmer or Ted Bundy, receiving a long prison sentence or the death penalty for a particularly heinous crime, each of us has a distinct reaction. Some of us are gratified that a truly evil person "got just what he deserved"; many people feel safer because a dangerous person is now "where he can't harm any other innocent victims"; others hope the punishment serves as a warning to potential criminals that "everyone gets caught in the end"; some may actually feel sorry for the defendant ("He got a raw deal; he needs help, not punishment"); and still others hope that "when he gets out, he'll have learned his lesson." And when an offender is forced to pay a large fine, we say, "What goes around comes around."

Each of these sentiments may be at work when criminal sentences are formulated. After all, sentences are devised and implemented by judges, many of whom are elected officials and share the general public's sentiments and fears. The objectives of criminal sentencing today can generally be grouped into six distinct areas: general deterrence, incapacitation, specific deterrence, retribution (just desert), rehabilitation, and restitution (equity).

General Deterrence

What effect does punishing a criminal offender have on the community? By punishing an offender severely, the state can demonstrate its determination to control crime and deter potential offenders. Too lenient a sentence might encourage criminal conduct; too severe a sentence might reduce the system's ability to dispense fair and impartial justice and might actually encourage criminality. For example, sometimes the public cries out for vengeance in a particularly brutal case of child rape. But if even the most heinous cases of rape were punished with death, rapists might be encouraged to kill their victims to dispose of the one person who could identify them. Since they would already be facing the death penalty for rape, they would have nothing more to lose. Maintaining a balance between fear and justice is an ongoing quest in the justice system.

Sentencing for the purposes of general deterrence, then, is designed to give a signal to the community at large: Crime does not pay! As a result, prison sentences are lengthening and the prison population is increasing.

Multiple choice 8
Essay 1

PERSPECTIVES ON JUSTICE

Crime control advocates believe that the threat of severe punishment will eventually bring crime rates down. They call for a "get tough" policy featuring long, mandatory prison terms with little chance for early release. Critics of the crime control perspective retort that the threat of punishment actually has little influence on crime rates. They believe that criminals may be too psychologically impaired by drugs and alcohol to be deterred by the threat of distant criminal punishment, or their economic circumstances may be too desperate for the threat of punishment to have an effect.

Incapacitation

Incapacitation of criminals by keeping them under state control so they cannot repeat their criminal acts is viewed as a justifiable goal of sentencing. Because an offending career is usually limited to a certain fixed period of time (between the ages of 15 and 45), each year that high-rate offenders serve behind bars significantly reduces their total lifetime offending opportunity. Sentencing high-rate offenders to a 10-year period of incarceration, for example, eliminates about one-third of their potential lifetime offenses; a 20-year sentence eliminates two-thirds of their entire offending career.

The current imprisonment boom, which has placed more than 2 million potential criminals behind bars, may be helping to lower crime rates. Opponents counter that this is a spurious relationship and that reductions in crime are just as likely related to other factors such as population makeup, police effectiveness, declining drug use, and a strong economy.

Multiple choice 9
Essay 2

incapacitation
The policy of keeping dangerous criminals in confinement to eliminate the risk of their repeating their offense in society.

PERSPECTIVES ON JUSTICE

Although the merits of incarcerating criminals are still open to debate, there is no question that incapacitation strategies that reflect the justice perspective are now in vogue. Mandatory life sentences for three-time felons—the so-called "three strikes and you're out" model—have been adopted in a number of states, including California. Sentencing laws that require a mandatory prison stay for people convicted of drug- and gun-related crimes are common. States have also toughened juvenile laws. Many young people who in the past would have been treated in the juvenile justice system are now being sent to adult courts and, if convicted, incarcerated in adult prisons.

Specific Deterrence

True/False 5
Multiple choice 10

Experiencing harsh criminal punishments should convince convicted offenders that crime does not pay and recidivism is not in their best interests. The suffering caused by punishment should inhibit future law violations.

Efforts to verify a specific deterrent effect on crime rates have produced mixed results. Chronic offender research indicates that arrest and punishment seem to have little effect on experienced criminals and may even increase the likelihood that first-time offenders will commit new crimes.[9] About 70 percent of prison inmates have had prior convictions, and more than 60 percent return to prison within three years of their release.[10] Incarceration may sometimes slow down or delay recidivism in the short term, but the overall probability of rearrest does not change following a period of incarceration.[11] Nor does leniency seem to help: Offenders who receive community sentences, such as probation, have rates of recidivism similar to those who are sentenced to prison.[12] Punishment may bring defiance rather than deterrence, and the stigma produced by apprehension may help lock offenders into a criminal career.

PERSPECTIVES ON JUSTICE

Although specific deterrence is a key element of the crime control perspective, questions of justice and propriety arise when punishment is designed to prevent future law violations, even though the person may never again violate the law. For example, executing a traitor serves no other practical purpose beyond vengeance: The damage has already been done, and even if released, the spy presents no future danger to society (because the person would never again have access to sensitive material).

Retribution/Just Desert

Fill in the blanks 5
True/False 6

According to the retributive goal of sentencing, the essential purpose of the criminal process is to punish offenders fairly and justly, in a manner that is proportionate to the gravity of their crimes.[13] If the law did not exact retribution, private citizens might be motivated to seek personal revenge.

From this perspective, offenders are punished simply and solely because they deserve to be disciplined for what they have done: "The punishment should fit the crime."[14] It would be wrong to punish people to set an example for others or to deter would-be criminals, as the general deterrence goal demands. Punishment should be no more or less than the offender's actions deserve; it must be based on how blameworthy the person is. This is referred to as the concept of **just desert**.[15]

PERSPECTIVES ON JUSTICE

Admired by advocates of the justice perspective, the just desert philosophy of punishment holds that criminal sentences should be proportional to the seriousness of an offender's criminal act. Offenders are punished for what they have already done, not for what they may do in the future or for what others may do unless they learn to fear punishment. Sentencing based on just deserts evaluates the weight of the criminal act, not the needs of the offender or the community. It demands that punishments be equally and fairly distributed to all people who commit similar illegal acts. Determining just punishments can be difficult because there is generally little consensus about the treatment of criminals, the seriousness of crimes, and the proper response to criminal acts.

just desert
The view that those who violate the rights of others deserve punishment commensurate with the seriousness of the crime.

Rehabilitation

True/False 7–8

Can criminal offenders be effectively treated so that they can eventually readjust to society? It may be fairer to offer offenders an opportunity for rehabilitation rather than harsh criminal punishments. In a sense, society has failed criminal offenders, many of whom have grown up in disorganized neighborhoods and dysfunctional families. They may have been the target of biased police officers, and once arrested and labeled, they are placed at a disadvantage at home, school, and in the job market.[16] Society is therefore obligated to help these unfortunate people who, through no fault of their own, experience social and emotional problems that are often the root of their criminal behavior.

The rehabilitation aspect of sentencing is based on a prediction of the future needs of the offender and not on the gravity of the current offense. For example, if a judge sentences a person convicted of a felony to a period of community supervision, the judge's actions reflect his or her belief that the offender can be successfully treated and presents no future threat to society. This faith is supported by studies showing that under the right circumstances rehabilitation efforts can be quite effective.[17]

The rehabilitation goal of sentencing has been criticized by those who find little conclusive evidence that correctional treatment programs can prevent future criminality.[18] The rehabilitative ideal has been undermined by such attacks, but surveys indicate that the general public still supports the treatment goal of sentencing.[19] Many people express preferences for programs that are treatment oriented, such as early childhood

Should a person's age or gender affect sentencing decisions? Faye Copeland, the nation's oldest woman on death row, is now 78 years old. Copeland's death sentence was commuted to life in prison by a federal judge on Aug. 10, 1999. She was convicted with her husband, Ray, of the murder of five men in a livestock swindle deal.

AP/Wide World Photos

intervention and services for at-risk children, over strict punishment and incarceration policies.[20]

Restitution/Equity

Because criminals gain from their misdeeds, it seems both fair and just to demand that they reimburse society for the losses caused by their crimes. In the early common law, wergild and fines represented the concept of **equity** by requiring the convicted offender to make restitution to both the victim and the state. Today, judges continue to require that offenders pay victims for their losses.

The equity goal of punishment means that convicted criminals must pay back their victims for their loss, the justice system for the costs of processing their case, and society for any disruption they may have caused. In a so-called victimless crime, such as drug trafficking, the social costs might include the expense of drug enforcement efforts, drug treatment centers, and care for infants born to drug-addicted mothers. In predatory crimes, the costs might include the services of emergency room doctors, lost workdays and productivity, and treatment for long-term psychological problems. To help defray these costs, convicted offenders might be required to pay a fine, forfeit any property acquired through illegal activity, do community service work, make financial restitution to their victims, and reimburse the state for the costs of the criminal process. Because the criminals' actions helped expand their personal benefits, rights, and privileges at society's expense, justice demands that they lose benefits, rights, and privileges to restore the social balance.[21]

The various goals that influence sentencing decisions are illustrated in Figure 13.1.

Fill in the blanks 6
Essay 3

equity
Sanction designed to compensate victims and society for the losses caused by crime; restitution.

FIGURE 13.1
THE GOALS
BEHIND
SENTENCING
DECISIONS

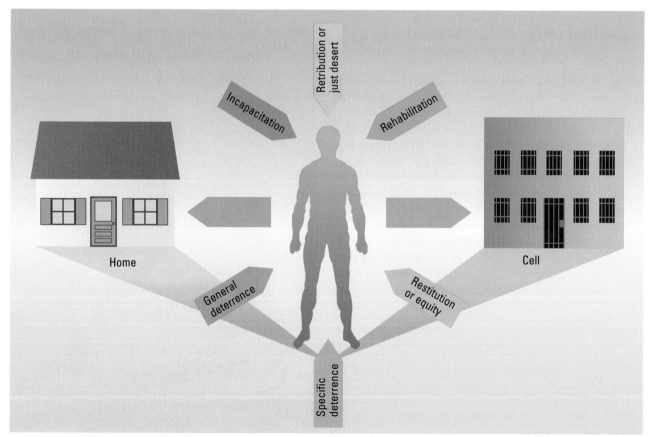

IMPOSING THE SENTENCE

Sentencing is one of the most crucial functions of a judge. Sentencing authority may also be exercised by a jury, or it may be mandated by statute (for example, a mandatory prison sentence for a certain crime).

In most felony cases, except where the law provides for mandatory prison terms, sentencing is based on a variety of information available to the judge. Some jurisdictions allow victims to make impact statements that are considered at sentencing hearings. Most judges also consider a presentence investigation report by the probation department. This report provides a social and personal history of the defendant, as well as an evaluation of his or her chances for rehabilitation within the community. Some judges give the presentence investigation report great weight; others may dismiss it completely or rely only on certain portions.

A defendant who is convicted of two or more charges must be sentenced on each charge. **Concurrent sentences** all begin on the same day and are completed when the longest term has been served. For example, suppose a defendant is convicted of burglarizing an apartment and assaulting its occupant. He is sentenced to 3 years on a charge of assault and 10 years for burglary, the sentences to be served concurrently. After 10 years in prison, the sentences would be completed.

A **consecutive sentence,** in contrast, means that only on completion of the sentence for one crime does the offender begin serving time for the other. If the defendant in the previous example had been sentenced consecutively, he would serve 3 years on the assault charge and then 10 for the burglary; therefore, the total term on the two charges would be 13 years. Concurrent sentences are the norm, but consecutive sentences may be requested for the most serious criminals and for those who are unwilling to cooperate with authorities. (See Figure 13.2.)

When a convicted offender is sentenced to prison, the statutes of the jurisdiction in which the crime was committed determine the penalties that may be imposed by the court. Over the years, a variety of sentencing structures have been used in the United States. They include indeterminate sentences, determinate sentences, and mandatory sentences.

Indeterminate Sentences

In the 1870s, prison reformers such as Enoch Wines and Zebulon Brockway called for the use of **indeterminate sentences** tailored to fit individual needs. Offenders, they argued, should be placed in confinement only until they were rehabilitated and then released on parole. Criminals were believed to be "sick" rather than bad; they could be successfully treated in prison. Rather than holding that "the punishment should fit the crime," reformers believed "the treatment should fit the offender."

Fill in the blanks 7
True/False 9
Multiple choice 11–12
Essay 4

concurrent sentence
Incarceration for more than one offense such that all sentences begin on the same day and are completed after the longest term has been served.

consecutive sentence
Incarceration for more than one offense such that each sentence begins only after the previous one has been completed.

indeterminate sentence
A term of incarceration with a stated minimum and maximum length; the prisoner is eligible for parole after serving the minimum.

Fill in the blanks 8
True/False 10–11
Multiple choice 13–14
Essay 5–6

FIGURE 13.2
CONSECUTIVE VERSUS CONCURRENT SENTENCES

Example: In state X	Consecutive Sentence	Concurrent Sentence
1. Rape is punishable by 10 years in prison 2. Possession of a handgun by 3 years 3. Possession of heroin by 4 years	Rape + Possession of a handgun + Possession of heroin 10 + 3 + 4 = 17 years (each sentence must be served)	Rape + Possession of a handgun + Possession of heroin 10 years (all sentences served simultaneously)

PERSPECTIVES ON JUSTICE

The indeterminate sentence is at the heart of the rehabilitation perspective on justice, because offenders may be released after a relatively short prison stay if they convince correctional authorities that they can forgo a criminal career. The view is that criminal offenders are "salvageable" and can be successfully treated by correctional authorities. Because many policymakers today believe that the rehabilitation of offenders has failed, more punitive sentencing schemes reflecting the crime control perspective are receiving greater consideration.

The indeterminate sentence is still the most widely used type of sentence in the United States. Convicted offenders are typically given a "light" minimum sentence that must be served and a lengthy maximum sentence that is the outer boundary of the time that can be served. For example, the legislature might set a sentence of a minimum of 2 years and a maximum of 20 years for burglary; the convicted offender must be sentenced to no less than 2 years but no more than 20 years in prison. Under this scheme, the actual length of time served by the offender is controlled both by the judge and by the correctional agency. If a judge sentences a burglar to "2 to 20," the inmate can be paroled from confinement soon after serving the minimum sentence if the correctional authorities believe that he or she is ready to live in the community; if the inmate accumulates good time, he or she could be released in 18 months. A troublesome inmate would be forced to serve the full 20 years.

The basic purpose of the indeterminate sentence is to individualize each sentence in the interests of rehabilitating the offender. This type of sentencing allows for flexibility not only in the type of sentence imposed but also in the length of time actually served. Following are some possible variations on the indeterminate sentence:

- The maximum sentence is set by the legislature and cannot be changed; the minimum is determined by the judge. For example, offender A might receive 1 to 20 years for burglary; offender B, 16 to 20; and offender C, 10 to 20.
- The judge sets both the maximum and the minimum sentence within guidelines set up by the legislature. For example, the minimum and maximum sentence for burglary might be 1 to 20 years. Offender A might get 1 to 20; offender B, 4 to 10; and offender C, 3 to 6. The maximum the judge imposes cannot exceed 20 years; the minimum cannot be less than 1 year.
- The maximum sentence is set by the judge within the upper limit, and the minimum is determined by the legislature. For example, all sentenced burglars must do at least 1 year in prison but no more than 20. Offender A might receive 1 to 10; offender B, 1 to 20; and offender C, 1 to 5.

Most jurisdictions that use indeterminate sentences have statutes that specify minimum and maximum terms but allow judges discretion to fix the actual sentence within those limits. The typical minimum sentence is at least 1 year; a few state jurisdictions require at least a 2-year minimum sentence for felons.[22]

The indeterminate sentence has come under attack in recent years for a variety of reasons. It is alleged to produce great disparity in the way people are treated in the correctional system. For example, one offender may serve 1 year and another may serve 20 for the same crime. Further, the indeterminate sentence is believed to take control of sentencing out of the hands of the judiciary and place it within the framework of corrections, especially when the minimum sentence is short. Every time an inmate granted early release via discretionary parole commits a violent crime, the call goes out to get tough on prison inmates. In contrast, many inmates feel cheated by the system when they are denied parole despite having a good prison record.

The protections of due process maintained in the courtroom are absent in the correctional setting. The 1970 publication of *Soledad Brother* by George Jackson exposed efforts to deny parole to a politically active inmate who campaigned for prison reform. Jackson served 11 years in the California correctional system after he was convicted on charges stemming from a $70 gas station robbery. Jackson's parole was continually denied because his political writings and activity indicated he had not yet been "rehabilitated." Jackson was convinced the authorities would never release him alive, and he was killed while trying to escape; his death was considered a political assassination by many of his supporters.[23]

Dissatisfaction with the disparity and uncertainty of indeterminate sentencing has prompted some states and the federal government to abandon it in favor of determinate or structured sentencing models.

Determinate Sentences

Fill in the blanks 9
True/False 12–13
Multiple choice 15–16

In 1969, Kenneth Culp Davis published *Discretionary Justice,* followed in 1972 by Judge Marvin Frankel's landmark study, *Law without Order.*[24] These works exposed the disparities in indeterminate sentencing and called for reform of the criminal law. Frankel wrote, "The almost wholly unchecked and sweeping powers we give to judges in the fashioning of sentences are terrifying and intolerable for a society that professes devotion to the rule to law."[25]

Concern focused on the degree of disparity in the sentencing process. Offenders with identical criminal records who were convicted of similar offenses were given widely disparate sentences. All too often, discretion seemed to aid the wealthy and powerful and harm the poor, the vulnerable, and members of minority groups.[26] Noted scholar Andrew von Hirsch argued that if the justice system could neither reform criminals nor bring down the crime rate, then it should at least be able to "do justice" in a fair and equitable manner.[27] James Q. Wilson called for sentencing reforms that would ensure that chronic criminal offenders would at least be incapacitated.[28] Conservative politicians wanted to control the rising crime rate by putting more offenders behind bars, whereas liberals emphasized the uncertainty of indeterminate sentencing and inequities in the parole process. The outcome was the adoption of **determinate sentences** in some of the nation's largest jurisdictions.

determinate sentence
A fixed term of incarceration.

Determinate sentences were actually the first kind used in the United States and are today employed in about ten jurisdictions. As originally conceived, a determinate sentence was a fixed term of years, up to a maximum set in law by the legislature, to be served by the offender sentenced to prison for a particular crime. For example, if the law provided for a sentence of up to 20 years for robbery, the judge might sentence a repeat offender to a 15-year term; another, less experienced felon might receive a more lenient sentence of 5 years.

Although determinate sentences specify a term of years to be served without benefit of parole, the actual time spent in prison can be reduced by "time off for good behavior." This concept was first used in 1817 in New York, and it was quickly adopted in most other jurisdictions. **Good time** is still in use today; inmates can accrue good time at a rate ranging from 10 to 15 days per month. In addition, some correctional authorities grant earned sentence reductions to inmates who participate in treatment programs, such as educational and vocational training, or who volunteer for experimental medical testing programs. More than half of a determinate sentence can be erased by accumulating standard and earned good time.

good time
Reduction of a prison sentence by a specified amount in exchange for good behavior within the institution.

Good time laws allow inmates to calculate their release date at the time they enter prison by subtracting the expected good time from their sentence. However, good time can be lost if inmates break prison rules, get into fights, or disobey correctional officers. In some jurisdictions, former inmates can be returned to prison to serve the balance of their unexpired sentence when their good time is revoked for failing to conform to conditions set down for their release (for example, not reporting to a postrelease supervisor or abusing drugs).

Sentencing Guidelines   To ensure that the new determinate sentences would be applied in a fair manner, those jurisdictions that embraced determinate sentencing have also sought to develop **sentencing guidelines** to control and structure the sentencing process and make it more "rational." Sentencing guidelines are usually based on the seriousness of a crime and the background of an offender: the more serious the crime and the more extensive the offender's criminal background, the longer the prison term recommended by the guidelines. For example, guidelines might require that all people convicted of robbery who had no prior offense record and who did not use excessive force or violence be given an average sentence of five years, and that those who used force and had a prior record have three years added to their sentence. Guidelines eliminate discretionary parole but still allow inmates to reduce their sentence through time off for good behavior. By eliminating judicial discretion, they are designed to reduce racial and gender disparity. [29]

A total of 17 states use some form of structured sentencing. Seven of these have *voluntary/advisory sentencing guidelines* (sometimes called *descriptive guidelines*) that merely suggest rather than mandate sentencing. The other 10 states have *presumptive sentencing guidelines* (sometimes called *prescriptive guidelines*). In these states, judges are required to use the guidelines to shape their sentencing decisions, and their sentencing decisions may be open to appellate review if they stray from the mandated sentences. Michigan, Washington, Oregon, Pennsylvania, Minnesota, North Carolina, and the federal government mandate that judges follow a set of comprehensive guidelines.[30]

Prescriptive guidelines are created by appointed sentencing commissions. The commission members determine what an "ideal" sentence would be for a particular crime and offender. There is a great deal of variation, however, within prescriptive sentencing. Some guidelines coexist with parole release; some do not. Some deal with all crimes; others, only with felonies. Some set narrow sentencing ranges; others set broad ones. Some address sentences of all types; others address only state prison sentences.[31] North Carolina, Pennsylvania, and Ohio have a *comprehensive structured sentencing* system, which sets sentencing standards for felonies and misdemeanors, and for prison, jail, intermediate, and community punishments. They also include mechanisms for tying sentencing policy to correctional capacity and for distributing state funds to stimulate and support local corrections programs.[32]

Configuring Guidelines   Guidelines can be formulated in a number of ways. One method is to create a grid with prior record and current offense as the two coordinates and then set out specific punishments; Minnesota's guidelines, shown in Table 13.1, are a good example. Note that as prior record and offense severity increase, so does recommended sentence length. After a certain point, probation is no longer an option, and the defendant must do prison time. A burglar with no prior convictions can expect to receive probation or an 18-month sentence for a house break-in; an experienced burglar with six or more prior convictions can get 54 months for the same crime, and probation is not an option.

The federal government uses a cookbook approach to determine the actual sentence. A magistrate must first determine the base penalty that a particular charge is given in the guidelines; for example, robbery has a base score of 20. The

---

sentencing guidelines
Specification of sentences based on the seriousness of the crime and the criminal background of the offender.

TABLE 13.1   MINNESOTA'S SENTENCING GUIDELINE GRID

Severity Level of Conviction Offense		Criminal History Score						
		0	1	2	3	4	5	6 or More
Murder, second degree (intentional murder; drive-by shootings)	X	306 *299–313*	326 *319–333*	346 *339–353*	366 *359–373*	386 *379–393*	406 *399–413*	426 *419–433*
Murder, third degree Murder, second degree (unintentional murder)	IX	150 *144–156*	165 *159–171*	180 *174–186*	195 *189–201*	210 *204–216*	225 *219–231*	240 *234–246*
Criminal sexual conduct, first degree Assault, first degree	VIII	86 *81–91*	98 *93–103*	110 *105–115*	122 *117–127*	134 *129–139*	146 *141–151*	158 *153–163*
Aggravated robbery, first degree	VII	48 *44–52*	58 *54–62*	68 *64–72*	78 *74–82*	88 *84–92*	98 *94–102*	108 *104–112*
Criminal sexual conduct, second degree	VI	21	26	30	34 *33–35*	44 *42–46*	54 *50–58*	65 *60–70*
Residential burglary Simple robbery	V	18	23	27	30 *29–31*	38 *36–40*	46 *43–49*	54 *50–58*
Nonresidential burglary	IV	12*	15	18	21	25 *24–26*	32 *30–34*	41 *37–45*
Theft crimes (over $2,500)	III	12*	13	15	17	19 *18–20*	22 *21–23*	25 *24–26*
Theft crimes ($2,500 or less) Check forgery ($200–$2,500)	II	12*	12*	13	15	17	19	21 *20–22*
Sale of simulated controlled substance	I	12*	12*	12*	13	15	17	19 *18–20*

NOTE: Italicized numbers within the grid denote the range within which a judge may sentence without the sentence being deemed a departure. Offenders with nonimprisonment felony sentences are subject to jail time according to law.

*One year and one day.

    Presumptive commitment to state imprisonment. First-degree murder is excluded from the guidelines by law and continues to have a mandatory life sentence.

    Presumptive stayed sentence; at the discretion of the judge, up to one year in jail and/or other nonjail sanctions can be imposed as conditions of probation. However, certain offenses in this section of the grid always carry a presumptive commitment to a state prison. These offenses include third-degree controlled substance crimes when the offender has a prior felony drug conviction, burglary of an occupied dwelling when the offender has a prior felony burglary conviction, second and subsequent criminal sexual conduct offenses, and offenses carrying a mandatory minimum prison term due to the use of a dangerous weapon (e.g., second-degree assault).

SOURCE: Minnesota Sentencing Guideline Commission, 1996.

base level can be adjusted upward if the crime was particularly serious or violent. For example, 7 points can be added to the robbery base if a firearm was discharged during the crime, and 5 points if the weapon was simply in the offender's possession. Similarly, points can be added to a robbery if a large amount of money was taken, a victim was injured, a person was abducted or restrained in order to facilitate an escape, or the object of the robbery was to steal weapons or drugs. Upward adjustments can also be made if the defendant was a ringleader in the crime, obstructed justice, or used a professional skill or position of trust (such as doctor, lawyer, or politician) to commit the crime. Offenders designated as "career criminals" by a court can likewise receive longer sentences.

Given the base score, judges determine the actual sentence by consulting a table that converts scores into months to be served. Offense levels are set out in the vertical column, and the criminal history (ranging from one to six prior

The duties of the United States Sentencing Commission, an independent federal agency in the judicial branch of government, include developing guidelines for sentencing in federal courts, collecting data about crime and sentencing, and serving as a resource on crime and sentencing policy for Congress, the executive branch, and the judiciary. Visit their Web site at http://www.ussc.gov/

For an up-to-date list of Web links, see http://www.wadsworth.com/product/0534573053s

Essay 7

offenses) is displayed in a horizontal column, forming a grid that contains the various sentencing ranges (similar to the Minnesota guidelines grid). By matching the applicable offense level to the criminal history, the judge can determine the sentence that applies to the particular offender.

How Effective Are Guidelines? Despite the widespread acceptance of guidelines, some nagging problems remain. A number of critics, including Michael Tonry, argue that they are rigid, harsh, overly complex, and disliked by the judiciary and should be substantially revised or totally eliminated![33] Though they were designed to eliminate racial and social disparity, the effects of race, gender, and economic status continue to be debated.[34] Evaluations of the Minnesota guidelines show that African American offenders are more likely to be charged with weapons violations and, consequently, more likely to receive prison terms than white offenders.[35] Similarly, possession of crack cocaine is punished far more severely by federal guidelines than possession of powdered cocaine. Critics charge that this amounts to racial bias because African Americans are much more likely to possess crack and whites, powder.[36] Some jurisdictions give enhanced sentences if the defendant had a prior juvenile conviction or was on juvenile probation or parole at the time of an arrest. African American offenders are more likely than white offenders to have a prior juvenile record and therefore receive harsher sentences for their current crime.[37]

Some defense attorneys oppose the use of guidelines because they result in longer prison terms, prevent judges from considering mitigating circumstances, and reduce the use of probation. Even the widely heralded federal guidelines have had and will continue to have some dubious effects. The use of probation has diminished and the size of the federal prison population is increasing because guideline sentences are tougher and defendants have very little incentive to plea bargain. The guidelines require incarceration sentences for minor offenders who previously would have been given community release; many of these petty offenders might be better served with cheaper alternative sanctions.[38] The amount of time served by offenders will almost double in the future as a result of guidelines coupled with sentencing enhancement statutes. For example, robbers who served approximately 45 months before the guidelines were implemented now serve 75; drug offenders will see their sentences increase on average from 23 months to 57 months. These sentencing enhancements will boost the federal prison population by up to 60,000 inmates by the year 2002.

These problems are not lost on the federal judiciary, many of whom dislike the guidelines, considering them too harsh, rigid, and mechanical. Some judges believe that the guidelines give too much power to prosecutors, who make the charging decision. They may even engage in "hidden" plea bargaining in order to manipulate the guidelines and allow offenders to plead to a lesser charge which they and the prosecutor believe is more appropriate. Because of these problems, sentencing expert Michael Tonry calls them "the most controversial and disliked sentencing reform initiative in United States history.[39] His vision is shared by legal experts Kate Stith and Jose Cabranes, who argue that the guidelines' zeal for equal treatment comes at the expense of deserved treatment.[40] By attempting to decree in advance what should count in sentencing, and how much, the guidelines ignore "the irreducible need for individualized judgment and for humanity as well as rationality in sentencing."[41] Efforts to create the proper sentence before someone actually commits a crime and is adjudicated, investigated, and sentenced is doomed to failure, because "no system of formal rules can fully capture our intuitions about what justice requires."[42]

In his important book *Sentencing Matters,* Tonry offers a prescription to improve structured sentencing guidelines. He calls for the creation of ongoing sentencing commissions, establishment of realistic guidelines, reliance on alternative

The Coalition for Federal Sentencing Reform is a private group of individuals and organizations united by a concern that the federal sentencing guidelines are not fulfilling their promise, and by a desire for reform. To find out their reasons, go to http://www.sentencing.org/

For an up-to-date list of Web links, see http://www.wadsworth.com/product/0534573053s

sanctions, and a sentencing philosophy that stresses the "least punitive and intrusive appropriate sentence."[43]

Mandatory Sentences

Another effort to limit judicial discretion and at the same time "get tough" on crime has been the passage of **mandatory sentence** laws. Some states, for example, prohibit people convicted of certain offenses, such as violent crimes, as well as multiple offenders (recidivists), from being placed on probation; they must serve at least some time in prison. Other statutes prohibit certain offenders from being considered for parole. Mandatory sentencing laws may impose minimum and maximum terms, but typically they require a fixed prison sentence. They can also serve as sentencing enhancement measures, requiring that people spend additional time behind bars if they commit a crime in a particular manner, such as carrying a firearm while committing a burglary.

Mandatory sentencing laws generally limit the judge's discretionary power to impose any disposition but that authorized by the legislature; as a result, they limit individualized sentencing and restrict sentencing disparity. They are designed to provide equal treatment for all offenders who commit the same crime, regardless of age, sex, or other individual characteristics.

Fill in the blanks 10
Multiple choice 17

mandatory sentence
A statutory requirement that a certain penalty be set and carried out in all cases on conviction for a specified offense or series of offenses.

PERSPECTIVES ON JUSTICE

Although crime control advocates applaud determinate and mandatory sentences, critics fear that they will swell prison populations, costing taxpayers additional billions and taking money away from more important public needs such as health care and education. Others fear that these sentencing policies will further exacerbate racial disparity in the prison population. What may work for crime control advocates draws cries of protest from due process advocates and sighs of resignation from rehabilitation advocates, who believe in offender treatment.

© Donna Binder/Impact Visuals

Prisoners on a chain gang work off their sentences. The "get tough" movement has prompted harsh penal measures as well as long and mandatory prison sentences. Even though these measures are often aimed at eliminating sentencing disparity, critics claim that African Americans are more likely to receive harsher punishment than whites.

The National Association of Criminal Defense Lawyers (NACDL) is a nonpartisan organization that encourages, at the federal, state, and local levels, a rational and humane criminal justice policy. Visit their Web site at http://www.criminaljustice. org/public.nsf/freeform/ legislativepriorities

For an up-to-date list of Web links, see http://www.wadsworth.com/ product/0534573053s

Essay 9

More than 35 states have already replaced discretionary sentencing with fixed-term mandatory sentences for such crimes as the sale of hard drugs, kidnapping, gun possession, and arson. As a result, many offenders who in the past might have received probation are now being incarcerated. The results have been mixed. Critics charge that mandatory sentences have helped increase the size of the correctional population to record levels and have failed to eliminate racial disparity from the sentencing process.[44]

It has also been suggested that mandatory sentences have failed as a crime deterrent. One reason may be that prosecutors and judges are sometimes reluctant to charge people with crimes that carry mandatory sentences if they fear that the resulting sentence may be too severe. Research shows, for example, that drug traffickers who are going to receive long sentences are rarely charged with possession of handguns, even though they are eligible for punishment under mandatory sentencing enhancement laws. Perhaps judges and prosecutors believe that the additional firearm penalty, given the already severe sentences for drugs, would be a matter of overkill.[45]

PATTERNS OF SENTENCING

How are people sentenced? Some of the most important information comes from national studies sponsored by the Bureau of Justice Statistics.[46] In 1996 (the most recent data available), state courts convicted more than 997,000 adults of murder, rape, robbery, drug trafficking, and other felony offenses. The likelihood of arrestees being convicted has increased (Table 13.2), helping in part to explain why the correctional population has been increasing while the crime rate has dropped.

In 1996, 38 percent of convicted felons were sentenced to a state prison, 31 percent were sentenced to a local jail (usually for a year or less), and the remaining 31 percent were sentenced to straight probation. The percentage of felons receiving a state prison sentence has been trending downward, from 45 percent in 1988 to about 38 percent today. The drop in prison sentences has been accompanied by an increase in the percentage receiving other types of sentences, particularly sentences to local jails (from 25 to 31 percent). (See Figure 13.3.)

Though fewer people are being sent to prison, the correctional population continues to rise. One reason may be that although the average court-imposed sentence has been decreasing, the amount of time actually spent behind bars before release is increasing (Tables 13.3). In 1988, the typical felon received a 6-year sentence and served about a third of that sentence, or 2 years, before being released. By contrast, in 1996, the typical felon received a 5-year sentence and served about half of that, or 2.5 years. In 1988, the average murderer spent 79 months in prison; by 1996, the average was 128 months. The increased time spent behind bars may be due in part to the passage of tough new sentencing laws, discussed in the Analyzing Criminal Justice Issues feature on page 416, which require offenders to remain incarcerated for a considerable portion of their sentence.

Factors That Affect Sentencing

What factors influence judges when they decide on criminal sentences? Crime seriousness and the

TABLE 13.2 THE LIKELIHOOD THAT A FELONY ARREST WILL RESULT IN CONVICTION

	1988	1992	1996
Murder	48%	65%	71%
Robbery	32	41	40
Aggravated assault	10	14	16
Burglary	33	41	41
Drug trafficking	39	55	66

SOURCE: David J. Levin, Patrick A. Langan, and Jodi M. Brown, *State Court Sentencing of Convicted Felons, 1996* (Washington, DC: Bureau of Justice Statistics, February 2000).

Percentage of convicted felons sentenced
to prison, jail, or probation

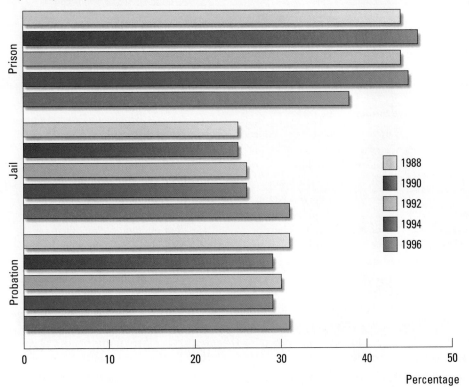

FIGURE 13.3
PERCENTAGE OF
CONVICTED
FELONS
SENTENCED TO
PRISON, JAIL, OR
PROBATION

SOURCE: *State Court Sentencing of Convicted Felons, 1996*, p. 50.

TABLE 13.3 AVERAGE PRISON SENTENCE, PERCENT SERVED, AND ACTUAL TIME TO BE SERVED BY FELONS: 1988, 1992, AND 1996

	Average Imposed Prison Sentence (in months)				Percent of Imposed Prison Sentence Actually Served				Estimated Actual Time to Be Served in Prison (in months)		
	1988	1992	1996		1988	1992	1996		1988	1992	1996
All offenses	76 mo	79 mo	62 mo	**All offenses**	32%	38%	45%	**All offenses**	24 mo	30 mo	28 mo
Murder	239	251	257	Murder	33	44	50	Murder	79	110	128
Robbery	114	117	101	Robbery	33	46	47	Robbery	38	54	48
Aggravated assault	90	87	69	Aggravated assault	36	48	54	Aggravated assault	32	42	38
Burglary	74	76	60	Burglary	30	35	42	Burglary	22	27	25
Larceny	50	53	40	Larceny	29	33	44	Larceny	15	17	17
Drug trafficking	66	72	55	Drug trafficking	30	34	42	Drug trafficking	20	24	23

SOURCE: *State Court Sentencing of Convicted Felons, 1996*, p. 7.

ANALYZING CRIMINAL JUSTICE ISSUES

Let's Get Tough: Truth in Sentencing and Three Strikes Laws

Public concern over crime has convinced lawmakers to toughen sentences for repeat offenders and those who commit serious crimes. Two efforts stand out: truth-in-sentencing laws and three-strikes laws.

Truth in Sentencing

Truth-in-sentencing laws, first enacted in 1984, require offenders to serve a substantial portion of their prison sentence behind bars. Parole eligibility and good time credits are restricted or eliminated. The movement was encouraged by the Violent Offender Incarceration and Truth-in-Sentencing Incentive Grants Program, part of the federal Crime Act of 1994, which offered states funds to support the costs involved in enforcing longer sentences. To qualify for federal funds, states must require persons convicted of a violent felony to serve not less than 85 percent of their prison sentence.

The provision is already having an effect. Violent offenders released from prison in 1996 had been sentenced to serve an average of 85 months in prison; prior to release, they had served about half their prison sentence, or 45 months. Under truth-in-sentencing laws requiring that 85% of a sentence be served, and given the average sentence for violent offenders admitted to prison in 1996, violent offenders would serve an average of 88 months in prison. Eleven states adopted truth-in-sentencing laws in 1995, the year after the 1994 Crime Act. By 1998, 27 states and the District

of Columbia met the federal Truth-in-Sentencing Incentive Grant Program eligibility criteria.

Three Strikes

Another new group of laws mandates lengthy periods of incarceration for repeat offenders, which in some cases can mean a life sentence for a minor felony. The new "three strikes and you're out" laws provide these lengthy terms for any person convicted of three felony offenses, even if the third crime is relatively trivial. California's three-strikes law is aimed at getting habitual criminals off the street. Anyone convicted of a third serious felony must do a minimum term of 25 years to life; the third felony does not have to be serious or violent. The Federal Crime Bill of 1994 also adopted a three-strikes provision, requiring a mandatory life sentence for any offender convicted of three felony offenses; 22 states have so far followed suit and passed some form of the three-strikes law.

Though welcomed by conservatives looking for a remedy for violent crime, the three-strikes policy remains controversial because it can mean that a person convicted of a minor felony can receive a life sentence. There are reports that some judges are defying three-strikes provisions because they consider them unduly harsh. Much to the chagrin of three-strikes advocates, the California Supreme Court has ruled that judges may disregard an earlier conviction if they believe that a life term is unjustified.

Three-strikes laws may in fact help put some chronic offenders behind bars, but can they realistically be expected to lower the crime rate? Marc Mauer of the Sentencing Project, a private group that conducts research on justice-related issues, finds that the three-strikes approach may satisfy the public's hunger for retribution but makes little practical sense. First, "three-time losers" are at the brink of aging out of crime; locking them up for life should have little effect on the crime rate. Second, current sentences for chronic violent offenders are already severe, yet their punishment seems to have had little influence on reducing national violence rates. Mauer also suggests that a three-strikes policy will enlarge an already overburdened prison system, driving up costs and, presumably, reducing resources available to house non-three-strikes inmates. Mauer also warns that African Americans face an increased risk of being sentenced under three-strikes statutes, expanding the racial disparity in sentencing. More ominous is the fact that police officers may be put at risk because two-time offenders would violently resist arrest, knowing that they face a life sentence.

Three-strikes laws have undeniable political appeal to legislators being pressured by their constituents to "do something about crime." Yet even if possibly effective against crime, any effort to deter criminal behavior through tough laws has its costs. A study by the Rand Corporation, a California-based think

Essay 8

Fill in the blanks 11–12
True/False 14–18
Multiple choice 18
Essay 10

offender's prior record are certainly considered. State sentencing codes usually list various factors that can legitimately influence the length of prison sentences, including:

- The severity of the offense
- The offender's prior criminal record
- Whether the offender used violence

tank, concluded that the state's three-strikes law may actually reduce serious felonies between 22% and 34%. However, the price of this reduction is an extra $4.5 to $6.5 billion per year in correctional costs in California alone. To put that in perspective, just the additional cost of the three-strikes policy would be sufficient to give more than 1 million students a full-tuition scholarship to the state university system!

Although many states have passed three-strikes laws, most rarely invoke the penalty. California is one of the few to have used it with thousands of offenders. Although many of these have committed serious crimes, as of 1996, 192 people had been sentenced to life in prison for possession of marijuana. Because of their application to petty offenders, three-strikes laws face ongoing legal challenges, and their future remains uncertain.

Although California officials attribute reduced crime rates to its three-strikes policy, others are skeptical about this approach. The Rand researchers argue that an alternative scheme would be to guarantee a full term in prison for serious felons without the possibility of probation, parole, or time off for good behavior. Their research shows that a guaranteed full-term policy would achieve the same benefits at a much lower cost.

As Mark Mauer points out, "Three-strikes policies tend to incarcerate people at the tail end of their offending career, at a point when they may be on the verge of spontaneously 'aging out' of crime." A three-strikes policy also suffers because criminals typically underestimate their risk of apprehension while overestimating the rewards of crime. Given their inflated view of the benefits of crime, coupled with a seeming disregard of the risks of apprehension and punishment, it is unlikely that a three-strikes policy can have a measurable deterrent effect on the crime rate. And even if such a policy could reduce the number of career offenders on the street, the drain on economic resources that might have gone for education and social welfare ensures that a new generation of young criminals will fill the offending shoes of their incarcerated brethren.

Critical Thinking Skills

1. Is a policy that calls for spending billions on incarceration throwing money into the wind? After all, the number of people in prison already exceeds 1 million, and there is little conclusive evidence that incarceration alone can reduce crime rates. Might the funds earmarked for prison construction be used elsewhere with greater effect?

2. A large portion of the prison population consists of drug offenders, and this group has seen the greatest overall increase during the past decade. While the number of people incarcerated for violent and property crimes has actually decreased in recent years, the number of incarcerated drug offenders has skyrocketed. Are the nation's interests best served by giving a life sentence to someone convicted of a third drug trafficking charge, even if the crime involves selling a small amount of cocaine?

InfoTrac College Edition Research

John DiIulio, one of the nation's most prominent conservative criminologists, is opposed to laws giving mandatory sentences to drug offenders. To find out why, read

John J. DiIulio, "Against Mandatory Minimums," *National Review,* 17 May 1999, v51 i9 p46(1)

SOURCES: Paula M. Ditton and Doris James Wilson, *Truth in Sentencing in State Prisons* (Washington: DC: Bureau of Justice Statistics, 1999), p. 108; "California Supreme Court Undercuts Three-Strikes Law," *Criminal Justice Newsletter,* 1 July 1996, p. 2; "Three-Strikes Laws Rarely Used, Except California's, Study Finds," *Criminal Justice Newsletter,* 17 September 1996, p. 4; "California Passes a Tough Three-Strikes-You're-Out Law," *Criminal Justice Newsletter,* 4 April 1993, p. 6; Rand Research Brief, *California's New Three-Strikes Law: Benefits, Costs and Alternatives* (Santa Monica, CA: Rand Corporation, 1994); Marc Mauer, testimony before the U.S. Congress House Judiciary Committee on "Three Strikes and You're Out," 1 March 1994 (Washington, DC: The Sentencing Project, 1994); Lois Forer, *A Rage to Punish: The Unintended Consequences of Mandatory Sentencing* (New York: Norton, 1994).

- Whether the offender used weapons
- Whether the crime was committed for money

Research studies do in fact show a strong correlation between these legal variables and the type and length of sentence received. For example, judges seem less willing to use discretion in cases involving the most serious criminal charges, such as terrorism, but use greater control in less serious cases.[47]

In addition to these legally appropriate factors, sentencing experts suspect that judges may also be influenced by the defendant's age, race, gender, and income. Consideration of such variables would be a direct violation of constitutional due process and equal protection, as well as of federal statutes such as the Civil Rights Act. Limiting judicial bias is one of the reasons that states have adopted determinate and mandatory sentencing statutes. Do extralegal factors actually influence judges when they make sentencing decisions?

Social Class Evidence supports an association between social class and sentencing outcomes: Members of the lower class may expect to get longer prison sentences than more affluent defendants. One reason is that poor defendants may be unable to obtain quality legal representation or to make bail, factors that influence sentencing.[48] Race may also influence the association between income and sentence length. At least in some jurisdictions, minorities receive longer sentences if they are currently indigent or unemployed than do Caucasians. It is possible that judges view their status as "social dynamite," considering them more dangerous and likely to recidivate than white offenders.[49]

Not all research efforts have found a consistent class–crime relationship, however, and the relationship may be more robust for some crime patterns than others.[50]

Johnny Lee Wilson served 10 years in prison before evidence proving his innocence came to light. Is it possible that indigent defendants get longer sentences than do affluent defendants because they cannot afford highly paid expert witnesses and expensive forensic tests?

Gender Does a defendant's gender influence how he or she is sentenced? Some theorists believe that females benefit from sentence disparity because the criminal justice system is dominated by males who have a paternalistic or protective attitude toward women; this is referred to as the **chivalry hypothesis**. Others argue that female criminals can be the victim of bias because their behavior violates what males believe is "proper" female behavior.[51]

Most research indicates that women receive more favorable outcomes the farther they go in the criminal justice system: They are more likely to receive preferential treatment from a judge at sentencing than they are from the police officer making the arrest or the prosecutor seeking the indictment.[52] Favoritism crosses both racial and ethnic lines, benefiting African American, Caucasian, and Hispanic women.[53] Gender bias may be present because judges perceive women as better risks than men. Women have been granted more lenient pretrial release conditions and lower bail amounts than men; women are also likely to spend less time in pretrial detention.[54]

Age Another extralegal factor that may play a role in sentencing is age. Judges may be more lenient with elderly defendants and more punitive toward younger ones.[55] Although sentencing leniency may be a result of judges' perception that the elderly pose little risk to society, such practices are a violation of the civil rights of younger defendants. On the other hand, judges may wish to protect the youngest defendants, sparing them the pains of a prison experience.

Research by Darrell Steffensmeier and his associates found that in fact judges often give the oldest and youngest offenders a break on their prison sentences while imposing the harshest terms on those ages 21–29.[56] Race and gender also influence the age–sentencing association: young African American males are sentenced more harshly than any other group.[57]

Victim Characteristics Victim characteristics may also influence sentencing. Victims may be asked to make a victim impact statement before the sentencing judge. This gives victims an opportunity to tell of their experiences and describe their ordeal; in the case of a murder trial, surviving family members can recount the

chivalry hypothesis
The idea that female defendants are treated more leniently in sentencing (and are less likely to be arrested and prosecuted in the first place) because the criminal justice system is dominated by men who have a paternalistic or protective attitude toward women.

Victims can play an important role in sentencing decisions. Here, Mark Dovey crosses the street in his wheelchair after attending the sentencing of Francisco Franco in Erie County Court, in Buffalo, N.Y., June 5, 2000. Franco shot and paralyzed Mark Dovey during a robbery. Franco was sentenced to 16½ to 23 years in prison.

AP/Wide World Photos

effect the crime has had on their lives and well-being.[58] The effect of witness statements on sentencing has been the topic of some debate. Some research finds that victim statements result in a higher rate of incarceration, but other studies have found the effect of witness statements to be insignificant.[59]

A victim's personal characteristics may influence sentencing. Sentences may be reduced when victims have negative personal characteristics or qualities. For example, rapists whose victims are described as prostitutes or substance abusers, or who have engaged in risky behaviors such as hitchhiking or going to bars alone, receive much shorter sentences than those who assault women without these negative characteristics.[60]

True/False 19

No issue concerning personal factors in sentencing is more important than the suspicion that race influences sentencing outcomes. Racial disparity in sentencing has been suspected because a disproportionate number of African American inmates are in state prisons and on death row. The war on drugs has been centered in African American communities, and politically motivated punitive sentencing policies aimed at crack cocaine have had a devastating effect on young African American men. If such punitive measures are allowed to continue or are even expanded, charges Michael Tonry, an entire cohort of young African Americans may be placed in jeopardy.[61] Because this issue is so important, it is the focus of a Race, Gender, and Ethnicity in Criminal Justice feature (see page 422).

CAPITAL PUNISHMENT

Multiple choice 19–20

The most severe sentence used in the United States is capital punishment, or execution. More than 14,500 confirmed executions have been carried out in America under civil authority, starting with the execution of Captain George Kendall in 1608. Most of these executions were for murder and rape. However, federal, state, and military laws have conferred the death penalty for other crimes, including robbery, kidnapping, treason (offenses against the federal government), espionage, and desertion from military service.

The death penalty for murder is used today in 38 states and by the federal government; public support of capital punishment is typically in the 75 to 80 percent range. Many years after abolishing it, New York reinstated the death penalty in 1995 and expanded its use to cover numerous acts, including serial murder, contract killing, and the use of torture.[62] (See Figure 13.4.)

**FIGURE 13.4
EXECUTIONS,
1930–1999**

In 1999, 98 inmates were executed, more than in any other year since the early 1950s.

SOURCE: *Capital Punishment 1999.* (Washington, DC: Bureau of Justice Statistics, 2000).

Number of executions, 1930–1999

If a person is to be sentenced to death, juries make the decision in 23 states, a judge in 5 states, and the judge with the recommendation of the jury in 7 states. In Missouri and New Mexico, either a jury or a judge may impose a sentence of death. In all states where the sentence is set by a jury, the decision must be unanimous. If the jury cannot reach agreement, life without parole is available in 12 states. A judge can alter a jury sentence of death in 12 states.[63]

In recent years, the Supreme Court has limited the death penalty to first-degree murder and then only when aggravating circumstances, such as murder for profit or murder with extreme cruelty, are present.[64] The federal government has provisions that impose the death penalty for espionage by a member of the armed forces, treason, and killing during a criminal conspiracy, such as drug trafficking. Some states still have laws assessing capital punishment for such crimes as aircraft piracy, ransom kidnapping, and the aggravated rape of a child, but it remains to be seen whether the courts will allow criminals to be executed today for any crime less than aggravated first-degree murder.

More than 3,500 people are currently on death row in the United States (see Figure 13.5). About 70 to 100 people are now executed each year; most have served 10 years on death row before their execution.[65] As of 2001, lethal injection was the predominant method of execution, though a number of states maintain the gas chamber and electric chair. In 1999, the Supreme Court refused to hear a case that challenged Florida's use of the electric chair as the sole means of execution. Even though the chair has malfunctioned several times, sending up smoke and flames, the Court refused to consider whether this amounted to cruel and unusual punishment. Of the 38 death penalty states, only Alabama, Georgia, and Nebraska still use the electric chair as the sole means of execution.[66]

Is the death penalty as popular overseas as it is in the United States? The International Justice feature on page 424 looks at the use of capital punishment worldwide.

No issue in the criminal justice system is more controversial or emotional than the implementation of the death penalty. Opponents and proponents have formulated a number of powerful arguments in support of their positions; these arguments are reviewed in the following sections.

Arguments for Retention

First, let's look at some of the most common arguments for retaining the death penalty in the United States.

The American Civil Liberties Union maintains a Web site that lists their various anti–capital punishment activities. You can access it at http://www.aclu.org/death-penalty/

For an up-to-date list of Web links, see http://www.wadsworth.com/product/0534573053s

Fill in the blanks 13
Essay 11–12

Prisoners on death row by race, 1968–1998

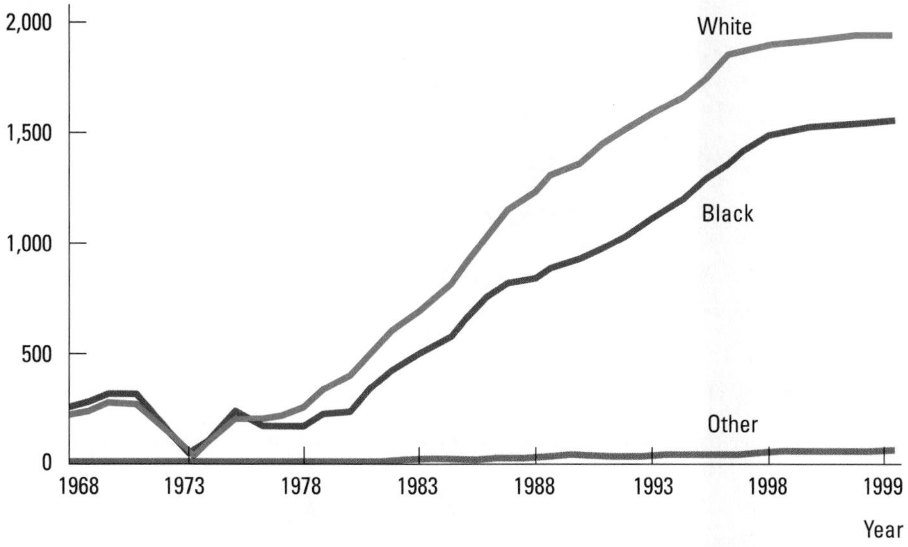

[Line graph showing prisoners on death row by race from 1968 to 1999. The vertical axis ranges from 0 to 2,000 in increments of 500. Three lines are shown: "White" rising to just under 2,000 by 1999, "Black" rising to about 1,500 by 1999, and "Other" remaining near 0 throughout. The horizontal axis shows years 1968, 1973, 1978, 1983, 1988, 1993, 1998, 1999 labeled "Year."]

FIGURE 13.5
PRISONERS ON DEATH ROW BY RACE, 1968–1999

Since the death penalty was reinstated by the Supreme Court in 1976, white inmates have made up the majority of those under sentence of death.

SOURCE: *Capital Punishment 1999.* (Washington, DC: Bureau of Justice Statistics, 2000).

Race and Sentencing

Although critics of American race relations may think otherwise, research on sentencing has failed to show a definitive pattern of racial discrimination. Some studies do indicate that a defendant's race has a direct impact on sentencing outcomes, but others find the influence of race on sentencing to be less clear-cut than anticipated. It is possible that the disproportionate number of minority inmates is a result of crime and arrest patterns, not racial bias by judges when they hand out criminal sentences. Members of racial and ethnic minorities commit more crime, the argument goes; therefore, they are more likely to wind up in prison. For example, the latest federal survey of sentencing in state courts shows that of those who were convicted, white felons were less likely than blacks to be sent to prison: 32 percent of convicted white defendants received a prison sentence, compared with 46 percent of black defendants. However, for those who were sent to prison, the average state prison sentence was about the same for white and black offenders (Figure A).

Despite the inconclusive evidence, racial disparity in sentencing has been suspected because a disproportionate number of minority inmates are in state prisons and on death row. Research shows that minority defendants suffer discrimination in a variety of court actions: They are more likely to be detained before trial than whites and, upon conviction, are more likely to receive jail sentences rather than fines. Prosecutors are less likely to divert minorities from the legal system than whites who commit the same crimes, and minorities are less likely than whites to win appeals.

The relationship between race and sentencing may be difficult to establish because their association may not be linear. Although minority defendants may be punished more severely for some crimes under some circumstances, they are treated more leniently for others. James Nelson, who studied misdemeanor sentencing in New York State,

found that minorities were given more lenient sentences than whites if they had no prior arrest record, but that African Americans with a prior arrest record received harsher sentences than whites with similar criminal backgrounds. Alexander Alverez and Ronet Bachman, who studied sentencing in Arizona, found that Native Americans received harsher sentences for robbery and burglary, but Caucasians were punished more harshly for homicide.

Sociologist Darnell Hawkins explains this phenomenon in terms of "appropriateness":

Certain crime types are considered less "appropriate" for blacks than for whites. Blacks who are charged with committing these offenses will be treated more severely than blacks who commit crimes that are considered more "appropriate." Included in the former category are various white collar offenses and crimes against political and social structures of authority. The latter groups of offenses would include various forms of victimless crimes associated with lower social status (e.g., prostitution, minor drug use, or drunkenness). This may

also include various crimes against the person, especially those involving black victims.

Race may affect sentencing because some race-specific crimes are punished more harshly than others. African Americans receive longer sentences for drug crimes than European Americans because (a) they are more likely to be arrested for crack possession and sale and (b) crack dealing is more severely punished by state and federal laws than other drug crimes. Because European Americans are more likely to use marijuana and metamphetamines, prosecutors are more willing to plea bargain and offer shorter jail terms.

Racial bias has also been linked to victim status. Minority defendants are sanctioned more severely if their victim is white than if their target is a fellow minority-group member. Judges may base sentencing decisions on the race of the victim, not the race of the defendant. For example, Charles Crawford, Ted Chiricos, and Gary Kleck found that African American defendants are more likely to be prosecuted under habitual

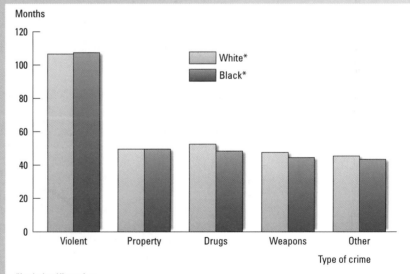

*Includes Hispanics

FIGURE A
LENGTH OF PRISON SENTENCE BY RACE

The average prison sentence imposed by state courts was nearly the same for whites and blacks in 1996.

SOURCE: *State Court Sentencing of Convicted Felons, 1996,* p. 8.

offender statutes if they commit crimes in which the victim is more likely to be white, such as larceny and burglary, than if they commit violent crimes that are largely intraracial. Where there is a perceived "racial threat" because of interracial crime, punishments are enhanced.

System Effects

Sentencing disparity may also reflect race-based differences in criminal justice practices and policies associated with sentencing outcome. Probation presentence reports may favor white over minority defendants, causing judges to award whites probation more often than minorities. Defendants who can afford bail receive more lenient sentences than those who remain in pretrial detention; minorities earn less on average and therefore are less likely to be able to make bail. Sentencing outcome is also affected by the defendant's ability to afford a private attorney and put on a vigorous legal defense that makes use of high-paid expert witnesses. These factors place the poor and minority-group members at a disadvantage in the sentencing process and result in sentencing disparity. And although prior record may be a legitimate consideration in sentencing decisions, there is evidence that minorities are more likely to have prior records because of organizational and individual bias on the part of police.

Jurisdictional Differences

The racial influence on sentencing varies significantly from state to state. Some states exhibit little racial bias, whereas others demonstrate a great deal. Studies that use multiple state data in their analyses may miss the effects of race on sentencing within particular states.

In a thorough review of sentencing disparity, Samuel Walker, Cassia Spohn, and Miriam Delone identify what they call *contextual discrimination*. This term refers to the practices of judges in some jurisdictions of imposing harsher sentences on African Americans who victimize whites or giving racial minorities prison sentences in "borderline" cases

for which whites get probation. It is also possible that sentencing disparity may be influenced by regional sentencing practices: The highest percentage of African Americans is in the South, where judges are more punitive to all defendants, regardless of race. According to their view, racism is very subtle and hard to detect but still exerts an influence in the court setting.

Are Sentencing Practices Changing?

If in fact racial discrepancies exist, new sentencing laws featuring determinate and mandatory sentences may be helping to reduce disparity. For example, Jon'a Meyer and Tara Gray found that jurisdictions in California that use mandatory sentences for crimes such as drunk driving also show little racial disparity in sentences between Caucasians and minority-group members. Similarly, a national survey of sentencing practices conducted by the Bureau of Justice Statistics found that, although white defendants are somewhat more likely to receive probation and other nonincarceration sentences than black defendants (34 percent versus 31 percent), there was little racial disparity in the length of prison sentences.

Critical Thinking Skills

Do you believe that sentences should be influenced by the fact that one ethnic or racial group is more likely to commit a given crime? For example, critics have called for changes in the way federal sentencing guidelines are designed, asking that the provisions that punish crack cocaine possession more heavily than powdered cocaine possession be repealed because African Americans are more likely to use crack and Caucasians powdered cocaine. Do you approve of such a change?

InfoTrac College Edition Research

Many African Americans are unwilling to cooperate with law enforcement and the courts because they believe

them to be racist.

Others believe that more enforcement is needed to protect African Americans from victimization. To read more on this debate, go to Carolyn Wolpert, "Considering Race and Crime: Distilling Non-partisan Policy from Opposing Theories," *American Criminal Law Review,* Spring 1999, v36 i2 p265(1)

SOURCES: David J. Levin, Patrick A. Langan, and Jodi M. Brown, *State Court Sentencing of Convicted Felons, 1996* (Washington, DC: Bureau of Justice Statistics, 2000); Travis Pratt, "Race and Sentencing: A Meta-Analysis of Conflicting Empirical Research Results," *Journal of Criminal Justice* 26 (1998): 513–525; Charles Crawford, Ted Chiricos, and Gary Kleck, "Race, Racial Threat, and Sentencing of Habitual Offenders," *Criminology* 36 (1998): 481–511; Jon'a Meyer and Tara Gray, "Drunk Drivers in the Courts: Legal and Extra-Legal Factors Affecting Pleas and Sentences," *Journal of Criminal Justice* 25 (1997): 155–163; Alexander Alvarez and Ronet Bachman, "American Indians and Sentencing Disparity: An Arizona Test," *Journal of Criminal Justice* 24 (1996): 549–561; Carole Wolff Barnes and Rodney Kingsnorth, "Race, Drug, and Criminal Sentencing: Hidden Effects of the Criminal Law," *Journal of Criminal Justice* 24 (1996): 39–55; Samuel Walker, Cassia Spohn, and Miriam DeLone, *The Color of Justice: Race, Ethnicity and Crime in America* (Belmont, CA: Wadsworth, 1996), pp. 145–146; Jo Dixon, "The Organizational Context of Sentencing," *American Journal of Sociology* 100 (1995): 1157–1198; Alfred Blumstein, "On the Racial Disproportionality of the United States Prison Population," *Journal of Criminal Law and Criminology* 73 (1982): 1259–1281; Celesta Albonetti and John Hepburn, "Prosecutorial Discretion to Defer Criminalization: The Effects of Defendant's Ascribed and Achieved Status Characteristics," *Journal of Quantitative Criminology* 12 (1996): 63–81; Jimmy Williams, "Race of Appellant, Sentencing Guidelines, and Decision Making in Criminal Appeals: A Research Note," *Journal of Criminal Justice* 23 (1995): 251–289; Joan Petersilia, *Racial Disparities in the Criminal Justice System* (Santa Monica, CA: Rand Corporation, 1983); Darnell Hawkins, "Race, Crime Type and Imprisonment," *Justice Quarterly* 3 (1986): 251–269; James Nelson, "A Dollar or a Day: Sentencing Misdemeanants in New York State," *Journal of Research in Crime and Delinquency* 31 (1994): 183–201; Robert Crutchfield, George Bridges, and Susan Pitchford, "Analytical and Aggregation Biases in Analyses of Imprisonment: Reconciling Discrepancies in Studies of Racial Disparity," *Journal of Research in Crime and Delinquency* 31 (1994): 166–182.

The International Use of the Death Penalty

The United States is not alone in using capital punishment; more than 90 countries still retain the death penalty. According to the latest data from watchdog group Amnesty International, executions were carried out in 34 countries and prisoners were under sentence of death in at least 55 countries.

During 1999, at least 1,813 prisoners were executed in 31 countries and 3,857 people were sentenced to death in 63 countries. In 1999, 85 percent of all known executions took place in China, Iran, Saudi Arabia, the Democratic Republic of Congo, and the United States. In China, the limited records available indicate that at least 1,077 people were executed; at least 165 executions were carried out in Iran, and about 100 in the Democratic Republic of Congo. In addition, hundreds of executions were reported in Iraq, but there is no way of calculating precise numbers.

Nations that operate under Islamic law routinely employ the death penalty and publicly execute convicted criminals. At least 103 executions were carried out in Saudi Arabia during 1999, for crimes ranging from murder and rape to drug smuggling. Those executed included 64 foreign nationals; at least three women were executed after being found guilty of drug smuggling. Hassan bin Awad al-Zubair, a Sudanese national, was beheaded after being convicted on charges of "sorcery" after he claimed the power to heal the sick and to "separate married couples."

While opposition to executions is growing some areas, in others, such as the Caribbean, the public is demanding increased use of the death penalty. The governments of Jamaica, Guyana, and Barbados have all expressed interest in speeding the use of the death penalty, and more than 250 prisoners are currently on death row across the English-speaking Caribbean. In July 1998, the twin-island federation of St. Kitts and Nevis executed its first prisoner since becoming independent in 1983, and Jamaica has ordered its first execution in a decade, that of a 29-year-old hitch-hiker convicted of strangling a business executive who gave him a ride.

Even Japan, a country that prides itself on low crime rates and nonpunitive forms of correction, executed five people in 1999. Some 99 prisoners were under sentence of death at the end of the year, at least 45 of whom had had their sentences upheld by the Japanese Supreme Court. Prisoners under sentence of death can receive visits only from one family member and are held in solitary confinement, sometimes for many years.

In Singapore, the death penalty remains a mandatory punishment for drug trafficking, murder, treason, and certain firearms offenses. Local newspapers reported that 11 executions by hanging were carried out between January and March 1999 alone. There have been at least 190 executions in Singapore since 1994, which means that in proportion to its population, Singapore has possibly one of the highest rates of executions in the world.

Incapacitation Supporters argue that death is the "ultimate incapacitation" and the only one that can ensure that convicted killers can never be pardoned or paroled or escape. Most states that do not have capital punishment provide a sentence of "life in prison without the possibility of parole." However, in 48 states, the chief executive has the power to grant clemency and commute a life sentence and may give "lifers" eligibility for various furlough and release programs.

Death penalty advocates believe that the potential for recidivism is a serious enough threat to require that murderers be denied further access to the public. Stephen Markman and Paul Cassell analyzed the records of 52,000 state prison inmates serving time for murder and found that 810 had previously been convicted of homicide and that these recidivists had killed 821 people following their first convictions.[67] More than 250 inmates on death row today had prior homicide convictions; if they had been executed for their first offense, close to 250 innocent people would still be alive.[68]

Deterrence Proponents of capital punishment argue that executions serve as a strong deterrent to serious crimes. Capital punishment probably cannot deter the few mentally unstable criminals, but it may have an effect on the cold, calculating

Abolition of the Death Penalty

More than half the countries in the world have abolished the death penalty in law or practice. Currently, 73 have abolished it for all crimes; 13 others have abolished it for ordinary crimes such as murder but may retain it for military use or crimes committed in exceptional circumstances. Another 22 have abolished it in practice, in that they have not executed anyone during the past 10 years and are believed to have a policy or established practice of not carrying out executions. During the past five years, the following nations have been added to the list: Azerbaijan, Belgium, Bulgaria, Canada, Djibouti, East Timor, Estonia, Georgia, Lithuania, Mauritius, Moldova, Nepal, Poland, South Africa, Spain, Turkmenistan, Ukraine, and the United Kingdom.

Executions of Juveniles

International human rights treaties prohibit anyone under 18 years old at the time of the crime from being sentenced to death. The International Covenant on Civil and Political Rights, the American Convention on Human Rights, and the UN Convention on the Rights of the Child all have provisions to this effect. More than 100 countries have laws specifically excluding the execution of juvenile offenders, or may be presumed to exclude such executions by being parties to one or another of the above treaties.

A small number of countries, however, continue to execute juvenile offenders. Since 1990, six countries are known to have executed prisoners who were under 18 years old at the time of the crime: Iran, Nigeria, Pakistan, Saudi Arabia, the United States, and Yemen. The country that carried out the greatest number of known executions of child offenders was the United States (13 since 1990).

Critical Thinking Skills

The movement for abolition of the death penalty in the United States is encouraged by the fact that so many nations have abandoned the practice. Should we model our own system of punishment after other nations, or is our crime problem so unusual that it requires the use of capital punishment?

InfoTrac College Edition Research

Are there really innocent people on death row? To find out, read Peter Vilbig, "Innocent on Death Row," *New York Times Upfront,* 18 September 2000, v133 i2 p10

SOURCES: Amnesty International USA, *Annual Report 2000: The Death Penalty: An Affront to Our Humanity* (Washington, DC: Amnesty International, 2000); Amnesty International, "The Death Penalty: List of Abolitionist and Retentionist Countries," 1 January 2000; Amnesty International, "Facts and Figures on the Death Penalty," April 2000; Larry Rohter, "In Caribbean, Support Growing for Death Penalty," *New York Times,* 4 October 1998, p. A1; Associated Press, "Chechen Pair Executed in Public," *Boston Globe,* 19 September 1997, p. A9; Reuters, "Saudi Beheadings over 100 for 1997," *Boston Globe,* 28 September 1997, p. A29.

---

murderer, such as the hired killer or someone who kills for profit. The fear of death may convince felons not to risk using handguns during armed robberies.

Proponents argue that the deterrent effect of an execution can produce a substantial decline in the murder rate.[69] In one analysis of 16 well-publicized executions, Steven Stack found that they may have saved 480 lives by immediately deterring potential murderers.[70] In a more recent survey, he concluded that well-publicized executions of criminals in California reduced the homicide rate by 12 percent during the month of the execution.[71]

Moral Correctness   Advocates of capital punishment justify its use on the grounds that it is morally correct because it is mentioned in the Bible and other religious works. Although the Constitution forbids "cruel and unusual punishments," this prohibition could not include the death penalty because capital punishment was widely used at the time the Constitution was drafted. The "original intent" of the Founding Fathers was to allow the states to use the death penalty; capital punishment may be cruel, but it is not unusual.

The death penalty is morally correct because it provides the greatest justice for the victim and helps alleviate the psychic pain of the victim's family and friends.

It has even been accepted by criminal justice experts who consider themselves humanists, concerned with the value and dignity of human beings. David Friedrichs, a noted humanist, argues that a civilized society has no choice but to hold responsible those who commit horrendous crimes. The death penalty makes a moral statement: Some behavior is so unacceptable to a community of human beings that one who engages in such behavior forfeits his or her right to live.[72]

Proportionality Putting dangerous criminals to death also conforms to the requirement that punishment be proportional to the seriousness of the crime. Since we use a system of escalating punishments, it follows that the most serious punishment should be used to sanction the most serious crime. And before the brutality of the death penalty is considered, the cruelty with which the victim was treated should not be forgotten.

Public Support Those who favor capital punishment point out that a majority of the public believes that criminals who kill innocent victims should forfeit their own lives. Recent public opinion polls show that up to 80 percent of the public favors the death penalty, almost double the percentage of 20 years ago (though some surveys indicate that public approval may now be in decline).[73] Public approval is based on the rational belief that the death penalty is an important instrument of social control, can deter crime, and is less costly than maintaining a murderer in prison for his or her life.[74] Alexis Durham and his associates found that the 80 percent approval rating may actually be low—that almost everyone (95%) would give criminals the death penalty under some circumstances, and the most heinous crimes are those for which the public is most likely to approve capital punishment.[75]

Unlikelihood of Error The many legal controls and appeals currently in use make it almost impossible for an innocent person to be executed or for the death penalty to be used in a racist or capricious manner. Although some unfortunate mistakes may have been made in the past, the current system makes it virtually impossible to execute an innocent person. Federal courts closely scrutinize all death penalty cases and rule for the defendant in an estimated 60 to 70 percent of the appeals. Such judicial care should ensure that only those who are both truly guilty and deserving of death are executed.

In sum, those who favor the death penalty argue that it is a traditional punishment for serious crimes, that it can help prevent criminality, that it is in keeping with the traditional moral values of fairness and equity, and that it is highly favored by the public.

Arguments for Abolition

Many experts believe that the death penalty is wrong and should be abolished. What arguments do they offer?

Possibility of Error Critics of the death penalty believe that capital punishment has no place in a mature democratic society.[76] They point to the finality of the act and the real possibility that innocent persons can be executed. Examples of people wrongfully convicted of murder abound. Critics point to miscarriages of justice such as the case of Rolando Cruz and Alejandro Hernandez who, wrongfully convicted of murder, were released in 1995 after spending more than a decade on death row in the Illinois prison system. Three former prosecutors and four deputy sheriffs who worked on the case were charged with fabricating evidence against

Critics claim that the possibility of executing a single innocent person is reason enough to end the use of the death penalty. Mumia Abu-Jamal is perhaps the most famous person on death row. He began his career as a journalist with the Black Panther Party. By age 25, he was one of the top names in local radio, interviewing such luminaries as Jesse Jackson and winning a Peabody Award for his coverage of the Pope's visit. Then, in what supporters say was a political vendetta, he was convicted of killing a Philadelphia police officer in 1981. From death row he managed to attract supporters and a defense team, which has been able to cast doubt on his guilt, although he has not been given a new trial.

the pair.[77] Cruz and Hernandez are certainly not alone. Jeffrey Blake went to prison for a double murder in 1991 and spent seven years behind bars before his conviction was over turned in 1998.[78] These wrongful convictions would have been even more tragic if those convicted had been executed for their alleged crimes. A congressional report cited 48 cases in the past two decades in which people who served time on death row were released because of evidence of their innocence; one Maryland man spent 9 years on death row before DNA testing proved that he could not have committed the crime.[79] These findings show that even with the best intentions, there is grave risk that an innocent person can be executed.[80] Consequently, a number of states including Virginia (2001) are now requiring DNA testing in all capital cases. Some states, such as Illinois (2001) have placed moratoriums on carrying out capital punishment sentences while the process of administration is studied.

According to research by Michael Radelet and Hugo Bedeau, there have been about 350 wrongful murder convictions this century, of which 23 led to executions. They estimate that about three death sentences are returned every two years in cases where the defendant has been falsely accused. More than half the errors stem from perjured testimony, false identifications, coerced confessions, and suppression of evidence. In addition to the 23 who were executed, 128 of the falsely convicted served more than 6 years in prison, 39 served more than 16 years in confinement, and 8 died while serving their sentence.[81] Although there is careful review of death penalty sentences, relatively few stays of execution are actually granted (about 2 out of 50); obviously, there is room for judicial error.[82]

Unfair Use of Discretion Critics also frown on the tremendous discretion used in seeking the death penalty and the arbitrary manner in which it is imposed. Of the approximately 10,000 persons convicted each year on homicide charges, only 250 to 300 are sentenced to death; an equal number receive a sentence of probation or community supervision only.[83] It is true that many convicted murderers do not commit first-degree murder and therefore are ineligible for execution. However, it is also likely that many serious criminals who could have received the death penalty are not sentenced to death because of prosecutorial discretion. Some escape death by cooperating or giving testimony against their partners in the crime. A person who commits a particularly heinous crime and knows full well that he will receive the death penalty if convicted may be the one most likely to plea bargain to avoid capital punishment. Is it fair to spare the life of a dangerous killer who cooperates with the prosecutor while executing another who does not?

Abolitionists also argue that juries use inappropriate discretion when make capital punishment recommendations. The ongoing Capital Jury Project has been interviewing members of juries involved in making death penalty decisions and finds that many are motivated by ignorance and error (see Exhibit 13.2).

Intent versus Result Some vicious criminals who grievously injure victims during murder attempts are spared death because of a physician's skill. Some notable cases come to mind. Lawrence Singleton used an axe to cut off the arms of a woman he raped, yet he served only 8 years in prison because the victim's life was saved by prompt medical care. (After being released from prison, Singleton killed a female companion in 1997 and was sentenced to death.) "David," a boy severely burned in a murder attempt, lives in fear because his assailant—his father, Charles Rothenberg—was paroled from prison after serving a short sentence.[84] Although these horrific crimes received national attention and the intent to kill the victim was present, the death penalty could not be applied because of the availability of effective medical treatment. Research shows that areas that have superior medical resources actually have lower murder rates than less well equipped areas; for example, ambulance response time can reduce the death rate by expeditiously transporting victims to an appropriate treatment center.[85] It makes little sense to execute someone for an impulsive murder while sparing the life of those who intentionally maim and torture victims who happen by chance to live because of prompt medical care.

EXHIBIT 13.2 THE CAPITAL JURY PROJECT (CJP)

The Capital Jury Project (CJP), begun by sociologist William Bowers in 1990, has sent research teams to 15 states to interview jurors in death penalty cases. The three-hour-plus interviews are taped and coded for analysis.

CJP findings show that the decision making in capital cases often strays from legal and moral guidelines. Some express overwhelming racial prejudice in making their decisions. Others say that they have decided on the punishment before the trial is completed and the defendant found guilty!

Others are confused about the law and influenced by factual misconceptions. For example, many believe that prison terms are far shorter than they really are, often underestimating the time served for murder by 10 years or more. Many jurors mistakenly believe that the death penalty is mandatory in cases when it is not, while others reject capital punishment in situations in which the law clearly mandates its use. The greater the factual errors, the most likely it is that the juror will vote for death.

Many capital jurors are unwilling to accept primary responsibility for their punishment decisions. They vote for the death penalty in the mistaken belief that most defendants will never be executed, absolving them of responsibility. They often place responsibility for the defendant's punishment elsewhere, such as with the judge or other jurors. For example, one female juror who had recommended death told CJP interviewers that she had voted only to go along with the other jurors and that she had never believed the man should be executed. "I really had no thought about it," she said. "It wasn't my choice to make. It was a judgment call. It really doesn't mean a whole lot what I say because it's ultimately up to the judge." These feelings were expressed most often in states where the law allows judges to override a jury's decision and either impose or reject a capital sentence.

The CJP findings indicate that jurors often rely on faulty information and use extralegal criteria in making what is truly a "life or death" decision.

SOURCES: William J. Bowers, "The Capital Jury Project: Rationale, Design, and Preview of Early Findings," *Indiana Law Journal* 70 (1995): 1043–1102; William J. Bowers, Marla Sandys, and Benjamin Steiner, "Foreclosed Impartiality in Capital Sentencing: Jurors' Predispositions, Guilt Trial Experience, and Premature Decision Making," *Cornell Law Review* 83 (1998): 1476–1556; Margaret Vandiver, "Race in the Jury Room: A Preliminary Analysis of Cases from the Capital Jury Project," unpublished paper presented to the American Academy of Criminal Justice Sciences, March 1997.

Misplaced Vengeance While acknowledging that the general public approves of the death penalty, critics maintain that prevailing attitudes reflect a primitive desire for revenge. Public acceptance of capital punishment has been compared to the approval of human sacrifice practiced by the Aztecs in Mexico 500 years ago.[86] It is ironic that many death penalty advocates oppose abortion on the grounds that it is the taking of human life.[87] The desire to be vengeful and punitive outweighs their concern about taking life.

Even if a majority of the general public favors the death penalty, support has been associated with prejudice against racial minorities and the approval of revenge as a rationale for punishment.[88] Nor is public support as strong as death penalty advocates believe. When surveys offer a choice of punishments, including life without parole, support for the death penalty declines from 80 percent to 50 percent.[89] Public opinion is influenced by such factors as the personal characteristics of the offender and the circumstances of the offense. Therefore, the public does not support death in many cases of first-degree murder.[90] It is possible that politicians favor the death penalty in the mistaken belief that the public favors such harsh punishments for criminal offenders.[91]

No Deterrent Effect Those opposed to the death penalty also find little merit in the argument that capital punishment deters crime. They see little evidence that the threat of a death sentence can convince potential murderers to forgo their criminal activity. Most murders involve people who know each other, very often friends and family members. Since murderers are often under the influence of alcohol or drugs or are suffering severe psychological turmoil, no penalty will likely be a deterrent. Most research concludes that the death penalty is not an effective deterrent.[92]

Hope of Rehabilitation The death sentence also rules out any hope of offender rehabilitation. There is evidence that convicted killers actually make good parole risks; convicted murderers are actually model inmates and, once released, commit fewer crimes than other parolees.

Racial Bias One of the most compelling arguments against the death penalty is that it is applied in a racially discriminatory fashion. Evidence suggests that prosecutors are more likely to recommend the death sentence for African Americans who kill white victims than for any other racial combination of criminal and victim, such as whites who kill blacks.[93] It is not surprising, then, that since the death penalty was first instituted in the United States, a disproportionate number of minority-group members have been executed. Charges of racial bias are supported by the disproportionate numbers of blacks who have received the death sentence, are currently on death row, and have been executed (53.5% of all executions). Racism was particularly blatant when the death penalty was invoked in rape cases: 90 percent of those receiving death sentences for rape in the South and 63 percent of those in the North and West were black.[94] Today, about 40 percent of the inmates on death row are black, a number disproportionate to their representation in the population.

White criminals arrested for homicide actually have a slightly greater chance of getting the death penalty than blacks do, and a majority of murderers executed since 1980 have also been white.[95] Does this statistical anomaly mean either that discrimination in the use of the death penalty has ended or that it never actually existed? The answer may be that simply calculating the relative proportion of each racial group sentenced to death does not tell the whole story. A number of researchers have found that the death penalty is associated with the race of the victim rather than the race of the offender. In most instances, prosecutors are more likely to ask for the death penalty if the victim was white. The fact that most murders involving a white victim also involve a white attacker (86%) accounts for the higher death sentence rate for white murderers.[96] With few exceptions, the relatively infrequent interracial murder cases involving a black criminal and a white victim (14%) are the most likely to result in the death penalty.[97] In contrast, since 1976, only two white criminals have been executed for murdering a black victim—the most recent being Kermit Smith, who was executed on January 24, 1995, in North Carolina for the kidnap, rape, and murder of a 20-year-old college cheerleader.[98]

Brutality Abolitionists believe that executions are unnecessarily cruel and inhumane and come at a high moral and social cost. Our society does not punish criminals by subjecting them to the same acts they themselves committed. Rapists are not sexually assaulted, and arsonists do not have their house burned down; why, then, should murderers be killed?

Robert Johnson has described the execution process as a form of torture in which the condemned are first tormented psychologically by being made to feel powerless and alone while on death row; suicide is a constant problem among those on death row.[99] The execution itself is a barbaric affair marked by the smell of burning flesh and stiffened bodies. The executioners suffer from delayed stress reactions, including anxiety and a dehumanized personal identity. Even a lethal injection, a so-called humanitarian method of execution, can turn into a brutal affair. Burl Cain, warden of Louisiana's Angola Prison, has administered lethal injections to a number of men. He tells of one who had heroin track marks so bad they had to shoot the poison into his neck; he kept bolting upright, so Cain had to push his shoulder down with his right hand while letting the man hold his left for comfort.[100]

brutalization effect

The belief that capital punishment creates an atmosphere of brutality, reinforces the view that violence is an appropriate response to provocation, and thus encourages rather than deters the criminal use of violence.

The brutality of the death penalty may actually produce more violence than it prevents—the so-called **brutalization effect**.[101] Executions may increase murder rates because they raise the general level of violence in society and because violence-prone people actually identify with the executioner, not the person being executed. When such individuals come into conflict with someone who challenges their authority, they may execute this person in the same manner that the state executes people who violate its rules.[102]

John Cochran, Mitchell Chamlin, and Mark Seth encountered this brutalization effect when they studied the influence of a well-publicized execution in Oklahoma: After the execution, murders of strangers actually increased by one per month.[103] Follow-up research by William Bailey found that the brutalization effect extends also to nonstranger murder. They also found evidence of a vicarious brutalization effect, with people in states without capital punishment being influenced by news reports of executions in death penalty states.[104]

Because of its brutality, many enlightened nations have abandoned the death penalty, with few ill effects. Abolitionists point out that such nations as Denmark and Sweden have long abandoned the death penalty and that 40 percent of the countries with a death penalty have active abolitionist movements.[105] It is ironic that citizens of countries that have abolished the death penalty sometimes find themselves on death row in the United States. Angel Francisco Breard, a 32-year-old citizen of Paraguay, was executed on April 14, 1998, in Virginia for murder and attempted rape, despite a plea from the International Court of Justice that he be spared and intense efforts by the government of Paraguay to stay the execution.[106]

Expense Some people complain that they do not want to support "some killer in prison for 30 years." Abolitionists counter that legal appeals drive the cost of executions far higher than years in prison. If the money spent on the judicial process were invested, the interest would more than pay for the lifetime upkeep of death row inmates. For example, in 1998, there were 508 men and 9 women on death row in California. Because of numerous appeals, the median time from conviction by a jury and sentencing by a judge to execution averages 14 years. The cost of processing appeals is extremely high; the annual budget for the state's public defender staff of 45 lawyers who represent inmates in death penalty cases is $5 million.[107]

At least 30 states now have a sentence of life in prison without parole, and this can fully substitute for execution. Being locked up in a hellish prison with no chance of release (barring a rare executive reprieve) may be a worse punishment than a painless death by lethal injection. If vengeance is the goal, life without parole may eliminate the need for capital punishment.

Legal Issues Surrounding the Death Penalty

The death penalty has raised a number of legal issues, including the constitutionality of its application and the process of jury selection.

Fill in the blanks 14–15
True/False 20
Multiple choice 21–26

Constitutionality   The constitutionality of the death penalty has been a major concern for both the courts and concerned social scientists. In 1972, the Supreme Court in *Furman v. Georgia*[108] decided that the discretionary imposition of the death penalty was cruel and unusual punishment under the Eighth and Fourteenth Amendments of the Constitution. This case not only questioned whether capital punishment is a more effective deterrent than life imprisonment but also challenged the very existence of the death penalty on the grounds of its brutality and finality. The Court did not completely rule out the use of capital punishment as a penalty; rather, it objected to the arbitrary and capricious manner in which it was imposed.

After *Furman,* many states changed statutes that had allowed jury discretion in imposing the death penalty. In some states, this was accomplished by enacting statutory guidelines for jury decisions; in others, the death penalty was made mandatory for certain crimes only. Despite these changes in statutory law, no further executions were carried out while the Supreme Court pondered additional cases concerning the death penalty.

Then, in July 1976, the Supreme Court ruled on the constitutionality of five state death penalty statutes. In the first case, *Gregg v. Georgia,*[109] the Court found valid the Georgia statute, which required a finding by the jury of at least one "aggravating circumstance" out of ten before imposing the death penalty for murder. In the *Gregg* case, the jury had imposed the death penalty after finding beyond a reasonable doubt two aggravating circumstances: (1) the offender was engaged in the commission of two other capital felonies, and (2) the offender committed the offense of murder for the purpose of receiving money and other financial gains (such as an automobile).[110]

In probably the most important death penalty case of the past few decades, *McClesky v. Kemp,* the Court upheld the conviction of a black defendant in Georgia despite social science evidence that black criminals who kill white victims have a significantly greater chance of receiving the death penalty than white offenders who kill black victims. The Court ruled that the evidence of racial patterns in capital sentencing was not persuasive without a finding of racial bias in the immediate case.[111] Many observers believe that *McClesky* presented the last significant legal obstacle that death penalty advocates had to overcome and that, as a result, capital punishment will be a sentence in the United States for years to come (McClesky was executed in 1991).

Although the Court has generally supported the death penalty, it has also placed some limitations on its use. Rulings have promoted procedural fairness in the capital sentencing process. For example, the Court has prohibited prosecutors from presenting damaging evidence about the defendant's background unless it is directly relevant to the case.[112] The Court has also limited capital punishment to first-degree murder cases, ruling that it is not permissible to punish lesser offenses, such as rape, with death.[113] Some states, such as Louisiana, have recently introduced laws that would make some forms of aggravated rape, such as those involving children, punishable by death, but it is unlikely that the Supreme Court would permit such punishment.[114]

The Court has also reinforced the idea that mental and physical conditions such as age, while not excusing criminal behavior, can be considered as mitigating factors in capital sentencing decisions. In *Wilkins v. Missouri* and *Stanford v. Kentucky,* the Court set a lower limit of 16 on the age of defendants who could be sentenced to death.[115] (Eight inmates who committed their crimes at age 17 or younger are currently on death row.) These rulings effectively barred the use of capital punishment for minors under the age of 16 who have been waived or transferred from the juvenile to the adult court system.

The Court seems committed to maintaining the death penalty within boundaries of fairness and due process. It has reduced a defendant's ability to reappeal a capital case by raising claims that were not included in the original legal motion.[116] It now permits victim impact statements, describing how victims will be missed by their family and friends, and gives prosecutors the right to include such statements in their closing arguments.[117] A judge now may, when the law allows, ignore a jury's recommendation for leniency and impose the death penalty.[118] And the Court has recently said it is not willing to overturn cases if a judge complies with the letter of the law; there is no legal requirement to go beyond minimum legal requirements when instructing juries.[119] These rulings, plus the failure to grant stays in numerous capital cases, underscore the Court's willingness to retain the death sentence.

death-qualified jury
A jury formed to hear a capital case, with any person opposed in principle to capital punishment automatically excluded.

Death-Qualified Juries   In forming a jury to hear a capital case, any person opposed in principle to capital punishment is removed during voir dire. The result is known as a **death-qualified jury**. Defense attorneys are opposed to death qualification because it excludes from juries citizens who oppose the death penalty and who may also be more liberal and less likely to convict defendants. Death qualification creates juries that are nonrepresentative of the 20 percent of the public that opposes capital punishment.

In *Witherspoon v. Illinois* (1968), the Supreme Court upheld the practice of excusing jurors who are opposed to the death penalty.[120] The Court has made it easier to convict people in death penalty cases by ruling that any juror can be excused if his or her views on capital punishment are deemed by a trial judge to "prevent or substantially impair the performance of their duties."[121] The Court has also ruled that jurors can be removed because of their opposition to the death penalty at the guilt phase of a trial, even though they would not have to consider the issue of capital punishment until a separate sentencing hearing. In *Lockhart v. McCree* (1986), the Court also ruled that removing anti–capital punishment jurors does not violate the Sixth Amendment's provision that juries represent a fair cross-section of the community, nor does it unfairly tip the scale toward juries who are prone to convict people in capital cases.[122] So, it appears that for the present, prosecutors will be able to excuse jurors who believe that the death penalty is wrong or immoral.

Essay 13

Does Capital Punishment Deter Murder?

The key issue in the capital punishment debate is whether it can actually lower the murder rate and save lives. Despite its inherent cruelty, capital punishment might be justified if it proved to be an effective crime deterrent that could save many innocent lives. Abolitionists claim it has no real deterrent value; advocates claim that it does. Who is correct?

Considerable empirical research has been carried out on the effectiveness of capital punishment as a deterrent. In particular, studies have tried to discover whether the death sentence serves as a more effective deterrent than life imprisonment for capital crimes such as homicide. Three methods have been used:

- *Immediate impact studies,* which calculate the effect a well-publicized execution has on the short-term murder rate
- *Time-series analysis,* which compares long-term trends in murder and capital punishment rates
- *Contiguous-state analysis,* which compares murder rates in states that have the death penalty with those in similar states that have abolished capital punishment

Using these three methods over a 60-year period, most researchers have failed to show any deterrent effect of capital punishment.[123] These studies show that murder rates do not seem to rise when a state abolishes capital punishment nor decrease when the death penalty is adopted. The murder rate is also quite similar in states that use the death penalty and neighboring states that have abolished capital punishment. Finally, there is little evidence that executions can lower the murder rate. For example, a recent test of the deterrent effect of the death penalty in Texas found no association between the frequency of execution during the years 1984–1997 and murder rates.[124]

A few studies have found that the long-term application of capital punishment may actually reduce the murder rate.[125] However, these results have been disputed by researchers who have questioned the methodology used and suggest that the deterrent effects uncovered are simply an artifact of the statistical methods used in the research.[126]

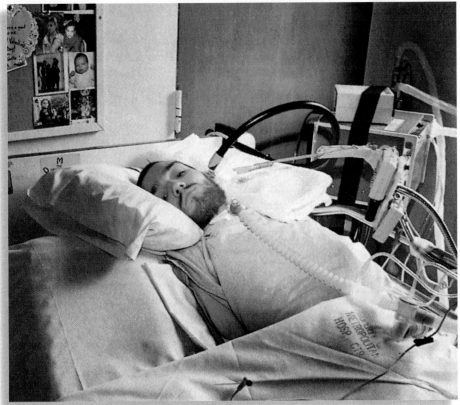

Crack dealer Eddie Matos lies in a hospital bed, shot by an assailant who he says "got his." Payback, revenge, and urban conflict are not easily deterred by the threat of capital punishment. People involved in the drug trade may find that violence and conflict are expected consequences of "doing business," making them the least likely to fear government retribution.

© Nicole Bengiveno/Matrix

The general consensus among death penalty researchers today is that the threat of capital punishment has little effect on murder rates. Although it is still unknown why capital punishment fails as a deterrent, the cause may lie in the nature of homicide. As noted earlier, murder is often a crime of passion involving people who know each other, and many murders are committed by people under the influence of alcohol and drugs (more than 50 percent of all people arrested for murder test positive for drug use). People involved in interpersonal conflict with friends, acquaintances, and family members and who may be under the influence of drugs and alcohol are not likely to be capable of considering the threat of the death penalty.

Murder rates have also been linked to the burdens of poverty and income inequality. Desperate adolescents caught up in the cycle of urban violence who become members of criminal groups and gangs may find that their life situation gives them little choice except to engage in violent and deadly behavior. They have few chances to ponder the deterrent impact of the death penalty.

The failure of the "ultimate deterrent" to deter the "ultimate crime" has been used by critics to question the value of capital punishment.

Despite the less than conclusive empirical evidence, many people still hold to the efficacy of the death penalty as a crime deterrent, and recent Supreme Court decisions seem to justify its use. Of course, even if the death penalty were no greater a deterrent than a life sentence, some people would still advocate its use on the grounds that it is the only way to permanently rid society of dangerous criminals who deserve to die.

SUMMARY

Punishment and sentencing have gone through various phases throughout the history of Western civilization. Initially, punishment was characterized by retribution and the need to fix sentences for convicted offenders. Throughout the middle years of the twentieth century, individualized sentencing was widely accepted, and the concept of rehabilitation was used in sentencing and penal codes. During the 1960s, however, experts began to become disenchanted with rehabilitation and concepts related to treating the individual offender. There was less emphasis on treatment and more on the legal rights of offenders. A number of states returned to the concept of punishment in terms of mandatory and fixed sentences.

Theorists suggest that the philosophy of sentencing has thus changed from a concentration on rehabilitation to a focus on incapacitation and deterrence. The goal is to achieve equality of punishment and justice in the law and to lock up dangerous criminals for as long as possible.

Sentencing in today's criminal justice system is based on deterrence, incapacitation, and rehabilitation. Traditional dispositions include fines, probation, and incarceration, with probation being the most common choice.

A number of states have developed determinate sentences that eliminate parole and attempt to restrict judicial discretion. Methods of making dispositions more uniform include the development of sentencing guidelines that establish uniform sentences based on offender background and crime characteristics. Despite these changes, most states continue to use indeterminate sentences, which give convicted offenders a short minimum sentence after which they can be released on parole if they are considered "rehabilitated." Jurisdictions that use either determinate or indeterminate sentences allow inmates to be released early on good behavior.

The death penalty continues to be the most controversial sentence, with more than half the states reinstituting capital punishment since the *Furman v. Georgia* decision of 1972. Although there is little evidence that the death penalty deters murder, supporters still view it as necessary in terms of incapacitation and retribution and cite the public's support for the death penalty and the low chance of error in its application. Opponents point out that mistakes can be made, that capital sentences are apportioned in a racially biased manner, and that the practice is cruel and barbaric. Nonetheless, the courts have generally supported the legality of capital punishment, and it has been used more frequently in recent years.

Key Terms

transportation	concurrent sentence	sentencing guidelines
incarceration	consecutive sentence	mandatory sentence
incapacitation	indeterminate sentence	chivalry hypothesis
just desert	determinate sentence	brutalization effect
equity	good time	death-qualified jury

Discussion Questions

1. Do you believe that too many people are now being sentenced to prison? Will the current get-tough approach create an extremely large pool of ex-offenders who are at risk for further crime?
2. Compare the various types of incarceration sentences. What are the similarities and differences? Why are many jurisdictions considering the passage of mandatory sentencing laws?
3. Discuss the issue of capital punishment. In your opinion, does it serve as a deterrent? What new rulings has the

U.S. Supreme Court made on the legality of the death penalty?
4. Why does the problem of sentencing disparity exist? Do programs exist that can reduce disparity? If so, what are they? Should all people who commit the same crime receive the same sentence?
5. Should convicted criminals be released from prison when correctional authorities are convinced they are rehabilitated?

A CLOSER LOOK

Will Manning and Jacqueline Rhoden-Trader have analyzed the death penalty and believe not only that it is growing less popular among the general population but also that it contains procedural problems that undercut its use:

> While most Americans support the death penalty, polls have begun to show some slippage. According to a June 2000 Gallup Poll, public support for the death penalty has declined from 80 percent to 66 percent since 1994. This slippage in support stems from increased doubt about the moral, ethical and racial disparity issues surrounding the death penalty. As was evident in 1972, when the most prominent death penalty case, *Furman v. Georgia*,

was brought before the Supreme Court, this subject again has become hotly debated and has polarized people, provoked international debate and stirred consciences. A number of factors have given rise to the general philosophical interest in the ultimate penalty for the ultimate crime.

To read what they have to say, go to InfoTrac College Edition and look up
Will Manning and Jacqueline Rhoden-Trader, "Rethinking the Death Penalty," *Corrections Today*, October 2000, v62 i6 p22

Notes

1 Dan McGraw, "Texan's Test Says Guilty," *U.S. News & World Report*, 24 July 2000, p. 26.
2 Frank Bruni with Richard Oppel, Jr., "The 2000 Campaign: The Texas Governor: Bush Delays an Execution for the 1st Time in 5 Years," *New York Times*, 2 June 2000, p. A3.
3 Michel Foucault, *Discipline and Punishment* (New York: Vintage Books, 1978).
4 Graeme Newman, *The Punishment Response* (Philadelphia: Lippincott, 1978), p. 13.

5 Peter Greenwood with Allan Abrahamse, *Selective Incapacitation* (Santa Monica, CA: Rand Corporation, 1982).
6 Kathleen Auerhahn, "Selective Incapacitation and the Problem of Prediction," *Criminology* 37 (1999): 703–734.
7 Kathleen Daly, "Neither Conflict nor Labeling nor Paternalism Will Suffice: Intersections of Race, Ethnicity, Gender, and Family in Criminal Court Decisions," *Crime and Delinquency* 35 (1989): 136–168.

8 Among the most helpful sources for this section are Benedict Alper, *Prisons Inside-Out* (Cambridge, MA: Ballinger, 1974); Gustave de Beaumont and Alexis de Tocqueville, *On the Penitentiary System in the United States and Its Applications in France* (Carbondale: Southern Illinois University Press, 1964); Orlando Lewis, *The Development of American Prisons and Prison Customs, 1776–1845* (Montclair, NJ: Patterson-Smith, 1967); Leonard Orland, ed., *Justice, Punishment, and Treatment* (New York: Free Press, 1973); J.

Goebel, *Felony and Misdemeanor* (Philadelphia: University of Pennsylvania Press, 1976); George Rusche and Otto Kircheimer, *Punishment and Social Structure* (New York: Russell & Russell, 1939); Samuel Walker, *Popular Justice* (New York: Oxford University Press, 1980); Newman, *The Punishment Response*; David Rothman, *Conscience and Convenience* (Boston: Little, Brown, 1980); George Ives, *A History of Penal Methods* (Montclair, NJ: Patterson-Smith, 1970); Robert Hughes, *The Fatal Shore* (New York: Knopf, 1986); Leon Radzinowicz, *A History of English Criminal Law,* vol. 1 (London: Stevens, 1943), p. 5.

9 Christina Dejong, "Survival Analysis and Specific Deterrence: Integrating Theoretical and Empirical Models of Recidivism," *Criminology* 35 (1997): 561–576; Paul Tracy and Kimberly Kempf-Leonard, *Continuity and Discontinuity in Criminal Careers* (New York: Plenum, 1996).

10 Allen Beck and Bernard Shipley, *Recidivism of Prisoners Released in 1983* (Washington, DC: Bureau of Justice Statistics, 1989).

11 Dejong, "Survival Analysis and Specific Deterrence," p. 573.

12 David Weisburd, Elin Waring, and Ellen Chayet, "Specific Deterrence in a Sample of Offenders Convicted of White-Collar Crimes," *Criminology* 33 (1995): 587–607.

13 Charles Logan, *Criminal Justice Performance Measures for Prisons* (Washington, DC: Bureau of Justice Statistics, 1993), p. 3.

14 Alexis Durham, "The Justice Model in Historical Context: Early Law, the Emergence of Science, and the Rise of Incarceration," *Journal of Criminal Justice* 16 (1988): 331–346.

15 Andrew von Hirsh, *Doing Justice: The Choice of Punishments* (New York: Hill and Wang, 1976).

16 Shawn Bushway, "The Impact of an Arrest on the Job Stability of Young White American Men," *Journal of Research in Crime and Delinquency* 35 (1998): 454–479.

17 For a review, see Arnulf Kolstad, "Imprisonment as Rehabilitation: Offenders' Assessment of Why It Does Not Work," *Journal of Criminal Justice* 24 (1996): 323–335.

18 Charles Logan and Gerald Gaes, "Meta-Analysis and the Rehabilitation of Punishment," *Justice Quarterly* 10 (1993): 245–264.

19 Richard McCorkle, "Research Note: Punish and Rehabilitate? Public Attitudes Toward Six Common Crimes," *Crime and Delinquency* 39 (1993): 240–252; D. A. Andrews, Ivan Zinger, Robert Hoge, James Bonta, Paul Gendreau, and Francis Cullen, "Does Correctional Treatment Work? A Clinically Relevant and Psychologically Informed Meta-Analysis," *Criminology* 28 (1990): 369–404; Francis Cullen, John Cullen, and John Wozniak, "Is Rehabilitation Dead? The Myth of the Punitive Public," *Journal of Criminal Justice* 16 (1988): 303–316.

20 Francis Cullen, John Paul Wright, Shayna Brown, Melissa Moon, Michael Blankenship, and Brandon Applegate, "Public Support for Early Intervention Programs: Implications for a Progressive Policy Agenda," *Crime and Delinquency* 44 (1998): 187–204.

21 Jacob Adler, *The Urgings of Conscience: A Theory of Punishment* (Philadelphia: Temple University Press, 1991).

22 Patrick Langan, *State Felony Courts and Felony Laws* (Washington, DC: Bureau of Justice Statistics, 1987), p. 6.

23 George Jackson, *Soledad Brother* (New York: Bantam Books, 1970).

24 Kenneth Culp Davis, *Discretionary Justice: A Preliminary Inquiry* (Baton Rouge: Louisiana State University Press, 1969); Marvin Frankel, *Criminal Sentences: Law without Order* (New York: Hill and Wang, 1972).

25 See Frankel, *Criminal Sentences: Law without Order,* p. 5.

26 American Friends Service Committee, *Struggle for Justice: A Report on Crime and Punishment in America* (New York: Hill and Wang, 1971).

27 Andrew von Hirsch, *Doing Justice: The Choice of Punishments* (New York: Hill and Wang, 1976).

28 James Q. Wilson, *Thinking about Crime* (New York: Random House, 1975), p. 236.

29 Jo Dixon, "The Organizational Context of Criminal Sentencing," *American Journal of Sociology* 100 (1995): 1157–1198.

30 Michael Tonry, *Reconsidering Indeterminate and Structured Sentencing Series: Sentencing and Corrections: Issues for the 21st Century* (Washington, DC: National Institute of Justice, 1999).

31 Michael Tonry, *The Fragmentation of Sentencing and Corrections in America* (Washington, DC: National Institute of Justice, 1999).

32 Ibid., p.11.

33 Michael Tonry, "The Failure of the U.S. Sentencing Commission's Guidelines," *Crime and Delinquency* 39 (1993): 131–149.

34 Terance Miethe and Charles Moore, "Socioeconomic Disparities under Determinate Sentencing Systems: A Comparison of Preguideline and Postguideline Practices in Minnesota," *Criminology* 23 (1985):337–363.

35 Ibid.

36 Michael Tonry, "Racial Politics, Racial Disparities, and the War on Crime," *Crime and Delinquency* 40 (1994): 475–494.

37 Joan Petersilia and Susan Turner, *Guideline-Based Justice: The Implications for Racial Minorities* (Santa Monica, CA: Rand Corporation, 1985).

38 Elaine Wolf and Marsha Weissman, "Revising Federal Sentencing Policy: Some Consequences of Expanding Eligibility for Alternative Sanctions," *Crime and Delinquency* 42 (1996): 192–205.

39 Tonry, "The Failure of the U.S. Sentencing Commission's Guidelines," p. 131.

40 Kate Stith and Jose A. Cabranes, *Fear of Judging: Sentencing Guidelines in the Federal Courts* (Chicago: University of Chicago Press, 1998).

41 Ibid., p. 170.

42 Ibid., p. 169.

43 Michael Tonry, *Sentencing Matters* (New York: Oxford University Press, 1996), p. 5.

44 Henry Scott Wallace, "Mandatory Minimums and the Betrayal of Sentencing Reform: A Legislative Dr. Jekyll and Mr. Hyde," *Federal Probation* 57 (1993): 9–16.

45 Paul J. Hofer, "Federal Sentencing for Violent and Drug Trafficking Crimes Involving Firearms: Recent Changes and Prospects for Improvement," *American Criminal Law Review* 37 (2000): 41–74.

46 David J. Levin, Patrick A. Langan, and Jodi M. Brown, *State Court Sentencing of Convicted Felons, 1996* (Washington, DC: Bureau of Justice Statistics, 2000).

47 Brent Smith and Kelly Damphouse, "Terrorism, Politics, and Punishment: A Test of Structural-Contextual Theory and the 'Liberation Hypothesis,'" *Criminology* 36 (1998): 67–92.

48 For a general look at the factors that affect sentencing, see Susan Welch, Cassia Spohn, and John Gruhl, "Convicting and Sentencing Differences among Black, Hispanic, and White Males in Six Localities," *Justice Quarterly* 2 (1985): 67–80.

49 Tracy Nobiling, Cassia Spohn, and Miriam DeLone, "A Tale of Two Counties: Unemployment and Sentence Severity," *Justice Quarterly* 15 (1998): 459–486.

50 Stewart D'Alessio and Lisa Stolzenberg, "Socioeconomic Status and the Sentencing of the Traditional Offender," *Journal of Criminal Justice* 21 (1993): 61–77.

51 Cecilia Saulters-Tubbs, "Prosecutorial and Judicial Treatment of Female Offenders," *Federal Probation* 57 (1993): 37–41.

52 See, generally, Janet Johnston, Thomas Kennedy, and I. Gayle Shuman, "Gender Differences in the Sentencing of Felony Offenders," *Federal Probation* 87 (1987): 49–56; Cassia Spohn and Susan Welch, "The Effect of Prior Record in Sentencing Research: An Examination of the Assumption That Any Measure Is Adequate," *Justice Quarterly* 4 (1987): 286–302; David Willison, "The Effects of Counsel on the Severity of Criminal Sentences: A Statistical Assessment," *Justice System Journal* 9 (1984): 87–101.

53 Cassia Spohn, Miriam DeLone, and Jeffrey Spears, "Race/Ethnicity, Gender, and Sentence Severity in Dade County, Florida: An Examination of the Decision to Withhold Adjudication," *Journal of Crime and Justice* 21 (1998): 111–132.

54 Ellen Hochstedler Steury and Nancy Frank, "Gender Bias and Pretrial Release: More Pieces of the Puzzle," *Journal of Criminal Justice* 18 (1990): 417–432.

55 Dean Champion, "Elderly Felons and Sentencing Severity: Interregional Variations in Leniency and Sentencing Trends," *Criminal Justice Review* 12 (1987): 7–15.

56 Darrell Steffensmeier, John Kramer, and Jeffery Ulmer, "Age Differences in Sentencing," *Justice Quarterly* 12 (1995): 583–601.

57 Darrell Steffensmeier, Jeffery Ulmer, and John Kramer, "The Interaction of Race, Gender, and Age in Criminal Sentencing: The Punishment Cost of Being Young, Black, and Male," *Criminology* 36 (1998): 763–798.

58 *Payne v. Tennessee,* 501 U.S. 808, 111 S.Ct. 2597, 115 L.Ed.2d 720 (1991).

59 Robert Davis and Barbara Smith, "The Effects of Victim Impact Statements on Sentencing Decisions: A Test in an Urban Setting," *Justice Quarterly* 11 (1994): 453–469; Edna Erez and Pamela Tontodonato, "The Effect of Victim Participation in Sentencing on Sentence Outcome," *Criminology* 28 (1990): 451–474.

60 Rodney Kingsworth, Randall MacIntosh, and Jennifer Wentworth, "Sexual Assault: The Role of Prior Relationship and Victim Characteristics in Case Processing," *Justice Quarterly* 16 (1999): 276–302.

61 Michael Tonry, *Malign Neglect: Race, Crime and Punishment in America* (New York: Oxford University Press, 1995), pp. 105–109.

62 "Many State Legislatures Focused on Crime in 1995, Study Finds," *Criminal Justice Newsletter,* 2 January 1996, p. 2.

63 David B. Rottman, Carol R. Flango, Melissa T. Cantrell, Randall Hansen, and Neil LaFountain, *State Court Organization, 1998* (Washington, DC: Bureau of Justice Statistics, 2000).

64 *Coker v. Georgia,* 433 U.S. 584, 97 S.Ct. 2861, 53 L.Ed.2d 982 (1977).

65 Tracy L. Snell, *Capital Punishment 1999* (Washington, DC: Bureau of Justice Statistics, 2000).

66 *Lopez v. Singletary,* No. 98-6065.

67 Stephen Markman and Paul Cassell, "Protecting the Innocent: A Response to the Bedeau-Radelet Study," *Stanford Law Review* 41 (1988): 121–170.

68 Snell, *Capital Punishment 1999,* p. 2.

69 Stephen Layson, "United States Time-Series Homicide Regressions with Adaptive Expectations," *Bulletin of the New York Academy of Medicine* 62 (1986): 589–619.

70 Steven Stack, "Publicized Executions and Homicide, 1950–1980," *American Sociological Review* 52 (1987): 532–540; for a study challenging Stack's methods, see William Bailey and Ruth Peterson, "Murder and Capital Punishment: A Monthly Time-Series Analysis of Execution Publicity," *American Sociological Review* 54 (1989): 722–743.

71 Steven Stack, "The Effect of Well-Publicized Executions on Homicide in California," *Journal of Crime and Justice* 21 (1998): 1–12.

72 David Friedrichs, "Comment: Humanism and the Death Penalty: An Alternative Perspective," *Justice Quarterly* 6 (1989): 197–209.

73 Kathleen Maguire and Ann Pastore, *Sourcebook of Criminal Justice Statistics, 1995* (Washington, DC: U.S. Government Printing Office, 1996), p. 183.

74 For an analysis of the formation of public opinion on the death penalty, see Kimberly Cook, "Public Support for the Death Penalty: A Cultural Analysis,"

paper presented at the annual meeting of the American Society of Criminology, San Francisco, November 1991.

75 Alexis Durham, H. Preston Elrod, and Patrick Kinkade, "Public Support of the Death Penalty: Beyond Gallup," *Justice Quarterly* 13 (1996): 705–736.

76 See, generally, Hugo Bedeau, *Death Is Different: Studies in the Morality, Law, and Politics of Capital Punishment* (Boston: Northeastern University Press, 1987); Keith Otterbein, *The Ultimate Coercive Sanction* (New Haven, CT: HRAF Press, 1986).

77 "Illinois Ex-Prosecutors Charged with Framing Murder Defendants," *Criminal Justice Newsletter,* 2 January 1997, p. 3.

78 Jim Yardley, "Convicted in Murder Case, Man Cleared 7 Years Later," *New York Times,* 29 October 1998, p. A6.

79 House Subcommittee on Civil and Constitutional Rights, *Innocence and the Death Penalty: Assessing the Danger of Mistaken Executions* (Washington, DC: U.S. Government Printing Office, 1993).

80 David Stewart, "Dealing with Death," *ABA Journal* (1994): 53.

81 Michael Radelet and Hugo Bedeau, "Miscarriages of Justice in Potentially Capital Cases," *Stanford Law Review* 40 (1987): 121–181.

82 Stewart, "Dealing with Death."

83 Patrick Langan and John Dawson, *Felony Sentences in State Courts, 1988* (Washington, DC: Bureau of Justice Statistics, 1990), p. 2.

84 "A Victim's Progress," *Newsweek,* 12 June 1989, p. 5.

85 William Doerner, "The Impact of Medical Resources on Criminally Induced Lethality: A Further Examination," *Criminology* 26 (1988): 171–177.

86 Elizabeth Purdom and J. Anthony Paredes, "Capital Punishment and Human Sacrifice," in *Facing the Death Penalty: Essays on Cruel and Unusual Punishment,* ed. Michael Radelet (Philadelphia: Temple University Press, 1989), pp. 152–153.

87 Kimberly Cook, "A Passion to Punish: Abortion Opponents Who Favor the Death Penalty," *Justice Quarterly* 15 (1998): 329–346.

88 Steven Barkan and Steven Cohn, "Racial Prejudice and Support for the Death Penalty by Whites," *Journal of Research in Crime and Delinquency* 31 (1994): 202–209; Robert Bohm and Ronald Vogel, "A Comparison of Factors Associated with Uninformed and Informed Death Penalty Opinions," *Journal of Criminal Justice* 22 (1994): 125–143.

89 Kathleen Maguire and Ann Pastore, *Sourcebook of Criminal Justice Statistics, 1995* (Washington, DC: U. S. Government Printing Office, 1996), p. 183.

90 Gennaro Vito and Thomas Keil, "Elements of Support for Capital Punishment: An Examination of Changing Attitudes," *Journal of Crime and Justice* 21 (1998): 17–25.

91 John Whitehead, Michael Blankenship, and John Paul Wright, "Elite versus Citizen Attitudes on Capital Punishment: Incongruity Between the Public and Policy

Makers," *Journal of Criminal Justice* 27 (1999): 249–258.

92 William Bowers and Glenn Pierce, "Deterrence or Brutalization: What Is the Effect of Executions?" *Crime and Delinquency* 26 (1980): 453–484.

93 Jon Sorenson and Donald Wallace, "Prosecutorial Discretion in Seeking Death: An Analysis of Racial Disparity in the Pretrial Stages of Case Processing in a Midwestern County," *Justice Quarterly* 16 (1999): 559–578.

94 Lawrence Greenfield and David Hinners, *Capital Punishment, 1984* (Washington, DC: Bureau of Justice Statistics, 1985).

95 Gennaro Vito and Thomas Keil, "Capital Sentencing in Kentucky: An Analysis of the Factors Influencing Decision Making in the Post-*Gregg* Period," *Journal of Criminal Law and Criminology* 79 (1988): 493–503; David Baldus, C. Pulaski, and G. Woodworth, "Comparative Review of Death Sentences: An Empirical Study of the Georgia Experience," *Journal of Criminal Law and Criminology* 74 (1983): 661–685; Raymond Paternoster, "Race of the Victim and Location of Crime: The Decision to Seek the Death Penalty in South Carolina," *Journal of Criminal Law and Criminology* 74 (1983): 754–785.

96 Raymond Paternoster, "Prosecutorial Discretion and Capital Sentencing in North and South Carolina," in *The Death Penalty in America: Current Research,* ed. Robert Bohm (Cincinnati: Anderson, 1991), pp. 39–52.

97 Vito and Keil, "Capital Sentencing in Kentucky," pp. 502–503.

98 David Brown, "Man Is Executed in Carolina: Second of a White Who Killed Black," *Boston Globe,* 25 January 1995, p. 3.

99 Robert Johnson, *Death Work: A Study of the Modern Execution Process* (Belmont, CA: Wadsworth, 1990).

100 Joel Stein, "The Lessons of Cain: Warden Burl Cain Has His Own System for Managing Inmates Who Will Never Go Home," *Time,* 10 July 2000, p. 84.

101 William Bailey, "Disaggregation in Deterrence and Death Penalty Research: The Case of Murder in Chicago," *Journal of Criminal Law and Criminology* 74 (1986): 827–859.

102 Gennaro Vito, Pat Koester, and Deborah Wilson, "Return of the Dead: An Update on the Status of *Furman*-Commuted Death Row Inmates," in *The Death Penalty in America: Current Research,* ed. Robert Bohm (Cincinnati: Anderson, 1991), pp. 89–100; Gennaro Vito, Deborah Wilson, and Edward Latessa, "Comparison of the Dead: Attributes and Outcomes of *Furman*-Commuted Death Row Inmates in Kentucky and Ohio," *The Death Penalty in America: Current Research,* ed. Robert Bohm (Cincinnati: Anderson, 1991), pp. 101–112.

103 John Cochran, Mitchell Chamlin, and Mark Seth, "Deterrence or Brutalization? An Impact Assessment of Oklahoma's Return to Capital Punishment," *Criminology* 32 (1994): 107–134.

104 William Bailey, "Deterrence, Brutalization, and the Death Penalty: Another Examination of Oklahoma's Return to Capital Punishment," *Justice Quarterly* 36 (1998): 711–734.

105 Joseph Schumacher, "An International Look at the Death Penalty," *International Journal of Comparative and Applied Criminal Justice* 14 (1990): 307–315.

106 David Stout, "Clemency Denied, Paraguayan Is Executed," *New York Times,* 15 April 1998, p. A3.

107 Don Terry, "California Prepares for Faster Execution Pace," *New York Times,* 17 October 1998, p. A7.

108 *Furman v. Georgia,* 408 U.S. 238, 92 S.Ct. 2726, 33 L.Ed.2d 346 (1972).

109 *Gregg v. Georgia,* 428 U.S. 153, 96 S.Ct. 2909, 49 L.Ed.2d 859 (1976).

110 Ibid., at 205–207, 96 S.Ct. at 2940–2941.

111 *McClesky v. Kemp,* 481 U.S. 279, 107 S.Ct. 1756, 95 L.Ed.2d 262 (1987).

112 *Dawson v. Delaware,* 503 U.S. 159, 112 S.Ct. 1093, 117 L.Ed.2d 309 (1992).

113 *Coker v. Georgia,* 433 U.S. 584, 97 S.Ct. 2861, 53 L.Ed.2d 393 (1977).

114 Annaliese Flynn Fleming, "Louisiana's Newest Capital Crime: The Death Penalty for Child Rape," *Journal of Criminal Law and Criminology* 89 (1999): 717–741.

115 *Wilkins v. Missouri* and *Stanford v. Kentucky,* 492 U.S. 361, 109 S.Ct. 2969, 106 L.Ed.2d 306 (1989).

116 *McClesky v. Zant,* 499 U.S. 467 (1991).

117 *Payne v. Tennessee,* 501 U.S. 808, 111 S.Ct. 2597, 115 L.Ed.2d 720 (1991).

118 *Harris v. Alabama,* 513 U.S. 504, 115 S.Ct. 1031, 130 L.Ed.2d 1004 (1995).

119 *Weeks v. Angelone, Director, Virginia Department of Corrections,* No. 99-5746, affirmed January 19, 2000.

120 *Witherspoon v. Illinois,* 391 U.S. 510, 88 S.Ct. 1770, 20 L.Ed.2d 776 (1968).

121 *Wainwright v. Witt,* 469 U.S. 412, 105 S.Ct. 844, 83 L.Ed.2d 841 (1985).

122 *Lockhart v. McCree,* 476 U.S. 162, 106 S.Ct. 1758, 90 L.Ed.2d 137 (1986).

123 Walter C. Reckless, "Use of the Death Penalty," *Crime and Delinquency* 15 (1969): 43; Thorsten Sellin, "Effect of Repeal and Reintroduction of the Death Penalty on Homicide Rates," in *The Death Penalty,* ed. Thorsten Sellin (Philadelphia: American Law Institute, 1959); Robert H. Dann, "The Deterrent Effect of Capital Punishment," *Friends Social Service Series* 29 (1935): 1; William Bailey and Ruth Peterson, "Murder and Capital Punishment: A Monthly Time-Series Analysis of Execution Publicity," *American Sociological Review* 54 (1989): 722–743; David Phillips, "The Deterrent Effect of Capital Punishment," *American Journal of Sociology* 86 (1980): 139–148; Sam McFarland, "Is Capital Punishment a Short-Term Deterrent to Homicide? A Study of the Effects of Four Recent American Executions," *Journal of Criminal Law and Criminology* 74 (1984): 1014–1032; Richard Lempert, "The Effect of Executions on Homicides: A New Look in an Old Light," *Crime and Delinquency* 29 (1983): 88–115.

124 Jon Sorenson, Robert Wrinkle, Victoria Brewer, and James Marquart, "Capital Punishment and Deterrence: Examining the Effect of Executions on Murder in Texas," *Crime and Delinquency* 45 (1999): 481–493.

125 Isaac Ehrlich, "The Deterrent Effect of Capital Punishment: A Question of Life or Death," *American Economic Review* 65 (1975): 397.

126 For a review, see William Bailey, "The General Prevention Effect of Capital Punishment for Non-Capital Felonies," in *The Death Penalty in America: Current Research,* ed. Robert Bohm (Cincinnati: Anderson, 1991), pp. 21–38.

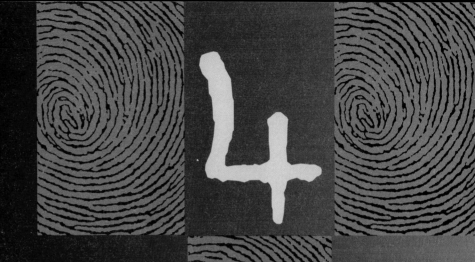

CORRECTIONS

Is it possible that in an enlightened nation such as the United States correctional inmates may be subdued with painful jolts of electricity? Hard to believe, but the use of stun belts, which deliver up to 50,000 volts of electricity, has become a somewhat routine practice in American correctional institutions. Critics of the practice, such as Amnesty International, have called for the abolition of a device that they view as a form of torture. The use of stun belts is just one of the many important issues facing the correctional system. Other critical topics reviewed in this part include the staggering rise in the inmate population, sexual exploitation of female inmates, and boot camps.

© Jacques Chenet/Woodfin Camp & Associates

PROBATION AND
INTERMEDIATE SANCTIONS

On November 23, 1999, Walter Turnbull, founder of the internationally known Boys Choir of Harlem, was spared a prison sentence for tax evasion when federal District Court Judge Barbara Jones sentenced him to one year of probation. The 54-year-old Turnbull had been convicted for failing to report $55,000 in income on his 1990 tax return. In rendering her decision, Judge Jones said, "Dr. Turnbull isn't just someone who does his job excellently.

He goes way beyond that, contributing his own personal money at times to keep the choir going." The court had received 35 letters of support for Turnbull who, while overseeing the choir for the past 30 years, helped it grow into an institution that provides special musical training as well as educational and personal counseling for hundreds of inner-city children. Under federal sentencing guidelines, Turnbull could have received up to 8 months in prison.

Chapter 14

Dr. Turnbull's sentencing represents some the core values of the probation sentence: Many of those convicted in criminal courts are deserving of a second chance; they present little threat to society; having learned their lesson, they are unlikely to recidivate. Under these circumstances, it seems foolish to incarcerate them in an overcrowded and dangerous prison system, which inmates describe as "criminal universities" where deviant identities are reinforced.[1] It may be both more effective and less costly to have them remain in the community under the supervision of a trained court officer, where they can receive treatment that will help them turn around their lives.

Considering the potential benefits and cost effectiveness of a probation sentence, it is not surprising that the number of probationers is at an all-time high. In addition, the need to create effective and efficient methods of controlling offenders in the community has prompted correctional policymakers to develop new forms of community-based intermediate sanctions: fines, forfeiture, restitution, shock probation and split sentencing, intensive probation supervision, house arrest, electronic monitoring, and residential community corrections. These programs are designed to provide greater control over an offender and increase the level of sanction without resorting to a prison sentence.

Both traditional probation and the newer intermediate sanctions have the potential to become reasonable alternatives to many of the economic and social problems faced by correctional administrators: They are less costly than jail or prison sentences; they help the offender maintain family and community ties; they can be structured to maximize security and maintain public safety; and they can be scaled in severity to correspond to the seriousness of the crime. No area of the criminal justice system is undergoing more change and greater expansion than probation and intermediate sanctions.

This chapter reviews these types of community based criminal sanctions. It begins with a brief history of probation and covers probation as an organization, sentence, and correctional practice. Then it examines such intermediate sanctions as intensive supervision, house arrest, and electronic monitoring.

PROBATION

probation
A sentence entailing the conditional release of a convicted offender into the community under the supervision of the court (in the form of a probation officer), subject to certain conditions for a specified time.

Fill in the blanks 1
True/False 1–2

judicial reprieve
In medieval England, a judge's suspension of punishment, enabling a convicted offender to seek a pardon, gather new evidence, or demonstrate reformed behavior.

recognizance
Medieval practice of letting convicted offenders remain free if they agreed to enter a debt relation with the state to pay for their crimes.

Probation is a criminal sentence mandating that a convicted offender be placed and maintained in the community under the supervision of a duly authorized agent of the court. Once on probation, the offender is subject to certain rules and conditions that must be followed to remain in the community. The probation sentence is managed by a probation department that supervises offenders' behavior and treatment and carries out other tasks for the court. Although the term has many meanings, *probation* usually indicates a nonpunitive form of sentencing for convicted criminal offenders and delinquent youth, emphasizing maintenance in the community and treatment without institutionalization or other forms of punishment.[2]

The History of Probation

The roots of probation can be traced back to the traditions of the English common law. During the Middle Ages, judges wishing to spare deserving offenders from the pains of the then commonly used punishments of torture, mutilation, and death used their power to grant clemency and stays of execution. The common law practice of **judicial reprieve** allowed judges to suspend punishment so that convicted offenders could seek a pardon, gather new evidence, or demonstrate that they had reformed their behavior. Similarly, the practice of **recognizance** enabled convicted offenders to remain free if they agreed to enter into a

PERSPECTIVES ON JUSTICE

Probation is at the heart of both the rehabilitation and noninterventionist perspectives. It rests on the assumption that the average offender is not actually a dangerous criminal or a menace to society and can be rehabilitated without further risk to the community. When offenders are institutionalized, the prison community becomes their new reference point; they are forced to interact with hardened criminals, and the "ex-con" label prohibits them from making successful adjustments to society. Probation provides offenders with the opportunity to prove themselves, gives them a second chance, and allows them to be closely supervised by trained personnel who can help them reestablish proper forms of behavior in the community.

debt obligation with the state. The debt would have to be paid only if the offender was caught engaging in further criminal behavior. Judges sometimes required **sureties**—people who made themselves responsible for the behavior of a released offender.

Early U.S. courts continued the practice of indefinitely suspending sentences of criminals who seemed deserving of a second chance, but it was John Augustus of Boston who is usually credited with originating the modern probation concept.[3] As a private citizen, Augustus began in 1841 to supervise offenders released to his custody by a Boston judge. Over an 18-year period, Augustus supervised close to 2,000 probationers and helped them get jobs and establish themselves in the community. Augustus had an amazingly high success rate, and few of his charges became involved in crime again.

Inspired by Augustus's work, the Massachusetts Legislature in 1878 passed a law authorizing appointment of a paid probation officer for the city of Boston. In 1880 probation was extended to other jurisdictions in Massachusetts, and by 1898 the probation movement had spread to the superior (felony) courts.[4] The Massachusetts experience was copied by Missouri (1887), by Vermont (1898), and soon after by most other states. The probation concept soon became the most widely used correctional mechanism in the United States.[5]

In 1925, the federal government established a probation system for the U.S. district courts. Because they were few in number, these federal officers had more cases than their contemporary peers. Common cases involved illegal immigration, mail fraud, car theft, and during World War II, military impersonation.[6]

The Concept of Probation

Probation usually involves suspension of the offender's sentence in return for a promise of good behavior in the community under the supervision of the probation department. As practiced in all 50 states and by the federal government, probation implies a contract between the court and the offender in which the former promises to hold a prison term in abeyance and the latter promises to adhere to a set of rules or conditions mandated by the court (see Exhibit 14.1). If the rules are violated, and especially if the probationer commits another criminal offense, probation may be revoked. **Revocation** means that the contract is terminated and the original sentence is enforced. If an offender on probation commits a second offense that is more serious than the first, he or she may also be indicted, tried, and sentenced on that second offense. However, probation may be revoked simply because the rules and conditions of probation have not been met; it is not necessary for an offender to commit another crime.

---

sureties
During the Middle Ages, people who made themselves responsible for people given release or a reprieve.

Fill in the blanks 2
True/False 3–4
Multiple choice 1–2

Fill in the blanks 3–4
True/False 5
Multiple choice 3–5

revocation
Removing a person from probation (or parole) in response to a violation of law or of the conditions of probation (or parole).

AP/Wide World Photos

Probation provides an opportunity for nondangerous offenders to receive treatment in the community. A probation sentence is often combined with a variety of other sentencing alternatives. Here, former Ashland county clerk Juanita Wright is comforted by her daughter Paula Hughes prior to her sentencing on embezzlement charges May 17, 2000, in Ashland County Common Pleas Court in Ashland, Ohio. The 78-year-old grandmother pleaded guilty to embezzling $178,000 in county funds over a 10-year period. She received 30 days in jail, 11 months house arrest, 400 hours of community service, 5 years probation, and a $5,000 fine and repayment of the embezzled funds out of her retirement account. In addition, she must undergo treatment for a gambling addiction, take financial management classes, and get a job.

Each probationary sentence is for a fixed period of time, depending on the seriousness of the offense and the statutory law of the jurisdiction. Probation is considered served when the offender fulfills the conditions set by the court for that period of time, after which state supervision is ended.

Awarding Probation

True/False 6
Multiple choice 6–10

Probationary sentences may be granted by state and federal district courts and state superior (felony) courts. In some states, juries may recommend probation if the case meets certain legally regulated criteria (for example, if it falls within a certain class of offenses as determined by statute). Even in those jurisdictions that allow juries to recommend probation, judges have the final say in the matter and may grant probation at their discretion. In nonjury trials, probation is granted solely by judicial mandate.

In most jurisdictions, all juvenile offenders are eligible for probation, as are most adults. Some state statutes prohibit probation for certain types of adult offenders, usually those who have engaged in repeated and serious violent crimes, such as murder or rape, or those who have committed crimes for which mandatory prison sentences have been legislated.

EXHIBIT 14.1 SPECIAL PROBATION RULES SUGGESTED FOR CONVICTED SEX OFFENDERS

- Your employment must be approved by the probation agency.
- You shall participate in treatment with a therapist approved by the probation department.
- You shall participate in periodic polygraph examinations.
- You shall not have contact with children under age 18.
- You shall not frequent places where children congregate, such as schoolyards, parks, playgrounds, and arcades.
- You shall maintain a driving log (mileage; time of departure, arrival, return; routes traveled and with whom; etc.).
- You shall not drive a motor vehicle alone without prior permission of your supervising officer.

- You shall not possess any pornographic, sexually oriented, or sexually stimulating visual, auditory, telephonic, or electronic media and computer programs or services that are relevant to your deviant behavior pattern.
- You shall reside at a place approved by the supervising officer, including supervised living quarters.
- You shall abide by a curfew imposed by the supervising officer and comply with electronic monitoring, if so ordered.
- You shall not have contact, directly or through third parties, with your victims.
- You shall abstain from alcoholic beverages and participate in periodic drug testing.

SOURCE: Adapted from Kim English, Suzanne Pullen, and Linda Jones, *Managing Adult Sex Offenders in the Community—a Containment Approach* (Washington, DC: National Institute of Justice, 1997), p. 5.

Direct sentencing to probation is used in about half of all cases. Alternatively, a judge may formulate a prison sentence and then suspend it if the offender agrees to obey the rules of probation while living in the community; this is known as a **suspended sentence**.[7] The term of a probationary sentence may extend to the limit of the suspended prison term, or the court may set a time limit that reflects the sentencing period. For misdemeanors, probation usually extends for the entire period of the jail sentence; for felonies, the probationary period is actually likely to be shorter than the suspended prison sentence. About 10 percent of offenders receive some form of "split sentence," in which they must first serve a jail term before being released on probation. In about 10 percent of all cases, the probation sentence is suspended. This step is usually taken to encourage the defendant to pursue a specific rehabilitation program, such as treatment for alcohol abuse. If the program is successfully completed, further legal action is not usually taken.

suspended sentence
A sentence of incarceration that is not carried out if the offender agrees to obey the rules of probation while living in the community.

The Extent of Probation

There are approximately 2,000 adult probation agencies in the United States. Slightly more than half are associated with a state-level agency, and the remainder are organized at the county or municipal level of government. About 30 states combine probation and parole supervision into a single agency.

At last count, about 4 million adults, or about two-thirds of all adults under some form of correctional supervision, were on probation. More than half of all offenders on probation have been convicted of a felony; 40 percent are on probation for a misdemeanor.[8] Only 1.1 million people were on probation in 1980, meaning that the number of probationers has almost quadrupled in two decades (see Figure 14.1). Some states, such as Texas and California, are now maintaining hundreds of thousands of probationers in their caseloads. Without probation, the correctional system would rapidly become even more overcrowded, expensive, and unmanageable.

Women make up about 22 percent of the nation's probationers, men 78 percent. Women are more likely to be on probation for property offenses, men for drug offending. Approximately 64 percent of the adults on probation are white, and 35 percent are black; Hispanics represent 14 percent of probationers.[9]

About 77 percent of those on probation are being actively supervised by a probation officer; about 10 percent are classified as inactive. Probation officers do not know the whereabouts of 9 percent of their cases, classified as "absconded." During 1999, about 1.9 million people were discharged from probation. Of these, 14 percent (244,700) were incarcerated because of a rule violation or new offense.

Eligibility for Probation

Several criteria are used in granting probation. The statutes of many states specify the factors that a judge should take into account when deciding whether to grant probation. Some states limit the use of probation in serious felony cases and for specific crimes whose penalties are controlled by mandatory sentencing laws. However, the granting of probation to serious felons is quite common; more than half of all probationers were convicted on felony offenses.

Some states have attempted to control judicial discretion by creating guidelines for granting probation. Although judges often follow these guidelines, probation

FIGURE 14.1
PROBATION
POPULATIONS
IN THE UNITED
STATES,
1980–2000

Source: Joan Petersilia, *Probation in the United States* (Washington, DC: National Institute of Justice, 1997); updated 2000.

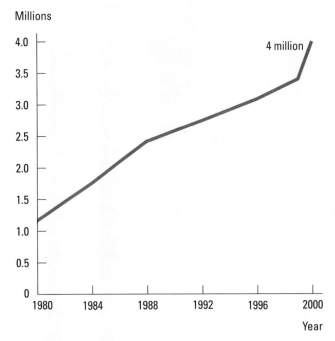

Fill in the blanks 5–6
True/False 7
Multiple choice 11

decision making is quite varied: An individual offender granted probation in one jurisdiction might not be if tried in another. Probation is most often granted by a discretionary decision based on the beliefs and attitudes of the presiding judge and the probation staff.

A significant issue involving eligibility for probation is community supervision of convicted felons. Many people believe that probation is given to minor or first offenders who are deserving of a break. This is not actually the case. Many serious criminal offenders are given straight probation sentences, including people convicted on homicide, rape, and robbery charges.[10] As Table 14.1 shows, many serious offenders are granted probationary sentences even when they are convicted of three or more criminal acts, including murder and sexual assault!

Originally conceived as a way to provide a second chance for young offenders, probation today is also a means of reducing the population pressures on an overcrowded and underfunded correctional system. Thus, there are two distinct sides to probation—one involving the treatment and rehabilitation of nondangerous offenders deserving of a "second chance," and the other the supervision and control of criminals who might otherwise be incarcerated.

Fill in the blanks 7–8
True/False 8–10

Conditions of Probation

When probation is fixed as a sentence, the court sets down certain conditions for qualifying for community treatment. Some conditions—for example, do not leave the jurisdiction—are standard and are applied in every probation case, but the sentencing judge usually has broad discretion to set specific conditions on a case-by-case basis. A presiding judge may not, of course, impose capricious or cruel conditions, such as requiring an offender to make restitution out of proportion to the seriousness of the criminal act.[11] In one Illinois case, for example, an appeals

TABLE 14.1 PERCENTAGE OF CONVICTED FELONS SENTENCED TO PROBATION

Most Serious Conviction Offense	Percent of Felons Sentenced to Probation When Their Conviction Offenses Numbered . . .			
	One or More	One	Two	Three or More
All offenses	58%	59%	56%	56%
Violent offenses	47%	49%	45%	39%
Murder	16	18	14	6
Sexual assault	49	50	51	39
Robbery	34	35	32	27
Aggravated assault	57	58	54	55
Other violent	59	60	56	50
Property offenses	61%	62%	59%	65%
Burglary	55	55	54	53
Larceny	59	60	55	58
Fraud	71	72	69	76
Drug offenses	60%	61%	57%	60%
Possession	65	65	60	73
Trafficking	57	57	57	58
Weapons offenses	57%	58%	56%	53%
Other offenses	61%	61%	61%	66%

SOURCE: David Levin, Patrick Langan, and Jodi Brown, *State Court Sentencing of Convicted Felons, 1996* (Washington, DC: Bureau of Justice Statistics, 2000).

court ruled that requiring a probationer to make a public apology in the local newspaper for driving drunk was too punitive and a more drastic requirement than those authorized by the state's probation laws.[12]

Judges, however, may legally impose restrictions tailored to fit the probationer's individual needs or to protect society from additional harm. For example, a child molester can be forbidden to associate with minor children.[13] In one case, a probationer was actually banished from the county in which he lived on the grounds that he was a popular figure among drug-using adolescents to whom he sold cocaine; barring him from his residence also gave him an opportunity for a fresh start.[14] The most common of these special conditions include residential placement, alcohol- or drug-abuse treatment and testing, mental health counseling, house arrest, and community service (the last two conditions are discussed later in this chapter); almost half of all probationers are given one or more special conditions.[15] Probationers' community supervision may be revoked if they fail to comply with these conditions and to obey the reasonable requests of the probation staff to meet their treatment obligations.[16]

Probationers can be ordered to abstain from using alcohol and illegal drugs and to take chemical tests at the request of their probation officer to determine whether they have recently used controlled substances.[17] Some courts have permitted probation officers to demand drug tests even though such testing was not part of the original conditions of probation.[18] Probationers can be required to cooperate with legal authorities; for instance, they may be required to testify against others in grand jury hearings.[19] Similarly, probation rules can require periodic reporting of personal practices; for example, tax violators can be required to submit their tax returns.[20] A common procedure today is to require probationers to make restitution to the victims of their crimes (restitution will be discussed later in this chapter).

Courts have upheld probation conditions as long as they are reasonably related to the purposes of probation. Probation conditions may even infringe on some constitutional rights, as long as they are not capricious or cruel.[21] Probationers have a right to challenge rules imposed at the time of sentencing or others imposed later by the court (for example, if the original rules are violated). Some courts have ruled that probationers may bring legal challenges to rules even before they have been charged with their violation.[22]

Administration of Probation Services

Probation services are organized in a variety of ways, depending on the state and the jurisdiction in which they are located. Some states have a statewide probation service, but each court jurisdiction actually controls its local department. Other states maintain a strong statewide authority with centralized control and administration. Thirty states combine probation and parole services in a single unit; some combine juvenile and adult probation departments, while others maintain these departments separately.

The typical probation department is situated in a single court district, such as a juvenile, superior, district, or municipal court. The relationship between the department and court personnel (especially the judge) is extremely close.

In the typical department, the chief probation officer (CPO) sets policy, supervises hiring, determines training needs, and may personally discuss sentencing with the judge or made recommendations. In state-controlled departments, some of the CPO's duties are mandated by the central office; training guidelines, for example, may be determined at the state level. If, however, the department is locally controlled, the CPO is invested with great discretion in the management of the department.

Most large probation departments also have one or more assistant chiefs. In departments of moderate size, each of these middle managers may be responsible

True/False 11
Multiple choice 12
Essay 1

for a particular aspect of probation services: One assistant chief will oversee training; another will supervise treatment and counseling services; another will act as a liaison with police or other agencies. In smaller departments, the CPO and the executive officers may also maintain a caseload or investigate cases for the court. For example, the chief may handle a few of the most difficult cases personally. In larger municipal departments, however, the probation chief is a purely administrative figure.

The line staff, or probation officers (POs), may be in direct personal contact with the entire supervisory staff, or they may be independent of the chief and answer mainly to the assistant chiefs. Line staff perform the following major functions:

1. They supervise or monitor cases assigned to them to ensure that the rules of probation are followed.
2. They attempt to rehabilitate their cases through specialized treatment techniques.
3. They investigate the lives of convicted offenders to enable the court to make intelligent sentencing decisions.
4. They occasionally collect fines due the court or oversee the collection of delinquent payments, such as child support.
5. They interview complainants and defendants to determine whether criminal action should be taken, whether cases can be decided informally, whether diversion should be advocated, and so on. This last procedure, called intake, is common in juvenile probation.

Some officers view themselves as "social workers" and maintain a treatment orientation; their goal is to help offenders adjust in the community. Others are "law enforcers" who are more concerned with supervision, control, and public safety. An officer's style is influenced by both personal values and the department's general policies and orientation toward the goals of probation.[23] In some major cities, the probation department is quite complex, controlling detention facilities, treatment programs, and research and evaluation staffs. In such a setting, the CPO's role is similar to that of a director of a multiservice public facility. This CPO rarely comes into direct contact with clients, and his or her behavior, attitudes, and values are quite different from those of the rural CPO who sometimes maintains a full caseload.

Duties of Probation Officers

Staff officers in probation departments are usually charged with four primary tasks: investigation, intake, diagnosis, and treatment supervision.

In the investigation stage, the probation officer conducts an inquiry within the community to discover the factors related to the offender's criminality. The **presentence investigation** is conducted primarily to gain information for judicial sentences, but in the event that the offender is placed on probation, the investigation becomes a useful basis for treatment and supervision.

Intake is a process by which probation officers interview cases that have been summoned to the court for initial appearances. Intake is most commonly used with juvenile offenders but may also be used in adult misdemeanor cases. During juvenile court intake, the petitioner (the juvenile) and the complainant (the private citizen or the police officer) may work with the probation officer to determine an equitable resolution of the case. The PO may settle the case without further court action, recommend restitution or other compensation, initiate actions that result in a court hearing, or recommend unofficial or informal probation.

 State and county probation departments sponsor a number of Web sites. The New York State Probation Officers Association (NYSPOA) is a professional organization formed more than three decades ago to represent the interests of line officers working in the field of probation. You can access their site at http://www.nyspoa.com/

For an up-to-date list of Web links, see http://www.wadsworth.com/product/0534573053s

Fill in the blanks 9–12
True/False 12

presentence investigation
A postconviction investigation, performed by a probation officer attached to the trial court, of the defendant's background, education, employment, family, acquaintances, physical and mental health, prior criminal record, and other factors that may affect sentencing.

intake
The process by which a probation officer settles cases at the initial court appearance, before the onset of formal criminal proceedings.

Probation may be revoked if the probationer either commits a new crime or violates the rules set down by the court. Here a Los Angeles probation officer talks to a client who has violated probation, while police officers look on.

© A. Ramey/Woodfin Camp & Associates

Diagnosis is the analysis of the probationer's personality and the subsequent development of a personality profile that may be helpful in treating the offender. Diagnosis involves evaluating the probationer based on information from an initial interview (intake) or the presentence investigation for the purpose of planning a proper treatment program. The diagnosis should not merely label the offender as, for example, neurotic or psychopathic, but should "codify all that has been learned about the individual, organized in such a way as to provide a means for the establishment of future treatment goals."[24]

diagnosis
Evaluation of a probationer's personality and other information for the purpose of planning a proper treatment program.

Treatment Supervision Based on a knowledge of psychology, social work, or counseling and the diagnosis of the offender, the probation officer plans a treatment program that will, it is hoped, allow the probationer to fulfill the probation contract and make a reasonable adjustment to the community.

In years past, the probation staff had primary responsibility for supervision and treatment. Probation officers today rarely have hands-on treatment responsibility and instead employ the resources of the community to carry out this function. Attitudes toward treatment also seem to be changing. Probation officers seem less interested today in treating clients than in controlling their behavior.[25] Some experts have called for totally eliminating the personal involvement of probation officers in supervising treatment.[26] However, the increasing number of narcotics abusers in probation caseloads often overwhelms the availability of community-based substance abuse programs; as a result, some probation departments are making greater efforts to deal directly with substance abuse.[27] Some maintain a substance abuse specialist, a senior-level probation officer responsible for the clinical treatment of offenders, some of whom suffer both from addiction and from other character, personality, or cultural problems.[28]

The diagnostic, treatment, and investigative skills needed for effective probation work are hard to find in a single individual. Probation officers often have social work backgrounds, and a master's degree in counseling or criminal justice may be a prerequisite for hiring or advancement in large departments. Today, most jurisdictions require officers to have a background in the social sciences and to hold at least a bachelor's degree.

Fill in the blanks 13
True/False 13

Presentence Investigations An important task of probation officers is the investigation and evaluation of defendants coming before the court for sentencing. The court uses presentence investigation reports in deciding whether to grant probation, incarcerate, or use other forms of treatment.

The style and content of presentence investigations may vary among jurisdictions and also among individual probation officers within the same jurisdiction. Some departments require voluminous reports covering every aspect of the defendant's life; other departments, which may be rule-oriented, require that officers stick to the basic facts, such as the defendant's age, race, sex, and previous offense record. Each department also has its own standards for presentence investigations.

At the conclusion of most presentence investigations, a recommendation is made to the presiding judge that reflects the department's sentencing posture on the case at hand. This is a crucial aspect of the report because the probation department's recommendation is followed in many, though not all, cases. Probation officers make critical decisions when recommending sentences to a judge, and a number of environmental and situational factors are thought to influence their decisions.

Presentence investigations are extremely important, as the recommendations developed out of them are followed closely by the sentencing judge.[29] Federal courts have prohibited defendants from suing probation officers who have made errors in their presentence investigations, on the grounds that liability "would seriously erode the officers' independent fact-finding function and would as a result impair the sentencing judge's ability to carry out his judicial duties."[30]

Fill in the blanks 14
True/False 14
Multiple choice 13

risk classification
Assigning probationers to a level and type of supervision based on their particular needs and the risks they pose for the community.

Risk Classification Probation officers classify and assign cases to a level and type of supervision on the basis of the clients' particular needs and the risks they present to the community. Based on this **risk classification**, some clients may receive frequent (intensive) supervision, while others are assigned to minimum monitoring by a probation officer.

A number of risk assessment approaches are used, but most employ such objective measures as the offender's age, employment status, drug abuse history, prior felony convictions, and number of address changes in the year prior to sentencing

Larry Wayne Harris, in prison garb and chains, giving "thumbs up" after his arrest in 1998 on suspicion of possession of a deadly virus. After his arrest, it was found that Harris had been on probation for illegally obtaining the bacteria that causes bubonic plague. Should people such as Harris be granted probation?

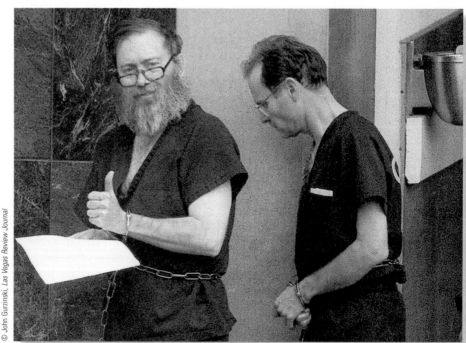

© John Gurzinski, *Las Vegas Review Journal*

EXHIBIT 14.2 RISK PREDICTION SCALE

Automatic Component: Automatically places an individual in low-activity supervision if two conditions are satisfied:

A. Offender has a 12th-grade education or better.
B. Individual has a history free of opiate usage.

If the two conditions are not met, the remaining items are scored:

C. 28 years of age or older at time of offense: 7 points. If not, score as 0.
D. Arrest-free period of five or more consecutive years: 4 points. If not, score as 0.
E. Few prior arrests (none, one, or two = 10 points). If not, score as 0.
F. History free of opiate usage: 9 points. If not, score as 0.
G. At least four months of steady employment immediately prior to arraignment for present offense: 3 points. If not, score as 0.

Risk Score	Supervisor Level	Minimum Personal Contacts	Maximum Personal Contacts	Collateral Contacts
Automatic assignment or 20–33	Low activity	1 per quarter	1 per quarter	Unlimited
0–19	High activity	1 per month	No maximum	Unlimited

SOURCE: Adapted from the Classification and Supervision Planning System, Probation Division, Administrative Office, U.S. Courts, January 1981.

(see Exhibit 14.2).[31] Efforts are under way to create more effective instruments using subjective information obtained through face-to-face interviews and encounters.[32]

Does classification make a dramatic difference in the success of probation? There is little clear-cut evidence that classification has a substantial impact on reducing recidivism. But although probation administrators are often skeptical about their validity, they continue to use these scales and believe they may be a useful tool in case management and treatment delivery. The scales may validate the probation officer's self-perception of being a rational and scientific decision maker.[33] The classification of offenders aids the most important goal of supervision: reducing the risk the probationer presents to the community. In addition, classification schemes fit well with desert-based sentencing models: The most serious cases get the most intensive supervision.[34]

How Successful Is Probation?

True/False 15
Multiple choice 14–15

Probation is the most commonly used alternative sentence for a number of reasons: It is humane, it helps offenders maintain community and family ties, and it is cost-effective. Incarcerating an inmate costs more than $20,000 a year; probation costs less than one-tenth that amount per year.[35]

Probation may be inexpensive, but is it successful? If most probation orders fail, the costs of repeated criminality would certainly outweigh the cost savings of a probation sentence. Overall, most probation orders do seem successful. According to the most recent Bureau of Justice Statistics survey (1999), about 61 percent of adults leaving probation were considered "successful." Among the rest, 14 percent had been returned to prison, 3 percent had absconded from the jurisdiction, and another 11 percent were ruled unsuccessful for unknown reasons.

Felony Probation Although the typical client completes probation successfully, the most serious felony offenders may be the ones most likely to commit new crimes. Since felons are commonly granted probation today, this issue is an important one. To track the outcome of felony probation, Joan Petersilia and her colleagues at the Rand Corporation, a private think tank, traced 1,672 men convicted of felonies who had been granted probation in Los Angeles and Alameda counties in California.[36] They found that 1,087 (65%) were rearrested; of those rearrested, 853 (51%) were convicted; and of those convicted, 568 (34%) were sentenced to jail or prison! Of the probationers who had new charges filed against them, 75 percent were charged with burglary, theft, robbery, and other predatory crimes; 18 percent were convicted of serious violent crimes.

The Rand researchers found that probation is by far the most common sentencing alternative to prison, used in about 60 to 80 percent of all criminal convictions. What is disturbing, however, is that the crimes and criminal records of about 25 percent of all probationers are indistinguishable from those of offenders who go to prison.

Who Fails on Probation? Young males who have no job or a very low income, a prior criminal record, and a history of instability are most likely to be rearrested. In contrast, probationers who are married with children, have lived in the area for two or more years, and are adequately employed are the most likely to be successful on probation.[37] Among female probationers, those who have stable marriages, who are better educated, and who are employed full- or part-time are more likely to successfully complete probation orders than male probationers or those who are single, less educated, and unemployed. Prior record is also related to probation success: Clients who have a history of criminal behavior, prior probation, and previous incarceration are the most likely to fail.[38]

Essay 2

Why Do People Fail on Probation? Probationers bring with them a great deal of emotional baggage that may reduce their chances of successful rehabilitation. Many are felons with long histories of offending; more than 75 percent of all probationers have had prior convictions. Others suffer from a variety of social and psychological disabilities. Recent surveys conducted by the federal government indicate that a significant number (16%) suffer from mental illness.[39] Whether mentally ill or mentally sound, probationers are likely to have grown up in households in which family members were incarcerated and to have lived part of their lives in a foster home or state institution. Many had parents and/or guardians who abused drugs; they also suffered high rates of physical and sexual abuse. They are now unemployed or underemployed, and almost half were substance abusers. Considering their harsh and abusive backgrounds and their current economic distress and mental illness, it comes as no surprise that many may find it difficult to comply with the rules of probation and forgo criminal activity.

Although the recidivism rate of probationers seems high, it is still somewhat lower than the recidivism rate of prison inmates.[40] To improve probation effectiveness, it could be supplemented with more stringent rules, such as curfews, and closer supervision. Even though such measures can dramatically increase the cost of probation, they would still be far less expensive than the cost of incarceration.

Probationers in Prison What types of acts cause probation to be terminated? One federally sponsored survey of more than 160,000 incarcerated probation violators found that 74 percent had been convicted of a new offense and the remaining 26 percent had violated a technical condition.[41] Most had been arrested for a new offense, but others had tested positive for drug use, failed to report for drug testing/treatment, failed to report for counseling, left the jurisdiction without telling their probation officer, neglected to make restitution payments, made contact with known offenders, or failed to report a change in address.

These "probation failures" were responsible for a significant number of highly serious crimes. They had committed at least 6,400 murders, 7,400 rapes, 10,400 assaults, and 17,000 robberies while under supervision in the community.[42] These offenders are referred to as **avertable recidivists**—people whose crimes could have been avoided if they had been sent to prison in the first place.

avertable recidivist
Repeat offender whose new crime could have been prevented if he or she had been incarcerated rather than released on bail, probation, or parole.

Legal Rights of Probationers

Multiple choice 16–21

The Supreme Court has ruled that probationers have a unique status and therefore are entitled to fewer constitutional protections than other citizens. Two cases illustrate this status. In *Minnesota v. Murphy,* a probationer was ordered to seek psychological counseling. During his therapy session, he admitted to his counselor that he had committed a rape; the counselor reported this admission to Murphy's probation officer. The probation officer confronted Murphy about the rape and murder, he admitted his crimes, and the information was turned over to prosecutors.[43] Murphy contested his subsequent conviction on rape and murder on the grounds that the information he gave the probation officer was an in-custody interrogation and that therefore he should have been given the *Miranda* warning. However, the Supreme Court ruled that requiring a probationer to show up for an appointment is not equivalent to an arrest and, therefore, self-incrimination protections do not apply. The Court held that, unlike doctor–patient or attorney–client relationships, the probation officer–client relationship is not confidential. Furthermore, the *Murphy* decision held that a probation officer could even use trickery or psychological pressure to get information and turn it over to police.

In *Griffin v. Wisconsin,* the Supreme Court held that a probationer's home may be searched without a warrant, on the grounds that probation departments "have in mind the welfare of the probationer" and must "respond quickly to evidence of misconduct." The usual legal standards did not apply to probation because to do so "would reduce the deterrent effect of the supervisory arrangement," and "the probation agency must be able to act based upon a lesser degree of certainty than the Fourth Amendment would otherwise require in order to intervene before a probationer does damage to himself or society."[44]

Probation Revocation

If a probationer violates the rules or terms of probation or commits a new crime, probation can be revoked and the offender placed in an institution. Revocation is often not an easy decision, because it conflicts with the treatment philosophy of most probation departments.

When revocation is chosen, the offender is notified and a formal hearing scheduled. If the charges against the probationer are upheld, the offender can then be placed in an institution to serve the remainder of the sentence. Most departments will not revoke probation unless the offender commits another crime or seriously violates the rules of probation.

Because placing a person on probation implies that probation will continue unless the probationer commits some major violation, the defendant has been given certain procedural due process rights at this stage of the criminal process. In three significant decisions, the U.S. Supreme Court provided procedural safeguards that apply at proceedings to revoke probation (and parole). In *Mempa v. Rhay* (1967), the Court unanimously held that a probationer was constitutionally entitled to counsel in a revocation-of-probation proceeding where the imposition of sentence had been suspended.[45] Then, in *Morrissey v. Brewer* (1972), the Court held that parolees were entitled to an informal inquiry to determine whether there was probable cause to revoke their parole; the same standard has been applied to probationers."[46] Finally, in the 1973 case of *Gagnon v. Scarpelli,* the Supreme Court held that both probationers and parolees have a constitutionally limited right to counsel in revocation proceedings.[47]

In *United States v. Granderson* (1994), the Supreme Court helped clarify what can happen to a probationer whose community sentence is revoked. Granderson was eligible for a 6-month prison sentence but instead was given 60 months of probation. When he tested positive for drugs, his probation was revoked. The statute he was sentenced under required that he serve one-third his original sentence in prison. When the trial court sentenced him to 20 months, he appealed. Was his original sentence 6 months or 60 months? The Court found that it would be unfair to force a probationer to serve more time in prison than he would have if originally incarcerated and ruled that the proper term should have been one-third of 6 months, or 2 months.[48]

PERSPECTIVES ON JUSTICE

The revocation of probation represents the inherent conflict between its rehabilitation and crime control aspects. On the one hand, probation is viewed as a "second chance" that enables deserving offenders to rehabilitate themselves in the community. On the other hand, probationers are convicted offenders who must obey stringent rules unless they want to be sent to prison. Rehabilitation advocates may not want to pull the "revocation trigger" unless it is absolutely necessary, whereas those who espouse a crime control approach may be less charitable toward breaches of probation rules.

Essay 3

The Future of Probation

Probation will likely continue to be the most popular alternative sentence used by U.S. courts; if anything, its use as a community-based correction will continue to grow. Part of its appeal stems from its flexibility, which allows it to be coupled with a wide variety of treatment programs, including residential care. As prison overcrowding has grown worse, more than half the states have taken measures to change their probation guidelines to help reduce the prison population.[49] It is unlikely that the treatment and rehabilitation potential of probation will be abandoned in the twenty-first century.[50]

Probation will continue to be a sentence of choice in both felony and misdemeanor cases because it holds the promise of great savings in cost at a time when many state budgets are being reduced. In fact, it is possible to help defray the cost of probation by asking clients to pay fees for probation services, a concept that would be impossible with prison inmates. At least 25 states now impose some form of fee on probationers to defray the cost of community corrections. Massachusetts has initiated day fees, which are based on the probationer's wages (the usual fee is between one and three days' wages each month).[51] An analysis of the probation fee system found that it may actually improve the quality of services afforded clients.[52] Texas requires judges to impose supervision fees unless the offender is truly unable to pay; fees make up more than half the probation department's annual budget.[53]

Probation is unquestionably undergoing dramatic changes. During the past decade, it has been supplemented and used as a restrictive correctional alternative. Expanding the scope of probation has created a new term, **intermediate sanctions**, to signify penalties that fall between traditional community supervision and confinement in jail or prison. These new correctional services are discussed in detail in the remainder of this chapter.

intermediate sanctions
A group of punishments falling between probation and prison; community-based sanctions including house arrest and intensive supervision.

INTERMEDIATE SANCTIONS

Community correction has traditionally emphasized offender rehabilitation. The probation officer has been viewed as a caseworker or counselor whose primary job is to help the offender adjust to society. Offender surveillance and control have seemed more appropriate for law enforcement, jails, and prisons than for community corrections.[54]

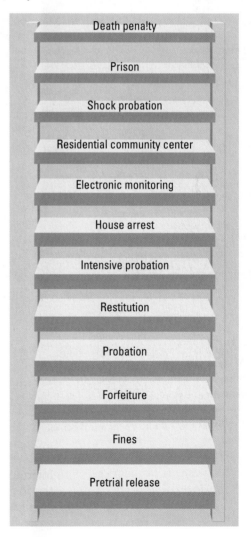

PERSPECTIVES ON JUSTICE

Since 1980, a more conservative justice system has reoriented toward social control. The rehabilitative ideals of probation have not been abandoned, but new programs have been developed that add a control dimension to community corrections. These programs can be viewed as "probation plus," because they add restrictive penalties and conditions to community service orders. More punitive than probation, intermediate sanctions can be sold to conservatives while remaining attractive to liberals as alternatives to incarceration.

Multiple choice 22

Intermediate sanctions include programs typically administered by probation departments: intensive probation supervision, house arrest, electronic monitoring, restitution orders, shock probation or split sentences, and residential community corrections.[55] Some experts also include high-impact shock incarceration, or "boot camp" experiences, within the definition of intermediate sanctions, but since these programs are typically operated by correctional departments, they are discussed separately in Chapter 15. Intermediate sanctions also include sentences administered independently of probation staffs: fines and forfeiture, pretrial programs, and pretrial and posttrial residential programs. Intermediate sanctions thus range from the barely intrusive, such as restitution orders, to the highly restrictive, such as house arrest accompanied by electronic monitoring and a stay in a community correctional center (see Figure 14.2).

What are the advantages of creating a system of intermediate sanctions? Primary is the need to develop alternatives to prisons and jails, which have proved to be costly, ineffective, and injurious. Research indicates that more than 60 percent of all prison inmates are rearrested and returned to prison, many within a short period after their release.[56] Little evidence exists that incapacitation is either a general deterrent to crime or a specific deterrent against future criminality. Some correctional systems have become inundated with new inmates. Even states that have extensively used alternative sanctions have experienced rapid increases in their prison population; the pressure on the correctional system if alternative sanctions had not been an option is almost inconceivable.[57] Other nations have embraced alternative sanctions and, despite rising crime rates, have not experienced the explosion in the prison population that has occurred in the United States. This issue is explored further in the International Justice feature.

Intermediate sanctions also have the potential to save money. Though more expensive than traditional probation, they are far less costly than incarceration. If those offenders given alternative sanctions were incarcerated instead, the extra cost would be significant. In addition, offenders given intermediate sanctions generate income, pay taxes, reimburse victims, perform community service, and provide other cost savings that would not exist had they been incarcerated. Although it is unlikely that intermediate sanctions will pay an immediate "corrections dividend," as many correctional costs are fixed, they may reduce the need for future prison and jail construction.

FIGURE 14.2
THE PUNISHMENT
LADDER

Death penalty

Prison

Shock probation

Residential community center

Electronic monitoring

House arrest

Intensive probation

Restitution

Probation

Forfeiture

Fines

Pretrial release

INTERNATIONAL JUSTICE

Community Sentencing Abroad

Although the crime rate has been declining in the United States for nearly a decade, "get tough" measures such as "three strikes and you're out" have resulted in a steadily increasing prison population. Western European countries have crime rates similar to those in the United States, but their incarceration rates are much lower; criminal penalties there are not nearly as harsh as they are in the United States. This disparity in punishment has not been lost on researchers such as legal scholar Michael Tonry, who has explored the differences between the United States and other Western democracies.

Tonry points out that crime trends seem to have an important impact on U.S. incarceration policies. As the crime rate goes up, so too does media coverage of crime stories. Political figures, especially those running for office, feed off the media coverage and make crime an election focus. These events fuel public anxiety, producing an outcry for punitive measures against criminals. Politicians are happy to oblige their constituents and pass tough sanctions against criminals to show their sensitivity to the voters.

Tonry finds that crime has taken on increasing political importance since the 1964 presidential election. Since the 1990s, the overused phrase "get tough on crime" has crossed party lines, as lawmakers promise to implement harsh measures against criminals regardless of whether they will actually reduce crime or if they are really needed. As crime rates fall, both the politicians and the public credit the "get tough" stance for

success, even though there is little evidence that draconian measures actually reduce crime. Crime rates were already trending downward before harsh reform laws such as mandatory minimum sentencing and truth in sentencing were passed; yet conservatives believe that these get-tough measures helped reduce crime rates.

Western European nations have taken a different approach to crime control. When crime rates rose in European democracies, lawmakers focused on making punishment fair rather than harsh. Rather than mandatory sentencing, individual circumstances and the reasons for committing a crime are considered. Western European lawmakers also focus on punishments that are utilitarian and effective in reducing crime, rather than punitive and retributive. They often rely on community sentences, such as day fines based on the offender's earnings and economic circumstances. The money collected from day fines not only punishes the offender but also serves to benefit society.

Western European judges have also been more likely to sentence offenders to community service. Community service, which ironically was created in the United States, has quickly become the sentence of choice for minor crimes in European nations. Whereas community service hours can number in the thousands in the United States for criminals, European sentences often limit the number of hours to 240.

Incarceration sentences in Europe are substantially shorter than in the United States. No European country has implemented mandatory sentences or

truth in sentencing. Almost all efforts to control or reduce judicial discretion have been met with disapproval. Tonry points out that Western European judges and prosecutors are career civil servants, free from political concerns. Not having to worry about an upcoming election allows them to focus on what they believe is just rather than on what is politically expedient.

Critical Thinking Skills

The use of community service in Europe is commendable, but is it practical in the United States, where recidivism rates are very high? A significant percentage of all criminal acts are committed by avertable recidivists—people who are out on bail, probation, or parole. Considering this, should we try to hold suspected and convicted criminals as long as possible by toughening bail requirements, restricting probation, and/or eliminating parole? Would the cost of such a "get tough" policy outweigh the benefits of a lowered crime rate?

InfoTrac College Edition Research

To learn more about these programs, use "probation" and "community treatment" as key terms in InfoTrac College Edition.

SOURCES: Michael Tonry, "Why Are U.S. Incarceration Rates So High?" *Crime and Delinquency* 45 (1999): 419–438; Michael Tonry, "Parochialism in U.S. Sentencing Policy," *Crime and Delinquency* 45 (1999): 48–66.

Multiple choice 23

Fines

Intermediate sanctions also help courts in their efforts to collect fines.

In most jurisdictions, little guidance is given to the sentencing judge regarding the imposition of fines. Judges often have inadequate information on the offender's ability to pay, resulting in defaults and contempt charges; it has been estimated that defendants fail to pay upwards of $2 billion in fines each year.[58]

Fines are the most common criminal sentence and are sometimes used in conjunction with other sentences. Here, Daniel Troyer, 39, is led away after his sentencing in Salt Lake City, June 11, 1999. Troyer, a career criminal who was charged with murdering two elderly Salt Lake City women, was given two consecutive life sentences and a $10,000 fine in a plea-bargain agreement. Why would a judge fine a criminal who has just received a life sentence?

AP/Wide World Photos

Because the standard sanction for nonpayment is incarceration, many offenders held in local jails are confined for nonpayment of criminal fines. Although the U.S. Supreme Court in *Tate v. Short* (1971) recognized that incarcerating a person who is financially unable to pay a fine discriminates against the poor, many judges continue to incarcerate offenders for noncompliance with financial orders.[59]

Research indicates that, given the facts of a case, judges do seem to use fines in a rational manner. Low-risk offenders are the ones most likely to receive fines instead of a jail sentence. Offenders who are fined seem less likely to commit new crimes than those who receive a jail sentence.[60]

The more serious the crime, the higher the amount of the fine. Because judges rely so heavily on offense seriousness to fix the level of fines, financial penalties may have a negative impact on success rates. The more serious the offense and the higher the fine, the greater the chances that the offender will fail to pay the fine and risk probation revocation. To overcome this sort of problem, some jurisdictions, such as New York City, are experimenting with **day fines**.[61]

A concept that originated in Europe, day fines are geared to an offender's net daily income. In an effort to make them equitable and fairly distributed, fines are based on the severity of the crime weighted by a daily-income value taken from a chart similar to an income tax table; the number of the offender's dependents is also taken into account. The day fine concept means that the severity of punishment is geared to the offender's ability to pay.

An evaluation of the Staten Island, New York, project indicates that it is generally successful, enabling judges to increase the amount of fines collected while reducing the number of arrest warrants issued for failure to appear at postsentencing hearings; even if the fine could not be paid in full, more offenders paid something as opposed to nothing.[62] Day fines hold the promise of becoming an

day fine
A fine geared to an offender's net daily income, as well as number of dependents and the seriousness of the crime, in an effort to make sentences more equitable.

equitable solution to the problem of setting the amount of a fine according to the offender's ability to pay.

True/False 16
Multiple choice 24–26

forfeiture
The seizure of personal property by the state as a civil or criminal penalty.

Forfeiture

Another alternative sanction with a financial basis is criminal (in personam) and civil (in rem) **forfeiture**. Both involve the seizure of goods and instrumentalities related to the commission or outcome of a criminal act. For example, federal law provides that after arresting drug traffickers, the government may seize boats used to import the narcotics, cars used to carry the drugs overland, warehouses in which the drugs were stored, and homes paid for with the drug profits; on conviction, the drug dealers lose permanent ownership of these "instrumentalities" of crime.

Forfeiture is not a new sanction. During the Middle Ages, "forfeiture of estate" was a mandatory result of most felony convictions. The Crown could seize all of a felon's real and personal property. Forfeiture derived from the common law concept of "corruption of blood" or "attaint," which prohibited a felon's family from inheriting or receiving his or her property or estate. The common law mandated that descendants could not inherit property from a relative who may have obtained the property illegally: "The Corruption of Blood stops the Course of Regular Descent, as to Estates, over which the Criminal could have no Power, because he never enjoyed them."[63]

Forfeiture was reintroduced to U.S. law with the passage of the Racketeer Influenced and Corrupt Organizations (RICO) and the Continuing Criminal Enterprises acts, both of which allow the seizure of any property derived from illegal enterprises or conspiracies. Although these acts were designed to apply to ongoing criminal conspiracies, such as drug or pornography rings, they are now being applied to a far-ranging series of criminal acts, including white-collar crimes. More than 100 federal statutes use forfeiture of property as a punishment.

Although law enforcement officials at first applauded the use of forfeiture as a hard-hitting way of seizing the illegal profits of drug law violators, the practice has been criticized because the government has often been overzealous in its application. For example, million-dollar yachts have been seized because someone aboard possessed a small amount of marijuana; this confiscatory practice is referred to as zero tolerance. This strict interpretation of the forfeiture statutes has come under fire because it is often used capriciously, the penalty is sometimes disproportionate to the crime involved, and it makes the government a "partner in crime."[64] It is also alleged that forfeiture unfairly targets a narrow range of offenders. For example, it is common for government employees involved in corruption to forfeit their pensions; employees of private companies are exempt from such punishment.[65]

The Supreme Court has expanded the ability of government agents to seize property in some instances and restricted it in others. For example, in the recent case of *United States v. Ursery* (1996), the Court settled the issue of whether a person can both have his assets seized and be prosecuted for the same criminal offense. Jerome Ursery paid a fine of $13,250 to settle a civil forfeiture claim against his home after police seized 147 marijuana plants on the premises. He was later criminally prosecuted and sentenced to prison. In its opinion, the Court held that the Constitution bars successive prosecutions for the same crime, not successive punishments.[66] In another case that expanded police power to seize property, *Bennis v. Michigan,* the Supreme Court ruled that a person's property could be seized and confiscated if used in a crime even if the owner had no knowledge of the crime; an "innocent owner" cannot recover his or her property.[67]

Some commentators maintain that the use of (civil) forfeiture has allowed the government to impose what in essence are fines that are unreasonable and severely disproportionate to the seriousness of the offense.[68] And, in fact, the Supreme

Court limited confiscatory practices in two recent cases, *Austin v. United States* and *Alexander v. United States,* in which it held that the seizure of property must be proportional to the seriousness of the crime in both civil and criminal forfeitures.[69] In the *Alexander* case, the government seized an entire chain of adult bookstores and ordered the destruction of the entire inventory of 100,000 items after the owner was convicted of selling seven obscene items; *Austin* involved the civil seizure of the defendant's home and business after he was convicted of possessing two grams of cocaine. Despite this setback, it is likely that forfeiture will continue to be used as an alternative sanction against such selective targets as drug dealers and white-collar criminals.

Restitution

Another popular intermediate sanction is **restitution**, requiring either that offenders pay back the victims of their crimes (**monetary restitution**) or that they serve the community to compensate for their criminal acts (**community service restitution**).[70] Restitution programs offer offenders a chance to avoid a jail or prison sentence or a lengthier probationary period. It may help them develop a sense of allegiance to society, better work habits, and some degree of gratitude for being given a second chance. Restitution also gives the community something of value without asking it to foot the bill for incarceration and helps victims regain lost property and income.[71]

If monetary restitution is called for, the probation department typically makes a determination of victim loss and develops a plan for paying fair compensation. To avoid the situation in which a well-heeled offender can fill a restitution order by merely writing a check, judges will sometimes order that compensation be paid out of income derived from a low-paid social service or public works job.

Community service orders usually require duty in a public nursing home, homeless shelter, hospital, drug treatment unit, or public works program; some young vandals may find that they must clean up the damage they caused to the school or the park. Judges sometimes have difficulty gauging the length of community service orders. One suggestion is that the maximum order should be no more than 240 hours and that this should be considered the equivalent of a 6- to

True/False 17
Multiple choice 27
Essay 4

restitution
Criminal sanction that requires the offender to repay the victim and/or society for damage caused by the criminal act.

monetary restitution
Criminal sanction that requires the offender to compensate the victim for property damage, lost wages, medical costs, or other losses.

community service restitution
Criminal sanction that requires the offender to work in the community at such tasks as cleaning public parks or helping handicapped children as an alternative to incarceration.

Restitution is a common alternative sanction. These Austin, Texas, probationers are loading relief supplies as part of their court-ordered restitution.

12-month jail term.[72] Whether these terms are truly equivalent remains a matter of personal opinion.

Judges and probation officers have embraced the concept of restitution because it appears to benefit the victim of crime, the offender, the criminal justice system, and society.[73] Financial restitution is inexpensive to administer, helps avoid stigma, and provides compensation for victims of crime. Offenders ordered to do community service work have been placed in schools, hospitals, and nursing homes. Helping them avoid a jail sentence can mean saving the public thousands of dollars that would have gone to maintaining them in a secure institution, frees up needed resources, and gives the community the feeling that equity has been returned to the justice system.

Does restitution work? Most reviews rate it as a qualified success.[74] It is estimated that almost 90 percent of the clients successfully complete their restitution orders and 86 percent have no subsequent contact with the justice system. Most restitution orders are met by a majority of program clients.[75] Other research indicates that those receiving restitution sentences have recidivism rates that are equal to or lower than those of control groups, including those receiving incarceration sentences.[76] One evaluation of community service orders in a federal district court in northern California found that groups of offenders receiving community service were no more likely to commit new crimes than equivalent groups who received incarceration. If this finding is valid, community service would be an effective and less expensive alternative to a jail or prison sentence.[77]

Although these findings are encouraging, the original enthusiasm for the restitution concept has been dampened somewhat by concern that it has not lived up to its promise of being a true alternative to incarceration. Critics charge that restitution merely serves to "widen the net" and increase the proportion of persons whose behavior is regulated and controlled by the state.[78] Instead of helping defendants avoid the pains of imprisonment, restitution orders are believed to add to the burden of people who would ordinarily have been given a relatively lenient probation sentence instead of a prison term.[79]

Shock Probation and Split Sentencing

Multiple choice 28–29
Essay 5

Shock probation and split sentences are alternative sanctions that allow judges to grant offenders community release only after they have sampled prison life. These sanctions are based on the premise that if offenders are given a taste of incarceration sufficient to shock them into law-abiding behavior, they will be reluctant to violate the rules of probation or commit another crime.

In a number of states and in the Federal Criminal Code, a jail term can actually be a condition of probation. About 30 percent of probationers are now given such **split sentences**, including 11 percent of people convicted of murder and 29 percent of rapists.[80] The **shock probation** approach involves resentencing an offender to probation after a short prison stay. The shock comes because the offender originally receives a long maximum sentence but is then eligible for release to community supervision at the discretion of the judge (usually within 90 days of incarceration). About one-third of all probationers in the 14 states that use the program (including Ohio, Kentucky, Idaho, New Jersey, Tennessee, Utah, and Vermont) receive a period of confinement.[81]

split sentence
Giving a brief term of incarceration as a condition of probation.

shock probation
A sentence in which offenders serve a short term in prison to impress them with the pains of incarceration before they begin probation.

Some states have linked the short prison stay with a boot camp experience, referred to as *shock incarceration,* in which young inmates undergo a brief but intense period of military-like training and hard labor designed to impress them with the rigors of prison life.[82] Boot camp programs will be discussed in greater detail in Chapter 15.

Shock probation and split sentencing have been praised as ways to limit prison time, reintegrate the client quickly into the community, maintain family ties, and reduce prison populations and the costs of corrections.[83] Advocates believe that an initial jail sentence probably makes offenders more receptive to the conditions of probation, because it amply illustrates the problems they will face if probation is violated. However, research examining shock programs has provided little evidence of a deterrent effect. Studies have found that shock probationers have the same recidivism rates as other probationers; in some cases, the shock probationers have done demonstrably worse.[84]

Split sentences and shock probation programs have been criticized by those who believe that even a brief period of incarceration can interfere with the purpose of probation, which is to provide the offender with nonstigmatizing, community-based treatment. Even a short-term commitment subjects probationers to the destructive effects of institutionalization, disrupts their life in the community, and stigmatizes them for having been in jail.

Intensive Probation Supervison

Intensive probation supervision (IPS) programs are another important form of intermediate sanction. IPS programs involve small caseloads of 15 to 40 clients who are kept under close watch by probation officers. Such programs have been implemented in some form in about 40 states and today include about 100,000 clients.[85]

The primary goal of IPS is decarceration: Without intensive supervision, clients would normally be sent to already overcrowded prisons or jails.[86] The second goal is control: High-risk offenders can be maintained in the community under much closer security than traditional probation efforts can provide. A third goal is reintegration: Offenders can maintain community ties and be reoriented toward a more productive life while avoiding the pains of imprisonment.

In general, IPS programs rely on a great degree of client contact to achieve the goals of diversion, control, and reintegration.[87] Most programs have admissions criteria based on the nature of the offense and the offender's criminal background. Some programs, such as New Jersey's, exclude violent offenders; others will not take substance abusers. In contrast, some jurisdictions, such as Massachusetts, do not exclude offenders based on their prior criminal history. About 60 percent of existing programs exclude offenders who have already violated probation orders or have otherwise failed on probation.

IPS programs are used in several ways. In some states, IPS is a direct sentence imposed by a judge; in others, it is a postsentencing alternative used to divert offenders from the correctional system. A third practice is to use IPS as a case management tool to give the local probation staff flexibility in dealing with clients. Other jurisdictions use IPS in all three ways and also apply it to probation violators to bring them "halfway back" into the community without resorting to a prison term.

Numerous IPS programs operate around the United States. The best known is Georgia's, which serves as a model for many other states' efforts. Georgia's program includes such measures as

- Five face-to-face contacts per week
- 132 hours of mandatory community service
- Mandatory curfew
- Mandatory employment
- Weekly check of local arrest records
- Automatic notification of arrest via the State Crime Information Network listing
- Routine and unannounced drug and alcohol testing[88]

An evaluation of the Georgia program gave it generally high marks: It reached its target audience and resulted in a 10 percent reduction in the number of felons

True/False 18
Essay 6–7

intensive probation supervision (IPS)
A type of intermediate sanction involving small probation caseloads and strict daily or weekly monitoring.

incarcerated without a significant increase in the recidivism rate.[89] While an IPS program is more expensive than a straight probation sentence, it is far less costly than prison. IPS averages about $16 per day, compared to about $60 for prison; in addition, IPS clients are employed, enabling them to pay taxes, make victim restitution, and support their families.[90]

Evaluations of IPS programs have yielded mixed results. Evaluations often ignore such issues as whether the program met its stated goals, whether IPS is more attractive than other alternative sanctions, and which types of offenders are particularly suited for IPS. For example, IPS seems to work better for offenders with good employment records than it does for the underemployed or unemployed.[91] Younger offenders who commit petty crimes are the most likely to fail on IPS; ironically, people with these characteristics are the ones most likely to be included in IPS programs.[92]

The failure rate in IPS caseloads seems to be quite high, in some cases approaching 50 percent; IPS clients may actually have a higher rearrest rate than other probationers.[93] IPS clients fail more often because they are more serious criminals who might otherwise have been incarcerated and are now being watched and supervised more closely than probationers. Probation officers may also be more willing to revoke the probation of IPS clients because they believe these clients are a risk to the community and, under normal circumstances, would have been incarcerated. Why risk the program to save a few "bad apples"?

In an important analysis of IPS programs in three California counties, Joan Petersilia and Susan Turner found that IPS clients were less dangerous than those sent to prison and just as likely to commit new crimes as clients in traditional probation caseloads.[94] Another nationwide study also found that IPS clients were just as likely to get arrested for new offenses as those in traditional correctional caseloads and more likely to have probation revoked for a technical violation; IPS is a waste of taxpayers' money if it works no better than traditional probation and serves a similar clientele.[95]

Although evidence that it can significantly reduce offending rates is still insufficient, there are some hopeful signs that IPS could one day become an attractive alternative to traditional secure correctional methods. Petersilia and Turner found that IPS clients are more likely to seek treatment and counseling; correctional clients who pursue such help are the most likely to succeed in the long run.[96] A similar evaluation of Arizona's IPS programs found that IPS clients, while they were being supervised, were less likely to commit new crimes than those under standard probation; it was only after termination of supervision that recidivism began to increase.[97] After thoroughly reviewing the impact of IPS, Betsy Fulton and her associates concluded that although IPS programs have not provided a solution to prison crowding, they offer a useful intermediate sanction for those who do not merit imprisonment but pose too high a risk for probation.[98]

Fill in the blanks 15
True/False 19

house arrest
A sentence that requires convicted offenders to spend extended periods of time in their own home as an alternative to incarceration.

House Arrest

The **house arrest** concept requires convicted offenders to spend extended periods of time in their own home as an alternative to an incarceration sentence. For example, persons convicted on a drunk driving charge might be sentenced to spend between 6 P.M. Friday and 8 A.M. Monday and every weekday after 5:30 P.M. in their home, for a period of six months. Current estimates indicate that more than 10,000 people are under house arrest.

As with IPS programs, house arrest initiatives vary widely. Some are administered by probation departments; others are simply judicial sentences monitored by surveillance officers. Some (such as the Florida Community Control Program)

One of the benefits of alternative sanctions such as house arrest is that they allow offenders to maintain a somewhat normal lifestyle. Here, former Republican state Sen. Bill Slocum is shown with his ankle bracelet on during the Crooks Farm Festival in Limestone, Pa., Aug. 26, 2000. Slocum was required to wear the device while he was under house arrest for five months. Slocum campaigned to return to the Senate seat he gave up last year when he was sentenced on federal pollution charges, making him the first candidate in recent Pennsylvania history to campaign while serving a sentence of home confinement.

AP/Wide World Photos

check clients 20 or more times a month; others do only a few curfew checks. Some use 24-hour confinement; others allow offenders to attend work or school. Regardless of the model used, house arrest programs are designed to be more punitive than IPS or any other community supervision alternative and are considered a "last chance" before prison.[99]

No definitive data exist indicating that house arrest is an effective crime deterrent, nor is there sufficient evidence to conclude that it has utility as a device to lower the recidivism rate. One evaluation of the Florida program found that nearly 10 percent of the house arrest sample had their probation revoked for technical violations within 18 months of sentencing.[100] Another evaluation of the same program found that recidivism rates were almost identical to those of a matched sample of inmates released from secure correctional facilities; 4 out of 5 offenders in both forms of correction recidivated within five years.[101]

Criticisms of house arrest also include charges that it has little deterrent value and seems more like being "grounded" than real punishment. They point to such cases as that of convicted Saudi arms dealer Adnan Khashoggi, whose "punishment" required him to be in his 30,000-square-foot luxury home—with its own swimming pool—between the hours of 1 A.M. and 8 A.M., with permission to take trips to Aspen and Fort Lauderdale.[102] While these findings are troublesome, the advantages of house arrest in reducing costs and overcrowding in the correctional system probably make further experimentation inevitable.

electronic monitoring (EM)
Technology that enables probation officers to monitor the location of those under house arrest or other forms of supervision.

Electronic Monitoring

For house arrest to work, sentencing authorities must be assured that arrestees are actually at home during their assigned times. Random calls and visits are one way to check on compliance with house arrest orders. However, one of the more interesting developments in the criminal justice system has been the introduction of **electronic monitoring (EM)** devices to manage offender obedience to home confinement orders.[103]

Electronic monitoring programs have been around since 1964, when Ralph Schwitzgabel of Harvard University experimented with linking offenders with a central monitoring station.[104] As Figure 14.3 shows, EM can be used with offenders at a number of points in the criminal justice system, ranging from pretrial release to parole. Today, about 14,000 probationers are being monitored electronically.[105] However, in all, approximately 1,500 programs exist and 95,000 EM units are in use, including those being used by individuals on pretrial status, home detention, probation, and parole, as well as in juvenile detention.[106]

The electronically monitored offender wears a device around the ankle, wrist, or neck that sends signals back to a control office. Two basic types of systems are used: active and passive. Active systems constantly monitor the offender by continuously sending a signal back to the central office. If the offender leaves home at an unauthorized time, the signal is broken and the "failure" recorded. In some cases, the control officer is automatically notified electronically through a beeper. Passive systems usually involve random phone calls generated by a computer to which the offender must respond within a specified time (such as 30 seconds). Some passive systems require that the offender place the monitoring device into a verifier box that sends a signal back to the control computer; another approach is to have the arrestee repeat words that are analyzed by a voice verifier and compared to tapes of the client's voice. Other systems use radio transmitters that receive a signal from a device worn by the offender and relay it back to the computer monitoring system via telephone lines.

**FIGURE 14.3
KEY DECISION
POINTS WHEN
ELECTRONIC
MONITORING
PROGRAMS ARE
BEING USED**

SOURCE: James Byrne, Arthur Lurigio, and Christopher Baird, *The Effectiveness of the New Intensive Supervision Programs*, Research in Corrections Series, vol. 2, no. 2 (preliminary unpublished draft; Washington, DC: National Institute of Corrections, 1989).

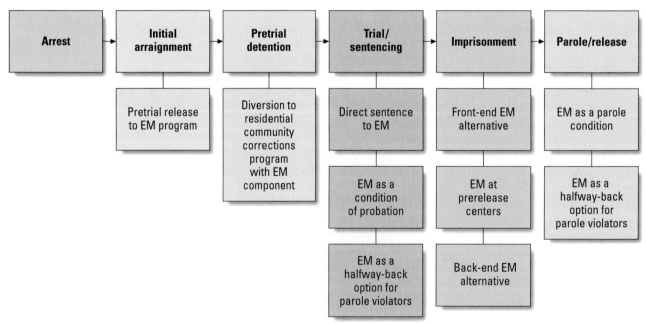

Supporters of EM point to its relatively low cost and high security, while helping offenders avoid the pains of imprisonment in overcrowded, dangerous state facilities. Electronic monitoring is capital- rather than labor-intensive. Since offenders are monitored by computers, an initial investment in hardware rules out the need for hiring many more supervisory officers to handle large numbers of clients. It is not surprising, then, that the public supports EM as a cost-effective alternative to prison sentences.[107]

There are some indications that EM can be an effective addition to the galaxy of alternative sanctions, providing the judiciary with an enhanced supervision tool.[108] Program evaluations with pretrial, probation, and parole groups indicate that recidivism rates are no higher than in traditional programs, costs are lower, and system overcrowding is reduced.[109] For example, one study of the cost savings potential of using house arrest with EM as an alternative to incarceration for drunk drivers in a Pennsylvania county found that the program was able to save money and avoid new construction costs without widening the net of social control.[110]

Research shows that although many EM clients are cited for program violations, recidivism rates are low, clients find the program valuable, and many use the opportunity to obtain jobs and improve family relationships.[111] If the program can service defendants who would otherwise have been incarcerated (for example, people convicted of driving while intoxicated in jurisdictions that have mandatory incarceration sentences), it will prove to be an efficient correctional option that works as well as, if not better than, a probation sentence.[112]

Electronic monitoring holds the promise of becoming a widely used intermediate sanction in the new millennium. Nevertheless, a few critics charge that the concept has drawbacks that can counterbalance its advantages as a form of low-cost confinement.

First, current technology is limited. Existing systems can be affected by faulty telephone equipment; by radio beams from powerful transmitters, such as those located at airports or radio stations; by storms and weather disturbances; and even by large concentrations of iron and steel, which can block signals or cause electromagnetic interference. There have also been cases of EM's being "defeated" by people using call-forwarding systems and prerecorded messages to fool monitors.[113] Assessing what the proper response should be when tracking equipment reveals a breach of home confinement is difficult: Can we incarcerate someone for what might be an equipment failure? As the Criminal Justice and Technology feature shows, new methods are now being developed to improve the efficiency of EM.

Second, it may be inaccurate to assume that electronic monitoring can provide secure confinement at a relatively low cost. In addition to the initial outlay for the equipment, other expenses involved with electronic monitoring include overtime pay for control officers who must be on duty nights or weekends, the cost of training personnel to use the sophisticated equipment, and the cost of educating judges in the legality of home confinement. The cost of home confinement with electronic monitoring is estimated to be four times greater than that of traditional probation.[114]

Third, most electronic monitoring or house arrest programs do not provide for rehabilitation services; the focus is on guaranteeing the secure incapacitation of offenders, not their treatment. Thus, electronic monitoring may lack the deterrent power of a prison sentence while offering little of the rehabilitative effect of traditional probation.

It is assumed that EM will be used as a cost-saving alternative to jail or prison. Unfortunately, alternative sanctions are often directed at offenders who might otherwise have received more lenient sentences, thereby "widening the net" of the criminal system of justice.[115] Electronic monitoring will not save money unless it

To read all about EM, see "Keeping Track of Electronic Monitoring," published by the National Law Enforcement Corrections Technology Center: http://www.nlectc.org/txtfiles/ElecMonasc.html

For an up-to-date list of Web links, see http://www.wadsworth.com/product/0534573053s

Pro-Tech Monitoring is a Florida-based firm that manufactures global positioning monitoring equipment and software to track offenders. Visit their Web site at http://www.ptm.com/

For an up-to-date list of Web links, see http://www.wadsworth.com/product/0534573053s

CRIMINAL JUSTICE AND TECHNOLOGY

Using Technology to Monitor Offenders at Home

Since 1997, the Florida Department of Corrections has been testing a Global Positioning Satellite (GPS) system that enables probation officers to track the movement and location of probationers 24 hours a day; the device notifies probation officers of violations as they occur. GPS is a network of satellites, used by the U.S. Department of Defense, that pinpoints targets anywhere in the world. With GPS, an officer can track an offender on a computer screen and can tell probation officers what street the offender is on, anywhere in the state. GPS currently operates in 18 of the 20 probation circuits in Florida.

Before this technology became available, probation officers had no way of providing early warnings to victims and no way of making certain areas off-limits. To complete the linkup to GPS, an offender straps a pager-size unit to an ankle and carries a lunch-box-size personal tracking device (PTD). Officers can send messages to the offender via the PTD, which has a display area for text. If an offender is in an exclu-sion zone—for example, when the court has ordered a sex offender to have no contact with the victim—the officer can warn the offender to immediately leave that zone. The victim can also be notified by pager that the offender is in the area. With GPS, everything is archived, so if an officer needs to know an offender's whereabouts in the past, that information is readily available.

The GPS is still in the experimental stage. Future home detection systems may incorporate video technology, enabling supervisors to keep visual tabs on offenders. Random telephone calls can then be placed to the offender, who has a video camera in his or her home with a telephone line video adaptor. The offender may be told to perform an action, such as holding up two fingers; the picture is transmitted to the central station, where it is date and time stamped.

Critical Thinking Skills

1. Do these systems smack of a "Big Brother" who can keep tabs on people at any time? Is this an invasion of privacy, or a reasonable alternative to prison?

2. Are there other types of people who might be monitored with these devices—for example, the mentally ill? Can the use of such technology get out of hand?

InfoTrac College Edition Research

To find out more about the use of advanced EM systems, use "home detention" and "electronic monitoring of prisoners" as key terms in Info-Trac College Edition.

SOURCES: Ron Mercer, Murray Brooks, and Paula Tully Bryant, "Global Positioning Satellite System: Tracking Offenders in Real Time," *Corrections Today* 62 (2000): 76–79; Dan Bowers, "Home Detention Systems," *Corrections Today* 62 (2000): 102–106.

---

eliminates the need for new jail and prison construction, as it is unlikely that staff in existing institutions will be let go because offenders are being monitored in their homes.[116]

Finally, some civil libertarians are troubled by EM's potential to erode privacy and liberty. Do we really want U.S. citizens watched over by a computer? What are the limits of electronic monitoring? Can it be used with mental patients? HIV carriers? Suicidal teenagers? Those considered high-risk future offenders? While promising to reduce the correctional population, EM actually has the potential to substantially increase it by turning homes into prisons.[117]

EM seems to hold great promise, but neither its effectiveness nor its virtue has been determined. It is not yet clear whether EM is a correctional savior or a temporary fad.[118]

Residential Community Corrections

The most secure intermediate sanction is a sentence to a **residential community correction (RCC)** facility. Such a facility has been defined as

residential community correction (RCC)
An intermediate sanction, as well as a parole or pretrial option, in which convicted offenders are housed in a nonsecure facility from which they go to work, attend school, and/or participate in treatment activities and programs.

a freestanding nonsecure building that is not part of a prison or jail and houses pretrial and adjudicated adults. The residents regularly depart to work, to attend school, and/or participate in treatment activities and programs.[119]

Traditionally, the function of community corrections has been served by the nonsecure halfway house, designed to reintegrate soon-to-be-paroled prison inmates back into the community. Inmates spend the last few months of their prison term in the halfway house finding employment, building up cash reserves, obtaining an apartment, and developing a job-related wardrobe.

The traditional concept of community corrections has expanded recently. Today, the community correctional facility is a means of providing intermediate sanctions as well as a prerelease center for those about to be paroled from the prison system. RCC may be used as a direct sentencing option by judges who believe that particular offenders need a correctional alternative halfway between traditional probation and a stay in prison. Placement in an RCC center can be used as a condition of probation for offenders who need a nonsecure community facility that provides a more structured treatment environment than traditional probation. It is quite commonly used in the juvenile justice system for youths who need a more secure environment than can be provided by traditional probation yet who are not deemed a threat to the community requiring a secure placement.

Probation departments and other correctional authorities have been charged with running RCC centers that serve as a preprison sentencing alternative. In addition, some RCC centers are operated by private, nonprofit groups that receive referrals from the county or district courts and from probation or parole departments. For example, Portland House, a private, nonprofit residential center in Minneapolis, operates as an alternative to incarceration for young adult felony offenders. The 25 adult male residents regularly receive group therapy and financial, vocational, educational, family, and personal counseling. Residents must work to earn a high school equivalency degree. With funds withheld from their earnings at work-release employment, residents pay room and board, family and self-support, and income taxes. Portland House appears to be successful. It is significantly cheaper to run than a state institution, and the recidivism rate is much lower among its clients than among those who have gone through traditional correctional programs.[120]

For more information on Portland House, go to their Web site: http://www.lssmn.org/portland.htm
For an up-to-date list of Web links, see http://www.wadsworth.com/product/0534573053s

Another well-known RCC program is Nexus, which has facilities in Onamia, Minnesota, and in Onarga and Manteno, Illinois. All told, it has more than 300 clients, approximately 10 percent of them female. Nexus accepts youths between the ages of 13 and 18 who have an intensive history of involvement in the criminal justice system. The Nexus program has a mixed population but provides primary treatment for young sex offenders. Services include treatment for chemical dependency as well as educational, financial, and vocational counseling. Each resident receives a comprehensive individual diagnosis of treatment needs. The program philosophy stresses adoption of treatments that have a proven record of success. Residents are often asked to make restitution to the victims of their crimes.[121]

For more information on the Nexus program, visit their Web site at http://www.nexustreatment.org
For an up-to-date list of Web links, see http://www.wadsworth.com/product/0534573053s

Besides being sole sentence and halfway houses, RCC facilities have also been used as residential pretrial release centers for offenders who are in immediate need of social services and as halfway-back alternatives for parole and probation violators who might otherwise have to be imprisoned. In this capacity, RCC programs serve as a base from which offenders can be placed in outpatient psychiatric facilities, drug and alcohol treatment programs, job training, and so on. Some programs make use of both inpatient and outpatient programs to provide clients with specialized treatment, such as substance abuse management.[122]

Fill in the blanks 17
True/False 20–22
Essay 9

EXHIBIT 14.3 EVALUATION OF METROPOLITAN DAY REPORTING CENTER, BOSTON, MASSACHUSSETTS

- Inmates who participate in the Metropolitan Day Reporting Center are twice as likely to remain crime free after their release from the program than inmates released directly from the county house of correction.
- Only 6 (1.3%) of 466 clients committed a new crime while in the program.
- Notably, 8 out of every 10 clients are either working or involved in a job search as part of their responsibilities as participants in the MDRC program.
- Nearly 17% (84 clients) were able to obtain their GED while in the MDRC program.
- A small number of MDRC clients (12.3%) have had three or more previous incarcerations. This indicates that the MDRC provides service equally to what could be considered a traditional parole clientele as well as many clients who resemble a traditional probation client.
- More than half (54.8%) of the clients have no prior offense. This indicates that criminal justice agencies are viewing the MDRC as a useful community correctional alternative for clients early in their criminal career.
- Most clients (59.7%) participate in some form of substance abuse treatment in addition to the two required AA or NA meetings.
- As clients age, their likelihood of recidivating decreases. Clients living with a spouse or children had very low recidivism rates (4.9% and 0.0%, respectively); clients living with parents and siblings had significantly higher rates (25.4% and 16.7%, respectively).
- A majority (approximately 60.0%) of MDRC clients with three or more prior incarcerations do not recidivate.

SOURCE: Jack McDevitt, Marla Domino, Katrina Baum, and K. Suzanne Armfield, "MDRC: An Evaluation," The Center for Criminal Justice Policy Research, College of Criminal Justice, Northeastern University, Boston, April 1997.

day reporting center (DRC)
Nonresidential, community-based treatment program.

One recent development has been the use of RCC facilities as **day reporting centers (DRCs)**.[123] First begun in Great Britain in the 1970s, day reporting centers provide a single location to which a variety of clients can report for supervision and treatment. Now operating in more than 80 locations, DRCs use existing RCC facilities to service nonresidential clients. They can be used as a step up for probationers who have failed in the community and a step down in security for jail or prison inmates.[124] Although some evaluations indicate that DRCs can be effective (see Exhibit 14.3), others question their ability to lower recidivism rates. It is possible that the rehabilitation opportunities provided by DRCs are sometimes counterbalanced by their increased surveillance and security.[125]

More than 2,000 state-run community-based facilities are in use today. In addition, up to 2,500 private, nonprofit RCC programs operate in the United States. About half also have inmates who have been released from prison (halfway houses) and use the RCC placement to ease back into returning to society. The remainder are true intermediate sanctions, including about 400 federally sponsored programs.[126]

Despite the thousands of traditional and innovative RCC programs in operation around the United States, relatively few efforts have been made to evaluate their effectiveness. Those evaluations that do exist suggest that many residents do not complete their treatment regimen in RCC facilities, violating the rules or committing new offenses. Those who do complete the program have lower recidivism rates than the unsuccessful discharges.[127]

One reason it is so difficult to assess RCC is that programs differ considerably with respect to target population, treatment alternatives, and goals. Some are rehabilitation-oriented and operate under loose security; others are control-oriented and use such security measures as random drug and alcohol testing. Although critics question their overall effectiveness, RCC facilities appear to work for some types of offenders, and some treatment orientations seem to work better than others. It is possible that rather than being used as a "last resort" community alternative before sentencing to a jail or prison, RCC placement might actually work better with first-time offenders who have relatively little experience with the criminal or juvenile justice system.[128]

CAN ALTERNATIVE SANCTIONS WORK? Essay 10

Alternative, community-based sanctions hold the promise of providing cost-effective crime control strategies without widening the net of the criminal justice system.[129] They reduce overreliance on incarceration and exploding correctional construction costs.[130] Nonetheless, there are indications that, as currently applied, alternative sanctions are no more effective in reducing recidivism than traditional forms of probation and, because of the more intense monitoring involved, may result in more offenders' committing technical violations.[131] Revocation for technical reasons helps increase rather than decrease the correctional population, an outcome contrary to the stated goals of alternative sentencing.[132]

Some criminal justice professionals welcome the use of intermediate sanctions as a practical alternative to prison, while others are skeptical about the ability of community sentences to significantly reduce the correctional population. Skeptics John DiIulio and Charles Logan argue that it is a "myth" that prison crowding can be reduced, that new construction can be avoided, and that annual operating costs can be cut if greater advantage is taken of alternative sanctions. The great majority of those under correctional supervision, they argue, have already been on probation and will eventually be supervised in the community.[133] Of course, alternative sanctions could be toughened sufficiently to match or even exceed the punitive level of prisons—for example, by making them longer and requiring heavy fines and long counseling sessions. But then people convicted of crime may find prison or jail preferable to a community sentence. This issue is explored in the Analyzing Criminal Justice Issues feature on pages 470–471.

In contrast to this view, Michael Tonry and Mary Lynch suggest that alternative sanctions can be a useful correctional tool. Not everyone who commits a crime is the same, and not everyone should receive the same punishment. Clients for alternative sanction programs might be chosen from those already incarcerated, eliminating the threat of "net widening." It might be possible, they suggest, to create "exchange rates" that define equivalent sentences for prison and community alternatives—for example, three days in home confinement instead of one day in jail. Intermediate sanctions are not a panacea for all offenders—as Tonry and Lynch put it, "there is no free lunch"—but for offenders who do not present unacceptable risks of violence, well-managed intermediate sanctions offer a cost-effective way to keep them in the community.[134]

Restorative Justice

Restorative justice principles are a perfect fit to serve as the basis of alternative sanctions. Maintaining "ownership" or jurisdiction over the conflict means that resolution of the conflict between criminal and victim should take place in the community in which it originated and not in some far-off prison. Victims should be given a chance to voice their stories, and offenders can help compensate them financially or provide some service, such as fixing damaged property. Citizens and victims are asked to participate in conferences or sentencing circles or to help mediate conflicts whenever possible.[135] The goal is to enable offenders to appreciate the damage they have caused, to make amends, and to be reintegrated back into society.

Alternative programs based on restorative principles hold great promise and may provide the key to developing effective programs. A few of these programs are described in the Analyzing Criminal Justice Issues feature on page 472.

ANALYZING CRIMINAL JUSTICE ISSUES

Is Probation Becoming More Punitive Than Prison?

Richard Moran, a highly re-garded sociologist and crimi-nal justice expert, has uncovered a dis-turbing trend: If given a choice, more and more defendants are now choosing jail over a restrictive probation sentence, even though it means living behind bars rather than in the community. He gives as an example the case of Raymond "Ray Dog" Scott, leader of the rap group Made Men, who was convicted in a Massachusetts district court in Octo-ber 2000 on a charge of disorderly con-duct. When the judge let him choose his own sentence—30 days in jail or a year of probation—Scott chose jail! The probation sentence would have in-cluded 10 weeks of anger management sessions and biweekly meetings with a probation officer, conditions that Scott considered more onerous than a short period of incarceration.

According to Moran, while most law-abiding citizens think that proba-tion is a mere slap on the wrist, many criminals have come to view it as worse than prison. Why? First, during the last decade, probation has become much tougher. Second, many criminals have lost their fear of prison. In fact, for those heavily involved in street culture,

prison has become a significant status symbol.

Moran cites recent surveys of con-victed criminals in Oregon and Texas that underscore the trend. When con-victed criminals in Oregon were given the choice between prison and intensive probation, about a third chose prison. In Texas, a majority of prison-bound felons said that they preferred prison sentences of as long as 3 to 5 years over compara-ble periods of intensive probation super-vision. Criminal justice professionals and others have recently begun to notice that many street criminals— especially young inner-city black males—are no longer afraid of going to prison.

How did this happen? According to Moran, there are a number of compet-ing explanations, but the "underclass thesis" has the most currency among scholars who study crime. Recent re-search suggests that inner-city blacks, al-ready familiar with the harsh realities and random violence of their neighbor-hoods, adjust more easily to imprison-ment than most members of other racial or ethnic groups. Black males who are involved in street life have learned to take care of themselves, to affect an ap-pearance of physical and mental tough-

ness, and to value violence as an end in itself. These characteristics enable them to dominate other inmates. Prison is one of the few places in America that poor black men rule.

Because so many inner-city blacks are in jail, having a prison record is no longer seen as socially stigmatizing. In fact, it can often be status enhancing—tangible evidence of a commitment to the values and code of the streets. Many convicts consider a prison sentence a "badge of honor," something to boast about when they return to the streets. Perhaps this is why so many inmates steal state-issued prison clothing. Wear-ing prison issue on the streets lets every-one know that they are not to be messed with, not to be dissed, or disre-spected. Indeed, ex-convicts helped set the fashion for today's young people, not only in the inner city but increas-ingly in the suburbs. Shaved heads, tat-toos, baggy pants worn below the hips, and unlaced sneakers, all owe their ori-gin to the prison, where heads are fre-quently shaved, belts and shoelaces con-fiscated to prevent suicides, and jailhouse tattoos readily acquired.

Nor is prison socially isolating. In-mates are not randomly selected from

The Future of Alternative Sanctions

Essay 11

The rapid increase in the use of community corrections and the variety of alter-native sanctions now available reflect the dual correctional concerns of economy and control. On the one hand, the public is concerned about the cost of the criminal justice system. Existing facilities are overcrowded, and budget cutbacks in many states promise little chance of relief. On the other hand, people want to feel safe in their homes and protected from predatory criminals. Alternative, community-based sanctions hold the promise of satisfying both needs. They allow judges to reserve the most restrictive sanctions for the most dangerous offenders while offering a ready alternative for less violent criminals, reducing overreliance on incarceration, and helping control exploding correctional construction costs.[136] The use of alternative sanctions, then, is likely to grow and evolve.

the general population, but are drawn heavily from certain neighborhoods. Baltimore, for example, makes up only 13 percent of Maryland's population, yet it contributes 56 percent of that state's prisoners.

Since 90 percent of prisoners are released back into the community after serving an average of two years, there is a constant flow of young males between the prison and certain inner-city neighborhoods. This two-way street exposes everyone, especially young minority males, to the norms and values of prison life, and has resulted in a merging of the two cultures.

New arrivals are often reunited with friends, relatives, fellow gang members, parents, and on rare occasions, even grandparents. They have a ready-made social network that provides personal security and access to drugs and material goods. This is borne out by research which indicates that once a person has been to prison, his fear of returning is much reduced.

Moran sees the fact that many street criminals no longer fear prison, and that some even prefer it to probation, as a terrible indictment of our social and economic policy toward the urban un-

derclass. It is also a measure of how desperate life has become for many Americans. When life on the inside is seen as no worse, and in some cases better, than life on the outside, there is little the threat of imprisonment can do to deter crime. In the end, he suggests, the best way to restore the punitive punch of a prison sentence is to improve the living conditions and life chances of the young men who inhabit the inner city.

Critical Thinking Skills

1. It may seem strange that offenders might find prison a more attractive alternative than intermediate sanctions. What can be done to reverse this trend? One approach might be to create a treatment continuum ranging from the most basic to the most intensive services. It is assumed that all potential clients require at least the most basic treatment; once on probation, they can be moved up or down the treatment continuum according to needs.

2. Should community-based services be recast as a form of voluntary help, not a form of coercion? Should treatment be implemented in such a way that it does not compromise the

integrity of community-based sanctioning but is not punitive or coercive? Or does this approach defeat the purpose of intermediate sanctions?

InfoTrac College Edition Research

Although some offenders do not mind going to jail, suicide is still the leading cause of death behind bars. To read about this phenomenon, and its prevention, go to Lindsay M. Hayes, "Suicide in Adult Correctional Facilities: Key Ingredients to Prevention and Overcoming the Obstacles," *Journal of Law, Medicine & Ethics,* Fall 1999, v27 i3 p260

SOURCE: Richard Moran is a professor of sociology and criminology at Mount Holyoke College.

PERSPECTIVES ON JUSTICE

The premise of alternative sanctions is attractive, but there is still little evidence that they reduce recidivism. Increased monitoring and surveillance almost guarantee a higher rate of probation failure and incarceration, because more offenders will be caught committing technical violations. In this sense, alternative sentencing programs may work counter to the noninterventionist perspective that underpins traditional probation; rather than resocialize offenders, they may help to widen the net.

ANALYZING CRIMINAL JUSTICE ISSUES

Restorative Justice in the Community

A number of new and innovative community programs based on restorative justice principles are now being tested around the nation. Three of these initiatives are discussed below.

Minnesota

Minnesota has been a groundbreaker in restorative justice. Its Department of Corrections created the Restorative Justice Initiative in 1992, and in 1994 hired Kay Pranis as a full-time Restorative Justice Planner—the first such position in the United States. The initiative offers training in restorative justice principles and practices, provides technical assistance to communities in designing and implementing practices, and creates networks of professionals and activists to share knowledge and provide support.

Sentencing Circles

Besides promoting victim–offender mediation, family group conferencing, and neighborhood conferencing, the Minnesota Department of Corrections has introduced sentencing circles. Citizen volunteers and criminal justice officials from Minnesota have participated in training in the Yukon Territory, where peacemaking circles have been held since the late 1980s. In Minnesota, the circle process is used by the Mille Lacs Indian Reservation and in other communities in several counties. The circle process usually has several phases. First, the Community Justice Committee conducts an intake interview with offenders who want to participate. Then, separate healing circles are held for the victim (and others who feel harmed) and the offender. The committee tries to cultivate a close personal relationship with victims and offenders and to create support networks for them. In the end, a sentencing circle, open to the community, meets to work out a sentencing plan.

Vermont

A pilot reparative probation program began in Vermont in 1994, and the first cases were heard by a Reparative Citizen Board the following year. Three features distinguish this restorative justice initiative from most others in the United States: The Department of Corrections designed the program; it is implemented statewide; and it involves a sizable number of volunteer citizens. The process is straightforward. Following an adjudication of guilt, the judge sentences the offender to probation, with the sentence suspended and only two conditions imposed: The offender will commit no more crimes and will complete the reparative program.

The volunteer board members meet with the offender and the victim and together discuss the offense, its effects on victim and community, and the life situations of victim and offender. All participants must agree on a contract, to be fulfilled by the offender, based on five goals: The victim is restored and healed; the community is restored; the offender understands the effects of the crime; the offender learns ways to avoid reoffending; and the community offers reintegration to the offender.

Reparative probation targets minor crimes; it is not meant as a prison diversion program. In 1998, the 44 boards handled 1,200 cases, accounting for more than one-third of the probation caseload. Ten coordinators handle case management and organization for the boards, and more than 300 trained volunteers serve as board members. The goal is to have the boards handle about 70 percent of the targeted probation cases. That only about 17 percent of offenders fail to complete their agreements or attend follow-up board meetings is a measure of the program's success. These offenders are referred back to court.

Critical Thinking Skills

Restorative justice may be the model that best serves alternative sanctions. How can this essentially humanistic approach be sold to the general public, which now supports more punitive sanctions? For example, can it be argued that using restoration with nonviolent offenders frees up resources for the relatively few dangerous people in the criminal population?

InfoTrac College Edition Research

InfoTrac College Edition has a number of papers on restorative justice models. Use "restorative justice" as a subject guide to access these articles.

SOURCE: Leena Kurki, *Incorporating Restorative and Community Justice into American Sentencing and Corrections* (Washington, DC: National Institute of Justice, 1999).

SUMMARY

Probation can be traced to the common-law practice of granting clemency to deserving offenders. The modern probation concept was developed by John Augustus of Boston, who personally sponsored 2,000 convicted inmates over an 18-year period. Today, probation is the community supervision of convicted offenders by order of the court. It is a sentence reserved for defendants who the magistrate views as having potential for rehabilitation without needing to serve prison or jail terms. Probation is practiced in every state and by the federal government and includes both adult and juvenile offenders.

In the decision to grant probation, most judges are influenced by their personal views and the presentence reports of the probation staff. Once on probation, the offender must follow a set of rules or conditions, violation of which may lead to revocation of probation and reinstatement of a prison sentence. These rules vary from state to state but usually involve such demands as refraining from using alcohol or drugs, obeying curfews, and terminating past criminal associations.

Probation officers are usually organized into countywide departments, although some agencies are statewide and others are combined parole/probation departments. Probation departments have instituted a number of innovative programs designed to bring better services to their clients. These include restitution and diversionary programs, intensive probation, and residential probation.

In recent years, the U.S. Supreme Court has granted probationers greater due process rights. Today, when the state wishes to revoke probation, it must conduct a full hearing on the matter and provide the probationer with an attorney when such assistance is warranted.

To supplement probation, a whole new family of alternative sanctions have been developed. These range from pretrial diversion to residential community corrections. Other widely used alternative sanctions include fines and forfeiture, house arrest, and intensive probation supervision. Electronic monitoring (EM) involves a device worn by an offender under home confinement. Although some critics complain that EM smacks of a "Big Brother Is Watching You" mentality, it would seem an attractive alternative to a stay in a dangerous and deteriorated secure correctional facility. A stay in a community correctional center is one of the most intrusive alternative sentencing options. Residents may be eligible for work and educational release during the day while attending group sessions in the evening. Residential community correction is less costly than more secure institutions and seems to be equally effective.

Although it is too soon to determine whether these programs are successful, they provide the hope of providing low-cost, high-security alternatives to traditional corrections. Alternatives to incarceration can help reduce overcrowding in the prison system and spare nonviolent offenders the pains of a prison experience. Alternatives may not be much more effective than a prison sentence in reducing recidivism rates, but they are far less costly and can free up needed space for more violent offenders. One promising approach is to use principles of restorative justice to shape intermediate sanctions.

Key Terms

probation	diagnosis	community service restitution
judicial reprieve	risk classification	split sentence
recognizance	avertable recidivist	shock probation
sureties	intermediate sanctions	intensive probation supervision (IPS)
revocation	day fine	house arrest
suspended sentence	forfeiture	electronic monitoring (EM)
presentence investigation	restitution	residential community correction (RCC)
intake	monetary restitution	day reporting center (DRC)

Discussion Questions

1. What is the purpose of probation? Identify some conditions of probation, and discuss the responsibilities of the probation officer.
2. Discuss the procedures involved in probation revocation. What are the rights of the probationer?
3. Is probation a privilege or a right?
4. Should a convicted criminal make restitution to the victim? When is restitution inappropriate?
5. Should offenders be fined based on the severity of what they did or according to their ability to pay? Is it fair to gear day fines to wages? Should offenders be punished more severely because they are financially successful?
6. Does house arrest involve a violation of personal freedom? Does wearing an ankle bracelet smack of "Big Brother"? Would you want the government monitoring your daily activities? Could this be expanded, for example, to monitor the whereabouts of AIDS patients?
7. Would you want a community correctional center located in your neighborhood?

A CLOSER LOOK

Brian McKay, a community supervision officer with the Hunt County Community Supervision and Corrections Department in Greenville, Texas, and Chief Barry Paris of the Greenville, Texas, Police Department believe that a partnership between probation and law enforcement is a key component of crime control:

> One resource seldom tapped by police agencies remains the local probation department. Perhaps as a result of interdepartmental rivalry or a perceived conflict of missions, many police departments have little, if any, contact or communication with the probation department serving the same jurisdiction. However, many law enforcement investigators who have explored this route have found that probation officers can become valuable resources and willing allies. For example, the Boston, Massachusetts, Police Department developed an effective gang program by actively working with local probation officers. Other programs have sprung up across the country to increase cooperation between probation and police departments, including a joint effort in Texas between the Greenville Police Department and the Hunt County Community Supervision and Corrections Department.

To learn more about this issue, go to InfoTrac College Edition and read
Brian McKay and Barry Paris, "Forging a Police–Probation Alliance," *FBI Law Enforcement Bulletin,* November 1998, v67 i11 p27(6)

Notes

1 Arnulf Kolstad, "Imprisonment as Rehabilitation: Offenders' Assessment of Why It Does Not Work," *Journal of Criminal Justice* 24 (1996): 323–335.
2 See, generally, Todd Clear and Vincent O'Leary, *Controlling the Offender in the Community* (Lexington, MA: Lexington Books, 1983).
3 For a history of probation, see Edward Sieh, "From Augustus to the Progressives: A Study of Probation's Formative Years," *Federal Probation* 57 (1993): 67–72.
4 Ibid.
5 David Rothman, *Conscience and Convenience* (Boston: Little, Brown, 1980), pp. 82–117.
6 Merrill A. Smith, "The Way It Was," *Federal Probation* 61 (1997):76–80.
7 Lawrence Bonczar and Lauren Glaze, *Probation and Parole, 1998* (Washington, DC: Bureau of Justice Statistics, 1999).
8 "U.S. Correctional Population Reaches 6.3 Million Men and Women: Represents 3.1 Percent of the Adult U.S. Popula-

tion," Bureau of Justice Statistics press release, July 23, 2000.
9 Ibid.
10 Jodi Brown and Patrick Langan, *Felony Sentences in the United States, 1996* (Washington, DC: Bureau of Justice Statistics, 1999).
11 *Higdon v. United States,* 627 F.2d 893 (9th Cir. 1980).
12 *People v. Johnson,* 175 Ill.App.3d 908, 125 Ill. Dec. 469, 530 N.E.2d 627 (1988).
13 *Ramaker v. State,* 73 Wis.2d 563, 243 N.W.2d 534 (1976).
14 *United States v. Cothran,* 855 F.2d 749 (11th Cir. 1988).
15 Patrick Langan and Mark Cuniff, *Recidivism of Felons on Probation, 1986–1989* (Washington, DC: Bureau of Justice Statistics, 1992).
16 *United States v. Gallo,* 20 F.3d 7 (1st. Cir., 1994).
17 *State v. McCoy,* 45 N.C.App. 686, 263 S.E.2d 801 (1980).
18 *United States v. Duff,* 831 F.2d 176 (9th Cir. 1987).

19 *United States v. Pierce,* 561 F.2d 735 (9th Cir. 1977), cert. denied 435 U.S. 923, 98 S.Ct.1486, 55 L.Ed.2d 516 (1978).
20 *United States v. Kahl,* 583 F.2d 1351 (5th Cir. 1977); see also Harvey Jaffe, "Probation with a Flair: A Look at Some Out-of-the-Ordinary Conditions," *Federal Probation* 33 (1979): 29.
21 *United States v. Williams,* 787 F.2d 1182 (7th Cir. 1986).
22 *United States v. Ofchinick,* 937 F.2d 892 (3d Cir. 1992).
23 Todd Clear and Edward Latessa, "Probation Officers' Roles in Intensive Supervision: Surveillance Versus Treatment," *Justice Quarterly* 10 (1993): 441–462.
24 Ibid.
25 Patricia Harris, Todd Clear, and S. Christopher Baird, "Have Community Supervision Officers Changed Their Attitudes Toward Their Work?" *Justice Quarterly* 6 (1989): 233–246.
26 John Rosencrance, "Probation Supervision: Mission Impossible," *Federal Probation* 50 (1986): 25–31.

27 David Duffee and Bonnie Carlson, "Competing Value Premises for the Provision of Drug Treatment to Probationers," *Crime and Delinquency* 42 (1996): 574–592.

28 Edward Read, "Challenging Addiction: The Substance Abuse Specialist," *Federal Probation* 61 (1997): 25–26.

29 *Turner v. Barry,* 856 F.2d 1539 (D.C. Cir. 1988).

30 Ibid., at 1538.

31 Mark Cuniff, Dale Sechrest, and Robert Cushman, "Redefining Probation for the Coming Decade," paper presented at the annual meeting of the American Society of Criminology, San Francisco, November 1991.

32 Patricia Harris, "Client Management Classification and Prediction of Probation Outcome," *Crime and Delinquency* 40 (1994): 154–174.

33 Anne Schneider, Laurie Ervin, and Zoann Snyder-Joy, "Further Exploration of the Flight from Discretion: The Role of Risk/Need Instruments in Probation Supervision Decisions," *Journal of Criminal Justice* 24 (1996): 109–121.

34 Clear and O'Leary, *Controlling the Offender in the Community,* pp. 11–29, 77–100.

35 Joan Petersilia, "An Evaluation of Intensive Probation in California," *Journal of Criminal Law and Criminology* 82 (1992): 610–658.

36 Joan Petersilia, Susan Turner, James Kahan, and Joyce Peterson, *Granting Felons Probation: Public Risks and Alternatives* (Santa Monica, CA: Rand Corporation, 1985).

37 Kathryn Morgan, "Factors Influencing Probation Outcome: A Review of the Literature," *Federal Probation* 57 (1993): 23–29.

38 Kathryn Morgan, "Factors Associated with Probation Outcome," *Journal of Criminal Justice* 22 (1994): 341–353.

39 Paula M. Ditton, *Mental Health and Treatment of Inmates and Probationers* (Washington, DC: Bureau of Justice Statistics, 1999).

40 Langan and Cuniff, *Recidivism of Felons on Probation, 1986–1989*; Allen Beck and Bernard Shipley, *Recidivism of Prisoners Released in 1983* (Washington, DC: Bureau of Justice Statistics, 1989).

41 Robyn L. Cohen, *Probation and Parole Violators in State Prison, 1991* (Washington, DC: Bureau of Justice Statistics, 1995).

42 Ibid.

43 *Minnesota v. Murphy,* 465 U.S. 420, 104 S.Ct. 1136, 79 L.Ed.2d 409 (1984).

44 *Griffin v. Wisconsin,* 483 U.S. 868, 107 S.Ct. 3164, 97 L.Ed.2d 709 (1987).

45 *Mempa v. Rhay,* 389 U.S. 128, 88 S.Ct. 254, 19 L.Ed.2d 336 (1967).

46 *Morrissey v. Brewer,* 408 U.S. 471, 92 S.Ct. 2593, 33 L.Ed.2d 484 (1972).

47 *Gagnon v. Scarpelli,* 411 U.S. 778, 93 S.Ct. 1756, 36 L.Ed.2d 656 (1973).

48 *United States v. Granderson,* 511 U.S. 39, 114 Ct. 1259, 127 L.Ed.2d 611 (1994).

49 Peter Finn, "Prison Crowding: The Response of Probation and Parole," *Crime and Delinquency* 30 (1984): 141–153.

50 Richard Sluder, Allen Sapp, and Denny Langston, "Guiding Philosophies for Probation in the 21st Century," *Federal Probation* 58 (1994): 3–7.

51 "Law in Massachusetts Requires Probationers to Pay 'Day Fees,'" *Criminal Justice Newsletter,* 15 September 1988, p. 1.

52 Gerald Wheeler, Therese Macan, Rodney Hissong, and Morgan Slusher, "The Effects of Probation Service Fees on Case Management Strategy and Sanctions," *Journal of Criminal Justice* 17 (1989): 15–24.

53 Peter Finn and Dale Parent, *Making the Offender Foot the Bill: A Texas Program* (Washington, DC: National Institute of Justice, 1992).

54 Richard Lawrence, "Reexamining Community Corrections Models," *Crime and Delinquency* 37 (1991): 449–464.

55 For a thorough review of these programs, see James Byrne, Arthur Lurigio, and Joan Petersilia, eds., *Smart Sentencing: The Emergence of Intermediate Sanctions* (Newbury Park, CA: Sage, 1993). Hereinafter cited as *Smart Sentencing.*

56 Beck and Shipley, *Recidivism of Prisoners Released in 1983.*

57 S. Christopher Baird and Dennis Wagner, "Measuring Diversion: The Florida Community Control Program," *Crime and Delinquency* 36 (1990): 112–125.

58 George Cole, "Monetary Sanctions: The Problem of Compliance," in *Smart Sentencing.*

59 *Tate v. Short,* 401 U.S. 395, 91 S.Ct. 688, 28 L.Ed.2d 130 (1971).

60 Margaret Gordon and Daniel Glaser, "The Use and Effects of Financial Penalties in Municipal Courts," *Criminology* 29 (1991): 651–676.

61 "'Day Fines' Being Tested in a New York City Court," *Criminal Justice Newsletter,* 1 September 1988, pp. 4–5.

62 Laura Winterfield and Sally Hillsman, *The Staten Island Day-Fine Project* (Washington, DC: National Institute of Justice, 1993), pp. 5–6.

63 C. Yorke, *Some Consideration on the Law of Forfeiture for High Treason,* 2nd ed. (1746), p. 26; cited in David Freid, "Rationalizing Criminal Forfeiture," *Journal of Criminal Law and Criminology* 79 (1988): 329–346 at p. 329.

64 Freid, "Rationalizing Criminal Forfeiture," p. 326.

65 James B. Jacobs, Coleen Friel, and Edward O'Callaghan, "Pension Forfeiture: A Problematic Sanction for Public Corruption," *American Criminal Law Review* 35 (1997): 57–92.

66 *United States v. Ursery,* 518 U.S. 267 (1996).

67 *Bennis v. Michigan,* 517 U.S. 1163, 116 S.Ct. 994, 58 Cr.L. 2060 (1996).

68 Eric Jensen and Jurg Gerber, "The Civil Forfeiture of Assets and the War on Drugs: Expanding Criminal Sanctions While Reducing Due Process Protections," *Crime and Delinquency* 42 (1996): 421–434.

69 *Austin v. United States,* 509 U.S. 602 (1993); *Alexander v. United States,* 509 U.S. 544 (1993).

70 For a general review, see Burt Galaway and Joe Hudson, *Criminal Justice, Restitution, and Reconciliation* (New York: Criminal Justice Press, 1990); Robert Carter, Jay Cocks, and Daniel Glazer, "Community Service: A Review of the Basic Issues," *Federal Probation* 51 (1987): 4–11.

71 Douglas McDonald, "Punishing Labor: Unpaid Community Service as a Criminal Sentence," in *Smart Sentencing.*

72 Norval Morris and Michael Tonry, *Between Prison and Probation: Intermediate Punishments in a Rational Sentencing System* (New York: Oxford University Press, 1990), pp. 171–175.

73 Frederick Allen and Harvey Treger, "Community Service Orders in Federal Probation: Perceptions of Probationers and Host Agencies," *Federal Probation* 54 (1990): 8–14.

74 Peter Schneider, Anne Schneider, and William Griffith, *Monthly Report of the National Juvenile Restitution Evaluation Project V* (Eugene, OR: Institute for Policy Analysis, 1981).

75 Sudipto Roy, "Two Types of Juvenile Restitution Programs in Two Midwestern Counties: A Comparative Study," *Federal Probation* 57 (1993): 48–53.

76 Anne Schneider, "Restitution and Recidivism Rates of Juvenile Offenders: Four Experimental Studies," *Criminology* 24 (1986): 533–552.

77 Malcolm Feeley, Richard Berk, and Alec Campbell, "Community Service Orders in the Northern District of California," paper presented at the annual meeting of the American Society of Criminology, San Francisco, November 1991.

78 James Austin and Barry Krisberg, "The Unmet Promise of Alternatives to Incarceration," *Crime and Delinquency* 28 (1982): 374–409.

79 Alan Harland, "Court-Ordered Community Service in Criminal Law: The Continuing Tyranny of Benevolence," *Buffalo Law Review* (Summer 1980): 425–486.

80 David Levin, Patrick Langan, and Jodi Brown, *State Court Sentencing of Convicted Offenders, 1996* (Washington, DC: Bureau of Justice Statistics, 2000), p. 24.

81 Louis Jankowski, *Probation and Parole, 1990* (Washington, DC: Bureau of Justice Statistics, 1991), p. 2.

82 Joan Petersilia, *The Influence of Criminal Justice Research* (Santa Monica, CA: Rand Corporation, 1987).

83 Ibid.

84 Lawrence W. Sherman, Denise Gottfredson, Doris MacKenzie, John Eck, Peter Reuter, and Shawn Bushway, *Preventing*

Crime: What Works, What Doesn't, What's Promising: A Report to the United States Congress (Washington, DC: National Institute of Justice, 1999).

85 Jodi Brown, *Correctional Populations in the United States, 1996* (Washington, DC: Bureau of Justice Statistics, 1999), p. 39.

86 Stephen Gettinger, "Intensive Supervision: Can It Rehabilitate Probation?" *Corrections Magazine,* April 1983, pp. 7–18.

87 James Byrne, Arthur Lurigio, and S. Christopher Baird, *The Effectiveness of the New Intensive Supervision Programs,* Research in Corrections Series, vol. 2, no. 2 (Washington, DC: National Institute of Corrections, 1989).

88 Billie Erwin and Lawrence Bennett, *New Dimensions in Probation: Georgia's Experience with Intensive Probation Supervision (IPS)* (Washington, DC: National Institute of Justice, 1987).

89 Ibid.

90 Frank Pearson and Alice Glasel Harper, "Contingent Intermediate Sentences: New Jersey's Intensive Supervision Program," *Crime and Delinquency* 36 (1990): 75–86.

91 James Byrne and Linda Kelly, "Restructuring Probation as an Intermediate Sanction: An Evaluation of the Massachusetts Intensive Probation Supervision Program," final report to the National Institute of Justice, Research Program on the Punishment and Control of Offenders, Washington, DC, 1989.

92 James Ryan, "Who Gets Revoked? A Comparison of Intensive Supervision Successes and Failures in Vermont," *Crime and Delinquency* 43 (1997): 104–118.

93 Peter Jones, "Expanding the Use of Noncustodial Sentencing Options: An Evaluation of the Kansas Community Corrections Act," *Howard Journal* 29 (1990): 114–129; Michael Agopian, "The Impact of Intensive Supervision Probation on Gang Drug Offenders," *Criminal Justice Policy Review* 4 (1990): 214–222.

94 Joan Petersilia, "Comparing Intensive and Regular Supervision for High-Risk Probationers: Early Results from Experiment in California," *Crime and Delinquency* 36 (1990): 87–111.

95 Joan Petersilia and Susan Turner, *Evaluating Intensive Supervision Probation/Parole: Results of a Nationwide Experiment* (Washington, DC: National Institute of Justice, 1993).

96 Ibid., p. 7.

97 General Accounting Office, *Intensive Probation Supervision: Crime-Control and Cost-Saving Effectiveness* (Washington, DC: U.S. Government Printing Office, 1993).

98 Betsy Fulton, Edward Latessa, Amy Stichman, and Lawrence Travis, "The State of ISP: Research and Policy Implications," *Federal Probation* 61 (1997): 65–75.

99 Joan Petersilia, *Expanding Options for Criminal Sentencing* (Santa Monica, CA: Rand Corporation, 1987), p. 32.

100 S. Christopher Baird and Dennis Wagner, "Measuring Diversion: Evaluation of the Florida Community Control Program," *Crime and Delinquency* 36 (1990): 112–125.

101 Linda Smith and Ronald Akers, "A Comparison of Recidivism of Florida's Community Control and Prison: A Five-Year Survival Analysis," *Journal of Research in Crime and Delinquency* 30 (1993): 267–292.

102 Cited in Stephen Rackmill, "An Analysis of Home Confinement as a Sanction," *Federal Probation* 58 (1994): 45–48.

103 Robert N. Altman, Robert E. Murray, and Evey B. Wooten, "Home Confinement: A '90s Approach to Community Supervision," *Federal Probation* 61 (1997): 30–32.

104 Marc Renzema, "Home Confinement Programs: Development, Implementation, and Impact," in *Smart Sentencing.*

105 Jodi Brown, *Correctional Populations in the United States, 1996* (Washington, DC: Bureau of Justice Statistics, 1999), p. 39.

106 *Keeping Track of Electronic Monitoring* (Washington, DC: National Law Enforcement Corrections Technology Center, 1999).

107 Preston Elrod and Michael Brown, "Predicting Public Support for Electronic House Arrest: Results from a New York County Survey," *American Behavioral Scientist* 39 (1996): 461–474.

108 Joseph Papy and Richard Nimer, "Electronic Monitoring in Florida," *Federal Probation* 55 (1991): 31–33.

109 James Beck, Jody Klein-Saffran, and Harold Wooten, "Home Confinement and the Use of Electronic Monitoring with Federal Parolees," *Federal Probation* 54 (1990): 22–31.

110 Kevin E. Courtright, Bruce L. Berg, and Robert J. Mutchnick, "The Cost Effectiveness of Using House Arrest with Electronic Monitoring for Drunk Drivers," *Federal Probation* 61 (1997): 19–22.

111 Terry Baumer and Robert Mendelsohn, "Electronically Monitored Home Confinement: Does It Work?" in *Smart Sentencing.*

112 J. Robert Lilly, Richard Ball, G. David Curry, and John McMullen, "Electronic Monitoring of the Drunk Driver: A Seven-Year Study of the Home Confinement Alternative," *Crime and Delinquency* 39 (1993): 462–484.

113 James Davis, "Electronic Monitoring in the Criminal Justice System," paper presented at the American Society of Criminology meeting, Miami, November 1994, p. 3.

114 Joan Petersilia, "Exploring the Option of House Arrest," *Federal Probation* 50 (1986): 50–55.

115 Morris and Tonry, *Between Prison and Probation.*

116 Annesley Schmidt, "Electronic Monitors—Realistically, What Can Be Expected?" *Federal Probation* 55 (1991): 47–53, at p. 51.

117 Richard Rosenfeld, "The Scope and Purposes of Corrections: Exploring Alternative Responses to Crowding," *Crime and Delinquency* 37 (1991): 500–551.

118 For a more complete analysis of the EM controversy, see Ronald Corbett and Gary Marx, "Critique: No Soul in the New Machine: Technofallacies in the Electronic Monitoring Movement," *Justice Quarterly* 8 (1991): 399–414.

119 Edward Latessa and Lawrence Travis III, "Residential Community Correctional Programs," in *Smart Sentencing,* p. 48.

120 Personal correspondence with Joseph Travis, Director, November 13, 2000.

121 Phone conversation with Tim Hammelman, Controller, Nexus, November 13, 2000.

122 Harvey Siegal, James Fisher, Richard Rapp, Casey Kelliher, Joseph Wagner, William O'Brien, and Phyllis Cole, "Enhancing Substance Abuse Treatment with Case Management," *Journal of Substance Abuse Treatment* 13 (1996): 93–98.

123 Dale Parent, *Day Reporting Centers for Criminal Offenders: A Descriptive Analysis of Existing Programs* (Washington, DC: National Institute of Justice, 1990); Jack McDevitt and Robyn Miliano, "Day Reporting Centers: An Innovative Concept in Intermediate Sanctions," in *Smart Sentencing.*

124 David Diggs and Stephen Pieper, "Using Day Reporting Centers as an Alternative to Jail," *Federal Probation* 58 (1994): 9–12.

125 Liz Marie Marciniak, "The Addition of Day Reporting to Intensive Supervision Probation: A Comparison of Recidivism Rates," *Federal Probation* 64 (2000): 34–37.

126 For a description of these programs, see Edward Latessa and Lawrence Travis III, "Residential Community Correctional Programs," in *Smart Sentencing*; see also Byrne and Kelly, "Restructuring Probation as an Intermediate Sanction."

127 David Hartmann, Paul Friday, and Kevin Minor, "Residential Probation: A Seven-Year Follow-Up of Halfway House Discharges," *Journal of Criminal Justice* 22 (1994): 503–515.

128 Banhram Haghighi and Alma Lopez, "Success/Failure of Group Home Treatment Programs for Juveniles," *Federal Probation* 57 (1993): 53–57.

129 Peter R. Jones, "Community Corrections in Kansas: Extending Community-Based Corrections or Widening the Net?" *Journal of Research in Crime and Delinquency* 27 (1990): 79–101.

130 Richard Rosenfeld and Kimberly Kempf, "The Scope and Purposes of Corrections: Exploring Alternative Responses to Crowding," *Crime and Delinquency* 37 (1991): 481–505.

131 For a thorough review, see Michael Tonry and Mary Lynch, "Intermediate Sanctions," in *Crime and Justice: A Review of Research,* vol. 20, ed. Michael Tonry

(Chicago: University of Chicago Press, 1996), pp. 99–144.

132 Francis Cullen, "Control in the Community: The Limits of Reform?" paper presented at the meeting of the International Association of Residential and Community Alternatives, Philadelphia, November 1993.

133 John DiIulio and Charles Logan, "The Ten Deadly Myths About Crime and Punishment in the U.S.," *Wisconsin Interest* 1 (1992): 21–35.

134 Michael Tonry and Mary Lynch, "Intermediate Sanctions," *Crime and Justice: A Review of Research,* vol. 20, ed. Michael Tonry (Chicago: University of Chicago Press, 1996), pp. 99–144.

135 Gordon Bazemore and Curt Taylor Griffiths, "Conferences, Circles, Boards, and Mediations: The "New Wave" of Community Justice Decisionmaking," *Federal Probation* 61 (1997): 25–37.

136 Richard Rosenfeld and Kimberly Kempf, "The Scope and Purposes of Corrections: Exploring Alternative Responses to Crowding," *Crime and Delinquency* 37 (1991): 481–505.

AP/Wide World Photos

Chapter

15

CORRECTIONS: HISTORY,
INSTITUTIONS, AND POPULATIONS

Arthur Shawcross, one of the nation's most notorious serial killers, has been obsessed by sex and violence most of his life. Known today as the Genesee River Killer, he is currently serving a life sentence within the New York State correctional system.

Shawcroft's early childhood was filled with violence and sexual abuse; he has told authorities of sexual relationships he had with his sister and aunt. As a young man, he was continually in trouble with the law. In Vietnam, he reveled in killing prostitutes and mutilating captured Vietcong. When he came home, Shawcross began to experience violent flashbacks and nightmares. His anger led him to commit arson at his place of employment, and he was sentenced to five years in prison. He was raped and brutalized in prison, an experience that did not help his already shaky psyche.

Upon his early release, Shawcroft's behavior deteriorated further, and he was linked to several brutal child killings. In 1972, he admitted to raping, mutilating, and killing 8-year-old Karen Ann Hill and was sentenced to 25 years in prison. While in prison, he continued to behave in a violent and bizarre manner. Though correctional mental health professionals considered him highly dangerous and unstable, especially under stress, he was paroled in 1987. He soon began a murder spree during which he killed 11 women, mainly prostitutes, and he was sentenced to life in prison.

In 1999, Shawcroft was in the news once again when it was revealed that he had been using Ebay, the Internet auction site, to sell drawings, oil paintings, portraits, and autographs. Because it is illegal for inmates to run any kind of business in prison, Shawcross was charged with soliciting goods or services and selling personal articles without approval. Officials revoked his arts and crafts privileges and placed him in solitary confinement.

Shawcroft's story, though unique, raises a number of questions about the correctional system. Why would a confessed child killer be paroled, especially after mental

478

Chapter

15

AP/Wide World Photos

Arthur J. Shawcross is brought in chains to the
Wayne County Courthouse in Lyons, New York. He
had been convicted of killing 10 women and was beginning trial for an eleventh murder.

health professionals had labeled him dangerous and disturbed? Should convicted murderers such as Shawcross
ever be released from confinement? How was it possible
for a highly dangerous offender to establish an online business and sell artworks without the knowledge of prison officials? Does this indicate that even highly secure prisons
are not secure enough?

479

penitentiary
A state or federal correctional institution for the incarceration of felony offenders for terms of one year or more; prison.

prison
A state or federal correctional institution for the incarceration of felony offenders for terms of one year or more; penitentiary.

jail
A county correctional institution used to hold people awaiting trial or sentencing, as well as misdemeanor offenders sentenced to a term of less than one year.

The American Correctional Association is a multidisciplinary organization of professionals representing all facets of corrections and criminal justice, including federal, state, and military correctional facilities and prisons, county jails and detention centers, probation/parole agencies, and community corrections/halfway houses. It has more than 20,000 members. To learn about what they do, see http://www.corrections.com/aca/
For an up-to-date list of Web links, see http://www.wadsworth.com/product/0534573053s

Although the Shawcross case is unusual, it is not totally atypical. Many prisoners in the vast American prison system come from trouble backgrounds; many have serious emotional problems and grew up in abusive households. A majority are alcohol and drug dependent at the time of their arrest. Is it realistic to expect that a significant portion of these troubled individuals will successfully adjust to society after a lengthy stay in an overcrowded and dangerous penal institution? Are the personal and social forces that engulfed a person in a life of crime likely to be counteracted or nourished by a stay in a correctional facility?

The contemporary correctional system has branches at the federal, state, and county levels of government. Felons may be placed in state or federal **penitentiaries** (**prisons**), which are usually isolated, high-security structures. Misdemeanants are housed in county **jails**, sometimes called reformatories or houses of correction. And juvenile offenders have their own institutions, sometimes euphemistically called schools, camps, ranches, or homes. These are typically nonsecure facilities, often located in rural areas, that provide both confinement and rehabilitative services for young offenders.

Other types of correctional institutions include ranches and farms for adult offenders and community correctional settings, such as halfway houses, for inmates who are about to return to society. Today's correctional facilities encompass a wide range, from "maxi-maxi" security institutions, such as the federal prison at Florence, Colorado, where the nation's most dangerous felons are confined, to low-security camps that house white-collar criminals convicted of such crimes as insider trading and mail fraud.

One of the great tragedies of our time is that correctional institutions, whatever form they may take, do not seem to correct. Prisons seem to be part of another age and, according to correctional expert Vivien Stern, no longer fit the needs of modern society.[1] They are an inefficient use of resources, she argues, and provide a setting for constant human rights abuses. Prisons are essentially counterproductive: Those coming out present a greater threat than when they entered. These institutions are, in most instances, overcrowded, understaffed, outdated warehouses for social outcasts. Prisons and jails now contain more than 2 million inmates. They are more suited to control, punishment, and security than to rehabilitation and treatment. It is a sad but unfortunately accurate observation that today's correctional institution has become a revolving door and that all too many of its residents return time and again. Although no completely accurate statement of the recidivism rate is available, it is estimated that more than half of all inmates will be back within six years of their release.[2]

PERSPECTIVES ON JUSTICE

Despite the apparent lack of success of penal institutions, great debate continues over the direction of their future operations. Those who embrace the justice perspective maintain that prisons and jails should be used to keep dangerous offenders apart from society and give them the "just deserts" for their crimes. Inmates should be made to believe that their treatment is fair and proportionate. People who commit similar crimes should spend equivalent amounts of time behind bars.

In this chapter, we will explore the correctional system, beginning with the history and nature of correctional institutions. In Chapter 16, we will examine institutional life in some detail.

HISTORY OF CORRECTIONAL INSTITUTIONS

As you may recall, the original legal punishments were typically banishment or slavery, restitution, corporal punishment, and execution. The concept of incarcerating convicted offenders for long periods of time as a punishment for their misdeeds did not become the norm of corrections until the nineteenth century.[3]

Although the use of incarceration as a routine punishment began much later, some early European institutions were created specifically to detain and punish criminal offenders. Penal institutions were actually constructed in England during the tenth century to hold pretrial detainees and those waiting for their sentence to be carried out.[4] During the twelfth century, King Henry II of England constructed a series of county jails to hold thieves and vagrants prior to the disposition of their sentence. In 1557, the workhouse in Brideswell, England, was built to hold people convicted of relatively minor offenses who would work to pay off their debt to society; those committing more serious offenses were held there pending execution.

Fill in the blanks 1–2
True/False 1–2
Multiple choice 1–2

Le Stinche, a prison in Florence, Italy, was used to punish offenders as early as 1301.[5] Prisoners were enclosed in separate cells, classified on the basis of gender, age, mental state, and crime seriousness. Furloughs and conditional release were permitted, and perhaps for the first time, a period of incarceration replaced corporal punishment for some offenses. Although Le Stinche existed for 500 years, relatively little is known about its administration or whether this early example of incarceration was unique to Florence.

The first penal institutions were foul places devoid of proper care, food, or medical treatment. The jailer, usually a **shire reeve** (sheriff)—an official appointed by king or noble landholder as chief law enforcement official of a county—ran the jail under a fee system, whereby inmates were required to pay for their own food and services. Those who could not pay were fed scraps until they literally starved to death:

shire reeve
In early England, the chief law enforcement official in a county, forerunner of today's sheriff.

> In 1748 the admission to Southwark prison was eleven shillings and four pence. Having got in, the prisoner had to pay for having himself put in irons, for his bed, of whatever sort, for his room if he was able to afford a separate room. He had to pay for his food, and when he had paid his debts and was ready to go out, he had to pay for having his irons struck off, and a discharge fee.... The gaolers [jailers] were usually "low bred, mercenary and oppressive, barbarous fellows, who think of nothing but enriching themselves by the most cruel extortion, and have less regard for the life of a poor prisoner than for the life of a brute."[6]

Jail conditions were deplorable because jailers ran them for personal gain; the fewer the services provided, the greater their profit. Early jails were catchall institutions that held not only criminal offenders awaiting trial but vagabonds, debtors, the mentally ill, and assorted others.

From 1776 to 1785, a growing inmate population that could no longer be transported to North America forced the English to house prisoners on **hulks**, abandoned ships anchored in harbors. The hulks became infamous for their degrading conditions and brutal punishments but were not totally abandoned until 1858. The writings of John Howard, the reform-oriented sheriff of Bedfordshire, drew attention to the squalid conditions in British penal institutions. His famous book, *The State of the Prisons* (1777), condemned the lack of basic care given English inmates awaiting trial or serving sentences.[7] Howard's efforts to create humane standards in the British penal system resulted in the Penitentiary Act, by which Parliament established a more orderly penal system, with periodic inspections, elimination of the fee system, and greater consideration for inmates.

hulk
Mothballed ship used to house prisoners in eighteenth-century England.

The Origin of Corrections in the United States

Multiple choice 3–4

Although Europe had jails and a variety of other penal facilities, it was in the United States that correctional reform was first instituted. The first American jail was built in James City in the Virginia colony in the early seventeenth century. However, the "modern" American correctional system had its origin in Pennsylvania under the leadership of William Penn.

At the end of the seventeenth century, Penn revised Pennsylvania's criminal code to forbid torture and the capricious use of mutilation and physical punishment. These penalties were replaced with imprisonment at hard labor, moderate flogging, fines, and forfeiture of property. All lands and goods belonging to felons were to be used to make restitution to the victims of their crimes, with restitution being limited to twice the value of the damages. Felons who owned no property were required by law to work in the prison workhouse until the victim was compensated.

Penn ordered that a new type of institution be built to replace the widely used public forms of punishment—stocks, pillories, gallows, and branding irons. Each county was instructed to build a house of corrections similar to today's jails. County trustees or commissioners were responsible for raising money to build the jails and providing for their maintenance, although they were operated by the local sheriff. Penn's reforms remained in effect until his death in 1718, when the criminal penal code was changed back to open public punishment and harsh brutality.

It is difficult to identify the first American prison. Alexis Durham has described the opening of the Newgate Prison of Connecticut in 1773 on the site of an abandoned copper mine. Newgate, which closed in the 1820s, is often ignored by correctional historians.[8] In 1785, Castle Island prison was opened in Massachusetts and operated for about 15 years.

The Pennsylvania System

Fill in the blanks 3
True/False 3–4
Multiple choice 5–6
Essay 1

The origin of the modern correctional system, however, is usually traced to eighteenth-century developments in Pennsylvania. In 1776, postrevolutionary Pennsylvania again adopted William Penn's code, and in 1787, a group of Quakers led by Benjamin Rush formed the Philadelphia Society for Alleviating the Miseries of Public Prisons. The aim of the society was to bring some degree of humane and orderly treatment to the growing penal system. The Quakers' influence on the legislature resulted in limiting the use of the death penalty to cases involving treason, murder, rape, and arson. Their next step was to reform the institutional system so that the prison could serve as a suitable alternative to physical punishment.

The only models of custodial institutions at that time were the local county jails that Penn had established. These facilities were designed to detain offenders, to securely incarcerate convicts awaiting other punishment, or to hold offenders who were working off their crimes. The Pennsylvania jails placed men, women, and children of all ages indiscriminately in one room. Liquor was often freely sold.

Under pressure from the Quakers to improve these conditions, the Pennsylvania State Legislature in 1790 called for the renovation of the prison system. The ultimate result was the creation of a separate wing of Philadelphia's Walnut Street Jail to house convicted felons (except those sentenced to death). Prisoners were placed in solitary cells, where they remained in isolation and did not have the right to work.[9] Quarters that contained the solitary or separate cells were called the *penitentiary house*, as was already the custom in England.

The new Pennsylvania prison system took credit for a rapid decrease in the crime rate—from 131 convictions in 1789 to 45 in 1793.[10] The prison became known as a school for reform and a place for public labor. The Walnut Street Jail's equitable conditions were credited with reducing escapes to none in the first four years of its existence (except for 14 on opening day).

The Walnut Street Jail was not a total success. Overcrowding undermined the goal of solitary confinement of serious offenders, and soon more than one inmate was placed in each cell. Isolation had a terrible psychological effect on inmates, and eventually inmates were given in-cell piecework on which they worked up to 8 hours a day. Despite these difficulties, similar institutions were erected in New York (Newgate in 1791) and New Jersey (Trenton in 1798).

The Auburn System

Fill in the blanks 4–5
True/False 5
Multiple choice 7–8
Essay 2

As the nineteenth century got under way, both the Pennsylvania and the New York prison systems were experiencing difficulties maintaining the ever-increasing numbers of convicted criminals. Initially, administrators dealt with the problem by increasing the use of pardons, relaxing prison discipline, and limiting supervision.

In 1816, New York built a new prison at Auburn, hoping to alleviate some of the overcrowding at Newgate. The Auburn Prison design became known as the *tier system*, because cells were built vertically on five floors of the structure. It was also referred to as the *congregate system*, because most prisoners ate and worked in groups. In 1819, construction began on a wing of solitary cells to house unruly prisoners. Three classes of prisoners were then created: One group remained continually in solitary confinement as a result of breaches of prison discipline; the second group was allowed labor as an occasional form of recreation; and the third and largest class worked and ate together during the day and were separated only at night.

The philosophy of the **Auburn system** was crime prevention through fear of punishment and silent confinement. The worst felons were to be cut off from all contact with other prisoners, and although they were treated and fed relatively well, they had no hope of pardon to relieve their solitude or isolation. For a time, some of the worst convicts were forced to remain totally alone and silent during the entire day. This practice, which led to mental breakdowns, suicides, and self-mutilations, was abolished in 1823.

Auburn system
Prison system, developed in New York during the nineteenth century, based on congregate (group) work during the day and separation at night.

The combination of silence and solitude as a method of punishment was not abandoned easily. Prison officials sought to overcome the side effects of total isolation while maintaining the penitentiary system. The solution adopted at Auburn was to keep convicts in separate cells at night but allow them to work together during the day under enforced silence. Hard work and silence became the foundation of the Auburn system wherever it was adopted. Silence was the key to prison discipline: It prohibited the formulation of escape plans, it prevented plots and riots, and it allowed prisoners to contemplate their infractions.

Perspectives on Punishment

Fill in the blanks 6–7
True/False 6–9
Multiple choice 9–11
Essay 3

Why did prisons develop at this time? One reason, of course, was that during this period of "enlightenment," a concerted effort was made to alleviate the harsh punishments and torture that had been the norm. The interest of religious groups, such as the Quakers, in prison reform was prompted in part by humanitarian ideals. Another factor was the economic potential of prison industry, viewed as a valuable economic asset in times of short labor supply.[11]

The concept of using harsh discipline and control to "retrain" the heart and soul of offenders was the subject of an important book on penal philosophy, *Discipline and Punish* (1978) by French sociologist Michel Foucault.[12] Foucault's thesis was that as societies evolve and become more complex, they create increasingly more elaborate mechanisms to discipline their recalcitrant members and make them docile enough to obey social rules. In the seventeenth and eighteenth centuries, discipline was directed toward the human body itself, through torture. However, physical punishment and torture turned some condemned men into heroes and martyrs. Prisons presented the opportunity to rearrange, not diminish,

Inmates in a nineteenth-century prison return from a work detail in "lock step."

Stock Montage, Inc.

The Eastern State Penitentiary became the most expensive and most copied building of its time. It is estimated that more than 300 prisons worldwide are based on its wagon-wheel or radial floor plan. Some of America's most notorious criminals were held in this penitentiary's vaulted, sky-lit cells, including Al Capone. After 142 years of consecutive use, Eastern State Penitentiary was completely abandoned in 1971. http://www.EasternState.com/

For an up-to-date list of Web links, see http://www.wadsworth.com/product/0534573053s

Pennsylvania system
Prison system, developed in Pennsylvania during the nineteenth century, based on total isolation and individual penitence.

punishment—to make it more effective and regulated. In the development of the nineteenth-century prison, the object was to discipline the offender psychologically; "the expiation that once rained down on the body must be replaced by a punishment that acts in the depths of the heart."[13]

Regimentation became the standard mode of prison life. Convicts did not simply walk from place to place; rather, they went in close order and single file, each looking over the shoulder of the preceding person, faces inclined to the right, feet moving in unison. The lockstep prison shuffle was developed at Auburn and is still used in some institutions today.[14]

When discipline was breached in the Auburn system, punishment was applied in the form of a rawhide whip on the inmate's back. Immediate and effective, Auburn discipline was so successful that when 100 inmates were used to build the famous Sing Sing Prison in 1825, not one dared try to escape, although they were housed in an open field with only minimal supervision.[15]

In 1818, Pennsylvania took the radical step of establishing a prison that placed each inmate in a single cell for the duration of his sentence. Classifications were abolished, because each cell was intended as a miniature prison that would prevent the inmates from contaminating one another.

The new Pennsylvania state prison, called the Western Penitentiary, had an unusual architectural design. It was built in a semicircle, with the cells positioned along its circumference. Built back to back, some cells faced the boundary wall while others faced the internal area of the circle. Its inmates were kept in solitary confinement almost constantly, being allowed out for about an hour a day for exercise. In 1829, a second, similar penitentiary using the isolate system was built in Philadelphia and called the Eastern Penitentiary.

Supporters of the **Pennsylvania system** believed that the penitentiary was truly a place to do penance. By totally removing the sinner from society and allowing the prisoner a period of isolation in which to reflect alone on the evils of crime, the Pennsylvania system reflected the influence of religion and religious philosophy on corrections. Its supporters believed that solitary confinement with in-cell labor would make work so attractive that upon release that the inmate would be well suited to resume a productive existence in society.

The Pennsylvania system eliminated the need for large numbers of guards or disciplinary measures. Isolated from one another, inmates could not plan escapes or collectively break rules. When discipline was a problem, however, the whip and the iron gag were used.

Many fiery debates occurred between advocates of the Pennsylvania system and adherents of the Auburn system. Those supporting the latter claimed that it was the cheapest and most productive way to reform prisoners. They criticized the Pennsylvania system as cruel and inhumane, suggesting that solitary confinement was both physically and mentally damaging. The Pennsylvania system's devotees, on the other hand, argued that their system was quiet, efficient, humane, and well ordered and provided the ultimate correctional facility.[16] They chided the Auburn system for tempting inmates to talk by putting them together for meals and work and then punishing them when they did talk. Finally, the Auburn system was accused of becoming a breeding place for criminal associations by allowing inmates to get to know one another.

The Auburn system eventually prevailed and spread throughout the United States; many of its features are still used today. Its innovations included congregate working conditions, the use of solitary confinement to punish unruly inmates, military regimentation, and discipline. In Auburn-like institutions, prisoners were marched from place to place; their time was regulated by bells telling them to wake up, sleep, and work. The system was so like the military that many of its early administrators were recruited from the armed services.

Although the prison was viewed as an improvement over capital and corporal punishment, it quickly became the scene of depressed conditions; inmates were treated harshly and routinely whipped and tortured. Prison brutality flourished in these institutions, which had originally been devised as a more humane correctional alternative. In these early penal institutions, brutal corporal punishment took place indoors where, hidden from public view, it could become even more savage.[17]

The Late Nineteenth Century

The prison of the late nineteenth century was remarkably similar to that of today. The congregate system was adopted in all states except Pennsylvania. Prisons were overcrowded, and the single-cell principle was often ignored. The prison, like the police department, became the scene of political intrigue and efforts by political administrators to control the hiring of personnel and dispensing of patronage.

Prison industry developed and became the predominant theme around which institutions were organized. Some prisons used the **contract system,** in which officials sold the labor of inmates to private businesses. Sometimes the contractor supervised the inmates inside the prison itself. Under the **convict-lease system,** the state leased its prisoners to a business for a fixed annual fee and gave up supervision and control. Finally, some institutions had prisoners produce goods for the prison's own use.[18]

The development of prison industry quickly led to the abuse of inmates, who were forced to work for almost no wages, and to profiteering by dishonest administrators and businessmen. During the Civil War era, prisons were major manufacturers of clothes, shoes, boots, furniture, and the like. Beginning in the 1870s, opposition by trade unions sparked restrictions on interstate commerce in prison goods.

The National Congress of Penitentiary and Reformatory Discipline, held in Cincinnati in 1870, heralded a new era of prison reform. Organized by penologists

Fill in the blanks 8
True/False 10–11
Multiple choice 12

contract system
System whereby officials sold the labor of prison inmates to private businesses, for use either inside or outside the prison.

convict-lease system
Contract system in which a private business leased prisoners from the state for a fixed annual fee and assumed full responsibility for their supervision and control.

Multiple choice 13

 The Oregon State Penitentiary is the oldest prison and the only maximum security institution currently operated in Oregon. To read about its history, go to http://www.doc.state.or.us/institutions/osp/histidx.htm

For an up-to-date list of Web links, see http://www.wadsworth.com/product/0534573053s

INTERNATIONAL JUSTICE

The Development of Parole

Parole was a concept that developed overseas and was later brought to the United States. The term *parole* itself comes from the French word for "promise," referring to the practice of releasing captured enemy soldiers if they promised not to fight again with the threat that they would be executed if recaptured.

In the early seventeenth century, English judges began to spare the lives of offenders by banishing them to the newly formed overseas colonies. In 1617, the Privy Counsel of the British Parliament standardized this practice by passing an order granting reprieves and stays of execution to convicts willing to be transported to the colonies. Transportation was viewed as an answer to labor shortages caused by war, disease, and the opening of new commercial markets.

By 1665, transportation orders were modified to include specific conditions of employment and to provide for reconsideration of punishment if the conditions were not met—for example, if the person returned to England before the expiration of the sentence. In 1717, the British Parliament passed legislation creating the concept of *property in service*, which transferred control of prisoners to a contractor or shipmaster until the expiration of their sentences. When the prisoners arrived in the colonies, their services could be resold to the highest bidder. After sale, the offender's status changed from convict to indentured servant.

Transportation quickly became the most common sentence for theft offenders. In the American colonies, property in service had to be abandoned after the revolution. Thereafter, Australia, claimed as a British colony in 1770, became the destination for most transported felons. From 1815 to 1850, large numbers of inmates were shipped to Australia to serve as indentured servants working for plantation owners, in mines, or on sheep stations.

In England, opposition to penal servitude and the deprivations associated with transportation produced such organizations as the Society for the Improvement of Prison Discipline. This group asked the famous reformer Alexander Maconochie to investigate conditions in Australia. Maconochie condemned transportation and eventually helped end the practice. Later, when appointed director of the infamous Australian prison on Norfolk Island, Maconochie instituted reforms, such as classification and rehabilitation programs, that became models for the treatment of convicted offenders. Recalled from Australia, Maconochie returned to England, where his efforts led to the English Penal Servitude Act of 1853, which all but ended transportation and substituted imprisonment as a punishment.

Part of this act made it possible to grant a *ticket-of-leave* to those who had served a sufficient portion of their prison sentence. This form of conditional release permitted former prisoners to be at large in specified areas. The conditions of their release were written on a license that the former inmates were required to carry with them at all times; conditions usually included sobri-

---

Multiple choice 14–15

parole
The early release of a prisoner from incarceration subject to conditions set by a parole board.

Enoch Wines and Theodore Dwight, the congress provided a forum for corrections experts from around the nation to call for the treatment, education, and training of inmates.

One of the most famous people to attend the congress, Z. R. Brockway, warden at the Elmira Reformatory in New York, advocated individualized treatment, the indeterminate sentence, and **parole**. The development of parole is discussed in the International Justice feature.

The reformatory program initiated by Brockway included elementary education for illiterates, designated library hours, lectures by faculty members of the local Elmira College, and a group of vocational training shops. From 1888 to 1920, Elmira administrators used military-like training to discipline the inmates and organize the institution. The military organization could be seen in every aspect of the institution: schooling, manual training, sports, supervision of inmates, and even parole decisions.[19] The cost to the state of the institution's operations was to be held to a minimum.

Although Brockway proclaimed Elmira to be an ideal reformatory, his actual achievements were limited. The greatest significance of his contribution was the

ety, lawful behavior, and hard work. Many releasees violated these provisions, prompting criticism of the system. Eventually, prisoner aid society members helped supervise and care for releasees.

In Ireland, Sir Walter Crofton, a disciple of Maconochie's reforms, liberalized Irish prisons. He instituted a mark system in which inmates could earn their ticket-of-leave by accumulating credits for good conduct and hard work in prison. Crofton also instituted a system in which private volunteers or police agents could monitor ticket-of leave offenders in the community. Crofton's work is considered an early form of parole.

The concept of parole spread to the United States. As early as 1822, volunteers from the Philadelphia-based Society for Alleviating the Miseries of Public Prisons began to help offenders once they were released from prison. In 1851, the society appointed two agents to work with inmates discharged from Pennsylvania penal institutions. Massachusetts appointed an agent in 1845 to help released inmates obtain jobs, clothing, and transportation.

In the 1870s, using a carefully weighted screening procedure, Z. R. Brockway selected "rehabilitated" offenders from Elmira Reformatory for early release under the supervision of citizen volunteers known as *guardians*. The guardians met with the parolees at least once a month and submitted written reports on their progress. The parole concept spread rapidly. Ohio created the first parole agency in 1884. By 1901, as many as 20 states had created some type of parole agency. By 1927, only three states, Florida, Mississippi, and Virginia, had not established some sort of parole release. Parole had become institutionalized as the primary method of release for prison inmates, and half of all inmates released in the United States were paroled.

Critical Thinking Skills

The new sentencing models attempt to restrict parole and early release. Does this do a disservice to offenders by restricting the rewards given to rehabilitation efforts?

InfoTrac College Edition Research

The National Parole Board of Canada is preparing to celebrate 100 years of conditional release. Read about the history of parole in Canada in Donald Evans, "One Hundred Years of Conditional Release in Canada," *Corrections Today*, August 1999, v61 i5 p132(3)

SOURCES: William Parker, *Parole: Origins, Development, Current Practices, and Statutes* (College Park, MD: American Correctional Association, 1972); Samuel Walker, *Popular Justice* (New York: Oxford University Press, 1980).

injection of a degree of humanitarianism into the industrial prisons of that day (although there were accusations that excessive corporal punishment was used and that Brockway personally administered whippings).[20] Although many institutions were constructed across the nation and labeled reformatories based on the Elmira model, most of them continued to be industrially oriented.[21]

Prisons in the Twentieth Century

The early twentieth century was a time of contrasts in the U.S. prison system.[22] At one extreme were those who advocated reform, such as the Mutual Welfare League led by Thomas Mott Osborne. Prison reform groups proposed better treatment for inmates, an end to harsh corporal punishment, the creation of meaningful prison industries, and educational programs. Reformers argued that prisoners should not be isolated from society and that the best elements of society—education, religion, meaningful work, self-governance—should be brought to the prison. Osborne went so far as to spend a week in New York's notorious Sing Sing Prison to learn firsthand about its conditions.

The penitentiary movement spread around the world. In Australia, Fremantle Prison was built by convicts between 1850 and 1860. Convicts were brought to Western Australia to help in the building of roads, bridges, port facilities, and public buildings. To read about the history of the institution and get a virtual tour, go to http://www.fremantleprison.com.au/home.htm

For an up-to-date list of Web links, see http://www.wadsworth.com/product/0534573053s

Fill in the blanks 9–10
True/False 12
Multiple choice 16–17

Elmira Reformatory, training course in drafting, 1909. Inmates stand at drafting tables as guards watch and supervisor sits at fenced-off desk at front of hall. Elmira was one of the first institutions to employ education and training programs.

American Correctional Association

PERSPECTIVES ON JUSTICE

Prison reform challenged the crime control orientation of prisons. Opposed to the reformers were conservative prison administrators and state officials who believed that stern disciplinary measures were needed to control dangerous prison inmates. They continued the time-honored system of regimentation and discipline. Although the whip and the lash were eventually abolished, solitary confinement in dark, bare cells became a common penal practice.

In time, some of the more rigid prison rules gave way to liberal reform. By the mid-1930s, few prisons required inmates to wear the red-and-white-striped convict suit; nondescript gray uniforms were substituted. The code of silence ended, as did the lockstep shuffle. Prisoners were allowed "the freedom of the yard" to mingle and exercise an hour or two each day.[23] Movies and radio appeared in the 1930s. Visiting policies and mail privileges were liberalized.

A more important trend was the development of specialized prisons designed to treat particular types of offenders. In New York, for example, the prisons at Clinton and Auburn were viewed as industrial facilities for hard-core inmates, Great Meadow was an agricultural center for nondangerous offenders, and Dannemora was a facility for the criminally insane. In California, San Quentin housed inmates considered salvageable by correctional authorities, while Folsom was reserved for hard-core offenders.[24]

Prison industry also evolved. Opposition by organized labor helped put an end to the convict-lease system and forced inmate labor. By 1900, a number of states had restricted the sale of prisoner-made goods on the open market. The worldwide Depression that began in 1929 prompted industry and union leaders to further pressure state legislators to reduce competition from prison industries. A series of ever more restrictive federal legislative initiatives led to the Sumners–Ashurst Act (1940), which made it a federal offense to transport in interstate commerce goods made in prison for private use, regardless of the laws of the state receiving the goods.[25] The restrictions imposed by the federal government helped to severely curtail prison industry for 40 years. Private entrepreneurs shunned prison investments because they were no longer profitable; the result was inmate idleness and make-work jobs.[26]

Despite some changes and reforms, the prison in the mid-twentieth century remained a destructive total institution. Although some aspects of inmate life improved, severe discipline, harsh rules, and solitary confinement were the way of life in prison.

The Modern Era

Multiple choice 18
Essay 4

The modern era has been a period of change and turmoil in the nation's correctional system. Three trends stand out. First, between 1960 and 1980, came the prisoners' rights movement. After many years of indifference (the so-called *hands-off doctrine*), state and federal courts ruled in case after case that institutionalized inmates had rights to freedom of religion and speech, medical care, procedural due process, and proper living conditions. Inmates won rights unheard of in the nineteenth and early twentieth centuries. Since 1980, however, an increasingly conservative judiciary has curtailed the growth of inmate rights.

Second, violence within the correctional system became a national concern. Well-publicized riots at New York's Attica Prison and the New Mexico State Penitentiary drew attention to the potential for death and destruction that lurks in every prison. Prison rapes and killings have become commonplace. The locus of control in many prisons shifted from the correctional staff to violent inmate gangs. In reaction, some administrators have tried to improve conditions and provide innovative programs that give inmates a voice in running the institution. Another reaction has been to tighten discipline and build new super-maximum-security prisons to control the most dangerous offenders. The problem of prison overcrowding has made attempts to improve conditions extremely difficult.

Third, the view that traditional correctional rehabilitation efforts have failed has prompted many penologists to reconsider the purpose of incarcerating criminals. Between 1960 and 1980, it was common for correctional administrators to cling to the **medical model**, which viewed inmates as "sick people" who were suffering from some social malady that prevented them from adjusting to society. Correctional treatment could help "cure" them and enable them to live productive lives once they returned to the community. In the 1970s, efforts were also made to help offenders become reintegrated into society by providing them with new career opportunities that relied on work release programs. Inmates were allowed to work outside the institution during the day and return in the evening; some were given extended furloughs in the community. Work release became a political issue when Willie Horton, a furloughed inmate from Massachusetts, raped a young woman. Criticism of the state's "liberal" furlough program helped George Bush defeat Massachusetts Governor Michael Dukakis for the U.S. presidency in 1988; in the aftermath of the Horton case, a number of states, including Massachusetts, restricted their furlough policies.

medical model
The view that convicted offenders are victims of their environment who need care and treatment to be transformed into valuable members of society.

Prisons have come to be viewed as places for control, incapacitation, and punishment, rather than as sites for rehabilitation and reform. Advocates of the "no frills" or "penal harm" movement believe that if prison is a punishing experience, would-be criminals will be deterred from crime and current inmates will be encouraged to "go straight." Nonetheless, efforts to use correctional institutions as

The Corrections Connection's mission is to provide a comprehensive and unbiased online community for professionals and businesses working in the corrections industry and to "inform, educate and assist" corrections practitioners by providing best practices, online resources, weekly news, products and services, career opportunities, access to post and review bids, partnership opportunities, innovative technologies, and educational tools. Contact them at http://www.corrections.com

For an up-to-date list of Web links, see http://www.wadsworth.com/product/0534573053s

treatment facilities have not ended, and such innovations as the development of private industries on prison grounds have kept the rehabilitative ideal alive.

PERSPECTIVES ON JUSTICE

The alleged failure of correctional treatment coupled with constantly increasing correctional costs has prompted advocates of the nonintervention perspective to develop alternatives to incarceration, such as intensive probation supervision, house arrest, and electronic monitoring. The idea is to move as many nonviolent offenders as possible out of the correctional system by means of community-based programs. These efforts have been compromised by a growing get-tough stance in judicial and legislative sentencing policy, including mandatory minimum sentences for gun crimes and drug trafficking.

In the following sections, we review the main types of correctional facilities in use today.

JAILS

Fill in the blanks 11
Multiple choice 19–21
Essay 5

Jails are institutional facilities with five primary purposes: (1) They detain accused offenders who cannot make or are not eligible for bail prior to trial. (2) They hold convicted offenders awaiting sentence. (3) They serve as the principal institution of secure confinement for offenders convicted of misdemeanors. (4) They hold probationers and parolees picked up for violations and waiting for a hearing. (5) They house felons when state prisons are overcrowded.

A number of formats are used to jail offenders. About 15,000 local jurisdictions maintain short-term police or municipal lockups that house offenders for no more than 48 hours before a bail hearing can be held; thereafter, detainees are kept in the county jail. In some jurisdictions, such as New Hampshire and Massachusetts, a house of corrections holds convicted misdemeanants, while a county jail is used for pretrial detainees. Today, the jail is a multipurpose correctional institution whose main functions are set out in Exhibit 15.1.

According to the most recent statistics, about half of jailed inmates are unconvicted, awaiting formal charges (arraignment), bail, or trial. The remaining half

EXHIBIT 15.1 JAIL FUNCTIONS AND SERVICES

- Receive individuals pending arraignment and hold them awaiting trial, conviction, or sentencing
- Readmit probation, parole, and jail-bond violators and absconders
- Temporarily detain juveniles pending transfer to juvenile authorities
- Hold mentally ill persons pending their movement to appropriate health facilities
- Hold individuals for the military, for protective custody, for contempt, and for the courts as witnesses
- Release convicted inmates to the community on completion of sentence
- Transfer inmates to federal, state, or other authorities
- House inmates for federal, state, or other authorities because of crowding of their facilities
- Relinquish custody of temporary detainees to juvenile and medical authorities
- Sometimes operate community-based programs as alternatives to incarceration
- Hold inmates sentenced to short terms (generally under one year)

SOURCE: Darrell K. Gilliard and Allen J. Beck, *Prison and Jail Inmates at Midyear 1996* (Washington, DC: Bureau of Justice Statistics, 1997).

are convicted offenders who are serving time, are awaiting parole or probation revocation hearings, or have been transferred from a state prison because of overcrowding.

Jails are typically a low-priority item in the criminal justice system. Because they are usually administered on a county level, jail services have not been sufficiently regulated, nor has a unified national policy been developed to mandate what constitutes adequate jail conditions. Consequently, many jails have developed into squalid, crumbling holding pens.

Jails are considered to be holding facilities for the county's undesirables, rather than correctional institutions that provide meaningful treatment. They may house indigents who, looking for a respite from the winter's cold, commit a minor offense; the mentally ill who will eventually be hospitalized after a civil commitment hearing; and substance abusers who are suffering the first shocks of confinement. The jail rarely holds professional criminals, most of whom are able to make bail.[27] Instead, the jail holds people considered detached from and disreputable in local society and who are frequently arrested because they are considered "offensive" by the local police. A recent survey in New York City found that on any given day more than 2,800 people with serious mental illness were being confined in jail, about 20 percent of the total inmate population.[28] The purpose of the jail is to "manage" these persons and keep them separate from the rest of society. By intruding in their lives, jailing them actually increases their involvement with the law.

Jail Population

A national effort has been made to remove as many people as possible from local jails through the adoption of both bail reform measures and pretrial diversion. Nonetheless, jail populations have been steadily increasing, due in part to the increased use of mandatory jail sentences for such common crimes as drunk driving and the use of local jails to house inmates for whom there is no room in state prisons.

Approximately 600,000 people are being held in local jails throughout the United States, a figure that has been increasing about 5 percent per year.[29] Another 70,000 people are assigned to jail but are being supervised in the community on work release, electronic monitoring, weekend programs, and the like. On an annual basis, about 10 million people are admitted to jail and slightly fewer are released.

The number of jails has declined from a high of 4,037 in 1970 to about 3,500 today, but the number of inmates has increased about 400 percent (from 160,683); the trend is thus toward fewer but larger jails. In 1970, there were 79 inmates per 100,000 population; by 1990, that number had risen to 163 per 100,000; today, it is more than 220 per 100,000. The increase in the jail population is a direct function of the nation's get-tough policy against drug offenders and offenses.

Jail Inmate Characteristics

Although the removal of juveniles from adult jails has long been a national priority, it is likely that more than 50,000 youths are admitted to adult jails each year.[30]

Fill in the blanks 12
Multiple choice 22

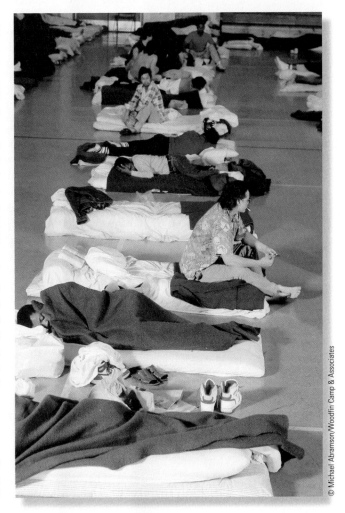

Inmates are sometimes forced to sleep outside of cells in overcrowded jails. Here inmates rest on a long line of floor mattresses in Illinois's Cook County Jail.

Fill in the blanks 13
Multiple choice 23–24

Close to 10,000 persons under age 18 are housed in adult jails on a given day. More than two-thirds of these young inmates have been convicted or are being held for trial as adults in criminal court.

Male inmates make up about 90 percent of the local jail population. However, the female population, like the female crime rate, has been growing at a faster pace. On average, the female jail population has grown 7 percent annually since 1990, whereas the male inmate population has grown by 4 percent per year.

A majority of local jail inmates are either black or Hispanic. White non-Hispanics make up about 40 percent of the jail population; black non-Hispanics, 40 percent; Hispanics, 16 percent; and other groups (Asians, Pacific Islanders, American Indians, and Alaska Natives), about 2 percent. Relative to their proportion of the U.S. population, black non-Hispanics are six times more likely than white non-Hispanics, more than twice as likely as Hispanics, and more than eight times more likely than persons of other races to have been held in a local jail.

Most inmates are either doing time or awaiting trial on property crime charges, such as burglary, larceny, or motor vehicle theft. However, the number of drug offenders has increased markedly. In 1983, about 9 percent of the total jail population was there for drug-related crimes; that number has now increased to about 24 percent of all jail inmates. Many inmates are repeaters: More than 70 percent had a prior criminal record, and more than half had a criminal justice status (probationer, bailee, parolee) at the time of their arrest. About 40 percent were under the influence of alcohol at the time of their arrest, and an equal number had been at one time or were currently being treated for abuse problems. There is also a strong association between prior physical and sexual abuse and jail inmate status: About 13 percent of male and 47 percent of female inmates report either physical or sexual abuse.[31] Not surprisingly, perhaps, about 16 percent of those in local jails report either having a mental condition or having had an overnight stay in a mental hospital at least once in their lives.[32]

Fill in the blanks 14

New Generation Jails

To relieve overcrowding and improve effectiveness, a jail building boom has been under way. Many of the new jails are using modern designs to improve effectiveness; these are referred to as new generation jails.[33] Traditional jails are constructed according to a linear/intermittent surveillance model. Jails using this design are rectangular, with corridors leading to either single- or multiple-occupancy cells arranged at right angles to the corridor. Correctional officers must patrol to see into cells or housing areas, and when they are in a position to observe one cell, they cannot observe others; unobserved inmates are essentially unsupervised.

The new generation jails allow for continuous observation of residents. There are two types of supervision, direct and indirect. Direct supervision jails contain a cluster of cells surrounding a living area or "pod," which contains tables, chairs, televisions, and other materials. A correctional officer stationed within the pod can observe inmates visually and relate to them on a personal level. Having an officer in the pod increases awareness of the inmates' behaviors and needs, resulting in a safer environment for both staff and inmates. Since interaction between inmates is constantly and closely monitored, dissension can be quickly detected before it escalates.

During the day, inmates stay in the open area (dayroom) and typically are not permitted to go into their rooms except with permission of the officer in charge. The officer controls door locks to cells from a control panel. In case of trouble, or if the officer leaves the station for an extended period of time, command of this panel can be switched to a panel at a remote location, known as central control. The officer usually wears a device that permits immediate communication with central control in case of trouble, and the area is also covered by a video camera monitored by an officer in the central control room.

Indirect supervision jails use similar construction, but the correctional officer's station is located in a secure room. Microphones and speakers inside the living unit permit the officer to hear and communicate with inmates.

Although these institutions have not yet undergone extensive evaluation, research shows that they may help reduce postrelease offending in some situations.[34]

THE PRISON SYSTEM

The Federal Bureau of Prisons and every state government maintain closed correctional facilities known as prisons, penitentiaries, or reformatories. It is a vast and costly system. According to the Bureau of Justice Statistics, the various states and the District of Columbia spend about $22 billion annually to build, staff, and maintain their prison facilities and to house the prisoners. The Federal Bureau of Prisons spends an additional $2.5 billion, or about $20,000 per year per inmate. Prison costs have escalated rapidly. State prison expenditures increased 83 percent from 1990 to 1996, an average of about 11 percent per year. Federal prison expenditures rose 160 percent during the same period, or an average of about 17 percent per year.[35]

True/False 13

Types of Prisons

Usually, prisons are organized or classified on three levels—maximum, medium, and minimum security—and each has distinct characteristics.

Fill in the blanks 15–18
Multiple choice 25
Essay 6

Maximum Security   Housing the most famous criminals and the subjects of films and stories, **maximum-security prisons** are probably the institutions most familiar to the public. Famous "max prisons" have included Sing Sing, Joliet, Attica, Walpole, and the most fearsome of all, the now-closed federal facility on Alcatraz Island known as The Rock.

A typical maximum-security facility is fortresslike, surrounded by stone walls with guard towers at strategic places. These walls may be 25 feet high, and sometimes inner and outer walls divide the prison into courtyards. Barbed wire or electrified fences are used to discourage escapes. High security, armed guards, and stone walls give the inmate the sense that the facility is impregnable and reassure the citizens outside that convicts will be completely incapacitated.

Inmates live in interior, metal-barred cells that contain their own plumbing and sanitary facilities and are locked securely either by key or electronic device. Cells are organized in sections called blocks; in large prisons, a number of cell blocks make up a wing. During the evening, each cell block is sealed off from the others, as is each wing. Thus, an inmate may be officially located in, for example, Block 3 of E Wing.

Every inmate is assigned a number and a uniform on entering the prison system. Unlike the striped, easily identifiable uniforms of old, the maximum-security inmate today wears khaki attire not unlike military fatigues. Dress codes may be strictly enforced in some institutions, but closely cropped hair and other regimenting features are vestiges of the past.

During the day, the inmates engage in closely controlled activities: meals, workshops, education, and so on. Rule violators may be confined to their cells; working and shared recreational activities are viewed as privileges.

The byword of the maximum-security prison is security. Guards and other correctional workers are made aware that each inmate may be a dangerous criminal or violent individual and that the utmost in security must therefore be maintained. In keeping with this philosophy, prisons are designed to eliminate hidden corners where people can congregate, and passages are constructed so that they can be easily blocked off to quell disturbances.

maximum-security prison
A correctional institution that houses dangerous felons and maintains strict security measures, including high walls, guard towers, and limited contact with the outside world.

 Alcatraz is now a National Park Service site. Visit their Web page at http://www.nps.gov/alcatraz/ For an up-to-date list of Web links, see http://www.wadsworth.com/product/0534573053s

Some states have constructed maxi-maxi prisons to house the most predatory criminals. These high-security institutions can be independent correctional centers or locked wings of existing prisons. Some maxi-maxi prisons lock inmates in their cells 22 to 24 hours a day, never allowing them out unless they are shackled. Threat of transfer to the maxi-maxi institution is used to deter inmate misbehavior in less restrictive institutions.

Civil rights watchdog groups charge that these maxi-maxi prisons violate United Nations standards for the treatment of prisoners.[36] For example, California's Pelican Bay State Prison is designed to hold the most violent criminals. Inmates are not permitted to hold jobs, attend educational or training sessions, or mingle with other prisoners. They spend almost the entire day in windowless cells. During the 90 minutes allowed outside their cell, inmates can exercise in a concrete space measuring 10 by 26 feet that has no athletic equipment. Whenever possible, the maxi-maxi prison is designed to limit contact between inmates and with staff; however, a lawsuit filed by residents charges that overcrowding forces inmates to be housed two to a cell, resulting in many violent assaults.[37] The Criminal Justice and Technology feature (pages 496–497) discusses these ultra-maximum-security prisons.

medium-security prison
A correctional institution that houses nonviolent offenders, characterized by a less tense and vigilant atmosphere and more opportunities for contact with the outside world.

Medium Security Medium-security prisons are similar in appearance to maximum-security prisons, but the security and atmosphere are neither so tense nor so vigilant. Medium-security prisons are also surrounded by walls, but there may be fewer guard towers or other security precautions. Visitor privileges may be more extensive and personal contact may be allowed, whereas in a maximum-security prison visitors may be separated from inmates by Plexiglas or other barriers (to prohibit the passing of contraband). Most prisoners are housed in cells, but individual honor rooms are used to reward those who make exemplary rehabilitation efforts. Finally, medium-security prisons promote greater treatment efforts, and the relaxed atmosphere allows freedom of movement for rehabilitation workers and other therapeutic personnel.

minimum-security prison
A correctional institution that houses white-collar and other non-violent offenders, characterized by few security measures and liberal furlough and visitation policies.

Minimum Security Operating without armed guards or walls, **minimum-security prisons** usually house the most trustworthy and least violent offenders; white-collar criminals may be their most common occupants. Inmates are allowed a great deal of personal freedom. Instead of being marched to activities by guards, they are summoned by bells or loudspeaker announcements and assemble on their own. Work furloughs and educational releases are encouraged, and vocational training is of the highest level. Dress codes are lax, and inmates are allowed to grow beards or mustaches or demonstrate other individual characteristics.

Minimum-security facilities may have dormitories or small private rooms for inmates. Prisoners are allowed quite a bit of discretion in acquiring or owning personal possessions, such as radios, that might be deemed dangerous in a maximum-security prison.

Minimum-security prisons have been scoffed at for being too much like "country clubs"; some federal facilities catering to white-collar criminals even have tennis courts and pools (they are called derisively "Club Fed"). Yet they remain prisons, and the isolation and loneliness of prison life deeply affects the inmates at these facilities.

Prison Inmates: A Profile

Fill in the blanks 19
True/False 14–17

As might be expected, the personal characteristics of prison inmates reflect those of arrestees: Inmates tend to be young, single, poorly educated, disproportionately male, and minority-group members.[38] Many were either underemployed or unemployed prior to their arrest; many had incomes of less than $10,000 and suffered from drug abuse and other personal problems.

A disproportionate number of minority males are now behind prison walls. This disturbing trend has prompted calls for sentencing reforms, such as guidelines that eliminate race as a factor in decision making.

Gender Gender differences in the prison population are considerable. Women are actually underrepresented in prison, and not only because they commit less serious crimes. The Uniform Crime Reports arrest statistics indicate that the overall male/female arrest ratio is today about 3.5 male offenders to 1 female offender; for violent crimes, the ratio is closer to 6 males to 1 female. Yet female inmates account for only about 10 percent of the prison population, for a ratio of 9 to 1. Whereas the typical male inmate committed a violent crime, most female inmates committed property offenses.

Minorities The prison system is populated disproportionately by minorities; black males in the United States are now incarcerated at a higher rate than in South Africa before the election of Nelson Mandela. This situation severely decreases the life chances of African American men, has a devastating effect on the black community, and is an ongoing national concern.

Crime What did the inmates do to earn their sentence? About half of all prison inmates are serving time for violent crimes. The number of offenders incarcerated for drug and violent crimes has increased significantly during the past decade. This increase probably reflects the effect of mandatory minimum sentences for violent and drug offenders and the increased emphasis that law enforcement agencies are putting on control of the drug trade.

Substance Abuse A strong association exists between substance abuse and inmate status. For example, one study of 400 Texas inmates found that almost 75 percent suffered from lifetime substance abuse or dependence disorder, defined by psychologists as (a) abuse of drugs for at least one continuous month (or repeated symptoms to occur over a longer period), (b) "failure to fulfill major role obligations" and (c) "substance-related legal problems."[39] About 80 percent of inmates report using drugs sometime during their lives, and more than 60 percent are regular users. About half of the inmates report being drunk, high, or both when they committed the crime that landed them in prison. Considering this background, it should come as no surprise that more inmates die from HIV-related disease than from prison violence.[40]

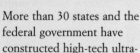

CRIMINAL JUSTICE AND TECHNOLOGY

Ultra-Maximum-Security Prisons

More than 30 states and the federal government have constructed high-tech ultra-maximum-security prisons to house the most dangerous predatory criminals. These high-security institutions may be independent correctional centers or locked wings of existing prisons, operating under such names as the "secure housing unit" or "maximum control unit." However, there is no agreed-upon definition of these units, so that what is considered "supermax" in one jurisdiction may not be "supermax" in another.

This development represents a shift from previous correctional policy, which favored dispersing the most troublesome inmates to different prisons in order to prevent them from joining forces or planning escapes. The supermax model finds that housing the most dangerous inmates in an ultra-secure facility eases their control while reducing violence levels in the general prison population.

The first federal maxi-prison, located in Marion, Illinois, was infamous for its tight security and isolate conditions. Marion has since been supplanted by a new 484-bed facility in Florence, Colorado. This new prison has the most sophisticated security measures in the United States, including 168 videocameras and 1,400 electronically controlled gates. Inside the cells, all furniture is unmovable; the desk, bed, and TV stand are made of cement. All potential weapons, including soap dishes, toilet seats, and toilet handles, have been re-

moved. The cement walls are 5,000-pound quality, and steel bars are placed so they crisscross every 8 inches inside the walls. Cells are angled so that inmates can see neither each other nor the outside scenery (see Figure A). This cuts down on communications and denies inmates a sense of location, in order to prevent escapes.

Escaping from this prison seems impossible. There are six guard towers at different heights to prevent air attacks. To get out, an inmate would have to pass through seven 3-inch-thick steel doors, each of which can be opened only after the previous one has closed. If a guard tower is ever seized, all controls are switched to the next station. If the whole prison is seized, it can be controlled from the outside. The only way out is via good works and behavior, through which an inmate can earn transfer to another prison within three years.

A national survey of supermax prisons conducted by the American Correctional Association found that although the cost of running these institutions is generally higher than in less secure facilities, they tend to be popular with correctional administrators, who believe that isolating troublemakers helps them maintain order. The survey's major findings include the following:

- Thirty-four prison systems are now operating or will soon open supermax facilities/units. Four others are considering the need for supermax facilities or are actively pursuing construction funds.

- Thirty-six prison systems cited the need to better manage violent and seriously disruptive inmates as a major factor in their jurisdictions' development of supermax housing; 17 of these systems include gang members as appropriate candidates for supermax housing.

- Jurisdictions vary greatly in the length of time inmates are confined in supermax facilities and the criteria for admission and release. Approval authority for admission and release of inmates varies from the warden or superintendent to the director/commissioner of the prison system.

- Programs in supermax facilities range from "none available" to "cell-front only" television/video programming or limited group programming.

- Jurisdictions differ in whether mentally ill and/or developmentally disabled inmates are placed in supermax housing.

- Transitional programming is available only in some jurisdictions.

Threat of transfer to a maxi-maxi institution is used to deter inmate misbehavior in less restrictive institutions. Civil rights watchdog groups charge that these maxi-maxi prisons violate the United Nations standards for the treatment of prisoners. They are typically located in rural areas, which makes staffing difficult in the professional areas of dentistry, medicine, and counseling. Senior officers would rather not work in these institutions, leaving the most difficult inmates in the hands of

Physical Abuse Like jail inmates, prisoners report a long history of physical abuse and mental health problems. About 19 percent report some form of physical abuse, including 57 percent of female prisoners (see Table 15.1 on page 498).[41] In addition, about 16 percent (283,000) of state prison inmates report having some form of mental problems.[42] Mentally ill inmates are more likely to be arrested for

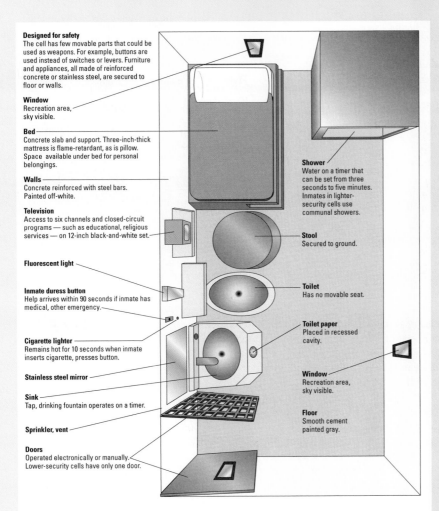

Designed for safety
The cell has few movable parts that could be used as weapons. For example, buttons are used instead of switches or levers. Furniture and appliances, all made of reinforced concrete or stainless steel, are secured to floor or walls.

Window
Recreation area, sky visible.

Bed
Concrete slab and support. Three-inch-thick mattress is flame-retardant, as is pillow. Space available under bed for personal belongings.

Walls
Concrete reinforced with steel bars. Painted off-white.

Television
Access to six channels and closed-circuit programs — such as educational, religious services — on 12-inch black-and-white set.

Fluorescent light

Inmate duress button
Help arrives within 90 seconds if inmate has medical, other emergency.

Cigarette lighter
Remains hot for 10 seconds when inmate inserts cigarette, presses button.

Stainless steel mirror

Sink
Tap, drinking fountain operates on a timer.

Sprinkler, vent

Doors
Operated electronically or manually. Lower-security cells have only one door.

Shower
Water on a timer that can be set from three seconds to five minutes. Inmates in lighter-security cells use communal showers.

Stool
Secured to ground.

Toilet
Has no movable seat.

Toilet paper
Placed in recessed cavity.

Window
Recreation area, sky visible.

Floor
Smooth cement painted gray.

FIGURE A
TYPICAL CELL IN A SUPER-MAXIMUM-SECURITY PRISON

Some of the toughest felons in the federal prison system are held in a new penitentiary in Florence, Colorado. It is designed to be the most secure ever built by the government. Many inmates live in isolation, except for an hour a day of recreation. A high-security cell in the 575-bed facility has these features.

SOURCE: Louis Winn, United States Penitentiary, Administrative Maximum, Florence, Colorado.

the least experienced correctional officers.

Critical Thinking Skills

Ultra-maxi prisons are reminiscent of the old Pennsylvania system, which made use of solitary confinement and high security. Is this inhumane in our more enlightened age? Why or why not?

InfoTrac College Edition Research

For a look into the Florence Penitentiary, go to InfoTrac College Edition and read "The Bomber Next Door: What Are the Most Dangerous Men in America Talking About at the Supermax Prison in Colorado?" *Time*, 22 March 1999, v153 i11 p55(1)

SOURCES: Richard H. Franklin, "Assessing Supermax Operations," *Corrections Today* 60 (1998): 126–128; Chase Riveland, *Supermax Prison: Overview and General Considerations* (Longmont, CO: National Institute of Corrections, 1998); Federal Bureau of Prisons, *State of the Bureau, 1995* (Washington, DC: U.S. Government Printing Office, 1996); Dennis Cauchon, "The Alcatraz of the Rockies," *USA Today*, 16 November 1994, p. A6.

violent offenses and to have suffered a variety of personal and emotional problems than the general prison population. The picture that emerges is that prisons hold those people who face the toughest social obstacles in society. Only a few members of the educated middle-class wind up in prison, and these people are usually held in minimum-security, "country club" institutions.

TABLE 15.1 PRIOR ABUSE OF CORRECTIONAL POPULATIONS, BY SEX

| Ever abused before admission | Total | Percent Experiencing Abuse Before Sentence | | | |
| | | Ever | | Before 18 | |
		Male	Female	Male	Female
State prison inmates	18.7%	16.1%	57.2%	14.4%	36.7%
Federal prison inmates	9.5	7.2	39.9	5.8	23.0
Jail inmates	16.4	12.9	47.6	11.9	36.6
Physically abused					
State prison inmates	15.4%	13.4%	46.5%	11.9%	25.4%
Federal prison inmates	7.9	6.0	32.3	5.0	14.7
Jail inmates	13.3	10.7	37.3	—	—
Sexually abused					
State prison inmates	7.9%	5.8%	39.0%	5.0%	25.5%
Federal prison inmates	3.7	2.2	22.8	1.9	14.5
Jail inmates	8.8	5.6	37.2	—	—

—Not available.

- A third of women in state prison, a sixth in federal prison, and a quarter in jail said they had been raped before their sentence. Another 3% to 6% reported that someone had tried unsuccessfully to rape them.
- More than half of the abused women said they were hurt by spouses or boyfriends, and less than a third, by parents or guardians. More than half of the abused men in correctional populations identified parents or guardians as abusers.
- Among state prison inmates, 1 in 20 men and 1 in 4 women said they had been sexually abused before age 18; 1 in 10 men and 1 in 4 women, physically abused.
- Among state prisoners reporting prior abuse, 89% had ever used illegal drugs; 76% of the men and 89% of the women had used them regularly. Of those not reporting prior abuse, 82% had used illegal drugs; 68% of the men and 65% of the women had used them regularly.

SOURCE: Caroline Wolf Harlow, *Prior Abuse Reported by Inmates and Probationers* (Washington, DC: Bureau of Justice Statistics, 1999), p. 2.

ALTERNATIVE CORRECTIONAL INSTITUTIONS

In addition to prison and jails, a number of other correctional institutions are in operation around the United States. Some have been in use for quite some time, while others have been developed as part of an innovative or experimental program.

Prison Farms and Camps

Prison farms and camps are found primarily in the South and the West, where they have been in operation since the nineteenth century.

Today, about 40 farms, 40 forest camps, 80 road camps, and more than 60 similar facilities (vocational training centers, ranches, and so on) exist in the United States. Prisoners on farms produce dairy products, grain, and vegetable crops that are used in the state correctional system and other government facilities, such as

Fill in the blanks 20
True/False 18
Multiple choice 26
Essay 7–8

hospitals and schools. Forestry camp inmates maintain state parks, fight forest fires, and do reforestation work. Ranches, primarily a western phenomenon, employ inmates in cattle raising and horse breeding, among other activities. Road gangs repair roads and state highways.

Shock Incarceration/Boot Camps

A recent approach to correctional care that is gaining popularity around the United States is **shock incarceration** in **boot camps**. Such programs typically include youthful, first-time offenders and feature military discipline and physical training. The concept is that short periods (90 to 180 days) of high-intensity exercise and work will "shock" the inmate into going straight. Tough physical training is designed to promote responsibility and improve decision-making skills, build self-confidence, and teach socialization skills. Inmates are treated with rough intensity by drill masters, who may call them names and punish the entire group for the failure of one of its members (see Figure 15.1). Discipline is so severe that some critics warn it can amount to "cruel and unusual punishment" and generate costly inmate lawsuits.[43]

The more than 75 programs now operating around the United States vary widely.[44] Some programs also include educational and training components,

shock incarceration
A short prison sentence served under military discipline at a boot camp facility.

boot camp
A short-term militaristic correctional facility in which inmates, usually young first-time offenders, undergo intensive physical conditioning and discipline.

Rita finishes 50 sit-ups and springs to her feet. At 6 A.M. her platoon begins a 5-mile run, the last portion of this morning's physical training. After 5 months in New York's Lakeview Shock Incarceration Correctional Facility, the morning workout is easy. Rita even enjoys it, taking pride in her physical conditioning.

When Rita graduates and returns to New York City, she will face 6 months of intensive supervision before moving to regular parole. More than two-fifths of Rita's platoon did not make it this far; some withdrew voluntarily, and the rest were removed for misconduct or failure to participate satisfactorily. By completing shock incarceration, she will enter parole 11 months before her minimum release date.

The requirements for completing shock incarceration are the same for male and female inmates. The women live in a separate housing area of Lakeview. Otherwise, men and women participate in the same education, physical training, drill and ceremony, drug education, and counseling programs. Men and women are assigned to separate work details and attend network group meetings held in inmates' living units.

Daily Schedule

A.M.
5:30	Wake up and standing count
5:45-6:30	Calisthenics and drill
6:30-7:00	Run
7:00-8:00	Mandatory breakfast/cleanup
8:15	Standing count and company formation
8:30-11:55	Work/school schedules

P.M.
12:00-12:30	Mandatory lunch and standing count
12:30-3:30	Afternoon work/school schedule
3:30-4:00	Shower
4:00-4:45	Network community meeting
4:45-5:45	Mandatory dinner, prepare for evening
6:00-9:00	School, group counseling, drug counseling, prerelease counseling, decision-making classes
9:00	Count while in programs
9:15-9:30	Squad bay, prepare for bed
9:30	Standing count, lights out

FIGURE 15.1 SHOCK INCARCERATION

Typical daily routines and schedule in a boot camp program

SOURCE: Cherie Clark, David Aziz, and Doris Mackenzie, *Shock Incarceration in New York: Focus on Treatment* (Washington, DC: National Institute of Justice, 1994), p. 5.

Boot camps use strict discipline regimes, which some critics find demeaning to inmates. Here at the Prison Boot Camp in Illinois, one correctional officer bangs the metal waste basket against the cement floor. Two officers yell at the new inmate, demanding that he hurry and gather his newly-cut hair into the basket. They hurl a barrage of nonprofane insults at him. Profanity by correctional officers as well as inmates is forbidden at the boot camp.

© *Jacksonville Courier/Zuzana Killian/The Image Works*

counseling sessions, and treatment for special-needs populations, while others devote little or no time to therapeutic activities. Some receive program participants directly from court sentencing, while others choose potential candidates from the general inmate population. Some allow voluntary participation and others, voluntary termination.[45]

Shock incarceration programs can provide some important correctional benefits. New York houses inmates in these programs in separate institutions and provides most (but not all) "graduates" with extensive follow-up supervision. Recidivism rates for these programs in New York are similar to those of traditional prisons, but there are indications that both inmates and staff view shock incarceration as a positive experience.[46] It is estimated that the New York program has saved taxpayers hundreds of millions of dollars, because boot camps are cheaper to build and maintain than traditional prisons. Other evaluations have found that a boot camp experience can improve inmates' attitudes and may enhance their postcorrection lifestyle.[47]

Shock incarceration has the advantage of being a lower-cost alternative to overcrowded prisons, as inmates are held in nonsecure facilities and sentences are short. Both staff and inmates seem excited by the programs, and even those who fail on parole report that they felt the shock incarceration was a valuable experience.[48] Of course, if shock incarceration is viewed as an exciting or helpful experience by its "graduates," they may be encouraged to recidivate, because the threat of the prison experience has been weakened.

Is shock incarceration a correctional panacea or another fad doomed to failure? The results so far are mixed. The costs of boot camps are no lower than those of traditional prisons, but because sentences are shorter, they do provide long-term savings. Some programs suffer high failure-to-complete rates, which makes program evaluations difficult (even if those who complete the program are successful, it is possible that success is achieved because troublesome cases drop out and are placed back in the general inmate population). What evaluations exist indicate that the recidivism rates of inmates who attend shock programs are in some cases no lower than for those released from traditional prisons.[49] Doris Mackenzie's extensive evaluations of the boot camp experience generate little evidence that they can significantly lower recidivism rates. Programs that seem to work best, such as those in New York, stress treatment and therapeutic activities, are voluntary, and are longer in duration.[50]

Community Correctional Facilities

One of the goals of correctional treatment is to help reintegrate the offender back into society. Placing offenders in a prison makes them more likely to adopt an inmate lifestyle than to reassimilate conventional social norms. As a result, the community corrections concept began to take off in the 1960s. State and federal correctional systems created community-based correctional models as an alternative to closed institutions. Many are **halfway houses** to which inmates are transferred just before their release into the community. These facilities are designed to bridge the gap between institutional living and the community. Specialized treatment may be offered, and the residents use the experience to cushion the shock of reentering society.

As you may recall, commitment to a community correctional center may also be used as an intermediate sanction and sole mode of treatment. An offender may be assigned to a community treatment center operated by the state department of corrections or to probation. Or the corrections department can contract with a private community center. This practice is common in the treatment of drug addicts and other nonviolent offenders whose special needs can be met in a self-contained community setting that specializes in specific types of treatment.

Halfway houses and community correctional centers can look like residential homes and in many instances were originally residences; in urban centers, older apartment buildings can be adapted for the purpose. Usually, these facilities have a central treatment theme—such as group therapy or reality therapy—that is used to rehabilitate and reintegrate clients.

Another popular approach in community-based corrections is the use of ex-offenders as staff members. These individuals have made the transition between the closed institution and society and can be invaluable in helping residents overcome the many hurdles they face in proper readjustment.

Despite the encouraging philosophical concept presented by the halfway house, evaluation of specific programs has not led to a definite endorsement of this type of treatment.[51] One significant problem has been a lack of support from community residents, who fear the establishment of an institution housing "dangerous offenders" in their neighborhood. Court actions and zoning restrictions have been brought in some areas to foil efforts to create halfway houses.[52] As a result, many halfway houses are located in decrepit neighborhoods in the worst areas of town—certainly a condition that must influence the attitudes and behavior of inmates. Furthermore, the climate of control exercised in most halfway houses, where rule violation can be met with a quick return to the institution, may not be one that the average inmate can distinguish from his or her former high-security penal institution.

halfway house
A community-based correctional facility that houses inmates before their outright release so that they can become gradually acclimated to conventional society.

Private Prisons

Essay 9

Correctional facilities are now being run by private firms as business enterprises. In some instances, a private corporation will finance and build an institution and then contract with correctional authorities to provide services for convicted criminals. Sometimes the private concern will finance and build the institution and then lease it outright to the government. This model has the advantage of allowing the government to circumvent the usually difficult process of getting voters to approve a bond issue and raising funds for prison construction. Another common method of private involvement is through specific service contracts; for example, a private concern might be hired to manage the prison health care system, food services, or staff training.

On January 6, 1986, the U.S. Corrections Corporation opened the first private state prison in Marion, Kentucky—a 300-bed minimum-security facility for inmates who are within three years of parole. Today, more than 20 companies are trying to enter the private prison market; five states are contracting with private companies to operate facilities, and more than 10 others—including Oregon, New Mexico, and Florida—have passed laws authorizing or expanding the use of private prison contractors.[53]

Although privately run institutions have been around for a few years, their increased use may present a number of problems. Will private providers be able to evaluate programs effectively, knowing that a negative evaluation might cause them to lose their contract? Will they skimp on services and programs in order to reduce costs? Might they not skim off the "easy" cases and leave the hard-core inmates to the state's care? Will the need to keep business booming require "widening the net" to fill empty cells? Must they maintain state-mandated liability insurance to cover inmate claims?[54] So far, private and state institutions cost about the same to operate.

Private corrections firms also run into opposition from existing state correctional staff and management, who fear the loss of jobs and autonomy. Moreover, the public may be skeptical about an untested private concern's ability to provide security and protection.

Private corrections also face administrative problems. How will program quality be controlled? To compete on price, a private facility may have to cut corners to beat out the competition. Determining accountability for problems and mishaps will be difficult when dealing with a corporation that is a legal fiction and protects its officers from personal responsibility for their actions. And legal problems can emerge quickly: Can privately employed guards patrol the perimeter and use deadly force to stop escape attempts? The Supreme Court has recently ruled that private correctional officers have less immunity from lawsuits than state employees.

The very fact that individuals can profit from running a prison may also prove unpalatable to large segments of the population. Should profit be made from human tragedy and suffering? However, is a private correctional facility really much different from a private hospital or mental health clinic that provides services to the public in competition with state-run institutions? The issue that determines the future of private corrections may be one of efficiency and cost effectiveness, not fairness and morality.

In the abstract, a private correctional enterprise may seem an attractive alternative to a costly correctional system, but these legal, administrative, and cost issues need to be resolved before private prisons can become widespread.[55] A balance must be reached between the need for a private business to make a profit and the integrity of a prison administration that must be concerned with such complex issues as security, rehabilitation, and dealing with highly dangerous people in a closed environment.[56] Research indicates that private prisons are no more economical than public institutions and that other factors, such as the size and security level of an institution, are the key indicators of an institution's actual costs.[57]

CORRECTIONAL POPULATIONS

The nation's vast system of penal institutions now holds about 2 milllion people (counting jail and community correction populations) and employs more than 250,000 to care for and guard them.

The U.S. prison population has had a number of cycles of growth and decline.[58] Between 1925 and 1939, it increased about 5 percent a year, reflecting the

True/False 19–20
Multiple choice 27

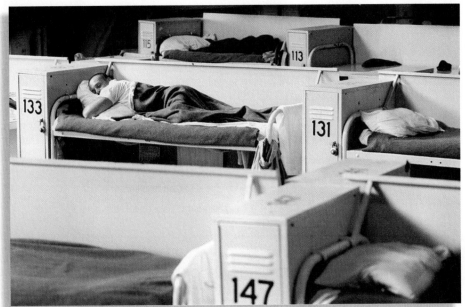

There is an ongoing correctional crowding crisis. Here, an inmate naps on a bunk-bed in a gym that has been converted to house prisoners at Deuel Vocational Institute near Tracy, Calif. More than 600 inmates are crammed into the half-century-old structure as part of measures to cope with prison system overcrowding.

AP/Wide World Photos

nation's concern for the lawlessness of that time. The incarceration rate reached a high of 137 per 100,000 U.S. population in 1939. During World War II, the prison population declined by 50,000, as potential offenders were drafted into the armed services. By 1956, the incarceration rate had dropped to 99 per 100,000 U.S. population.

The late 1950s saw a steady increase in the prison population until 1961, when 220,000 people were in custody, a rate of 119 per 100,000. From 1961 to 1968, with the escalation of the Vietnam War, the prison population declined by about 30,000. The incarceration rate remained fairly stable until 1974, when the current dramatic rise began. As Table 15.2 shows, the number of inmates has continued to increase steadily, until today well over 400 people per 100,000 population are in prison.

The Growth of the Prison Population

How can this dramatic rise in the prison population be explained? Prison administrators have linked the growth of the correctional population to a change in public opinion, which has demanded a more punitive response to criminal offenders. Public concern about drugs and violent crime has not been lost on state lawmakers. Mandatory sentencing laws, which have been implemented by a majority of states and the federal government, increase eligibility for incarceration and limit the availability of early release via parole. Although probation and community sentences still predominate, structural changes in criminal codes and crime rates have helped produce an expanding correctional population. The growing punitiveness of sentencing has significantly increased the amount of time served in prison, and efforts are now under way to adopt truth-in-sentencing laws that require inmates to serve at least 85 percent of their sentence behind

TABLE 15.2 PRISON POPULATION, 1990–1999

December 31	Number of Inmates		Sentenced Prisoners per 100,000 Resident Population	
	Federal	State	Federal	State
1990	65,526	708,393	20	272
1995	100,250	1,025,624	32	379
1998	123,041	1,177,532	38	423
1999	135,246	1,231,475	42	434

SOURCE: Allen Beck, *Prisoners in 1999* (Washington, DC: Bureau of Justice Statistics, 2000).

FIGURE 15.2
TRUTH-IN-
SENTENCING LAWS
REQUIRE INMATES
TO SERVE MORE
OF THEIR
SENTENCES

SOURCE: Paula Ditton and Doris James Wilson, *Truth in Sentencing in State Prisons* (Washington, DC: Bureau of Justice Statistics, 1999), p. 1.

State Prisons, 1996

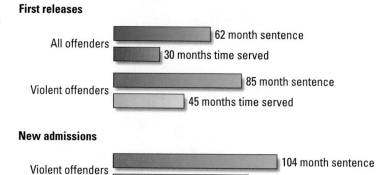

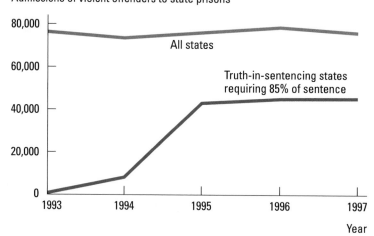

bars (see Figure 15.2).[59] Also swelling the prison population is an increasing number of ex-inmates who have failed on community release. About one-third of new admissions to prison in 1999 were parole or other conditional release violators, up from 29 percent in 1990.

As you may recall from Chapter 12, the conviction rate is increasing for crimes that are traditionally punished with a prison sentence, such as robbery and burglary. At the same time, get-tough policies have helped curtail the use of parole and have reduced judicial discretion to impose nonincarceration sentences.[60]

States fed up with juvenile crime have passed strict laws mandating that violent juveniles be waived or transferred to the adult court for treatment.[61] More than 20,000 juveniles are being tried as adults each year, making them eligible for incarceration in adult facilities.

As Table 15.3 shows, the number of state inmates being sentenced to prison underwent a slight decline between 1994 and 1996 (the most recent data available). It is possible that this trend may herald an eventual reduction in prison populations.

Because of the vast numbers of people in prison, there is an increasing need to maintain security in overcrowded facilities. As the Criminal Justice in Technology feature on page 506 shows, correctional administrators may rely on high-tech advances to maintain order.

TABLE 15.3   WHO GOES TO PRISON?

Percentage of felons convicted in state courts who received a prison sentence

	1988	1990	1992	1994	1996	Probation Only Sentences (1996)
All offenses	44%	46%	44%	45%	38%	29%
Murder	91	91	93	95	92	5
Rape	69	67	68	71	63	21
Robbery	75	73	74	77	73	13
Aggravated assault	45	45	44	48	42	28
Burglary	54	54	52	53	45	29
Larceny	39	40	38	38	31	37
Drug trafficking	41	49	48	48	39	29

SOURCES: Patrick A. Langan and Jodi M. Brown, *Felony Sentences in State Courts, 1994* (Washington, DC: Bureau of Justice Statistics, 1997); Brown and Langan, *Felony Sentences in State Courts, 1996* (Washington, DC: Bureau of Justice Statistics, 1999).

What the Future Holds

Multiple choice 28–29

The U.S. prison system now costs in excess of $25 billion annually, accounting for about 80 percent of all state correctional expenditures (the remaining 20 percent goes to juvenile justice activities, probation and parole services, and community-based corrections).

Incarceration rates are so high that the federal government estimates that about 5 percent of the U.S. population, or more than 13 million people, will serve a prison sentence sometime during their life. Men are more than eight times as likely as women to be imprisoned at least once during their life. Among men, blacks (28.5%) are about twice as likely as Hispanics (16.0%) and six times as likely as whites (4.4%) to be admitted to prison during their life. Among women, 3.6 percent of blacks, 1.5 percent of Hispanics, and 0.5 percent of whites will enter prison at least once.[62] The extreme racial differences in the imprisonment rate are a key concern of the justice system. Do these differences reflect racial discrimination in the sentencing process?

Despite these ominous statistics, the nation's prison population may be "maxing out." First, with the downtrend in crime rates, there are simply fewer criminals to incarcerate. For example, the waning of the crack cocaine epidemic in large cities may lower incarceration rates because fewer offenders will be eligible for the long penalties associated with crack possession.[63]

Budget cutbacks and belt tightening may halt the expansion of prison construction and the housing of ever more prisoners in already crowded prison facilities.[64] New modular construction techniques and double and triple bunking of inmates make existing prisons expandable, but the secure population probably cannot expand endlessly. As costs skyrocket, some states are now spending more on prisons than on higher education. The general public may begin to question the wisdom of a strict incarceration policy. In the 2000 election, California voters passed Proposition 36, which sends first- and second-time nonviolent drug offenders into treatment. The law provides probation and drug treatment for people convicted of possession, use, and transporting for personal use of controlled substances; those caught selling or manufacturing drugs are excluded from the treatment mandate, as are offenders also arrested on non-drug-related

CRIMINAL JUSTICE AND TECHNOLOGY

Using Technology to Increase Prison Security

A number of new and developing technologies are being used to increase prison safety, reduce escapes, and control contraband. A few of these advances are described here.

Preventing Escapes

Ground Penetrating Radar

The Special Technologies Laboratories (STL) has developed a new technology called ground penetrating radar (GPR), that can locate tunnels inmates use to escape. The system transmits energy into the ground, and by measuring the time it takes for that energy to be reflected, detects changes in ground material. GPR works almost like an old-fashioned Geiger counter, held in the hand and swept across the ground by an operator. Instead of detecting metal, however, the GPR system detects changes in ground composition, including voids, such as those created by a tunnel.

Heartbeat Monitoring

The weakest security link in any prison has always been the sally port, where trucks unload their supplies and where trash and laundry are taken out of the facility. Over the years, inmates have hidden in loads of trash, old produce, laundry—any possible container that might be exiting the facility. Now it is possible to prevent escapes by monitoring inmates' heartbeats! The Advanced

Vehicle Interrogation and Notification System (AVIAN)—being marketed by Geo Vox Security—works by identifying the shock wave generated by the beating heart, which couples to any surface the body touches. The system takes all the frequencies of movement, such as the expansion and contraction of the engine, and rain hitting the roof, and determines if there is a pattern similar to a human heartbeat.

Sticky Shocker

This less-than-lethal projectile uses stun gun technology to temporarily incapacitate a person at stand-off range. The Sticky Shocker is a low-impact, wireless projectile fired from compressed gas or powder launchers and is accurate to within 10 meters.

Finding Weapons and Other Contraband

Pulsed Radar

The ground penetrating radar developed by Special Technologies Laboratories, which detects changes in ground composition, can locate not only tunnels but also contraband buried in the recreation yard.

Back-Scatter Imaging

This system uses a back-scatter imager to detect weapons and contraband. Its major advantage over current walk-through portals is that it can detect

nonmetallic as well as metallic weapons. It uses low-power X-rays equivalent to about 5 minutes of exposure to the sun at sea level. These X-rays penetrate clothing but do not penetrate the body.

Body Scanning

This stationary screening system can detect nonmetallic weapons and contraband in the lower body cavities. It uses simplified magnetic resonance imaging (MRI) as a noninvasive alternative to X-ray and physical body cavity searches.

Critical Thinking Skills

Should an ever-increasing amount of money be spent on hardware to improve prison security, or should these resources be devoted to rehabilitation efforts?

InfoTrac College Edition Research

Use "prison security" as a key term to read more about efforts to improve safety within correctional settings.

Sources: Steve Morrison, "How Technology Can Make Your Job Safer," *Corrections Today* 62 (2000): 58–60; Gabrielle deGroot, "Hot New Technologies," *Corrections Today* 59 (1997): 60–63.

Essay 10

charges such as theft or gun possession. The law, which is scheduled to take effect in July 2001, will reduce the prison population by as many as 36,000 inmates a year.[65]

In the final analysis, change in the correctional population may depend on the faith judges and legislators place in incarceration as a crime control policy. As long as policymakers believe that incarcerating predatory criminals can bring crime rates down, the likelihood of a significant decrease in the institutional population seems remote. If there is little evidence that this costly system does anything to lower crime rates, less costly and equally effective alternatives may be sought.

SUMMARY

Today's correctional institutions trace their development from European origins. Punishment methods developed in Europe were modified and improved by American colonists, most notably William Penn, who replaced the whip and other methods of physical punishment with confinement in county institutions or penitentiaries.

Later, as needs grew, the newly formed states created their own large facilities. Discipline was harsh, and most enforced a code of total and absolute silence. The Auburn system of congregate working conditions during the day and isolation at night has been retained in the present U.S. penal system.

A number of institutions currently house convicted offenders. Jails are used for misdemeanants and minor felons. Because conditions are so poor in jails, they have become a major trouble spot for the criminal justice system.

Federal and state prisons—classified as minimum, medium, and maximum security—house most incarcerated felons. However, their poor track record has spurred the development of new correctional models, including the boot camp, the halfway house, and the community correctional center. Nonetheless, the success of these institutions has been challenged by research efforts indicating that their recidivism rates are equal to those of state prisons.

One recent development has been the privately run correctional institution. These are jails and prisons operated by private companies that receive a fee for their services. Used in a limited number of jurisdictions, they have been the center of some controversy: Can a private company provide better management of what has traditionally been a public problem?

The correctional population has grown dramatically in the past few years. Although the number of inmates diminished in the late 1960s and early 1970s, it has since hit an all-time high. This development may reflect a toughening of sentencing procedures nationwide. As a result, the greatest problem facing the correctional system today is overcrowding, which has reached a crisis level. To help deal with the problems of overcrowding, corrections departments have begun to experiment with modular prison construction and the use of alternative sanctions.

Key Terms

penitentiary	Pennsylvania system	medium-security prison
prison	contract system	minimum-security prison
jail	convict-lease system	shock incarceration
shire reeve	parole	boot camp
hulk	medical model	halfway house
Auburn system	maximum-security prison	

Discussion Questions

1. Should pretrial detainees and convicted offenders be kept in the same institution?
2. What can be done to reduce correctional overcrowding?

3. Should private companies be allowed to run correctional institutions?
4. What are the drawbacks to shock incarceration?

A CLOSER LOOK

Ken Adams, a noted correctional expert, is skeptical about the rush to build prisons and increase correctional budgets. He chides "law and order" types who are scaring the public:

The fundamentals of the prison industry are very solid. The estimated cost of incarcerating 1.3 million inmates is $26.8 billion annually, and at least six states have a prison budget greater than $1 billion. Consumer demand has been strongly trending upward for well over a decade and shows no signs of abating. Demand is driven by sophisticated marketing strategies, and key market makers, legislators, judges, and policy wonks are trying to outdo each other, vying for the public's admiration. Bill Bennett, former secretary of education, has been riding around the nation with his lock 'em up gang, trying to stir up support for more record-breaking increases in prison construction. (Schools and prisons must have more in common than we think!) His chief gunslinger, John DiIulio, who prefers pen to pistol, stands ready to shoot it out with anyone who challenges the desirability of massive increases in

prison spending. In what may be the greatest advertising gimmick of the decade, second perhaps only to Joe Camel, DiIulio has been promoting the "superpredator"—a fatherless, godless, jobless, armed to the teeth, gang-involved urban teenager—as the compelling reason for more prisons. Having raised the art of fear mongering to an all-time high, the beauty of this promotional strategy is that it comes at a time when crime rates are going down, thereby fending off the possibility that other competitors for the taxpayers' money, such as education, commerce, and health, may divert the revenue stream. Never mind that the superpredator is about as elusive as the Loch Ness monster. The image is so terrifying that even otherwise sensible Nebraska farmers are willing to pay for more prison construction. Look for a CLIO award next year.

To read more of what Dr. Adams has to say, go to InfoTrac College Edition and read his paper:
Kenneth Adams, "The Bull Market in Corrections," *Prison Journal,* December 1996, v76 i4 p461(7)

Notes

1 Vivien Stern, *A Sin Against the Future: Imprisonment in the World* (Boston: Northeastern University Press, 1998).

2 Allen Beck and Bernard Shipley, *Recidivism of Young Parolees* (Washington, DC: Bureau of Justice Statistics, 1987); see also John Wallerstedt, *Returning to Prison* (Washington, DC: Bureau of Justice Statistics, 1984).

3 Among the most helpful sources in developing this section were Mark Colvin, *Penitentiaries, Reformatories, and Chain Gangs* (New York: St. Martin's Press, 1997); David Duffee, *Corrections: Practice and Policy* (New York: Random House, 1989); Harry Allen and Clifford Simonsen, *Correction in America,* 5th ed. (New York: Macmillan, 1989); Benedict Alper, *Prisons Inside-Out* (Cambridge, MA: Ballinger, 1974); Harry Elmer Barnes, *The Story of Punishment,* 2nd ed. (Montclair, NJ: Patterson-Smith, 1972); Gustave de Beaumont and Alexis de Tocqueville, *On the Penitentiary System in the United States and Its Applications in France* (Carbondale: Southern Illinois University Press, 1964); Orlando Lewis, *The Development of American Prisons and Prison Customs, 1776–1845* (Montclair, NJ: Patterson-Smith, 1967); Leonard Orland, ed., *Justice, Punishment, and Treatment* (New York: Free Press, 1973); J. Goebel, *Felony and Misdemeanor* (Philadelphia: University of Pennsylvania Press, 1976); Georg Rusche and Otto Kircheimer, *Punishment and Social Structure* (New York: Russell & Russell, 1939); Samuel Walker, *Popular Justice* (New York: Oxford University Press, 1980); Graeme Newman, *The Punishment Response* (Philadelphia: J. B. Lip-

pincott, 1978); David Rothman, *Conscience and Convenience* (Boston: Little, Brown, 1980).

4 F. Pollock and F. Maitland, *History of English Law* (London: Cambridge University Press, 1952).

5 Marvin Wolfgang, "Crime and Punishment in Renaissance Florence," *Journal of Criminal Law and Criminology* 81 (1990): 567–584.

6 Margaret Wilson, *The Crime of Punishment,* Life and Letters Series, no. 64 (London: Johnathon Cape, 1934), p. 186.

7 John Howard, *The State of Prisons,* 4th ed. (1792; reprint ed., Montclair, NJ: Patterson-Smith, 1973).

8 Alexis Durham III, "Newgate of Connecticut: Origins and Early Days of an Early American Prison," *Justice Quarterly* 6 (1989): 89–116.

9 Lewis, *Development of American Prisons and Prison Customs,* p. 17.

10 Ibid., p. 29.

11 Dario Melossi and Massimo Pavarini, *The Prison and the Factory: Origins of the Penitentiary System* (Totowa, NJ: Barnes and Noble, 1981).

12 Michel Foucault, *Discipline and Punish* (New York: Vintage Books, 1978).

13 Ibid., p. 16.

14 David Rothman, *The Discovery of the Asylum* (Boston: Little, Brown, 1970).

15 Orland, *Justice, Punishment, and Treatment,* p. 143.

16 Ibid., p. 144.

17 Walker, *Popular Justice,* p. 70.

18 Ibid., p. 71.

19 Beverly Smith, "Military Training at New York's Elmira Reformatory, 1880–1920," *Federal Probation* 52 (1988): 33–41.

20 Ibid.

21 See Z. R. Brockway, "The Ideal of a True Prison System for a State," in *Transactions of the National Congress on Penitentiary and Reformatory Discipline,* reprint ed. (Washington, DC: American Correctional Association, 1970), pp. 38–65.

22 This section leans heavily on Rothman, *Conscience and Convenience.*

23 Ibid., p. 23.

24 Ibid., p. 133.

25 18 U.S.C. 1761.

26 Barbara Auerbach, George Sexton, Franlin Farrow, and Robert Lawson, *Work in American Prisons: The Private Sector Gets Involved* (Washington, DC: National Institute of Justice, 1988), p. 72.

27 John Irwin, *The Jail: Managing the Underclass in American Society* (Berkeley: University of California Press, 1985).

28 Correctional Association of New York, *Prison and Jails: Hospitals of Last Resort* (New York: Correctional Association of New York, 1998).

29 Allen J. Beck, *Prison and Jail Inmates at Midyear 1999* (Washington, DC: Bureau of Justice Statistics, 2000).

30 Ibid.

31 Caroline Wolf Harlow, *Prior Abuse Reported by Inmates and Probationers* (Washington, DC: Bureau of Justice Statistics, 1999).

32 Paula M. Ditton, *Mental Health and Treatment of Inmates and Probationers* (Washington, DC: Bureau of Justice Statistics, 1999).

33 Brandon Applegate, Ray Surette, and Bernard McCarthy, "Detention and Desistance From Crime: Evaluating the Influence of a New Generation of Jail on

Recidivism," *Journal of Criminal Justice* 27 (1999): 539–548.

34 Ibid.

35 James J. Stephan, *State Prison Expenditures, 1996* (Washington, DC: Bureau of Justice Statistics, 1999).

36 Human Rights Watch, *Prison Conditions in the United States* (New York: Human Rights Watch, 1991).

37 "Suit Alleges Violations in California's 'Super-Max' Prison," *Criminal Justice Newsletter,* 1 September 1993, p. 2.

38 Allen Beck, Darrell Gilliard, Lawrence Greenfeld, Caroline Harlow, Thomas Hester, Louis Jankowski, Tracy Snell, James Stephan, and Danielle Morton, *Survey of Prison Inmates, 1991* (Washington, DC: Bureau of Justice Statistics, 1993).

39 Roger Peters, Paul Greenbaum, John Edens, Chris Carter, and Madeline Ortiz, "Prevalence of DSM-IV Substance Abuse and Dependence Disorders Among Prison Inmates," *American Journal of Drug and Alcohol Abuse* 24 (1998): 573–580.

40 Craig Hemmens and James Marquart, "Fear and Loathing in the Joint: The Impact of Race and Age on Inmate Support for Prison AIDS Policies," *Prison Journal* 78 (1998): 133–152.

41 Harlow, *Prior Abuse Reported by Inmates and Probationers,* p. 1.

42 Ditton, *Mental Health and Treatment of Inmates and Probationers,"* p. 1.

43 Faith Lutze and David Brody, "The Eighth Amendment and Boot Camp Prison: Mental Abuse as Cruel and Unusual Punishment," *Crime and Delinquency* 45 (1999): 242–255.

44 Doris Layton Mackenzie, Robert Brame, David McDowall, and Claire Souryal, "Boot Camp Prison and Recidivism in Eight States," *Criminology* 33 (1995): 327–357.

45 Ibid., pp. 328–329.

46 "New York Correctional Groups Praises Boot Camp Programs," *Criminal Justice Newsletter,* 1 April 1991, pp. 4–5.

47 Velmer Burton, James Marquart, Steven Cuvelier, Leanne Fiftal Alarid, and Robert Hunter, "A Study of Attitudinal Change Among Boot Camp Participants," *Federal Probation* 57 (1993): 46–52.

48 Doris Layton Mackenzie, "Boot Camp Prisons: Components, Evaluations, and Empirical Issues," *Federal Probation* 54 (1990): 44–52; see also "Boot Camp Programs Grow in Number and Scope," NIJ Reports, November/December 1990, pp. 6–8.

49 Doris Layton Mackenzie and James Shaw, "The Impact of Shock Incarceration on Technical Violations and New Criminal Activities," *Justice Quarterly* 10 (1993): 463–487.

50 Mackenzie et al., "Boot Camp Prisons and Recidivism in Eight States," pp. 352–353.

51 Correctional Research Associates, *Treating Youthful Offenders in the Community: An Evaluation Conducted by A. J. Reiss* (Washington, DC: Correctional Research Associates, 1966).

52 Kevin Krajick, "Not on My Block: Local Opposition Impedes the Search for Alternatives," *Corrections Magazine,* October 1980, pp. 15–27.

53 "Many State Legislatures Focused on Crime in 1995, Study Finds," *Criminal Justice Newsletter,* 2 January 1996, p. 2.

54 Ira Robbins, *The Legal Dimensions of Private Incarceration* (Chicago: American Bar Foundation, 1988).

55 Lawrence Travis, Edward Latessa, and Gennaro Vito, "Private Enterprise and Institutional Corrections: A Call for Caution," *Federal Probation* 49 (1985): 11–17.

56 Patrick Anderson, Charles Davoli, and Laura Moriarty, "Private Corrections: Feast or Fiasco," *Prison Journal* 65 (1985): 32–41.

57 Travis Pratt and Jeff Maahs, "Are Private Prisons More Cost-Effective Than Public Prisons? A Meta-Analysis of Evaluation Research Studies," *Crime and Delinquency* 45 (1999): 358–371.

58 Data in this section come from Bureau of Justice Statistics, *Prisoners, 1925–1981* (Washington, DC: U.S. Government Printing Office, 1982).

59 Todd Clear, *Harm in American Penology: Offenders, Victims and Their Communities* (Albany: State University of New York Press, 1994).

60 Daniel Nagin, "Criminal Deterrence Research: A Review of the Evidence and a Research Agenda for the Outset of the 21st Century," in *Crime and Justice: An Annual Review,* ed. Michael Tonry (Chicago: University of Chicago Press, 1997).

61 For more on this issue, see Marcy Rasmussen Podkopacz and Barry Feld, "The End of the Line: An Empirical Study of Judicial Waiver," *Journal of Criminal Law and Criminology* 86 (1996): 449–492.

62 Thomas P. Bonczar and Allen J. Beck, *Lifetime Likelihood of Going to State or Federal Prison* (Washington, DC: Bureau of Justice Statistics, 1997).

63 Andrew Lang Golub, Farrukh Hakeem, and Bruce Johnson, *Monitoring the Decline in the Crack Epidemic with Data from the Drug Use Forecasting Program: Final Report* (Washington, DC: National Institute of Justice, 1996).

64 Timothy Noah, "Prison Population Boom Sputters to Halt as States Lack Funds to House Criminals," *Wall Street Journal,* 3 February 1992, p. A7.

65 Evelyn Nieves, "California Gets Set to Shift on Sentencing Drug Users," *New York Times,* 10 November 2000, p. 3.

AP/Wide World Photos

THE PRISON EXPERIENCE: LIVING IN AND LEAVING PRISON

On November 3, 2000, seven federal prison correctional officers, members of a group called the Cowboys, were indicted on charges that they kicked inmates, smashed their heads into walls, and mixed human waste into their food. The 52 acts of abuse against 20 inmates listed in the indictment included an incident in which a handcuffed inmate was choked until his eyes were bulging and another in which an inmate's head was slammed repeatedly into a wall. The indictment followed a two-year investigation into the Cowboys, who allegedly held the prison in a reign of terror. One inmate told investigators, "I'm scared to death every day I'm in here. It's like I'm in a lion's mouth."

Some members of the Cowboys have already plead guilty in exchange for testimony against fellow officers. One said that members regularly beat inmates for infractions as minor as kicking a door. It was common for them to enter cells and punch or kick prisoners, some of whom were handcuffed. It is also alleged that the Cowboys had a "green light" from prison authorities to "take care of business." If convicted, the correctional officers could receive up to 10 years in prison and fines of up to $250,000.[1]

Chapter

16

Criminal Justice Links

Criminal Justice Viewpoints

Inmates must learn to cope with a strange, hostile environment. Sometimes they find themselves far from home because the correctional department employs the practice of out-of-state placement of prisoners. Randi Taylor, left, leads chants outside the Waterbury, Conn., Superior Court July 18, 2000. Alice Tracy, second from right, is the mother of David Tracy, who she said died at the Wallens Ridge Prison in Big Stone Gap, Va. Family and friends demonstrated against Connecticut's policy of reducing prison inmate overcrowding by sending inmates to prisons in Virginia.

AP/Wide World Photos

Fill in the blanks 1
True/False 1
Multiple choice 1–2

The saga of the Cowboys is an extreme instance of prison brutality, but it helps explain why many inmates find their correctional experience extremely damaging and also why many recidivate. A majority of ex-inmates return to prison soon after their release. The spotty record of correctional rehabilitation is not surprising considering how overcrowded the system is. A significant percentage of facilities are old, decrepit, archaic structures: 25 prisons were built before 1875, 79 between 1875 and 1924, and 141 between 1925 and 1949. In fact, some of the first prisons ever constructed, such as the Concord Reformatory in Massachusetts, are still in operation.

Although a majority of prisons are classified as medium security, more than half of all inmates are being held in large, maximum-security institutions. Despite the continuous outcry by penologists against the use of fortresslike prisons, institutions holding a thousand or more inmates still predominate. Prison overcrowding is a significant problem, and many institutions are operating above stated capacity. Recreation and workshop facilities have been turned into dormitories housing 30 or more inmates in a single room. Most prison experts agree that a minimum of 60 square feet is needed for each inmate, but many prisons fail to reach this standard.

This giant, overcrowded system designed to reform and rehabilitate offenders is undergoing a crisis of massive proportions. Institutions are so overcrowded that meaningful treatment efforts are often a matter of wishful thinking, and recidivism rates are shockingly high. Inmates are resentful of the deteriorated conditions, and correctional officers fear that the institution is ready to explode. At the same time, correctional administrators have begun to adopt a no-frills policy in prison, removing privileges and making prisons truly places of punishment. The no-frills movement is a response to lawmakers' claims that crime rates are high because inmates no longer fear imprisonment. This chapter presents a brief review of some of the most important issues confronting the nation's troubled correctional system.

Fill in the blanks 2

total institution
A regimented, dehumanizing institution, such as a prison, in which like-situated people are kept in social isolation, cut off from the world at large.

MEN IMPRISONED

According to prevailing wisdom, prisons in the United States are **total institutions**. This means that inmates locked within their walls are segregated from the outside world, kept under constant scrutiny and surveillance, and forced to obey strict of-

TABLE 16.1 INCARCERATED PARENTS AND THEIR CHILDREN

In 1999, an estimated 721,500 state and federal prisoners were parents to 1,498,800 children under age 18.
- About 40 percent of fathers and 60 percent of mothers in state prison reported weekly contact with their children.
- A majority of both fathers (57%) and mothers (54%) in state prison reported never having a personal visit with their children since admission.
- More than 60 percent of parents in state prison reported being held more than 100 miles from their last place of residence.

Minor Children	Percent of Prisoners, 1997			Type of Contact	Percent of State Inmate Parents Reporting Monthly Contact with Their Children, 1997	
	State	Federal			Male	Female
Any	55.4%	63.0%		Any	62.4%	78.4%
1	23.8	24.0		Phone	42.0%	53.6%
2	15.8	18.5		Mail	49.9	65.8
3 or more	15.8	20.5		Visits	21.0	23.8
None	44.6%	37.0%				
Estimated number of minor children, 1999	1,324,900	173,900				

SOURCE: Christopher Mumola, "Incarcerated Parents and Their Children" (Washington, DC: Bureau of Justice Statistics, 2000).

ficial rules to avoid facing formal sanctions. Their personal possessions are taken from them, and they must conform to institutional dress and personal appearance norms. Many human functions are strictly curtailed; heterosexual relationships and sex, friendships, family relationships, education, and participation in groups become privileges of the past. More than half of all inmates report never having a personal visit with their children (see Table 16.1).

Imprisonment is a disheartening experience for most men, one that causes their lives to be disrupted, their relationships to be suspended, their ambitions and dreams to go sour. Few prisoners have experienced comparable stress on the outside and so have not developed coping strategies that can shield them from prison problems. Although prisoners differ from one another and may feel the pressures of confinement somewhat differently, they concur on the extraordinarily stressful nature of life in maximum-security penal institutions.

Living in Prison

Fill in the blanks 3
True/False 2–3

Inmates quickly learn what the term *total institution* really means. When they arrive at the prison, they are stripped, searched, shorn, and assigned living quarters. Before they get there, though, their first experience occurs in a classification or reception center, where they are given a series of psychological and other tests and are evaluated on the basis of their personality, background, offense history, and treatment needs. Based on the classification they are given, they will be assigned to a permanent facility. Hard-core, repeat, and violent offenders will go to a maximum-security unit; offenders with learning disabilities may be assigned to an institution that specializes in educational services; mentally disordered offenders will be held in a facility that can provide psychiatric care; and so on.

Once they arrive at the long-term facility, inmates may be granted a short orientation period and then given a permanent cell assignment in the general population. Because of overcrowding, they may be sharing a cell designed for a single inmate with one or more others. All previous concepts of personal privacy and dignity are soon forgotten. Personal losses include liberty, goods and services, heterosexual relationships, autonomy, and security.[2] Inmates may be subject to verbal and physical attack and threats, with little chance of legal redress. The criminal law applies to inmates as it does to any other citizen, but it is rarely enforced within prison walls.[3] Therefore, part of living in prison involves learning to protect oneself and developing survival instincts.

Inmates in large, inaccessible prisons may find themselves physically cut off from families, friends, and associates. Visitors may find it difficult to travel great distances to see them; mail is censored and sometimes destroyed.

Fill in the blanks 4
True/False 4

Adjusting to Prison Inmates may go through a variety of attitude and behavior changes, or cycles, as their sentence unfolds. During the early part of their prison stay, inmates considering the long duration of the sentence and the loneliness and dangers of prison life may easily become depressed. Their preprison life and roles must be forgotten and a new self, adapting to the institution, reconstructed.[4] This may mean taking on a new identity, ranging from "merchant," who can supply goods in exchange for cash or services, to "punk," who quickly becomes involved in sexuality.[5] They must learn the ins and outs of survival in the institution: Which persons can be befriended, and which are best avoided? Who will grant favors, and for what repayment? Some inmates will demand regular payments in exchange for protection from rape and beatings. Inmates must learn to adopt a lifestyle that shields them from victimization.[6] They must discover areas of safety and danger. Some learn how to fight back to prove they cannot be taken advantage of. Some kill their attackers and get even longer sentences; others join cliques and gangs that provide protection and power within the institution.

Inmates may find cliques or groups based on ethnic backgrounds or personal interests. They are likely to encounter Mafia-like or racial terror groups that must be dealt with, and they may be the victim of homosexual attacks. They may find that power in the prison is shared by terrified correctional officers and inmate gangs; the only way to avoid being beaten and raped may be to learn how to beat and rape.[7] If they are weak and unable to defend themselves, new inmates may find that they are considered a "punk"; if they ask a correctional officer for help, they are labeled a "snitch." After that, they may spend the rest of their sentence in protective custody, sacrificing the "freedom of the yard" and rehabilitation services for personal protection.[8]

Fill in the blanks 5

hustle
The underground prison economy.

Hustling Part of new inmates' early adjustment involves becoming familiar with and perhaps participating in the black market—the hidden economy of the prison known as the **hustle**. Hustling provides inmates with a source of steady income and the satisfaction that they are beating the system.[9] Hustling involves sales of such illegal commodities as drugs (uppers, downers, marijuana), alcohol, weapons, or illegally obtained food and supplies. When prison officials crack down on hustled goods, it merely serves to drive the price up—giving hustlers greater incentive to promote their activities. Drugs and other contraband are smuggled into prison by visitors, carried in by inmates who are out on furlough or work-release programs, or bought from corrupt prison officials. In some insititutons, the entire prison revolves around gang control of the contraband economy, and there are constant power struggles for control of the markets.[10] Control of the prison drug trade is often the spark that ignites violence and conflict.

Racial Conflict Inmates must also learn to deal with the racial conflict that is a daily fact of life. Prisoners tend to segregate themselves, and if peace is to reign in the institution, they learn to stay out of each other's way. Often racial groupings are quite exact; for example, Hispanics will separate themselves according to their national origin (Mexican, Puerto Rican, Colombian, and so on). Because racial disparity in sentencing is common in many U.S. courts, prisons are one place where "minorities" often hold power.

Social Support Inmates may find that the social support of inmate peers can make incarceration somewhat less painful. They may begin to take stock of their situation and enter into educational or vocational training programs, if they are available. Many turn to religion and take Bible classes. They heed the inmate grapevine to determine what the parole board considers important in deciding to grant community release. They may become more politically aware in response to the influence of other inmates, and the personal guilt they may have felt may be shifted to society at large. Why should they be in prison when those equally guilty go free? They learn the importance of money and politics. Eventually, they may be called on by new arrivals to aid them in adapting to the system.

Coping Behavior Despite all these hardships, many inmates learn to adapt to the prison routine. Each prisoner has his own method of coping; he may stay alone, become friends with another inmate, join a group, or seek the advice of treatment personnel. New inmates soon learn that their lifestyle and activities can contribute to their being vicitmized by more aggressive inmates: The more time they spend in closely guarded activities, the less likely they are to become the victims of violence; the more they isolate themselves from others who might protect them, the greater their vulnerability to attack; the more visitors they receive, the more likely they are to be attacked by fellow inmates jealous of their relationship with the outside world.[11]

Fill in the blanks 6
Multiple choice 3–5

New inmates must learn to deal with the correctional officers and other correctional personnel; these relationships will determine whether the inmates do "hard time" or "easy time." Younger inmates, especially minority-group members, report that they have more difficulty with correctional officers, whom they claim are likely to use excessive force; younger inmates of all races say they are treated as being "less than human."[12]

Erik Freeland/U.S. News & World Report

Counselor Charlie Doty talks to an inmate in a Kentucky prison. Counseling and treatment are standard fare in most prisons. Whether prison-based rehabilitation can succeed in reducing recidivism rates is the subject of constant debate. The so-called "failure" of rehabilitation has encouraged harsh penal measures such as mandatory life sentences for "three-time losers."

Regardless of adaptation style, the first stage of the inmates' prison cycle is marked by a growing awareness that they can no longer depend on their traditional associates for help and support and that, for better or worse, the institution is a new home to which they must adjust. Unfortunately for the goal of rehabilitation, the predominant emotion that inmates must confront is boredom. The absence of anything constructive to do—the forced idleness—is what is often so frustrating and so damaging.[13]

Even in the harsh prison environment, inmates may learn to find a niche for themselves. Inmates may be able to find a place, activity, or group in which they can feel comfortable and secure.[14] An inmate's niche is a kind of insulation from the pains of imprisonment, enabling him to cope and providing him with a sense of autonomy and freedom. Finding a niche may insulate inmates from attack; in fact, recent research indicates that prison victimization may be less prevalent than commonly believed. Not surprisingly, the relatively few victims of prison violence seem less psychologically healthy, more fearful than nonvictims, and less able to avoid the pains of imprisonment.[15]

Of course, not all inmates learn to cope. Some inmates repeatedly violate institutional rules; more than 10 percent of all inmates have six or more such infractions yearly.[16] While it is difficult to predict who will become an institutional troublemaker, rule-breaking behavior has been associated with being a younger inmate with a low IQ and numerous juvenile convictions, being a repeat offender, and having victimized a stranger. Inmates who have limited intelligence and low self-control may not be able to find adaptive coping mechanisms and manage the stress of being in prison.[17]

The Inmate Social Code

True/False 5–6
Multiple choice 6–7

For many years, criminal justice experts maintained that prisoners formed their own world with a unique set of norms and rules, known as the **inmate subculture**.[18] A significant aspect of the inmate subculture was a unique social code—unwritten guidelines that expressed the values, attitudes, and type of behavior that older inmates demanded of young ones. Passed on from one generation of inmates to another, the inmate social code represented the values of interpersonal relations within the prison.

inmate subculture
The loosely defined culture that pervades prisons and has its own norms, rules, and language.

National attention was first drawn to the inmate social code and subculture by Donald Clemmer's classic book *The Prison Community,* in which he presented a detailed sociological study of life in a maximum-security prison.[19] Referring to thousands of conversations and interviews, as well as to inmate essays and biographies, Clemmer was able to identify a unique language, or *argot,* that prisoners use. In addition, Clemmer found that prisoners tend to group themselves into cliques on the basis of such personal criteria as sexual preference, political beliefs, and offense history. He found complex sexual relationships in prison and concluded that many heterosexual men will turn to homosexual relationships when faced with long sentences and the loneliness of prison life.

prisonization
Assimilation into the separate culture in the prison that has its own rewards and behaviors.

Clemmer's most important contribution may have been his identification of the **prisonization** process. This he defined as the inmate's assimilation into the existing prison culture through acceptance of its language, sexual code, and norms of behavior. Those who become the most "prisonized" will be the least likely to reform on the outside.

Using Clemmer's work as a jumping-off point, a number of prominent sociologists have set out to explore more fully the various roles in the prison community. The most important principles of the dominant inmate culture are described in Exhibit 16.1.

Although some inmates violate the code and exploit their peers, the "right guy" is someone who uses the inmate social code as his personal behavior guide.

EXHIBIT 16.1 THE PRINCIPLES OF THE TRADITIONAL INMATE CULTURE

1. Don't interfere with inmates' interests. Never betray another inmate to authorities; grievances must be handled personally. "Don't be nosy," "Don't have a loose lip," "Keep off the other inmates' backs," and "Don't put another inmate on the spot."

2. Don't lose your head. Inmates are cautioned to refrain from arguing, quarreling, or engaging in other emotional displays with fellow inmates. "Play it cool" and "Do your own time."

3. Don't exploit inmates. Prisoners are warned not to take advantage of one another: "Don't steal from cons," "Don't welsh on a debt," "Be right."

4. Be tough, and don't lose your dignity. If conflict starts, an inmate must be prepared to deal with it effectively and thoroughly. "Don't cop out," "Don't weaken," "Be tough; be a man."

5. Don't be a sucker. Inmates are cautioned not to make fools of themselves and support the correctional officers or prison administration over the interests of the inmates: "Be sharp."

SOURCE: Gresham Sykes and Sheldon Messinger, "The Inmate Social Code," in *The Sociology of Punishment and Corrections*, ed. Norman Johnston et al. (New York: Wiley, 1970), pp. 401–408.

He is always loyal to his fellow prisoners, keeps his promises, is dependable and trustworthy, and never interferes with inmates who are conniving against the officials.[20] The right guy does not go around looking for a fight, but he never runs away from one; he acts like a man.

Not all experts believe that the prison culture reflects the deprivation and harsh conditions of a total institution. In a classic paper, John Irwin and Donald Cressey conceded that a prison culture exists but claimed that its principles are actually imported from the outside world.[21] According to their **importation model**, the inmate culture is affected as much by the values of newcomers as it is by traditional inmate values.[22] Irwin and Cressey found that the inmate world is actually divided into three groups, each corresponding to a role in the outside world. The *thief subculture* is made up of professional criminals who stick to themselves and always try to "do your own time." Members of the *convict subculture* try to gain power in the prison and control others for their own ends. The *conventional subculture* is made up of inmates who try to retain legitimate elements of the outside world in their daily life (that is, they identify with neither of the deviant prison subcultures).

Irwin and Cressey's research showed that the inmate culture could be influenced by outside events and that the values that inmates held on the outside could be imported into the prison. Recent research by Candace Kruttschnitt, Rosemary Gartner, and Amy Miller has found support for the importation model through interviews with female offenders in two California prisons. Women's social class background, age, and history of abuse shape their prison experiences. Not surprisingly, lower-class women, especially those who lived on the street, were able to adapt to the prison experience better than their more affluent peers, who had little experience with personal or institutional deprivation. Women who had been abused were extremely sensitive to control efforts by correctional officers that seemed in any way reminiscent of the abuse they had suffered on the outside.[23]

It is possible that both socialization and importation help define the way inmates adopt to the prison culture. For example, inmates who viewed violence as an acceptable alternative before entering prison are the ones most likely to adopt the inmate social code.[24]

The effects of prisonization may be long term and destructive. Many imates become hostile to the legal system, learn to use violence as a means of solving problems, and come to value criminal peers.[25] For some, this change may be permanent; for others, it is temporary—they may revert to their "normal" life after release.

True/False 7
Multiple choice 8

importation model
The view that the violent prison culture reflects the criminal culture of the outside world and is neither developed in nor unique to prisons.

True/False 8
Multiple choice 9

The New Inmate Culture

The importation of outside values into the inmate culture has had a dramatic effect on prison life. The "old" inmate subculture may have been harmful because its norms and values insulated the inmate from change efforts, but it also helped create order within the institution and prevented violence among the inmates. People who violated the code and victimized others were sanctioned by their peers. An understanding developed between correctional officers and inmate leaders: The correctional officers would let the inmates have things their own way; the inmates would not let things get out of hand and draw the attention of the administration.

The old system may be dying or already dead in most institutions. The change seems to have been precipitated by the Black Power movement of the 1960s and 1970s. Black inmates were no longer content to fill a subservient role and challenged the power of established white inmates. As the Black Power movement gained prominence, racial tension in prisons created divisions that severely altered the inmate subculture. Older, respected inmates could no longer cross racial lines to mediate disputes. Predatory inmates could victimize others without fear of retaliation. Consequently, more inmates than ever are now assigned to protective custody for their own safety.

In the new culture, African American and Latino inmates are much more cohesively organized than whites.[26] Their groups sometimes form out of religious or political affiliations, such as the Black Muslims; out of efforts to combat discrimination in prison, such as the Latino group La Familia; or from street gangs, such as the Vice Lords or Gangster Disciples in the Illinois prison system and the Crips in California. Where white inmates have successfully organized, it is in the form of a neo-Nazi group called the Aryan Brotherhood. Racially homogenous gangs are so cohesive and powerful that they are able to supplant the original inmate code with one of their own. Consider the oath taken by new members of Nuestra Familia (Our Family), a Latino gang operating in California prisons: "If I go forward, follow me. If I hesitate, push me. If they kill me, avenge me. If I am a traitor, kill me."[27]

These groups not only provide protection to their members but also act as a bloc to make demands on prison administrators. Although their members may adhere to principles of the traditional inmate code (such as "Don't inform"), allegiance is always to members of their own group.

The current state of prisons may also be responsible for eroding the traditional inmate culture. Prisons are crowded, and it is common to move inmates from one unit to another. With the population in such a state of flux, a stable prison society cannot be achieved. Moreover, there are now a significant number of state-raised convicts—young, institutionally experienced individuals who often use violence to satisfy their urges and who have little use for an inmate code.[28] Rape has become an ever-increasing problem. At one time it was suggested that heterosexual men in prison might turn to homosexual relations because of the absence of female partners, but today rape as a means of expressing dominance, power, and anger is an accepted prison norm.[29]

WOMEN IMPRISONED

Before 1960, few women were in prison. Women's prisons were relatively rare and were usually an outgrowth of male institutions. Only 4 institutions for women were built between 1930 and 1950; in comparison, 34 women's prisons were constructed during the 1980s.

At the beginning of the twentieth century, female inmates were viewed as morally depraved people who flaunted conventional rules of female behavior. New

True/False 9
Multiple choice 10–11

prisons began to be built for women. One result of the establishment of these reformatories was the application of sentences that proportionately were actually harsher than those given to males. Feminist scholar Nicole Rafter has found that during World War I, in women's reformatories from Connecticut to Arkansas, women were imprisoned whose only offense was having a venereal disease.[30] Some women were sentenced for an indeterminate amount of time, which often meant that they were kept in an institution until they were "cured"—a condition that might have taken years, if ever, to achieve. The treatment of white and black women differed significantly. In some states, white women were placed in female-only reformatories designed to improve their deportment; black women were placed in male prisons, where they were subject to the chain gang and beatings.[31]

The place of women in the correctional system has changed dramatically. Today, more than 90,000 women are incarcerated in the state and federal systems, about 7 percent of the total population. Although still small compared to the male inmate population, the female population has grown at a faster pace. Since 1986, the percentage of the male population behind bars has risen 50 percent (from 3.3% to 4.9%) while the percentage of the female population behind bars has risen 100 percent (from 0.4% to 0.8%). Between 1990 and 1999, the number of males in prison increased 60 percent while the number of females increased 84 percent.[32]

The female offender population has increased so rapidly for a number of reasons. Female crime rates have accelerated at a faster pace than male crime rates. The get-tough policies that produced mandatory and determinate sentencing statutes also helped reduce the judicial discretion that has traditionally benefited women. As Meda Chesney-Lind points out, women are swept up in the get-tough movement and no longer receive the benefits of male chivalry. The use of sentencing guidelines means that such factors as family ties and employment record, two elements that usually benefit women during sentencing, can no longer be considered by judges.[33] Chesney-Lind notes that judges seem willing once again to view female offenders as "depraved" and outside the ranks of "true womanhood." Her work is discussed in greater detail in the Race, Gender, and Ethnicity in Criminal Justice feature.

Female Institutions

State jurisdictions have been responding to the influx of female offenders into the correctional system by expanding the facilities for housing and treating them.[34] Women's prisons tend to be smaller than those housing male inmates.[35] Although some female institutions are strictly penal, with steel bars, concrete floors, and other security measures, the majority are nonsecure institutions similar to college dormitories and group homes in the community. Women's facilities, especially those in the community, commonly offer a great deal of autonomy to inmates and allow them to make decisions affecting their daily life in the institution.

Like men's prisons, women's prisons suffer from a lack of adequate training, health, treatment, and educational facilities. Psychological counseling often takes the form of group sessions conducted by laypeople, such as correctional officers. Most trained psychologists and psychiatrists restrict their activities to conducting intake classifications and court-ordered examinations and prescribing mood-controlling medication. In fact, there is evidence that female inmates are subjected to medication in custody with much greater frequency than male inmates.[36] Although many female inmates are parents and had custody of their children before their incarceration, little effort is made to help them develop better parenting skills.

The lack of meaningful work opportunities is also a problem. Where vocational training exists, it is in areas with limited financial reward, hindering adjustment on release. Female inmates, many of whom were on the economic

Fill in the blanks 7
True/False 10–11
Essay 1

RACE, GENDER, AND ETHNICITY IN CRIMINAL JUSTICE

Women in Prison: Vengeful Equity

According to Meda Chesney-Lind, a highly respected feminist scholar, the soaring number of women in prison is not simply a product of the increasing reliance on imprisonment as a sanction. Women's proportional share of the prison population has increased because of a significant change in society's response to women's crime. In the past, the status of a female defendant—usually a nonviolent offender who was also a wife and mother—might be taken into account, but this is no longer possible under new mandatory sentences.

Many female offenders are involved in drug offenses, which are now heavily sanctioned. The "war on drugs" has placed an extremely harsh burden on poor and marginalized women. Though its intent was to get tough on drug kingpins and dealers, mandatory drug sentencing, especially in federal courts, has produced an explosion in the female inmate population. The war on drugs, Chesney-Lind claims, has become a "war on women": More than one-third of incarcerated women are serving time solely for possession of illegal drugs. In addition, the new technologies being developed for drug testing have resulted in more parole and probation violations, further increasing the number of female inmates.

The result has been a dramatic change in the way the country responds to female offending. The nation is becoming more punitive and is treating men and women more equally. However, this has harmed women by increasing their share of the prison population; it is "equality with a vengeance."

The effort to treat men and women more equally has also triggered abuse of incarcerated females in male-dominated institutions. When male inmates in New York were videotaped while being strip-searched, the state instituted a policy of also taping women's strip searches. The videotaping was done while male officers were in the vicinity, and the female inmates sued and won damages when they suspected that the videos were being watched by prison officials. Such sexually charged situations are particularly damaging to women who have a history of sexual and physical abuse. Because male correctional officers now are commonly assigned to women's prisons, there have also been major scandals involving the sexual exploitation and rape of female inmates. Few if any of these incidents are reported, and perpetrators rarely go to trial. Institutional workers cover for each other, and women who file complaints are offered little protection from vengeful correctional officers.

At the same time that women are suffering because of this misguided effort at equity, they are also being victimized because of perceived gender differences. Women are much more likely than men to suffer disciplinary complaints for trivial offenses and more likely to be punished with solitary confinement and other severe sanctions. There is clear evidence that women in prison are overpoliced and overcontrolled.

Critical Thinking Skills

Chesney-Lind concludes that women in modern prisons suffer the "worst of both worlds"—sometimes suffering because of gender differences, sometimes receiving "equity with a vengeance" that results in their sexual exploitation. Would an alternative approach, stressing community care and support, be a more effective method of reducing female crime rates and helping indigent women achieve their potential? Should prison be a last resort for female offenders?

InfoTrac College Edition Research

To learn more about women in prison, use "female inmates" and "female prisons" as key terms in InfoTrac College Edition.

SOURCE: Meda Chesney-Lind, "Vengeful Equity: Sentencing Women to Prison," in *The Female Offender: Girls, Women and Crime,* ed. Meda Chesney-Lind (Thousand Oaks, CA: Sage, 1997), pp. 1–27.

margin before their incarceration, find little means for improvement during their prison experience.[37] Surveys indicate that the prison experience does little to prepare women to reenter the workforce after their sentence has been completed. Gender stereotypes still shape vocational opportunities.[38] Female inmates are still being trained for "women's roles," such as child rearing, and not given the programming to make successful adjustments in the community.[39]

Fill in the blanks 8
True/False 12

Female Inmates

Like their male counterparts, female inmates tend to be young (most are under age 30), minority-group members, unmarried, undereducated (more than half are high school dropouts), and either unemployed or underemployed.

Incarcerated women are also likely to have had a troubled family life. Significant numbers were at-risk children, products of "broken homes" and the welfare system; more than half had received welfare at some time during their adult lives. They have often experienced a pattern of harsh discipline and physical abuse. Many claim to have been physically or sexually abused at some point in their lives. This pattern has continued in their adult life: Many female inmates are victims of domestic violence.

A serious problem for women in prison is the disruption of their families. About three-fourths of all female inmates are mothers, and most were living with their children before their incarceration. Who takes care of the children while their mothers are in prison? Most children of incarcerated women are placed with their father, grandparent, other relative, or a family friend; about 10 percent wind up in foster homes or state facilities.

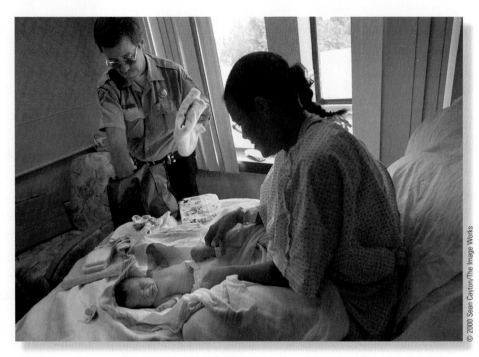

It is common for female inmates to have young children or even to give birth while in prison. Female institutions may have a maternity ward to provide services to the newborn infants and their inmate mothers.

A significant number of female inmates report having substance abuse problems. About three-fourths had used drugs at some time in their lives, and almost half were involved with addictive drugs, such as cocaine, heroin, or PCP. There is actually little difference in major drug use between male and female offenders, whether measured over their life span or at the time of their current arrest. The incarceration of so many women who are low criminal risks yet face a high risk of exposure to HIV and other diseases because of their prior history of drug abuse presents a significant challenge for correctional authorities.

The picture that emerges of the female inmate is troubling. After a lifetime of emotional turmoil, physical and sexual abuse, and drug use, it seems improbable that overcrowded, underfunded correctional institutions can effect a dramatic turnaround in the behavior of at-risk female inmates.

Sexual Exploitation

Daily life in the women's prison differs somewhat from that in male institutions. Unlike male inmates, women usually do not present an immediate physical danger to staff and fellow inmates. Relatively few engage in violent behavior, and incidents of inmate-initiated sexual aggression, so common in male institutions, are quite rare in women's prisons.[40] Nevertheless, there are numerous reports of female prisoners' being sexually abused and exploited by male correctional workers, who use either brute force or psychological coercion to gain sexual control over inmates.[41]

Staff-on-inmate sexual misconduct covers a wide range of behaviors, from lewd remarks to voyeurism to assault and rape. A 1999 survey by the federal government's General Accounting Office (GAO) found that the federal government, 41 states, and the District of Columbia had passed laws criminalizing some types of staff sexual misconduct in prisons. The GAO's in-depth analysis of the three correctional systems with the largest number of female inmates—the Federal Bureau of Prisons, the California Department of Corrections, and the Texas

Department of Criminal Justice—found that sexual misconduct persists despite efforts to correct problems and train staff. Between 1995 and 1998, female inmates made 506 allegations of staff sexual misconduct; 92 of them were sustained, generally resulting in staff firings or resignations. Each of these jurisdictions was involved in at least two civil lawsuits arising from staff sexual misconduct during this period.[42]

Although sexual exploitation may be banned, the duties of male correctional workers often include conduct that is not prohibited by law but that greatly distresses female inmates—most notably, searches for contraband that require male staff to touch their bodies, and surveillance when they are dressing.[43] Under U.S. antidiscrimination laws, prisons and jails cannot refuse to employ men to supervise female inmates (or women to supervise male inmates), and in many states there are few restrictions on their duties. It is estimated that about 40 percent of the correctional officers working with female inmates are men.[44]

Adapting to Prison

Fill in the blanks 9
True/False 13

The rigid, antiauthority inmate social code found in many male institutions does not exist in female insitutions.[45] Confinement for women, however, may produce severe anxiety and anger, because of separation from families and loved ones and the inability to function in normal female roles. Unlike men, who direct their anger outward, female prisoners may turn to more self-destructive acts to cope with their problems. Female inmates are more likely than males to mutilate their own bodies and attempt suicide. For example, one common practice among female inmates is self-mutilation or "carving." This ranges from simple scratches to carving the name of a boyfriend, or even complex statements or sentences ("To mother, with hate"), on one's body.[46]

make-believe family
A peer unit containing mother and father figures that is formed by women in prison to compensate for the loss of family and loved ones.

Another form of adaptation to prison used by women is the **make-believe family**. This group contains masculine and feminine figures acting as fathers and mothers; some even act as children and take on the role of brother or sister. Formalized marriages and divorces may be conducted. Sometimes one inmate holds multiple roles, so that a "sister" in one family may "marry" and become the "wife" of another inmate. It is estimated that about half of all female inmates are members of make-believe families.[47]

Why do make-believe families exist? Experts suggest that they provide the warm, stable relationships otherwise unobtainable in the prison environment. People both in and out of prison have needs for security, companionship, affection, attention, status, prestige, and acceptance that can be filled only by having primary group relationships. Friends fill many of these needs, but the family better represents the ideal or desire for these qualities in a stable relationship.

INSTITUTIONAL TREATMENT PROGRAMS

Almost every prison facility uses some mode of treatment for inmates. This may take the form of individual or group therapy programs or educational or vocational training.

Fill in the blanks 10
True/False 14

Despite good intentions, rehabilitative treatment within prison walls is extremely difficult to achieve. Trained professional treatment personnel usually command high salaries, and most institutions do not have sufficient budgets to adequately staff therapeutic programs. Usually, a large facility may have a single staff psychiatrist or a few social workers. A second problem revolves around the philosophy of **less eligibility**, which has been interpreted to mean that prisoners should always be treated less well than the most underprivileged law-abiding citizen. Translated into today's terms, less eligibility usually raises the question "Why

less eligibility
The view that prisoners should always be treated less well than the most underprivileged law-abiding citizen.

should inmates be treated to expensive programs denied to the average honest citizen?" Enterprising state legislators use this argument to block expenditures for prison budgets, and some prison administrators may actually agree with them.

Finally, correctional treatment is hampered by the ignorance surrounding the practical effectiveness of one type of treatment program over another: What constitutes proper treatment has not yet been determined. Studies evaluating treatment effectiveness have suggested that few, if any, of the programs currently used in prisons actually produce significant numbers of rehabilitated offenders. Several of the therapeutic methods that have been used nationally in correctional settings are discussed here.

To read about programs in the California prison system, go to http://www.cdc.state.ca.us/index.htm

For an up-to-date list of Web links, see http://www.wadsworth.com/product/0534573053s

Counseling Programs

Essay 2

Prison inmates typically suffer from a variety of cognitive and psychosocial deficits, such as poor emotional control, social skills, and interpersonal problem solving; these deficits are often linked to long-term substance abuse. Modern counseling programs can help people control their emotions (understand why they feel the way they do, how not to get too nervous or anxious, how to solve problems creatively); communicate with others (understand what people tell them, communicate clearly when they write); deal with legal concerns (keep out of legal trouble, avoid breaking laws); manage general life issues (find a job, deal with difficult co-workers, be a good parent); and develop and maintain social relationships (have good relations with others, make others happy, make others proud).[48] To achieve these goals, correctional systems use a variety of intensive individual and group techniques, including behavior modification, aversive therapy, milieu therapy, reality therapy, transactional analysis, and responsibility therapy.

Counseling is a major component of correctional treatment policy, but the personnel and resources needed to carry out effective programs are often lacking. Many institutions maintain a unit for the emotionally disturbed and offer psychological services tied in with state hospitals and mental health services. Yet the number of trained mental health professionals employed in the correctional system is far less than what is needed. This problem becomes even more acute when a significant percentage of the prison population may be suffering from acute mental problems, such as schizophrenia, while others suffer from adaption problems marked by nervousness, sleeplessness, and depression.

Treating the Special-Needs Inmate

True/False 15
Multiple choice 12

One of the challenges of correctional treatment is to care for **special-needs inmates**. These individuals can have a variety of social problems. Some are mentally ill but have been assigned to prison because the state has toughened its insanity laws. Others develop serious mental problems during their imprisonment. Nationally, from 1 to 6 percent of the inmate population is mentally retarded. Treating the mentally ill inmate has required the development and use of new therapies in the prison environment. Although some critics warn of the overuse of "chemical straitjackets"—psychotropic medications—to keep disturbed inmates docile, prison administrators have been found to have a genuine concern for these special-needs inmates.[49]

Restrictive crime control policies have also produced another special-needs group: elderly inmates who require health care, diets, and work and recreational opportunities that are quite different from those of the general population. Some correctional systems have responded to the growing number of elderly inmates by creating facilities tailored to their needs.[50] The most recent data available indicate that 3 percent of all inmates, or about 40,000, are age 55 or older, an increase of more than 40 percent since 1990.[51]

special-needs inmate
A prisoner distinguished by a particular problem such as mental illness, advanced age, drug dependence, or HIV infection.

Two other types of special-neeeds inmates—those who are drug dependent and those who are infected with the AIDS virus—will be discussed in greater detail.

The Drug-Dependent Inmate

The Drug-Dependent Inmate Although most institutions attempt to provide treatment for drug and alcohol dependence, these efforts are often inadequate. Government-sponsored surveys have found that an estimated 500,000 state inmates are in need of drug treatment, but because of lack of funding and inadequate security measures, only 100,000 receive adequate treatment.[52] Nearly 60 percent of all correctional facilities nationwide do not provide on-site substance abuse treatment to inmates or residents.[53]

Although the ideal drug treatment has yet to be identified, experimental efforts around the country use counseling sessions, instruction in coping strategies, employment counseling, and strict security measures featuring random urinalysis.

The AIDS-Infected Inmate The AIDS-infected prisoner is another acute special-needs inmate. Two groups of people at high risk of contracting the human immunodeficiency virus (HIV) that causes AIDS are intravenous drug users who share needles and males who engage in homosexual sex—two lifestyles common in prison. Although the numbers are constantly changing, the rate of HIV infection among state and federal prisoners seems to have stabilized at around 2 percent (5 times higher than in the general population). At last count, there were about 25,000 HIV-infected inmates, and both the number of infected inmates and the AIDS mortality rate have been in decline.[54]

Correctional administrators have found it difficult to arrive at effective policies to confront AIDS. All state and federal jurisdictions do some AIDS testing, but only 18 states and the Federal Bureau of Prisons conduct mass screenings of all inmates. Most states test inmates only if there are significant indications that they are HIV positive. About 40 percent of all state prison inmates have ever been tested for AIDS.

Most correctional systems are now training staff about AIDS. Educational programs for inmates are often inadequate, because administrators are reluctant to give them information on the proper cleaning of drug paraphernalia and safe sex (since both drug use and homosexual sex are forbidden in prison).

Many questions remain about the proper treatment of AIDS-infected inmates. Should they be given the full range of treatment, including multiple doses of expensive medications such as AZT? Although most jurisdictions report that they provide this care, many fail to provide treatment to all infected inmates. Should AIDS-infected inmates be isolated from the general population and held in restricted areas? About 30 percent of state correctional systems have some type of segregation policy, but most inmates with AIDS are in the general inmate population. Cases challenging segregation policies have been filed. In one important California case, *Gates v. Deukmejian,* a court upheld a one-year experimental program in which 20 to 30 HIV-infected inmates would live in a closed unit but be mainstreamed with the general population in all programs and activities.[55] Prison administrators have been sued over incidents in which staff or inmates were bitten or spit on by HIV-infected inmates.

What steps should be taken to limit the HIV infection risk to inmates and staff? A majority of institutions now provide AIDS information and education to both groups. Most encourage the proper handling of inmates to reduce the risk of infection. Controversy exists over whether condoms should be provided to inmates. Only five correctional systems currently take that step; the majority of officials believe condom distribution encourages and condones behavior that is illegal and, some feel, immoral.

To read how corrections departments are trying to treat drug-dependent inmates in the prison setting, go to http://www.ojp.usdoj.gov/docs/psrsa.txt
For an up-to-date list of Web links, see http://www.wadsworth.com/product/0534573053s

True/False 16
Multiple choice 13

Educational and Vocational Programs

In addition to treatment programs stressing personal growth through individual analysis or group process, inmate rehabilitation is also pursued through vocational and educational training. These two kinds of training sometimes differ in style and content, but may overlap when, for example, education involves practical, job-related study.

The first prison treatment programs were in fact educational. A prison school was opened at the Walnut Street Jail in 1784. Elementary courses were offered in New York's prison system in 1801 and in Pennsylvania's in 1844. An actual school system was established in Detroit's House of Corrections in 1870, and Elmira Reformatory opened a vocational trade school in 1876.

Today, most institutions provide some type of educational program. At some prisons, inmates can obtain a high school diploma or a general educational development (GED) certificate through equivalency exams. Other institutions provide an actual classroom education, usually staffed by certified teachers employed full-time at the prison or by part-time teachers who also teach full time at nearby public schools.

The number of hours devoted to educational programs and the quality and intensity of these efforts vary greatly. Some are full-time programs employing highly qualified and concerned educators; others are part-time programs without any real goals or objectives. Although worthwhile attempts are being made, prison education programs often suffer from inadequate funding and administration. The picture is not totally bleak, however. In some institutions, programs have been designed to circumvent the difficulties inherent in the prison structure. They encourage volunteers from the community and local schools to tutor willing and motivated inmates. Some prison administrators have arranged flexible schedules for inmate students and actively encourage their participation in these programs. In

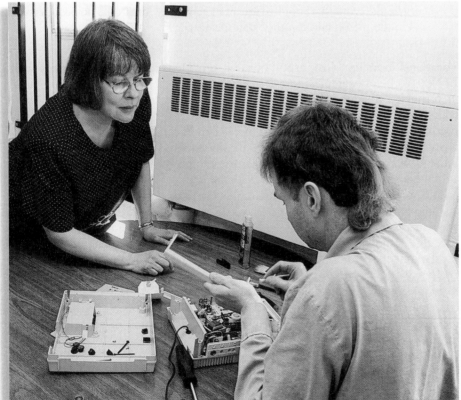

Prison vocational programs help train inmates in job skills that may be applied in the work environment upon their release. Here, a prisoner cleans and repairs cassette recorders that are used by vision-impaired people as part of a talking-book program.

AP/Wide World Photos

several states, statewide school districts serving prisons have been created. Forming such districts can make better-qualified staff available and provide the materials and resources necessary for meaningful educational programs.

All state correctional systems also have some job-related services for inmates. Some offer elaborate training programs within the institution; others have instituted prerelease and postrelease employment services. Inmates who hope to obtain parole need to participate in prison industry. Documenting a history of stable employment in prison is essential if parole agents are to convince prospective employers that the ex-offender is a good risk; postrelease employment is usually required for parole eligibility.[56]

A few of the more important work-related services are discussed in the following sections.

Fill in the blanks 11

Basic Prison Industries Prisoners are normally expected to work within the institution as part of their treatment program. Aside from saving money for the institution, prison work programs are supposed to help inmates develop good habits and skills. Most prominent among traditional prison industries are those designed to help maintain and run the institution and provide services for other public or state facilities, such as mental hospitals. These prison industries include the following:

- *Food services.* Inmates are expected to prepare and supply food for prisoners and staff. Duties include baking bread, preparing meat and vegetables, and cleaning and maintaining kitchen facilities.
- *Maintenance.* The buildings and grounds of most prisons are cared for by the inmates. Electrical work, masonry, plumbing, and painting are all inmate activities. Of a less skilled nature are such duties as garbage collection, gardening, and cleaning.
- *Laundry.* Most prisons have their own inmate-run laundries. Quite often, prison laundries will also furnish services to other state institutions.
- *Agriculture.* In western and southern states, many prisons farm their own land. Dairy herds, crops, and poultry are all managed by inmates. The products are used in the prison and in other state institutions.

The State of Iowa has a program that uses manufacturing processes to teach inmates job skills and work attitudes in an effort to reduce recidivism. They produce high-quality goods that can be purchased online. For example, the shop at Fort Madison offers a complete line of wood office products, desks, bookcases, dormitory furniture, textiles, clothing, mattresses, pillows, towels, linen, furniture restoration, state surplus sales, inbound telemarketing, and help desk. Visit their Web site at http://www.iaprisonind.com/ For an up-to-date list of Web links, see http://www.wadsworth.com/product/0534573053s

Vocational Training Most institutions also provide vocational training programs. In New York, for example, more than 42 trade and technical courses are provided in organized training shops under qualified civilian instructors. Some of these courses not only benefit the inmate but also provide services for the institution. For example, New York has trained inmates to become dental laboratory technicians; this program provides dentures for inmates and saves the state money. Another New York program trains inmates to become optical technicians and has the added benefit of providing eyeglasses for inmates. Other New York correctional training programs include barber training, computer programming, auto mechanics, auto body work, and radio and television repair. The products of most of these programs save the taxpayers money, while the programs provide the inmates with practical experience. Many other states offer this type of vocational programming.

Despite the promising aspects of such programs, they have also been seriously criticized: Inmates often have trouble finding skill-related, high-paying jobs on their release; equipment in prisons is often secondhand, obsolete, and hard to come by; some programs are thinly disguised excuses for prison upkeep and maintenance; and unions and other groups resent the intrusion of prison labor into their markets.

Essay 4

Work Release To supplement programs stressing rehabilitation via in-house job training or education, more than 44 states have attempted to implement **work re-**

lease (furlough) programs. These programs allow deserving inmates to leave the institution and hold regular jobs in the community.

Inmates enrolled in work release may live at the institution at night and work in the community during the day. However, security problems (for example, contraband may be brought in) and the usual remoteness of prisons often make this arrangement difficult. More typical is the extended work release, where prisoners are allowed to remain in the community for significant periods of time. To help inmates adjust, some states operate community-based prerelease centers where inmates live while working. Some inmates may work at their previous jobs; others seek new employment.

Like other programs, work release has its good and bad points. Inmates are sometimes reluctantly received in the community and find that certain areas of employment are closed to them. Citizens are often concerned about prisoners "stealing" jobs or working for lower than normal wages; consequently, such practices are prohibited by Federal Public Law 89-176, which controls the federal work release program.

On the other hand, inmates gain many benefits from work release, including the ability to maintain work-related skills, to maintain community ties, and to make an easier transition from prison to the outside world. For those who have learned a skill in the institution, work release offers an excellent opportunity to test out a new occupation. For others, the job may be a training situation in which new skills are acquired. A number of states have reported that few work release inmates abscond while in the community.

Helping Female Offenders Critics have charged that educational and vocational programs are especially deficient in female institutions, which typically have offered only remedial-level education or occasional junior college classes. Female inmates have not been provided with the tools needed to succeed on the outside because the limited vocational training stresses what was traditionally considered "women's work": cosmetology, secretarial work, and food services.

Today, all but three states have instituted some sort of vocational training programs for women; the other three provide supplemental services for their few female inmates. The traditional vocation of sewing remains the most common industrial program, but correctional authorities are beginning to teach data processing, and female inmates are involved in such other industries as farming, printing, telemarketing, and furniture repair. Clearly, greater efforts are needed to improve the quality of work experiences for female inmates (see Table 16.2).

Private Prison Enterprise Although opposition from organized labor ended the profitability of commercial prison industries, a number of interesting efforts have been made to vary the type and productivity of prison labor.[57] The federal government helped put private industry into prisons when it approved the Free Venture program in 1976. Seven states, including Connecticut, South Carolina, and Minnesota, were given grants to implement private industries within prison walls. This successful program led to the Percy Amendment (1979), federal legislation that allowed prison-made goods to be sold across state lines if the projects complied with strict rules, such as making sure unions were consulted and preventing manufacturers from undercutting the existing wage structure.[58] The new law authorized a number of Prison Industry Enhancement pilot projects. These were certified as meeting the Percy Amendment operating rules and were therefore free to ship goods out of state; by 1987, 15 projects had been certified.

Today, private prison industries use a number of models. One approach, the *state-use model,* makes the correctional system a supplier of goods and services for state-run institutions. For example, the California Prison Industry Authority (PIA)

Essay 4

work release (furlough)
A prison treatment program in which inmates leave the institution to work in the community, sometimes returning to prison or another supervised facility at night.

TABLE 16.2 PROGRAM ELEMENTS BELIEVED TO WORK FOR FEMALE INMATES

Program Element	Measures of Program Element
Program staff	Dedicated and caring staff Staff members are ex-addicts or ex-offenders Qualified staff Staff members are female and serve as role models
Specific/multiple needs are met	Comprehensive or multiple focus Addresses a rudimentary or major need Establishes a continuum of care
Program participation	Program participants like the program High inmate participation Participation is self-initiated Participants responsible for helping to run program
Peer influence	Positive influence by other program participants Peer pressure to be a good mom Support from other participants
Program is individualized and structured	Clear, measurable goals are established Individualized treatment plans and programming Intensity and duration of program Screening and assessment
Technology and resources	Equipment Space Money and resources
Acquisition of skills	Acquire "real" job skills (e.g., marketable, nontraditional) Teaches parenting skills Addresses thinking and reasoning Anger management Life skills
Program environment	"Homey" atmosphere and nice climate for visits Open communication and confidentiality Good rapport with other participants Participants are separated from the general population Small size of the program
Victimization issues	Addresses self-esteem Women are treated like human beings Addresses domestic violence Addresses empowerment and self-sufficiency
Administrative and staff interaction	Administrative support and communication Nonaggressive management style Supportive and an understanding security staff
Assistance from outside the facility	Outside private/public partnerships Interagency coordination Staff members from outside, not department of corrections

SOURCE: Barbara Koons et al., "Expert and Offender Perceptions of Program Elements Linked to Successful Outcomes for Incarcerated Women," *Crime and Delinquency* 43 (1997): 512–532, at p. 524.

provides work assignments for approximately 7,000 inmates and operates 70 service, manufacturing, and agricultural industries at 23 prisons. These industries produce a variety of goods and services, including flags, printing services, signs, binders, eyewear, gloves, office furniture, clothing, cell equipment, and much more. PIA products and services are available to government entities, including

Some employers have created programs for ex-offenders. Ronald Cook works at the Bellagio Hotel in Las Vegas. A former inmate in a Nevada Boot Camp, he took a job as a cook's assistant and has worked his way up the ladder. The opportunity has helped him turn his life around.

federal, state, and local governmental agencies. Court-ordered restitutions/fines are deducted from the wages earned by PIA inmates and are transferred to the Crime Victims' Restitution Fund. PIA inmates receive wages of $.30 to $.95 per hour, before deductions.[59] In another approach, the *free enterprise model,* private companies set up manufacturing units on prison grounds or purchase goods made by inmates in shops owned and operated by the corrections department. In the *corporate model,* a semi-independent business is created on prison grounds whose profits go to the state government and inmate laborers.[60]

Postrelease Programs   A final element of job-related programming involves helping inmates obtain jobs before they are released and keep them once they are on the outside. A number of correctional departments have set up employment services designed to ease the transition between institution and community. Employment program staff assess inmates' backgrounds to determine their abilities, interests, goals, and capabilities. They also help them create job plans essential to receiving early release (parole) and successfully reintegrating into the community. Some programs maintain community correctional placements in sheltered environments that help inmates bridge the gap between institutions and the outside world. Services include job placement, skill development, family counseling, and legal and medical assistance.

Conjugal Visits

Essay 5

Research studies generally agree that inmates who are able to maintain family ties have a better chance of succeeding on the outside after they have been released.[61] Correctional systems have developed programs that help inmates maintain their emotional stability by maintaining closer ties with their families and living in an environment that is more "normal" than that provided in the typical correctional facility. For example, some women's prisons now allow inmates who give birth in prison to keep the child in a nursery in the institution for up to a year, followed by liberal visitation rights. Others allow male and female inmates home visitation privileges if they show exemplary behavior in the institution. Some programs

conjugal visit
A prison program that allows inmates to receive visits from spouses for the purpose of maintaining normal interpersonal relationships.

provide direct support to families, such as by involving them in self-help groups, providing counseling, helping them obtain transportation to the prison, and finding them overnight lodging.

The **conjugal** (or family) **visit** enables prisoners to have completely private meetings with their spouse and family on a regular basis. The explicit purpose of the program is to grant inmates access to normal family and sexual outlets and thereby counteract the pains of imprisonment. Some institutions have even set up an on-grounds camping facility where inmates can stay overnight with their families.[62]

Those who favor family visitation argue that, if properly administered, it can provide a number of important benefits: reducing inmate frustration levels, strengthening family ties, and maintaining normal sexual patterns. However, problems associated with conjugal visitation include the following:

1. Such visits can serve only the minority of inmates who are married; there is a question of fairness.
2. Appropriate facilities are almost universally lacking.
3. Administrative problems abound: security, staff abuses of power, jealousy.
4. Administrative support is lacking.
5. Spouses may feel embarrassment at openly sexual visits.
6. Children may be born to parents who cannot support them.[63]

Essay 6

coed prison
A penal institution that houses both male and female inmates, who share work and recreational facilities.

Coed Prisons

Since 1973, **coed prisons** have proliferated throughout the United States.[64] Most are minimum-security institutions, but coed prisons are also found at the medium- and maximum-security levels, and some institutions operate with a mix of security levels. Officials report that male and female inmates commonly share food services, recreation, educational programs, and jobs.

The typical coed prison is a small, low-security institution, predominantly of one sex (either mostly male or mostly female), and populated by nonviolent, carefully screened offenders. In most instances, males and females live in physically separate housing—either in different buildings or in separate cottages—but they participate jointly in most institution activities, such as work, recreation, and vocational and educational programs.

The benefits of coed prisons include the ease and cost effectiveness of a joint operation, the more normal environment produced by heterosexual contact, the expansion of programs available to women because of joint participation, greater flexibility in staffing, alleviation of overcrowding at male institutions, and the ability to house some inmates closer to home. Coed prisons also have their drawbacks. The greatest problems listed by administrators are illicit relationships, supervisory and disciplinary problems, negative staff attitudes, developing similar and equal programs without joint participation, and security.

Inmate Self-Help

Recognizing that the probability of failure on the outside is high, inmates have attempted to organize self-help groups to provide the psychological support needed to prevent recidivism.[65] Membership in these programs is designed to improve inmates' self-esteem and help them cope with common problems, such as alcoholism, narcotics abuse, or depression.

Some groups are chapters of broad-based national organizations, such as Alcoholics Anonymous. Other groups are organized along racial and ethnic lines. For example, there are chapters of the Chicanos Organizados Pintos Aztlan, the Afro-American Coalition, and the Native American Brotherhood in prisons stretching from California to Massachusetts. These groups try to establish a sense of brotherhood so members will work together for individual betterment. They hold literacy, language, and religious classes and offer counseling, legal advice, and prerelease support. Ethnic groups seek ties with outside minority organizations, such as the National Association for the Advancement of Colored People (NAACP), Muslims, the Urban League, La Raza, and the American Indian Movement, as well as the religious and university communities.

A third type of self-help group helps inmates find the strength to make it on the outside. The best known is the Fortune Society, which claims more than 7,000 members. Staffed by ex-offenders, the Fortune Society provides counseling, education, and vocational training to parolees. It even helps supervise offenders in the community as an alternative to incarceration. It runs a substance abuse treatment unit that provides individual and group counseling to clients sent by the New York City Department of Probation, provides HIV prevention information, and works as an advocate group to improve prison conditions.[66]

Can Rehabilitation Work?

Fill in the blanks 12
Essay 7

Despite the variety and number of treatment programs in operation, questions remain about their effectiveness. In their oft-cited research, Robert Martinson and his associates (1975) found that a majority of treatment programs were failures.[67] Martinson found in a national study that, with few exceptions, rehabilitative efforts seemed to have no appreciable effect on recidivism; his research produced a "nothing works" view of correctional treatment.

Martinson's work was followed by efforts showing that some high-risk offenders were more likely to commit crimes after being placed in treatment programs than before the onset of rehabilitation efforts.[68] A slew of reviews have claimed that correctional treatment efforts aimed at youthful offenders provide little evidence that rehabilitation can occur within correctional settings. Evidence is scant that treatment efforts, even those that include vocational, educational, and mental health services, can consistently lower recidivism rates.[69]

The seeming failure of correctional treatment has helped promote a conservative view of corrections in which prisons are considered places of incapacitation and punishment, not treatment centers. Some ways in which this view has been implemented are described in the Analyzing Criminal Justice Issues feature. Current policies stress eliminating the nonserious offender from the correctional system while increasing the probability that serious, violent offenders will be incarcerated and serve longer sentences. This view supports the utility of mandatory and determinate sentences for serious offenders and the simultaneous use of intermediate sanctions, such as house arrest, restitution, and diversion, to limit the nonserious offender's involvement in the system.

Despite this pessimism, recent reviews show that it is much too early to give up on correctional treatment. A number of researchers have found that rehabilitation efforts can be successful under some circumstances and with some inmates. Exhibit 16.2 lists some of the factors that have been associated with successful correctional rehabilitation efforts.

EXHIBIT 16.2   WHAT WORKS IN CORRECTIONAL REHABILITATION?

Rehabilitation is effective in reducing the criminal behavior of at least some offenders. The evidence suggests that effective correctional treatment programs follow some basic principles. In order to effectively reduce recidivism, treatment programs need to:

- Be carefully designed to target the specific characteristics and problems of offenders that can be changed in treatment (dynamic characteristics) and those that are predictive of the individual's future criminal activities (criminogenic), such as antisocial attitudes and behavior, drug use, and anger responses
- Be implemented in a way that is appropriate for the participating offenders and uses therapeutic techniques that are known to work (e.g., designed by knowledgeable individuals, programming provided by appropriately educated and experienced staff, use of adequately evaluated programs) and require offenders to spend a reasonable length of time in the program considering the changes desired (deliver sufficient dosage)
- Give the most intensive programs to offenders who are at the highest risk of recidivism
- Use cognitive and behavioral treatment methods based on theoretical models such as behaviorism, social learning, or cognitive behavioral theories of change that emphasize positive reinforcement contingencies for prosocial behavioral and is individualized as much as possible.

SOURCES: Lawrence W. Sherman, Denise Gottfredson, Doris MacKenzie, John Eck, Peter Reuter, and Shawn Bushway, *Preventing Crime: What Works, What Doesn't, What's Promising: A Report to the United States Congress* (Washington, DC: National Institute of Justice); Doris Layton MacKenzie, "Evidence-Based Corrections: Identifying What Works," *Crime and Delinquency* 46 (2000): 457–471.

ANALYZING CRIMINAL JUSTICE ISSUES

The No-Frills Movement

There is little question that some treatment does work and that the quest for offender rehabilitation should not be abandoned. Yet some correctional administrators and politicians believe that prisons should be places of punishment only and that all inmate privileges and treatment programs should be curtailed. Inmates in some states have suffered reduced visiting hours, removal of televisions and exercise gear, and substitution of cold sandwiches for hot meals. One county in Maryland plans to reintroduce chain gangs; instead of being shackled to prevent flight, inmates will be forced to wear *stun belts.* After detonation, the belts give fleeing inmates an eight-second, 50,000-volt jolt of electricity, which renders them helpless for up to 10 minutes. Developed by Stun Tech Inc., more than 1,000 belts have been sold to law enforcement and correctional agencies. Amnesty International has asked Congress to ban the belts, in part because they can be used for torture. Amnesty charges that the belts are "cruel, inhuman, and degrading."

Advocates of the *no-frills* or *penal harm* movement claim to be responding to the public's desire to get tough on crime. They are tired of hearing that some prison inmates get free education, watch cable TV, or get special educa-

tional programs. Some of the efforts to restrict inmates' rights include the following:

- The Alabama Department of Corrections (DOC) introduced no-frills chain gangs in each of the state's three prisons in 1994. Inmates in the gangs do not have telephones or visitation privileges, and recreation is limited to basketball on the weekends. Chain gang members include primarily parole violators and repeat offenders, especially offenders who are former gang members. After six months of good behavior, chain gang members return to the general population and are given standard inmate privileges.
- Throughout the 1990s, the Arizona DOC, supplementing the legislature's ban on weightlifting equipment, reduced the amount of property and clothing inmates may keep in their cells, the number of items for sale in the store, the number and types of movies and television programs they may watch, and the frequency of telephone calls.
- Effective January 1, 1996, the Kansas DOC introduced a formal incentive program in which incoming inmates have to earn a range of privileges, including television, handicrafts, use of outside funds, canteen expenditures,

personal property, and visitation. Under a three-level system, new inmates who spend their first 120 days (Incentive Level I) without disciplinary reports and participate in educational programs or work assignments earn increased privileges (Incentive Level II). After another 120 days of similar behavior, additional privileges are made available (Incentive Level III). Inmates are reduced one level for misbehavior. Furloughs were the only privilege the DOC banned permanently for all inmates.

- Complementing the action of the state's governor, the commissioner of corrections in Wisconsin reduced the amount of personal property inmates may own, established limits on the amount of personal clothing and electronic equipment they may keep, and introduced monitoring of telephone calls.
- A number of sheriffs have eliminated privileges in their jails. Seven sheriffs in Florida have eliminated television and weightlifting; seven jails in Los Angeles County have also eliminated weightlifting equipment; the Niagara County, New York, sheriff has eliminated free coffee. The sheriff of Maricopa County (Phoenix) has eliminated "girlie" magazines, hot

Although the concept of correctional rehabilitation is facing serious challenges, many experts still believe strongly in the rehabilitative ideal. Some believe that rehabilitation has just not been given a realistic chance because of inadequate budgets and programs.[70] Even where programs exist, the level of participation in work, vocational, mental health, substance abuse, and parent counseling programs has been low for both male and female inmates.[71] Studies have shown that programs that teach interpersonal skills, offer individual counseling, and make use of behavioral modification techniques have produced positive results both in the community and within correctional institutions.[72] Other research has shown that although not all programs are successful for all inmates, many treatment programs are effective and that participants, especially younger clients, have a better chance of success on the outside than those who forgo treatment. If administered properly, cor-

lunches, most hot breakfasts, and coffee, and has reduced recreation time, television programming, visitation, and the number of items in the commissary.

- In 1995, the Federal Bureau of Prisons ordered—and federal legislation now requires—wardens to stop purchasing or repairing new televisions in individual cells.

In 1999, Rep. Bob Franks introduced into Congress a No Frills Prison Bill that would make a state eligible for truth-in-sentencing incentive grants only if it demonstrates that it

(1) provides living conditions and opportunities within its prisons that are not more luxurious than those that the average prisoner would have experienced if not incarcerated; (2) does not provide to any such prisoner specified benefits or privileges, including earned good time credits, less than 40 hours a week of work that either offsets or reduces the expenses of keeping the prisoner or provides resources toward restitution of victims, unmonitored phone calls (with exceptions), in-cell television viewing, possession of pornographic materials, instruction or training equipment for any martial art or bodybuilding or weightlifting equipment, or dress or hygiene other than as is uniform or standard in the prison; and (3) does not provide, for a prisoner serving a sentence for a

crime of violence which resulted in serious bodily injury to another, housing other than in separate cell blocks intended for violent prisoners, less than nine hours a day of physical labor (with exceptions), any release from the prison for any purpose unless under physical or mechanical restraint, any viewing of television, any inter-prison travel for competitive sports, more than one hour a day spent in sports or exercise, or possession of personal property exceeding 75 pounds in total weight or that cannot be stowed in a standard size U.S. military issue duffel bag.

Although this bill has not yet been enacted into law, many politicians embrace the no-frills prison idea to appeal to their vengeful, conservative constituents. Wardens and prison administrators are more wary of a policy that restricts inmate activities, increases boredom, and threatens their control over inmates. One approach is to limit privileges at first but return them as rewards for good behavior. Whether the no-frills approach is a political fad or a long-term correctional policy trend remains to be seen.

Critical Thinking Skills

Do you believe that inmates should be "harmed" by their prison experience in order to shock them into conformity? The penal harm movement is the an-

tithesis of the rehabilitation ideal. By "harming" inmates and taking away privileges, are correctional administrators giving up on the prison as a place of reform?

InfoTrac College Edition Research

The no-frills movement is not unique to the United States. To read about the Canadian counterpart, go to InfoTrac College Edition and read Brian Stewart, "Not a Country Club: Most Inmates Do Hard Time behind Twenty Rows of Razor Wire." *MacLean's,* April 9, 2001, p. 34.

SOURCES: H.R. 370, a bill to amend the Violent Crime Control and Law Enforcement Act of 1994 to prevent luxurious conditions in prisons (1999); Peter Finn, "No-Frills Prisons and Jails: A Movement in Flux," *Federal Probation* 60 (1996): 35–49; W. Wesley Johnson, Katherine Bennett, and Timothy Flanagan, "Getting Tough on Prisoners: Results from the National Corrections Executive Survey, 1995," *Crime and Delinquency* 43 (1997): 24–41; Peter Kilborn, "Revival of Chain Gangs Takes a Twist," *New York Times,* 11 March 1997, p. A18.

---

rectional treatment programs have success rates on the order of 20 to 35 percent.[73] Characteristics associated with the most successful programs include the following:

- Services are intensive, lasting only a few months.
- Programs are cognitive, aimed at helping inmates learn new skills to better cope with personality problems such as impulsivity.
- Program goals are reinforced in a firm, fair manner, making use of rewards rather than punishments.
- Therapists relate to clients in a sensitive and positive way. Therapists are trained and supervised in an appropriate manner.
- Clients are insulated from disruptive interpersonal networks and placed in environments where prosocial activities predominate.

CRIMINAL JUSTICE AND TECHNOLOGY

Technocorrections: Contemporary Correctional Technology

Contemporary technological forces are today converging with the forces of law and order. The correctional establishment—the managers of the jail, prison, probation, and parole systems—and their sponsors in elected office are seeking more cost-effective ways to increase public safety as the number of people under correctional supervision continues to grow. Taking advantage of all the potential offered by the new technologies to reduce the costs of supervising criminal offenders and minimize the risk they pose to society will define the field of *technocorrections*. A few recent advances, some of which have been deployed and others still in the development stage, are described here.

Currently Available Technology

The following high-tech devices are close to implementation or already in use in some correctional facilities.

Personal Health Status Monitor

It may be getting easier to monitor inmates who pose a suicide risk. Correc-tional authorities are now developing a personal health status monitor that, in its initial form, will use acoustics to track the heartbeat and respiration of a person in a cell. The monitor does not need to be attached to the person being monitored; the size of two packs of cigarettes, it can be placed on the ceiling or just outside a cell. This device is similar to ones that are installed inside the cribs of infants in hospitals.

More advanced health status monitors now being developed can monitor five or more vital signs at once, and based on the combination of findings, produce an assessment of an inmate's state of health. Although this more advanced version of the personal health status monitor may take another decade to develop, the current version can help save lives that would otherwise be lost to suicide.

All-in-One Drug Detection Spray

For the past several years, Mistral Security of Bethesda, Maryland, has marketed drug detection sprays for marijuana, methamphetamines, heroin, and cocaine. A specially made piece of paper is wiped on a surface; when sprayed with one of the aerosol sprays, it changes color within 15 seconds if as little as 4 to 20 micrograms of the target drug is present. A new detection device now being developed will use a single spray to test for all four drugs at once. The test paper will turn different colors depending on which drug or drugs the spray contacts.

Radar Vital Signs Monitor/Radar Flashlight

Researchers at Georgia Tech have developed a handheld radar flashlight that can detect the respiration of a human in a cell from behind a 20-centimeter hollow-core concrete wall or an 8-inch cinder block wall. It instantly gives the user a bar-graph readout that is viewed on the apparatus itself. Other miniature radar detectors give users heartbeat and respiration readings. The equipment is expected to be a useful tool in searches for people who are hiding; the only thing that successfully blocks its functioning is a wall made of metal or conductive material in the direction it is

Fill in the blanks 13

GUARDING THE INSTITUTION

Control of a prison is a complex task, as illustrated in the Criminal Justice and Technology feature. On the one hand, a tough, high-security environment may meet the goals of punishment and control but fail to reinforce positive behavior changes. On the other hand, too liberal an administrative stance can lower staff morale and place inmates in charge of the institution.

Prison Correctional Officers

For many years, prison correctional officers were viewed as ruthless people who enjoyed their position of power over inmates, fought rehabilitation efforts, were racist, and had a "lock psychosis" developed from years of counting, numbering, and checking on inmates. This view has changed in recent years. Correctional officers are now viewed as public servants who are seeking the security and financial rewards of a civil service position.[74] Most are in favor of rehabilitation efforts

pointed. These radar devices can also be used in telemedicine and for individuals to whom electrodes would be difficult to apply.

Future applications for this technology include advanced lie detectors and using the human heartbeat as a biometric for personnel identification.

Personal Alarm Location System

It is now possible for prison employees to carry a tiny transmitter linking them with a computer in a central control room. In an emergency, they can hit an alarm button that transmits to a computer, which automatically records whose distress button had been pushed. An architectural map of the facility instantly appears on-screen showing the exact location of the staff member.

Although sensors are placed only inside the prison, the Personal Alarm Location System (PALS) works up to 300 feet outside prison walls. It locates within a range of 4 meters inside the room where the duress button is pushed, and also locates signals in between floors. The system also has an option that tracks the movement of employees who have pressed their duress buttons. If an officer moves after hitting the duress button, the red dot that represents him or her on the computer screen will move as well. The PALS system is now being used in six correctional institutions in the United States and Canada and is scheduled to be adopted in more.

Future Technology

Not yet employed but in the planning stage are the following technological breakthroughs.

The Angel Chip

This microchip, containing vital and identifying information, would be implanted underneath the skin of the user. To avoid future legal entanglements, it is being developed by Sun Microsystems with the assistance of the American Civil Liberties Union.

The Noninvasive Body Cavity Scanner

Eliminating the necessity of a physical search, this machine uses Magnetic Resonance Imaging (MRI) technology to scan body cavities.

Noninvasive Drug Detection

A swab or patch is being developed that, when placed on the skin, absorbs perspiration and detects the presence of illegal drugs.

InfoTrac College Edition Research

To learn more about high-tech security in prisons, go to Info-Trac College Edition. Enter "Correctional Institutions" as a subject and go to the subsection "Safety and Security Measures."

SOURCES: Tony Fabelo, "Technocorrections," *Sentencing and Corrections: Issues for the 21st Century* (Washington, DC: National Institute of Justice, 2000); Irwin Soonachan, "The Future of Corrections: Technological Developments Are Turning Science Fiction into Science Fact," *Corrections Today* 62 (2000): 64–66.

and do not hold any particular animosity toward inmates, even as the general public has turned punitive.[75] The correctional officer has been characterized as a "people worker" who must be prepared to deal with the problems of inmates on a personal level and also a member of a complex bureaucracy who must be able to cope with its demands.

Corrections officers play a number of roles within the institution. They supervise cell houses, dining areas, shops, and other facilities, as well as perch up on the walls armed with rifles to oversee the yard and prevent escapes. Corrections officers also sit on disciplinary boards and escort inmates to hospitals and court appearances.

The greatest problem faced by prison correctional officers is the duality of their role: maintainers of order and security, and advocates of treatment and rehabilitation. Added to this basic dilemma is the changing inmate role. Where before corrections officers could count on inmate leaders to help them maintain order, they are now faced with a racially charged atmosphere in which violence is a way of life. Today, correctional work is filled with danger, tension, boredom, and little evidence that efforts to help inmates lead to success.

A correctional worker's life can be stressful. Working in dangerous, overcrowded institutions can take a toll. Halfway into his 10-hour shift, prison guard Sgt. Jeffrey Clark takes a moment to rest his eyes. The Texas prison system is facing a shortage of about 2,292 guards, raising safety risks for guards and inmates.

AP/Wide World Photos

Multiple choice 14–15

Unlike police officers, correctional workers apparently do not form a close-knit subculture with unique values and a sense of group loyalty. Correctional officers experience alienation and isolation from the inmates, the administration, and each other. Interestingly, this sense of alienation seems greatest in younger officers; evidence suggests that later in their careers, officers enjoy a revival of interest in their work and take great pride in providing human services to inmates.[76]

Not surprisingly, correctional officers perceive significant levels of stress related to such job factors as lack of safety, inadequate career opportunities, and work overload.[77] These and other difficulties faced by correctional officers have been captured in a new book called *Newjack* (slang for a rookie officer), discussed in the Analyzing Criminal Justice Issues feature. Many state prison authorities have developed training programs to prepare correctional officers for the difficulties of prison work, and officers have formed unions to negotiate wages and working conditions with corrections departments.

The issue of female correctional officers in male institutions comes up repeatedly. Today, it is common for women to be assigned to all-male institutions.[78] The employment of women as correctional officers in close contact with male inmates has spurred many questions of privacy and safety, and a number of legal cases. In one important case, *Dothard v. Rawlinson* (1977), the Supreme Court upheld Alabama's refusal to hire female correctional officers on the grounds that it would put them in significant danger from the male inmates.[79]

Despite such setbacks, women now work side by side with male correctional officers in almost every state, performing the same duties. Research indicates that discipline has not suffered because of the inclusion of women in the correctional officer force. Sexual assaults have been rare, and more negative attitudes have been expressed by the female correctional officers' male peers than by inmates. Most commentators believe that the presence of female correctional officers can have an important beneficial effect on the self-image of inmates and improve the correctional officer–inmate working relationship. However, female correctional officers experience role conflict from trying to cope with being a woman in a traditionally male occupation in a primarily male institution.[80] Some manage by adopting the role of "counselor" within their jobs.

ANALYZING CRIMINAL JUSTICE ISSUES

Newjack

Ted Conover, a well-known author (*Whiteout, Coyotes*), wanted to understand what it meant to be a correctional officer in a maximum-security prison. He soon found out that there is no way a civilian (especially a writer) would be allowed to enter a prison and be given needed access to inmates and correctional personnel. So, to get the data he needed, he applied to become a correctional officer, was given a position, and underwent seven weeks of preparation at the Correctional Officer Training Academy in Albany, New York. After graduation he was ready, so he thought, to become a *Newjack*—a rookie correctional officer. He was assigned as a gallery officer, who oversees a prison pod, in Sing Sing prison. This infamous 170-year-old institution, one of the first built in the United States, is the kind of maximum-security institution where men instantly size each other up to see who can be dominated and who will dominate.

On his first day on the job, Conover is asked to stand before a camera, holding a piece of paper showing his name and Social Security number. When he asks why, he is told that the pictures are "hostage shots," kept on file in case a correctional officer is injured or taken hostage, at which time the photographs are released to the press. He at first laughs but then realizes that "hostage shots" aren't all that funny—that correctional officers can be injured or killed at any moment. It comes as no surprise that while some of his colleagues are hardworking and sincere, others are brutal and vicious.

Conover soon learns that correctional officers can't show a trace of fear because it attracts abuse from inmates and the loss of respect of fellow officers. Inmates will grant respect if the correctional officer is firm but willing to make an exception to the rules once in a while. Too many exceptions, and the respect vanishes as the residents start taking advantage.

He can feel the aggression, frustration at the procedures, and perpetually tense interaction between inmates and correctional personnel that permeate the institution. Officers brag that at some institutions unruly inmates are savagely beaten and they wouldn't mind doing the same at Sing Sing. Horrified at first, he soon realizes that he too has a violent side that he never knew existed and learns the tricks he can use to protect himself when his aggression emerges. He learns to yell "stop resisting" as he roughs up an inmate in order to avoid brutality charges; he is shown how logbooks can be fudged to conceal undeserved discipline. He considers some of his duties demeaning and ugly, especially body cavity searches. He is attacked and punched in the head by an inmate and forced to wrestle with powerful muscle-bound men. All this for about $23,000 per year.

Conover experiences what he considers to be the essence of correctional life: unending tedium interrupted by a sudden adrenaline rush when an "incident" occurs. He begins to understand why correctional officers develop the feeling that they are in confinement themselves. It is a consequence of dealing all day and night with men who can do almost nothing on their own and depend on their gallery officer to take care of their most personal needs. Instead of feeling tough and in control, at the end of the day the correctional officer feels like a "waiter" who has served a hundred tables or a mother with too many dependent children. Because of their dependence, the inmates are often made to feel like infants, and those who do not take it well may resort to violence to ease their frustrations. The potential for violence in the prison setting is so great that it makes even routine assignments seem dangerous. Conover is astonished that there are not even more violent incidents, considering that 1,800 rapists, murderers, and assaulters

are trapped together in a hellish environment.

Conover finds that some inmates are intelligent and sensitive. One named Lawson points out that the United States is now planning prisons that will be built in 12 years. By planning that far into the future, he tells Conover, the government is preparing to imprison people who are currently children. Instead of spending millions on future prisons, why not spend thousands on education and social services to ensure that child will not be just another statistic? Conover cannot think of an adequate answer.

Probably most disturbing is the effect the institution has on Conover's personal life. Though he gets to go home to his wife and children, he cannot leave his prison experiences at the "gate." Prison gets into your skin, he says; if you stayed long enough, "some of it seeped into your soul." His wife is troubled by the changes she sees in him and begs him to quit; he in turn has to beg her to let him finish out the year.

Critical Thinking Skills

If a man like Conover experiences such personal stress, knowing that he is a writer incognito on temporary assignment, what must the stress be like for professional officers who do not share the luxury of having another career waiting over the horizon?

InfoTrac College Edition Research

To read more about the life of correctional workers, use "correctional officer" as a key term in InfoTrac College Edition.

SOURCE: Ted Conover, *Newjack: Guarding Sing Sing* (New York: Random House, 2000).

Interestingly, little research has been conducted on male correctional officers in female prisons, although almost every institution housing female offenders employs male officers. What research there is indicates that male officers are generally well received. Although there is evidence of sexual exploitation and privacy violations, female inmates generally believe that the presence of male correctional officers helps create a more natural environment and reduce tension. Both male and female inmates are concerned about opposite-sex correctional workers' intruding on their privacy, such as observing inmates dressing or bathing or coming into physical contact, as during searches or pat-downs.

Prison Violence

Conflict, violence, and brutality are ever-present facts of institutional life. Violence can involve individual conflict: inmate versus inmate, inmate versus staff, staff versus inmate. One common threat is sexual assault. Research has shown that prison rapes usually involve a victim viewed as weak and submissive and a group of aggressive rapists who can dominate the victim through their collective strength. Sexual harassment leads to fights, social isolation, fear, anxiety, and crisis. Nonsexual assaults may stem from an aggressor's desire to shake down the victim for money and personal favors, may be motivated by racial conflict, or may simply be used to establish power within the institution.

Violence can also involve large groups of inmates, such as the famous Attica riot in 1971, which claimed 39 lives, or the New Mexico state prison riot of February 1980, in which the death toll was 33. More than 300 prison riots have occurred since the first one in 1774, 90 percent of them since 1952.[81]

A number of factors can spark such damaging incidents. They include poor staff–inmate communications, destructive environmental conditions, faulty classification, and promised but undelivered reforms. The 1980 New Mexico State Penitentiary riot drew national attention to the problem of prison riots. The prison was designed for 800 but actually held 1,136 prisoners; precipitating conditions included overcrowding, squalor, poor food, and lack of medical treatment. The state government, which had been called on to improve correctional officer training, upgrade the physical plant, and provide relief from overcrowding, was reluctant to spend the necessary money.

Essay 8

Individual Violence A number explanations have been offered for individual violence by prisoners.[82] One position holds that inmates are often violence-prone individuals who have always used force to get their own way. In the crowded, dehumanizing world of the prison, it is hardly surprising that some inmates resort to force to exert their dominance over others.

A second view is that prisons convert people to violence by their inhuman conditions, including overcrowding, depersonalization, and the threat of sexual assault. Even in the most humane prisons, life is a constant put-down, and prison conditions are a threat to the inmates' sense of self-worth. Violence is a predictable consequence of these conditions.

Violence may also result because prisons lack effective mechanisms for handling grievances against either prison officials or other inmates fairly and equitably. Prisoners who complain about other inmates are viewed as "rats" or "snitches" and are marked for death by their enemies. Similarly, complaints or lawsuits filed against the prison administration may result in the inmate's being placed in solitary confinement—"the hole." The frustration caused by living in a prison with a climate that promotes violence—that is, one that lacks physical security and adequate mechanisms for resolving complaints and where the "code of silence" protects violators—is believed to promote individual violence by inmates who might otherwise be controlled.

Collective Violence There are two distinct theories of collective disturbances. The first, called the *inmate-balance theory,* suggests that riots and other forms of collective action occur when prison officials make an abrupt effort to take control of the prison and limit freedoms. Crackdowns occur when officials perceive that inmate leaders have too much power and take measures to control their illicit privileges, such as gambling or stealing food.[83]

Essay 9

According to the *administrative-control theory,* collective prison violence may be caused by prison mismanagement, lack of strong security, and inadequate control by prison officials. Poor management may inhibit conflict management and set the stage for violence. Repressive administrations give inmates the feeling that nothing will ever change, that they have nothing to lose, and that violence is the only means of change.

Overcrowding caused by rapid increases in the prison population has also been linked to prison violence. As the prison population continues to climb, unmatched by expanded capacity, prison violence may increase.

Controlling Violence Can prison violence be controlled, despite the fact that the inmate population is not likely to decline significantly or to become less hostile and aggressive? In his book *Governing Prisons,* John DiIulio suggests that reform of prison management can help alter the violent institutional climate.[84]

Essay 10

After studying prisons in three states, DiIulio found that management could be classified into three types. The *consensual model,* practiced in California, is based on the notion that prison government rests on the consent of the governed, the inmates. This model fails to provide a coherent basis for dealing with violence because it allows inmates a say in the management process. Under the *responsibility model,* used in Michigan, rehabilitation is keyed to inmates' participation in prison operations, with staff members required to facilitate the process. The responsibility model has also failed, because it offers weak controls on inmate behavior and produces disillusionment and alienation among the staff.

In DiIulio's view, the *control model* used in the Texas prison system offers the greatest promise for reducing violence. The Texas system stresses clearly defined rules of behavior, inmate conformity with rules and regulations, and strong, independent, top-down leadership. DiIulio believes that the bureaucratic organization that works in large private corporations and government agencies can save prisons. In this approach, prison administrators act in a caring yet efficient manner without prejudice and bias, and experienced correctional leaders create and enforce clear and fair rules.

PERSPECTIVES ON JUSTICE

Rehabilitation advocates scoff at the notion that a get-tough, "firm, but fair" approach can cure the ills of the nation's prison system. The Texas prison system that DiIulio so admires was the scene of such overcrowding and brutality that it was subjected to court-ordered reform. Even then, prison officials were reluctant to change and attempted to undermine reform efforts. The control model may seem appealing to some experts, but it remains to be seen whether it can work in the real world.

Prisoners' Rights

Before the early 1960s, it was accepted that on conviction, an individual forfeited all rights not expressly granted by statutory law or correctional policy; inmates

Multiple choice 16
Essay 11

were "civilly dead." The Supreme Court held that convicted offenders should expect to be penalized for their misdeeds and that part of their punishment was the loss of freedoms that free citizens take for granted.

One reason that inmates lacked rights was that state and federal courts were reluctant to intervene in the administration of prisons unless the circumstances of a case clearly indicated a serious breach of the Eighth Amendment's protection against cruel and unusual punishment. This judicial policy is referred to as the **hands-off doctrine**. The courts used three basic justifications for their neglect of prison conditions:

hands-off doctrine
The judicial policy of not interfering in the administrative affairs of prisons.

1. Correctional administration was a technical matter best left to experts rather than to courts ill equipped to make appropriate evaluations.
2. Society as a whole was apathetic to what went on in prisons, and most individuals preferred not to associate with or know about offenders.
3. Prisoners' complaints involved privileges rather than rights. Prisoners were considered to have fewer constitutional rights than other members of society.[85]

As the 1960s drew to a close, the hands-off doctrine was eroded. Federal district courts began seriously considering prisoners' claims concerning conditions in the various state and federal institutions and used their power to intervene on behalf of the inmates. In some ways, this concern reflected the spirit of the times, which saw the onset of the civil rights movement, and subsequently was paralleled in such areas as student rights, public welfare, mental institutions, juvenile court systems, and military justice.

Beginning in the late 1960s, such activist groups as the NAACP Legal Defense Fund and the American Civil Liberties Union's National Prison Project began to search for appropriate legal vehicles to bring prisoners' complaints before state and federal courts. The most widely used device was the federal Civil Rights Act, 42 U.S.C. 1983:

> Every person who, under color of any statute, ordinance, regulation, custom, or usage of any State or Territory subjects, or causes to be subjected, any citizen of the United States or other person within the jurisdiction thereof to the deprivation of any rights, privileges, or immunities secured by the Constitution and laws shall be liable to the party injured in an action at law, suit in equity, or other proper proceeding for redress.

The legal argument went that as U.S. citizens, prison inmates could sue state officials if their civil rights were violated—for example, if they were the victims of racial or religious discrimination.

The Supreme Court first recognized the right of prisoners to sue for civil rights violations in cases involving religious freedom brought by the Black Muslims. This well-organized group had been frustrated by prison administrators who feared its growing power and desired to place limits on its recruitment activities. In the 1964 case of *Cooper v. Pate,* the Supreme Court ruled that inmates who were being denied the right to practice their religion were entitled to legal redress under 42 U.S.C. 1983.[86] Although *Cooper* applied to the narrow issue of religious freedom, it opened the door to providing other rights for inmates.

The subsequent prisoners' rights crusade, stretching from 1960 to 1980, paralleled the civil rights and women's movements. Battle lines were drawn between prison officials hoping to maintain their power and resenting interference by the courts and inmate groups and their sympathizers, who used state and federal courts as a forum for demanding better living conditions and personal rights. Each decision handed down by the courts was viewed as a victory for one side or the other; this battle continues today.

substantive right
A specific right, such as the right to medical care or freedom of religion.

Through a slow process of legal review, the courts have granted inmates a number of **substantive rights** that have significantly influenced the entire correctional system. The most important of these rights are discussed in the following sections.

Access to Courts, Legal Services, and Materials Without the ability to seek judicial review of conditions causing discomfort or violating constitutional rights, the inmate must depend solely on the slow and often insensitive administrative mechanism of relief within the prison system. Therefore, the right of easy access to the courts gives inmates hope that their rights will be protected during incarceration. Courts have held that inmates are entitled to have legal materials available and to be provided with assistance in drawing up and filing complaints. Inmates who help others, so-called **jailhouse lawyers**, cannot be interfered with or harassed by prison administrators. Federal courts have expanded this right to include virtually all inmates with various legal problems, as the following cases show:

1. *DeMallory v. Cullen* (1988). An untrained inmate paralegal is not a constitutionally acceptable alternative to law library access.[87]
2. *Lindquist v. Idaho State Board of Corrections* (1985). Seven inmate law clerks for a prison population of 950 were sufficient legal representation since they had a great deal of experience.[88]
3. *Smith v. Wade* (1983). An inmate who has been raped can have access to the state court to sue a correctional officer for failing to protect the inmate from aggressive inmates.[89]
4. *Bounds v. Smith* (1977). State correctional systems are obligated to provide inmates with either adequate law libraries or the help of people trained in the law.[90]

Freedom of the Press and of Expression Correctional administrators have traditionally placed severe limitations on prisoners' speech and expression. For example, they have read and censored inmate mail and restricted their reading material. With the lifting of the hands-off doctrine, courts have consistently ruled that only when a compelling state interest exists can prisoners' First Amendment rights be modified; correctional authorities must justify the limiting of free speech by showing that granting it would threaten institutional security. The following list of cases related to prisoners' freedom of speech rights indicates current policy on the subject:

1. *Turner v. Safley* (1987). Prisoners do not have a right to receive mail from one another. Inmate-to-inmate mail can be banned if the reason is "related to legitimate penological interests."[91]
2. *Ramos v. Lamm* (1980). The institutional policy of refusing to deliver mail in a language other than English is unconstitutional.[92]
3. *Procunier v. Martinez* (1974). Censorship of a prisoner's mail is justified only when (a) there exists substantial government interest in maintaining the censorship to further prison security, order, and rehabilitation, and (b) the restrictions are not greater or more stringent than is demanded by security precautions.[93]
4. *Nolan v. Fitzpatrick* (1971). Prisoners may correspond with newspapers unless their letters discuss escape plans or contain contraband or otherwise objectionable material.[94]

Freedom of Religion Freedom of religion is a fundamental right guaranteed by the First Amendment. In general, the courts have ruled that inmates have the right to assemble and pray in the religion of their choice but that religious symbols and practices that interfere with institutional security can be restricted. Administrators can draw the line if religious needs become cumbersome or impossible to carry out for reasons of cost or security. Granting special privileges can also be denied on the grounds that they will cause other groups to make similar demands.

Some of the issues surrounding religious practices in prison are highlighted in the following cases:

Multiple choice 17–20

jailhouse lawyer
An inmate trained in law or otherwise educated who helps other inmates prepare legal briefs and appeals.

Multiple choice 21–24

Multiple choice 25–27

1. *Mumin v. Phelps* (1988). If there is a legitimate penological interest, inmates can be denied special privileges to attend religious services.[95]
2. *O'Lone v. Estate of Shabazz* (1987). Prison officials can assign inmates work schedules that make it impossible for them to attend religious services as long as no reasonable alternative exists.[96]
3. *Rahman v. Stephenson* (1986). A prisoner's rights are not violated if the administration refuses to use the prisoner's religious name on official records.[97]

Multiple choice 28–29

class action
A suit brought on behalf of all individuals affected by similar circumstances.

Medical Rights In early prisons, inmates' right to medical treatment was restricted through the *exceptional circumstances doctrine.* Using this policy, the courts would hear only those cases in which the circumstances totally disregarded human dignity, while denying hearings to less serious cases. The cases that were allowed access to the courts usually involved a total denial of medical care.

To gain their medical rights, prisoners have resorted to **class actions**—suits brought on behalf of all individuals affected by similar circumstances, such as poor medical attention. In the most significant case, *Newman v. Alabama* (1974), the entire Alabama prison system's medical facilities were declared inadequate.[98] The federal court cited the following factors as contributing to inadequate care: insufficient physician and nurse resources; reliance on untrained inmates for paramedical work; intentional failure in treating the sick and injured; and failure to conform to proper medical standards. The *Newman* case forced corrections departments to upgrade prison medical facilities.

It was not until 1976, in *Estelle v. Gamble,* that the Supreme Court clearly mandated an inmate's right to medical care.[99] Gamble had hurt his back in a Texas prison and filed suit because he contested the type of treatment he had received and questioned the lack of interest prison correctional officers had shown in his case. The Supreme Court said, "Deliberate indifference to serious medical needs of prisoners constitutes the 'unnecessary and wanton infliction of pain,' proscribed by the Eighth Amendment."[100] Gamble was allowed to collect monetary damages for his injuries. The *Gamble* decision means that lower courts can decide, on a case-by-case basis, whether "deliberate indifference" to an inmate's medical needs occurred and to what damages the inmate is entitled.

The issue of medical rights of prisoners appears to be reemerging as correctional departments have sought relief from spiraling medical costs. Some prison systems are now contracting with health maintenance organizations (HMOs) or managed care organizations (MCOs) to provide medical services for inmates.[101] The MCOs hire physicians and other health care providers and supervise their provision of health care in prisons much as they do in the general population. To date, 14 private sector firms are providing inmate health care, and approximately 29 states have managed care in all or part of their prison health care systems.

The goals of this medical outsourcing are typically efficiency and cost cutting. To contain costs, contracts may have a fee-per-offender provision that limits the amount the health care provider must spend on each inmate. Some critics, such as Ira Robbins, have charged that this approach often results in treatment decisions that are based less on the inmates' needs and more on saving money.[102]

Essay 12

Cruel and Unusual Punishment The concept of cruel and unusual punishment is founded in the Eighth Amendment of the U.S. Constitution. The term itself has not been specifically defined by the Supreme Court, but the Court has held that treatment constitutes cruel and unusual punishment when it

- Degrades the dignity of human beings[103]
- Is more severe (disproportional) than the offense for which it has been given[104]
- Shocks the general conscience and is fundamentally unfair[105]

- Is deliberately indifferent to a person's safety and well-being[106]
- Punishes people because of their status, such as race, religion, or mental state[107]
- Is in flagrant disregard of due process of law, such as punishment that is capriciously applied[108]

State and federal courts have placed strict limits on disciplinary methods that may be considered inhumane. Corporal punishment all but ended after the practice was condemned in *Jackson v. Bishop* (1968).[109] Although the solitary confinement of disruptive inmates continues, its prolonged use under barbaric conditions has been held to be in violation of the Eighth Amendment. Courts have found that inmates placed in solitary have the right to adequate personal hygiene, exercise, mattresses, ventilation, and rules specifying how they can earn their release.

Overall Prison Conditions Prisoners have long had a right to the minimal conditions necessary for human survival, such as the food, clothing, shelter, and medical care necessary to sustain human life. A number of attempts have been made to articulate reasonable standards of prison care and make sure they are carried out. Courts have held that although people are sent to prison for punishment, it does not mean that prison should be a punishing experience.[110] Inmates are entitled to reasonable care, protection, and shelter. In the 1994 case of *Farmer v. Brennan,* the Court ruled that prison officials are legally liable if, knowing that an inmate faces a serious risk of harm, they disregard that risk by failing to take measures to avoid or reduce it. Furthermore, officials should be able to infer the risk from the evidence at hand; they need not be warned or told.[111]

Although inmates retain the right to reasonable care, if there is a legitimate purpose for government restrictions, they may be considered constitutional. For example, prison officials may be permitted to restrict reading material, conduct strip searches, and prohibit inmates from receiving packages from the outside if the restrictions are legitimate security measures. Similarly, if overcrowded conditions require it, inmates may be double-bunked in cells designed for a single inmate.[112]

Courts have also reviewed entire correctional systems to determine whether practices are unfair to inmates. In a critical case, *Estelle v. Ruiz,* the Texas Department of Corrections was ordered to provide new facilities to alleviate overcrowding; to abolish the practice of using inmate trustees; to lower the inmate-to-staff ratio; to improve treatment services, such as medical, mental health, and occupational rehabilitation programs; and to adhere to the principles of procedural due process in dealing with inmates.[113] A court-ordered master was appointed to oversee the changes and served from 1981 to 1990, when the state was deemed in compliance with the most critical of the court-ordered reforms.[114] A period of tension and violence followed this decision, in part perhaps because the staff and administration felt that the court had undermined their authority. It took more than 18 years for the case to be settled.

Because of the large numbers of lawsuits filed by inmates, the federal government has moved to limit inmate access to the courts. The Prison Litigation Reform Act (PLRA) of 1996 limited the number of prison cases in federal court by providing that "no action shall be brought with respect to prison conditions" by an inmate in either state or federal prison "until such administrative remedies as are available are exhausted."[115] The PLRA includes a new form of "three strikes and you're out": If a prisoner has filed three suits that are dismissed because they fail to state a claim for relief (or are frivolous), he or she is barred from filing future actions unless in imminent danger of serious physical harm. Although such measures are designed to limit litigation, it is likely that the overcrowding crisis will prompt additional litigation requesting overall prison relief.

Fill in the blanks 14
True/False 17
Multiple choice 30

LEAVING PRISON

True/False 18–19

At the expiration of their prison term, most inmates return to society and try to resume their life there. In a few instances, inmates are released after their sentence has been commuted by a board of pardons or directly by a governor or even the president of the United States. About 15 percent of prison inmates are released after serving their entire maximum sentence without any time excused or forgiven. And despite the efforts of correctional authorities, about 7,000 inmates escape every year from state and federal prisons (the number of escapes is actually declining, due in part to better officer training and more sophisticated security measures).[116]

For many inmates, however, their reintegration into society comes by way of parole—the planned community release and supervision of incarcerated offenders before the expiration of their full prison sentences. In states where determinate sentencing statutes have eliminated discretionary parole, offenders are released after having served their determinate sentence, less time off for good behavior and other credits designed to reduce the term of incarceration. Their release may involve supervision in the community, and rule violations can result in return to prison for the balance of their unexpired sentence. The U.S. parole population today is more than 700,000, having increased more than 150,000 in the past decade.[117]

Regardless of the method of their release, former inmates face the formidable task of having to readjust to society. This means regaining legal rights they may have lost upon conviction, reestablishing community and family ties, and finding employment. After being in prison, these goals are often difficult to achieve.

The Parole Process

Most correctional administrations allow inmates to become eligible for parole after completing their minimum sentence less good time. Parole is considered a way of completing a prison sentence in the community under the supervision of the correctional authorities. It is not the same as a pardon; paroled offenders can be legally recalled to serve the remainder of their sentence in an institution if the parole authorities deem the offenders' adjustment inadequate because they fail to obey the conditions of their release or commit another crime while on parole.

The decision to parole is determined by statutory requirement and usually occurs on completion of a minimum sentence less any good time or special release credits. In about 40 percent of all prison-release decisions, parole is granted by a **parole board**, a duly constituted body of men and women who review inmate cases and determine whether offenders have reached a rehabilitative level sufficient to deal with the outside world. The board also dictates what specific parole rules parolees must obey.

Once released into the community, the offender is supervised by a trained staff of parole officers who help the offender search for employment and monitor the parolee's behavior and activities to ensure that the conditions of parole are met.

Parolees are subject to strict rules, standardized and personalized, that guide their behavior and set limits on their activities. If these rules are violated, they can be returned to the institution to serve the remainder of their sentence; this is known as a **technical parole violation**. Parole can also be revoked if the offender commits another offense while in the community. The offender may even be tried and sentenced for this subsequent crime.

In recent years, the parole system has come under increasing criticism from those who believe that it is inherently unfair to inmates and fails to protect the public. It is unfair to the inmate because the decision to release is based on the discretion of parole board members who are forced to make predictions about

parole board
Group that reviews inmate cases, determines whether offenders are ready for supervised release, and dictates the specific rules that parolees must obey.

technical parole violation
Revocation of parole because conditions set by correctional authorities have been violated.

the inmate's future behavior, an uncertain activity at best. It fails to protect the public because predatory criminals released before the expiration of their sentence are free to attack innocent victims once again. The movement toward determinate and mandatory sentences has limited the availability of parole and restricted the discretion of parole boards.

PERSPECTIVES ON JUSTICE

Parole is generally viewed as a privilege granted to deserving inmates on the basis of their good behavior while in prison; it is a cornerstone of the noninterventionist philosophy, in that it supports removal of as many people from the system as possible. Parole has two conflicting sides, however. On the one hand, according to a rehabilitation view, the paroled offender is someone who has been reformed and should be allowed to serve part of the sentence in the community. On the other hand, crime control advocates warn that parole is a "privilege and not a right," and the parolee is viewed as a dangerous criminal who must be carefully watched and supervised. The conflict between the treatment and enforcement aspects of parole has not been reconciled by the criminal justice system, and the parole process still contains elements of both.

Mandatory Parole Release   In addition to the inmates released at the discretion of correctional authorities, a significant number are released via mandatory parole. These are inmates whose discharge is required by determinate sentencing statutes or good-time reductions but whose release is supervised by parole authorities. Mandatory release begins when the unserved portion of the maximum prison term equals the inmate's earned good time (plus time served in jail awaiting trial). In some states, determinate sentences can be reduced by more than half through a combination of statutory and earned good time. If the conditions of their release are violated, mandatory releasees can have their good time revoked and be returned to the institution to serve the remainder of their unexpired term.

True/False 20

The remaining inmates are released for a variety of reasons, including expiration of their term, commutation of their sentence, and court orders to relieve overcrowded prisons.

The movement to create mandatory and determinate sentencing statutes has significantly affected parole. The number of people leaving prison via discretionary parole has declined substantially in the past few years. At one time, more than 70 percent of releasees were released by a parole board; that number has declined to 40 percent. In contrast, mandatory releases from prison as a result of a sentencing statute or good-time provision comprised more than 50 percent of those entering parole in 1998, compared with 41 percent in 1990.[118] Almost all the mandatory parole releasees are in jurisdictions that rely heavily on determinate sentences, such as Washington and Minnesota. As the new truth-in-sentencing laws take effect, the number of parolees should decline. People who are spending more of their time in prison will have less time left to spend on parole.

The Parole Board   In those states that have maintained discretionary parole, the authority to release inmates is usually vested in the parole board. State parole boards have four primary functions:

Essay 13

1. To select and place prisoners on parole
2. To aid, supervise, and provide continuing control of parolees in the community

Parole-board members bring their life experiences to the job, which helps shape their decision making. Nancy Conn McCreary, who was beaten, stabbed, and left for dead 29 years ago, is the newest member of the Alabama state parole board, a board she campaigned against when it decided to release the man who attacked her and killed her cousin. McCreary admitted it took years of praying and helping other crime victims before she could forgive her attacker and get to the point where she could even think about letting a criminal walk out a prison door before the end of his or her sentence.

AP/Wide World Photos

3. To determine when the parole function is completed and to discharge from parole
4. If violations of conditions occur, to determine whether parole should be revoked

Most parole authorities are independent agencies with their own staff and administration; a few are part of the state department of corrections. Arguments for keeping the board within a corrections department usually include improved communication and the availability of more intimate knowledge about offenders. Most boards are relatively small, usually numbering fewer than 10 members. Their small size, coupled with their large caseloads and the varied activities they are expected to perform, can prevent board members from becoming as well acquainted with the individual inmates as might be desired.

True/False 21

Parole Hearings The actual (discretionary) parole decision is made at a parole grant hearing. At this hearing, the full board or a selected subcommittee reviews information, may meet with the offender, and then decides whether the parole applicant has a reasonable probability of succeeding outside prison. Each parole board has its own way of reviewing cases. In some, the full board meets with the applicant; in others, only a few members do that. In a number of jurisdictions, a single board member can conduct a personal investigation and submit the findings to the full board for a decision.

At the hearing, parole board members consider such information as police reports of the crime, the presentence investigation, psychological testing and scores developed by prison mental health professionals, and institutional reports of disciplinary actions, treatment, and adjustment.[119] Letters may be solicited from the inmate's friends and family members. In some jurisdictions, victims may appear and make statements of the losses they have suffered. By speaking directly to the applicant, the board can also promote and emphasize the specific types of behavior and behavior changes it expects to see if the inmate is to eventually qualify for or successfully serve parole.

The inmate's specific rights at a parole grant hearing also vary from jurisdiction to jurisdiction. In about half the parole-granting jurisdictions, inmates are permitted counsel or are allowed to present witnesses on their behalf; other jurisdictions do not permit these privileges. Because the federal courts have declared that the parole applicant is not entitled to any form of legal representation, the inmate may have to pay for legal services where this privilege is allowed. In almost all discretionary parole-granting jurisdictions, the reasons for the parole decision must be given in writing; in about half the jurisdictions, a verbatim record of the hearing is made.

In a recent case, *Pennsylvania Board of Probation and Parole v. Scott,* the U.S. Supreme Court held that the exclusionary rule for illegally obtained evidence did not apply to parole revocation proceedings. The Court reasoned that the social costs of excluding incriminating evidence outweigh any benefits of protecting the parolee from invasion of privacy. *Scott* thus allows evidence to be used in a parole revocation hearing that would be excluded from a criminal prosecution.[120]

Parole Rules Before release into the community, a parolee is given a standard set of rules and conditions that must be obeyed and conformed to. As with probation, the offender who violates these rules may have parole revoked and be sent back to the institution to serve the remainder of the sentence.

Parole rules may curtail or prohibit certain types of behavior while encouraging or demanding others. Some rules tend to be so moralistic or technical that they severely inhibit the parolee's ability to adjust to society. By making life unnecessarily unpleasant without contributing to rehabilitation, such parole rules reflect the punitive side of community supervision. Rules may prohibit marriage, ban the use of motor vehicles, or forbid the borrowing of money. Often, parolees must check in and ask permission to leave their residences. They may also be barred from associating with friends with criminal records, which, in some cases, severely limits their social life.

The way in which parole rules are stated, the kinds of activities they forbid or encourage, and their flexibility vary between jurisdictions. Some states may expressly forbid a certain type of behavior; others may require permission to engage in it.

Each item in the parole conditions must be obeyed lest the offender's parole be revoked for a technical violation. In addition, the parole board can impose specific conditions for a particular offender, such as requiring that the parolee receive psychiatric treatment.

Parole Supervision Once released into the community, the offender normally comes under the control of a parole officer who enforces parole rules, helps the parolee gain employment, and meets regularly with the parolee for purposes of treatment and rehabilitation.

Parole supervision is quite similar to probation in some respects. Both types of supervision attempt to help clients attain meaningful relationships in the community, using similar enforcement, counseling, and treatment skills. However, some major differences exist.

Parole officers deal with more difficult cases. The parolee has been institutionalized for an extended period of time and must now adjust to the community, which at first can seem a strange and often hostile environment. The person's family life has been disrupted, and the parolee may find it difficult to resume employment. A presentence report may already have classified this person as dangerous or as a poor risk for community adjustment, and a prison sentence probably does little to improve the offender's chances for rehabilitation.

Fill in the blanks 15

To overcome these roadblocks to success, the parole officer may have to play a much greater role than the probation officer in directing and supervising clients' lives. As a result, a significant number of parolees are sent back to prison for technical rule violations.

Intensive Supervision Parole   Some jurisdictions are implementing systems that classify offenders on the basis of their supervision needs. Typically, a point or guideline system (sometimes called a *salient factor score*), based on prior record and prison adjustment, divides parolees into three groups: (1) those who require intensive surveillance, (2) those who require social service rather than surveillance, and (3) those who require only limited supervision.

In some jurisdictions, parolees in need of closer surveillance are placed on **intensive supervision parole (ISP)**. These programs use limited caseload sizes, treatment facilities, the matching of parolee and supervisor by personality, and shock parole (which involves immediate short-term incarcerations for parole violators to impress them with the seriousness of a violation).

Intensive supervision parole clients are supervised in smaller caseloads and are required to attend more office and home visits than routine parolees. ISP may also require frequent drug testing, a term in a community correctional center, and electronic monitoring in the home. More than 17,000 parolees are under intensive supervision; 1,400 of them are monitored electronically by computer.

Although ISP seems like an ideal way of limiting already overcrowded prison populations, there is little evidence that ISP programs are effective; in fact, they may produce a higher violation rate than traditional parole supervision. Limiting caseload size allows parole officers to supervise their clients more closely and spot infractions more easily.[121]

intensive supervision parole (ISP)
A form of parole characterized by smaller caseloads and closer surveillance; may include frequent drug testing or, in some cases, electronic monitoring.

Essay 14

The Effectiveness of Parole

Parole recidivism rates are very high—approaching 50 percent or more—and the social cost is enormous. One federal survey of 156,000 parole violators serving time in the nation's prison system estimated that these offenders had committed at least 6,800 murders, 5,500 rapes, 8,800 assaults, and 22,500 robberies while under supervision in the community for an average of 13 months. Of the parole violators in prison, 80 percent were in confinement following conviction for a new crime; the remaining 20 percent had been imprisoned for a technical violation. More than 40 percent of these technical violators, though not convicted of a new crime, had been arrested for a new crime while on parole supervision in the community. (An arrest for violating parole conditions was not counted as an arrest for a new crime.) Technical parole violators in prison who said they had not been arrested for a new crime while on parole made up about 3 percent of the prison population.[122] Of 565,000 state prison admissions in 1998, 206,000 were parole violators.

Reasons for Failure   Why do so many released inmates end up back behind prison walls? The specter of recidivism is especially frustrating to the U.S. public: It is so difficult to apprehend and successfully prosecute chronic offenders that it seems foolish to grant them early release so they can prey on more victims.

A strong association exists between prior and future offending: The parolees most likely to fail on release are the ones who have failed in the past; chronic offenders are the ones most likely to reoffend. Most research efforts indicate that a long history of criminal behavior, an antisocial personality, a record of substance abuse, and childhood experiences with family dysfunction are all correlated with postrelease recidivism.[123] Other factors that seem to predict parole violations include family criminality, criminal companions, and interpersonal conflict.[124] Many parolees were prior drug users and once released may revert to substance abuse. For example, a recent study of 237 parolees in Maryland found that 58 percent of those deemed successful on parole and 82 percent of the parole failures tested positively for drugs within a few months of their release.[125] Other parolees have mental health problems, and more than 10 percent exhibit both mental illness and substance abuse (see Table 16.3).

Parolees fail because the psychological and economic reasons that led them to crime probably have not been eliminated by a stay in prison. Despite rehabilitation efforts, the typical ex-convict is still the same undereducated, unemployed, substance-abusing lower-class male he was when arrested. For example, one study of 400 Texas inmates found that almost 75 percent suffered from lifetime substance abuse or dependence disorder.[126] It seems naïve to think that incarceration alone can help someone overcome these lifelong disabilities.

TABLE 16.3 LEVELS OF SUBSTANCE ABUSE AND MENTAL ILLNESS AMONG STATE PRISONERS REENTERING SOCIETY

	Percent of Reentering Inmates
Drug/alcohol involved	73.6%
Drug use	
In month before offense	59.2%
At time of offense	33.7
Intravenous use in past	22.2
Alcohol abuse	
Binge drinkers	41.8%
Alcohol dependent	25.2
At time of offense	35.7
Identified as mentally ill	14.4%
Co-occurring disorders (substance abuse and mentally ill)	11.4%

SOURCE: Allen Beck, "State and Federal Prisoners Returning to the Community: Findings from the Bureau of Justice Statistics," unpublished paper presented at the First Reentry Courts Initiative Cluster Meeting, Washington, DC, April 2000.

Social and Economic Consequences The prison experience—being separated from friends and family, not sharing in conventional society, associating with dangerous people, and adapting to a volatile lifestyle—probably does little to improve offenders' personality or behavior. And when they return to society, it may be to the same destructive neighborhood and social groups that prompted their original law-violating behavior. Some ex-inmates may have to prove that the prison experience has not changed them: Taking drugs or being sexually aggressive may show friends that they have not lost their "heart."[127]

Ex-inmates may find their home life torn and disrupted. Wives of inmates report that they must face the shame and stigma of having an incarcerated spouse while withstanding a barrage of calls from jealous husbands on the "inside" who try to monitor their behavior and control their lives. Family visits to the inmate become traumatic and strain interpersonal relationships because they often involve strip searches and other invasions of privacy.[128] Sensitive to these problems, some states have instituted support groups designed to help inmates' families adjust to their loneliness and despair.[129]

Even if familial and spousal support are present, former inmates soon find that imprisonment reduces their income and employment opportunities.[130] Ex-convicts by law are denied the right to work in certain occupations. And even if a criminal record does not automatically prohibit employment, many employers are reluctant to hire people who have served time. Why would someone hire an ex-con when other applicants are available? If ex-offenders lie about their prison experience and are later found out, they will be dismissed for misrepresentation. The stress of economic deprivation, in turn, can lead to family breakup and to less involvement with children.[131] Research shows that former inmates who gain and keep meaningful employment are more likely to succeed on parole than those who are unemployed or underemployed.[132]

Loss of Rights During the 2000 presidential election, the media caught onto an amazing fact: Nationally, about 4.2 million Americans—some still behind bars, others freed long ago—were not allowed to vote because of felony disenfranchisement

EXHIBIT 16.3 RIGHTS LOST BY CONVICTED FELONS

- Fourteen states permanently deny felons the right to vote; 18 suspend the right until after the correctional sentence has been completed.
- Nineteen states terminate parental rights.
- Twenty-nine states consider a felony conviction to be legal grounds for divorce.
- Six states deny felons the opportunity for public employment.
- Thirty-one states deny convicted felons the right to serve on juries.
- Twenty-five states prevent convicted felons from holding public office.
- Federal law prevents ex-convicts from owning guns. All states except Vermont employ additional legal measures to prevent felons from possessing firearms.
- Forty-six states now require that felons register with law enforcement agencies. This requirement is up sharply in recent years; in 1986, only eight states required felons to register.
- Civil death, or the denial of all civil rights, is still practiced in four states.

SOURCE: Kathleen Olivares, Velmer Burton, and Francis Cullen, "The Collateral Consequences of a Felony Conviction: A National Study of State Legal Codes 10 Years Later," *Federal Probation* 60 (1996): 10–17.

laws. About 7 percent of all African Americans are barred from voting because of felony convictions, compared to 2.1 percent of the general population.[133]

Losing voting rights is one among many obstacles inmates face when they leave the institution. One reason that ex-inmates find it so difficult to make it on the outside is the legal restrictions they are forced to endure. These may include bars on certain kinds of employment, limits on obtaining licenses, and restrictions on their freedom of movement. One survey found that a significant number of states still restrict the activities of former felons.[134] Some of the more important findings are contained in Exhibit 16.3.

In general, states have placed greater restrictions on former felons as part of the get-tough movement. However, courts have considered individual requests by convicted felons to have their rights restored. It is common for courts to look at such issues as how recently the criminal offense took place and its relationship to the particular right before deciding whether to restore it. A number of experts and national commissions have condemned the loss of rights of convicted offenders as a significant cause of recidivism. Consequently, courts have generally moved to eliminate the most restrictive elements of post-conviction restrictions.[135]

SUMMARY

On entering prison, offenders must make tremendous adjustments to survive. Usual behavior patterns or lifestyles are radically changed. Opportunities for personal satisfaction are reduced. Passing through a number of adjustment stages or cycles, inmates learn to cope with the new environment.

Inmates also learn to obey the inmate social code, which dictates proper behavior and attitudes. If inmates break the code, they may be unfavorably labeled.

Inmates may be eligible for a large number of treatment programs designed to help them readjust to the community once they are released. These include educational programs on the basic, high school, and even college levels, as well as vocational training programs. In addition, inmates may be offered individualized and group psychological counseling. Work furloughs, conjugal visits, and coed prisons have also been employed.

Despite such measures, prisons remain forbidding structures that house desperate men and women. Violence is common in prisons. Women often turn their hatred inward and hurt themselves; male inmates engage in individual and collective violence against others. The Attica and New Mexico riots are examples of the most serious collective prison violence.

In years past, society paid little attention to the incarcerated offender. The majority of inmates confined in jails and prisons were basically deprived of the rights guaranteed them under the Constitution. Today, however, the judicial system is actively involved in the administration of correctional institutions. Inmates can now take their grievances to courts and seek due process and equal protection under the law. The courts have recognized that persons confined in correctional institutions have rights, including access to the courts and legal counsel, the exercise of religion, the rights to correspondence and visitation, and the right to adequate medical treatment.

Most inmates return to society before the completion of their prison sentence. The majority earn early release through time off for good behavior or other sentence-reducing mechanisms. In addition, about 40 percent of all inmates are paroled before the completion of their maximum term. Most state jurisdictions maintain an independent parole board whose members decide whether to grant parole. Their decision making is discretionary and is based on many factors, such as the perception of the needs of society, the correctional system, and the client. Once paroled, the client is subject to control by parole officers, who ensure that the conditions set by the board (the parole rules) are maintained. Parole can be revoked if the offender violates the rules of parole or commits a new crime.

Inmates have a tough time adjusting on the outside, and the recidivism rate is disturbingly high. One reason is that many states restrict inmate rights and take away privileges granted to other citizens.

Key Terms

total institution	less eligibility	substantive right
hustle	special-needs inmate	jailhouse lawyer
inmate subculture	work release (furlough)	class action
prisonization	conjugal visit	parole board
importation model	coed prison	technical parole violation
make-believe family	hands-off doctrine	intensive supervision parole (ISP)

Discussion Questions

1. What are the benefits and drawbacks of coed prisons? Of conjugal visits?
2. Should women be allowed to work as correctional officers in male prisons? What about male correctional officers in female prisons?
3. Should prison inmates be allowed a free college education while noncriminals are forced to pay tuition? Do you believe in less eligibility for prisoners?
4. Define parole, including its purposes and objectives. How does it differ from probation?
5. What is the role of the parole board?
6. Should a former prisoner have all the civil rights afforded the average citizen? Should people be further penalized after they have paid their debt to society?

A CLOSER LOOK

Robert J. Gagliardo is a drug and alcohol treatment specialist for the Commonwealth of Pennsylvania Department of Corrections. He is involved in a prison counseling program geared specifically to help inmates adjust to parole release:

In a perfect world, a relationship between therapy and parole eligibility merit systems would not exist. Parole-Centered Counseling (PCC) is a set of motivational and behavioral techniques that provides the necessary separation between therapy and merit systems, enabling therapy groups to function as they were intended. It accomplishes this by teaching inmates how to develop human relations skills and how to project a positive influence. When used properly, these methods can be the cornerstone of a stable, pro-

ductive life. Prison therapy groups are a mandatory requirement in most cases. Inmates attend therapy for the sake of meeting the requirements of their perspective program plan. PCC appeals to an inmate's self interest; an inmate wants to come for the information, not for the requirement.

To read more about this program, go to InfoTrac College Edition and look up
Robert J. Gagliardo, "Parole-Centered Counseling: Motivating Inmates by Addressing Their Primary Concerns," *Corrections Today,* August 2000, v62 i5 p16

Notes

1 Judith Kohler, "7 Colo. Prison Guards Indicted in Abuse Probe," *Boston Globe,* 4 November 2000, p. A4.

2 Gresham Sykes, *The Society of Captives* (Princeton, NJ: Princeton University Press, 1958).

3 David Eichenthal and James Jacobs, "Enforcing the Criminal Law in State Prisons," *Justice Quarterly* 8 (1991): 283–303.

4 Brent Paterline and David Petersen, "Structural and Social Psychological Determinants of Prisonization," *Journal of Criminal Justice* 27 (1999): 427–441.

5 Ibid., p. 439.

6 John Wooldredge, "Inmate Lifestyles and Opportunities for Victimization," *Journal of Research in Crime and Delinquency* 35 (1998): 480–502.

7 David Anderson, *Crimes of Justice: Improving the Police, Courts, and Prison* (New York: New York Times Books, 1988).

8 Robert Johnson, *Hard Time: Understanding and Reforming the Prison* (Monterey, CA: Brooks/Cole, 1987), p. 115.

9 Sandra Gleason, "Hustling: The Inside Economy of a Prison," *Federal Probation* 42 (1978): 32–39.

10 Paterline and Petersen, "Structural and Social Psychological Determinants of Prisonization, p. 440.

11 Wooldredge, "Inmate Lifestyles and Opportunities for Victimization."

12 Craig Hemmens and James Marquart, "Friend or Foe? Race, Age, and Inmate Perceptions of Inmate–Staff Relations," *Journal of Criminal Justice* 28 (2000): 297–312.

13 Kevin Wright, *The Great American Crime Myth* (Westport, CT: Greenwood Press, 1985), p. 167.

14 Hans Toch, *Living in Prison* (New York: Free Press, 1977), pp. 179–205.

15 Angela Maitland and Richard Sluder, "Victimization and Youthful Prison Inmates: An Empirical Analysis," *Prison Journal* 77 (1998): 55–74.

16 J. Stephan, *Prison Rule Violators* (Washington, DC: Bureau of Justice Statistics, 1989).

17 Leonore Simon, "Prison Behavior and Victim–Offender Relationships Among Violent Offenders," paper presented at the annual meeting of the American Society of Criminology, San Francisco, November 1991.

18 John Irwin, "Adaptation to Being Corrected: Corrections from the Convict's Perspective," in *Handbook of Criminology,* ed. Daniel Glazer (Chicago: Rand McNally, 1974), pp. 971–993.

19 Donald Clemmer, *The Prison Community* (New York: Holt, Rinehart, and Winston, 1958).

20 Gresham Sykes and Sheldon Messinger, "The Inmate Social Code," in *The Sociology of Punishment and Corrections,* ed. Norman Johnston et al. (New York: Wiley, 1970), pp. 401–408.

21 John Irwin and Donald Cressey, "Thieves, Convicts, and the Inmate Culture," *Social Problems* 10 (1962): 142–155.

22 Ibid., 145.

23 Candace Kruttschnitt, Rosemary Gartner, and Amy Miller, "Doing Her Own Time? Women's Responses to Prison in the Context of the Old and the New Penology," *Criminology* 38 (2000): 681–718.

24 Paterline and Petersen, "Structural and Social Psychological Determinants of Prisonization."

25 Ibid., p. 439.

26 James B. Jacobs, ed., *New Perspectives on Prisons and Imprisonment* (Ithaca, NY: Cornell University Press, 1983); "Street Gangs Behind Bars," *Social Problems* 21 (1974): 395–409; "Race Relations and the Prison Subculture," in *Crime and Justice,* vol. 1, ed. Norval Morris and Michael Tonry (Chicago: University of Chicago Press, 1979), pp. 1–28.

27 Stanley Penn, "Prison Gangs Formed by Racial Groups Pose Big Problem in West," *Wall Street Journal,* 11 May 1983, p. A1.

28 Maitland and Sluder, "Victimization and Youthful Prison Inmates: An Empirical Analysis."

29 Helen Eigenberg, "Homosexuality in Male Prisons: Demonstrating the Need for a Social Constructionist Approach," *Criminal Justice Review* 17 (1992): 219–223.

30 Nicole Hahn Rafter, *Partial Justice* (New Brunswick, NJ: Transaction Books, 1990), p. 67.

31 Ibid., pp. 181–182.

32 Allen J. Beck, *Prisoners in 1999* (Washington, DC: Bureau of Justice Statistics, 2000).

33 Meda Chesney-Lind, "Patriarchy, Prisons and Jails: A Critical Look at Trends in Women's Incarceration," paper presented at the International Feminist Conference on Women, Law and Social Control, Mont Gabriel, Quebec, July 1991.

34 Elaine DeCostanzo and Helen Scholes, "Women Behind Bars, Their Numbers Increase," *Corrections Today* 50 (1988): 104–106.

35 This section synthesizes the findings of a number of surveys of female inmates, including DeCostanzo and Scholes, "Women Behind Bars, Their Numbers Increase"; Ruth Glick and Virginia Neto, *National Study of Women's Correctional Programs* (Washington, DC: U.S. Government Printing Office, 1977); Ann Goetting and Roy Michael Howsen, "Women in Prison: A Profile," *Prison Journal* 63 (1983): 27–46; Meda Chesney-Lind and Noelie Rodrigues, "Women Under Lock and Key: A View from Inside," *Prison Journal* 63 (1983): 47–65; Contact, Inc., "Women Offenders," *Corrections Compendium* 7 (1982): 6–11.

36 Kathleen Auerhahn and Elizabeth Dermody Leonard, "Docile Bodies? Chemi-

cal Restraints and the Female Inmate," *Journal of Criminal Law and Criminology* 90 (2000): 599–634.

37 Merry Morash, Robin Harr, and Lila Rucker, "A Comparison of Programming for Women and Men in U.S. Prisons in the 1980s," *Crime and Delinquency* 40 (1994): 197–221.

38 Pamela Schram, "Stereotypes About Vocational Programming for Female Inmates," *Prison Journal* 78 (1998): 244–271.

39 Morash, Harr, and Rucker, "A Comparison of Programming for Women and Men in U.S. Prison in the 1980s."

40 Candace Kruttschnitt and Sharon Krmpotich, "Aggressive Behavior Among Female Inmates: An Exploratory Study," *Justice Quarterly* 7 (1990): 370–389.

41 "Sex Abuse of Female Inmates Is Common, Rights Group Says," *Criminal Justice Newsletter,* 16 December 1996, p. 2.

42 General Accounting Office, *Women in Prison: Sexual Misconduct by Correctional Staff* (Washington, DC: U.S Government Printing Office, 1999).

43 Amnesty International, United States of America Rights for All, *Not Part of My Sentence: Violations of the Human Rights of Women in Custody* (Washington, DC: Amnesty International, 1999).

44 "Female Offenders: As Their Numbers Grow, So Does The Need for Gender-Specific Programming," *Corrections Compendium,* March 1998, p. 1.

45 Edna Erez, "The Myth of the New Female Offender: Some Evidence from Attitudes Toward Law and Justice," *Journal of Criminal Justice* 16 (1988): 499–509.

46 Robert Ross and Hugh McKay, *Self-Mutilation* (Lexington, MA: Lexington Books, 1979).

47 Alice Propper, *Prison Homosexuality* (Lexington, MA: Lexington Books, 1981).

48 Dianna Newbern, Donald Dansereau, and Urvashi Pitre, "Positive Effects on Life Skills Motivation and Self-Efficacy: Node-Link Maps in a Modified Therapeutic Community," *American Journal of Drug and Alcohol Abuse* 25 (1999): 407–410.

49 Ira Sommers and Deborah Baskin, "The Prescription of Psychiatric Medication in Prison: Psychiatric Versus Labeling Perspectives," *Justice Quarterly* 7 (1990): 739–755.

50 Judy Anderson and R. Daniel McGehee, "South Carolina Strives to Treat Elderly and Disabled Offenders," *Corrections Today* 53 (1991): 124–127.

51 Allen Beck, *Correctional Populations in the United States, 1997* (Washington, DC: Bureau of Justice Statistics, 2000).

52 "Few Inmates Get Drug Treatment, But Most Need It, GAO Finds," *Criminal Justice Newsletter,* 1 November 1999, p. 3.

53 Substance Abuse and Mental Health Services Administration, *Substance Abuse Treatment in Adult and Juvenile Correc-*

tional Facilities: Findings from the Uniform Facility Data Set 1997 Survey of Correctional Facilities (Washington, DC: U.S. Government Printing Office, 2000).

54 "Rates of HIV Infection and AIDS-Related Deaths Drop Among T\the Nation's Prisoners," news release, Wednesday, November 3, 1999, Bureau of Justice Statistics, p. 2.

55 *Gates v. Deukmejian* (U.S.D.C., E.D. Cal.) CIVS 87-1636 (1990).

56 Howard Skolnik and John Slansky, "A First Step in Helping Inmates Get Good Jobs After Release," *Corrections Today* 53 (1991): 92.

57 This section leans heavily on Barbara Auerbach, George Sexton, Franklin Farrow, and Robert Lawson, *Work in American Prisons: The Private Sector Gets Involved* (Washington, DC: National Institute of Justice, 1988).

58 Public Law 96-157, sec. 827, codified as 18 U.S.C. sec. 1761(c).

59 Courtesy of the Prison Industry Authority, 560 East Natoma Street, Folsom, CA 95630.

60 Diane Dwyer and Roger McNally, "Public Policy, Prison Industries, and Business: An Equitable Balance for the 1990s," *Federal Probation* 57 (1993): 30–35.

61 Barbara Bloom, "Families of Prisoners: A Valuable Resource," paper presented at the annual meeting of the Academy of Criminal Justice Sciences, St. Louis, March 1987.

62 Norma Stumbo and Sandra Little, "Campground Offers Relaxed Setting for Children's Visitation Program," *Corrections Today* 53 (1991): 136–144.

63 Donald Johns, "Alternatives to Conjugal Visits," *Federal Probation* 35 (1971): 48–50.

64 "Coed Prisons," *Corrections Compendium* 10 (1986): 7, 14–15.

65 Mark Hamm, "Current Perspectives on the Prisoner Self-Help Movement," *Federal Probation* 52 (1988): 49–56.

66 For more information, contact The Fortune Society, 39 West 19th Street, New York, NY 10011, (212) 206-7070. Their email address is info@fortunesociety.org.

67 Douglas Lipton, Robert Martinson, and Judith Wilks, *The Effectiveness of Correctional Treatment: A Survey of Treatment Evaluation Studies* (New York: Praeger, 1975).

68 Charles Murray and Louis Cox, *Beyond Probation: Juvenile Corrections and the Chronic Delinquent* (Beverly Hills, CA: Sage, 1979).

69 Steven Lab and John Whitehead, "An Analysis of Juvenile Correctional Treatment," *Crime and Delinquency* 34 (1988): 60–83.

70 Ted Palmer, "The Effectiveness of Intervention: Recent Trends and Current Issues," *Crime and Delinquency* 37 (1991): 330–346.

71 Morash, Harr, and Rucker, "A Comparison of Programming for Women and Men in U.S. Prisons in the 1980s."

72 Mark Lipsey and David Wilson, "Effective Intervention for Serious Juvenile Offenders: A Synthesis of Research," in *Serious and Violent Juvenile Offenders: Risk Factors and Successful Interventions,* ed. Rolf Loeber and David Farrington (Thousand Oaks, CA: Sage, 1998), pp. 81–98.

73 Paul Gendreau and Claire Goggin, "Principles of Effective Correctional Programming," *Forum on Correctional Research* 2 (1996): 38–41.

74 Lucien X. Lombardo, *Guards Imprisoned* (New York: Elsevier, 1981); James Jacobs and Norma Crotty, "The Guard's World," in *New Perspectives on Prisons and Imprisonment,* ed. James Jacobs (Ithaca, NY: Cornell University Press, 1983), pp. 133–141.

75 Mary Ann Farkas, "Correctional Officer Attitudes Toward Inmates and Working with Inmates in a 'Get Tough' Era," *Journal of Criminal Justice* 27 (1999): 495–506.

76 John Klofas and Hans Toch, "The Guard Subculture Myth," *Journal of Research in Crime and Delinquency* 19 (1982): 238–254.

77 Ruth Triplett and Janet Mullings, "Work-Related Stress and Coping Among Correctional Officers: Implications from the Organizational Literature," *Journal of Criminal Justice* 24 (1996): 291–308.

78 Peter Horne, "Female Correction Officers," *Federal Probation* 49 (1985): 46–55.

79 *Dothard v. Rawlinson,* 433 U.S. 321 (1977).

80 Farkas, "Correctional Officer Attitudes Toward Inmates and Working with Inmates in a 'Get Tough' Era," pp. 503–504.

81 David Duffee, *Corrections, Practice and Policy* (New York: Random House, 1989), p. 305.

82 Randy Martin and Sherwood Zimmerman, "A Typology of the Causes of Prison Riots and an Analytical Extension to the 1986 West Virginia Riot," *Justice Quarterly* 7 (1990): 711–737.

83 Bert Useem and Michael Resig, "Collective Action in Prisons: Protests, Disturbances, and Riots," *Criminology* 37 (1999): 735–760.

84 John DiIulio, *Governing Prisons: A Comparative Study of Correctional Management* (New York: Free Press, 1987).

85 National Advisory Commission on Criminal Justice Standards and Goals, *Corrections* (Washington, DC: U.S. Government Printing Office, 1973), p. 18.

86 *Cooper v. Pate,* 378 U.S. 546 (1964).

87 *DeMallory v. Cullen,* 855 F.2d 422 (7th Cir. 1988).

88 *Lindquist v. Idaho State Board of Corrections,* 776 F.2d 851 (9th Cir. 1985).

89 *Smith v. Wade,* 461 U.S. 30, 103 S.Ct. 1625 (1983).

90 *Bounds v. Smith,* 430 U.S. 817 (1977).

91 *Turner v. Safley,* 482 U.S. 78, 107 S.Ct. 2254 (1987) at 2261.

92 *Ramos v. Lamm,* 639 F.2d 559 (10th Cir. 1980).

93 *Procunier v. Martinez,* 411 U.S. 396 (1974).

94 *Nolan v. Fitzpatrick,* 451 F.2d 545 (1st Cir. 1971); see also *Washington Post Co. v. Kleindienst,* 494 F.2d 997 (D.C. Cir. 1974).

95 *Mumin v. Phelps,* 857 F.2d 1055 (5th Cir. 1988).

96 *O'Lone v. Estate of Shabazz,* 482 U.S. 342, 107 S.Ct. 2400 (1987).

97 *Rahman v. Stephenson,* 626 F.Supp. 886 (W.D. Tenn. 1986).

98 *Newman v. Alabama,* 503 F.2d 1320 (5th Cir. 1974).

99 *Estelle v. Gamble,* 429 U.S. 97 (1976).

100 Ibid.

101 Ira P. Robbins, "Managed Health Care in Prisons as Cruel and Unusual Punishment," *Journal of Criminal Law and Criminology* 90 (1999): 195–234.

102 Ibid.

103 *Trop v. Dulles,* 356 U.S. 86, 78 S.Ct. 590 (1958); see also *Furman v. Georgia,* 408 U.S. 238, 92 S.Ct. 2726, 33 L.Ed.2d 346 (1972).

104 *Weems v. United States,* 217 U.S. 349, 30 S.Ct. 544, 54 L.Ed. 793 (1910).

105 *Lee v. Tahash,* 352 F.2d 970 (8th Cir. 1965).

106 *Estelle v. Gamble,* 429 U.S. 97 (1976).

107 *Robinson v. California,* 370 U.S. 660, 82 S.Ct. 1417, 8 L.Ed.2d 758 (1962).

108 *Gregg v. Georgia,* 428 U.S. 153, 96 S.Ct. 2909, 49 L.Ed.2d 859 (1976).

109 *Jackson v. Bishop,* 404 F.2d 571 (8th Cir. 1968).

110 *Bell v. Wolfish,* 441 U.S. 520, 99 S.Ct. 1873, 1974 (1979); see *"Bell v. Wolfish:* The Rights of Pretrial Detainees," *New England Journal of Prison Law* 6 (1979): 134.

111 *Farmer v. Brennan,* 511 U.S. 825, 144 S.Ct. 1970 (1994).

112 *Rhodes v. Chapman,* 452 U.S. 337 (1981); for further analysis of *Rhodes,* see Randall Pooler, "Prison Overcrowding and the Eighth Amendment: The Rhodes Not Taken," *New England Journal of Criminal and Civil Confinement* 8 (1983): 1–28.

113 *Estelle v. Ruiz,* No. 74-329 (E.D. Texas 1980).

114 *"Ruiz* Case in Texas Winds Down: Special Master to Close Office," *Criminal Justice Newsletter,* 15 January 1990, p. 1.

115 Prison Litigation Reform Act of 1995, Pub. L. No. 104-134 (codified as amended in scattered titles and sections of the U.S.C.); see also H.R. 3019, 104th Cong. (1996).

116 Prison Escape Survey (Lincoln, NE: Corrections Compendium, 1991).

117 Thomas Bonczar and Lauren Glaze, *Probation and Parole in the United States, 1998* (Washington, DC: Bureau of Justice Statistics, 1999).

118 Ibid.

119 Ronald Burns, Patrick Kinkade, Matthew Leone, and Scott Phillips, "Perspectives on Parole: The Board Members' Viewpoint," *Federal Probation* 63 (1999): 16–22.

120 *Pennsylvania Board of Probation and Parole v. Scott,* 524 U.S. 357 (1998); see also Duncan N. Stevens, "Off the Map: Parole Revocation Hearings and the Fourth Amendment," *Journal of Criminal Law and Criminology* 89 (1999): 1047–1460.

121 Thomas Hanlon, David N. Nurco, Richard W. Bateman, and Kevin E.

O'Grady, "The Response of Drug Abuser Parolees to a Combination of Treatment and Intensive Supervision," *Prison Journal* 78 (1998): 31–44; Susan Turner and Joan Petersilia, "Focusing on High-Risk Parolees: An Experiment to Reduce Commitments to the Texas Department of Corrections," *Journal of Research in Crime and Delinquency* 29 (1992): 34–61.

122 Robyn L. Cohen, *Probation and Parole Violators in State Prison, 1991: Survey of State Prison Inmates, 1991* (Washington, DC: Bureau of Justice Statistics, 1995).

123 James Bonta, Moira Law, and Karl Hanson, "The Prediction of Criminal and Violent Recidivism Among Mentally Disordered Offenders: A Meta-Analysis," *Psychological Bulletin* 123 (1998): 123–142.

124 Paul Gendreau, Tracy Little, and Claire Goggin, "A Meta-Analysis of the Predictors of Adult Offender Recidivism: What Works?" *Criminology* 34 (1996): 575–607.

125 Hanlon, Nurco, Bateman, and O'Grady, "The Response of Drug Abuser Parolees to a Combination of Treatment and Intensive Supervision."

126 Roger Peters, Paul Greenbaum, John Edens, Chris Carter, and Madeline Ortiz, "Prevalence of DSM-IV Substance Abuse and Dependence Disorders Among Prison Inmates," *American Journal of Drug and Alcohol Abuse* 24 (1998): 573–580.

127 J. E. Ryan, "Who Gets Revoked? A Comparison of Intensive Supervision Successes and Failures in Vermont," *Crime and Delinquency* 43 (1997): 104–118.

128 Laura Fishman, *Women at the Wall: A Study of Prisoners' Wives Doing Time on the Outside* (New York: State University of New York Press, 1990).

129 Leslee Goodman Hornick, "Volunteer Program Helps Make Inmates' Families Feel Welcome," *Corrections Today* 53 (1991): 184–186.

130 Jeffrey Fagan and Richard Freeman, "Crime and Work," in *Crime and Justice: A Review of Research,* vol. 25, ed. Michael Tonry (Chicago: University of Chicago Press, 1999), pp. 211–229.

131 John Hagan and Ronit Dinovitzer, "Collateral Consequences of Imprisonment for Children, Communities, and Prisoners," in *Crime and Justice: A Review of Research,* vol. 26, ed. Michael Tonry and Joan Petersilia (Chicago: University of Chicago Press, 1999) pp. 89–107.

132 Hanlon, Nurco, Bateman, and O'Grady, "The Response of Drug Abuser Parolees to a Combination of Treatment and Intensive Supervision."

133 Somini Sengupta, "Felony Costs Voting Rights for a Lifetime in 9 States," *New York Times,* 3 November 2000, p. A3.

134 Kathleen Olivares, Velmer Burton, and Francis Cullen, "The Collateral Consequences of a Felony Conviction: A National Study of State Legal Codes 10 Years Later," *Federal Probation* 60 (1996): 10–17.

135 See, for example, *Bush v. Reid,* 516 P.2d 1216 (Alaska 1973); *Thompson v. Bond,* 421 F.Supp. 878 (W.D. Mo. 1976); *Delorne v. Pierce Freightlines Co.,* 353 F.Supp. 258 (D.Or. 1973); *Beyer v. Werner,* 299 F.Supp. 967 (E.D. N.Y. 1969).

THE HISTORY AND NATURE OF THE JUVENILE JUSTICE SYSTEM

CHAPTER 17
Juvenile Justice

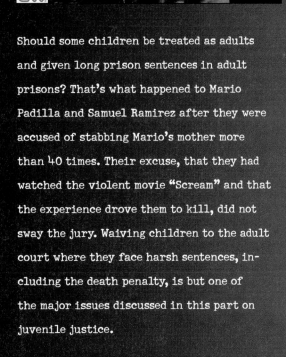

Should some children be treated as adults and given long prison sentences in adult prisons? That's what happened to Mario Padilla and Samuel Ramirez after they were accused of stabbing Mario's mother more than 40 times. Their excuse, that they had watched the violent movie "Scream" and that the experience drove them to kill, did not sway the jury. Waiving children to the adult court where they face harsh sentences, including the death penalty, is but one of the major issues discussed in this part on juvenile justice.

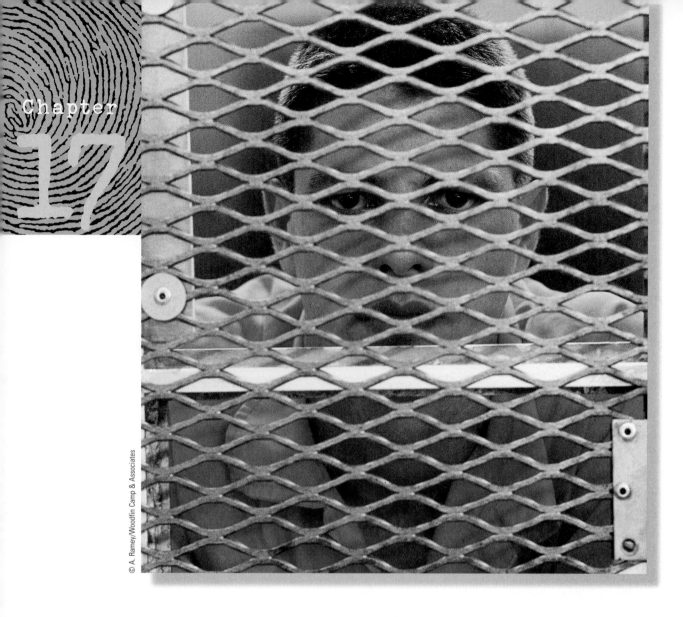

© A. Ramey/Woodfin Camp & Associates

JUVENILE JUSTICE

At 13 years old, Nathaniel Abraham was the youngest person ever to be charged with murder as an adult in the state of Michigan.[1] Abraham was 11 years old when, on October 29, 1997, he fired a shot from a .22-caliber rifle, fatally wounding 18-year-old Ronnie Lee Greene, Jr., who was standing 288 feet away. As his trial began, Abraham's defense attorney told jurors in his opening statement that the shooting was a "very tragic, tragic accident" and that Abraham had the developmental abilities of a boy 6 to 8 years old at the time of the killing. He argued that Abraham, one of the youngest people ever to face murder charges as an adult in the United States, was not capable of forming the

intent to kill, as is required for a first-degree murder conviction. However, the prosecutor retorted that Abraham later bragged to friends about the killing. Prosecutors noted that Abraham had had 22 scrapes with police and that his mother had tried to have him ruled incorrigible in juvenile court.

After his conviction for murder, prosecutors sought a blended sentence of incarceration in a juvenile facility until age 21, followed by imprisonment in an adult facility. However, the sentencing judge ordered him to be held in juvenile detention until age 21, when he will be released. "While there is no guarantee Nathaniel will be rehabilitated at 21, it is clear 10 years is enough to accomplish this goal," said Judge Eugene Moore at the sentencing hearing. Moore went on to say that if society is committed to preventing future criminal behavior, rehabilitation through the juvenile system is the answer. "You clearly need to learn to think before you act. You have probably done the worst thing that can be done . . . you are going to have to come to terms with this," Moore told the boy.[2]

In September 2000, Jonathan Lebed, age 15, made headlines when he became the youngest person ever charged with breaking securities laws. Lebed used a computer in his bedroom to buy thousands of shares of penny

Nathaniel Abraham, shown here talking to his attorney, was 11 years old when he committed murder.

stocks. He then used a variety of screen names to hide his identity and post fictitious messages in chat rooms, talking up the stock. Meanwhile, he would place a "limit order" with his broker, setting a higher price at which he wanted to unload the investment. Investors who reacted to Lebed's hot tips would invariably push the stock price up until it reached the limit order, at which time he would sell his large block of shares, pocket the profits, and send the price plummeting again.

Lebed's case is only one of hundreds of Web-based stock fraud cases, but it stands out because of the defen-dant's age. Lebed agreed to repay the $285,000 he made from his illegal trades in what is known as a "pump and dump" scheme. Lebed's white-collar crime cannot be com-pared in magnitude to the Abraham murder case, yet it too raises a host of questions. How can the Securities and Ex-change Commission and other Internet fraud groups pro-tect the public from such schemes? What punishment should such juvenile offenders receive? Who is responsi-ble for any permanent damage to the stock price of the companies traded by the juvenile offender?

Fill in the blanks 1–2
True/False 1
Essay 1

juvenile justice system
The system of agencies and organizations that deal with youths who engage in crime (juvenile delinquency) or noncriminal behaviors such as truancy and incorrigibility (status offenses).

parens patriae
The power of the state to act on behalf of a child and provide care and protection equivalent to that of a parent.

balanced and restorative justice model
A model of juvenile justice that seeks to involve offenders, victims, and the community in a process of victim restoration, program development, and community protection.

Fill in the blanks 3
Multiple choice 1

Independent of, yet interrelated with, the adult criminal justice system, the **juvenile justice system** is primarily responsible for dealing with juvenile and youth crime, as well as with incorrigible and truant children and runaways. When the juvenile court was originally conceived at the turn of the century, its philosophy was based on the idea of **parens patriae**: The state was to act on behalf of the parent in the interests of the child. In the 1960s, however, the theme changed when the U.S. Supreme Court began ensuring legal rights for juveniles. In the 1980s, the emphasis of the juvenile justice system shifted to controlling chronically delinquent youths.

Today, the U.S. juvenile justice system is in the midst of reexamining its fundamental operations and institutions. Although more than a century has passed since the first independent juvenile court was established, a comprehensive and comprehensible statement of its goals and purposes has yet to be developed. On the one hand, some authorities still hold to the original social welfare principles of the juvenile justice system. They argue that the juvenile court is primarily a treatment agency that acts as a wise parent, dispensing personalized, individual justice to needy children who seek guidance and understanding. On the other hand, those with a crime control orientation suggest that the juvenile court's parens patriae philosophy has neglected the victims of delinquents and that serious offenders should be punished and disciplined, rather than treated and reha-bilitated. A third approach to juvenile justice takes the position that court pro-cessing has a potentially adverse effect on children, who are denied some of the constitutional rights afforded adult offenders. Advocates of this position believe that juvenile courts should dispense impartial justice and increase the due process rights of children who, depending on the outcome of their trial, may be subjected to extended periods of confinement or transferred to the adult court.[3] A fourth approach advocates a **balanced and restorative justice model**, which calls for ac-countability, program development, and community protection.[4]

This chapter reviews the history of juvenile justice and discusses the justice system's processing of youthful offenders.

HISTORY OF JUVENILE JUSTICE

The modern practice of legally separating adult and juvenile offenders can be traced to two developments in English custom and law: the poor laws and the chancery court. Both were designed to allow the state to take control of the lives of needy, but not necessarily criminal, children.[5]

Poor Laws As early as 1535, the English passed statutes known as **poor laws**. These laws provided for the appointment of overseers to indenture destitute or neglected children as servants. Such children were forced to work during their minority for families who trained them in agriculture, trade, or domestic service. The Elizabethan poor laws of 1601 became a model for dealing with poor children for more than 200 years. These laws created a system of church wardens and overseers who, with the consent of the justices of the peace, identified vagrant, delinquent, and neglected children and took measures to put them to work. Often this meant placing them in poorhouses or workhouses or, more commonly, apprenticing them to masters—adults who taught them a trade. Parents or guardians who wanted to secure training for their children put them into voluntary apprenticeships.

poor laws
Seventeenth-century English laws under which vagrants and abandoned and neglected children were bound to masters as indentured servants.

Chancery Courts A medieval institution, chancery courts were concerned primarily with protecting property rights, but their authority extended to the welfare of children in general. The major issues that came before the medieval chancery courts involved guardianship, the uses and control of property, and the relationship of the people to the monarchy. These courts were founded on the proposition that children and other incompetents were under the protective control of the king. Thus, the Latin phrase *parens patriae* referred to the role of the king as the father of his country. In the famous English case *Wellesley v. Wellesley,* a duke's children were taken from him in the name of parens patriae because of his scandalous behavior.[6] Thus, the concept of parens patriae became the theoretical basis for the chancery courts acting on behalf of the crown.[7]

Multiple choice 2–3

The chancery courts dealt with the property and custody problems of the wealthier classes. They never had jurisdiction over children charged with criminal conduct; juveniles who violated the law were handled within the regular criminal court system. Nevertheless, the concept of parens patriae came to refer primarily to the responsibility of the courts and the state to act in the best interests of the child. The idea that the state—and particularly the juvenile court—should act to protect the young, the incompetent, the neglected, and the delinquent subsequently became a major influence on the development of the U.S. juvenile justice system in the twentieth century.

Care of Children in Early America

Multiple choice 4

The poor laws and the forced apprenticeship system were brought from England to colonial America. Poor laws were passed in Virginia in 1646 and in Connecticut and Massachusetts in 1678. To accommodate dependent and destitute youths, local jurisdictions developed almshouses, poorhouses, and workhouses. Crowded and unhealthy, these accepted the poor, the insane, the diseased, and vagrant and destitute children. Forced apprenticeship of poor and destitute youths continued until the early nineteenth century. However, youths who committed serious criminal offenses continued to be treated the same as adults.

Increased urbanization and industrialization led to the belief that certain segments of the population—namely, youths in urban areas and immigrants—were particularly prone to criminal deviance and immorality. The children of these classes were regarded as persons who might be "saved" by state intervention. Such intervention, primarily by middle-class organizations and groups, became the basis of the **child-saving movement**. Wealthy, civic-minded citizens attempted to alleviate the burdens of the unfortunate urban classes and immigrants by sponsoring shelter care for youths, educational and social activities, and the development of settlement houses. Their main focus, however, was on extending government

child-saving movement
Nineteenth-century American reformers who developed programs for troubled youths and influenced legislation creating the juvenile justice system.

control over a whole range of youthful activities that previously had been left to private or family control, including idleness, drinking, vagrancy, and delinquency.[8]

The Child-Saving Movement

Although various legislatures enacted laws giving courts the power to commit children who had committed criminal acts or were runaways or out of the control of their parents, specialized institutional programs were also created. One example was the House of Refuge in New York in 1825.[9] Its aim was to protect youths by taking potential criminals off the streets and reforming them in a family-like environment.

When the House of Refuge opened, the majority of children were admitted because of vagrancy or neglect. The institution was run more like a prison, however, with work and study schedules, strict discipline, and total separation of the sexes. So many children ran away from this harsh program that the House of Refuge was forced to adopt a more lenient approach. Children were placed in the house by court order, sometimes over parental objections, for vagrancy or delinquency. Their stay depended on their needs, age, and work skills. While there, they were required to do piecework provided by local manufacturers or to work part of the day in the community.

Boys on the steps of an abandoned tenement building in New York City, about 1889. The child-savers were concerned that children such as these if left alone would enter a life of crime. Critics accused them of class and race discrimination and thought they sought to maintain control over the political system.

The Granger Collection, New York, NY

Despite criticisms, the concept enjoyed widespread popularity. In 1826, the Boston City Council founded the House of Reformation for juvenile offenders. Similar reform schools were opened in Massachusetts and New York in 1847.[10] To these schools, which were both privately and publicly funded, the courts committed children found guilty of criminal violations, as well as those beyond the control of their parents. Because the child-saving movement viewed convicted offenders and parents of delinquent children in the same light, they sought to have the reform schools establish control over the children. By training destitute and delinquent children and by separating them from their natural parents and adult criminals, refuge managers believed they were preventing poverty and crime.[11]

The child-savers influenced state and local governments to create increasing numbers of reform schools devoted exclusively to the care of vagrant and criminal youths. State institutions opened in Westboro, Massachusetts, in 1848 and in Rochester, New York, in 1849. Other states soon followed suit—Ohio in 1850, and Maine, Rhode Island, and Michigan in 1860. Children lived in congregate conditions and spent their days working at institutional jobs, learning a trade where possible, and receiving some basic education. They were racially and sexually segregated, discipline was harsh and often involved whipping and isolation, and the physical care was of poor quality.

Some viewed houses of refuge and reform schools as humanitarian answers to poorhouses and prisons for vagrant, neglected, and delinquent youths, but many others disagreed. For example, as an alternative, New York philanthropist Charles Brace helped develop the Children's Aid Society in 1853. Brace's formula for dealing with neglected and delinquent youths was to rescue them from the harsh environment of the city and provide them with temporary shelter and care. He then sought to place them in private homes throughout the nation. This program was very similar to today's foster home programs.

Establishment of the Illinois Juvenile Court: 1899

Multiple choice 6

The influence of the child-savers prompted development of the first comprehensive **juvenile court** in Illinois in 1899. The Illinois Juvenile Court Act set up an independent court to handle criminal law violations by children under 16 years of age, as well as to care for neglected, dependent, and wayward youths. The act also created a probation department to monitor youths in the community and to direct juvenile court judges to place serious offenders in secure schools for boys and industrial schools for girls. The ostensible purpose of the act was to separate juveniles from adult offenders and provide a legal framework in which juveniles could get adequate care and custody. By 1925, most states had developed juvenile courts. The enactment of the Juvenile Court Act of 1899 was a major event in the history of the juvenile justice movement in the United States (see Exhibit 17.1).

juvenile court
A court with original jurisdiction over persons defined by statute as juveniles and alleged to be delinquents or status offenders.

Although the efforts of the child-savers were originally viewed as liberal reforms, modern scholars commonly view them as attempts to control and punish. Justice historians such as Anthony Platt have suggested that the reform movement actually expressed the vested interests of the "ruling class."[12] According to this revisionist view, the reformers applied the concept of parens patriae for their own purposes, including the maintenance of middle- and upper-class values, control of the political system, and a child labor system consisting of lower-class workers with marginal skills.

EXHIBIT 17.1 SHIFTING PHILOSOPHIES OF JUVENILE JUSTICE

Pre-1899	Juveniles treated similarly to adult offenders. No distinction by age or capacity to commit criminal acts.
1899 to 1950s	Children treated differently, beginning with the Illinois Juvenile Court Act of 1899. By 1925, juvenile court acts established in virtually every state.
1950s to 1970s	Recognition by experts that the rehabilitation model and the protective nature of parens patriae had failed to prevent delinquency.
1960s to 1970s	Introduction of constitutional due process into the juvenile justice system. Punishing children or protecting them under parens patriae requires due process of law.
1970s to 1980s	Failure of rehabilitation and due process protections to control delinquency leads to a shift to a crime control and punishment philosophy similar to that of the adult criminal justice system.
Early 1990s	Mixed constitutional protections with some treatment. Uncertain goals and programs. Reliance on punishment and deterrence.
Mid-1990s to 2000	Focus on stemming threat of juvenile crime and expanding options for handling juvenile offenders. Emphasis on "what works" and implementing the best intervention and control programs. Calls for use of the restorative justice model.

Multiple choice 7–8

due process
Constitutional safeguards against arbitrary and unfair state procedures in judicial or administrative proceedings.

The Development of Juvenile Justice

The juvenile court movement quickly spread across the United States. In its early form, it provided youths with quasi-legal, quasi-therapeutic, personalized justice. The main concern was the "best interests of the child," not strict adherence to legal doctrine, constitutional rights, or **due process** of law. The court was paternalistic, rather than adversarial. For example, attorneys were not required. Hearsay evidence, inadmissible in criminal trials, was admissible in the adjudication of juvenile offenders. Verdicts were based on a "preponderance of the evidence," rather than proof "beyond a reasonable doubt," and children were often denied the right to appeal their convictions. These characteristics allowed the juvenile court to function in a nonlegal manner and to provide various social services to children in need.

The major functions of the juvenile justice system were to prevent juvenile crime and to rehabilitate juvenile offenders. The roles of the two most important parts of the system—the juvenile court judge and the probation staff—were to diagnose the child's condition and to prescribe programs to alleviate it. Until 1967, judgments about children's actions and consideration for their constitutional rights were secondary.

Reform Schools Juvenile corrections also underwent considerable change. Early reform schools were generally punitive and based on the concept of rehabilitation or reform through hard work and discipline. In the second half of the nineteenth century, the emphasis shifted from massive industrial schools to the cottage system. Juvenile offenders were housed in a series of small cottages in a compound, each one holding 20 to 40 children. Each cottage was run by "cottage parents," who attempted to create a homelike atmosphere. It was felt that this would be more conducive to rehabilitation than the rigid bureaucratic organization of massive institutions. The first cottage system was established in Massachusetts, the second in Ohio. The system was generally applauded as a great improvement over the industrial training schools. The general movement was away from punishment and toward rehabilitation by implementing complex programs of diagnosis and treatment.

By the 1950s, the influence of such therapists as Karen Horney and Carl Rogers promoted the introduction of psychological treatment in juvenile corrections. Group counseling techniques became standard procedure in most juvenile institutions.

One of the best sources of information on juveniles and the law is the National Center for Youth Law: http://www.youthlaw.org
For an up-to-date list of Web links, see http://www.wadsworth.com/product/0534573053s

Legal Change In the 1960s and 1970s, the U.S. Supreme Court radically altered the juvenile justice system when it issued a series of decisions that established the due process rights of juveniles: *Kent v. United States* (1966), *In re Gault* (1967), *In re Winship* (1970), and *Breed v. Jones* (1975).[13] Figure 17.1 presents a timeline of some of the most important legal cases bringing procedural due process to the juvenile justice system. These and other Supreme Court decisions involving such issues as preventive detention, the death penalty, and search and seizure law are discussed in this chapter.

The post-1970 period also saw an alarming rise in juvenile crime and revealed obvious inequities in the juvenile justice system. In addition to the legal revolution brought about by the Supreme Court, Congress passed the Juvenile Justice and Delinquency Prevention Act of 1974 (JJDP Act) and established the federal Office of Juvenile Justice and Delinquency Prevention (OJJDP).[14] This legislation was enacted to identify the needs of youths and to fund programs in the juvenile justice system. Its main goals were to remove wayward, nondangerous youths from institutions housing delinquents and to remove adolescents from institutions housing adult offenders.

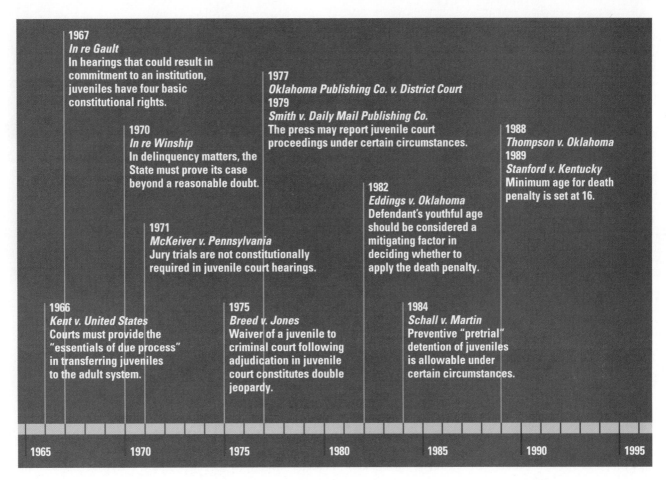

1967
In re Gault
In hearings that could result in commitment to an institution, juveniles have four basic constitutional rights.

1977
Oklahoma Publishing Co. v. District Court
1979
Smith v. Daily Mail Publishing Co.
The press may report juvenile court proceedings under certain circumstances.

1988
Thompson v. Oklahoma
1989
Stanford v. Kentucky
Minimum age for death penalty is set at 16.

1970
In re Winship
In delinquency matters, the State must prove its case beyond a reasonable doubt.

1982
Eddings v. Oklahoma
Defendant's youthful age should be considered a mitigating factor in deciding whether to apply the death penalty.

1971
McKeiver v. Pennsylvania
Jury trials are not constitutionally required in juvenile court hearings.

1966
Kent v. United States
Courts must provide the "essentials of due process" in transferring juveniles to the adult system.

1975
Breed v. Jones
Waiver of a juvenile to criminal court following adjudication in juvenile court constitutes double jeopardy.

1984
Schall v. Martin
Preventive "pretrial" detention of juveniles is allowable under certain circumstances.

1965   1970   1975   1980   1985   1990   1995

FIGURE 17.1

A series of U.S. Supreme Court decisions made juvenile courts more like criminal courts but maintained some important differences.

SOURCE: Howard Snyder and Melissa Sickmund, *Juvenile Offenders and Victims: 1999 National Report* (Washington DC: Department of Justice, Office of Juvenile Justice and Delinquency Prevention, 1999), p. 91.

juvenile delinquency
Commission of an illegal act by a child younger than a statutory age limit.

status offense
Noncriminal behavior, such as truancy and incorrigibility, that falls within the jurisdiction of a juvenile court.

JUVENILE COURT JURISDICTION

The modern juvenile court is a specialized court for children. It may be organized as an independent statewide court system, as a special section of a lower court, or even as part of a broader family court. Juvenile courts are normally established by state legislation and exercise jurisdiction over two distinct categories of juvenile offenders: delinquents and status offenders.[15]

Juvenile delinquency refers to the commission of acts in violation of the penal code by children under a jurisdictional age limit, which varies from state to state. **Status offenses**, on the other hand, include truancy and being habitually disobedient or uncontrollable. State statutes commonly refer to status offenders as persons in need of supervision (PINS) or children in need of supervision (CHINS). Most states distinguish status offenses from delinquency to lessen any stigma resulting from a child's involvement with the juvenile court. In addition, juvenile courts generally have jurisdiction over situations involving conduct directed at (rather than committed by) juveniles, such as parental neglect, deprivation, abandonment, and abuse.

Juvenile court jurisdiction is established by state statute and is based on several factors, the first of which is age. The states have set different maximum ages below which children fall under the jurisdiction of the juvenile court. Many states set the upper limit at 18, others at 17, and still others at 16.

A juvenile court's jurisdiction is also affected by state statutes that exclude certain offenses from its consideration. Based on the premise that the rehabilitative resources and protective processes of the juvenile court are not appropriate

Teens behind bars in Florida. The juvenile justice system can maintain control over delinquent youths or transfer their jurisdiction to the adult court.

in cases of serious criminal conduct, various states have excluded certain offenses, such as those punishable by death or life imprisonment, from the juvenile court's jurisdiction. A more common exclusionary scheme involves transfer provisions, whereby juvenile courts waive jurisdictions to the criminal court (waiver is discussed later in this chapter). Having once obtained jurisdiction over a child, the juvenile court ordinarily retains it until the child reaches a specified age, usually the age of majority.

THE JUVENILE COURT TODAY

The juvenile court is the centerpiece of the juvenile justice system. It plays a major role in controlling juvenile behavior and delivering social services to children in need. Efforts to control juvenile crime depend largely on how the juvenile court is organized and on what laws apply to those who appear before it. In 1997 (the most recent data available), U.S. courts with juvenile jurisdiction handled about 1.8 million cases involving delinquency charges and another 155,000 cases involving status offenses.[16] Figure 17.2 illustrates the place of the juvenile court within the structure of the juvenile justice system.

Over the past century, the juvenile court has been shaped by

- State statutes
- U.S. Supreme Court decisions
- Federal legislation
- Social science theories and programs
- Social trends and problems such as poverty, violence, and single-parent households

It has struggled to provide treatment for juvenile offenders, protect the public, and guarantee juveniles constitutional due process, all at the same time. But the system has been so overwhelmed by the increase in violent juvenile crime and family breakdown that some judges and politicians have suggested abolishing the juvenile system. Almost everywhere juvenile courts are starved for money, record keeping is often primitive, and young offenders often fail to get adequate legal representation.

All the troubles with the juvenile court have sparked a movement to restructure the system. Conservative politicians and lawmakers want laws to allow most

Multiple choice 9
True/False 3–5
Essay 2
Fill in the blanks 5

One group that has struggled to upgrade the juvenile court system is the National Council of Juvenile and Family Court Judges. Learn about this important organization at http://www.ncjfcj.unr.edu

For an up-to-date list of Web links, see http://www.wadsworth.com/product/0534573053s

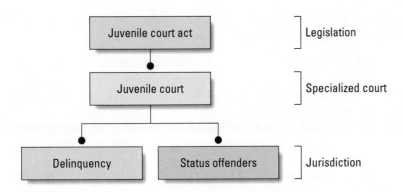

FIGURE 17.2
JUVENILE
JUDICIAL SYSTEM

juveniles charged with serious crimes to be tried in adult courts. Liberal scholars suggest trying some children in adult courts but giving them a lighter sentence depending on their age. Children's advocates suggest that the court scale back its judicial role and transfer its functions to community groups and social service agencies. According to Ira Schwartz, an expert on juvenile justice policy, "What we have now in the juvenile court is chaos, with every state moving piecemeal on its own."[17]

The juvenile court was created and is governed by individual state statutes. Despite the system's limitations, many jurisdictions have at least adequate resources to meet future challenges and goals—to install values and discipline in children, punish and hold them accountable if they commit serious crimes, and then help rehabilitate them. Judge Leonard Edwards of the Santa Clara (California) Superior Court, a former juvenile court judge with extensive experience, believes the juvenile court will remain a critical societal institution because there is no viable alternative. The question is not whether there will be a juvenile court but what form it will take. Changes in court jurisdiction might include

- Elimination of some of the court's delinquency function by transferring more jurisdiction to adult criminal court
- Removal from juvenile court of status offenses
- Expansion of the court's role over abuse and neglect cases

In addition to these jurisdictional trends, other major recommendations are

- Restructuring the juvenile court into a unified family court
- Using alternative dispute resolution (ADR) techniques
- Integrating the juvenile court with the private sector and volunteer resources
- Creating a comprehensive juvenile justice system where there is an appropriate response for each child who comes before the court[18]

PERSPECTIVES ON JUSTICE

What was unique about the original juvenile justice system was its philosophy of protecting children from the criminal law. The development of a personal rapport between the juvenile court judge and the child was particularly significant; courts considered what was best for the child, often filing no formal charge against the child. Because the parens patriae philosophy ignored legal procedures used in the adult justice system, the rehabilitative perspective lost support and the juvenile court became a court of law. Today, the juvenile justice system is using many different programs, policies, and perspectives to solve the juvenile crime problem, including the due process, crime control, and rehabilitative perspectives.

POLICE PROCESSING OF THE JUVENILE OFFENDER

To find the latest facts and figures on juvenile justice, delinquency prevention, and violence and victimization, contact the Juvenile Justice Clearinghouse at http://www.ojjdp.ncjrs.org/facts/facts.html

For an up-to-date list of Web links, see http://www.wadsworth.com/product/0534573053s

For the past several years, about 2.7 million youths under 18 years of age have been arrested each year.[19] The total number of juvenile arrests is no longer growing, but juvenile arrests for violent crimes are continuing to climb, and arrests for drug offenses are increasing once again.

When a juvenile is found to have engaged in delinquent or incorrigible behavior, police agencies are charged with the decision to release or to detain the child and refer him or her to juvenile court. This discretionary decision—to release or to detain—has been found to be based not only on the nature of the offense but also on police attitudes and the child's social and personal conditions at the time of the arrest. The following is a partial list of factors believed to be significant in police decision making regarding juvenile offenders:

- The type and seriousness of the child's offense
- The ability of the parents to be of assistance in disciplining the child
- The child's past contacts with police
- The degree of cooperation obtained from the child and parents and their demeanor, attitude, and personal characteristics
- Whether the child denies the allegations in the petition and insists on a court hearing

The police may adjust a case by simply releasing the child at the point of contact on the street, giving an official warning and releasing the offender to the parents at the station house or the child's home, or referring the child to a social services program. Generally, cases involving violence and serious property offenses are most often referred to court. On the other hand, police often attempt to divert from court action minor disputes between juveniles, school and neighborhood complaints, petty shoplifting cases, runaways, and ungovernable children. Because of the state's interest in the child, the police generally have more discretion in the investigatory and arrest stages of the juvenile process than they do when dealing with adult offenders.

School Searches

Once a juvenile has been taken into custody, the child has the same Fourth Amendment right to be free from unreasonable searches and seizures as an adult does. A major current issue of search and seizure in juvenile law is the right of school officials to search students and their possessions on school grounds. School

Children in police custody can be detained prior to trial, interrogated, and placed in lineups. However, because of their youth and inexperience, children are generally afforded more protection than that given adults. Police must make sure they understand their constitutional rights before talking to them and, in most cases, will have a parent or guardian present to protect their interests.

© Sherman Zent/Palm Beach Post

Multiple choice 10–11

officials often assume quasi-police powers over children. They may search students to determine whether they are in possession of contraband, such as drugs or weapons; search their lockers and desks; and question them about illegal activities. Such actions are comparable to the acts of the regular police.

In *New Jersey v. T.L.O.* (1985), the U.S. Supreme Court held that a school official had the authority to search a student's purse, even though no warrant was issued and there was no probable cause that a crime had been committed, only a suspicion that T.L.O. had violated school rules.[20] This important case involved an assistant principal's search of the purse of a 14-year-old student observed smoking a cigarette in a school lavatory. The search was prompted when the principal found cigarette rolling papers as the pack of cigarettes was removed from the purse. A further search revealed marijuana and several items indicating marijuana selling; as a result, T.L.O. was adjudicated as a delinquent. The Supreme Court held that the Fourth Amendment protections against unreasonable searches and seizures apply to students but that the need to maintain an orderly educational environment modified the usual Fourth Amendment requirements of warrants and probable cause. Thus, the court relaxed the usual probable cause standard and found the search to be reasonable.[21] It declared that the school's right to maintain discipline on school grounds allowed it to search students and their possessions as a safety precaution. Thus the Court, which had guarded the warrant requirement and its exceptions in the past, now permits warrantless searches in school, based on the lesser standard of "reasonable suspicion." This landmark decision did not deal with other thorny issues, however, such as the search and seizure of contraband from a student's locker or desk.

Faced with increased crime by students in public schools, particularly illicit drug use, school administrators today are prone to enforce drug control statutes and administrative rules.[22] Some urban schools are using breathalyzers, drug-sniffing dogs, hidden video cameras, and routine searches of students' pockets, purses, lockers, and cars.[23] In general, courts consider such searches permissible when they are not overly offensive and where there are reasonable grounds to suspect that the student may have violated the law.[24] School administrators are walking a tightrope between a student's constitutional right to privacy and school safety.

In 1995, the U.S. Supreme Court held that public school athletes in middle and high school may be required to submit to random drug testing without violating their Fourth Amendment rights. James Acton, a seventh-grader, was kept off a football team because his parents refused to sign a urinalysis consent form. In *Vernonia School District v. Acton* (1995), the Court held that such testing is constitutional even though the student does not engage in suspicious behavior. This type of case represents the contemporary dilemma of the nation's drug scourge versus privacy rights. It remains for future Court decisions to indicate how far the state may go in curbing school crime before privacy rights are violated.[25]

Juveniles and the *Miranda* Decision

True/False 6

Another issue related to the exclusion of evidence in juvenile matters is the use of statements made by juvenile offenders to police officers. In the past, police often questioned juveniles in the absence of their parents or an attorney. Any incriminatory statements or confessions made by juveniles could be placed in evidence at their trials. The *Miranda* warning, which lists the adult defendant's Fifth Amendment rights against self-incrimination, has now been made applicable to children.[26]

Today, children in the juvenile justice system generally receive almost as much procedural protection as adults tried in criminal court. Exhibit 17.2 lists the basic similarities and differences between the juvenile and adult justice systems; Table 17.1 shows how the language used in the juvenile court differs from that used in the adult system.

EXHIBIT 17.2 SIMILARITIES AND DIFFERENCES BETWEEN JUVENILE AND ADULT JUSTICE SYSTEMS

Similarities

- Discretion used by police officers, judges, and correctional personnel
- Right to receive *Miranda* warning
- Protection from prejudicial lineups or other identification procedures
- Procedural safeguards when making an admission of guilt
- Advocacy roles of prosecutors and defense attorneys
- Right to counsel at most key stages of the court process
- Availability of pretrial motions
- Plea negotiation/plea bargaining
- Right to a hearing and an appeal
- Standard of proof beyond a reasonable doubt
- Pretrial detention possible
- Detention without bail if considered dangerous
- Probation as a sentencing option
- Community treatment as a sentencing option

Differences

- The primary purpose of juvenile procedures is protection and treatment; with adults, the aim is to punish the guilty.
- Jurisdiction is determined by age in the juvenile system, by the nature of the offense in the adult system.
- Juveniles can be apprehended for acts that would not be criminal if committed by an adult (status offenses).

- Juvenile proceedings are not considered criminal; adult proceedings are.
- Juvenile court proceedings are generally informal and private; adult court proceedings are more formal and are open to the public.
- Courts cannot release to the press identifying information about a juvenile, but must release information about an adult.
- Parents are highly involved in the juvenile process but not in the adult process.
- The standard of arrest is more stringent for adults than for juveniles.
- Juveniles are released into parental custody; adults are generally given bail.
- Juveniles have no constitutional right to a jury trial; adults do. Some states extend this right to juveniles by statute.
- Juveniles can be searched in school without probable cause or a warrant.
- A juvenile's record is generally sealed when the age of majority is reached; an adult's record is permanent.
- A juvenile court cannot sentence juveniles to county jails or state prisons, which are reserved for adults.
- The U.S. Supreme Court has declared that the Eighth Amendment prohibits the death penalty for juveniles ages 15 and under, but not for juveniles ages 16 and 17.

TABLE 17.1 COMPARISON OF TERMS USED IN ADULT AND JUVENILE JUSTICE SYSTEMS

	Juvenile Terms	Adult Terms
The Person and the Act	Delinquent child	Criminal
	Delinquent act	Crime
Preadjudicatory Stage	Take into custody	Arrest
	Petition	Indictment
	Agree to a finding	Plead guilty
	Deny the petition	Plead not guilty
	Adjustment	Plea bargain
	Detention facility; child-care shelter	Jail
Adjudicatory Stage	Substitution	Reduction of charges
	Adjudicatory or fact-finding hearing	Trial
	Adjudication	
Postadjudicatory Stage	Dispositional hearing	Sentencing hearing
	Disposition	Sentence
	Commitment	Incarceration
	Youth development center; treatment center; training school	Prison
	Residential child-care facility	Halfway house
	Aftercare	Parole

THE PRETRIAL STAGE OF JUVENILE JUSTICE

After arrest and before trial, the juvenile defendant is processed through a number of important stages of the juvenile justice system. These may include intake, detention, bail, waiver hearing, and diversion programs. Each of these stages and processes is discussed in the following sections.

Fill in the blanks 6
Essay 4

Since its creation, the juvenile justice system has sought to maintain its independence from the adult justice system. Nonetheless, the institutions, processes, and law of the two systems exhibit a number of similarities.

The Intake Process

Fill in the blanks 7
Multiple choice 12

Juveniles coming into contact with the police and juvenile courts can generally be categorized into two major groups: those accused of committing crimes (juvenile delinquency) and those accused of noncriminal behavior (status offenses). Police officers who confront children committing a crime or behaving in a manner that could be dangerous to themselves or others must decide whether the situation warrants court attention or not. Thus, the police exercise a certain amount of discretion in dealing with children. A police officer who decides not to initiate court action may give the child a warning, advise the parents to refer the child to a welfare agency, or refer the child's case to a social agency.

When the police department believes the child needs a court referral, the police become involved in the **intake** division of the court. The term *intake* refers to the screening of cases by the juvenile court system. Intake probation officers review and initially screen the child and the family to determine if the child needs to be handled by the juvenile court. The intake stage is when the child can receive treatment in a most efficient and timely manner. It represents an opportunity to place a child in informal programs both within the court and in the community. The intake process is critically important because more than half of all referrals to the juvenile courts never go beyond this stage.

intake
The screening process in which a juvenile is referred to the juvenile court, referred elsewhere, or released.

Detention

After a juvenile is formally taken into custody, either as a delinquent or as a status offender, a decision is made whether to release the child to the parent or guardian or detain the child in a shelter pending trial. The child is usually released to the parent or guardian. In the past, far too many children were routinely placed in **detention** while awaiting court appearances. Detention facilities were inadequate; in many parts of the country, county jails were used to detain juvenile offenders. The emphasis in recent years has been on reducing the number of children placed in detention, although the practice continues.

detention
Temporary care of a child alleged to be a delinquent or status offender who requires secure custody pending court disposition.

Most state statutes require a hearing on the appropriateness of detention if the initial decision is to keep the child in custody. At this hearing, the child has a right to counsel and may be given other procedural due process safeguards, notably the privilege against self-incrimination and the right to confront and cross-examine witnesses. Most state juvenile court statutes provide criteria to support a decision to detain the child. These include (1) the need to protect the child, (2) whether the child presents a serious danger to the public, and (3) the likelihood that the juvenile will return to court for adjudication.

Essay 5

Whereas in adult cases the sole criterion for pretrial release may be the offender's availability for trial, juveniles may be detained for other reasons, including their own protection. Normally, the finding of the judge that the child should be detained must be supported by factual evidence. When a valid reason for a child's detention has not appeared on the records, courts have mandated release from temporary custody. In the 1984 case of *Schall v. Martin,* the U.S. Supreme

True/False 7
Essay 6

Court upheld the right of the states to detain a child before trial to protect his or her welfare and the public safety.[27]

The use of juvenile detention involves three important issues. The first has been the effort, mostly successful, to remove status offenders from lockups containing delinquents. After decades of effort, almost all states have passed laws requiring that status offenders be placed in shelters rather than detention facilities.

Another serious problem is the detention of youths in adult jails. The practice is quite common in rural areas, where there are relatively few separate facilities for young offenders. Although the federal government, through the OJJDP, has actively supported removing detained youths from adult jails, the practice still continues. In fact, under the JJDP Act, states receiving federal funds were compelled to revise their jail practices and separate juveniles from adults.[28] The OJJDP has given millions of dollars in aid to encourage the removal of juveniles from adult lockups. These grants have helped many jurisdictions develop intake screening procedures, specific release or detention criteria, and alternative residential and nonresidential programs for juveniles awaiting trial. By 1980, amendments to the act mandating the absolute removal of juveniles from jails had been adopted. Despite such efforts, many states are not complying with the removal provisions, and some experts estimate that more than 100,000 youths annually are detained in adult jails.

Eliminating the confinement of juveniles in adult institutions remains a difficult task. In a comprehensive study of the jailing of juveniles in Minnesota, Ira Schwartz and his associates found that even in a state recognized nationally for juvenile justice reform, the rate of admission of juveniles to adult jails remains high.[29] Their research also revealed that the rate of admission is not related to the seriousness of the offense, and that minority-group juveniles are spending greater amounts of time in jail than white offenders for the same offense. Schwartz suggests that

- Government enact legislation prohibiting the confinement of juveniles in jail
- Appropriate juvenile detention facilities be established
- Funds be allocated for such programs
- Racial disparity in detention be examined
- Responsibility for monitoring conditions of confinement be fixed by statutes and court decisions[30]

A third problem is overcrowding caused by a tremendous increase in the number of juveniles detained. The number of youths held in short-term detention facilities has grown significantly since 1995. In addition, the number of minority-group children (African Americans and Hispanics) held in detention facilities has risen more than 30 percent, which has caused considerable concern to juvenile justice practitioners.[31]

Experts believe the steady increase in detention use may result from (1) more serious crime by juveniles; (2) a growing link between juveniles and drug-related crimes; and (3) the involvement of younger children in the juvenile justice system. A declining juvenile crime rate may help reduce these problems.

Bail

If a child is not detained, the question of bail arises. Federal courts have not found it necessary to rule on the issue of a juvenile's constitutional right to bail because

A juvenile detainee confers with a detention officer. Detention centers tend to be overcrowded, and all too often youths are still detained in adult jails, where they may be subject to physical and sexual abuse.

© A. Ramey/Woodfin Camp & Associates

liberal statutory release provisions act as appropriate alternatives. Only a few state statutes allow release on money bail, but many others have juvenile code provisions that emphasize the release of the child to the parents as an acceptable substitute. A constitutional right to bail that on its face seems to benefit a child may have unforeseen results. For example, money bail might impose a serious economic strain on the child's family while simultaneously conflicting with the protective and social concerns of the juvenile court. Considerations of economic liabilities and other procedural inequities have influenced the majority of courts confronting this question to hold that juveniles do not have a right to bail.

True/False 8

Plea Bargaining

A child may plead guilty or not guilty to a petition alleging delinquency. Today, states tend to minimize the stigma associated with the use of adult criminal standards by using other terminology, such as "agree to a finding" or "deny the petition." When the child makes an admission, juvenile court laws and rules of procedure in numerous jurisdictions require the following procedural safeguards:

• That the child knows of the right to a trial
• That the plea or admission is made voluntarily
• That the child understands the charges and consequences of the plea

The same requirements for adult offenders have been established in a series of decisions by the U.S. Supreme Court. Although these standards have not been established by constitutional law for juveniles, they carry equal weight in juvenile cases because the guilty plea constitutes a waiver of the juvenile's Fifth Amendment privilege against self-incrimination.

THE WAIVER OF JURISDICTION

Before the first modern juvenile court was established in Illinois in 1899, juveniles were tried for violations of the law in adult criminal courts. The consequences were devastating; children were treated as criminal offenders and often sentenced to adult prisons. Although the subsequent passage of state legislation creating juvenile courts eliminated this problem, the juvenile justice system did recognize that certain forms of conduct require that children be tried as adults. Today, most jurisdictions provide by statute for **waiver**, or transfer of juvenile offenders to the criminal courts. The decision of whether to waive a juvenile to the adult, or criminal, court is made in a **transfer hearing**.

The transfer of a juvenile to the criminal court is often based on statutory criteria established by the state's juvenile court act, and waiver provisions vary considerably among jurisdictions. The two major criteria for waiver are the age of the child and the type of offense alleged in the petition. For example, some jurisdictions require that the child be over a certain age and be charged with a felony before being tried as an adult. Others permit waiver of jurisdiction to the criminal court if the child is above a certain age, regardless of the offense. Still other states permit waiver under any conditions.

Because of the nature of the waiver decision and its effect on the child in terms of status and disposition, the U.S. Supreme Court has imposed procedural protections for juveniles in the waiver process. *Kent v. United States* (1966), the first major case before the Court on this issue, challenged the provisions of the District of Columbia code, which stated that the juvenile court could waive jurisdiction after a full investigation.[32] The Supreme Court in *Kent* held that the waiver proceeding is a critically important stage in the juvenile justice process, and that juveniles must be afforded minimum requirements of due process of law at such proceedings.

True/False 9
Multiple choice 13–14

waiver
Transfer of a juvenile offender to criminal court for prosecution as an adult.

transfer hearing
A preadjudication hearing in juvenile court to determine whether a juvenile offender should be transferred (waived) to criminal court for prosecution as an adult.

In *Breed v. Jones* (1975), another significant decision on juvenile waiver proceedings, the Supreme Court held that the prosecution of a juvenile as an adult in the California Superior Court, following an adjudicatory proceeding in juvenile court, violated the double jeopardy clause of the Fifth Amendment as applied to the states through the Fourteenth Amendment.[33] The Court concluded that jeopardy attaches when the juvenile court begins to hear evidence at the adjudicatory hearing; therefore, the waiver hearing must take place prior to any adjudication.

True/False 10
Essay 7

Youths in Adult Courts

The problem of youths processed in adult courts is a serious one. An estimated 11,000 juvenile delinquency cases were transferred to criminal court by judicial waiver in 1996 (the most recent data available).[34] Today, all states allow juveniles to be tried as adults in criminal courts in one of three ways:

- *Concurrent jurisdiction.* The prosecutor has the discretion of filing charges for certain offenses in either juvenile or criminal court.
- *Excluded offenses.* The legislature excludes from juvenile court jurisdiction certain offenses that are either very minor, such as traffic or fishing violations, or very serious, such as murder or rape.
- *Judicial waiver.* The juvenile court waives its jurisdiction and transfers the case to criminal court (the procedure is also known as "binding over" or "certifying" juvenile cases to criminal court). All of the states, the District of Columbia, and the federal government have judicial waiver provisions.

Barry Feld, a juvenile law scholar, suggests that waiver to adult court should be mandatory for juveniles committing serious crimes.[35] He argues that mandatory waiver would jibe with popular sentencing policy and eliminate potential bias and disparity in judicial decision making, because it eliminates discretion. In a recent extensive study of legislative changes in juvenile statutes, Feld found that most states rely on the seriousness of the current offense as the major factor in deciding whether to waive a youth to adult court. However, as Feld points out, youths transferred under excluded offenses statutes may not be as criminally responsible as their adult counterparts.[36] Legislatures often transfer large numbers of youth offenders to criminal court by statutorily excluding them from juvenile court jurisdiction.[37] State statutes mandating transfers based on age and offense preclude consideration of the individual circumstances of each case.

> ## PERSPECTIVES ON JUSTICE
>
> The juvenile waiver is the current "hot" issue in handling violent juvenile offenders. Nearly every state has provisions for handling juveniles in adult criminal courts, and the trend is to make waiver broader. Crime control advocates believe that the overriding purposes of the juvenile waiver are protection of the public, deterrence of violent juvenile behavior, and the incarceration of serious youthful offenders in the adult criminal justice system.

The Effect of Waiver

What is accomplished by treating juvenile offenders as adults? Studies of the impact of the recent waiver statutes have yielded inconclusive results.[38] Some juveniles whose cases are waived to criminal court are sentenced more leniently than they would have been in juvenile court. In many states, even when juveniles are tried in criminal court and convicted on the charges, they may still be sentenced to a juvenile or youthful offender institution, rather than to an adult prison. The laws may allow them to be transferred to an adult prison when they reach a certain age. Some studies show that only a small percentage of juveniles tried as adults are incarcerated for periods longer than the terms served by offenders convicted of the same crime in the juvenile court. Moreover, judges tend to sentence 16-year-olds appearing in adult court to probation, rather than prison. In the end, what began as a get-tough measure has had the opposite effect, while costing taxpayers more money.

The findings of a study of juvenile transfers to criminal courts in four states in the 1990s can be summarized as follows:

- Juvenile court judges generally concur with prosecutors as to which juveniles should be transferred to criminal court.
- Transfer criteria used by the court are consistent with common interpretations of the law in that transfer is reserved for the most serious juvenile offenders.
- The juvenile justice system adapts to change in response to the public's concern about the increase in juvenile violence.
- Certain characteristics of the waiver incident (age, weapon use, victim injury, and nature of court history) are critical variables in transfer decision making.[39]

Critics view these new methods of dealing with juvenile offenders as inefficient, ineffective, and philosophically out of step with the original concept of the juvenile court. Supporters view the waiver process as a sound method of getting the most serious juvenile offenders off the streets while ensuring that rehabilitation plays a less critical role in the juvenile justice system. No area of juvenile justice has received more attention recently than efforts to redefine the jurisdiction of the juvenile court.[40]

THE JUVENILE TRIAL

Juvenile courts dispose of an estimated 1,755,000 delinquency cases a year.[41] During the adjudicatory or trial process, often called the *fact-finding hearing* in juvenile proceedings, the court hears evidence on the allegations stated in the delinquency petition.

True/False 11
Multiple choice 15–17

In the early years of its development, the juvenile court did not emphasize judicial rule making similar to that of the criminal trial process. Absent were such basic requirements as the standard of proof, rules of evidence, and similar adjudicatory formalities. Rather, the juvenile system was designed to diagnose and rehabilitate children appearing before the court. The court was seen as social service–oriented; proceedings were to be nonadversarial, informal, and noncriminal.

Gradually, however, the juvenile court movement became the object of much criticism. Juvenile courts seemed unable to rehabilitate juvenile offenders, while at the same time failing to safeguard their constitutional rights. Under the guise of being social service agencies, juvenile courts were punishing children but arguing that constitutional protections were unnecessary because the juveniles were being helped in the name of the state. Under the parens patriae philosophy, the adjudicatory proceedings, as well as subsequent dispositions, were seen as being in the child's best interests. Thus, the philosophy of the juvenile court saw no need for legal rules and procedures, as in criminal process, nor for the introduction of prosecutors or defense attorneys.

These views and practices have been changed by the U.S. Supreme Court. In 1966, with *Kent v. United States,* the Court began to consider the constitutional

A thirteen-year-old sits with his attorneys in juvenile court. Juvenile trials are held before a judge, who weighs the evidence to determine whether there is proof beyond reasonable doubt that the child actually committed the delinquent act.

AP/Wide World Photos

adjudication
The juvenile court hearing at which the juvenile is declared a delinquent or status offender, or no finding of fact is made.

validity of transfer proceedings. This process culminated in the landmark case of *In re Gault* (1967).[42] In *Gault,* the Court ruled that the concept of fundamental fairness is applicable to juvenile delinquency proceedings. The Court held that the due process clause of the Fourteenth Amendment requires certain procedural guarantees in the **adjudication** of delinquency cases.

The *Gault* decision, particularly as it applies to the constitutional right of a juvenile to the assistance of counsel, has completely altered the juvenile justice system. Instead of dealing with children in a benign and paternalistic fashion, the court must process juvenile offenders within the framework of appropriate constitutional procedures. Although *Gault* was technically limited to the adjudicatory stage, it has spurred further legal reform throughout the juvenile system. Today, the right to counsel, the privilege against self-incrimination, the right to treatment in detention and correctional facilities, and other constitutional protections are applied at all stages of the juvenile process, from investigation through adjudication to parole. Because of the importance of the *Gault* case in juvenile proceedings, it is discussed in greater detail in the Law in Review feature.

After *Gault,* the Supreme Court continued its trend toward legalizing and formalizing the juvenile trial process with its decision in *In re Winship* (1970).[43] Relying on the "preponderance of the evidence" standard required by the New York Family Court Act, a judge found Winship, a 12-year-old boy, guilty of the crime of larceny. In reviewing the case, however, the Supreme Court held that the standard of proof beyond a reasonable doubt, which is required in a criminal prosecution, is also required in the adjudication of a delinquency petition.

Although the traditional juvenile court was severely altered by *Kent, Gault,* and *Winship,* the trend of increased rights for juveniles was somewhat curtailed by the Supreme Court's decision in *McKeiver v. Pennsylvania* (1971).[44] In *McKeiver,* the Court held that trial by jury in a juvenile court's adjudicative stage is not a constitutional requirement. This decision does not prevent the various states from granting juveniles a trial by jury as a state constitutional right or by state statute. In the majority of states, however, a child has no such right.

Once an adjudicatory hearing has been completed, the court is normally required to enter a judgment against the child. If found guilty of the allegation, the

LAW IN REVIEW

In re Gault

Facts

Gerald Gault, age 15, was taken into custody by the sheriff of Gila County, Arizona, because a woman complained that he and another boy had made an obscene telephone call to her. At the time, Gerald was under a six-month probation as a result of being found delinquent for stealing a wallet. As a result of the woman's complaint, Gerald was taken to a children's home. His parents were not informed that he was being taken into custody. His mother appeared in the evening and was told by the superintendent of detention that a hearing would be held in juvenile court the following day. On the day in question, the police officer who had taken Gerald into custody filed a petition alleging his delinquency. Gerald, his mother, and the police officer appeared before the judge in his chambers. Mrs. Cook, the complainant, was not at the hearing. Gerald was questioned about the telephone calls and sent back to the detention home, then released a few days later.

On the day of Gerald's release, Mrs. Gault received a letter indicating that a hearing would be held on Gerald's delinquency a few days later. A hearing was held, and again the complainant was not present. No transcript or recording was made of the proceedings. The juvenile officer stated that Gerald had admitted making the lewd telephone calls. Neither the boy nor his parents were advised of any right to remain silent, the right to be represented by counsel, or any other constitutional rights. At the conclusion of the hearing, the juvenile court committed Gerald as a juvenile delinquent to the state industrial school in Arizona for the period of his minority.

This meant that, at the age of 15, Gerald was sent to the state school until he reached the age of 21, unless discharged sooner. The maximum punishment for an adult charged with the same crime was a $50 fine or two months in prison.

Decision

Gerald's attorneys filed a writ of habeas corpus, which was denied by the Superior Court of the state of Arizona. That decision was subsequently affirmed by the Arizona Supreme Court. On appeal to the U.S. Supreme Court, Gerald's counsel argued that the juvenile code of Arizona under which Gerald was found delinquent was invalid because it was contrary to the due process clause of the Fourteenth Amendment. In addition, Gerald was denied the following basic due process rights: (1) notice of the charges with regard to their timeliness and specificity, (2) right to counsel, (3) right to confrontation and cross-examination, (4) privilege against self-incrimination, (5) right to a transcript of the trial record, and (6) right to appellate review.

In deciding the case, the Supreme Court had to determine whether procedural due process of law within the context of fundamental fairness under the Fourteenth Amendment applies to juvenile delinquency proceedings in which a child is committed to a state industrial school. The Court, in a far-reaching opinion written by Justice Abe Fortas, agreed that Gerald's constitutional rights had been violated. Notice of charges was an essential ingredient of due process of law, as were the right to counsel, the right to confront and cross-examine witnesses, and the privilege against self-incrimination. The Court did not answer the questions of appellate review and right to a transcript in this case.

Significance of the Case

The *Gault* case established that a child has the procedural due process constitutional rights listed above in delinquency adjudication proceedings where the child could be committed to a state institution. While recognizing the history and development of the juvenile court, the Court sought to reconcile the motives of rehabilitation and treatment with children's rights. It recognized the principle of fundamental fairness of the law for children as well as for adults.

Although the *Gault* decision was confined to proceedings at the adjudication stage of the juvenile process, it has had a far-reaching impact throughout the entire juvenile justice system. *Gault* initiated the development of due process standards at the pretrial, trial, and posttrial stages of the juvenile process. Judged in the context of today's juvenile justice system, *Gault* redefined the relationships between juveniles, their parents, and the state. It remains the single most significant constitutional case in the area of juvenile justice.

SOURCE: *In re Gault,* 387 U.S. 1; 87 S.Ct. 1248 (1967).

---

child may be declared delinquent or a ward of the court; in some cases, however, judgment may be suspended to avoid the stigma of a juvenile record. Following the entering of a judgment, the court can begin its determination of possible **dispositions** for the child.

disposition
The treatment decision for a juvenile offender, equivalent to the sentencing of an adult.

DISPOSITION AND TREATMENT

Fill in the blanks 8
True/False 12–13

At the dispositional hearing, the juvenile court judge imposes a sentence on the juvenile offender based on his or her offense, prior record, and family background. Normally, the judge has broad discretionary power to issue a range of dispositions, from dismissal to institutional commitment. In theory, the dispositional decision is an effort by the court to serve the best interests of the child, the family, and the community. In many respects, this postadjudicative process is the most important stage in the juvenile court system because it represents the last opportunity for the court to influence the child and control his or her behavior.

Most jurisdictions have statutes that require the court to proceed with disposition following adjudication of the child as a delinquent or status offender. This may be done as part of the adjudicatory process or at a separate dispositional hearing. Statutory provisions that use a two-part hearing process are preferred, because different evidentiary rules apply at each hearing. The basic purpose of having two separate hearings is to ensure that only evidence appropriate to determining whether the child committed the alleged offense is considered in the adjudication. If evidence relating to the presentence report of the child were used in the adjudicatory hearing, it would normally result in a reversal of the court's delinquency finding because it is inadmissible evidence. On the other hand, the social history report is essential for court use in the dispositional hearing. Thus, the two-part hearing process seeks to ensure that the adjudicatory hearing is used solely to determine the merits of the allegations, whereas the dispositional hearing determines whether the child is in need of rehabilitation.

In theory, the juvenile court seeks to provide a disposition that represents an individualized treatment plan for the child. This decision is normally based on a presentence investigation by the probation department, reports from social agencies, and possibly a psychiatric evaluation. The judge generally has broad discretion in dispositional matters but is limited by the provisions of the state's juvenile court act. The prevailing statutory model provides for the following types of alternative dispositions:

- Dismissal of the petition
- Suspended judgment
- Probation
- Placement in a community treatment program
- Commitment to the state agency responsible for juvenile institutional care

In addition, the court may place the child with parents or relatives, make dispositional arrangements with private youth-serving agencies, or order the child committed to a mental institution.

Essay 8

Juvenile Sentencing Reform

Over the past decade, juvenile justice experts and the general public have become aroused about the serious juvenile crime rate in general and about violent acts committed by children in particular. As a result, reformers, especially law enforcement officials and legislators, have demanded that the juvenile justice system take a more serious stand with dangerous juvenile offenders. Many state legislatures have responded by amending their juvenile codes and passing harsh laws. Other jurisdictions have passed mandatory or determinate prison sentences for juveniles convicted of serious felonies. The get-tough approach even allows the use of the death penalty for minors transferred to the adult system.[45]

A second reform movement involves status offenders. This approach suggests that status offenders and other minor juvenile offenders be removed from the juvenile justice system and kept out of institutional programs. With the develop-

Boys in a juvenile institution sit down for their evening meal. Despite efforts to treat delinquents in the community, the institutional population is at an all-time high; more than 100,000 youths are in closed facilities.

ment of numerous diversion programs, many children involved in truancy and incorrigible behavior who would previously have been sent to a closed institution are now being placed in community programs.

A third reform effort emanates from the American Bar Association's development of standards for the juvenile justice system on dispositions, dispositional procedures, juvenile delinquency and sanctions, and corrections administration.[46] The standards recommend that juveniles be given determinate or "flat" sentences without the possibility of parole, rather than indeterminate sentences.

As early as 1977, the State of Washington passed one of the first determinate sentencing laws for juvenile offenders; other states have since adopted similar statutes.[47] All children convicted of juvenile delinquency are evaluated on a point system based on their age, prior juvenile record, type of crime committed, and other factors. Minor offenders are handled in the community. Those committing more serious offenses are placed on probation. Children who commit the most serious offenses are subject to institutional penalties. Institutional officials, who in the past had total discretion on releasing children, now have limited discretion. As a result, juvenile offenders who commit such crimes as rape or armed robbery are being sentenced to institutionalization for two, three, and four years. This approach is sharply different from indeterminate sentencing, under which children who have committed a serious crime may be released from institutions in less than a year if correctional authorities believe they have been rehabilitated.

Of late, many states have developed a system of graduated sentencing sanctions. Graduated sanctions provide a range of options, moving from the least to the most restrictive placement for different offenders. This trend toward comprehensive juvenile justice reform is explored later in this chapter.

In sum, the most popular piece of juvenile crime legislation has been tougher sentences for repeat juvenile offenders of serious and violent crimes (see Exhibit 17.3).

EXHIBIT 17.3 TYPES OF LAWS PASSED TO CRACK DOWN ON JUVENILE CRIME

- **Jurisdictional authority** laws remove increasing numbers of violent juvenile offenders from the juvenile justice system to criminal court prosecution.
- **Sentencing authority** laws give courts new sentencing options.
- **Confidentiality** laws changed traditional juvenile court confidentiality provisions to make records and proceedings more open to the public.
- **Victims' rights** laws increase the role of victims of juvenile crime in the process.
- **Corrections** administrators have developed more programs to hold juveniles accountable for their actions as a result of new transfer and sentencing laws.

Fill in the blanks 9–11
True/False 14–15

Juvenile Probation

The most commonly used formal sentence for juvenile offenders is probation. Many states require that, except for very serious crimes, probation must be tried before a youth is sent to an institution.

Probation involves placing the child under the supervision of the juvenile probation department for the purpose of community treatment. Conditions of probation are normally imposed on the child by either statute or court order. General conditions, such as those that require the child to stay away from other delinquents or to obey the law, are often vague, but they have been upheld by the courts. More specific conditions of probation include requiring the child to participate in a vocational training program, to attend school regularly, to obtain treatment at a child guidance clinic, or to make restitution. Restitution may be in the form of community service; for example, a youth found in possession of marijuana might be required to work 50 hours in a home for the elderly. Monetary restitution requires delinquents to pay back the victims of their crimes. Restitution programs have proven quite successful and have been adopted around the country.[48]

In recent years, some jurisdictions have turned to a *balanced probation* approach in an effort to enhance the success of probation.[49] Probation systems that integrate community protection, the accountability of the juvenile offender, competency, and individualization incorporate the treatment values of this balanced approach. Some of these juvenile protection programs offer renewed promise for community treatment.

Juvenile probation is a major component of the juvenile justice system. Juvenile courts place more than 82 percent of adjudicated delinquents on some form of probation. It is the most widely used method of community treatment. Approximately 550,000 youths are on probation in any given year.[50] The cost savings of community treatment, coupled with its nonpunitive intentions, are likely to keep probation programs growing.

INSTITUTIONALIZATION

The most severe of the statutory dispositions available to the juvenile court involves **commitment** of the child to an institution. The committed child may be sent to a state training school or private residential treatment facility. These are usually minimum-security facilities with small populations and an emphasis on treatment and education. Some states, however, maintain facilities with populations of more than 1,000 youthful offenders.

State statutes vary when determining the length of a child's commitment. Traditionally, many jurisdictions committed the child up to the age of majority, which usually meant age 21. This normally deprived the child of freedom for an extended period of time—sometimes longer than an adult sentenced for the same offense would be confined. As a result, some states have passed legislation under which children are committed for periods ranging from one to three years.

To better handle violent juvenile offenders, some states have created separate or intermediate juvenile systems. Under such statutes, 14- to 17-year-olds charged with certain violent felonies are treated as adults, and if convicted, sentenced to new intermediate prisons, separated from both adult and regular juvenile offenders, for terms of two to five years.[51]

commitment
Decision to place an adjudicated juvenile offender in a correctional facility.

Fill in the blanks 12–14
True/False 16–17
Multiple choice 18–19

Profile of Incarcerated Youth

The most recent available census of juvenile institutions (1997) indicates that about 125,805 young persons were being held in 1,121 public and 2,310 private residential facilities nationwide.[52] Although the typical inmate was a white male, residential placement custody rates for black juveniles were substantially higher than rates for other groups. For every 100,000 non-Hispanic black juveniles in the population, 1,018 were in a residential placement facility; that rate was five times higher than the white incarceration rate of about 200 per 100,000 population. The overall proportion of minorities in the juvenile population in 1997 was 34 percent.

The disproportionate number of minority youths incarcerated may mean that African American, Hispanics, and other minorities are more likely to be arrested and charged with serious crimes than are white youths.[53] However, researchers question whether the seriousness of the offense alone can explain differences in incarceration rates among racial groups. Minority youths are being incarcerated at a far greater rate than their representation in the general population. Some experts believe the overrepresentation of minorities in the nation's juvenile justice corrections system is even greater than previously thought and may be 10 times that of whites in some states. The Juvenile Delinquency Act now requires states to assess disproportionate minority representations and racial issues at any level of the system. Minority representation remains disproportionately high, but it is actually being reduced by federal initiatives that combat racism in the juvenile justice system.

Ninety-five percent of incarcerated juveniles are held for delinquent offenses—offenses that would be crimes if committed by adults. About 35 percent are held for person-oriented offenses; about 20 percent for alcohol, drug, and public order offenses; and more than 40 percent for property crimes.[54] Just over 5 percent are confined for a juvenile status offense, such as truancy, running away, or incorrigibility. The efforts made in recent years to keep status offenders out of institutions seem to have paid off.

The Right to Treatment

The question has been raised as to whether children committed to juvenile institutions have a constitutional or statutory right to **treatment**. Advocates of this right claim that the state must provide treatment for juvenile offenders if it intends to exercise control over them.

Because the system of dealing with juvenile offenders is similar to the system of commitment for the mentally ill, in that both are based on the parens patriae philosophy, juveniles have sought a right to treatment. The case of *Martarella v. Kelly* (1972) established that when juveniles judged to be "persons in need of supervision" are not furnished with adequate treatment, the failure to provide such treatment violates the Eighth and Fourteenth Amendments.[55] In *Inmates v. Affleck* (1972), the federal court recognized the right to treatment on statutory grounds and also required that minimum standards of treatment be implemented for juvenile offenders under institutional care.[56] Similar to *Affleck* was *Morales v. Turman* (1973), where the federal court specifically found that juveniles at a training school in Texas have a statutory right to treatment.[57] In accordance with these holdings, the Seventh U.S. Circuit Court of Appeals in *Nelson v. Heyne* (1974) upheld a constitutional right to treatment for institutionalized juveniles under the Fourteenth Amendment.[58]

The *Nelson* case is significant because it was the first federal appellate court decision to affirm a constitutional right to treatment. Although the U.S. Supreme Court has not yet declared that juveniles have such a right, these decisions seem to indicate that juveniles do have a right, be it statutory or constitutional, to receive

Multiple choice 23–25

treatment
The rehabilitative method, such as therapy or educational or vocational programs, used to effect a change of behavior in the juvenile offender.

treatment and to be assured of a minimum standard of physical care if committed to an institution.

Fill in the blanks 15
True/False 18

Deinstitutionalization

Some experts in delinquency and juvenile law question the policy of institutionalizing juvenile offenders. Many believe that large institutions are too costly to operate and only produce more sophisticated criminals. This dilemma has produced a number of efforts to remove youths from juvenile facilities and replace large institutions with smaller community-based facilities. For example, Massachusetts closed all of its state training schools more than 25 years ago (subsequently, however, public pressure caused a few secure facilities to be reopened). Many other states have established small residential facilities operated by juvenile care agencies to replace larger units.

Despite the daily rhetoric on crime control, public support for community-based programs for juveniles still exists. Although such programs are not panaceas, many experts still recommend more treatment and less incarceration for juvenile offenders. Utah, Maryland, Vermont, and Pennsylvania, for example, have dramatically reduced their reform school populations while setting up a wide range of intensive treatment programs for juveniles. Many large, impersonal, and expensive state institutions with unqualified staff and ineffective treatment programs have been eliminated. Figure 17.3 suggests the range of placement alternatives used for adjudicated youths.

Another problem involves the treatment of status offenders. It has been almost 30 years since the movement to deinstitutionalize status offenders (DSO) began.[59] Since its inception, the DSO approach has been hotly debated. Some have argued that early intervention is society's best hope of forestalling future delinquent behavior and reducing victimization. Others have argued that legal control over status offenders is a violation of youths' rights. Still others have viewed status-offending behavior as a symptom of some larger trauma or problem that requires attention. These diverse opinions still exist today.

The twin concepts of *treatment* and *normalization* form the framework for the DSO approach. Since Congress passed the JJDP Act in 1974, all 50 states have complied with some aspect of the deinstitutionalization mandate. Millions of federal, state, and local dollars have been spent on the DSO movement as a result of the act. Vast numbers of programs have been created around the country to reduce the number of juveniles in secure confinement.

FIGURE 17.3
PLACEMENT
OPTIONS FOR
ADJUDICATED
YOUTHS

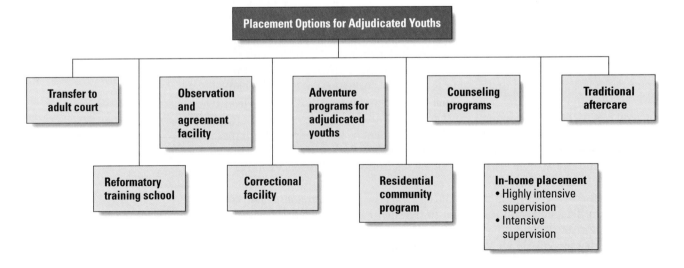

Chronic and Violent Offenders

True/False 19
Multiple choice 20–22

One of the top priorities of recent years has been treating hard-core chronic delinquents while removing nonviolent and noncriminal youths from the juvenile correctional system. Juvenile courts currently concentrate their resources on chronic juvenile offenders—youths who have appeared in court four, five, or six times and are the most likely to continue their law-violating behavior.

A recent study of court careers of juvenile offenders has shed new light on this issue. The study's major finding—that youths who were referred to juvenile court for a second time before age 16 were likely to continue their law-violating behavior—indicates that juveniles may be identified as chronic offenders as early as their second or third offense. Thus, the study suggests that juvenile courts have the opportunity to intervene in the lives of a large number of youths at a time when problems first become apparent. In addition, the study implies that courts should not wait until the youth has returned for the fourth or fifth time before taking strong remedial action.[60]

A related problem is the juvenile court's response to violent youth crime. Violent crime represents a relatively small, though significant, part of a juvenile court's total delinquency caseload. With such offenses as criminal homicides, violent sexual assaults, robberies, and aggravated assaults, the juvenile court detains larger numbers of youths before trial, has more adjudicatory hearings, initiates more transfer petitions to adult courts, and orders significantly more serious dispositions.

A greater percentage of young people are arrested for violent crimes today than 30 years ago, and adolescents 15 years old and younger are involved in more violent behavior than ever before. Much of the increase in youth violence has been linked to drug and gang activities and occurred from 1988 to 1994. Although the soaring violent crime rate has slowed, the level of juvenile violent crime remains unacceptably high.

Chronic and violent juvenile offenders represent a small proportion of the nation's juvenile population but commit a disproportionate amount of juvenile crime. Gun violence, for instance, is on the rise in many areas of the country. More dispositional alternatives aimed at this target population can only increase the effectiveness of the juvenile court system. Others recommend banning handguns, enforcing liquor laws, and keeping children in school. Today's juvenile justice system needs community crime prevention programs as well as punitive measures.

Programs around the country have attempted to use swift prosecution, high-security incapacitation, and intensive treatment to reduce serious juvenile crime.[61] One such program, the Habitual Serious and Violent Juvenile Offender Program, allows prosecutors to target youths defined as chronic, serious, and violent offenders.[62] Undertaken in many jurisdictions, such programs result in speedier outcomes, more findings of guilt, more correctional commitments, and fewer plea bargaining dispositions. These programs suggest that special targeting and prosecution of serious and habitual juvenile offenders may prove successful.

The International Justice feature indicates that violent juvenile crime is also a serious problem in other countries.

POSTDISPOSITION

True/False 20

A juvenile may be released from an institution to serve the rest of the sentence in **aftercare**, or parole. A juvenile parole officer provides the child with counseling, school referral, vocational training, and other services. Children who violate the conditions of parole may have their parole revoked and be returned to the institution.

Unlike the adult postconviction process, where the U.S. Supreme Court has imposed procedural protections in probation and parole revocations, juveniles do

aftercare
Juvenile equivalent of parole, designed to help youths make the transition from residential or institutional settings back into the community; may include counseling, treatment referrals, education, vocational training, or other services.

INTERNATIONAL JUSTICE

Juvenile Violent Crime in Canada

Delinquency is considered a major social problem in the United States. Are other countries plagued by the same problem? Alison Hatch and Curt Griffiths examined the delinquency problem in Canada. Although Canada has a lower overall crime rate than the United States, it has its share of youth problems. Among the types of youth crime emerging in Canada, Hatch and Griffiths found reports of violent, thrill-seeking behavior by middle-class youths. Youth gangs were becoming a problem in large cities, and economic problems have resulted in overrepresentation of minorities in drug abuse cases.

According to Sickmund, Snyder, and Poe-Yamagata, the juvenile arrest rate for violent crime was much higher in the United States than in Canada in 1994. Between 1986 and 1994, however, the juvenile violent crime arrest rate increased more in Canada (105%) than in the United States (66%). During this period, the difference between U.S. and Canadian arrest rates for juveniles diminished. By 1994, although the juvenile crime arrest rate in Canada was only half the U.S. rate, the juvenile property crime arrest rates were relatively similar.

With regard to the justice system, juvenile courts in the United States handle a greater proportion of cases informally than in Canada. This pattern reflects a far greater use of diversion in the U.S. juvenile courts. Canadian courts adjudicated delinquent youths in

65 percent of all formally processed person-oriented cases, compared with 54 percent in the United States. In both countries, about 3 in 10 adjudicated juvenile offenders were placed out of the home; most were placed on probation.

The U.S. juvenile court system transfers cases to a criminal court at 11 times the rate in Canada. Canada has only one path to the criminal court—transfer by a juvenile court judge. In the United States, juveniles may be transferred to criminal court by order of the court, the discretion of a prosecutor, or legislative mandate. The transfer process in the United States has become one of the most important methods used by states to crack down on juvenile crime.

Delinquency is not a problem confined to the United States. Many of the factors that contribute to delinquency— alienation, family problems, and school failure—may also contribute to delinquency in Canada and other industrial nations. The international experience suggests that societies with similar problems may have similar rates of delinquency.

Critical Thinking Skills

1. The American system of juvenile justice is based on U.S. history, culture, and beliefs. Recently, Americans have begun to examine the justice system of other cultures. Do you believe that information available about other juvenile justice systems could assist the United States in dealing with its delinquency problem?

2. Social, cultural, and political variations make it difficult to understand comparative international juvenile justice systems. Similarly, statistical reporting practices limit our understanding of crime data. How do juvenile crime rates reflect political and cultural bias? What factors explain the differences in the juvenile violent crime rate between the United States and Canada?

InfoTrac College Edition Research

How the public perceives crime and justice may contribute to the development of policies and procedures for controlling juvenile and adult crime. To read more about perception of crime in Canada, see Catherine Kaukinen and Sandra LoLavecctia, "Public Perceptions of the Courts: An Examination of Attitudes Toward the Treatment of Victims and Accused," *Canadian Journal of Criminology,* 1999, v41 p365

SOURCES: Alison Hatch and Curt Griffiths, "Youth Crime in Canada: Observations for Cross-Cultural Analysis," *International Journal of Comparative Criminal Justice* 16 (1992): 165–179; Melissa Sickmund, Howard Snyder, and Eileen Poe-Yamagata, *Juvenile Offenders and Victims: 1997 Update on Violence* (Washington DC: U.S. Department of Justice, Office of Juvenile Justice and Delinquency Prevention, 1997), p. 36.

not have such due process rights. State courts have also been reluctant to grant juveniles rights in this area, and those that have generally refuse to grant the whole array of rights available to adult offenders. Since the *Gault* decision, however, many states have adopted administrative regulations requiring juvenile agencies to incorporate due process, such as proper notice of the hearing and the right to counsel, in postconviction proceedings.

Aftercare marks the final stage of the formal juvenile justice process. Its purpose is to help youths make the transition from residential or institutional settings back into the community. Effective aftercare programs provide adequate supervision and support services to help juvenile offenders avoid criminal activity. Examples of programs include electronic monitoring, counseling, treatment and community service referrals, education, work training, and intensive parole supervision.

CURRENT AND FUTURE ISSUES IN JUVENILE JUSTICE

Essay 10

What are the remedies for the current juvenile court system? Some suggest changing the jurisdiction of the juvenile courts. Others want to strengthen the legal rights of juveniles. The vast majority of experts believe there is an urgent need to develop successful dispositional programs. Over the last century, the juvenile court system has been transformed from a rehabilitative to a quasi-criminal court. With limited resources and procedural deficiencies, there is little likelihood of much change in the near future.[63]

A serious crisis exists in the U.S. juvenile justice system. How to formulate new policies and meet the needs of large numbers of children in trouble remains one of the most controversial issues facing the American legal system. The National Juvenile Justice Action Plan of the federal government is a comprehensive response to this critical challenge (see Exhibit 17.4).[64]

For the complete information presented in *Juvenile Offenders and Victims: 1999 National Report,* go to the OJJDP Web site at http://www.ojjdp.ncjrs.org

For an up-to-date list of Web links, see http://www.wadsworth.com/product/0534573053s

Comprehensive Juvenile Justice Reform

At a time when much attention is focused on the small group of serious juvenile offenders, the National Conference of State Legislatures has called for a **comprehensive juvenile justice** strategy to deal with all aspects of juvenile crime. This strategy focuses on crime prevention and expanded options for handling juvenile offenders. Its components include (1) prevention in early childhood; (2) intervention methods for at-risk teenage youths; (3) graduated sanctions to hold juvenile offenders accountable for juvenile crimes; (4) proper utilization of juvenile detention and confinement; and (5) the placement of serious juvenile offenders into adult courts.[65]

comprehensive juvenile justice
A reform model that seeks to combine and balance early childhood prevention, adolescent intervention, graduated sanctions, institutional reform, and judicial waiver for the most serious juvenile offenders.

Early Childhood Prevention Research has identified certain risk factors that may possibly suggest future delinquency. For young children, these factors include abuse and neglect, domestic violence, family conflict, unpreparedness for school, and health problems. Early childhood services may therefore prevent delinquency from occurring and make a child less vulnerable to future criminality. State legislatures are increasingly investing in state-funded early education programs such as Head Start, as a way to reduce juvenile crime, as well as Smart Start, designed to make certain children are healthy before starting school. Home-visiting programs for new parents target families at risk because of child abuse and neglect.

Essay 9

Adolescent Intervention Many jurisdictions are developing new programs for teenage youths. An example of a national program that has been effective is the Big Brother/Big Sister Program, a structured relationship that matches a volunteer adult with a youngster. More and more cities are finding

EXHIBIT 17.4 NATIONAL JUVENILE JUSTICE ACTION PLAN OBJECTIVES

- Provide immediate intervention and appropriate sanctions and treatment for delinquent juveniles.
- Prosecute certain serious, violent, and chronic juvenile offenders in criminal court.
- Reduce youth involvement with guns, drugs, and gangs.
- Provide opportunities for children and youth.
- Break the cycle of violence by addressing youth victimization, abuse, and neglect.
- Strengthen and mobilize communities.
- Support the development of innovative approaches to research and evaluation.
- Implement an aggressive public outreach campaign on effective strategies to combat juvenile violence.

SOURCE: Sarah Ingersoll, "The National Juvenile Justice Action Plan," *Juvenile Justice* 2 (1997): 11.

that night curfews can also reduce gang violence and vandalism. Curfews may also contribute to a feeling of safety among residents of high-crime neighborhoods. The actual impact of curfew laws on juvenile crime control is hard to document, however, and more research is needed to determine their effectiveness. Efforts are also being made to deter young people from becoming involved with gangs. Gang members ordinarily have higher rates of serious violent behavior.

Graduated Sanctions Graduated sanction programs for juveniles are another solution being explored by states across the country. Types of graduated sanctions include (1) immediate sanctions for nonviolent offenders; (2) intermediate sanctions, which target repeat minor offenders and first-time serious offenders; and (3) secure care, which is reserved for repeat serious offenders and violent offenders. (See, for example, the Indiana Juvenile Corrections Placement Matrix, shown in Table 17.2.) A survey of more than 3,000 intervention programs found that about 425 of them demonstrated success in juvenile treatment and control.[66] As a result, states have considerable information available on which to base comprehensive graduated sanctions.

Institutional Reform Many experts believe that juvenile incarceration is overused, particularly for nonviolent offenders. The Juvenile Justice and Delinquency Act of 1974 established the principle of deinstitutionalization. Considerable research suggests that warehousing juveniles without proper treatment does little to deter future delinquent and criminal behavior. The most effective secure detention and corrections programs are those that provide individual services for a small number of participants. Large training schools have not reduced recidivism.

Judicial Waiver Treating juveniles as adults is the final component of an overall strategy for juvenile justice. At issue here are the number and types of juvenile cases going to adult courts. Little is known about what happens to juveniles sent to criminal courts. In the meantime, new laws have expanded the pool of cases eligible for judicial waiver. As a result, more juvenile offenders are being sentenced as adults and incarcerated in adult prisons.

TABLE 17.2 INDIANA JUVENILE CORRECTIONS PLACEMENT MATRIX

	Risk Level		
Severity of Offense	**High**	**Medium**	**Low**
Violent Offenses	Violent offender program Assaultive sex offender program Staff secure residential	Violent or sex offender program Staff secure residential	Boot camp Intermediate sanctions program
Serious Offenses	Boot camp Staff secure residential Job corps Intermediate sanctions program	Intermediate sanctions program	Intermediate sanctions program Day treatment Specialized group home
Less Serious Offenses	Intermediate sanctions program Day treatment Specialized group home	Proctor program Tracking Community service	Community supervision Community service Mentors
Minor Offenses	Proctor program Tracking Community supervision	Community supervision Mentors	Mentors

SOURCE: Indiana Department of Corrections.

Getting tough on juvenile crime is the primary motivation for moving cases to the adult criminal justice system. Some commentators argue that transferring juveniles is a statement that juvenile crime is taken seriously by society; others believe the fear of being transferred will serve as a deterrent. Whatever the stated purpose of moving cases to the adult court, more research is needed to substantiate the claim that the transfer process reduces crime and to determine what role it should play in a comprehensive crime control strategy.[67]

Ongoing Juvenile Justice Issues

Beyond reform of the juvenile court system, what are some of the major programs affecting juvenile justice today?

 The Office of Juvenile Justice and Delinquency Prevention (OJJDP) is a branch of the U.S. Department of Justice charged with shaping national juvenile justice policy. Explore their Web site at http://www.ojjdp.ncjrs.org

For an up-to-date list of Web links, see http://www.wadsworth.com/product/0534573053s

Parental Responsibility Statutes   Related to the get-tough philosophy about juvenile crime are new laws that hold parents criminally and civilly responsible for the crimes of their children. The goal of these statutes is to prevent juvenile crime by requiring parents to be more accountable for their children. Some laws also require parents to participate with the juvenile in counseling programs or community service work.

Privacy of Juvenile Records   For most of the twentieth century, juvenile records were kept confidential by case law or statute. The general rule was that juvenile court records—both legal and social—were considered confidential and thus inaccessible. Today, however, the record itself or the information contained in it can be opened by court order in many jurisdictions on the basis of statutory exception.

Many states have enacted laws authorizing a central repository for juvenile arrest records. Some states allow a juvenile adjudication for a criminal act, such as rape, to be used as evidence in a subsequent adult criminal proceeding for the same act to show predisposition or criminal nature. In addition, a juvenile's records may be used during the disposition or sentencing stage of an adult criminal trial in some states.

Juvenile Gun Violence   Easy availability of guns is a significant contributor to teen violence. Research indicates a close tie between gun use, control of drug markets, and teen violence. Gang-related homicides almost always involve firearms. Unless significant efforts are made to control the spread of handguns, teenage murder rates should continue to rise.

At least 35 states have adopted legislation dealing with guns and children. Nineteen states have passed laws requiring schools to expel or suspend students for possessing weapons on school grounds.[68] Federal laws now restrict the possession, sale, and transfer of guns to juveniles. The Gun-Free Schools Act of 1994 requires local educational agencies receiving financial assistance to expel for one year any student who brings a firearm to school. The Youth Handgun Safety Act (part of the Omnibus Violent Crime Control and Law Enforcement Act of 1994) prohibits the possession or private transfer of a handgun to a juvenile. Although this legislation was enacted by the federal government, it is the state and local officials who can deal most effectively with juvenile gun violations.

Gang Reemergence   Juvenile gangs have become a serious and growing problem in many major metropolitan areas throughout the United States. Ethnic youth gangs, consisting mostly of males ages 14 to 21, appear to be increasing in areas such as Los Angeles, Chicago, Boston, and New York. National surveys of gang activity estimate a total of about 670,000 gang members in the United States, belonging to about 25,000 gangs, up sharply over the last 20 years.[69]

One view of gang development postulates that such groups serve as a bridge between adolescence and adulthood in communities where adult social control is not available. Another view suggests that gangs are a product of lower-class social disorganization and that they serve as an alternative means of economic advancement for poorly motivated and uneducated youths. Today's gangs are often commercially rather than culturally oriented, and the profit motive may be behind increasing memberships. States predict rapid growth in gangs when the current adolescent population matures and limited job opportunities encourage gang members to prolong their involvement in illegal activities. Two basic methods are used to control gang activity: (1) priority targeting by law enforcement and (2) implementation of a variety of social service programs.

SUMMARY

The juvenile justice system is concerned with delinquent children, as well as with those who are beyond the care and protection of their parents. Juveniles involved in antisocial behavior come under the jurisdiction of juvenile or family court systems. These courts belong to a system of juvenile justice agencies, including law enforcement, child care, and institutional services.

When a child is brought to the juvenile court, the proceedings are generally nonadversarial and informal. Representatives from different disciplines, such as lawyers, social workers, and psychiatrists, all play major roles in the judicial process.

In recent years, the juvenile court system has become more legalistic as U.S. Supreme Court decisions have granted children procedural safeguards. However, neither rehabilitation programs nor the application of due process rights has stemmed the growing tide of juvenile antisocial behavior. Perhaps the answer lies outside the courthouse in the form of job opportunities for juveniles, improved family relationships, and more effective school systems. How to cope with the needs of children in trouble remains one of the most controversial and frustrating issues in the justice system.

In the immediate future, the goals of the juvenile justice system are likely to be (1) reorganization of the juvenile system; (2) increased use of the juvenile waiver; (3) development of intermediate juvenile systems to handle violent offenders; and (4) tougher sentences. The comprehensive juvenile justice strategy to reduce youth violence discussed in this chapter may be the most appropriate response to juvenile crime.

Key Terms

juvenile justice system	juvenile delinquency	disposition
parens patriae	status offense	commitment
balanced and restorative justice model	intake	treatment
poor laws	detention	aftercare
child-saving movement	waiver	comprehensive juvenile justice
juvenile court	transfer hearing	
due process	adjudication	

Discussion Questions

1. Should status offenders be treated by the juvenile court? Should they be placed in confinement for running away or cutting school?
2. Should a juvenile ever be waived to adult court if the juvenile might be incarcerated with adult felons?
3. Do you support the death penalty for juveniles?
4. Should juveniles be given mandatory incarceration sentences for serious crimes, as adults are?
5. Is it fair to deny juveniles a jury trial?
6. Do you think the trend toward treating juveniles like adult offenders is desirable?

A CLOSER LOOK

Barry C. Feld raises the issue of whether a separate juvenile justice system is still needed. Considering the arguments for and against the abolition of the juvenile court, he notes that modern-day juvenile courts have grown increasingly indistinguishable from adult courts. He describes the various procedures enacted by legislatures to impose crime-based rather than individual sanctions on young offenders. No longer is the juvenile court delivering on the promise of rehabilitation. Reflecting on these problems, Feld challenges juvenile justice practitioners to alter the traditional system.

To read more, go to InfoTrac College Edition and look up

Barry C. Feld, "Abolish the Juvenile Court: Youthfulness, Criminal Responsibility, and Sentencing Policy," *Journal of Criminal Law and Criminology,* 1997, v99 p68

Notes

1 Al Koski, "Trial Starts for Michigan Boy Charged with Murder," *Reuters Internet News,* 11 October 1999; also Keith Bradsher, "Boy Who Killed Gets 7 Years," *New York Times,* 14 January 2000, p. 1.

2 Scott Nelson, "Online, A Sucker's Just a Click Away," *Boston Sunday Globe,* 24 September 2000, p. G4.

3 Ralph Weisheit and Diane Alexander, "Juvenile Justice Philosophy and Demise of *Parens Patriae,*" *Federal Probation* 86 (December 1988): 56–64; also Judge Lindsay Arthur, "Abolish the Juvenile Court," *Juvenile and Family Court Journal* 49 (1998): 51–59.

4 Gordon Bazemore, "What's 'New' about the Balanced Approach," *Juvenile and Family Court Journal* 48 (1997): 1–21; see also Office of Justice Programs, *Balanced and Restorative Justice for Juveniles: A Framework for Juvenile Justice in the 21st Century* (Washington, DC: U.S. Department of Justice, Office of Juvenile Justice and Delinquency Prevention [OJJDP], 1997).

5 Material in this section depends heavily on Sanford J. Fox, "Juvenile Justice Reform: A Historical Perspective," *Stanford Law Review* 22 (1970): 1187–1205; Lawrence Stone, *The Family, Sex, and Marriage in England: 1500–1800* (New York: Harper & Row, 1977); Philippe Aries, *Century of Childhood: A Social History of Family Life* (New York: Vintage Press, 1962); Douglas R. Rendleman, *"Parens Patriae:* From Chancer to the Juvenile Court," *South Carolina Law Review* 23 (1971): 205–229; Wiley B. Sanders, "Some Early Beginnings of the Children's Court Movement in England," *National Probation Association Yearbook* (New York: National Council on Crime and Delinquency, 1945); Anthony Platt, "The Rise of the Child-Saving Movement: A Study in Social Policy and Correctional Reform," *Annals of the American Academy of Political and Social Science* 381 (1979): 21–38; Anthony M. Platt, *The Child Savers: The Intervention of Delinquency* (Chicago: University of Chicago Press, 1969); Robert S. Pickett, *House of Refuge: Origins of Juvenile Reform in New York State, 1815–1857* (Syracuse, NY: Syracuse University Press, 1969).

6 4 Eng.Rep. 1078 (1827).

7 Rendleman, *"Parens Patriae,"* p. 209.

8 Platt, *The Child Savers,* pp. 11–38.

9 Fox, "Juvenile Justice Reform," p. 1188.

10 Pickett, *House of Refuge.*

11 Robert Mennel, *Thorns and Thistles* (Hanover, NH: University Press of New England, 1973); also Paul Cromwell, "Quaker Origins of Juvenile Justice Reform," *Juvenile and Family Court Journal* 38 (1987): 9–15.

12 Platt, *The Child Savers,* p. 116.

13 *Kent v. United States,* 383 U.S. 541, 86 S.Ct. 1045, 16 L.Ed.2d 84 (1966); *In re Gault,* 387 U.S. 1, 87 S.Ct. 1428, 18 L.Ed.2d 527 (1967): *In re Winship,* 397 U.S. 358, 90 S.Ct. 1068, 25 L.Ed.2d 368 (1970): *Breed v. Jones,* 421 U.S. 519, 95 S.Ct. 1779, 44 L.Ed.2d 346 (1975).

14 Public Law 93–415 (1974).

15 For a comprehensive view of juvenile law, see, generally, Joseph J. Senna and Larry J. Siegel, *Juvenile Law: Cases and Comments,* 2d ed. (St. Paul, MN: West, 1992).

16 Howard Snyder and Melissa Sickmund, *Juvenile Offenders and Victims: 1999 National Report* (Washington, DC: OJJDP). Hereinafter cited as *Juvenile Offenders and Victims: 1999.*

17 Fox Butterfield, "Justice Besieged," *New York Times,* 21 July 1997, p. A16.

18 The Center for the Future of Children, *The Juvenile Court* (Los Altos, CA: David and Lucille Packard Foundation, 1996).

19 Federal Bureau of Investigation, *Crime in the United States, 1998* (Washington, DC: U.S. Government Printing Office, 1999).

20 469 U.S. 325, 105 S.Ct. 733, 83 L.Ed.2d 720 (1985).

21 See D. A. Walls, "*New Jersey v. T.L.O.:* The Fourth Amendment Applied to School Searches," *Oklahoma University Law Review* 11 (1986): 225–241.

22 K. A. Bucker, "School Drug Tests: A Fourth Amendment Perspective," *University of Illinois Law Review* 5 (1987): 275.

23 M. Meyers, *"T.L.O. v. New Jersey*: Officially Conducted School Searches and a New Balancing Test," *Juvenile Family Journal* 37 (1986): 27–37.

24 J. Braverman, "Public School Drug Searches," *Fordham Urban Law Journal* 14 (1986): 629–684.

25 *Vernonia School District v. Acton,* 515 U.S. 646, 115 S.Ct. 2386, 132 L.Ed.2d 564 (1995).

26 *Miranda v. Arizona,* 384 U.S. 436, 86 S.Ct. 1602, 16 L.Ed.2d 694 (1966). *Miranda* held that accused individuals in police custody must be given the following warning: (1) They have a right to remain silent; (2) any statements made can be used against them; (3) they have a right to counsel; and (4) if they cannot afford counsel, one will be furnished at public expense.

27 *Schall v. Martin,* 467 U.S. 253, 104 S.Ct. 2403, 81 L.Ed.2d 207 (1984).

28 See Juvenile Delinquency and Prevention Act of 1974, 42 U.S.C. § 5633.

29 Ira Schwartz, Linda Harris, and Laurie Levi, "The Jailing of Juveniles in Minnesota," *Crime and Delinquency* 34 (1988): 131–140; also Barry Krisberg and Robert DeComo, *Juveniles Taken into Custody, 1991* (San Francisco: National Council on Crime and Delinquency, 1993), p. 25.

30 See Schwartz, Harris, and Levi, "The Jailing of Juveniles in Minnesota," p. 134.

31 Eugene Rhoden, "Disproportionate Minority Representation: First Steps to a Solution," *Juvenile Justice* 2 (1994): 9–12; see also *Juvenile Offenders and Victims: 1999,* p. 192; and U.S. Department of Justice, *Minorities in the Juvenile Justice System* (Washington, DC: OJJD, 1999).

32 383 U.S. 541, 86 S.Ct. 1045, 16 L.Ed.2d 84 (1966).

33 421 U.S. 519, 528, 95 S.Ct. 1779, 44 L.Ed.2d 346 (1975).

34 *Juvenile Offenders and Victims: 1999,* p. 170.

35 Barry Feld, "Delinquent Careers and Criminal Policy," *Criminology* 21 (1983): 195–212.

36 Barry Feld, "The Juvenile Court Meets the Principle of the Offense: Legislative Changes in Juvenile Waiver Statutes," *Journal of Criminal Law and Criminology* 78 (1987): 126–160; Kristin Choo, "Minor Hardships: Jailing Youths as

Adults Gaining Ground," *American Bar Association Journal* 87(2000): 20.

37 Alan Karpelowitz, *State Legislative Priorities, 1995* (Denver: National Conference of State Legislatures, 1995): 10.

38 Peter Greenwood, *Juvenile Offenders* (Washington, DC: National Institute of Justice, 1986), P. 3.

39 Howard Snyder et al., *Juvenile Transfers to the Criminal Court in the 1990's* (Washington, DC: OJJDP, 2000).

40 Dale Parent et al., *Key Issues in Criminal Justice: Transferring Serious Juvenile Offenders to Adult Courts* (Washington, DC: National Institute of Justice, 1997).

41 Anne L. Stahl, *Delinquency Cases in Juvenile Courts, 1999,* Fact Sheet #4 (Washington, DC: OJJDP, 2000).

42 387 U.S. 1, 87 S.Ct. 1428, 18 L. Ed. 2d 527 (1967).

43 397 U.S. 358, 90 S.Ct. 1068, 25 L.Ed.2d 368 (1970).

44 403 U.S. 528, 91 S.Ct. 1976, 29 L.Ed.2d 647 (1971).

45 Victor Streib, *Death Penalty for Juveniles* (Bloomington: Indiana University Press, 1987); also Paul Reidinger, "The Death Row Kids," *American Bar Association Journal* 70 (April 1989): 78–80; "The Death Penalty and the 8th Amendment: An Analysis of *Stanford v. Kentucky,*" *Yale Law Review* 35 (1990): 641.

46 Stanley Fisher, "The Dispositional Process under the Juvenile Justice Standards Project," *Boston University Law Review* 57 (1977): 732–760. See also American Bar Association, *Juvenile Justice Standards Project* (Chicago: IJA/ABA, 1980); this is a set of 23 volumes aimed at improving the juvenile justice system.

47 A. Schneider and D. Schram, *Assessment of Juvenile Justice Reform in Washington State,* vols. 1–4 (Washington, DC: U.S. Department of Justice, Institute of Policy Analysis, 1983); T. Castellano, "Justice Model in the Juvenile Justice System:

Washington State's Experience," *Law and Policy* 8 (1986): 479–486.

48 Anne Schneider, *Guide to Juvenile Restitution* (Washington, DC: U.S. Department of Justice, 1985).

49 Dennis Mahoney, Dennis Romig, and Troy Armstrong, "Juvenile Probation: The Balanced Approach," *Juvenile and Family Court Journal* 39 (1988): 26–36. See also Ted Palmer and Robert Wedge, "California's Juvenile Probation Camps: Findings and Implications," *Crime and Delinquency* 35 (1989): 234–240; National Council on Crime and Delinquency, *Juvenile Intensive Probation Programs: The State of the Art* (San Francisco: National Council on Crime and Delinquency, 1991).

50 *Juvenile Offenders and Victims: 1999,* p. 159.

51 "Colorado OKs New Way to Handle Violent Juvenile Offenders," *Criminal Justice Newsletter* 9 (1993): 4.

52 *Juvenile Offenders and Victims: 1999,* p. 190.

53 U.S. Department of Justice, *Minorities in the Juvenile Justice System* (Washington, DC: OJJDP, 1999).

54 Melissa Sickmund, Howard Snyder, and Eileen Poe-Yamagata, *Juvenile Offenders and Victims: 1997 Update on Violence* (Washington, DC: OJJDP, 1997), p. 18.

55 349 F.Supp. 575 (S.D. N.Y. 1972).

56 346 F.Supp. 1354 (D. R.I. 1972).

57 364 F.Supp. 166 (E.D. Tex.1973).

58 491 F. 2d 352 (7th Cir. 1974).

59 National Conference of State Legislatures, *A Legislator's Guide to Comprehensive Juvenile Justice, Juvenile Detention, and Corrections* (Denver: National Conference of State Legislators, 1996).

60 Office of Juvenile Justice and Delinquency Prevention, "Study Sheds New Light on Court Careers of Juvenile Offenders," *Juvenile Justice Bulletin,* August 1988, p. 1; also Grant Grissom, "Disposi-

tional Authority and Future of the Juvenile Justice System," *Juvenile and Family Court Journal* 42 (1991): 25–30.

61 Mark Lipsey, David Nilson, and Lynn Cuthern, *Effective Intervention for Serious Juvenile Offenders* (Washington, DC: OJJDP, 2000).

62 American Institute for Research, *Evaluation of the Habitual Serious and Violent Juvenile Offender Program* (Washington, D.C.: OJJDP, 1988); see also U.S. Department of Justice, Office of Juvenile Justice and Delinquency Prevention, "Targeting Serious Juvenile Offenders Can Make a Difference," *Juvenile Justice Bulletin,* December 1988, pp. 1–10; Patricia Torbet and Howard Snyder, "Juvenile Violence: A New Perspective Today," *Juvenile and Family Justice* 7 (1998): 8–9.

63 Fox Butterfield, "Justice Besieged: Two Part Series on Juvenile Courts," *New York Times,* 21 and 22 July 1997, p. A1.

64 Sarah Ingersoll, "The National Juvenile Justice Action Plan," *Juvenile Justice* 2 (1997): 11–21.

65 National Conference of State Legislatures, *A Legislator's Guide to Comprehensive Juvenile Justice, Juvenile Detention, and Corrections,* p. 1.

66 James Howell, ed., *Guide for Implementing the Comprehensive Strategy for Serious, Violent, and Chronic Juvenile Offenders* (Washington DC: OJJDP, 1995).

67 James Howell, *Youth Gang Programs and Strategies: U.S. Department of Justice* (Washington, DC: OJJDP, 2000).

68 Office of Justice Programs, *Reducing Youth Gun Violence* (Washington DC: OJJDP, 1996).

69 Carol J. DeFrances and Kevin Strom, *Juveniles Prosecuted in State Criminal Courts* (Washington DC: Bureau of Justice Statistics, 1997).

CAREERS IN CRIMINAL JUSTICE

The criminal justice system provides numerous career opportunities. Some people who choose the field are motivated by the desire to help people and do social service work. Others are more interested in law enforcement and policing, and some choose teaching and research. Others want to supplement their criminal justice education with legal studies to take on the role of defense counsel, prosecutor, or magistrate. Of course, some enterprising people are able to take on a number of these endeavors at various times during their criminal justice career: A police officer might earn a doctorate and go into teaching; a probation officer might go to law school and become a prosecutor; a professor might be appointed head of a state corrections department; and so on. Let us now examine some of the specialties within the field of criminal justice to get an idea of some of these career alternatives.

Law Enforcement

More than half a million people are employed in policing and law enforcement in the United States at the municipal, county, state, and federal levels.

The majority of people in law enforcement work for city police departments. The work of the patrol officer, traffic cop, and detective is familiar to anyone who watches television or goes to movies (although the accuracy of the portrayal by those entertainment vehicles is highly suspect). Beyond these familiar roles, however, police work also includes a great many administrative and service jobs, such as officer training, communications, records management, purchasing, and so on. Salaries in municipal police agencies are competitive and entry-level officers earn in the vicinity of $25,000. However, larger cities may offer higher starting salaries and provide a full range of benefits. For example, the Dallas police department has the following pay scales:

Trainee	$33,382–$34,582
Apprentice	$33,716
Probationary Status	$34,053
Starting salary	$36,002
after 2 years	$37,802
after 3 years	$39,692
after 5 years	$41,677

after 7 years	$43,760
after 9 years	$45,948
after 11 years	$48,246
after 13 years	$50,658
after 15 years	$53,191
Senior Corporal	
Starting salary	$37,022
after 14 years	$59,643
(5% step increases at the 2, 4, 6, 8, 10, 12, 14 year anniversary)	
Sergeant	
Starting salary	$42,528
after 10 years	$64,225
Lieutenant	
Starting salary	$46,672
after 8 years	$70,349

In addition, officers can get salary increases for completing college courses and becoming language specialists. In Massachusetts, salaries start at about $30,000 a year. However, under the Quinn Bill, if police officers earn an undergraduate degree, they get an extra 20 percent on their base pay; a master's or law degree increases their starting pay by 25 percent. Overtime and special detail pay can add to this sum. It is not uncommon for uniformed police officers to top $100,000 in a single year.

Civilian Employees   In addition to sworn personnel, many police agencies hire civilian employees who bring special skills to the department. For example, it is common in the computer age for departments to employ information resource managers who are charged with improving data processing; integrating the department's computer information database with others in the state; operating computer-based fingerprint identification systems and other high-tech investigation devices; and linking with national computer systems such as the FBI's national crime information system, which holds the records of millions of criminal offenders.

State and County Law Enforcement   In addition to city police agencies, state and county governments also provide career opportunities in law enforcement. The state police and county sheriff's department do much the same work as city police agencies—traffic, patrol, and investigation—depending on their area of jurisdiction. These agencies commonly take on a greater law enforcement role in more rural areas and provide ancillary services, such as running the local jail or controlling traffic, in urban centers. State agencies also hire investigators as part of their enforcement mandate. For example, the California Department of Insurance employs fraud investigators to conduct felony investigations of insurance fraud and related statutes. They also employ property controllers to handle property seized in investigations of insurance fraud. Similarly, the California Division of Consumer Affairs employs investigators to enforce rules and regulations relating to consumer protection. State investigators carry out many of the tasks of other law enforcement officers, including serving warrants, making arrests, and conducting undercover investigations.

Federal Law Enforcement   The federal government also employs thousands of law enforcement personnel in such agencies as the Federal Bureau of Investigation, the Drug Enforcement Agency, the Secret Service, and so on. These agencies are often considered the elite of the law enforcement profession, and standards for entry are quite high. The duties of these federal agencies include upholding federal laws controlling counterfeiting, terrorism, espionage, bank robbery, and importation and distribution of controlled substances, among others.

Private Security   The field of private security also offers many career opportunities. Some positions are in large security companies, such as Pinkerton or Wackenhut. Others are in company security forces, such as those maintained by large retail chains, manufacturing companies, and railroads. Public institutions such as hospitals, airports, and port facilities also have security teams. For example, large retail chains typically employ loss prevention agents who are responsible for the protection of company assets.

Other private companies maintain their own enforcement branches. Insurance firms hire field investigators to determine the origin and cause of accidents, fires, and other events for which the company is liable. Insurance investigators also handle claims in which client fraud is suspected.

These are but a few of the many careers in law enforcement. Table A provides a more complete list of opportunities.

Starting a Career in Law Enforcement

What are the best ways to begin a career in law enforcement? Plan your career as best you can by keeping current on employment trends and job descriptions. Both are available from the Bureau of Labor Statistics at their Employment Projections Site and their Occupational Outlook Handbook site, where you can find the fastest growing jobs in the nation (a frequently requested table). Look at state-by-state analyses, and avoid states where there have been cutbacks in law enforcement (or courts and correctional agencies). Make use of the Career Services center at your local college or library. Utilize the people you know: faculty, alumni, fellow students, and professionals. Trade magazines can be informative. Attend a professional association meeting such as the Academy of Criminal Justice Sciences (ACJS). Consider joining one of these or other professional associations (as a student member with reduced fees) as their newsletters will be invaluable to you. Subscribe to Internet discussion groups and post questions. There are also monthly newsletters that list jobs (although they require a fee):

Public Safety Recruitment
802 Maple St.
East Jordan, MI 49727
1-800-880-9018

Police Career Digest
P.O. Box 7772, Dept. GA
Winter Haven, FL 33883
1-800-359-6260

Try to be as certain as you can about what's important to you on the job; for example, geographic location, freedom, pay, security, praise, promotion, chances to learn, chances to do something worthwhile.

Choosing a Particular Career Option Each level of government (federal, state, county, local) has its own benefits and costs, and all the different job titles have different pay grades. Federal and state jobs have the most pay and prestige, but you will almost certainly have to relocate. Here are some entry-level minimums to make sure you don't sell yourself short:

Federal jobs should start at at least $33,000
State jobs should start at at least $27,000
County jobs should start at at least $22,000
City jobs should start at at least $24,000

Try to maximize your salary potential by choosing large agencies with lots of job titles, especially civilian ones. Big cities are your best bet, but bigger is not necessarily better in some cases. Expect to start out no less than $24,000 in a metropolitan department, and as high as $38,000 in others.

Getting Prepared for a Career in Law Enforcement
The ten steps to getting an appointment include: (1) application, (2) entrance exam, (3) physical testing, (4) medical examination, (5) interview, (6) psychological testing, (7) background check, and *after* appointment (8) academy training, (9) field training, and (10) civil service exam (for promotional purposes).

Steps 3 and 4 are the most critical in terms of general preparation. Find a sport or exercise regimen that you are comfortable with and develop your physical fitness. Fitness is one of the most important criteria for

TABLE A LAW ENFORCEMENT JOB TITLES

Arson investigator	Instructor
Attache/police liaison officer	Intelligence analyst
	Investigator
Ballistics expert	Jailer
Booking officer	Juvenile specialist
Border patrol agent	K-9 handler
Chaplain	Lawyer
Chief of police	Law enforcement planner
Chief of staff	Law enforcement representative
Commander	
Commissioner	Manpower allocation specialist
Communications specialist	
Community policing officer	Narcotics officer
Community safety officer	Patrol officer
Community service officer	Personnel specialist
Conservation officer	Photographer
Crime prevention specialist	Pilot
Crime lab technician	Polygraph examiner
Crime scene technician	Psychologist/psychiatrist/ psychometrician
Customs agent	
Data processing specialist	Public relations officer
Deputy chief	Public safety director
Deputy sheriff	Radio communications
Detective	Records management
Detention officer	School liaison
Document examiner	Scientist
Director of research/development	Secret service
	Security specialist
Director of scientific services	Serologist
	Sheriff
Director of standards and training	Street crimes investigator
	Superintendent
Dispatcher	S.W.A.T. officer
Drug enforcement agent	T.A.C. officer
EMS coordinator	Technologist
Evidence technician	Traffic analyst
FBI special agent	Trainer
Fingerprint expert	Treasury agent
Firearms instructor	Trooper
Forensic scientist	Undercover operative
Gaming enforcement officer	Undersheriff
	U.S. marshal
Gang crimes investigator	Water patrol officer
Inspector	Witness protection

obtaining a job in criminal justice, and you can't achieve it overnight. Plan to impress employers with your stamina and strength. Here are some of the tougher (federal) standards:

Pull-ups (palms out) average 10, maximum 25 in 1 minute
Sit-ups (alt.) average 70, maximum 100 in 1 minute
Push-ups average 40, maximum 85 in 1 minute

300-yd run average 60 sec, maximum 50 sec
2-mile run average 12 min, maximum 10 min

If you have any kind of functional or organic disorder such as high blood pressure, high cholesterol level, smoking status, drug use, diabetes, or epilepsy, it becomes the duty of your medical examiner to qualify or disqualify you. If you smoke, stop, since recently quitting tobacco is not held against you. If you used drugs (including alcohol abuse, casual use of marijuana, or psychotropic medication), you will be excluded in about 75 percent of agencies. Some will accept the fact you experimented with marijuana as long as it was not prolonged or recent usage, but they are generally not forgiving of the slightest experimentation with hallucinogens, cocaine, and so on. Most agencies will accept corrected vision (no worse than 20/40 uncorrected, but in some cases as bad as 20/100 if at least one eye is correctable to 20/20) but not color blindness or deafness. The Americans with Disabilities Act allows anyone to apply and prohibits any disability-related inquiry prior to a conditional job offer. The job offer will be conditioned on the results of a confidential medical exam, which is used to determine if the department can make reasonable accommodations.

Your criminal history should be clear of felonies and serious misdemeanors (anything punishable by one year or more). Many people have had run-ins with the law sometime in their lives, so most examiners are sympathetic, but expect sympathies and interpretations of what constitutes a "serious misdemeanor" to vary. Above all, don't try to hide anything. In general, agencies are more forgiving the younger you were when the incident occurred. Some agencies still use a "moral turpitude" clause, which includes any sexual offense, indecent liberties, use, sale, or manufacture of any controlled substance, or any offense addressing public morality. The Criminal Records division of the State Police will allow you to look at your record beforehand and assist you with correcting errors, but to wipe something out will more than likely require a petition for expungement with the District Attorney from the jurisdiction where it was recorded. It is a definite plus to have a clean driving record as the time of appointment rolls around. You should also have a clean credit history, or at least no signs of continual poor financial responsibility, such as records of late payments, wage garnishments, or bankruptcy.

Although some jurisdictions have outlawed polygraph evidence in courts of law, most police agencies still rely on it for employment purposes. Try to breathe steadily and act normally; your best bet is to be honest about your past. Some agencies have substituted other types of assessment exercises to get at your honesty and integrity. You may find that someone "accidentally" left his or her wallet in the restroom (to see if you turn it in); you may be asked how serious a colleague's misconduct has to be before you would report him or her; or you may have to address hypothetical scenarios such as if your senior patrol partner disappears into a tavern for over an hour. In general, examiners like it when you show a willingness to be tough and hard, but they also don't like whistle-blowers and snitches.

Anticipate that finding the ideal job will take at least three months of hard work. For this effort, you may have to wait approximately six months to two years before the agency actually hires you. Since some places make you wait as long as two years, you should begin a serious job search sometime in your sophomore or junior year of college. Anything you can do to get your foot in the door or build up some experience (which often substitutes for education) during this waiting period is useful. Does the agency need volunteers? Does it have a police auxiliary or a reserve program? Can you voluntarily attend classes and workshops held at their training center?

Ads and Applications Often, a job ad will appear one day only in a newspaper, usually the Sunday edition. Such ads will usually say respond with a cover letter and résumé, and you should respond in such manner by the required date, but remember that some agencies don't treat you as having technically filed unless you fill out their application form. If a job exists, a document called the "Job Announcement" will list detailed instructions for applicants. Remember that the purpose of filling out an application is to be notified by mail when and where to appear for the entrance examination.

In responding to an ad, your cover letter should be specific to the job advertised, and addressed to an individual, if possible. Keep the cover letter to one page, match your qualifications to any requirements listed in the ad, and strive for a combination of modesty and self-confidence. One- to two-page résumés are sufficient for entry-level positions; three to four pages for management jobs. Education and training (dates, course titles, and degrees) should be listed first in an easy-to-read format. Then provide your job experience, but be cautious with job titles. If you once attended a neighborhood watch meeting, don't put down that you were a crime prevention specialist. Copies of diplomas and photographs are usually unnecessary. It is better to provide names and means of contacting your references on the résumé instead of simply saying "available on request." Consider sending your material by a priority mail service as this indicates you are concerned enough to make sure it arrived, and don't rule out the option of hand-delivering your material. Remember, including too much data is the main fault of résumés. Keep it brief, but well documented, with no gaps in employment dates. And don't forget a follow-up letter about a week or two later.

The following is a sample cover letter.

December 1, 2001
Capt. Robert Jones
Director of Training and Recruitment
Anytown Police Department
Anytown, Anystate 00000

Dear Capt. Jones:

I am applying for a police officer position with your department. Enclosed is my résumé. As my résumé indicates, I will have a Bachelor's degree in criminal justice next May, and I have had considerable work experience while attending college. Although I have gained valuable experience in a variety of areas, my particular interest is in a police career. Your ad said that applicants should be academy-certified or certifiable, and I would be more than willing to attend the academy you send your recruits to as this would further develop the skills and abilities I can already bring to your department.

Please inform me if there are any further requirements to the application process. I look forward to hearing from you at your earliest convenience. My telephone number is 555-1234 and my mailing address is listed below.

Thank you for your consideration.
Respectfully submitted,

Jack Smith
1116 Collegetown Apts
Anytown, USA 00000
504-555-1234

Correctional Service Work

A significant number of people who work in the field of criminal justice become involved in its social service side. Many opportunities are available to provide direct service to people both before they actually get involved with the law and after they have come to the attention of criminal justice agencies.

Salaries in the correctional field vary widely based on skill level, experience, responsibilities, and the size of the institution. Correctional pay varies tremendously from state to state. States with big prison systems like New York and New Jersey may start their entry-level correctional officers as high as $32,000. Jobs in probation and parole also have salaries that vary widely. Federal probation has some of the highest salaries in corrections, usually around $40,000 or more to start, and some states such as Massachusetts offer similar wages. The various correctional positions are described in Table B.

Probation Officer Probation officers supervise offenders who have been placed under community supervision by the criminal court. Their duties include counseling clients to help them adjust to society. This may be done through family counseling, individual counseling, or group sessions. Probation officers are trained to use the resources of the community to help their clients. Their work involves them in the personal, family, and work problems of their clients.

Community Correctional Counselor There are thousands of community-based correctional facilities around

TABLE B CORRECTIONAL JOB TITLES

Administrator	Juvenile detention officer
Affirmative action officer	Juvenile worker
Budget analyst	Leisure time activities
Business office manager	specialist
Chaplain	Medical records supervisor
Chief of programs	Ombudsman
Chief of security	Personnel officer
Computer specialist	Placement officer
Correctional clerk	Psychiatrist/psychologist
Correctional counselor	Public relations officer
Correctional officer	Records office manager
Employee development	Teacher
specialist	Trainer
Facility manager	Transport officer
Food service supervisor	Unit manager
Health systems	Vocational specialist
administrator	Warden

the country. These house nonviolent criminals serving out their prison sentences and inmates transferred from high-security institutions near the completion of their prison terms; separate facilities are maintained for juvenile offenders. These settings also provide ample opportunity for direct service work, because the overwhelming majority of programs emphasize the value of rehabilitation and treatment. Community-based corrections provide the setting for some of the most innovative treatment techniques used in the criminal justice system. There are numerous job opportunities in community corrections.

Secure Correctional Work Numerous opportunities exist for working in secure correctional settings. Although some may view correctional work as a matter of guarding incarcerated inmates, that narrow perspective is far from accurate. Correctional workers are charged with overseeing a great variety of activities that may involve them in budgeting, management, training, counseling, classification, planning, and human services. Correctional treatment staff engage in such tasks as vocational and educational training, counseling, recreational work, and so on. Almost every correctional institution has a social service staff that helps inmates adjust to the institution and prepare for successful reentry into the outside world. In addition, correctional settings require security staff, maintenance workers, medical staff, clergy, and other types of personnel.

Parole and Aftercare Parole and aftercare workers supervise offenders upon their release from correc-

tional treatment. This work involves helping individuals find jobs, achieve their educational objectives, sort out their family problems, and so on. Parole officers employ various counseling techniques to help clients clarify their goals and find ways of surmounting obstacles so that they can make a successful readjustment to the community.

Law and the Courts

The criminal justice system provides many opportunities for people interested in working in the legal system and the courts. Of course, in most instances, these careers require postgraduate education, such as law school or a course in court management. The various court-related positions are described in Table C.

Prosecutor Prosecutors represent the state in criminal matters. They bring charges against offenders, engage in plea bargaining, conduct trials, and help determine sentences. Prosecutors work at the local, county, state, and federal levels of government. For example, an assistant U.S. Attorney General would prosecute violations of federal law in one of the U.S. District Courts.

Defense Counsel All criminal defendants are entitled to legal counsel. Therefore, agencies such as the public defender's office have been created to provide free legal services to indigent offenders. In addition, private attorneys often take on criminal cases without compensation as a gesture of community service or are assigned cases by the court for modest compensation (referred to as pro bono cases). Defense attorneys help clients gather evidence to support their innocence; represent them at pretrial, trial, and sentencing hearings; and serve as their advocate if an appeal is filed upon conviction. A legal career is, of course, quite desirable and lucrative, with starting salaries in major big-city firms in excess of $100,000. Law school admissions are highly competitive, and students interested in attending are cautioned to maintain the highest levels of academic achievement.

Judge Judges carry out many functions during the trial stage of justice. They help in jury selection, oversee the admission of evidence, and control the flow of the trial. Most important, they are entrusted with the duty of ensuring that the trial is conducted within the boundaries of legal fairness. Although many criminal defense attorneys and prosecutors aspire to become judges, few are actually chosen for this honor. As might be expected, senior judges are paid quite well, and six-figure salaries for senior court judges are not uncommon.

Staff Counsel A number of public agencies will hire a staff counsel to give legal advice, prepare legal memoranda and reports, respond to inquiries, draft proposed legislation, and advise administrators on the legal ramifications of policy changes. Staff counsel typically are paid in the $50,000 range to start, depending on their experience and specialized knowledge; more senior staff counsel might be hired at $60,000 plus.

Court Administrator Most court jurisdictions maintain an office of court administration. These individuals help in case management and ensure that the court's resources are used in the most efficient manner. Court administrators are usually required to receive advanced education in programs that specialize in court management and are involved in financial management, human resources, case flow management, and statistical analysis, among other duties. Pay is quite high, typically between $75,000 and $100,000.

Research, Administration, and Teaching

In addition to work within the agencies of justice themselves, it is also possible to make a career in criminal justice that involves teaching, research, or administration.

Private Sector Research A number of private sector institutes and research firms—such as the Rand corporation in Santa Monica, California, and the Battelle Institute in Columbus, Ohio—employ research scientists who conduct criminal justice-related research. In addition, a number of private nonprofit organizations are devoted to the study of criminal justice issues, including the Police Executive Research Forum, the Police Foundation, and the International Association of Chiefs of Police, all located in the Washington, D.C., area, and the National Council on Crime and Delinquency in San Francisco. Many universities also maintain research centers that for many years have conducted ongoing efforts in criminal justice, often with funding from the government and private foundations. For example, the Institute for Social Research at the University of Michigan has conducted an annual survey of teenage substance abuse; the Hindelang Research Center at the University at Albany produces the *Sourcebook of Criminal Justice Statistics,* an invaluable research tool; the National Neighborhood Foot Patrol Center at Michigan State University conducts research on community policing.

Most people who work for these research centers hold advanced degrees in criminal justice or other applied social sciences. Some of the projects carried out by these centers, such as the study of career criminals conducted by Rand corporation scientists and the Po-

TABLE C COURT-RELATED JOB TITLES

Arbitrator	Grants administrator
Assistant administrator	Investigator
Assistant prosecutor	Judicial assistant
Background investigator	Law clerk
Bailiff	Lawyer
Bondsman	Legal research
CJ systems planner	Manager
Court clerk	Mediation specialist
Court reporter	Paralegal
Courthouse security	Parole officer
Defense attorney	Probation officer
Deputy assistant	Process server
Diversion specialist	Sentencing analyst
Expert witness	Victim restitution

lice Foundation's study of the deterrent effect of police patrol, have had a profound effect on policymaking within the criminal justice system.

Public Sector Research Most large local, state, and federal government agencies contain research arms that oversee the evaluation of ongoing criminal justice programs and plan for the development of innovative efforts designed to create positive change in the system. For example, most state corrections departments have planning and research units that monitor the flow of inmates in and out of the prison system and help evaluate the effectiveness of prison programs, such as work furloughs. On a local level, larger police departments commonly employ civilian research coordinators who analyze police data to improve the effectiveness and efficiency of police services.

The most significant contribution to criminal justice research made by the public sector is probably that of the federal government's Bureau of Justice Statistics and National Institute of Justice (NIJ), which are the research arms of the U.S. Justice Department. In recent years, these agencies have supported some of the most impressive and important of all research studies on criminal justice issues, such as sentencing, plea bargaining, and victimization. Research salaries are generally high, typically $65,000 and up.

System Administration It is also common for the federal and state governments to maintain central criminal justice planning offices that are responsible for setting and implementing criminal justice policy or for distributing funds for policy implementation. For example, the NIJ sets priorities for criminal justice research and policy on an annual basis, then distributes funds to local and state applicants willing to set up and evaluate demonstration projects. The NIJ has targeted the following areas: apprehension, prosecution, and adjudication of criminal offenders; public safety and security; punishment and control of offenders; victims of crime; white-collar and organized crime; criminal careers; drugs and alcohol and crime; forensic science; offender classification; and violent criminal behavior.

A number of states also have criminal justice administrative agencies that set policy agendas and coordinate state efforts to improve the quality of the system. Planners and analysts working for these agencies are expected to hold a master's degree and are typically hired in the $40,000 to $50,000 range.

College Teaching There are more than six hundred criminal justice education programs in the United States. These include specialized criminal justice programs, programs in which criminal justice is combined with another department (such as sociology or political science), and programs that offer a concentration in criminal justice as part of another major.

Criminal justice educators have a career track similar to that of most other teaching specialties. Regardless of the level at which they teach—associate, baccalaureate, or graduate—their courses will reflect the core subject matter of criminal justice, including courses on policing, the courts, and the correctional system. Starting salaries for assistant professors typically range from $35,000 to $50,000, and senior full professors at prestigious universities average in the $100,000 range.

Note

This material was prepared with the aid of Dr. Tom O'Connor, Assistant Professor of Justice Studies, North Carolina Wesleyan College, 3400 N. Wesleyan Blvd, Rocky Mount, NC 27804. We really appreciate his help in this project.

THE CONSTITUTION OF THE UNITED STATES

Preamble

We the People of the United States, in Order to form a more perfect Union, establish Justice, insure domestic Tranquility, provide for the common defence, promote the general Welfare, and secure the Blessings of Liberty to ourselves and our Posterity, do ordain and establish this Constitution for the United States of America.

Article I

Section 1 All legislative Powers herein granted shall be vested in a Congress of the United States, which shall consist of a Senate and House of Representatives.

Section 2 The House of Representatives shall be composed of Members chosen every second Year by the People of the several States, and the Electors in each State shall have the Qualifications requisite for Electors of the most numerous Branch of the State Legislature.

No Person shall be a Representative who shall not have attained to the Age of twenty five Years, and been seven Years a Citizen of the United States, and who shall not, when elected, be an Inhabitant of that State in which he shall be chosen.

Representatives and direct Taxes shall be apportioned among the several States which may be included within this Union, according to their respective Numbers, which shall be determined by adding to the whole Number of free Persons, including those bound to Service for a Term of Years, and excluding Indians not taxed, three fifths of all other Persons. The actual Enumeration shall be made within three Years after the first Meeting of the Congress of the United States, and within every subsequent Term of ten Years, in such Manner as they shall by Law direct. The Number of Representatives shall not exceed one for every thirty Thousand, but each State shall have at Least one Representative; and until such enumeration shall be made, the State of New Hampshire shall be entitled to choose three, Massachusetts eight, Rhode Island and Providence Plantations one, Connecticut five, New York six,

New Jersey four, Pennsylvania eight, Delaware one, Maryland six, Virginia ten, North Carolina five, South Carolina five, and Georgia three.

When vacancies happen in the Representation from any State, the Executive Authority thereof shall issue Writs of Election to fill such Vacancies.

The House of Representatives shall choose their Speaker and other Officers; and shall have the sole Power of Impeachment.

Section 3 The Senate of the United States shall be composed of two Senators from each State, chosen by the Legislature thereof, for six Years; and each Senator shall have one Vote.

Immediately after they shall be assembled in Consequence of the first Election, they shall be divided as equally as may be into three Classes. The Seats of the Senators of the first Class shall be vacated at the Expiration of the second Year, of the second Class at the Expiration of the fourth Year, and of the third Class at the Expiration of the sixth Year, so that one third may be chosen every second Year; and if Vacancies happen by Resignation, or otherwise, during the Recess of the Legislature of any State, the Executive thereof may make temporary Appointments until the next Meeting of the Legislature, which shall then fill such Vacancies.

No Person shall be a Senator who shall not have attained to the Age of thirty Years, and been nine Years a Citizen of the United States, and who shall not, when elected, be an Inhabitant of that State for which he shall be chosen.

The Vice-President of the United States shall be President of the Senate, but shall have no Vote, unless they be equally divided.

The Senate shall choose their other Officers, and also a President pro tempore, in the Absence of the Vice-President, or when he shall exercise the Office of President of the United States.

The Senate shall have the sole Power to try all Impeachments. When sitting for that Purpose, they shall be on Oath or Affirmation. When the President of the United States is tried the Chief Justice shall preside: And no Person shall be convicted without the Concurrence of two thirds of the Members present.

Judgment in Cases of Impeachment shall not extend further than to removal from Office, and disqualification to hold and enjoy any Office of honor, Trust or Profit under the United States: but the Party convicted shall nevertheless be liable and subject to Indictment, Trial, Judgment, and Punishment, according to Law.

Section 4 The Times, Places and Manner of holding Elections for Senators and Representatives, shall be prescribed in each State by the Legislature thereof; but the Congress may at any time by Law make or alter such Regulations, except as to the Places of choosing Senators.

The Congress shall assemble at least once in every Year, and such Meeting shall be on the first Monday in December, unless they shall by Law appoint a different Day.

Section 5 Each House shall be the Judge of the Elections, Returns and Qualifications of its own Members, and a Majority of each shall constitute a Quorum to do Business; but a smaller Number may adjourn from day to day, and may be authorized to compel the Attendance of absent Members, in such Manner, and under such Penalties as each House may provide.

Each House may determine the Rules of its Proceedings, punish its Members for disorderly Behaviour, and, with the Concurrence of two thirds, expel a Member.

Each House shall keep a Journal of its Proceedings, and from time to time publish the same, excepting such Parts as may in their Judgment require Secrecy; and the Yeas and Nays of the Members of either House on any question shall, at the Desire of one fifth of those Present, be entered on the Journal.

Neither House, during the Session of Congress, shall, without the Consent of the other, adjourn for more than three days, nor to any other Place than that in which the two Houses shall be sitting.

Section 6 The Senators and Representatives shall receive a Compensation for their Services, to be ascertained by Law, and paid out of the Treasury of the United States. They shall in all Cases, except Treason, Felony and Breach of the Peace, be privileged from Arrest during their Attendance at the Session of their respective Houses, and in going to and returning from the same; and for any Speech or Debate in either House, they shall not be questioned in any other Place.

No Senator or Representative shall, during the Time for which he was elected, be appointed to any civil Office under the Authority of the United States, which shall have been created, or the Emoluments whereof shall have been increased during such time; and no Person holding any Office under the United States, shall be a Member of either House during his Continuance in Office.

Section 7 All Bills for raising Revenue shall originate in the House of Representatives; but the Senate may propose or concur with Amendments as on other Bills.

Every Bill which shall have passed the House of Representatives and the Senate, shall, before it become a Law, be presented to the President of the United States; If he approve he shall sign it, but if not he shall return it, with his Objections to that House in which it shall have originated, who shall enter the Objections at large on their Journal, and proceed to reconsider it. If after such Reconsideration two thirds of that House shall agree to pass the Bill, it shall be sent, together with the Objections, to the other House, by which it shall likewise be reconsidered, and if approved by two thirds of that House, it shall become a Law. But in all such Cases the Votes of both Houses shall be determined by Yeas and Nays, and the Names of the Persons voting for and against the Bill shall be entered on the Journal of each House respectively. If any Bill shall not be returned by the President within ten Days (Sundays excepted) after it shall have been presented to him, the Same shall be a Law, in like Manner as if he had signed it, unless the Congress by their Adjournment prevent its Return, in which Case it shall not be a Law.

Every Order, Resolution, or Vote to which the Concurrence of the Senate and House of Representatives may be necessary (except on a question of Adjournment) shall be presented to the President of the United States; and before the Same shall take Effect, shall be approved by him, or being disapproved by him, shall be repassed by two thirds of the Senate and House of Representatives, according to the Rules and Limitations prescribed in the Case of a Bill.

Section 8 The Congress shall have Power To lay and collect Taxes, Duties, Imposts and Excises, to pay the Debts and provide for the common Defence and general Welfare of the United States; but all Duties, Imposts and Excises shall be uniform throughout the United States;

To borrow Money on the credit of the United States;

To regulate Commerce with foreign Nations, and among the several States, and with the Indian Tribes;

To establish an uniform Rule of Naturalization, and uniform Laws on the subject of Bankruptcies throughout the United States;

To coin Money, regulate the Value thereof, and of foreign Coin, and fix the Standard of Weights and Measures;

To provide for the Punishment of counterfeiting the Securities and current Coin of the United States;

To establish Post Offices and post Roads;

To promote the Progress of Science and useful Arts, by securing for limited Times to Authors and Inventors the exclusive Right to their respective Writings and Discoveries;

To constitute Tribunals inferior to the supreme Court;

To define and punish Piracies and Felonies committed on the high Seas, and Offences against the Law of Nations;

To declare War, grant Letters of Marque and Reprisal, and make Rules concerning Captures on Land and Water;

To raise and support Armies, but no Appropriation of Money to that Use shall be for a longer Term than two Years;

To provide and maintain a Navy;

To make Rules for the Government and Regulation of the land and naval Forces;

To provide for calling forth the Militia to execute the Laws of the Union, suppress Insurrections and repel Invasions;

To provide for organizing, arming, and disciplining, the Militia, and for governing such Part of them as may be employed in the Service of the United States, reserving to the States respectively, the Appointment of the Officers, and the Authority of training the Militia according to the discipline prescribed by Congress;

To exercise exclusive Legislation in all Cases whatsoever, over such District (not exceeding ten Miles square) as may, by Cession of particular States, and the Acceptance of Congress, become the Seat of the Government of the United States, and to exercise like Authority over all Places purchased by the Consent of the Legislature of the State in which the Same shall be, for the Erection of Forts, Magazines, Arsenals, dock-Yards, and other needful Buildings;—And

To make all Laws which shall be necessary and proper for carrying into Execution the foregoing Powers, and all other Powers vested by this Constitution in the Government of the United States, or in any Department or Officer thereof.

Section 9 The Migration or Importation of such Persons as any of the States now existing shall think proper to admit, shall not be prohibited by the Congress prior to the Year one thousand eight hundred and eight, but a Tax or duty may be imposed on such Importation, not exceeding ten dollars for each Person.

The privilege of the Writ of Habeas Corpus shall not be suspended, unless when in Cases of Rebellion or Invasion the public Safety may require it.

No Bill of Attainder or ex post facto Law shall be passed.

No Capitation, or other direct, Tax shall be laid, unless in Proportion to the Census or Enumeration herein before directed to be taken.

No Tax or Duty shall be laid on Articles exported from any State.

No Preference shall be given by any Regulation of Commerce or Revenue to the Ports of one State over those of another: nor shall Vessels bound to, or from, one State be obliged to enter, clear, or pay Duties in another.

No Money shall be drawn from the Treasury, but in Consequence of Appropriations made by Law; and a regular Statement and Account of the Receipts and Expenditures of all public Money shall be published from time to time.

No Title of Nobility shall be granted by the United States: And no Person holding any Office of Profit or Trust under them, shall, without the Consent of the Congress, accept of any present, Emolument, Office, or Title, of any kind whatever, from any King, Prince, or foreign State.

Section 10 No State shall enter into any Treaty, Alliance, or Confederation; grant Letters of Marque and Reprisal; coin Money; emit Bills of Credit; make any Thing but gold and silver Coin a Tender in Payment of Debts; pass any Bill of Attainder, ex post facto Law, or Law impairing the Obligation of Contracts, or grant any Title of Nobility.

No State shall, without the Consent of the Congress, lay any Imposts or Duties on Imports or Exports, except what may be absolutely necessary for executing its inspection Laws: and the net Produce of all Duties and Imposts, laid by any State on Imports or Exports, shall be for the Use of the Treasury of the United States; and all such Laws shall be subject to the Revision and Control of the Congress.

No State shall, without the Consent of Congress, lay any Duty of Tonnage, keep Troops, or Ships of War in time of Peace, enter into any Agreement or Compact with another State, or with a foreign Power, or engage in War, unless actually invaded, or in such imminent Danger as will not admit of delay.

Article II

Section 1 The executive Power shall be vested in a President of the United States of America. He shall hold his Office during the Term of four Years, and, together with the Vice-President, chosen for the same Term, be elected, as follows:

Each State shall appoint, in such Manner as the Legislature thereof may direct, a Number of Electors, equal to the whole Number of Senators and Representatives to which the State may be entitled in the Congress; but no Senator or Representative, or Person holding an Office of Trust or Profit under the United States, shall be appointed an Elector.

The Electors shall meet in their respective States, and vote by Ballot for two Persons, of whom one at least shall not be an Inhabitant of the same State with them-

selves. And they shall make a List of all the Persons voted for, and of the Number of Votes for each; which List they shall sign and certify, and transmit sealed to the Seat of Government of the United States, directed to the President of the Senate. The President of the Senate shall, in the Presence of the Senate and House of Representatives, open all the Certificates, and the Votes shall then be counted. The Person having the greatest Number of Votes shall be the President, if such Number be a Majority of the whole Number of Electors appointed; and if there be more than one who have such Majority, and have an equal Number of Votes, then the House of Representatives shall immediately choose by Ballot one of them for President; and if no Person have a Majority, then from the five highest on the List the said House shall in like Manner choose the President. But in choosing the President, the Votes shall be taken by States, the Representation from each State having one Vote; A quorum for this Purpose shall consist of a Member or Members from two thirds of the States, and a Majority of all the States shall be necessary to a Choice. In every Case, after the Choice of the President, the Person having the greatest Number of Votes of the Electors shall be the Vice-President. But if there should remain two or more who have equal Votes, the Senate shall choose from them by Ballot the Vice-President.

The Congress may determine the Time of choosing the Electors, and the Day on which they shall give their Votes; which Day shall be the same throughout the United States.

No Person except a natural born Citizen, or a Citizen of the United States, at the time of the Adoption of this Constitution, shall be eligible to the Office of President; neither shall any Person be eligible to that Office who shall not have attained to the Age of thirty five Years, and been fourteen Years a Resident within the United States.

In Case of the Removal of the President from Office, or of his Death, Resignation, or Inability to discharge the Powers and Duties of the said Office, the same shall devolve on the Vice-President, and the Congress may by Law provide for the Case of Removal, Death, Resignation or Inability, both of the President and Vice-President declaring what Officer shall then act as President, and such Officer shall act accordingly, until the Disability be removed, or a President shall be elected.

The President shall, at stated Times, receive for his Services, a Compensation, which shall neither be increased nor diminished during the Period for which he shall have been elected, and he shall not receive within that Period any other Emolument from the United States, or any of them.

Before he enter on the Execution of his Office, he shall take the following Oath or Affirmation: "I do solemnly swear (or affirm) that I will faithfully execute the Office of President of the United States, and will to the best of my Ability, preserve, protect and defend the Constitution of the United States."

Section 2 The President shall be Commander in Chief of the Army and Navy of the United States, and of the Militia of the several States, when called into the actual Service of the United States; he may require the Opinion, in writing, of the principal Officer in each of the executive Departments, upon any Subject relating to the Duties of their respective Offices, and he shall have Power to grant Reprieves and Pardons for Offenses against the United States, except in Cases of Impeachment.

He shall have Power, by and with the Advice and Consent of the Senate, to make Treaties, provided two thirds of the Senators present concur; and he shall nominate, and by and with the Advice and Consent of the Senate, shall appoint Ambassadors, other public Ministers and Consuls, Judges of the supreme Court, and all other Officers of the United States, whose Appointments are not herein otherwise provided for, and which shall be established by Law; but the Congress may by Law vest the Appointment of such inferior Officers, as they think proper, in the President alone, in the Courts of Law, or in the Heads of Departments.

The President shall have Power to fill up all Vacancies that may happen during the Recess of the Senate, by granting Commissions which shall expire at the End of their next Session.

Section 3 He shall from time to time give to the Congress Information of the State of the Union, and recommend to their Consideration such Measures as he shall judge necessary and expedient; he may, on extraordinary Occasions, convene both Houses, or either of them, and in Case of Disagreement between them, with Respect to the Time of Adjournment, he may adjourn them to such Time as he shall think proper; he shall receive Ambassadors and other public Ministers; he shall take Care that the Laws be faithfully executed, and shall Commission all the Officers of the United States.

Section 4 The President, Vice-President and all civil Officers of the United States, shall be removed from Office on Impeachment for, and Conviction of, Treason, Bribery, or other high Crimes and Misdemeanors.

Article III

Section 1 The judicial Power of the United States, shall be vested in one supreme Court, and in such inferior Courts as the Congress may from time to time ordain and establish. The Judges, both of the supreme and inferior Courts, shall hold their Offices during good Behaviour, and shall, at stated Times, receive for their Services a Compensation which shall not be diminished during their Continuance in Office.

Section 2 The judicial Power shall extend to all Cases, in Law and Equity, arising under this Constitution, the Laws of the United States, and Treaties made, or which shall be made, under their Authority;—to all Cases affecting Ambassadors, other public Ministers and Consuls;—to all Cases of admiralty and maritime Jurisdiction;—to Controversies to which the United States shall be a Party;—to Controversies between two or more States;—between a State and Citizens of another State;—between Citizens of different States;—between Citizens of the same State claiming Lands under Grants of different States, and between a State, or the Citizens thereof, and foreign States, Citizens or Subjects.

In all Cases affecting Ambassadors, other public Ministers and Consuls, and those in which a State shall be Party, the supreme Court shall have original Jurisdiction. In all the other Cases before mentioned, the supreme Court shall have appellate Jurisdiction, both as to Law and Fact, with such Exceptions, and under such Regulations as the Congress shall make.

The Trial of all Crimes, except in Cases of Impeachment, shall be by Jury; and such Trial shall be held in the State where the said Crimes shall have been committed; but when not committed within any State, the Trial shall be at such Place or Places as the Congress may by Law have directed.

Section 3 Treason against the United States shall consist only in levying War against them, or in adhering to their Enemies, giving them Aid and Comfort. No Person shall be convicted of Treason unless on the Testimony of two Witnesses to the same overt Act, or on Confession in open Court.

The Congress shall have Power to declare the Punishment of Treason, but no Attainder of Treason shall work Corruption of Blood, or Forfeiture except during the Life of the Person attainted.

Article IV

Section 1 Full Faith and Credit shall be given in each State to the public Acts, Records, and judicial Proceedings of every other State. And the Congress may by general Laws prescribe the Manner in which such Acts, Records and Proceedings shall be proved, and the Effect thereof.

Section 2 The Citizens of each State shall be entitled to all Privileges and Immunities of Citizens in the several States.

A Person charged in any State with Treason, Felony, or other Crime, who shall flee from Justice, and be found in another State, shall on Demand of the executive Authority of the State from which he fled, be delivered up, to be removed to the State having Jurisdiction of the Crime.

No Person held to Service or Labour in one State, under the Laws thereof, escaping into another, shall, in Consequence of any Law or Regulation therein, be discharged from such Service or Labour, but shall be delivered up on Claim of the Party to whom such Service or Labour may be due.

Section 3 New States may be admitted by the Congress into this Union; but no new State shall be formed or erected within the Jurisdiction of any other State; nor any State be formed by the Junction of two or more States, or Parts of States, without the Consent of the Legislatures of the States concerned as well as of the Congress.

The Congress shall have Power to dispose of and make all needful Rules and Regulations respecting the Territory or other Property belonging to the United States; and nothing in this Constitution shall be so construed as to Prejudice any Claims of the United States, or of any particular State.

Section 4 The United States shall guarantee to every State in this Union a Republican Form of Government, and shall protect each of them against Invasion; and on Application of the Legislature, or of the Executive (when the Legislature cannot be convened) against domestic Violence.

Article V

The Congress, whenever two thirds of both Houses shall deem it necessary, shall propose Amendments to this Constitution, or, on the Application of the Legislatures of two thirds of the several States, shall call a Convention for proposing Amendments, which, in either Case, shall be valid to all Intents and Purposes, as Part of this Constitution, when ratified by the Legislatures of three fourths of the several States, or by Conventions in three fourths thereof, as the one or the other Mode of Ratification may be proposed by the Congress; Provided that no Amendment which may be made prior to the Year One thousand eight hundred and eight shall in any Manner affect the first and fourth Clauses in the Ninth Section of the first Article; and

that no State, without its Consent, shall be deprived of its equal Suffrage in the Senate.

Article VI

All Debts contracted and Engagements entered into, before the Adoption of this Constitution, shall be as valid against the United States under this Constitution, as under the Confederation.

This Constitution, and the Laws of the United States which shall be made in Pursuance thereof; and all Treaties made, or which shall be made, under the Authority of the United States, shall be the supreme Law of the Land; and the Judges in every State shall be bound thereby, any Thing in the Constitution or Laws of any State to the Contrary notwithstanding.

The Senators and Representatives before mentioned, and the Members of the several State Legislatures, and all executive and judicial Officers, both of the United States and of the several States, shall be bound by Oath or Affirmation, to support this Constitution; but no religious Test shall ever be required as a Qualification to any Office or public Trust under the United States.

Article VII

The Ratification of the Conventions of nine States shall be sufficient for the Establishment of this Constitution between the States so ratifying the Same.

Done in Convention by the Unanimous Consent of the States present the Seventeenth Day of September in the Year of our Lord one thousand seven hundred and Eighty seven and of the Independence of the United States of America the Twelfth IN WITNESS whereof We have hereunto subscribed our Names,

Amendment 1 [1791]

Congress shall make no law respecting an establishment of religion, or prohibiting the free exercise thereof; or abridging the freedom of speech, or of the press; or the right of the people peaceably to assemble, and to petition the Government for a redress of grievances.

Amendment 2 [1791]

A well regulated Militia, being necessary to the security of a free State, the right of the people to keep and bear Arms, shall not be infringed.

Amendment 3 [1791]

No Soldier shall, in time of peace be quartered in any house, without the consent of the Owner, nor in time of war, but in a manner to be prescribed by law.

Amendment 4 [1791]

The right of the people to be secure in their persons, houses, papers, and effects, against unreasonable searches and seizures, shall not be violated, and no Warrants shall issue, but upon probable cause, supported by Oath or affirmation, and particularly describing the place to be searched, and the persons or things to be seized.

Amendment 5 [1791]

No person shall be held to answer for a capital, or otherwise infamous crime, unless on a presentment or indictment of a Grand Jury, except in cases arising in the land or naval forces, or in the Militia, when in actual service in time of War or public danger; nor shall any person be subject for the same offence to be twice put in jeopardy of life or limb; nor shall be compelled in any criminal case to be a witness against himself, nor be deprived of life, liberty, or property, without due process of law; nor shall private property be taken for public use, without just compensation.

Amendment 6 [1791]

In all criminal prosecutions, the accused shall enjoy the right to a speedy and public trial, by an impartial jury of the State and district wherein the crime shall have been committed, which district shall have been previously ascertained by law, and to be informed of the nature and cause of the accusation; to be confronted with the witnesses against him; to have compulsory process for obtaining witnesses in his favor, and to have the Assistance of Counsel for his defence.

Amendment 7 [1791]

In Suits at common law, where the value in controversy shall exceed twenty dollars, the right of trial by jury shall be preserved, and no fact tried by a jury, shall be otherwise re-examined in any Court of the United States, than according to the rules of the common law.

Amendment 8 [1791]

Excessive bail shall not be required, nor excessive fines imposed, nor cruel and unusual punishments inflicted.

Amendment 9 [1791]

The enumeration in the Constitution, of certain rights, shall not be construed to deny or disparage others retained by the people.

Amendment 10 [1791]

The powers not delegated to the United States by the Constitution, nor prohibited by it to the States, are reserved to the States respectively, or to the people.

Amendment 11 [Jan. 8, 1798]

The Judicial power of the United States shall not be construed to extend to any suit in law or equity, commenced or prosecuted against one of the United States by Citizens of another State, or by Citizens or Subjects of any Foreign State.

Amendment 12 [Sept. 25, 1804]

The Electors shall meet in their respective states, and vote by ballot for President and Vice-President, one of whom, at least, shall not be an inhabitant of the same state with themselves; they shall name in their ballots the person voted for as President, and in distinct ballots the person voted for as Vice-President, and they shall make distinct lists of all persons voted for as President, and of all persons voted for as Vice-President, and of the number of votes for each, which list they shall sign and certify, and transmit sealed to the seat of the government of the United States, directed to the President of the Senate;—The President of the Senate shall, in the presence of the Senate and House of Representatives, open all the certificates and the votes shall then be counted;—The person having the greatest number of votes for President, shall be the President, if such number be a majority of the whole number of Electors appointed; and if no person have such majority, then from the persons having the highest numbers not exceeding three on the list of those voted for as President, the House of Representatives shall choose immediately, by ballot, the President. But in choosing the President, the votes shall be taken by states, the representation from each state having one vote; a quorum for this purpose shall consist of a member or members from two-thirds of the states, and a majority of all the states shall be necessary to a choice. And if the House of Representatives shall not choose a President whenever the right of choice shall devolve upon them, before the fourth day of March next following, then the Vice-President shall act as President, as in the case of the death or other constitutional disability of the President.—The person having the greatest number of votes as Vice-President, shall be the Vice-President, if such number be a majority of the whole number of Electors appointed, and if no person have a majority, then from the two highest numbers on the list, the Senate shall choose the Vice-President; a quorum for the purpose shall consist of two-thirds of the whole number of Senators, and a majority of the whole number shall be necessary to a choice. But no person constitutionally ineligible to the office of President shall be eligible to that of Vice-President of the United States.

Amendment 13 [Dec. 18, 1865]

Section 1 Neither slavery nor involuntary servitude, except as a punishment for crime whereof the party shall have been duly convicted, shall exist within the United States, or any place subject to their jurisdiction.

Section 2 Congress shall have power to enforce this article by appropriate legislation.

Amendment 14 [July 28, 1868]

Section 1 All persons born or naturalized in the United States, and subject to the jurisdiction thereof, are citizens of the United States and of the State wherein they reside. No State shall make or enforce any law which shall abridge the privileges or immunities of citizens of the United States; nor shall any State deprive any person of life, liberty, or property, without due process of law; nor deny to any person within its jurisdiction the equal protection of the laws.

Section 2 Representatives shall be apportioned among the several States according to their respective numbers, counting the whole number of persons in each State, excluding Indians not taxed. But when the right to vote at any election for the choice of electors for President and Vice-President of the United States, Representatives in Congress, the Executive and Judicial officers of a State, or the members of the Legislature thereof, is denied to any of the male inhabitants of such State, being twenty-one years of age, and citizens of the United States, or in any way abridged, except for participation in rebellion, or other crime, the basis of representation therein shall be reduced in the proportion which the number of such male citizens shall bear to the whole number of male citizens twenty-one years of age in such State.

Section 3 No person shall be a Senator or Representative in Congress, or elector of President and Vice-President, or hold any office, civil or military, under the United States, or under any State, who, having previously taken an oath, as a member of Congress, or as an officer of the United States, or as a member of any State legislature, or as an executive or judicial officer of any State, to support the Constitution of the United States, shall have engaged in insurrection or rebellion against the same, or given aid or comfort to the enemies

thereof. But Congress may by a vote of two-thirds of each House, remove such disability.

Section 4 The validity of the public debt of the United States, authorized by law, including debts incurred for payment of pensions and bounties for services in suppressing insurrection or rebellion, shall not be questioned. But neither the United States nor any State shall assume or pay any debt or obligation incurred in aid of insurrection or rebellion against the United States, or any claim for the loss or emancipation of any slave; but all such debts, obligations and claims shall be held illegal and void.

Section 5 The Congress shall have power to enforce, by appropriate legislation, the provisions of this article.

Amendment 15 [March 30, 1870]

Section 1 The right of citizens of the United States to vote shall not be denied or abridged by the United States or by any State on account of race, color, or previous condition of servitude.

Section 2 The Congress shall have power to enforce this article by appropriate legislation.

Amendment 16 [Feb. 25, 1913]

The Congress shall have power to lay and collect taxes on incomes, from whatever source derived, without apportionment among the several States, and without regard to any census or enumeration.

Amendment 17 [May 31, 1913]

Section 1 The Senate of the United States shall be composed of two Senators from each State, elected by the people thereof, for six years; and each Senator shall have one vote. The electors in each State shall have the qualifications requisite for electors of the most numerous branch of the State legislatures.

Section 2 When vacancies happen in the representation of any State in the Senate, the executive authority of such State shall issue writs of election to fill such vacancies: Provided, That the legislature of any State may empower the executive thereof to make temporary appointments until the people fill the vacancies by election as the legislature may direct.

Section 3 This amendment shall not be so construed as to affect the election or term of any Senator chosen before it becomes valid as part of the Constitution.

Amendment 18 [Jan. 29, 1919; repealed Dec. 5, 1933]

Section 1 After one year from the ratification of this article the manufacture, sale, or transportation of intoxicating liquors within, the importation thereof into, or the exportation thereof from the United States and all territory subject to the jurisdiction thereof for beverage purposes is hereby prohibited.

Section 2 The Congress and the several States shall have concurrent power to enforce this article by appropriate legislation.

Section 3 This article shall be inoperative unless it shall have been ratified as an amendment to the Constitution by the legislatures of the several States, as provided in the Constitution, within seven years from the date of the submission hereof to the States by the Congress.

Amendment 19 [Aug. 26, 1920]

Section 1 The right of citizens of the United States to vote shall not be denied or abridged by the United States or by any State on account of sex.

Section 2 Congress shall have power to enforce this article by appropriate legislation.

Amendment 20 [Feb. 6, 1933]

Section 1 The terms of the President and Vice-President shall end at noon on the 20th day of January, and the terms of Senators and Representatives at noon on the third day of January, of the years in which such terms would have ended if this article had not been ratified; and the terms of their successors shall then begin.

Section 2 The Congress shall assemble at least once in every year, and such meeting shall begin at noon on the third day of January, unless they shall by law appoint a different day.

Section 3 If, at the time fixed for the beginning of the term of the President, the President elect shall have died, the Vice-President elect shall become President. If a President shall not have been chosen before the time fixed for the beginning of his term, or if the President elect shall have failed to qualify, then the Vice-President elect shall act as President until a President shall have qualified; and the Congress may by law provide for the case wherein neither a President elect nor a Vice-President elect shall have qualified, declaring who shall then act as President, or the manner in which one who is to act shall be selected, and such person shall act accordingly until a President or Vice-President shall have qualified.

Section 4 The Congress may by law provide for the case of the death of any of the persons from whom the House of Representatives may choose a President whenever the right of choice shall have devolved upon them, and for the case of the death of any of the persons from whom the Senate may choose a Vice-President whenever the right of choice shall have devolved upon them.

Section 5 Sections 1 and 2 shall take effect on the 15th day of October following the ratification of this article.

Section 6 This article shall be inoperative unless it shall have been ratified as an amendment to the Constitution by the legislatures of three-fourths of the several States within seven years from the date of its submission.

Amendment 21 [Dec. 5, 1933]

Section 1 The eighteenth article of amendment to the Constitution of the United States is hereby repealed.

Section 2 The transportation or importation into any State, Territory, or possession of the United States for delivery or use therein of intoxicating liquors, in violation of the laws thereof, is hereby prohibited.

Section 3 This article shall be inoperative unless it shall have been ratified as an amendment to the Constitution by conventions in the several States, as provided in the Constitution, within seven years from the date of the submission hereof to the States by the Congress.

Amendment 22 [March 1, 1951]

Section 1 No person shall be elected to the office of the President more than twice, and no person who has held the office of President, or acted as President, for more than two years of a term to which some other person was elected President shall be elected to the office of the President more than once. But this Article shall not apply to any person holding the office of President when this Article was proposed by the Congress, and shall not prevent any person who may be holding the office of President, or acting as President, during the term within which this Article becomes operative from holding the office of President or acting as President during the remainder of such term.

Section 2 This article shall be inoperative unless it shall have been ratified as an amendment to the Constitution by the legislatures of three-fourths of the several States within seven years from the date of its submission to the States by the Congress.

Amendment 23 [April 3, 1961]

Section 1 The District constituting the seat of Government of the United States shall appoint in such manner as the Congress may direct:

A number of electors of President and Vice-President equal to the whole number of Senators and Representatives in Congress to which the District would be entitled if it were a State, but in no event more than the least populous State; they shall be in addition to those appointed by the States, but they shall be considered, for the purposes of the election of President and Vice-President, to be electors appointed by a State; and they shall meet in the District and perform such duties as provided by the twelfth article of amendment.

Section 2 The Congress shall have power to enforce this article by appropriate legislation.

Amendment 24 [Feb. 4, 1964]

Section 1 The right of citizens of the United States to vote in any primary or other election for President or Vice-President, for electors for President or Vice-President, or for Senator or Representative in Congress, shall not be denied or abridged by the United States or any State by reason of failure to pay any poll tax or other tax.

Section 2 The Congress shall have power to enforce this article by appropriate legislation.

Amendment 25 [Feb. 10, 1967]

Section 1 In case of the removal of the President from office or his death or resignation, the Vice-President shall become President.

Section 2 Whenever there is a vacancy in the office of the Vice-President, the President shall nominate a Vice-President who shall take the office upon confirmation by a majority vote of both houses of Congress.

Section 3 Whenever the President transmits to the President pro tempore of the Senate and the Speaker of the House of Representatives his written declaration that he is unable to discharge the powers and duties of his office, and until he transmits to them a written declaration to the contrary, such powers and duties shall be discharged by the Vice-President as Acting President.

Section 4 Whenever the Vice-President and a majority of either the principal officers of the executive departments, or of such other body as Congress may by law provide, transmit to the President pro tempore of the Senate and the Speaker of the House of Representatives their written declaration that the President is unable to discharge the powers and duties of his office, the Vice-President shall immediately assume the powers and duties of the office as Acting President.

Thereafter, when the President transmits to the President pro tempore of the Senate and the Speaker of the House of Representatives his written declaration that no inability exists, he shall resume the powers and duties of his office unless the Vice-President and a majority of either the principal officers of the executive department, or of such other body as Congress may by law provide, transmit within four days to the President pro tempore of the Senate and the Speaker of the House of Representatives their written declaration that the President is unable to discharge the powers and duties of his office. Thereupon Congress shall decide the issue, assembling within forty-eight hours for that purpose if not in session. If the Congress, within twenty-one days after receipt of the latter written declaration, or, if Congress is not in session, within twenty-one days after Congress is required to assemble, determines by two-thirds vote of both Houses that the President is unable to discharge the powers and duties of his office, the Vice-President shall continue to discharge the same as Acting President; otherwise, the President shall resume the powers and duties of his office.

Amendment 26 [June 30, 1971]

Section 1 The right of citizens of the United States, who are eighteen years of age or older, to vote shall not be denied or abridged by the United States or any state on account of age.

Section 2 The Congress shall have power to enforce this article by appropriate legislation.

Amendment 27 [May 7, 1992]

No law, varying the compensation for the services of Senators and Representatives, shall take effect until an election of Representatives shall have intervened.

GLOSSARY

accountability system A method of dealing with police corruption by making superiors responsible for the behavior of their subordinates.

actus reus An illegal act, or failure to act when legally required.

adjudication (adult) The determination of guilt or innocence; a judgment concerning criminal charges.

adjudication (juvenile) The juvenile court hearing at which the juvenile is declared a delinquent or status offender, or no finding of fact is made.

adversarial procedure Method of determining truth in the adjudication of guilt or innocence in which the prosecution advocates for the state, the defense advocates for the accused, and the judge is a neutral arbiter of the legal rules.

aftercare Juvenile equivalent of parole, designed to help youths make the transition from residential or institutional settings back into the community; may include counseling, treatment referrals, education, vocational training, or other services.

aging out The reduction in criminal behavior as people get older.

anomie The absence or weakness of rules, norms, or guidelines as to what is socially or morally acceptable.

appeal A review of lower court proceedings by a higher court.

appellate court Court that reconsiders a case that has already been tried to determine whether the lower court proceedings complied with accepted rules of criminal procedure and constitutional doctrines.

arraignment Initial trial court appearance at which accused is read the charges, advised of his or her rights, and asked to enter a plea.

arrest Taking a person into legal custody for the purpose of restraining the accused until he or she can be held accountable for the offense at court proceedings.

arrest warrant Written court order authorizing and directing that an individual be taken into custody to answer criminal charges.

assigned counsel A private attorney appointed by the court to represent a criminal defendant who cannot afford to pay for a lawyer.

attorney general The chief legal officer and prosecutor of each state and of the United States.

Auburn system Prison system, developed in New York during the nineteenth century, based on congregate (group) work during the day and separation at night.

avertable recidivist Repeat offender whose new crime could have been prevented if he or she had been incarcerated rather than released on bail, probation, or parole.

bail A monetary amount set by a judge as a condition of pretrial release, to ensure the defendant's appearance at subsequent proceedings; if the defendant fails to appear, bail is forfeited.

bail bond An instrument executed by another party promising to forfeit money to the court if the defendant fails to appear for future criminal proceedings.

bail bonding The business of providing bail to needy offenders, usually at very high rates of interest.

balanced and restorative justice model A model of juvenile justice that seeks to involve offenders, victims, and the community in a process of victim restoration, program development, and community protection.

beat A designated police patrol area.

bench trial The trial of a criminal matter by a judge without a jury.

beyond a reasonable doubt Standard of proof required for conviction of a criminal defendant; conclusive proof of guilt, with no realistic possibility of innocence.

blue curtain The secretive, insulated police culture that isolates officers from the rest of society.

bobbies Members of the London police force, named after its founder, Sir Robert Peel.

booking The administrative record of an arrest listing the offender's name, address, physical description, date of birth, employer, time of arrest, offense, and name of arresting officer; also includes photographing and fingerprinting of the offender.

boot camp A short-term militaristic correctional facility in which inmates, usually young first-time offenders, undergo intensive physical conditioning and discipline.

broken windows model Role of the police as maintainers of community order and safety.

brutalization effect The belief that capital punishment creates an atmosphere of brutality, reinforces the view that violence is an appropriate response to provocation, and thus encourages rather than deters the criminal use of violence.

bus sweep Police investigation technique in which officers board a bus or train without suspicion of illegal activity and question passengers, asking for identification and seeking permission to search their baggage.

career criminal A persistent repeat offender who organizes his or her lifestyle around criminality.

challenge for cause Dismissal of a prospective juror by either the prosecution or the defense because he or she is biased, has prior knowledge about a case, or for other reasons that demonstrate the individual's inability to render a fair and impartial judgment.

charge Instructions to a jury on the principles of law that ought to guide their decision; also, the specific crime a defendant is accused of committing.

chief of police The head of a police agency who sets policy and has control over operations.

child-saving movement Nineteenth-century American reformers who developed programs for troubled youths and influenced legislation creating the juvenile justice system.

chivalry hypothesis The idea that female defendants are treated more leniently in sentencing (and are less likely to be arrested and prosecuted in the first place) because the criminal justice system is dominated by men who have a paternalistic or protective attitude toward women.

chronic offender As defined by Wolfgang, a delinquent arrested five or more times before the age of 18 who commits a disproportionate amount of all criminal offenses.

circumstantial evidence Indirect evidence from which a fact may be inferred.

civil law All law that is not criminal, including tort, contract, personal property, maritime, and commercial law.

class action A suit brought on behalf of all individuals affected by similar circumstances.

coed prison A penal institution that houses both male and female inmates, who share work and recreational facilities.

cohort study A study using a group of subjects who share a common characteristic, such as place and time of birth.

commitment Decision to place an adjudicated juvenile offender in a correctional facility.

common law Early English law, developed by judges, that incorporated Anglo-Saxon tribal customs, feudal rules and practices, and the everyday rules of behavior of local villages; basis of U.S. criminal law.

community prosecution A prosecutorial philosophy that emphasizes community support and cooperation with other agencies in preventing crime, and a less centralized and more proactive role for local prosecutors.

community service restitution Criminal sanction that requires the offender to work in the community at such tasks as cleaning public parks or helping handicapped children as an alternative to incarceration.

community-oriented policing (COP) A police strategy that emphasizes fear reduction, community organization, and order maintenance rather than crime fighting.

complaint A sworn written statement addressed to a court or judge by the police, prosecutor, or individual alleging that an individual has committed an offense and requesting indictment and prosecution.

comprehensive juvenile justice A reform model that seeks to combine and balance early childhood prevention, adolescent intervention, graduated sanctions, institutional reform, and judicial waiver for the most serious juvenile offenders.

concurrent sentence Incarceration for more than one offense such that all sentences begin on the same day and are completed after the longest term has been served.

conflict theory The view that crime results from the imposition by the rich and powerful of their own moral standards and economic interests on the rest of society.

conflict view The view that law is an instrument of control used by those who hold economic and political power to further their own interests.

confrontation clause The constitutional right of a criminal defendant to see and cross-examine all the witnesses against him or her.

conjugal visit A prison program that allows inmates to receive visits from spouses for the purpose of maintaining normal interpersonal relationships.

consecutive sentence Incarceration for more than one offense such that each sentence begins only after the previous one has been completed.

consensus view The view that the majority of people in a society share common ideals and work toward a common good; crimes are behaviors that conflict with the rules of the majority and the good of society.

constable In early English towns, an appointed peacekeeper who organized citizens for protection and supervised the night watch.

continuance Adjournment of a court case to a future time.

contract system (court) Provision of legal services to indigent defendants by private attorneys under contract to the state or county.

contract system (prison) System whereby officials sold the labor of prison inmates to private businesses, for use either inside or outside the prison.

convict-lease system Contract system in which a private business leased prisoners from the state for a fixed annual fee and assumed full responsibility for their supervision and control.

corpus delicti The body of the crime; all the elements that together constitute a crime, including the criminal act, criminal intent, and the relationship between the two.

court of general jurisdiction A court that tries felony cases and more serious civil matters.

court of last resort A court that handles the final appeal on a matter; in the federal system, the U.S. Supreme Court.

court of limited jurisdiction A court that handles misdemeanors and minor civil complaints.

courtroom work group All parties in the adversary process working together in a cooperative effort to settle cases with the least amount of effort and conflict.

crime control perspective A model of criminal justice that emphasizes the control of dangerous offenders and the protection of society through harsh punishment as a deterrent to crime.

Crime Fighter A style of policing that stresses dealing with serious crimes and arresting dangerous criminals.

criminal justice system The various sequential stages through which offenders pass, from initial contact with the law to final disposition, and the agencies charged with enforcing the law at each of these stages.

criminal law The body of rules that define crimes, set out their punishments, and mandate the procedures for carrying out the criminal justice process.

criminology The scientific study of the nature, extent, cause, and control of criminal behavior.

cross-examination The questioning of a prosecution witness by the defense, or of a defense witness by the prosecution.

cruel and unusual punishment Treatment that degrades human dignity, is disproportionately severe, or shocks the general conscience; prohibited by the Eighth Amendment to the U.S. Constitution.

culture of poverty The view that people in the lower class of society form a separate culture with its own values and norms that are in conflict with those of conventional society.

curtilage Grounds or fields attached to a house.

cynicism The belief that most people's actions are motivated solely by personal needs and selfishness.

DARE Drug Abuse Resistance Education, a school-based program designed to give students the skills to resist peer pressure to experiment with tobacco, alcohol, and illegal drugs.

Daubert test A rule that gives courts wider discretion in admitting scientific evidence if it helps the judge or jury to understand the evidence.

day fine A fine geared to an offender's net daily income, as well as number of dependents and the seriousness of the crime, in an effort to make sentences more equitable.

day reporting center (DRC) Nonresidential, community-based treatment program.

deadly force Police killing of a suspect who resists arrest or presents a danger to an officer or the community.

death-qualified jury A jury formed to hear a capital case, with any person opposed in principle to capital punishment automatically excluded.

decriminalization Reducing the penalty for a criminal act without actually legalizing it.

defeminization The process by which policewomen become enculturated into the police profession at the expense of their feminine identity.

defense attorney Legal counsel for the defendant in a criminal case, representing the accused person from arrest to final appeal.

deinstitutionalization The movement to remove as many offenders as possible from secure confinement and treat them in the community.

demeanor The way in which a person outwardly manifests his or her personality.

Department of Justice (DOJ) The legal arm of the U.S. government, headed by the attorney general, empowered to enforce federal laws, represent the federal government in court, and conduct independent investigations.

deposit bail System in which the state acts as a bonding agency; defendants put up 10 percent of the total bail but are responsible for paying the entire amount if they abscond.

desistance The reduction in criminal behavior as people get older; aging out.

detention Temporary care of a child alleged to be a delinquent or status offender who requires secure custody pending court disposition.

determinate sentence A fixed term of incarceration.

deterrent Preventing crime before it occurs by means of the threat of criminal sanctions.

diagnosis Evaluation of a probationer's personality and other information for the purpose of planning a proper treatment program.

differential association theory The view that criminal acts are related to a person's exposure to antisocial attitudes and values.

direct examination The initial questioning of one's own (prosecution or defense) witness during a trial.

directed verdict A judge's order directing a jury to acquit a defendant because the state has not proven the elements of the crime or otherwise has not established guilt according to law.

discretion The use of personal decision making and choice in carrying out operations in the criminal justice system.

disposition The treatment decision for a juvenile offender, equivalent to the sentencing of an adult.

district attorney The county prosecutor who is charged with bringing offenders to justice and enforcing the criminal laws of the state.

diversion The use of a noncriminal alternative to trial, such as referral to treatment or employment programs.

DNA profiling The identification (or elimination) of criminal suspects by comparing DNA samples (genetic material) taken from them with specimens found at crime scenes.

double marginality According to Nicholas Alex, the social burden African American police officers carry by being both minority-group members and law enforcement officers.

drug court A specialty court with jurisdiction over cases involving illegal substances, often providing treatment alternatives for defendants.

Drug Enforcement Administration (DEA) The federal agency that enforces federal drug control laws.

due process Constitutional safeguards against arbitrary and unfair state procedures in judicial or administrative proceedings.

due process perspective A model of criminal justice that emphasizes individual rights and constitutional safeguards against arbitrary or unfair judicial or administrative proceedings.

electronic monitoring (EM) Electronic equipment that enables probation officers to monitor the location of those under house arrest or other forms of supervision.

entrapment A legal defense that maintains the police originated the criminal idea or initiated the criminal action.

equity Sanction designed to compensate victims and society for the losses caused by crime; restitution.

ex post facto law A law that makes an act criminal after it was committed or retroactively increases the penalty for a crime.

exclusionary rule The principle that prohibits using illegally obtained evidence in a trial.

expressive crime A criminal act that serves to vent rage, anger, or frustration.

Federal Bureau of Investigation (FBI) The arm of the Justice Department that investigated violations of federal law, gathers crime statistics, runs a comprehensive crime laboratory, and helps train local law enforcement officers.

federal district court A trial court of the federal system.

felony A more serious crime that carries a penalty of incarceration in a state or federal prison, usually for one year or more.

focal concerns Central values and goals that, according to Miller, differ by social class.

foot patrol Police patrol that takes officers out of cars and puts them on a walking beat to strengthen ties with the community.

forfeiture The seizure of personal property by the state as a civil or criminal penalty.

Frye test A rule that allows scientific evidence to be admitted in court only if the technique used has general acceptance in its field.

general deterrence A crime control policy that depends on the fear of criminal penalties.

general intent Action that on its face indicates a criminal purpose.

good faith exception The principle that evidence may be used in a criminal trial even though the search warrant used to obtain it was technically faulty, so long as the police acted in good faith when they sought the warrant from a judge.

good time Reduction of a prison sentence by a specified amount in exchange for good behavior within the institution.

grand jury A group of citizens chosen to hear charges against persons accused of crime and to determine whether there is sufficient evidence to bring the persons to trial.

grass eater A term used for a police officer who accepts payoffs when everyday duties place him or her in a position to be solicited by the public.

halfway house A community-based correctional facility that houses inmates before their outright release so that they can become gradually acclimated to conventional society.

hands-off doctrine The judicial policy of not interfering in the administrative affairs of prisons.

hearsay evidence Testimony that is not firsthand but relates information told by a second party.

house arrest A sentence that requires convicted offenders to spend extended periods of time in their own home as an alternative to incarceration.

hue and cry In medieval England, a call for mutual aid against trouble or danger.

hulk Mothballed ship used to house prisoners in eighteenth-century England.

hundred In medieval England, a group of 100 families responsible for maintaining order and trying minor offenses.

hung jury A jury whose members are unable to agree on a verdict.

hustle The underground prison economy.

importation model The view that the violent prison culture reflects the criminal culture of the outside world and is neither developed in nor unique to prisons.

in forma pauperis An appeal "in the form of a pauper"; if granted, a criminal defendant is entitled to assistance of counsel at state expense.

incapacitation The policy of keeping dangerous criminals in confinement to eliminate the risk of their repeating their offense in society.

incarceration Confinement in a correctional institution, such as a jail or prison.

incorporation theory The view that all provisions of the Bill of Rights are incorporated into the Fourteenth Amendment's due process clause and are therefore binding on the states.

indeterminate sentence A term of incarceration with a stated minimum and maximum length; the prisoner is eligible for parole after serving the minimum.

index crimes The eight serious crimes—murder, rape, assault, robbery, burglary, arson, larceny, and motor vehicle theft—whose incidence is reported in the annual Uniform Crime Reports (UCR).

indictment A written accusation returned by a grand jury, charging an individual with a specified crime after determination of probable cause.

indigent A poor defendant who lacks the funds to hire a private attorney and is therefore entitled to free counsel.

information A formal charging document, similar to an indictment, based on probable cause as determined at a preliminary hearing.

initial hearing Appearance before a magistrate that occurs within 24 hours after a defendant's arrest, at which the defendant is informed of the charge, counsel is appointed, a plea is taken, and bail is considered.

inmate subculture The loosely defined culture that pervades prisons and has its own norms, rules, and language.

innovative neighborhood-oriented policing (INOP) A model in which police solve problems at the neighborhood level.

insanity A legal defense that maintains that the defendant was incapable of forming criminal intent owing to a defect of reason or mental illness.

instrumental crime A criminal act intended to improve the financial or social position of the criminal.

intake The process by which a probation officer settles cases at the initial court appearance, before the onset of formal criminal proceedings; the screening process in which a juvenile is referred to the juvenile court, referred elsewhere, or released.

intensive probation supervision (IPS) A type of intermediate sanction involving small probation caseloads and strict daily or weekly monitoring.

intensive supervision parole (ISP) A form of parole characterized by smaller caseloads and closer surveillance; may include frequent drug testing or, in some cases, electronic monitoring.

interactionist view The view that crime is defined by people who hold social power and mold the law to reflect their own ideas of right and wrong.

intermediate sanctions A group of punishments falling between probation and prison; community-based sanctions including house arrest and intensive supervision.

internal affairs Unit that investigates allegations of police misconduct.

International Association of Chiefs of Police (IACP) The professional organization of local police agencies.

jail A county correctional institution used to hold people awaiting trial or sentencing, as well as misdemeanor offenders sentenced to a term of less than one year.

jailhouse lawyer An inmate trained in law or otherwise educated who helps other inmates prepare legal briefs and appeals.

judicial reprieve In medieval England, a judge's suspension of punishment, enabling a convicted offender to seek a pardon, gather new evidence, or demonstrate reformed behavior.

just desert The view that those who violate the rights of others deserve punishment commensurate with the seriousness of the crime.

justice of the peace Official appointed to act as the judicial officer in a county.

justice perspective A model of criminal justice that favors determinate sentencing, seeks to abolish parole, and sees prisons as places of punishment, not rehabilitation.

juvenile court A court with original jurisdiction over persons defined by statute as juveniles and alleged to be delinquents or status offenders.

juvenile delinquency Commission of an illegal act by a child younger than a statutory age limit.

juvenile justice system The system of agencies and organizations that deal with youths who engage in crime (juvenile delinquency) or noncriminal behaviors such as truancy and incorrigibility (status offenses).

Knapp Commission A public body that conducted an investigation into police corruption in New York City in the early 1970s and uncovered a widespread network of payoffs and bribes.

labeling theory The view that society produces criminals by stigmatizing certain individuals as deviants, a label which they come to accept as a personal identity.

landmark decision A decision of the Supreme Court that establishes a significant precedent for similar legal issues.

Law Enforcement Assistance Administration (LEAA) Agency funded by the federal Safe Streets Act that provided technical assistance and hundreds of millions of dollars in aid to local and state justice agencies between 1969 and 1982.

Law Enforcer A style of policing that stresses the detection and apprehension aspects of police work, enforcement of all statutes and ordinances, and going "by the book."

left realism A branch of conflict theory that accepts the reality of crime as a social problem and stresses its impact on the poor.

legalization The removal of all criminal penalties from a previously outlawed act.

less eligibility The view that prisoners should always be treated less well than the most underprivileged law-abiding citizen.

lineup Placing a suspect in a group for the purpose of being viewed and identified by a witness.

longitudinal cohort study Research that tracks the development of a group of subjects over time.

lower criminal court A court that has jurisdiction over misdemeanors and conducts preliminary investigations of felony charges.

M'Naghten rule A legal test that defines insanity as not knowing what one is doing or being unable to distinguish between right and wrong.

make-believe family A peer unit containing mother and father figures that is formed by women in prison to compensate for the loss of family and loved ones.

mandatory sentence A statutory requirement that a certain penalty be set and carried out in all cases on conviction for a specified offense or series of offenses.

masculinity hypothesis The view that women who commit crimes have biological and psychological traits similar to those of men.

maximum-security prison A correctional institution that houses dangerous felons and maintains strict security measures, including high walls, guard towers, and limited contact with the outside world.

meat eater A term used to describe a police officer who actively solicits bribes and vigorously engages in corrupt practices.

medical model The view that convicted offenders are victims of their environment who need care and treatment to be transformed into valuable members of society.

medium-security prison A correctional institution that houses nonviolent offenders, characterized by a less tense and vigilant atmosphere and more opportunities for contact with the outside world.

mens rea A guilty mind; the intent to commit a criminal act.

methadone A synthetic narcotic used as a substitute for heroin in drug-control efforts.

minimum-security prison A correctional institution that houses white-collar and other nonviolent offenders, characterized by few security measures and liberal furlough and visitation policies.

misdemeanor A less serious crime usually punishable by a fine or incarceration in a local jail for less than one year.

Missouri Plan A method of judicial selection that combines a judicial nominating commission, executive appointment, and nonpartisan confirmation elections.

Mollen Commission An investigative unit set up to inquire into police corruption in New York City in the 1990s.

monetary restitution Criminal sanction that requires the offender to compensate the victim for property damage, lost wages, medical costs, or other losses.

moral entrepreneurs Interest groups that use their economic, social, and political influence to impose their own moral values on the rest of the population.

National Crime Victimization Survey (NCVS) Annual survey conducted jointly by the U.S. Census Bureau and the Department of Justice that questions a large national sample about their experiences as victims of crime.

no bill The action by a grand jury when it votes not to indict an accused suspect.

nolle prosequi Decision by a prosecutor to drop a case after a complaint has been made; reasons may include insufficient evidence, witness reluctance to testify, police error, or office policy.

nolo contendere A plea of "no contest"; the defendant submits to sentencing without any formal admission of guilt that could be used against him or her in a subsequent civil suit.

nonintervention perspective A model of criminal justice that favors the least intrusive treatment possible: decarceration, diversion, and decriminalization.

official crime statistics Criminal behavior that has been recorded by the police.

order maintenance (peacekeeping) Maintaining order and authority without the need for formal arrest; "handling the situation"; keeping things under control by means of threats, persuasion, and understanding.

parens patriae The power of the state to act on behalf of a child and provide care and protection equivalent to that of a parent.

parole The early release of a prisoner from incarceration subject to conditions set by a parole board.

parole board Group that reviews inmate cases, determines whether offenders are ready for supervised release, and dictates the specific rules that parolees must obey.

particularity The requirement that a search warrant state precisely where the search is to take place and what items are to be seized.

peacemaking criminology A branch of conflict theory that stresses humanism, mediation, and conflict resolution as means to end crime.

penitentiary A state or federal correctional institution for the incarceration of felony offenders for terms of one year or more; prison.

Pennsylvania system Prison system, developed in Pennsylvania during the nineteenth century, based on total isolation and individual penitence.

peremptory challenge Dismissal of a prospective juror by either the prosecution or the defense for unexplained, discretionary reasons.

plain view doctrine Evidence that is in plain view of police officers may be seized without a search warrant.

plea negotiation/plea bargaining Discussions between defense counsel and prosecution in which the accused agrees to plead guilty in exchange for certain considerations, such as reduced charges or a lenient sentence.

pledge system In early England, the system in which neighbors aided each other and protected the settlement.

police brutality Actions such as using abusive language, making threats, using force or coercion unnecessarily, prodding with nightsticks, and stopping and searching people to harass them.

police-community relations (PCR) Programs designed to bring police and the public closer together and create a more cooperative working environment between them.

poor laws Seventeenth-century English laws under which vagrants and abandoned and neglected children were bound to masters as indentured servants.

preliminary hearing (probable cause hearing) Hearing before a magistrate to determine if the government has sufficient evidence to show probable cause that the defendant committed the crime.

preponderance of the evidence Standard of proof in civil cases; greater weight of evidence on one side than the other.

presentence investigation A postconviction investigation, performed by a probation officer attached to the trial court, of the defendant's background, education, employment, family, acquaintances, physical and mental health, prior criminal record, and other factors that may affect sentencing.

presentment The report of a grand jury investigation, which usually includes a recommendation of indictment.

pretrial detention Holding a defendant in jail without bail to ensure his or her appearance at trial.

pretrial diversion Informal, community-based treatment programs that are used in lieu of the formal criminal process.

pretrial services Programs that screen arrestees and provide judges with information relevant to the granting of bail or other pretrial release.

preventive detention Holding without bail a defendant believed to be dangerous or likely to commit a crime if released before trial.

prison A state or federal correctional institution for the incarceration of felony offenders for terms of one year or more; penitentiary.

prisonization Assimilation into the separate culture in the prison that has its own rewards and behaviors.

pro bono The practice by private attorneys of taking the cases of indigent offenders without fee as a service to the profession and the community.

pro se To present one's own defense in a criminal trial; self-representation.

probable cause The evidentiary criterion necessary to sustain an arrest or the issuance of an arrest or search warrant; a set of facts, information, circumstances, or conditions that would lead a reasonable person to believe that an offense was committed and that the accused committed that offense.

probation A sentence entailing the conditional release of a convicted offender into the community under the supervision of the court (in the form of a probation officer), subject to certain conditions for a specified time.

problem-oriented policing A style of police management that stresses proactive problem solving rather than reactive crime fighting.

procedural law The rules that define the operation of criminal proceedings, from obtaining a warrant or making an arrest through trial, sentencing, and appeal.

prosecutor The public official who presents the government's case against a person accused of a crime.

psychopath A person whose personality is characterized by a lack of warmth and feeling, inappropriate behavioral responses, and an inability to learn from experience; also called *sociopath* or *antisocial personality*.

public defender An attorney employed by the government to represent criminal defendants who cannot afford to pay for a lawyer.

Racketeer Influenced and Corrupt Organization Act (RICO) Federal legislation that enables prosecutors to bring additional criminal or civil charges against people whose multiple criminal acts constitute a conspiracy.

radical feminism A branch of conflict theory that focuses on the role of capitalist male dominance in female criminality and victimization.

real evidence Any object, such as a weapon or a photograph, produced for inspection at a trial; physical evidence.

reasonable competence standard Minimally required level of functioning by a defense attorney such that defendants are not deprived of their rights to counsel and to a fair trial.

reasonableness Requirement, under the Fourth Amendment, for a search and seizure; there must be probable cause to believe that the item being searched for was involved in criminal activity and is located at the place to be searched.

recidivism Repetition of criminal behavior; habitual criminality.

recognizance Medieval practice of letting convicted offenders remain free if they agreed to enter a debt relation with the state to pay for their crimes.

recoupment Process by which the state later recovers some or all of the cost of providing free legal counsel to an indigent defendant.

rehabilitation perspective A model of criminal justice that sees crime as an expression of frustration and anger created by social inequality that can be controlled by giving people the means to improve their lifestyle though conventional endeavors.

release on recognizance (ROR) A pretrial release in which a defendant with ties to the community is not required to post bail but promises to appear at all subsequent proceedings.

residential community correction (RCC) An intermediate sanction, as well as a parole or pretrial option, in which convicted offenders are housed in a nonsecure facility from which they go to work, attend school, and/or participate in treatment activities and programs.

restitution Criminal sanction that requires the offender to repay the victim and/or society for damage caused by the criminal act.

revocation Removing a person from probation (or parole) in response to a violation of law or of the conditions of probation (or parole).

risk classification Assigning probationers to a level and type of supervision based on their particular needs and the risks they pose for the community.

routine activities theory The view that crime is a product of three everyday factors: motivated offenders, suitable targets, and a lack of capable guardians.

search and seizure The legal term, contained in the Fourth Amendment to the U.S. Constitution, that refers to the searching for and carrying away of evidence by police during a criminal investigation.

search incident to a lawful arrest An exception to the search warrant rule; limited to the immediate surrounding area.

search warrant An order, issued by a judge, directing officers to conduct a search of specified premises for specified objects or persons and to bring them before the court.

selective incorporation The view that the rights and privileges in the Bill of Rights can be applied to the states through the due process clause of the Fourteenth Amendment, but only on a case-by-case basis.

self-defense A legal defense that claims a criminal act was justified by an imminent and unavoidable threat to oneself or another person.

self-incrimination A person's spoken or written statement that can be used against him or her as evidence in a criminal matter; such statements may not be coerced.

self-report survey A research approach that questions large groups of subjects, typically high school students, about their own participation in delinquent or criminal acts.

sentence The criminal sanction or punishment imposed by the court on a convicted defendant, usually in the form of a fine, incarceration, or probation.

sentencing guidelines Specification of sentences based on the seriousness of the crime and the criminal background of the offender.

sequester To insulate jurors from the outside world so that their decision making cannot be influenced or affected by events outside the courtroom.

sheriff The chief law enforcement officer in a county.

shire reeve In early England, the chief law enforcement official in a county, forerunner of today's sheriff.

shock incarceration A short prison sentence served under military discipline at a boot camp facility.

shock probation A sentence in which offenders serve a short term in prison to impress them with the pains of incarceration before they begin probation.

Social Agent A style of policing that sees police work as a helping profession involved in a wide range of activities, not just law enforcement.

social capital Positive relations with individuals and institutions that foster self-worth and inhibit crime.

social control The ability of society and its institutions to control, manage, restrain, or direct human behavior.

social control theory The view that most people do not violate the law because of their social bonds to family, peer group, school, and other institutions; if these bonds are weakened or absent, they become free to commit crime.

social learning theory The view that human behavior is learned through observation of human social interactions, either directly from those in close proximity or indirectly from the media.

social structure The stratifications, classes, institutions, and groups that characterize a society.

source control Attempting to cut off the supply of illegal drugs by destroying crops and arresting members of drug cartels in drug-producing countries.

special-needs inmate A prisoner distinguished by a particular problem such as mental illness, advanced age, drug dependence, or HIV infection.

specific deterrence Punishment severe enough to convince convicted offenders never to repeat their criminal activity.

specific intent The intent to accomplish a specific criminal purpose.

split sentence Giving a brief term of incarceration as a condition of probation.

stare decisis To stand by decided cases; the legal principle by which the decision or holding in an earlier case becomes the standard by which subsequent similar cases are judged.

state police Agencies that enforce state law outside of metropolitan areas and have jurisdiction over highway patrol.

status offense Noncriminal behavior, such as truancy and incorrigibility, that falls within the jurisdiction of a juvenile court.

stigma An enduring label that taints a person's identity and changes him or her in the eyes of others.

sting An undercover police operation in which police pose as criminals to trap law violators.

stop and frisk The situation in which police officers who are suspicious of an individual run their hands lightly over the suspect's outer garments to determine if the person is carrying a concealed weapon; also called a threshold inquiry or pat-down.

strain The emotional turmoil and conflict caused when people believe they cannot achieve their desires and goals through legitimate means.

strict liability crime A criminal violation—usually one that endangers the public welfare—that is defined by the act itself, irrespective of intent.

style Working attitude through which a police officer approaches policing. Four styles that have been identified are the Crime Fighter, the Social Agent, the Law Enforcer, and the Watchman.

subpoena A court order requiring a witness to appear in court at a specified time and place.

substantive criminal law A body of specific rules that declare what conduct is criminal and prescribe the punishment to be imposed for such conduct.

substantive right A specific right, such as the right to medical care or freedom of religion.

sureties During the Middle Ages, people who made themselves responsible for people given release or a reprieve.

suspended sentence A sentence of incarceration that is not carried out if the offender agrees to obey the rules of probation while living in the community.

technical parole violation Revocation of parole because conditions set by correctional authorities have been violated.

thief takers In eighteenth-century London, organized groups of private police who earned a living by catching wanted felons.

threshold inquiry A term used to describe a stop and frisk.

time-in-rank system The promotion system in which a police officer can advance in rank only after spending a prescribed amount of time in the preceding rank.

tithings During the Middle Ages, groups of about ten families responsible for maintaining order among themselves and dealing with disturbances, fire, wild animals, or other threats.

tort law The law of personal wrongs and damage; includes negligence, libel, slander, assault, and trespass.

total institution A regimented, dehumanizing institution, such as a prison, in which like-situated people are kept in social isolation, cut off from the world at large.

transfer hearing A preadjudication hearing in juvenile court to determine whether a juvenile offender should be transferred (waived) to criminal court for prosecution as an adult.

transportation Exile of convicted criminals to overseas colonies in lieu of execution.

treatment The rehabilitative method, such as therapy or educational or vocational programs, used to effect a change of behavior in the juvenile offender.

true bill The action by a grand jury when it votes to indict an accused suspect.

U.S. circuit court A court that handles the first level of appeal in the federal system.

Uniform Crime Reports (UCR) The official crime data collected by the FBI from local police departments.

venire The group called for jury duty from which jury panels are selected.

verdict The finding of a trial jury or judge on the question of fact: guilty or not guilty.

vice squad Police officers assigned to enforce morality-based laws, such as those on prostitution, gambling, and pornography.

victim precipitation The role of the victim in provoking or encouraging criminal behavior.

victimless crime Public order crime that has no specific victim, such as public drunkenness or vagrancy.

vigilantes In the Old West, members of a vigilance committee or posse called upon to capture cattle thieves or other felons.

voir dire The process in which a potential jury panel is questioned by the prosecution and the defense to select jurors who are unbiased and objective.

waiver The voluntary and deliberate relinquishing of a known right, such as those guaranteed under the Fifth and Sixth Amendments; the transfer of a juvenile offender to criminal court for prosecution as an adult.

watch system In medieval England, men organized in church parishes to guard at night against disturbances and breaches of the peace under the direction of the local constable.

Watchman A style of policing that reacts to calls for service rather than aggressively pursuing crime.

widen the net To enmesh more offenders for longer periods in the criminal justice system—a criticism of pretrial diversion programs.

work release (furlough) A prison treatment program in which inmates leave the institution to work in the community, sometimes returning to prison or another supervised facility at night.

writ of certiorari An order of a superior court requesting that a record of an inferior court (or administrative body) be brought forward for review or inspection.

writ of habeas corpus A judicial order requiring a review of the legal reasons for a person's detention and confinement.

TABLE OF CASES

NAME INDEX

SUBJECT INDEX

PHOTO CREDITS

Chapter 1. 1: Cable News Network 2: © Kelley Chinn/*The Fort Worth Star Telegram*/Sipa 3: © Sean Cayton/The Image Works 9: AP/Wide World Photos 17: © Rob Nelson/Black Star 19: Universal/MGM/Shooting Star 21: © Brooks Kraft/CORBIS-Sygma 22: © Brooks Kraft/CORBIS-Sygma 27: AP/Wide World Photos

Chapter 2. 36: AP/Wide World Photos 37: Tribune photo by Piol Velasquez/Copyright 2001 *Chicago Tribune*. World rights reserved. 38: Ted Thai, Time, Inc. 47: © Mark Peterson/SABA 55: AP/Wide World Photos

Chapter 3. 68: AP/Wide World Photos 69: AP/Wide World Photos 73: AP/Wide World Photos 75: AP/Wide World Photos 79: © Christopher Morris/Black Star 85: © Jim Avelis/*Tribune Star*/Sipa Press 93: Courtesy of DARE America 100: © Greg Lovett/*Palm Beach Post*

Chapter 4. 108: A.C. Cooper Ltd., by permission of The Inner Temple, London 112: AP/Wide World Photos 119: © Ted Fitzgerald/*The Boston Herald* 124: AP/Wide World Photos 125: AP/Wide World Photos 129: AP/Wide World Photos 135: © John Kuntzer/Sipa Press 141: © Ken Heinen

Chapter 5. 145: Cable News Network 146: © Nancy Richmond/The Image Works 147: AP/Wide World Photos 152: Thomas Nast, Jr. "The Position of Police Inspector—Nothing to 'Do' But—Everybody," 1907. #47.242.4. © Museum of the City of New York 154: © Dennis Brack/Black Star 157: AP/Wide World Photos 160: AP/Wide World Photos 161: AP/Wide World Photos 169: AP/Wide World Photos

Chapter 6. 174: AP/Wide World Photos 180: © David Butow/SABA 187: © Dan Lamont/Matrix 190: © Kathy McLaughlin/The Image Works 195: © Albert Fanning/The Image Works 198: AP/Wide World Photos

Chapter 7. 204: AP/Wide World Photos 205: © Steve Jacobs/*Albany Times Union*/The Image Works 207: ABC/Shooting Star 218: © Alan Weiner/Liaison Agency 221: AP/Wide World Photos 227: © Tony Sovino/Sipa Press 233: AP/Wide World Photos

Chapter 8. 242: © Alon Reininger/Contact Press Photos 245: © Bob Strong/The Image Works 251: © Rick Maiman/CORBIS/Sygma 254: © Bob Strong/Sipa Press 256: AP/Wide World Photos 264: PhotoDisc, Inc.

Chapter 9. 271: Cable News Network 272: Alinari/Regione Umbria/Art Resource, NY 273: Copyright 1994 Globe Newspaper Company, Inc. Republished with permission of Globe Newspaper Company, Inc. 279: © Paul Milette/*Palm Beach Post* 285: © Mark Graham/CORBIS/Sygma 290: AP/Wide World Photos 292: AP/Wide World Photos

Chapter 10. 298: AP/Wide World Photos 299: AP/Wide World Photos 303: Ben Shahn, Passion of Sacco and Vanzetti, from the Sacco-Vanzetti series, 1931–1932. Tempera on canvas. Whitney Museum of American Art. Gift of Edith and Milton Lowenthal in memory of Juliana Force [49.22]. Photograph Copyright © 2001: Whitney Museum of American Art, New York. Photography by Sandak, Inc./Macmillan Publishing. 310: AP/Wide World Photos 315: © Henry A. Barrios/*The Bakersfield Californian* 321: AP/Wide World Photos 324: AP/Wide World Photos

Chapter 11. 332: © Mark Richards/Contact Press Images 333: © M. Tully/CORBIS-Sygma 338: AP/Wide World Photos 345: © Alon Reininger/Contact Press Images 350: AP/Wide World Photos 351: AP/Wide World Photos 360: AP/Wide World Photos

Chapter 12. 364: AP/Wide World Photos 368: AP/Wide World Photos 372: Photo reproduced by permission of the *San Francisco Examiner,* print courtesy of AP/Wide World Photos 375: AP/Wide World Photos 386: © Philip Kamrass/*Albany Times Union*/The Image Works 389: AP/Wide World Photos

Chapter 13. 398: AP/Wide World Photos 399: AP/Wide World Photos 405: AP/Wide World Photos 413: © Donna Binder/Impact Visuals 418: © Kevin Horan 419: AP/Wide World Photos 427: © Lisa Terry/Liaison Agency 433: © Nicole Bengiveno/Matrix

Chapter 14. 439: Cable News Network 440: © Jacques Chenet/Woodfin Camp & Associates; 444: AP/Wide World Photos 449: © A. Ramey/Woodfin Camp & Associates 450: © John Gurzinski/*Las Vegas Review Journal* 457: AP/Wide World Photos 459: © Bob Daemmrich/The Image Works 463: AP/Wide World Photos

Chapter 15. 478: AP/Wide World Photos 479: AP/Wide World Photos 484: Stock Montage, Inc. 488: American Correctional Association 491: © Michael Abramson/Woodfin Camp & Associates 495: © Shelly Katz/Liaison Agency 500: © *Jacksonville Courier*/Zuzana Killiam/The Image Works 503: AP/Wide World Photos

Chapter 16. 510: AP/Wide World Photos 512: AP/Wide World Photos 515: Erik Freeland/*U. S. News & World Report* 521: © 2000 Sean Cayton/The Image Works 525: AP/Wide World Photos 529: © Hank Delespinasse 536: AP/Wide World Photos 546: AP/Wide World Photos

Chapter 17. 555: Cable News Network 556: © A. Ramey/Woodfin Camp & Associates 557: AP/Wide World Photos 560: The Granger Collection, New York, NY 564: © Lui Xin/*Palm Beach Post* 566: © Sherman Zent/*Palm Beach Post* 570: © A. Ramey/Woodfin Camp & Associates 574: AP/Wide World Photos 577: © A. Ramey/Woodfin Camp & Associates